ENCYCLOPEDIA OF THE
AMERICAN MILITARY

ENCYCLOPEDIA OF THE
AMERICAN MILITARY

———— ☆ ————

Studies of the History, Traditions, Policies,
Institutions, and Roles
of the Armed Forces in War and Peace

John E. Jessup
Editor in Chief

Louise B. Ketz
Executive Editor

Volume II

CHARLES SCRIBNER'S SONS
NEW YORK

MAXWELL MACMILLAN CANADA
TORONTO

MAXWELL MACMILLAN INTERNATIONAL
NEW YORK • OXFORD • SINGAPORE • SYDNEY

Charles Scribner's Sons   Maxwell Macmillan Canada, Inc.
Macmillan Publishing Company   1200 Eglinton Avenue East
866 Third Avenue   Suite 200
New York, New York 10022   Don Mills, Ontario M3C 3N1

Library of Congress Cataloging-in-Publication Data
Encyclopedia of the American military : studies of the history,
    traditions, policies, institutions, and roles of the armed forces in
    war and peace / John E. Jessup, editor in chief, Louise B. Ketz,
    executive editor.
        p.   cm.
    Includes bibliographical references and index.
    ISBN 0-684-19255-1 (set) — ISBN 0-684-19695-6 (v. 1)
    — ISBN 0-684-19696-4 (v. 2) — ISBN 0-684-19697-2 (v. 3)
    1. United States—Defenses—History.   2. United States—History,
Military.   3. Military art and science—United States—History.
I. Jessup,   John E.
UA23.E56   1994
355'.00973—dc20   93-49621
                                                   CIP

1 3 5 7 9 11 13 15 17 19   V/C   20 18 16 14 12 10 8 6 4 2

PRINTED IN THE UNITED STATES OF AMERICA.

The views expressed in the essays in the *Encyclopedia of the American Military* are those of the authors and do
not reflect official policy or history of any United States government agency, department, bureau, or
educational institution, or that of the U.S. armed services.

∞ The paper used in this publication meets the minimum requirements of the American National Standard
for Information Sciences—Permanence of Paper for Printed Library Materials, ANSI Z39.48-1984.

CONTENTS

PART 4   THE AMERICAN MILITARY IN WAR AND PEACE

PART 5   MILITARY ARTS AND SCIENCES

PART 6 MILITARY PRACTICES

ENCYCLOPEDIA OF THE
AMERICAN MILITARY

THE WAR WITH MEXICO

Odie B. Faulk

On 18 April 1846 Mexican President Mariano Paredes y Arrillaga wrote a blunt order to the commander of his Army of the North, General Pedro de Ampudia: "At the present time I suppose you to be at the head of our valiant army, either fighting already or preparing for the operations of the campaign. . . . It is indispensable that hostilities be commenced, yourself taking the initiative against the enemy." Five days later, long before his letter to Ampudia could have been taken from Mexico City to Matamoros and a reply received, President Paredes issued a proclamation declaring "defensive war" against the United States.

The following day, 24 April, Ampudia was replaced as commander of the Army of the North by General Mariano Arista, a militant, who immediately issued orders for sixteen hundred cavalry to cross the Rio Grande and attack U.S. forces on the north side of the river. That same afternoon part of this cavalry detachment came upon Captain Seth B. Thornton and sixty-three American dragoons, who were investigating a report of a large-scale Mexican crossing of the river onto Texas soil. Following intensive skirmishing, in which sixteen Americans were killed or wounded, Thornton was forced to surrender.

Thus began a war that would redraw political boundaries, bring dramatic change to the officer corps of the U.S. Army and U.S. Navy, produce lingering hatreds between neighboring nations, and generate an endless argument in assessing blame for causing the conflict.

CAUSES OF THE WAR

The order from President Paredes to commence hostilities was a result of a deep political division that had developed in Mexico after it won its independence from Spain in 1821. The two major parties in Mexico were the Centralists and the Federalists, the former wanting a strong national government, with appointed state and local officials, and the latter a federal republic similar to the United States. In 1822 the Centralists had installed an emperor, Agustín de Iturbide, only to see him quickly ousted and replaced by a Federalist regime, inaugurated under the Mexican constitution of 1824. That regime lasted, albeit with several revolutions, until 1835, when Antonio López de Santa Anna, president since 1833, overthrew the constitution and installed himself as a Centralist dictator, causing Texas and six other Mexican states to revolt. Santa Anna lost power after he was captured by Texans at the Battle of San Jacinto in April 1836.

Federalism returned to power in Mexico in 1842 with the election of a constituent assembly that restored the constitution of 1824, and Santa Anna again became president, only to dissolve the assembly in 1843 and reinstall himself as a Centralist dictator. Revolution began anew in 1844 with Federalist José Joaquin Herrera installed as president in December and Santa Anna forced into exile in Cuba. It was at this juncture that the question of Texas became a major issue while the Centralists fought to regain power.

Texas had been a province in the Spanish viceroyalty of New Spain and then had been joined with Coahuila to form the state of Coahuila-Texas under the Mexican constitution of 1824. The previous year colonists had been allowed to settle in Texas from the United States and elsewhere, and by 1835 about thirty thousand Americans had moved into the province. Santa Anna's overthrow of the 1824 constitution caused Texas, along with six other Mexican states, to rise in rebellion to restore federalism. On 2 March 1836 the Texas rebels, both American and Mexican, declared their independence and created an interim government for the Republic of Texas. This independence was ratified on 21 April 1836 at the Battle of San Jacinto, where General Sam Houston and a force of 783 Texans defeated Santa Anna and a Mexican force of about fifteen hundred. The Mexican dictator was captured in the uniform of a private soldier and quickly signed the Treaties of Velasco, which recognized Texas independence and ordered Mexican troops to withdraw south of the Rio Grande.

Texas subsequently maintained its status as a republic for almost ten years, but it clearly preferred annexation to the United States. On 28 February 1845 the U.S. Congress adopted a joint resolution calling for the annexation of Texas as a state, and on 1 March President John Tyler signed it.

On 6 March the Mexican ambassador to the United States, Juan Nepomuceno Almonte, a Centralist not yet recalled following the overthrow of Santa Anna's dictatorship in December 1844, demanded his passport and stormed out of Washington. He asserted that the annexation of Texas was tantamount to a declaration of war. In reality, his action was intended to embarrass the new Federalist regime in Mexico City and to inflame Mexican patriotism. His declaration was popular in Mexico and became a rallying cry for Centralist opposition to Herrera and the Federalists.

Moreover, Federalist support waned when it became known that Herrera had indicated he would receive a minister plenipotentiary from the United States. In October 1845, amid Centralist cries for war to preserve the spurious Mexican claim to Texas, the Mexican congress met in secret session and approved a declaration that it would receive a representative from the United States "with full powers to settle the present dispute." President James K. Polk then named John Slidell to negotiate with the Herrera government. Slidell was given instructions to settle not only the dispute over Texas but also several other points of disagreement between the two nations, including the claims question.

During the continuing political unrest south of the Rio Grande, many U.S. citizens had filed claims against both state and national governments in Mexico for property taken or destroyed. During his eight years in office, President Andrew Jackson made repeated attempts to have these claims paid, leading to the severing of diplomatic relations between the two countries in 1836.

In 1839 Powhatan Ellis reopened the U.S. embassy in Mexico City (after France had attacked Mexico in 1838 to recover what was owned by its citizens, and British gunboats had forced payment of claims to British subjects). Early in 1840 the United States and Mexico agreed to binding arbitration of the U.S. claims. Delegates from the two countries met, with Baron Roenne of Prussia acting as umpire. After months of haggling, the baron adjourned the session in disgust early in 1842. Of the $11 million in claims, $7 million was discussed, $2 million was awarded, and $5 million was tabled. By this time Santa Anna was back in power and, short on money, refused to pay these claims. Arbitration was scheduled to begin anew in 1843, but

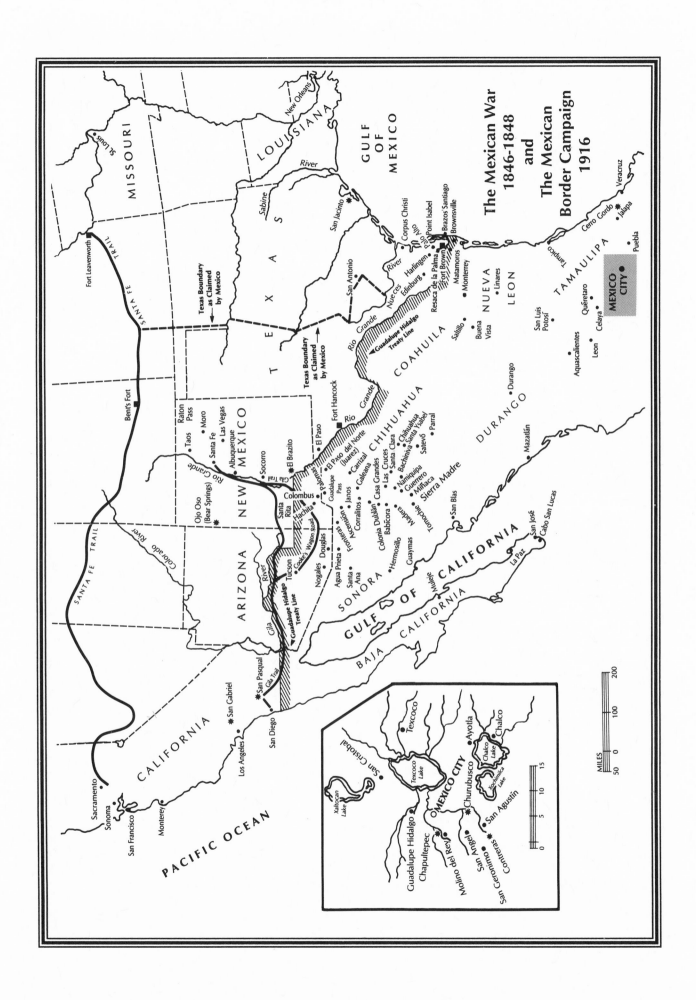

The Mexican War
1846-1848
and
The Mexican
Border Campaign
1916

broke down after three of twenty payments were made on the earlier settlement.

Another issue that Slidell was empowered to negotiate was that of California. By 1845 California was virtually independent of Mexico. The British consul there wrote that separation was inevitable, while the French minister to Mexico asserted that it was a moot question whether Great Britain or the United States would get the Pacific Coast territory. In 1845 the United States was negotiating with England over the boundary between Oregon and Canada, and British intrigue was evident in California. Polk instructed Thomas O. Larkin, the U.S. consul at Monterey, California, to support any movement for separation from Mexico. Polk also had Lieutenant John Charles Frémont and a detachment of sixty-two armed men stationed just north of the forty-second parallel in Oregon awaiting developments in California.

In short, Polk was protecting U.S. interests in California, which was reflected in his instructions to Slidell to attempt to purchase California from Mexico. The minister plenipotentiary was empowered to accept the Nueces River as the southern boundary of Texas if Mexico would agree to a prompt settlement of the claims; to assume payment by the United States of the claims of its citizens if Mexico would accept the Rio Grande as far north as El Paso del Norte as the boundary; to pay $5 million if Mexico would cede New Mexico to the United States; to pay an additional $5 million for northern California; and to give as much as $25 million for all of California to San Diego.

During the months in which Herrera agreed to receive U.S. minister and Polk dispatched Slidell, the annexation of Texas moved forward rapidly. In October 1845 the voters of the Lone Star Republic agreed to the terms of the joint congressional resolution of annexation and elected a convention, which drafted a state constitution. After Congress approved this constitution, Polk signed the Texas Admission Act on 29 December 1845, making Texas the twenty-eighth state in the Union.

Earlier in December Slidell arrived in Mexico City to be informed that Herrera would not receive a minister from the United States until Texas was returned to Mexico. By this point the Centralists had so inflamed Mexican public opinion that no government in Mexico could even negotiate with the United States. On 14 December Paredes raised the standard of revolt by proclaiming that Herrera repeatedly had kept the Mexican army from attacking the Americans in Texas. On the same day that Polk signed the Texas Admission Act, Paredes was able to enter Mexico City and take power without firing a shot. A revolutionary junta named him president and rewarded Almonte with appointment as secretary of war. It also reiterated an intention to make war on the United States to recover Texas—indeed, it was claimed that a state of war already existed between the two countries.

The new Centralist president began mobilizing his forces for a war that he and his cabinet members fervently believed would be won by Mexico. They expected aid from Great Britain in the event of war because of the U.S.-British quarrel over Oregon. They also had convinced themselves that France likewise would send aid to Mexico.

Most foreign military observers assured Paredes and his Centralist ministers that the Mexican regular army was superior to U.S. troops, because it was more than four times larger, well-armed, well-disciplined, and experienced. Lewis Pakenham, the British minister to Mexico, declared it would be impossible for U.S. troops to defeat Mexican soldiers on their own territory. Because the U.S. army was so small, the bulk of its fighting would have to be done by volunteers, and it was axiomatic among military observers that regulars could defeat volunteers in any contest of arms.

In addition, Mexican Centralist leaders counted on their side geography and political divisiveness in the United States. Should U.S. troops invade Mexico, they would find themselves in a thinly populated desert, a land of vast distances, barren mountains, and ever-lengthening supply lines, where they would be cut to pieces by guerrilla warfare and local resistance.

Just as important were the political divisions that Almonte and other observers reported in the United States. The former ambassador to the United States assured Paredes that U.S. northern abolitionists would not support the war, that internal conflict would destroy American morale, and that Indians in the American Southwest and slaves in the South would rise up to join the Mexican army when it invaded and marched toward Washington, D.C.

For all these reasons President Paredes assured his fellow countrymen that he would see the Eagle and Serpent of Mexico flying over the White House in Washington before he would negotiate anything. Privately he believed that at the first news of a victory in the north, his countrymen would rise up and proclaim him king of Mexico.

Thus, it was not a dispute over the southern boundary of Texas—the Nueces or the Rio Grande—that led to the outbreak of hostilities between the United States and Mexico. No Mexican politician ever asserted that the Nueces was the boundary; rather they were unanimous in claiming that the Sabine River (the present boundary between Texas and Louisiana) was the true boundary. Nor was the war caused by any American feelings of Manifest Destiny—a belief that the Divine Being intended for the United States to extend its rule over all of North America. The war was also not a result of a conflict of cultures.

The conflict began in 1846 because President Paredes and his Centralist advisers wanted a war—in fact, deliberately provoked a war—to achieve their goals. The accusations that Polk plotted war in order to acquire New Mexico and California were the inventions of Whigs bent on winning victory in the election of 1848.

TAYLOR'S CAMPAIGN

When President Polk learned of the deteriorating political condition in Mexico and that Slidell's mission had been rejected, he ordered Brevet Major General Zachary Taylor to move to the mouth of the Rio Grande to protect American interests.

"Old Rough and Ready," as Taylor was known, was commander of the Department of the Southwest. On 28 May 1845 he had been ordered by Polk to repel any Mexican effort to invade Texas and had moved from Louisiana to the mouth of the Nueces River (the site of present-day Corpus Christi). He next moved to the mouth of the Rio Grande, where he arrived with four thousand men on 23 March 1846, and established a depot at Point Isabel, where his supplies could land by ship from New Orleans. Named Fort Polk after the president, it was fortified by hastily constructed earthen breastworks. Taylor also had his troops erect Fort Texas, another earthen fortification, some thirty miles inland and opposite the Mexican town of Matamoros.

Second in command to sixty-two-year-old Taylor was Brigadier General William J. Worth, ten years younger and with an appetite for alcohol and bad decisions. Other high officers included colonels William G. Belknap, David E. Twiggs, and William Whistler and Lieutenant Colonel James S. McIntosh. All were more than fifty years old and, as one journalist wrote, "prepared to fight in 1846. . . . as [the] army had fought in 1812." Among the junior officers at the mouth of the Rio Grande were Ulysses S. Grant, then a lieutenant of infantry, and Ephraim Kirby Smith, an infantry captain and brother of Civil War General Edmund Kirby Smith.

When Taylor received word that Captain Thornton's dragoons had been attacked on 24–25 April, he had 3,880 troops, of whom about five hundred were disabled with amebic dysentery, diarrhea, yellow fever, and a host of other diseases arising from the unsanitary conditions at Fort Polk, Fort Texas, and other encampments.

Across the river in Mexico was forty-four-year-old General Mariano Arista. He arrived at Matamoros on 24 April 1846 to take command of the Army of the North, which consisted of more than eight thousand soldiers. Some of the elements of the Army of the North were crack units, such as the Tampico veterans, the Second Light Infantry, the Fourth and Tenth infantries, and General Anastasio Torrejón's lancers; these were all experienced men who had demonstrated competence in battle, veterans of discipline and courage. Arista's troops also included, however, poorly trained and equipped raw conscripts and convict soldiers who lacked experience and were prepared to desert at the first opportunity. Arista's subordinate officers included generals Torrejón, Luis Noriega, and José María García and Colonel José López Uraga.

The first commander of the Army of the North had been General Francisco Mejía, a twenty-four-year-old political appointee filled with bombast and self-importance. When he did not attack Taylor's army on the north side of the Rio Grande, after an order dated 4 April from President Paredes, he was replaced by General Ampudia. The new commander of Mexican forces at Matamoros ordered Taylor to withdraw as far north as the Nueces River and told all American civilians to leave Matamoros because a state of war existed. Ampudia, however, like Mejía, did not take the initiative, and on 24 April he was superseded by General Arista. lt was Arista who at last ordered troops north of the Rio Grande, attacking Captain Thornton and his dragoons.

Meanwhile, on 23 April President Paredes had issued a curious proclamation: "At the time Mr. Slidell presented himself [in Mexico] the troops of the United States occupied our territory [Texas]. . . . Hostilities then have been commenced by the United States of the north. . . . I solemnly announce that I do not declare war on the United States. . . . From this day commences a defensive war."

President Polk, after learning of the ambush on Captain Thornton, sent a message to Congress on 11 May to ask for recognition that a state of war existed between the United States and Mexico and for authority to raise fifty thousand twelve-month volunteers, stating that "American blood had been shed upon American soil." That same day the House of Repre-

sentatives passed the bill by a vote of 174 to 14, and the next day the Senate concurred by a vote of 40 to 2. Every vote against the declaration of war was cast by a Whig, and all of them northerners. Angry abolitionists in the Senate were able to delay temporarily an appropriations bill of $10 million for the war, charging that the war was being promoted to acquire more slave territory, but on 13 May the bill went to Polk for his signature. A Mexican congress assembled by President Paredes on 1 July voted a declaration of "offensive war," a declaration made public five days later.

These political actions were unknown to the U.S. troops at the mouth of the Rio Grande. On 1–2 May, General Taylor, who had advanced to a point opposite Matamoros to establish Fort Texas, left five hundred men there and returned to Point Isabel. At 3:00 P.M. on 7 May he began marching back to Fort Texas with supplies and two 18-pound siege guns. The next day, at about noon, he and his estimated twenty-two hundred effectives were confronted at Palo Alto by Arista and about six thousand Mexican troops, the entire Army of the North having crossed the Rio Grande. Despite the advice of his officers, Taylor placed his sixteen batteries of artillery in the center of his formation and his infantry on the flanks; his 932 artillerymen were regulars, and he felt he could depend on them.

Stand firm the artillery did, cutting the Mexican army to pieces with explosives and canister, as well as fighting occasionally as infantry. The cannon fire was so devastating that huge holes appeared in the Mexican ranks. After an hour Arista ordered Torrejón's lancers to charge the American right, with the intent of taking the supply wagons. Colonel Twiggs and the Fifth Infantry, drawn up in a square, met the Mexican charge, which was in column not line. The lancers were repulsed, and repulsed again when they charged a second time.

When the two U.S. 18-pounders, under command of Lieutenant William Churchill, opened fire with grape and canister, the Mexicans several times tried to charge and halt the devastation. They were repulsed each time, however, and by 7:00 that evening the Americans were preparing to charge when darkness intervened. A count that evening showed nine American dead and forty-seven wounded; Arista later reported 250 dead or wounded.

The light of day on 9 May revealed that the Mexican army had retreated. Despite a vote of seven to three by his senior officers to entrench and wait, Taylor ordered an advance. The Mexicans, he learned, had retreated seven miles toward the Rio Grande until they had entered a thick woods and found Resaca de la Palma, an ancient channel of the Rio Grande. There Arista had implanted his artillery and scattered his troops along both sides of the road.

When U.S. scouts determined the Mexican location, Taylor advanced with seventeen hundred men. After several skirmishes, Taylor ordered Colonel Belknap and the Eighth Infantry to capture the Mexican artillery, saying, "Take those guns, and by God keep them." With fiendish yells the infantry charged, captured the guns, and held them, thereby demoralizing Arista's force.

Seeing his artillery lost, Arista fled to the Rio Grande and crossed. His soldiers followed as fast as possible, dropping weapons, supplies, and clothing in their haste. By the time they reached the river, they were in total panic, believing that the Americans were following with their deadly artillery. Most crowded into boats for the crossing, some of which overturned, while other soldiers tried to swim, resulting in the death of many men by drowning. Resaca de la Palma was another decided American victory, because Arista's army had dwindled to four thousand when it finally regrouped.

Taylor made no attempt to cross the Rio Grande immediately, choosing instead to regroup and resupply. He then began preparations to invade Mexican territory. Arista, meanwhile, found himself with scant funds, panicky troops, and little ammunition. On 17 May he requested an armistice from Taylor, only to have the American general reply, "I must have Matamoros even if I am forced to batter the entire town." His terms were blunt: "The city must capitulate; all property must be surrendered; then and only then may the Mexican army march out and retire." A reply was demanded by 3:00 P.M. on 17 May.

Told by his officers that Matamoros was indefensible, Arista fled the city, leaving behind his wounded and part of his supplies. The next day a delegation of leading citizens from Matamoros called on Taylor to ask for terms. Taylor responded that the Americans would respect persons and property. When the Mexicans agreed, Taylor's troops crossed the river, entered without opposition what had been called Fort Paredes, and raised the Stars and Stripes as they sang "Yankee Doodle."

Arista's army, fleeing southward, was in almost total panic. His route to Linares was lined with dead animals and soldiers who had dropped out in exhaustion and despair. Arista arrived in Linares with 2,638 troops and made his report, placing himself in as favorable a light as possible after the disasters at the mouth of the Rio Grande. Because of drought in northern Mexico that summer, the Army of the North soon moved on to Monterrey, the nearest major city.

In Mexico City the Centralists were stunned at the news from the north, because they had been predicting a quick victory over the Americans. When confidence plummeted, President Paredes blamed Arista for the defeat and replaced him with General Mejía.

The reaction in the United States to news of Taylor's victories was soaring confidence and hordes of young men seeking to fill the quota for volunteers in each state. A call for twenty-eight hundred men in Tennessee saw a response by thirty thousand, some of the disappointed trying to buy a billet. In Maine the Aroostook County boys sang gaily as they marched off to war, while in Connecticut there were twice as many volunteers as needed. Texans were especially enthusiastic during the war, seeing an opportunity to strike once again at the nation from which they had fought for their independence. Texas Governor James Pinckney Henderson took a leave of absence to accept a commission as a colonel and fight. Taylor was the great hero of the hour, Congress voting him two gold medals, while Whigs talked of running him for president in 1848.

There was little rejoicing for the U.S. army in Matamoros, as more and more volunteers swarmed to the city. Young officers, trained at West Point, cursed Taylor as inept, bumbling, old, and foolish, saying he was incapable of using the information given him by Texas Ranger scouting companies. The enlisted men were bivouacked in poorly planned locations, drinking brackish water and sweating out fevers as they watched many of their companions die of disease. Out of boredom they flocked to the gambling halls, cantinas, and brothels for entertainment.

Still the volunteers came, many of them signing up for only three or six months. Taylor sent some of them home, but by 1 August he had almost twenty thousand men under his command. At last Taylor decided to move his army inland, in part to get away from the fleshpots of Matamoros and in part to press the war.

Captain Ben McCulloch and a company of Texas Rangers scouted the route toward Monterrey, where the Mexican Army of the North was rebuilding. The move from Matamoros began on 6–7 July toward a place known as Camargo, forty miles up the Rio Grande from Matamoros and in the general direction of Monterrey. Taylor and his staff arrived there by steamer on 8 August.

Camargo proved a place of death for fifteen hundred Americans, because of heat, poor sanitation, and diseases brought from Matamoros. Lieutenant George B. McClellan wrote of the encampment at Camargo, "I have seen more suffering since I came out here than I could have imagined to exist. It really is awful. I allude to the suffering of the volunteers. They literally die like dogs." Lew Wallace, a volunteer from Indiana, commented, "I cannot recall another instance of a command so wantonly neglected and so brutally mislocated."

The march to Monterrey began on 19 August in two parallel (later converging) columns consisting of two divisions of regulars and one division of volunteers, a total of 6,640 men. Commanding the regulars were Major General Worth and Brigadier General Twiggs, while the volunteers served under Brevet Major General William O. Butler, a Kentucky lawyer. There was little Mexican opposition to this march, the Texas Rangers enthusiastically clearing the route.

Unknown to the Americans, Monterrey was heavily defended. Command of the Army of the North had passed from Mejía to the far more formidable General Ampudia, who awaited Taylor with ten thousand soldiers. Monterrey, located on the north bank of the Rio Santa Catarina, was a natural fortress with mountains on the south and west and forts on the north and northeast. To the west of the city, atop Independence Hill, was the strongly fortified Bishop's Palace. Ampudia believed he could hold off Taylor and his army.

The fight for Monterrey on 21–24 September was sharp and bitter, but Texas Rangers turned the tide of battle by storming the Bishop's Palace and other fortresses on high ground. U.S. artillerists then turned their pieces on the city while the infantry moved into town on 23 September for house-to-house fighting. The next day Ampudia sent an emissary under a flag of truce to ask for an armistice. Colonel Jefferson Davis, commanding a regiment of Mississippi volunteers, along with General Worth and Colonel Henderson, negotiated an agreement that allowed the Mexican army to retire with their sidearms and accoutrements, along with six pieces of artillery. The agreement also stipulated that U.S. troops would not advance farther into Mexico for eight weeks. Ampudia and the Mexican troops withdrew on 25 September, after which Taylor and his army raised the U.S. flag. The supposedly impregnable city of Monterrey had been taken with a loss of eight hundred Americans killed and wounded.

News of Taylor's latest victory caused celebrations in the United States, but not everyone was happy. Because of increasing talk among Whigs of running Taylor for the presidency, many Democrats criticized the terms of the armistice granted at Monterrey. President Polk declared, "In agreeing to this armistice General Taylor violated his express orders." Late in November he wrote in his diary, "I am now satisfied that he is . . . wholly unqualified for the command he holds." Therefore, on 26 January 1847 he issued orders for Taylor to remain in Monterrey and to dispatch four-fifths of his troops to accompany General Winfield Scott, who was to invade Mexico at Veracruz. Taylor and his remaining men were to remain on the defensive.

When Ampudia led the remains of the Army of the North south from Monterrey, he retreated all the way to San Luis Potosí, arriving in that city in mid-October. He learned that the army had been renamed the Army of Liberation and that he had been replaced as commander by General Santa Anna. When the war broke out, Santa Anna used diplomatic channels from his exile in Cuba to promise a quick end to the war on U.S. terms if he was allowed to return to Mexico. Issued a safe-conduct pass through the U.S. naval blockade of the Mexican coast by Polk, Santa Anna reached Mexico City on 14 September. Three days later José Mariano Salas, acting president after Paredes had been deposed, named Santa Anna commander of the Army of Liberation.

As always, Santa Anna proved efficient at raising men, and soon he had twenty thousand troops. When his scouts intercepted a letter from Winfield Scott to Zachary Taylor ordering Taylor to send all but six thousand of his men to the coast for embarkation, Santa Anna decided to go north to fight Taylor. He knew that the U.S. troops would consist mainly of volunteers and that they would be largely untrained. With visions of a quick victory and the Mexican presidency that would follow, Santa Anna marched his army north, his promises to make peace forgotten.

Meanwhile, Taylor chose to ignore Polk's order to remain on the defensive. On 8 November 1846 he ordered General Worth to begin a march to Saltillo, seventy-five miles southwest of Monterrey. His daring was made possible by the arrival of fourteen hundred fresh troops under the command of Brigadier General John E.

Wool. Learning that Santa Anna was advancing toward him, Taylor and his troops took up a defensive position just south of Saltillo on the road to San Luis Potosí. At this encampment he had 4,759 men, of whom only two squadrons of cavalry and three batteries of artillery were regulars, a total of 476 men.

When Santa Anna approached on 21 February 1847, Taylor withdrew his troops to the hacienda of Buena Vista, seven miles south of Saltillo. On the morning of 22 February, Santa Anna sent a note to Taylor demanding an unconditional surrender, stating, "You are surrounded by twenty thousand men, and cannot in any human probability avoid suffering a rout." He also gave Taylor just one hour to reply. Old Rough and Ready's response was brief: "In reply to your note . . . summoning me to surrender my forces at discretion, I beg leave to say that I decline acceding to your request."

Santa Anna hurried to start the battle despite the poor condition of his men, who had been rushed north with little chance for rest or hot food. On the first day of battle, repeated Mexican charges failed to breach the U.S. lines, thanks mainly to withering artillery fire directed by Captain John Paul Jones O'Brien. Shortly after darkness Santa Anna brought forward the San Patricio Battalion, a small unit composed of American deserters, mainly Irish-Catholics, who were fighting on the Mexican side. That night a cold, drizzling rain fell, and both sides got little sleep because of repeated rumors of attack.

The second day of fighting saw the Mexicans again halted in their attacks by withering artillery fire. At a critical juncture in the battle, Colonel Davis and the Mississippi volunteers charged and turned the Mexicans back. When the Mexicans regrouped and came forward again, the Illinois infantry charged into them; among their dead were Colonel John J. Hardin and Lieutenant Colonel Henry Clay (son of the politician). When this charge faltered, Captain O'Brien and the artillery again turned the tide of battle, opening holes in the Mexican lines with grape and canister. By nightfall the center of the

Mexican line had collapsed, and the Americans were advancing.

During the night of 23–24 February, Taylor counseled with his generals. His casualties that day had been 673 killed and wounded, and General Wool and other top aides advised a retreat. At about 3:00 A.M. on 24 February, however, about four hundred men and two 18-pound guns arrived from Saltillo, and Taylor decided to continue the fight.

To Taylor's delight, the light of day revealed that Santa Anna had quit the field of battle. Twice the Mexican army seemingly had victory within its grasp after brave charges, and twice it had been routed by deadly artillery fire. Santa Anna's men were without food and exhausted, their ammunition largely expended. Realizing his men could not fight again, the Mexican general had ordered a retreat, the wounded to be left behind. What started as an orderly retreat became a rout as conscripts fled the scene of death. Men discarded weapons and fled into the hills. By the time the Army of Liberation returned to San Luis Potosí, there were nine thousand men unaccounted for.

Taylor's troops gave food and water to the Mexican wounded on the field of battle, while Taylor and Wool hugged each other with relief. Taylor wrote to his brother, "The great loss on both sides . . . has deprived me of everything like pleasure." He remained in northern Mexico through most of 1847, after Congress voted him yet another gold medal, while President Polk criticized his actions. Late in 1847 he returned to the United States expecting both Whigs and Democrats to nominate him for the presidency and election by near acclamation.

NEW MEXICO AND CHIHUAHUA

While Taylor was winning his stunning victories in northern Mexico, a second major U.S. offensive was taking place in the Southwest.

New Mexico east of the Rio Grande had been claimed by Texas prior to the outbreak of war, a claim with little legitimacy. Santa Fe traders, however, had shown the commercial value of this Mexican state, and President Polk was determined to have it. There was no great national patriotism in New Mexico, and its citizens had received little protection from Indian raids, taxes were exorbitantly high, and government was arbitrary. Thus, Polk's move to take New Mexico was strategically sound.

On 13 May 1846, shortly after the U.S. declaration of war, the president called on the governor of Missouri to raise eight companies of dragoons and two companies of light artillery for the conquest of New Mexico. Command of this Army of New Mexico was given to Colonel Stephen Watts Kearny, commander of the Third Military Department in 1846. Recruiting proved easy, and the First Regiment of Missouri Mounted Volunteers, 856 men, was soon filled to capacity. Elected commander of this unit was Alexander W. Doniphan, who was given the rank of colonel. Other units, including the 1st Dragoons of the regular army, brought Kearny's total strength to 1,658. After twenty days of drill, the move toward Santa Fe began on 5 June. A month later, on 5 July, the first units reached Council Grove, where a halt was called for the men to rest before beginning the five hundred-mile trek to Bent's Fort (in present-day southeast Colorado), at which point the first elements arrived on 22 July.

Accompanying the soldiers west from Missouri was a wagon train of 414 vehicles belonging to civilian traders anxious to do business in Santa Fe and another one hundred wagons loaded with provisions and supplies for the soldiers, along with eight hundred cattle for food.

At Bent's Fort, Kearny allowed his weary men to rest from the hardships of the trail. Informants had brought him word that New Mexico Governor Manuel Armijo had called twenty-five hundred men to defend Santa Fe and that another army was assembling at Taos, making a total enemy force of more than three thousand. These troops, however, mainly were raw recruits with little inclination to fight, but thanks to geography they stood a real chance of victory. A short distance east of Santa Fe was Apache Canyon, a narrow mountain pass through which the Americans would have to pass in order to reach Santa Fe. A handful of loyal Mexicans, even those with few military skills, could hold off Kearny's army until heat, hunger, and thirst forced their retreat or surrender.

As Kearny pondered his options, a wagon arrived on 27 July bringing James Wiley Magoffin, a Santa Fe trader who spoke fluent Spanish and was a friend of Governor Armijo. He brought Kearny letters from President Polk and Secretary of War William L. Marcy, which instructed Kearny to allow Magoffin to go ahead of the Army of the West to negotiate with Governor Armijo.

A man of cunning and greed, Armijo, said Magoffin, was not courageous. In fact, one of the New Mexican governor's favorite sayings was, "It is better to be thought brave than to be so." In short, he might be persuaded to surrender the province without a shot being fired.

After conferring with Magoffin, Kearny announced that he would protect the property of all New Mexicans who did not resist the U.S. occupation and that New Mexicans would have full civil and religious freedom. On 31 July, Magoffin departed ahead of Kearny's army for Santa Fe accompanied by twelve dragoons under the command of Captain Philip St. George Cooke. On 1–2 August, Kearny's army left Bent's Fort to march south through Raton Pass and enter New Mexico.

Magoffin was hospitably received in Santa Fe on 12 August by Armijo, who soon was persuaded that resistance was useless. Some reports indicate the method of persuasion was a satchel filled with gold brought by Magoffin from Washington. The governor never stated his intentions. The military commander in New Mexico, Colonel Diego Archuleta, was told that the Americans intended to take only that part of the province east of the Rio Grande and that an enterprising officer might make himself governor of that part of the province west of the river. The conference adjourned on a cordial note.

The next morning, 13 August, Magoffin prepared a sealed packet for Kearny, which Captain Cooke set out to deliver.

Meanwhile, Kearny and the Army of the West had been making its way south, arriving at Las Vegas on 15 August, just after a courier arrived with dispatches from Washington and Kearny's commission as a brigadier general, with date of rank from 30 June. Kearny proclaimed that New Mexico was part of the United States and to the assembled citizens of Las Vegas promised them freedom of religion and security of property. Everyone then was administered an oath of allegiance to the United States.

The next day, 16 August, just west of Las Vegas, Kearny received Magoffin's report from Captain Cooke. Whatever its content, Kearny continued his march westward. Armijo, meanwhile, did lead his army from Santa Fe to Apache Canyon, taking up a position there on 16 August. The next morning, however, he ordered his troops home, spiked eight cannon and hid them in the woods, and fled south to the neighboring Mexican state of Chihuahua. That afternoon the U.S. army reached Apache Canyon and were able to march through it the next morning without opposition.

On 18 August, in a driving rain, Kearny read General Order Thirteen to his troops, which declared New Mexico east of the Rio Grande annexed to the United States as part of Texas and ordered the soldiers to respect persons and property in New Mexico. That evening the army entered Santa Fe without firing a shot. The U.S. flag was raised in the central plaza on a makeshift flagpole accompanied by a salute of thirteen shots from a howitzer.

The next morning, 19 August, Kearny issued a formal proclamation to the people of New Mexico from the plaza in Santa Fe. In this he declared himself governor of the province, which was declared part of the United States. He then administered an oath of loyalty to local officials, whom he left in office. Three days later another proclamation announced that all of New Mexico had been annexed. Subsequently, he issued a code of laws (known as the Kearny Code), and a territorial constitution was drafted. William Bent was named acting governor along with a slate of civil officials.

This work done, Kearny then divided his command into four parts. A significant portion of the troops, under the command of Colonel Sterling Price, would remain in New Mexico as an army of occupation. Kearny personally would lead three hundred dragoons to California to conquer that province, while Colonel Doniphan and his Missouri Mounted Volunteers were to subdue troublesome Indians in New Mexico, particularly the Navajo, then march southward to Chihuahua City, after which they were to move east to link up with General Taylor's force.

The fourth part of the Army of the West consisted of a curious sidelight to the war with Mexico. On 25 September, after Kearny had departed Santa Fe for California, word reached him of the arrival in Santa Fe of a special unit of troops, which consisted of about five hundred Mormons, members of the Church of Jesus Christ of Latter-Day Saints, who had been enlisted into the U.S. Army at the request of their leader, Brigham Young. Their pay would go directly to the church to help finance the epic trek of the Mormons from Illinois to Utah. These men, known as the Mormon Battalion, had followed Kearny down the Santa Fe Trail and were in that city awaiting orders. Kearny decided that the Mormon Battalion should follow him to California, blazing a wagon road on the way. At Kearny's orders, Colonel Cooke took command of this unique battalion.

The units under Kearny, Doniphan, and Cooke had just departed Santa Fe when trouble began. Price's troops, unhappy at being left behind for garrison duty, began drinking, gambling, and cursing the local population. By 1 December Colonel Archuleta found willing recruits for an uprising to reclaim the province for Mexico. The conspirators gathered arms and ammunition in secret, planning an uprising for 19 December, then postponed it to Christmas Eve. U.S. authorities learned of the uprising, however, and arrested some of the conspirators, whereupon Archuleta and others fled to

Chihuahua. On 5 January 1847 Governor Bent issued a proclamation describing what had transpired and asked the people to remain loyal.

Thinking all danger past, Bent went to Taos to visit his family. On 19 January the rebellion finally began under the leadership of Pablo Montoya, a self-styled "Santa Anna of the North," and Tomasito, an Indian; most of their followers were from Taos Pueblo, along with some Mexican sympathizers. On the first day of the uprising, Governor Bent was killed and scalped, as were five other men, while seven more Americans were killed at Turley's Mill and a similar number at the town of Mora.

Colonel Price heard of the outbreak on 20 January and quickly gathered a force to crush the rebels. Marching 279 men north through bitter cold, he met fifteen hundred insurgents at La Canada on 24 January and won a decisive victory. Five days later Price won another battle against six hundred to seven hundred Mexicans and Indians. On 3 February he entered Taos to find the remaining seven hundred rebels had taken refuge inside Taos Pueblo, which was stormed in a battle in which seven of Price's force were killed and approximately 150 rebels died. The fifteen ringleaders of the revolt, including Montoya, were tried by a makeshift court and hanged, bringing an end to the New Mexican uprising.

Doniphan's Missouri Mounted Volunteers, meanwhile, set out in October 1846 to negotiate a peace treaty with the Navajo, who had raided in New Mexico for centuries. Marching west in three columns that converged at Ojo Oso (Bear Springs, near present-day Gallup), these volunteers had not been paid, they had no supply train, and they were without winter clothing. Despite snowstorms, typhoid fever, and other problems, they made their rendezvous, and on 21–22 November, Doniphan conferred with Navajo leaders at Ojo Oso. On 26 November, Doniphan held another conference, this one with Zuni leaders. His message to the leaders of both tribes was the same—New Mexico had become part of the United States, the Indians were to cease raiding on pain of severe punishment, and they should learn to trade. He persuaded both the Navajo and Zuni to sign treaties with the United States.

His task with the Indians concluded, Doniphan on 1 December began moving his men down the Rio Grande to fulfill the remaining part of his orders. His ragged army was accompanied by 315 wagons of traders anxious to penetrate Chihuahua. George Ruxton, an English observer, commented that the Missouri Mounted Volunteers did not look like an army, saying they sat about in the evening "playing cards, and swearing and cursing, even at the officers." Doniphan dressed in ragged clothing, pitched his own tent, cooked his own meals, and swore like the rest of the men.

Subsisting on half rations, Doniphan's men nevertheless managed to march about fifty miles a day. As they approached El Paso del Norte (present-day Juárez, Mexico), they learned that a Mexican force of about five hundred men and one two-pound howitzer were waiting for them about thirty miles north of El Paso at El Brazito. On 25 December their commander, Brevet Lieutenant Colonel Juan Ponce de León, sent a lieutenant forward under a flag of truce to demand Doniphan's surrender or else his force would charge and annihilate the Missourians. Doniphan calmly replied, "Charge and be damned!"

When Ponce de León ordered his men forward, the Missourians patiently waited, then opened fire with devastating result. The enemy soon was in disorganized retreat. Seven Americans were slightly wounded, while Ponce de León had lost approximately one hundred men and his howitzer. The fleeing Mexican force did not halt at El Paso, but chose to continue southward to Chihuahua City. A delegation of leading citizens from El Paso then invited Doniphan into town, where his men soon were feasting to make up for the lost rations, drinking the strong local brew, and fighting the town's men for the affections of their women.

It was in El Paso that Doniphan learned of the uprising at Santa Fe, which, if successful, would cut him off from supplies and a route of retreat.

He also learned that the Mexicans three hundred miles to the south at Chihuahua City were preparing a stout defense if he advanced. Without waiting to learn the fate of Price and his men, he chose to march south. The advance began on 8 February 1847 with 924 effectives and approximately three hundred wagons driven by traders. This march was one of great hardship—cold nights, hot days, storms that battered tents, shortages of food and water, and even a grass fire.

At Chihuahua City a confident Mexican force of twelve hundred cavalry and fifteen hundred infantry, all well-armed, along with one thousand ranch workers armed with lances and machetes, awaited Doniphan. Breastworks were erected fifteen miles north of town on the south bank of the Sacramento River, and ten cannon, ranging from 4- to 9-pounders, were in place. Commanding these troops was Brigadier General José Antonio de Heredia with Governor Angel Trías Alvarez as his second. Before the battle commenced, Brigadier General Pedro García Condé, a professional soldier and diplomat, arrived on the scene. Because of their superior numbers, an entrenched position, ten cannon, and good leadership, morale was high among the Mexican troops.

The Missourians and their entourage of traders approached the Sacramento River on the morning of 28 February 1847. Viewing the Mexican defenses, Doniphan chose to execute a flanking movement, ordering his men to turn right and then cross downriver, bringing them against the Mexicans from a not-so-stoutly-defended position. This maneuver was executed despite the hardship of steep river banks, even by the traders and their wagons.

About 3:00 that afternoon both sides opened fire with their artillery, the Americans using solid and chain shot, their shells demoralizing the Mexican lancers who charged. The Mexican artillery was using locally made gunpowder, which proved so inferior that their shots reached the American lines only on the bounce, easily seen and dodged. After this opening artillery duel, Doniphan called for a charge that quickly breached the Mexican lines. By 5:00 the shooting was almost over. A count of casualties showed four Americans dead and eight wounded, while the Mexicans had lost three hundred killed and another three hundred wounded. Governor Trías and General Heredia fled toward Mexico City, and the next morning, 1 March, Doniphan and his men entered Chihuahua City unopposed.

Within a few weeks almost 30 percent of the Missourians were on the sick list, many with venereal disease, the rest with diarrhea and assorted fevers. The small scouting party Doniphan sent east found General Taylor at Saltillo, and on 23 April the scouts returned to Chihuahua City with orders for Doniphan to join the larger American force to the southeast.

In late April the Missourans began a march in two sections, arriving at Saltillo on 21 May in ragged condition. After a brief rest, they marched on to Monterrey and then to the mouth of the Rio Grande. There they boarded ship for New Orleans, where they were taken aboard steamboats for a return to Saint Louis to be mustered out of service—and to be paid for the first time since they had volunteered. They had marched six thousand miles, had fought and won two major battles, had promoted trade and commerce, and had helped conquer and annex New Mexico to the United States, all without uniforms, government supplies, commissary, or paymaster.

THE PACIFIC COAST

Before the war with Mexico began, President Polk had taken steps to protect U.S. interests in California. On 17 October 1845, to offset British and French intrigues there, he had appointed Thomas 0. Larkin, U.S. consul at Monterey, a confidential agent in the province. Larkin was told to work against any transfer of ownership to France or England. Polk's instructions had been communicated by Secretary of State James Buchanan and were very clear: "Whilst the President will make no effort and use no influence to induce California to become one of the free and independent States of this Union, yet if the people should desire to unite their destiny with ours, they would be received as brethren, whenever this can be done without affording Mexico just cause of complaint." The U.S. policy, Secretary Buchanan wrote, was to "let events take their course, unless an attempt should be made to transfer them [Californians] without their consent either to Great Britain or France. This they ought to resist."

Polk also had taken precautions to see that U.S. aid was readily available should the Californians rise up in rebellion in order to join the United States or if force was needed to prevent a transfer to British ownership. In 1845 Polk had sent an officer of the Corps of Topographical Engineers, Captain John Charles Frémont, west with a party of sixty-two soldiers ostensibly on a mapping expedition. Guided by the scout Kit Carson, Frémont had arrived in California late in 1845 only to be ordered out of the province. Early in 1846 he and his soldiers were encamped near Klamath Lake on the California-Oregon border, obviously waiting to intervene at a moment's notice.

Also ready to intervene was the Pacific Squadron of the U.S. Navy. The navy at this time was deployed in two squadrons, the Home Squadron, operating in the Atlantic and the Gulf of Mexico, and the Pacific Squadron. The West Coast squadron consisted of two seventy-gun warships and six lesser vessels and were under the command of Commodore John D. Sloat. Taking command on 18 November 1845, Sloat remained in the harbor at Mazatlán waiting for orders.

Such was the situation in the spring of 1846 when U.S. Marine Corps Lieutenant Archibald Gillespie was sent by Polk with secret instructions, some written, some oral, for Sloat, Larkin, and Frémont. Traveling under the guise of a Boston company's commercial agent, Gillespie set out late in 1845 and made his way to Veracruz, thence overland to Mazatlán, where he found Sloat and elements of the Pacific Squadron. The orders Sloat received from Gillespie were to cruise within striking distance of Monterey and to avoid aggression, but he was to seize and hold the ports of California on first word of an outbreak of war with Mexico.

Sailing on to Monterey, Gillespie next met with Larkin, after which he set out overland to find Frémont. He found him on 9 May 1846, the same day that Taylor's troops were rejoicing after their victory at Resaca de la Palma. Gillespie later said the oral orders he transmitted from the president to Frémont were "to watch over the interests of the United States, and counteract the influence of any foreign agents who might be in the country with objects prejudicial to the United States."

Frémont's response to Gillespie's arrival was immediate. He resigned his commission in the army and set out for California, sending Gillespie to rendezvous with a U.S. warship at San Francisco to procure arms and supplies for the insurgents Frémont intended to raise. At the town of Sonoma on 14 June, a group of U.S. civilians who had moved to California earlier, led by Ezekiel Merritt and William B. Ide, seized a store of arms and ammunition, devised a flag decorated with the Lone Star of Texas and a grizzly bear, and began what came to be known as the Bear Flag Revolt.

On hearing of this declaration, the military commander governing the northern portion of the province, General José Castro, sent men north to disperse the revolutionists. A brief skirmish on 24 June, called the Battle of Olompali, forced the Mexicans to retreat. It was then that Frémont assumed command of the Bear Flag Revolt, seized the ungarrisoned fort at San Francisco, and spiked its guns. On 5 July he formally organized the California Battalion with himself as commander and Gillespie as his adjutant.

At this juncture Commodore Sloat and the U.S. Navy intervened. Arriving at Monterey on 2 July aboard the *Savannah*, Sloat counseled with Larkin. On 6 July he sent Captain John B. Montgomery and the *Portsmouth* to take San Francisco, and the next day ordered Captain William Mervine ashore at Monterey with 165 sailors and eight-five marines. After the U.S. flag was raised over the customshouse on 9 July, Mervine read Sloat's proclamation, which stated

that California henceforth "was a portion of the United States" and that its residents were U.S. citizens who would be protected in their religion and property. Castro and his adherents fled southward to Los Angeles to link up with California Governor Pío Pico.

On 16 July, British Admiral Sir George E. Seymour arrived at Monterey aboard the eighty-gun *Collingwood*. A week later he sailed away, reporting to his superiors that there was nothing he could do. His presence and the content of his message clearly indicated that British designs on California had been thwarted by the measures taken by Polk.

At this juncture Commodore Robert Field Stockton arrived in California, and on 23 July he officially assumed command of the Pacific Squadron, replacing Sloat. That same day he enrolled the California Battalion as a volunteer force in the U.S. Army, naming Frémont its major and Gillespie its captain. He then loaded Frémont and the volunteers aboard the *Cyane* and sent them to San Diego to attack Castro, Governor Pico, and loyalist Mexican forces from the rear. With Frémont in command at San Diego and advancing toward Los Angeles and with another U.S. force coming from San Pedro, landed there by the navy, Castro and Pico realized that they had lost. On 10 August they fled southeastward to Sonora, thereby ending all Mexican resistance.

On 17 August, Stockton issued another proclamation, this one declaring all of California to be under martial law. He divided the province into two parts with Frémont at Monterey in charge of the northern half and Gillespie administering the southern portion. Kit Carson was sent overland to Washington, D.C., with dispatches reporting all that had transpired.

On 6 October at the New Mexican village of Socorro, sixty miles south of Albuquerque, Carson met General Kearny and his three hundred dragoons bound for California. On learning of the conquest of California, Kearny sent two hundred dragoons back to Santa Fe and proceeded westward with one hundred men guided by Carson, whom he persuaded to accompany him. His intent was to go to California and assume control over the new U.S. territory, believing he needed only a token force.

Passing the ancient copper mines at Santa Rita and crossing the Continental Divide, this column marched to the headwaters of the Gila River, which they followed to the Colorado River. Near the junction of the Gila and Colorado on 22 November, Kearny learned that a counterrevolution was under way in California under the leadership of José María Flores.

These Mexican patriots had driven Gillespie out of Los Angeles in September and soon had control of the entire southern part of the province except for San Diego and San Pedro, which were under the protection of guns aboard U.S. naval vessels. The exultant Mexicans then convened a legislative body in Los Angeles to name Flores governor and commanding general and to declare martial law.

The army of this body met Kearny's dragoons at San Pasqual on 6 December, thirty-five miles northeast of San Diego, under the command of Captain Andrés Pico, brother of the departed governor. Incredibly, the U.S. soldiers had allowed their powder to get wet and their horses were jaded. Nevertheless, Kearny ordered a charge. Pico's men used lances with deadly precision to kill eighteen Americans and wound a similar number. That evening Carson and Lieutenant Edward Fitzgerald Beale slipped through the enemy lines, reached San Diego, and informed Commodore Stockton of Kearny's plight. Stockton sent two hundred marines, which enabled Kearny to break out of his encirclement on 10 December and to reach San Diego two days later.

The combined forces at San Diego marched out as a land force on 29 December with Stockton commanding and Kearny as executive officer. They met Governor Flores and a force of 450 Mexicans on 8 January 1847 at Bartolo Ford on the San Gabriel River (twelve miles from Los Angeles). After brief skirmishing that day and the next, Flores fled to Mexico, and U.S. forces once again victoriously entered Los Angeles. Frémont, advanced to the rank of brevet lieutenant colonel, came south from Sacramento

and on 13 January received the surrender of Andrés Pico and the remaining insurgents, signing the Treaty of Cahuenga. The war for California was over, but the battle to govern it had just begun.

Stockton's orders from the Navy Department concerning the government of California were vague, but he interpreted them broadly and named Frémont governor of the territory before departing. Kearny's orders from the War Department were not vague; he had been told to take and govern California, and he refused to recognize Frémont's appointment. The headstrong, politically ambitious Frémont refused to relinquish the governor's office despite repeated orders from Kearny to do so.

When orders came from Washington on 7 March 1847 upholding Kearny's claim, he arrested Frémont, charged him with mutiny and insubordination, and sent him to Washington for court-martial. The court found Frémont guilty on 31 January 1848 and sentenced him to dismissal from the army. President Polk approved the verdict but remitted the penalty, whereupon Frémont in anger resigned his commission. He returned to California, where he acquired a large land grant, and 1850 became a senator when California entered the Union.

While these events were unfolding, the Mormon Battalion was opening a wagon road from New Mexico to California. Departing Santa Fe on 19 October 1846, this battalion came down the Rio Grande to a point below Socorro, then turned to the southwest to Playas Lake and followed an ancient Spanish-Mexican road to Janos, Chihuahua. From there the column turned westward to the valley of the Santa Cruz River, then went north down this river toward Tucson, which it entered unopposed on 18 December. Continuing north to the Gila, the Mormons then went down this stream to Yuma Crossing and California soil. Crossing the final mountain range, the coastal sierra, the Mormons suffered mightily before reaching San Diego on 29 January 1847. In his final report Cooke wrote, ''Marching half naked and half fed, and living upon wild animals, we have discovered and made a road of great value to our country." Indeed they had, for Cooke's Wagon Road, later called the Gila Trail, would become a principal route to the gold fields for the forty-niners.

The Pacific Squadron did more than merely assist in the conquest of California. It also blockaded Guaymas, Sonora, the major Mexican port in the Gulf of California. On 22 January 1847, before Stockton could take further measures, he was replaced by Commodore William Branford Shubrick, who exercised command from January to March of 1847 and from 19 July 1847 to the end of the war. When he arrived in California, Shubrick found that the Pacific Squadron consisted of seven warships and two supply vessels. He supplemented the squadron by commandeering commercial ships, whose owners subsequently filed exorbitant claims for their services. Between March and July 1847 the Pacific Squadron was commanded by Commodore James Biddle.

On Commodore Biddle's orders, Commander John B. Montgomery sailed the *Portsmouth* to San José, at the tip of Baja California, and a landing party of 140 men occupied the city on 30 March 1847. Another landing party went ashore unopposed at Cabo San Lucas, and a third party took the port of La Paz on 14 April. The mainland ports of Guaymas and San Blas were blockaded despite inclement weather, and that fall they and Mazatlán were occupied by landing parties, as was Muleje in Baja California. The only battle occurred at Guaymas, when troops came ashore on 17 October. At Mazatlán on 10 November the twelve hunderd Mexican soldiers in the city at first threatened to fight, but when Shubrick sent 750 men ashore, the Mexicans withdrew without firing a shot.

In almost two years of warfare (July 1846 to May 1848), the Pacific Squadron was a decisive factor on the West Coast of North America. Shubrick's final report to the secretary of the navy proudly noted his men had occupied twelve Mexican Pacific port cities and had destroyed or confiscated forty enemy ships, mostly coastal vessels. He had accomplished this with never more than ten naval vessels at his command, and his men had collected sufficient customs duties in those port cities to offset the cost of his operations.

GULF COAST OPERATIONS

The Home Squadron of the U.S. Navy, with a supply depot at Pensacola, Florida, numbered seven steamers, three frigates, six sloops, one schooner, five brigs, seven gunboats, and four bomb vessels. The largest was the fifty-gun *Raritan*. Commanding the Home Squadron at the outbreak of hostilities was Commodore David Conner. His first task was to blockade Mexican Gulf ports in order to prevent the arrival of arms and munitions from Europe, to wage war on any privateers that might try to operate out of Mexico, and to support General Taylor. Despite the fact that the mouth of the Rio Grande was nine hundred miles from Pensacola, ships of the Home Squadron actively aided Taylor, even contributing five hundred sailors and marines for combat and continuously landing supplies for Taylor's troops at Point Isabel during 1846 and 1847.

To make the blockade truly effective, Conner knew he had to occupy the principal Mexican ports. Moreover, if these ports were captured, his men could collect the customs duties and use the money to buy supplies for his fleet. Thus, on 8 June 1846 a naval expedition attacked Tampico, which was taken on 10 November. On 23 October, Conner's second-in-command, Captain Matthew C. Perry, occupied Frontera, a port at the mouth of the Tabasco River and an important source of cattle. In addition, Conner was effective in obtaining the neutrality of the Mexican state of Yucatán. Conner sent Perry with four ships to occupy the major port of Carmen in this state, which was accomplished on 2 December.

Conner's most important service, however, was transporting Major General Scott and more than twelve thousand soldiers to land at Veracruz in February 1847. President Polk ordered this invasion as much because of politics as for reasons of military strategy. By late 1847 Zachary Taylor had become so popular that the president decided to order him to halt at Monterrey and to send most of his regular troops for an invasion of Mexico at Veracruz. The officer chosen to head this new effort was Scott, the commanding general of the army.

On 18 November 1846 Polk gave his orders to "Old Fuss and Feathers," as the troops called Scott, who since the outbreak of hostilities had argued that Mexico could be conquered only by the occupation of its capital. Moreover, he said this could not be done by invading across the northern deserts, but rather would have to follow the route of Hernando Cortes in his conquest of the Aztecs—a thrust from Veracruz to Mexico City. Polk's orders to Scott, delivered through Secretary of War William L. Marcy on 23 November, were purposefully vague: "The President, several days since, communicated in person to you his orders to repair to Mexico, to take the command of the forces there assembled, and particularly to organize and set on foot an expedition to operate on the Gulf coast, if, on arriving at the theater of action, you shall deem it practicable." Responsibility for any failure clearly would fall on the general, not the president.

Shortly after Scott sailed for New Orleans and then to Brazos Santiago at the mouth of the Rio Grande, intrigues began in Washington to name Senator Thomas Hart Benton a lieutenant general, thereby having him outrank Major General Scott. Congress refused to approve this, but President Polk satisfied his partisan feelings by refusing to give Scott adequate financial and logistic support for the campaign.

The army of invasion was delayed at Brazos Santiago because the president failed to order the necessary transport vessels. When the ships did arrive, most were sailing vessels despite Polk's promise to Scott that all would be steam-powered. The army finally embarked the second week in February 1847 and paused briefly at Tampico on 19–20 February. While at Tampico, Scott issued General Order No. 20 (later reissued at Veracruz, Puebla, and Mexico City),

which was designed to prevent atrocities. It said that soldiers committing what would have been civil crimes at home would be punished in military courts. In effect, the order meant Scott had established martial law in all areas occupied by U.S. troops.

Scott arrived on 7 March at Antón Lizardo, an anchorage thirty miles south of Veracruz that was to be the staging area for the invasion. Scott faced a need for haste, for the heat of late spring would mark the beginning of the deadly yellow fever season. Knowing Veracruz to be heavily defended, Scott conferred with his generals about a course of action. The fortress of San Juan de Ulúa in the harbor was formidable, and it was known that there were more than three hundred serviceable cannon and mortars in the city pointing seaward to defend it against naval invasion. His staff advised a frontal assault, one certain to win public admiration for heroics, but Scott feared that such an assault would so decimate his ranks that he would have insufficient troops to continue to the interior of Mexico. He also could not rely on a siege to accomplish his purpose because the port could be reprovisioned from the interior.

His decision was daring. He would put ashore his 12,803 men, along with horses, cannon, and supplies, by amphibious landing at the beach of Collado, three miles southeast of Veracruz, thereby bypassing San Juan de Ulúa and the other defenses by attacking Veracruz from the undefended rear. Scott and Commodore Conner devised an elaborate flag system of communication between the army and the fleet of approximately one hundred ships, and at sunrise on 9 March the operation began, the first amphibious landing in U.S. history. Using sixty-seven whale boats that transported sixty to eighty men each, the first wave of forty-five hundred men went ashore at 6:00 P.M., and by 10:00 more than ten thousand men had been landed along with their equipment and supplies. The entire operation took only sixteen hours and was completed without a casualty. The following day the remaining men and equipment were brought ashore, and by 15 March Veracruz was surrounded by land and blockaded by sea. On 21 March, just as the battle was about to be joined, Conner was succeeded as commodore of the Home Squadron by Perry. He loaned Scott some of his siege guns, which were manned by navy crews after being hauled ashore and wrestled into position.

After Scott went through the formality of asking the commander of Veracruz to surrender, the siege began on 22 March with a roar of cannon from both land and Perry's fleet. On 27 March, Scott halted the shelling to inform the Mexican commander, General Juan Morales, that if he did not surrender by 6:00 the following morning, the town would be stormed. Morales saw no reason to fight and on 28 March signed articles of capitulation. The Mexicans were allowed the honors of war—soldiers were paroled on oath not to fight again and persons and property were to be respected. Scott had taken the city with only nineteen Americans killed and sixty-three wounded in skirmishing. On 29 March, Conner sailed for Washington with dispatches telling of this astonishing victory.

In Mexico City news of the defeat caused little panic, because, in the past, armies invading Mexico usually paused long enough at Veracruz for yellow fever to decimate their ranks. Scott, however, wasted no time. Buying supplies from Mexican merchants, who preferred U.S. Treasury drafts to the confiscation methods of Mexican officials, he sent Brigadier General Twiggs and the First Division marching inland on 8 April, soon followed by most of the remainder of his force, a total of eighty-five hundred men. Only a small garrison was left behind to hold Veracruz. The remainder of the army brought ashore at Veracruz were volunteers whose term of service had expired and they were sent home. As Scott marched inland, he was plagued constantly by problems of supply and manpower, because President Polk was slow to send either to support the campaign of the Whig general.

POLITICAL MANEUVERING

In the United States both Democrats and Whigs were seeking in every way to gain political advantage from the conflict. Polk's war message to Congress in May 1846 had triggered the outbreak of this bickering. The Whig-abolitionist position was that the Texas Revolution had been the result of a conspiracy among southern slaveowners to steal Texas from Mexico, that Polk's order moving Taylor from the mouth of the Nueces River to the mouth of the Rio Grande was a provocation, and that southern Democrats were promoting the war in order to gain additional slave territory, especially California.

The charge that the Nueces was the real boundary received the most Whig-abolitionist play. Most abolitionists were forced to admit that the Texas Revolution and annexation were accomplished facts, and the California question was intertwined in the Oregon boundary dispute then under negotiation with England. The claim that the Nueces was the true boundary of Texas, however, was made entirely in the United States, because the Mexican position was that all of Texas belonged to Mexico and that the Sabine River was the boundary. Despite these charges, the war bill passed, and the response in all parts of the United States was enthusiastic. There was continuing Whig-abolitionist opposition that was vocal but not violent, but the overwhelming majority of Americans supported Polk and the war.

The abolitionists found a champion in Congressman David Wilmot of Pennsylvania. Elected in 1844 as a Polk Democrat, he nevertheless introduced an amendment to a $2 million war appropriation bill in August 1846 providing that no slavery should ever exist in any territory acquired as a result of negotiations or war with Mexico. Debate on the amendment was especially bitter, raising questions of constitutionality that would not be resolved until the end of the Civil War. The Wilmot Proviso caused a split in both the Whig and Democratic parties, nearly 40 percent of Democrats voting for it in the House and 30 percent of the Whigs voting against it. The bill was passed in the House and went to the Senate, which adjourned without voting on it, but the Wilmot Proviso did not die. When reintroduced in the next session of Congress, beginning in December 1846, it passed the House by a vote of 115 to 106, but it failed in the Senate by a vote of 31 to 21, with splits in both parties and heated debate. The proviso had delayed a much-needed war appropriation by six months, and it continued to be introduced as an amendment to dozens of bills. Abraham Lincoln, then serving in the House of Representatives, later said he voted for the Wilmot Proviso at least forty times.

In the bitter off-year election of 1846, Whigs won control of the House of Representatives, and they smelled victory in the upcoming presidential election of 1848. Despite their opposition to any extension of slavery as a result of the war, northern Whigs joined their southern brethren in talking openly of nominating a military hero—someone such as Taylor or Scott—as their candidate for the presidency, which created great difficulty for Polk and the Democrats. They wanted to win the war, but neither Scott nor Taylor could be allowed to develop a heroic public image. Thus, neither general ever got the political and logistical support he deserved, especially Scott. Because Taylor had been the early hero of the war, Polk had ordered him to halt in northern Mexico and had taken most of his troops from him, giving command of the invasion at Veracruz to Scott.

Moreover, there were various peace movements in the United States creating some opposition to the war, including such organizations as the Non-Resistant Peace Society founded by abolitionist William Lloyd Garrison and others. These peace groups denounced Polk and his administration and demanded an end to war. Among religious sects, the most unwavering opposition came from Quakers, Unitarians, and Congregationalists. Because these denominations were strongest in New England, it was from there that they harangued the president and deluged the public with antiwar propaganda.

Because of such opposition, as well as political considerations Polk repeatedly tried to negotiate peace treaty with Mexico. In May 1846 he asked Bishop John Joseph Hughes of New York to influence the Catholic church in Mexico to

help in restoring peace. In July 1846, Secretary of State Buchanan sent dispatches to Mexico suggesting negotiations for peace, but these were rejected. Other efforts also came to naught.

Following the off-year elections in November 1846, in which the Whigs gained control of the House, and because of the vocal minority of peace advocates in the United States, Polk decided on a major peace initiative. He appointed Nicholas P. Trist, chief clerk in the State Department, to secretly accompany Scott to Mexico. Carrying a variety of proposals for ending the war with him, Trist slipped out of Washington on 16 April 1847 for New Orleans and then went by ship to Veracruz, arriving on 6 May. From Veracruz he was to make his way to Scott's headquarters and accompany the army as it marched inland to Mexico City.

In Mexico the opposition to war was far more vocal, leading to continued political instability. After they provoked an outbreak of hostilities, Paredes and his advisers found that their hopes for aid from England and France had been ill-founded. After the defeats at Palo Alto and Resaca de la Palma, public opinion welled up against the regime. Various Mexican commanders resorted to pamphlets to "explain" their actions, and Arista was arrested and later court-martialed.

When Taylor crossed the Rio Grande and took Matamoros in April 1846, Paredes was confronted with a separatist movement and by Federalist plots. In northern Mexico there had been separatist efforts since 1835 and the Texas Revolution. In 1839 Federalists had organized the Republic of the Rio Grande (immediately south of Texas), which failed to win independence. As early as September 1845 Taylor was receiving messages from Federalists in Tamaulipas, Nuevo León, and Coahuila, saying that if war broke out these states would support the United States. Moreover, most of Taylor's supplies came from Mexican merchants anxious to take drafts on the U.S. Treasury. While Taylor was in northern Mexico, there was also talk of rebellion against the Centralist regime throughout the region. Most local citizens never gave outright military cooperation to the Americans, but there was little overt opposition.

Another area of separatist sympathies was in Yucatán, whose citizens had rebelled against centralism in 1839 and had declared their independence from Mexico in 1842. Because of its geographical isolation from the rest of Mexico, no Mexican attempt to reconquer this area had been made when war broke out. In November 1846 the Mexican government offered concessions to Yucatán if it would rejoin the nation, whereupon U.S. naval forces occupied key ports in that state. In January 1847 insurgents in Yucatán again declared independence and even sent a delegation to Washington to discuss annexation to the United States with Secretary of State Buchanan. The idea was rejected, but the hostility in Yucatán to centralism was another factor in weakening the Mexican war effort.

Following Taylor's victories on the Rio Grande, in July 1846 Paredes was faced with several uprisings in central Mexico, some of them Federalist, some personally directed against him. From Havana, Cuba, came word that Santa Anna was opposed to the monarchical tendencies of Paredes, causing Almonte to swing his allegiance to Santa Anna. Moreover, Gómez Farías, leader of a radical group of Federalists, began planning a coup. On 28 July Paredes announced that he was leaving Mexico City to take personal command of the army, but stayed in hiding in the city. His de facto resignation allowed the reins of government to fall to Vice-president Nicolas Bravo.

On 3 August, Bravo proclaimed the restoration of constitutional government, but that same day the garrison at Veracruz pronounced in favor of Santa Anna. The next day in Mexico City the commander of local troops, General Salas, also announced for Santa Anna, and on 6 August Bravo resigned. On 22 August, Salas, guided by Farías and Federalists, announced the restoration of the constitution of 1824. It was at this juncture that Santa Anna returned to Mexico, passing through the U.S. naval blockade after assuring the Polk administration that if allowed to do so he would conclude an immediate peace. Landing at Veracruz on 16 August,

he declared his support of federalism and the constitution of 1824. Shortly afterward he assumed command of the Army of Liberation and began raising troops for it, eventually doing battle with Taylor at Buena Vista in February 1847.

Under the restored constitution, elections were held in November for delegates to a congress that was to name a new president. The man selected on 22 December 1846 was Farías, who took office two days later. He found an empty treasury, despite the millions of pesos that had been raised for the war effort by Paredes. There were so many charges of widespread corruption that efforts to levy new taxes and float new loans proved futile. Santa Anna's Buena Vista campaign was financed by a forced loan.

The only institution with wealth in Mexico was the Catholic church, and on 11 January 1847 the Mexican congress passed a law authorizing the president to use church lands as collateral for a loan, if lenders could be found, and to sell church lands if the president could not borrow. Priests were threatened with excommunication if they implemented the law, and opposition to the Federalist anticlerical policy snowballed. The militia of Mexico City turned against the regime, as did regular army units shortly afterward. By the end of February 1847 Farías was no longer able to govern and was forced from power.

At this opportune moment, Santa Anna returned from the disaster of Buena Vista to find everyone welcoming him as a potential savior of Mexico. On 23 March he formally assumed the presidency with a vote of thanks from congress for his "victory" at Buena Vista. Milking two million pesos from the church in return for an annulment of the laws of 11 January, Santa Anna then marched east from Mexico City to confront Scott, who in early April had begun marching inland from Veracruz.

SCOTT'S DECISIVE CAMPAIGN

Santa Anna's chosen site for a battle with the invading Americans was Cerro Gordo, one of those places that nature seemingly created for a defensive army. Just east of the little village of Plan del Rio, the road wound upward six to seven miles through a rocky defile from the hot and malarial coastal plain to the cool inland plateau. On the way up, the road passed between steep hills, from whose tops artillery could stop an invading army with both direct and cross fire. It was here that Santa Anna located his army, his reserves at the rear, thirty-five of his artillery pieces atop the high ground and others at strategic points, and his fifty-six hundred regulars and more than six thousand national guardsmen from the capital manning the high ground. He was confident that he and his men would win the victory that had eluded him at Buena Vista. Morale was high as they waited.

On the morning of 12 April 1847 Scott's advance unit of twenty-six hundred men commanded by General Twiggs began climbing through the gorge. Fortunately for them the Mexican artillery opened fire too soon, and they withdrew to safety. Twiggs, however, was prepared to order a charge the next morning, but his staff persuaded him to wait. Scott and additional soldiers arrived the next day—to the cheers of Twiggs's nervous soldiers—and that afternoon all were joined by General Worth and another sixteen hundred men, bringing the total U.S. force to eighty-five hundred.

Rather than order a suicidal charge into the Mexican guns, Scott sent two engineering officers into the ravines of each side, Captain Robert F. Lee and Lieutenant George H. Derby. They found a trail that bypassed the road, a difficult task because it was overgrown with cactus and chaparral, and up this trail were hauled by hand the heavy 24-pound howitzers.

Scott's major attack came on the morning of 18 April, as Americans stormed the summit and, using bayonets, pistols, and muskets as clubs, drove off the Mexicans and raised the U.S. flag. Just as Santa Anna was about to rally a counterattack, Brigadier General James Shield and three hundred men, who had circled the Mexican camp, attacked them from the rear, which threw the Mexicans into panic, and they fled, amid cries of "Everyone for himself." By

10:00 A.M. the battle was over, Santa Anna and his staff fleeing westward over the road to Mexico City. A final count of casualties showed sixty-four American dead and 353 wounded. Mexican casualties were estimated at between one thousand and twelve hundred, and another three thousand had been captured along with forty-three cannon and some four thousand small arms.

Scott could not mount an effective pursuit because he had too few cavalry, but his infantry and artillerymen advanced despite having rations for only two days in their knapsacks. The fleeing Mexicans were pursued to within four miles of Jalapa, the next village along the road to Mexico City, but the Mexican army did not halt there or at the next village, La Hoya, choosing instead to fall back toward Puebla.

Scott's soldiers entered Jalapa the morning of 19 April to an absence of hostility. In fact, the church bells were rung as if in celebration. Fortunately for his troops, Scott was able to buy supplies from Mexican merchants, because nothing was coming from the United States. It was at Jalapa that U.S. troops began to suffer terribly because of the climate. In the hot, low country, many had discarded blankets and heavy clothing. Now in the mountains, they shivered at night and many fell ill. Scott tried to send the sick back to Veracruz, but those who went found it ravaged by yellow fever. On 4 June, Scott reported to Secretary of War Marcy that he had one thousand bedridden at Veracruz and another one thousand ill at Jalapa.

Another problem Scott faced the farther he marched into the interior was keeping the road open to Veracruz. Mexican irregulars committed atrocities on stragglers and attacked supply trains, couriers, and small detachments. Scott's answer was to assign Captain Samuel H. Walker, a former Texas Ranger and designer of the six-shooter that bore his name, the Walker-Colt, to patrol the road. A regiment of Texas Rangers sent by President Polk and the secretary of war was also on patrol. Commanded by Texas Ranger Captain John Coffee Hays, these rangers did their task with such ferocity that Mexicans soon were referring to them as *los Te-*

janos sangrietes ("those bloody Texans"). When the rangers once brought in a prisoner, a soldier noted in his diary that this was considered "one of the seven wonders."

While at Jalapa, Scott sent General Worth and a division after the retreating Mexicans. Worth pursued them as far as Perote Castle, once a fortified position on the Veracruz—Mexico City road, but in use as a prison prior to the war. Worth found fifty cannon, five hundred muskets, and twenty-five thousand rounds of cannon and musket shot in the castle. He halted to await further orders.

Scott's position at this time was precarious. Food, clothing, and ammunition were in short supply, and he knew he could expect little help from Polk. Moreover, many of the enlistments of his volunteers were ending around the middle of June. When his pleas for them to reinlist failed, he sent them to the coast for shipment home, leaving him with 7,113 men. He continued his advance the first week in May, after issuing a proclamation to the Mexican people, in which he praised the valor of Mexican soldiers and blamed their defeats on generals who had lived "in idleness." He noted that his troops had given fair treatment to churches and clergy.

Santa Anna, meanwhile, had retreated to Puebla, arriving there on 11 May, and began trying to raise another army. He was facing a sullen population that finally realized that Buena Vista had been a defeat. He did manage to raise a force that he claimed numbered four thousand, but that was much nearer to twenty-five hundred. Unknown to him, however, the clergy and leading citizens in Puebla did not want a battle to take place there. They had heard that when Scott arrived in a town, the hated Mexican taxes were abolished, that the U.S. troops respected persons and property, that religion and churches were left alone, and that Scott paid for supplies with valid drafts drawn on the U.S. treasury. Therefore, they sent word to the advancing Americans that the city would be open to them.

Santa Anna did his utmost, seizing horses, conscripting men, and forcing loans, but when

Worth and General John Anthony Quitman approached with a U.S. force, the Mexican leader was able to make only a token attack with about two thousand men. Seeing many of his men desert under cover of battle, Santa Anna fled toward Mexico City. Worth and Quitman entered Puebla unopposed on the morning of 15 May.

At Puebla, Scott was able to provision his troops from the countryside, as well as to purchase clothing and shoes for them from merchants in the city. Had it not been for Mexicans who hated their own government and were willing to trade with the Americans, Scott would have been forced to withdraw. Moreover, Scott chose to wait at Puebla until volunteers began arriving from the United States. By 3 July he had 8,061 effectives and 2,215 sick at Puebla. On 6 August twenty-five hundred men arrived from Veracruz under command of Brigadier General Franklin Pierce, by which time Scott's army had grown to almost fourteen thousand (of whom twenty-five hundred were ill and another six hundred convalescent and unable to perform their duties).

As Scott waited in Puebla, confusion reigned in Mexico City. Plan followed plan for defense of the city, and orders went out to the Mexican states for a loan of twenty million pesos, which never was delivered. The states were also sent quotas to bring thirty-two thousand men to the capital's defense, but few responded. Santa Anna arrived into this troubled situation on 19 May with three thousand men. The next day he announced that, despite his wishes to the contrary, he would assume the presidency. He tried to win popular support by announcing freedom of the press, but when bitter attacks resulted he announced his resignation, only to retract it on 2 June, suspend freedom of the press, and lock up his political opponents. He had become a virtual dictator with little popular support.

With great energy, however, Santa Anna set about preparing his defenses. Cannon were cast from melted bells, arms were confiscated from private citizens, gunpowder was manufactured, and bullets were molded. He united the three thousand men he had brought with him with the two thousand regulars and eight thousand militia in the capital. This army was augmented by all the able-bodied men he could conscript, bringing his force to twenty-five thousand. His strategy was to concentrate his troops to defend the city en masse. The perimeter would be rimmed with fortifications guarded by militia, while regulars would rush to any threatened point. General Juan Alvarez, commanding the Army of the South outside the city, was ordered to move behind Scott and harass his advance and destroy him when he retreated.

The president-general ordered outlying villages emptied, laborers were conscripted, and the prisons emptied. All the men were used to dig gun emplacements, parapets, breastworks, and trenches to be filled with water, which Santa Anna decreed must be completed in just eight days. By 9 August all was in readiness, and Santa Anna issued a proclamation designed to increase morale: "Blinded by pride the enemy have set out for the capital. For this, Mexicans, I congratulate myself and you."

Meanwhile in England, the Duke of Wellington was following Scott's campaign closely, and he commented to his junior officers, "Scott is lost. He cannot capture the city and he cannot fall back upon his base."

On 7 August, Scott began his advance from Puebla, with Twiggs's division in the lead and other units following, a total of 10,738 men and officers. The road crested at 10,500 feet about thirty-six miles outside Mexico City and before them lay the beautiful valley of Mexico, unconquered by a foreign army since Cortes had defeated the Aztecs in 1519–1521. On 9 August the advance halted at Ayotla, fifteen miles outside the capital. Scott looked at his maps and listened to the reports of his scouts on the fortifications ahead.

Scott's decision was to avoid the bulk of Santa Anna's defenses by swinging most of his army to the south around Lake Chalco through unguarded wastelands, cold lava flows called *pedregals*, which the Mexicans thought impassable. The route the Americans followed had been scouted by engineering officers Lee and

Pierre G. T. Beauregard. After three days of slogging through "mud, mud, mud," the main body of Scott's force arrived on 18 August at the village of San Agustín, ten miles to the south of Mexico City, but they could not tarry long. They had only four days of rations on hand.

When Santa Anna realized what Scott was doing, he rushed troops to take up a position between San Agustín and Mexico City under the command of General Gabriel Valencia. Morale was slipping among the Mexican troops, however, because of Scott's surprise march to the south.

At San Agustín on 19 August the U.S. commander divided his force, leaving Worth and Quitman, along with his artillery and baggage, while he and the remainder of the troops continued through the cold lava flows and wastelands to the village of Padierna, where light American guns commanded by John B. Magruder, Jesse Lee Remo, and Thomas Jonathan Jackson were silenced by Mexican artillery, which included several 68-pounders. The village was eventually taken, however, thanks to the outstanding courage of charging American troops.

Padierna was immediately north of Contreras, where Valencia's troops awaited the Americans, and it was just south of the village of San Geronimo where Santa Anna had arrived with a force that, in effect, caught the Americans in the middle. That night of 19 August a violent storm hit, during which Santa Anna's troops withdrew north to San Angel. The Americans then slipped out of their camp at 3:00 A.M. on 20 August and three hours later attacked the unprepared Valencia from behind. The Battle of Contreras lasted only seventeen minutes and caused approximately seven hundred Mexican casualties. The remainder fled in panic toward the capital and were joined by Santa Anna's soldiers. Brigadier General James Shield, waiting on the road to San Angel, captured eight hundred Mexicans, including four generals. U.S. losses amounted to sixty dead and wounded.

Santa Anna rallied what men he could, falling back to the convent of Churubusco and declaring Valencia a traitor to be shot on sight. He then ordered General Manuel Rincón and former President Pedro María Anaya to hold the convent against the Americans. They had almost the remainder of Santa Anna's forces outside Mexico City for this effort, including two hundred members of the San Patricio Battalion, Irish-Catholic deserters from the American army fighting for Mexico. Churubusco was a natural fortress with stout walls, a parapeted roof, breastworks to the south and west, and a ditch twenty feet wide filled four feet deep with water.

Expecting no stiff resistance, Scott ordered his two columns to converge at Churubusco, one coming from its victory at Contreras, the other from San Agustín, where it had waited with artillery and baggage. Arriving at Churubusco, the Americans were allowed to advance until they were in musket range before both they and Mexican cannon opened fire. For a time the American advance halted almost in panic, but individual and unit courage asserted itself and the Americans moved forward. Lieutenant Richard Stoddert Ewell had two horses killed under him, while others were less fortunate and were killed. First Lieutenant James Longstreet was adjutant of the Eighth Infantry that day, while Second Lieutenant Winfield Scott Hancock charged with the Sixth Infantry. Finally, the parapet of the convent was breached by a battery of artillery commanded by Captain James Duncan and the Americans swarmed inside.

When the shooting halted, a count of Mexican losses showed 4,297 killed or wounded and 2,637 prisoners, among whom where eight generals, two of them former presidents of the republic. Additional thousands of Mexican troops had deserted, bringing Santa Anna's total loss to more than a third of his entire army. Thirty-two Mexican cannon were captured and added to the U.S. batteries. American losses that day were 133 killed, 865 wounded, and 40 missing. One of Scott's first orders, after the cheering for him had stopped, was to execute the captured members of the San Patricio Battalion.

Next, he wrote a note calling for a peaceful surrender of Mexico City, to which Mexican officials responded with a request for an armistice. On 24 August Quitman and Twiggs met with General Mora y Villamil and agreed to an armistice while a peace treaty was drafted. Scott used these days to reprovision his army through purchases from Mexican merchants in the capital city and the surrounding area. Santa Anna likewise used the truce to augment his army by conscription and to strengthen his defenses of the city.

Santa Anna bragged that the U.S. agreement to an armistice was the result of a Mexican victory, and thus Mexican demands during peace talks were unrealistic. The Mexican congress arrogantly resolved that no peace treaty would be considered until all U.S. forces were withdrawn from Mexican soil and Mexico had been indemnified for the entire cost of the war. On 6 September the Mexican commissioners offered to accept the annexation of Texas if the United States paid for the territory, which was to have the Nueces as its southern boundary. These demands were so outrageous that Scott declared the armistice at an end on 7 September.

The next day Santa Anna assumed command of a large Mexican force in the vicinity of the castle of Chapultepec. Half a mile away were stone buildings a quarter of a mile long known as El Molino del Rey (the King's Mill). Spies had said that this was a foundry where bells were being melted to cast cannon that reportedly were stored five hundred yards away in a powder magazine known as Casa Mata.

On 8 September, General Worth moved forward to take these two sites. After only a brief cannonade he ordered five hundred men forward in a charge, because Worth had a fondness for the bayonet. Despite heavy losses in bloody fighting, the mill and powder magazine were taken, only to find no evidence of cannon-casting. U.S. losses in the Battle of Molino del Rey were 117 killed and 658 wounded, along with 18 missing, out of a total of 3,447 engaged. Mexican casualties were estimated at twenty-seven hundred. Ethan Allen Hitchcock echoed the sentiments of several U.S. officers when he wrote in his diary that this battle had been "a sad mistake."

On 11 September, Scott counseled with his staff about his next move, stating he preferred to attack Mexico City through its western gate, which would require taking the castle of Chapultepec. Lee and all engineering officers except one argued for an attack through the southern gate. The other engineering officer, Beauregard, along with Twiggs and Riley, preferred the western route. After all had expressed an opinion, Scott concluded, "Gentlemen, we will attack by the western gate." Quitman and General Gideon J. Pillow took troops to make a feint at the eastern gate as a diversion, then abandoned that position during the night of 12 September.

The Mexican fortification of Chapultepec had gone forward since May 1847 despite shortages of money and supplies. Rising two hundred feet above the plain and protected by steep cliffs on its northern and eastern faces, Chapultepec was a formidable obstacle. The approach to it on its southern side was steep and ended at a fifteen-foot wall; on the west the Americans would have to advance up a steep, rough hillside strewn with land mines into the face of fire from troops atop a steep masonry wall. Chapultepec originally had been built as the summer palace for viceroys of New Spain, but by 1846 was the home of the Military Academy of Mexico. Inside were a hundred cadets and 240 regular troops along with the crews of twelve guns; six hundred infantry and artillerymen guarded the outworks, and another four thousand soldiers were on the causeways close to the eastern side of the castle hill. Commanding these men was General Nicolas Bravo.

The U.S. artillery assembled to bombard Chapultepec was formidable, consisting of 8-, 12-, 16-, and 24-pounders as well as howitzers and mortars, which opened fire on the morning of 12 September and continued throughout the day with demoralizing effect on the Mexicans. Bravo sent a request to Santa Anna for reinforcements, but was told these would be sent only at a critical moment.

On the morning of 13 September, the American bombardment commenced anew at 5:30, then halted at 8:00 as Pillow and Twiggs advanced with infantry. Ninety minutes later the battle was over, Bravo surrendering his sword when Santa Anna failed to send him reinforcements. U.S. casualties numbered slightly under five hundred, while the Mexicans had eighteen hundred dead, wounded, and captured.

After this victory Scott did not hesitate. He sent Quitman's division hurrying across the Belén causeway into the city. Santa Anna, half mad with fury, tried to rally resistance, but demoralized Mexican troops would not stand. By 1:20 P.M. the U.S. flag was flying inside the city walls, and Worth's troops were crossing the Veronica causeway. That night, despite having approximately twelve thousand men, Santa Anna decided his cause was lost. At 1:00 A.M. on the morning of 14 September he ordered Mexico City evacuated, saying Mexican honor had been satisfied. He took what troops he could muster north with him to the town of Guadalupe Hidalgo. Just after dawn on 14 September, Quitman marched troops into the grand plaza of Mexico City and raised the U.S. flag.

Scott's next act was to organize some kind of government, because looting broke out in parts of the city. General Quitman was named governor of the city, and troops and Texas Rangers began patrolling. These men had to be severe, for Scott had only a small army in a city of 180,000 people. So effectively did the U.S. troops and Texas Rangers restore order in Mexico City that a delegation of leading Mexican citizens asked Scott to become dictator of the nation. He refused.

In the weeks immediately after Mexico City surrendered, Scott faced anxious moments. He had only six thousand effective troops, and along every road into the city there were guerrilla bands, little more than bandits but a threat to couriers, small detachments, and supply trains. By mid-December 1847, however, replacements began arriving and Scott's force increased to more than thirteen thousand, but these new men fell victim to the same diseases that had riddled U.S. troops earlier.

Among those who died of camp fever was Edward Webster, son of the great Massachusetts orator Daniel Webster. Some of those who came to be part of the army of occupation were good men, such as young West Point graduates Ambrose E. Burnside and John Gibbon, but many of the newly arrived soldiers were ready for any opportunity to plunder and desert.

Scott tried to find duties that would keep these men busy. From December 1847 to the following May, for example, his soldiers levied assessments in various cities and collected the customs duties to make Mexico pay for the costs of the war. His men were able to collect about $3 million to defray part of the $23 million the war actually cost the United States.

For a brief time there was no real Mexican government. On 22 September Santa Anna resigned the presidency and retired to his plantation, but two weeks later, he had raised an army of four thousand, with which he attacked the U.S. garrison at Puebla. He believed a victory there would cause the Mexican people to rise up and proclaim him dictator. Defeated at Puebla on 9 October, he quit the war and departed the country with an escort of U.S. soldiers to protect him from Texans who remembered him from the massacres he had inflicted during the Texas Revolution.

In London, the Duke of Wellington, after reading the details of Scott's invasion and conquest of Mexico, urged young English officers to study the details, saying "His [Scott's] campaign was unsurpassed in military annals. He is the greatest living soldier." Unfortunately for Scott, the Democratic administration in Washington did not want a military hero, especially one who was a Whig.

THE TREATY OF GUADALUPE HIDALGO

The Mexican congress, which met in Querétaro on 11 November 1847, elected Anaya the acting president. He, in turn, formed a cabinet that included Manuel de Peña y Peña as minister of foreign affairs. There were some Centralists in Querétaro that favored a continuation of war, but Anaya was a moderate and a realist. There-

fore, negotiations for a peace treaty with the United States began on 15 November. The Mexican commissioners were José Bernardo Cuoto, Miguel Atristán, Manuel Rincón, and Luís Gonzaga Cuevas. Negotiating for the United States was Nicholas Trist.

Trist had hardly begun serious negotiations when an order arrived from Washington on 16 November recalling him, along with a rebuke for his prolonged quarrels with Scott during the march toward Mexico City. By this time he and Scott had patched over their dispute and become friends. Nevertheless, the recall order left him without any authority to negotiate, and he packed his bags to return to the United States.

At this juncture he was asked to stay and negotiate by the British ambassador and by Scott, both of whom realized that the collapse of peace talks would be followed by the collapse of Mexican government itself. Trist knew that if he stayed and negotiated, he could prepare a treaty that would include most of what he had been instructed to obtain—Texas with the Rio Grande as the boundary and a cession of New Mexico and California in return for a cash indemnity. He decided to stay, and on 2 January 1848 he met the Mexican commissioners in Mexico City and began secret negotiations.

The haggling was endless and tediously slow and Anaya's term as acting president expired, whereupon Peña y Peña assumed the mantle of chief executive. At last the two sides settled on the Rio Grande as the boundary of Texas, in return for which the United States would assume the claims owed U.S. citizens. New Mexico and California would become part of the United States in return for $15 million. On 2 February the treaty was signed at the suburb of Guadalupe Hidalgo and sent by swift courier to Washington for the president's consideration.

A week after the Treaty of Guadalupe Hidalgo was signed, Scott learned that President Polk intended to bring him before a court of inquiry for his conduct during the late war. This situation was a result of the president playing partisan politics and because of the ambitions and jealousies of some of Scott's staff, particularly Worth and Pillow. Following the battles of

Contreras and Chapultepec, Pillow's reports had been so self-glorifying that Scott asked him to modify them. Pillow did so, but there soon appeared in U.S. newspapers letters under the pen names "Leonidas" and "Veritas," heaping praise on Pillow. One letter laughably stated that Pillow belonged "in the first rank of American generals." A former law partner of President Polk and a political general, Pillow had been responsible for some of the greatest blunders of Scott's campaign.

Old Fuss and Feathers responded with a general order dated 12 November 1847 that the authors of these letters were guilty of "despicable self puffings" and demanded to know if the letters were meant to demean his own contributions. General Worth, feeling himself the object of this general order, accused Scott of conduct unbecoming an officer, whereupon Scott placed Worth, Pillow, and Colonel James Duncan under arrest and asked Washington that they be court-martialed. Duncan had admitted writing one of the letters in question, a violation of army regulations.

On receiving notification of these arrests, the President concluded that Pillow was being persecuted because he was a Democrat and that the charges against Worth and Duncan were unwarranted. He wrote that these charges came "more by the vanity and tyrannical temper of General Scott, and his want of prudence and common sense, than from any other cause." After discussing the matter with his cabinet, Polk ordered that Major General William O. Butler, a veteran of the Battle of New Orleans, as well as a Democrat, should take command in Mexico City; that Pillow, Worth, and Duncan should be released from arrest; and that Scott should face a court of inquiry in Mexico City. As for Trist, whom the president in January had learned was negotiating with the Mexicans despite the order recalling him, he concluded that the State Department clerk was staying at Scott's "insistence and dictation" and that General Butler was to order him home.

The court of inquiry met in Mexico City on 14 March 1848, but nothing came of it. Worth asked that his charges against Scott be with-drawn, and Scott decided he would not press his charges against Pillow. Moreover, many of the witnesses already had departed for the United States, making any full inquiry difficult. Pillow, however, insisted that the charges be examined, because he believed his friend in the White House would not let him be convicted. Lee, Hitchcock, and Longstreet, among other junior officers, testified to the extravagance of Pillow's claims.

The court adjourned on 21 April to return to the United States to take additional testimony. Scott, leaving Mexico the next day, returned to a vote of thanks from Congress and its request that the president have a gold medal struck for him. He did attend the further session of the court of inquiry when it met at Frederick, Maryland, to hear testimony from Quitman, Twiggs, and others, and on 1 July it delivered its report. It found that Pillow had exaggerated his own importance, but recommended no punishment for him. President Polk promptly approved the court's findings and, realizing that Scott was a great hero to most Americans, invited him and his wife to the White House for dinner.

Trist's treaty arrived at the White House on the evening of 19 February, just seventeen days after it was dated at Guadalupe Hidalgo. The next day, a Sunday, Polk met with his cabinet to discuss the agreement, whose negotiator, Trist, he wanted "severely punished" if some legal means could be found. Polk wrote that Trist was "arrogant, impudent, and very insulting."

The Treaty of Guadalupe Hidalgo presented Polk with difficulty. By the time the treaty was concluded, there was a growing movement in the United States to annex all of Mexico or, at least, several additional north Mexican states. Some proponents of this all-of-Mexico movement were idealistic, arguing that it would be beneficial to Mexicans to have a stable, republican government extended over them. Others were covetous of the mines of Guanajuato and northern Mexico, while yet others wanted an opportunity to grab huge landed estates. There were also many Protestant ministers who thought they might make millions of converts from Catholicism. This movement gained momentum in direct proportion to news of Scott's victories, and by late 1847–early 1848 the stance of the Polk administration toward Mexico was hardening.

Then Trist's treaty arrived. The State Department clerk had overlooked (or conveniently forgotten) some of his instructions. He had not gotton agreement for a U.S. canal across the Isthmus of Tehuantepec. He had not obtained a favorable railroad route to the West Coast by way of the Gila Valley, instead agreeing that no railroad along this route could be built save by mutual consent of both nations. Nor was there a U.S. outlet to the Gulf of California, and, contrary to orders, he had agreed to recognize land grants made in the ceded territory after the declaration of war in 1846. Finally, he had agreed both to an **indemnity** of $15 million to Mexico and to the **assumption** of claims against Mexico by private U.S. citizens.

Despite these drawbacks, however, Polk found the treaty to be worth serious consideration. It had been made with only the pretense of an existing government in Mexico and to reject it would mean a long and bloody battle to conquer all of the rest of that nation. The treaty did, however, contain most of what Polk originally had demanded: the Rio Grande was to be the boundary of Texas; New Mexico and California would become part of the United States in return for only $15 million rather than the $30 million the Mexicans wanted; and the claims issue was settled at long last (at the expense of U.S. taxpayers).

On 21 February, Polk told his cabinet that he would submit the Treaty of Guadalupe Hidalgo to the Senate. He said it was the best that could be obtained without additional fighting, and he believed the Congress would not vote more men and money for that. The only cabinet member to speak against the treaty was Secretary of State Buchanan.

The treaty met a storm of criticism in the Senate. For some it took too much land, for others too little. Abolitionists were against it because they felt it would add probable slave territory to the country. Reflection, however brought a realization that the alternative was a continuation of

war, and on 10 March the Senate gave its consent, thirty-eight to fourteen.

As for the negotiator of the treaty, Trist was arrested in Mexico on 17 March 1848 and escorted under guard out of Mexico. He was never brought to trial, although his job in the State Department was forfeited. The expenses he had incurred on his mission and his salary for that period of time were not paid until 1874. shortly before his death.

There was also discontent in Mexico over ratification of this treaty. There was an outburst of indignation everywhere when the terms of the agreement became known, and there appeared dozens of vituperative pamphlets. Peña y Peña and the peace advocates, however, argued that this agreement saved Mexico's honor. The country had not been forced to beg for peace terms, and the $15 million it was to receive in return for the ceded territory, already lost to Mexico, would restore the country to fiscal solvency. New elections were held, a new congress convened, and what one historian called a "quorum of shaking legislators" ratified the treaty.

A formal exchange of ratifications of the treaty took place at Querétaro on 30 May 1846. At that time the Mexican secretary of state and relations, Luís de la Rosa, asked that the U.S. army of occupation remain in Mexico City until Mexican authorities could take precautions to avoid disorders. At 6:00 on the morning of 12 June 1848, the U.S. flag was replaced by the Mexican tricolor above the National Palace in Mexico City, and that same day U.S. troops began withdrawing from Veracruz. The signed copy of the treaty was returned to Washington and delivered to President Polk on the morning of 4 July, and he ordered the secretary of state to proclaim it on that anniversary of the Declaration of Independence.

RESULTS OF THE WAR

The number of casualties in the war with Mexico made it the deadliest conflict in U.S. history in terms of the total deaths per thousands who served per year. Of the 100,182 soldiers, sailors, and marines who participated, 1,548 were killed in action, but another 10,970 died from disease and various other complications—a mortality rate of 110 per 1,000 per annum (as compared with the Civil War rate of 85 and the World War II rate of 30). Moreover, additional thousands died as a result of diseases contracted in Mexico in the months and years after the war. J. J. Oswandel, a veteran of the conflict, wrote in 1885, "After the close of war we returned . . . with a disease contracted in a strange climate, which, in a few years after the war had taken from their homes more than half of those who returned."

Other results of the war were numerous. It made the United States a Pacific power. It led to a Whig victory in the election of 1848, as Zachary Taylor was swept into office over Democrat Lewis Cass. It brought a renewal of intense debate with regard to slavery in the territories, leading to the Compromise of 1850—which, in turn, would lead to the doctrine of squatter sovereignty, the Dred Scott decision, Bleeding Kansas, John Brown's raid, the formation of the Republican party, the election of Abraham Lincoln, and the Civil War. In that bloody "Brother's War," many of the officers who commanded had won their spurs on the field of battle in the conflict with Mexico.

BIBLIOGRAPHY

Alcaraz, Ramón, et al. *The Other Side*, trans. by Albert C. Ramsey (1850).

Bauer, Karl Jack. *Surfboats and Horse Marines: U.S. Naval Operations in the Mexican War* (1969).

Bill, Alfred Hoyt. *Rehearsal for Conflict: The War With Mexico* (1947).

Brooks, Nathan C. *A Complete History of the Mexican War* (1849).

Chidsey, Donald Barr. *The War with Mexico* (1968).

Clarke, Dwight L. *Stephen Watts Kearny: Soldier of the West* (1961).

Connor, Seymour V., and Odie B. Faulk. *North America Divided: The Mexican War, 1846–1848* (1971).

Cooke, Philip St. George. *The Conquest of New Mexico and California* (1878).

Dufour, Charles L. *The Mexican War: A Compact History* (1968).

Dyer, Brainerd. *Zachary Talor* (1946).

Elliott, Charles Winslow. *Winfield Scott: The Soldier and the Man* (1937).

Faulk, Odie B., and Joseph A. Stout, Jr., eds. *The Mexican War: Changing Interpretations* (1973).

Fuller, John D. P. *The Movement for the Acquisition of All Mexico, 1846–1848* (1936).

Furber, George C. *The Twelve Months Volunteer, or, Journal of a Private in the Tennessee Regiment . . .* (1848).

George, Isaac. *Heroes and Incidents of the Mexican War* (1982).

Greer, James K. *Colonel Jack Hays* (rev. 1974).

Hamilton, Holman. *Zachary Taylor: Soldier of the Republic* (1941).

Hammond, George P., ed. *The Treaty of Guadalupe Hidalgo, February Second, 1848* (1949).

Henry, Robert Selph. *The Story of the Mexican War* (1950).

Hitchcock, Ethan Allen. *Fifty Years in Camp and Field*, ed. by William A. Croffut (1909).

Hughes, John Taylor. *Doniphan's Expedition* (1848).

Jenkins, John Stilwell. *History of the War Between the United States and Mexico* (1848).

Johannsen, Robert W. *To the Halls of the Montezumas: The Mexican War in the American Imagination* (1985).

Lavender, David. *Climax at Buena Vista: The American Campaigns in Northeastern Mexico, 1846–47* (1966).

Lawson, Don. *The United States in the Mexican War* (1976).

McAfee, Ward, and J. Cordell Robinson, eds. *Origins of the Mexican War*, 2 vols. (1982).

Merk, Frederick. *The Monroe Doctrine and American Expansionism, 1843–1849* (1966).

Morrison, Chaplain W. *Democratic Politics and Sectionalism: The Wilmot Proviso Controversy* (1967).

Myers, William S., ed. *The Mexican War Diary of General George B. McClellan* (1917).

Nevins, Allan, *Frémont: Pathmarker of the West* (1939).

Nevin, David. *The Mexican War* (1978).

Nichols, Edward J. *Zach Taylor's Little Army* (1963).

Owsandel, J. Jacob. *Notes of the Mexican War* (1885).

Pletcher, David M. *The Diplomacy of Annexation: Texas, Oregon, and the Mexican War* (1973).

Price, Glenn W. *Origins of the War With Mexico* (1967).

Quaife, Milo M., ed. *The Diary of James K. Polk, During His Presidency, 1845 to 1849*, 4 vols. (1910).

Ripley, Robert S. *The War With Mexico*, 2 vols. (1849).

Rippy, James Fred. *The United States and Mexico* (rev. 1931).

Schroeder, John H. *Mr. Polk's War* (1973).

Sellers, Charles G. *James K. Polk: Continentalist: 1843–1846* (1966).

Singletary, Otis A. *The Mexican War* (1960).

Smith, Justin H. *The War With Mexico*, 2 vols. (1919).

Stephenson, Nathaniel W. *Texas and the Mexican War: A Chronicle of the Winning of the Southwest* (1919).

Villa-Amor, Manuel. *Biografia del General Santa-Anna* (1847, rev. 1857).

Weems, John Edward. *To Conquer a Peace: The War Between the United States and Mexico* (1974).

Weinberg, Albert K. *Manifest Destiny: A Study of Nationalist Expansionism in American History* (1935).

EXPANSION AND THE PLAINS INDIAN WARS

Robert Wooster

For most Americans, the war with Mexico (1846–1848) reaffirmed the supremacy of the traditional military system of the nation. A small regular army, agreed President James K. Polk and Congress, could in times of war be supplemented by state militias and volunteers. These citizen-soldiers had indeed performed well in the recent conflict. Thus, while the Treaties of Guadalupe-Hidalgo and Buchanan-Pakenham, which secured Texas, New Mexico, California, and Oregon, had increased the total area of the United States by 50 percent, the military establishment of the nation would remain relatively stable. A small standing army was still sufficient to defend national security at minimal cost.

Indeed, a large permanent military would remain an anathema to most Americans throughout the latter half of the nineteenth century. Fears that a regular army might threaten the democratic Republic and the desire to limit the power of the federal government dominated discussions concerning the size of the military. Protected by the Atlantic and Pacific oceans to the east and west, and with Mexico and British Canada posing minimal threats to the south and north, the United States had little reason to fear a surprise invasion. The navy would discourage enemy raids and harass any major amphibious assaults, the army would patrol the frontiers and garrison coastal defenses, and state militias and assembled volunteers would overwhelm any intruders.

These assumptions would not be seriously challenged until the Spanish-American War, but the new territorial acquisitions would call into question the traditional frontier defensive policies. Earlier military and political officials had assumed that Indians could be removed to lands undesirable to white settlers. Several eastern tribes had thus been moved to the Indian Territory, on the fringes of what many still believed to be the Great American Desert. To separate these and other Indians from whites, small army detachments had garrisoned a line of forts established well in advance of American settlements. According to such designs, reserve forces, concentrated at inner posts, such as Jefferson Barracks, Missouri, were to use military roads and water transportation to converge upon any threat.

The new land acquisitions, however, shattered these assumptions. Texas, with its long heritage of white-Indian violence, retained state control over its public lands. In an age of limited federal budgets, this would severely restrict the

U.S. government's military efforts in the Lone Star State. Elsewhere, the central government could build posts and establish Indian reservations at minimal cost. In Texas, however, such tracts would have to be leased or purchased from the state.

The new Pacific outposts also presented a problem because settlers would no longer follow the neat east-to-west progression envisioned by earlier defensive schemes. More significant were the astonishing numbers involved in this disorderly migration. Fewer than twenty thousand Americans lived in Oregon and California before 1848; the discovery of gold at Sutter's Mill that year unleashed a massive overland emigration that numbered at least 250,000 by 1860. Thousands more came by sea, boosting the population of California to nearly 380,000. Another sixty-four thousand lived in Washington and Oregon, with Utah boasting about forty thousand residents by 1860. These new arrivals needed protection, thus necessitating more military posts in the Far West.

Economy in all things dominated the status of the antebellum army. To cut expenses troops were hired out on extra duty (at between twenty and forty cents per day) as construction workers, rather than hire civilians to build the frontier posts necessary for continued expansion. Because the War Department could not afford to purchase extra ammunition and gunpowder, target practice for regular troops was not conducted on a regular basis. To reduce commissary and transportation costs at the far-flung western outposts, Secretary of War Charles M. Conrad ordered each garrison to plant a post garden in 1851. In an effort to improve mobility at low cost, several experiments in mounting infantry on horses and mules, all of which proved unsuccessful, were conducted during the 1850s.

The need to reduce expenditures also influenced larger policy decisions. On the advice of Lieutenant Colonel Edwin V. ("Bull") Sumner, Secretary Conrad estimated the annual military expenses in New Mexico to be nearly one-half the real estate value of the territory. Rather than continue the tenuous defense of the region,

Conrad proposed that the government buy up all the property of every citizen in New Mexico. With the non-Indian population thus removed, the army might also be withdrawn. According to Conrad, the change would rid the military of a tremendous burden, allow the army to reinforce more valuable areas, and save money.

Although Conrad's proposal was soon forgotten, skyrocketing expenses especially affected the Quartermaster's Department. Before the mid-1840s, all military posts had been accessible by water, but with the recent expansion, many inland forts could only be reached by wagon. The effects were painfully obvious. In 1845 the annual costs to the army to transport men and supplies had been $130,000; in 1851, the cost exceeded two million dollars, with further increases in the coming years. Money that might have been spent on training or recruitment was instead devoted to transportation.

Financial limitations often delayed deployment of new weapons to the frontiers. In 1855 the army adopted a new .58-caliber rifle-musket, a nine-pound weapon that boasted a new primer system and used the recently developed minié balls, replacing the 1842 percussion musket. The War Department also adopted several models of Colt repeating pistols. Those troops equipped with such weapons posed formidable challenges to the Indians, whose bows, arrows, and muskets could match neither the range nor the accuracy of the newer firearms. Army inspectors in the late 1850s frequently bemoaned the fact that soldiers at western posts had not yet received these more modern tools of war and had rarely if ever taken target practice.

In addition to garrisoning the coastal fortifications and attempting to quell violence along the frontiers, the army was also responsible for a wide array of nonmilitary tasks. The regulars had long been pressed into service in building and improving military roads, and the years after 1848 would not alter this practice. With transportation costs so high, it was not surprising that the army took a particularly keen interest in the developing railroad system. As early as 1838, General Edmund P. Gaines presented a detailed plan for frontier defense that featured

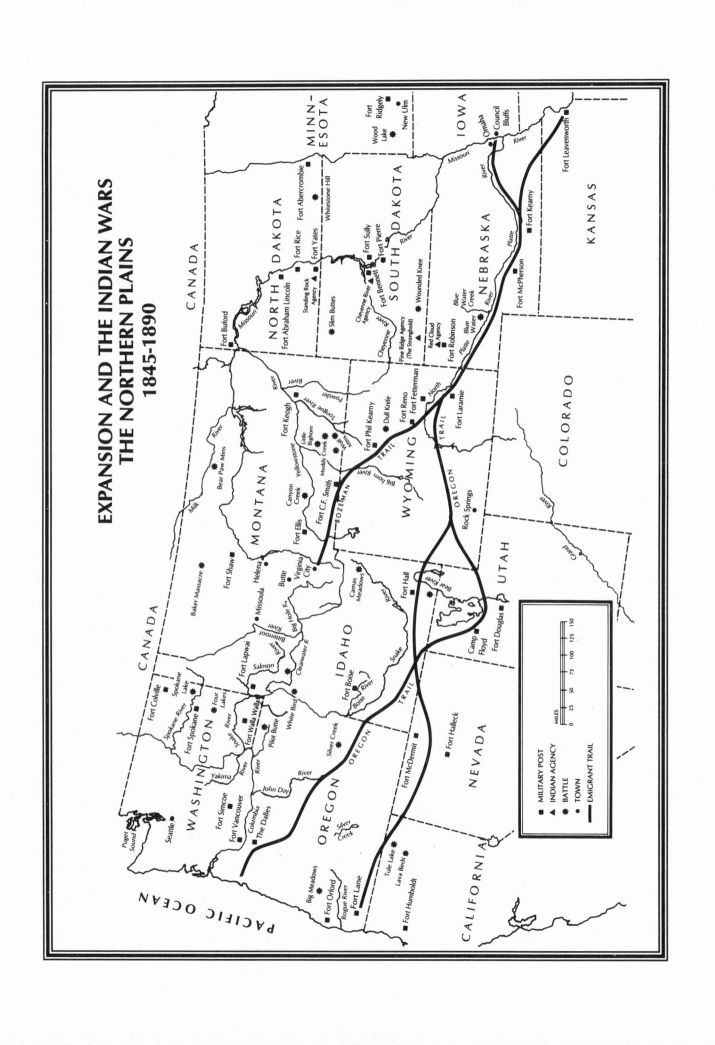

EXPANSION AND THE INDIAN WARS
THE NORTHERN PLAINS
1845-1890

MAP LABELS:

CANADA

MINN-ESOTA

NORTH DAKOTA

SOUTH DAKOTA

MONTANA

WYOMING

IDAHO

WASHINGTON

OREGON

NEVADA

CALIFORNIA

UTAH

COLORADO

NEBRASKA

KANSAS

IOWA

PACIFIC OCEAN

Fort Ridgely
New Ulm
Wood Lake
Fort Abercrombie
Whitestone Hill
Fort Rice
Fort Yates
Fort Sully
Fort Pierre
Fort Buford
Fort Abraham Lincoln
Standing Rock Agency
Slim Buttes
Cheyenne River Agency
Fort Bennett
Wounded Knee
Pine Ridge Agency (The Stronghold)
Red Cloud Agency
Fort Robinson
Blue Water Creek
Blue Water
Fort McPherson
Fort Kearny
Council Bluffs
Omaha
Fort Leavenworth
Missouri River
Platte River
North Platte
South Platte
Fort Laramie
Fort Fetterman
Fort Reno
Fort Phil Kearny
Dull Knife
Fort Keogh
Fort C.F. Smith
Fort Ellis
Canyon Creek
Little Bighorn
Muddy Creek
Wolf Mtn.
Yellowstone River
Powder River
Tongue River
Big Horn River
Bear Paw Mtns
Milk River
Baker Massacre
Fort Shaw
Helena
Butte
Virginia City
Missoula
Big Hole R.
Bitterroot River
Fort Lapwai
Salmon
Clearwater R.
Four Lakes
Spokane Lake
Fort Colville
Fort Spokane
Spokane River
Snake River
Fort Walla Walla
White Bird
Pilot Butte
Silver Creek
Fort Boise
Boise River
Camas Meadows
Fort Hall
Snake River
Bear River
Camp Floyd
Fort Douglas
Rock Springs
Grand River
Fort Halleck
Fort McDermit
Tule Lake
Lava Beds
Fort Humboldt
Fort Lane
Big Meadows
Fort Orford
Rogue River
Silver Creek
The Dalles
Fort Vancouver
Columbia
John Day River
Yakima River
Fort Simcoe
Seattle
Puget Sound
BOZEMAN TRAIL
OREGON TRAIL

LEGEND:

■ MILITARY POST
▲ INDIAN AGENCY
✳ BATTLE
● TOWN
— EMIGRANT TRAIL

MILES
0 25 50 75 100 125 150

an extensive system of railroads, to be constructed by soldiers during peacetime.

Military officials continued to study means of reducing transportation costs. In addition to roads and railroads, some urged a massive system of river improvements. Some observers, such as Quartermaster General Thomas S. Jesup, speculated that the Rio Grande might be transformed into a waterway to supply posts in west Texas and New Mexico.

Most of these antebellum river improvements failed, and other officials suggested more esoteric plans. Secretary of War Jefferson Davis sponsored a program to replace army mules and oxen with camels. More than seventy of the ungainly beasts were imported to the Southwest, and, in a series of tests, they proved their ability to carry larger loads at lower costs than more traditional work animals. Their handlers, however, found it nearly impossible to deal with the acute halitosis and voluminous sneezing of the camels, plus their fierceness during rutting season. The camels lost their most powerful advocate when Davis resigned as secretary of war, and they were largely forgotten amidst the growing sectional crisis of the late 1850s.

In a more general sense, the army had long recognized the importance of western emigration. By facilitating the expansion of the frontiers, the military might also secure a few friends in Congress or the executive branch. Carrying the brunt of this work was the Corps of Topographical Engineers, reorganized in 1838 under the leadership of Colonel John J. Abert. John C. Frémont, a brash young topographical officer who had married the daughter of Senator Thomas Hart Benton, led three western expeditions that helped bring the corps, and Frémont himself, wide popular acclaim.

Other engineers provided useful services during the war with Mexico, but the heyday of the Corps of Topographical Engineers came in the late 1840s and 1850s. Eager young officers, most full of the dreams that would conquer a continent, helped map the vast expanses of west Texas and the Mexican cession. The corps took a special interest in railroads, and when

Congress authorized Secretary of War Davis to survey rail routes to the Pacific Ocean, he assigned many of its best officers to his newly established Bureau of Explorations and Surveys. In 1854 army officers headed scientific parties that examined four potential routes along the forty-eighth, thirty-eighth, thirty-fifth, and thirty-second parallels. Each team reported enthusiastically about its survey, but Davis, a Mississippian, threw his weight behind the southernmost route. Whatever the merits of that survey, however, sectional rivalries quickly combined to block congressional support for any transcontinental railroad.

The army also committed significant resources to check civil disturbances in Kansas and Utah. To restore peace between proslavery and antislavery forces in Kansas, most of the First Cavalry Regiment was deployed to that bloody territory in 1856. Fear of Mormon hegemony led Secretary of War John B. Floyd to dispatch Colonel Albert Sidney Johnston, two infantry regiments, the Second Dragoons, and a battery of artillery into Utah in late 1857. The Mormons initially readied to resist the army, and their extensive defenses and scorched-earth strategy would have cost Johnston's column dearly if some skillful last-minute diplomacy had not brought peace. Upon occupying Utah in June 1858, Johnston was able to support emigrant trains bound for Oregon and California, but these distractions hindered the army's efforts against the Indians of the American West.

Only grudgingly did Congress recognize the added responsibilities and importance of the army in westward expansion. The volunteers who had swelled the ranks during the war against Mexico were quickly disbanded—by 1849 only 10,744 officers and men were in uniform, a figure roughly equivalent to that of the previous decade. The army was then reconstituted to include eight infantry, two dragoon, and four artillery regiments, as well as the Regiment of Mounted Riflemen, which had been created in 1846. The mounted and infantry units each included ten companies, the artillery twelve. An act of 1850 increased the army by authorizing companies stationed on the frontier to expand to seventy-four privates each. A captain, assisted by two lieutenants and assorted noncommissioned personnel, headed each unit. Regimental staffs included one colonel, one lieutenant colonel, two majors, two sergeants, and a few musicians. Two officers, drawn from the line companies, served as regimental adjutant and quartermaster.

Plagued by chronic shortages in recruiting and rapid turnover, the army never reached these authorized unit levels. A survey in 1853 showed that of the 13,821 men allowed by law, only 10,417 were actually in uniform. Slightly more than eight thousand men were assigned to the fifty-four western posts, but fewer than seven thousand were actually present at those forts. Desertion rates were about 15 percent per year, while another 12 percent of the men died or were discharged annually.

The survey also found that the western forts boasted an average garrison of 128, but even this figure was inflated, because sickness, extra duty assignments, and recruiting details further stripped available forces. A typical army inspector's assessment was that made in 1860 of Fort Davis, Texas, a strategic post guarding the road between El Paso and San Antonio. One company of the Eighth Infantry garrisoned the fort, but the commanding officer and an escort were away on court-martial duty. A lieutenant and twenty-two enlisted men were on detached service at nearby Fort Quitman. Another officer was temporarily at San Antonio, thus leaving Fort Davis with one commissioned officer, one sergeant, two corporals, twenty-six privates, and a musician. Of those present, seven privates were in confinement and another ten enlisted men were assigned to extra duty, leaving a total disposable force of one officer and twelve men—hardly enough to strike fear into the hearts of the region's Indian tribes.

As a U.S. senator, Jefferson Davis, also a West Point graduate and Mexican War veteran, supported the increase of 1850 and was well aware of the army's dilemma. Appointed secretary of war by Franklin Pierce in 1853, he proved to be one of the most effective champions of the regular military establishment during the antebellum years. Davis pressed hard for another increase, pointing out that the army had expanded by fewer than three thousand men in forty-five years, during which time the population of the nation had grown by eighteen million and the territories by a million square miles. Dispersed in tiny pockets across the vast frontiers, Davis argued, the army's obvious weakness invited Indian attacks. In 1855 he convinced Congress to raise two new infantry and two new cavalry regiments, thus bringing the strength of the regular army to nearly sixteen thousand men.

The officers who comprised the backbone of this force remained a mixed lot. An increasing number—73 percent by the mid-1850s—were graduates of the U.S. Military Academy. Many were well-read and most had won recognition for their gallantry in action during the war with Mexico. The mid-level ranks bulged with men who would rise to greatness in the coming years. Lieutenant Philip H. Sheridan served with the First and Fourth Infantry regiments in Texas and Oregon. Lieutenant Colonel Robert E. Lee helped patrol the frontiers with the Second Cavalry, as did fifteen other men who would become general officers during the Civil War.

Other commissioned personnel, however, left much to be desired. Lieutenant George Crook, who became one of the premier Indian fighters after the Civil War, described the typical post commanders of the 1850s as "petty tyrants" whose long years of frontier isolation narrowed "their habits and minds . . . down to their surroundings." One young lieutenant found in Major John S. Simonsen, a veteran of the War of 1812, "a simple, but kind old fellow . . . deficient in reason, cramped in his understanding and warped in his judgment." Monotony, low pay, poor food, and decrepit housing drove many to drink. Others left the army, including such future Civil War leaders as William T. Sherman, Ulysses S. Grant, and Thomas E. Jackson, disgusted with not only their miserable living conditions but also the slow rate of promotion that resulted from the refusal of Congress to set mandatory retirement ages.

Enlisted personnel reflected equally diverse elements of American society. Official regulations provided that prospective recruits be white males between the ages of eighteen and thirty-five, speak English, and be at least five feet four and a half inches tall. Commissioned personnel complained that many of their soldiers failed to meet even these minimal requirements; indeed, except in times of extreme economic distress (such as the depression of 1857–1859), enlisted life offered few attractions. Immigrants thus dominated the ranks, with Ireland and Germany providing the largest share of recruits.

The army made little effort to develop tactical doctrine applicable to Indian warfare before the Civil War. *The Elements of Military Art and Science* by Henry W. Halleck, first published in 1846, became a staple military primer, but included little notice of nontraditional conflicts. Contemporary tactical manuals, including *Infantry Tactics* (1855) by Captain William J. Hardee and *Cavalry Tactics* (officially adopted in 1861) by Colonel Philip St. George Cooke also concentrated on European-style warfare.

West Point offered little assistance. Mathematics and sciences, rather than tactics and strategy, comprised the bulk of the curriculum. The most celebrated course at the academy, an offering by Professor Dennis Hart Mahan on military and civil engineering and the science of war, briefly emphasized the use of superior firepower and the employment of Indians to fight Indians, but spoke little to the subject of fighting indigenous peoples.

Zealous officers might pick up bits and pieces from more popular accounts, namely Cooke's *Scenes and Adventures in the Army: or, Romance of Military Life*. A few colleagues probably knew something of the report by Captain George B. McClellan on his tour of the Crimean War, in which he suggested that the U.S. Army develop a light cavalry designed to combat western Indians. McClellan's report was relegated to an obscure government document and failed to attract a wide audience.

In fact, conflicts between commanding General Winfield Scott and Secretary of War Davis seemed to take precedence over discussions of strategy and tactics. Scott, a pompous, punctilious man who nonetheless possessed great military talent, saw his position as being independent from the secretary's authority. Several years before Davis even took the cabinet post, Scott declared his independence by moving his offices to New York. Equally proud and difficult, Davis sought to control his testy subordinate, but failing in this, he simply acted without bothering to consult General Scott.

THE ARMY AND THE INDIANS, 1848–1861

With all of its distractions and problems, the United States Army remained a formidable fighting force, with, if emergencies arose, a nearly inexhaustible pool of volunteer reserves. Reasonably well-disciplined and representing a nation determined to fulfill what it believed to be its manifest destiny—expansion to the Pacific Ocean—the regular military faced about 360,000 Indians in the trans–Mississippi West. Approximately eighty-four-thousand of these belonged to the Five Civilized Tribes of the Indian Territory, and another seventy-five thousand roamed what had once been the Louisiana Territory. An estimated twenty-five thousand Indians lived in Texas, with a similar number in the Oregon Country. One hundred and fifty thousand probably inhabited the areas recently secured from Mexico. Most of these Indians had scant regard for the strange laws of the United States and little appreciation for the determination of Americans to dominate the West.

Bent on encouraging white expansion into the West, the U.S. government nonetheless hoped to avoid warfare. In an effort to improve relations with the tribes, the Indian Bureau was separated from the War Department and incorporated into the newly created Home Department (later the Department of the Interior) in 1849. Civilians, it was hoped, would be more successful than the military had been in negotiating treaties and removing Indians to areas not desired by whites.

Access to the newly acquired regions had to be guaranteed. Therefore, Indian ownership to lands suitable for white development, argued the government, had to be extinguished. Because the tribes were thought to represent inferior cultures, it was believed that they could be removed in the name of progress. Once placed on reservations, the Indians would, in theory, be protected from the evil effects of white society, taught the blessings of Christian civilization, and transformed into thrifty farmers. It was determined that treaties had to be concluded with the various tribes, and although some effort should be made to do so peacefully, the army was seen as a legitimate tool in the work of Indian removal.

The Pacific Northwest.

U.S. troops made a less than auspicious entry into the Pacific Northwest, where the murders of Reverend Marcus Whitman, his wife, and a dozen others by Cayuse Indians disrupted the uneasy peace in 1847. Counterstrikes by Oregon volunteers the following year failed, and as late as October 1849, only six companies of regulars were present for duty in the region. Lieutenant Colonel William W. Loring, the one-armed commander of the Eleventh Department (merged with the Tenth Department to form the Pacific Division in 1851), was almost immediately faced with the en masse desertion of a third of his troops to the burgeoning mining camps of southern Oregon and northern California. The newly arrived Regiment of Mounted Riflemen, which was to have comprised the bulk of Loring's command, was broken up in 1851, to the delight of a civilian populace because its ill-disciplined actions had terrorized rather than protected.

Violent encounters with the Indians increased as gold-hungry whites poured into the mountains along the California-Oregon boundary line. In keeping with standard practice, the army established a line of forts designed to keep the two groups apart while government negotiators attempted to convince the tribes to move to reservations to the east. Logistical and manpower shortages limited the regulars, however, as ill-disciplined volunteers took it upon themsevles to rid the country of Indians. In 1853 a series of treaties carved out temporary reservations in the Rogue River area, but neither whites nor Indians respected the official lines of separation. The arrival of fiery Brigadier General John E. Wool to the Department of the Pacific in 1854 exacerbated the civil-military tensions, because Wool blamed the troubles squarely on the antics of local volunteers. His efforts to protect a few of the Indians only incurred the wrath of the settlers.

In October 1855, full-scale war broke out in the Rogue River valley. Oregon volunteers initiated the bloodletting with attacks against three Indian camps. About five hundred Rogue, Shasta, Scoton, Klamath, Grave Creek, Umpqua, and Cow Creek Indians retaliated with a quick strike before fleeing to the mountains. White citizens bent on extermination launched a series of campaigns; two companies of beleaguered regulars at Fort Lane scrambled to protect those Indians who still sought peace, at the same time assisting efforts against those tribes that had joined the hostilities.

In the spring of 1856, Wool was determined to crush the Rogue River uprising. Columns from Forts Humboldt, Lane, and Orford converged against those tribes deemed hostile; further expeditions of Oregon volunteers, along with a sharp action with the regulars at the Battle of Big Meadows (28 May 1856), convinced the Indians to surrender. Twelve hundred persons were eventually removed from the southern Oregon–northern California coastal regions.

Even more formidable military opponents awaited the army east of the mountains. The proud Nez Perce roamed the Columbia and Snake rivers. In the valleys drained by the Snake River resided the Yakima, Klikitat, Palouse, Umatilla, and Walla Walla tribes. To the north lived the Spokane, Coeur d'Alene, Pend d'Oreilles, and Flatheads. These tribes, most of whom owned considerable horse herds, lived seminomadic lives, exchanging the fisheries of the spring and fall for the mountain berries and roots of the summer harvest. Long familiar with the traders of Hudson's Bay Company, they had acquired firearms, but were often split between progressive factions that espoused Christianity and more conservative groups that followed traditional beliefs.

In 1855 government agents initiated a determined effort to place these people on defined reservations. Isaac I. Stevens, governor of Washington Territory, led the campaign. A West Point graduate and confirmed supporter of a transcontinental railroad, Stevens wanted clear title to the Pacific Northwest from the Indians. A few tribes signed treaties, even as gold discoveries near Fort Colville, along the border with British Canada, led to another torrent of intruders across the Cascade Mountains and up the Columbia River. Sparked by the leadership of Kamaiakin, other Indians determined to resist the encroachments. Major Gabriel J. Rains sought to overawe the tribes with a demonstration of force in the fall of 1855, but hundreds of angry warriors checked the three companies sent to do the job. A mixed column of regulars and territorial militia that penetrated the Yakima River country in the closing months of 1855 only drove more tribes into the opposing camp, as did a subsequent volunteer sweep through the Walla Walla Valley.

As General Wool feuded with Governor Stevens over the incendiary actions of the volunteers, Colonel George Wright and the Ninth Infantry poured into the Pacific Northwest. The regulars cleared the Puget Sound region of Indians in the spring of 1856. Meanwhile, Wright pushed into the Yakima country and, in a bloodless campaign that satisfied neither whites nor Indians, concluded an uneasy peace. From the newly established Fort Simcoe and Fort Walla Walla, the army maintained a semblance of order until spring 1858, when Spokane, Coeur d'Alene, and Palouse warriors nearly an-

nihilated three companies of dragoons near Spokane Lake.

Wool, whose order closing eastern Washington to white settlement had irritated many, had been transferred to a quieter eastern station in 1857. His replacement, Colonel Newman S. Clarke, was determined to crush all Indian resistance and thus expedite new westward migration. Major Robert S. Garnett would push out from Fort Simcoe while Wright marched north from Fort Walla Walla. Garnett struck a camp of Yakima and forced their surrender, but Wright, a superb tactician and regimental commander, inflicted even more telling blows. With two mountain howitzers and nearly six hundred men, many of whom carried the new model 1855 Springfield .58-caliber rifled muskets, Wright dealt the Indians a pair of stinging defeats at the Battles of Four Lakes (1 September 1858) and Spokane River (5 September). The regulars reported only one man wounded in the unequal duels, while the Indians, whose muskets could not match the ranges of the new rifles in these conventional battles, were routed with heavy losses. Wright ordered several Indian leaders hung, and the remaining tribes were forced to accept the Stevens treaties of 1855.

The Army in Texas. Texas posed unique problems for the U.S. Army. Its enormous size brought huge transportation costs and made communication between scattered frontier stations extremely difficult. The long border with Mexico presented innumerable opportunities for Indian raiders, petty thieves, and revolutionaries to escape pursuers by crossing the Rio Grande. The thousands of California-bound immigrants also demanded protection and forced the army to extend its defenses far past existing non-Indian settlements. The Treaty of Guadalupe-Hidalgo had also obliged the U.S. government to prevent incursions into Mexico from the American side. Not to be forgotten was the Lone Star republic's virulent expansionism and anti-Indian policies, which left the remaining indigenous people determined to fight for their tribal lands.

General George Mercer Brooke began establishing a string of forts across central Texas in the late 1840s and early 1850s. He also proposed a three-pronged offensive against the Plains tribes, but the chronic shortage of manpower precluded such a move. With Brooke's death, Brevet Major General Persifor Smith succeeded to department command in 1851. By the mid-1850s, Smith's soldiers had erected another line of federal posts. According to theory, mounted troops would man the inner line and chase down enemy intruders; at the same time, infantry garrisons at the outer posts would cut off Indian retreat onto the Great Plains.

In practice, this plan left much to be desired. The regulars were too few, the distances too great, and the Indian raiders too crafty to fall victim to the army's traps. Texans howled for action and derided the regulars, particularly the infantry. Although another chain of posts was established along the road between San Antonio and El Paso during the mid-1850s, Texans made little effort to hide their displeasure with the federal government. Only locally raised and mounted rangers, argued the Texans, could effectively combat the mobile warriors of the southern Plains.

Secretary of War Davis dispatched the crack Second Cavalry Regiment to Texas, but also urged state officials to set aside public lands for Indian reservations. Reluctantly, the state established two reserves along the upper Brazos River in 1854; continued violence and loud protests by Texas congressmen, however, led the federal government to abort the experiment five years later. A similar project west of the Pecos River never got off the ground.

Far more satisfactory to Texans were a series of military operations during the late 1850s. A contingent of Texas Rangers led by Captain John S. ("Rip") Ford struck first. Operating independently of the regulars, Ford's Rangers, aided by one hundred Indian auxiliaries, splashed across the Red River in the early spring of 1858. At the Battle of Antelope Hills (11 May), the Texans routed several hundred Comanche. Rather than overawing the tribesmen, however, the action inspired bitter retalia-

tory raids. With the entire Second Cavalry Regiment conveniently gathered at Fort Belknap (orders to transfer the horse soldiers to Kansas had only recently been cancelled), Brigadier General David E. Twiggs, having assumed command of the Department of Texas in May 1857, opted for another offensive.

To lead the campaign, Twiggs selected Brevet Major Earl Van Dorn, a battle-hardened combat veteran of wars against Mexico and the Florida Seminole. With four troops of cavalrymen and several dozen Indian auxiliaries from the short-lived Brazos Reservation, Van Dorn left Fort Belknap on 15 September 1858. Establishing their base in the southwest corner of Indian Territory, the command received word that Buffalo Hump and his Comanche were encamped at Rush Spring. A series of forced marches allowed Van Dorn to approach the enemy unnoticed. Taking advantage of his surprise, the major led three companies directly into the village while the fourth company and the Indian allies went after the horses just after daybreak on 1 October. Four soldiers were killed and twelve others, including Van Dorn and the leader of the auxiliaries, were wounded in the swirling melee. Enemy losses were much heavier—fifty-eight dead, 120 lodges burned, three hundred horses captured, and irreplaceable winter supplies lost to the soldiers.

In strictly military terms, Rush Spring had been a complete success for the U.S. military. The aftermath of the battle, however, dramatically symbolized the western dilemma of the army. Unknown to Van Dorn, several Comanche chiefs had concluded a treaty six weeks before the fight. Buffalo Hump had freely admitted that he intended to lead raids into Texas that summer, but the federal government's actions—extending one hand of friendship while using the other as a mailed fist—had seemed no less duplicitous.

The Comanche reacted vigorously, launching raid after raid onto the northern Texas frontiers. Van Dorn's victory at Crooked Creek the following year (13 May 1859) almost completely annihilated an entire Comanche village of nearly one hundred inhabitants, but did no more than the

Battle of Rush Spring to bring peace. Troopers from Kansas, New Mexico, and Fort Cobb, Indian Territory, swept the southern Plains again in 1860, but only seemed to further antagonize the tribes.

The army also erected a series of military posts in New Mexico. With the transfer of Sumner, Brigadier General John Garland took command of the Department of the West and initiated several offensive thrusts during the mid-1850s. The Jicarilla Apache were humbled by late 1854; although the Mescalero Apache dodged several army columns, they too accepted a reservation in south central New Mexico when confronted by three hundred infantrymen commanded by Lieutenant Colonel Dixon Miles. After three months of hard campaigning, mixed volunteer-regular columns led by Colonel Thomas T. Fauntleroy and trapper Cerán St. Vrain defeated the Ute in spring 1855.

The Army in New Mexico.

Despite these efforts, other Indians continued to harass non-Indian emigrants and settlers in New Mexico and Arizona. Colonel Benjamin L. E. Bonneville surprised a large camp of Coyotero Apache along the Gila River on 27 June 1857, killing or wounding nearly forty warriors and taking forty-five women and children captive. Brevet Lieutenant Colonel William Hoffman's seven infantry companies were enough to impress the Mohave, who had earlier driven back a large emigrant party, to sue for peace in 1859.

The more numerous Navaho proved more resilient. Several military thrusts into their homelands produced a temporary truce in late December 1858, but open warfare again erupted thirteen months later. In an unusually bold move, several hundred Navaho warriors attacked Fort Defiance in April 1860. The garrison held and reinforcements raced to New Mexico. Three army columns pushed west from Fort Defiance into Arizona. Failing to secure a decisive victory, the troops nonetheless inflicted great damage upon the Navaho herds and crops. The onset of the secession crisis in 1860–1861, however, prevented local commanders from implementing the subsequent winter campaign envisioned by Washington officials.

The Great Plains.

The War Department had long analyzed the military problems associated with expansion into the Great Plains. During the 1830s Secretaries of War Lewis Cass and Joel R. Poinsett had based their plans for western defense on the idea of a permanent Indian frontier. As settlers streamed west, however, it became evident that static defense was impracticable. Small dragoon expeditions thus began to comb the vast lands west of the Mississippi River during the late 1830s. Hoping that a show of force might overawe the Plains tribes before violence against white overlanders became commonplace, Colonel Stephen Watts Kearny led five companies of horsemen from Fort Leavenworth, Kansas, to the Rocky Mountains in 1845. Similarly, Congress attempted to protect emigrants on the Oregon Trail by creating the Regiment of Mounted Riflemen the following year.

Kearny's mounted force had met representatives of several tribes in its 2,200-mile roundtrip journey. Convinced that this display of American military might have impressed the Indians, Kearny argued that periodic mounted columns might dispel the need for permanent military posts in the Great Plains. During the war against Mexico, regular and volunteer columns continued to patrol the Santa Fe and Oregon trails. Notably, however, one of the most vocal leaders of these battalions, William Gilpin, had concluded that key strategic positions must be occupied if the migrants were to be protected. At the urging of Adjutant General Roger Jones and Secretary of War George W. Crawford, troops erected Fort Atkinson (1950) and Fort Union (1851) to guard the Santa Fe Trail. Colonel Loring had already begun the process on the route to Oregon, establishing Fort Kearny (1846) and garrisoning older trading posts at Forts Laramie, Hall, and Vancouver.

Several government officials questioned the reversion to a fixed-post strategy. Indian agent Thomas Fitzpatrick joined commanding General Scott and Colonel Fauntleroy in advocating the abandonment of the costly, manpower-intensive forts in favor of roving columns launched from a strategic base, a concept also supported by Quartermaster General Jesup.

Fort Riley, established in 1853 near the junction of the Kansas and Republican rivers, was intended to replace Forts Leavenworth, Scott, Atkinson, Kearny, and Laramie, but abandoning military posts proved politically unpalatable to western congressmen, who saw each site as an uncommonly good source of patronage and federal contracts. The small forts also served as helpful way stations for travelers and stimulated settlement, and the army dared not antagonize its western supporters.

Diplomacy, it was hoped, might substitute for immediate military action. Chiefs of the northern tribes signed treaties with Indian Bureau agents at Fort Laramie in 1851; two years later, negotiations with southern tribes resulted in similar pacts at the Fort Atkinson conferences. Lured by gifts and promises of future annuities, few chiefs realized that they had promised to end their intertribal feuds and to allow the U.S. government to build overland trails and military posts across their tribal homelands.

However earnest the supplications of the diplomats might have been, good intentions could not hide the clear and present danger on the Great Plains. The white intruders, convinced of their own moral and cultural righteousness, made little effort to understand the tribal ways of the indigenous peoples. Equally sure of their own superiority, the Indians failed to comprehend the zeal with which the newcomers approached the American West. With garrisons at many of the Plains forts reduced to a single company, tensions increased when a Miniconjou Sioux fired a shot at a soldier outside Fort Laramie in June 1853. Only a year out of West Point and anxious to make his mark in the army, Lieutenant Hugh Fleming and a squad of twenty-three men attempted to arrest the wayward marksman. The soldiers killed six Indians but failed to bring back their captive.

With the Sioux still in an ugly mood the following year, Brevet Second Lieutenant John L. Grattan, fresh out of West Point and still awaiting his permanent appointment, determined to show the Sioux the supremacy of white military techniques. Backed by two howitzers, Grattan, an interpreter, two NCOs, and twenty-seven privates, moved into a Brulé Sioux village and demanded that a young warrior accused of slaughtering a stray cow be given up. Enraged at the defiance of the Indians, Grattan unlimbered the cannons and fired. The shells went high and the Indians swarmed over the outnumbered soldiers. One mortally wounded regular struggled back to Fort Laramie to report the events.

The Plains Wars had begun. Secretary of War Davis recalled Brevet Brigadier General William S. Harney, veteran of the Black Hawk, Seminole, and Mexican wars, from leave in Paris to direct the army's response. At the head of six hundred men as he rode out of Fort Kearny in August 1855, Harney determined to strike first and negotiate later. "By God, I'm for battle—no peace," roared the colonel. Discovering a Brulé camp of two hundred and fifty persons in western Nebraska along Blue Water Creek, Harney took his infantry straight at the Indian lodges and sent four troops of mounted men to hit the enemy rear. The soldiers routed the Sioux, killing or capturing well over half of the village's inhabitants.

Harney then pushed north into the Dakotas, wintering along the Missouri River at the dilapidated old fur trading post of Fort Pierre. The following spring, the colonel received promises of peace from seven Sioux tribes. Although the Senate refused to ratify the soldier-chief's treaties, the Indians of the upper Missouri had been cowed for nearly a decade.

To the south, several violent incidents in 1856 between the Cheyenne and whites convinced both sides to take to the warpath the following year. With a semblance of order having been restored among proslavery and abolitionist factions in Kansas, Colonel Sumner's First Cavalry Regiment spearheaded the thrust from Fort Leavenworth. After nearly two months of campaigning, Sumner encountered three hundred mounted Cheyenne on 29 July 1857. With their left flank resting comfortably on the Solomon Fork of the Kansas River and their spirits buoyed by the assurances of a medicine man that the enemy's bullets had been rendered harmless, the warriors braced for battle. Sumner deployed his own forces, of roughly equal size. Both sides thundered forward on a collision course; the colonel, to the surprise of his own command, ordered his men to sling their carbines and draw sabers.

The medicine man's magic had no power over the flashing swords. The Cheyenne hesitated, then broke. Savage individual combats followed as the cavalry horses galloped after the fleeing ponies. Although Sumner reported only nine Indians killed (his own wounded included the dashing young cavalier J. E. B. Stuart), the Battle of the Solomon was a dramatic psychological victory for the cavalry. During the following winter, the Cheyenne, whose lands had been violated and whose battlefield supremacy had been challenged, remained quiet despite the intrusions of prospectors heading toward new mining camps west of Denver.

THE CIVIL WAR

The secession of eleven southern states and the onset of the Civil War had a dramatic effect upon the American West. Three hundred and thirteen officers, including such stalwart Indian fighters as Lee, Stuart, Van Dorn, and John Bell Hood, resigned their commissions and joined the ranks of the Confederacy. The vast majority of enlisted men, however, remained loyal to the Union. Most of the regulars marched east to confront the rebellion, to be replaced by state and territorial volunteers. The exodus of the southern states, which had often opposed the creation of new governments in the West, allowed Congress to create several new territories—Colorado, Dakota, and Nevada in 1861 (with Nevada securing statehood in 1864), Idaho and Arizona in 1863, and Montana in 1864.

The Civil War wreaked havoc on the Texas frontiers. The withdrawal of federal forces left the state vulnerable to attack by Indians whose cultural proclivities toward warfare had been fired by motives of revenge. As thousands of Texans joined Confederate armies in Virginia, Tennessee, and Arkansas, Texas officials scraped together a few mounted regiments for frontier duty. These poorly supplied units, however, could not protect every western settlement. Texans living in exposed counties often banded together to erect crude defensive stockades for self-protection, but the Battle of Dove Creek (8 January 1865), in which fourteen hundred migratory Kickapoo routed a 370-man ranger force led by Captain Henry Fossett, seemed indicative of the crisis.

Wartime mobilization did allow white expansionists to secure major gains in New Mexico. After driving back a Confederate invasion force in 1862, federal troops there turned their attention to the Indians. The Department of New Mexico commander, Colonel James Henry Carleton, an autocratic professional who determined to make no concessions with any Indians, found in frontiersman Christopher ("Kit") Carson an ideal man for his uncompromising policies. Most of the Mescalero Apache were removed to the Bosque Redondo Reservation. After dodging Carson's columns for nearly nine months in 1863–1864, the Navaho also succumbed to reservation life. Carson also struck a large Kiowa village on 25 November 1864; in a fiercely fought engagement with the Kiowa and a nearby Comanche camp, Carson destroyed the lodges and with artillery support from two howitzers managed to escape with his own force largely intact. Only in Arizona, where the Yavapai and Chiricahua Apache continued to harass would-be miners who flocked to the mining camps of southern Arizona, were Carleton's legions unable to force a temporary peace.

In Brigadier General Wright's Department of the Pacific, volunteer forces managed to preserve the long communication lines through California, Oregon, Nevada, and Utah. On 27 January 1863, California troops under Colonel Patrick E. Connor won a signal victory by storming Bear Hunter's fortified Shoshone village, located along the Bear River in southeastern Idaho. More than two hundred Shoshone were killed in the bloody assault, which cost nearly seventy California casualties. Nearly three months later, another column scattered two hundred Ute at Spanish Fork Canyon, Utah (15 April 1863). The remaining Shoshone, Ute,

Bannock, and Gosiute quickly made peace. Other campaigns in northern California, southern Oregon, and central Nevada also proved largely successful.

Conditions to the north deteriorated badly during the Civil War. In Minnesota, Little Crow's Santee Sioux had long suffered at the hands of white intruders. Repeated delays in annual annuities and chronic food shortages created a tempest that boiled over in August 1862. A two-day bloodletting left four hundred whites dead. Assaults on Fort Ridgely and New Ulm, however, were repulsed with severe loss. An attempted ambush of Colonel Henry H. Sibley's Minnesota volunteers at Wood Lake (23 September 1862) also failed, with about two thousand Sioux subsequently turning themselves in. The most belligerent fled west, with Sibley inflicting heavy casualties upon an informal Sioux coalition in a summer campaign in 1863. A second volunteer column from Nebraska and Iowa, headed by the experienced Brigadier General Alfred Sully, drove into present-day North Dakota. At the Battle of Whitestone Hill (3 September 1863), Sully's legions killed over three hundred Sioux and captured another two hundred and fifty women and children.

Violence also spread to the central Plains, where the expeditionary columns of 1860 had failed to encounter significant resistance. Although the overland and emigrant mail routes had been subjected to some harassment, most tribes remained relatively tolerant of the intruders during the early stages of the Civil War. Colorado officials, such as district commander Colonel John M. Chivington, however, feared a major Indian uprising, and launched a series of probing actions in spring 1864. The Plains tribes struck back against the trails with a savage fury, leading to another flurry of volunteer expeditions that cost a great deal of money and energy but failed to locate many Indians.

As winter approached peace factions regained the initiative among several tribes. Led by Black Kettle, some Cheyenne and Arapaho opened negotiations with government officials, but Chivington declared all Indians to be hostile, and attacked Black Kettle's village near Sand Creek, Colorado, on 28 November 1864. Disregarding the U.S. flag that flew over Black Kettle's tepee, the Colorado volunteers swept through the village, slaughtering two hundred Indians, two-thirds of whom were women and children.

Ripples from the Sand Creek massacre swept the Plains. More than fifteen hundred Cheyenne, Oglala, Brulé, and Arapaho warriors gathered to launch a wave of attacks through the Platte and Powder River valleys. To deal with the crisis, Lieutenant General Grant created a large new command, the Division of the Missouri, which would consolidate the entire Plains regions into a single administrative unit. To command the new division, Grant selected Major General John Pope, a failure against the Confederates but still considered by fellow officers a solid Indian fighter. Pope immediately began planning a major offensive, which some speculated might include twelve thousand men.

Originally slated to begin in April 1865, supply foul-ups, contract problems, and a new peace initiative coming from Senator James R. Doolittle's congressional committee on Indian relations delayed Pope's offensive until the summer. In the meantime, the Indian coalition had ambushed a small escort just outside the Platte Bridge Station in central Wyoming. On 26 July the Indians, at the cost of sixty killed and more than one hundred wounded, finally succeeded in destroying an approaching wagon train. To the south, because most of the Plains tribes were opting for peace, one projected offensive was abandoned by the army.

Three columns, commanded by Brigadier General Connor, finally pushed out from Omaha and Fort Laramie in July and early August. Collectively totaling twenty-five hundred soldiers, the expeditions scoured the Powder River region for two months. An early blizzard, the rugged terrain, and poor army leadership, however, combined to largely thwart the effort. Another eight hundred men under Sully pushed up the Missouri River into the northern Dakotas, but once again produced few tangible results. At a cost of well over $20 million, the summer campaigns of 1865 had killed no more than one hundred Indians.

THE POST–CIVIL WAR ARMY

In May 1865 the combined armies of the United States had numbered more than one million men. Swift demobilization followed the defeat of the Confederacy, as the volunteers were mustered out and the regulars slowly returned to the frontiers. In July 1866 Congress cut the peacetime army to 54,302; further reductions in 1869, 1870, and 1874 trimmed the maximum authorized regular force to just over twenty-seven thousand. The reconstituted army would include ten cavalry, twenty-five infantry, and five artillery regiments. In partial recognition of the service provided by black volunteers during the Civil War, two cavalry (the Ninth and Tenth) and two infantry (the Twenty-fourth and Twenty-fifth) regiments would be comprised of black enlisted personnel. Black officers, however, remained virtually unknown during the postbellum years, with the first black graduate of West Point, Lieutenant Henry O. Flipper, court-martialed for dubious cause in 1882.

Although even the force of twenty-seven thousand represented an increase over the antebellum military, the growing national population and continued westward expansion would have made the army's task extremely difficult, and circumstances were less than ideal. From 10 to 15 percent of the soldiers guarded the arsenals and coastal defenses of the east, and were as such unavailable for service against the Indians. In 1885 a special board headed by Secretary of War William C. Endicott recommended major improvements in the seaboard defenses. Congress refused to fund all the proposals, but further attention was nonetheless paid to such defensive needs in the wake of the Endicott plan.

From 1865 to 1877, Reconstruction drained even more manpower. Federal forces occupied the South immediately after the war, but their powers and authority remained unclear until the Reconstruction Act of 1867, which carved the unreconstructed states into five military districts. In that year duties involved nearly 40 percent of the army, and even as late as 1876, about 15 percent of the regulars were stationed in the South. The army's efforts to supervise the new governments and to guarantee the rights of freedmen proved immensely unpopular among white southerners. Congressional Democrats also challenged the military's activist role, and the resurgence of the Democrats would not augur well for advocates of a stronger military establishment in following years.

Although the Civil War had confirmed the supremacy of the federal government, lawmakers generally proved reluctant to assert this authority, particularly after the end of Reconstruction. The number of federal agencies thus remained small. Rather than creating new offices to handle emerging problems, Congress and the executive branch continued to rely upon the U.S. Army, which seemed to many politicians a convenient alternative to new bureaucracy. As such, the regulars undertook a variety of quasi-military responsibilities in the late nineteenth century.

These duties encompassed a wide array of tasks. Civilian scientists and explorers in the American West required military escorts. In addition, under the direction of the Signal Service and Corps of Engineers, the army conducted extensive surveys and observations of its own throughout the period. The United States Weather Bureau, for example, was created in 1870 from one branch of the Signal Service. Likewise, the army served as official custodian of the Yellowstone, Yosemite, General Grant, and Sequoia national parks during the 1880s and 1890s. Squads of cavalry policed these natural wonders, protecting wildlife and suppressing vandalism by careless tourists. In the absence of federal relief agencies, troops distributed food, blankets, and shoes to civilians rendered destitute by natural disaster. Similarly, when a fire destroyed much of Chicago in 1871, four companies of regulars were called in to help restore order to the city.

The army also took an active role in quelling the internal disorders of the late nineteenth century. Nearly four thousand soldiers participated in the government's efforts to reopen the railroads during the strikes of 1877. Federal troops occupied Seattle, Washington; Omaha, Nebraska; and Rock Springs, Wyoming, during a wave of anti-Chinese riots during the 1880s. In 1894 nearly two-thirds of the army stood poised to intervene against domestic unrest; in Chicago, General Nelson A. Miles used his troops to assist railroad management during the Pullman strikes. Still fearful of the power of the Mormons in Utah, the government also dispatched troops into Deseret on several occasions.

The diversion of so many troops away from duties along the Indian frontiers posed major hurdles. Civilian demands for protection against Indian attack or for offensive campaigns against tribes deemed hostile could not always be met while quasi-military responsibilities siphoned off available units. The army remained committed to national expansion, but limited manpower made it impossible to garrison every area and prevented the military from opening simultaneous offensives throughout the West.

Problems of organization and administration, doctrine, and politics added to the dilemma. As had been the case before the Civil War, the military divided the American West into a series of districts, departments, and divisions, including the Division of the Missouri (generally encompassing Texas, New Mexico, and the lands drained by the Missouri River and its tributaries) and the Division of the Pacific (the Pacific coast plus Arizona), which were the prime commands for Indian duty. The commands were organized largely for convenience, with the number of divisions usually equal to the number of two-star generals. Brigadier generals typically handled the departments, with periodic administrative changes being tailored to fit personnel rather than military necessity.

In theory, the secretary of war, after consultation with the president, would set general policy for the commanding general, who would then lend his military expertise in refining and issuing more detailed instructions to division commanders, who would add their own endorsements in forwarding orders to the respective department chiefs. Had everyone followed proper military procedure, had the respective authorities of the secretary of war and commanding general been clearly delineated, and had the separation of responsibilities between staff and line officers been clear, the system might have worked reasonably well.

The post–Civil War military establishment, however, benefited from none of these routine procedures or definitions in authority. The long-standing dispute between war secretaries and commanding generals grew worse, the latter position remaining ill-defined, even though it was held by such tested Civil War veterans as William T. Sherman (1869–1883), Philip H. Sheridan (1883–1888), John M. Schofield (1888–1895), and Nelson A. Miles (1895–1903). Of these individuals, only Schofield, who had briefly served as secretary of war from 1868 to 1869, opted not to challenge the secretary's authority. Disgusted with his rivalry with Secretary William W. Belknap, Sherman transferred the offices of the commanding general to Saint Louis in 1874. For the next two years, during which some of the largest campaigns against Indians took place, the senior general was virtually removed from discussions regarding his troops. Belknap's subsequent resignation to avoid charges of selling post sutlerships allowed Sherman to return to Washington, D.C., but the fundamental problem remained unresolved. Sheridan subsequently tested, without success, Secretary of War Robert T. Lincoln; Miles would later confront Elihu Root, who responded by abolishing the commanding general's office altogether.

Controversies between staff and line officers also divided the army. The brigadier generals in command of the War Department's ten staff bureaus after the Civil War (Adjutant General's Office, Inspector General's Department, Judge-Advocate General's Office, Quartermaster Department, Subsistence Department, Ordnance Department, Corps of Engineers, Medical Department, Signal Bureau, and Pay Department) controlled their petty fiefdoms with virtual impunity. Staff personnel, often protected by strong political alliances, controlled logistics and weapons development. Line officers, jealous of the influence and privileges of their rivals, demanded a system of rotation between staff and line positions. Staff officers, they charged, had grown soft and cared little for the welfare of men in the field and in combat.

Confusion over proper doctrine against Indians also hampered the army. Few officers showed much interest in questions of strategy; those who did concerned themselves almost entirely with issues related to traditional, European-style foes. Those who hoped to reform the U.S. military system found a limited audience during the nineteenth century. The most notable reformer, Emory Upton, compiled a manuscript, "The Military Policy of the United States," which eventually served as an important guide for Secretary Root, who led a major renaissance in organizational thinking after the war against Spain. Upton's work, however, contained little of interest to those fighting Indians, and although compiled before his death in 1881, was not published until 1904. Although a few commissioned personnel supported new postgraduate educational programs, the typical officer continued to scorn the proverbial schoolbook soldier.

In the absence of formal doctrine, experience and tradition provided a few generally accepted means of dealing with Indians and assisting expansion. Fixed posts, as had been the case before the Civil War, again provided the basis for these efforts. Railroad and telegraph lines also continued to receive the army's close attention. Decisive results could only be obtained, argued military leaders, through offensive action, but the army faced a cruel dilemma, because mounted warriors from the military societies of the Plains tribes comprised a growing percentage of those Indians deemed hostile by the federal government. Forcing these skilled tribesmen to fight posed a major problem. Horses were too expensive to maintain in the field, thus prohibiting the military from mounting all of its soldiers, and the sheer vastness of the American West made it difficult for even the most determined columns to track down their foes.

Only the most perceptive officers learned to overcome these obstacles. To increase mobility, the regulars often abandoned their wagons in favor of the more ambulatory mules. Miles, one of the ablest of the Indian fighters, mounted his Fifth Infantry Regiment on captured ponies and even managed to deploy light mountain howitzers. More widespread was the employment of Indian auxiliaries, essential in tracking and defeating their brethren declared hostile by federal authorities. Converging columns also proved their worth, at tactical as well as strategic levels. By threatening Indian villages from several directions, such columns often forced the warriors to stand and fight under unfavorable tactical conditions.

Political hurdles severely hindered military effectiveness. "The army," wrote Sherman in 1873, "has no 'policy' about Indians or anything else. It has no voice in Congress, but accepts the laws as enacted." Following Sherman's apolitical lead, the army neglected to mount an effective lobbying campaign, a failure that contrasted starkly with the determined efforts of the navy during the period to enlist public and congressional support for modern warships. Private traders, contractors, and local interests thus weighed more immediately in the minds of most congressmen than did the nation's army. With Civil War veterans offering eloquent testimony to the effectiveness of volunteers, the traditional fears of a standing military establishment detracted from efforts to build a larger regular force. The army's political weakness was perhaps nowhere better demonstrated than in June 1877, when a congressional impasse over appropriations left officers without pay for nearly five months.

Conflicts with other governmental agencies and civilian reformers further complicated the task of the War Department. Few tribes respected the artificial boundaries with Mexico and Canada, and the army demanded permission to pursue Indians accused of depredations across these lines. International cooperation, argued officers on the scene, was also necessary. To secure these ends, the army depended upon the State Department, whose agents viewed the military effort against Indians as only one part of a much broader range of international relations. Thus, securing a reciprocal crossing agreement with Mexico (such agreements were concluded in 1880 and 1882) remained only a secondary goal of the State Department's diplomacy.

The Department of Interior proved even more recalcitrant. The essential problem remained the same as before the Civil War—the military jurisdiction of the army did not extend to the reservations, which were administered by a branch of the Interior Department, the Bureau of Indian Affairs. Military men claimed that Indians committed depredations off their reservations, then fled back to the reserves for safety just ahead of their army pursuers. Emphasizing the corruption that infected many Indian Bureau agencies, the army also asserted that its officers could better distribute supplies and administer justice on the reservations than the political hacks who had received government jobs by virtue of their personal connections. All Indian affairs, claimed nearly every general officer, should be consolidated under the aegis of the Department of War.

Interior Department officials denied such accusations. Army officers trained in the arts of war could scarcely be qualified to initiate peaceful efforts with the tribes, which required men who espoused Christian morality. Transferring Indian affairs to the War Department, argued Interior officials, would merely legitimize a large standing army and threaten democratic institutions. Most of the self-styled "Indian reformers" of the period—well-meaning if somewhat paternalistic individuals, such as Indian Rights Association secretary Herbert Welsh, Episcopal clergyman Henry B. Whipple, Secretary of the Interior Carl Schurz, and Senator Henry L. Dawes—also opposed the transfer to the War Department. Congressional challenges to the existing system therefore failed, leaving in their wake a legacy of tense relations and mistrust between the War and Interior departments.

THE WARS AGAINST THE INDIANS, 1865–1891

In November 1865, General Sherman, inexperienced in handling Indian affairs, predicted that the return of the regulars would quickly overwhelm the Indians. Although Sherman had demonstrated his leadership abilities during the Civil War, he and many fellow veterans, who had served some time on the frontier, did not have much command experience in the West. In a futile gesture to defend westward emigrants immediately after the war, Sherman suggested that commanders at Forts Ridgely (Minnesota), Abercrombie (North Dakota), Kearny (Nebraska), and Riley and Larned (Kansas) organize travelers into groups that each included at least thirty armed men.

The Bozeman Trail. Such stopgap measures could hardly be expected to bring peace to the frontier. Slowed by the Civil War, western migration would increase dramatically after 1865. New problems arose as the overlanders threatened the traditional hunting grounds of the proud Plains Indians. Relations were particularly tense in Wyoming and Montana along the recently opened Bozeman Trail, which offered the shortest route to the Montana gold fields near Virginia City, Butte, and Helena. In 1866 Fort Reno, Wyoming, was reoccupied and Forts Phil Kearny, Wyoming, and C. F. Smith, Nebraska, were established to guard the Bozeman Trail.

Colonel Henry B. Carrington, a patient, literate individual who had spent most of the Civil War behind a desk, commanded the isolated garrison at Fort Phil Kearny. Junior officers chafed under Carrington's inactivity, and, when one of the post's woodgathering parties was attacked on 21 December, Brevet Lieutenant Colonel William J. Fetterman was selected to lead an eighty-man relief force. Decoyed into a superbly laid ambush, Fetterman's command was annihilated and the entire region rendered unsafe for all but the strongest patrols. Paralyzed by the crisis, Carrington was transferred to a quieter position in Colorado. Heavy snows delayed a retaliatory strike until the following February.

As commander of the crucial Division of the Missouri, Sherman was working on more general plans for the Great Plains. The federal government he believed needed to establish an Indian-free belt between the Arkansas and Platte rivers, which would allow unimpeded continued construction of the Kansas Pacific and Union Pacific railroads, which were vital to western expansion. The southern tribes, in Sherman's view, had to be kept east of Fort Union, New Mexico, and the Sioux restricted to an area west of the Missouri River and east of the Bozeman Trail. Expecting reinforcements to bolster his division, Sherman hoped to launch major offensives in spring 1867. The Fetterman massacre only stiffened his resolve. "We must act with vindictive earnestness against the Sioux," he reported, "even to their extermination, men, women, and children".

However exaggerated such a statement (Sherman's subsequent actions suggest that he never advocated complete physical extermination), his bombastic rhetoric certainly confirmed suspicions of military inhumanity. The Senate refused to transfer the Indian Bureau to the War Department. Indeed, President Andrew Johnson dispatched a new peace commission to speak with the Sioux. Rather than the offensives promised by Sherman, the army was thus relegated to a defensive posture on the northern Plains even as the number of raids increased against the Bozeman Trail. In 1867 detachments from Forts C. F. Smith and Phil Kearny turned back determined attacks by the Sioux and northern Cheyenne in the Hayfield (1 August) and Wagon Box (2 August) fights, respectively, while other soldiers erected several forts on the outskirts of the Sioux country.

The Southern Plains.

The diplomatic initiatives in the north did not deter a major campaign to the south. Winfield Scott Hancock, an able Civil War veteran who later made a deter-

mined bid for the presidency, led a column that eventually totaled fourteen hundred men out of Fort Riley in April 1867. Cursory discussions convinced Hancock that the Indians had opted for war; he burned a large Cheyenne and Sioux village near Pawnee Fork, Kansas, and detached Lieutenant Colonel George Armstrong Custer on a wildly unsuccessful pursuit of the warriors. Although Sherman credited the Hancock expedition with having broken up a massive coalition, the regulars had not brought peace to the region. Peace commissioners blamed the campaign for having ruined their efforts, and Kansans and Nebraskans felt the wrath of angry Indian attacks throughout the summer.

Congress responded by forming another commission, which included three generals—Sherman, Alfred H. Terry, and retired Brigadier General Harney—among its seven members. Meetings with a variety of Indian delegations confirmed the civilian majority's belief that the government should adopt a more pacific policy. Treaties signed at Medicine Lodge Creek, Kansas, in 1867 established two large reservations in western Indian territory for the Cheyenne, Arapaho, Kiowa, and Comanche. The agreements reached at Fort Laramie, Wyoming, in 1868 defined another large reserve for the Sioux in western South Dakota. Extensive hunting privileges were also promised, and the army agreed to abandon its posts along the Bozeman Trail. In both sets of agreements, the Indians relinquished most of their other rights off the reservations in return for government annuities.

Although conducted with the full support of President Grant, Sherman was certain the new peace policy would fail. Indeed, fiercely independent southern Plains warriors continued to launch raids while Congress delayed funding the Indian appropriations. Therefore, the army began patroling Kansas, Nebraska, and Colorado more actively in August 1868. Skirmishing culminated in the Battle of Beecher Island (17–25 September), during which Brevet Colonel George A. Forsyth and a company of fifty volunteer scouts fended off a week-long Oglala

Sioux and Cheyenne siege along the Arikara River.

Sherman concluded that major offensive actions were needed. To oversee the campaigns, he selected Sheridan, a pugnacious battler whose temperament had nearly prevented him from graduating from West Point and who had been an unrelenting campaigner against the Cascade and Yakima Indians during the mid-1850s. Brilliant service during the Civil War had culminated in his masterly conquest of the Shenandoah Valley in 1864–1865 and catapulted him to the rank of major general. After the close of the war, however, his heavy-handed rule of Texas and Louisiana had antagonized President Andrew Johnson, who transferred him from Reconstruction duties to the Department of the Missouri in 1868. When Sherman took the office of commanding general the following year, Sheridan stepped up to command the Division of the Missouri. Sheridan's willingness to make enemy noncombatants feel the hard hand of war, his insensitive view of Indians, and a determination to protect white expansion ideally suited him to Sherman's purposes.

As army columns scoured the region between the Red and Republican rivers, the peace commission reconvened in early October 1868. The absence of Senator John Henderson and the subsequent appointment of Brigadier General Christopher C. Augur gave the military a working majority on the commission. Seizing this opportunity to dictate government policy, the generals sharply increased the authority of the army, thus enabling Sheridan and Sherman to put their offensives into motion. All the Indians who wanted peace were instructed to gather near Fort Cobb, Oklahoma, under the loose protective custody of Colonel William B. Hazen. Those who did not report to Hazen were declared hostile and subject to attacks timed to coincide with the onset of winter.

Three columns took the field in November 1868. Major Andrew W. Evans led over five hundred men out of Fort Bascom, New Mexico, eastward down the South Canadian River. From Fort Lyon, Colorado, Major Eugene A. Carr commanded a slightly larger force that pushed south and east toward the Red River. From a new base at Camp Supply in Indian Territory, Sheridan accompanied a third column, which boasted a strong infantry escort and most of Lieutenant Colonel Custer's Seventh Cavalry Regiment. It was hoped that the cold weather would restrict Indian movement and that the convergence of Evans and Carr would force the enemy to retreat into the jaws of the heavy column spearheaded by Custer's cavalry.

Custer indeed struck first. Upon locating a large Indian village along the Washita River, he ordered a dawn assault on 27 November. Eager to recoup his fortunes (he had been court-martialed for having left his command during a reckless visit to his wife during the Hancock campaign of 1867), the lack of information as to the dispositions of the enemy did not dispel the ambitious officer. Custer assumed that his Seventh Cavalry could defeat any opposition. Dividing his command into four detachments in an effort to trap the entire camp, Custer thundered into the village as surprised inhabitants rushed from their lodges.

Although the delayed arrival of two of the columns allowed many of the Indians to escape, Custer's men enjoyed complete surprise. Pockets of resistance were eliminated as Custer gained control of the village within ten minutes. To the east, however, Major Joel H. Elliott's battalion had encountered an unforeseen enemy. Elliott and his nineteen men were never heard from again as hundreds of fresh warriors from camps Custer had not yet found ringed the original Indian encampment. Still ignorant of Elliott's whereabouts, Custer, after destroying the Indian lodges and winter stores and slaughtering the captured pony herd, pulled back toward Camp Supply.

The army's victory at the Washita was full of irony. The village had been that of Black Kettle, the Cheyenne chief who had barely escaped from the disaster at Sand Creek. Seeking peace, Black Kettle had attempted to gain succor with Hazen earlier in the month, but the chief's followers had not been without blame, as witnessed in the four white captives and assorted wartime spoils found in the village. Custer emerged an even more controversial figure. Supporters pointed out that he had destroyed an Indian village and inflicted more than one hundred casualties, while his critics emphasized his willingness to depart the field without determining Elliott's fate and to the high number of Indian noncombatants killed in the action.

The army kept up the pressure all winter. Colonel Benjamin Grierson's black Tenth Cavalry began constructing strategic Fort Sill along the eastern face of the Wichita Mountains. In December, Evans razed a Comanche camp at Soldier Spring, in the southwestern corner of the Indian Territory. Casualties were light, but the soldiers once again burned the invaluable winter stores of their foes. Thousands of southern Cheyenne, Kiowa, and Comanche turned themselves in as the winter took its cruel toll. After briefly pausing to refit their strike forces, Custer, Evans, and Carr continued to comb suspected Indian haunts through the early spring. In a final fling, Carr destroyed an encampment of Cheyenne Dog Soldiers at Summit Springs, Colorado, on 11 July 1869.

By striking at the homes of their foes, the army had forced the Indians to fight on less than favorable terms during the campaigns of 1868–1869. Although the battles had not always been decisive, the ceaseless pressure had shattered Indian morale. The tribes could no longer rely on their traditional winter security blanket. Of course, the cold weather campaigns also displayed critical army weaknesses. Severe supply shortages plagued every army column, and hundreds of horses and mules died of exposure and starvation. Several officers had displayed neither the skill nor the determination to track down and engage their foes. The effort to distinguish peaceful and hostile Indians had not worked, and Sheridan never forgave Hazen for having promised safe haven to so many Indians. (The two had clashed earlier over their respective roles in the Battle of Missionary Ridge during the Civil War.)

The Pacific Northwest.
Violence also disrupted non-Indian expansion into the Pacific Northwest. Gold discoveries in the Boise Basin region of southwestern Idaho had attracted thousands of prospectors during the Civil War. Placer yields in eastern Oregon also drew large migrant populations. Others headed east for Helena and Virginia City in Montana. The Snake River Paiute vigorously resisted these encroachments, and desultory campaigns by state and territorial volunteers failed to clear the region of its native inhabitants.

For expansion to continue unabated, it fell to the bewhiskered Lieutenant Colonel Crook to defeat the northern Paiute. A stubborn campaigner, Crook's legendary feats of stamina were rivaled only by his determination to fulfill every promise he made to his Indian foes. Using pack mules to bring up supplies, Crook also took great pains to enlist qualified scouts, many of whom were recruited from the nearby Shoshone. For twenty-one months his command engaged in forty battles and skirmishes with the Paiute, who finally gave up the cause by summer 1868.

Events in Montana the following winter gave the army less cause for self-congratulation. Mountain Chief's band of Piegan Indians had harassed white intruders for several years. Tired of the clamor for action, Sheridan urged a winter strike and suggested Brevet Colonel Eugene M. Baker as an excellent man to do the job. "Tell Baker to strike them hard," concluded Sheridan. Eager to comply, Baker found a Piegan camp near the Big Bend of the Marias River in mid-January 1870.

At dawn on the twenty-third, the regulars swept through the surprised village with a vengeance; official army figures state that fifty-three of the 173 Indians reported killed had been women and children. Another three hundred captives were turned loose to face the winter blizzards without their belongings, which had been destroyed by the soldiers. The Piegan had not been followers of Mountain Chief; instead, they adhered to the peaceful leadership of Heavy Runner, who had been killed early in the slaughter.

The Army and the Peace Policy.
Eager to cut military spending and appalled by reports of the Baker massacre, Congress determined to rein in the army. Expansion had to continue but

the peace policy of newly elected President Grant needed a chance to succeed. The Indians would become self-sufficient, argued the reformers, by adopting agriculture on the reservations. Christian virtue and forgiveness would replace the sword in dictating Indian policy. Because the army needed to secure Interior Department permission before entering the reservations, a ten-man board of commissioners was created to advise the secretary of the interior. Church groups would send dedicated agents to the reservations to help the tribes achieve the white man's version of civilization.

Reformers concentrated their efforts on the Great Plains, where the peace policy had halted army offensives. In Arizona, however, the regulars continued to strike various Apache bands whose defiance of government authority threatened non-Indian settlers and travelers. The terrain and sparse population of the territory rendered impossible defense of each ranch, mining camp, settlement, and overland party. In response to a chorus of demands for action, the War Department carved out a separate Department of Arizona in April 1870.

Officers stationed in the region decried Apache culture and urged that they be allowed to stamp out all Indian resistance, but implementing such harsh policies demanded more effort than many were willing to give. The first head of the Department of Arizona, Colonel George Stoneman, for example, found no solace in the stark physical isolation of the Far Southwest and set up headquarters near Los Angeles, California. Desultory campaigns in the winter of 1870–1871 pleased few Arizonans, who demanded that the Indians be removed to make room for white immigrants. As usual, special criticisms were reserved for the infantrymen, whose immobility often relegated them to garrison duty.

Intense pressure from western politicians led President Grant to transfer the able Crook to command the department. Before he arrived, however, a group of Tucson vigilantes, joined by a contingent of Papago Indians, slaughtered at least eighty-five Apache at Camp Grant, Arizona. The hue and cry raised by eastern reformers to the Camp Grant massacre forced

Crook to delay his offensives until peace delegations were given another chance. Crook publicly supported such initiatives, but privately he believed that he should be allowed to "conquer a lasting peace" in Arizona.

Although more than five thousand Apache and Yavapai accepted terms and government rations, the violence continued. Indian raiders killed forty-four persons between September 1871 and September 1872, with more than five hundred head of livestock reported stolen. An impatient Crook received permission to take the offensive in late 1872. Encouraging subordinates to study the terrain and the people with whom they were dealing, he signed up swarms of Indian auxiliaries to scout for and fight with his regulars. His remorseless columns swept through suspected enemy haunts, forcing most of the Indians onto reservations by the close of 1873.

A far different scenario disrupted the peace policy in Oregon. The Modoc had ceded their lands along the northern California–southern Oregon boundary in 1864, but now chafed under reservation life in which they were dominated by the more numerous Klamath. Kintpuash (Captain Jack) led about seventy warriors and their families back to their Lost River homelands; by 1871, white settlers in the area demanded that the military remove the Modoc back to their reservation.

An attack on Kintpuash's village the following year forced the issue. The Modoc, although badly outnumbered by army forces (which eventually totaled nearly one thousand men), retreated into the lava beds south of Tule Lake and set up virtually impregnable defenses. Clumsy attempts to storm the natural stronghold having failed, Brigadier General Edward R. S. Canby was authorized to seek a peaceful settlement. Militants within the Modoc camp, presumably buoyed by what some considered a sign of government weakness, demanded that Kintpuash kill the peace commissioners in a desperate attempt to secure a reservation at Lost River.

On 11 April 1873, Canby and three delegates met with Modoc leaders in a tent between the two lines. Jack drew a pistol and murdered

Canby, the only regular army general to be killed by Indians during the long history of Indian-white conflicts in the United States. Two of the other commissioners also fell dead, with the third severely wounded. Subsequent efforts to close the siege again reflected poorly on the army, with a strong reconnaissance commanded by Captain Evan Thomas nearly annihilated on 26 April.

Only with the arrival of Colonel Jefferson C. Davis did the shaken regulars regain the initiative. Some of the Modoc began surrendering in May, with Kintpuash and his family, at the behest of deserters from his own tribe, giving up in early June. Kintpuash and three advisers were hung by order of a military court-martial; 155 of his followers were escorted to Indian Territory that October. The campaign painted a dismal picture of army tactics. Well-led, determined Modoc warriors had enjoyed superb positions, but poor marksmanship and timid leadership had plagued the regular attackers. Junior officers seemed incapable even of properly deploying a skirmish line. Concluded one blunt critic, "Those men don't know how to fight Indians."

In Texas western travelers and non-Indian frontier settlers were voicing bitter complaints about Indian depredations. Delayed by the Civil War, thousands poured into north central and southwestern Texas during the late 1860s and the 1870s. Others headed to New Mexico, Arizona, and California via the roads across the trans-Pecos. Immediately following the Civil War, the regulars were more closely involved with Reconstruction than western expansion. By the late 1860s, however, the army had reoccupied its frontier posts and stepped up its patrols.

Kickapoo, Lipan, and Mescalero Apache raiders had long terrorized settlers along both sides of the Rio Grande. U.S. Army officers demanded permission to cross the border into Mexico, but officials of that nation remained reluctant to authorize such military excursions. Still chafing under the dictates of Grant's peace policy, division commander Sheridan searched for some means of eliminating the Indian

threats. Colonel Ranald S. Mackenzie and his Fourth Cavalry Regiment were transferred to the Texas borderlands in early 1873; his fine Civil War record and good relationship with President Grant augured well for those who hoped for decisive action.

Texans did not have to wait long. Sheridan visited Mackenzie at Fort Clark in April 1873. Verbally assuring the young colonel of presidential support, he encouraged Mackenzie to take any steps necessary to bring peace to the borderlands. Mackenzie drilled his men for several weeks before implementing Sheridan's suggestions. On 17 May 1873, a squad of hand-picked scouts guided nearly four hundred regulars across the Rio Grande. Burning three Indian villages near Remolino, Mexico, they splashed back across the river two days later. Several smaller border crossings followed that summer, although the international furor resulting from the Remolino raid convinced Sheridan to rein in his eager subordinate.

Violence on the southern Plains soon shifted attention away from Mackenzie's raid and called into question the entire peace policy. Although the region's major tribes were still drawing rations from their respective agencies, raids into Kansas and Texas intensified as memories faded of the winter campaigns of 1868–1869. The danger posed by these attacks was made abundantly clear in May 1871, when, during an inspection tour of north Texas, General Sherman and a small escort narrowly escaped a Kiowa war party outside Fort Richardson, Texas. Satank, Satanta, and Big Tree, among the most outspoken of the Indian war leaders, were arrested soon thereafter.

Satank later died while trying to escape; a Texas jury sentenced Satanta and Big Tree to death, only to have their sentences commuted to life imprisonment by Governor Edmund J. Davis. As the two Indians whiled away their hours in a Huntsville prison, army columns crisscrossed the Llano Estacado (Staked Plain) in the summer of 1872. On 29 September, Mackenzie routed a Comanche village near McClellan Creek, killing fifty Indians and taking another 124 captive. Officials still hoped, however, that a final gesture of diplomacy might convince the Indians to lay down their arms. In a move designed to end the raids against Texas, Satanta, Big Tree, and the Comanche prisoners were freed in fall 1873.

The Red River War. Instead of bringing peace, the act prompted a series of Kiowa and Comanche raids into Texas. Infuriated by what they considered to be the gullibility of the Christian agents and the corruption of the Interior Department, army officers demanded the opportunity to take the field. Only by disarming and dismounting the tribes, argued military men, could western expansion be freed from the threat of Indian attack. Sheridan drew up plans for a winter offensive in 1873–1874, only to be rebuffed by a hesitant Department of the Interior. Indian attacks continued the following year, culminating in an unsuccessful assault on a camp of buffalo hunters at Adobe Walls, Texas, in June 1874. On 18 July Secretary of the Interior Columbus Delano gave the army permission to enter the reservations.

Having anticipated Delano's decision, Sheridan had already encouraged his key department commanders, Augur (Department of Texas) and Pope (Department of the Missouri) to draw up plans for an offensive. Augur did so, but Pope remained reluctant, arguing instead that the army should wait until the onset of winter to launch its columns. Premature attacks, maintained Pope, would only waste the cavalry and that it would be better to wait until the timing was right and do the job properly.

But Sheridan held firm. The army had to move immediately, he believed, or it would risk having the Interior Department retract its decision to allow troops to enter the reservations. As such, sketchy plans for a late summer offensive slowly materialized despite Pope's objections. As division commander, Sheridan took little direct role except as cheerleader and chief logistical officer. "I will not sketch out any plan of operations for your cavalry," he told Pope on 22 July, "leaving you to exercise your good judgment in this respect." Pope and Augur could thus organize their efforts as they saw fit,

a policy that gave wide latitude for flexibility and initiative, but that discouraged efforts to coordinate the various columns. To further complicate planning, Sherman, in his flight from Secretary of War Belknap, had recently transferred his headquarters to Saint Louis, thereby removing him from any effective role in the upcoming campaign.

Augur and Pope also opted to give their field commanders optimum freedom of action. From the Department of the Missouri, Pope organized columns under Colonel Nelson A. Miles and Major William R. Price. Miles was to move south from Fort Dodge, Kansas, then operate west of the Wichita Mountains, attacking hostile Indians wherever they might be located. He should not, suggested Pope, be bound by any more specific guidelines. Price was to march down the Canadian River from Fort Bascom, New Mexico, then link up with Miles. Again, however, Pope cautioned his subordinate to fit his actions to the circumstances as they presented themselves.

Augur braced his forces for a similar effort. Mackenzie and the veteran Fourth Cavalry, recently transferred from the borderlands to Fort Concho, would spearhead the thrust. Other forces, commanded by Lieutenant Colonels George Buell, John W. Davidson, and Thomas H. Neill, would operate north of Mackenzie. Davidson and Neill, assigned to separate friendly from hostile Indians at Fort Sill and the Darlington Agency, respectively, had particularly difficult assignments. Other than warning his commanders that the campaign would be prolonged, Augur declined to issue detailed instructions, relying chiefly upon the abilities of Mackenzie as a combat leader.

Skirmishing began in August as Davidson unsuccessfully tried to disarm the Kiowa and Comanche near Fort Sill. Some five thousand southern Cheyenne, Comanche, and Kiowa, about one-quarter of them warriors, fled the reservations in confusion. Price, Miles, Mackenzie, Buell, and Davidson had also taken the field, collectively mounting about two thousand men capable of offensive action. Moving south of the Canadian River through the drought-ravaged southern Plains, Miles struck a strong Cheyenne force near the Salt Fork of the Red River on 30 August. In a running battle, he drove the Indians back in disrepair, only to see his pursuit ended by supply shortages. Raids against his rearguard areas nearly annihilated several detached escorts, even as Price's forces linked up with the main body.

Davidson and Buell set forth from Fort Sill in September, encountering little organized resistance at the onset. More determined was Mackenzie, who had established a supply depot on the upper Brazos River. His 471-strong force threw back a night assault on 26 September, then hurried ahead to Palo Duro Canyon, where Tonkawa scouts had located a large camp of Cheyenne, Kiowa, and Comanche. At daybreak of 28 September, Mackenzie's veterans scrambled down the canyon slopes. Warning shots fired by sleepy Indian pickets enabled most of the inhabitants to flee, but the soldiers seized the lodges and ponies left behind in the rush to freedom. Mackenzie's troopers burned the camp, and the following day his men replaced their jaded mounts, then slaughtered the remainder of the herd.

The army maintained the pressure through the fall. Buell burned two Indian villages, collectively numbering more than five hundred lodges, on 11–12 October. A detachment from Miles' main force led by Lieutenant Frank D. Baldwin dealt a Cheyenne camp another stinging blow near McClellan Creek on 8 November. The onset of winter forced Davidson, Buell, and Mackenzie to break up their expeditions in December, but Miles remained indefatigable despite the icy blizzards. At the head of three companies, the colonel set out in early January 1875 on a final drive through the headwaters of the Red River.

Although combat casualties had been relatively light, the Red River campaigns had taken a severe toll among the Indians. Shorn of their mobility by the forageless winter, the destruction of so many ponies, and the relentless pursuits of the army, tattered bands had started to turn themselves in the previous October. Most of those remaining out surrendered in the early

spring of 1875. A final group of four hundred Comanches came in as late as 2 June.

The regulars had also suffered, because of the army's dependence upon private contractors for logistical support, particularly the transportation of supplies from depots to the field columns. The failure to establish unity of command also hampered their efforts. Sheridan had designed the general plan, but then concerned himself largely with trying to resolve the supply morass. Troops from two departments (Texas and Missouri), therefore, struck out with only vague notions of where their comrades might be. Critics also speculated that the competition between Miles and Mackenzie had needlessly endangered the lives of their men, for each of these able but ambitious leaders had failed to cooperate as well as might have been expected.

The Great Sioux War. The Red River War, in leaving behind a defeated, demoralized Plains peoples, had shattered the peace policy in the south. With the full support of the military, the government had opted to back the interests of those who sought western development over the objections of the earlier inhabitants of the region. Blatant expansionism would more directly end the brief peace initiatives on the northern Plains. The Fort Laramie Treaties had left to the Sioux a huge reservation comprising much of western South Dakota, but large numbers of Sioux, northern Arapaho, and northern Cheyenne, proud of their independent heritage, continued to deny government sovereignty. The tense situation was exacerbated by the seemingly inexorable advance of the Northern Pacific Railroad, which by the early 1870s neared the Yellowstone River valley.

As railroad parties approached lands that the Sioux considered theirs (the recent treaties were unclear as to whether the Indian cessions extended as far as the Yellowstone), Indian resistance grew more apparent. Military escorts accompanied railroad surveying parties in 1871 and 1872. Mounting pressure led to an even larger army effort the following year; Colonel David S. Stanley, fifteen hundred troops, and four hundred civilians comprised the 1873 summer expedition. Near the mouth of the Tongue River, several hundred warriors engaged detachments of Stanley's command led by Custer on 4 August. Another sharp skirmish occurred a week later.

Although the Northern Pacific was thrown into bankruptcy by the panic of 1873, rumors of rich mineral deposits heightened interest in the Black Hills. The army also wanted to establish a large new military post in the region. To investigate both possibilities, Custer mounted another strong expeditionary force in the summer of 1874. Nearly one hundred wagons, three Gatling guns, one cannon, a military band, four scientists, and a photographer accompanied the two companies of infantrymen and ten troops of horse soldiers as they wound their way through western Dakota and the Black Hills.

Custer was able to find a good location for a fort. His reports also stressed the potential economic value of the region's hunting, lumbering, and grazing areas. Although the lieutenant colonel played down the mineral prospects, thousands of prospectors seized upon more inflated press reports and began rushing to the Black Hills. The *New York Tribune* noted, "If there is gold in the Black Hills, no army on earth can keep the adventurous men of the west out of them." The army was sincere if ineffective in preventing the onslaught of white trespassers onto the Great Sioux Reservation.

To have attempted to check white expansion would have been incongruent with army policy. In early November 1875, Sheridan and Crook joined President Grant and Interior Department officials in determining to end the efforts to block trespassers and to force the Indians to sign new treaties. Declaring that diplomacy had failed, on 1 February 1876, Secretary of the Interior Zachariah Chandler authorized the War Department to send the army in against the Sioux and the northern Cheyenne.

The military scrambled to take advantage of the diplomatic opening, with hastily formulated plans that month calling for a two-pronged invasion of the Black Hills. From the Department of the Platte, Colonel Joseph J. Reynolds led nearly nine hundred men out of Fort Fetterman,

Wyoming, on 1 March. Crook accompanied the column in an observer's role. To the east and from the Department of Dakota, General Terry prepared to mount an expedition from Fort Abraham Lincoln. Although the troops were to come from different departments, Sheridan, whose Division of the Missouri encompassed both regions, declined to coordinate movements.

Winter snows forced Terry to abandon the campaign even before it began. Reynolds and Crook were slightly more persistent, but retired after less than a month in the field. The latter force had managed to capture one pony herd, only to see the Indians recapture their animals in a night raid. Acknowledging the failure of the winter campaign, Sheridan ordered his subordinates to try again when weather and supplies permitted. As usual, the general declined to outline specific campaign plans; he did, however, assure his field commanders of "the impossibility of any large numbers of Indians keeping together as a hostile body for even one week."

On 30 March, Colonel John Gibbon and 450 men left Fort Ellis, Montana, pushing through the remaining snows to the Yellowstone River valley. Terry led a larger column, spearheaded by Custer and the Seventh Cavalry, out of Fort Lincoln on 17 May. Crook rejoined the chase from Fort Fetterman twelve days later. Bitter experience led each officer to agree with Sheridan's claim about potential opposition. Finding the enemy, and then forcing that enemy to fight, had traditionally been the most difficult challenge on the western Plains.

Crook fought the campaign's first engagement. On 17 June, his column met determined resistance at the Battle of Rosebud Creek. Claiming victory, Crook nonetheless fell back to his field depot to await reinforcements. Terry in the meantime was still struggling to locate the enemy. Suspecting that a large Indian camp lay along the Little Bighorn River, Terry dispatched Custer and the Seventh to drive up the Rosebud and approach the enemy from the south. Gibbon would block any retreat to the north. Mindful of the need for flexibility, Terry's orders were vague, as was customary during such campaigns.

Early on 25 June, Custer's Indian scouts verified Terry's suspicions about an Indian presence along the Little Bighorn. Fearful that the Sioux and northern Cheyenne would retreat unscathed and certain that the enemy must be aware of his regiment, Custer pushed his tired troopers ahead. Replicating his tactics of nearly eight years ago at the Washita, he divided his forces. Three companies under the acerbic yet talented Captain Frederick Benteen would screen the advance to the south. Major Marcus A. Reno took three more companies to hit the village; Custer and five companies would complete the pincer movement against the enemy, about whose dispositions he still knew little.

But Custer's luck had run out. Contrary to Sheridan's prediction, the northern Cheyenne, a few Arapaho, and five Sioux tribal circles—Sans Arc, Miniconjou, Hunkpapa, Blackfoot, and Oglala—had stayed together this summer. Numerical estimates vary wildly, from a conservative guess of ten thousand to as many as fifteen thousand Indians with between fifteen hundred and four thousand warriors. Ably led by men such as Crazy Horse, Sitting Bull, Gall, Lame Deer, and Hump, the Sioux and northern Cheyenne, their confidence buoyed by the recent action against Crook, began swarming from their lodges to attack the intruders.

Reno's troopers were checked well short of the village. With great difficulty Reno managed to withdraw across the Little Bighorn, where he hung on until joined by Benteen. The Indians kept up the pressure against Reno's men through the following evening, killing forty-seven soldiers and wounding another fifty-three. Custer suffered an even worse fate—all 215 of his men fell, after a spirited defense, among the broken, grassy ridges north of the huge Indian encampment.

Terry and Gibbon came up on 27 June. Shocked by the carnage on the Custer battlefield, they withdrew to the mouth of the Rosebud to refit and await reinforcements, which brought Terry's combined command up to seventeen hundred men. Crook, his force now boasting nearly two thousand men and a large pack train, rejoined the campaign on 5 August. He blundered into Terry five days later near the Rosebud. Still shaken by the defeats of the early summer, Terry and Crook unified their command as they drove eastward toward the Powder River. Morale sunk ever lower as the leadership's temerity became more obvious; in late August, the two columns again went their separate ways.

Miles and the Fifth Infantry had been among the reinforcements bound for Terry. Anxious to leave the joint column, which he believed too large to find any Indians, Miles had jumped at the opportunity to take his regiment north to hold the Yellowstone River against a possible Indian flight toward Canada. In early September a thoroughly baffled Terry broke up his remaining command, but instructed Miles to occupy the Yellowstone through the winter. Crook continued the pursuit, and on 9 September fought an extended skirmish at Slim Buttes, South Dakota, but even Crook retired back to Fort Fetterman without having beaten his Sioux antagonists.

The military braced for a long war. In a cruel preventive measure, reservation peoples at the Red Cloud, Standing Rock, and Cheyenne River agencies were disarmed and dismounted. The burden of the campaigning now fell to two colonels, both relative newcomers to the northern Plains. Colonel Miles, with five hundred infantrymen of his Fifth Regiment and two companies of the Twenty-second, had established his base on the mouth of the Tongue River, from which he patrolled the Yellowstone fords. Heavy Montana snows failed to deter his probes, which drove off all Indian attempts to interdict his supply lines. On 7 January 1877 Miles captured a number of Cheyenne women and children, then fended off attacks by Crazy Horse's Sioux and the Cheyenne that night and the following day at the Battle of Wolf Mountain.

Colonel Mackenzie had also been transferred north, where he joined another massive command that Crook led out from Fort Fetterman into central Wyoming on 14 November. Mackenzie's cavalrymen and Indian auxiliaries hit Dull Knife's Cheyenne village, consisting of nearly two hundred lodges, eleven days later. Savage fighting ensued as the Cheyenne withdrew, leaving twenty-five dead; government casualties numbered thirty-two soldiers and scouts. Mackenzie reproached himself for not pursuing the Cheyenne, but his troops, in capturing five hundred ponies and destroying the village and the winter stores, had in fact dealt the Indians another harsh blow.

In the spring of 1878, large numbers of Sioux and northern Cheyenne began turning themselves in to military authorities. By April about three thousand had come in at the Red Cloud, Spotted Tail, and Cheyenne River agencies. Another three hundred Cheyenne surrendered at the Tongue River cantonment; on 6 May Crazy Horse led most of the Oglala into the Red Cloud Agency. Miles whipped Lame Deer's band at the Little Muddy Creek on 7 May. Scattered remnants of the northern Plains peoples gave up during the summer, although Sitting Bull and a few hundred followers fled into Canada.

Large new army posts throughout the region symbolized the determination of the government to occupy the high Plains. Tension remained high among the Indians who had surrendered. Crazy Horse was killed in captivity and the northern Cheyenne were allowed to return to their homelands only after desperate escape attempts from the Indian Territory. Miles continued to patrol the Canadian border, with a sharp engagement at Milk River, Montana, on 17 July 1879. After numerous defections, Sitting Bull finally turned himself in at Fort Buford, North Dakota in July 1781.

The Nez Perce Campaign.

As the wars against the Sioux continued, the army was also called upon to expedite white expansion into the Wallowa Valley in Oregon, where the Nez Perce had attempted to coexist with their new neighbors. In 1877, however, the government determined that the Indians must be removed in order to preempt future violence. Leading the mission was Brigadier General Oliver O. Howard, a battle-scarred veteran of the Civil War and Reconstruction. Chief Joseph and his followers opted instead to make their way to the Salmon River, where they hoped to join a group of fellow tribesmen. Wayward warriors killed several whites en route, and Captain David Perry set out with a hundred troopers and a swarm of volunteers from Fort Lapwai to defend the settlers. At White Bird Canyon, Idaho, however, the Nez Perce repulsed Perry with heavy casualties on 17 June.

Commanding the Department of the Columbia, Howard assembled four hundred men and set out after Joseph. Another botched effort to negotiate with Looking Glass and his followers, who as yet remained neutral, only convinced this group to join Joseph. After a tortuous march, Howard caught his foes near the Clearwater River on 11 July. The battle again reflected poorly on the regulars as the Indians escaped to the northeast in good order.

Howard reorganized his command and rejoined the pursuit after a three-week delay, but it seemed unlikely that his column of infantry, cavalry, Bannock scouts, and civilian packers could catch Joseph's people. From Missoula, Colonel Gibbon prepared to cut off the Nez Perce escape. Assembling 161 regulars and forty-five volunteers, he pushed down the Bitterroot Valley and surprised the Indians near the mouth of the Big Hole River on 9 August 1877. Once again, the Nez Perce proved resourceful fighters, quickly recovering from the initial shock to dominate the battlefield. Indian sharpshooters pinned down the troops as their families made good their escape. One-third of Gibbon's men had fallen casualty, while eighty-nine Nez Perce, many of them women and children slain during the first onslaught, also littered the field.

Howard and a small escort joined Gibbon's bloodied command two days later. They resumed the chase only after messages from General Sherman and Colonel Miles, who had been alerted at Tongue River about Joseph's eastern flight into Montana, goaded a dispirited Howard into action. As Miles took the field, the Nez Perce continued to confound his fellow officers, on 13 September escaping efforts by Colonel Samuel D. Sturgis to block the Yellowstone Valley passes at the Battle of Canyon Creek. Miles, however, proved to be of sterner stuff. The tired Nez Perce slowed enough as they neared the Canadian border for Miles to jump their camp near the Bear Paw Mountains on the morning of 30 September.

Stiff resistance forced Miles to call off the attack after suffering sixty casualties, but his soldiers and hired Sioux and Cheyenne auxiliaries had seized most of the Nez Perce ponies and settled in for a siege. Miles ignored rumors that Sitting Bull was coming to spring the trap as the winter snows continued. Howard, accompanied by a small escort, arrived on 4 October. The constant skirmishing and winter snows had taken their toll upon the Nez Perce, and about four hundred men, women, and children joined Joseph in surrendering the following day. "I will fight no more forever," pledged the chief. Canadian officers later reported that about three hundred Nez Perce had escaped to Canada.

The Bannock, Sheepeater, and Ute Campaigns.
Embarrassed during the campaigns against the Nez Perce, General Howard redeemed himself the following year. In spring 1878 the Bannock Indians of Idaho, Oregon, and Nevada found that the livestock of white farmers and ranchers had nearly devastated their favored Camas Prairie, a site rich in camas roots and tribal tradition. To check the plundering that followed, Howard organized three columns to converge upon the Bannock, estimated to have amassed 450 warriors. Captain Reuben F. Bernard struck the first blow, surprising an Indian village at Silver Creek, Oregon, and capturing most of the Bannock supplies on 23 June.

Howard himself took up the pursuit as the chase wound through the tangled ravines of the John Day River. On 8 July a strike force, again led by Bernard, bested the coalition at Pilot Butte. Displaying tactical skills rarely equaled during the long wars against the Indians, Bernard's cavalrymen drove the well-placed warriors from the field. The pursuit resumed thereafter, with the Bannock still unable to shake the army columns. By now, expeditionary forces led by Colonel Frank Wheaton and Miles had also taken the field, blocking escape routes and cementing the collapse of the coalition.

In the summer of 1879, about thirty Sheepeater Indians and their families led another prolonged chase, this time through the Salmon River Mountains of Idaho. Pursuit teams scoured the rugged ranges for three months, with a small detachment led by Lieutenant Edward S. Farrow forcing the surrender of the Sheepeater in early October. In the same year there was an uprising among the Ute at the White River Agency, Colorado, where the tribe had resisted the demands of agent Nathan C. Meeker that his charges give up their culture for the ways of the white man. After he was assaulted by an Indian, he called upon the army to enforce his new order. The Ute checked the first column, led by Major Thomas T. Thornburgh, in a bloody encounter near Milk Creek on 29 September. Thornburgh himself was killed during the action. On the same day other Ute attacked the agency, killing Meeker and seven others. The Ute then extended the violence to nearby settlements along White Creek. The army rushed in reinforcements, and only the determined intercession of Secretary of the Interior Schurz averted a full-scale war. Still threatening to resist any further encroachments, the Ute eventually gave up and accepted a new reservation.

The Far Southwest.
Wars against the Indians also continued in the Far Southwest, but the army had sometimes been less enthusiastic about guaranteeing white expansion in that region. During the 1850s, Lieutenant Colonel Sumner and Secretary of War Conrad had urged the nation to sell rather than defend the arid regions of New Mexico and Arizona. Two decades later, commanding General Sherman seemed to espouse a similar policy. "The occupation of Arizona by Whites I am satisfied was premature and the cost of maintaining troops there is all out of proportion to the result," he concluded in 1870. Like his predecessors, the

general saw the region as an inhospitable desert that should be abandoned by the army and left to the Indians.

Political pressure had forced a reluctant Sherman to allow the transfer of Crook to the Department of Arizona in 1872. Crook exploited his unusual familiarity with the ways of the Apache to enforce a peace upon most of the region by the mid-1870s. His replacement, Colonel August V. Kautz, proved less able to balance the competition between military, interior, and political officials for jurisdiction over the Indian reservations, which had become a profitable source of federal contracts. The army's top brass, however, reasoned that demands for offensive action in regions better suited to white development required their best field commanders. If the theory held true, even mediocre talents like Kautz and Colonel Orlando B. Willcox could do little to hinder the prospects of this forlorn region.

Contrary to army prognostications, however, the 1870s brought much economic development to the Far Southwest. The Tombstone silver strike and increasing capital investments in the copper mines of the region lured settlers and entrepreneurs alike. Construction of the Santa Fe and Southern Pacific railroads added further luster. By 1880 Arizona and New Mexico boasted a collective population of 160,000 people. Even Sherman was convinced that the recent years had transformed the prospects of the region.

New army policy accompanied the new appreciation for the Far Southwest. The top officials concluded that efforts to stamp out Indian resistance had to be intensified. Victorio, the dynamic Warm Springs Apache, broke from the Mescalero Agency in 1879, followed by a number of his fellow tribesmen and a smattering of Mescalero and Chiricahua. With nearly one hundred and fifty warriors, Victorio avoided Mexican and U.S. soldiers as he skipped back and forth across the international boundary. To reduce the threat, troops from New Mexico and Texas disarmed the reservation Mescalero in April 1880. Efforts to track down the recalcitrant Victorio having failed, Colonel Grierson suggested a new tactic—by holding the strategic water holes of the dry trans-Pecos region, the army could save itself the wear and tear of the fruitless desert treks and drive Victorio from Texas.

Victorio acted as Grierson had expected and tangled with army detachments at Tinaja de las Palmas (30 July) and Rattlesnake Springs (6 August). The Indians fell back into Mexico in some confusion. Colonels Carr and Buell pushed across the border under agreement that allowed reciprocal crossings in hot pursuit of hostile Indians. A strong column of Mexican soldiers under Colonel Joaquin Terrazas eventually dealt the Indians a crushing blow, with Victorio dying during the fighting.

Even these blows, however, failed to bring about a peaceful solution to problems stemming from white expansion. On 30 August, the near-annihilation of Colonel Carr's two troops of Sixth Cavalrymen at Cibicu Creek, Arizona, by Chiricahua and Warm Spring's Apache suggested the need for new leadership. Mackenzie seemed a perfect candidate to inject new life into the dispirited southwestern garrisons. Slated for command of the Department of New Mexico, Mackenzie's outbursts of insanity led military officials instead to spirit him away to a New York asylum. Consistent with the new importance attributed to the region, Crook was returned to Arizona in 1882.

Crook implemented what he hoped to be a comprehensive policy based on a rigorous adherence to treaty promises. Officers replaced civilian agents at several reservations; scores of Apache scouts were hired to assist the government. Those Indians who resisted the reservation system were subjects for intense campaigning, but small bands led by Geronimo, Chato, and other raiders continued to elude government forces and wreak terror upon the non-Indian citizens of Sonora, Chihuahua, Arizona, and New Mexico. Crook led a force of forty-five regulars and nearly two hundred scouts deep into the Sierra Madre in May 1883. After a series of exhausting marches and skirmishes, success seemed imminent that June, when most of the leading warriors agreed to turn themselves in.

A brief peace followed as various Apache bands drifted in to the San Carlos Reservation, but Geronimo and about ninety followers (including forty-two men) again broke from the reservation in May 1885. To recapture the fugitives, Crook deployed three thousand men to occupy key water holes, patrol the Sierra Madre, and protect the Southern Pacific Railroad. Grueling chases into Mexico, keyed by Captains Emmet Crawford and Wirt Davis and Indian scouts, finally located Geronimo's camp about two hundred miles into Mexico in January 1886, but just as Crawford secured a meeting with Geronimo, a strong force of Mexican militia struck the soldiers, killing Crawford and forcing the expedition back into the United States.

Stunned by Crawford's death but convinced that Geronimo and the others wanted to talk, Crook arranged a meeting just south of the border two months later. Tired of the struggle, Geronimo, Nachez, and Chihuahua agreed to surrender if allowed to make their own way back to Fort Bowie. Overjoyed, Crook hastened back with the news, only to learn that Geronimo, twenty men, and thirteen women made yet another break on the way north. Sheridan, who upon Sherman's retirement had assumed the office of commanding general in 1883, had long questioned Crook's reliance upon Indian scouts and quickly accepted his subordinate's request for a transfer.

Nelson Miles replaced Crook as commander of the Department of Arizona in April 1886. A frustratingly ambitious yet inordinately talented combat leader, Miles assured Sheridan that he would change Crook's tactics. Heliograph stations would improve communications, regulars would replace the Apache scouts, and no preliminary discussions with the Indians would be sanctioned. An ineffective summer campaign by the regulars, guided by less able scouts recruited from other tribes, led Miles to quietly reintroduce Crook's methods. It thus came as little surprise to experienced southwestern hands that Lieutenant Charles B. Gatewood, one of Crook's favorites, made the first significant contact with Geronimo in August.

Miles had adopted one innovation that would prove crucial to the negotiations. He had recently orchestrated the removal of the reservation Chiricahua (including many of the same scouts who had formerly worked for Crook) from Arizona to Florida. Stunned by the enforced transfer of their fellow tribesmen, Geronimo and his followers surrendered to Miles at Skeleton Canyon, Arizona, on 4 September. War Department orders that these people be held in Arizona for civil trial arrived too late to be implemented, and the fugitive bands were packed off to Florida. The confusing denouement, however, embarrassed Miles before government officials and led many to question whether the general had made unauthorized guarantees to secure Geronimo's surrender.

The Ghost Dance. Isolated incidents would keep soldiers in Arizona, New Mexico, and Texas on edge for years to come, but the next major encounter with Indians broke out on the northern Plains, scene of relative peace during the 1880s. The effects of white expansion in the region were clearly apparent among the Indians. Relegated to their reservations and stripped of their pride, many Plains peoples had grown dispirited during the late 1880s. The decline of the buffalo, years of drought, and the ravages of disease accelerated their physical decline. Cuts in promised annuities and the surrender of nearly half of their reservation by the Sioux Act of 1889 had taken a heavy toll.

The spread of the Ghost Dance among the Indians seemed to fire forgotten hopes. Initially propagated as a peaceful movement by the prophet Wovoka, many Sioux accepted a more violent version of the movement that promised the destruction of the white people. Interior Department agents, spooked by visions of this Indian millennium, called for army assistance in November 1890. Recently promoted to head the Division of the Missouri, Miles tried to contain the outbreak by sending strong garrisons to the most excited agencies in South Dakota and Nebraska. A plan to arrest Sitting Bull at Standing Rock in December was botched; his death at the hands of Indian police sent to capture him only hastened the panicky flight from the reserves.

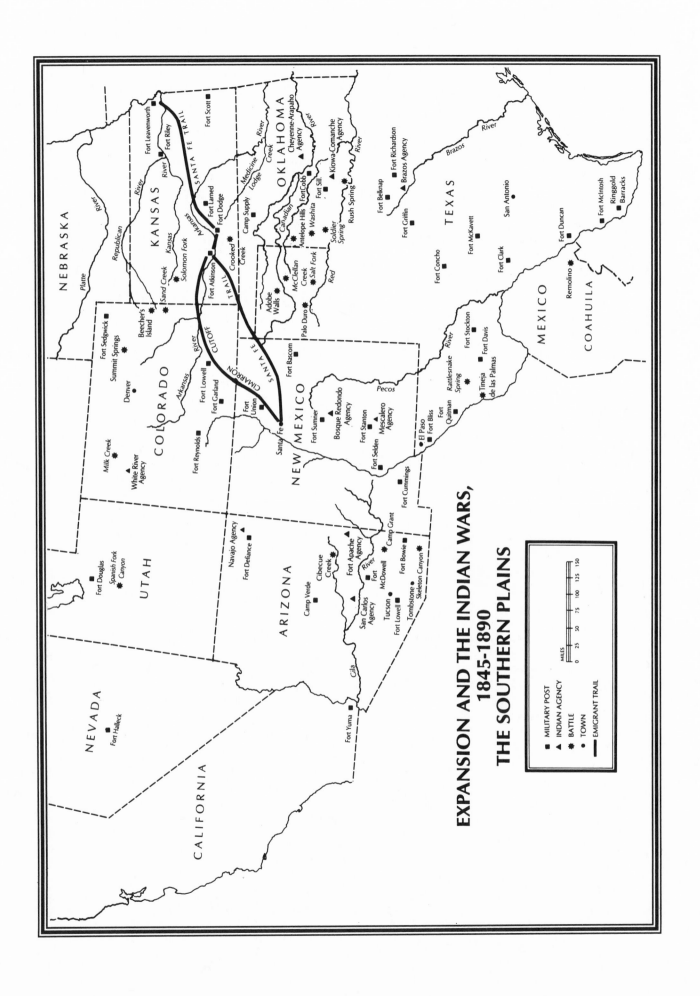

EXPANSION AND THE INDIAN WARS, 1845-1890
THE SOUTHERN PLAINS

- ■ MILITARY POST
- ▲ INDIAN AGENCY
- ✳ BATTLE
- ● TOWN
- ── EMIGRANT TRAIL

MILES
0 25 50 75 100 125 150

Reinforcements poured into western South Dakota and northern Nebraska. Many Oglala and Brulé Sioux took refuge in a defensible plateau north of the Pine Ridge Reservation, known as the Stronghold. Three hundred and ten Miniconjou, led by the respected Big Foot and joined by about forty Hunkpapa from Grand River, had also fled from their reservation on the Cheyenne River and were by late December heading toward Pine Ridge. Eluding Lieutenant Colonel Sumner, Big Foot's people were caught by another army column on 28 December. That night, Colonel James W. Forsyth arrived at the camp near Wounded Knee Creek with orders to disarm the tribes. Both the Indians and the troopers of Forsyth's regiment—ironically, the Seventh Cavalry, so ignominiously defeated fourteen and a half years ago along the banks of the Little Bighorn—spent a tense wintry night.

Disarming 120 warriors without violence would have tested the most grizzled Indian campaigner. Forsyth, although a competent staffer, had never faced the tribes in battle. He had at his disposal five hundred soldiers and four Hotchkiss cannon, but only 110 of his troops were in direct contact with the warriors. A scuffle broke out and the firing became general. Men, women, and children alternately fought back and fled for cover as the troops poured volley after volley into the melee. Twenty-five soldiers lay dead, with another thirty-nine wounded; Indian losses were more than 150 dead and about fifty wounded.

The bloody carnage at Wounded Knee nearly precipitated a general conflict. On 30 December, Forsyth again blundered, allowing his command to stumble into an ambush near the Drexel Mission. Several troops of black cavalrymen rode in to save Forsyth's command from an embarrassing situation. Only the cool direction of the campaign by Miles and the overwhelming numerical superiority of the thirty-five hundred government forces (those fighting men declared "hostile" probably numbered less than one thousand) prevented an even greater calamity.

The Wounded Knee campaign would be the last major conflict associated with the Indian wars of the nineteenth century, but the army remained attuned to potential Indian difficulties throughout much of the West for years. Only with the onset of the Spanish-American War in 1898 and the retirement of Miles as commanding general in 1903 did the United States Army truly recognize that its service as a frontier constabulary had ended.

THE ARMY AND WESTERN EXPANSION

Frederick Jackson Turner pronounced the American frontier to be closed in his essay "The Significance of the American Frontier in American History," which he read at the 1893 meeting of the American Historical Association. The essay argued that the uniqueness of the American character was explained through the frontier experience and would dominate historical thought in the United States for nearly a half century. Turner's much-debated work largely ignored the army; only belatedly have historians come to recognize the multifaceted role of the military in the nation's westward march.

Few military officials of the nineteenth century doubted the cause of expansion. Winfield Scott, commanding general from 1841 to 1861, triggered the territorial expansion of 1848 by capturing Mexico City. Secretary of War Jefferson Davis worked hard to conquer the newly acquired lands of the Far West, spurring efforts to increase the size of the army, supporting the Gadsden Purchase, and sponsoring the railroad explorations of the mid-1850s. After the Civil War, commanding Generals Sherman (1869–1883), Sheridan (1884–1888), John M. Schofield (1888–1895), and Miles (1895–1903) all championed the rights of white settlers to occupy huge portions of the trans-Mississippi West.

After years of campaigning, the army ultimately established its military supremacy over the Indians. Of course, civilian activities greatly assisted this process. Most important were the millions of settlers themselves; by occupying vast regions of the West, these immigrants significantly reduced the amount of land available to the native tribes. Hunters and sportsmen furthered the ultimate success of the United States government. Their destruction of the great buffalo herds severely weakened the Plains peoples. The railroads were also crucial in facilitating this westward push. As Sherman noted in his last annual report, "The recent completion of the last of the four great transcontinental lines of railway has settled forever the Indian question."

Thus, only when analyzed in conjunction with civilian activities can the army's role in the westward expansion of the United States be properly assessed, but the multipurpose army of the nineteenth century was more than a military force. Its forts attracted entrepreneurs, encouraged settlement, and at least indirectly supplied the buffalo hunters; its escorts guarded railroad construction and overland wagon trails; and its officers espoused an optimistic view of the western environment that helped attract the millions of immigrants.

Few in the army espoused physical extermination of the Indians. At the same time, however, most military leaders accepted the racism and paternalism that accentuated white approaches to the native peoples of the late nineteenth-century frontiers. The reservation system, therefore, is in part an army legacy, just as are the cities, towns, and dramatic history of the American West.

BIBLIOGRAPHY

General Histories

Clendenen, Clarence C. *Blood on the Border: The United States Army and the Mexican Irregulars* (1969).

Coffman, Edward M. *The Old Army: A Portrait of the American Army in Peacetime, 1784–1898* (1986).

Dunlay, Thomas W. *Wolves for the Blue Soldiers: Indian Scouts and Auxiliaries with the United States Army, 1860–1890* (1982).

Ellis, Richard N. "The Humanitarian Generals." *Western Historical Quarterly* 3 (1972).

Frazer, Robert W. *Forts of the West: Military Forts and Presidios, and Posts Commonly Called Forts, West of the Mississippi River to 1898* (1965).

Hutchins, James S. "Mounted Riflemen: The Real Role of Cavalry in the Indian Wars." In *Probing the American West: Papers from the Santa Fe Conference on the History of Western America*, edited by Kenneth Ross Toole et al. (1962).

Hutton, Paul A. "The Indians' Last Stand: A Review Essay." *New Mexico Historical Review* 59 (1984).

Leckie, William H. *The Military Conquest of the Southern Plains* (1963).

Myres, Sandra L. "Romance and Reality on the American Frontier: Views of Army Wives." *Western Historical Quarterly* 13 (1982).

Russell, Don. "How Many Indians Were Killed? White Man Versus Red Man: The Facts and the Legend." *American West* 10 (July 1973).

Smith, Sherry L., "A Window on Themselves: Perceptions of Indians by Military Officers and Their Wives." *New Mexico Historical Review* 64 (1989).

Tate, James P. ed. *The American Military on the Frontier: The Proceedings of the 7th Military History Symposium* (1978).

Tate, Michael L. "The Multi-purpose Army on the Frontier: A Call for Further Research." In *The American West: Essays in Honor of W. Eugene Hollon*, edited by Ronald Lora (1980).

Utley, Robert M. *The Indian Frontier of the American West, 1846–1890* (1984).

Wade, Arthur P. "The Military Command Structure:. The Great Plains, 1853–1891." *Journal of the West* 15 (1976).

Wooster, Robert. "'A Difficult and Forlorn Country': The Military Looks at the American Southwest, 1850–1890." *Arizona and the West* 28 (1986).

Antebellum and Civil War Years

Bender, Averam. "The Soldier in the Far West, 1848–1860." *Pacific Historical Review* 8 (1939).

———. *The March of Empire: Frontier Defense in the Southwest, 1848–1860* (1952).

Bischoff, William N. "The Yakima Indian War, 1855–1856: A Problem in Research." *Pacific Northwest Quarterly* 41 (1950).

Goetzmann, William H. *Army Exploration in the American West, 1803–1863* (1959).

Prucha, Francis Paul. *Broadax and Bayonet: The Role of the United States Army in the Development of the Northwest, 1815–1860* (1953).

Sievers, Michael A. "Sands of Sand Creek Historiography." *Colorado Magazine* 49 (1972).

Skelton, William B. "Army Officers' Attitudes Toward Indians, 1830–1860." *Pacific Northwest Quarterly* 67 (1976).

Thompson, Gerald. *The Army and the Navajo* (1976).

Trafzer, Clifford E. *The Kit Carson Campaign: The Last Great Navajo War* (1982).

Utley, Robert M. *Frontiersmen in Blue: The United States Army and the Indian, 1848–1865* (1967).

Wooster, Robert. "Military Strategy in the Southwest, 1848–1860." *Military History of Texas and the Southwest* 15 (1979).

Biographies

Athearn, Robert G. *William Tecumseh Sherman and the Settlement of the West* (1956).

Hutton, Paul A. *Phil Sheridan and His Army* (1985).

Hutton, Paul A., ed. *Soldiers West: Biographies from the Military Frontier* (1987).

King, James T. "George Crook: Indian Fighter and Humanitarian." *Arizona and the West* 9 (1967).

Kroeker, Marvin E. *Great Plains Command: William B. Hazen in the Frontier West* (1976).

Smith, Sherry L. *Sagebrush Soldier: Private William Earl Smith's View of the Sioux War of 1876* (1989).

Utley, Robert M. *Cavalier in Buckskin: George Armstrong Custer and the Western Military Frontier* (1988).

Young, Otis E. *The West of Philip St. George Cooke, 1809–1895* (1955).

The Post–Civil War Years

Fite, Gilbert. "The United States Army and Relief to Pioneer Settlers, 1874–1875." *Military Affairs* 29 (1965).

Gates, John M. "The Alleged Isolation of U.S. Army Officers in the Late 19th Century." *Parameters* 10 (1980).

Gray, John S. *Centennial Campaign: The Sioux War of 1876* (1976).

Greene, Jerome A. *Slim Buttes, 1876: An Episode of the Great Sioux War* (1982).

Haley, James L. *The Buffalo War: The History of the Red River Indian Uprising of 1874* (1976).

Hedren, Paul L. *Fort Laramie in 1876: Chronicle of a Frontier Post at War* (1988).

Jackson, Donald D. *Custer's Gold: The United States Cavalry Expedition of 1874* (1966).

Josephy, Alvin M. *The Nez Perce Indians and the Opening of the Northwest* (1965).

Leckie, William H. *The Buffalo Soldiers: A Narrative of the Negro Cavalry in the West* (1967).

Miller, Darlis A. *Soldiers and Settlers: Military Supply in the Southwest, 1861–1885* (1989).

Rickey, Don. *Forty Miles a Day on Beans and Hay: The Enlisted Soldier Fighting the Indian Wars* (1963).

Thompson, Erwin N. *Modoc War: Its Military History and Topography* (1971).

Utley, Robert M. *The Last Days of the Sioux Nation* (1963).

———. *Frontier Regulars: The United States Army and the Indian, 1866–1891* (1973).

Wooster, Robert. *The Military and United States Indian Policy, 1865–1903* (1988).

———. "The Army and the Politics of Expansion: Texas and the Southwestern Borderlands, 1870–1886." *Southwestern Historical Quarterly* 93 (1989).

THE CIVIL WAR

Frank E. Vandiver

THE COMING OF WAR

What caused the Civil War is a question that both puzzles and fascinates and answers are as numerous as questioners. North and South were split over slavery, economic systems, and ways of life and each had different ideas about democracy and freedom. It seemed that by the election of 1860 the United States had nearly ruptured already, so angry were the words heard in Congress and read in the daily press. Aggressive northern pursuit of progress caused some of the problem. Burgeoning with money and people, the North rushed into the Industrial Age almost as a reward for good Yankee business sense. All sections of the nation except the agrarian South followed in pursuit of the power of wealth. The South had lagged woefully in the traces of the plantation system, in the thrall of slavery, and shackled to the land. And the South nagged at northern consciences.

Democracy, progress, and the graces come from money all blessed the land of the "free and the brave." But what about slavery? The "peculiar institution," which persisted from colonial times, had a place in the U.S. Constitution and spread with the Cotton Kingdom. Slaves worked in gangs, in teams, and sometimes alongside their masters and were the labor source in the South. Because they were essential to the agrarian way, the South adapted a society around slavery, and as abolitionism grew in the American conscience to the focus of all reform, the South stood at bay.

Increasingly through the nineteenth century, the cotton states turned away from the future; their citizens looked backward toward a calmer, slower time. Not a great proportion of them owned slaves, and according to 1860 figures, from a total southern population of 9,103,332, some 365,000 owners held 3,953,696 slaves. Even small owners, certainly in their own eyes, were part of the elite planter class—the class that set the tone of southern life—but many of the elite were uneasy with their social order and freeing slaves was not uncommon. There were 132,760 free blacks in the cotton states.

As abolition rhetoric rose, Southerners felt threatened, isolated, and resentful and turned from guilt to pride in slavery. Politicians began to speak of slavery's "positive good" and point to plantation paternalism as superior to the sweatshop exploitation of northern labor. Some planters boasted of the idyllic southern way of life and railed against the crass materialism they saw tarnishing existence north of Mason and Dixon's Line. Both sections looked at each other's stereotypes and saw evil, although neither North nor South cared about what was going on in the other section. Prejudices were fully made up and by election time in 1860, two belligerents stared in anger across American ballot boxes. The splintering of the Democratic party during the campaign wrecked the last national political organization and made way for the triumph of the sectional Republicans and their presidential candidate, Illinois lawyer Abraham Lincoln.

Lincoln's election ignited secession sentiment. Southerners saw him as the embodiment of "black republicanism," a man determined to end slavery in the south. His debates with Democrat Stephen A. Douglas during the 1858 Illinois senatorial campaign seemed to confirm his antislavery views and his studied ambiguity during the 1860 presidential campaign to justify the worst suspicions. South Carolina adopted an ordinance of secession on 20 December 1860. A combination of admiration for the Palmetto State's dedication and fear of the possible economic and social policies of Lincoln spurred secession conventions across the south. Mississippi seceded on 9 January 1861, followed by Florida on the 10th, Alabama on the 11th, Georgia on the 19th, and Louisiana on the 26th. Texas submitted its secession ordinance to voters on 23 February, but the state had withdrawn from the Union on 1 February.

As moderates were crowded out by zealots, secession had its own momentum and eliminated the fence sitters; many people who doubted the wisdom of disunion went with their native states. Most Unionists in the South shared the view that loyalty lay with the closest government and that the Union had second claim on their patriotism. Those straggling few who remained steadfast to the United States would soon be the "Tories" of the southland and would suffer like their earlier counterparts.

Leaders of the seceded states congregated at Montgomery, Alabama, on 4 February 1861, to form a government. Despite the wash of independence across the South, there was general agreement that a new confederation would have to be formed to face the Union and that the new government would have to be a good deal stronger than the one created under the Articles of Confederation. Delegates to Montgomery were not all "fire-eaters" (southern proslavery extremists) and a sense of moderation tinged their doings in convention. They were, they thought, the legitimate inheritors of traditional strains of American political freedom, and they wanted to show that the nation they were creating came more in evolution than revolution. They adopted a provisional constitution that resembled the United States document in everything save the fact that the new congress would be unicameral and worked to perfect a permanent constitution that would be better than the U.S. model. Drafted in a few days, the Confederate Constitution did show such wisdoms as the item veto and six-year terms for the president and vice-president.

Montgomery's delegates decided on a name for their nation that conformed to conservative views of states' rights—the Confederate States of America. For national leaders, they selected Alexander H. Stephens of Georgia as vice-president, and Jefferson Davis of Mississippi as president. Stephens, a well-known Unionist, dragged his feet toward secession and represented the "Tory" minority. Davis, a long-time U.S. senator (1847–1851, 1857–1861), held John C. Calhoun's mantle as national spokesman for the South. A states' righter and defender of slavery, Davis nonetheless took a cautious stand on secession and quit his senate seat with high hopes and great fears for the Confederacy.

Davis seemed almost the embodiment of the southland he so loved. A tall man with a chiseled, ascetic face ravaged by neuralgia that clouded one eye, he had graciousness blended with the reserve of the severely shy. Warm and winning in person, he showed a chilly public exterior. A devoted Confederate patriot, he found the petty bickering of many Southerners unfathomable. For him, patriotism had no limits and he had a zealot's stout heart and short patience. Nevertheless, he was the best man the South could call to fashion independence. Davis knew far better than most fellow Southrons the fragility of his new country. Long political experience gave him perspective on the economic anomalies of an agrarian state in an industrializing world; experience as secretary of war (1853–

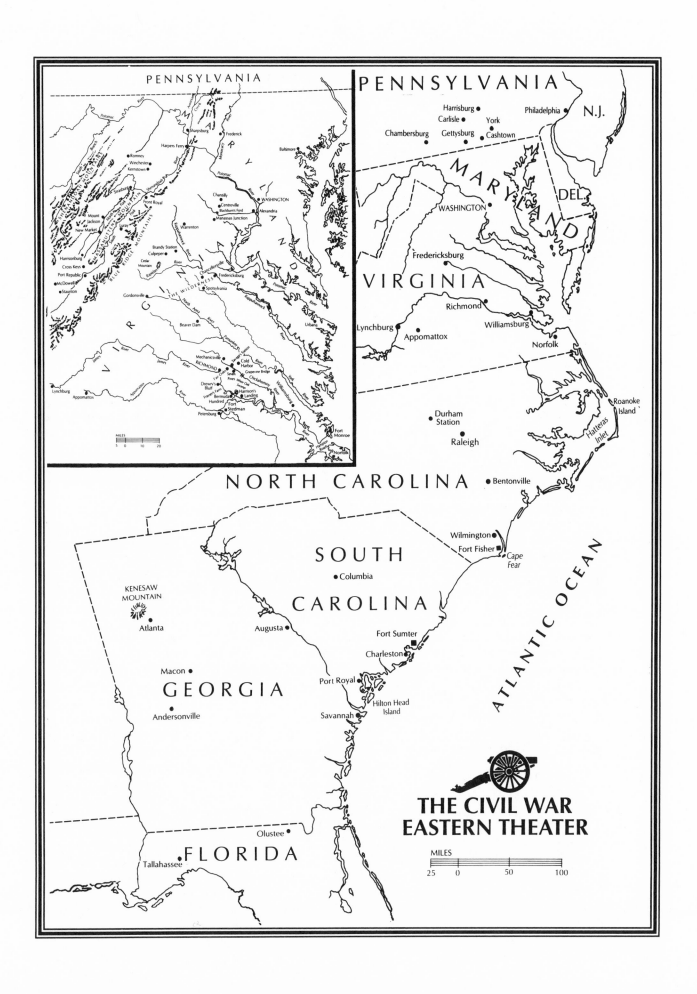

PENNSYLVANIA

MARYLAND

Potomac River

Sharpsburg
Frederick
Harpers Ferry
Romney
Winchester
Kernstown
Strasburg
Front Royal
Mount Jackson
Luray
New Market
Harrisonburg
Cross Keys
Port Republic
McDowell
Staunton

SHENANDOAH MOUNTAINS
MASSANUTTEN MOUNTAIN
BLUE RIDGE MOUNTAINS
North Fork
South Fork
Shenandoah River

Baltimore

Chantilly
Centreville
Blackburn's Ford
Manassas Junction
WASHINGTON
Alexandria

Warrenton
Rappahannock River

Brandy Station
Culpeper
Cedar Mountain
Chancellorsville
Fredericksburg
Spotsylvania

Gordonsville
THE WILDERNESS

Rapidan River

VIRGINIA

North Anna River
Beaver Dam
Pamunkey River

Mechanicsville
Savage Station
Cold Harbor
Seven Pines
Fair Oaks
Gaines' Mill
Grapevine Bridge
Chickahominy River
RICHMOND
Drewry's Bluff
Frazier's Farm
Bermuda Hundred
Fort Stedman
Petersburg

James River
Appomattox River

Lynchburg
Appomattox

Urbana

York River
Williamsburg

Fort Monroe
Hampton Roads
Norfolk

MILES
5 0 10 20

PENNSYLVANIA

Harrisburg
Carlisle
York
Chambersburg
Gettysburg
Cashtown
Philadelphia
N.J.

MARYLAND

DEL.

WASHINGTON

Fredericksburg

VIRGINIA

Richmond
Lynchburg
Appomattox
Williamsburg
Norfolk

Durham Station

Raleigh

Roanoke Island

Hatteras Inlet

NORTH CAROLINA

Bentonville

Wilmington
Fort Fisher
Cape Fear

SOUTH

Columbia

CAROLINA

KENESAW MOUNTAIN
Atlanta

Augusta

Fort Sumter
Charleston

ATLANTIC OCEAN

Macon

GEORGIA

Port Royal

Andersonville

Hilton Head Island

Savannah

THE CIVIL WAR
EASTERN THEATER

Olustee

FLORIDA

Tallahassee

MILES
25 0 50 100

1857) in President Franklin Pierce's administration gave him acute awareness of the Confederacy's military weaknesses. In his inaugural address on 18 February 1861, he put forth the best hope for a collection of new '"'republics" flushed with the bravado of independence. He hoped for peaceful separation from the Union, but expected war, and tried to brace Southerners for a long and costly conflict.

As Abraham Lincoln stood on the Capitol's steps and gave his own inaugural on 4 March 1861, he shared some of Davis' qualms. His trip to Washington from Springfield, Illinois, had been awkward. Detective Allan Pinkerton warned of southern plotters everywhere, kept the president-elect's travel plans secret, and ushered him covertly into the capital near dawn on Saturday, 23 February 1861. Nine crowded days before the inauguration gave Lincoln a measure of the confusion facing the Union. A peace convention wrangled over proposals to save the United States, Congress wrestled with various amendments, and waves of office-seekers filled the Willard Hotel lobby for a word with the incoming president. Lincoln shuffled candidates for his cabinet, listened to varying views on how to save the country, and perhaps realized fully the reality of the crisis he had casually called "artificial." Everyone wondered what the mysterious Illinoisan would do; rumors preceded him and they ran from admiration to derision. Since the election he had kept quiet and ambiguous counsel. Washington, D.C., saw a tall, plain, and ungainly rustic, thin in political experience, rich in western jokes, and altogether out of place at a crossroads of history.

Impressions shifted after the inauguration on 4 March. He did not, said Lincoln, have any intent to interfere with slavery where it existed, would not object to the proposed constitutional amendment forbidding federal interference, and supported enforcement of the Fugitive Slave Act of 1850. He also assured Southerners that he would be lenient in administering the government and would not put "obnoxious strangers" in the South to enforce the laws. The South, he argued, had no real grievances—dif-

ferences could be settled by the next election—but the Union was "perpetual," and "the central idea of secession is the essence of anarchy." Nor could the states physically separate—trade and political relations would continue. Would legal separation make anything easier? Let passions cool, he urged. "If the Almighty Ruler of nations, with his eternal truth and justice, be on your side of the North, or on yours of the South, that truth and that justice, will surely prevail by the judgment of this great tribunal of the American people." Responsibility for trouble would be clear. "In *your* hands, my dissatisfied fellow countrymen, and not in *mine*, is the momentous issue of civil war. The government will not assail *you*. You can have no conflict, without being yourselves the aggressors. *You* have no oath registered in Heaven to destroy the government, while *I* shall have the most solemn one to 'preserve, protect and defend' it."

Memories caught some poetry in his heart as he made an emotional call for caution. "I am loath to close. We are not enemies, but friends. We must not be enemies. Though passion may have strained, it must not break our bonds of affection. The mystic chords of memory, streching [*sic*] from every battlefield and patriot grave, to every living heart and hearthstone, all over this broad land, will yet swell the chorus of the Union, when again touched, as surely they will be, by the better angels of our nature." Lincoln's address rewards careful study. In this one speech, he proclaimed a policy of preserving the Union, focused on slavery as the evil in dispute, and fixed any war guilt on the South. In addition, he had tried to put America's crisis in a rational frame of legal reference and put it in terms of political reason. Reason, however, ran differently in this crisis time, as words played tricks in meaning and symbols stood for facts.

Consequently, reaction to Lincoln's inaugural address ran according to prejudice. To radicals, North and South, it sounded either too weak or too strong. Some border-state moderates liked it and for a time the border stood firm, but many in the North found scant leadership in what they heard. To sober southern readers, however, the inaugural came as a declaration of

COMPARISON OF NORTH AND SOUTH

	North	South
Number of states	23	11
Population	22,000,000	9,000,000*
Cities over 100,000 population	8	1 (New Orleans)
Cities over 50,000 population	7	1
Railroad mileage	22,000	9,000
Annual shipping tonnage**	13,654,925	737,901
Horses	4,417,130	1,698,328
Mules	328,890	800,663
Industrial establishments	110,274	18,026
Industrial workers	1,300,000	110,000
Annual product	$1,754,650,000	$145,350,000

* Including 3.5 million slaves
** June 1860 to June 1861

war. Although Lincoln might allow interruptions in local administration, he would keep the forts and other properties of the Union, a fact that negated Confederate sovereignty.

Both sides prepared for war. Rationally, the South had no chance in a war against the North and the statistics were chilling (see chart "Comparison of North and South"). Although the South boasted its cotton culture and lead in cottage industry, the North had a large lead in cash crops from improved farmland. The South manufactured only 3 percent of all arms produced in the United States, and in 1861 could count only $27 million in specie. The South's chances looked grimmer still in a counting of military manpower. The Confederacy had about 1 million men ready for service in 1861, and the North, about 3.5 million. Slaves were not expected to be used, save for personal service and labor, but slave numbers were important to both sides.

After the war, some critics argued that southern leaders ignored all the odds in a vain attempt for glory. Convenient as this charge is to believers in the cynical theory of history, it ignores the cause of independence, the South's strategic position, and especially cotton and courage, two tangibles of value.

President Davis and his cabinet—men of greater substance than most accounts allow—

agreed from the beginning that cotton would be the Confederacy's best fulcrum for success. Most of the industrial nations, particularly Great Britain and France, supported large textile industries that relied heavily on southern cotton. Foreign recognition and intervention might come in direct response to the need for "King Cotton." Although Davis and his advisers counted the odds against the South realistically, they did not ignore the rising tide of rebel sentiment that spurred a new patriotic zeal.

Lincoln followed his inaugural with a cautious attitude toward two United States forts. Fort Sumter, an old coastal bastion athwart Charleston Harbor, South Carolina, was held by a small U.S. garrison that had moved into the fort in December 1860. Fort Pickens, in Florida's Pensacola Harbor, had been garrisoned in January 1861. Both were old, designed for forgotten sieges from the sea, and of dubious military value. Suddenly, however, they had awesome symbolic power, because they stood as Union anchors against secession tides, especially Fort Sumter. Southern authorities wanted Sumter most of all, because of its threat to international commerce, and demanded its evacuation. Several members of Lincoln's cabinet thought Sumter too hard to hold and a risk beyond its worth. They also believed that there might be a chance to trade off Sumter if Pickens were held. Lincoln groped toward a policy to uphold federal honor and reduce southern fears. Southern concern made these forts useful tokens in an opening game of wits. Davis sent three commissioners to treat with Lincoln's government about peaceful separation and about public property scattered across the Confederacy, especially the forts. Maneuvering to win northern support for a war to coerce southern loyalty, Lincoln cannily avoided Davis's emissaries. He let his shrewd secretary of state, William H. Seward, deal with them in varying guises of cooperation.

Frustration tinged Confederate cabinet meetings as reports arrived of Seward's delaying tactics. Davis, however, began to learn that diplomacy can be a system of deceit and came to suspect that the forts might be pawns in a game to push the South into firing the first shot. Aware of uncertain northern opinion, Davis also knew that the Confederacy could not boast full independence unless at least Fort Sumter flew the new rebel banner. How long could the South wait? On 6 April, Seward told the southern commissioners that the United States would defend its property only when attacked, and on that same day a messenger from Lincoln informed Governor Francis Pickens of South Carolina that Fort Sumter would be resupplied, but reinforced only in case of resistance.

Rumors of a large relief expedition moving toward Charleston in early April caused serious war jitters. After anguished cabinet consultation, Davis authorized action. Secretary of War Leroy P. Walker telegraphed the Confederate commander in Charleston, General Pierre G. T. Beauregard, that once he knew Sumter would be resupplied, "you will at once demand its evacuation, and if this is refused proceed, in such manner as you may determine, to reduce it." Beauregard worked to complete and garrison the works and batteries surrounding Fort Sumter. On 11 April a small boat under a white flag took three men out to Sumter. They carried a message to Major Robert Anderson, commanding the fort, demanding evacuation. After long talks with his officers, Anderson refused, but said that he would be starved out in a few days. Beauregard reported this to Montgomery

and was told that the Confederate government did not "desire needlessly to bombard Fort Sumter," and that, if Anderson would say when he would quit the fort without a fight, "you are authorized thus to avoid the effusion of blood." Anderson, informed of the new terms, replied that he would leave at noon on the 15th unless he received reinforcements or new orders. The southern negotiators rejected this reply and announced that firing would begin in an hour. At 4:30 A.M. on 12 April 1861, one of Beauregard's guns signaled the start of the Civil War.

Surrender of the fort on the 13th triggered swift northern reaction. Lincoln carefully crafted a call for seventy-five thousand volunteers to put down the insurrection, which had the effect of a declaration of war and fixed the nature of the conflict—Southerners had rebelled, hence their new "confederacy" did not exist. Lincoln knew that Northerners might lag to coerce the South but would flock to save the Union. He also knew that the call for men would force the border states to make some decisions. Lincoln hoped, too, that defining the coming conflict as a rebellion would prevent foreign recognition of the Confederacy, which would mean a southern victory. Queen Victoria's proclamation of neutrality on 13 May comforted Lincoln and Seward, but her concession of Confederate belligerency angered them, because belligerency gave legality to southern armies, ships, and commissions and was just a step short of full recognition.

Although technicalities tinged some border state withdrawals, Lincoln's proclamation of insurrection and call for volunteers pushed Virginia out of the Union on 17 April, Arkansas on 6 May, Tennessee on 7 May, and North Carolina on 20 May. Later critics would see Lincoln's proclamation of insurrection as a great mistake, one that lost him the best chance to save the Union short of war. While some border state governors were rejecting the Union call for men, Davis issued a proclamation calling 100,000 men into Confederate service, and, when the Confederate Provisional Congress convened on 29 April, he requested more

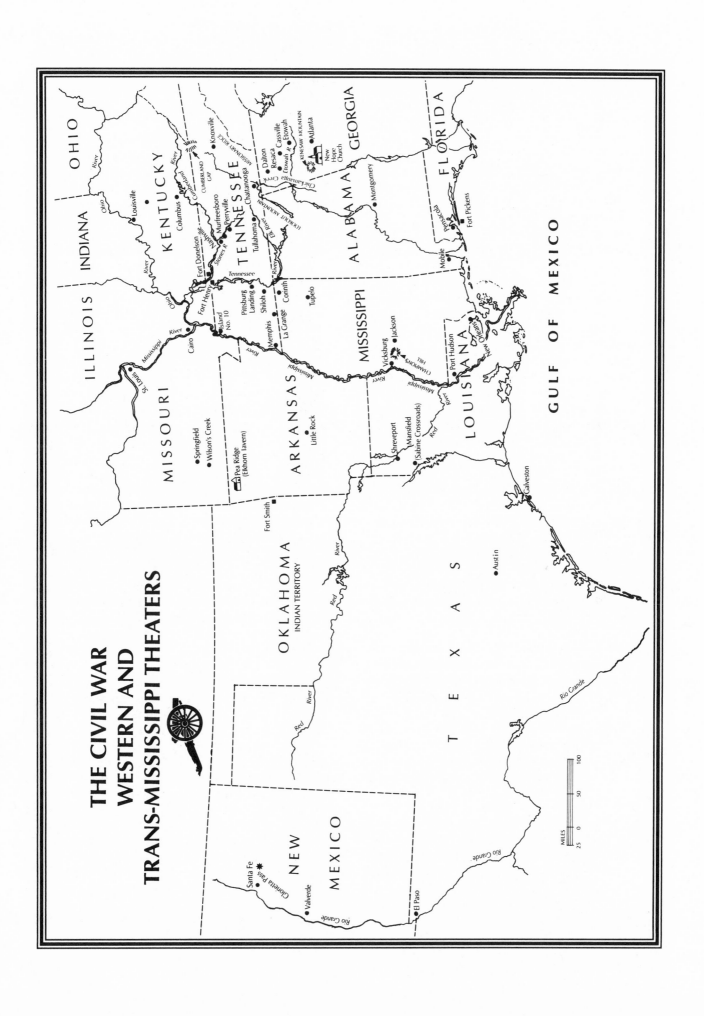

THE CIVIL WAR
WESTERN AND
TRANS-MISSISSIPPI THEATERS

money to prosecute the war and to organize the War and Navy departments.

By the end of April 1861, nothing seemed the same. War had come—a war to run beyond all bounds of reckoning and all previous American experience. Small armies led by individual generals operating in isolation were gone forever. North and South edged toward the first war of the industrial revolution, the first modern war of machines—not just the traditional machines of conflict, such as artillery and digging tools and wagons, but such new machines as rolling mills, railroads, ironclad warships, rapid-fire guns, torpedoes, chemical agents, workable submarines, balloons, telegraphs, battlefield semaphore signals, massed fire, and sophisticated trenches. It would be a total war of peoples, nations, and resources that smashed traditions as it forged a new power in the world.

BEGINNING OF THE WAR

North and South began with the same ideas of war. Because the South rejected revolution, it followed federal military precedents. Both sides faced problems of handling vast numbers of recruits; of supplying, training, and organizing them into armies; and, most urgently, of providing competent officers. The North had an army in being, and therefore faced an apparently easy problem of expansion, but the South faced vexing issues of creating a national war machine from fragmented state efforts.

Northern military preparations were the responsibility of Simon Cameron, a canny Pennsylvania politico and the new secretary of war. A crafty dealer and maneuverer, he had no art for War Department bureaucracy. Uncertain, equivocating, and a slow decider, Cameron added confusion to red tape. Fortunately, he had good professional officers heading the small national army of the Union.

General Winfield Scott, veteran of the War of 1812 and hero of the Mexican War whose experience weighed against his age (seventy-five) and lent wisdom to his portents, served as general in chief of the army. He grasped quickly that expanding existing offices, bureaus, and army units would be much more difficult than expected and sought highly competent men to head various departments. He put western Virginia, a highly pro-Union section, under command of the dashing, young Major General George Brinton McClellan, who proceeded to wage an extremely effective campaign with a relatively small army that preserved his area for the North and defeated several Confederate forces.

Lincoln and Scott offered the vital position of commanding the main Union army to Colonel Robert E. Lee of Virginia, a judicious soldier whose commands had included the illustrious Second Cavalry and who boasted wide engineering experience. Lee pondered the offer, but resigned his U.S. commission because he could not war against his native Virginia. Scott considered several other officers, in various department commands, as he looked for someone else to take charge of the large federal army gathering near Washington, D.C. On 28 May 1861, Brigadier General (soon to be Major General) Irvin McDowell received command of the Department of Northeastern Virginia, which included the troops mustering at Alexandria and in the Union capital and the major federal army. A competent professional, McDowell's experience suffered the limitations of long service in a small U.S. army, but he quickly showed ability as an organizer.

As recruits gathered around Washington, McDowell and his staff struggled to use regulars to mold volunteers and militiamen into soldiers and fashion an army from an amalgam of enthusiasts. This difficult task was complicated by a growing demand to attack the rebels. President Lincoln, not yet a patient paragon, also demanded action. McDowell, still learning his job and his army, wisely delayed advancing into Virginia until strength, training, and prudence allowed. Problems abounded. Not only did receiving and training men occupy every day, but logistical tangles confused everything. The Eleventh Massachusetts Infantry had twenty-five wagons for the baggage of 950 men—a fairly typical ratio. Thousands of horses and mules had to be tended and distributed. Rifles, ammunition, cannon, wagons, harness, uniforms, shoes—all the staff of armies—had to be sorted, inventoried, and issued. Field hospitals were new and untested and the number of doctors too few. Officers were usually as raw and untrained as their men. Everywhere McDowell looked, chaos roiled his camps.

Gradually a kind of order arrived. Streets could be seen amidst the sea of tents; men marched in semblance of formations; artillery batteries took shape; and cavalry galloped without undue damage. Unlikely as it seemed, McDowell's army came into being, a huge force of nearly thirty-five thousand men. Lincoln pressed for action because further delay might cool Yankee ardor. At a cabinet meeting on 29 June, McDowell revealed his plan to attack Confederate positions at Manassas, Virginia. At that meeting, General Scott proposed his Anaconda Plan, an expedition down the Mississippi River to cut the Confederacy in two and make possible a squeezing operation around the coast and interior borders of the eastern seceded states. The cabinet and Lincoln decided to deal first with the Virginia rebels.

Lincoln understood the need for a grand strategic plan, but political pressure focused his eye toward the enemy capital, which had moved from Montgomery to Richmond, Virginia, on 29 May. On 16 July, McDowell's army moved west from the Potomac toward Centreville and Manassas in response to the rising cry of "'On to Richmond" and to open the summer campaign of 1861. His columns were long, at first somewhat confused, and made scarcely six miles that first day, but he had advanced, and the North writhed in justifiable excitement because scattered military operations along the Potomac boundary of Virginia and in Missouri and Kentucky had gone the North's way. A few reverses in the Far West could be glossed over in the wash of success.

In the meantime, successes were being claimed by the South. As secession continued in the border areas and in some of the Indian nations, boundaries and resources expanded.

Much pro-Confederate sentiment persisted in Missouri, and that state's plight stood stark and clear during rioting in St. Louis in May and in the removal of the state government to the southwestern corner of the state. When the Confederate capital shifted to Richmond, it marked the addition of a good deal more than territory or industrial strength. The ancient ambience of the Old Dominion gave a special imprimatur to the reseated Confederate government.

Shifting the government moved the focus of the Confederacy and also the war. Virginia's exposed position demanded some Confederate commitment. With the government came trainloads of recruits from the deeper South to pass through Richmond and muster near Manassas, some thirty miles southwest of Washington. Thousands of variously garbed and eager troops went through the new capital on the way to join the army commanded by the hero of Fort Sumter, Brigadier General Beauregard.

News of McDowell's advance brought a quick call for help to the army around Manassas. Westward, in the Shenandoah Valley of Virginia, Brigadier General Joseph E. Johnston, with about twelve thousand men, had been holding the area near Harpers Ferry and was ordered to move rapidly to aid Beauregard. In the first strategic use of railroads in the war, Johnston began to move his army on 18 July, and his leading elements reached Manassas on the 19th, in time for the approaching battle. By that time, Beauregard had about thirty-thousand men in his Army of the Potomac.

On the 18th, McDowell's men had probed Beauregard's right flank and became embroiled in unexpected action at Blackburn's Ford. They were repulsed and that shifted McDowell's attention to the Confederate left. He prepared to throw some thirteen thousand men against the northwestern end of Beauregard's line early on the morning of 21 July. As it happened, that section of front would be lightly held, because Beauregard planned to attack McDowell's left at roughly the same time, and had both plans carried, the armies might well have switched position. Beauregard's boldness came with Johnston's arrival. With about thirty-five thousand rebels on the field, an attack seemed feasible. The Battle of Bull Run or Manassas (the federals named battles after the nearest body of water; the Confederates, after the nearest town or community), was about to start.

A mix-up in orders delayed the southern attack and by mid-morning on the 21st, McDowell's flanking force struck a small Confederate brigade near Sudley Springs Ford and began to move eastward toward Beauregard's bunched legions. Unchecked, this advance would sweep up the whole Confederate line in a rolling defeat. Beauregard's grandiose plans awry, he and Johnston devoted themselves to a defensive battle. As the main battle unfolded, they fed reinforcements to their left, especially the Virginia brigade commanded by Brigadier General Thomas J. Jackson, a somber and devout former professor of artillery tactics at the Virginia Military Institute. While the thin Confederate flank guard grudgingly retreated in front of the Union attack, Jackson's brigade anchored a growing force atop the Henry House hill. Around 2 P.M., McDowell launched a heavy drive against the hill. As Confederates retired, Brigadier General Barnard E. Bee of South Carolina saw Jackson's line and rallied his retreating men with immortal last words: "There is Jackson standing like a stone wall. Let us determine to die here, and we will conquer. Follow me."

McDowell's men were repulsed but surged forward again and again. By 4 P.M., both sides were exhausted. The timely arrival of Confederate reinforcements finally turned the Union right. McDowell's men halted, withdrew, and then stampeded toward Centreville. As the rout gathered momentum, all kinds of flotsam were swept in its wake, including a group of Union congressmen and ladies who had come out to watch the "Bull Run races." Confederate cavalry nudged the retreaters, but confusion in gray ranks impeded proper pursuit. The victors were stunned by success, and many survivors wandered over the field looking for comrades, some to pilfer from the dead, others simply to bask in living. The costs of the Battle of Bull Run were high: Union losses amounted to some twenty-eight hundred killed, wounded, and captured; Confederate casualties came to about nineteen hundred.

News of the battle was received differently in the North and the South. Richmond basked in expected triumph, its citizens wrapped in winners' rectitude. Washington huddled in gloomy fear, Lincoln shocked by the disarmed and dispirited rabble that thronged the streets. These different reactions were measures of the attitudes toward the prosecution of the war. Southerners were confirmed in confidence and knew that one rebel soldier could whip ten Yankees. Northerners suddenly knew the seriousness of the war and the toughness of the rebels. In the aftermath, the South relaxed and the North girded.

Small operations continued in the remaining summer weeks. President Davis reorganized his army's command by appointing eight generals on 31 August; since the appointees took their rank on different dates, jealousies were instant. The South still boasted about Manassas, but Yankee incursions around Confederate coasts and borders were disturbing. By the end of the year, the war's writ ran for the Union.

Confederate morale sagged as Port Royal in South Carolina fell on 7 November, when Hilton Head Island passed to the Yankees on the 8th, and especially when Roanoke Island off North Carolina was lost on 8 February 1862. These losses, most particularly Roanoke, seemed to be the fruits of a piecemeal strategy, weak leadership, or indefensible stupidity. They crowned a winter of bleak discoveries: railroad weaknesses that compounded the rustic backwardness of highway development across the South; financial errors that robbed the South of monetary confidence; logistical problems almost beyond belief and made worse by the blockade of southern ports announced by Lincoln back on 19 April 1861; and strategical errors that called presidential wisdom into question. Instead of concentrating smaller numbers of Confederate troops for the strategic offensive, Davis had scattered soldiers in a doomed attempt to hold the entire borderline of the Confederacy. There were not enough men to do this, proved by steady losses of important coastal areas. Davis confessed his error but explained that strategic weakness forced boundary bravado. Men and supplies were inadequate to taking the offensive. By the time he took the oath of office as the permanent president of the Confederacy on 22 February 1862, he had already developed a strategy for the war—the offensive-defensive—just the kind of plan that the weaker side needed to husband scarce resources until a chance came for decisive concentration at a vital point in the war. At that point, Confederate strength, saved for the moment, could be used decisively. Davis followed the plan throughout the war to far better advantage than allowed by critics.

Although things looked generally better in the North, Lincoln wallowed in worry that first winter. Bull Run continued to rankle, and, despite successes on the periphery, Confederates still kept the field and more sacrifice would be needed to end an insurrection that was growing into one of history's big wars.

To those concerned with war planning, it seemed clear that the conflict would be waged in four sectors—east, middle, west, and on the seas. Each sector seemed equally important, with special significance, in Lincoln's view, hinging on operations in and around northern Virginia. Many others, however, said the war would be decided along the Mississippi, that old river of commerce that seemed now to offer inroads of doom or opportunity to either side. What of Scott's Anaconda Plan? According to that scheme, each sector offered opportunities to use the North's superiority in men and materiel and chop the Confederacy up bit by bit. Not actively pushed by anyone, Scott's plan seemed to be working itself out. Christmas holidays in the North were frantic and tinged with dread in 1861, and the new year seemed clouded in an endless mist of carnage.

CONCENTRATION IN THE EAST, 1862

Scarcely one hundred miles separated the opposing national capitals, and the corridor between Washington and Richmond was to become America's most contested stretch of earth. Ground between the cities had military advantages for both sides. Rolling Virginia country was cut by myriad streams and rivers and much lay hidden by forests and scrub timberland, the right type of geography for breaking up big infantry formations and slicing cavalry brigades into small scouting groups. Each side sought the way to put northern Virginia to martial advantage, especially when armies grew wary of frontal assaults and tried increasingly the ancient art of field entrenchment.

After the Battle of Manassas, Johnston and Beauregard held the Bull Run line, collected additional men, and sought to strengthen their positions with fieldworks. Above them, again around Washington, the federals rebuilt their army and found the second in a long roll of generals to lead it back toward Richmond. George McClellan's ego matched the size of his new command the Military Division of the Potomac, which came under his charge on 27 July 1861. He accepted the assignment of leader of the Army of the Potomac as homage for brilliance and then proceeded to collect McDowell's wretched troop remnants and whip them into a large, flashy army and to perfect Washington's defenses in case the rebels pressed their post-Bull Run advantage. As he gathered men and supplies and confidence, his dapper figure on an imposing charger was seen prancing around the capital daily. His posturing angered some, but McClellan collected men like flies, trained them zealously, and won a fervent loyalty with paternal care and flamboyance.

All indicators ran well for "Little Mac"—an affectionate sobriquet conferred by his men. His operations in western Virginia showed him to be a good organizer, sound planner, a competent strategist, and a tactician of promise. While McClellan's manner may have gone against the plain grain of the president, Lincoln liked his record and hoped for the best. McClellan had no doubt of success as he prepared to invade Virginia, determining to use the Union's growing strength to advantage. With that in mind, he proposed to bypass Confederate lines by transporting his army by water to Urbana on the Rappahannock, disembark, and march rapidly to Richmond before Johnston could cover the capital. Lincoln had qualms but welcomed an aggressive idea. When Winfield Scott took reluctant retirement in November 1861, McClellan took his place as general in chief of the army. If Lincoln had misgivings, Scott assuaged them with firmer warlike words. Still, Lincoln chafed at delays in fear of flagging northern zeal and of too much time presented to the enemy.

Carefully McClellan built his legions, consuming time and mountains of supplies. Success, he believed, would reward care, and when he moved he wanted overwhelming superiority in his favor. McClellan's slowness through the winter sorely tried Lincoln's patience. Aware that campaigning usually stopped for the winter, the president certainly expected the campaign of 1862 to begin as soon as roads dried and temperatures moderated. Still McClellan honed his army and fended demands to attack until spring had almost gone. The Confederate government, on the other hand, worked earnestly through the winter of 1861 to fill ranks thinning from expiring enlistments; to procure and distribute arms, munitions, and other supplies; and especially to forward men to Johnston's army north of Richmond.

There were interesting blends of similarities between Johnston, Beauregard, and McClellan; in fact, a combination of Johnston's and Beauregard's personalities nicely duplicated Little Mac's methodical conceit. As grayclads clustered along Bull Run through the fall and winter, both Johnston and Beauregard fussed in isolation and in some rivalry over who commanded the army. Davis detested the silly command arguments and solved them by sending Beauregard, known as the "Great Creole" to the west early in 1862 as Johnston's second in command. Davis matched Johnston's contentiousness until relations between them chilled with the season. Johnston did organize well and kept his army supplied, and Davis shared his worries about federal intentions. Whenever McClellan moved, it seemed likely to be too soon. Men and munitions came slowly to northern Virginia, and Richmond seemed increasingly exposed.

Southern planners were not unaware of invasion avenues open to McClellan. A flanking move southeast of the capital had logic, and the Bull Run positions were too far north to permit swift adjustment. Johnston wanted to retire closer to the capital. On 9 March he fell back behind the Rappahannock River and neatly negated McClellan's Urbana plan.

Another rebel general also intruded on McClellan's hopes—the strange, solemn, Presbyterian deacon "Stonewall" Jackson, whose winter operations had confused a good many people. Against all precedent, Jackson decided on a winter campaign west of the Shenandoah Valley. Sent to the valley after the Battle of Manassas, he had collected some militia forces, received a few reinforcements, and harassed federal troops in the lower (northern) end of what was known as the "granary of Virginia." As winter set in, however, he knew that Union forces dominated most of the state from the Ohio River to the Shenandoah Valley. How best to thwart them? A glance at a map showed that a Confederate force posted at Romney, across the Alleghenies in the South Branch (Potomac) Valley, would disrupt federal railroad and highway communications and dominate northwestern Virginia.

Winter marching in the mountains would be severe, but the chance to lure McClellan into attacking Johnston before the Union army had finished preparation and the chance to clear western Virginia of the enemy were opportunities too good to ignore—or so thought a general who measured risks against rewards. General Johnston, the department commander, and Secretary of War Judah P. Benjamin approved Jackson's scheme and sent him a few more men. On 1 January 1862, with eighty-five hundred men, Jackson marched on Romney. Some of his untrained militia and recently attached men suffered, but the campaign fuddled the federals and satisfied Jackson. Some of his subordinates complained directly to the War Department about hardship and Jackson's "lunatic" strategy. Benjamin and President Davis blundered badly by listening out of channels and especially in giving Jackson a direct order to bring some of his men back from Romney. Complying instantly with the order, he also offered his resignation in the face of such lack of confidence. Johnston urged charity in the midst of crisis, while the governor of Virginia and many of Jackson's clerical friends urged restraint as they tried to explain to the government the chaos inherent in so "ruinous" a policy. In time, Jackson withdrew his resignation, his important point about command channels amply made.

Jackson could take consolation in knowing that activity in the Shenandoah Valley did indeed disturb Union forces. The enemy sent nearly twenty-five thousand men against his forty-five hundred. The ratio pleased him because he was attracting attention. Johnston wanted Jackson's little band to guard his flank, to stay between him and the federals, delay them in the valley, and keep reinforcements away from McClellan. Jackson could attract more Yankees if he had more men but he agreed to do what he could. With news that the federals were leaving the valley, Jackson took the offensive. At Kernstown on 23 March, inadequate intelligence led him to attack a superior force and he lost, and Jackson never again neglected field intelligence.

Although a defeat, the Battle of Kernstown had the strategic advantage of stopping the movement of federal troops toward McClellan and brought more men against Jackson. As Johnston withdrew closer to Richmond, Jackson received some reinforcements and made plans to engage the enemy and continue his Valley Campaign, a dazzling series of actions in which Jackson fought several groups of federal forces and beat them in detail, a campaign that gave Jackson lasting rank among the world's great captains.

While Jackson prepared, so did McClellan. Lincoln kept harassing McClellan, and at one point, with unvarnished irony, the president allegedly mused that if the general was not using the army, he would like to borrow it. Although keeping outward confidence in his boisterous general's new plan to embark his army for the Virginia Peninsula between the York and James rivers, Lincoln took the unusual step of con-structing "President's General War Order No. 1," on 27 January, which declared "that the 22d of February 1862, be the day for a general movement of the Land and Naval forces of the United States against the insurgent forces." Lest McClellan missed the point, the president issued the "President's Special War Order No. 1" on 31 January, which directed McClellan's Army of the Potomac to move south of Manassas.

McClellan's plans were not all bad, but they were confounded by phantoms. Convinced he was opposed by no less than 100,000 rebels north of Richmond, McClellan wanted at least 250,000 men in his area. Although he counted nearly 150,000 by March, he felt insecure about advancing. Lincoln, concerned that the "Young Napoleon" had too much to do, relieved him of all but his army command on the 11th, and at last McClellan moved. On 17 March the leading elements of his army embarked at Alexandria. Lincoln insisted on troops being left to defend Washington, and pressures from other sectors induced the president to siphon a few men from McClellan, but a peremptory presidential order on 3 April retaining McDowell's fine corps of thirty thousand men to watch Stonewall Jackson enraged McClellan. He knew Washington's safety hinged on his own success, but he had more than 100,000 men and rebel defenses around Yorktown and Williamsburg seemed thinner than expected. As he moved glacially toward Richmond, his spirits rose with his rhetoric. He would have been less enthused if he had known of Stonewall Jackson's doings.

The little Army of the Valley had moved up the Shenandoah to camps near Mount Jackson. Reorganization and refitting proceeded, and General Jackson kept an eye on General Nathaniel P. Banks, who moved south from Winchester with about fifteen thousand men and counted on help from scattered Union units. Talks with General Lee, now commanding Confederate operations outside Richmond, brought Jackson encouragement and the temporary aid of General Richard S. Ewell's six-thousand-man brigade. Lee admired Jackson's dogged determination—despite rising odds, he wanted to pin all the Yankee forces west of the Blue Ridge (even west of the Alleghenies) in the mountain theater and keep them away from Richmond.

In a sense, Lee measured Jackson by his achievements with a small force. Not only was General Banks returning in strength to the valley, but General John C. Frémont was also inching eastward toward the Shenandoah from his Mountain Department. Lincoln, responding to Frémont's calls, detailed General Louis Blenker's division from the Army of the Potomac to Frémont's army. Later, because of rising concerns about Jackson's movements, which were shrouded in mystery, he kept McDowell's corps to guard the capital. Therefore, with a few more men Jackson could hope for large results, but Lee could not promise more, because Johnston needed all the reinforcements available around Richmond.

Patiently, Jackson fell back up the valley and made a close study of its geography and geometry. In the area north of his main base at Staunton, Virginia, the valley sat between the Blue Ridge and the Alleghenies, varied in width from ten to thirty miles, and ran northward nearly one hundred miles to the Potomac. The Shenandoah River also ran northward, and divided at the southern base of Massanutten Mountain, a fifty-mile-long north-south range that created two valleys, the one to the east named Luray. Roads were not too good, although the six-foot-wide Valley Pike, connecting Staunton and Winchester, was "metalled" (macadamized). A skein of other dirt roads and traces created a rough parallelogram around Massanutten Mountain and in the upper and lower valley, which gave some maneuvering room to creative strategists.

Jackson lacked skill in understanding ground, but his brilliant topographical engineer, Jedediah Hotchkiss, provided maps that spread the valley clearly before Jackson. All kinds of chances beckoned, but chances shifted as Banks moved south to the end of Massanutten and threatened Staunton. In an unexpected series of moves at the end of April 1862, Jackson apparently took part of his army toward Richmond and left Ewell in observation at a strategic Blue Ridge mountain pass, put his infantry on the "cars," and raced through Staunton toward McDowell, Virginia, where he joined forces with General Edward ("Allegheny") Johnson's army of two thousand. On 8 May, Jackson's ten thousand defeated General Robert H. Milroy's force of six thousand at McDowell and pursued them down the South Fork Valley, sealing mountain passes eastward as they went. On 12 May, Jackson moved back toward Bank's force near Harrisonburg.

Banks was in trouble. He had detached James Shields and his ten thousand men toward Fredericksburg; with scarcely nine thousand left he feared Jackson's movements. He withdrew slowly northward toward Strasburg, which he fortified, and sent a flanking force eastward to Front Royal in hopes of reserving a reinforcement route. Meanwhile, he lost Jackson and Turner Ashby's splendid Confederate cavalry thoroughly screened the valley army. Stonewall had crossed the Massanutten, moved swiftly north down the Luray Valley, and on 23 May struck and smashed Banks's outpost at Front Royal, then sent his rebels racing to cut off Banks's retreat toward Winchester. A running engagement took the federals into their works at Winchester, where Banks made a stand. Jackson wasted no time—his men stormed the fortifications on 25 May, and Yankee remnants streamed for Harpers Ferry with Jackson in pursuit. A romantic figure of speech had it that the Shenandoah Valley pointed like a rifle barrel at the heart of the Union, but the figure now took the shape of Stonewall Jackson. He lurked in that barrel as a seemingly unstoppable charge. As his worn and weary legions crowded toward the Potomac, the Shenandoah was clear of the enemy and, with Shields on his way back to Banks, no help had gone to McClellan.

While Union commanders fumed at Jackson's quick marching—he had set up a system of ten minutes rest each hour and steady pacing through a whole day—Lincoln saw a Euclidean solution to the valley problem. If Jackson's army was at Winchester, the apex of a triangle, and if Shields was coming into the valley at Front Royal at the right base angle, Frémont could approach the left base angle and the two could close the base line at Strasburg and cut Jackson off as he tried to escape southward. It was, Lincoln saw, "a question of legs," and he hoped that shorter angles would put his men ahead of Jackson's "foot cavalry." Not quite. Jackson escaped, moved to the upper valley, and engaged the two forces of Frémont and Shields at Cross Keys on 8 June and Port Republic on 9 June. A double victory numbed federal initiative in the valley and forced them back on Banks beyond Massanutten. Stonewall reported to Lee that "God blessed our arms with victory."

The Valley Campaign remains a military classic, one still studied as a matchless example of what sound strategy combined with mobility, surprise, logistical planning, and determination can accomplish. In a period of forty-eight marching days, Jackson's army covered more than 650 miles, fought five major battles and countless combats and skirmishes. His 16,500 men kept three enemy armies, numbering more than sixty thousand, separated and away from Richmond, captured hundreds of Union wagons with precious supplies, and revived the rebel victory spirit when it seemed buried in bad news. By the time the Army of the Valley went into Blue Ridge for a rest, it had become legendary to South and North alike. Jackson ranked as a new American hero. His men told affectionate jokes about him and said they expected any day to be ordered to march to the gates of Hell and take them by storm. A proud biblical parody captured a great deal about the general and his men:

> Man that is born of woman,
> And enlisteth in Jackson's Army,
> Is of few days and short rations.

Jackson had kept an eye on operations around the capital during the valley fighting to protect Richmond. He knew that McClellan had landed a big army at Fort Monroe and had eased toward Yorktown. He knew, too, that Johnston had countered by moving the main Confederate army toward Richmond and sent some units to support Yorktown and Williamsburg.

By the second week of June, Jackson had learned that Johnston had been severely wounded in the Battle of Seven Pines (Fair Oaks), near Richmond, on 31 May, and that the fifty-five-year old Lee now commanded the main army, which pleased Jackson because he trusted Lee completely. Meanwhile, McClellan, moving with customary caution, inched up the peninsula between the York and James rivers. Because Johnston's attack at Seven Pines had failed, Lee reconcentrated and replanned the battle for Richmond and suggested that Jackson come at once, keeping an eye out for McDowell's corps, which might come to join McClellan from the north. Lee thought Jackson should hit the federal right, north of the Chickahominy River, cut communications, and pressure the flank while Lee's men attacked in front. Lee's call was discretionary and Jackson should decide. He went.

McClellan's amphibious movement to Fort Monroe was well planned, but he made the reckless assumption that the Union navy would be able to prevent interference from the CSS *Virginia* (formerly the USS *Merrimac*), which threatened Hampton Roads and help take Yorktown. As it happened, federal naval forces could only neutralize the *Virginia*. That unexpected deficiency slowed the campaign, but men and supplies did get to the proposed area of operations and McClellan had reason for some satisfaction. Army organization and management were his strengths and the movement to Virginia showed them to best advantage.

Strategy usually came in grandiose ways to McClellan, but peninsular geography and weather conditions focused his vision. Overflowing rivers and streams reduced maneuverability in the lowlands south of the Chickahominy River, which bisected the peninsula north of Williamsburg. Despite poor maps, McClellan saw he might get between Johnston and Richmond by concentrating between the Pamunkey and Chickahominy rivers, a route that would protect his base at West Point on the York River and leave an opening for McDowell, coming from the north. He wanted to work south of the Chickahominy, however, to attack Richmond's weaker defenses.

General J. E. B. Stuart's three-day cavalry ride around the Union army, 13–15 June, dismayed the northern public as well as some of McClellan's men, but, oddly enough, not the general. He thought that the raid had glamour but little military value other than reconnaissance, although it did alert him to his exposed communications and he prepared to change base. The raid also alerted Lee to the fact that the Yankee right could be turned, which helped bring Jackson to Richmond. Lee, suffering a drop in reputation because of the West Virginia defeats, planned a brilliant attack, but one that probably required too much sophistication on the part of inexperienced generals and staffs. He had noted McClellan's gradual shift south of the Chickahominy after the Battle of Seven Pines and noted particularly that one federal corps, General Fitz-John Porter's of thirty thousand men, remained virtually isolated north of that torrent. Assuming McClellan's caution, Lee schemed to hold the main Union force in place with twenty-five thousand men, put the bulk of his army, sixty-five thousand, north of the Chickahominy, crush Porter, and roll up the Union flank in what would have been sound examples of mass and economy of force.

Jackson was to hit Porter's right flank early on the morning of 26 June. As soon as he heard Jackson's guns, General A. P. Hill was to advance against Mechanicsville and Porter's Union line at Beaver Dam Creek. Generals D. H. Hill and James Longstreet were to bring their divisions through Mechanicsville, the former going to aid Jackson, the latter to support A. P. Hill. Generals John B. Magruder and Benjamin Huger, holding in front of Richmond, were to demonstrate heavily and convince McClellan that he dare not attack. Only the demonstrations went according to plan.

Jackson arrived late and got lost; an impatient A. P. Hill attacked Porter's entrenchments almost alone and was repulsed. While Lee pondered his next day's battle, McClellan overcame the aggressive urging of some of his generals and decided that he not only could not attack Richmond, he should hasten his change of base to the James River and consolidate his positions.

Lee, on 27 June, again ordered a flank attack on Porter and again saw his plans delayed. A. P. Hill advanced at 2:00 P.M., but Jackson did not attack with his three divisions until 4:00 P.M. Porter's corps fought fiercely and skillfully but his line finally broke as darkness fell. His fine artillery and two brigades from General E. V. Sumner's corps covered Porter's crossing of the Chickahominy at 4:00 in the morning of 28 June.

McClellan's situation had advantages. He knew that only one of his five corps had been engaged and that it fought well. He knew, too, that a new army, consisting of the commands of McDowell, Banks, and Frémont, had been organized under Major General John Pope and was ordered to his support. If the intact federal army held where it was on 28 June, Lee would soon find himself facing strong enemy forces in his front and rear. McClellan decided to retreat to his new base at Harrison's Landing on the James. If that decision seemed inexplicable, it hardly surprised Lee, who counted on his opponent's caution. For the moment, however, McClellan's movements baffled the Confederate leader. Where was he going? That question paralyzed southern movements during 28 June. If the bulk of the Union army moved South toward the James, Lee could cross the Chickahominy and attack. If, on the other hand, McClellan moved his men toward Fort Monroe and crossed the river downstream, Lee would have problems recrossing. Stuart's cavalry was off raiding instead of scouting and not until late in the day did Lee decide where McClellan was. Longstreet and A. P. Hill were sent to hit the federals in flank and Jackson was ordered to press the enemy rear. Magruder and Huger's men were to push southeastward.

McClellan himself seems to have lost interest in the battle for a time, but at least his subordinates were untrammeled by his leadership during three large actions. The bulk of his force—the Second, Third, and Sixth corps—struggled on 29 June to find crossings through White Oak Swamp. Magruder, hoping for help from Jackson, hit the three enemy corps at Savage Station in the afternoon; his action allowed the federals to get through the swampy barrier. Again the question ran Confederate ranks: What happened to Jackson? He apparently spent the day resting his men and rebuilding Grapevine Bridge while he could hear Magruder's battle in the distance. Why his atypical procrastination? The obvious explanation was slow bridge repair, but that would not excuse Jackson ignoring the sound of Magruder's fight. The real reason for the delay was an order from headquarters, signed by Lee's adjutant general, ordering Stuart's cavalry to guard bridges against enemy attempts to recross, and ordering Jackson to stay at the Grapevine crossing for the same reason—and to stay put until released. Jackson obeyed, telling one of Magruder's subordinates who asked for help that he had "other important duty to perform." While Jackson waited, federals retreated and fought with Magruder.

The next day, 30 June, after crossing the swamp, the Yankees kept moving toward the James. Lee hoped to get Jackson and Huger into action to press the enemy rear from the north, and have Magruder and Longstreet pick up the attack west of the federals as they bunched toward their base. Again Jackson delayed, this time in front of White Oak Swamp, despite the sound of battle in the near distance. Longstreet and A. P. Hill were in desperate combat at Frayser's Farm, but Jackson made no strong move to press on through the swamp. Instead, he dozed most of the day, apparently a victim of pent-up fatigue and short rations.

A sort of weirdness tinged 30 June, a Monday of errors and missed chances for the Confederates and hard fighting for the federals, who struggled to move their wagon trains and most of their army to Malvern Hill. This strong defensive position had height for Union cannon and the advantage of proximity to the base at Harrison's Landing. McClellan's men settled atop the hill under protection of artillery and bloodily repulsed another rebel attack on 1 July—an attack poorly organized and haphazardly delivered. McClellan retired that night to his base, ending his Peninsula Campaign against Richmond.

The casualties in the Seven Days' Battles were appalling to a people unprepared for a war of modern artillery and improved rifles. Lee had

more than 20,000 (some 4,000 killed, 15,000 wounded, and 1,000 missing) out of a total of nearly 88,000 men engaged from an army of nearly 90,000 men. Union losses amounted to 16,000 (about 2,000 killed, 8,000 wounded, and 6,000 missing) out of a total of 83,000 engaged from an army of more than 115,000 men.

Some reputations were casualties as well, especially that of McClellan. A storm of recrimination burst over him, but he continued preaching to President Lincoln on military as well as political matters. Lincoln visited the Army of the Potomac and tried to encourage the men. McClellan was through, however, despite his boast that he was still near Richmond and might resume the offensive in time. Jackson, too, suffered. So lately a national hero, he seemed almost a failure in some eyes. During the battles, Lee had scolded Jackson in his gentlemanly way but appeared to have no lingering ill feelings. President Davis seemed to have some doubts about the strange, dowdy-looking soldier, and so did some Richmond newspapers, which were remarkably fickle. A few days before they had cried for deliverance, and now that the enemy no longer thronged the gates, they carped. Far from savior, Lee was pictured as nearly a villain, blamed for badly planned battles, wasted opportunities, and heavy losses.

Lee and his generals, however, had no time for rebuttals. While McClellan floundered around the peninsula, General John Pope had collected Union troops and issued grandiloquent orders and proclamations, which irritated his army and angered Virginia civilians about to be subjected to illegal martial law. Originally created to help McClellan, Pope's Army of Virginia now had a new mission. When Pope moved east of the Blue Ridge in mid-July, he threatened the Gordonsville rail hub. Adhering to the basic strategy of the offensive-defensive, Lee sent Jackson to do something about Pope.

Lincoln had appointed Major General Henry W. Halleck to the revived post of general in chief of the Union armies on 11 July. Halleck had field experience in the west and the confidence of military men. "Old Brains" (Halleck's sobriquet) decided to bring McClellan's forlorn legions from the peninsula to strengthen Pope's army—a decision McClellan detested and one that Pope did not clearly understand. By the time McClellan's army began a move to Aquia Creek, Jackson had a new lease on glory.

On July 13, Jackson led his divisions toward Gordonsville. Reinforcements went to Jackson until he counted almost twenty-five thousand bayonets. He made good time on his march and beat Pope to Gordonsville. Rashly, Pope decided not to wait for McClellan's reinforcements and moved south. Unexpectedly, his advance under General Banks ran into Jackson's vanguard at Cedar Mountain on 9 August and a major battle developed. Badly managed on both sides, the battle ended in Banks's withdrawal, but Jackson did not pursue against all of Pope's army.

McClellan's men were arriving at Aquia by early August and were routed to Pope. Lee, knowing that Pope would be reinforced, wanted to beat him before all of McClellan's men joined. He devised a plan to fix Pope along the Rappahannock while Jackson secretly went around his right to occupy the large Union supply base at Manassas Junction—near the old battlefield. During 27 August, Jackson's men occupied Bristoe Station and Manassas Junction. Gorging on the mountainous Union supply dumps, Jackson's men filled ammunition wagons, packed four-days rations, and moved that night to a strong position in a unfinished railroad cut not too far from the Henry House hill.

Pope lost control of the situation, confused by conflicting reports, short of cavalry, and some of his men short of ammunition. By the afternoon of 28 August, he decided that Jackson was at Centreville and directed his various corps there. Late in the afternoon Jackson's men attacked a Union force crossing their front, because he wanted to bring Pope's army down on him so that Longstreet's divisions could hit the enemy on the left flank and perhaps achieve a double envelopment. Now certain of Jackson's location, Pope concentrated. Jackson's men stood off several attacks on the 29th and narrowly held the field at nightfall. Pope misconceived the situation and thought the Confeder-

ates were withdrawing; he ordered a pursuit that subjected Jackson's weary men to another series of attacks. At the crucial moment, Longstreet's artillery swept across the Union advancing front, and late in the afternoon his five divisions hit Pope's army on the left rear. Pope managed to extract his troops and retreated toward Centreville, toward which Jackson was also moving. Through a drenched 31 August, both armies groped to new positions, and on 1 September a pitched engagement at Chantilly produced only casualties. But Pope was beaten. Receiving permission to fall back into the Washington defenses, his sodden legions reached the capital on 2 September 1862.

During this Second Battle of Bull Run (Second Manassas), from 27 August through 2 September, Pope had a total of 16,000 casualties, Lee, a total of 9,500. The war had grown costlier with practice. If Confederates boasted fewer losses, they also faced a shrinking manpower pool—a cause of growing alarm in Richmond.

Alarm about dwindling numbers of men and enemy incursions around southern borders forced President Davis and the new secretary of war, George W. Randolph, to ask the Confederate congress to draft men for the armies. By March 1862, however, attempts to encourage reenlistments had increased morale problems in the army—liberal furlough policies had riddled the ranks and many on leave would not come back. Rebels had learned, like their stout enemies, that war was hard. Many of them resented the physical labor of digging trenches and latrines, and slaves were sometimes impressed into labor service. Both armies had learned that life in the field lacked glamour. There were proud, parading moments, but mostly things were dirty, wet, hot, or cold, and disease stalked camps with grim impartiality. Both sides had recruiting problems after the first winter, but the Confederacy's armies seemed to be melting away as spring 1862 gave way to the dog days of summer and the Yankees appeared to be winning everywhere. The Confederate congress enacted the first draft law in American history on 16 April 1862, calling to the colors all white men between eighteen and thirty-five; a liberal exemption law watered down the effect, but the armies were saved for the moment. Union armies were saved, too, as Lincoln's repeated calls for men boosted enlistments in the Army of the Potomac. Lincoln pondered ways to defend Washington and kept a wary eye on Maryland, which might be a Confederate objective.

TROUBLES IN THE FAR WEST, 1861–1862

Both Lincoln and Davis looked on the middle border as a strategic area. Lincoln felt that losing Tennessee, Kentucky, and Missouri might be tantamount to losing the war. Davis knew that the Confederacy needed some of those states—preferably all—to solidify the northern border and Confederate national spirit.

Lincoln counted on a groundswell of unionism to hold the border, while Davis relied on sweeping southern nationalism. Both were right and wrong. There were divided loyalties in each of the border states. People in east Tennessee thought much like west Virginians, but prosecessionists prevailed and the state joined the Confederacy. Kentucky, with sentiments spread fairly evenly across the state and a secessionist governor, sought a neutral's profiteering status, which persisted until Confederates entered the state in September and triggered Union occupation. A rump Kentucky government joined the Confederacy in December. Missouri had a prosecessionist governor and majority in the legislature; St. Louis, however, claimed a pro-Union majority and was the state's power center. Federal troops held that city firmly for the Union. The state government, exiled to southwestern Missouri, joined the Confederacy late in November 1861.

A divided Arkansas became a Confederate state with modest difficulty in May 1861, which made easier friendly relations with the Five Civilized Tribes and some of the Plains Indians.

Several treaties of Confederate alliance not only helped solidify the turbulent western frontier but also brought many good troops into rebel ranks. Military operations in the Far West began with secession and spread from the Mississippi to Arizona. With rare exceptions, operations in the Far West were peripheral and of slight effect.

One of the two most important western campaigns in the first year started in Texas. Confederate General Henry Hopkins Sibley led an expedition of twenty-five hundred men into New Mexico during February–April 1862, in an attempt to secure that area and to open routes to the far west; it was a confederate dream to hold all the southwest to California. At Valverde on 21 February 1862, his men skirmished with troops under Colonel E. R. S. Canby and marched on to Santa Fe. Sibley sent a probing column eastward toward Las Vegas, New Mexico, where it had an engagement on 28–29 March 1862 with federal troops moving toward Santa Fe. The Yankees retreated until part of their force got behind the rebel lines and burned their supply and ammunition wagons. With the withdrawal of this force, Sibley began a bitter winter retreat to Texas and the Confederate dream of a western empire faded. Scattered fights in Arizona that were aimed at political results were abortive.

The other important campaign centered in northwestern Arkansas and was a result of the union defeat at Wilson's Creek, near Springfield, Missouri, on 10 August 1861. A resultant federal buildup threatened Arkansas and induced President Davis to send the dashing, competent cavalry general, Earl Van Dorn to the trans-Mississippi. With an army of fourteen thousand, including a brigade of Indians, Van Dorn, who hoped to capture St. Louis, fought a confused, two-day battle against the army of twelve thousand under General S. R. Curtis at Pea Ridge (Elkhorn Tavern), Arkansas, 7–8 March 1862. Defeated, Van Dorn gave up hope of invading Missouri and was unable to help General Albert Sidney Johnston, then in northern Mississippi.

THE KENTUCKY-TENNESSEE LINE, 1861–1862

All through the winter of 1861, pressure steadily mounted against the thin Confederate defense lines in Kentucky and Tennessee. Unconsciously pushing the Anaconda Plan, Lincoln saw the war in geographical and geometrical terms, and he read maps with a strategist's eye. When he looked at a map of the middle of the country, he was instantly struck by the rivers. The Mississippi bisected the rebel states; if it could be forced, the trans-Mississippi Confederacy would be cut off, and Davis' eastern armies dealt with piecemeal. The Ohio River ran like the lifeline of the Union from western Pennsylvania to its junction with the Mississippi at Cairo, Illinois.

To Southerners, the Ohio seemed a natural northern border for the Confederacy. To Lincoln, some of its tributaries were open arteries to the rebel heartland. As increasing numbers of gunboats joined the Union naval inventory along the Mississippi, Lincoln envisioned amphibious operations on the Tennessee and Cumberland rivers and eventually along the "Father of Waters," but he had a familiar problem—aggressive commanders were hard to find. The president had approved General in Chief McClellan's suggestion that two departments be created in the west: the first, the Department of Missouri, including western Kentucky, should be commanded by Halleck; the second, the Department of the Ohio, encompassing the rest of Kentucky and Tennessee, should be under General Don Carlos Buell. A moment's pondering might have raised an important question in Lincoln's mind: Did McClellan pick generals like himself? If so, the new co-command structure would confound rather than coordinate.

Jefferson Davis shared Lincoln's unease about activities in the west. Too many little actions persisted, conducted by too many disorganized units. Perceiving that the area west of the mountains offered great advantages as well as weaknesses to the South, Davis grasped the need for unified command in that key sector.

He had, he thought, just the man for the job—Albert Sidney Johnston. A highly trusted friend of Davis, Johnston boasted illustrious careers in the armies of the United States and the Republic of Texas. He resigned his U.S. commission on 10 April 1861 and was appointed a full general in the Confederate regular army. Confident that Sidney Johnston could organize a cohesive defense of the Tennessee-Kentucky line, in September, Davis gave him command of all Confederate forces from Arkansas to the Cumberland Gap, some fifty thousand men.

Johnston knew that Halleck and Buell combined in their departments about 130,000 widely scattered men. Confederate advantages were few; the best was good lateral communications. The federals, however, now counted on heavy naval support on the rivers and could infiltrate swiftly. Johnston's position hinged on three key points—big Fort Donelson on the Cumberland River, the smaller Fort Henry on the Tennessee, and Columbus, Kentucky, on the Mississippi. He had small forces at each of these places and at several others, but delayed concentration as he pondered logistics and the moves of the army under General Ulysses S. Grant.

Halleck sent Grant against the two river forts, and after an opéra bouffe affair on 6 February at Fort Henry (which sat so close to the river that Union gunboats floated by and fired down into the works), Grant thoroughly dominated the timid commanders of Fort Donelson and took it on 16 February 1862, along with 11,500 men and forty cannon. With his center broken, his lateral communications cut, and an opportunity to defeat Grant's smaller force wasted, Johnston pondered a disaster created in part by his vacillation.

General Beauregard arrived to aid Johnston and soon convinced him to concentrate the scattered Confederate units to wrest the initiative from the federals. Johnston selected Corinth, Mississippi, as the junction point, and Beauregard departed to take command of all rebel troops between the Tennessee and Mississippi rivers. Beauregard used the telegraph to coerce reinforcements from across the Mississippi and urged help from the Deep South. He also saw the danger posed by Johnston's two main forces being separated by Grant and Buell, who had moved to Nashville. He urged Johnston to hasten the concentration at Corinth, and moved the Columbus force in that direction, leaving a garrison at Island No. 10 in the Mississippi to delay twenty-five thousand Union troops. Johnston, oddly enough, did not move with any special sense of urgency.

Command problems hampered federal efforts to take advantage of their inner lines. Halleck talked of attacking such strategic points as Memphis or Corinth and bragged about Grant's operations, but he squandered the splendid opportunity to destroy Johnston's forces in detail. Buell saw the chance and wanted to join Grant and attack before Johnston got his men together. Halleck sent Grant's force up the Tennessee to raid rebel rail lines. Lincoln solved the command tangle on 11 March 1862 by giving Halleck command of the central theater, and, once in charge, Halleck acted. He ordered Buell to join Grant's force near Pittsburg Landing (Shiloh), Tennessee, where the combined forces could threaten Memphis. Buell moved casually and took thirteen days to cover thirty-five miles to Columbus; a wrecked bridge there again delayed him considerably.

Fortunately for Sidney Johnston, he had Beauregard to goad him and Davis to plan for him. Davis, as much a student of war as vaunted "Old Brains" Halleck, saw the chance to hit Grant's army in its relatively isolated position near Shiloh. He began a strategic concentration of reinforcements using the latest military technology in a Napoleonic application of the offensive-defensive. Davis telegraphed for reinforcements from Charleston and New Orleans, released Bragg from Mobile with his ten thousand troops, and pushed them all forward by an innovative use of railroads and river steamers. By early April, Johnston had forty-thousand men at Corinth. Grant, unaware of enemy concentration, had encamped at Pittsburg Landing without bothering about security.

Johnston, hoping for surprise, moved his men forward under heavy security. A skirmish on 4 April 1862 seemed to have compromised the attack, but the Confederates pressed on. They found Grant's position circumscribed by the Tennessee to their right, with Owl and Snake creeks to their left. They would be attacking into a sack but both flanks were protected and the enemy had no place to run. An early morning attack on 6 April 1862 caught most of the federals unprepared.

Johnston wanted to turn the enemy left and cut them off from the river. Federal positions and terrain dictated a frontal assault, weighted to the right. Beauregard had overall command of the field and botched his tactical dispositions by deploying in two lines of division with a corps in reserve. As the battle progressed, bunching along the blazing battle lines confused organization. Beauregard fed in his reserves almost evenly across the front, so there were no tactical emergency forces available to exploit opportunities. Johnston had gone forward to encourage the front. Fatally wounded, he died about 2:30 P.M. Beauregard continued to manage the advance, which had been halted by several strong points of resistance. By nightfall, the Union left had been turned, but rebel troops were too scattered and too weary to exploit their advantage, especially against freshly massed Union cannon. During the night, Buell's men began arriving on the field. Grant counterattacked on 7 April and slowly drove the rebels back to the original Union positions. Beauregard retreated at the end of the day. Losses were appalling in what was the hardest fighting of the war—nearly fourteen thousand Union casualties, and eleven thousand Confederate.

Disaster threatened the Confederacy. Beauregard's strength was gone, Union troops controlled the Mississippi almost to Memphis, and Halleck, with a large army near Corinth, had decisive victory in his grasp—but it eluded him. Beauregard's optimism persisted and he collected reinforcements, many of them on the way, but too late for Shiloh. He soon commanded about 70,000 men at Corinth, but Halleck had also collected troops and was nearby with no fewer than 120,000. Beauregard wisely decided not to try holding heavily fortified Corinth, because he might simply find himself bottled up. Instead, he retired to Tupelo. Halleck, happy with having taken Corinth, left the enemy army alone. Davis was furious over the wasted opportunities in the west, and Beauregard resigned his command and took sick leave. Davis gave the Army of Tennessee to General Braxton Bragg on 27 June, as crises compounded for the South.

Even before the impact of the Battle of Shiloh could be fully felt, a decisive federal success crowned joint naval and land efforts at the southern end of the Mississippi. For months, the Confederate commander of New Orleans, General Mansfield Lovell, had called for reinforcements to strengthen the defenses of the South's largest city and most important port. Instead, he had been repeatedly ordered to send men to help Sidney Johnston. Lovell watched anxiously a buildup of Union ships, mortar boats and transports under Flag Officer David Glasgow Farragut and General Benjamin F. Butler. To defend the mouth of the Mississippi, the Confederates counted on two large brick forts on the river below New Orleans and on a barrier of hulks and chain across the river. A small rebel river fleet of wooden boats supporting the new ironclad ram *Manassas* was expected to hamper Union operations. At 2:00 A.M. on 24 April 1862, Farragut's fleet ran past the forts, broke through the barrier boom, fended off rebel fire rafts, and reached New Orleans's docks.

A daring gamble had brought the biggest Union prize of the war. The fall of New Orleans not only had military and economic impact but heartened the Union. If the South could not protect so vital a city, it must be weak indeed. With efforts apparently succeeding to clear the Mississippi from both ends, Lincoln felt that soon the Confederacy would be cut in two. Once that was accomplished, it might be chopped up as envisioned by Winfield Scott. Davis became increasingly aware of the impossibility of defending every threatened point and sought a different strategy to make the offensive-defensive more effective.

In moments of dark reflection, Davis might also have pondered the qualities of his generals in the West. The Shiloh campaign showed good logistical planning on his own part and that of railroad and quartermaster officers. If Davis had been able to surmount his personal likes and dislikes, he would also have seen that Beauregard had sound strategic sense and certainly more energy than Sidney Johnston. Bauregard's mercurial nature sometimes undermined his tactical sense, but he had values worth using. Bragg's part in the battle had been commendable enough and his men fought well and shared no shame in defeat. Davis hoped that Bragg, "who had shown himself equal to the management of volunteers and at the same time commanded their love and respect,'" might somehow hold the sagging central front. The president would try to send men from the interior, but they were scarce and demands constant.

For the moment, the best southern defense came from federal inaction. Leaving two divisions to hold Grant in place, on 21 July, Bragg began to move thirty-five thousand men by rail from Tupelo, Mississippi, via Mobile to Chattanooga. Buell had been ordered there on 10 June, but his march on inner lines was slow and plagued by logistical troubles. Bragg reached Chattanooga before Buell and developed a plan to carry the war into Kentucky. While he gathered ammunition and other supplies, Lee cleared Virginia of federal troops.

With Lee victorious and Bragg planning boldly, President Davis enjoyed a rare opportunity to rise above daily war necessities to think strategically. He evolved a scheme for a major two-pronged Confederate offensive in the east and west. Lee, who wanted to invade Maryland, would do so; Bragg would march for Kentucky, aided by General Edmund Kirby Smith's force of ten thousand men at Knoxville. Davis promised to comb the Confederacy for men in the hope that a combined attack on the Union's right and left fronts would prevent constant shuttling of troops and tend to equalize numbers. Although risky, his plan had great potential for wresting the initiative from the Union, for clearing Tenneessee, and for shifting pressure into vital federal territory. Davis also added a political dimension to his planning—overtures would be made to the people of those states to induce them to join rebel ranks and to perhaps entice other states into the Confederacy. The invading generals would renew the southern call for peace, independence, and free trade and offer liberal terms of alliance. Such a bold program would commit every reserve of Confederate men and supplies into one venture. Failure in the west could lose the Mississippi Basin; failure in the east could uncover Richmond. Success, however, could change the strategic balance of the war.

Things looked good at the start for the Confederates. As Bragg moved north from Chattanooga at the end of August and Lee crossed into Maryland in early September, Union forces were abruptly thrown on the defensive and faced depressing possibilities. Should Louisville fall, all of Indiana and Ohio would be threatened, the Baltimore and Ohio rail link would break, and Bragg might reach the Great Lakes. If Lee was not stopped, Washington might be captured and the war lost.

Lee would be bold enough, but what of Bragg? Union commanders who had met him knew his personal courage, his spit and polish discipline and his McClellan-like capacity to weld an army out of broken remnants. They also knew he had some kind of restless force in him, but a few surely guessed he lacked the essential fighter's spark. As he advanced from Chattanooga on 30 August 1862, he had the rhetoric for the moment. "This campaign," he said, "must be won by marching, not fighting." If this seemed a bravado's boast, Bragg at least tried to make it true. He maneuvered Buell almost back to the Ohio without fighting, but command problems and political realities negated Bragg's great venture. Kirby Smith, an independent commander, did not join Bragg. People were not flocking to rebel banners. Buell, who had admirably cooperated by caution, finally began to concentrate. A sharp engagement at Perryville, Kentucky, on 8–9 October bruised both armies indecisively, but Bragg lost heart, abandoned his campaign, and marched through the Cumberland Gap all the way to Murfreesboro. General William S. Rosecrans relieved Buell, and Halleck, now called to Washington as general in chief, pushed him to occupy east Tennessee.

Rosecrans moved against Bragg in late December and in the big, confused Battle of Stones River (Murfreesboro), 30 December 1862–2 January 1863, he won a victory of sorts. Each army suffered nearly ten thousand casualties and Bragg withdrew toward Tullahoma, Tennessee. Rosecrans had at least held middle Tennessee, but he did not advance for another six months.

In all of his campaigning, Bragg underused his cavalry. His mounted arm, under such able leaders as Joseph Wheeler and Nathan Bedford Forrest (probably the greatest natural soldier of the nineteenth century) could have done much better duty than allowed by Bragg's limited thinking. The left prong of Davis' joint offensive had been stopped and bent back. Bragg could boast of many supplies captured, of holding the initiative for months, and of not losing the Confederate center altogether, but the writ for 1862 in the west ran for the Union. What of the other prong of Davis' offensive?

EASTERN CAMPAIGNS AND COMMAND CHANGES, SEPTEMBER 1862–JULY 1863

Pope's army straggled into Washington in August 1862 and spilled through the city, ragged, demoralized veterans clotting the streets and shocking the populace. Lincoln also felt the shock. Pressure of northern public opinion burdened him now; how many more defeats would the country tolerate? McDowell had marched off to finish the rebels at Bull Run, McClellan to finish them at Richmond, Banks to smash Stonewall Jackson in the Shenandoah Valley, and Pope had taken his "headquarters in the saddle" into Virginia to help McClellan finish Lee. Now remnants of all those finishing schools were flotsam roaming through the capital. Things might look good in the west, but the main armies had been driven from Virginia and criticism mounted.

Although Pope had done a reasonably competent job, Lincoln knew he would have to go, but who could organize the wreckage of the Army of the Potomac and shove it into battle against Lee's victorious legions thronging along the Potomac, possibly about to invade the North? McClellan's organizational skills were acknowledged even by his enemies and the men in the ranks loved and trusted him. Lincoln now considered him a fine army builder but not a fighter. He could refit the army, prepare adequate defenses for the capital, but would probably be replaced when an offensive opportunity came. McClellan, ignorant of presidential misgivings, took the assignment while Lee pondered a new campaign.

President Davis' military-political application of his offensive-defensive strategy clarified some of Lee's thinking. Logistical facts lent impetus to the idea of invading Maryland. Virginia had been scavenged mercilessly by all the armies and had little left worth taking. Food, forage, and other supplies awaited in abundance across the Potomac. A Confederate army in Maryland would give loyal Marylanders a chance to join the southern colors—as Davis firmly hoped. One possible negative was that the Confederacy had repeatedly said that all it wanted was to be left alone in independence, that it had no territorial interests outside its own boundaries. Would the joint invasions make mockery of that claim? Possibly, but it could be reasonably argued that Maryland, and Kentucky, were really part of the Confederacy and that gray legions would be operating within legitimate borders.

Lee really had no choice and wasted little time preparing for the Maryland incursion, which left several things dangling. He did not seem to have a clear objective save the vague possibility of moving on Harrisburg, Philadelphia, or Baltimore, cutting important Union rail communications and hitting targets of opportunity. In his hasty planning, Lee committed an unprofessional error in judgment. When he learned that McClellan again would be the opponent, he made the complacent assumption that his old foe would move with typical sloth. This time he was wrong.

Screened by Jeb Stuart's cavalry, Lee's men crossed the Potomac on 4 September 1862 and were near Frederick, Maryland, by the 7th. McClellan moved slowly northwestward with 85,000 men, but had overestimated Lee's 55,000 into 120,000. Lee divided his force. Jackson went to capture Harpers Ferry, possibly to secure the Shenandoah as a supply line, and Longstreet was sent to meet a threatened federal militia force. By 10 September, Lee had scattered his army in the face of the enemy. Why this dangerous gamble? Probably because Lee believed that McClellan could not bring himself to move quickly enough to make a difference. That was a likely assumption, but on 13 September, McClellan received a copy of Lee's Special Order No. 191, which outlined his whole plan of dispersal. For sixteen hours McClellan did not move and digested the information, but then he moved with unwonted speed.

Lee, quickly alerted to McClellan's intelligence coup, made hasty efforts to reconcentrate. He sent a force to block South Mountain and ordered concentration at Sharpsburg on Antietam Creek. McClellan struck Lee's men at South Mountain while Longstreet moved toward Sharpsburg. Jackson besieged Harpers Ferry, which fell to him on 15 September, and could not join immediately. When McClellan forced the mountain, Lee prepared to hold along Antietam in relatively weak positions unstrengthened by fieldworks and with scarcely twenty-thousand men on the field. McClellan arrived late on 15 September. Had he attacked vigorously on the 16th, Lee would probably have been crushed, but McClellan waited and planned himself into fragmentation. On the 17th, after Lee had been reinforced by Jackson's men from Harpers Ferry, McClellan watched as his army delivered a series of bold and tactically sound attacks from the right, to the center, and then on the left. McClellan took no personal part in coordinating his attacks and they went in piecemeal, nearly succeeded, and at length all were repulsed because Lee was allowed to shift men from attack to attack. Lee was saved almost at the moment of defeat by the arrival of reinforcements.

Both commanders mismanaged the Battle of Antietam (Sharpsburg). Lee's determination to stand with inferior numbers on weak ground seemed uncharacteristic and was certainly dangerous. McClellan's typical hesitancy confounded his subordinates, who were frequently frustrated in attempts to take advantage of Confederate weaknesses. Every battle seems to have its swaying moments of crisis and usually one of real decision, and Antietam had many moments of Confederate crises, several of real decision, and McClellan missed every one of those chances.

Against the advice of his subordinates, Lee held the field during 18 September, apparently hoping to lure McClellan into another attack, which probably would have eliminated the Army of Northern Virginia. Not only did McClellan have an unused corps available, he had received reinforcement, but he did not attack and Lee retired to Virginia during the night. Of about 39,000 Confederate men on the field, there were about 13,700 casualties; of 70,000 Union troops, there were about 12,500 casualties. On the threadbare victory at Antietam, Lincoln issued his Preliminary Emancipation Proclamation on 22 September and changed the nature of the war. Great Britain began to turn slowly to the northern side.

Now that the right prong of Davis' offensive had been clipped, what strategy could retain the initiative and somehow negate the rising tide of Union numbers? Davis learned from his double offensive. Unwilling to believe that Bragg had failed because of resolution, Davis fixed on faulty command arrangements as the cause of western problems. With Bragg and Kirby Smith coequal commanders, cooperation had been difficult and coordination from Richmond impossible. Davis, guided by the brilliant new War Secretary James A. Seddon, recognized that command arrangements for the Army of Northern Virginia needed no tinkering. The west, however, posed vast problems that caused the two war planners to consider a new concept in military delegation, one that indicated the president and the secretary were original organizational theorists. Because geographical departments had not solved issues of rank and seniority in the field, Davis began to think of what is now called a "theater command" in the west.

Despite the telegraph, distance still wrapped battlefields in the fog of war, the west in particular because of widely scattered forces. A deputy war leader was needed out there, a general of experience equal to the broadest authority. If he rose to his chance he would coordinate all rebel forces and all logistical efforts in his domain and intrude on state and local politics to military purpose. The right man would seize the heartland and rule it as his satrapy. Lee was in exactly the right niche; Bragg, Davis hated to admit, was marred by defeat; Beauregard—too flamboyant for the president's austerity—was back in Charleston doing brilliant work in defending the city, leaving only one man of proper experience, the man Seddon had in mind, Joseph E. Johnston. Davis had qualms and Johnston may have had some, but he wanted to be back in the field and accepted the assignment.

Lincoln also pondered command problems. He thought he had arrived at the right command structure with McClellan installed as general in chief, then he thought Halleck could do the job. McClellan's plans were obscurantist classics and Halleck wrapped himself in minutiae. Therefore, like it or not, Lincoln was still a practicing commander in chief, but he looked for some competent military man to run the war for him. It had not yet occurred to him that he was fast becoming a master strategist as he kept his eye fixed on the whole conflict and on the enemy's armies.

In November, Lincoln fired McClellan for the last time. Who could pick up the pieces after Antietam and get after Lee? Who had the sense to know that the North had more of everything, the sense to mobilize it, and overwhelm the rebels? Despairingly, he turned to a gentleman soldier, a fine corps commander in the Army of the Potomac, General Ambrose E. Burnside, whose tonsorial sweep gave a word to the English language, "sideburns." A rightfully humble man, Burnside said he was incompetent to command a large army and, lamentably, would prove his point. Taking command on 7 November 1862, he reorganized the Army of the Potomac and moved south toward Fredericksburg.

Lee hated losing the initiative and after Sharpsburg stayed close to the Potomac, hoping to lure McClellan into an attack. Reorganizing his army into two corps (Longstreet commanding the First Corps and Stonewall Jackson the Second Corps), Lee left Jackson in the valley, threatening the Union right flank, and went with Longstreet to Culpeper Court House, to confront the main enemy thrust.

Dividing the army had dangers, but McClellan would not likely take advantage of it, nor would Burnside. Burnside ranked as a competent corps commander but was hardly fervent. Lee might impose on him as he had his predecessor. Burnside, however, had a coherent plan of operations—not brilliant, but coherent. He wanted to concentrate near Warrenton, threaten a dash to the valley to cut off Jackson, and move the main army to Fredericksburg, where he would be between Lee and Richmond. Lee would have to come to him, and Burnside could either fight or take the enemy capital. Skeptical, Lincoln approved with the caveat that speed was essential. Burnside moved quickly to Falmouth, north of Fredericksburg, by 17 November and caught Lee out of position. General E. V. Sumner urged a swift river crossing, but Burnside called for pontoon bridges and Halleck failed to urge haste on supply officers. It was not until 25 November that the first bridges arrived, but by then Longstreet's men resisted Rappahannock crossings.

Burnside might still have gotten between Lee's corps by a quick march up the river because Jackson could not arrive for several days. Like so many Civil War generals, Burnside focused on the wrong objective. His eye was fixed on Richmond, not on Lee's army, so he waited to control the river and cross closer to the enemy capital. That decision is indefensible on almost any ground—Longstreet's men were in front, and although the federals might well have overwhelmed them, the price would have

been high. Waiting for more bridges simply gave Jackson time to reach the field. Obviously, the Union commander should have moved upriver and threatened both wings of Lee's army, or crossed the river and moved on Richmond via the Rapidan River and Gordonsville. As Burnside waited for more pontoons in front of Fredericksburg, Lee's lines grew stronger in men and entrenchments.

A kind of eerie fatalism hung over Burnside's headquarters while Lee's legions gathered and opportunities faded. The road to Richmond seemed to lead straight through the Army of Northern Virginia, which was perched mainly on high ground behind frowning earthworks. Burnside believed the erroneous reports of balloon observers that Lee had posted his army south of Fredericksburg, with his left resting opposite the town. Burnside skewed the strength of his three "grand divisions" to his right, arraying Hooker and Sumner against formidable Marye's Heights and General William B. Franklin on the left in open ground fronting Jackson's Second Corps. He counted on superb artillery support from the high ground across the river to sustain an attack against massed men and guns. The attack began on the cold morning of 13 December 1862. Repeated assaults on Marye's Heights and its grisly sunken road piled up Union casualties; Franklin's attack on the left made early progress but was finally driven back without result. By nightfall the attacks waned at a cost of nearly twelve thousand Union casualties to about five thousand Confederates killed, wounded, and a few missing.

In Washington an anxious president dogged the military telegraph and once more heard of high hopes dashed in gore—another defeat, another wasted campaign, and thousands more dead as winter seemed to freeze the nation's hope. In Richmond, a grateful President Davis congratulated a victorious general as he rested his legions and begged for food, firewood, and simple comforts for men suffering a Valley Forge–type winter on the Rappahannock. Lee hoped fighting had ended for the year, but Burnside, scorched to the high anger of a timid man, tried one more tilt for glory. Late in January 1863, he ordered a flanking movement up-river from Lee, only to endure a charade of his men losing the campaign to Virginia mud. Derisive comments from his subordinates nearly maddened Burnside, who lashed out with threats of dismissal. Sadly, Lincoln relieved the humble general on 25 January in favor of General Joseph Hooker, proudly known as "Fighting Joe." Lincoln hoped for truth in the sobriquet.

Hooker received an intriguing order of appointment, one filled with the president's personal brand of honest criticism, one aimed at bristling pride. Lincoln told him

> There are some things in regard to which, I am not quite satisfied with you. . . . You are ambitious, which, within reasonable limits, does good rather than harm. But I think that during General Burnside's command of the Army, you have taken counsel of your ambitions, and thwarted him as much as you could, in which you did a great wrong to the country, and to a most meritorious and honorable brother officer. I have heard . . . of your recently saying that both the Army and the Government needed a Dictator. Of course it was not for this, but in spite of it, that I have given you the command. Only those generals who gain successes can set up Dictators. What I now ask of you is military success, and I will risk the Dictatorship. . . . I much fear that the spirit which you have aided to infuse into the Army, of criticizing their Commander, and withholding confidence from him, will now turn upon you. I shall assist you as far as I can, to put it down. Neither you nor Napoleon if he were alive again, could get any good out of an Army, while such a spirit prevails in it. . . . And now, beware of rashness.—Beware of rashness, but with energy and sleepless vigilance, go forward, and give us victories.

Hooker overlooked this presidential homily in the fullness of fortune. With characteristic energy, he plotted Lee's destruction—and he plotted well. He would fix Lee in the Fredericksburg lines with part of his army, take the main body to an upriver crossing, swing around the Confederate left, and get between Lee and Richmond. Aware that much of Longstreet's corps

had been detached to the south, Hooker determined to use his much larger numbers to force the rebels to fight on Yankee terms. He began his campaign swiftly in late April 1863 as spring greened the Rappahannock Valley, roads dried, and spirits rose.

Anticipating action from Hooker, Lee quickly grasped his strategy, and on 30 April ordered Jackson to intercept the enemy in or near the Wilderness of Virginia, a great, gloomy, wooded area stretching west and south from Fredericksburg. When Jackson's men moved into the Wilderness to catch Hooker before he cleared the woods, the Battle of Chancellorsville began—a battle that is now famous as a classic in maneuver and applied psychology.

Hooker's dispositions were excellent, and when he reached Chancellorsville, he might be able to get between Jackson's men and General Jubal Early's screening force at Fredericksburg. Greatly outnumbering both enemy forces, Hooker could beat them in detail. He squandered the opportunity as the dank, dripping woodland worked its alchemy of dread. Jackson's probe on 1 May stalled the Yankees; Hooker entrenched and yielded the initiative. Lee and Jackson sought ways to negate the heavy log works constructed by the Yankees. Could a way around Hooker's right be found? Yes. A fairly well-covered road led all the way around the Union army. Jackson received his most exciting orders from Lee—take twenty-eight thousand men and flank Hooker while Lee held the front with a scant sixteen thousand grayclads.

One of the great flank marches of military history began at 8:00 A.M. on 2 May 1863. The Second Corps of the Army of Northern Virginia marched fifteen miles across Hooker's front and around his army and hit it from behind. Security cracked several times during the march; some federal troops attacked the column and reported a mass of rebel infantry to Hooker, who, surprisingly, concluded that Lee was retreating to Richmond. When Jackson attacked at 5:15 P.M., the Union right crumbled and spilled into Hooker's rear area. He tried to rally an artillery defense, but the rebel attack rolled on remorselessly. At a critical point in the action, "Fighting Joe" was leaning against a column on the porch of his headquarters when it was struck by a rebel shell. Knocked senseless, Hooker recovered slowly but refused to yield command. Although competent subordinate leadership saved his army and provided an opportunity to attack, Hooker lost his nerve.

Jackson's attack stalled with night and he rode ahead of his lines to find enemy positions. Riding back to his troops, he was fired on by nervous infantry, wounded, and carried from the field. Command passed to Jeb Stuart as the senior general present. Stuart renewed the attack with morning, as did Lee. Hooker's men were now fortifying and fighting stubbornly. Hearing that Major General John Sedgwick's corps had driven Early out of the Fredericksburg lines, and convinced that Hooker had gone on the defensive, Lee left Stuart with twenty-five thousand men to hold the Wilderness and took twenty-one thousand to deal with Sedgwick. With speed and daring, a whole Union corps might be cut up and captured.

Battle weary, hungry, and working in hard ground, Lee and Early's men were slow and ragged in their attack on Union positions west of Fredericksburg. Sedgwick escaped, but Lee still hoped to finish Hooker and planned a final attack for 6 May—a rash idea because the entire federal line now was heavily entrenched. Hooker, however, recrossed the Rappahannock during the night of 5–6 May, and his great venture to Richmond cost seventeen thousand casualties to Lee's thirteen thousand.

How to assess the Battle of Chancellorsville? It crowned the cooperation between Lee and Jackson and stands as a signal southern victory. Hooker never used all his force and had lost his nerve; the knock on the head only addled an already broken psyche. When Lincoln heard the news he cried out in anguish: "My God! My God! What will the country say?" The North would rage, but the South would mourn the costliest victory of the war. On 10 May 1863, Stonewall Jackson, thirty-nine years old, died, having been shot by his own troops in the confusion of battle on 2 May.

Lincoln pondered a complex problem of morale versus failed men, failed opportunities, and failed ideas. The Army of the Potomac, beaten again, was made of firm stuff—its body battered but heart sound—and it would fight for a good leader. Some of the man wanted McClellan back, because he, at least, had stopped the rebs at Antietam. Some of the men wanted to go home, the war seeming hopeless. There were some who thought they could whip Lee, however, given a fighting chance. For a time after Chancellorsville, Hooker acted like a general. A thorough refitting and reorganization put his army in top shape and he kept a close watch on Lee. Hooker, Halleck, and Lincoln all thought Lee would do something aggressive, but what and where?

Those questions engaged President Davis, his cabinet, and senior military advisers while Lee recruited, refurbished, and reorganized the Army of Northern Virginia. Jackson's death left a chasm in command. Lee now divided his army into three corps: Longstreet kept his solid First; Jackson's famed Second went to his trusted lieutenant, Richard Stoddert Ewell; the new Third was given to A.P. Hill. Ranks swelled with conscripts and new units from the Deep South; supplies filled the depots—though rations were thin—and Stuart's horses were rejuvenated. What should this reinvigorated army do?

Longstreet, noting that the South still had interior lines, suggested that Bragg be reinforced to crush Rosecrans. That would surely call Grant from Vicksburg. Beauregard thought relief of General John C. Pemberton, besieged in Vicksburg, essential to defeat Grant and save the Mississippi. Lee saw logic in both schemes but kept his own focus on the Virginia theater and suggested that an invasion of Pennsylvania would relieve his army as well as Vicksburg by putting pressure on the sorest point of the Union—Washington. Lee's power prevailed and he prepared to move north.

Hooker understood strategy and sifted intelligence well, and by late May he suspected Lee planned to move down the Shenandoah, either to flank him back to Washington or to recross the Potomac. General Alfred Pleasonton's horsemen went in search of Lee and had an engagement with Stuart's full force at Brandy Station on 9 June. Brandy Station swirled into the biggest cavalry battle in American history. Confused, seesawing, and hectic, the battle engaged about ten thousand men on each side in shooting, hacking and charging until late in the day, when Stuart's men began to prevail, especially after some foot soldiers arrived to help. Pleasonton retired, encouraged by near victory, and gave Hooker the vital information that the rebels were in force near Culpeper and it looked as though Stuart was preparing to move.

Lee's vanguard crossed the Potomac in mid-June, headed for Chambersburg, Pennsylvania. Hooker, using his own inner lines, took his army toward Frederick, Maryland, which covered Washington and threatened Lee's communications. Hooker's reactions to Lee were sound, but Lincoln had lost confidence in him, and he was losing his grip on himself. Clearly, he was afraid to fight Lee. Like McClellan, he fantasized about enemies in Washington, felt hugely outnumbered, and resented interference with his army. In a fit of pique he asked to be relieved and Lincoln hastily complied. On 27 June 1863, the command went to General George Gordon Meade, a Pennsylvanian, veteran corps commander, and a competent, plodding soldier of nervous demeanor, fiery temper, and considerable personal fortitude. Surprised at the assignment, Meade took it on as a duty. Ordering the army north from Frederick, he hoped to catch Lee at a scattered disadvantage, which summed up Lee's situation fairly well.

Lee's army was spread across a big part of southern Pennsylvania, from Chambersburg to Carlisle to Harrisburg and York, and his troops were wallowing in the rich farmland's food and forage. They heard rumors of hats and shoes at Gettysburg, which stirred trouble. Rumors were curiously hard to check. Stuart, acting under Lee's usually permissive orders, had gone off on a wagon hunt in Maryland—probably trying to heal the scars of Brandy Station—and the cavalry that remained with the main army had been spread too thinly for sound reconnaisance.

Lee pulled his army toward Cashtown, which had strong defensive positions and sat on the flank of an advancing Union force, but some of A. P. Hill's men wandered on toward Gettysburg to "get those shoes." At about 8:00 A.M. on 1 July, Hill's men ran into strong resistance just northwest of Gettysburg. A Union cavalry division, carefully deployed with good artillery support, confronted the Confederates. Troops of both armies piled up around the town and a major battle began without either army commander's intent.

For three days a bitter, bloody battle raged around Gettysburg. Several times Lee attacked, several times he was repulsed—once in the bare nick of time. A fearsome, grueling testing of both armies finally culminated in one of gallantry's last great gestures—Pickett's Charge. George Edward Pickett led fifteen thousand men against Meade's well-entrenched center on 3 July. It was a splendid effort, one of flying banners, precision marching, storms of grape and canister sweeping over the attackers, of gaps and fallen, and a few men who broke through the blue lines, and of the shattered survivors who streamed back, shocked, torn, and maimed. It was America's greatest battle.

It was Lee's worst. Confederate casualties neared twenty-one thousand to the federals twenty-three thousand—almost a third of Lee's army had been killed, wounded, or captured. He escaped total destruction only because Meade failed to counterattack or to push the Confederate retreat, failure that grievously wounded President Lincoln. It seemed to be another Antietam, another great chance gone. Who could win a decisive battle?

Jefferson Davis rejected Lee's suggestion of relief—he had no greater general—but surely the Confederate president was troubled. What had gone wrong? Word had been received of a different Lee at Gettysburg, a petulant, stubborn man, heedless of Longstreet's proposal to flank Meade, an ill man the day that Pickett's men marched into death and history, a superior sharply demanding obedience to orders some found futile. When those broken five thousand came back down from Cemetery Ridge, the old

Lee snapped back in tender, guilty anguish. "It is all my fault," he quietly confessed to those who still would follow him. Lee's return to normal loomed more vital now than ever. Not only did the South suffer Gettysburg that week, but also it suffered the loss of Vicksburg, Mississippi, and its thirty-thousand-man garrison. With that bastion went effective connection with the trans-Mississippi.

VITALITY AT VICKSBURG: WESTERN CAMPAIGNS, JANUARY-JULY 1863

Meade's failure put Lincoln in a deep gloom. He poured out furious anguish to Navy Secretary Gideon Welles, in the wake of Lee's escape after Gettysburg. "We had them within our grasp. We had only to stretch forth our hands and they were ours." He had expected this news, he despondently told Welles. "And that, my God, is the last of this Army of the Potomac! There is bad faith somewhere. . . . What does it mean, Mr. Welles? Great God! What does it mean?" In a familiar way of teaching and venting, Lincoln wrote a long letter to Meade, probably the toughest he ever wrote to a general. He filed it, unmailed, probably fearing it would do more harm than good to an earnest, willing soldier. The letter, however, showed that the president was advanced far beyond most military minds in a firm grasp of the war. Lincoln knew the first week of July was the turning point in the war— two rebel armies were exposed, and armies were the main objectives. Had Lee been smashed as Vicksburg fell, the stuffing would have gone out of the Confederacy. "As it is," Lincoln mourned, "the war will be prolonged indefinitely." He did not relieve Meade, but he had little faith that the Army of the Potomac could do more in Virginia than it had in Pennsylvania. He doubted Meade could win in an offensive battle with Lee.

As Lincoln looked for consolation, he saw one bright sign. Ulysses S. Grant had gumption. When he fixed on an enemy, he stuck. A grizzled, disheveled soldier without grace or much couth, he chewed on his cold cigar as he chewed on the enemy and kept going forward. Once detached from Buell, Grant fixed on Vicksburg and tried various ways to capture it. A great Confederate bastion with heavy cannon dominating the Mississippi, combined with the smaller, no less vital, Port Hudson downriver, Vicksburg served to hinge the Trans-Mississippi Department to the eastern Confederacy. Vicksburg truly deserved all the attention both sides offered.

While Grant had his own schemes for taking this key site of the South, he had considerations other than military necessity working on him. Forced to react to political and journalistic carping, he tried four different approaches to the South's vital Mississippi bastion; all four failed, one to a daring cavalry raid by General Earl Van Dorn, but Grant kept at it. By late April his cooperating gunboat fleet had passed Vicksburg's batteries, and he moved a large force along the west bank of the Mississippi to find a promising crossing point where he would use his gunboats again. By 1 May, Grant had recrossed the Mississippi and turned north to get between General John C. Pemberton's defenders of Vicksburg and Joseph E. Johnston's small force at Jackson, Mississippi. In all of these operations, he had fuddled Confederate reactions by the unexpected. During late April, he had pushed a daring cavalry raid under General Benjamin H. Grierson, to damage rail communications with Vicksburg and to alarm and scatter Pemberton's thin mounted force all the way from La Grange, Tennessee, to Baton Rouge, Louisiana. Grant had produced.

Productive aggressiveness set him far apart from his colleagues. Lincoln always looked for generals who did well on their own and kept grinding on the rebels. If Grant took Vicksburg, he would achieve the greatest strategic victory since the fall of New Orleans in May 1862. It took a good deal of marching and some hot fighting, but he finally did it. He fought Pemberton in a pitched battle at Champion's Hill, won it, and invested the Confederate fortress city on 18 May. He made a quick, violent assault on Pemberton's formidable works on 19 May and was bloodily repulsed. Grant wanted to beat Pemberton quickly, not only so that he could hit Johnston before he was strengthened, but also so that he could swing south to aid General Nathaniel P. Banks in his siege of Port Hudson, the last Confederate fort commanding the Mississippi. A renewed attack on Vicksburg's strong works failed on 22 May, costing Grant thirty-two hundred casualties.

Grant now moved to get between Johnston's force and that of Pemberton. Johnston, trying to save the garrison, pondered how to relieve Vicksburg. Pushed out of Jackson, he gathered a thin force north of Mississippi's capital at the apex of a right-angle triangle with Jackson and Vicksburg the right and left anchors of the base line. About thirty-five miles from Pemberton's works, Johnston strove to build up his army and, on 17 May, ordered Pemberton to evacuate Vicksburg and save his army. A council of war and President Davis advised Pemberton to stay put—Vicksburg had strategic and morale importance far beyond its military potential. Johnston continued working to scavenge men from a War Department trying to help both Lee and Bragg.

Grant's siege ground on until 4 July, when Pemberton surrendered, hoping for generous terms on Independence Day. He got none save the paroling of himself and his army. On 9 July, the small, heroic garrison of Port Hudson surrendered to Banks. Johnston, moving toward Vicksburg with some thirty thousand men, retreated beyond Jackson.

Grant had determined to get Vicksburg, and he kept to the siege despite enemy and friendly distractions. Grant parried Confederate efforts to relieve the bastion with fortitude. Attacks from the northern press and the rumors that eddied congressional halls did more harm. Siege operations were too slow, carpers said, and Grant lost too many men to the joint fogs of war and of deep delta country. Lincoln ignored calls for Grant's removal. "I rather like the man," he said, because "he doesn't worry and bother me. He isn't shrieking for reinforcements all the time. He takes what troops we can safely

give him . . . and does the best he can with what he has."

In the afterglow of success at Vicksburg, Lincoln wrote Grant one of most graceful confessions ever made by a commander in chief. Writing a week after Vicksburg's surrender, Lincoln's letter said: "I write this . . . as a grateful acknowledgment for the almost inestimable service you have done the country." Grant must have seen how much he and the president thought alike about the war. Lincoln said he had watched Grant's operations with growing approval. He had thought Grant should go river, march south, recross, and operate below Vicksburg, but he thought that then Grant should have turned south to help General Banks at Port Hudson. "I now wish to make the personal acknowledgment that you were right and I was wrong."

The Vicksburg campaign had opened the Mississippi at a relatively small cost. Since 1 May, Grant's casualties came to ninety-five hundred men. The Confederacy had not only lost control of the river but also a good field army. Combined with Lee's defeat at Gettysburg, in the first week of July the Confederacy, had lost some fifty thousand men and sixty-five thousand stands of arms, many of them fine British Enfield rifles. Men and arms were running out in the South. More than that, the Confederacy, now cut in twain, began a precarious dual existence, with Richmond's span of control clearly atrophying.

On Jefferson Davis' side of things, post-Gettysburg analyses were cold indeed. His great hopes for the Department of the West under Johnston had been dashed by the general's incapacity to rise to his powers. Instead of taking charge, ordering armies and supplies where he wanted, taking command of a field army when circumstances dictated, Johnston served more as a coordinator than commander. He knew the Army of Tennessee had lost faith in Bragg and should have removed him, but he felt unable to do that to so staunch a friend of the president—and he was probably right in his fears. Still, Johnston hewed to old fancies of his own—to him an army command was the highest post a general could have—and he wanted that more than some amorphous post as facilitator of bits and dribbles. Thus, he missed what was probably the greatest chance of the conflict.

Halleck and others, knowing Lincoln's views about the victorious Grant, schemed to get the command of new western hero Meade, but Grant, who wanted to keep moving on Mobile, dodged the eastern army. "Whilst I would disobey no order I should beg very hard to be excused before accepting that command," he confessed. The Army of the Potomac seemed to wallow in bad luck. Certainly it battled formidable odds and enemies.

General William Starke Rosecrans faced lesser obstacles but acted with greater timidity. It was not until 26 June 1863 that he finally moved his army from Murfreesboro. Halleck had prodded him restlessly since January. Bragg, his army starved for men as all aid went to Vicksburg, held on below Murfreesboro and kept pressure on the enemy by cavalry raids that earned little, and on one of those, the famed rebel raider John Hunt Morgan was captured. Rosecrans countered with equally fruitless mounted expeditions.

Bragg's main concern was Chattanooga—he had to hold that strategic city. A rail center that anchored one of the Confederacy's main east-west trunks, Chattanooga also anchored the mountain barrier to Alabama and Georgia. If the federals took it, they would have interior lines for advancing in almost any direction. When Rosecrans started, he moved with deceptive speed, and he ran Bragg's Kentucky campaign in reverse. Maneuvering instead of fighting, by 30 June he had forced the rebels back to Tullahoma, Tennessee. Again swift marches almost trapped Bragg north of Elk River. By 4 July, Bragg fell back on Chattanooga.

In the woeful news of those first July days, Jefferson Davis understood better than most the strategic portent of Bragg's failure but had little mourning time. Critical blows at Vicksburg and Gettysburg overshadowed the slow agony of the Army of Tennessee. With Vicksburg's garrison and important arms supplies gone, Bragg's

beleaguered force propped the Confederacy's sagging left shoulder.

In a way, the fall of Vicksburg unburdened Confederate planning. Most of the time, Davis and Seddon had been forced to defend wrong objectives to satisfy local commands, but this time they were right to concentrate on saving a city. Chattanooga's logistical and morale value could not be exaggerated. Even Johnston acted like a theater commander when he sent Bragg some units he had collected near Jackson. He knew Bragg's scant forty-four thousand, including fourteen thousand cavalry, had to hold several possible Tennessee River crossings against Rosecrans' sixty-five thousand, which might be reinforced by Grant.

Only scattered bodies of men could be stripped from such places as Mobile. A strategic crisis faced Davis' government. Lee showed reluctance to take a western command. What could be done to sustain Bragg? The old idea of detaching Longstreet's corps from Lee's army reappeared. Longstreet was for it; he wanted an independent chance for glory. Lee reluctantly approved; the want of men made it about the only workable option, if Bragg was to be quickly strengthened. Bragg's recent call for S. B. Buckner's nine thousand-man corps from Knoxville yielded the main rail line from Richmond to Chattanooga. Longstreet's move would have to be made on roundabout rail routes. On 6 September, Longstreet received his coveted orders. He wanted Bragg's command; victory might win it, if the First Corps could arrive in time.

Bragg's situation had good and bad potential. By the end of August, he had virtually forted up in Chattanooga and deployed General Forrest's cavalry as a screening force along the east bank of the Tennessee, which all but eliminated any chance to discover enemy movements. Rosecrans began crossing on 20 August and aimed to sever Bragg's supply line below the city. Bragg's cavalry greatly outnumbered their mounted foes and brought Bragg copious intelligence of enemy moves through various mountain passes south of Chattanooga. News of "rats from so many holes" baffled him and not until 8 September did he realize the threat to his rear. He evacuated Chattanooga that night—outmaneuvered, he left without a fight, but he planned one.

Victorious and overconfident, Rosecrans stumbled into trouble. Part of it came from the terrain, the rest from unexpected rebels. Rosecrans knew that east of the Tennessee and below Chattanooga various mountains and ridges covered approaches to the city. Cut by various passes and defiles, the ridges were real and puzzling barriers. Bad maps and scarce cavalry left "Rosy" more ignorant of terrain than he guessed.

Bragg had sound strategic sense, once he found out what was happening. He plotted the destruction of the Army of the Cumberland. Rosecrans had split his force into three widely separated units. Bragg, suddenly seized with aggressiveness, concentrated to pick off these exposed units piecemeal. Everything went wrong with his proposed attack on 10 September. General Thomas C. Hindman failed to move speedily, other subordinates wallowed in timidity, and Rosecrans escaped during the next several days. Bragg nearly isolated several federal forces but lost them to slow obedience to good orders. He complicated his problem by not being close enough to the front personally to insist on quick action. He kept to the offensive, however, never yielding initiative to his opponent.

Longstreet's First Corps had moved with remarkable speed, despite the long circuit through the Deep South. His lead elements, under General John B. Hood, arrived early on 18 September, in time to join an attempt to turn the Union left, resting nearly ten miles south of Chattanooga, along Chickamauga Creek. Delays again frustrated rebel hopes, but more men arrived during the night, and Bragg planned to press on the next day. Bitter, confused, and uncertain fighting took up most of the 19th, with Bragg unaware of what happened. He stubbornly held to the attack. During the night Rosecrans strengthened his line and ordered fieldworks erected on the left. When the rebels

lauched their drive at about 9:30 A.M. on 20 September, federal resistance slowed them from the start.

Bragg stuck to his flanking plan and ordered an echelon attack on a close timetable. Early rebel success against General George H. Thomas on the left prompted Rosecrans to send help from his right, but in sending it, he left a gap in his line that Longstreet exploited expertly late in the morning. Rosencrans' battle went to pieces, and some of his men bolted the field. Swept up in the confused retreat himself, Rosecrans did not know of the heroic stand on the left that earned Thomas his battle name, 'The Rock of Chickamauga." Thomas finally had to retreat becasue he was left virtually alone.

Bragg had won but he failed to pursue, much to Forrest's frustration. As Rosecrans pulled his remnants into Chattanooga, both sides counted Chickamauga's costs. Rosecrans sustained 16,170 casualties out of some 58,000 engaged, while Bragg, with about 66,000 engaged, lost 18,454—nearly 28 percent on both sides. Rosecrans lost more than men, of course; he had lost the initiative and huddled in Chattanooga's defenses. Bragg partially surrounded the town and cut federal supply lines down to one uncertain road. Rosecrans faced starvation as Bragg's men and cannon sat atop such surrounding heights as Missionary Ridge and Lookout Mountain. Neither command could boast about Chickamauga. True, Bragg won, but failure to reinforce his attack at crucial times on the 20th robbed him of the smashing victory he designed. Thomas had saved Rosecrans from the disaster his own tactical errors almost ensured.

Bragg still had the initiative. He could stay where he was and maintain the investment; he could cross the river and flank Rosecrans out of the city and force him to fight; or he could leave an observation force in front of Rosecrans and move quickly to beat Burnside's small force at Knoxville. His unwonted daring gone, he chose to sit and besiege.

Lincoln read dispatches from Chattanooga in mounting gloom. He thought that Rosecrans had acted "stunned like a duck hit on the head." The president wanted Chattanooga held at all costs—he easily grasped its strategic value—and ordered reinforcements from Meade's idle army. In a sweeping reorganization, Lincoln put all western departments and armies under General Grant. Directing Grant to look at the Chattanooga situation, the president gave him full authority to do whatever seemed best. In effect, he copied Davis' theater command scheme. Grant replaced Rosencrans with Thomas.

Energy, audacity, and courage were Grant's contribution to his new post. Wasting no time, he organized several attacks on Bragg's lines, each time gaining an advantage. Bragg, apparently confident of his lofty lines, had detached Longstreet to take Knoxville and had to go on the defensive against Grant. In a dazzling series of attacks, Grant's army unexpectedly carried Bragg's at Lookout Mountain on 24 November and smashed through the main front along Missionary Ridge the next day. Grant failed to pursue. Bragg's army fled to the southeast, leaving sixty-six hundred casualties behind. Grant's losses amounted to fifty-eight hundred.

President Davis had reason to regret his earlier decision to overlook criticism by Bragg's generals and keep him in command after the Kentucky campaign. As the Army of Tennessee retreated into northwest Georgia, Davis accepted Bragg's resignation. Despite personal reservations, on 16 December 1863, Davis appointed Johnston to replace Bragg. It was Johnston's proudest moment.

Longstreet failed to take Knoxville. Grant, using the full logistical powers of his new command, sent help to Burnside, which forced the besiegers to abandon their task. Longstreet fell back to Greeneville, Tennessee, where he could either rejoin Lee or threaten Grant's left. His withdrawal signaled the end of the western campaign in 1863, a year that saw Grant win two of the Union's major objectives—control of the Mississippi and possession of Chatanooga—which ensured control of Tennessee and a good route to the heart of Dixie.

Out of the year's turmoil, Grant emerged and Bragg faded. The Union grew stronger in the west and the Confederacy's power ebbed as the Trans-Mississippi Department went into a kind of semi-independence. Lincoln stated the main import of the western year from the North's standpoint: "The Father of Waters again goes unvexed to the sea." Davis could point to nothing positive from the year in the west save the continued presence of the Army of Tennessee, an army of lost battles and opportunities, led by incompetents and sometimes by fools, that still survived and fought and stayed to its steadfast duty.

COMING THUNDER DRUMS: WINTER 1863–SUMMER 1864

As was the Army of Tennessee, the Union Army of the Potomac was labeled unlucky, badly officered, and slackly run, an army of wasted lives and chances and cast against the fates and Lee. Still, it stood bulwark to Washington. The ranks had almost abandoned hope of good leaders when they lost McClellan and events had not disabused such thoughts. Meade, however, had a kind of following, and after Gettysburg, like all of Lee's opponents, settled the army into rebuilding and refitting. The army liked that because "getting after Lee" had never been a winning game. Waiting to throw him back had always been best. Meade clearly agreed.

Halleck and Lincoln wanted something done in those post-battle days, with Longstreet absent and Lee's army licking its wounds, but Meade had the stubbornness of his predecessors. He needed men, supplies, and horses before he could move. Despairing of an offensive against Lee, Lincoln ordered the detachment of some of Meade's army to Rosecrans, and Lee tried to take advantage of a weakened opponent.

In early October 1863, the Army of Northern Virginia crossed the Rapidan, in a familiar try to get around Meade's right and move on

Washington. Meade, despite the detachments, largely outnumbered Lee, but the old Napoleonic flanking threat made him retreat. Lee saw his chance: He would hit Meade's retreating columns at Bristoe Station, break them up, take their trains, and give battle on the old Manassas grounds. It did not happen. Lee's command structure had lost its nimbleness; orders went slowly and were even more slowly obeyed. The Army of Northern Virginia showed alarming signs of attrition at almost every level. None marked the import more clearly than Lee.

Both armies found no opportunity to strike a decisive blow and the rebels retired. Meade picked up the gauntlet, as good weather held in Virginia. Halleck and Lincoln hazed him into crossing the Rapidan with about eighty-five thousand men on 26 November 1863 in a campaign to turn Lee's right. Meade, much to Lincoln's chagrin, still aimed at Richmond, not at Lee's army. He hoped to maneuver Lee into a retreat to his capital. With slightly fewer than fifty thousand men—Longstreet had not yet returned—Lee move quickly to meet the enemy and occupied strong positions along the brook Mine Run. So strong were Lee's works that Meade found no point of attack and his campaign failed aborning.

Operations along Mine Run confirmed a new element that was shaping battles—field entrenchments. Wherever armies halted, they now threw up heavy works. It should have been done earlier, considering the engineering background of all West Pointers. For the early years, however, marching and stand-up fighting were the ways of American combat. Some students suggest that this passion for open formation attacks reflected the Celtic element in both armies. Whatever the cause, discretion overcame foolish valor. Improved weapons brought a fearsome growth in firepower. Massed rifles and vastly improved field artillery shattered old European attack formations. Immense slaughter forced entrenching. Fieldworks sprang up on western battlefields earlier than in Virginia, but by winter 1863, veteran troops were deft diggers.

They were also superior scavengers, especially Lee's men. Virginia had been picked clean for three years by various hordes. Fervent efforts by commissary and quartermaster agents to supply the Army of Northern Virginia during the cold winter of 1863–1864 produced starvation rations. The men foraged a bare landscape. Lee constantly requested supplies in letters increasingly like George Washington's missives from Valley Forge. Davis gave all he could, but scarcity crippled the logistical chain. By mid-1863 the effects of attrition were widespread across the Confederacy.

Attrition in the South affected not only manpower but also facilities and transportation. With repeated drives to fill ranks, some supply officers and men were shifted and often replaced by the less skilled and able-bodied. Shortages of shops and equipment retarded repair of war-worn trains and tracks. Rickety wagons, patched harness, and thinned horses and mules became standard equipment by mid-1863—all symptoms of scarcity. Sometimes these symptoms came from poor administration. Bad planning occasionally piled up supplies at one point, while starving another. Coordination came hard to a laissez-faire government. War pressure finally led Davis' government to limited nationalization of transportation, an essential policy, although damned as dictatorial.

Men were in shortest supply. The Confederacy's military population was running out. Various schemes were tried to fill the ranks—amnesty for deserters, bounties, special leave consideration—but as the war ground on morale sagged and even a slight wound became a discharge. Confederate congressmen had understood the manpower crisis and passed the first draft law in American history in April 1862. Approved by most state courts, often opposed by such ardent states' rights governors as Georgia's Joseph E. Brown and North Carolina's Zebulon B. Vance, the act produced too few men. Increasingly stiff draft acts were enacted, attacking the sacrosanct substitution system, expanding eligible years to from seventeen to fifty, and cutting exemptions. Slaves were enrolled for work on fortifications; too late in the war, they were accepted as soldiers, and a few actually donned the gray just at the end.

In the government's view, conscription's special value came from its control of the national manpower pool. Under War Department regulations, the war secretary could manage the talent of the Confederacy and put men where they could best serve the cause. Without the draft, however, rebel ranks would probably have disintegrated by the end of 1862. Modern estimates indicate about eighty-two thousand conscripts enrolled east of the Mississippi from 16 April 1862 until war's end.

Even with vast manpower superiority, the United States had difficulty in keeping up the armies. Early glamour quickly tarnished; volunteers wrote brothers to avoid camps as places of pestilence, vermin, and corruption. Religious youths were horrified at the army's coarse secular tone. Patriotism became a selective thing. After Lincoln's first call for volunteers, a visible drop in response prompted the so-called "draft of 1862." A mishmash of state and national programs, this early conscription effort kept responsibility at the state level; where states had no laws drafting the militia, national orders were to prevail. Liberal exemptions and a general lack of enthusiasm vitiated these early efforts. It was not until 3 March 1863 that the U.S. Congress adopted conscription. Enforcement wallowed in problems. New York City—where Mayor Fernando Wood supported the South—writhed in draft riots, 13–15 July, and resistance sparked across the North.

As in the South, control of national manpower ranked as an important result of northern conscription. Additions to the ranks, however, were vital to the federal cause. Best estimates are that 249,259 men were drafted and that 86,724 paid to be exempted. Consequently 162,535 men actually were drafted. Federal numbers were swelled in July 1862 by the acceptance of blacks in the ranks. Some 179,000 served in many regiments during the war. Conscription's value to both sides came more from suasion than from force. Even though a draft law lurked in the background, volunteering and reenlistments continued.

As cold clamped on the armies' camps at the end of 1863, mere existence took precedence over war, and as a new campaign season approached, Lincoln reshaped his entire command structure. After years of groping, he recognized in Grant just the general to run the war. On 10 March 1864, the president promoted Grant, who was forty-one years old, to the revived rank of lieutenant general and made him general in chief of the Union armies. More than half a million men were in Grant's charge, and he could hardly handle the heavy minutiae of so many and happily accepted Lincoln's notion that Halleck be chief of staff to handle relations between the civilian president and his general and between the general and his various department commanders. This arrangement, as historian T. Harry Williams observed in *Lincoln and His Generals* (1952), marked the beginning of a modern command system.

Grant knew his headquarters had to be close to Washington but did not want to stay in the city. He went to the field with the Army of the Potomac. Meade remained in command, but Grant's tent always stood close by. This potentially volatile arrangement worked well because both generals cooperated. Grant gave overall strategic directions and left tactics to Meade. As a result, an aggressive spirit permeated the army as it began to believe in victory.

The new general in chief shared President Lincoln's understanding of power and pressure. He knew the United States had vastly more war resources than the Confederacy and worked to use that superiority. As Winfield Scott proposed much earlier and Lincoln often repeated, Grant wanted to put as many troops in the field as possible and press the Confederates everywhere—a program one modern student has called "Operation Crusher." Recognizing that uncoordinated federal operations permitted the enemy to shift troops from one army to another on inner lines, Grant intended to put all federal forces into some kind of action;

those not fighting could menace by maneuver. Lincoln had a metaphor for that: "Those not skinning can hold a leg."

Grant projected three major offensives for the 1864 campaign. The Army of the Potomac under Meade (whom Grant came to admire greatly) would stick to Lee's army and not let go, while smaller forces would threaten Richmond from the James River side and the Shenandoah Valley. A big western army under one of Grant's favorites, William T. Sherman, would press the Army of Tennessee through north Georgia, into Atlanta. While pressing Johnston, Sherman would also destroy southern war resources in the state. As Sherman moved south, an army under General Banks would march from New Orleans to Mobile, where it might link with Sherman and at last secure one of Grant's pet objectives, the Chattanooga-Mobile line.

These good plans quickly skewed. Banks started an expedition of his own up the Red River in Louisiana in April. Using gunboats, he hoped to capture Shreveport, headquarters of the Trans-Mississippi Department and bring war to Texas. Everything went wrong. He lost the major Battle of Mansfield (Sabine Crossroads) on 8 April 1864, had to abandon his campaign, and was unable to make the Mobile move. An infuriated Grant wanted Banks removed, but Lincoln needed that general's considerable political support in the upcoming presidential election. He put Banks on the shelf at New Orleans.

Sherman continued to get his army of more than ninety thousand ready to move against Johnston, and Meade collected more than one hundred thousand to hurl against Lee. These coordinated offensives would stress the Confederacy at its weakest point—manpower. Unable to shift troops from one army to the other, Davis would have to scrape the barrel for men. This situation put a premium on killing in the coming campaigns, because the North had replacements aplenty while the South had few.

Anxious but not despondent, Davis also modified his command structure. He brought the unemployed Bragg to Richmond as his chief of staff—an absurdity in the eyes of Bragg's widening circle of critics—but Bragg had good strategic sense. Davis would have preferred advice from Lee on all Confederate fronts, but Lee's attention fixed on Meade. Bragg, at least, knew logistical fundamentals and the odd ways of rebel soldiers. After that key appointment, Davis rejoiced in Banks's failure and in the limited successes of Forrest at Okolona, Mississippi, and also of General Joseph Finnegan's victory over a federal expedition into Florida's interior (the Battle of Olustee) in late February 1864. Glad of some good news, the Confederate president had done valiantly in sending help to both Lee and Johnston. Despite the heavy threat hanging over the Confederacy, the new year had promise. If Sherman and Grant (Meade) could be checked, the coming Union election might change the character of the war; another Union stalemate might finally induce foreign recognition. There were reasons for hope as Johnston received men from Alabama and Mississippi and the coast until he counted nearly sixty thousand, and Lee, supported again by Longstreet's corps, counted almost seventy thousand.

Meade advanced just after midnight on Wednesday, 4 May 1864, and began a desperate series of battles in the Virginia Wilderness, near the old Chancellorsville fields. Fearsome fighting on the 6th found Lee going forward to encourage his men and hearing them cry "Lee to the rear! General Lee to the rear!" Longstreet took a serious wound as carnage among the generals shook command. Opportunities came to both sides, were seized and missed, and light fieldworks proved their value. By the end of the day, opposing lines were stabilized. More than 100,000 federals were in the fight and 17,666 of them were casualties. Across from them, Lee lost 7,500 from his 60,000 engaged. Unlike his predecessors, Meade did not turn back to Washington. Grant, holding the strategic initiative, ordered continued pressure on the rebel right. Lee hurried troops to intercept the enemy at Spotsylvania Court House, an important road hub.

Running into unexpected rebel entrenchments at the court house on 8 May, Meade's men were repulsed and fighting faded. Grant ordered General Philip H. Sheridan to take the cavalry on a raid to hit Lee's communications and so divert Stuart's riders. Light encounters the next day underscored a general field readjustment and further entrenching. General John Sedgwick, one of Meade's corps commanders, fell. Meade ordered a morning attack.

A general assault on rebel works in late afternoon on 10 May was repulsed, but some dents were made at cost. Light skirmishing took up most of the next day, and Grant determined to exploit one of the dents in Lee's works by a major attack on 12 May. Furious assaults and counterattacks occupied the day. General Ewell's corps of Lee's army lost some four thousand prisoners in before-dawn fighting. The "bloody angle" consumed men for most of the afternoon and into the night. This day ranks as one of the costliest of the war—federal casualties ran to sixty-eight hundred, and five thousand Confederate troops were killed or wounded. All the rage and fury cost men and gained little, but attrition stalked Lee's ranks. Hard war resumed in the Wilderness on 18 May, when a series of Union attacks failed against strengthened rebel works. So strong were the enemy lines at Spotsylvania that Grant decided to shift the battle further to Lee's right. Actions around the court house cost more than 17,500 federal casualties out of 110,000 engaged. Confederate losses were much less (about 8,000) but not reliably counted. In both the Wilderness and Spotsylvania engagements, Meade lost 33,000 men—a terrible price for slow progress.

Lee guessed Grant's moves and also turned toward the southeast. Some good news came from the James River front. Beauregard, brought up to command in southern Virginia, had pretty well bottled up General Benjamin F. Butler's army at Bermuda Hundred neck. Richmond's situation need not worry Lee, for the moment, but he worried about Grant. Along the North Anna River, confused fighting won Lee a chance to hit a divided federal army. Lee was sick, subordinates confused, and the opportu-

nity passed. By 26 May, Grant ordered another flank move, far to Lee's right, but rebels got to Cold Harbor first and began a maze of fortifications. On 1 and 2 June, Meade's men concentrated at Cold Harbor. Many bluecoats, seeing the awesome strength of Lee's trenches, wrote their names on slips of papers and pinned them on their uniforms to avoid being listed among the "unknown." Meade attacked on 3 June at 4:30 A.M. in a pell-mell rush to smash through Lee's lines. Three Union corps stormed toward rebel works and in little more than a half hour were repulsed at probably the highest cost of any day in the war. Numbers are disputed, but Unions losses are put at seven thousand to fifteen hundred Confederates. Lee remarked that the concentrated Confederate rifle fire sounded like wet sheets tearing in the wind.

Grant's stubborn campaign raised high criticism at home. One prominent Northerner rightly wrote that the Army of the Potomac "has literally marched in blood and agony from the Rapidan to the James." At last Grant halted. So strong were opposing entrenchments that neither side could attack. Grant was of different stuff than McClellan and the others and would not quit. What would he do and where?

Being closer to Richmond gave Lee logistical advantages. As he fell back on his base, he received some reinforcements and reorganized. Beauregard's situation grew bothersome, however, because Butler outnumbered him two to one. Nevertheless, Lee hoped Beauregard could put some men in front of Richmond, between the James and the Chickahominy.

Sticking to the scheme of pressing Lee from various quarters, Grant engineered several incursions into Virginia. One, led by General David Hunter, would probe the upper end of the Shenandoah, take Staunton, destroy crops and shops, pin down scattered Confederate forces and perhaps force Lee to detach forces to stop him. Hunter's threat came after Lee had brought General John C. Breckinridge's small force from the Shenandoah Valley to help fill the Cold Harbor lines. With Sheridan's cavalry on the way to Hunter, Lee sent Breckinridge back, but his twenty-one hundred men seemed a hollow threat to Hunter's eighteen thousand. Breckinridge and Lee guessed Lynchburg would be Hunter's objective, a supply center vital to Lee. Something would have to be done about Hunter.

Desperately short of men and eager to avoid a siege of the capital or its consort city, Petersburg, some thirty miles south, Lee knew that any further detachments from his ranks would commit him to the heavy works ringing Richmond. He had to act, however, and sent Early to deal with Hunter. It seemed a good choice. Early commanded Jackson's Second Corps, including remnants of the Army of the Valley, had drive and gall, and liked fighting. Lee gave him wide discretion.

Early dealt with Hunter at Lynchburg, then moved boldly down the Shenandoah to threaten Harpers Ferry, crossed the Potomac, and moved directly on Washington. Only the stubborn defense of the Monacacy River in Maryland by General Lew Wallace on 9 July prevented Early's twelve thousand from possibly wandering the streets of Washington. Early's raid in June and July 1864 was in the best offensive-defensive tradition. Lee hoped it would force Grant to send troops to protect the Union capital; it did, but not enough to change the odds compounding at Richmond and Petersburg. At its high point, Early's campaign reached the outskirts of Washington—even fired on President Lincoln in a redoubt—and convinced some foreign observers that "the Confederacy is more formidable as an enemy than ever." The raid scared Lincoln and Halleck and cleared the valley of federals at a crucial time. Early remained a threat as Lee left him there to protect the granary of the army.

By the end of the first week in June, Lincoln and Grant were disappointed. Grant, who intended to fight on to Richmond if it took all summer, found that it would take that time and more. After all the carnage, his campaign had failed. True, he was seven miles from Richmond, but Lee's army remained intact. No good way seemed open to flank the rebels away from Richmond's formidable entrenchments. Grant told the president he intended to give up the direct approach, cross south of the James, and hit Richmond from its supposedly soft underbelly. He wanted to get Lee out in the open for a decisive blow. Lee would not come out of his lines to fight Grant's battle; hence, he magnified his numbers.

Grant, for once, however, fooled the wily rebel leader. He began crossing the James on 12 June and Lee lost him for several days. Expecting a move south of the James, Lee nevertheless lacked definite information of Grant's movements. A large part of the Army of the Potomac crossed beyond the river, and by 15 June, sixteen thousand Yankees attempted to attack Beauregard's three thousand men defending Petersburg. Bad maps, combined with botched orders and short rations, confused the advance, and Beauregard's brilliant countermeasures staved off ruin.

If Lee was confused about Grant's whereabouts and intentions, Beauregard was not—he kept reporting mounting Union numbers to Lee, and kept asking for help. Lee remained unconvinced of Grant's doings. Beauregard held against mounting numbers, contracted his lines, called for help, stripped his Bermuda Hundred line, and by 17 June had done about all he could to hold Petersburg. On that day Lee sent heavy reinforcements and saved the southern gateway to Richmond. The siege of Petersburg began on 18 June 1864. Over the next months Lee's lines would extend some thirty miles and be held by scarcely more than 60,000 men against Meade's 110,000. The four-day defense of Petersburg had been bloody—Meade lost about 8,000 killed and wounded. Confederate losses were less in number, more in portent.

ON TO HISTORY

Although many Northerners thought Grant's new strategy had failed, it was working. While Meade battled his way through northern Virginia, Sherman moved from Chattanooga against the Army of Tennessee. As both Lee and Johnston called for men, Davis and Seddon found fewer and fewer; the pool of eligible white males had about gone dry. Some brigades were scraped together in the spring and summer of 1864 from outlying posts and stations, usually from exposed coastal areas, and each shipment brought loud complaints from fearful governors.

Large sections of the southern heartland had no men left. Part of the manpower problem stemmed from the need to protect the armies' lines of communication against Union raiders, even against disaffected Southerners and organized deserters. When such hard war measures as conscription and impressment drained morale, trouble sprang up behind the lines, and Confederate troops were detached for rear-area security. As summer fighting ground on, casualties could not be replaced. Grant's suspension of prisoner exchanges hit the South harder than the North—there were more than 150,000 rebels in Union prisons who were badly needed in the ranks.

All of the logistical support network of the Confederacy wobbled under Grant's joint offensives. Ammunition and clothing could be had but distribution to the armies became problematical as federal cavalry wrecked railroads and bridges. Rations grew thinner as agricultural areas went to the enemy. An iron shortage crippled cannon production while scarcity of copper cut percussion cap manufacture. When would all these shortages coalesce into defeatism?

Hard campaigns vastly consumed Union manpower as well. As the staggering casualty lists filled northern papers, a great spasm of agony and anger racked the country. Lincoln, as well as Grant, were hotly criticized, so much so that Lincoln thought he might lose the election of 1864, might not even get the Republican nomination. He would stay the course, but his opponent might not. The cause might be lost by ballots. Signs of war weariness and apathy multiplied.

No signs of defeatism showed in the field. Hope and determination fired Sherman's one hundred thousand men, divided into three armies, as they began moving on 7 May 1864. Sherman launched a great raid, aimed at smashing Johnston's army and at cutting Georgia in two

with a sixty-mile wide incursion to the sea. It became a surprisingly effective logistical campaign that threatened key Confederate arsenals, armories, and depots. The first rush stalled, however, because Johnston's lines were too strong. Johnston always had a good eye for holding ground, and he had entrenched his sixty thousand devoted men along a ridge near Dalton, Georgia. Sherman tried turning the Confederate left. Johnston began one of history's great retreats. Grudgingly, he backed down the Western and Atlantic Railroad toward Atlanta, entrenching where he could, standing when he had a chance to fight, slipping away from flankers with sure control of his men and superb sense of timing. The retreat became a kind of offense; Sherman repeatedly deployed, skirmished, flanked, only to see Johnston's rear guard still ahead. From 13 to 28 May, battles at Resaca, Cassville, the Etowah River, and New Hope Church each stalled Sherman's march. At Kenesaw Mountain, 27 June 1864, Johnston bloodily repulsed a major attack.

To a worried Lincoln, Sherman's operations offered vast potential. If Johnston's army was destroyed, Lee would be finished quickly and the war would end. By the end of June, however, Sherman seemed to be emulating Grant's tactics—pushing the enemy back on his base while extending federal supply lines. At last, Johnston fell back into Atlanta's strong defenses and awaited battle.

Through the weeks of Johnston's retreat President Davis watched in mounting frustration. How far would he go? When and where would he fight? These understandable presidential questions Johnston either ignored or parried with some excuse about security. Silence might have been prudent because Johnston would have had to say that the army took precedence over cities or ground and he would keep it between Sherman and the sea. Still, the president had a right to know what the commander of one of the South's main armies had in mind. When Johnston pulled his men into the Atlanta lines, Davis made a mistake. Unable to find out what his general planned, save retreat, the president replaced him with General

John Bell Hood, one of Lee's best division leaders and a corps commander in the Army of Tennessee. The army seethed because the men loved "Old Joe" and many felt that Hood had undermined him and frustrated chances to attack Sherman. There was truth to the thought, but the deed stood, and fear chilled veterans so often pawns to ambition.

Davis had asked Lee's advice and heard cautionary words about leaving a good man in command, about Hood being a fighter but perhaps not quite of army command caliber. Hood knew that Davis wanted a fight for Atlanta. Two hard attacks, on 20 and 22 July failed, and Hood abandoned the city on 1 September 1864. This disaster crowned a grinding summer for the south. Atlanta's fall proved the value of Grant's "Operation Crusher." Sherman wasted no time as he prepared a march through the industrial heart of Georgia and on to the coast, finally on to Charleston, the "Cradle of Secession."

Hood made a good attempt to recoup his fortunes. Guessing that a march up Sherman's communications toward Nashville would force him to follow, Hood started for Tennessee in November. Sherman followed only a short way, left Hood to others, and on 14 November marched on to the sea. Hood wasted the flower of his army in a useless frontal attack on 30 November at Franklin, Tennessee, then limped on to clamp a partial siege on Nashville. General Thomas broke the siege on 15–16 December and also broke Hood's army. Bits and pieces of the army drifted back to Georgia, where Johnston tried to rebuild it as some kind of a buffer to Sherman. Out from Sherman's army had gone clouds of "bummers," who burned, pillaged, and degraded young and old as they carried freedom's flag. A gallant remnant of the Army of Tennessee later fought Sherman at Bentonville, North Carolina, on 19–21 March 1865, and surrendered at Durham Station, North Carolina, on 26 April 1865.

Lee hated the defensive. As siege lines snaked ever longer south and west along the Appomattox River early in 1865, as more of his men were confined in burgeoning labyrinths of trenches, he knew the initiative had firmly passed to Grant. Now the Army of Northern Virginia faced the daily routine of attrition—the slow death Lee had so fiercely fended. Petersburg had to be held because important rail lines joined there from the Deep South that sustained the army's thin rations and supplies. Federal cavalry raided the lines and others coming directly to Richmond, but Fitzhugh Lee, who took over from the dead Jeb Stuart, kept them at bay, even though his horsemen had to forage almost forty miles from the Confederate army. Supplies grew fewer as enemy thrusts into the logistical heart of the Confederacy sapped resources. Rickety trains ran slower and more unreliably when winter dug the army deeper into its strange dirt warrens.

From mid-June 1864 to 2 April 1865, the siege distracted Lee. Desperately, he wanted to maneuver, to get out and attack Grant with some chance of flanking him, turning him back toward the Potomac. Grimly, Grant stuck to his trenching, steadily extending westward to thin out Lee's defenders. These long months saw raids and frontal assaults, charges, skirmishes, and the endless, dreary burrowing. Occasionally the lines twitched. A Union attempt to blow up part of the rebel trenches east of Petersburg, the Battle of the Crater on 30 July 1864, changed the veteran feelings of respectful animosity into one of real bitterness against black troops, who gallantly led the way into an inferno. Several times during the winter of 1864–1865, Lee tried to gain a strategic advantage along the trench lines, but heavy Union strength in men and guns usually prevailed.

Slowly Grant moved to his left, until Lee's forty-five thousand men were stretched to cover nearly thirty miles of line. Caught in the geometry of a closing circle, Lee, who had been made commander in chief of the Confederate armies in February 1865 by a congress angry at Davis, planned a desperate gamble. If, somehow, he could cripple Grant's army, he would leave a holding force at Petersburg and join Johnston to defeat Sherman. The combined Confederate armies would then return to deal with Grant. The plan had the forlorn logic of fantasy, but Lee tried. At 4 P.M. on 25 March 1865, he launched an attack on Fort Stedman at the north end of the Union lines, a costly failure—five thousand casualties. Grant followed that battle with a major effort on Lee's attenuated right, and on 2 April 1865 the Confederate line broke. Lee evacuated Petersburg and Richmond and began marching southwestward with the hope of finding rations and perhaps of joining Johnston.

On 9 April 1865, with federal columns front and rear, Lee went to the house of Wilmer McLean, who had moved when the first Battle of Bull Run overran his residence, and surrendered the Army of Northern Virginia. Terms were generous. Horsemen kept their horses, officers their side arms, the men got Union rations, and everyone was paroled on Grant's authority. With Lee's surrender the remaining Confederate fragments yielded everywhere, and by the end of May the first of the modern wars was over. The Confederacy went on to legend and the United States to world power.

President Lincoln toured a smoking, subdued Richmond on 5 April 1865. Crowds of cheering former slaves swirled around him. He visited the Confederate White House, listened to an old friend, former Supreme Court Justice John A. Campbell, suggest that the Virginia legislature might withdraw Virginia from the Confederacy—and approved the idea—then walked around a bit. Stopping at George Edward Pickett's house, he found he had missed his friend, who was with General Lee.

At Ford's Theater in Washington on the evening of 14 April 1865, the Lincolns were watching a performance of "Our American Cousin." During the performance, the actor John Wilkes Booth shot the president, who died at 7:22 A.M. the next day. Lincoln had lived to see victory. Problems of Reconstruction passed to President Andrew Johnson.

THE NAVAL WAR, 1861–1865

Lincoln's proclaimed blockade of the southern coasts on 19 April 1861 looked good on paper and nowhere else. The United States Navy had only forty-two ships in commission and many of those were in repair. Many of the warships were flung far around the globe. Lincoln expected more diplomatic than commercial results from his announced policy. Although the Declaration of Paris of 1856 held that blockades had to be effective to be honored, Lincoln had some hope that Great Britain and European nations might find it advantageous to respect his paper interdiction of the Confederacy. He was right. Great Britain, whose concern with maritime rights had helped cause the War of 1812, chose to honor the blockade. When Queen Victoria proclaimed neutrality soon after Lincoln's call for volunteers, she also enjoined her subjects not to defy the blockade. Many did, but the precedent had been set. There might come a time when Albion would want a paper cordon acknowledged by the Yankees.

Davis and his secretary of state, Robert A. Toombs, expecting support from signatories to the Declaration of Paris, took pains to compile statistics on the sieve-like nature of the blockade in the first months of application. Beyond that, the government strove to create a navy strong enough to keep the harbors open to the world's cotton trade. King Cotton would change everything. A shortage in British and European mills would force not only foreign recognition, but also foreign help in mocking Lincoln's empty prohibition.

Both sides raced to build a fleet. Although small, the mere existence of the Union navy carried great advantages. Dry docks and shipyards existed on the East Coast, which suggested a possibly easy conversion from commercial vessels to warships. Naval stores abounded in both North and South, but skilled builders clustered north of Mason and Dixon's Line. More than that, facilities for making marine engines capable of propelling giant wooden warships, or perhaps the heavy new ironclads, existed only in the North. Even with these advantages and a rich industrial base, the possible effectiveness of the Union navy depended on the skill and drive of its leaders.

President Lincoln selected Gideon Welles to be secretary of the Union navy. An unlikelier appointment could hardly have been fantasized. A former Democrat and a New England newspaper publisher, Welles had a doleful man's acerbic tongue and a look of melancholy. Welles brought surprising ability and zeal to his office and a captiousness reflected in the biting wit of his diary to Cabinet meetings. About ships and sailors he had little knowledge, perhaps less interest, but Lincoln saw in him a fine organizer and administrator who might learn. His challenges were fearsome, but he learned.

First among the problems was the blockade and how to enforce it. With more than thirty-five hundred miles of insurrectionary coastline to cover, the Union navy needed massive help. Welles ordered a blockade semblance immediately, and the steam frigate *Minnesota* and the sail frigate *Cumberland* anchored at Hampton Roads, which would become the main base for the North Atlantic Blockading Squadron. Two ships patrolled North Carolina waters in May 1861. Welles rushed a naval acquisition program that emphasized not only construction, but also purchase of all potentially useful vessels—from sailboats to tugs—and pushed production of naval ordnance. Slowly the Union ship inventory grew and more vessels deployed along the Atlantic seaboard. Welles went further. Major construction of big ships-of-the-line received attention, and unusual orders were entered for some of the new ironclads already in use in foreign navies. Recruiting also received attention from the top.

Welles and senior naval officers quickly grasped the new tactics of sea-land cooperation in attacking southern coastal areas, and specially designed gunboats were ordered to expand that effort. Marines usually participated, as amphibious operations became one of the most important and successful efforts of the Union navy. With so much of the south Atlantic coast protected by inland waterways, Confederate shipping, including potential runners of the nascent blockade, could sail inside the barrier islands until a clear inlet was found. A quick rush out would foil blockaders sitting around major harbors. Navy-army cooperation brought three important Union victories: the closure of

Hatteras Inlet on 29 August 1861, the capture of Roanoke Island on 8 February 1862, and the signal victory at New Orleans in April 1862.. These joint efforts not only foreclosed many options for the rebels, but also provided fine bases for blockading squadron operations. Similar cooperative efforts greatly helped Grant's Tennessee and Vicksburg campaigns. Indeed, without the ironclad gunboats bombarding Confederate fortifications, army efforts to take Forts Henry and Donelson or to storm Vicksburg would have been much costlier, if successful at all.

Experience tightened and improved all navy enterprises, particularly antiblockade activity. As more ships cruised the southern coasts, Confederate efforts to break the cordon intensified. Specially designed blockade runners—small, speedy, light-draught vessels painted to blend with the sea—plied the trade and were attacked by new or updated gunboats and cruisers. Lincoln and Welles understood the importance of shutting off foreign supplies to the beleaguered South. Blockade runners were never entirely stopped, but trade slackened gradually to a point of diminishing returns. When Fort Fisher, the formidable bastion guarding the entrance to Cape Fear River and hence to Wilmington, North Carolina, fell to amphibious attack on 15 January 1865 the Confederacy's last Atlantic port closed.

Officers and men on blockading service wallowed in the troughs of boredom. Weeks of uninterrupted sea duty, sometimes moving, sometimes not, galled the hottest patriots. Mail deliveries were scarce, the food monotonous, men were cold in winter, stifled on summer station, and there were no women. "Adventure! Bah!" complained one frustrated buccaneer. "The blockade is the wrong place for it."

Boredom might be relieved by capturing a blockade runner and sharing the prize money. Boredom could be totally conquered in the derring-do of such officers as Commander Charles Wilkes, whose capture of two Confederate diplomatic commissioners, James Mason and John Slidell, from the British mail steamer *Trent* almost caused a foreign war in November 1861. Reckless and finally humiliating to the United

States, the venture caught northern enthusiasm and made Wilkes a passing hero. Opportunities abounded for thrill seekers. Various small excursions along the southern coasts involved volunteers in high danger, such as the small but spectacular expedition of Lieutenant William B. Cushing, 27–28 October 1864, in which he rammed and sank the feared rebel ironclad *Albemarle*. Standard naval doctrine expected navies to fight navies in big sprawling battles between heavy-gunned ships-of-the-line, a theory that narrowed some naval views in the early years of the war. Most Union operations were on blockading station or in combined river operations, but there were some real battles.

Secretary Welles contracted for some of the new ironclads shortly after he took office and that visionary gamble brought important results at Hampton Roads, where the first battle between ironclads occurred. When the Confederates captured Norfolk Navy Yard, they raised the *Merrimack*, encased it in armor, renamed it the CSS *Virginia*, and sent it to clear off coastal blockaders. On 8 March 1862, this giant, commanded by Captain Franklin Buchanan, steamed to attack the Union blockading squadron at Hampton Roads. Moving right into the large wooden ships, the *Virginia* rammed and shelled the USS *Cumberland*, sank it, and then destroyed the USS *Congress*. Apparently impervious to enemy fire, the *Virginia* became, for that day, queen of the Civil War at sea. One of the Union's ironclads appeared in Hampton Roads the next day. The *Monitor* was a small, low-lying craft with its flat deck almost awash and crowned with a round turret (it looked like a "cheese box on a raft" to some, to others like a "tin can on a shingle"). Almost unseaworthy, the *Monitor* nearly foundered on the way to Hampton Roads, but on 9 March it engaged the *Virginia* for several hours in a close-fought duel that resulted in both vessels withdrawing without real injury. The day of the iron warship had arrived—all wooden navies were suddenly obsolete.

Another classic encounter involved Admiral David G. Farragut in the Battle of Mobile Bay on 5 August 1864. During that battle against both rebel ironclads and mines (then called "torpedoes"), Farragut had himself lashed to his flagship's rigging and gave the famous attack order, "Damn the torpedoes! Full speed ahead."

Confederate cruisers posed one of the most difficult challenges to the Union navy. Buying some ships and ordering others abroad, the Confederate navy concentrated on commerce raiding. Some of the ships in this service were fine fighting vessels, often commanded by daring and resourceful captains. These cruisers usually avoided battle against heavier warships but not always. Various efforts were made to track them and trap them in neutral harbors and fight them when found. In one case, a raider was taken out of a Brazilian harbor, with diplomatic repercussions, and while these campaigns were exciting, they were also time-consuming and of limited value.

Diplomatic issues compounded some federal naval activities. Lincoln, and particularly Secretary of State Seward, wanted to deprive the Confederacy of any foreign aid. Doing so involved some high-tension clandestine activity in foreign capitals, where southern agents sought to buy blockade runners and warships. Occasionally, Union warships would lay off neutral ports to intercept Confederates vessels, or presumed Confederate vessels, often to the irritation of host countries. The practice, however, did often inhibit southern activities and showed considerable international deference to the U.S. Navy.

Welles deserves much credit for his even-handed, progressive administration of the Navy Department. Organization and management were his strengths, and he created and ably led a huge bureaucratic structure with minimum confusion. Perhaps his amateur sailor's status helped; for him, there were no sacrosanct precedents and innovations held no terrors.

Audacity counted far more poignantly in Confederate navy leaders. As with the army, inferior numbers demanded vision and innovation. Jefferson Davis' choice of Stephen R. Mallory as navy secretary irritated some members of the Provisional Congress. Born in Trinidad, Mallory grew up in Key West and had been one of Florida's senators when the state seceded. As chairman of the U.S. Senate Committee on Naval Affairs, he had worked to modernize a service rusted in the past. Unfortunately, he had a look of slowness to him that bred more anxiety than faith. Many students of the Confederacy consign him to the usual middling rummage of Davis' cabinet. Viewed from the standpoint of the resources he commanded and the loom of his opponents, Mallory's achievements rank him among the best navy secretaries in American history.

Without shipbuilding facilities of consequence once Norfolk and New Orleans fell, without machine shops capable of making sound marine engines, with ample but scattered naval stores, and with most men wanting to join the army, Mallory's challenges dwarfed those facing Welles. Aware that the South could not compete with the United States in conventional ways, Mallory became one of the true naval innovators. He had a kind of restless intuition that sometimes led to outlandish things but mostly steered him to sound ideas and brilliant novelties.

Early in his tenure he said that "I regard the possession of an iron-armored ship as a matter of the first necessity," and when the *Merrimack* came into Confederate hands, he pressed its speedy conversion. Other ironclads received his money and attention, including the iconoclastic railroad ironclad *Arkansas*, until the small southern navy had a respectable number of the latest things in naval combat, albeit most of them lacked efficient engines. Naval ordnance also earned Mallory's early eye, and he stimulated development of the Torpedo Bureau, which produced numbers of mines that did deadly duty against many federal hulls. More ships were lost to these "infernal machines" than to regular combat.

Confronted with the fact that the South could not compete with the Union war fleet, Mallory supported President Davis' reliance on the old American practice of privateering. Because the United States had not agreed to banning privateers under the Declaration of Paris, the Confederacy legitimately inherited the right to use

these "militia of the sea." Northern outrage against this "inhumane" practice merely cloaked irritation at its being used against the Union. Many would-be privateers signed up as soon as allowed in May 1861, and initial seizures were impressive; but the practice faded as coasts were interdicted and prizes could not be brought into the Confederacy.

Mallory tried to have the navy cooperate in resisting combined federal river operations. Some Confederate naval gunners served important land batteries, notably Drewry's Bluff near Richmond, and Confederate marines helped protect ships under construction from Union raiders. If the Confederacy could hit commercial shipping hard enough, federal ships might be diverted from the blockade to relieve the merchantmen. With that in view, and also with a view to unfurling the Confederate banner around the world, Mallory supported the construction and purchase abroad of commerce raiders. They were not unknown to war; their success depended on leadership, morale, and the stoutness of the ships. Many were commissioned and some reached the high seas. Famed far and wide were the *Sumter, Alabama, Florida, Shenandoah,* and *Stonewall.*

Their captains are inseparable from these fast, well-armed, rakish cruisers that accounted for many northern ships and millions in prizes. The *Sumter* and *Alabama* were commanded by Raphael Semmes, an officer of long and prosaic duty in the "old navy." Much like Stonewall Jackson, Semmes rested on arms for his moment, and when it came, he seized it and became one of the great sea raiders of history. He sailed in the *Sumter* for six months in the Atlantic and Caribbean, received honors from neutral ports, and captured eighteen ships. Trapped at Gibraltar, Semmes abandoned the *Sumter*. His great days were ahead.

President Davis had dispatched Captain James D. Bulloch to England in May 1861 to contact for warships, cruisers, and blockade runners. His surprisingly successful activities in the nether world of diplomatic infighting produced contracts for big and little warships and for myriad blockade runners from Liverpool and Glasgow. The Laird Rams, two double-turret ironclads ordered from John Laird and Sons, were his prime hope, frustrated when the United States frightened Great Britain into impounding them. His great success was a stray ship constructed in the Laird yards under its way number, *290*. Federal agents suspected the purpose of the *290* but could not prove it before it left on a shakedown cruise. A modern vessel, the *290* had every essential for a cruiser—1,000 tons, more than 200 feet long, and, most important, two 300-horsepower engines in addition to sail. Making quickly for the Azores, it received its armament and ammunition and a mixed crew (with many Yankees). On 24 August 1862, off the island of Terceira, its new captain, Semmes, took charge of the *290*, now the *Alabama*.

For two years Semmes and the *Alabama* scourged the high seas. He coursed the Atlantic, the Gulf of Mexico (where he sank the USS *Hatteras*), to Oriental waters, to Cape Town in Africa, and back to the Azores, and finally lost the ship in a fight with the USS *Kearsarge*, 19 June 1864, off Cherbourg, France. He might have been consoled by his record, as he and his men sought ways back to the Confederacy: one ironclad warship (100 tons heavier) sunk; sixty-two vessels captured.

Other cruisers did direct damage, too, but their real impact was on creating fear in the North. Insurance rates soared and a general "flight from the flag'" took more than seven hundred American ships to the protection of the British ensign. These raiders set an important precedent that the Russian czar's navy tried to emulate before the First World War.

Blockade running posed a special problem for the Confederate navy. Nominally a private matter, in which great fortunes were often the order of one or two successful trips to and from Bermuda and Wilmington or Nassau and Wilmington, occasionally Havana to Mobile or Galveston, several government agencies became involved in running their own ships through the blockade. Control of free space on these vital runners intruded on the freedom of commerce, but a beleaguered Confederate Congress approved partial nationalization of space on incoming and outgoing ships in early 1864. When the Ordnance Department, under the remarkably able General Josiah Gorgas, bought several runners and ran them in conjunction with the Medical and Quartermaster departments of the War Department, Mallory worked to enhance their efforts. He encouraged the participation of Confederate naval officers in the blockade-running effort by granting official leaves. Several served as captains on harrowing voyages through the Union naval curtain. Not only were the trips important to sustaining a flow of essential supplies, but also in boosting the zest of participants. A careful organization underlay the blockade-running effort. Depots in Bermuda and Nassau received freight from England and the Continent, and the shipments were then transferred to blockade runners for the run to the Confederacy.

The high profits and higher risks of blockade running were run by a kind of shadow cast of captains and crews unknown save to sponsors and to daring. A successful run in and out might pay for the ship, several runs would indemnify disaster, and anyone whose blood ran high never got enough. Tom Taylor of the blockade runner *Banshee* recalled:

> The night proved dark, but dangerously clear and calm. No lights were allowed—not even a cigar; the engine-room hatchways were covered with tarpaulins, at the risk of suffocating the unfortunate engineers and stokers in the almost insufferable atmosphere below. But it was absolutely imperative that not a glimmer of light should appear. Even the binnacle was covered, and the steersman had to see as much of the compass as he could through a conical aperture carried almost up to his eyes. . . . We steamed on in silence except for the stroke of the engines and the beat of the paddle-floats, which in the calm of the night seemed distressingly loud; all hands were on deck, crouching behind the bulwarks; and we on the bridge, namely, the captain, the pilot, and I, were straining our eyes into the darkness. . . . And fortunate it was for us we so

near. Daylight was already breaking, and before we were opposite the fort [Fisher] we could make out six or seven gunboats, which steamed rapidly towards us and angrily opened fire. Their shots were soon dropping close around us; an unpleasant sensation when you know you have several tons of gunpowder under your feet.

Such excitement roiled the blood and made addicts of even the careful men.

How important was blockade running? Ratios of successful runs are impressive: in 1861 blockaders caught one out of ten runners; in 1862, one out of eight; in 1863, one out of four; in 1864, one out of three; in 1865, after most Confederate Atlantic ports were gone, one out of two. Only estimates can be made, but they indicate it was one of the Confederacy's most successful ventures: 330,000 small arms imported for the government from 1861 to 1865; 624,000 pairs of boots; 378,000 blankets. During the one-year period from December 1863 to December 1864, blockade runners brought in 1,933,000 pounds of saltpeter, 1,507,000 pounds of lead, 8,632,000 pounds of meat, 520,000 pounds of coffee, plus much more uncategorized material. Some commercial freighters reached Matamoros, Mexico, which remained open throughout the war, and almost-direct shipments from there to Texas helped sustain the Confederate Trans-Mississippi Department. Quite simply, blockade running extended the Confederacy's life for at least two years.

Did Mallory's efforts fail? In the sense that they did not prevail over federal fleets, yes. An overall view shows that Mallory's innovative efforts, including the rudimentary submarine *Hunley*, which sank the Union corvette *Housatonic* in February 1864, changed the nature of naval war and opened the vision of navies around the world. If he did not secure Confederate independence, he did free naval minds from shackling inhibitions.

Important to the story of the Confederate navy is the fact that last rebel banner flew on the *Shenandoah*'s mast. It ranged the Atlantic and Pacific beginning in September 1864, was sec-

ond only to the *Alabama* in destruction, and struck its colors at Liverpool on 6 November 1865.

WHAT KIND OF WAR?

The Civil War began as an old-fashioned war of armies against armies and had evolved, as Bruce Catton observed, into a "war against"— against the enemy, against even civilians. Building its own momentum, it became a great rolling agent of change that freed the slaves; reworked social, economic and political seams in the North and South; and left America forever different.

It was a war of more than 10,500 fights. It was also the first war of the industrial revolution: of machinery and firepower and engineering beyond imaginings; of railroads and iron ships and submarines and rifled cannon; of telegraphs and rudimentary air observation; of massed firepower and the end of massed charges; of machines against gallantry. The costs were also commensurate with new machinery and with new ways of killing. Estimates vary, but adjusted statistics indicate on the Union side 110,100 killed and mortally wounded, 224,580 dead of disease, plus 275,175 wounded and 30,192 prisoner-of-war dead, for 642,427 total casualties of all causes. Confederate figures are more conjectural (no naval figures are available), but a fair assessment gives 94,000 Confederates killed or mortally wounded, 164,000 dead of disease, plus 194,026 wounded and from 26,000 to 31,000 prisoner-of-war dead, for 483,026 total casualties of all causes. Total Civil War deaths from all causes are estimated at least at 623,026, with minimum wounded totals at 471,427, and an overall war casualty figure of 1,125,453. More than 25 percent of the 1861 available manpower of the North and South became casualties of some kind.

Numbers alone do not tell the whole wages of the war. Vast areas of the South stood scorched, ravaged, pillaged, and wrecked by friendly and hostile armies. In both North and South the returning veterans were not the same men as before the war. A dread scythe of maiming and disfiguring passed across their ranks; whole men were hard to find. The lame, broken, and blind lingered as mutant hostages of conflict.

Numbers do offer interpretive aid in assessing the monetary costs of America's great war. Again, figures are disputed, but careful students estimate that northern costs ran to about $8.5 billion and that southern costs could hardly have been less than $6 billion. In addition, there were, of course, intangible horrors to count in hope, pride, courage, and faith that affected psyches, North and South, for generations to the present. In that terrible expense of blood and treasure and intangibles, Americans tested whether they had the courage of their convictions in democracy.

More than anything else, it had been a war about democracy, a war to test whether human freedom or political liberty were the main themes of the American Revolution. Out of the crucible of carnage came an iron decision—all men were forever free. That decision reforged old themes of brotherhood into a new and stronger America. There were scars and sorrows and anguish mixed in a strange, surging thirst for destiny. The Civil War was actually the war of American unification.

BIBLIOGRAPHY

Official Publications

Journal of the Congress of the Confederate States of America, 7 vols. (1904–1905).

Official Records of the Union and Confederate Navies in the War of the Rebellion, 31 vols. (1894–1927).

War of the Rebellion: A Compilation of the Official Records of the Union and Confederate Armies, 128 vols. (1881–1901).

Matthews, James M., ed. *The Statutes at Large of the Confederate States of America* (1862–1864).

———. *The Statutes at Large of the Provisional Government of the Confederate States of America* (1864).

Ramsdell, Charles W., ed. *Laws and Joint Resolutions of the Last Session of the Confederate Congress (November 7, 1864–March 18, 1865) Together with the Secret Acts of Previous Congresses* (1941).

Bibliographies and Atlases

Atlas to Accompany the Official Records of the Union and Confederate Armies (1891–1895, new ed. 1958).

Coletta, Paolo E. *A Bibliography of American Naval History* (1981).

Esposito, Vincent J., ed. *The West Point Atlas of American Wars*, 2 vols. (1959).

Kennedy, Frances H., ed. *The Civil War Battlefield Guide* (1990).

Mitchell, Joseph B. *Decisive Battles of the Civil War* (1955).

Nevins, Allan, Bell I. Wiley, and James I. Robertson. *Civil-War Books: A Critical Bibliography*, 2 vols. (1967–1969).

Steele, Matthew F. *American Campaigns*, 2 vols. (1909).

Photographic Collections

Davis, William C., ed. *The Image of War, 1861–1865*, 6 vols. (1981–1984).

———. *Touched by Fire: A Photographic Portrait of the Civil War*, 2 vols. (1985–1986).

Ketchum, Richard M., ed. *The American Heritage Picture History of the Civil War*. Text by Bruce Catton (1960).

Milhollen, Hirst D., and Milton Kaplan, eds. *Divided We Fought: A Pictorial History of the War, 1861–1865*. Narrative by David Donald (1956).

Miller, Francis T. *The Photographic History of the Civil War*, 10 vols. (1911).

Ward, Geoffrey C., Ric Burns, and Ken Burns. *The Civil War: An Illustrated History* (1990).

Biographies

Ambrose, Stephen E. *Halleck: Lincoln's Chief of Staff* (1962).

Bushong, Millard K. *Old Jube: A Biography of General Jubal A. Early* (1965).

Cleaves, Freeman. *Rock of Chickamauga: The Life of General George H. Thomas* (1948).

———. *Meade of Gettysburg* (1960).

Current, Richard N., ed. *Advance and Retreat: The Memoirs of John Bell Hood* (1959).

Davis, Varina Howell. *Jefferson Davis, Ex-President of the Confederate States of America: A Memoir by His Wife*, 2 vols. (1890).

Dodd, William E. *Jefferson Davis* (1907).

Dowdey, Clifford. *Lee* (1965).

Durkin, Joseph T. *Stephen R. Mallory: Confederate Navy Chief* (1954).

Dyer, John P. *The Gallant Hood* (1950).

Eaton, Clement. *Jefferson Davis* (1977).

Freeman, Douglas Southall. *R. E. Lee: A Biography*, 4 vols. (1934–1935).

———. *Lee's Lieutenants*, 3 vols. (1942–1944).

Fuller, J. F. C. *Grant and Lee: A Study in Personality and Generalship* (1938; rev. ed. 1982).

Gosnell, Harpur A. *Rebel Raider: Being an Account of Raphael Semmes' Cruise in the C.S.S. Sumter* (1948).

Govan, Gilbert, and J. W. Livingood. *A Different Valor: The Story of General Joseph E. Johnston, C.S.A.* (1956).

Grant, U. S. *Personal Memoirs of U. S. Grant*, 2 vols. (1885–1886).

Hart, B. H. Liddell. *Sherman: Soldier, Realist, American* (1929).

Hassler, Warren W. *General George B. McClellan: Shield of the Union* (1957).

Haupt, Herman. *Reminiscences* (1901).

Hebert, Walter H. *Fighting Joe Hooker* (1944).

Heleniak, Roman J., and Lawrence L. Hewitt, eds. *The Confederate High Command and Related Topics: The 1988 Deep Delta Civil War Symposium: Themes in Honor of T. Harry Williams* (1990).

Henderson, G. F. R. *Stonewall Jackson and the American Civil War*, 2 vols. (1919; rev. ed. 1936).

Lamers, William M. *The Edge of Glory: A Biograhy of General William S. Rosecrans* (1961).

Lewis, Lloyd. *Sherman, Fighting Prophet* (1932).

Luthin, Reinhard H. *The Real Abraham Lincoln* (1960).

McFeely, William S. *Grant: A Biography* (1981).

McMurry, Richard M. *John Bell Hood and the War for Southern Independence* (1982).

McWhiney, Grady. *Braxton Bragg and Confederate Defeat* (1969).

Maurice, Frederick. *Robert E. Lee, the Soldier* (1925).

Meade, George G. *The Life and Letters of George Gordon Meade, Major General United States Army*, 2 vols. (1913).

Merrill, J. M. *William Tecumseh Sherman* (1971).

Niven, John. *Gideon Welles: Lincoln's Secretary of the Navy* (1973).

Oates, Stephen B. *With Malice Toward None: The Life of Abraham Lincoln* (1977).

Parks, Joseph H. *General Edmund Kirby Smith, C.S.A.* (1954).

Piston, William G. *Lee's Tarnished Lieutenant: James Longstreet and His Place in Southern History* (1987).

Poore, Ben P. *The Life of Ambrose E. Burnside* (1882).

Randall, James G., and Richard Current. *Lincoln the President*, 4 vols. (1945–1955).

Roberts, W. Adolphe. *Semmes of the Alabama* (1938).

Robertson, James I., Jr. *General A. P. Hill: The Story of a Confederate Warrior* (1987).

Roland, Charles P. *Albert Sidney Johnston: Soldier of Three Republics* (1964).

Roman, Alfred. *The Military Operations of General Beauregard in the War Between the States, 1861–1865*, 2 vols. (1884).

Sandburg, Carl. *Abraham Lincoln: The Prairie Years*, 2 vols. (1926).

———. *Abraham Lincoln: The War Years*, 4 vols. (1939).

Sanger, D. B., and T. R. Hay. *James Longstreet* (1952).

Sears, Stephen W. *George B. McClellan: The Young Napoleon* (1988).

Seitz, Don. *Braxton Bragg: General of the Confederacy* (1924).

Sherman, William T. *Memoirs of William T. Sherman, Written by Himself*, 2 vols. (1875).

Strode, Hudson. *Jefferson Davis*, 3 vols. (1955–1964).

Tate, Allen. *Jefferson Davis: His Rise and Fall* (1929).

Thomas, Benjamin. *Abraham Lincoln: A Biography* (1952).

Thomas, Benjamin P., and Harold M. Hyman. *Stanton: The Life and Times of Lincoln's Secretary of War* (1962).

Thomas, Emory M. *Bold Dragoon: The Life of J. E. B. Stuart* (1986).

Vandiver, Frank E., *Mighty Stonewall* (1957).

Vandiver, Frank E., ed. *Narrative of Military Operations Directed During the Late War Between the States: The Memoirs of Joseph E. Johnston* (1959).

———. *War Memoirs: Autobiographical Sketch and Narrative of the War Between the States: The Memoirs of Jubal A. Early* (1960).

Warner, Ezra J. *Generals in Gray: Lives of the Confederate Commanders* (1959).

———. *Generals in Blue: Lives of the Union Commanders* (1964).

Weigley, Russell F. *Quartermaster-General of the Union Army: A Biography of Montgomery C. Meigs* (1959).

Welles, Gideon. *Diary of Gideon Welles: Secretary of the Navy Under Lincoln and Johnson,* 3 vols. (1911).

Williams, T. Harry. *P. G. T. Beauregard: Napoleon in Gray* (1955).

General Histories of the Civil War

Adams, Michael C. C. *Our Masters, the Rebels: A Speculation on Union Military Failure in the East, 1861–1865* (1978).

Boatner, Mark Mayo, III. *The Civil War Dictionary* (1959).

Catton, Bruce. *This Hallowed Ground* (1956).

———. *The Centennial History of the Civil War,* 3 vols. (1961–1965).

Commager, Henry Steele, ed. *The Blue and the Gray: The Story of the Civil War as Told by Participants,* 2 vols. (1950).

Dornbusch, C. E., comp. *Regimental Publications and Personal Narratives of the Civil War: A Checklist,* 2 vols. (1961–1971).

Dupuy, R. Ernest, and Trevor N. Dupuy. *The Compact History of the Civil War* (1960).

Dyer, Frederick. *A Compendium of the War of the Rebellion* (1959).

Foote, Shelby. *The Civil War: A Narrative,* 3 vols. (1958–1974).

Griess, Thomas E., ed. *The American Civil War* (1980).

Hattaway, Herman, and Archer Jones. *How the North Won: A Military History of the Civil War* (1986).

Long, E. B., and Barbara Long. *The Civil War Day by Day: An Almanac, 1861–1865* (1971).

Luraghi, Raimondo. *Storia della Guerra Civile Americana* (1966)

McPherson, James M. *Battle Cry of Freedom: The Civil War Era* (1988).

Nevins, Allan. *The War for the Union,* 4 vols. (1959–1971).

Randall, J. G., and David Herbert Donald. *The Civil War and Reconstruction,* 2nd ed. (1969).

Roland, Charles P. *An American Iliad: The Story of the Civil War* (1991).

Thomas, Emory M. *The Confederate Nation: 1861–1865* (1979).

Vandiver, Frank E. *Their Tattered Flags: The Epic of the Confederacy* (1970).

Wakelyn, Jon L., ed. *Biographical Dictionary of the Confederacy* (1977).

Campaigns and Battles

Barrett, John G. *Sherman's March Through the Carolinas* (1956).

Bigelow, John. *The Campaign of Chancellorsville* (1910).

Carter, Samuel, III. *The Final Fortress: The Campaign for Vicksburg* (1980).

Catton, Bruce. *A Stillness at Appomattox* (1953).

Coddington, Edwin B. *The Gettysburg Campaign: A Study in Command* (1968).

Connelly, Thomas L. *Army of the Heartland: The Army of Tennessee, 1861–1862* (1967).

———. *Autumn of Glory: The Army of Tennessee. 1862–1865* (1971).

Dowdey, Clifford. *The Seven Days* (1964).

Downey, Fairfax. *Storming the Gateway: Chattanooga, 1863* (1960).

Glatthaar, Joseph T. *The March to the Sea and Beyond: Sherman's Troops in the Savannah and Carolina Campaigns* (1987).

Haskell, Frank A. *The Battle of Gettysburg* (1908).

McDonough, James L. *Shiloh: In Hell Before Night* (1977).

———. *Stones River: Bloody Winter in Tennessee* (1980).

Miers, Earl Schenck. *Web of Victory: Grant at Vicksburg* (1955).

Murfin, J. V. *The Gleam of Bayonets: The Battle of Antietam and the Maryland Campaign of 1862* (1965).

Sears, S. W. *Landscape Turned Red: The Battle of Antietam* (1983).

Sommers, Richard. *Richmond Redeemed: The Siege at Petersburg* (1981).

Stewart, George R. *Pickett's Charge: A Microhistory of the Final Attack at Gettysburg* (1959).

Sword, Wiley. *Shiloh: Bloody April* (1974).

Walker, Peter F. *Vicksburg: A People at War* (1960).

Strategy, Tactics, and Theories of War

Connelly, T. L., and Archer Jones. *The Politics of Command: Factions and Ideas in Confederate Strategy* (1973).

Fuller, J. F. C. "The Place of the Civil War in the Evolution of War." *Army Quarterly* 26 (1933).

Hagerman, Edward. *The American Civil War and the Origins of Modern Warfare* (1988).

Jones, Archer. *Confederate Strategy from Shiloh to Vicksburg* (1961).

———. "Jomini and the Strategy of the American Civil War: A Reinterpretation." *Military Affairs* 34 (Winter 1970).

———. *The Art of War in the Western World* (1987).

McWhiney, Grady, and Perry D. Jamieson. *Attack and Die: Civil War Military Tactics and Southern Heritage* (1982).

Moore, John G. "Mobilization and Strategy in the Civil War." *Miltary Affairs* 24 (Summer 1960).

The Armies

Cook, Adrian. *The Armies of the Streets: The New York City Draft Riots of 1863* (1974).

Hernon, Joseph. *Celts, Catholics, and Copperheads* (1968).

Jimerson, Randall C. *The Private Civil War: Popular Thought During the Sectional Conflict* (1988).

Linderman, Gerald. *Embattled Courage: The Experience of Combat in the American Civil War* (1987).

Lonn, Ella. *Desertion During the Civil War* (1928).

Martin, Bessie. *Desertion of Alabama Troops from the Confederate Army* (1932).

Meneely, Alexander H. *The War Department, 1861* (1928).

Mitchell, Reid. *Civil War Soldiers: Their Expectations and Experiences* (1988).

Shannon, Fred A. *The Organization and Administration of the Union Army, 1861–1865*, 2 vols. (1928).

Robertson, James I., Jr. *Soldiers Blue and Gray* (1988).

Tatum, Georgia L. *Disloyalty in the Confederacy* (1934).

Wiley, Bell I. *The Life of Johnny Reb: The Common Soldier of the Confederacy* (1943).

———. *The Life of Billy Yank: The Common Soldier of the Union* (1952).

The Navies

Cochran, Hamilton. *Blockade Runners of the Confederacy* (1958).

Gosnell, H. A. *Guns on the Western Waters: The Story of River Gunboats in the Civil War* (1949).

Jones, Virgil C. *The Civil War at Sea*, 3 vols. (1960–1962).

Mahan, A. T. *The Gulf and Inland Waters* (1883).

Perry, Milton F. *Infernal Machines: The Story of Confederate Submarine and Mine Warfare* (1965).

Reed, Rowena. *Combined Operations in the Civil War* (1978).

Scharf, John T. *History of the Confederate States Navy* (1887).

Soley, James R. *The Blockade and the Cruisers* (1883).

Still, W. N. *Confederate Shipbuilding* (1969).

———. *Iron Afloat: The Story of the Confederate Armorclads* (1971).

Wells, Tom H. *The Confederate Navy: A Study in Organization* (1971).

Wise, Stephen R. *Lifeline of the Confederacy: Blockade Running During the War* (1988).

Vandiver, Frank E., ed. *Confederate Blockade Running Through Bermuda, 1861–1865; Letters and Cargo Manifests* (1947).

Black Troops and Slaves

Brewer, James H. *The Confederate Negro: Virginia's Craftsmen and Military Laborers, 1861–1865* (1969).

Cornish, Dudley T. *The Sable Arm: Negro Troops in the Union Army, 1861–1865* (1956).

Durden, Robert F. *The Gray and the Black: The Confederate Debate on Emancipation* (1972).

Genovese, Eugene. *Roll, Jordan, Roll: The World the Slaves Made* (1974).

Glatthaar, Joseph T. *Forged in Battle: The Civil War Alliance of Black Soldiers and White Officers* (1990).

McPherson, James M. *The Struggle for Equality: Abolitionists and the Civil War and Reconstruction* (1964).

———. *The Negro's Civil War: How American Negroes Felt and Acted During the War for Union* (1965).

McPherson, James M., et al. *Blacks in America* (1971).

Mohr, Clarence L. *On the Threshold of Freedom: Masters and Slaves in Civil War Georgia* (1986).

Quarles, Benjamin. *The Negro in the Civil War* (1953).

Wiley, Bell I. *Southern Negroes, 1861–1865* (1938).

Technology

Black, Robert C., III. *The Railroads of the Confederacy* (1952).

Broun, W. LeRoy. "The Red Artillery." *Southern Historical Society Papers* 26 (1898).

Fuller, Claude. *The Rifled Musket* (1958).

Goff, Richard D. *Confederate Supply* (1969).

Gorgas, Josiah. "Ordnance of the Confederacy, I, II." *Army Ordnance* 16 (1936).

Naisawald, L. Van Loan. *Grape and Canister: The Story of the Field Artillery of the Army of the Potomac, 1861–1865* (1960).

Nichols, James L. *The Confederate Quartermaster in the Trans-Mississippi* (1964).

Turner, George E. *Victory Rode the Rails: The Strategic Place of the Railroads in the Civil War* (1953).

Vandiver, Frank E. *Ploughshares into Swords: Josiah Gorgas and Confederate Ordnance* (1952).

Weber, Thomas. *The Northern Railroads in the Civil War, 1861–1865* (1952).

Wise, Jennings Cropper. *The Long Arm of Lee: The History of the Artillery of the Army of Northern Virginia* (1959).

RECONSTRUCTION AND AMERICAN IMPERIALISM

Joseph G. Dawson III

In 1897 the United States Army operated on a limited budget and mustered only about twenty-eight thousand officers, noncommissioned officers, and enlisted men. Many of the senior officers had entered the army as volunteers in the Civil War thirty-five years earlier and were no longer fit for arduous field service. Five years earlier the army had adopted a new rifle, the Krag-Jörgensen, and gradually distributed the five-shot-magazine shoulder weapon modeled on a Danish design, but some soldiers considered the Krag to be inferior to the standard rifles of the Spanish and German armies. For an industrialized nation populated by 70 million people and having thousands of miles of vulnerable coastline, the U.S. Army was not very imposing.

Not surprisingly, when the German General Staff issued a report in 1897 covering modern military forces, it failed to include the U.S. Army. The report evaluated the armies of most Western countries—among them modest Portugal and little Montenegro—but the U.S. Army was absent from its pages. It would be illuminating to have the German evaluation of the U.S. Army on the eve of the War with Spain in 1898 and deployment to Cuba, Puerto Rico, and the Philippines, events that helped spur the

United States to institute a series of military reforms that modernized the army. Some of those reforms had been debated for thirty years.

In contrast to the imperial adventures of 1898, during the 1870s, 1880s, and 1890s, the U.S. Army had fallen back on the varied duties it had fulfilled before the Civil War, including patrolling borders, guarding the coasts, exploring and mapping the West, and fighting Indians. In addition, the army took on new or less familiar responsibilities, such as operating military governments in the South and Alaska, suppressing wide-scale labor strikes, and conducting a social experiment of sorts—recruiting and maintaining regular regiments of African-American soldiers under the leadership of white officers. In other words, the army was a multipurpose organization that performed several jobs simultaneously, the nation's "obedient handyman," according to historian Samuel Huntington (1957).

Many army officers, however, wanted to be more than handymen and as early as the 1870s, reform-minded soldiers called for such measures as tripling the size of the army, developing new weapons, and creating a reliable reserve, steps that would prepare the army to conduct war against Europeans or other conventional adversaries. These calls came even before the campaigns against the trans-Mississippi Indian tribes drew to a close. Critics of these reforms—they might be termed "traditionalists"—harped on the high cost of reform and the low chance of such a conventional conflict. Where was the threatening enemy? Would the threat take the form of bombarding North America's coastal cities? The army's fortifications and U.S. Navy coastal defense ships could meet such threats. Might a potential crisis involve a significant deployment of U.S. Army units into a contested Latin American nation in defense of the Monroe Doctrine? Taking such action, the reformers argued, would overtax the military capabilities of the United States. They proposed that the army be designed to meet a conventional enemy, not just the scattered and uncoordinated Indian tribes.

For the last third of the nineteenth century the traditional advocates of a low-cost, multipurpose army had their way. They saw no need for the United States to maintain an up-to-date army commensurate with its economic strength. If a threat arose, they reckoned that the nation would have several months to respond and that thousands of volunteers would spring to the colors. In the meantime, a small, inexpensive army took orders from its civilian leaders—the president and the secretary of war. Claiming fiscal responsibility, and recognizing both historical American concerns over a large standing army and distrust of the officer corps as a military elite, the traditionalists merely sought to keep the kind of army expected by most Americans.

By 1897, however, the picture was changing. Colonial unrest in the Caribbean indicated an increasing possibility of war. As newsboys hawked tabloids on street corners, influential newspaper owners promoted the notion of war for nationalist and imperialist goals. The war they wanted led to the first major overseas deployment of the U.S. Army since Winfield Scott's invasion of Mexico in 1847. The experimental black units contributed to the war's major campaign. When a treaty ended the fighting, the army again operated postwar military gov-ernments. After years of functioning as a frontier constabulary and part-time internal police force, and amidst the controversy and confusion of island expeditions, the U.S. Army began to come of age.

RECONSTRUCTION

Postwar military occupations are seldom easy or popular, either with the soldiers on duty or the civilians whose land they occupy. Military forces often have occupied territory after a war using martial law—short-run suspensions of civil government—and sometimes by establishing military governments that supplant civil officials altogether for longer stretches of time. During much of their history, the British and Americans have displayed a deep distrust of standing armies as engines of tyranny. The English provided a specific example of military government at work following the English Civil Wars (1642–1646 and 1648–1651). After ordering the execution of King Charles in 1649, General Oliver Cromwell established a dictatorship, disbanded Parliament, and in 1655 divided the nation into eleven military districts, each administered by a general. Cromwell's protectorate was a short-lived aberration in England's heritage of constitutional government and civil law.

Two centuries later, northerners and southerners faced the daunting task of binding up the self-inflicted wounds resulting from the American Civil War. In contrast to the traumatic English example, U.S. civil government continued to function on the national level. Congress met in regular sessions, and Vice President Andrew Johnson succeeded to the office of president, as called for in the U.S. Constitution, after the assassination of Abraham Lincoln. The southern situation was more chaotic. Confederate armies surrendered in the spring of 1865, and thousands of ex-Confederate soldiers began returning home. The war's campaigns had devastated some southern cities and parts of several states. Nearly 4 million African-Americans had discarded the shackles of slavery, but their new

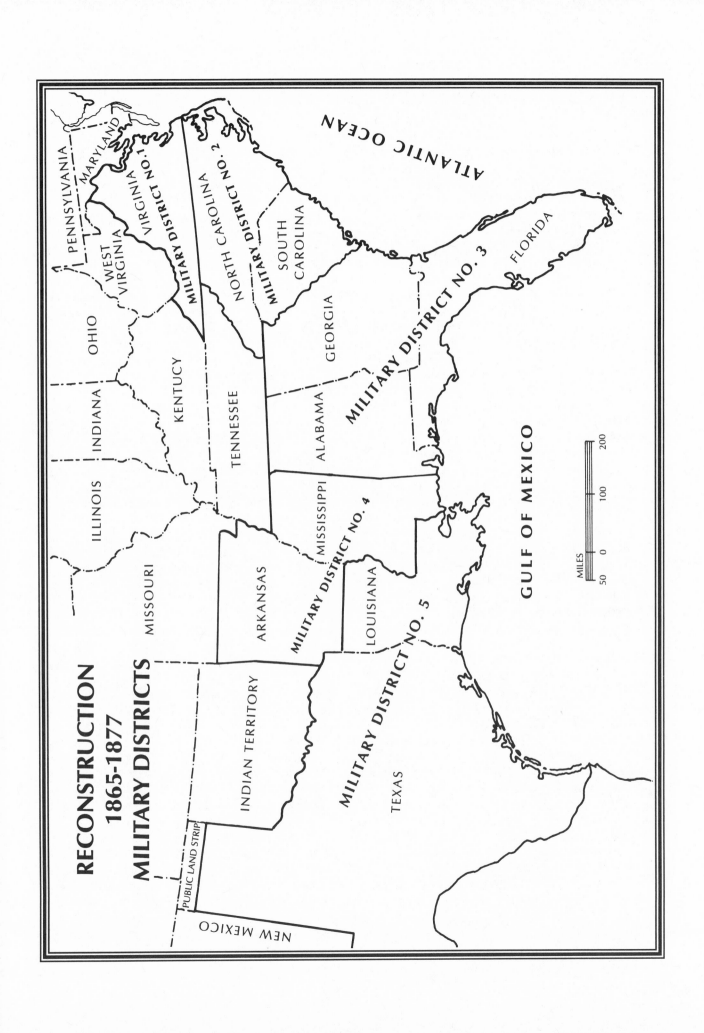

RECONSTRUCTION
1865-1877
MILITARY DISTRICTS

freedom was ill-defined. In Louisiana, Arkansas, and Tennessee, governments approved by Lincoln himself had been laboratories of Reconstruction, a contemporary term denoting the steps that would have to be taken to restore the Union. Elsewhere in the South, the collapse of the Confederacy had disrupted southern government and judicial process at the local and state levels.

Across the nation more than one million soldiers wore the blue uniform of the Union army, and they were the logical force to carry out Reconstruction. There were not enough U.S. marshals or agents of the Treasury Department to act either as temporary federal policemen or as administrators. In other words, under the pressures of the time, no existing federal agency other than the army possessed the size or strength to reconstruct the South.

Although the influence of the army over civil affairs was unique in U.S. history, it was not without precedent. After the Mexican War (1846–1848), U.S. Army units occupied parts of Mexico, including the capital, Mexico City. For several months they operated under martial law, supervising local elections, policing saloons and streets, and holding courts-martial to hear cases involving U.S. soldiers and Mexican nationals. When negotiators completed the Treaty of Guadalupe Hidalgo, the U.S. Army gladly left Mexico. Meanwhile, other army officers administered a territorial government in California, part of the land taken from Mexico in the war. Military governors there enforced the law, suppressed civil unrest, and drafted a constitution, paving the way for California statehood in 1850. No field manual was ever produced describing the successes and pitfalls of military administration in either Mexico or California. In retrospect this is not surprising, given the lack of attention to formal doctrine in the army during the nineteenth century.

Without written doctrine for guidance, Union army officers—often volunteers or political appointees, such as Benjamin F. Butler and Nathaniel P. Banks—undertook Reconstruction duties in Louisiana, Arkansas, and Tennessee before the end of the Civil War. The generals acted independently with little direction from Washington. As the need arose, they removed mayors and councilmen, jailed newspaper editors, cleaned city gutters to protect public health, and ordered units to patrol streets and roads. Moreover, the army issued thousands of its rations to the destitute, both black and white. Military officers in several southern states also operated banks and railroads, arranged for labor contracts between planters and the freedmen, supervised orphanages and almshouses, and licensed gaming establishments.

After Johnson took the oath as president, he moved quickly to take control of Reconstruction. A southerner, former slaveholder, and lifelong Democrat, Johnson acted without consulting Congress. On 29 May 1865 he issued his Proclamation of Pardon and Amnesty, designed to accomplish a speedy restoration of the Union. Accordingly, he recognized the Lincoln governments in Louisiana, Arkansas, and Tennessee, moved exiled Unionist Virginians from West Virginia to Richmond, and appointed provisional governors for the rest of the Confederate states. The president wanted the army to cooperate with the provisional governors while continuing to perform its ad hoc roles as part-time police force, occasional judge and jury, and short-term administrator for various banks and businesses.

Johnson needed the presence of the army in the South for his plan to work. He required the civil governors to act promptly in registering voters and ensuring that new state constitutions were drafted to abolish slavery, void Civil War debts, and nullify ordinances of secession. Statewide elections would then be held for all offices. His aim was to have all this done by the time Congress reconvened in the winter. In pushing for a quick Reconstruction, Johnson specified nothing for the former slaves and opposed the recently created Freedmen's Bureau as unnecessary and unconstitutional.

On the other hand, Johnson treated the Union's enemies leniently. The president gave a blanket pardon to most southerners who fought in the rebellion but excepted many high-ranking civil officials, senior rebel military officers (colonel and above), and anyone who, in his words, "voluntarily participated in said rebellion and the estimated value of whose taxable property was over $20,000." Johnson aimed this barb of his plan at rich southern planters, but there was a loophole. Anyone denied a pardon (and therefore denied participation in politics) was permitted to apply for a personal pardon from Johnson. In the next six months he gave out hundreds of pardons to ex-Confederate officials and planters, the very men who had favored secession or led the war to break up the Union. Thus, the president let slip the opportunity to temporarily exclude the economic, political, and military leadership of the Confederacy from the process of forming and operating new governments in the South. Johnson's indulgent pardoning scheme drew opposition from moderate Republicans in Congress, emboldened ex-Confederates, and made the soldiers' roles as policemen and managers of civil affairs more difficult.

Meanwhile, the army cooperated with the Bureau of Refugees, Freedmen, and Abandoned Lands, a federal agency established on 3 March 1865. Major General Oliver Otis Howard served as commissioner of the Freedmen's Bureau. Other army officers or former officers filled slots as state superintendents and local agents. The Freedmen's Bureau fulfilled many functions, including arranging employment for blacks and determining their wages, opening special courts to hear cases involving freedmen, operating schools, and handing out rations. Had the president supported the bureau, it no doubt would have accomplished even more than it did. Nevertheless, as an agency of the War Department, the Freedmen's Bureau was a remarkable experiment in social welfare.

A small, experimental agency was one thing, but even Republicans in Congress could not support retaining a one-million-man army now that the war was over. During the summer of 1865, the War Department began mustering out the Union army. Not even the short-lived prospect of war with France over its occupation of Mexico slowed the process. By Christmas of 1865 most of the volunteers who had marched under Ulysses S. Grant, George G. Meade,

Philip H. Sheridan, and William T. Sherman were civilians again. In January 1866 only 123,000 soldiers remained in uniform.

Many of the soldiers still on duty were African-Americans, who had made up more than 10 percent of Union forces. Hundreds of black volunteers found soldiering to their liking and wanted to stay in the nation's service. Subsequently (in July 1866), the War Department gained authorization from Congress to create the first black units in the regular army, four regiments of infantry and two of cavalry. These units represented an unusual social experiment. Although conservative politicians tried to have them disbanded, the segregated black regiments, under the command of white officers, remained a part of the army until the Korean War. In these regiments black citizens demonstrated their abilities as soldiers and were a visible reminder that blacks were no longer slaves.

In the meantime, relations between President Johnson and Congress grew tense and antagonistic. Congress exercised its prerogative to determine the validity of its own members, and in December 1865 rejected the southern representatives, including several notable former Confederates, elected under Johnson's state governments. Thus, Congress rejected the president's Reconstruction plan. Early the next year he vetoed both a civil rights bill and a bill to extend the Freedmen's Bureau. Congress later passed the two measures over the president's veto, but both moderate and radical Republicans had reason to be concerned.

Encouraged by Johnson's restricted view of federal power, the southern state legislatures separately enacted Black Codes, which restricted the rights of freedmen. Race riots occurred in Norfolk, Virginia (April), Memphis, Tennessee (May), and New Orleans, Louisiana (July), each with particular local causes but all sharing the themes of conflict between the races and white desperation at the thought of blacks holding offices or jobs that had been denied to them in the days of slavery. In each case, army commanders acted hesitantly and failed to head off the violence.

The race riots, Johnson's vetoes and lenient restoration plan, and the South's recalcitrant attitude—including passing the Black Codes, electing former Confederates, and rejecting the proposed Fourteenth Amendment—prompted Republicans in Congress to pass a series of laws that took the reins of Reconstruction from the president. On 2 March 1867 congressional Republicans passed over Johnson's veto the first Military Reconstruction Act, officially styled "An Act to Provide for the More Efficient Government of the Rebel States." Subsequent Military Reconstruction Acts clarified or added powers not well-defined in the first one. Collectively, these laws divided the former Confederate states into five military districts. (Tennessee, which had ratified the Fourteenth Amendment, was exempted.) Each of these districts would be commanded by an army general appointed by the president, but the civil governments cobbled together under Johnson's original plan would no longer have legal standing. Civilian officials and state judges would keep their posts only at the sufferance of the army and could be removed from office by the district commanders.

The Reconstruction Acts conferred considerable responsibility on the generals. Military courts could supplant civil courts if necessary, and the generals supervised the drafting of new state constitutions in conventions. All adult males (including blacks) would be able to vote for delegates to these conventions, except former Confederates temporarily denied the right to hold office under the terms of the proposed Fourteenth Amendment. Furthermore, the Reconstruction Acts required that the new state constitutions enfranchise the freedmen. After the delegates drafted the state's constitution, elections would take place for approving or rejecting the constitution and electing men to state offices and the U.S. Congress. The new state legislatures would have to ratify the Fourteenth Amendment before a state's congressional leaders would be eligible to assume their places in Washington. When Congress gave permission for southern congressmen and senators to take their seats, military reconstruction would end and the state's civil government could begin exercising its legal authority.

The use of the U.S. Army by Congress to implement Reconstruction's unusual political changes was a radical step in U.S. history. Certainly, it seemed that way to many nineteenth-century Americans, especially most white southerners and many northern Democrats. Congressional Reconstruction instituted political changes that carried significant social implications, requiring that state constitutions give certain types of persons (African-American men) the right to vote. Moreover, in order for a state's senators and congressmen to regain their voices, Congress demanded that state legislatures ratify a proposed amendment to the U.S. Constitution.

No doubt it would have **been** possible to make the process more radical. **Congress** could have included provisions **banning** top Confederates from voting and holding office for many years. Confiscated or federal lands might have been given to the freedmen, and a federally supported system of schools and colleges for blacks could have been provided. These steps, in addition to the radical ones that were taken, probably would have meant greater results for Reconstruction and, likewise, a longer involvement of the army in the South.

As it was, congressional leaders were unable to put their plan into effect without President Johnson. In his role as commander in chief, he chose the generals who supervised the military districts. General Grant exerted some influence on Johnson's choices, which included John M. Schofield for the First District (Virginia), Daniel E. Sickles for the Second District (North and South Carolina), John Pope for the Third District (Georgia, Florida, and Alabama), Edward O. C. Ord for the Fourth District (Mississippi and Arkansas), and Sheridan for the Fifth District (Louisiana and Texas).

These and other generals were divided in their attitudes toward Reconstruction. A conservative at heart, Schofield opposed black suffrage and doubted the propriety of the congressional acts, but he enforced them unflinchingly and removed pro-Confederate politicians, including a governor. Ord was moderate on the race issue but evolved into a stern administrator. Pope, Sickles, and Sheridan favored congressional Reconstruction. Sheridan removed the governors of both Texas and Louisiana. The radical trio enforced the acts of Congress in a scrupulous fashion and therefore ran afoul of Johnson in the coming months. General Sherman was uncomfortable with military Reconstruction but believed that ex-Confederates had failed to accommodate themselves to the outcome of the war. General Grant concluded that the Republicans, and not Johnson, had the right idea about the nation's needs during Reconstruction and acted in concert with the leaders of Lincoln's party. Other generals, such as Winfield Scott Hancock and Meade, either were Democrats or wished for a speedy and easy restoration.

During 1867 and into 1868, the generals pushed to complete the congressional plan. Showing their disgust for the Reconstruction Acts, various southern state and local officials resigned. The district commanders removed others, usually after they had obstructed federal laws, discriminated against blacks, or in some other way had been "impediments to Reconstruction," in the phrase used by the generals. Local and state offices of all kinds thus fell vacant, and the district commanders filled them with their appointees.

Johnson demonstrated his opposition to congressional Reconstruction by removing four of the district commanders. At the president's order, in August 1868, General Edward R. S. Canby stepped in for Sickles, and General Hancock, an outspoken conservative, took over for Sheridan. Reversing or watering down some of Sheridan's directives in the Fifth District, Hancock scored points with his Democratic supporters. Canby turned out to be one of the most evenhanded district commanders, but he enforced the letter of the law and southerners did not like him. In December, again at Johnson's order, Major General Meade, recognized as a moderate, replaced Pope, and Major General Alvin Gillem took Ord's place. To Johnson's surprise, and demonstrating how difficult it was

to predict a general's actions, Meade deposed the governor of Georgia and made an army officer acting governor.

On top of his reassignments of Sheridan, Sickles, Pope, and Ord, Johnson removed Secretary of War Edwin M. Stanton in August and replaced him with temporary substitutes, including Generals Grant and Schofield. Stanton protested Johnson's actions, and the radicals in Congress had hoped to protect Stanton with the Tenure of Office Act, a law of dubious constitutionality passed over Johnson's veto on 2 March. As Harold Hyman argues in a landmark essay (1960), with military forces in both the West and the South, Johnson was commander in chief of what were essentially two distinct armies, so different were their missions. The Republicans let the president control the Indian-fighting army but opposed him when he began interfering with the Reconstruction army.

The showdown resulted in Johnson's impeachment on 24 February 1868. According to the U.S. Constitution, impeachment proceedings could be applied to any federal officeholder for "treason, bribery, or other high crimes and misdemeanors." Two-thirds of the House of Representatives were needed to impeach (indict) an official and two-thirds of the Senate needed to convict and remove him. The impeachment power had been used sparingly since 1789. Eight of the eleven items on the Johnson bill of impeachment dealt in some way with the removal of Stanton. The ninth item concerned the president's supposed violation of another dubious law, passed on 2 March 1867, the Command of the Army Act, which supposedly required the president to send all orders to the army by way of General of the Army Grant. The two other items were poorly phrased or vaguely worded catchalls drawn up to snare the votes of senators who might not go along with the first nine. In May 1868, Johnson escaped conviction and removal by only one vote in the Senate, but the impeachment and trial combined to restrain the president. His personal political aspirations now curtailed, Johnson had slowed the process but failed to block the path of the nation's Reconstruction.

The army guided the southern states down that path, but violence marred the process prescribed by Congress. Shootings, assaults, and arson took place in numbers that indicated the army had too few soldiers to police the entire region. Former Confederates realized that they could commit these crimes with impunity. At the same time, while they prosecuted a form of guerrilla warfare, southern Democrats complained loudly about "bayonet rule" and "military despotism." By using such loaded terms, the Democrats were implying that the U.S. Army was acting illegally or improperly to carry out the Reconstruction Acts passed by Congress. If violence threatened or occurred, the army usually responded as a *posse comitatus.* Marching or riding with local sheriffs or U.S. marshals who requested their aid, the soldiers assisted the civilian lawmen in making arrests. Sometimes the army acted on its own and arrested suspects without civilian officials present, although mayors, governors, or state attorneys-general could call for the army's assistance.

In June 1868, seven former Confederate states had completed the requirements of the Military Reconstruction Acts. At one stroke Alabama, Arkansas, Florida, Georgia, Louisiana, North Carolina, and South Carolina all regained their representation in Congress and thereby were readmitted to the Union. Army units remained stationed in the South, not only garrisoning posts, forts, and arsenals that they had used in the antebellum years, but also occupying barracks in some of the region's larger cities.

In both the recently readmitted states and those that had not yet met the requirements, the army guarded the southern polls during the presidential election of 1868. The Republicans nominated General Grant, and former Governor Horatio Seymour of New York was the choice of the Democrats. In several states vigilante groups such as the Ku Klux Klan intimidated white Republicans and the newly enfranchised freedmen. The Klan and similar organizations, such as the Knights of the White Camelia in Louisiana, presented a significant challenge to the army. By the fall of 1868, fewer than eighteen thousand soldiers occupied the South, and they were unable to guard every ballot box, protect the life of each Republican, or patrol every highway. The Klan rode, day and night, threatening or shooting Republicans, burning houses and schools, escaping ahead of army patrols. Brigadier General Lovell H. Rousseau, one of Hancock's successors and President Johnson's political friend, commanded troops in Louisiana during the election. Rousseau's tardy actions were either inept or disingenuous, and despite a large black voting population, Louisiana and Georgia went for Seymour in his losing bid for the presidency.

After Grant's election, the army was still faced with the task of preparing the remaining southern states for readmission. Texas, by virtue of its size, frontier conditions, and confused political circumstances, was particularly troublesome. Military commanders had to worry about hostile Indians in the central and western parts of the state. Following Sheridan's departure, General Joseph J. Reynolds eventually commanded the troops in Texas, and although he devoted considerable time to the Indians and the frontier, he became involved in state politics as a Republican and sought election as U.S. senator from Texas. Reynolds ordered his troops to suppress Klanlike groups in east Texas. In some cases the lawless men were simply bandits, and the army assisted U.S. marshals in tracking them down. In a few cases politically motivated vigilantes directly confronted the army, but usually they dispersed or escaped before the soldiers arrived on the scene. Until Texas was readmitted in 1870, trials for some lawbreakers were held before military commissions.

Georgia was another difficult test for the army. The Georgia legislature balked at seating some elected black representatives, and in December 1869 the state went back under military control. The Freedmen's Bureau had documented more than three hundred cases of politically inspired assault in Georgia during 1868. In 1870, President Grant sent General Alfred H. Terry to replace Meade. Terry established a special three-officer board to hear the cases involving the disputed legislative seats. Eventually the

Georgia legislature was reconstituted, and, after it ratified the Fifteenth Amendment, which prohibits the denial of suffrage on account of race, the state's congressmen and senators were reseated in 1870. Virginia also completed Reconstruction in 1870.

After the readmission of the southern states, the army's role in the South diminished, but it never was completely without influence, especially in South Carolina and Louisiana. The generals no longer operated military commissions, but Republican governors (and sometimes Democratic ones) called on the army to enforce civil law and keep the peace. During the 1870s the army continued to provide guards at polling places on election days, and occasionally soldiers acted as referees between rival claimants to gubernatorial offices in southern states.

During the 1870s the army's duties were made more difficult by the declining numbers of troops available for duty in the South. At the time of the Military Reconstruction Acts, more than twenty-thousand soldiers were in the southern states. One year later there were fewer than eighteen thousand, and by late 1869 there were only slightly more than eleven thousand troops occupying the territory of the old Confederacy. The number continued to decline in succeeding years for three reasons. First, and perhaps most important, was the need for more soldiers to fight the Indians on the Plains. The second reason was that the longer Reconstruction lasted, the less support it received from northerners and Congress as they turned their attention to the Indian wars, western settlement, and business expansion. The third reason for declining troop strength in support of Reconstruction also pertained to economics. The nineteenth-century Congress was much more tightfisted than the free-spending solons of the twentieth century. Politicians, especially Democrats, minutely scrutinized War Department budgets and often reduced them to the bare minimum to allow operations. Congress demanded reductions in the size of the regular army from sixty thousand in 1865 to about thirty thousand in 1871, and to about twenty-seven thousand in 1876. When all the former Confed-

erate states gained readmission in 1870, there were fewer and fewer troops to go around.

Increasingly, officers avoided Reconstruction duty by taking extended leaves, going on recruiting duty, or accepting assignments away from their regiments. In letters or in testimony before congressional committees, they expressed their desire to be out of the South and serving instead on the frontier. Officers who later wrote memoirs described at length their experiences in the West, but often skipped over their service in the South altogether or mentioned it only briefly. After 1870 some army officers became impatient with escorting U.S. marshals, arresting moonshiners who refused to pay federal revenue taxes, or chasing down white-sheeted Klansmen in South Carolina. Such actions offered no opportunity for glory or advancement, and many officers thought it was duty without honor.

Despite these attitudes, however, officers and soldiers carried out their assigned tasks in the latter part of Reconstruction, rendering invaluable aid to black and white Republicans and supporting the legally elected state governments. Moreover, the officers in the South often had to act with very little guidance from their superiors in Washington. The secretary of war, the adjutant general, and President Grant all usually left important decisions to the officer on the scene.

For a time it appeared that organizations like the Ku Klux Klan would sweep the South and remove all the Republicans from their elected offices. General Terry suggested that the army pick one state and kill the Klan at the roots. Acting under Enforcement Acts passed by Congress in 1870–1871, to enforce the Fourteenth and Fifteenth Amendments, President Grant singled out South Carolina. The army went to work there with a vengeance against the Klan; army units also acted in other states. Several companies of the Seventh Cavalry were sent into nine South Carolina counties where the president had declared martial law. Patrols were constant and U.S. marshals with strong military escorts arrested hundreds of Klansmen. The Klansmen stood trial in regular federal courts and dozens were convicted. Others were set free, but at least for a time they had been incarcerated and out of circulation.

Army patrols and federal prosecutors broke the power of the Klan, but former Confederates switched tactics. They formed "gun clubs" that claimed to be "hunting" on election days when actually they were stalking their quarry near polling places. Other Democrats used economic threats against blacks—reduced wages, loss of jobs, or the like—to get them to vote for Democrats or to sit out elections. Despite Democratic sniping, murder, and arson, brave Republican precinct leaders (white and black), vocal newspaper editors, and courageous elected officials continued to hold out in several southern states. As historian George C. Rable emphasizes (1984), the Democrats fine-tuned their use of violence in order to bring down Republican administrations in the South.

As for election duty in the 1870s, the army's main job was to keep the peace. Commanders did not always wait for civil authorities to invite them to act. In the larger cities military commanders paraded their soldiers through the main streets to discourage violence. Troops watched voters in selected precincts or patrolled entire wards where violence was likely to occur. After the election was over, soldiers usually guarded the ballot boxes themselves to prevent tampering or fraud.

The General Amnesty Act of 1872 allowed more ex-Confederates to participate legally in politics once again. They registered to vote in great numbers, and, combined with their selective use of terror and intimidation, the Democrats won back control of southern state governments one by one. Furthermore, revelations of corruption in the Grant administration and a lessening in Republican radicalism resulted in what some historians later termed a "retreat from Reconstruction."

Rivalry between claimants to governorships involved the army in two states before the election turmoil of 1876–1877. Two Republicans in Arkansas, Joseph Brooks and Elisha Baxter, claimed to have been elected governor in 1872.

Democrats supported Baxter, if only to divide the Arkansas Republican party. Baxter held office from 1872 until 1874, when he was ousted by Brooks. The commander of the army garrison at Little Rock, Captain Thomas E. Rose, believed at first that he could maintain order until the authorities in Washington decided which of the claimants deserved the office, but he had a difficult time keeping the militias of the two "governors" apart. Outside of Little Rock the two sides clashed in several bloody encounters and Rose was helpless. Finally, President Grant recognized Baxter and ordered both militias to disperse. Rose breathed a sigh of relief when the antagonists did as the president ordered.

In Louisiana the situation was even more complex, but in the final analysis both the army and the Grant administration supported the Republican claimants to office. Fearing a yellow-fever epidemic in 1874, the army garrisoned Louisiana with only a handful of soldiers. These few failed to stop the overthrow of the Republican governor, William Pitt Kellogg, in September 1874. Several thousand armed men attacked the state militia and took possession of the state capitol in New Orleans. Only one company (about forty soldiers) was in the city at the time, and they elected to remain out of the fighting, in which twenty-five men were killed and more than one hundred wounded.

In a matter of hours the telegraph lines were buzzing between Washington and General William Emory's temporary headquarters in Mississippi. Troops were sent from Mississippi to New Orleans, arriving within a matter of hours after the fighting. President Grant issued a executive proclamation demanding that the rebels disperse within five days or face the might of the U.S. Army. The Democrats who had engineered the coup denied that they were usurping the government and boldly asked for recognition from Grant. Two days after the takeover, General Emory arrived in New Orleans, and soon he was supported by more than seven hundred soldiers from three regiments. The Democrats reluctantly yielded possession of the capitol and other state buildings they had captured and occupied. Kellogg resumed his office a couple of days later, after army Colonel John R. Brooke had temporarily acted as military governor.

By 1876 only three southern states still had Republican governors—Louisiana, South Carolina, and Florida. Following the disputed presidential election of 1876—when Republicans successfully challenged the votes of four states accused of irregularities, leading to the election of their candidate Rutherford B. Hayes—soldiers protected the Republican claimants to the governorships of South Carolina and Louisiana until the new president decided to withdraw the army's support and allow the Democratic candidates to become governors of the two states. In each state before the election the Democrats had carried out programs of intimidation against black and white Republicans. The results of each election are shrouded in the fog of fraud and violence, and the debate will continue as to who would have won in a fair, open, and nonviolent contest. Hayes, however, allowed the Democrats to take office, and Reconstruction and the army's unique role in it finally came to an end in April 1877.

Reconstruction was the army's second significant experience with military government, but it lasted much longer than such duties after the Mexican War. During Reconstruction the army had to occupy some of the states of its own nation, contribute to rebuilding their economies, and support the creation of a new social order, imperfect as it was. A few officers, such as Sheridan and Pope, enforced the Military Reconstruction Acts to the letter, and a few others, such as Hancock and Rousseau, tried to circumvent the laws or sided with the Democrats. Most officers, however, tried to administer the extraordinary laws evenhandedly. The federal government's policies on Reconstruction changed from president to president and from year to year. After the ratification of the Fourteenth and Fifteenth Amendments and the readmission of the former Confederate states, many northerners and members of Congress lost interest in Reconstruction, leaving small

army detachments to stand between resurgent ex-Confederates and vulnerable Republicans. All of that made Reconstruction the most difficult peacetime duty in the army's history.

THE INDIAN-FIGHTING ARMY

By 1870 the army had completed its legally mandated duties called for under the Military Reconstruction Acts, and senior military officers began turning their attention to other matters—a war in Europe, reform of the services, and Indian-fighting in the trans-Mississippi West. For its traditional, dangerous, and thankless task of fighting Indians, the army had developed no doctrine either before or after the Civil War. Having no set of accepted tactical guidelines for Indian wars, and no strategy for that matter, the burden again fell on individual commanders and resulted in haphazard application of military force.

As was the case with Reconstruction in the South, the army dealt regularly with civilians in the West. Southern duties brought the army into contact with the Freedmen's Bureau, its agents, teachers, and, of course, the freedmen themselves. High-ranking officers met with members of Congress and the cabinet and eastern reformers who wanted to improve the lot of the freedmen. Soldiers interracted with southerners from all walks of life as well as with politicians of both parties. In a similar fashion, western duties called for the army to work with the agents of the Bureau of Indian Affairs (part of the Interior Department, not the War Department) and, of course, with the Indians themselves. In Washington, senior officers, especially Commanding General of the Army Sherman and the adjutant general, met with members of Congress and the cabinet and eastern philanthropic organizations who debated how to protect, educate, and "civilize" the Indians. Local, state, and territorial politicians in the West alternately condemned the army for its timidity or complimented its field campaigns. In most cases these same politicians sought to gain or keep forts or army depots in the area they represented. On many occasions soldiers came in contact with ranchers, settlers, businessmen, railroad workers, and miners between the Canadian and Mexican borders. Western expansion and settlement called for the army to build roads, map the country, guard railroads, purchase goods and services, deliver the mail, provide medical care to civilians, and protect Indian reservations. After the collapse of the wartime and immediate postwar treaties with several Indian tribes, the army demonstrated its flexibility in numerous ways in the West, even as some of its main units, such as the Seventh Cavalry, remained on duty in the South. As in the southern states, the army in the West had too few soldiers to accomplish everything that everyone wanted. The territory it covered was too vast and the demands too many.

The army approached Indian warfare by combining several factors. Soldiers built forts and depots and set up temporary cantonments to keep pace with the settlers and railroad construction. In fact, railroad resupply often helped maintain and move army units in the trans-Mississippi. The forts and supply depots provided bases from which expeditions took the field. Typical forts, unlike the ones in Hollywood films or television melodramas, were not surrounded by wooden palisades. Instead, rows of clapboard buildings clustered around a large parade ground. Usually garrisoned by a combination of infantry and cavalry units, most forts had a lifespan of ten or fifteen years before they were closed and their units consolidated at a larger post, often near a town or city.

When a crisis loomed or a clash occurred between Indians and whites, the soldiers, usually the cavalry but sometimes a joint column of horse and infantry units, sortied from the fort to restore order. They arrested whites who illegally crossed onto Indian lands and returned marauding Indians to their reservations. Routinely, small detachments of ten to twenty troopers went on patrols (called "scouts"), checking for signs of Indian raiders or wayward hunting parties, watching for white miners or settlers who trespassed on the reservations, and

making maps of the region. Like modern police cars cruising sectors of urban terrain in order to deter or detect criminal activity, army units typically performed a police function rather than preparing for and conducting large-scale combat operations.

In the unusual event of a major campaign, the army's senior officer in the West outlined a plan of action for four or five heavy columns of soldiers. Lieutenant General Sheridan sketched out the opening movements of the multicolumn campaigns of 1874–1875 and 1876–1878, the two largest such efforts in the trans-Mississippi Indian wars. He left most of the details of the 1870s campaigns to the column commanders and their subordinates and declined to take the field in either case. Although Sheridan relied on multiple columns, the tactic had been suggested before the Civil War by Winfield Scott and Montgomery Meigs. When they caught Indians ensconced in a lightly guarded winter encampment (as happened in 1868 and 1874), soldiers inflicted devastating defeats on the tribes.

To patrol the West the army recruited volunteers, as was the standard practice in times without a major war. At any one time, perhaps 50 percent of U.S. soldiers were European-born immigrants recently arrived in eastern cities. The typical enlistment was for five years, and military service allowed the immigrant-soldiers, mostly Irish, to become acclimated to America, earn some money (about $13 a month for a private), and receive free transportation to the West.

In the months following the Civil War the army's Ordnance Department concluded that a new standard issue rifle was needed for the service—a breechloader rather than the old-style muzzleloader. Accordingly, after testing several weapons, the Ordnance Department adopted the Model 1873 Springfield rifle, originally a .50–.70 caliber. After additional experimenting, the caliber was changed to .45–.70 for the infantry version and .45–.55 for the shorter cavalry carbine. The Model 1873 possessed advantages over the standard issue infantry shoulder weapon of the Civil War, the .58-caliber Springfield Model 1855 (modified in 1861). The

Model 1873 was breechloaded rather than muzzleloaded, and it accepted a centerfire copper cartridge rather than using a tear-open paper cartridge that contained the so-called minié ball. The cartridges for the Model 1873 still used heavy-grain black powder, however, rather than a fine-grain fast-burning powder, and, like the earlier Springfield rifles, was only single shot. A soldier fed one round at a time through a pop-up door in the top of the barrel, thus giving the Model 1873 its distinctive nickname, the "trapdoor" Springfield. Until the changeover was complete, some cavalry units still carried other carbine models, including the seven-shot Spencer.

Although the trapdoor Springfield had some advantages, there was a problem with its ejector mechanism. After a soldier fired ten or fifteen shots, the barrel became hot, sometimes causing the soft copper base of the cartridge to stick in the breech. The trooper needed a knife to pry out the spent shell before inserting a new round. Having to take such action in the midst of combat was, of course, both disconcerting and potentially dangerous. Nevertheless, the trapdoor Springfield became the army's standard shoulder weapon. The rifle possessed tremendous stopping power: When its large bullet hit either man or beast, the target came down. It provided the added advantage of uniformity of ammunition among infantry and cavalry units. The Ordnance Department expected the single-shot rifle to reduce ammunition expenditure and therefore cost less to use than an updated version of the seven-shot Spencer carbine, which had been issued to some Union cavalry regiments in the Civil War.

Not every soldier was satisfied with the trapdoor Springfield, but an overwhelming number responded favorably to the Ordnance Department's selection of other items. The .45-caliber 1872 Colt pistol became the standard-issue sidearm. Popular with civilians as well as soldiers, the "Peacemaker," as the pistol was called, had been issued to most units by 1874. Some troopers obtained canvas or leather cartridge belts on their own, but by 1876 such belts were general issue, replacing the old-style, flip-open cartridge boxes. In the years to come, the Ordnance and Quartermaster departments continued to make modifications in weapons, uniforms, and equipment.

Utilizing this equipment against the Sioux, Cheyenne, Comanche, Apache, or other tribes severely tested the army and its conventional, constabulary organization. When the army changed from police patrols to larger campaigns, it demonstrated spotty performance against the guerrillalike tribesmen. Although Indians seldom used prearranged battle plans, they naturally sought any advantage that terrain or weather provided and relied upon stealth, surprise, speed of movement, and deception. Combining such concepts or military principles sometimes produced victories for the Indians, especially against isolated or poorly led army detachments. At other times the Indians abandoned their villages and fought rearguard actions, using their tactics to stave off a severe defeat. From the point of view of the Indians, staying to fight in a disadvantageous circumstance only invited defeat in detail at the hands of the army. Dispersing and reassembling for another opportunity for combat was a typical Indian maneuver. Therefore, army officers, frustrated after numerous scouts produced nothing, concluded that locating a sizable force of warriors or an entire village was half the contest; bringing the warriors to battle or destroying the logistical resources contained in the village was the other half. Consequently, in major campaigns the army moved its conventional units in such strength that it focused on making contact, fighting the engagement, and pursuing the enemy, rather than showing concern about being outnumbered, cut off, or defeated.

The post–Civil War campaigns started badly for the army. At a time when many of the top officers were serving in the South, Captain William J. Fetterman brazenly proclaimed that he could lead two companies of soldiers into the heart of Sioux territory. Stationed at Fort Phil Kearny in Wyoming Territory in late 1866 to help guard the Bozeman Trail, Fetterman and other officers had opportunities to observe the Sioux in action. Colonel Henry B. Carrington,

Fort Phil Kearny's senior officer, believed in acting cautiously away from the safety of the fort. Rather than studying the enemy's capabilities, however, Fetterman decided that other detachment commanders lacked élan. Using an attack on a wood-gathering detail from the fort as a decoy, the Sioux planned to ambush the force that sortied to rescue the workers. Itching to take a crack at the Sioux, Fetterman picked a detachment of mounted infantry (fifty men) and cavalry (twenty-eight men); two civilians also accompanied the impetuous officer. An unknown number of Sioux wiped out Fetterman's command on 21 December only a few miles from the fort. A combat officer with battlefield experience against Confederates in the Civil War, Fetterman underestimated and misjudged the Sioux. To commemorate the captain's aggressive spirit (but presumably not his faults), in 1867 the army named a new post in Wyoming Fort Fetterman.

In 1867 the army fought two other notable skirmishes on the North Plains, the so-called Hayfield Fight (1 August), near Fort C. F. Smith in Montana Territory, and the Wagon Box Fight (2 August), near Fort Phil Kearny. In both instances, large groups of Sioux or Cheyenne attacked isolated detachments less than half the size of Fetterman's but failed to defeat them. These fights seemed to indicate that determined soldiers armed with breechloaders could stand off hundreds of Indians and may have offset some of the negative consequences of the Fetterman defeat. Such defensive stand-offs, however, were not going to clear the northern Plains for the wave of white settlers, miners, ranchers, farmers, and railroaders.

In the same year, Major General Winfield Scott Hancock initiated a campaign against the Cheyenne and Kiowa in Kansas. Those Indians had been buying weapons from traders and had used them in response to Hancock's attack on the Indian village at Pawnee Fork in western Kansas. Commanding units from the Seventh Cavalry and the Thirty-seventh Infantry (about fourteen hundred soldiers altogether), Hancock and his officers chased the warriors from Fort Riley in central Kansas to Colorado Territory

and back again. Hancock's top subordinate, Lieutenant Colonel George A. Custer, received his introduction to Indian warfare in Kansas. From April to July 1867, Custer rode far, skirmished occasionally, and accomplished little. Mostly the campaign created ill-will between the army on the one hand and the Indians and the Indian Bureau on the other. It also tarnished Hancock's lustrous military reputation. As one of the Union's heroes of the Battle of Gettysburg, Hancock's major generalcy was secure, but his fumbling behavior on the Plains demonstrated again that most army officers found it difficult to make the transition from conventional combat to Indian-fighting. Despite Hancock's efforts and the signing of the major treaty of Medicine Lodge at Barber County, Kansas, in October 1867, groups of Cheyenne and warriors from other tribes continued their attacks on settlers and ranchers.

Consequently, the following year the army mounted one of its most important post–Civil War campaigns, the South Plains campaign of 1868–1869. Sheridan conferred with Sherman and drew up a plan, which called for Sheridan himself (then commanding the Military Department of the Missouri) to take the field. In its destructive potential the plan bore a similarity to Sherman's march to the sea and Sheridan's Shenandoah Valley campaign. As the weather chilled, strong army columns set out from forts in Kansas, Colorado Territory, and New Mexico Territory, converging on the suspected locations of winter campsites of hostile bands. The soldiers were to engage the warriors and damage or destroy their villages—in other words, the Indians' logistics bases. If it was not total war, it was something close to it. The Indians could not survive the winter without tepees, blankets, stored food, weapons, and horses. Their alternatives were either to surrender, accept the government's rations, and be confined on restricted reservations, or to die—which some preferred to do. A plan on paper was one thing, but finding and defeating the Indians was another matter. Cold-weather campaigning strained the army's heavy-wagon supply system and ruined many of its grain-fed horses. In contrast to previous efforts, however, the South Plains campaign produced devastating results.

On the snowy morning of 27 November, Custer and the Seventh Cavalry (about seven hundred soldiers) located and attacked the large Cheyenne village of Chief Black Kettle on the Washita River in Indian Territory (Oklahoma). As was his custom from Civil War days, Custer disdained much reconnaissance and struck precipitously. A brisk skirmish resulted, forcing most of the Cheyenne out of the camp. Finding evidence that some of the village's warriors had committed raids on settlements in Kansas, Custer ordered his soldiers to set fire to the village. Meanwhile, Major Joel H. Elliott and fifteen troopers had galloped off in pursuit of the fleeing Cheyenne. When threatened by hundreds of warriors from other nearby Indian camps (who were closer than he realized), Custer ordered his men to kill more than eight hundred Indian horses, destroying the transportation and offensive capability of the Cheyenne. Custer thereupon abandoned the ruined camp (and Major Elliott), escaping with his regiment from a potential Indian trap. Elliott and his detachment were later found, all dead. Even a large rescue party might have met the same fate, but Elliott's death and Custer's refusal to send help to him inflamed animosities among officers in the Seventh Cavalry.

The Washita engagement and Custer's subsequent punitive patrols indicated the army's destructive power in this conflict between two cultures. It showed that the army could put two thousand soldiers in the field and sustain them under adverse weather conditions. The Plains Indians found it impossible to abide by Anglo-American notions of boundaries and restrictions. The army, for its part, often found itself attempting to prevent white encroachment on Indian lands at the same time it was seeking out Indian raiding parties. The unstoppable wave of white settlers—whether ranchers, European immigrants, railroad builders, or workers from eastern cities—had little regard for the Indians or the sanctity of their lands. This inexorable wave of settlement transformed the trans-Mississippi landscape and destroyed the buffalo, on

which the Plains Indians depended for their livelihood. Hunters slaughtered the buffalo nearly to the point of extinction. If the Indians resisted, in their uncoordinated fashion, they suffered at the hands of the army and the settlers. When the Indians decided not to resist, they were shunted off to ever-smaller, less-desirable reservation lands.

Winter or summer, the army was determined to find and fight bands or whole tribes that rejected the white man's law or stood in the way of the expansion of the rival culture. As needed, the army shifted its forces to deal with particular tribes. For example, soldiers nearly wiped out the Piegan in a winter attack in Montana (1870), suppressed the Modoc on the West Coast (1872–1873), and several times pursued the Kiowa and Lipan-Apache across the border into Mexico (1873–1877).

To complete the subjugation of the South Plains tribes, the army conducted another multicolumn campaign, the Red River War of 1874–1875. Five powerful army expeditionary forces marched in Texas, New Mexico Territory, and Indian Territory. The most damage was inflicted by the column under Colonel Ranald S. Mackenzie, commander of the Fourth Cavalry, who developed into one of the army's most successful Indian fighters. In September 1874, Mackenzie's men rode into a large encampment of Comanche, Kiowa, Arapaho, and Cheyenne at Palo Duro Canyon in the Texas Panhandle. The Indians sustained only a handful of casualties before they escaped. Mackenzie took over the village and, like Custer at the Washita, destroyed the Indian supplies, food, weapons, blankets, and tepees and killed or captured one thousand horses. During the next six months, hundreds of tribesmen and their families surrendered themselves at army posts or Indian reservations. Subsequently, some of their main leaders were imprisoned in Florida. With the exception of scattered outbreaks of violence, the power of the South Plains tribes was broken.

On the North Plains, railroad builders and mining entrepreneurs coveted rights-of-way and access to tribal lands held sacred by the Sioux. Military exploring parties pointed out the best routes and confirmed rumors of gold in the Black Hills of the Dakotas. Intrusions on Indian lands and evident Anglo-American intent to acquire the lands in question pushed most of the Teton Sioux and Northern Cheyenne, as well as some Arapaho and other Sioux bands, to the brink of war in the winter of 1875–1876. Some left the reservations, and others, who had never come into the agencies, assembled along the Little Bighorn River.

In some ways this extraordinary gathering of Indians helped the army. Its size made it easier for civilian scouts or Indian auxiliaries to track and locate the enemy. Initially, Sheridan's outline of campaign called for another winter-weather success. Various problems, including severe weather, lack of cooperation among subordinate commanders, and strong Indian resistance, turned the army's main effort into a summer expedition. Sheridan allowed distractions to occupy his time and failed to coordinate the campaign.

Adhering to Sheridan's outline, three powerful columns, totaling about twenty-six hundred soldiers and Indian auxiliaries, aimed to crush the Plains tribes in Montana Territory. One column marched eastward from Fort Ellis, Montana, including several companies each from the Seventh Infantry and Second Cavalry (about five hundred soldiers), commanded by the doughty Brevet Major General John Gibbon, colonel of the Seventh Infantry Regiment. The second column moved northward from its base at Fort Fetterman, Wyoming Territory, and was led by Brevet Major General George Crook, holder of a controversial but productive record against the Apache in Arizona Territory. Crook's forces totaled eleven hundred soldiers and more than two hundred Indian auxiliaries. Brigadier General Alfred Terry, the senior field commander, led the third column, marching westward from Fort Abraham Lincoln, Dakota Territory. Terry's column contained all of Custer's Seventh Cavalry (750 officers and men) plus units of the Sixth Infantry (one company), Seventeenth Infantry (two companies), Twentieth Infantry (a detachment of thirty-one men with Gatling guns), and Terry's headquarters

(twelve soldiers), nearly nine hundred officers and men altogether. This was the largest and most capably led of all the army's post–Civil War Indian campaigns, although small when contrasted to Civil War armies. Lacking only Sheridan's central coordination, it became the most sustained conventional campaign of the Indian wars.

The number of Indian combatants assembled in the Yellowstone River–Little Bighorn vicinity remains in dispute. The estimates vary from around fifteen hundred to more than four thousand, or even perhaps six thousand. In any event, the Plains had never seen such a multitribal gathering before, and a reasonable estimate is approximately fifteen hundred warriors from the extraordinary Indian encampments. Furthermore, these Indians, the Sioux especially, planned to fight, not to hit and run or skirmish and withdraw.

Led by Crazy Horse, an exceptional warrior who used all of his influence to keep the warriors together, the Sioux already had defeated Crook's column in southern Montana along Rosebud Creek. On 17 June 1876, Crook's troopers fought for six hours (a remarkable engagement itself) and suffered more than twenty killed and fifty wounded before retreating all the way back to a base camp in Wyoming. The tenacity and unexpected belligerence of the Indians shook Crook's self-confidence, deflecting his column southward and out of the battle on the Little Bighorn, where his men were needed to complete the ring around the Indians. Had Crook resumed his march toward the Yellowstone River, at least word of his advance might have undermined the Indian alliance. At best, some of his troops could have contributed to the Battle of the Little Bighorn itself or been available to mount a proper pursuit. Instead, after taking less than 10 percent casualties among his soldiers, Crook abandoned the field, failed to inform Terry of his whereabouts, and left open the southern area of the campaign.

Receiving no word from Crook as to his decision to retreat, Terry, Gibbon, and Custer met on 21 June in the cabin of a steamboat to discuss the campaign. Terry authorized Custer to forge ahead, giving the Seventh Cavalry's field commander flexible orders to use his own discretion about engaging the enemy. Echoing Fetterman's boast, but elevating it to an epic scale, Custer reputedly stated that he could "whip all the Indians on the continent with the Seventh Cavalry." Minus the band and others on detached duty, the regiment mounted 647 men who rode toward the Little Bighorn.

On 25 June, more than twenty-four hours ahead of the forces of Gibbon and Terry, Custer found the huge Indian assemblage. Interpreting his orders to his own satisfaction, he decided to attack—in part, at least, because he was concerned that the Indians might flee before battle could be joined—but Custer made four decisions that compounded the problems in the battle before him. First, prior to riding ahead of the main column, Custer rejected Terry's offer of taking several companies of the Second Cavalry from Gibbon's command; Custer wanted the glory that awaited only for himself and the Seventh Regiment. Second, as was his habit, he had disdained much reconnaissance for fear of alerting the Indians and perhaps scaring them away. Third, in the face of a superior enemy force of unknown numbers, Custer divided his regiment into four parts; probably he became aware of the enemy's strength only after the battle was underway. Finally, by dividing his regiment, Custer kept with his battalion the officers who were his best and most dependable subordinates. If his brothers and friends, however, had been with the other battalions, an argument can be made that they would have responded to the sounds of heavy firing and to Custer's scribbled messages to come quickly and bring more ammunition. Custer and almost one-third of his regiment (212 officers and soldiers) were killed in the battle. The other battalions suffered losses totaling fifty-three killed and sixty wounded.

The Battle of the Little Bighorn marked the high point of Indian resistance to Anglo-American encroachment on their lands. It also prompted an exceptional response from the United States and its army. Grant, Sherman, and Sheridan all had been enjoying the festivities celebrating the nation's Centennial in Philadelphia. Custer's defeat forced them to turn some of their attention to the war at hand. Congress authorized an increase of twenty-five hundred soldiers for the regular army. Terry, Gibbon, Crook, and other officers reorganized their columns, and reinforcements arrived in the North Plains. The army's pursuit of the Indians who won at the Little Bighorn lasted for twenty-four months and drove the battle's victors onto reservations or across the Canadian border. Crazy Horse was killed on 7 September 1877 at Camp Robinson, Nebraska, and Sitting Bull fled into Canada. In addition, Colonel Nelson A. Miles and General O. O. Howard launched a campaign against the Nez Percé through Montana and into Idaho, forcing that tribe and its renowned leader, Chief Joseph, to surrender on 5 October 1877. Using conventional field forces, in winter and summer, by the end of 1879 the army had broken the power of the North Plains tribes.

Although soldiers fought occasional skirmishes and rode on dozens of patrols on the North Plains after 1879, the army began shifting its attention to the Southwest, where the Apache blocked white expansion. Under the leadership of Crook and Miles, the campaign to completely defeat the Apaches took seven more years. The Apache wars challenged the army with the most grueling guerrilla-style combat since the poorly conducted Second Seminole War in Florida (1835–1842).

From 1871 to 1875, Crook had built a creditable record in Arizona; he knew the terrain and the tribesmen intimately. Taken off this familiar ground and moved to the North Plains in 1876, he had failed to win the kind of glorious victory that might have earned him a major-generalcy and changed much else besides. Had Crook's column defeated Crazy Horse at the Rosebud, all that came after that battle might have been quite different. Following a defeat, Crazy Horse's leadership might have waned and the fragile Indian alliance might have weakened or fallen apart, thus affecting the outcome of the Battle of the Little Bighorn a few days later. Furthermore, speculation abounds about Custer's objectives in 1876: If he had scored a spectacular battlefield victory, he surely would have won promotion to brigadier general and perhaps would have sought the Democratic presidential nomination in 1880 (which went instead to Hancock).

In contrast to Custer, Crook was not a high-profile public figure, and a political career for him was unlikely. Crook's earlier success against the Apache had earned him respect from those Indians but no more than grudging acknowledgment from his fellow officers and little recognition from the public. Crook did not help his own cause. He was irascible, possessed of complete self-assurance that he was right and most other officers were wrong when it came to fighting Indians. Crook and his peers parted company over his consistent reliance on Indian auxiliaries and his use of mobile pack mules rather than heavy wagons to carry supplies. Furthermore, these and other professional differences had estranged Crook from Sheridan, his longtime friend and former West Point classmate. The two had had a falling out over allocation of credit for portions of Union victories in Sheridan's Shenandoah Valley campaign, in which Crook served as a valued corps commander. The Crook-Sheridan feud was one of several that undercut the harmony of the officer corps of the U.S. Army in the 1870s and 1880s. Such animosities often were connected to disagreements originating in the Civil War.

Therefore, when Crook resumed the fight against the Apache in September 1882 (after a stint in the Department of the Platte), he had something to prove. He aimed to refurbish his reputation and achieve promotion to major general by fighting the type of Indian warfare he knew best. Crook called the Apache "the tigers of the human race." Led by the warrior Geronimo, the Apache operated on both sides of the U.S.-Mexican border and played off the Mexican government, the U.S. Army, and the Indian Bureau against one another. Crook, however, may have led the army in patience as well as innovation, and Apache guerrilla tactics did not dismay him. Moreover, Crook wanted to conclude the wars leaving the Apache their self-respect and some of their traditional lands,

views not shared by other senior officers, especially Sheridan, who was appointed commanding general of the army in 1883.

During 1883–1884, Crook and his subordinates, usually commanding units in the field at company strength (about fifty soldiers plus numerous Apache auxiliaries) suppressed an uprising in the Sierra Madre led by Chato, Nana, and Geronimo. Skirmish by skirmish, patrol after patrol, parley by parley, Crook's small mobile units pursued the enemy. These tactics temporarily persuaded many Apache bands to return to reservations under army supervision.

Another outbreak undermined Crook's reputation and again called his tactics into question. Warm Springs and Chiracahua Apache conducted several raids, killing more than thirty settlers. In the resulting Sierra Madre campaign of 1885–1886, Crook again employed his mule-pack trains, small mobile units, and helpful Apache auxiliaries. Sheridan, however, wanted a line of stationary posts along the border and, to resolve the issue, a plan to deport from the Southwest to confinement in the East all Apache, even those who had fought alongside the army. Crook had one more chance to end things his way.

Units composed mostly of Apache auxiliaries led by army captains and lieutenants fanned out into the mountains and across the border into Mexico. Captain Emmet Crawford, one of Crook's best field officers, and Lieutenant Britton Davis led the most effective counterstrikes. Although Crawford was killed in a skirmish, his efforts led to a conference between Geronimo and Crook in Mexico in March 1886. Crook promised to keep up the pursuit until the last hostile Apache was subdued—even "if it takes fifty years," he concluded. Giving in partly to Sheridan's wishes, Crook indicated that some Apache leaders would be locked up for several months in an eastern prison when they surrendered. Heeding Crook's words, Geronimo and other leaders pledged to surrender, but instead resumed fighting a few days later, after Crook had telegraphed Sheridan the news that the campaign had ended.

As far as Sheridan was concerned, Crook had lost his chance. The commanding general applied pressure and expressed doubts about Crook's methods and capabilities. Such pressure produced the result Sheridan desired— Crook requested that he be reassigned. Replacing him in Arizona was the ambitious and aggressive Miles, who had been one of Crook's strongest critics.

Ironically, once Miles had been in Arizona a few days, he saw the wisdom of most of Crook's unorthodox methods, including putting reinforced mobile companies in the field, operating on both sides of the border, and, especially, using Apache auxiliaries to track down the renegades. Miles, too, rejected Sheridan's notion of depending upon a line of fixed positions along the Mexican border. Four months after he took over, Miles forced Geronimo's surrender in September 1886. According to Sheridan's wishes, the most important Apache leaders and warriors went into exile in a Florida prison. The Apache wars were finished.

Often listed as the final battle of the trans-Mississippi wars, the confrontation at Wounded Knee, South Dakota, between reservation Sioux and elements of the Seventh Cavalry in December 1890 was not much more than a police assignment gone awry. In the process of disarming several potentially hostile Sioux, an altercation led to guns being fired on both sides, including four mountain howitzers that the cavalry had set up on a nearby hill. For several minutes the two sides exchanged shots. The soldiers killed 150 Indians and wounded 50 others. The cavalry lost 25 dead and 39 wounded. The mismatch gave the Seventh Cavalry a small measure of revenge for the Little Bighorn, and ended the army's Indian-fighting in a familiar, constabulary role. In the years to come—even into the early twentieth century, the army could not reject completely the possibility of another Indian war.

THE ARMY AND REFORM

By 1890 most officers had put aside Indian-fighting and turned their attention to other concerns. Indeed, twenty years before the tragic events at Wounded Knee, a handful of officers wanted to reject the traditional task of Indian-fighting as the army's primary function. Throughout the 1870s these reformers, mid-ranking officers as well as Sherman and other top generals, sought ways to increase professionalism within the service. Unfortunately for these reformers and their political allies in Congress, the active Indian campaigns of the 1870s, among other things, diluted or distracted the reform efforts. Even as late as the mid-1890s, on the eve of a war with Spain, the reformers could not agree on what needed to be done. Nevertheless, the army took incremental steps toward maturing into a force that would be capable of conducting conventional war in the twentieth century.

From the 1870s to the 1890s, as it considered and adopted some reforms, the army demonstrated a remarkable elasticity in its ability to fulfill multiple purposes. U.S. soldiers have never lacked jobs. Some of the tasks they undertook after Reconstruction were traditional, some were new, others were short-lived, and still others lasted longer than expected and were handed over to another federal agency. For example, the army operated a weather service from 1870 to 1890, at which point it was taken over by the newly established Department of Agriculture. Thus, for twenty years the army kept records on a variety of meteorological and climatological data across the nation. In 1867, President Johnson ordered Brevet Major General Rousseau to lead the official delegation that received Alaska from the Russians. The army stayed on to administer and explore the territory for ten years before giving the duties to civilians. Beginning with Meriwether Lewis and William Clark in 1803, army explorers had gathered a variety of information about the trans-Mississippi. Many post–Civil War patrols acquired valuable geological, botanical, and geographical information while fulfilling their more immediate military orders. Notable among such efforts were those of Colonel William R. Shafter in his numerous scouts during the 1870s across the Llano Estacado (Staked Plain) in Texas and New Mexico.

Few outside the army knew of Shafter's patrols, but more controversial activities caught the public's attention. The Yellowstone expeditions of 1871, 1872, and 1873, the last one led by Colonel David S. Stanley, guarded surveying parties searching for the best railroad route through the Sioux country. The Black Hills expedition of 1874, promoted by Lieutenant Colonel Custer, confirmed the location of gold in the sacred Indian promontories, including the Black Hills, causing prospectors to flood the area and bringing on the Great Sioux War of 1876. On the other hand, scientific and geographical data were the goals of the Wheeler Survey and the Greely Arctic Expedition. Led by Lieutenant George M. Wheeler, a team of soldiers made fourteen field trips between 1871 and 1879 from the Great Plains to the Pacific. Wheeler went on to compile two large volumes describing these activities before the U.S. Geological Survey, a new civilian agency, took over the work. In 1881 Lieutenant Adolphus W. Greely volunteered to take charge of a twenty-five-man scientific group planning to set up a meteorological station in the Arctic. Severe conditions cut the scientists off from resupply. In 1884 a relief party led by a flamboyant naval officer, Commander Winfield Scott Schley, rescued Greely and five other desperate survivors. Two years later, the War Department ordered army officers to administer and protect the priceless handful of U.S. national parks. As the park system grew, the army maintained this responsibility until the nascent National Park Service stepped in in 1918.

Such diverse accomplishments called into question whether the army had a paramount purpose. An unsought adjunct to Indian-fighting and a follow-up to Reconstruction presented itself in the railroad strikes of 1877. In the closest thing that the United States has had to a general strike, thousands of workers walked off their jobs to protest working conditions and low wages. President Rutherford B. Hayes ordered several regiments, some from barracks or forts in the South, to relocate to the East, Midwest, and the trans-Mississippi, where they guarded railyards, locomotives, and rolling stock; they also allowed strikebreakers to cross the picket lines. The president's orders established a precedent. Although the army had been used to restore order in various domestic disturbances be-

fore and during the Civil War, for the next several years the army's strikebreaking duties complemented its constabulary duties against the Indians.

Had the army found its métier as a national police force? Several officers wrote articles in military journals indicating the need to maintain order across the country. Such articles also gave indications of the authors' support for the business community—which abhorred the disruptions and violence that the strikes engendered—and carried antilabor overtones. From 1877 to the mid-1890s, in railyards and coal mines from Pennsylvania to Coeur d'Alene, Idaho, and in Chicago's Pullman Strike of 1894, soldiers acted as strikebreakers, under orders from President Grover Cleveland. Throughout these deployments, the War Department developed no official doctrine for the army to use in labor disturbances. Most officers eventually concluded that their future did not lie with an army that acted as a national police force. Carrying out such duties later moved Colonel William A. Ganoe to label the 1870s as the army's "Dark Ages."

By the late 1870s, the commander of the Military Division of the Atlantic at Governors Island in New York City, General Hancock, had had his fill of Reconstruction and strikebreaking. Hancock and several subordinate officers began discussing the broader roles of the U.S. Army. They were familiar with Great Britain's Royal United Service Institution and knew, of course, that U.S. naval officers had established the U.S. Naval Institute in 1873. Encouraged by Sherman, in September 1878 Hancock helped to form the Military Service Institution (MSI) of the United States, an organization to improve army professionalism. Less than two years later, the MSI had enrolled 550 members (about one-fourth of the officer corps) and published the first issue of its *Journal of the Military Service Institution* (JMSI). Until World War I, *JMSI* was an unofficial but respected means for army officers to express ideas, arguments, and observations on a wide variety of political as well as military subjects. Another similar professional journal, *United Service*, began publication in April 1879.

These journals were the most sophisticated U.S. military periodicals of the nineteenth century and were the forerunners of such twentieth-century publications as *Army* and *Military Review*. *United Service* and *JSMI* included articles on topical matters, such as equipment and Indians, but other essays pointed toward the future. Officers wrote about such issues as field training, multiunit maneuvers, mandatory officer retirement, and developments in European armies.

The Franco-Prussian War of 1870, for example, attracted the attention of U.S. Army officers. During the short conflict General Sheridan obtained official permission to travel in Europe as an observer. Despite this expression of interest in European warfare, however, Sheridan never contributed significantly to army reforms in America. In sharp contrast to Sheridan, General Sherman set the example for army reformers in the post–Civil War era. By necessity he had to devote attention to the West and, like Sheridan, supported the construction of railroads there for military as well as civilian use. Unlike Sheridan, Sherman disapproved of Reconstruction and increasingly spent time trying to make the army a more professional organization and seeking ways to improve military education.

Following the Franco-Prussian War, Sherman and other officers made European tours, visiting several nations, including England, Russia, and Germany. When Sherman inspected the battlefields in France, he gained a favorable impression of Prussian military victories. Preceding Sherman to Europe, Colonel William B. Hazen wrote a book about his own tour entitled *The School of the Army in Germany and France* (1872). Sherman's protégé, Colonel Emory Upton, later made the most thorough inspection of Asian and European military forces by an American in the nineteenth century. Sherman did not endorse all of the suggestions Upton had to offer when he returned, but he did put some of them on the reform agenda.

Reform-minded, practical, but cautious, Sherman faced several political challenges as commanding general of the army from 1869 to 1883. A budget-conscious Congress reduced the army's authorized strength to 27,400 in 1876 and threatened further cuts. Sherman watched as Congress debated a series of bills that contained some "reform" features but which, if passed, might have crippled the army.

From 1876 to 1878 Congressman Henry Banning (a Democrat from Ohio) proposed a series of omnibus bills that provided for reducing the number of army officers, cutting the pay of officers (especially that of lieutenants), eliminating the black regiments, preventing soldiers from supervising elections, establishing examination boards for officer promotion, and setting compulsory retirement for officers at age sixty-five. The first version of the bill passed the House of Representatives in 1876 but failed in the Senate. Banning and other Democrats then salted the proposed legislation with enough features to make it appear that reform or thrift inspired them, when in actuality vindictiveness and racism motivated them to weaken the army and remove freedmen from the service. News of Custer's defeat at the Little Bighorn, however, turned another likely reduction of the service into a twenty-five-hundred-man increase.

In 1878, Senator Ambrose Burnside (a Republican from Rhode Island) chaired a congressional committee on army reorganization. Burnside was a West Point graduate and former Union general who took a serious interest in reforming the army. In 1879 the Burnside committee, which included Banning, issued a seven-hundred-page report. The resulting bill revealed the need to compromise with Banning and the Democrats in order to obtain some worthwhile changes. Among its many articles, the Burnside bill recommended reducing the number of officers by three hundred, consolidating and reducing some staff departments, setting officer retirement at age sixty-two, encouraging officer rotation from the staff to line units, requiring staff officers to report to the commanding general rather than to secretary of war, restructuring infantry regiments to allow for wartime expansion, increasing the pay for noncommissioned officers, and shrinking the army to a size that probably would have meant disbanding some or all of the black regiments. The Burnside bill split the army, with some line officers favoring and most staff officers opposing it. Sheridan was against it, but Sherman, Hancock, Upton, and Schofield all found provisions they liked well enough to justify their support. Because of these divisions, in 1879 the Burnside bill failed to pass in Congress. It probably tried to change too much in one stroke.

The multiple agendas behind the Banning and Burnside bills and the flagrant abuse of the army during these congressional debates (the service went unpaid during much of 1877) only deepened Sherman's conviction that most politicians were not trustworthy. Banning and Burnside each claimed the reform mantle, but some of the provisions of their bills could have had negative consequences for the army. Political leaders seemed to agree: With no foreign wars or invasions likely, the primary goal of reform was to reduce the strength of the army and the number of its officers. Military leaders winced at the prospect of further cutbacks because promotion in the army was difficult enough, limited as it was to vacancies by death or retirement in an officer's regiment. Accordingly, Sherman laid out a practical agenda to do what he could within the army's existing structure and budget to improve the service.

Sherman's reforms stressed military education, and he first looked to the existing specialty schools and sought to modernize them. The Artillery Schools at Fortress Monroe, Virginia, had operated from 1824 to 1860 and reopened in 1868. Sherman ordered improvements in the curriculum and sent Upton to serve on its staff. That same year the Signal School began holding classes at Fort Greble in Washington, D.C. Sherman hoped one day to have an advanced school covering practical and theoretical instruction for each of the army's branches, all crowned by a "war college."

Sherman's most important contribution to military education came in 1881 when he authorized the School of Application for Infantry and Cavalry at Fort Leavenworth, Kansas. The school opened the next year with an initial class of forty-two lieutenants who not only took courses in a variety of military subjects, but also studied mathematics and geography and brushed up on their grammar and reading. At the outset, Sherman expressed both public optimism and private skepticism about the Leavenworth school and what good it might accomplish; it was an experiment, the U.S. Army's first attempt at post–graduate education, as opposed to training, for its officers. Sherman wanted students to have the opportunity to study the higher art of war and to familiarize themselves with the responsibilities of various levels of command—captains as company commanders, colonels as regimental commanders, and brigadier generals as brigade commanders. Undergoing several name and curriculum changes in succeeding years, the school began to take root. Sherman had planted the seeds of what would eventually become known as the Command and General Staff College and in so doing filled a yawning gap in army professionalism. By 1914 the "Leavenworth experience" of studying strategy and staff duties created a pool of capable officers who provided leadership for millions of U.S. soldiers in World War I.

To accomplish all—and more—that Sherman expected of the new school, the army needed a handful of educated, intellectually gifted professors at Leavenworth in the 1880s and 1890s. Two officers in particular came forward and left a lasting impression on the experimental military school, Arthur L. Wagner and Eben Swift. Wagner joined the staff at Leavenworth in the fall of 1886, concerned about the deficiencies in the U.S. Army's size, training, and weapons when contrasted to several European armies. He provided the Leavenworth schools and the army at large with badly needed textbooks and other reference works, including *The Service of Security and Supply (1893), Organization and Tactics* (1894), and *Elements of Military Science* (1898). Wagner taught at Leavenworth from 1886 to 1898 and served there again when it resumed classes in 1902, after a break caused by the Spanish-American War. Swift served as an instructor at the Leavenworth schools from 1893 to 1898 and devised a series of challenging war games using maps and field exercises. He also developed the standardized five-paragraph field order that became uniform throughout the army and has been in use ever since. In 1902, Secretary of War Elihu Root reopened the school and renamed it the General Service and Staff College.

Sherman's other notable contribution was to advance the career and writings of Upton. A combat veteran of the Civil War, Upton detested Indian-fighting and saw no future in it. Defeating the western tribes simply added to the list of thankless duties that detracted from what he believed was the army's true calling—preparing for the next war with a conventional opponent. Upton's star burned white-hot in the 1870s. He served as commandant of cadets at West Point from 1870 to 1875. He wrote down his ideas at a feverish pace, publishing *Cavalry Tactics* in 1874 and *Artillery Tactics* in 1875 to supplement his earlier work, *A New System of Infantry Tactics* (1867). Recognizing the changes brought on by improved weapons, his tactics incorporated looser, more flexible formations, stronger skirmish lines, and allowed more responsibility for noncommissioned officers and the soldiers themselves. Returning as a reform zealot after his year abroad evaluating the armies of other countries, he published *The Armies of Asia and Europe* in 1878, emphasizing the accomplishments and techniques of the German army in particular.

According to Upton, German techniques had to be incorporated in the reformation of the U.S. Army. He supported the parts of the Burnside bill that provided for consolidating staff departments (a first step toward a more sophisticated, German-style general staff), setting an age or length of service for mandatory officer retirement, and redesigning regiments to allow for expanding them in wartime. Beyond these reasonable changes, he deplored America's past reliance on inadequate volunteers to round out the officer corps after a war began and urged the adoption of the German system of always maintaining a corps of well-educated officers on active duty to meet the needs of wartime mobilization. A modification of John C. Calhoun's "expansible army" plan (which itself relied on even earlier proposals), Upton's reform scheme was grandiose and seemed too dependent on a foreign model. He stridently promoted his reforms and insisted on their worth. He wanted them adopted as a package and the sooner the better. All of these factors combined to make Upton's scheme unacceptable to politicians of both parties and to a number of army officers as well.

Disappointed by the rejection of his ideas, Upton again turned to his writing, this time producing his magnum opus, *The Military Policy of the United States,* a book that was not published until 1904. In it he emphasized the mistakes of U.S. wartime civilian leadership and was especially critical of what he considered interference in military matters by President Lincoln. He also decried the traditional military unpreparedness of the United States, the error of relying on an inadequate militia, and the indiscipline of volunteer officers. Unfortunately for Upton, such disrespect for presidents and heroic volunteers negated much of his effort at reforming the army. Despite being Sherman's protégé, he failed to make flag rank in 1880; he was promoted to full colonel but did not receive the brigadier's star he thought he deserved. He grew despondent over the lack of congressional support for his sweeping reforms. Other officers, such as Hazen, favored some of what he wanted, but accepted the slow pace of such changes. Upton's health complicated these disappointments, and he committed suicide on 15 March 1881.

Upton's personality and impatience put off both reform-minded officers such as Hancock and traditionalists such as Sheridan. He rejected the concept of working gradually for his goals; in his opinion, everyone—officers, politicians, newspaper editors—should have seen the wisdom of what he proposed. Neither his sincerity nor his intensity overcame his failure to understand and to work within the U.S political system. Consequently, his actions and the manner in which he proselytized on behalf of his reforms embittered civil-military relations in the years to come. Had he demonstrated more patient, sagacious leadership, he might have increased the chances of obtaining some of his goals.

Upton had found time to write two of his books while serving as commandant of cadets at the U.S. Military Academy, but neither he nor Sherman dwelt on reforming West Point. Overall, Sherman appeared to be satisfied with his alma mater. As commanding general, Sherman was lenient toward misbehaving cadets accused of hazing. He also declined to diversify the academy faculty by adding new civilian professors, and the curriculum remained much the same as it had been when Sherman graduated in 1840. Perhaps the most important academic change at West Point came in 1871, when Colonel Dennis Hart Mahan, who had taught at West Point for more than forty years and had made a personal impression on the army officer corps, was forced to retire.

Another significant change at West Point in the post–Civil War years was the admission in 1870 of the first African-American cadet, James W. Smith. After suffering through racist epithets, isolation, and other forms of mistreatment, Smith was dismissed for academic deficiencies in 1873. Tracing the lives of other black cadets at West Point and the few black officers in the period indicates how unwelcome they were in the army. Between 1870 and 1889 twenty-five blacks received appointments to the academy. Twelve passed the tests and gained admission, but only three graduated. After persevering under trying circumstances, in 1877 Henry O. Flipper became the first black to graduate from West Point and earn a commission. Flipper served with the Tenth Cavalry from 1877 to 1882, when he was hounded out of the army by Colonel William Shafter on charges of "conduct unbecoming an officer" stemming from misuse of military funds. The most deplorable case of mistreatment was that of Johnson C. Whittaker, a black cadet from South Carolina. Whittaker was found beaten and tied to his bunk, but the superintendent, General John M. Schofield, ruled that the bruises and cuts were self-inflicted and that Whittaker had roped himself to his bed. An academy review board dismissed Whittaker in 1882 for a failing grade. Two other African-Americans graduated from West Point and served with the Ninth Cavalry,

John H. Alexander (class of 1887) and Charles Young (class of 1889), the last black graduate until Benjamin O. Davis, Jr., in 1936.

Despite the grim record of African-Americans who aspired to become officers, the fact that black enlisted men served in the regular army set a significant example for the future. The Reconstruction Congress established six units for them in 1866—the Ninth and Tenth Cavalry regiments, and the Thirty-eighth, Thirty-ninth, Fortieth, and Forty-first Infantry regiments. The four infantry regiments were consolidated in the army reduction of 1869 into the Twenty-fourth and Twenty-fifth regiments. These units made up about 10 percent of the army's enlisted strength, slightly less than the percentage of black troops in Union service in 1865. Commanded mostly by white officers (with the few exceptions noted above), the black units not only earned the distinction of having the lowest desertion rates in the army, but also boasted high reenlistment rates. They performed a variety of duties, including fighting Indians, breaking strikes, and garrisoning western outposts. These black regulars—nicknamed "buffalo soldiers" by the Indians—established a creditable record of more than thirty years of service by the time of the Spanish-American War. Although the buffalo soldiers and their white officers suffered indignities, insults, assaults, and discrimination, they paved the way for other African-Americans to serve in U.S. forces in the major wars of the twentieth century. These experimental army units therefore made an important contribution to civil rights for blacks in the United States.

There were several other positive developments in the service during the Gilded Age. A federal law set sixty-four as the standard retirement age for army officers in 1882. The Engineer School of Application at Willett's Point, Long Island, New York, opened in 1885, and the School of Cavalry and Light Artillery at Fort Riley, Kansas, was authorized in 1887. Several officers formed the U.S. Cavalry Association in 1885, which supported the publication of the *Cavalry Journal*, launched in 1888. Adjutant General Robert C. Drum supervised preparation of the *Soldier's Handbook* in 1884, a valuable reference covering a variety of duties and details pertaining to the lives of enlisted men. At the end of the 1880s, the army changed the traditional Sunday-morning inspections of enlisted men's barracks, uniforms, and bunks to Saturday morning, thus allowing soldiers some time for recreation and personal activities on the weekend.

In the late 1880s, a number of officers, including Miles, Crook, and Wesley Merritt, planned and conducted regimental field-training exercises, some of which were supplemented by soldiers from other infantry, cavalry, and artillery outfits. Following an example set by the navy when it established the Office of Naval Intelligence in 1882, the army established its own intelligence-gathering agency, the Bureau of Military Information, in 1885. Army attaches assigned to several U.S. embassies began sending data to this bureau, which changed its name to the Military Information Division in 1890. These modest reforms were carried out in the 1880s despite Sheridan's lack of interest. Schofield replaced Sheridan as commanding general in August 1888.

According to federal law, the commanding general held no direct control over either line units or staff bureaus, but he could attempt to use his influence or powers of persuasion to affect military legislation and, like Sherman, carry out special projects, such as establishing the Leavenworth schools. The background Schofield brought to this task was exceptional. In addition to holding standard departmental commands, Schofield had served as a special U.S. representative to negotiate the withdrawal of French forces in Mexico in 1866, a district commander during Reconstruction, interim secretary of war from June 1868 to March 1869, and superintendent of West Point in the late 1870s. Schofield also had traveled to Europe for a year (1881–1882). No other post–Civil War commanding general had such breadth of experience.

Although he was not an Uptonian, Schofield was acutely interested in army reform. In particular, he wanted to improve and standardize the working relationship between the secretary of war and the commanding general, which he believed should be a position more like that of a European chief of staff. Unlike Upton, Schofield understood the need to subordinate the U.S. military to its civilian leadership—the president and the secretary of war. In his memoirs, *Forty-six Years in the Army* (1897), Schofield concluded: "Nothing is more absolutely indispensable to a good soldier than perfect subordination and zealous service to him whom the national will may have made the official superior for the time being." Furthermore, he encouraged professionalism in the army and stressed that officers must keep abreast of technological changes in arms, munitions, and equipment.

As head of the army's Board of Ordnance and Fortification, Schofield had the duty of implementing some of the recommendations made by the joint army-navy Endicott Board on Fortifications. Chaired by Secretary of War William C. Endicott, the board included four army officers, two navy officers, and two civilians, and met several times in 1885. It issued a lengthy report in January 1886 calling for elaborate coastal defenses. In coordination with the navy, these defenses would protect the twenty-seven primary U.S. harbors as well as points along the Great Lakes, employ hundreds of modern breechloading cannons, and cost more than $127 million, a huge expenditure for the time. Because of its cost, the Endicott defense system was never fully funded and construction progressed slowly, but the public tolerated these expenditures, whereas it might have blanched at spending the same money for new infantry or field artillery weapons and increasing the number of regiments in the army. Althoug the usefulness of the Endicott defense system was questionable, the army did not reject the money sent its way for the traditional role of coastal defense.

In the late nineteenth century, life at the army's coastal forts and interior posts gradually improved as the number of forts decreased. As the Indian wars drew to an end, the War Department closed posts throughout the trans-Mississippi. By 1890 the army maintained 103 posts across the nation, contrasted with 167 posts in 1870 and 130 in 1880. Garrisoning dozens of one-, two-, or three-company forts during Reconstruction and the Indian wars undercut regimental integrity and discouraged officers who wanted to turn their attention to broader questions of national defense. Nevertheless, the army never lost contact with civilians and civilian society. In the West, army doctors, libraries, stores, mail delivery, and social activities such as band concerts drew civilians and travelers to the forts. Even near the smaller forts, towns grew and developed symbiotic relationships with the posts. In the South, most forts were located near towns or cities. Seeking a break from routine, soldiers naturally gravitated to the shops, saloons, restaurants, and bordellos of nearby towns.

Based on the research of historian John M. Gates, students of the period must reconsider the interpretation advanced by Samuel P. Huntington in his valuable and influential *The Soldier and the State* (1957). Huntington argues that the army was isolated from civilian society in the late-nineteenth century. Gates shows that by 1891, however, 20 percent of the army's officers held assignments in or near eastern cities such as New York and Washington, D.C. Another 28 percent occupied billets in midwestern or western cities such as Chicago, Denver, Omaha, Portland, St. Paul, San Antonio, San Francisco, and Salt Lake City. The percentage of officers stationed in or near urban centers increased in the 1890s. These figures reinforce the conclusion that army officers were not isolated from society, and were aware of the progressive reforms under way in the late 1890s. Reform-minded officers, such as Colonel August V. Kautz, wanted to see steps taken to advance the army's professional standing much the same way that reformers in other areas of society advocated improved professional accreditation of physicians, attorneys, schoolteachers, civil-service employees, social workers, and policemen, among others.

The years 1890–1901 saw several beneficial changes for the army. In October 1890 a federal law changed the outmoded system of army-officer promotions. Thereafter, officers would be promoted within their branch of service (infantry, artillery, cavalry) rather than within their regiment. This modernizing step was one of the most important reforms of the late nineteenth century. In addition, the School for Cavalry and Light Artillery opened at Fort Riley in 1892 and the *Journal of United States Artillery* began publication that year. The following year officers formed the Infantry Society (which changed its name to the Infantry Association in 1904) and the *Infantry Journal* began publication in 1894. In the mid-1890s, about one hundred army officers served as instructors of tactics or military science at civilian colleges and universities around the nation. Overseas, the army stationed officers as attaches in sixteen U.S. embassies, including those in London, Berlin, Paris, Vienna, Rome, St. Petersburg, Brussels, Mexico City, and Tokyo.

The army accomplished another step toward modernization in the 1890s by adopting the new Krag-Jörgensen rifle. Picking a rifle based on a foreign (Danish) rather than a U.S. design caused opposition by Americans who pulled political strings to delay the Krag's manufacture. They hoped to rescind the choice and reopen testing. Therefore, although the Ordnance Department approved it in 1892, the Krag did not swing into production until 1894. By 1898 the arsenal at Springfield, Massachusetts, had turned out 53,000 rifles and 14,800 Krag carbines, more than enough to equip the regular army of 28,000. Nevertheless, Congress declined to appropriate money to begin issuing the new rifle to National Guard units, and guardsmen had to make do with the Model 1873 Springfield. Guard units carried the venerable trapdoor rifle into the Spanish-American War.

There were still many aspects of the army that needed improvement. For example, the army required no standard medical examinations for senior officers to remain on active duty. There were no pension or retirement plans for noncommissioned officers or officers, so they remained in uniform for as long as possible. Other matters needed attention. Throughout the second half of the nineteenth century, desertion rates remained high, averaging almost 15 percent of the enlisted force per year, but in the 1870s it exceeded 30 percent in some years. By contrast, the desertion rate in the British army was only about 2 percent. Observers and critics offered numerous explanations for so many deserters—low pay, poor food, inadequate amenities at some posts, dangerous assignments, or lack of excitement. The adjutant general took some steps to better the enlisted men's lot, and desertion rates dipped to about 5 percent in the 1890s, a considerable improvement. Furthermore, training and military planning left much to be desired. The United States lacked a European-style general staff to draw up contingency plans, and there was no army-wide doctrine for field-training exercises. The War Department addressed some of these matters after the War with Spain.

In August 1899, Russell Alger resigned as secretary of war and President William McKinley replaced him with Elihu Root. An astute corporate attorney who brought to the post energy, progressive attitudes, and a willingness to consider changes for the War Department, Root was receptive to some army officers' ideas for reform. Reversing the post–Civil War trend, Root became a civilian reformer who sought an increase, rather than a reduction, in the size of the army. Deployments to China and the Philippines during Root's administration helped bolster his advocacy of a larger force. Root supported some Uptonian concepts and later authorized the publication of the colonel's *Military Policy of the United States*. Particularly important among Root's early steps was his call for the approval of the Army Reorganization Act, subsequently passed by Congress on 2 February 1901. This law limited the tour of duty for most army staff officers to four years, thus instituting a rotation between line units and staff bureaus that had been an ideal sought by reform-minded officers even before Upton's time. This important law nullified the earlier practice of some officers who had secured for themselves an entrenched staff billet in Washington away from regimental duties in garrison and field.

The Reorganization Act of 1901 indicated the direction that Root's later, more famous reforms

would take. He began considering numerous other changes, such as establishing a war college, reforming the National Guard, improving the Leavenworth schools, and creating a new general staff. The latter would have a chief of staff similar to that found in European armies, but also like the one John Schofield, among other American officers, had recommended some years before. Thus, the Root reforms culminated years of debate among politicians and military officers by combining American and European ideas that led to a rejuvenated army.

THE U.S. NAVY: FROM "DARK AGE" TO "NEW NAVY"

For the U.S. Navy and its officer corps, fighting the Confederacy had been a professional challenge successfully met. Over the four years of the Civil War the navy increased the number of warships and other vessels in service from 42 in 1861 to about 700 by 1865. Personnel on duty grew accordingly, from 7,600 enlisted men and 1,300 officers in 1861 to 51,500 sailors and 7,000 officers by 1865. Many of the warships in service in 1865 were based on the innovative *Monitor*. Like their namesake, they sported modernistic turrets, low freeboard, armor protection, and were highly maneuverable. These design features would be incorporated into the major warships of all nations in years to come.

Furthermore, the U.S. Navy Department had grown to accommodate the demands of the service, managed by the capable Secretary of the Navy Gideon Welles and by a newly created office, assistant secretary of the navy, filled admirably by Gustavus Fox. This administrative tandem supervised the blockade of the enemy's coast, a traditional navy responsibility in wartime. The blockade had been one of several causes contributing to the Confederacy's demise. Moreover, the Union navy's river gunboats had worked with the army to defeat the South in the war's western theater. The navy had fallen short in only one category—failing to suppress the South's *guerre de course* ("war of the chase," or attacks on cargo ships), even though the most infamous Confederate commerce raider, the *Alabama*, had been destroyed by the USS *Kearsarge*. Indeed, the *Alabama* made such an impression on U.S. naval officers that some of the navy's cruisers in the postwar years would be prepared as commerce raiders, ready to prey upon the cargo ships of potential enemies. Altogether, then, by 1865 the U.S. Navy had reached a high point of strength, pride, and sense of accomplishment, and made the United States one of the world's major naval powers.

This elevated status could not last. Within eighteen months after the Civil War ended the government began selling off ships, some of which, after all, had been merchant vessels converted to wartime use. Innovative monitor-style ships, some with two turrets, demonstrated their greatest usefulness in harbors and rivers. Their postwar ocean voyages only proved the point. In other words, traditional wooden war steamers still formed the heart of the blue-water navy, and by the 1870s the navy had dropped to only one hundred warships and about fifteen support vessels of various kinds. This drastic reduction came as no surprise, but what really stung America's navalists was its speed. U.S. political leaders saw no external threats and therefore no need to continue funding an expensive modern navy to keep pace with European navies. The American sea service had entered its own "dark age."

Within a decade after the Civil War, the U.S. Navy was stigmatized for relying on ships and guns that Europeans considered obsolescent or obsolete. By the 1880s, American wooden-hulled warships mounting smoothbore, muzzleloading Dahlgren cannon looked like dinosaurs when they dropped anchor near new metal-hulled British or French ships carrying rifled, breechloading guns. Because of the shortage of overseas coaling stations and reduced funds for buying coal, archconservative Admiral David Porter opposed using steam power and issued orders requiring U.S. Navy ships to use their sails when on patrol. Porter also used his clout as a hero of the Civil War to oppose

progress in steam engineering, maintaining a feud with Benjamin Franklin Isherwood, chief of the navy's Bureau of Steam Engineering. Although this bitter rivalry involved personality as well as professional ideology, it revealed the first of several postwar contests in the naval officer corps between progressives who wanted the United States to build a European-style navy and traditionalists willing to accept wooden ships and antique cannon as the best the U.S. Navy could get out of Congress in a time of stringent budgets.

For two decades after the Civil War, it appeared as if technology had left the U.S. Navy behind, but its ships still "showed the flag" at a number of distant stations around the world. In the mid-1870s ten wooden war steamers sailed in the North Atlantic Squadron (that is, off the East Coast), while only five patrolled in the European Squadron, based for part of the time at Villefranche, France. The navy assigned nine ships to the Asiatic Squadron and seven to the Pacific Ocean. A point to note in these squadron assignments is that while they varied slightly in number from year to year, the United States had approximately twice as many ships patrolling in foreign wars in the 1870s as it had in the 1840s, even if the ships were obsolescent. In other words, the nation, as represented by its navy, was somewhat more visible and involved around the world, although it was arguable how much respect was earned by the wooden ships.

As the years passed, the navy, like the army, remained top-heavy with officers who were Civil War veterans. During the 1880s and 1890s younger officers complained about slow promotion and called for regular medical examinations to determine the fitness of commanders, proposed that Congress pass a retirement pay plan to encourage geriatric leaders to retire, and wanted more ships added to the service, thus opening up command assignments and sea time for junior and mid-level officers. As new ships were commissioned this pressure for promotion eased somewhat, but overage, infirm officers still dotted the naval list by the time of the Great White Fleet in 1906.

Traditional ideas dominated strategic thinking among many of the older officers. Reflecting wisdom or fossilization, some senior commanders recognized that appropriations could be had for defense from a tight-fisted Congress skeptical of offensive schemes against imaginary foes. During 1885 the Endicott Board, including navy Commander William T. Sampson, met over a period of several months and then issued a report in January 1886. The lengthy report indicated, among several conclusions, that coastal defense would continue to be a joint army-navy responsibility. The army would garrison forts near major cities and the navy would guard the coasts and the merchant marine. Commander Sampson specified the variety of vessels that might be used in a comprehensive coastal defense plan, including gunboats and new, modern torpedo boats, as well as the employment of submarine mines in harbors. Furthermore, the Endicott Board called for U.S. industry to improve its capability to manufacture high quality steel needed for shipmaking and artillery production.

While the Endicott Board report combined traditional themes and new ideas, changes already had begun that led the way to a "new navy." In 1881, Secretary of the Navy William H. Hunt picked several officers to serve on the unofficial Naval Advisory Board that gave advice to the secretary on a wide range of subjects. Hunt, who served only from March 1881 to April 1882, took the advice of the board and recommended that several new ships of steel be built, despite their high cost. Republican President Chester A. Arthur listened to Hunt and pressed Congress to allocate money for the ships. Congress failed to designate such funds in 1882 but passed the Naval Appropriations Act of 1883 providing for the so-called "ABC" ships, three all-steel cruisers named for the cities of Atlanta, Boston, and Chicago, and the dispatch boat *Dolphin*. Coal-burning steam engines powered the ships, which were capable of 17 knots, but they also had a full complement of masts and sails. The new cruisers also had "protected" steel decks designed for improved defense against plunging fire from enemy shells.

The *Atlanta*, *Boston*, and *Chicago* did not have full armor defensive belts, however, and carried guns of smaller caliber in contrast to similar ships in European navies. Nevertheless, the ABC ships signified the turn from wood to steel for the U.S. Navy. As these new ships were commissioned, the U.S. Navy could be ranked above such nations as Chile and Bolivia.

Additional congressional appropriations during the rest of the 1880s permitted construction of other steel ships. Led by Secretary of the Navy William Whitney, under Democratic President Grover Cleveland, Congress funded nine more steel cruisers—six without sails—which carried stronger armor similar to the ships of European navies. Included in this group were the *Maine* and the *Texas*. The trend to a modern navy with bipartisan support was now unmistakable.

In addition to new ships, the 1880s saw other important steps in U.S. naval modernization. In 1882 Secretary Hunt got approval from Congress to establish the Office of Naval Intelligence (ONI). Its duties involved collecting and studying information on foreign navies in order to assess their capabilities. To assist in the collection of data, attachés were sent to major European and Asian nations and reported their observations to Washington, D.C By the 1890s, ONI maintained files on every major navy in the world and drew up contingency plans addressing the possibility for war between the United States and several countries, notably Great Britain and Spain. The Naval Institute, a private organization for naval officers and interested civilians, had been founded in 1873. By the mid-1880s the institute's journal, *Proceedings*, had been published for ten years, allowing navalists to offer ideas for discussion in an unofficial forum.

Yet another step in modernization began in 1884. A three-officer board, composed of Commodore Stephen B. Luce, Commander Sampson, and Lieutenant Commander Casper Goodrich, reported to Secretary of the Navy William E. Chandler, urging him to support a postgraduate college for naval officers. In their report, the three officers pointed out that in an age of new inventions and changing technology, military leaders needed to "bring to the investigation of the various problems of modern naval warfare the scientific methods adopted in other professions." Chandler approved the officers' recommendation and obtained funding for the Naval War College, which began its first classes in September 1885 at Newport, Rhode Island, with Luce serving as it first president.

Luce had maintained a long interest in naval education. An Annapolis graduate (class of 1849), Luce originally had gained his midshipman's papers in 1841 and served at sea before going to the Naval Academy. During his long career (1841 to 1889), he devoted attention to improving the training of enlisted men as well as the education of officers. He taught at the Naval Academy, commanded a training ship and a training squadron, and advocated programs for naval cadets at the state land-grant colleges where the Morrill Act authorized training army cadets. Becoming president of the Naval War College in 1885 was a capstone to his career, but he also held the position of president of the Naval Institute from 1887 to 1898, guiding the institute for a decade after his retirement. While in uniform Luce wrote many magazine articles calling for naval reform and professional education. Promoted to the rank of rear admiral in 1885, Luce was an unusual combination of intellectual and administrator. Subsequently, after retiring in 1889, he returned to active duty and served an exceptional ten-year stint on special assignment at the Naval War College.

One of Luce's first appointments to the college's faculty was also his most important. The admiral tapped Captain Alfred Thayer Mahan to teach naval history. He was the son of West Point professor Dennis Hart Mahan. From his Annapolis graduation in 1859 to 1883, Alfred Mahan's naval career combined patience and ennui. New horizons opened with the publication of his first book, *The Gulf and Inland Waters* (1883), a volume in the Scribner's History of the Civil War series. In 1885 Luce directed Mahan to prepare lectures in naval history and to begin delivering them in 1886. Mahan not only taught, he succeeded Luce as president of the

college (1886–1888 and 1892–1893). He helped shape the study of naval history, not only in the United States but also in other nations, including Great Britain, Germany, and Japan, by the publication of his seminal work, *The Influence of Seapower upon History, 1660–1783* (1890), which book made Mahan the most important U.S. writer on military affairs.

Mahan remains an important author worthy of study. In his writings (especially in the long introductory section of *The Influence of Seapower upon History*) he proposed that nations may have a certain aptitude for the sea, based upon several factors, such as geographical area, length of coastline, number of ports, overseas outposts, resources applicable to maritime endeavors, and the maritime "character" of the population. Furthermore, he asserted that a nation pretending to international leadership must maintain modern naval forces in existence to protect its interests and gain "command of the sea" in wartime, precepts that became fundamentals of modern military thought. According to Mahan, navies existed for offensive capabilities beyond blockades, the *guerre de course*, and coastal defense. Naval forces should be prepared to seek out, engage, and destroy enemy navies in fleet action. Most of his writings on naval tactics, however, soon became outdated and his stress, along the lines of Antoine Henri Jomini, of concentrating entire national fleets no longer became applicable. Likewise. his dictum that the *guerre de course* (destroying an enemy nation's commerce-carrying ships) could never be decisive was severely tested by the German successes with submarines in the world wars of the twentieth century. This highlighted that Mahan limited his strategic view to one dimension—war on the sea—not in the air above it or in the water beneath the surface.

Mahan's writings described the maturation of the British Royal Navy and how Britain relied upon its navy to become a great imperial power. It was ironic that books by an American naval officer greatly enhanced the reputation of the Royal Navy. Mahan implied that for any nation to have similar imperial success, it must also possess a strong navy. Indeed, he showed that building a powerful navy was one of the prerequisites of being a great power. Mahan went on to produce a series of successful volumes, including *The Influence of Seapower upon the French Revolution and Empire* (2 vols., 1892), *Seapower in its Relation to the War of 1812* (2 vols., 1905), *The Major Operations of the Navies in the War of American Independence* (1913), as well as biographies of David G. Farragut (1892) and Horatio Nelson (1897) and a work titled *Naval Strategy* (1911).

A number of British military and political leaders delighted in Mahan's broad conclusions, emphasizing as they did the accomplishments of the Royal Navy. Mahan's writings could also be used to confirm the verisimilitude of a large navy of capital ships and lend credence to the European imperialistic system during another round of competition for colonies, this time in Africa and the Pacific Ocean. Accordingly, U.S. leaders came to see America's need for a modern navy if their nation was to join this imperialistic contest, and to give the United States an improved status among the Western nations.

Adding endeavors in journalism not only brought Mahan financial comfort but boosted his national standing. His essays on naval subjects, imperialism, and contemporary affairs were published in such widely circulated magazines as *Collier's, North American Review, Atlantic, Century, McClure's,* and *Harper's Monthly.* Political, military, business, and religious leaders were pleased to use Mahan's name and conclusions to bolster their own agenda, such as building a bigger navy, acquiring colonies, expanding U.S. trade abroad, or increasing Protestant missionary activities in foreign lands. Although Mahan had been skeptical of imperialistic ventures in the 1870s, he pushed for U.S. procurement and consolidation of colonial possessions from the 1890s to his death in 1914. The U.S. control of a canal in Panama became one of his pet projects. Theodore Roosevelt, Henry Cabot Lodge, and others had already been advocating a larger role for the United States in international affairs and they applauded Mahan and his writings.

Mahan, of course, favored regular forces, so

an unusual aspect in naval activities began in 1888 when Congressman Washington C. Whitthorne (a Democrat from Tennessee) proposed to establish "the enrollment of a naval militia and the formation of a naval reserve in the several sea and lake board States." According to the *Report of the Secretary of the Navy* for 1889, Whitthorne's bill did not pass through Congress in 1888, but he brought it up again the next year. In the meantime, the legislatures of Massachusetts, Rhode Island, and New York passed state laws anticipating the approval of a national naval militia, which could be considered a complement to the army's National Guard. In 1889, Secretary of the Navy Benjamin F. Tracy supported the Whitthorne bill, but Congress disappointed Tracy again. Acting on his own, Tracy authorized the New York and Massachusetts state naval militiamen to conduct drills on a navy ship for a few days of summer training. He continued to lobby Congress for support of a bill that would provide surplus federal arms and equipment for the naval militias. Tracy concluded that hundreds of naval militia could be trained to supplement the active forces, which were limited by law to seventy-five hundred sailors. Some militiamen might serve in frontline ships in wartime, but in Tracy's view most would be involved in harbor defense.

Tracy's diligence was rewarded by the Naval Appropriations Act of 1891, which allocated $25,000 annually for the support of state naval militias, funds to be distributed by the secretary of the navy. State governors would make requisitions for arms and equipment from the Navy Department based on the number of naval militia enrolled. Based on the *Report of the Secretary of the Navy* for 1891, California led all states by enlisting 371 men into its naval militia, followed by New York (342), Massachusetts (238), North Carolina (101), Rhode Island (54), and Texas (43). In the next few years, other states initiated naval militia programs and eastern states expanded theirs. For example, in 1892 New York surpassed all states with 401 naval militiamen. California, Massachusetts, North Carolina, South Carolina, and Maryland tallied 376, 331, 296, 208, and 124, respectively. Pennsylvania and Illinois announced their intentions to recruit naval militia battalions, while Texas disbanded its company.

During the 1890s the naval militia program was not uniform from state to state. Secretary of the Navy Hilary A. Herbert placed Assistant Secretary of the Navy William G. McAdoo in charge of the Navy Department's relations with these new state organizations, which went by various names. The Naval Militia of the National Guard of California drilled haphazardly and usually without the benefit of an active duty navy ship. The Naval Brigade, Ohio National Guard was established in 1896 and enrolled 174 men in 1897. The Naval Militia of Illinois recruited most of its 448 men in the Chicago area in 1897 and was considered by the navy to be "a valuable naval auxiliary in time of war." The First Naval Battalion of the Louisiana State National Guard received an excellent rating for discipline and activity from the regular navy officer assigned to evaluate it in New Orleans in 1897. On the other hand, another officer rated the discipline of the Naval Force of the State of Pennsylvania only "as good as can be expected of such an organization." Other states dubbed their units variously, such as the Naval Reserve of New Jersey and the Michigan State Naval Brigade.

Putting the best face on his duties, in 1896 Assistant Secretary McAdoo found most naval militia he inspected to be patriotic, interested in their avocation, and enthusiastic about the naval service. McAdoo also found a need, however, for more weapons, equipment, and boats and noted that, although it differed state by state, between 50 percent and 85 percent of the militia in the states attended their summer drills, but not enough navy ships were available for all militiamen to see how things were done in an active duty vessel. Secretary Herbert concluded that most militiamen possessed "limited knowledge and experience" about the shipboard duties they could be asked to assume in wartime.

In 1897, on the eve of war with Spain, Assistant Secretary of the Navy Theodore Roosevelt called for more congressional appropriations for naval militia summer drills. Its enrollment had been increasing year by year, and in 1897 totaled 3,703 men in fifteen states, six in the Northeast (Massachusetts, Rhode Island, Connecticut, New York, New Jersey, and Pennsylvania), five in the South (Maryland, North Carolina, South Carolina, Georgia, and Louisiana), three in the Midwest (Illinois, Michigan, and Ohio), and California in the West. (At about this time the army enrolled some 105,000 citizens across the country in the National Guard.) Roosevelt personally visited naval militia units in New York and the three Midwest states and noted that there was "a great variety in the condition of efficiency reached by the different organizations." In the conflict with Spain some naval militiamen were brought on active duty, but the naval militia units provided proof to businessmen and politicians, especially on the eastern seaboard, that the navy was paying attention to their needs for local defense in time of war.

Far more important than the naval militia to the "new navy" were the modern warships commissioned in the 1890s. Secretary of the Navy Tracy served from 1889 to 1893 under Republican President Benjamin Harrison. When Tracy took office some European observers ranked the U.S. Navy twelfth in the world. Beginning with the Naval Appropriations Act of 1891, Tracy recommended construction of several new ships, including three battleships and supporting cruisers. He also expanded the Naval War College and developed a tactical training unit called the "squadron of evolution." Congress was still skeptical of so-called offensive weapons and therefore Tracy classified his largest new vessels as "coastal defense" battleships. Comparable in some respects to their European cousins, the coastal defense battleships displaced 10,000 tons, reached speeds up to 17 knots, menaced potential opponents with 13-inch guns, and were fully armored. The battleships (named for states) included the *Indiana*, *Oregon*, and *Massachusetts*, supplemented by the cruisers (named for cities) *Brooklyn* and *Minneap-*

olis. All of them served in the U.S. Navy's confrontation with Spanish forces near the end of the decade. Secretary of the Navy Herbert endorsed new construction for additional battleships during President Grover Cleveland's second term (1893–1897). Especially notable was the completion of the 11,000-ton battleship *Iowa* in 1897, but five other battleships were under construction by the time Cleveland left office.

Thus, in 1898 the U.S. Navy possessed sturdy new battleships and modern armored cruisers as well as older battleships and protected cruisers. Taken together with torpedo boats and other auxiliaries, they would not overawe such first-class navies as those of Great Britain or France, but they presented a formidable array against a second-class power, such as Spain. The U.S. Navy's ships had the advantage of newness, most having been commissioned during the years 1886–1897 and incorporating some of the era's best technology, such as range finders, automated ammunition hoists, and sophisticated electrical systems. Some of these innovations had been invented or developed by an exceptional U.S. naval officer Bradley A. Fiske.

While European opinions varied, and taking numerous factors into account, the ranking of the U.S. Navy had moved up from twelfth in 1889 to around sixth or seventh in 1898. It ranked behind the navies of Great Britain, France, Russia, Germany, and Italy and just above or below that of Spain. Whatever its international ranking, the navy certainly justified its traditional claim of being the nation's first line of defense. Based on such factors as gunnery, ammunition quality, serviceability of ships' engines, and general seaworthiness of the fleet, the U.S. Navy compared favorably with European navies. As events showed, in all of these specifics, the U.S. Navy proved to be ranked above the Spanish navy.

The U.S. Navy had made great strides in the 1880s and 1890s. On such comparable points as overall capability, level of training, and use of modern technology it surpassed the U.S. Army. Officers on the German General Staff could (and did) disregard the U.S. Army in their 1897 report on military forces in other nations, but the U.S. Navy deserved to be ranked as a high-quality military force.

See also THE DEVELOPMENT OF AN AMERICAN MILITARY PHILOSOPHY; THE AMERICAN MILITARY AS AN INSTRUMENT OF POWER; MILITARY GOVERNANCE AND OCCUPATION; *and* POLITICAL OBJECTIVES AND THE DEVELOPMENT OF MILITARY STRATEGY.

BIBLIOGRAPHY

General Works

Coffman, Edward M. *The Old Army: A Portrait of the American Army in Peacetime, 1784–1898* (1986).

Dawson, Joseph G., III. *The Late 19th Century U.S. Army, 1865–1898: A Research Guide* (1990).

Ganoe, William A. *The History of the United States Army* (1924).

Hagan, Kenneth J., and William R. Roberts, eds., *Against All Enemies: Interpretations of American Military History from Colonial Times to the Present* (1986).

Millett, Allan R., and Peter Maslowski. *For the Common Defense: A Military History of the United States of America* (1984).

Spiller, Roger J., Joseph G. Dawson III, and T. Harry Williams, eds., *Dictionary of American Military Biography*, 3 vols. (1984).

Weigley, Russell F. *Towards an American Army: Military Thought from Washington to Marshall* (1962).

———. *History of the United States Army* (1967, rev. 1984).

Reconstruction

Clendenen, Clarence C. "President Hayes' 'Withdrawal' of the Troops—An Enduring Myth." *South Carolina Historical Magazine* (1969).

Coakley, Robert W. *The Role of Federal Military Forces in Domestic Disorders, 1789–1878* (1988).

Dawson, Joseph G., III. *Army Generals and Reconstruction: Louisiana, 1862–1877* (1982).

Hyman, Harold M. "Johnson, Stanton, and Grant: A Reconsideration of the Army's Role in the Events Leading to Impeachment." *American Historical Review* 66 (1960).

Rable, George C. *But There Was No Peace: The Role of Violence in the Politics of Reconstruction* (1984).

———. "William T. Sherman and the Conservative Critique of Radical Reconstruction." *Ohio History* 93 (1984).

Richter, William L. *The Army in Texas During Reconstruction, 1865–1870* (1987).

Sefton, James E. *The United States Army and Reconstruction, 1865–1877* (1967).

The Indian Wars

Ambrose, Stephen E. *Crazy Horse and Custer* (1975).

Athearn, Robert G. *William Tecumseh Sherman and the Settlement of the West* (1956).

Fowler, Arlen. *Black Infantry in the West, 1869–1891* (1971).

Gates, John M. "Indians and Insurrectos: The U.S. Army's Experience with Insurgency." *Parameters* 13 (1983).

Gray, John S. *Centennial Campaign: The Sioux War of 1876* (1976).

Haley, James L. *The Buffalo War: The History of the Red River Indian Uprising of 1874* (1976).

Hutton, Paul A. *Phil Sheridan and His Army* (1985).

Knight, Oliver. *Life and Manners in the Frontier Army* (1978).

Leckie, William H. *The Buffalo Soldiers: A Narrative of the Negro Cavalry in the West* (1967).

Rickey, Don, Jr. *Forty Miles a Day on Beans and Hay: The Enlisted Soldier Fighting the Indian Wars* (1963).

Stewart, Edgar I. *Custer's Luck* (1955).

Thrapp, Dan L. *The Conquest of Apacheria* (1967).

Tate, Michael L. "The Multi-Purpose Army on the Frontier: A Call for Further Research." In *The American West*, edited by Ronald Lora (1980).

Utley, Robert M. *Frontier Regulars: The United States Army and the Indian, 1866–1891* (1973).

———. *Cavalier in Buckskin: George Armstrong Custer and the Western Military Frontier* (1988).

Wooster, Robert. *Soldiers, Sutlers, and Settlers: Garrison Life on the Texas Frontier* (1987).

———. *The Military and United States Indian Policy, 1865–1903* (1988).

Army Reforms

Abrahamson, James L. *America Arms for a New Century: The Making of a Great Military Power* (1981).

Ambrose, Stephen E. *Upton and the Army* (1964).

Browning, Robert S., III. *Two if By Sea: The Development of American Coastal Defense Policy* (1983).

Coffman, Edward M. "The Long Shadow of *The Soldier and the State*." *Journal of Military History* 55 (1991).

Cooper, Jerry M. *The Army and Civil Disorder: Federal Military Intervention in Labor Disputes, 1877–1900* (1980).

Cosmas, Graham A. *An Army for Empire: The United States Army in the Spanish-American War* (1971; rev. ed. 1993).

Foner, Jack D. *The United States Soldier Between Two Wars: Army Life and Reforms, 1865–1898* (1970).

Gates, John M. "The Alleged Isolation of U.S. Army Officers in the Late 19th Century." *Parameters* 10 (1980).

———. "The 'New' Military Professionalism." *Armed Forces and Society* 11 (1985).

Hacker, Barton C. "The United States Army as a National Police Force: The Federal Policing of Labor Disputes, 1877–1898." *Military Affairs* 33 (1969).

Hampton, Duane H. *How the U.S. Cavalry Saved Our National Parks* (1971).

Huntington, Samuel P. *The Soldier and the State: The Theory and Politics of Civil Military Relations* (1957).

Karsten, Peter. "Armed Progressives: The Military Reorganizes for the American Century." Peter Karsten, ed., *The Military in America* (1980).

Nenninger, Timothy K. *The Leavenworth Schools and the Old Army: Education, Professionalism, and the Officer Corps of the United States Army, 1881–1918* (1978).

The U.S. Navy, 1865–1890s

Alden, John D. *The American Steel Navy* (1972).

Allin, Lawrence C. *The United States Naval Institute: Intellectual Forum of the New Navy, 1873–1889* (1978).

Bradford, James C. *Admirals of the New Steel Navy* (1990).

Buhl, Lance C. "Maintaining 'An American Navy,' 1865–1889." In *In Peace and War*, edited by Kenneth Hagan (1984).

———. "Mariners and Machines: Resistance to Technological Change in the American Navy, 1865–1869." *Journal of American History* 59 (December 1974).

Cooling, Benjamin F. *Benjamin Franklin Tracy: Father of the Modern American Fighting Navy* (1973).

———. *Gray Steel and Blue Water Navy: The Formative Years of America's Military-Industrial Complex, 1881–1917* (1979).

Dorwart, Jeffrey M. *The Office of Naval Intelligence: The Birth of America's First Intelligence Agency, 1865–1918* (1979).

Herrick, Walter B., Jr. *The American Naval Revolution* (1966).

Karsten, Peter. *The Naval Aristocracy: The Golden Age of Annapolis and the Emergence of Modern American Navalism* (1972).

Livezey, William E. *Mahan on Sea Power* (1947; rev. ed. 1980).

Ransom, Edward. "The Endicott Board of 1885–86 and the Coast Defenses." *Military Affairs* 31 (1967).

Seager, Robert, III. *Alfred Thayer Mahan: The Man and His Letters* (1977).

Spector, Ronald. *Admiral of the New Empire: The Life and Career of George Dewey* (1974).

———. *Professors of War: The Naval War College and the Development of the Naval Profession* (1977).

———. "The Triumph of Professional Ideology: The U.S. Navy in the 1890s." In *In Peace and War*, edited by Kenneth Hagan (1984).

Still, William N. *American Sea Power in the Old World: The United States Navy in European and Near Eastern Waters, 1865–1917* (1980).

THE SPANISH-AMERICAN WAR AND ITS AFTERMATH

David F. Trask

Although the briefest of American conflicts, the Spanish-American War of 1898, otherwise known as the War with Spain, was nevertheless of considerable significance. It began as a humanitarian enterprise, but it led to the acquisition of a measurable insular empire. Moreover, it marked the beginning of the nation's transformation from an isolated nation indifferent to events in Europe and Asia to an interventionist power implicated in developments throughout the world. Finally, the war led to a new mission for the armed forces, the administration and protection of the new empire.

ORIGINS OF THE WAR

The Spanish-American War stemmed from the failure of Spain to put down an insurgency in Cuba. This revolt, beginning in February 1895, constituted a resumption of the Ten Years War (1868–1878), an earlier uprising that ended unsuccessfully. A Cuban junta in New York augmented by others in Latin America raised funds to support the insurgents and attempted to run arms to them past Spanish naval vessels guarding the coast of Cuba. The principal Cuban rebel

general, Máximo Gómez, adopted a scorched-earth strategy, seeking to disrupt the island's principal enterprise, the sugar industry, and force affluent Cubans to support the insurgency. Recognizing that he could not defeat the superior Spanish army by waging conventional war, he avoided pitched battles, preferring to make surprise raids on sugar plantations and then to seek refuge in heavily forested or mountainous locations. This partisan warfare was designed to wear out the opposition; the *insurrectos* hoped that Spain would eventually tire and give up the struggle. Gómez never had more than forty thousand lightly armed troops under his command at any one time. The Spanish army and its Cuban auxiliaries numbered about 230,000 troops. Tropical diseases—malaria, dysentery, and yellow fever—seriously impaired the efficiency of the Spanish organizations.

Having decided to pacify Cuba, the Spanish government sent the victor of the Ten Years War, General Arsenio Martínez de Campos, to lead the campaign against Gómez. His strategy was to construct a defensive line (*trocha*) from the northern coast of Cuba to the southern coast between Morón and Júcaro to isolate the eastern province of Oriente, stronghold of the insurgents. This essentially defensive scheme did not work. The insurgents easily penetrated the *trocha* and operated at will to the west.

A more vigorous commander, General Valeriano Weyler y Nicolau, soon replaced Martínez de Campos and immediately issued an order of reconcentration. This measure gathered all civilians (*reconcentrados*) into camps and halted movement in the countryside. Its chief objective was to deny arms and supplies to the enemy. Weyler then built another *trocha*, this one in the west from Mariel to Majana, isolating the province of Pinar del Río, which he planned to pacify and then move against Oriente. Unfortunately for Weyler, his measures proved no more successful than those of his predecessor. The insurgents remained free to operate at will throughout the Cuban countryside.

Weyler's activities stimulated considerable criticism in the United States, imparting new impetus to the generally anti-Spanish sentiment of the public. The suffering of the *reconcentrados* aroused general sympathy. President Grover Cleveland at first ignored the insurgency, but, in response to congressional pressure, he eventually tendered his good offices to Spain. Madrid's answer defended Spanish policy in Cuba without reserve and rejected all proposals for reform. As his term ended, Cleveland adopted a more advanced policy, calling for some form of home rule or autonomy for Cuba and suggesting that Spain's failure to take action might lead to American intervention.

Like his predecessor, Republican President William McKinley, who took office in March 1897, did not want to involve himself in the struggle between Spain and Cuba, preferring to concentrate on a domestic agenda that included reform of the tariff and the currency. Growing publc support for the Cuban revolutionaries, however, forced him to take action. He sent a new minister to Spain, General Stewart L. Woodford, to urge autonomy upon a new government in Madrid headed by the Liberal party leader, Práxedes Mateo Sagasta. McKinley indicated, as had Cleveland before him, that delay might lead to U.S. intervention on the side of the insurgents. The Liberals had agreed to autonomy for Cuba, but they were constrained by strong Spanish opinion favoring the retention of Cuba, the jewel of their decaying empire. Sagasta's conduct reflected his fear that any sign of undue weakness on his part might result in a powerful domestic reaction, perhaps a revolution that would overthrow the Restoration monarchy established in 1875. His policy was doomed to failure because it encouraged the insurgents to sustain their operations. Why accept autonomy when independence was within sight?

In February 1898 two events suddenly transformed the situation. One was the publication of a private letter written by Enrique Dupuy de Lôme, the Spanish minister in Washington, which included several derogatory comments about President McKinley. The Cuban junta in New York had stolen the letter and given it to the press, and the American public was instantly inflamed. Dupuy de Lôme admitted authorship and resigned, bringing to an end an embarrassing affair.

A few days later, however, on 15 February, the U.S. battleship *Maine*, lying at anchor in the harbor at Havana, blew up and sank, killing 266 crew members and wounding many others. The ship had been sent to Cuba to provide protection for U.S. citizens and their property. A U.S. investigation concluded that an explosion of external origin had caused the disaster, strengthening the instinctive public assumption that Spain had been at fault. A Spanish commission found that an internal explosion had occurred, which placed the responsibility with the Americans. Decades later, careful inquiry proved with near-certainty that the forward coal bunkers had caught fire and caused adjacent magazines to explode, but few Americans reached that conclusion in 1898.

Before 15 February, the Cuban question had been one of many important public issues in the United States, but the destruction of the *Maine* dwarfed all other matters. A great outburst of public opinion that favored the expulsion of Spain from Cuba, fed by inflammatory yellow journalism in the American press, found ex-

THE SPANISH-AMERICAN WAR
Caribbean Theater

Advance on Santiago and Battle of El Caney

pression in insistent calls for action from Congress. McKinley, who hoped to find a peaceful solution, tried to obtain sufficient concessions from Madrid, working through Minister Woodford. To exert pressure on Sagasta, McKinley gained congressional authority on 9 March to expend $50 million for national defense. On 27 March, McKinley instructed Woodford to seek independence for Cuba, recognizing that he could no longer defy public opinion without grievously undermining his political position.

Sagasta proved unresponsive despite energetic efforts to move him from autonomy to independence. He retained the belief that a grant of independence to Cuba under U.S. pressure would lead to domestic revolution and the destruction of the Restoration monarchy. Ironically, both Sagasta and McKinley desired peace, but public opinion denied them the freedom of action necessary to produce such a result. Sagasta renewed efforts to obtain support for his position from other European states, but no

help was forthcoming. Spain lacked claims on other nations, having followed a foreign policy of isolation for many years, and none of the great powers wished to alienate the United States.

On 11 April, having exhausted all his diplomatic options, President McKinley sent a message to Congress asking for authority to intervene in Cuba on the side of the insurgents, a step that soon led to war. He did not, however, call for recognition of the Cuban insurgent government, seeking to retain as much flexibility as possible. During the congressional debate, Senator Henry M. Teller, a Democrat from Colorado, offered an amendment that sought to establish the purity of U.S. motives. This self-denying ordinance disclaimed any intent to annex Cuba. On 19 April, Congress passed a joint resolution providing for intervention. McKinley signed the resolution on 20 April, and an ultimatum was then sent to Madrid, demanding that Spain act by noon on 23 April.

Spain had already determined its course. The Spanish minister in Washington was ordered home on 21 April and Spain declared war on 23 April. In Washington, on 25 April, the president asked congress for a declaration of war as of 21 April. This step reflected the need to legitimize certain acts of war that had already taken place, particularly the establishment on 22 April of a naval blockade against Havana.

WAR PLANS

It was evident to both countries long before the outbreak of hostilities that a Spanish-American conflict would turn largely on naval warfare. The Spanish minister of marine, Admiral Segismundo Bermejo y Merolo, envisioned dispatch of a naval squadron composed of six armored vessels—a battleship and five cruisers—to Cuban waters, where it would join eight lesser vessels stationed at Havana. After destroying the U.S. naval base at Key West, Florida, it would blockade the eastern seaboard. Rear Admiral Pascual Cervera y Topete, the commander of the proposed expedition, protested the plan, noting worriedly that some of his ships were under repair and that the vessels at Havana were useless. Economic difficulties at home had interfered with the growth and readiness of the navy. The U.S. naval forces were three times stronger than those of Spain, and Cervera had to assume a defensive posture. When further pressures for offensive action came from the Ministry of Marine, Cervera insisted that the United States would exercise command of the sea and that a sortie to the Caribbean Sea would "surely cause the total ruin of Spain."

Bermejo remained adamant and, like all too many in the Spanish government, underestimated the capabilities of the United States. He gave orders to locate one squadron near Cádiz in home waters and to send another to Cuba. Early in April he arranged to concentrate a squadron under Cervera in the Portuguese Cape Verde Islands. When all ships arrived at St. Vincent, the Spanish squadron consisted of four armored cruisers—*Cristóbal Colón, Infanta*

María Teresa, Vizcaya, and *Almirante Oquendo*—and three destroyers. The *Cristóbal Colón* was potentially stronger than any armored cruiser in the U.S. North Atlantic Squadron, but the Spanish vessel lacked its main batteries of ten-inch guns and could not participate in a squadron engagement. Despite continuing protests from Cervera, who wanted to return to Spain, his squadron remained in the Cape Verdes prepared to depart for the Caribbean Sea.

Spain did not make plans to reinforce its land forces in Cuba, Puerto Rico, and the Philippines. The army in Cuba was much larger than any force the United States could hope to send for many months. A sizable army was also stationed in the Philippines, where Spanish troops, numbering about twenty-six thousand, were augmented by fourteen thousand Filipino militia. Twenty-three thousand men were on the main island of Luzon, nine thousand of them assigned to the defense of Manila. For the moment, nothing was done to reinforce the weak Spanish naval squadron at Manila despite the pleas of Admiral Patricio Montojo, who feared that the U.S. Asiatic Squadron, then anchored at Hong Kong, would mount an early attack. Montojo had only two unprotected cruisers and five gunboats. These ships carried just thirty-seven modern guns, of which the largest were seven 6.3-inch rifles. Spain's insular possessions would have to make do with the land forces available at the start of hostilities. Madrid staked everything on the hope that it could prevent the United States from establishing command of the sea and interdicting communications between the insular empire and the homeland, an achievement that would prevent eventual reinforcement and resupply of the overseas forces and interrupt all maritime commerce.

Much more extensive planning took place in the United States. Officers at the Naval War College in Newport, Rhode Island, had interested themselves in a possible conflict with Spain as early as 1894, but the initial war plan was not prepared until 1896. Lieutenant William Warren Kimball, an intelligence officer assigned to the Naval War College, concocted a scheme that contemplated a naval war only. U.S. forces would seize control of the Straits of Florida and help the Cuban insurgents. If necessary, an army expedition would move against Havana. While operations unfolded in the main theater of war, secondary campaigns would develop, including a naval demonstration in Spanish waters to prevent the dispatch of reinforcements to the Caribbean and a naval strike against Manila to exert pressure on Spain to end the war. Later plans reflected the general ideas included in the early scenarios. Among them were a blockade of Cuba and Puerto Rico, an attack by land forces against Cuba, the occupation of Puerto Rico, a naval attack on Manila, and naval operations in Spanish home waters.

After the sinking of the *Maine*, actions were taken to put these ideas into effect. On 25 February 1898, Assistant Secretary of the Navy Theodore Roosevelt sent a message to Commodore George Dewey, commander of the Asiatic Squadron, ordering him to move his squadron from Japan to Hong Kong. If war came, he was to prevent the Spanish squadron from leaving Asiatic waters, an order that reflected prior planning. Dewey's movement to Manila Bay would provide a base for the Asiatic Squadron, which could not remain long in neutral ports during time of war, and preclude Spanish attacks on U.S. merchant shipping in the Pacific Ocean. The Navy Department then ordered the first-class battleship *Oregon*, stationed on the West Coast, to steam around Cape Horn and join the North Atlantic Squadron, a move intended to assure naval superiority in the principal theater of war. Also, the department began a strenuous search for suitable auxiliary vessels and launched an effort to purchase ships of war from various foreign powers.

During March 1898, the navy prepared to take action against Cuba. To guard against possible Spanish naval raids on eastern U.S. ports, a "flying squadron," able to move rapidly to threatened locations, was organized and stationed initially at Hampton Roads in Virginia. Commanded by Commodore Winfield S. Schley, it included three armored vessels, the battleships *Texas* and *Massachusetts* and the ar-

mored cruiser *Brooklyn*. Most of the vessels available in the Atlantic, however, were placed under Captain William T. Sampson, commander of the North Atlantic Squadron, whose orders were to blockade Cuba and Puerto Rico. His ships included the battleships Iowa, Indiana, and Oregon, the latter en route from the West Coast, and the armored cruiser *New York*. When combined, the seven armored ships in the Atlantic vastly outclassed the modern armored vessels available to Spain.

In March 1898, Secretary of the Navy John D. Long organized the Naval War Board, which directed naval intelligence and provided advice on important naval matters. One of its three members was Captain Alfred Thayer Mahan, the renowned naval historian, recalled to active duty during the emergency. Adopting a principle that would guide later activities, the board soon decided that the navy should concentrate on Spain's vulnerable insular possessions. Operations would take place in Spain's home waters only after victory had been assured in the Caribbean theater. Early naval operations would buy time for the army, which needed to mobilize a large volunteer force before it could undertake serious operations against the large Spanish force around Havana.

Meanwhile, Commodore Dewey prepared for operations against Montojo at Manila. Dewey's Asiatic Squadron included the protected cruisers *Olympia*, *Raleigh*, and *Baltimore*, the unprotected cruisers *Concord* and *Boston*, the gunboat *Petrel*, the revenue cutter *McCulloch*, and three auxiliary vessels. Although he did not have a modern armored ship, his squadron was much superior to the decrepit enemy force at Manila. He had fifty-three heavy guns, including ten 10-inch breechloading rifles that outranged all the Spanish naval guns.

The prewar planning and preparations of the U.S. Army reflected the general presumption that it would play a subordinate role in a war with Spain. It was assigned only $19 million from the $50 million appropriation voted by Congress in March, and the secretary of war, Russell Alger, decided that he could use the special fund only for defensive purposes, such as coast defense. When the War Department began to consider land operations in support of the navy, it contemplated small hit-and-run raids on the Cuban coast, recognizing the limitations that stemmed from the size of the regular army, only about twenty-eight thousand men. Ultimately, it would prepare a volunteer force of about a hundred thousand recruits from which, if necessary, it could draw men for a strike at strong enemy troop concentrations such as those around Havana.

These ideas guided decisions about the army's mobilization in 1898. The first step was to concentrate most of the regular army in the southeastern United States at three ports—New Orleans, Mobile, and Tampa. Other troops went to Camp Thomas at Chickamauga Park, Tennessee. Meanwhile, Congress passed legislation on 22 April that provided for the volunteer army. This measure reflected the considerable political influence of state-controlled militia units. An initial call for volunteers would be confined to members of the National Guard, who would enter the federal service, quotas being established for each state. Guard units could volunteer en masse and serve under their officers. The president was authorized to appoint staff officers and general officers, but state governors retained the right to select officers of lower rank. The act of 22 April also permitted recruitment of three thousand national volunteers, a provision that led to the formation of the First United States Volunteer Cavalry Regiment, better known as the Rough Riders, and several other similar organizations. The volunteer army would be formed into corps of three divisions, each of which included no more than three brigades. The brigades contained no more than three regiments.

In a flurry of activity the government soon completed preparations for the mobilization of the army. President McKinley immediately issued a call for 125,000 volunteers, approximately the strength of militia units. On 26 April, Congress agreed to expand the regular army to 65,000 men. On 11 May, Congress approved a plan calling for the organization of ten regiments of men immune from tropical disease;

black men from the South supposedly would not contract diseases such as malaria and yellow fever, an assumption later proved unfounded. On 25 May, McKinley called for an additional 75,000 volunteers. Eventually about 200,000 volunteers entered the service, of whom only about 65,000 were sent overseas. Congress thus authorized a combined force of about 280,000 men, of whom 216,500 were volunteers and 65,700 regulars.

The tardy provisions for mobilization of a volunteer army ensured that the navy would have to bear the burden of early operations. Fortunately, the navy was prepared to take immediate action in the Caribbean Sea and in the South China Sea. If successful, the initial operations of the navy would prepare the way for army expeditions as troops became available.

INITIAL NAVAL OPERATIONS

On 27 April, Commodore Dewey left Mirs Bay, China, where he had anchored after leaving Hong Kong, following orders received on 25 April that directed him to attack the Spanish squadron at Manila. Having received intelligence that Admiral Montojo intended to make his defense at Subic Bay, outside the entrance to Manila Bay, Dewey and his squadron of five cruisers and a gunboat sailed in column across the South China Sea and arrived off Subic Bay on the afternoon of 30 April.

Meanwhile, Admiral Montojo maneuvered in preparation for the expected American onslaught. Believing that planned fortifications at Subic Bay had been carried out, Montojo had indeed intended to make his defense at Subic Bay, rejecting alternatives, such as the entrance to Manila Bay and the naval station at Cavite south of Manila, because neither place was appropriately fortified with artillery and mines. When he arrived at Subic Bay, however, he discovered that the fortifications had not been completed. With his options thus narrowed, he elected to fight at the Cavite naval station after all, where he could anchor in shallow water and gain at least some artillery assistance from a bat-

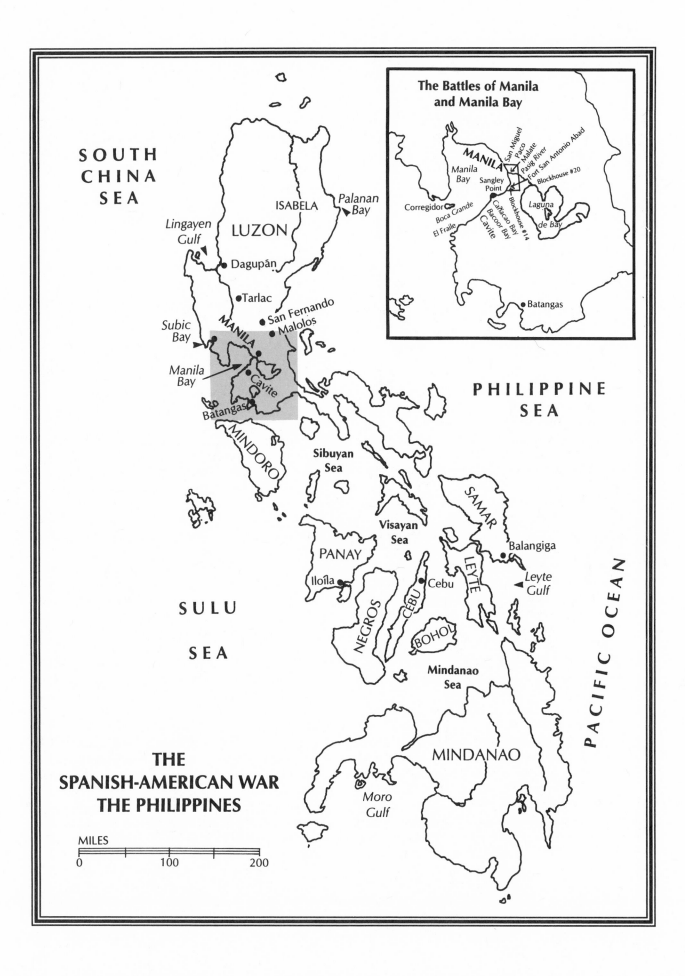

SOUTH
CHINA
SEA

**The Battles of Manila
and Manila Bay**

MANILA

*Manila
Bay*

San Miguel
Paco
Malate
Pasig River
Fort San Antonio Abad
Blockhouse #20

Sangley
Point

Corregidor

Boca Grande

El Fraile

Cañacao Bay
Bacoor Bay
Cavite
Blockhouse #14

*Laguna
de Bay*

• Batangas

*Palanan
Bay*

*Lingayen
Gulf*

ISABELA

LUZON

• Dagupán

• Tarlac

• San Fernando
Malolos

*Subic
Bay*

MANILA

*Manila
Bay*

Cavite

Batangas

MINDORO

**PHILIPPINE
SEA**

*Sibuyan
Sea*

SAMAR

**Visayan
Sea**

PANAY

• Balangiga

LEYTE

◄ *Leyte
Gulf*

Iloíla •

• Cebu

CEBU

SULU

NEGROS

BOHOL

SEA

**Mindanao
Sea**

MINDANAO

PACIFIC OCEAN

*Moro
Gulf*

**THE
SPANISH-AMERICAN WAR
THE PHILIPPINES**

MILES

0   100   200

tery on Sangley Point. This decision reflected Montojo's belief in the superiority of the U.S. squadron. If his ships foundered in shallow water, his crews could hope to survive.

Theoretically, there were other options. Montojo might have accepted battle in the open sea, but this course would almost certainly have led to defeat. He also could have fled Manila and sent his ships to various widely separated ports, at least denying an early victory to the Americans. The governor-general at Manila, Basilio Augustín, vetoed this course, reflecting the wishes of the Spanish residents of Manila who thought that Montojo could overcome the U.S. squadron.

When Dewey ascertained that Montojo was not at Subic Bay, he immediately moved into Manila Bay. This operation required a dash past several artillery batteries at the entrance to the bay, some on the mainland and others on the islands of Corregidor and El Fraile. Although it seemed likely that the entrance was mined, Dewey discounted this as a serious obstacle. At midnight the U.S. squadron ran through Boca Grande, the entrance to the bay. Only three shots were fired from El Fraile. Apparently Dewey achieved surprise, the Spanish batteries assuming that he would attempt to enter in daylight. No mines were encountered.

After entering the bay, Dewey prepared for action. He arranged his ships in line—the four protected cruisers *Olympia, Baltimore, Raleigh,* and *Boston;* the unprotected cruiser *Concord;* and the gunboat *Petrel.* He first bore in on Manila, but then observed the Spanish squadron anchored to the south in a crescent-shaped line in Cañacao Bay. It consisted of two unprotected cruisers, *Reina Cristina* and *Castilla,* and five gunboats. Although the crew strengths of the two squadrons were roughly comparable, the U.S. ships were much heavier and were better protected, manned, and armed. Had Montojo anchored under the guns of Manila somewhat farther north, he would have enjoyed the support of powerful batteries, including four modern breech-loading 9.4-inch guns. He did not do so, hoping to avoid a U.S. bombardment of the city.

After closing to five thousand yards, Dewey

opened fire on the enemy squadron at 5:40 A.M. on 1 May, beginning the Battle of Manila Bay. The U.S. squadron turned to the right and brought its port batteries into action. It then returned on a parallel line, employing its starboard batteries. At 7:00 A.M. the Spanish flagship *Reina Cristina* made a valiant attack, but it was soon driven back to its anchorage. Montojo was then forced to move to the gunboat *Isla de Cuba.* At 7:30 Dewey broke off the battle temporarily, fearing that he was about to exhaust his ammunition. A check showed that he had plenty of rounds available. Enemy fire had been ineffective; only minor damage had been inflicted on the U.S. ships, but the Spanish vessels were afire. During the lull in the battle, Montojo moved his stricken ships to the roadstead at Bacoor Bay. The Americans resumed the attack at 11:16, and a white flag was raised at Cavite about 12:15 P.M. By this time, the enemy squadron had been destroyed. The two unprotected cruisers and one of the gunboats had been sunk, and the remaining gunboats were set on fire. Three were later salvaged and refitted.

The casualty lists revealed the extent of Dewey's victory. He suffered only nine wounded and none killed. Montojo's ships endured 371 casualties, 161 killed and 210 wounded, most of them on the *Reina Cristina.* The outcome assured Dewey of a base and gave him control of Manila Bay. He anchored off Cavite and occupied that location. After being refused the right to use the Manila cable to Hong Kong, he cut it. Service was not restored until after the end of hostilities in August; Dewey communicated by dispatch boat to Hong Kong. The Spanish garrison was able to send messages to the Visayan Islands south of Luzon by another cable unknown to Dewey; from there, boats carried dispatches to a cable station off the coast of Borneo, which in turn sent them to Madrid. Messages returned from Madrid along the same route.

Unconfirmed news of Dewey's victory reached Washington on 3 May, but official dispatches did not arrive until 7 May. The dramatic victory stimulated wild celebrations across the United States, and Dewey, now the object of national adulation, was immediately promoted to admiral. Although Dewey could maintain himself safely in Manila Bay for an indefinite time, he could not move against Manila itself because he lacked troops for this purpose. Nevertheless he had fulfilled his orders. The victory at Manila Bay destroyed Spanish naval power in the Pacific Ocean, assuring the safety of U.S. maritime commerce and providing a refuge for the U.S. squadron. Most important, Dewey's triumph accorded fully with the U.S. need to confront Spain with instant and unrelenting pressure, a means of encouraging an early turn to peace negotiations. McKinley entered the war reluctantly, but once in, he hoped to bring the struggle to a conclusion at the earliest possible moment. Early and sustained indications of American resolve would help lead to this outcome.

As Dewey conducted his operations in Manila Bay, Sampson, now promoted to rear admiral, established a blockade of Cuba. The North Atlantic Squadron moved from Key West to Havana on 22 April and immediately sent vessels to cover Matanzas and Cárdenas to the east and Mariel and Cabañas to the west. Soon he also blockaded the important port of Cienfuegos on the south coast, but he could not immediately cover all the ports of eastern Cuba, including Nuevitas, Sagua la Grande, and Caibarién on the north coast and Santiago de Cuba and Guantánamo on the south coast. As the weeks passed, Sampson was able to strengthen the blockade and extend it to cover additional ports. It proved exceedingly effective—only two vessels exited past the blockading ships at Havana and only eight ships entered Cuban ports without detection. Some minor engagements with Spanish vessels or shore batteries occurred at various ports during the war. Spain could never prove its claim that the blockade was ineffective, which under international law would have rendered it illegal. The North Atlantic Squadron ensured that Spain could not reinforce or resupply its army in Cuba.

As Sampson perfected his blockade, Admiral Cervera finally steamed westward across the Atlantic from the Cape Verde Islands, leaving St. Vincent on 29 April bound for San Juan, Puerto Rico. He had four armored cruisers and three torpedo-boat destroyers. The cruiser *Vizcaya* had a fouled bottom and slowed the pace of the squadron. The new *Cristóbal Colón* proved of little use without its main battery of 10-inch guns. Captain French E. Chadwick, commander of the U.S. cruiser *New York*, aptly described the pathetic condition of the Spanish force: "Spain was without the primal necessities of a fleet— without guns, without ammunition, without engineers, without coal, and even with the ships short of bread." Had Cervera remained in European waters, the Spanish navy could have functioned as a "fleet-in-being," avoiding engagements and restricting the freedom of action of the opposing navy. By moving to the Caribbean, he surrendered these options and played directly into the hands of Sampson.

When Sampson learned that Cervera had left the Cape Verdes, he took a strong detachment east to San Juan, assuming that the enemy was bound for that port. Not finding Cervera in the harbor at San Juan, he bombarded the city briefly on 12 May and returned to his station off Havana. Cervera wisely decided to avoid San Juan. He did not reach Martinique, his first port of call, until 10 May because of his slow steaming speed. He was forced to leave a damaged destroyer at Fort de France. Deciding against moving either to Santiago de Cuba, which had not been blockaded, or to Havana, where he would have to deal with Sampson, he proceeded instead to the Dutch island of Curaçao, hoping to find a collier there to refuel his vessels. This hope was dashed, and the Dutch governor allowed him only a few hundred tons of coal from local stocks, a decision following international law. He had to leave Curaçao, a neutral port, within twenty-four hours. Seeking to avoid contact with any U.S. vessels, Cervera now determined to go to Santiago de Cuba, a decision that largely decided the future course of the war. He arrived there on 19 May, one day after Sampson returned to Havana from San Juan. Sampson immediately learned of this landfall, and, on 22 May, Commodore Schley and the Flying Squadron, then on the way to blockade Cienfuegos, received orders to pen up Cervera in port. The bumbling Schley took eight days to establish the blockade, arriving off Santiago de Cuba on 26 May but failing to observe Cervera in the harbor. After moving westward, he finally returned to Santiago de Cuba and established a blockade on 28 May. Cervera was thus given an opportunity to escape, but he did not do so. Sampson was highly critical of Schley's decisions during this period. After the war a board of inquiry ruled that Schley had shown "vacillation, dilatoriness, and lack of enterprise."

When Sampson learned of the blockade, he left Havana for Santiago de Cuba with a force that included all his remaining armored ships. He was finally able to consolidate his principal vessels because he no longer had to worry about Spanish naval raids against either the U.S. East Coast or the blockading squadron in Cuba. Arriving at Santiago de Cuba on 1 June, he devoted himself to strengthening the close-in blockade of the harbor. He wished to storm the narrow entrance to the port and engage Cervera, but he feared electrical mines in the channel that could be triggered from the shore as well as five shore batteries. To prevent Cervera from attempting to run the blockade, he tried to sink a collier, the *Merrimac*, in the channel on the night of 3 June. Richmond Pearson Hobson, a naval constructor, undertook this mission. He managed to sink his ship, but it came to rest too far north to accomplish its purpose. Sampson then settled down to await land reinforcements from the United States, hoping that they would neutralize the defenses at the harbor entrance and allow him to attack Cervera. To secure a nearby protected anchorage where ships could coal, the First Marine Battalion landed at Guantánamo Bay on 10 June. It secured the eastern shore by 15 June, and Sampson's vessels were able to use the bay after that.

PREPARATIONS FOR ARMY OPERATIONS

Early U.S. planning for the employment of the army centered on the preparation of small expeditions to support the navy, it being recognized that no major operations could take place until the volunteer army had been mobilized, a mat-

ter of many months. Meanwhile, energetic but chaotic efforts were made to enroll volunteers and to send them to training camps. On 29 April, Major General William R. Shafter was ordered to prepare an expedition of six thousand men at Tampa, Florida, that would land on the south coast of Cuba to support the Cuban guerrillas, departing after a brief stay. This operation was dropped when news of Cervera's movement to the Caribbean reached the War Department, but Shafter continued to prepare for later unspecified operations.

On 2 May a council of war at the White House considered a plan to establish a base at Mariel and mount an attack on Havana, but no such operation was possible soon. This plan was cancelled when Cervera's arrival at Martinique became known, but Shafter continued to concentrate troops at Tampa. Also on 2 May, President McKinley directed the dispatch of troops to the Philippines to support Dewey. Major General Wesley Merritt was made commander of a force that eventually numbered twenty thousand men. Designated the Eighth Army Corps, Merritt's expedition was given the mission of conquering Manila. Troops for this purpose were gathered at San Francisco.

The complexity of affairs in the Philippines increased considerably because of the activities of the Filipino insurgent leader, Emilio Aguinaldo y Famy. He had been exiled to Hong Kong after the defeat of the Filipino insurgents in 1897 and had departed for Europe early in April 1898. When he stopped at Singapore, the American consul general there, E. Spencer Pratt, held conversations with him and arranged his return to Hong Kong. When Dewey was consulted, he urged this action, thinking that Aguinaldo might be of assistance at Manila. Aguinaldo reappeared in Hong Kong early in May, and at the insistence of his followers returned to the Philippines on 19 May, arriving on the dispatch boat *McCulloch*. Dewey then supplied some arms that Aguinaldo used to help equip an insurgent force near Manila. Aguinaldo later claimed that the Americans with whom he dealt in the Far East had offered Filipino independence in return for armed assistance. Evidence for this assertion is lacking;

Washington specifically ruled out any such promise, adopting a wait-and-see policy concerning the future of the Philippines. Although increasingly concerned about the ultimate intentions of the Americans, Aguinaldo collaborated with Dewey because no other course seemed appropriate. The first task was to throw out the Spaniards; he would deal with the Americans later.

With considerable U.S. assistance, Aguinaldo obtained a store of arms and soon gained control of the area just outside Manila, but he lacked sufficient strength to storm the city, defended by nine thousand Spanish troops. On 12 June he proclaimed the independence of the Philippines, and on 23 June he formed a provisional government, which took the form of a military dictatorship. Such was the situation when the first contingent of U.S. troops arrived at the end of June.

Meanwhile, after Cervera arrived at Santiago de Cuba, important decisions were being made concerning future U.S. operations in Cuba. Plans for a strike at Havana were suspended. On 26 May a council of war approved not one but two expeditions to the Caribbean Sea. Shafter's troops at Tampa would move immediately to Santiago de Cuba, and another force would occupy Puerto Rico. Shafter's orders were to land near Santiago de Cuba with twenty-five thousand troops and cooperate with the navy in measures to capture Cervera and the garrison defending the city.

Like some naval leaders, the commanding general of the army, Major General Nelson A. Miles, wanted to seize Puerto Rico because it would provide a convenient base from which to interdict possible Spanish efforts to reinforce Cuba. He also envisioned limited operations in the interior of Cuba designed in part to support the insurgents. On 9 April, more than two weeks before the declaration of war, he had ordered Lieutenant Andrew S. Rowan to contact the insurgent General Calixto García Iñiguez in eastern Cuba. Rowan did so just after war was declared. Early in June arrangements were made for insurgent support of a landing at Santiago de Cuba. Soon, however, President McKinley rejected Miles' plans for operations in

Cuba other than at Santiago de Cuba. After that the commanding general concentrated on preparations for the Puerto Rican expedition.

During the early days of June, a mad scramble followed at Tampa as Shafter attempted to load the troops concentrated there onto transports. Supplies were scattered along the rail line between Columbia, South Carolina, and Tampa, often in unmarked railroad cars. An attempt to leave about 7–8 June failed when false reports of Spanish naval vessels, the "ghost squadron," forced postponement. Finally, a convoy was formed outside Tampa Bay on 14 June, consisting of twenty-nine transports and six supporting vessels. Three naval vessels escorted the convoy to the Dry Tortugas, where other vessels, including the battleship *Indiana*, joined the covering force.

Shafter's troops, officially designated the Fifth Army Corps, numbered about seventeen thousand troops. Fewer than twenty-five hundred were volunteers, although subsequent reinforcements raised this number to about seventy-five hundred. The regular army dominated the expedition because its regiments were organized and ready for action. Among these were four black regiments, the Ninth and Tenth cavalries and the Twenty-fourth and Twenty-fifth infantries. The principal volunteer organization was the Rough Riders, commanded by Colonel Leonard Wood and his deputy, Lieutenant Colonel Theodore Roosevelt, who had left the Navy Department. Only four other volunteer units participated in the initial phases of the Cuban campaign—the Second Massachusetts, the Seventy-first New York, the Thirty-third Michigan, and one battalion of the Thirty-fourth Michigan. About twenty-three hundred horses and mules were taken along. Artillery being scarce, the force was equipped with only sixteen light field guns, eight field mortars, and a detachment of four Gatling guns.

EVOLUTION OF WAR AIMS

The United States began the war with but one political objective—independence for Cuba—but early successes led to additional demands. On 3 June, after confirmation that Cervera was bottled up at Santiago de Cuba, Secretary of State William R. Day communicated a list of war aims to the U.S. ambassador in London, John M. Hay. This information went through British channels to Vienna for transmission to Madrid. First, Spain must hand over Cuba to the United States, which would help the Cuban people establish a stable government. Second, Spain must cede Puerto Rico to the United States instead of a monetary indemnity to satisfy claims of U.S. citizens stemming from the war. Third, the Philippines would remain in Spanish hands with the exception of a port to be selected by the United States. Fourth, Spain must cede a port in the Mariana Islands with a harbor suitable for a coaling station. The acquisition of Puerto Rico would strengthen the ability of the United States to maintain command of the sea in the western Atlantic. A coaling station in the Marianas would improve maritime communications to East Asia. On 14 June, however, Hay modified the provision concerning the Philippines, noting that the Filipino insurgents had become a factor and that their situation must receive attention. "It is most difficult without further knowledge," he concluded, "to determine as to the disposition of the Philippine Islands."

Various considerations lay behind this secret diplomatic initiative to bring Spain to the peace table. The U.S. government hoped that Spain's honor had now been satisfied, its forces having offered resistance in the Caribbean Sea and in the Philippines. McKinley sought to end the war promptly with the least possible expenditure of blood and treasure. Recognizing the Spanish penchant for delay and obfuscation, Hay concluded his message with the warning that U.S. demands might expand, should Spain continue to fight. For the moment, Spain rejected negotiations on McKinley's terms. The Austrian foreign minister, Count Agenor Goluchowski, soon informed the British foreign secretary, Lord Salisbury, that the Spanish government was not ready to consider the U.S. terms. This result, which was made known to Ambassador Hay, meant that further operations would develop in the two theaters of war, the primary arena being the Caribbean Sea and the secondary one being the western Pacific Ocean.

The expansion of U.S. war aims did not yet suggest strong public or official desire for extensive territorial gains. In this respect, the most important development of the summer was the peaceful annexation of the independent Hawaiian Republic by joint resolution of Congress. Interest in absorbing the Hawaiian Islands had existed for many years, one motive being to deny the islands to Japan. A treaty of annexation proposed in 1897 had languished in the Senate until the need for improved communications to Asia became evident during the wartime summer of 1898. Broad public support for annexation developed, and large majorities in both the House of Representatives and the Senate voted for the joint resolution. The strategic argument for annexation had earlier emphasized the defensive value of the islands, which screened the West Coast, but events in 1898 drew attention to their utility as stepping stones across the broad Pacific to the Philippines. Thus, the war stimulated territorial ambitions that had not previously gained much support.

NAVAL EXPEDITION OF ADMIRAL CÁMARA

As the United States moved energetically against Cuba, Puerto Rico, and Manila, the Spanish government decided to send a naval squadron to the Philippines. Admiral Manuel de la Cámara was given command of this force. It included two armored vessels, the battleship *Pelayo* and the cruiser *Carlos V*, two auxiliary cruisers, two troop transports with four thousand men aboard, and four colliers. Cámara left Spain on 16 June, steaming eastward through the Mediterranean Sea to the Suez Canal. Once through the canal, he intended to go to Mindanao, where he would decide his later movements. Planning to leave the Suez area about 8 July, he could expect to arrive in the Philippines forty days later, around 17 August.

The departure of Cámara's squadron stimulated activity in the U.S. Navy Department. The initial response was to order two heavily armed seagoing monitors based on the West Coast, the *Monterey* and the *Monadnock,* to the Philippine Islands. These vessels, more than a match for Cámara's armored ships, were expected to reach Manila before the Spanish squadron. Another reaction was to begin preparation of an organization that became known as the Eastern Squadron. It was to include three armored vessels detached from Sampson's command (*Iowa, Oregon,* and *Brooklyn*) and four other vessels.

The mission of the Eastern Squadron was to operate in Spanish waters, should Cámara move beyond the Suez Canal, which would force Spain either to allow uncontested attacks on its coastal cities or to recall its expedition. Commodore John C. Watson was made commander of the Eastern Squadron. Admiral Sampson dragged his feet, loath to give up armored vessels as his responsibilities broadened in the Caribbean theater. This reaction raised an important question: Did the United States possess enough armored vessels to operate successfully in both the Caribbean Sea and Spanish waters? The Navy Department was never convinced that Cámara would move beyond the eastern Mediterranean Sea, but it pressed for the early designation of vessels for the Eastern Squadron as a prudent response to the Spanish naval initiative.

SANTIAGO DE CUBA CAMPAIGN

The Spanish force at Santiago de Cuba, commanded by General Arsenio Linares Pomba, was ill-prepared to make a stout defense against a determined enemy. Insurgent detachments had interdicted his land communications with Spanish forces, elsewhere in Cuba, especially at Havana, and the U.S. Navy had cut its maritime connections. Initially, Linares had only ninety-four hundred men, but a contingent of sailors from Cervera's squadron added another thousand. A third of the force was composed of Cuban militia, *voluntarios,* who were not deemed

fully effective. Linares organized his small command into a division with two brigades, one under General of Brigade Joaquín Vara del Rey and the other under General of Division José Toral. About twenty-five thousand Spanish troops were located elsewhere in eastern Cuba, garrisoned at Sagua de Tánamo, Baracoa, Guantánamo, Holguín, and Manzanillo. The governor-general of Cuba, Don Ramón Blanco y Erenas, did not order these troops to concentrate at Santiago de Cuba for several compelling reasons. It would have been impossible to supply so many troops, concentration would have left all eastern Cuba to the insurgents, and an enlarged force would have been vulnerable to naval gunfire from Sampson's powerful squadron.

The location of Santiago de Cuba dictated the U.S. Army's plan of campaign. It lay at the western end of a valley that stretched for twenty miles and widened to seven miles near El Caney and San Miguel, two towns northeast of the city. The San Juan River ran in a southerly direction about two and one-half miles east of Santiago de Cuba below elevations known as the San Juan Heights. The harbor was about four miles in length. A narrow one-mile channel, commanded by the Punta Gorda Heights, connected the harbor to the sea. Two elevations of about two hundred feet, the Morro and the Socapa heights, rose at the mouth of the channel.

Both the channel and the city were fortified. Two lines of electrical mines, controlled from the shore, were laid in the channel. Five artillery batteries were placed on the Socapa, Morro, and Punta Gorda heights to help deny entrance. If the batteries could be silenced, an attacking navy might force its way into the harbor, but only one ship could move through the channel at a time. General Linares constructed three lines of defense around the city. An outer screen was placed between Daiquirí and Siboney, where Linares anticipated a U.S. landing. The main line of fortifications ran close to the boundary of the city, passing southward through Ermitano, El Caney, San Miguel de Lajas, Quintero Hill, and the hills of Veguita and La Caridad. A line of blockhouses and forts about eight miles in length lay farther west, including strong points on the San Juan Heights. Linares spread his forces thinly, seeking not only to defend the city but to protect a rail connection that ran north to the Sierra Maestre and an aqueduct that supplied the city with water. He had to cover his entire perimeter because of the Cuban insurgents, although he expected the U.S. attack to come from the east.

The U.S. expedition arrived off Santiago de Cuba on 20 June, and General Shafter immediately contacted Cuban General Calixto García to plan his attack on the city. It was decided to land the Fifth Army Corps at Daiquirí on 22 June.

Contingents of insurgents would attack Cabañas to give the false impression that the Americans would land at that point. Meanwhile, Sampson's squadron would shell various other coastal locations, including Daiquirí.

Once ashore, Shafter planned to move against Santiago de Cuba by a route that would take his troops away from the shore, rejecting the navy's plan for an attack on the elevations at the entrance to the channel that would allow Sampson's squadron to enter the harbor. This interior route would deprive Shafter of support from the guns of the squadron. Sampson did not learn of this decision for several days. Shafter later insisted that he rejected the navy's suggestions because of delays that would result from movement through difficult terrain along the approach to the channel entrance. He felt compelled to move rapidly because of a historical precedent. In 1741 an English army had landed at Guantánamo and attempted to move overland against Santiago de Cuba, but before it could approach the city, it suffered more than two thousand deaths from tropical disease. Shafter's decision neglected the strength of the second line of fortifications around Santiago de Cuba, particularly those associated with the San Juan Heights.

There may have been another motive. Shafter's adjutant, Lieutenant Colonel Edward J. McClernand, reported later that the commander thought he could minimize casualties by investing the city and forcing its surrender rather than storming it. An attack on the heights at the channel entrance might have produced unacceptable losses. Still another concern may have influenced Shafter. The navy had monopolized the glory of the early campaigns. Shafter may have wished to seize Santiago de Cuba and Cervera's squadron by himself, denying the navy another opportunity to distinguish itself. In any event, Shafter's decision precluded effective coordination between the army and navy in a joint operation.

Shafter arranged with García to make use of the insurgent army. In addition to the Cuban troops around Santiago de Cuba, which helped to prevent Spanish troops from leaving or entering the city, large Cuban concentrations at other locations made certain that Spanish reinforcements at other locations, such as Guantánamo or Holguín, would be unable to move overland to Santiago de Cuba. Unfortunately, cooperation with García tended to break down because of growing U.S. dislike of the insurgents. Racial prejudice was part of the cause, as was distaste for the Cuban guerrilla tactics. On the Cuban side, concern developed that the United States might not honor its pledge of independence for Cuba.

A dramatic episode added to Cuban-American tensions. On 22 June, Spanish Colonel Federico Escario and thirty-seven hundred Spanish troops marched from Manzanillo to Santiago de Cuba, seeking to break through the Cuban cordon around the city and to reinforce the trapped garrison. This column had to traverse about 160 miles of difficult terrain, facing guerrilla harassment at every turn. The march turned into a remarkable achievement; the Spaniards fought as many as forty skirmishes with the Cuban insurgents along the route. On 2 July, the day after the battles of El Caney and the San Juan Heights, Escario entered Santiago de Cuba with thirty-three hundred men despite the attempts of García's troops to stop them. The Americans attributed this outcome to the inadequacies of the Cubans, but Shafter had vetoed García's proposal to reinforce the area of the perimeter through which Escario approached the city.

The Fifth Army Corps began its landing at Daiquirí on 22 June. Linares did not oppose the operation. When sufficient troops were ashore, they moved on Siboney. This coastal location was secured by 23 June, and elements of the Fifth Army Corps began coming ashore there. Shafter intended to concentrate his entire force at Siboney before moving forward, but Major General Joseph ("Fighting Joe") Wheeler, a former Confederate cavalryman commanding the dismounted cavalry division composed of the First and Tenth cavalries and the Rough Riders, decided to attack a concentration of about fifteen hundred Spanish troops at Las Guásimas, a few miles to the northwest along the road to Santiago de Cuba. He overrode orders to another commander that would have precluded such an engagement.

The Spanish force at Las Guásimas, occupying a strong position, had orders to withdraw when attacked, but before it abandoned the position a sharp skirmish took place on 24 June. This confused engagement heightened morale in the Fifth Corps, but it created serious problems. It further committed Shafter to an advance in the interior against Santiago de Cuba, but the route passed through difficult terrain along a very poor road. To prevent Wheeler from undertaking any more unauthorized adventures, Shafter forbade further advance until he had his troops well in hand.

The Fifth Army Corps lingered in the area of Sevilla, a small town near Las Guásimas, while Shafter prepared to attack Santiago de Cuba. He wanted to move as quickly as possible, fearing outbreaks of tropical disease, but he needed several days to build up for a strong assault on the city. The army suffered from a dearth of docks, transportation, and good roads, circumstances that slowed preparation, and the hasty departure from Tampa also had an adverse effect. It proved difficult to locate and land the supplies deemed most critical for the impending attack. Although Shafter had brought some heavy artillery, he decided to rely solely on four batteries of light artillery and the Gatling-gun detachment, a concession to the difficulties of moving equipment along the road from Siboney that passed through Las Guásimas and Sevilla.

The delay around Sevilla allowed General Linares to strengthen his defensive arrange-

ments. He gave special attention to the outer line of fortifications that ran through El Caney and the San Juan Heights and thence to the shore near Aguadores. About 4,760 troops occupied eleven strong points on this line, but they were divided into many small detachments. Only 520 men occupied El Caney, and on the crucial San Juan Heights there were but 137 men each on San Juan Hill and Kettle Hill. This force was later increased to 520 men. Linares used almost thirty-four hundred of the approximately ten thousand troops available to him to defend the western side of the bay.

Shafter decided to move quickly when he learned of Escario's approach. His intelligence was faulty, leading to the misapprehension that about eight thousand Spanish reinforcements were approaching Santiago de Cuba, more than twice the correct number. Shafter hastily reconnoitered the Spanish positions at El Caney and the San Juan Heights. El Caney lay about six miles to the northeast of Santiago de Cuba, where defenders manned six blockhouses and a stone fort known as El Viso. Troops could approach it by turning north off the main road to Santiago de Cuba at El Pozo. A road connected El Caney directly with Santiago de Cuba. About two miles east of the city, the San Juan Heights began their rise. Kettle Hill lay just to the north of the road from Sevilla and El Pozo. San Juan Hill, a higher point, was located about four hundred yards to the southwest.

Shafter decided to make his main assault on the San Juan Heights on 1 July, organizing two secondary attacks in support. After moving across the heights, he intended to storm Santiago de Cuba, which meant that he would encounter the city's main defense lines about a thousand yards farther on. Worried about the threat to his right flank from the direction of El Caney, he decided to have a division under Brigadier General Henry W. Lawton clear that location before it moved into position on the right of the line that would sweep across the San Juan Heights. To deceive Linares into thinking that his main attack would come against the elevations at the entrance to the channel, he planned to move the Michigan Volunteers under Brigadier General Henry M. Duffield along a coastal rail line and demonstrate at Aguadores on the coast. Two divisions, one under Brigadier General Jacob F. Kent to the south of the road to Santiago de Cuba and the other the dismounted cavalry under General Wheeler to the north of the road, would assault the San Juan Heights. Lawton's division would come on line on the right next to Wheeler's troops after reducing El Caney.

ACTIONS AT AGUADORES AND EL CANEY

The Michigan Volunteers made the first move on 1 July, advancing by train to the railroad bridge just west of Aguadores. Upon arriving, they discovered that the Spanish defenders had destroyed the western end of the bridge, an act that precluded further action. This demonstration was supposed to prevent Linares from reinforcing the San Juan Heights, but only 275 Spanish defenders faced Duffield's force of twenty-five hundred men. The move against Aguadores did not influence the battle.

Meanwhile, General Lawton attacked El Caney. He expected to begin at 7:00 A.M. and to reach his objectives two hours later, a schedule that would allow him to join the force below the San Juan Heights by 10:00 A.M., the time set for the main action of the day. Lawton assaulted El Caney with two of his three brigades, one under Brigadier General William Ludlow on the left and another under Brigadier General Adna R. Chaffee on the right. He kept his other brigade, commanded by Colonel Evan Miles, in reserve. A battery of light artillery, consisting of four 3.2-inch guns, was positioned about twenty-three hundred yards south of El Caney. The Spanish defenders lacked artillery, which would have allowed Lawton to locate the guns much closer to El Caney. In any event, Lawton's artillery fire was ineffective for much of the battle.

Lawton attacked at 7:00 A.M. as planned, but the 520 Spanish defenders under General Vara del Rey, armed only with Mauser rifles, made a valiant defense based on the fort of El Viso. This delay upset the timetable for the attack on the

San Juan Heights. The struggle at El Caney wore on through the morning. Lawton then committed his reserve brigade and the independent brigade under Brigadier General John C. Bates. Shortly after noon, Shafter decided to order Lawton to break off the engagement so that he could move to his position on the right of the line below the San Juan Heights. Lawton resisted this order, successfully requesting permission to complete his mission. He feared that withdrawal might be construed as defeat. Besides, his brigades were deeply engaged and therefore difficult to extract.

The Battle of El Caney continued into the afternoon. Finally, the artillery battery obtained the range on El Viso, which permitted the Twelfth Infantry, with help from other regiments, to overrun the fort at about 3:00 P.M. It took two more hours to mop up. The Spanish defenders suffered terribly, losing their commander, Vara del Rey, and all but about 100 of the 520 troops. Lawton lost 81 killed and 360 wounded.

The delay at El Caney kept Lawton's troops out of the main attack on the San Juan Heights. Critics of the operation argue that a small force could have held the Spanish garrison at El Caney in place, avoiding a frontal attack on a strong defensive position. Lawton could then have participated in the main attack, a contribution that might have led to the fall of Santiago de Cuba on 1 July. As it was, Secretary of War Russell Alger made the curious argument that the hand of Providence was at work. If Lawton had joined the rest of the Fifth Army Corps, he maintained, the assault on Santiago de Cuba might have been pressed to a conclusion, increasing the number of American casualties taken during the attack on the San Juan Heights for no good reason.

BATTLE OF THE SAN JUAN HEIGHTS

To defend the San Juan Heights, General Linares established a line about four thousand yards long anchored on San Juan Hill, the largest elevation in the area. He manned this position with about 1,700 men, of whom only 520 were on San Juan Hill and Kettle Hill In addition, a reserve of about 400 men with two artillery pieces, a 6.3-inch gun and a 4.7-inch gun, supported the troops on the two hills.

The division commanders, General Kent and General Sumner (who had replaced Wheeler as commander of the dismounted cavalry division), began their deployments at 7:00 A.M. A U.S. artillery battery of four 3.2-inch guns at El Pozo opened on the heights at 8:00 A.M. from a distance of twenty-six hundred yards. The black powder used by the Americans was clearly visible, and Spanish guns to the rear of the heights soon silenced the battery. This development meant that eight thousand attackers would have to move to their initial positions without benefit of artillery support along a single highly congested road.

Shafter made use of a hot-air balloon to provide observation, because he lacked good information about the terrain, not having conducted an adequate reconnaissance of the battlefield. The balloon was towed along the road and was visible above the trees, thus pinpointing the movement of the U.S. column and attracting enemy fire that caused many casualties.

The approach march did not go well. Kent's infantry division, moving west along the road from El Pozo, was supposed to turn south of the main road below the heights and move against San Juan Hill. Sumner's dismounted cavalry division, proceeding along the same route, was to turn north and move across Kettle Hill before joining Kent on the main elevation. A lagoon lay between the two hills. Unfortunately, one of Kent's regiments, the Seventy-first New York Volunteers, broke in the face of heavy enemy fire as it moved toward its starting position. Kent and others managed to stop the flight of the Seventy-first New York, which was held in place while the two regular army regiments of the brigade, the Sixth and Sixteenth infantries, passed through them. Another of Kent's brigades, which included the Ninth, Thirteenth, and Twenty-fourth infantries, got into position on the left. Kent's third brigade, composed of the Second, Tenth, and Twenty-first infantries,

came up just to the rear of the leading brigades. Meanwhile, the two brigades of Sumner's division, the first made up of the Third, Sixth, and Ninth cavalries and the second of the First and Tenth cavalries and the Rough Riders, moved into position below Kettle Hill.

At 1:00 P.M., three hours after the time set for the assault, Kent and Sumner began their movement against the San Juan Heights. Lieutenant John D. Miley, Shafter's aide, authorized the charge at the urging of General Sumner, although Lawton's troops had not arrived. As Kent's left brigade started up San Juan Hill, the most important event of the engagement took place. Second Lieutenant John H. Parker's Gatling-gun detachment opened on the Spanish positions at the summit, three weapons using .30-caliber ammunition at ranges between six hundred and eight hundred yards. Parker fired for about eight minutes, expending as many as thirty-six hundred rounds per minute, and his guns had an instant effect. The Spanish defenders fled down the opposite slope. Despite confusion, the Sixth and Sixteenth regiments, in the lead, occupied the abandoned hilltop, and the rest of Kent's division followed them into positions on the heights. Meanwhile, Sumner moved against Kettle Hill without benefit of supporting fire from artillery or Gatling guns. The Ninth Cavalry led the assault with the First Cavalry and the Rough Riders following. The defenders abandoned the crest before the Americans arrived, and the U.S. troops pressed on past the lagoon to the northern end of San Juan Hill.

After gaining control of the San Juan Heights, the two assault divisions halted and began to entrench, abandoning any thought of going on to Santiago de Cuba. Shafter feared a counterattack, but none happened, the enemy having retreated to the principal defensive positions of Santiago de Cuba. Although defeated, the Spanish defenders at El Caney, outnumbered twelve to one, and those at the San Juan Heights, outnumbered sixteen to one, made a brave defense. Only three thousand U.S. troops of the Fifth Corps reached the heights in the initial charge. Exhausted by their effort, these troops were in any event too few to continue toward Santiago de Cuba.

Both sides suffered many casualties. Shafter lost 205 men killed and 1,180 wounded at El Caney and the San Juan Heights. Including losses suffered during the two days immediately following the attack, about 10 percent of the Fifth Army Corps became casualties. The Spanish lost about 35 percent of the seventeen hundred men who defended the positions at El Caney and the San Juan Heights.

Shafter worked feverishly to reinforce the San Juan Heights, a confused effort because he had made no plans for it, having assumed that he would carry Santiago de Cuba in one grand leap. Some authorities do not think that Shafter intended to move on to Santiago de Cuba on 1 July, but the evidence clearly establishes this intention. After the battle, Shafter noted that the "hitch" in his operations, the cause of the failure to finish the assault, was Lawton's inability to reduce El Caney quickly. He concluded that "it was better as it was, for had he [Lawton] been on the right on the Caney road at 10 o'clock, we should have taken the city of Santiago that day, and would have had none of the territory or outside soldiers that we got later." As did Secretary Alger, he made a virtue out of Lawton's necessity.

Somehow the Fifth Army Corps occupied the heights in strength. Lawton's troops did not reach the front line until 2 July. As they marched along the road from El Caney to Santiago de Cuba during the evening of 1 July, the advance guard encountered enemy fire. Shafter's deputy, Colonel McClernand, then directed Lawton to return to El Pozo, greatly lengthening the distance that had to be covered. Meanwhile, the independent brigade under General Bates moved into the line at the extreme left next to Kent's division with Duffield's division of volunteers, which included the newly arrived Ninth Massachusetts. Some Cuban troops came into the line to the right of Lawton's brigade. Shafter also brought up the four light-artillery batteries and Parker's Gatling-gun detachment.

Many students of the battle have criticized both commanders. Linares did not concentrate

sufficient troops and artillery at the probable point of attack, and when his troops were forced off the San Juan Heights, he did not order a counterattack. Shafter has been faulted for using too many men against El Caney, for failing to make a good reconnaissance of the battlefield, and for not making the most effective use of his few artillery pieces. He also did not call upon the guns of Admiral Sampson, which could easily have fired on the Spanish positions. Of course, Admiral Cervera also could have fired on the Americans.

The stubborn resistance of the Spanish garrison, largely unexpected, had adverse effects on the confidence of the Fifth Army Corps and its commander. Shafter, who was in poor health, greatly overestimated his difficulties and as grossly underestimated those of the enemy. General Linares had been wounded on 1 July, and his successor, General Toral, quickly reinforced the positions between the Americans and the city, placing about fifty-five hundred troops along a line of about six miles with another thousand in reserve. His troops were short of ammunition and ill-fed, a situation that grew worse because the attacks of 1 July had cut off access to the water supply and cultivated regions to the north. Meanwhile, the Fifth Army Corps was well-positioned to fire on the city from protected locations on the San Juan Heights, and Admiral Sampson's squadron also could bombard the city. Shafter, however, worried mostly about his difficulties—the possibility that reinforcements might appear to bolster Toral, that his miserable supply line from Siboney and Daiquirí might break down, that tropical weather might inhibit operations, and that disease might overwhelm his command.

Bearing these problems in mind, Shafter cast about for a course of action. He first considered the operation he had rejected earlier, an attack on the elevations at the entrance to the channel, but General Wheeler counseled successfully against this proposal because it might produce many casualties, precisely what the commander of the Fifth Army Corps wished to avoid. Shafter then contemplated a withdrawal, reporting to Washington by cable that many officers thought it "absolutely necessary for us to retreat in order to save ourselves from being enfiladed by the Spanish lines and cut off from our supplies, as an attack by the Spanish with a few fresh troops would result in our utter defeat."

Meanwhile, Shafter asked Sampson to move against the channel entrance. The admiral refused, noting that the electrical mines were the chief threat to his ships, not the batteries. An attack by land would be necessary to effect their neutralization, pending countermining operations. The Navy Department was anxious to avoid risking the loss of any armored ships, recognizing that they were all required to support operations elsewhere, perhaps against Puerto Rico or in Spanish waters. Secretary of the Navy Long also considered the possibility that Spain might gain naval support from some European power.

When President McKinley received word of Shafter's inclination to withdraw to more secure positions, he immediately headed off any such initiative. Noting the adverse effect on public opinion that would stem from a retreat, he urged Shafter to hold fast. Brigadier General Henry Clark Corbin, the adjutant general, promised immediate reinforcements. McKinley also considered replacing Shafter because of his illness. When Shafter learned of Washington's interest in his health, he moved to dispel concern. He and Admiral Sampson arranged to confer on the morning of 3 July. He also decided to act on an idea that he had mentioned to his adjutant, McClernand, while on the voyage to Santiago de Cuba. After placing his troops in sound positions around the city, he would demand the surrender of the city. Accordingly, a message was dispatched to the enemy, warning Toral that the Fifth Army Corps would begin bombardment of the city unless it was surrendered.

NAVAL BATTLE OF SANTIAGO DE CUBA

On Sunday morning, 3 July, Sampson's flagship, the cruiser *New York*, left the blockading squadron to go to Siboney; from there the admiral intended to go on to Shafter's headquarters for their planned meeting. After steaming east about seven miles, however, he spotted gunsmoke at the entrance to the channel. Admiral Cervera's squadron was attempting to flee. The *New York* immediately turned to rejoin its squadron, but it missed much of the ensuing action. Commodore Schley, in whom Sampson lacked confidence, was the senior officer present on the blockade.

Admiral Cervera had actually received authority to leave Santiago de Cuba back on 23 June, but he had expended considerable energy attempting to avoid any such sortie. He had an excellent reason for his view, being fully aware that the U.S. blockading squadron was much stronger than his command. He stated to Linares, "I have considered the squadron lost ever since it left Cape Verde for to think anything else seems madness to me, in view of the enormous disparity which exists between our own forces and those of the enemy." Unfortunately, the governor-general in Havana, Blanco, thought differently, arguing that the moral effect of surrendering without a fight would have terrible consequences in Spain. Naval authorities in Madrid urged Cervera to attempt escape at night, but the Spanish commander noted later that the U.S. blockaders moved close to the entrance during the evening hours, not only illuminating the channel, but making it impossible for exiting ships to avoid running aground or colliding with other vessels. Nevertheless, on 28 June, Blanco ordered Cervera to depart, but Cervera had trouble recovering the seamen who had become part of Linares' defense. These men participated in the battles of El Caney and the San Juan Heights on 1 July.

After the battles, however, Cervera had been forced to decide his course of action. The fall of Santiago de Cuba appeared imminent, and consideration was given to an early departure of the garrison, which might march north to join forces from Holguín or Manzanillo. Blanco again ordered Cervera to leave, informing Toral that the loss of the squadron would mean that "Spain will be morally defeated and must ask for peace at mercy of enemy."

Thus it was that late on 2 July, Cervera issued

instructions for a sortie from the harbor at 9:00 A.M. on 3 July. The *Infanta María Teresa* would depart first, followed by the three armored cruisers. The two destroyers would come out last. The objective was escape; those vessels that could do so were to steam for Cienfuegos or Havana. Captain Víctor Concas y Palau, one of the Spanish ship commanders, noted the most harrowing aspect of the sortie. The narrow channel meant that Cervera's ships would have to exit one by one, allowing the U.S. squadron to concentrate its fire on each exiting vessel.

Spanish observations on the morning of 3 July revealed a gap in the western end of the U.S. blockade, a circumstance that led Cervera to order flight westward to Cienfuegos. Several U.S. vessels were absent. The battleship *Massachusetts*, two cruisers, and a converted tender had gone to Guantánamo to coal, and the armored cruiser *New York* with Sampson aboard and two small vessels had left for Siboney. Seven ships remained on station. At the east side of the semicircular formation was the converted yacht *Gloucester*. Next came the battleships *Indiana*, *Oregon*, *Iowa*, and *Texas* and the armored cruiser *Brooklyn*, Schley's flagship. At the western end was the converted yacht *Vixen*.

The U.S. squadron, as Cervera recognized, was much stronger than the Spanish force. Cervera's six vessels displaced less than thirty thousand tons and carried only forty-two big guns. Sampson's vessels displaced almost fifty thousand tons and carried seventy-six big guns. Only the crews were roughly similar in number. With Cervera's ships emerging one at a time, the U.S. advantage was all the more imposing.

At 9:35 A.M. the *Infanta María Teresa* came out with Admiral Cervera aboard, and the other ships followed at intervals of ten minutes, separated by eight hundred yards and moving at a speed of eight to ten knots. All turned west toward Cienfuegos, an act that Sampson later wrote "removed all tactical doubts or difficulties." When the Spanish flagship exited, it forced Commodore Schley on the *Brooklyn* into a serious error. Cervera hoped to engage the *Brooklyn* because it was the fastest of the U.S. ships. If it could be disabled, it might ease the

escape of other ships. Faced with Cervera's approach, Schley ordered his ship to turn northeastward away from the onrushing Cervera, passing behind the *Iowa* and the *Texas*, which screened him temporarily. This "loop" was so unexpected that the *Texas* had to reverse its engine to avoid a crash. Despite Schley's error, the *Infanta María Teresa* did not survive for long. It turned westward, but, mortally wounded, it was driven on the shore at Punta Cabrera only an hour after it came out of the channel.

The next two Spanish ships to exit, the *Vizcaya* and the *Cristóbal Colón*, benefited from the attention paid to the Spanish flagship. The fourth ship to appear, the *Almirante Oquendo*, was next to be destroyed. It also was driven on the shore just west of the *Infanta María Teresa* at 10:40 A.M. The remaining destroyers, *Furor* and *Plutón*, drew fire from the four U.S. battleships present, but the *Gloucester*, commanded by Lieutenant Commander Richard Wainwright, a survivor of the *Maine* disaster, finished off both vessels. The Plutón struck the shore at 10:45 A.M. west of Cabañas, and the *Furor* foundered somewhat nearer Cabañas offshore.

After two hours of battle, only two Spanish ships remained afloat, the speedy *Cristóbal Colón* and the *Vizcaya*. Although the *Vizcaya* exited first, the faster vessel soon passed it, but the U.S. squadron first concentrated its fire on the *Vizcaya*, which was beached on a reef at 11:15 A.M. near Asseraderos. At this point, the *New York* reached the scene of the battle, and the U.S. flagship conducted the pursuit of the *Cristóbal Colón*. Sampson ordered the *Iowa* and the *Indiana* to return to the blockade, fearing that two Spanish ships remaining at Santiago de Cuba might attack noncombatant ships unloading at Siboney. Thus, the cruisers *New York* and *Brooklyn* and three battleships chased the *Cristóbal Colón*. At full speed, the Spanish ship was faster than its pursuers, but it ran out of good coal and had to make use of an inferior grade that it had taken on at Santiago de Cuba. When it slowed and came within range of the *Oregon*, its captain decided to drive his ship on the shore, which he did near the Turquino River fifty miles west of Santiago de Cuba at 1:15 P.M.

Few sea battles have ended more disastrously for the loser. Sampson's squadron lost one sailor killed and another wounded, and three ships sustained minor damage. The Spanish squadron may have lost 323 killed and 157 wounded, about one in five of the crew members, the figure reported by Captain Concas. A large number of prisoners of war, 1,720 officers and men, were later detained in the United States, the officers at Annapolis, Maryland, and the enlisted men at Portsmouth, New Hampshire. The critical difference between the performance of the two squadrons was gunnery. Cervera's four armored ships were struck no less than 123 times, the *Almirante Oquendo* taking fifty-seven shells. Spanish gunnery suffered from lack of practice and deficient ammunition. Nevertheless, as at Manila Bay, the percentage of U.S. hits was low, an outcome that stimulated efforts to improve gunnery methods after the war.

Schley's performance during the battle, especially his loop turn away from the *Infanta María Teresa*, further lowered his standing with Sampson, and it influenced the postwar inquiry into the commodore's actions, which criticized him severely. Although fate kept Sampson out of most of the action, he deserves high praise for having prepared his squadron very well for the action of 3 July. An unfortunate postwar dispute between Sampson and Schley over credit for the victory at Santiago de Cuba did not add to the reputation of either officer.

Sampson's victory produced an immediate result that eased the navy's concerns in both the Caribbean and the Pacific—the recall back to Spain of Admiral Cámara, whose squadron was then in the Red Sea. As his squadron proceeded eastward across the Mediterranean Sea to Egypt, the U.S. Navy Department tracked its progress carefully and from time to time adjusted the list of vessels to be assigned to the Eastern Squadron. Eventually the list included three armored vessels—the *Oregon, Iowa,* and *Brooklyn*—a development that worried Sampson. When word of Cervera's catastrophe reached Spain, however, Cámara was brought back to Spanish waters because, as Spanish

Minister of Marine, Captain Ramón Auñón, later acknowledged, there was fear of a U.S. naval descent on the undefended Spanish coast. Sampson's concerns were thus allayed, and in the Philippines, Dewey no longer had to consider the possibility that he might have to face Cámara with only one armored vessel, the monitor *Monterey*, then en route to the Philippines and scheduled to arrive before the *Monadnock*, another monitor.

The Navy Department did not, however, immediately disband the Eastern Squadron. It considered sending naval reinforcements to Dewey via the Mediterranean Sea, seeking by this expedient to discourage other nations, especially Germany, that were thought to have an interest in acquiring the Philippines. Under this plan, Admiral Watson would take two armored ships to the Philippines. A powerful covering squadron would accompany him to Gibraltar, including all the remaining armored ships, and they would remain in the area until Watson had moved well to the east. This plan came to nothing, because the navy had to support operations against Puerto Rico, and in any case there were indications of an early end of the war.

SIEGE OF SANTIAGO DE CUBA

Sampson's naval triumph strengthened Shafter's preference for a siege, rather than an assault, of Santiago de Cuba. News that Spanish reinforcements were on the way added to the argument against storming the city. Shafter again demanded its surrender, but Toral did not respond favorably. The arrival of Escario's relief column in Santiago de Cuba heightened Shafter's interest in reinforcements and in the proposal for a naval attack on the channel entrance. Claiming that Escario's arrival had nearly doubled the strength of the enemy garrison, an exaggeration, he revealed a major concern to Sampson: "My present position has cost me 1,000 men, and I do not want to lose any more."

President McKinley and his advisers in Washington wanted action. Shafter received orders to plan an attack with the cooperation of the navy. The Navy Department and Sampson, however, opposed operations that might entail loss of armored vessels. The nation could replace troops, but it could not easily replace cruisers or battleships. Sampson wanted to use his marines to attack the western side of the channel while Shafter moved against the eastern side. Control of the elevations would permit removal of mines and other obstacles in the channel. In its final form, the plan of joint operations called for another demand for the surrender of Santiago de Cuba. If it was rejected, Sampson's ships would bombard the city. If the shelling did not produce results, an attack on the elevations at the entrance to the harbor would take place. This scheme again revealed Shafter's wish, to avoid further combat if possible.

Growing medical, logistical, and tactical complications reinforced Shafter's thinking. Although yellow fever did not appear, the troops began to contract malaria and dysentery. Adding to the difficulties of the Fifth Army Corps was the tenuous supply line between Siboney and the San Juan Heights and the shortage of transports to move personnel, equipment, and supplies from U.S. ports to Cuba. Finally, the War Department expressed concern about the failure to cover the flanks of the U.S. position adequately, to which observation Shafter responded with a plea for additional reinforcements.

As the U.S. grip on the city tightened, the two sides continued negotiations for the surrender of the city. On 8 July, Toral proposed to evacuate Santiago de Cuba in return for the right to march unmolested to Holguín. Shafter referred this deal to his superiors, correctly anticipating refusal. McKinley responded almost immediately, the adjutant general conveying his sentiments in unequivocal language: "You will accept nothing but unconditional surrender and should take extra precautions to prevent the enemy's escape." Meanwhile, however, Shafter had decided to recommend acceptance of Toral's proposition. It would convey the city to the Americans, minimize disruption of civil life, and allow the Fifth Army Corps to move elsewhere, presumably to Puerto Rico. The War

Department replied to this proposal with a clear veto, insisting on an assault at the proper time in language that implied considerable criticism of Shafter's hesitancy.

On 9 July, Shafter finally fell in with the instructions of the War Department and made the required dispositions. He notified Toral that he expected unconditional surrender. Otherwise, he would bombard the city. Reinforcements had arrived, which allowed the Fifth Army Corps to extend its right flank, a step intended to preclude Toral from breaking out to the north. Admiral Sampson was asked to bombard Santiago de Cuba, although Shafter enjoined him to make certain that his shells did not fall near the San Juan Heights, less than two miles from the town. The naval bombardment duly took place on 10–11 July. The navy destroyed some houses in the city, but many missiles appear to have missed their targets, a consequence of Sampson's endeavors to avoid hitting the U.S. positions. Shafter thought the bombardment ineffective, but it was not pressed to its limits. If the navy had used its larger armament extensively, the city could have been destroyed easily, but no further naval gunfire was ordered.

The bombardment nevertheless forced Toral into negotiations that led to the capitulation of Santiago de Cuba several days later. On 11 July, the War Department informed Shafter that should Toral accept unconditional surrender, the United States would bear the cost of transporting the Spanish garrison to Spain. At this point, General Nelson A. Miles arrived at Santiago de Cuba with the troops he had gathered to conduct an invasion of Puerto Rico. He did not supersede Shafter in command of the Fifth Army Corps but attempted to arrange for a joint army-navy attack on the channel entrance. Shafter disapproved of this initiative and Miles suspended it. Together the two generals again raised the idea of granting Toral safe conduct to Holguín, but President McKinley rejected this course, recognizing that it would likely elicit adverse public reaction at home and that Spain might interpret any such step as a sign of weakness.

In Madrid, Sagasta inclined strongly toward an end to the war. Spain had fought honorably, and could now negotiate a settlement acceptable to the public. Besides, the tactical situation at Santiago de Cuba appeared hopeless, and the U.S. Eastern Squadron might descend on the Canary Islands or the Balearic Islands. Governor-general Blanco urged continued resistance, but Sagasta ended the session of the Spanish parliament on 14 July and took steps to end the siege at Santiago de Cuba. When Blanco finally accepted McKinley's proposal to follow capitulation with repatriation of the Spanish garrisons, Toral acted immediately, proposing to Shafter the capitulation not only of the garrison at Santiago de Cuba but those located elsewhere in eastern Cuba.

Both sides appointed commissioners to negotiate the settlement and formal meetings began on 14 July. Various delays followed, and Shafter at one point considered allowing the Spanish troops to retain their arms, an initiative that elicited instant disapproval in Washington. Soon, however, Toral received formal permission to capitulate, and final arrangements were made on 16 July, including the surrender of the garrisons elsewhere in the region. Shafter later wrote that he had been "simply thunderstruck that of their own free will they should give me twelve thousand men that were absolutely beyond my reach." Shafter would not allow Admiral Sampson to sign the articles of capitulation, a further manifestation of the tension that had marked interservice relationships throughout the campaign.

The formal capitulation occurred on 17 July, an event that preceded the beginning of diplomatic attempts to end the war. On 18 July, the Duque de Almodóvar del Río, the Spanish foreign minister, moved through the French government to notify the United States of Spain's willingness to accept Cuban independence and to suspend hostilities. The Spanish government recognized that further delay might lead to more defeats because U.S. expeditions aimed at Puerto Rico and the Philippines were about to launch attacks. Delays postponed delivery of the Spanish proposal in Washington until 26 July, when French Ambassador Jules Cambon delivered it to the president. This development showed the importance of the naval and military victories at Santiago de Cuba. The action in southeastern Cuba fulfilled the president's wish for an early settlement, one that would come before much further expenditure of blood and treasure.

As the capitulation took place at Santiago de Cuba, the Fifth Army Corps experienced an alarming epidemic of tropical diseases. Despite various expedients, including frequent changes of campsites and rigorous sanitation measures, the number of men taken ill continued to rise. On 23 July, Shafter recommended the return of his command to the United States. On 24 July he reported 396 new illnesses and by 27 July a total of 3,770 on sick report. This number increased to 4,270 men on 28 July. When Shafter on 2 August warned of a likely outbreak of yellow fever, the War Department proposed that he move troops to high ground above the fever belt.

This action stimulated complaints from elements of the Fifth Army Corps that led to action. A round-robin letter signed by leading officers argued that the army must depart or suffer massive losses. Another letter signed by the surgeons at Santiago de Cuba expressed the same sentiments. Lieutenant Colonel Roosevelt wrote a private letter to Senator Henry Cabot Lodge in which he claimed that remaining in Cuba would "simply involve the destruction of thousands." When the round-robin and Roosevelt letters were leaked to the press, they generated a burst of public concern, but the War Department had already decided to act. Shafter received orders to return his command to the United States. Other troops would continue the occupation of Santiago de Cuba.

Arrangements were hurriedly made to construct a camp at Montauk Point on the eastern tip of Long Island, New York, a thinly populated location, where the Fifth Army Corps would recuperate after returning from Cuba. The first troops left Cuba on 7 August, and others followed when transportation became available. The hasty evacuation of Santiago de Cuba and the short warning at Montauk Point led to much confusion, but the Fifth Army Corps was saved from disaster. More than twenty thousand troops arrived at Camp Wikoff at Montauk, but only 257 died there compared with 514 deaths in Cuba. As soon as their health permitted, the men were released from service. On 3 October, the Fifth Army Corps was formally disbanded at Camp Wikoff.

PUERTO RICAN CAMPAIGN

Attention now turned to Puerto Rico and the expedition headed by General Miles that was organized to invade that island. The conquest of Puerto Rico would deprive Spain of a most useful base and provide an excellent eastern location from which to guard against Spanish naval or military movements to the Caribbean Sea. Perhaps more important, operations there would add to the pressure exerted upon Madrid to come to terms. Some military advisers, including Captain Alfred Thayer Mahan of the Naval War Board, had argued that Puerto Rico should come under attack before Cuba, but logistical considerations had doomed any such decision.

General Miles took a special interest in a Puerto Rican campaign, and he spearheaded preparations for an invasion of the island, an operation decided upon at the same time as the movement to Santiago de Cuba. Feverish preparations, particularly at Key West and Charleston, South Carolina, were made to prepare troops for the attack on Puerto Rico.

When difficulties developed at Santiago de Cuba, Miles was ordered to move the troops intended for Puerto Rico to that city, where he arrived on 11 July. While at Santiago de Cuba, Miles completed arrangements for his invasion of Puerto Rico. When arranging a naval escort, he said that he planned a landing at Fajardo, which was at the northeast corner of the island. From there he would move against San Juan. Miles sought a powerful naval escort for his transports, to which Sampson raised objections. President McKinley resolved this dispute summarily, evidently tired of interservice squabbling at Santiago de Cuba, asking Secretary of the Navy Long to assign sufficient ships—including a cruiser or battleship or both—to serve

as Miles' escort. Sampson then designated the battleship *Massachusetts*, the auxiliary cruiser *Dixie*, and the armed yacht *Gloucester* to this duty.

Miles cleared Guantánamo Bay on 21 July with three transports carrying about thirty-four hundred men, expecting other troops to join him. Major General James H. Wilson left Charleston on 20 July with thirty-six hundred troops, and Brigadier General Theodore Schwan departed from Tampa four days later with another twenty-nine hundred men. Eight thousand troops awaited transports at Newport News, Virginia, and Tampa, so that Miles anticipated a total force of about eighteen thousand men. He expected to deal with a Spanish garrison of about seventeen thousand members, more than half of them unreliable Puerto Rican volunteers. While on his way to Fajardo, Miles abruptly changed his plan of campaign. He decided not to land at Fajardo, but to continue to steam around Puerto Rico until he reached Guánica on the southwestern coast. A landing at this point, which possessed an excellent harbor, would gain surprise. He would then seize nearby Ponce, the largest city in Puerto Rico, and after that move north against San Juan. The commander of the *Massachusetts*, Captain Francis J. Higginson, raised objections, arguing the advantages of a landing at Fajardo, which included easy landing operations and the availability of coal and communications at the adjacent island of St. Thomas. When Miles persisted, Higginson gave in. This change of plan meant that the army would have to operate all the way across the mountainous interior of Puerto Rico to reach objectives on the north coast, including San Juan. Miles must have thought that the advantages of surprise would outweigh the difficulties that would stem from landing far from the enemy center of resistance.

The Spanish governor-general, General Manuel Macías y Casado, was well-informed of Miles' intended invasion, and he disposed his forces to sustain resistance, a means of strengthening Spain's bargaining power in forthcoming peace negotiations. Instead of concentrating all his forces around San Juan, Macías sent strong detachments to Ponce and Mayagüez and another to Caguas, which lay on the road from Ponce to San Juan.

Miles conducted successful landing operations and then established himself in force at several important southern locations before launching columns northward. Troops went ashore at Guánica without resistance and soon secured the place. He then moved against Ponce, somewhat to the east, taking possession of the city on 27–28 July. Shortly after that, reinforcements arrived from the United States, swelling his force to more than fifteen thousand men. A contingent of five thousand men commanded by Major General John R. Brooke landed at Arroyo, another port on the southeast coast of Puerto Rico, on 3–5 August.

Miles' decision to begin his campaign on the south coast led to a scheme initiated by Commander Charles H. Davis—a naval operation to capture San Juan without the help of the army. Sampson fell in with this idea, perhaps smarting from previous setbacks in controversies with army leaders. He sought permission from Secretary Long to attack San Juan from the sea. It could "be destroyed from the water and may yield without much resistance to a proper show of naval strength." Unfortunately for the navy, Miles learned of this plan and managed to scotch it. Like the attack on Santiago de Cuba, the Puerto Rican campaign stimulated unseemly interservice controversy.

Miles began his northern movement during the first week of August, following a plan of campaign that called for several sweeps across the interior of Puerto Rico to the north coast, eventually converging on San Juan. General Schwan was ordered to lead his Independent Regular Brigade of 1,450 troops, mostly infantry with a cavalry troop and two batteries of light artillery, to Mayagüez and from there through Lares to Arecibo, conquering western Puerto Rico. On the right flank, General Brooke was ordered to move against Cayey, a strong point on the route to San Juan. Meanwhile, General Wilson would move from Ponce against Aibonito. These two forces would then move north to Caguas and San Juan. Brigadier General George H. Garretson was to move toward Utuado north of Ponce.

Only a few engagements took place before word arrived that a protocol providing for a cessation of hostilities had been signed in Washington. Wilson's troops outflanked a Spanish force at Coamo on 9 August and opened the route to Aibonito. On 10 August, Schwan routed a Spanish force at Hormigueros a few miles south of Mayagüez, permitting him to occupy the latter city on 11 August before starting his march on Lares. The most difficult engagement of the campaign seemed destined to take place at Aibonito, where thirteen hundred Spanish defenders occupied a strong position. The battle, which was to take place on 13 August, never happened because of the cessation of hostilities the previous day.

Miles insisted that he would have conquered all Puerto Rico in four days. Although it might have taken longer to overcome the defenses at Aibonito and San Juan, Macías could not have mounted a serious defense. U.S. casualties were only seven killed and thirty-six wounded. The Spanish losses were perhaps ten times that many. If Miles had landed at Fajardo, he might have conquered Puerto Rico before the protocol of peace was signed. His general opposition to frontal assaults was understandable, given the likelihood of extensive casualties and uncertain results, but the U.S. plan of operations should have been governed by the weak defenses of Puerto Rico, not by unwarranted caution. In any event, Spain did not conduct a successful defense of the island, an outcome that might have influenced the protocol of peace in its favor.

MANILA CAMPAIGN

After his victory of 1 May, Admiral Dewey settled down to await the arrival of troops. Although his naval guns dominated Manila Bay and the city, he lacked sufficient manpower to deal with about nine thousand Spanish troops ashore. The governor-general, Basilio Augustín, decided not to call in garrisons located elsewhere, about twenty-three thousand men, including Filipino volunteers, thinking that they could retain control of the countryside. This assumption proved erroneous; the insurgents of Aguinaldo rapidly defeated all but a courageous garrison at Baler, which managed to hold out for almost a year. Augustín attempted to retain control of Cavite province but proved unable to do so. Only the city of Manila remained in his hands, but he recognized that he needed additional troops and supplies from Spain to hold out indefinitely.

It was in response to Augustín's situation that Madrid dispatched Admiral Cámara eastward toward Manila with the goal of reinforcing and resupplying the city. When he was recalled to Spain after the debacle at Santiago de Cuba, however, the two U.S. seagoing monitors *Monterey* and *Monadnock*, which were sent across the Pacific to give Dewey vessels that could cope with the armored ships in Cámara's squadron, continued on to the Philippines. They did not arrive until August—the *Monterey* on 4 August and the *Monadnock* four days after the end of the war on 16 August. When word of Cámara's recall reached Manila, morale plummeted in the city. The fall of the city could only be a matter of time.

Dewey's principal preoccupation at Manila while awaiting the U.S. Army was the German navy. By 27 June the German squadron at Manila included two armored vessels and three other ships, displacing almost twenty-five thousand tons, a much stronger force than Dewey's. Germany sent the ships to Manila to take advantage of any opportunity that might present itself to occupy the islands—but only, the Germans asserted, if the Americans decided to leave. Nevertheless, U.S. suspicions grew after a debate developed over certain questions of international law. Although Germany did not intend to dispute U.S. control of the islands, the suspicion, although unfounded, still lingers in some quarters.

When word of Dewey's victory reached the United States, President McKinley decided to send an army expedition to Manila. No evidence exists to support the view of some historians that this step was part of a conscious plan

to annex the Philippine Islands. The U.S. motive was to fulfill a prime strategic purpose—maintenance of constant and growing pressure on Spain's insular possessions to encourage early peace negotiations. Sentiment for annexation began to build later in the United States, but none existed before the war or at its outset.

Major General Wesley Merritt, a veteran of the Civil War, was designated commander of the force that became the Eighth Army Corps, and he mounted an expedition of considerable strength. It included units from the regular army and several regiments of volunteers mostly from western states. Merritt assembled his troops at the Presidio in San Francisco, California, managing to avoid much of the confusion that had characterized the buildup at Tampa for the expedition to Cuba. Merritt's orders merely required him to complete "the reduction of Spanish power" at Manila and to provide security for the Philippines while in U.S. hands. No one from President McKinley on down had yet decided the long-term fate of the distant archipelago.

A small contingent of troops commanded by Brigadier General Thomas M. Anderson left San Francisco on 25 May bound for Manila Bay with the unprotected cruiser Charleston as an escort. Three transports carried about twenty-five hundred men—elements of the Fourteenth Infantry, the First California, and the Second Oregon. This force arrived at Manila on 30 June. The *Charleston* was assigned a special mission to discharge while on the way—to stop at and take possession of Guam, the southernmost island in the Marian group owned by Spain. This island lay about thirty-three hundred miles west of Honolulu and from thirteen hundred to eighteen hundred miles east of the principal east Asian ports of Yokohama, Shanghai, Canton, Hong Kong and Manila. On 20–22 June the *Charleston* accomplished its mission, encountering no resistance from the minuscule Spanish garrison of sixty troops. Thus, the United States easily gained an important link in its line of communications to the Philippines.

Two other contingents of troops sent from San Francisco eventually reached the Philippines, making a total of approximately eleven thousand officers and men. A group of about thirty-six hundred men on three transports departed on 15 June under the command of Brigadier General Francis V. Greene and arrived at Manila on 17 July. Some elements of two regular army units, the Eighteenth and Twenty-third infantries, and four volunteer units—the First Colorado, the First Nebraska, the Tenth Pennsylvania, and two batteries of Utah Artillery—made up the force. The third contingent of almost forty-nine hundred troops under Brigadier General Arthur MacArthur left San Francisco on seven transports between 25 and 29 June and reached Manila on 31 July. This group included the remaining elements of the regular regiments sent earlier, a company of regular army engineers, and more volunteers—the First Idaho, the Thirteenth Minnesota, the First North Dakota, and the First Wyoming. Like Shafter's troops, the Philippine expedition did not have much artillery support, depending on sixteen light field guns, six mountain guns, and a few rapid-fire weapons. When General Merritt arrived at Manila, he set about preparing to attack the city, a task that posed difficulties because Aguinaldo's troops occupied positions around Manila that lay between the city and the Eighth Army Corps. Merritt wanted to avoid any action that might be construed as recognizing the insurgent government, following a policy like that of Shafter toward the Cuban insurgents. Accordingly, he arranged for General Greene, a subordinate, to deal directly with the local Filipino commander. This procedure worked well. The insurgents agreed to abandon trenches to the north of the U.S. camp near a suburb called Malate, opening the way to Manila.

On 29 July, Merritt occupied these field fortifications and then built another line facing two Spanish strong points, Fort San Antonio Abad and Blockhouse No. 14, both parts of a line of blockhouses that covered the southern and eastern outskirts of Manila. This act spurred an exchange of fire with the Spanish defenders on the night of 31 July. Ten Americans were killed and thirty-three were wounded. Other firefights during the following days caused more U.S. casualties—five killed and twenty wounded. Meanwhile, the U.S. position was extended for a thousand yards so that its right flank ended at an impassable swamp.

Merritt wanted to move quickly against Manila, and sought supporting naval gunfire from Dewey, but the admiral temporized. He wanted to await the arrival of the *Monterey* and its powerful weapons, including two twelve-inch and two ten-inch guns. He also hoped to negotiate a surrender of the city that would eliminate the need for a serious engagement. Attempts to arrange a capitulation took place on two levels. Formal demands were made on the new governor-general, Don Fermín Jáudenes y Alvarez, who had replaced the despairing Augustín. This effort culminated on 9–10 August with Jáudenes asking for time to consult Madrid, but Merritt and Dewey rejected this request. Meanwhile, secret discussions were held through the Belgian consul in Manila, Edouard C. André. Also involved was the Roman Catholic archbishop of Manila, one of a group of civilians organized to help in the defense of the city. Eventually, Jáudenes made an intriguing proposal: He would capitulate provided the Americans agreed to a sham battle that would preserve the garrison's honor and that they pledged to keep Aguinaldo's troops from entering the city. Dewey agreed, proposing to shell Fort San Antonio Abad briefly and then signal a request for surrender. The Spanish garrison would then display a white flag.

Dewey's informal deal with Jáudenes did not cover land forces, but General Merritt, although skeptical of the plan, agreed to board one of Dewey's supply ships, the *Zafiro*, taking with him six companies of the Second Oregon, which would occupy the walled city after the surrender. To assure the capture of the city should the secret arrangement break down, Merritt made plans for an assault. He did not inform his subordinate commanders of the Jáudenes-Dewey agreement.

Merritt's plan of operations entailed a frontal attack by two brigades. General MacArthur, with about five thousand men, would move at the right of the U.S. line against Blockhouse No. 14. General Greene and about thirty-eight hundred men would move at the left of the line against Fort San Antonio Abad after Dewey finished his bombardment of that position. General Anderson was to arrange for the evacuation of insurgents in front of Blockhouse No. 14, but if the insurgents proved uncooperative, the Americans were not to force them out. Artillery was placed to avoid firing on insurgent positions.

On 13 August, Dewey's squadron took positions opposite the fortifications of Manila. Four ships moved off Fort San Antonio Abad and began to bombard it at 9:35 A.M., firing slowly for an hour. At 10:25 General Greene approached Fort San Antonio Abad, but no Spanish troops were found within. Some firing came from Malate, however, and Greene's force took a few casualties, one killed and fifty-four wounded. On the right, MacArthur advanced when he heard gunfire on the left, and his troops became engaged in a sharp fight. He took Blockhouse No. 14 and then assaulted Blockhouse No. 20 at Singalong, where resistance continued until 1:30 P.M. Taking casualties of five killed and thirty-eight wounded, MacArthur moved through Paco into the walled city.

As these operations unfolded on land, Dewey tested the planned surrender. At 11:00 A.M., after completing his bombardment of Fort San Antonio Abad, he moved off Manila and there discovered a white flag displayed from the south bastion of the city walls. U.S. officers went ashore to arrange the details of the surrender with Jáudenes and Admiral Montojo, which were completed by 2:30 P.M. The companies of the Second Oregon assigned the task of occupying the walled city went ashore and acted as a provost guard, disarming the Spanish garrison. The sham battle produced the desired result. Unfortunately, some U.S. casualties were incurred after the display of the white flag on the Manila bastion.

Merritt ensured that Aguinaldo's forces were kept out of Manila. On 11 August, General Anderson informed the insurgents that they were not to enter the city, and he reiterated this notice forcefully on the day of the battle. Nevertheless, about four thousand insurgents moved into suburban areas, portending future difficulties.

Unlike the campaign in Cuba, operations in the Philippines proceeded very smoothly. Merritt's orderly preparations placed his troops in position to move quickly after their arrival at Manila. Dewey's efforts to avoid unnecessary bloodshed helped greatly to obtain an early capitulation without extensive bloodletting. The interservice wrangling that occurred at Santiago de Cuba did not happen at Manila. Nothing comparable to the epidemic of tropical diseases that struck the Fifth Army Corps developed in the Philippines. In both instances, the navy's ability to establish command of the sea determined the outcome. Land operations proved successful because Spain could not reinforce and resupply its garrisons.

TREATY OF PARIS

While General Merritt in the Philippines and General Miles in Puerto Rico accomplished their missions, negotiations in Washington between President McKinley and French Ambassador Jules Cambon at length produced a protocol of peace that ended hostilities. Consultations in Washington led to the formulation of the U.S. demands. Three were quickly specified—independence for Cuba, the cession of Puerto Rico instead of an indemnity, and cession of an island in the Marianas, probably Guam. Only the disposition of the Philippines occasioned debate because opinion was divided. Some opposed any territorial acquisition, and others wanted a naval base or Luzon or the entire island group. McKinley eventually decided simply to demand the retention of Manila and Manila Bay for the moment, leaving the final settlement to a postwar peace conference. Despite vigorous efforts by Cambon, McKinley would not budge from these requirements. Sagasta finally accepted the U.S. terms, recognizing that further delay would lead only to further exactions. The protocol ending the war was signed in the White House on 12 August, President McKinley acting for the United States and Cambon for Spain.

President McKinley soon chose commissioners to represent the United States at the peace conference scheduled to convene in Paris during September. Secretary of State William R. Day was selected to head the delegation. John Hay, the U.S. ambassador in London, was brought back to Washington to take Day's place at the State Department. Three senators were named, recognizing that the U.S. Senate must give advice and consent to a treaty of peace by a two-thirds majority. One was Senator George Gray of Delaware, the ranking Democratic member of the Senate Foreign Relations Committee. The fifth member was Whitelaw Reid, publisher of the *New York Tribune,* a highly partisan Republican whose expansionist views balanced those of the antiexpansionist Gray. McKinley showed his political acumen by selecting a commission that represented different currents of opinion and that would follow wherever he wished to lead them.

The negotiations at Paris during October and November 1898 reflected the dominant bargaining position of the United States. The only question of great importance decided during the peace negotiations was the disposition of the Philippine Islands. Spanish diplomats labored mightily to influence the outcome, but President McKinley controlled the settlement. Although the United States entered the war with only one war aim, independence for Cuba, expansionist sentiment soon developed. Puerto Rico and Guam were taken principally for strategic reasons, to strengthen the U.S. position in the Caribbean Sea and in the Pacific Ocean. The same motive dictated the peaceful annexation of the independent Hawaiian Republic during the summer of 1898. Therefore, expansionist aspirations after the end of the war centered on the Philippine Islands.

A significant body of opinion opposed annexation of the Philippines, but over time a clear majority of the American people came to favor this step. Those who argued against annexation offered many compelling arguments, among them the claim that annexation of a noncontiguous area was unconstitutional and that it violated the democratic principle of self-determination. Another argument reflected racial and religious prejudices—some objected to the acquisition of a largely nonwhite and Roman Catholic populace. Most influential, however, were the claims that the annexation of the Philippines would assure U.S. access to the China market and that imperialism was the natural policy for a great power. Psychological elements also developed. The quick victory over Spain engendered great enthusiasm and confidence. In this mood, overseas expansion seemed fully justified.

President McKinley hesitated, recognizing the complications that might result from annexation of the Philippines, and he took several weeks to decide. In search of guidance, he consulted some experts, among them General Greene, who had returned from the Philippines. Most important, he undertook a speaking tour to the Middle West during the period 11–21 October, encountering extensive support for the retention of the Philippines and developing three interrelated arguments for annexation that ultimately guided his decision. First, he decided, there were humanitarian responsibilities. Second, the United States, having intervened in Philippine affairs, had a certain obligation to the inhabitants. Third, destiny seemed to exert its influence. These powerful justifications undergirded a message sent to Paris on 26 October that instructed the peace commission to negotiate the annexation of the entire Philippine archipelago.

The Spanish delegation strenuously resisted this demand, but it could not carry the day, and the final terms of the Treaty of Paris reflected the president's desires. To sweeten the bitter pill, the United States agreed to pay $20 million in compensation for the Philippines. The undertakings specified in the protocol of 12 August, including independence for Cuba and the annexation of Puerto Rico and Guam, were formalized in the peace treaty. Some U.S. interest in the Caroline Islands had surfaced during the conference, but nothing came of it. Earlier, in September, Spain had made a secret agreement with Germany to sell the Caroline, Mariana, and Palau island groups, a deal completed on 10 December. Not having obtained an island such as Kusaie in the Carolines that would have improved its line of communications across the Pacific Ocean, the United States occupied Wake Island to serve that purpose.

A lively debate took place in the U.S. Senate over Treaty of Paris. Although the public clearly favored ratification of the treaty, a significant minority advanced the familiar arguments against this course. Given the requirement for a two-thirds majority of the Senate to give consent to treaties, the outcome appeared in doubt. Two developments provided sufficient votes to assure ratification. One was the influence of William Jennings Bryan, the Democratic candidate for the presidency in 1896 who wanted to run again in 1900. He argued that the Democratic party should support the treaty but after that seek independence for the Philippines. Another was the sudden outbreak of hostilities between the insurgents and U.S. forces near Manila on 4 February. McKinley recognized that this deed would agitate public opinion and strengthen his hand. On 6 February, the treaty received senatorial consent by a vote of fifty-seven to twenty-seven. Two more negative votes would have led to its defeat. In Spain, the treaty did not muster the necessary votes in the Cortes, but the Queen Regent decided to make use of her constitutional powers to override the legislature. The treaty was ratified on 19 March and proclaimed on 11 April 1899.

THE PHILIPPINE WAR

For approximately six months, while the Treaty of Paris was negotiated and discussed, relations between the U.S. occupation force and the Filipino insurgents continually worsened. The outcome of the postwar negotiations confirmed what the insurgents had suspected from the first, that the United States would take the Philippines. On 17 August 1898, the War Department has issued instructions to guide relations with the insurgents that would remain in force until February 1899. There was to be no joint occupation of Manila. The United States would preserve peace and protect the people and property within the zone of occupation, and the

insurgents must respect this policy. General Merritt then reached an agreement with Aguinaldo that allowed the insurgents to remain in several suburbs around Manila while denying them access to the city. Admiral Dewey was uneasy and requested reinforcements. The protocol of peace precluded any such measure, but the Navy Department decided to send the *Oregon* and the *Iowa* to Hawaii, from which point they could move quickly to Manila.

When General Merritt left to advise the peace commission at Paris, Major General Elwell S. Otis took command of the Eighth Army Corps. He had brought the last contingent of troops to Manila, landing on 21 August 1898, a force that included 172 officers and 4,610 enlisted men. An exceptionally hardworking officer, Otis found it difficult to delegate authority, leading one observer to note, "he lives in a valley and works with a microscope, while his proper place is on a hilltop with a spyglass." Otis remained in Manila throughout his tenure, a practice that annoyed troops in the field. Nevertheless, Otis was an efficient civil administrator who rapidly gained the respect of the Filipinos. Otis faced many problems during the early months of the occupation. One task was to force the withdrawal of insurgents to positions well outside Manila. Another was to provide effective security within the city itself. When possible, Otis, a lawyer, allowed local courts to hear civil cases and he set up military tribunals to hear criminal cases. Hoping to revive the economy, he resumed collection of the customs and established a fiscal system.

Meanwhile, Aguinaldo set up a capital at Malolos and strengthened his government and his armed forces. His authority was extended to much of Luzon, and he energized a junta in Hong Kong to conduct his foreign relations, which consisted of seeking aid for his regime. On 28 September, he named Antonio Luna director of war, and he soon designated other senior commanders. Luna, an Ilocoan *ilustrado* who had lived in Spain and undertaken a study of military affairs, set about creating a conventional army along European lines that would fight according to the strategy and tactics generally followed in the western world. His initial plans for war entailed conventional warfare in northern Luzon along the Manila-Dagupan railway. To prepare for these operations, he placed his troops on a line north of Manila that extended from Caloocan to Novaliches.

As the U.S. Army made its arrangements, factionalism within the insurgent camp led to a lively debate over the provisions of a constitution. The more conservative elements in the insurgency, including men such as Pedro Paterno and Felipe Buencamino, proved successful in frustrating the desires of a more radical faction led by Apolinario Mabini that advocated advanced social revolution. The Malolos constitution, promulgated on 31 January 1899, placed the executive and judicial branches largely under legislative control, frustrating the radical wish for a strong central administration that could act quickly and efficiently.

Although Aguinaldo gave many indications of his intention to resist U.S. authority, Otis hoped that a peaceful resolution could take place, making plans to maintain an army of occupation numbering about twenty-five thousand troops. He remained optimistic even after the terms of the Treaty of Paris became known.

On 21 December 1898 President McKinley issued a proclamation that established his policy for the future government of the Philippines. He ordered the extension of U.S. authority to all points in the Philippines, although the treaty was not yet ratified. The Americans would rule as friends and protectors rather than as invaders or conquerors. Municipal law would remain in force within the context of U.S. military authority. Public property would fall to the United States but private property would remain unaffected. The United States would collect taxes and ports would be opened to friendly nations. The president also ordered Otis to seek the support of the people by assuring them "that full measure of individual rights and liberties which is the heritage of free peoples." The mission of the United States was "benevolent assimilation, substituting the mild sway of justice and right for arbitrary rule." Otis was enjoined to conduct a "temperate administration" but nevertheless

to use "the strong arm of authority to repress disturbance."

The optimism of Otis may have led to misapprehension in Washington of the difficulties that lay ahead. The Americans held only Manila and Cavite; Aguinaldo was in control elsewhere. Many Filipinos were prepared to take up arms rather than acquiesce to benevolent assimilation. Otis himself delayed issuing the president's proclamation for two weeks and then expurgated it, using the word "beneficent" rather than "benevolent" and the term "temporary administration" rather than "temperate administration." He also added a promise of Filipino representation in the government. Seeking to extend his authority to the Visayan Islands, Otis sent an expedition to occupy the important port of Iloílo on the island of Panay. Before these troops arrived, an insurgent force took control of the city, and Otis decided to avoid trouble by postponing a landing. He explained his action to the War Department as an attempt to arrange a settlement with the more moderate elements of the insurgent leadership. McKinley accepted this policy, hoping to avoid developments that might prejudice consideration of the Treaty of Paris, which was before the Senate. Otis then engaged in secret negotiations, but his effort came to nothing. This outcome showed that the two positions were irreconcilable. The Filipino wish for independence clashed hopelessly with the U.S. policy of annexation. Although Otis has been criticized for his rigid negotiating position, it was unlikely that more flexibility would have led to a peaceful outcome.

To provide assistance to Otis and Dewey in dealing with the insurgents, President McKinley formed a group that became known as the First Philippine Commission. Jacob Gould Schurman, the president of Cornell University, served as its chairman. It was ordered to "facilitate the most humane, pacific, and effective extension of authority . . . and to secure, with the least possible delay, the benefits of a wise and generous protection of life and property to the inhabitants." After studying conditions in the Philippines, the commission was to make recommendations for the governance of the islands. Meanwhile, military government would continue. Before the commission reached Manila, however, accumulating tensions led to a passage at arms.

Otis became increasingly worried about an insurgent attack on his troops, although he did not convey his suspicions fully to his superiors. To assure a sound defense of the city, he placed a division under General Anderson to the north and east of Manila and another under General MacArthur to the south and the east, forming a front of about sixteen miles. His army consisted of about twenty thousand enlisted men and fewer than a thousand officers, more than two thousand of whom had been sent to Iloílo. Others were ill or assigned to a provost guard, leaving only ten thousand men to man the line facing the insurgent army. In addition to making arrangements for defense of the city, Otis prepared plans for operations against the waterworks east of Manila and the insurgent capital of Malolos to the north.

The Filipino regular army at this time consisted of about fourteen thousand men, eight thousand of whom faced the U.S. troops at Manila. Militia and irregular troops raised the total Filipino force to somewhere between twenty thousand and thirty thousand. The troops at Manila were divided into two groups, one on each side of the Pasig River four miles east of Manila. Despite Luna's efforts, the insurgent army was poorly trained and equipped, and it lacked organized operational plans. If attacked, Luna planned to hold his defensive positions, to create an uproar in the city, and to attack targets of opportunity.

At 8:30 P.M. on the evening of 4 February, a Filipino patrol approached the American line, an act that started the Philippine War (also known as the Philippino Insurrection and the Filipino-American War). A guard from the First Nebraska Volunteers challenged the patrol which passed 150 yards beyond the midpoint between the two armies. After the third challenge, the guard opened fire, killing one insurgent. Another U.S. soldier wounded a second insurgent, and firefight followed during the night on both the north and south sides of the Pasig River. Meanwhile, the provost guard in Manila dealt effectively with an insurgent uprising.

General Otis later claimed that the insurgent action represented a premature beginning to a planned assault, but Filipino commentators dispute this view. According to the U.S. commander, the incident on 4 February came several days before the insurgents planned to attack, but their initiative could not have been delayed long because of the need to move before significant U.S. reinforcements could arrive. Filipino observers claim that the insurgents did not inaugurate the action. Luna lacked plans for operations at the time, and he and his principal subordinates were absent on the night of 4 February. It seems probable that neither side intended to attack the other, but, once an exchange of fire took place, it was impossible to suppress further action. Aguinaldo may have attempted to halt hostilities, but the Americans, once engaged, made no such effort. Otis merely informed Aguinaldo that he would receive an insurgent proposition for suspension of the fighting. The Filipino leader made no response.

Otis reached his initial objectives without difficulty. He quickly seized the waterworks, and by 8 February had moved north to a line near Caloocan from which he planned to move on Malolos. To husband his available troops, Otis did not move farther south of Manila than the line Pasay–San Pedro Macatí.

Senator Henry Cabot Lodge of Massachusetts had called the Spanish-American War "a splendid little war," an apt characterization perhaps, but this description did not apply to the Philippine War, which lasted for more than three years. Of the more than 125,000 Americans who served in it, 4,224 died and 2,818 were wounded. The insurgent losses were much greater, perhaps sixteen thousand killed and wounded, and the civilian population may have endured as many as a hundred thousand fatalities from famine and disease.

Conventional Warfare in 1899. General Otis faced the task of engaging a large Filipino force with few troops. He led more than twenty thousand men, of whom about fifteen thousand were volunteers. The latter troops were due for discharge shortly, having served a year. During the early months of the war, Otis was forced to exchange many of his units for others arriving from the United States. As the volunteer regiments departed, regular regiments came in, including the Third, Fourth, Seventeenth, Twentieth, and Twenty-second infantries by the end of March. The new troops were deployed immediately, but Otis rarely could place more than ten thousand men in the field at any one time. Although General Otis was by nature a cautious commander, his limited available manpower explains the deliberate and controlled character of his operations north of Manila during 1899.

His task was made easier because General Luna persisted in treating his army as a conventional force that could conduct operations along European lines. Aguinaldo apparently preferred guerrilla warfare from the beginning, but his views did not prevail until Luna's approach was fully tested and found wanting. Guerrilla operations might have narrowed the gap between the two armies, but conventional warfare played into the hands of the much more experienced, better-trained, and better-equipped U.S. troops.

During the initial phase of the conventional war, February–March 1899, the Eighth Army Corps pursued two interrelated objectives. Otis began to project forces into the Visayan Islands, hoping by this measure to prevent Aguinaldo from gaining full control of the region. Meanwhile he pursued an attack on the insurgent capital of Malolos. In the Visayans, an expedition moved on the port of Iloílo almost immediately and seized it. Soon after, the gunboat *Petrel* succeeded in taking Cebu City, the largest port on the island of Cebu. Early in March an army expedition took the island of Negros. The Americans were unable to take further action in the Visayans during 1899, but another army expedition occupied the island of Joló in the Sulu group. Although difficulties arose in Mindanao, the huge southern island of the archipelago, Otis lacked sufficient strength to undertake operations in that quarter.

Most of Otis' troops were employed north of Manila in a drive on Malolos that began on 25 March. Otis deployed two divisions, one under MacArthur on the right and the other under Brigadier General Henry Lawton on the left. His plan was to envelop and capture the entire insurgent army of between six thousand and eight thousand troops. The envelopment failed, but the insurgents were driven back easily, and Malolos fell on 26 March. Casualties were light, amounting to only 139 killed and 891 wounded as of 1 April.

During May, Otis pushed farther north but then ceased offensive operations. MacArthur reached San Fernando and Lawton in the Ildefonso–San Miguel–San Isidro region, short of the new insurgent capital at Tarlac. This delay reflected the necessity to exchange more volunteer regiments for units coming out from the United States and the difficulties of campaigning in the torrid, rainy summer. Otis had contained the insurgents to the south and east of Manila and defeated them to the north, but he was forced to await a more propitious moment to resume the attack. This pause contributed to growing irritation with Otis among his troops. The commander did not communicate his strategic and tactical intentions effectively to his force. Another source of discontent was his continuing policy of maintaining extraordinarily close command and control from his headquarters in Manila. He even managed to alienate the American journalists congregated in Manila by maintaining stringent censorship.

Although Otis incurred growing criticism at this time, perhaps his only serious error was his delay in requesting sufficient reinforcements to complete the campaign. Eventually he stated that a force of thirty thousand troops could quell the insurgency. On 2 March 1899, Congress passed legislation that made additional troops available in the Philippines. The regular army was increased to a level of sixty-five thousand men, and the War Department was authorized to recruit thirty-five thousand volunteers from the nation at large, to be organized into twenty-seven infantry regiments and three cavalry regiments. Strength reports during the summer and fall of 1899 reflect the increase in the size of Otis' army. Effectives at the end of August numbered about twenty-eight thousand, but this figure rose to about thirty-six thousand by the end of October. By the end of December, the total strength mounted to more than fifty thousand troops.

While the army awaited reinforcements and the end of the rainy season, opposition to the war began to develop rapidly in the United States, a recrudescence of the antiimperialist movement that had opposed the Treaty of Paris. Many arguments—ideological, humanitarian, economic, religious, racial, constitutional, and political in nature—emanated from a diverse coalition of antiimperialists who urged that the United States withdraw from the Philippines and grant some form of self-government. Pressure from the antiimperialists led President McKinley to defend his policy energetically. So did Secretary of War Elihu Root, who in vigorous language disputed the antiimperialist view that the insurgency in the Philippines had legitimate origins and that it represented the best interests of the Philippine people. This outspoken official support at home strengthened the position of General Otis as he prepared to resume active operations in October–November 1899.

During the summer, General Luna had come to a violent end. His relations with Aguinaldo had become increasingly strained, leading him to resign, a gesture that was refused. On 5 June, however, members of an insurgent unit from Kawit, Aguinaldo's home town, assassinated Luna. Many have suspected Aguinaldo of ordering this deed, but direct proof is lacking. Intense rivalries among the insurgent leadership adversely affected the operations of the Philippine army. The death of Luna made it possible for Aguinaldo to adopt a different military strategy. An alternative to conventional operations was to wage guerrilla war, a means of postponing defeat and playing for time. McKinley would be standing for reelection in 1900, and his Democratic rival, the antiimperalist William Jennings Bryan, might win the presidency and end the war.

In the autumn of 1899, General Otis launched an attack in northern Luzon intended to destroy the insurgent army. He anticipated no difficulty in defeating the insurgents in the central plain of Luzon. His principal problem was to prevent the defeated enemy from fleeing into the adjacent mountains of the north. Otis decided upon a complicated plan of operations. MacArthur's division was ordered to attack north from the San Fernando–Baliaug line, seizing both the insurgent capital at Tarlac and Dagupan at the end of the railroad. Lawton's division would move in a northeasterly direction up the Rio Grande at the northeastern edge of the central plain, seeking to close mountain passes leading eastward out of the plain. He would link with MacArthur at Dagupan. Brigadier General Lloyd Wheaton would make an amphibious landing near San Fabian on the Lingayen Gulf. After gaining control of the coastal road that ran to the northern end of Luzon, he would move eastward to a junction with Lawton's division. The insurgent army, fleeing from MacArthur, would be driven onto the forces of Lawton and Wheaton.

The operation itself proved successful, although it did not follow the script exactly. Lawton began his attack on 12 October, and by mid-November he had reached most of his objectives, although the Rio Grande proved difficult to use. MacArthur's frontal attack began on 5 November. He captured Tarlac on 12 November and reached Dagupan on 20 November. Wheaton landed at San Fabian on 7 November, but he was delayed. Otis dispersed the regular Philippine army, but Aguinaldo and many of his troops managed to escape into mountainous regions. Even so, Otis was convinced that he had practically ended the war. MacArthur was ordered to provide small garrisons at various locations to guard against depredations by *ladrones* and any insurgent forces that might conduct local operations. Otis resisted proposals to offer a general amnesty, hoping instead to quell all resistance. To this end, during the first four months of 1900, he attempted to pacify southern Luzon and the Visayan Islands.

Throughout his tenure, Otis believed the insurrection was largely the doing of the Tagalog tribesmen in Luzon. Failing to recognize the extent of disaffection among the general populace and the broad base of support for Aguinaldo that had developed throughout the Philippines, he assumed that when Tagalog resistance was ended, the insurgency would collapse. All that was needed after that, he thought, was the establishment of an effective constabulary to protect the citizenry against *ladrones* and small detachments of insurgent bitter enders. To support this effort, Otis established four administrative districts, the Department of Northern Luzon north of the Pasig River, the Department of Southern Luzon south of the Pasig River, the Department of the Visayas, and the Department of Mindanao and Joló. A military governor directed affairs in Manila.

In April 1900, Otis asked for relief and soon left for the United States, believing that his pacification efforts has been successful. His superiors in Washington accepted this estimate of the situation. President McKinley promptly formed a second Philippine Commission to help create an efficient civilian government in the islands. Its chairman was a respected judge, William Howard Taft. General MacArthur, named to succeed Otis as military commander, proceeded to organize small garrisons throughout the Philippines to assure stability.

Guerrilla Warfare, 1900–1902. On 12 November 1899, even as the U.S. forces were capturing the insurgent capital of Tarlac, Aguinaldo issued orders just before his flight to the mountains that inaugurated a new phase of the war. Troops in central Luzon were now to "maneuver in flying columns and guerrilla bands." Although insurgent organizations in Luzon would not begin serious guerrilla operations until the summer of 1900, after a period of rest and preparation, it was clear to Aguinaldo that guerrilla warfare was the only means available to prolong the war. If insurgent forces could remain in the field, antiimperialist sentiment in the United States, intensified because of continuing losses of blood and treasure in a protracted conflict, might eventually force changes in policy and lead to independence for the Philippines. Aguinaldo especially hoped for the overthrow of McKinley and the Republican party in the

election of 1900. Various motives ranging from patriotism to profit energized the decentralized detachments of guerrillas that now prepared for an entirely new war, one that eventually would be fought throughout the Philippines.

In June 1900, MacArthur issued a proclamation of amnesty, assuming, as had Otis before him, that he had only to mop up the remaining resistance and to organize effective police protection. Only about five thousand insurgents took advantage of his offer, a disappointing result that led him to recommend retention of a substantial force. (By March 1901 that force would grow to forty-five thousand men.) Meanwhile, he emphasized construction of a road net to improve communications and created a constabulary made up of two thousand Filipinos to help police the archipelago.

By September 1900, MacArthur had established more than four hundred military stations, but by this time a much-diminished Filipino force held an enlarged number of U.S. troops in the field. The number of engagements with small groups of insurgents mounted rapidly as guerrilla leaders loyal to Aguinaldo, whose headquarters now moved from place to place, emerged in various locations and perfected their plans of operations. They benefited greatly from widespread assistance that came either voluntarily or by coercion from the civil population. Dual governments developed in some areas. Officials who worked for the Americans during the day served the guerrillas at night. Although the guerrilla bands fled into mountainous or jungle areas when necessary to avoid battle, they were usually based in towns, which kept them supplied.

Guerrilla operations greatly compromised the measures undertaken by the military to put benevolent assimilation into effect. These included education, road construction, sanitation, and other humanitarian enterprises. The military intent of these measures was to attenuate local support of guerrilla bands, but the insurgents used nationalist appeals and terrorism to thwart many of the army's efforts to pacify the islands.

At length General MacArthur decided to turn

away from the garrison policy of Otis and resume aggressive operations against the insurgents. This decision brought him into conflict with the Second Philippine Commission headed by Taft, which had reached Manila in June 1900. The army disliked civilian interference, an attitude reflected in a line of doggerel poetry popular among the troops who rejected patronizing talk of brown brothers: "He may be a brother of Big Bill Taft, but he ain't no brother of mine." Taft naturally advocated an early resumption of civil government, and he pursued what became known as "the policy of attraction," adoption of civil measures designed to wean support from the insurgents. The army did not oppose "attraction," but they objected to steps that might interfere with effective military operations in the field.

President McKinley and Secretary of War Root supported a policy that emphasized both attraction and aggressive military operations. Theodore Roosevelt summarized very well the attitude of the home government: "By every consideration of honor and humanity we are bound to stay in the Philippines and put down the insurrection, establish order and then give a constantly increasing measure of liberty and self-government, while ruling with wisdom and justice. Whenever the islands can stand alone, I should be only too glad to withdraw." This general posture met with public approbation. Aguinaldo's hopes for the election of Bryan in 1900 were disappointed, McKinley winning by an impressive majority.

Nothing had developed in the Philippines to counter the McKinley administration's assertion that the insurgents were under great pressure and doomed to defeat. Aguinaldo did not provide effective leadership. Had he avoided the debacle of 1899, preventing Luna's disastrous experiment with conventional operations, and had he organized an effective system of command and control for the conduct of coordinated guerrilla operations, the insurgency might have fared far better. The inadequacies of the insurgent organization for guerrilla warfare played directly into the hands of the Americans. Its weakness prevented a clear demonstration that the insurgents could remain in the field in-

definitely and exact a considerable cost in American lives and resources, a result that might have aroused considerable domestic opposition to the Philippine War. As it was, the antiimperialist movement in the United States, divided in purpose and leadership, never gained broad public support.

After the election of 1900, both Taft and MacArthur expanded their operations, the civilian emphasizing measures of political attraction and the soldier directing offensive operations in the field. Success in both areas would result in mutually reinforcing gains. Failure might encourage growing resistance.

MacArthur revised the initial U.S. assumptions about the proper means of ending the insurgency. He decided upon "an entirely new campaign . . . based on the central idea of detaching the towns from the immediate support of the guerrillas in the field, and thus also precluding . . . indirect support." On 20 December he issued a proclamation that showed his change of policy. The United States would no longer tolerate violations of the laws of war. Zones of military operations were placed under martial law. MacArthur's forces would protect citizens from guerrillas who would from now on be subject to condign punishment.

MacArthur also adopted a tactical innovation of great importance, an emphasis on untiring pursuit in the field. If the guerrillas could be denied support from towns, they would lack sufficient supplies and equipment. If kept constantly in flight, they would eventually be forced either to surrender or to leave the field. The tactics of untiring pursuit created a need for additional manpower, and it was forthcoming. After the U.S. force was built up to seventy thousand troops in 1901, MacArthur had sufficient strength both to protect civilians and maintain constant pressure on the guerrillas. To strengthen his intelligence, MacArthur developed a force of fifty-four hundred Philippine Scouts, an organization distinct from the Philippine Constabulary, and created the Division of Military Information to gather and distribute military intelligence. Perhaps the most striking evidence of MacArthur's willingness to press affairs to a conclusion was his experimentation with the concentration of civilians in camps, a means of depriving the guerrillas of support in the countryside. He sought to avoid the errors of Weyler in Cuba, arguing that concentration was "exclusively a military measure carried out without objectionable or offensive measures."

Although MacArthur advocated broad general changes in strategy and tactics, he allowed considerable freedom of action to local commanders, who adopted a variety of approaches, reacting to specific circumstances. In his 1989 study of the subject, Brian M. Linn shows conclusively that the counterinsurgency in Luzon, the critical arena, reflected regional variations rather than a centralized approach, although these measures were consistent with MacArthur's general directives. Decentralization reflected the regional character of the Filipino insurgency, which varied markedly from place to place.

MacArthur supplemented his counterinsurgency program with other measures designed to force an early end to Filipino resistance. He ordered a naval blockade of certain locations in the Visayas to prevent the insurgents from collecting levies on trading goods. He expedited the road-building program to improve his communications. He also authorized the banishment of captured insurgent leaders, among them Apolinario Mabini and Artemio Ricarte, who were detained on Guam. MacArthur's counterinsurgency operations occasionally led to U.S. violations of the laws of war. Antiimperialist opponents exaggerated the extent of these activities, but at times U.S. troops, goaded by Filipino terrorism, an unacceptable motivation, resorted to torture, especially the "water cure," forcing water down a victim's throat, and the "rope cure," which required the use of a garrote.

As the army put into effect the new military practices, Taft and the Philippine Commission strengthened the policy of attraction. Chief among its measures was support of a pro-American political organization, the Federal party. Its leaders were among the more circumspect, expediential, and politically conservative members of the Filipino opposition. It provided a workable means of exerting Filipino influence,

and it gained strength as U.S. military operations systematically dealt with guerrilla bands. The policy of attraction received a considerable boost when the daring U.S. General Frederick Funston managed to capture Aguinaldo. When it was learned that Aguinaldo was settled at Palinan, in Isabela Province near the northeastern coast of Luzon, Funston organized a small expedition of eighty Macabebe scouts disguised as guerrillas. He and a few other Americans posed as prisoners. The navy ferried Funston and his men to the east coast about a hundred miles south of Palinan. He then marched northward, sending forged messages ahead announcing his approach. On 23 March 1901, he reached Palinan and surprised Aguinaldo and his small bodyguard of fifty men. Funston's romantic and improbable scheme had worked to perfection. Once in American hands, Aguinaldo took an oath of loyalty and called for an end of the insurgency.

By the summer of 1901, the army had all but quelled organized insurgent operations in Luzon except in Batangas and emphasis shifted to the Visayas. Mopping-up operations against specific guerrilla bands in a few salient locations took place during the last phase of the Philippine War from the summer of 1901 to July 1902, when the insurgency was officially declared at an end. Major General Adna R. Chaffee had succeeded MacArthur in July 1901, presiding over the last operations. One by one the Visayans were pacified, Panay by March 1901, Cebu by September 1901, and Bohol by December 1901.

The most serious resistance came in Samar, where Vicente Lukban took advantage of difficult terrain to remain active. On 28 September 1901, Lukban succeeded in wiping out a garrison of seventy-four men at Balangiga—only twenty-six soldiers survived the attack—but this success turned into disaster. Brigadier General Jacob H. Smith, nicknamed "Hell-Roaring Jake," was ordered to run Lukban into the ground, which he did by a thorough application of the tactical principles that had been applied effectively in Luzon. Lukban finally surrendered on 18 February 1902, ending the last resistance in the Visayas. Smith's enthusiastic campaign led to the most ruthless measures of the Philippine conflict, including some violations of the laws of war. One of Smith's subordinates accused him of ordering troops to turn Samar into a "howling wilderness." Smith was eventually court-martialed and officially admonished. Soon after, the disgraced general retired from the service.

While Smith pacified Samar, Brigadier General J. Franklin Bell moved against the guerrilla forces of Miguel Malvar in Batangas province, the last resistance of any consequence. Malvar was Aguinaldo's successor as titular head of the insurgents. The most distinctive aspect of this campaign was the systematic application of concentration; some 300,000 Filipinos were enclosed in "zones of protection," while four thousand troops ran the guerrillas into the ground. Bell was careful to avoid the errors of Weyler, and concentration soon deprived Malvar of essential resources. On 16 April 1902 he was forced to surrender.

Bell's operations, like those in Samar, produced some atrocities, and these came to the attention of a committee of the U.S. Senate organized to investigate complaints about the conduct of the Philippine War. The committee identified some war crimes, but its activities also publicized the rationale for the counterinsurgency. The successful end of the war and the passage of the Philippine Organic Act, defining the future civil government for the Philippines, worked to minimize public reactions.

While Chaffee's troops ended the last resistance, Taft and his colleagues managed a successful transition from military to civil government. Taft had become civil governor on 4 July 1901 and had soon organized executive departments. In September he appointed several Filipinos to the Philippine Commission, a good example of attraction. The Organic Act for the Philippines went into effect on 4 July 1902, the official end of the Philippine War. By October of the following year, the army in the Philippines had been reduced to a force of about fifteen thousand men.

The Philippine War was brought to a successful conclusion because the United States adopted a sound program of counterinsurgency and executed it effectively in a minimum of time. The ill-coordinated and often flawed resistance of the insurgents lessened the difficulty of the task. The insular situation of the Philippines precluded effective outside assistance and use of protected sanctuaries. Attraction played an important role in the outcome, but if military operations in the field had not produced prompt and decisive results, it could not have been so influential. Public opposition to the Philippine War in the United States never seriously interfered with the conduct of the struggle because of the efficient conduct of the counterinsurgency on all levels.

The successful outcome of the Spanish-American War and the Philippine War equipped the armed services of the United States with a modified mission to replace those of the latter nineteenth century. Before 1898 the U.S. Army had devoted itself principally to constabulary activity in the American West, and the U.S. Navy had provided protection for U.S. maritime commerce. After 1898, until the coming of World War I, the two services devoted themselves primarily to the protection and administration of the modest insular empire annexed in 1898 and to the construction of the Panama Canal, completed in 1914.

Considerable growth and modernization accompanied the acceptance of this new mission. Perhaps the most significant achievements were the creation of a general staff system for the army in 1903 and the construction of several huge new armored vessels for the navy in 1906 and after. These accomplishments did not represent a national embrace of defense policies that would create armed services designed to engage the great armies and navies of Europe on equal terms. The emphasis was on hemispheric defense, a much different proposition. Nevertheless, the reforms of the years between 1898 and 1917 provided a useful foundation for the extraordinary revolution in national defense policy, strategy, and operations that resulted from the onset of the Great War in Europe. The small wars of 1898–1902 brought the armed services into extensive operations in the Caribbean Sea and in the western Pacific Ocean, an outcome that no one expected before the sudden burst of war fever that accompanied the destruction of the *Maine* in February 1898. Many officers who gained their first experience of warfare at the turn of the century rose to positions of high command during the ensuing two decades, and they led the army and navy during World War I.

BIBLIOGRAPHY

The Spanish-American War

Alger, Russell A. *The Spanish-American War* (1901).

Braisted, William R. *The United States Navy in the Pacific, 1897–1909* (1958).

Chadwick, French E. *The Relations of the United States and Spain: The Spanish-American War*, 2 vols. (1911).

Concas y Palau, Victor. *The Squadron of Admiral Cervera* (1900).

Cosmas, Graham A. *An Army for Empire: The United States Army in the Spanish-American War* (1971).

Dewey, George. *Autobiography of George Dewey: Admiral of the Navy* (1913).

Leech, Margaret. *In the Days of McKinley* (1959).

Linderman, Gerald F. *The Mirror of War: American Society and the Spanish-American War* (1974).

Long, John D. *The New American Navy*, 2 vols. (1903).

Mahan, Alfred Thayer. *Lessons of the War with Spain, and Other Articles* (1899).

May, Ernest R. *Imperial Democracy: The Emergence of America as a Great Power* (1961).

Millis, Walter. *The Martial Spirit: A Study of Our War with Spain* (1931).

Morgan, Howard Wayne. *America's Road to Empire: The War with Spain and Overseas Expansion* (1965).

Rickover, Hyman G. *How the Battleship Maine Was Destroyed* (1976).

Sargent, Herbert H. *The Campaign of Santiago de Cuba*, 3 vols. (1907).

Sargent, Nathan. *Admiral Dewey and the Manila Campaign* (1947).

Spector, Ronald. *Admiral of the New Empire: The Life and Career of George Dewey* (1974).

Trask, David F. *The War with Spain in 1898* (1981).

Trask, David F., Michael C. Meyer, and Roger R. Trask, comps. *A Bibliography of United States–Latin American Relations Since 1810*, ch. 5 (1968).

Venzon, Anne Cipriano. *The Spanish-American War: An Annotated Bibliography* (1990).

Wagner, Arthur L. *Report of the Santiago Campaign, 1898* (1908).

Wheeler, Joseph. *The Santiago Campaign* (1898).

The Philippine War

Agoncillo, Teodoro C. *Malolos: The Crisis of the Republic* (1960).

Gates, John M. *Schoolbooks and Krags: The United States Army in the Philippines, 1898–1902* (1973).

Linn, Brian M. *The U.S. Army and Counterinsurgency in the Philippine War, 1899–1902* (1989).

Miller, Stuart C. "Benevolent Assimilation": The American Conquest of the Philippines, 1899–1903* (1982).

Salamanca, Bonifacio S. *The Filipino Reaction to American Rule, 1901–1913* (1984).

Sexton, William T. *Soldiers in the Sun: An Adventure in Imperialism* (1939).

Welch, Richard E. *Response to Imperialism: The United States and the Philippine-American War, 1899–1902* (1979).

Wolff, Leon. *Little Brown Brother: How the United States Purchased and Pacified the Philippine Islands at the Century's Turn* (1961).

Zaide, Gregorio. *The Philippine Revolution*, rev. ed. (1968).

THE MEXICAN BORDER CAMPAIGN

Charles E. Kirkpatrick

Between 15 March 1916 and 5 February 1917, United States Army troops under the command of Brigadier General John J. Pershing conducted a punitive expedition into Mexico in pursuit of Francisco (Pancho) Villa, a charismatic revolutionary leader who was in rebellion against the constituted government of Mexico and whose men had attacked American border towns over a period of two months. Marching south of the Rio Grande with the grudging consent of the Mexican government, Pershing's forces not only skirmished with Villista bands but also encountered civilian hostility and, eventually, active opposition from the Mexican army. Pershing ultimately failed to capture Villa but secured the border region until the political situation stabilized and his troops could safely be recalled. Swiftly overshadowed by the mobilization for World War I a few months later, the Mexican Punitive Expedition and the entire border campaign revealed deficiencies in military organization, equipment, and training that provided many useful lessons for the U.S. Army as it entered the European war.

See THE MEXICAN WAR *map on page 679 for* THE MEXICAN BORDER CAMPAIGN *geography.*

THE POLITICAL BACKGROUND

The political situation that led to Pershing's expedition into Mexico in 1916 had its roots in the years of rebellion, revolution, and unrest that followed the overthrow of Porfirio Díaz in 1911. Mexico had enjoyed a degree of stability under Díaz, president since 1877, albeit one enforced by dictatorial methods. Although he had increased Mexican prestige abroad and made material progress in commerce, industry, and internal communications, Díaz had also favored policies that set the stage for social and political revolution. His economic practices fostered the concentration of wealth in the hands of a few large landowners and financiers and created peonage. Likewise, his concessions to foreigners, while stimulating investment in Mexico, debilitated the middle and working classes. By 1910, few Mexicans actually participated in their government, and widespread frustration became open revolt. In May 1911, Francisco I. Madero deposed Díaz and became president.

Madero was no more successful in resolving Mexico's political crises, however, and was himself overthrown on 18 February 1913 by General Victoriano Huerta, whom the army and twenty-five of Mexico's twenty-seven states immediately recognized as president. Although many foreign nations extended recognition to the Huerta government, the United States was not among them, because U.S. officials believed Huerta was responsible for Madero's death. Tensions between the two countries increased with a series of incidents, the most serious at Tampico in April 1914. Local officials arrested a U.S. naval officer and seven sailors and marines on shore. Although city officials released them and apologized, subsequent discussions between Admiral Henry J. Mayo and the Huerta government exacerbated the situation. President Woodrow Wilson directed Mayo to demand a 21-gun salute to the U.S. flag. When Huerta's government demurred, U.S. troops under Brigadier General Frederick Funston occupied Veracruz on 21 April. Ill will continued to build, but the Huerta government collapsed in July, and U.S. troops were withdrawn.

Refusal of the United States to recognize his government had made Huerta's situation almost impossible and encouraged his opponents. A movement headed by Venustiano Carranza, governor of Coahuila, had compelled Huerta's resignation, and one month later a Constitutionalist army under command of General Alvaro Obregón occupied Mexico City and made Carranza president, but he controlled only part of the country and found himself in the midst of a chaotic civil war in which major factions were led by Emiliano Zapata in the southwest and by Villa (once a supporter of Carranza), who virtually controlled the state of Chihuahua. Villa had held the capital for a short time in December, but was ousted by Obregón's troops on 27 January 1915.

Events in Mexico had early on persuaded President Wilson to adopt a wait-and-see policy in the matter of granting recognition to any government there. In the first quarter of 1915, General Hugh L. Scott, army chief of staff, had toured army garrisons in Texas and New Mexico to inspect troops in the southwest and assess the situation along the border. In the course of his travels, Scott met with Villa and arranged the release of U.S. funds seized by the revolu-

tionaries. The two men established a mutual respect that evidently led Villa to believe that the United States would eventually side with him. Events would prove otherwise.

With Carranza in firm possession of the government by midsummer, Mexican army troops began to show that they could defeat the rebels. Villa lost considerable prestige, and all hopes for the presidency, when General Obregón defeated him in a series of fights at Celaya, León, Agua Prieta, and Hermosillo. In August the diplomatic representatives of six Latin American countries met in Washington, D.C., to discuss the factional conflict in Mexico and took note of Carranza's strengthened position. They concluded that Carranza and his party represented the de facto government of the country and its best hope for stability. Accordingly, the United States recognized Carranza's government on 19 October, as did the Latin American powers. Diplomatic recognition led to some practical aid as well. The United States allowed Carranza to make use of American railroads in Arizona to move his troops during battles with Villa.

Angered by what he viewed as U.S. duplicity, Villa mustered his forces in western Chihuahua and decided to provoke the United States into armed intervention in Mexico. Broadly, his plan relied on pervasive anti-Americanism in the border state as a mobilizing sentiment that would make him the leader of the Mexican populace in a patriotic uprising against an invading American army. Having supplanted Carranza in popular opinion, Villa's thinking went, he would then be propelled to the presidency of Mexico. Villa began his two-pronged campaign against federal army forces under Carranza and against Americans in the opening months of 1916.

THE COLUMBUS RAID

A series of attacks on U.S. citizens and property—by Villistas and by Mexicans pursuing other political agendas—occurred in the opening months of 1916. On 10 January 1916, for example, some of Villa's troops halted a Mexican train at Santa Ysabel, just south of Chihuahua City, and forced off seventeen American mining engineers invited by Carranza's government to reopen mines in that area. The troops shot sixteen of the Americans, touching off a storm of outrage in the United States. Carranza offered apologies and promised to punish the criminals, a concession that allowed President Wilson to take no immediate action. Nor did cross-border forays that took place near Hachita, New Mexico (18 January), Fort Hancock, Texas (17 February), and Edinburg, Texas (7 March), among others, precipitate the American reaction Villa was seeking. What was needed, he decided, was a major raid into the United States.

Brigadier General Funston, commanding the Southern Department, which included the Mexican border from the Gulf of Mexico to the California state line, had the task of preventing or deflecting such raids and keeping order along the frontier. To do so, he divided his seventeen hundred-mile-long area of responsibility into cavalry patrol districts, establishing camps and garrisons at intervals along the international border. One of those districts was centered on Columbus, New Mexico, where Colonel Herbert J. Slocum patrolled sixty-five miles of terrain with the five hundred men of the Thirteenth Cavalry. Early in March 1916, rumors of pending Villa actions prompted Slocum to reinforce his garrisons in the vicinity of Columbus and to engage the services of paid spies who periodically brought him information about Villa's movements. Because local rumors continued to place the rebel leader in the vicinity, Slocum led a large patrol along the border on the night of 7–8 March but received assurances from the commander of local Carranza forces that Villa was not in the area. In fact, Villa was at that moment poised to attack into the United States.

Villa descended upon the little town of Columbus in the predawn hours of 9 March with about four hundred men. Converging on the town in separate columns about 4:00 A.M., Vil-

la's troops attacked both the town and the garrisons of the Thirteenth Cavalry. A scattered gunfight developed that lasted for a little more than an hour. As dawn broke, Villa's men retreated, having killed eight U.S. soldiers and eight civilians and wounded seven soldiers and three civilians. They also burned and looted several homes and stores. Major Frank Tompkins led a squadron of the Thirteenth Cavalry some fifteen or twenty miles into Mexico in pursuit, returning only when his ammunition was exhausted. Cavalrymen found sixty-seven Mexican dead around Columbus and estimated that seventy to one hundred were killed during the pursuit into Mexico.

Within hours of the Columbus attack, General Funston dispatched a telegram to General Hugh Scott at the War Department, asking permission to send his troops into Mexico after the raiders. It was clear, he thought, that there would be no security along the international frontier as long as Villa and similar bands of outlaws had freedom of action. Furthermore, he argued, the de facto government of Mexico lacked the ability to suppress the insurgents who were threatening American lives and property. He believed that further attacks were imminent. President Wilson quickly agreed, and on 10 March he directed Funston to send armed forces into Mexico to capture Villa and prevent further raids into the United States. Wilson cautioned Funston, however, to have a scrupulous regard for the sovereignty of Mexico. Secretary of War Newton Baker invited Funston to inform him of what the army needed to carry out the president's order.

Funston had appended to his telegram a plan for two columns of troops to enter Mexico from Columbus and Hachita, New Mexico, link up around Ascención, some sixty miles into Mexico, and then patrol to the south and west in search of Villa, whom Funston expected to draw back into his traditional stronghold of the mountains of Chihuahua. A general depot would be established at El Paso, Texas, and supplies forwarded to the troops by means of the Mexican Northwestern Railroad. Using the available four cavalry regiments, Funston intended to march a brigade of cavalry in each column and protect the line of the advance with a reinforced infantry brigade.

The next day the War Department approved the basic plan, but with several exceptions. Funston was not to assume that he could use Mexican railroads to transport and supply his forces and was not to permit his soldiers to enter Mexican towns or cities. The expedition was to leave Mexico as soon as it captured or broke up Villa's bands, or sooner if the Mexican government was able to relieve it of the task. General Scott and General Tasker H. Bliss recommended, and Secretary Baker approved, the appointment of Brigadier General John J. Pershing, at that time in El Paso in command of the Eighth Cavalry Brigade, to command the expedition. The War Department staff then turned to considering the problem of mobilizing the state militias, which would make up the greater part of any wartime army. While Scott prepared for war, diplomatic discussions continued.

While Funston was awaiting permission to enter Mexico, a note arrived in Washington from the Carranza government expressing its regret for the Columbus attack. The same note asked permission for Mexican troops to enter the United States in pursuit of Villa and granted similar privileges to the U.S. Army if there were any additional raids. In his reply to the Mexican proposal, President Wilson did not wait for another attack in the United States but agreed that the arrangement Carranza proposed was in force, and that he could exercise the privilege of sending U.S. forces across the border whenever he felt necessary. The War Department informed Pershing that the Mexican government would tolerate U.S. operations south of the Rio Grande, and two days later, on 17 March, Congress adopted a resolution approving Pershing's orders.

The situation in Mexico at that time was somewhat confused. Carranza's intention, obviously (and possibly deliberately) misunderstood by Wilson, was to allow U.S. troops to enter Mexico only when in hot pursuit of bandits. His subsequent actions make it clear that Carranza never meant to grant President Wilson carte blanche to mount a major expedition on Mexican soil. Conscious of the danger of misunderstandings, General Obregón, the Mexican secretary of war and navy, informed the governors of the northern states of the agreement into which the Mexican government had entered and asked them to advise commanders of Mexican army garrisons closer to the border. Conflicting instructions issued from Mexico City clouded the matter, however, and allowed Mexican officers to draw the conclusion that permission for U.S. troops to enter had not been granted after all. The matter continued to be a subject of discussion between the two governments as Pershing's troops began to move south. In any case, the control Carranza and Obregón exercised from the capital was tenuous at best, and they had some doubts about the essential loyalty of federal troops in Chihuahua. It began to seem possible that the appeal Villa had for the Mexican population at large was extending to the military as well.

THE U.S. ARMY IN 1916

With few exceptions, the last major ground battles U.S. troops had fought was in the Civil War, more than fifty years earlier. Over the intervening years of the Plains Indian wars, the army had become a frontier constabulary in which the largest tactical organization was typically the company, troop, or squadron. Only rarely did units as large as regiments or brigades come together, and there was little practical training in the art of commanding large bodies of troops. During the Spanish-American War in 1898, scattered units of the regular army, hastily mobilized militia units, and volunteers temporarily formed larger tactical organizations for the brief fighting in Cuba and the extended campaign in the Philippines. After that war, the service disbanded its volunteer units and returned the regular army to its peacetime garrisons. At the time of the Mexican revolution, the U.S. Army remained little changed in organizational terms from the days of the Indian wars.

Sharply increasing tensions along the U.S.-Mexico border in 1911 prompted Secretary of War Henry L. Stimson to make a show of strength in Texas. On 6 March 1911, he detailed Major General William H. Carter to command a "maneuver division" at San Antonio and issued orders to concentrate troops into three infantry brigades, a field artillery brigade, and an independent cavalry brigade, together with the necessary auxiliary service units and a brigade of coast artillery. The inevitable problems encountered in forming the maneuver division threw the inefficacy of a tactically efficient small-unit army into sharp relief. Funding constraints limited the duration of the experiment, and the division never managed to reach full strength before it was disbanded early in 1912. Inexperienced in mobilization planning, the War Department took several months, even using railroads, to get the last regiments to San Antonio. A failure in many ways, the maneuver division still offered army officers the chance to work with a modern-style division for the first time and to understand the complexities of maintaining and operating such a force. For the War Department, the maneuver division was a sobering experience in just how difficult mobilization could be. Because the division used nearly all of the units of the regular army then in the United States, it also graphically demonstrated the army's inability to confront any significant foreign armed force.

Border raids continued, however, and six cavalry regiments and other troops totaling about sixty-seven hundred men began patrolling the international border from Texas to Arizona and enforcing an embargo on shipments of arms and munitions to Mexico. By mid-1913, fighting between various Mexican factions in the northern territories had intensified to the point that the battles were spilling over into the United States. In response to the increased tension, the War Department ordered the creation of the Second Division at Texas City, under the command of General Carter. This time the organization of the division went smoothly, although it reached only a little more than half its planned strength. As with the maneuver divi-

sion, the army soon disbanded the Second Division.

During the Veracruz expedition the following year, General Funston commanded brigade-size units in the field, thus further training his officers in the handling of larger units. At Veracruz, however, the army and marines were chiefly an occupation force, albeit one that conducted regular patrols into the hinterlands around the city. By the beginning of 1915 the army had returned to the Mexican border, where its mobile troops dispersed into patrol districts along the frontier.

By the middle of 1915, the army had gained a certain amount of experience in operating division-size units. The service had thirty-one infantry regiments, fifteen cavalry regiments, and six field-artillery regiments available for field duty. Nearly all of the mobile combat units then in the United States were assigned to what amounted to war duties along the frontier. Well-trained and of high quality at the small-unit level, the army was not well-prepared in a material sense. There were only seven hundred field guns in the entire army, including units overseas, and no more than fifty-eight hundred rounds of ammunition. Quartermaster returns showed that the entire army had only enough rifle ammunition to fight for four days. There were very few field-service units, among which were only three battalions of engineers and eight companies of the Signal corps. The army also had barely begun to make the transition to motor transport and had only just started to experiment with the organization of an air service. It was from this slowly modernizing army that Pershing was to form his expeditionary force.

ORGANIZATION OF THE EXPEDITION

Funston gave Pershing his orders on 11 March and directed him to comply with the basic plan approved by the War Department. Until Pershing reached and established an advanced base in Mexico, Funston would maintain the line of communications from Columbus. After that time, the logistics responsibility, like the responsibility for tactical command, would devolve on Pershing. Meanwhile, Funston placed the troops of the Southern Department at Pershing's disposal. Roughly ten thousand men were available to organize a provisional division to be known as the Punitive Expedition, U.S. Army. In organizing his expedition, Pershing could refer to the recent experiments with the maneuver division and Second Division, in which some of his subordinates had been involved.

The theater of operations influenced Pershing's organizational decisions. Chihuahua, a large and sparsely populated state, had both a rugged terrain and a forbidding climate. Some 80 percent of the land was a high desert plateau ranging from three thousand to six thousand feet in elevation. Good water was scarce, and the land supported little vegetation for forage at any time of the year. The ground varied from gravel to a fine silt, making travel difficult. The peaks of the trackless mountains of the Sierra Madre in the west sometimes reached ten thou-

sand feet. Inaccessible except through hazardous rocky canyons, the Sierra Madre were the assumed refuge of Villa's bands. The area was extremely dry except in the midsummer months of late June through early August, when heavy rains were common. During the summer, Chihuahua was intensely hot during the day but often chillingly cold at night. In winter, temperatures plunged, with dust storms punctuated by ice and snowstorms. Most of the campaign took place on the plateau, a strip of plains and foothills fifty to one hundred miles wide and about five hundred miles long, bounded on the west by the mountains and on the east by the National and New Mexico Railroad.

On balance, a predominantly cavalry force seemed best to maneuver in such conditions, and Pershing organized his expedition around two provisional cavalry brigades that would enter Mexico in two columns. On the east, the First Provisional Cavalry Brigade, would march from Columbus, New Mexico, while to the west, the Second Provisional Cavalry Brigade

THE PUNITIVE EXPEDITION FORCES

First Provisional Cavalry Brigade (Colonel James Lockett)	Thirteenth Cavalry (Negro) (less one troop)
	Eleventh Cavalry (Negro)
	Battery C, Sixth Field Artillery
Second Provisional Cavalry Brigade (Colonel George A. Dodd)	Seventh Cavalry
	Tenth Cavalry (Negro)
	Battery B, Sixth Field Artillery
First Provisional Infantry Brigade (Colonel John H. Beacom)	Sixth Infantry
	Sixteenth Infantry
	Company E, Second Engineer Battalion
	Company H, Second Engineer Battalion
Service Troops	Ambulance Company Number Seven
	Field Hospital Number Seven
	Signal Corps Detachments
	First Aero Squadron
	Wagon Company Number One
	Wagon Company Number Two

would enter from the town of Hachita. One company of engineers and the First Aero Squadron were to advance with the First Provisional Cavalry Brigade from Columbus, and the remaining service troops marched from Columbus with the First Provisional Infantry Brigade, charged with protecting the expedition's lines of communication.

Once it was clear that Pershing would not be able to use the Mexican railways to supply his troops, he had to find means to sustain the expedition overland. In Washington, General Scott directed the acting quartermaster general, Brigadier General Henry G. Sharpe, to purchase enough trucks for that purpose. General Sharpe worked quickly, soliciting bids and awarding a contract at 5:00 A.M. on 14 March. By 16 March, the first consignment of trucks was shipped by train from Wisconsin, arriving at Columbus on 18 March. The army employed civilian drivers, who arrived in New Mexico at the same time the trucks were delivered. Quickly organizing motor convoys, supporting troops in Columbus shipped the first consignments across the border to Pershing before his command exhausted the supplies they had carried with them. The first truck company was quickly followed by two others. By June the army had placed ten such companies in operation to support Pershing and 588 trucks were in service on the lines of communication. Sharpe's department also established two auxiliary remount depots at El Paso and Fort Sam Houston to provide the expedition with animals to replace those that died or became unfit for service. For the moment, adequate supplies of food and other equipment were on hand. The quartermaster had earlier stocked depots at El Paso, Fort Sam Houston, Harlingen, Columbus, Nogales, and other towns against the possibility of trouble on the border.

Availability of supplies did not imply efficiency in their distribution. When Pershing arrived in Columbus from El Paso, the confusion he found there rivaled that at the Tampa, Florida, embarkation point during the Spanish-American War. There was no chief quartermaster or ordnance officer in Columbus, and the line officers detailed to duty in those depart-

ments had no experience and less knowledge of the complicated requisitioning and supply system. The quartermaster supplies, medical supplies, and ordnance matériel that arrived by train were unloaded and stored in no particular order. Wagons and trucks were also delivered promptly, but without instructions for their assembly. Through furious effort, Pershing and his staff imposed some order on the chaos, but the unsuitability of a supply system designed for small garrisons for an army in the field was already clearly apparent and became a gnawing problem as the expedition advanced into Mexico.

From the beginning, both motor trains and animal pack trains supplied Pershing's troops. The lack of good roads dictated the disposition of the logistical trains. The western column from Hachita, which Pershing expected to move most quickly, took with it only pack trains; the wagon transportation followed the eastern column from Columbus. Simultaneously, the two companies of engineers began to consider ways to improve the trails over which the truck trains would eventually have to drive. The problem was compounded by a lack of good maps of northern Chihuahua, and Pershing had to detail an engineer detachment to draw them, based on reports from scouts as the force advanced.

A variety of signal equipment sustained communications within the march columns and with the bases of supply. Lacking proper wire, Signal Corps troops improvised a telegraph line that paralleled the route of march. Radio sets with the marching cavalry columns were useful over short ranges, while the longer-range radios were mounted in wagons. Pershing planned to use Signal Corp airplanes both for scouting and for maintaining contact among his scattered forces.

Less than a week after the Columbus raid, General Pershing had completed preparations based on War Department and Southern Department orders and reported himself ready to cross into Mexico. In the interval, Funston had mustered remaining regular troops to replace the cavalry regiments along the border, and the War Department had acted to create a transportation service to replace the railroad that political considerations denied Pershing. It remained to be seen whether Villa could actually be caught.

THE CAMPAIGN IN MEXICO

There were six discernable stages of the campaign. In the first, Pershing's two columns marched to the Mormon colony of Colonia Dublán, in Chihuahua, where they met and established a base. Next, the general dispatched three independent cavalry columns from that base in search of Villa. In the third phase, four more independent cavalry detachments scoured the southern region of the state. Fourth, Pershing recalled his scattered troops to a central base. Fifth, having failed to find Villa, the U.S. troops began a policy of policing the northern part of Chihuahua by districts. The final stage, almost a year after the expedition began, was the evacuation of all troops to Columbus.

Approach March to Colonia Dublán. Despite the diplomatic discussions that had gone before, the reaction of the Mexican government to Pershing's march into Mexican territory was anything but certain. Nevertheless, Funston instructed Pershing to begin his operation no later than 6:00 A.M. on 15 March because he feared the effects of further delay. Among the other shortcomings of the expedition was a lack of definite information about the strength and intentions of the Mexican army in Chihuahua, estimated at around eight thousand men with additional militia forces available, and about the location and strength of Villa's forces, estimated at between five hundred and a thousand men.

Pershing had a letter from General Obregón that he could present to local authorities as authorization for his presence south of the frontier, but he still feared he might encounter opposition. He impressed on his men the need for calm and restraint in dealing with Mexican officials, especially during the border-crossing. Indeed, there very nearly was an incident when the commander of the garrison at Palomas, a few miles south of the border, objected to the intrusion. Explaining his intentions, Pershing managed to calm the belligerent Carranzista commander in part by hiring him as a guide for the expedition. Thus, the Columbus column entered Mexico a few minutes after noon on 15 March, camping that night at Las Palomas and arriving at Colonia Dublán on 20 March by way of Boca Grande, Ascensión, and Corralitos. The wagon trains that followed Colonel Lockett's Second Brigade could only travel twenty to forty miles per day and thus lagged behind.

Colonel Dodd's Second Provisional Cavalry Brigade marched from Culbertson's Ranch, about fifty miles west of Columbus, and crossed the border about 1:00 A.M. on 16 March. The brigade then marched 125 miles over the dusty alkali roads without incident in a column of twos, the Seventh Cavalry leading, and reached Colonia Dublán in the early evening of 17 March. Pershing established his advanced base about a mile north of the colony, adhering to War Department instructions to avoid towns or cities. With both brigades in camp, Pershing had a force of about forty-eight hundred men available and began to make detailed plans to pursue Villa.

Pershing presumed that Villa and his men had begun retreating to the south of Chihuahua as soon as they had learned the U.S. Army was in pursuit. To capture him would require extremely fast-moving columns, unencumbered by slow baggage trains or excessive equipment. Believing that Villa was somewhere in the vicinity of San Miguel de Babícora, a village about fifty miles south, Pershing determined that the best plan was to send three parallel columns after him. By so doing, the Americans could keep Villa from escaping into Sonora to the west or across the Mexican National Railway to the east. If the cavalry troopers moved fast enough, they might even get ahead of Villa before he could reach the mountains at Guerrero.

To implement the plan, the general organized three detachments of cavalry. In the west, Major Ellwood W. Evans left Colonia Dublán by train on 19 March with the First Squadron,

Tenth Cavalry. His objective was the village of Las Varas, near Madera, farthest to the south and not far from Guerrero. That same day, Colonel William C. Brown led the Second Squadron, Tenth Cavalry, to the San Miguel plateau in the center, taking the train as far as Rucio. The eastern column, comprising the Seventh Cavalry under Colonel James B. Erwin, left Colonia Dublán on the night of 17–18 March bound for the San Miguel plateau by way of Galeana and the region southwest of El Valle.

Pursuit by Major Columns. Erwin's Seventh Cavalry set out on horseback, but Pershing wanted the Tenth Cavalry columns to go at least part of the way by train. This was an attempt in part to gain time on Villa's forces, but an equally important consideration was the fatigue of animals that had already marched more than 250 miles in the past fortnight. Although Pershing could not resupply his men over the Mexican railways, he requested, and was granted permission, the use of the Mexican Northwestern Railway to move the Tenth Cavalry. When the train arrived at Colonia Dublán on the morning of the 19th, however, the dilapidated rail cars took so much time to repair that Colonel Brown and his men did not reach Rucio until the next morning. There he left the train and led his men over a mountain trail in the direction of the San Miguel plateau. Major Evans continued the rail journey but encountered worse fortune when the train wrecked, injuring eleven of his men. He also left the train and reached the vicinity of Las Varas on the 22nd.

Meanwhile Colonel Brown had arrived in the San Miguel area about noon on 21 March and found that intelligence reports were entirely wrong: Villa had not been there. Following a rumor (which subsequently proved false) that Carranzista troops had fought and had defeated Villa at Namiquipa, Brown continued southward to meet with Mexican Colonel Chico Cano there on 25 March. He learned that Villa was probably around El Oso or Santa Clara and proposed that if Cano could locate Villa, the Tenth Cavalry would attack. Cano agreed and promised to send out scouting parties. Brown re-

mained in camp near Namiquipa, where, in response to Pershing's orders, Major Evans joined him with the First Squadron on 24 March. Within a few days, Brown concluded that Cano had no intention of making the promised reconnaissance, and he moved his regiment toward San Diego del Monte and Le Quemada, where rumors placed the bandit.

The other column had more success. Colonel Dodd, the brigade commander, joined Colonel Erwin's Seventh Cavalry on 21 March and assumed command of the column. After reaching El Valle on 22 March, he conferred with Mexican General Salas, who reported that, contrary to the rumor that brought U.S. troops there, his men had in fact been defeated by Villa on the 19th at Namiquipa and had fallen back in a demoralized condition to El Valle, where they assumed defensive positions. Despite his defeat, Salas spurned any help from the Americans and disputed Dodd's right to be there, asserting that he had never heard of Obregón's proclamation. Salas declined to cooperate with Dodd in tracking Villa. Like Brown, Dodd determined to go on without assistance from the Mexican forces.

After a week of scouting over rough trails in the face of extremely cold weather, Dodd had virtually exhausted both forage and supplies. He reached the town of Bachiniva on the morning of 28 March and learned that a substantial force of Villistas was nearby at Guerrero. Dodd immediately marched his command in that direction, traveling all night with the hope of surprising the bandits at first light. He approached the town from the east with half his regiment, but placed Major Edward B. Winans with his Second Squadron to the west of the town to block the enemy's retreat.

Early on the morning of 29 March, the Villistas spotted Dodd's column approaching from the bluffs to the east and immediately began to flee. Dodd had surprised approximately 230 men, apparently commanded by Elicio Hernandez, one of Villa's principal lieutenants. Opening long-range rifle and machine-gun fire, the Seventh Cavalry began a four-hour running fight in which they killed thirty Villistas and captured a number of weapons, horses, and other equipment. The remainder of the Villa troops broke into small detachments and scattered into the mountains, carrying their wounded away with them. Dodd could not pursue his demoralized enemy because the Seventh Cavalry's horses were exhausted, having marched seventeen hours out of the previous twenty-four.

In the first phase of his operations, Pershing had enjoyed only modest success. Inadequate intelligence had kept his columns largely occupied chasing rumors, aside from Dodd's encounter at Guerrero. Convinced that Villa would retreat into the mountains as a result of that skirmish, and believing that only carefully selected cavalry detachments could follow him there, Pershing decided on a change in tactics and in his own methods of command.

Changes in Command Technique. Pershing knew that communications lay at the heart of command, but found that the available technology was not up to the task of controlling his far-flung cavalry columns. The regiments' pack-mounted radio sets proved so unreliable as to be useless. Radio sets carried on wagons worked better, but wagons could not keep up with the fast-marching cavalry, even when the horsemen kept to roads that the wagons could traverse. To direct his men, Pershing had to rely on mounted couriers and on the airplanes of the First Aero Squadron, under Captain Benjamin Foulois. Couriers, however, could move little faster than the columns they sought, and even then spent much precious time looking for the intended recipients of the messages. Airplanes, unfortunately, fared little better.

The First Aero Squadron took off from Columbus on 19 March with eight Curtiss JN-2 airplanes. One crashed en route to the advanced base and two others were forced down and arrived late. Eventually, seven reached the base at Casas Grandes near Colonia Dublán. During the first month of operations, the pilots kept busy carrying dispatches and messages to Columbus and among units of the expedition. On several occasions, pilots managed to find the scouting cavalry squadrons and deliver orders

to them; just as often, they failed. Underpowered aircraft were not up to some of the missions. On 20 March, for example, two aircraft turned back just twenty-five miles into a reconnaissance flight because they could not climb over the foothills of the Sierra Madre. Dust storms and gales often grounded the machines, and rough terrain took its toll when pilots tried to land near cavalry columns on the march.

The squadron made seventy-nine flights between 26 March and 4 April, but by the end of the first full month of flying operations, five of the airplanes had been wrecked and another was so badly damaged that its crew abandoned it far from the base. The remaining two flew back to Columbus, where they were condemned as unfit for further use. The squadron's occasional successes in reconnaissance and liaison showed the potential that aircraft offered, but the fragile machines of the First Aero Squadron could not realize that potential. Pershing had to find other means of tactical control.

Precarious communications thus forced a difficult decision on the expedition's commander. Pershing decided to divide his headquarters. The majority of his staff remained at the advanced base at Colonia Dublán, where it functioned under the direction of the chief of staff, Lieutenant Colonel DeRosy C. Cabell, and performed the logistical and administrative tasks necessary to keep the regiments in the field. The real general headquarters became Pershing's automobile, which the commander adopted as the only feasible means of coordinating cavalry operations. Around the end of March, Pershing began the practice of moving forward in a convoy of three automobiles, which carried his aides de camp, a small armed escort, his cook, and a couple of press correspondents. The party lived under the stars, regardless of the weather, and generally on short rations. When necessary, Pershing dispatched one of his aides—George Patton, J. Lawton Collins, and Martin C. Shallenberger—with a car to carry messages either to Colonia Dublán or to one of his subordinate commanders. Pershing kept moving forward, at considerable personal risk, so that he could stay reasonably close to his columns, keep up with their reports, and issue timely and appropriate orders.

The drawback to Pershing's method of command was that he had no good means of communicating with General Funston at Southern Department headquarters in San Antonio. Throughout the campaign, he faced the dilemma that he could either control his deployed columns or maintain satisfactory contact with his own superior, but not both. The telegraph line his signal troops had laid ended at Colonia Dublán, where Colonel Cabell could sustain communications with Columbus and thence with the department headquarters in San Antonio. Pershing was isolated from such rapid communications and could only respond to Funston's queries by messenger to Colonia Dublán, where Colonel Cabell in turn forwarded his dispatches. The inherent delays frustrated Funston and periodically created misunderstandings in San Antonio and in Washington about what was actually happening in Mexico.

Independent Cavalry Detachments.
While the Seventh and Tenth cavalries continued their search for Villa, Pershing moved his field headquarters to Namiquipa, where he would be better able to control the march columns to the south. Using the uncommitted portions of his two cavalry brigades, he organized four pursuit columns, each of approximately squadron strength. To enable them to move swiftly in the high country into which he expected Villa had fled, Pershing directed the soldiers to ride with minimum amounts of equipment. Pack-mule trains supported and supplied the columns, each of which also had a detachment of Apache Indian scouts for tracking and intelligence gathering. This happened to be the last time the army used an organized Indian scout unit in field operations.

Lieutenant Colonel Henry T. Allen and Major Robert L. Howze commanded provisional squadrons drawn from the Eleventh Cavalry. Major Frank Tompkins, who had pursued Villa into Mexico on the morning of the Columbus raid, commanded a provisional squadron of two troops each from the Tenth and Thirteenth cav-

alries. Major Elmer Lindsley led the Second Squadron, Thirteenth Cavalry. The first three columns left Colonia Dublán between 21 March and 29 March and all had arrived in Namiquipa by 2 April, where Pershing awaited them. Lindsley drew the task of screening the western flank from Namiquipa to Chuhuichupa to San José de Babícora, to keep Villa's men from escaping over the mountain trails into the state of Sonora. Supplied with five days' rations for men and horses and 150 rounds of ammunition per man, his squadron rode out of the base on 20 March and was in San José de Babícora ten days later, having struggled through a driving snowstorm during the latter part of the march.

The farther south Pershing's expedition moved, the worse the problem of unreliable information became. As the squadrons concentrated at Namiquipa, the Americans received reports that placed Villa in several different places at the same time. It also seemed likely that Villa's forces had split up into many small detachments and were dispersing before the advancing American columns. Several sources indicated that Villa was somewhere to the west of Bachiniva. In response, Pershing ordered Tompkins to take his men there on a night march by way of Santa Ana, in the west, while Howze and his men scouted the mountains to the east. Taking his small personal staff, the general went directly to Bachiniva, where Tompkins and Howze met him on 1 April, reporting that they had found nothing.

Lacking more substantial information, Pershing then decided to resort once again to advance by parallel columns. After making certain that the passes to the north and west were guarded, he sent all of his men to the south, hoping to catch Villa before he crossed the line into Durango. Tompkins led the advance, with Brown's Tenth Cavalry a day's march behind him and to his left rear. Howze and his squadron occupied a similar position to Tompkins' right rear, and Allen's column followed about three days' march directly behind. The force was lightly equipped and carried minimal supplies, but Pershing adjudged it strong enough to fight any hostile force it encountered. The flexible organization allowed the columns to cover a great deal of territory and to reinforce quickly any column that ran into trouble.

Those precautions appeared wise. As the expedition marched deeper into Chihuahua, the likelihood increased that Carranzista forces would resist its movement. Although the two armies were ostensibly working toward the same goal of putting down the Villa rebellion and pacifying the border region, the Mexican troops had never displayed much enthusiasm for working with Pershing's forces. As March turned into April, the indifference that Brown and Dodd had encountered in their first meetings with their Mexican counterparts was deepening into active hostility. Soon there was little question that, to the Carranzistas, ejecting the foreigners from Mexico was more important than capturing Villa.

During the month of April, Pershing's columns systematically searched the southern half of Chihuahua. As the four flying columns marched to the south, Colonel Dodd's column guarded the trails leading into the mountains to the west while Colonel Brown secured the eastern flank; gradually they would converge on a selected spot near the Chihuahua-Durango border. During those several weeks of hard riding in cold and difficult conditions, the Americans fought a series of skirmishes, but only a few were with Villa's men. Instead, their major battles were with units of the regular Mexican army.

Colonel Brown's Tenth Cavalry column, moving southward in a blizzard that interrupted communications both with Pershing and with Colonel Dodd, made the first contact. On 1 April, riding from San Diego del Monte toward Guerrero, Brown's men unexpectedly met a small band of Villistas near Agua Caliente, just across the Continental Divide. The troopers attacked under the overhead fire of machine guns (the first time the army had used that technique), killing two bandits and chasing the others out of the town. A pursuit over a half-dozen miles of timbered terrain ended at dusk. Major Evans, leading the remainder of the Tenth Cavalry, received orders to guard the

country between Santa Clara and El Oso. His detachment, so occupied until early May, encountered no action.

Brown took the remainder of his regiment on to San Antonia de los Arenales on 3 April, where Mexican General José Cavazos threatened that any further American advance would be considered a hostile act and treated accordingly. Sidestepping the Mexican forces, Brown continued south. On 6 April an airplane found his column and delivered orders from Pershing to secure the eastern border of the territory and advance to Parral. On 9 April, Brown reached Tres Hermanos, where General Juan Garza, a Carranzista commander, agreed to cooperate and sent out scouts. Hearing nothing from the Mexican reconnaissance, Brown set out on 10 April toward Parral, this time with the assistance of a Mexican liaison officer. By the afternoon of 12 April, he was encamped about ten miles from his objective.

Following Villa's trail on a route that led them through Agua Caliente, San Antonio de los Arenales, and San Francisco de Borja, Major Tompkins and his column were also nearing Parral. Like Brown, Tompkins had been threatened by Cavazos, who told him that further pursuit was fruitless in any case, because Villa had been killed. Following his orders to avoid a clash with the Carranzistas, Tompkins withdrew north to Cienguita and then east to Santa Rosalia, whence he continued his march to the south on 7 April.

Adhering to Pershing's plan for mutually supporting columns, Howze resupplied his squadron and pushed out to the southwest, passing by the village of Cusihuiriachic along a track that Brown and Tompkins had followed earlier. He then pursued a rumor that Villa, only wounded, was heading along the mountains to Durango. Avoiding Cavazos' units, on 9 April Howze reached the village of San José del Sitio, where locals fired into his camp during the night. The next day he skirmished with a group of Villistas at La Joya de Herrera, killing its commander and reporting that he had dispersed the surviving bandits. Two days later, on 11 April, he surrounded Santa Cruz de Herrera and fought with another force believed to be Villistas, most of whom escaped. It later turned out that Villa had been encamped about a mile away at the time.

While those columns advanced, Dodd continued to watch the passes to the west, skirmishing frequently but inconclusively with small, armed parties. He moved part of his command to Miñaca on 8 April to protect Howze's flank and to try to locate Villista bands reported in the area. As planned, Colonel Allen and his squadron trailed several days behind the advance columns. He left Namiquipa on 2 April, scouted El Oso, and joined the main body at San Geronimo Ranch. By 8 April, he had reached San Antonio de los Arenales and left there the following morning to scout the area for Villistas. After sixteen straight days in the saddle, Allen's men arrived at Satevó on 12 April, where Pershing had established a temporary command post and aerodrome.

Such was the disposition of forces when Tompkins' squadron approached Parral on 12 April. Tompkins knew that several thousand soldiers of the Mexican army were encamped in his vicinity and to his rear and had firm intelligence that some three hundred Villistas, including Villa and his staff, were scattered throughout the region. He was confident of rapid support, knowing that Howze was about three days' march behind him to one side, and Brown about a day and a half behind to the other side. Thus, he decided to go as far as Parral, where he intended to buy fodder and supplies, before striking farther south toward the Durango line.

Tompkins paused at the little town of Valle de Zaragosa on 10 April, where he was able to purchase clothing for his troopers, many of whom were literally in rags. While there, Tompkins met a Carranzista officer from the garrison at Parral, who agreed to deliver a message to the garrison commander, General Ismael Lozano, requesting a guide to a camp site and permission to purchase supplies. When the column reached Parral at noon on 12 April, Tompkins halted outside the town and then went to visit General Lozano at his headquarters. Suspicious that Lozano was directing his

men into a camp site where they could easily be attacked that night, Tompkins instead planned to move away from the town. While inspecting the site, a belligerent mob gathered, and Carranzista soldiers evidently began firing into the American column. The situation rapidly deteriorated, and General Lozano lost control of his men, who numbered five to six hundred.

Tompkins attempted to get the Mexicans to cease fire and, failing that, began to withdraw to the north, pursued by Mexican troops and skirmishing with them from around 1:30 to 4:00 in the afternoon, when his men reached defensible terrain near Santa Cruz de Villegas. Several hundred Mexican soldiers directed a sporadic fusillade at the American positions, but Tompkins' men easily kept them at a distance by accurate long-range rifle fire. U.S. losses were two killed, one missing, and six—including Major Tompkins—wounded. An estimated forty Mexican soldiers were killed and an unknown number wounded.

A rider sent in search of Colonel Brown's column returned with detachments of the Tenth Cavalry around 7 P.M., at which point the Mexicans broke off the action and retired into Parral. Brown assumed command, demanded explanations from the Mexican general commanding the region, and dispatched reports to General Pershing, then in his new headquarters at Satevó, eighty miles to the northwest. By the next day, both provisional squadrons of the Eleventh Cavalry under Allen and Howze had arrived, which relieved Brown's concern about Mexican attacks but exacerbated an already severe supply problem. In an unsatisfactory exchange of notes, Mexican authorities denied any responsibility for the attack. For his part, Pershing praised Tompkins for his attempt to avoid trouble and his restraint in dealing with the crisis. Nevertheless, in the face of escalating Mexican opposition, Pershing decided to withdraw his men from southern Chihuahua. The columns left Santa Cruz de Villegas on 22 April.

While events were developing around Parral, Colonel Dodd's security forces continued to scout for Villistas in the western highlands of the state. On 18 April he and his men, accompanied by a detachment of Carranzista cavalry, followed up a rumor that a large Villista band was in the vicinity of Yoquivo. Early in the march, the U.S. and Mexican forces became separated, and when Dodd reached Yoquivo on 20 April, he found that the Carranzistas had already been there and that the bandits had fled farther west. Convinced that the commander of the Mexican detachment had warned Villa's men of his approach, Dodd pushed on toward Tomochic, where he ran into about 150 Villistas under Candelario Cervantes on 22 April.

Dodd's men were fired on from the surrounding hills as they approached the village in the late afternoon. They found the bandits rapidly leaving the town and immediately opened fire. The cavalrymen quickly overcame the Villista rear guard and several scattered detachments in the hills around the village. The enemy main body was in the hills to the east. Because it was late in the day and there appeared to be no way to flank or get behind the enemy, Dodd ordered his men to attack frontally. By dark, they had driven the Villistas from their positions, killing or wounding some twenty-five of them, and the survivors fled. In Dodd's judgment, his attack had completely disintegrated the band.

He then returned with his men to Miñaca, where he continued patrolling until early June, when Pershing ordered the column back to El Valle. In July, Dodd reached his sixty-fourth birthday, was promoted to brigadier general, and retired from the army. Brigadier General Eben Swift replaced him in command.

REASSEMBLY OF THE PUNITIVE EXPEDITION

The fight at Parral marked both the southernmost advance of U.S. troops into Mexico and a turning point in the campaign. With the bulk of his cavalry in the vicinity of Parral, Pershing would have been in a position to control the southern half of Chihuahua, where support for Villa appeared to be particularly strong. Serious logistical problems, however, far outweighed the desirable tactical advantages of remaining so far south.

Relations between the governments of Mexico and the United States were increasingly strained, and the expeditionary force had no assurance that the hostility of the federal garrison at Parral would be an isolated occurrence. The civilian population was equally unfriendly, and there was little hope that his columns could purchase food, fodder, clothing, and other supplies locally. Pershing's own logistical system, rudimentary at best, was simply not up to the task of supplying two cavalry brigades that were 180 miles south of the advanced bases. Furthermore, such long lines of supply were extremely vulnerable to attack.

Although the expedition relied primarily on wagon and pack-mule train, which operated with customary, if slow, efficiency, motor trucks were also used for supply. This was a new experience, and the men assigned to the lines of communications had to improvise standard operating procedures. Skilled mechanics from the First Aero Squadron quickly overcame the initial muddle at Columbus when the trucks were delivered in parts and without instructions for assembly. Most of the personnel assigned to the truck trains were civilian drivers and mechanics, although some drivers were soldiers and each column had a detachment of infantry detailed for guard duty. Pershing ordered a maintenance shop set up at Columbus to inspect and overhaul trucks after each round trip, but it was soon evident that the rigors of the poor and nonexistent roads made it necessary for each truck train to carry along a good supply of repair parts.

Leaving the railhead at Columbus, the normal truck route extended due west to Gibson's Ranch, where it crossed the border, then led through Boca Grande, Espia, Ascensión, and Corrialitos to the expeditionary base at Colonia Dublán. From that point, trucks struck out to the advanced bases at Galeana, El Valle, Las Cruces, and Namiquipa. The White, FWD, and Jeffrey Quad trucks followed a trail defined by wagon ruts and the telegraph wire laid by the

Signal Corps troops between Colonia Dublán and Columbus. The steel and hard rubber wheels of the trucks soon churned the trails into an almost impassable morass of ruts and chuck holes. Consequently, wherever the land was reasonably flat, the drivers kept broadening the track until it was half a mile wide in some places. Once the rains began, those tracks became impassable. The expedition's two engineer companies were completely overwhelmed by the task of maintaining the primitive roads.

The daily cartage requirements were staggering. The expedition needed 223,000 pounds of forage, 120,000 pounds of fuel, 60,000 pounds of rations, 10,000 pounds of clothing and miscellaneous supplies, and 5,000 pounds of dry stores. Early in the campaign, Pershing's staff established an adequate rate of supply from the United States to the expedition's base at Colonia Dublán and made satisfactory arrangements for forwarding matériel to the advanced bases. The logistical system broke down, however, between the advanced bases and the marching cavalry columns, which rarely returned north to resupply. Pack and wagon trains could not keep up with the cavalry, and only periodically reached the squadrons. Supply difficulties multiplied the farther the cavalrymen rode. As a consequence, the scouting columns had to rely on the little they could carry with them and on foraging to supplement the meager quantities of food, fodder, and equipment provided by their pack trains. The barren countryside provided little for them in any case, even when the Mexican population did not recoil in hostility at their approach.

The usual foraging system relied on issuance of government receipts, which the seller presented to the army quartermaster for payment. Increasingly, Mexican civilians and businessmen were unwilling to accept such "scraps of paper" that could only be redeemed far in the north. Eventually, commanders found that only cash would produce the supplies their men needed, and some, lacking government funds, paid for the army's needs out of their own pockets. The experience of Colonel Brown, commanding the Tenth Cavalry, was typical. The

day his men rode out of Colonia Dublán was the last on which they had government rations until 20 April. Brown paid out more than $1,600 of his own money over that month to buy what little food the country had to offer. By and large his men subsisted on corn and beans, rarely getting sugar, coffee, or fruit. Poor food debilitated their health, although they did not always eat all they received. Following the old cavalry dictum of "the horse, the saddle, the man," they reserved their corn for their animals whenever necessary. Horses accustomed to grass and oats fared poorly on dry hay and corn, however, and the animals quickly thinned down.

Equipment suffered correspondingly. Clothing wore out rapidly, and officers only occasionally were able to buy civilian trousers, shirts, and hats to replace it. Stirrup cups soon disappeared, as soldiers used them to resole light issue shoes worn out while leading their horses over difficult terrain. Pieces of shelter halves soon appeared as patches on riding breeches, and some of the men replaced their tattered campaign hats with ones made from the linings of their saddle bags. No column had a forge, and periodic stops at ranches to use local blacksmith shops barely sufficed to keep the horses shod. As it was, there developed a dangerous shortage of horseshoes, and commanders ordered their men to contribute all their spares to a common pool and to pick up any they saw along the trail. It was no wonder that Pershing was so shocked at the gaunt, ragged appearance of his men and their mounts when they finally rode back into camp after the fight at Parral.

With those limitations in mind, Pershing sent his chief of staff, Colonel Cabell, to Santa Cruz de Villegas to determine whether the troops could stay there. Brown pointed out that his men and their animals needed a minimum of one ton of food, six tons of hay, and four and a half tons of grain every day. Cabell found no way to sustain such a rate of supply and quickly concluded that all of Pershing's apprehensions were justified. Thus, on 21 April, Brown was ordered to begin withdrawing by way of Satevó to San Antonio de los Arenales. By 22 April, the last column was on the march to the north.

Patrol of the Districts. Pershing perceived the actions of the Carranzista troops as simple treachery and became convinced that Mexican officers did not want him to find Villa. In messages to Funston, he decried the fiction of Carranza's cooperation with the expedition and suggested investing sufficient military force to control all of Chihuahua. The attack on Tompkins and his men at Parral alarmed Washington, however, and President Wilson opted instead for further negotiations with the Mexican government. While those talks progressed, Pershing was to make every effort to avoid confrontation.

At first, the pause in operations was a welcome one. As his tattered and weary columns reported into the encampment at San Antonio de los Arenales, Pershing realized that rest and refitting were the first priority for the cavalry troops. Within a week, however, the general had become impatient. Finding extended inactivity distasteful, he instituted a rigorous training program that kept the men occupied. While negotiations between Generals Scott and Obregón dragged on without result in Juárez, Pershing sought some way to continue his mission.

The campaign of the three columns and the subsequent operations of the four smaller columns had succeeded in catching a number of Villistas and, perhaps more important, dispersing and discouraging others. Villa was still at large in Chihuahua, however, and scattered bands of his supporters remained under arms. After withdrawing his troops from the southern part of the state and reestablishing his general headquarters at Namiquipa, Pershing decided on 29 April to adopt a system of patrol by district. The idea, strongly reminiscent of the methods successfully used by the British in policing the northwest frontier of India, was inspired by the work of Colonel Dodd's Seventh Cavalry. While busy securing the western passes, Dodd's men had remained essentially in the same area and had become familiar with both the terrain and the population. Such propinquity bred a mutual respect that allowed the cavalrymen to develop good sources of information about Villista bands. Dodd knew the reliability of his Carranzista counterpart and, well-informed about matters around Miñaca, had been able to sift probability from rumor. Diligently following up sound information had brought Dodd the success of Tomochic. Dodd's methods, Pershing reasoned, might bring similar successes to his other commanders.

As soon as his men were rested and reequipped, Pershing sent the cavalry regiments out to five patrol districts that covered all of central Chihuahua from Galeana, just south of his original base at Colonia Dublán, to the region just north of Parral.

Pershing tried to assign each cavalry regiment to the district with which it was most familiar because of its service, although that obviously could not apply to the Fifth Cavalry, newly arrived from the United States. He also based much of his infantry and artillery forward in the districts to support the cavalry regiments

MEXICAN DISTRICT PATROLS

District	Regiment	Commander
Satevó	Fifth Cavalry	Colonel Wilbur E. Wilder
Guerrero	Seventh Cavalry	Colonel George A. Dodd
Namiquipa	Tenth Cavalry	Major Ellwood W. Evans
San Francisco de Borja	Eleventh Cavalry	Colonel James Lockett
Bustillos	Thirteenth Cavalry	Colonel Herbert J. Slocum

when necessary. Pershing charged his commanders with organizing their own agents and services of information within their districts and taking independent action to pursue Villistas whenever the opportunity presented itself. Although civilians were to be treated with special consideration, he warned that U.S. troops were always in some danger of being attacked and ordered appropriate precautions to be taken. By 4 May, the regiments had moved into their districts.

Active patrolling quickly produced results. Reacting to a request from the local Carranzista commander for help, Major Howze rode with six troops of the Eleventh Cavalry to Ojos Azules, where approximately 120 Villistas under Julio Acosta, Cruz Dominguez, and Antonio Angel were still celebrating a victory over Mexican federal troops. After a long night march, Howze arrived at the town just after dawn on 5 May. Having achieved surprise, Howze ordered an immediate attack. His six troops of cavalry delivered a mounted pistol charge that broke the Villista resistance in little more than twenty minutes and rescued a group of Carranzista prisoners that the bandits had intended to execute. A two-hour fight followed, during which the Villistas separated into three groups and fled into the hills. Howze's men virtually wiped out one of the groups, killing sixty-two and capturing a large number of horses and mules. The Eleventh Cavalry suffered no casualties in an action that Pershing called "a brilliant piece of work" in his report to Funston.

Chance governed some of the encounters. Pershing's supernumerary aide de camp, Lieutenant George S. Patton, Jr., encountered a party of Villistas on 14 May while on an expedition to purchase corn. When Patton and his detachment of ten men from the Sixteenth Infantry drove up to the San Miguel Ranch near Rubio, a number of men ran out of the buildings and opened fire. In an action that newspaper reporters played up as an innovation in warfare, Patton and his men returned fire from their moving vehicles and killed several bandits, one of whom happened to be Julio Cárdenas, one of Villa's better commanders. In another brief fight near Las Cruces, Villistas ambushed a small U.S. detachment from the Seventeenth Infantry that was escorting a detail of engineers sketching roads. After the skirmish the patrol discovered that they had killed Candelario Cervantes, another of Villa's right-hand men. Slowly but surely, sustained pressure was eroding Villa's organization.

The Threat of War.

The Threat of War. Measurable and satisfactory progress in Pershing's district scheme was not accompanied by similar progress in U.S.-Mexican relations. The failure of talks between Scott and Obregón and the increasing hostility of the Mexican government spurred a flurry of telegrams between Pershing, Funston, and the War Department, debating what the expedition ought to do. Fearing the outbreak of general war, Secretary of State Robert Lansing had already warned U.S. consuls in Mexico to be ready to advise Americans to leave the country. In Chihuahua, swelling numbers of Mexican federal troops worried both Funston and the War Department, causing them to urge Pershing to withdraw his scattered regiments and shorten his exposed lines of communication. Receiving no reports from his district commanders of threatening Mexican troop movements, Pershing calmly advised against any withdrawal. Secretary of War Baker firmly believed that Pershing had to stay as long as the danger to the border remained, but warned him not to provoke the Mexican authorities and advised him to be ready, in the event of attack, to fall back with his entire command and join the Fifth Infantry Brigade.

By the end of May, Carranzista patrols had become more aggressive, and U.S. and Mexican armed detachments had the dual task of pursuing Villa and keeping careful watch on each other. Concerned about the possibility of accidentally firing on Mexican federal troops, Pershing emphasized discretion and restraint in his instructions to his officers. Through the month, the threat of war loomed larger as additional Mexican units arrived in Chihuahua and deployed along Pershing's lines of communications. By 1 June, approximately thirty thousand men were encamped to the east and west of

Pershing's expeditionary force. General J. B. Treviño wired Pershing on 16 June to inform him that the Mexican army would not permit movement of U.S. troops in any direction except north. Pershing defiantly replied the same day to the effect that he would follow the instructions originally issued by the United States government and conduct patrols to accomplish those instructions in accordance with his own best judgment. Thus, considerable anxiety attended the dispatch of more U.S. patrols in search of Villa. A few days later, a clash occurred, bringing the two nations to the brink of war.

In an attempt to keep tabs on the disposition of Mexican troops, Pershing ordered general reconnaissance, particularly to the east of the U.S. lines of communication. He had reports that Mexican troops were massing near Villa Ahumada, about eighty miles from Colonia Dublán. Troops C and K, Tenth Cavalry, marched out on 18 June with specific orders from Pershing to avoid trouble. Advancing along separate lines, the two troops met at Santo Domingo Ranch, where Captain Charles T. Boyd, as the senior of the two leaders, assumed overall command. For reasons that remain unclear, he decided to march directly through the town of Carrizal, which lay between the ranch and his objective of Villa Ahumada. Captain Lewis S. Morey argued against such a provocative move, because there were good roads around the town. Similarly, the American foreman of the ranch warned that there were Mexican troops in Carrizal who would surely oppose the U.S. troops. Boyd, however, insisted, and the hundred men of the two cavalry troops arrived at Carrizal about 6:30 A.M. on 21 June.

Boyd halted just short of the town and requested permission to march through. He consulted with General Felix Gomez, the garrison commander, who refused permission and emphasized General Treviño's orders that Americans were not to be permitted to move in any direction except toward the international border. As the two men talked, Mexican troops debouched from the town and took up positions along irrigation ditches and in front of the village. Boyd formed up his troops and dismounted to attack, believing that the Mexicans would not stand up to his men.

His estimate of the situation was incorrect. The Carranzistas opened fire and Captain Boyd was killed in the opening exchange. In the course of the next hour, Troop K fell back and the Mexicans turned the open flank of Troop C. In the ensuing debacle, seven Americans were killed, twelve wounded, twenty-four captured, and five reported as missing. The remainder of the two troops retired about one thousand yards to the west and then disengaged from the action and eventually reached a relieving column from the Eleventh Cavalry, led by Major Howze.

Captain Boyd had completely misjudged Mexican resolve and, expecting no resistance, had frittered away every tactical advantage by delaying action so long that the Mexicans had plenty of time to deploy in strong positions. Then, although he certainly observed the Mexican preparations, he ordered a frontal attack. Boyd's thoroughly bad judgment caused unnecessary casualties. Worse, it brought on a battle that Pershing wanted to avoid at all costs. Popular outrage over the Carrizal fight in the United States and the continued failure of talks between the United States and Mexico, both at the military and political levels, appeared to make open war inevitable.

Immediately, Chief of Staff Scott directed the War Department General Staff to frame plans for war with Mexico. In general, the plan envisioned an advance into the country by three major columns, to be commanded by Funston (eastern), Pershing (central), and General William H. Sage (western), then in Nogales. Overall command was to be vested in Leonard Wood. In Mexico, Pershing promptly fulfilled simultaneous War Department orders to concentrate his expeditionary division at Colonia Dublán and to prepare for offensive action. To provide the manpower for the other two columns, the War Department had nowhere to turn but to the states.

The previous month, Generals Scott and Funston had voiced concerns to the administration about the lack of security along the border. Despite the successes Pershing's men had enjoyed, periodic raids continued, although the evidence was far from clear that Villistas were always responsible for them. General Scott, having heard reports of extremist Mexican rhetoric about crushing the expeditionary force and riding into the United States far enough to "water their horses on the Potomac," was concerned that the Mexicans considered their long border with Texas to be undefended and therefore might be tempted to make an attack in force across it, thereby precipitating war. There were not enough regular army troops to guard against such an eventuality, and the two generals asked the president to call out the militia of the border states for additional protection. Scott did not pretend that the militia troops, whose standard of readiness and training was far below that of the regulars, could actually campaign against the Mexicans in the wastelands around the Rio Grande. He recognized, however, that the presence of a highly visible large group of uniformed armed men would serve as an effective deterrent. On 9 May 1916, President Wilson agreed and called the militias of Texas, New Mexico, and Arizona into federal service.

Those troops provided the nucleus for the second call-up of state troops and provided the bulk of the men to be assigned to Sage and Funston. The passage of the National Defense Act on 3 June made the process easier, because it clearly defined the relationship between the regular army and the state forces, now to be known as the National Guard. On 18 June, state forces were federalized and ordered to the Mexican border. Between then and the end of August, a total of 111,954 National Guardsmen from almost every state in the Union reached the Southwest, where they were stationed in large camps at El Paso, San Antonio, Brownsville, and Douglas, Arizona, in addition to smaller detachments all along the border.

Many units, overwhelmingly infantry, cavalry, and field artillery, reported for duty. Most were at far from full strength, however, and the National Guard mustered 155,971 fewer than called for by their tables of organization. Plans to employ the men in National Guard divisions and brigades foundered in the face of the same problems Pershing had already encountered in Mexico. There were not enough service troops—signal, engineer, medical, transportation, and quartermaster—to allow commanders to create and use large formations. As a consequence, most of the National Guard units functioned as independent regiments or battalions under a garrison command. While newspapers played up citizen-soldier complaints that they had to travel to Texas in cramped railway cars, War Department officials were quietly delighted that their movement had been, although probably uncomfortable, a rapid and efficient one. Colonel Chauncey Baker of the Quartermaster Department had studied the problems in concentrating troops for the maneuver division in 1911 and resolved them through special arrangements with the railroads.

Once the National Guard troops arrived in the Southern Department, they could begin sharpening their military skills, and regular army commanders began planning for their eventual use in case of war with Mexico. Funston and Scott were satisfied that the martial display of so many troops along the border would impress, and thus deter, any Mexican forces that might be tempted to raid the United States on a large scale.

EVACUATION

While soldiers prepared for war, diplomats sought a settlement. Negotiations that began in May continued through June. At first the positions of the two countries appeared too far apart for any orderly resolution. Mexico properly emphasized its sovereignty, while the State Department stressed the right of the United States to guarantee the safety and security of its citizens. On 29 June, the Mexican government took a step to ease tensions when it released the prisoners from the Tenth Cavalry taken during the fight at Carrizal. Early in July, the two governments set up a joint commission to resolve the conflict. While talks were going on in New London, Philadelphia, New York, and Washington, confrontations between the two armies virtually ceased.

By that time Pershing's command was concentrated at Colonia Dublán, where shorter supply lines improved the welfare and readiness of the troops. Villa had ceased to be a threat to the United States, lost most of his capable leaders, and found that his remaining supporters had been scattered by the diligent patrolling of the U.S. cavalry. His prestige, however, began to grow as soon as reports of a possible U.S. withdrawal began to be common knowledge. Villa again commenced limited operations against the Mexican federal troops farther south. Pershing dutifully reported those facts to Funston, along with his considered opinion that the Carranza government was incapable of managing the situation.

Expeditionary troops remained in Colonia Dublán over the next six months while the two governments painfully reached an accord, and Pershing spent the time developing his encampment into a regular military cantonment. After frustrating experiments, the Americans finally learned the art of making adobe bricks and built neat rows of huts, using their shelter halves for roofs. His staff laid out a logical arrangement of facilities that included a supply depot at the railhead, ordnance and engineering shops, truck parts, maneuver areas, baseball fields, and an airfield. With routine and relative comfort, however, came the boredom that can quickly blunt a soldier's readiness to fight. The remedy for that, Pershing knew, was training.

At Pershing's insistence, and with his close supervision, the expedition therefore filled the ensuing months in Mexico with an intensive and carefully thought-out training program that made those regulars among the most proficient men under arms in the nation's history. The campaign against Villa and its almost classical cavalry operations had nothing to do with modern warfare. It had toughened the men but not introduced them to, for example, the conditions under which men were even then fighting in France. Rigorous musketry courses were followed by machine-gun training, reflecting Pershing's ardent faith in marksmanship. Next were maneuver problems that stressed infantry tactics in open order, and the expeditionary force also learned to dig field fortifications and practiced fighting from trenches. Carefully planned exercises, followed by thoughtful critiques, drove the lessons home. By early winter, Pershing had a first-rate division at his disposal.

The need for retaining that division in Mexico, however, was fast disappearing. President Wilson worried that the United States might become involved in the war in France, and did not want the largest part of the regular army tied down on the Mexican border if that eventuality came to pass. While the U.S.-Mexican joint commission had reached no firm agreement, the U.S. members of the commission recommended to the president that Pershing's command be withdrawn from Mexico. Wilson agreed. Funston, acting on instructions from the War Department, directed Pershing on 18 January 1917 to return to the United States.

Funston left the exact date to Pershing, who organized his withdrawal in order to leave nothing behind. He began with the shipment of surplus equipment and supplies to Columbus, and followed on the night of 27–28 January 1917 with the evacuation of his men. Crews of soldiers demolished the orderly rows of huts and administrative buildings before leaving. The division marched north to Palomas, where the men halted on 5 February to clean up before reentering the United States. Pershing crossed the border first and reviewed his troops as they rode into Columbus, the last of them crossing out of Mexico at three o'clock in the afternoon.

SIGNIFICANCE OF THE CAMPAIGN

Withdrawal of the Punitive Expedition proved the final hurdle to normalizing relations between the United States and Mexico. In March, Carranza was elected president of Mexico, and in August, Wilson extended recognition of and reopened full diplomatic relations with Carranza's government. Even so, tensions between the two countries did not really abate until after World War I. During the war U.S. soldiers occasionally pursued Mexican raiders back across the international frontier. Villa remained a problem until July 1920, when he surrendered and, in return for retiring entirely from politics, was given vast estates in Chihuahua. He was assassinated in 1923.

Shortly after the return of the expedition, General Funston died of a heart attack, leaving Pershing commander of the Southern Department as of 20 February 1917. Summing up the successes and failures of the expeditionary force, Pershing regretted that he had failed to catch Villa, but concluded that, given the steadily growing opposition of all Mexicans to his operations, he had done well in dispersing Villista bands and returning a sense of security to the southern regions of Texas, New Mexico, and Arizona. Secretary of War Baker, noting that capturing Villa would have been desirable, shared Pershing's sentiments that the real purposes of the expedition in terms of U.S. security had been met. General Scott and senior officers in the War Department were as impressed with Pershing's restraint as with his military successes. They observed that he had accomplished his mission with very few casualties and had weathered numerous crises and provocations without allowing periodic clashes of arms to bring on war with Mexico.

The Punitive Expedition into Mexico was the United States Army's last great cavalry campaign, and cavalry supporters derived considerable satisfaction from the reliable and, at times, exciting performance of the mounted troopers. Some, such as Patton and Tompkins, saw the campaign as proof that the cavalry would continue to have a role in warfare and drew up careful lists of ways that the equipment and techniques of the arm could be improved. While the experience of World War I eventually proved supporters of the mounted arm wrong about their hopes for cavalry in general war, the Punitive Expedition continued to bear witness to the arm's utility in small-scale fighting, particularly over rough terrain. Throughout the

1920s and 1930s, U.S. war plans for defense of the Western Hemisphere continued to envisage such a role for the horse cavalry. The Cavalry School at Fort Riley, Kansas, was the legacy of the Punitive Expedition until World War II.

While the expedition suggested the continued utility of the horse cavalry, it also made clear that the days of fighting with saber and lance were past. Few of Pershing's cavalrymen bothered to carry the saber, which, despite the protestations of such vigorous supporters as Patton, clearly no longer had much use. Concerned about the loads their mounts had to carry and conscious that the saving of even a few ounces would significantly affect the endurance of their horses, troopers commonly preferred the more effective rifle and pistol. The doctrinal lesson of the Punitive Expedition was that the principal use of cavalry in the future would be as mounted rifles.

If it was the last great cavalry campaign, the Punitive Expedition was also the army's first modern campaign, presaging the mechanization of the service in the decades to come. Operations in Mexico forced doctrinal development in many areas, the most spectacular of which was the use of airplanes. Signal Corps airmen, observing the progress of the air war in Europe, believed that their airplanes should have been employed chiefly for reconnaissance and only incidentally for liaison. Foulois and his pilots saw that, given more reliable machines, they could have been invaluable to Pershing as scouts and that the information they provided would have multiplied many times over the value of the cavalry columns by directing them more efficiently. The thinking of the Air Service about the observation function of aircraft, founded in the experience in Mexico, developed dramatically over the next two years.

The brilliant small-unit actions fought by the cavalrymen could not, however, conceal the many shortcomings displayed by the army. Before the United States Army could fight a major war against a modern opponent, much thought would have to be given to reorganizing and expanding the administrative and logistical services. Quartermaster, signal, ordnance, and maintenance organizations demanded full-time, highly qualified specialists if combat soldiers equipped with modern weapons and machines were to be kept ready for battle. The army could not continue merely to detail line officers to organize logistical support, as had been tried at Columbus.

The expedition also served a useful purpose in testing airplanes, radios, machine guns, trucks, cars, and other equipment then entering the inventories of Western armies. U.S. soldiers learned many lessons about how much equipment suffers under the stress of constant use and quickly discovered which machines were too complicated, unreliable, or simply ill-suited for field service. Thus, the army replaced the JN-2 aircraft with more robust and powerful machines and discarded the Benet-Mercier machine gun that had failed as early as the night of Villa's raid on Columbus and never served satisfactorily thereafter. Pershing's command difficulties raised more serious problems, pointing to the need for more reliable field communications.

Service in Mexico was perhaps most valuable as a opportunity for hardening and training the regulars who would become the core of the national army a few months later. Pershing had the opportunity to train hard, without the usual distractions of garrison duty. Also, the campaign allowed many younger officers to lead large formations of troops for the first time in their careers and offered them the opportunity for independent action with the consequent difficult decisions such command implied. Many succeeded, others failed, and Pershing developed the system of merit by which he would award commands in France. In Mexico, Pershing concluded that modern war required young leaders—this despite the spectacular performances of men such as Dodd and Brown, well into their sixties, and of many company commanders and field officers who were forty and older.

Controversies surrounding passage of the National Defense Act of 1916 and later difficulties in manning the National Guard regiments detailed for border duty convinced Scott, Persh-

ing, and others that the nation could no longer rely solely on its militia in time of war. Conscription, they concluded, was the only way to guarantee enough men to field an appropriate fighting force. That decision—logical enough in view of the fact that less than half the National Guard's presumed strength ever appeared for duty—ignored the political clamor that selective service was certain to raise.

Although the National Guard did not serve in Mexico, the mobilization did reveal important deficiencies in its organization and training, as well as in its mobilization system. Inefficient leaders stood out, as did good ones. After he returned from Mexico, Pershing extended his training program in the Southern Department to include the National Guard until the regiments returned to state control. That training had important consequences after the United States declared war on Germany. The National Guard mobilization in 1916 was an important dress rehearsal that made the general national mobilization in 1917 a more successful and efficient procedure.

In sum, the Punitive Expedition into Mexico and the entire border campaign that began in 1911 helped to lay a sound foundation for the vast expansion of the U.S. Army in 1917. While the reforms of Secretary of War Elihu Root at the turn of the century improved the functioning of the War Department General Staff, the Punitive Expedition was the laboratory in which those reforms were worked out in practice.

The Punitive Expedition made Pershing the best and, perhaps, only choice to command the American Expeditionary Forces in France. By 1917 he had gained experience in handling large numbers of troops, which no one else in the army could claim. Further, he had the opportunity to think deeply about battle and, particularly in the period after June 1916, to experiment with various types of tactics. The confused political situation during the Punitive Expedition required him to deal tactfully with foreign officials and to consider the political implications of military actions. The entire experience was excellent training for a commander in chief of an army on foreign service. At the declaration of war, Pershing offered a combination of skill, experience, and proven ability unique in the officer corps.

BIBLIOGRAPHY

Blumenson, Martin, ed. *The Patton Papers, 1885–1940* (1972).

Braddy, Haldeen. *Pershing's Mission in Mexico* (1966).

Brimlow, George Francis. *Cavalryman Out of the West: Life of General William Carey Brown* (1944).

Campobello, Nellie. *Apuntes Sobre la Vida Militar de Francisco Villa* (1940).

Clendenen, Clarence C. *The United States and Pancho Villa: A Study in Unconventional Diplomacy.* (1961).

———. *Blood on the Border: The United States Army and the Mexican Irregulars* (1969).

Cramer, Stuart, Jr. "The Punitive Expedition from Boquillas." *Cavalry Journal* 27 (November 1916).

Dallam, Samuel F. "The Punitive Expedition of 1916." *Cavalry Journal* 36 (July 1927).

Elser, Frank B. "General Pershing's Mexican Campaign." *Century Magazine* (February 1920).

Evans, Ellwood W. "Cavalry Equipment in Mexico." *United States Cavalry Journal* 28 (November 1916).

Foulois, Benjamin. *From the Wright Brothers to the Astronauts* (1968).

Ganoe, William Addleman. *The History of the United States Army* (1942).

Greer, Thomas H. "Air Arm Doctrinal Roots, 1917–1918." *Military Affairs* 20 (Winter 1956).

Guzman, Martin Luis. *Memoirs of Pancho Villa*, translated by Virginia H. Taylor (1965).

Johnson, William Weber. *Heroic Mexico: The Violent Emergence of a Modern Nation* (1968).

Kreidberg, Marvin A., and Merton G. Henry. *History of Military Mobilization in the United States Army, 1775–1945* (1955).

Lister, Florence C., and Robert H. Lister. *Chihuahua: Storehouse of Storms* (1966).

Mason, Herbert Molloy, Jr. *The Great Pursuit* (1970).

Maurer, Maurer. *The U.S. Air Service in World War I*, 4 vols. (1978–1979).

Morey, Lewis S. "The Cavalry Fight at Carrizal." *Cavalry Journal* 27 (January 1917).

Page, Victor W. "Substituting Gasoline for Horseflesh: Work of Motor Trucks with the Army in Mexico." *Scientific American* (5 August 1916).

Palmer, Frederick. *Newton D. Baker, America at War* (1931).

Patton, George S., Jr. "Cavalry Work on the Punitive Expedition." *Cavalry Journal* 27 (January 1917).

Pickering, Abner. "The Battle of Agua Prieta." *United States Infantry Journal* 12 (January 1916).

Pool, William C. "Military Aviation in Texas, 1913–1917." *Texas Military History* 2 (February 1962).

Porter, John A. "The Punitive Expedition." *Quartermaster Review* 12 (January-February 1933).

Rippy, J. Fred. "Some Precedents of the Pershing Expedition into Mexico." *Southwestern Historical Quarterly* 24 (April 1921).

Scott, Hugh Lenox. *Some Memoirs of a Soldier* (1928).

Shunk, William A. "The Military Geography of Mexico." *United States Cavalry Journal* 6 (June 1893).

Smythe, Donald. *Pershing: General of the Armies* (1986).

Spaulding, Oliver Lyman. *The United States Army in War and Peace* (1937).

Swift, Eben, Jr. "Experiences in Mexico." *United States Cavalry Journal* 27 (November 1916).

Tompkins, Frank. *Chasing Villa: The Story Behind the Story of Pershing's Expedition into Mexico* (1934).

Toulmin, H. A., Jr. *With Pershing in Mexico* (1935).

Troxel, O. C. "The Tenth Cavalry in Mexico." *Cavalry Journal* 28 (October 1917).

Vandiver, Frank E. *Black Jack: The Life and Times of John J. Pershing*, 2 vols. (1977).

Weigley, Russell F. *History of the United States Army* (1967).

Weissheimer, J. W. "Field Ovens in Mexico." *United States Infantry Journal* 13 (February 1917).

Wharfield, H. B. "The Affair at Carrizal." *Montana, The Magazine of Western History* 18 (October 1968).

Williams, S. M. "The Cavalry Fight at Ojos Azules." *Cavalry Journal* 27 (January 1917).

WORLD WAR I

David R. Woodward

AMERICA ON THE EVE OF ENTRY INTO THE GREAT WAR

On 9 January 1917, the German war leadership held a momentous meeting at the castle of Pless on the border of Poland. This crown council finalized a policy—unrestricted submarine warfare against Allied and neutral maritime commerce—that would have profound consequences for the outcome of World War I. Frustrated by the exhausting military stalemate and nervous over signs of growing unrest on the home front, which the Allied naval blockade had exacerbated, the German army and naval leadership had for some time favored an all-out campaign of undersea assault to shorten the war. Pressure from the neutral United States previously had forced Germany to stay its hand.

In addition to Germany's army and naval leaders, this council of war included Kaiser Wilhelm II and Chancellor Theobold von Bethmann-Hollweg. The leaders of Germany's armed forces exuded confidence. The admiralty had prepared a two-hundred-page memorandum, one that was sustained more by faith than by the questionable tables and charts that sought to bolster its conclusions that the British would be starved out of the war before another harvest. An equally misguided assumption by the military was that Germany had nothing to

fear from forcing the United States into the war. When Bethmann-Hollweg spoke with the voice of caution, he was silenced by the confidence of the war lords. Having earlier assured victory through unrestricted submarine warfare, the chief of the Naval General Staff, Admiral Henning von Holtzendorff, was quick with another promise: "I guarantee on my word as a naval officer that no American will set foot on the Continent!" Field Marshal Paul von Hindenburg, the German supreme commander, was equally contemptuous of U.S. potential to influence the course of the global conflict. "We can take care of America," he blustered. "The opportunity for the U-boat war will never be as favorable again." The Kaiser, who in January was indifferent in word and deed toward the prospect of war with the United States, concluded the discussion by affixing his signature to a document: "I order that unrestricted submarine warfare be launched with the utmost vigor on the first of February."

German underestimation of the United States at first glance appears incredibly shortsighted, analogous to the Japanese decision to attack Pearl Harbor in December 1941. The United States had vast mineral and financial resources, with an industrial base on the verge of outproducing that of all the European states combined. With a population of about 100 million, the United States had the potential to provide more soldiers than either France or Great Britain. During the course of the war, almost 24 million Americans between the ages of eighteen and forty-five would register for the draft; by war's end the American Expeditionary Forces (AEF) in Europe would number just over 2 million. Supported by the U.S. Navy, with personnel numbering almost 500,000, and a Marine Corps of more than 60,000 men, the AEF would give the Allies clear military superiority.

It should be noted, however, that there is little agreement about the statistical data for the First World War. Figures vary considerably according to the sources consulted, official or otherwise. The figures given here for the AEF and its supporting forces are taken from Kreidberg and Henry (1955).

That the United States emerged in Europe by 1918 as a great military power was in truth a surprise for America's allies as well as for Germany. The British, who welcomed U.S. belligerency in April 1917 for the financial relief it provided, certainly did not initially expect U.S. arms to be an important factor in defeating the German army. The views of the British chief of the Imperial General Staff on U.S. military potential differed little from that of the German military authorities. General Sir William R. Robertson, whose sensible and down-to-earth military advice, strength of character, and force of personality had led to his elevation as the government's strategical adviser in late 1915, saw little direct military value in America's entry into the war. Two weeks after Berlin announced that it would resume unrestricted U-boat warfare, Robertson wrote a fellow general: "I do not think that it will make much difference whether America comes in or not. What we want to do is to beat the German Armies, until we do that we shall not win the war. America will not help us much in that respect."

Robertson's typically blunt assessment of the inability of the United States to play an extra-continental role was not an offhand comment. On the contrary, it was based on the British General Staff's evaluation of the existing U.S. military establishment and its leadership from

1914 to the beginning of 1917. What were the Allies to think of the U.S. commander in chief, the scholar-president Woodrow Wilson, who earlier had been "too proud to fight" after the sinking of the *Lusitania* in 1915. One manifestation of Wilson's hatred of war was his tepid interest in military matters. He appeared bored with questions of defense and was uncomfortable in the presence of soldiers. Convinced that the authors of the U.S. Constitution intended the president to be a civilian, he had been angered by a wartime etching that showed him dressed in a military uniform as commander in chief. His secretaries of war and the navy, the diminutive Newton D. Baker and the North Carolina newspaperman Josephus Daniels, were pacifists; the army chief of staff, Major General Hugh L. Scott, a former Indian fighter now in the twilight years of his career, oversaw an army that was ranked seventeenth in the world. The army's armament was obsolete, its supply of munitions hopelessly inadequate. The U.S. Army had enough rounds for its field artillery to sustain a bombardment on the western front for only a few minutes. The army had no tanks, poison gas, flamethrowers, mortars, hand and rifle grenades, heavy field howitzers, or aircraft fit for combat. As the global conflict being waged in Europe, Mesopotamia, Palestine, East Africa, and elsewhere threatened to entangle the United States, the army remained, in the words of former Secretary of War Henry L. Stimson, "a profoundly peaceful army."

Some of the shortcomings of the U.S. military establishment were vividly demonstrated when President Wilson dispatched the Punitive Expedition into Mexico in response to Francisco "Pancho" Villa's raid in March 1916 on Columbus, New Mexico. This expedition, which at its maximum strength numbered about eleven thousand troops, advanced three hundred miles into Mexico in its futile effort to capture the elusive Mexican bandit. There were breakdowns in the mobilization of units of the regular army and especially of the National Guard, whose training was shown to be rudimentary at best. Munitions shortages, poor logistics (com-

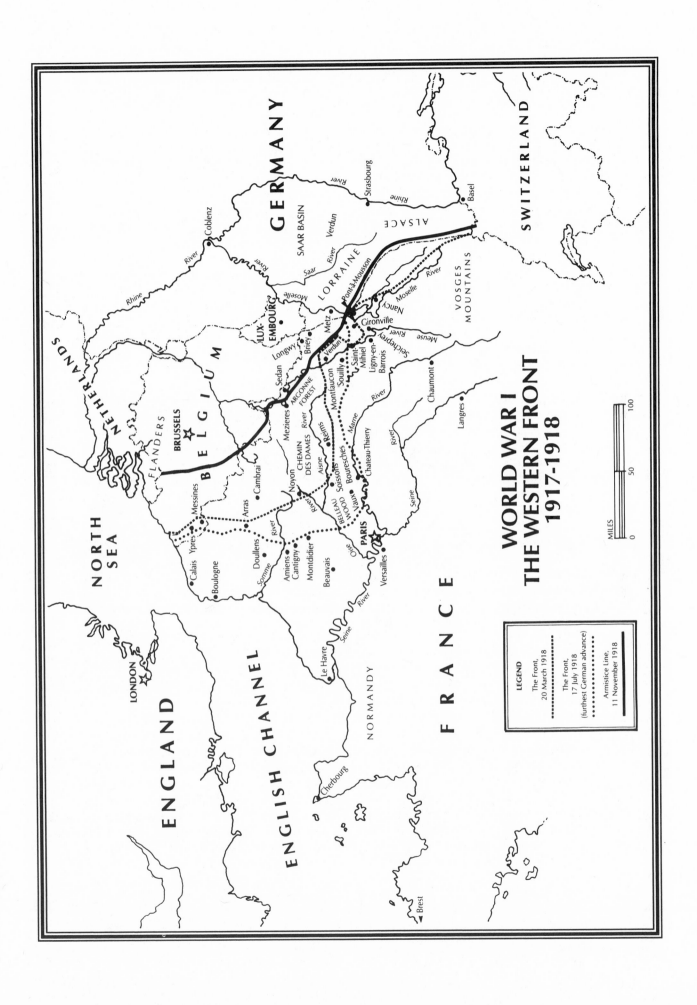

NORTH SEA

ENGLAND

ENGLISH CHANNEL

LONDON

NETHERLANDS

GERMANY

Coblenz

Rhine River

River

River

SAAR BASIN

Saar River

Moselle River

LUXEMBOURG

LORRAINE

ALSACE

Verdun

Strasbourg

Rhine River

Basel

SWITZERLAND

Pont-à-Mousson

Nancy

VOSGES MOUNTAINS

Moselle River

BELGIUM

BRUSSELS

FLANDERS

Messines

Ypres

Calais

Boulogne

Cambrai

Arras

Doullens

Somme River

Amiens

Cantigny

Montdidier

Beauvais

Noyon

Oise River

Oise River

CHEMIN DES DAMES

Aisne River

Soissons

Bouresches

BELLEAU WOOD

Vaux

Chateau-Thierry

Marne River

PARIS

Versailles

Seine River

Sedan

Mezieres

Reims

Longwy

Briey

ARGONNE FOREST

Montfaucon

Souilly

Verdun

Saint-Mihiel

Ligny-en-Barrois

Gironville

Seicheprey

Meuse River

Chaumont

Langres

Seine River

River

Le Havre

NORMANDY

Cherbourg

Brest

FRANCE

WORLD WAR I
THE WESTERN FRONT
1917-1918

LEGEND

The Front,
20 March 1918

The Front,
17 July 1918
(furthest German advance)

Armistice Line,
11 November 1918

MILES

0   50   100

pounded by the shortage of trucks), and an insufficient supply of machine guns also plagued this limited military venture.

On 3 June 1916, while U.S. troops were engaged in Mexico, Wilson signed the National Defense Act, which represented the first attempt by Congress to establish a comprehensive system of national security. In addition to the regular army, which had its peacetime strength increased to 175,000 men over a five-year period, future U.S. land forces were to be composed of reserves, the National Guard, and a volunteer force raised in the event of war.

This act reflected the political realities of 1916. Americans overwhelmingly opposed U.S. involvement in the war. Hence, the provisions for the expansion of the army were totally inadequate for U.S. participation in the gigantic battles taking place in Europe. The National Guard, politically popular but incapable of providing the training to fight a modern war, was expected to grow to more than 400,000 officers and men. (In April 1917, however, it numbered only 174,008 officers and men.) The cornerstone of U.S. land warfare thus became the militia, a primitive fighting force by European standards. Refusing to follow the example of the European powers, Congress rejected conscription and kept the regular army relatively small. Equally detrimental to adequate military preparedness was the refusal of Congress to sanction the plans and machinery necessary for national mobilization. As former Assistant Secretary of War Henry Breckenridge put it, the act was "either a comedy or a tragedy." In his blunt assessment, "surely the mountain has labored and brought forth a mouse."

The preparedness campaign of 1916 clearly was not designed to prepare the United States for the European war. The focus, rather, of U.S. leaders was defensive—to protect the nation's vital interests against the victors of the war. There is no better example of this than the Naval Act of 1916, which appropriated money for a battleship-dominated fleet, which would prove to be ineffective in containing Germany's most formidable threat on the high seas, the submarine. Besides being designed for a war quite different from the one it would actually fight, the U.S. Navy was woefully unprepared in 1917, entering the conflict with nine out of its ten warships inadequately manned and two of three not materially fit.

President Wilson's antimilitary views contributed to the army's ineffectiveness. He helped thwart conscription in 1916, and his views on the duties of soldiers in peacetime served to undermine the efforts of military authorities to prepare for the war they were likely to fight. Artificially separating civil and military responsibilities, Wilson insisted that the soldiers had no role to play in the formulation of national policy prior to the outbreak of war. In 1915 he had exploded in rage when the Baltimore Sun erroneously reported that the General Staff was considering calling up a million men to fight against Germany. The U.S. General Staff was not then contemplating intervention in Europe, and the president's heated response to such a charge guaranteed that it would not do so as long as the United States remained neutral.

Congress, reflecting the strong neutralist and isolationist sentiment of the country, also crippled strategic planning by including in the National Defense Act the stipulation that the General Staff, which was responsible for the mobilization and strategic deployment of U.S. forces, be restricted to a chief of staff, two general officers of the line, ten colonels, ten lieutenant colonels, fifteen majors, and seventeen captains—a total of fifty-five officers. No more than half of these officers could be posted to or near the District of Columbia. When the United States entered the war, there were in fact only nineteen officers attached to the General Staff in the War Department, with only eleven assigned to intelligence and the strategic deployment of U.S. forces. The staff officers were warned to make no public statements about the war; civilian employees were under orders to not even discuss the war while at work. Advances in tactics and the impact of the new military technology went unexamined up close because the War Department did not send observers to the front, as it had done during the Russo-Japanese War (1904–1905). Wilson's instructions to his countrymen to be "impartial in thought as well as in action" served to impose an ostrichlike position upon the military professionals who would largely be held responsible for the success or failure of U.S. arms in the event of war.

That is not to say that many U.S. officers did not think seriously about their profession in the prewar years. Professionalism was in fact growing in the U.S. Army. The overwhelming majority of U.S. commanders (although not their chiefs of staff) who engaged the German army in 1917–1918 were West Pointers. The Leavenworth School, founded in 1881, also afforded both graduates and nongraduates of the U.S. Military Academy a chance to study seriously the art of war, with the cream of the class being given an additional year of study at the Staff College. The final stage of an officer's education was at the Army War College, established in 1903. The future AEF leaders received valuable instruction in organizing and leading large military units.

The education of the U.S. military elite, however, did not prepare it for stalemated and industrialized trench warfare dominated by the machine gun and artillery. Through its concentration on the American Civil War, the Army War College reinforced an image of nineteenth-century warfare. As was the case with the European general staffs, the U.S. Army's officer corps emphasized offensive and maneuver warfare prior to the Great War. The new fire weapons, however, presented attacking forces with serious tactical problems. If U.S. officers had made a serious study of the killing fields of the western front from 1914 to 1916, they would have learned far more about modern warfare than they did from their extended studies of earlier wars or their tours of Civil War battlefields.

Given the strength of its adversary and the logistical difficulties of confronting an enemy some three thousand sea miles away, the United States found itself less prepared to fight on the eve of the Great War than it had been for the War of 1812 or even the American Revolution. The country had neither the plans, the army, the modern equipment, nor even the

transport ships to wage a European campaign. The German and British professional soldiers can be forgiven for believing that the war would be over before any U.S. expeditionary force could play an important military role in Europe.

On 2 April 1917, President Wilson, escorted by a troop of cavalry, made his way from the White House to Capitol Hill to end his country's armed neutrality with a war message. British blockade measures had impinged on the freedom of U.S. overseas commerce, but unrestricted German U-boat warfare had killed Americans, and war fever now swept the country. Just prior to President Wilson's meeting with his cabinet on 20 March, to decide on a response to Germany's provocative acts, the American people were told that three U.S. merchant ships had been sunk, with the loss of fifteen Americans. German outrages also included the foolhardy attempt by German Foreign Secretary Arthur Zimmermann to enlist the support of Mexico and Japan against the United States. The headline of the *New York Times* on 1 March 1917 announced:

GERMANY SEEKS ALLIANCE AGAINST U.S.
ASKS JAPAN AND MEXICO TO JOIN HER

During Wilson's pivotal discussion with his cabinet on 20 March, Albert S. Burleson, a Texan who headed the Post Office Department, asserted that Germany "woke up a giant." He and the other cabinet members wanted to teach the Kaiser a lesson.

Although Wilson decided soon after this meeting that he had no choice but to make war, he apparently did not fully comprehend the consequences of U.S. belligerency. He told Congress that the United States would "exert all its power and employ all its resources to bring the government of the German empire to terms and end the war." He apparently believed at this time, however, that the war was nearing a conclusion because of the exhaustion of the warring states and that the U.S. role would be that of a maritime rather than a land power. He thought of fighting with the navy, industrial might, and finance. In these circumstances, there might be little difference between armed neutrality and belligerency.

The General Staff in the War Department did not share Wilson's view that the war was rushing to a conclusion. Immediately following Germany's resumption of unrestricted submarine warfare, General Hugh Lenox Scott had asked the War College Division, the section of the General Staff responsible for war planning and intelligence, to "submit without delay a statement of a plan of action that should be followed by the United States in case hostilities with Germany occur in the near future." Four days before the president's war message, the General Staff produced its first strategic appreciations (memorandums) of a war on European soil.

Allowed for the first time to consider seriously the consequences of a forward policy in Europe, the War College Division initially considered independent U.S. operations either in Holland (if that neutral country were forced into the war) or in the Balkans in Macedonia. Both of these plans were, to be blunt, daft. The suggestion that U.S. forces could play a decisive and independent role in the Balkans was amateurish; the advocacy of U.S. "surprise" attack on the unprotected German flank via Holland even more so. After reviewing these plans, the chief of the War College Division, Brigadier General Joseph E. Kuhn, concluded that it was "impossible" for the United States to launch military operations against Germany except in cooperation with the Triple Entente powers.

The initial considerations of sending an expeditionary force to European theaters served a useful purpose, by highlighting the enormous difficulties facing the U.S. military establishment. For the first time, the General Staff came to grips with such vital questions as the size of an expeditionary force, where that force might fight, and the time it would take to deliver that force to the chosen theater.

The General Staff realistically argued that the essential first step for U.S. involvement in the war was the acceptance of conscription without delay. Secretary of War Baker agreed and lobbied the president, who, although he had not yet decided to send Americans to Europe, ac-

cepted the necessity of the draft. His adroit handling of the controversial issue of compulsory service in Congress represented what was perhaps his finest hour in the military realm during the war. Without this prompt decision it would have been impossible to have a U.S. army of 2 million men in Western Europe by the armistice.

Although Congress gave the War Department the ability to conscript a mass army with passage of the Selective Service Act on 18 May 1917, the training and equipping of that force seemed months, perhaps even years, away. Starting essentially from scratch, the United States had neither the training camps, equipment, nor officers for the rapid expansion of the army. The British War Office believed that the U.S. War Department was incapable of calling more than 100,000 men at any one time. As British General Staff appreciation noted, "When this 'call' has entered the field another 100,000 could be handled perhaps in five months or slightly less, after the 'first call.'" The pessimistic British conclusion was that it would take a full year for the Americans to put 250,000 men into the field.

As U.S. officers studied the possibility that arms would be deployed in Europe, they encountered an even greater problem than the creation of an American army to fight on Germany's level—the transport of that force to Europe and its supply. The United States did not have a merchant marine to match its industrial might, while Great Britain in 1917 had a merchant marine that was eight times larger. When the General Staff examined the logistics for an expeditionary force in the Balkans, it discovered that it would take at least ten months to transport an army of 500,000 men to the eastern Mediterranean if fully half the U.S. merchant marine were diverted for this task.

The all-out campaign of undersea assault by the U-boats in April highlighted the problems of sea transport for both London and Washington. The month that America entered the war was the most successful month for the German submarine in World War I. The Allies lost a staggering 881,027 gross tons, of which the British share was 500,000 gross tons, a fivefold increase over January. One out of every four ships departing England was sunk. On the day that the United States went to war, London informed Washington that "the most vital thing for the Allies at present is the provision of shipping."

The Allies, especially the French, also needed new recruits if they were to win what had become a war of attrition. The appeal of the marshal of France, Joseph Joffre, could not have been more direct: "We want men, men, men." Given its lack of military readiness, however, the United States seemed better prepared to build ships than to deploy large troop formations to Europe, especially if President Wilson followed the advice of his General Staff, which now advocated the creation of a large and modern army in the United States before sending it to Europe. The sea transport of an American army to Europe might take longer than its organization. Major General Tasker H. Bliss, the assistant chief of staff, concluded on the eve of U.S. belligerency that "the war must last practically two years longer before we can have other than naval and economic participation."

Several weeks after the passage of the war resolution on 6 April, British and French missions arrived in Washington with the intention of giving U.S. mobilization a sense of urgency. To enable American manpower to have an immediate impact on the war, the French and British made an extraordinary proposal: to feed American draftees and volunteers into British and French divisions, either as individuals or in small units. Americans, although serving under foreign flags, would then be able to fight in battle-tested armies, equipped with modern weapons of war and provided with sophisticated logistical and experienced staff support.

From a purely military point of view, this proposal had much to recommend it, but it asked much of a great nation. If amalgamation was accepted, there might never be an independent U.S. force with its own commander and sector of operations in Europe. More was at stake than national pride. President Wilson's efforts to create a new world order would be compromised if Americans fought in the armies of nations with annexationist objectives, and the president's voice in any peace settlement would be muffled if U.S. arms were given such a limited role in the war. Not surprisingly, this proposal, in the words of a British officer, had to be dropped "like a hot potato," but only for the moment. As the fortunes of the Allies declined in late 1917 and early 1918, the amalgamation issue resurfaced, creating serious friction between the United States and its war partners.

Wilson's desire to create a new world order decisively influenced his decision for war with Berlin. In order to achieve a liberal peace, he valued U.S. political and military independence just below the defeat of Germany. Determined to avoid any entanglement with Allied war objectives, he chose the designation of "associate" power rather than "ally." He also emphasized that he was fighting against Germany and not its allies. (On 7 December, however, the United States would declare war on Austria-Hungary.)

Despite his suspicion of the political objectives of his war partners, in early May President Wilson made another crucial military decision. Pressed by the British and French missions, who emphasized the political aspects of a symbolic show of U.S. arms in Europe, he told Marshal Joffre, the chief military representative of the French mission, "to take it for granted that such a force would be sent just as soon as we could send it." On 14 May, Baker and Joffre reached a formal agreement that called for U.S. military cooperation with the French army. The U.S. Navy was already moving to cooperate with the British Grand Fleet in European waters.

Even before the United States entered the war, Wilson had sought better communications with the British Admiralty. Secretary of Navy Daniels chose Vice Admiral William S. Sims, known for his forthrightness and independence of mind, as the U.S. Navy's man in London. When Congress declared war, Sims was en route to Great Britain. Soon the view in Washington was that the Canadian-born Sims, as commander of American Naval Forces in European Waters, did his job of coordinating the U.S. naval role with the British too well. Arguing that the United States should accept Britain's primacy on the high seas, Sims wanted the U.S. fleet to play a supportive naval role that emphasized the submarine threat to the Allies, especially Great Britain. On the other hand, Wilson, Daniels, and Admiral William S. Benson, chief of naval operations and responsible for advising the government on the strategic deployment of the navy, were reluctant to play second fiddle to the British Admiralty. The White House and Navy Department viewed the Royal Navy as an ally, but also as a future rival. "Don't let the British pull the wool over your eyes," Benson lectured Sims as the latter was about to depart for London. "It is none of our business pulling their chestnuts out of the fire. We would as soon fight the British as the Germans."

As late as 1889, the year before Alfred Thayer Mahan published his book on the importance of sea power, *The Influence of Sea Power upon History, 1660–1783*, the U.S. Navy ranked twelfth in the world in number of warships, behind such countries as Norway, China, and Turkey. The Wilson administration, however, challenged Britain's naval supremacy, and in 1916 Congress approved the largest U.S. naval expansion program in history. When Wilson learned that the British were concerned by this ambitious naval construction program, 168 warships, he asserted, "Let us build a navy bigger than hers and do what we please."

Given the grave menace of German undersea assault, Benson belatedly accepted Sims's advice to concentrate U.S. destroyers in the eastern Atlantic to prevent the economic strangulation of Great Britain by U-boats. More than 70 percent of the navy's modern destroyers in 1917 were located at Queenstown, Ireland, where they cooperated with the Royal Navy on antisubmarine patrols.

By the end of 1917, U.S. cooperation with the Royal Navy on the maritime front in Europe included a fleet of thirty-six destroyers (a number that grew to sixty-eight by the end of the war) and the Sixth Battle Squadron, five coal-burning battleships commanded by Rear Admiral Hugh Rodman, which represented a degree of amalgamation never achieved by U.S. land forces with the British and French. Despite this joint effort, which inevitably assigned the Americans a secondary role in the eastern Atlantic and Mediterranean, there were serious underlying conflicts about naval strategy and priorities between the Navy Department and British Admiralty.

Possessing a love for the sea, the president, who had once hoped to attend Annapolis, took a stronger interest in the sea war than in the land war in Western Europe. If the German U-boat campaign succeeded, as appeared possible in the spring of 1917, the United States, of course, would be unable to play a decisive part in the land war in Western Europe. To clear a path for U.S. transports across the sub-infested North Atlantic, Wilson pressed the British to accept the convoy system, which the Admiralty hitherto had vetoed in favor of anti–U-boat patrols in the danger zone around the British Isles. Advocates of the convoy system, including British Prime Minister Lloyd George, however, argued that better use could be made of destroyers as escorts for convoys of cargo ships. A convoy of twenty or thirty ships was almost as difficult for a submarine to locate as a single ship in the vast ocean. The destroyer also had a much better chance of engaging and destroying a submarine when it was attempting to attack a convoy. Many anxious months lay ahead, but the adoption of the convoy system eventually provided the answer to the submarine threat.

In an attempt to play a leading role in the naval campaign, Benson, Daniels, and Wilson pressed the British to be more aggressive in waging war against the submarine. On 11 August 1917, the president, accompanied by Daniels, spoke to naval officers aboard the USS *Pennsylvania*, the flagship of the Atlantic Fleet: "We are hunting hornets all over the farm and letting the nest alone. None of us knows how to go to the nest and crush it, and yet I despair of hunting for hornets all over the sea when I know where the nest is, and know that the nest is breeding hornets as fast as I can find them." Believing that the war would be won if German U-boat bases were neutralized, Wilson professed a readiness to lose half the U.S. and British naval strength in an assault against the bases of the "hornets." In opposition to U.S. naval leadership, the British, perhaps influenced by the Royal Navy's failed attack operation in the Dardanelles in 1915, opposed employing their battleships against German-controlled ports.

The Admiralty did, however, accept the U.S. proposal to build a great mine barrier from Scotland across the North Sea to Norwegian waters. Begun in the spring of 1918, this largely American enterprise led to the planting of fifty-seven thousand U.S. and sixteen thousand British mines by the end of the war. The effectiveness of the hugely expensive ($80 million) North Sea Mine Barrage remains a subject of controversy. Only four subs were destroyed and perhaps four more were damaged. On the other hand, this mine barrier may have discouraged many U-boats from using this route.

The United States also employed 110-foot wooden subchasers that were modeled after the sturdy New England fishing boat against the submarine. By the armistice of 11 November 1918, the navy had 120 wooden subchasers deployed in European waters, sailing in groups of three. One group of subchasers was based on the island of Corfu to block the Strait of Otranto between Italy and Greece. This so-called Splinter Fleet employed depth charges and an acoustic sounding device, the forerunner of sonar, to locate the submarines.

Despite the offensive-minded stance of the U.S. administration on the European maritime front, the foremost priority of the U.S. Navy was the protection of American troops and supplies crossing the Atlantic to Europe. Less than 15 percent of the navy's personnel was in the eastern Atlantic and Mediterranean for other purposes. In the words of Benson's assistant, Captain William Veazie Pratt: "The impelling reason of the British was protection to food and war supplies in transit. Our basic reason was protection to our military forces in crossing the seas."

The reluctance of U.S. political and naval leadership to accept an auxiliary part in the naval campaign was also characteristic of the AEF's military role in the land war in Western Europe. To command the AEF, Baker, with the president's verbal approval, chose Major General (soon General) John J. Pershing, the commander of the Punitive Expedition, which had been withdrawn from Mexico in early February 1917. Pershing had never commanded more than eleven thousand men, but no U.S. general officer in active service had ever led a force that large. Given the questionable physical condition of Brigadier General Leonard Wood, Pershing's only serious rival for the command, Baker's choice was an easy one. Pershing had many qualities to recommend him. He had taught tactics at the U.S. Military Academy, and he had been tested by fire even before the Punitive Expedition—in skirmishes with Apaches, at San Juan Hill in the Spanish-American War, and during the pacification of the Moros in the Philippines. He was a thoroughgoing professional, recognized for his integrity, dedication, and force of personality. Although he was only five feet, nine inches tall, his ramrod-straight bearing led many to think him six feet or taller.

Pershing initially had doubts about Wilson's war leadership, and when Wilson made his "too proud to fight" statement after the *Lusitania* went down, the rugged Missourian had exclaimed, "Isn't that the damnedest rot you ever heard a sane person get off?" When Wilson responded firmly to the German resumption of U-boat warfare, however, Pershing changed his mind, expressing unconditional admiration for the president as a war leader. Wilson met Pershing only once during the war. On 24 May 1917, Baker had Pershing with him when he called on Wilson at the White House. Except for a cursory mention of the tonnage problem in transporting U.S. troops to Europe and the bloody bludgeoning in the trenches, the president had nothing else to say directly at this meeting about the U.S. role in the war. Pershing's instructions came later, when he visited Baker in the War Department just prior to his departure for Europe. "Here are your orders, General," Baker allegedly told him. "The president has just approved them." Baker also told Pershing: "If you do not make good, they [the American people] will probably hang us both on the first lamppost they can find."

Until an independent American army was a reality, Pershing's instructions were to "cooperate as a component" of the Allied armies. Alarmed by the obvious desire of the French and British to incorporate U.S. troops into their forces, Wilson and Baker made a point of emphasizing that Pershing was to maintain the American "identity" of his forces serving with the Allies. Pershing's civilian superiors also gave him the authority to expand or limit the cooperation of U.S. armed forces according to his reading of the military situation. These instructions granted Pershing virtual control over the extent of U.S. commitment to the war in Western Europe. No American field commander in history has been given a freer hand from civilian control to plan and execute military operations. These powers were all the more remarkable in light of the fact that the United States was involved in a coalition war and had the interests of its war partners to consider as well as its own. Inevitably, Pershing would have to deal with military matters marked by strong political overtones.

On 28 May, Pershing, with a small contingent of officers and enlisted men, sailed from New York on the transport *Baltic*. During their voyage across the Atlantic, Pershing and his staff attempted to take stock of the colossal struggle and to explore the role that America might play. Units forming the First Division in Europe began embarking the following month. Pershing's most important initial appointment was Major James G. Harbord as AEF chief of staff. The cool and self-possessed Harbord, who had risen through the ranks after enlisting as a private in 1889, soon justified his reputation as one of the army's most able officers.

EUROPE ENGULFED

On 28 June 1914, in the Bosnian capital of Sarajevo, a nineteen-year-old Bosnian assassinated Archduke Franz Ferdinand, the heir to the throne of Austria-Hungary. With considerable justification, the Austrian government blamed this terrorist act on Serb nationalism and decided to punish Serbia. Having gained Berlin's firm support, Vienna provoked a war with Serbia. Germany and Austria-Hungary hoped to confine this conflict to the Balkans and avoid triggering the alliance system that divided Europe between the Triple Alliance (Germany, Austria-Hungary, and Italy) and the Triple Entente (France, Great Britain, and Russia). This proved impossible when Russia chose to back Serbia by ordering general mobilization on 29 July. Germany's response to Russian mobilization was to declare war on Russia (1 August) and France (3 August) and invade Belgium. By 4 August, when Great Britain declared war on Germany, all of the great European powers save Italy had been drawn into this war.

The military stalemate facing Pershing in Western Europe had its roots in the first weeks of the conflict. The Great War had begun in the west in August 1914 with the French and German armies on the offensive. The French frontally assaulted the German southeastern flank in Alsace-Lorraine while Germany violated the neutrality of Belgium in an attempt to envelop the French army—the Schlieffen Plan. The German offensive through Belgium was far more successful than the reckless and easily repulsed French attack along the German frontier. The German army reached the Marne River and threatened Paris, but an Anglo-French counterattack, the First Battle of the Marne, saved the French capital. More important, it shattered German hopes for a quick victory over France and the illusion of a short war.

Following this German setback, each side attempted to outflank the other in what came to be called the "race to the sea." When the sea was reached and there were no more flanks to turn, the armies began to dig in. Siege warfare replaced the war of movement. For the next three years, neither side succeeded in moving its opponent's front for more than ten miles at any point, despite heavy and prolonged attacks that resulted in horrendous slaughter. The war at sea was also a standoff, which worked in favor of the British Grand Fleet. Operating a distant blockade from bases in Scotland at Scapa Flow and the village of Rosyth, the British fleet kept German surface ships from threatening the world's sea lanes. Only one great sea battle occurred during the war, the Battle of Jutland on 31 May 1916. In this clash between the Grand Fleet and the German High Seas Fleet, 259 warships were engaged. Following this indecisive sea battle, the High Seas Fleet remained bottled up for the remainder of the war. "The German Fleet has assaulted its jailor; but it is still in jail," was a New York newspaper's accurate assessment.

The war inexorably spread to other corners of the globe, drawing in other powers that included Italy, who joined the Allies, and Bulgaria and Turkey, who cast their lots with the Central Powers. With Turkey a belligerent, new theaters opened in Egypt-Palestine, Mesopotamia, and the Caucasus. Czarist Russia, beleaguered and virtually isolated, now fought on a front that stretched from the Baltic almost to the Caspian. Hoping to mobilize the Balkan states against the Central Powers and to open better communications with Russia, the British in 1915 attempted to force their way through the Dardanelles, first by an unsuccessful naval attack, then by an amphibious assault on Gallipoli. Following the failure of the Dardanelles and Gallipoli ventures, the Allies, in a quixotic attempt to save Serbia, established a base in Salonika, Greece, the beginnings of a major campaign in the Balkans.

Despite these military operations in the outlying theaters, most Anglo-French military leaders believed in 1915–1916 that the war was going to be won or lost on the western front. These "westerners," as they are popularly known, opposed any indirect approach to defeating the major enemy, Germany.

While the British expanded their small volunteer force to a mass army capable of measuring up to the Continental conscript armies, the French bore the brunt of the fighting in the west until the summer of 1916. In February 1916 the Germans, having made great gains in league with Austria-Hungary against Russia the previous year, abandoned their defensive stance in the west, concentrating on the French army. During the next ten months, the French and Germans stained the churned earth of northeastern France around the fortress town of Verdun with their blood, with casualties reaching 1 million. Fearing that the French were about to crack, the British launched a massive attack along the Somme River in July. When winter brought the inconclusive Battle of the Somme to a halt, the British had suffered almost 500,000 casualties, approximately the same number they would lose fighting Germany during all of World War II.

The year of Verdun and Somme ended with neither side enjoying a clear military advantage. The world had never witnessed such large-scale slaughter, with casualties surpassing 1.75 million for these two battles. Although the Germans maintained their forward positions in Belgium and France, they were in danger of losing the attrition war. Some 4 million French, British, and Belgain soldiers confronted approximately 2.5 million Germans on the western front. In the east, however, the Central Powers were in the ascendancy. They occupied Russian Poland, dominated southeastern Europe, and it seemed only a matter of time before the collapse of the Russian Romanov dynasty. Russia's decline, however, was roughly offset by growing warweariness in Austria-Hungary, Allied military successes against Turkey, and the maintenance of a blockade that imposed severe hardships on the home fronts of the Central Powers. Allied plans for 1917 called for roughly simultaneous attacks on the Russian, western, and Italian fronts. Realistically, however, only the Allied forces in the west were capable of achieving a major strategical success. War-weary Italy and Russia were more likely to receive than to deliver a knockout punch.

A new French commander in chief, Robert Nivelle, rashly promised to end the military stalemate in the west with a breakthrough in twenty-four or forty-eight hours. His method was a sudden and violent attack, utilizing improved artillery tactics, especially the "rolling" or "creeping barrages," against the flanks of the huge Noyon bulge (the German-held salient in the French line). The British Expeditionary Force (BEF) was assigned the diversionary role of drawing off German reserves by an attack on Vimy Ridge. On 9 April 1917, three days after U.S. entry into the war, the BEF attacked along a broad front (the Battle of Arras). The resulting conquest of Vimy Ridge represented the greatest British success yet against the German army. The continuation of this battle into early May to assist the French, however, resulted in minor gains and heavy losses.

When finally launched on 16 April, Nivelle's offensive (Second Battle of the Aisne) was a crushing disappointment, in part because of the unrealistic expectations raised by the French commander in chief. Surprise had been lost, with Parisian taxi drivers openly talking of the day the offensive was scheduled to begin. Moreover, the Germans had just eliminated their vulnerable flanks by withdrawing their forces (thereby shortening their front by some twenty-seven miles) to a much strengthened defensive system in depth, the Siegfried Position (a section of what the Allies called the Hindenburg Line). Nivelle's assault with 1.2 million troops cost him 120,000 dead, wounded, or captured. His violent artillery bombardment failed to destroy the German machine gunners, who had been spaced in depth to mow down the advancing French soldiers.

Nivelle's stubborn continuation of his offensive despite his failure to break through the German defenses demoralized his tired poilus, and a series of mutinies, beginning in late May, rocked the French army. Many soldiers, including some officers, put aside their arms and refused to advance to the front. At Missy-aux-Bois, an infantry regiment established an antiwar "government" during the first week of June. In one of the best-kept secrets of the war, however, the French were able to mask this widespread mutiny from their Allies and the Germans.

"OVER THERE"

Pershing and his staff, after a brief visit to London, arrived at Boulogne, France, on 13 June 1917. The arrival of this tiny U.S. contingent coincided with a serious downturn in Allied fortunes and growing uncertainty about the future. The fall of the Romanov dynasty had not slowed the decline of the Russian army. If anything, the March Revolution unleashed a whirlwind of change that accelerated its demise. Sir William Robertson told the British leadership that the Russian army, which had "fallen to pieces," was incapable of putting pressure on the Germans and Austrians in Europe or the Turks in Asia. As for Great Britain's other vital ally, France, that country was badly shaken by Nivelle's failure and was inclined to defer action until the Americans arrived in force. But when might that be? Could the Americans get to Europe in sufficient strength to turn the tide before it was too late?

The answer appeared to be in the negative. Major General Tom Bridges, who had accompanied the British mission to Washington in late April and May, in June told the British War Cabinet (the small inner committee created to direct the war effort when Lloyd George became prime minister) that the United States was likely to have no more than 120,000 to 150,000 men in Europe by 1 January 1918 and that the number would probably not rise beyond 500,000 by the end of the year. If Bridges' prediction proved correct, the United States would not be able to play a decisive role until 1919 at the earliest. No wonder therefore that Lord Curzon, a member of the War Cabinet lamented that this was the "most depressing statement that the cabinet had received for a long time."

Aboard the *Baltic*, Pershing and his fellow officers addressed fundamental questions about U.S. participation in the war. Among other matters, they discussed logistics and lines of supply, possible theaters of operations, the limits of cooperation with the Allies, and the timetable for introducing U.S. units into combat. The most urgent matter to be decided was the size of the AEF. Pershing's messages to the War Department were soon echoing Joffre's earlier appeal for "men, men, men." Initially, the leaders of the AEF thought in terms of an army of 1 million men, which considerably exceeded the initial U.S. draft. The AEF planners expected this force ultimately to grow to 3 million, but before the war ended Pershing was asking for 5 million soldiers, a mighty force that would have dwarfed all other armies on the western front.

The War Department, although sometimes taken aback by Pershing's accelerating manpower demands, accepted the necessity of creating a great army on foreign soil. By mid-July, when Pershing's appeal for a million men reached Washington, the General Staff had reached a similar conclusion. To project American power to Europe as quickly as possible, the General Staff had also abandoned any thought of creating an army in the United States and then shipping it intact to Europe. The tonnage shortage necessitated shipping U.S. forces piecemeal, in a continuous flow, with training on both sides of the Atlantic.

Although Pershing was a commander without an army for many months, he never thought small. His gaze remained firmly fixed on the time when he would have the military muscle to defeat the German army. His choice of a front was greatly influenced by his desire to play the decisive role in the outcome of the war. The British lobbied for an American zone at the northern end of the British front in Belgium or at the junction of the British and French armies. Pershing, however, ultimately selected Lorraine, the area between the Argonne Forest and Vosges Mountains, as the American sector. He rightly suspected the British of attempting to harness U.S. power to their own. Proximity to the BEF would increase the pressures and dangers of amalgamation with their Anglo-Saxon cousins. In addition, any U.S. force, even if operating under its own flag and commander, would inevitably be assigned a secondary role if it fought alongside the British on the seaward side of the western front or at the point where the British and French defenses joined.

Logistics also contributed to Pershing's choice of an American sector on the southern end of the western front. The war had rapidly become a war of railroads as well as of artillery. A front to the southeast of Paris enabled the AEF to utilize its own ports of supply along the southwestern French coast; a railway network, running south of Paris, promised to provide the

Americans in Lorraine with less-congested although distant lines of supply.

At the beginning of September, Pershing and his fellow officers established in great secrecy ("somewhere in France") their headquarters at Chaumont, a small city in the rolling countryside of the headwaters of the Marne. While U.S. soldiers trickled across the Atlantic (the last elements of the First Division did not arrive in France until December), the Leavenworth-taught staff officers, occupying a four-story regimental barracks, turned their attention to the formulation of war-winning strategy (where to attack) and tactics (how to fight).

Pershing ordered his operations section to focus on German defenses running from Verdun to the Swiss frontier. The resulting memorandum, entitled "A Strategical Study on the Employment of the A.E.F. Against the Imperial German Government," dated 25 September 1917, decisively shaped the future U.S. role in the coalition war against Germany.

Pershing's operations staff, headed by the robust Colonel Fox Conner, was attracted to the strategic possibilities of an attack to the east and west of the fortress city of Metz. If the railway lines running laterally between the German right and left wings could be captured, the thinking went, the enemy's southern defenses would collapse, compelling the German army to retreat from northern France to eastern Belgium and perhaps even beyond the Rhine. A successful advance beyond Metz also would result in the capture of some of the enemy's important iron-ore deposits in Longwy-Briey and the coalfields of the Saar, which would cripple—or so it was believed—the German war economy.

As a prelude to this distant and extremely ambitious offensive, the operations section planned a minor offensive (with French assistance) that would take place in late 1918 to eliminate the pronounced salient of Saint-Mihiel, southwest of Metz. With the AEF's front shortened by the conquest of Saint-Mihiel and the threat of a German counterthrust from Metz neutralized, the next phase of the offensive would commence in 1919. In conjunction with other Allied attacks to the north to occupy German reserves, a massive war-winning assault by five U.S. corps (or 1,272,858 men when line of communications troops were included) would commence.

To spur his government to action, Pershing enlisted the support of the Allied commanders, and on 5 December 1917, a cablegram that reported the conclusions of an Allied military conference arrived at the War Department. The United States was asked as its minimum effort to send twenty-four divisions to France by the end of June. By autumn, if the required shipping tonnage was secured, the U.S. presence in Europe was expected to increase to thirty divisions, or five complete corps. This figure, not by chance, was precisely what Pershing's operations staff estimated would bring victory in 1919. With U.S. mobilization proceeding erratically and at a snail's pace, this request seemed unrealistic. "Is such a programme *possible*?" a shaken President Wilson asked Secretary of War Baker. Certainly the Allied generals, who had been prompted by Pershing to make their request, did not think it feasible. As late as January 1918, the French General Staff believed that it would be May 1919 before the AEF had sixteen trained divisions in Europe, with four or five of that number capable of holding a quiet sector of the front.

By European standards, U.S. divisions were unusual because of their size, approximately twice the size of German, British, and French divisions. Before the war, the U.S. Army had been built around regiments, and divisions existed only in theory or on paper. Hence, the leadership of the AEF had the freedom to experiment in the organization of the field army in Europe. Pershing's staff ultimately decided upon a large "square" division, commanded by a major general, consisting of four regiments of infantry, three regiments of artillery, fourteen machine-gun companies, one engineer regiment, one signal battalion, one troop of cavalry, and other auxiliary units. The total authorized strength, which included 17,666 rifles, was a little more than 28,000 men.

In deciding upon these oversized divisions, the AEF planners were at odds with many German, British, and French political and military authorities who were either recommending or implementing the downsizing of their divisions. The accelerating manpower crisis of every European belligerent, of course, pressured military planners to reduce the size of divisions to maintain their number, but there was another justification for smaller divisions. The revolution in firepower meant more emphasis on machine guns and artillery and less on infantry shock tactics. The organization of the AEF, however, did not always take the increased lethality of the battlefield into consideration. The infantry-rich U.S. divisions, although approximately double the size of Allied divisions, had no greater artillery complement per division, which in effect meant that artillery was undervalued. The same could be said for machine guns.

Defenders of the large U.S. division argued that its size would enable it to sustain losses and remain in the line longer than a smaller division. Perhaps, but this did not fully take into account the morale factor. As was demonstrated later in the war, AEF divisions in heavy combat needed relief after a short time no matter what their size. Another justification was that large divisions would enable the AEF to better utilize its limited supply of regular army commanders and staff, glossing over the fact that one of the greatest weaknesses of the prewar officers corps was its lack of exposure to large military formations. It was by no means certain that doubling the responsibilities of the leadership of a division would further either its tactical or logistical effectiveness. To the contrary, the size of U.S. divisions, when combined with inexperienced officers, contributed to serious command and control breakdowns. Dubious communications and an understandable lack of faith in its inexperienced officers encouraged GHQ (General Headquarters) AEF to adopt rigid schemes of fire and maneuver at a time when the more experienced European general staffs were abandoning such rigidity and the consequent heavy loss of attacking forces.

The goal toward which the AEF leaders directed their tactics was the complete destruction of the German Imperial Army. Influenced by the American Civil War, the U.S. military elite of 1917–1918 believed in total victory—the strategy of annihilation as opposed to a limited or indirect strategy that sought a favorable peace through conquering territory or destroying enemy morale through attrition or blockade. Both the War Department General Staff and AEF planners believed in concentration and mass on the western front, which would force Germany to collect its forces there. "The contest will then narrow down to a tug-of-war like Grant had against Lee until, by means of our unlimited resources, we are enabled to force a favorable conclusion," wrote one General Staff officer in Washington in September 1917.

The U.S. war planners consequently looked with disfavor upon the "easterners," or the Allied leaders who advocated a peripheral (or "knocking away the props") strategy against Berlin. U.S. political and military leaders saw this indirect approach as being predominantly political. It might add imperial plums to the European states in the Middle East and elsewhere, but it also might prolong the war. Putting its faith in the superiority of its men and morale, the AEF leadership sought total victory through a massive assault to rupture the strongly fortified German positions. The cost in human terms was almost certain to be high if the AEF's advance across the pulverized and shell-pocked battlefields on the western front paralleled the experiences of previous Allied offensives.

In 1914 most Allied generals had begun the war with images of heroic warfare; the courage of individual soldiers was given priority over the technological revolution that dramatically altered warfare. Senior officers initially viewed battles as rigidly structured and tactically simple. Decisive results would largely be achieved through offensive spirit. Illustrative of this emphasis on the fighting qualities of the foot soldier is the following account by a British officer who observed the first day of the Battle of the Somme (1 July 1916), in which few British soldiers survived to reach the enemy trenches. British infantry, he reported to his superiors, had advanced in "admirable order" into the teeth of German artillery and machine guns. "Yet not a man wavered, broke the ranks, or

attempted to come back." He had "never seen, indeed could never have imagined, such a magnificent display of gallantry, discipline and determination." As Tim Travers has astutely observed (1987): "What is striking about senior British army officers before and during the First World War was their ready acceptance of new weapons, but their emotional difficulty in coming to mental grips with the tactical and command changes implied by the new or improved technology." This emphasis on the psychological as opposed to the technical aspects of modern warfare contributed to the cult of the *offensive à l'outrance* ("offensive beyond anything else").

Before the United States entered the war, Allied generals launched repeated attacks against the much more sophisticated German defensive system. Foot soldiers were sent in waves across no-man's-land to occupy trenches that supposedly had been conquered by the artillery. The objective was to punch a hole or open a gap in the enemy defensive system. The horse soldier, which in reality had no place on a battlefield dominated by artillery, automatic weapons, and barbed wire, was expected to maintain the momentum of the advance to prevent the Germans from digging in once again. In 1914–1917, these offensives resulted in huge casualties and modest advances. The multiple German positions could not be fully penetrated and the decisive battle remained a chimera.

To end the stalemate, governments looked to scientists and engineers and mobilized the entire country for conducting war. New and vast quantities of war material were produced. High-explosive shells, rifle grenades, flamethrowers, poison gas, tanks, and airplanes, however, did not alone provide the solution to the deadlock. These weapons had to be applied intelligently. In 1917, the BEF, commanded by Sir Douglas Haig, launched four offensives—Arras, Messines, Ypres, and Cambrai—and the French one significant offensive, the disastrous Nivelle offensive on the Aisne. The results of these offensives had limited tactical success and failed to achieve their ultimate strategical goals. Nevertheless, lessons were learned. When success was achieved, it was primarily because of limited objectives for the infantry and the massive application of artillery to terrify the defenders and neutralize their machine guns and artillery. The artillery's success was not attributable to just the increased number of big guns and shells. Bombardments were now minutely orchestrated and delivered with timing and accuracy to provide cover for the advancing infantry. Robin Prior and Trevor Wilson (1992) explain how soldiers were learning to make artillery a part of a comprehensive system, with weapons ranging from heavy machine guns to poison gas to tanks. The stage was being set for victory in 1918. "This volume of weaponry," they argue, "and the development of an administrative structure capable of placing it on the battlefield in appropriate quantities and circumstances, served to produce a strike force against which the enemy ultimately could provide no effective resistance."

In their war planning, Pershing and his staff rejected the now cautious and increasingly technical Allied approach to fighting the German army. When a reporter challenged him at a press conference in the fall of 1917 as to whether he thought a breakthrough would be possible, he retorted: "Of course the western front can be broken. What are we here for?" Pershing's formula for ending the stalemate was to deploy fearless U.S. foot soldiers trained for open warfare. "An aggressive spirit must be developed until the soldier feels himself, as a bayonet fighter, invincible in battle," was the language he imposed on AEF training instructions.

Another consideration for Pershing was his fear that AEF acceptance of Allied tactics (which by necessity would give a leading role to foreign military instructors) would mean a loss of independence and a subordinate role in the fighting. In this he had the firm backing of Secretary Baker. When President Wilson's closest adviser, Colonel Edward House, expressed the fear that the AEF might repeat the costly blunders of the European generals, Baker responded by emphasizing the connection between U.S. pursuit of its own military doctrine and the maintenance of the AEF's separate "identity."

U.S. officers closer to the front proved much more adaptable to the realities of the new technology of warfare than their commander in chief. The Germans were not going to be driven from their sophisticated defensive systems by "bayonet fighters." The official doctrine of the AEF, however, never deviated from its reliance on riflemen and its advocacy of mobile warfare.

To help many U.S. officers overcome their lack of experience in modern large-scale warfare, Pershing sent them to school. At Langres, just south of this GHQ at Chaumont, he established the important General Staff College, under the direction of Brigadier General James W. ("Dad") MacAndrew, who eventually became his chief of staff. With some advice from French and British officers, the General Staff College did its best during the rapid buildup of U.S. forces in Western Europe to provide the AEF with competent staff officers.

Logistical problems as well as the handling of large bodies of troops were emphasized in the instruction of AEF officers at the school. Modern armies consumed an ever-increasing amount of war material. To distribute supplies, Pershing created a line of communications (LOC) headquarters (later called the Services of Supply, or SOS) under his direction. Almost one-third of Pershing's manpower was eventually delegated to the gigantic task of supplying the AEF with everything from tinned hash to cuspidors and condoms.

There were numerous breakdowns in the logistical support, especially during the summer of 1918. Many factors were to blame, including the insistence of the overburdened commander in chief to concern himself directly with both military and supply matters. Problems stemmed from lack of experience in logistical management as well as a rapid buildup of personnel that emphasized riflemen over stevedores and railwaymen. New leadership was also needed to head the Services of Supply. Pressed by the War Department in July to end the bottleneck of supplies, primarily at ports between Brest and Bordeaux, Pershing chose Harbord as chief of staff of the SOS.

Harbord was selected in part for his loyalty. "I am his man," he had once noted about Pershing. "He can send me to hell if he wants to."

Harbord reorganized the SOS, and his hands-on style improved the delivery of supplies from the ports to the trenches. During his first one hundred days, he spent fifty-five nights on a special train touring the AEF supply lifeline. Ports competed with each other in unloading cargo in a contest called the "Race to Berlin." Army bands played ragtime music to increase the tempo of the work of stevedore companies unloading ships. French ports were modernized, railway communications improved, and vast supply centers constructed. By the end of the war, 670,000 men were allocated to provisioning U.S. forces. Logistics improved, but the war ended before the SOS reached maturity and its full potential.

The Medical Department of the army had an important advantage over the SOS. Because most U.S. troops were not in combat until the last 110 days of the war, the Medical Department had time to provide for beds, evacuation trains, and operating facilities to care for the wounded. Working closely with the Red Cross and other civilian health agencies, the medical services were reasonably well prepared for the entry of the AEF into heavy combat during the last months of the war. The Medical Department's record in caring for the sick was also commendable. Compared with that of the Civil War, the mortality rate among Americans in World War I from disease was lowered from sixty-five to fifteen per thousand. The catastrophic influenza epidemic of 1918 that affected all armies, however, took a great toll of American lives. A soldier was almost as likely to die from disease as from gas, bullet, or shell. In the U.S. Army, influenza and pneumonia claimed almost as many victims (46,992) as combat with the Germans.

As Pershing and his staff at Chaumont made plans for the organization, training, and provision of an independent army capable of launching limited operations in late 1918 as the prelude for a major, war-winning campaign in Lorraine in 1919, the Allied position became extremely precarious. The war-weary French army, worn thin by more than three years of hard fighting, lost its offensive spirit. The Italian army, which had suffered heavy losses with little gain in eleven unsuccessful attacks in the mountainous terrain of Isonzo, was shattered by an Austro-German surprise attack (Battle of Caporetto) on 24 October 1917. French and British divisions had to be rushed south of the Alps to save Italy from being driven from the war.

More serious than either the setbacks to Italy and France was Russia's total collapse. On 7 November 1917 the Bolsheviks stormed the Winter Palace in Petrograd, overthrowing the democratic-minded Provisional Government. The triumph of communism in Russia and the subsequent demise of the eastern front dramatically altered the strategic landscape. Germany, by concentrating its forces in Western Europe, might achieve a numerical superiority on the western front for the first time since 1914. Conversely, Great Britain, which had become the cornerstone of the alliance after Nivelle's failed offensive, was nearing the end of its resources. The BEF offensives during the last half of 1917 had maintained pressure on the German army, but at a price that the British government believed it could no longer sustain. As winter led to a lull in the fighting, the strategic initiative passed into the hands of the Germans. U.S. participation perhaps offered hope for the future, but only if the flow of American manpower crossing the Atlantic substantially increased and if these fresh and unbloodied soldiers entered into the line as soon as possible.

Tasker H. Bliss, who in September had replaced Scott as chief of the General Staff in Washington, captured the increasingly desperate Allied mood and American predicament. "It is pitiful to see the undercurrent of feeling that the hopes of Europe have in the United States," he wrote his wife in a letter from London on 8 November, "pitiful because it will be so long before we can really do anything, although the very crisis seems to be at hand."

The AEF was not yet a factor in the war and would apparently not be for some time. After occupying a quiet section of French trenches near Nancy, elements of the First Division fired the first American shots of the war on 23 October 1917. In early November three Americans, Corporal James Bethel Gresham, Private Thomas F. Enright, and Private Merle D. Hay, were killed in a German trench raid, a portent of the many thousands to follow.

Mobilization on the home front during the first months of the war paralleled the disappointing projection of U.S. power abroad. This was to be expected, given the enormity of the task of rapidly moving from a peace to a war economy and creating a great army from almost nothing. Raw draftees and volunteers flocked to hastily built camps and cantonments, where frequently they did not receive adequate training, equipment, or even uniforms. At Camp Funston, Kansas, recruits attired in blue overalls drilled with wooden rifles. The shortage of officers was especially acute. Some 200,000 officers were required to lead the U.S. Army, which grew to 4 million by the end of the war, but there were only 18,000 regular and National Guard officers available when the war began. Thousands of "ninety-day wonders" were soon turned out by officer-training camps, many of which were established in colleges and universities across the United States.

Particular attention was devoted to clean living for those about to embark on what Theodore Roosevelt had called the "great adventure." Secretary of the Navy Daniels argued that "men must live straight if they would shoot straight." The War Department closed down bars near military bases in an effort to create "sin-free zones." Storyville, the legally established district for prostitution in New Orleans, was closed on 12 November 1917 because of Daniels' concern for its influence on a nearby naval institution. Men in uniform were forbidden to buy a drink. Sex, as well as temperance, engaged the interest of those responsible for preparing Americans to fight in a foreign war. Sex education and prophylactics were provided the trainees. One training-camp poster warned, "A German bullet is cleaner than a whore."

As young Americans prepared for war, U.S. industry failed to provide them with modern weapons. Although thousands of tanks were ordered, virtually none of them reached the AEF by the armistice. The AEF manned 2,250 artillery pieces on the western front, only about 100 of U.S. manufacture. Similarly, aircraft production fell far short of expectations, with no

U.S. combat airplanes arriving in Europe before the war's end. Even machine gun production was slow in developing. Eventually John M. Browning was responsible for a series of superior .30-caliber automatic weapons, the water-cooled heavy machine gun M1917, the air-cooled light machine gun M1919A1, and the Browning automatic rifle M1918, but none of these Brownings were available to the AEF at the front until September 1918. Most of the rapid-fire weapons of the AEF were of French production.

The breakdown in industrial mobilization with the most serious consequences, however, was the chaos in the U.S. shipbuilding program. The raising of an army received far more attention in Washington than its sea transport. "The United States shipbuilding programme had broken down very badly," British Prime Minister Lloyd George gravely informed his colleagues in early December 1917, "and it would be impossible to get the American troops over in American ships at the rate we had thought possible a short time ago." In Washington, Bliss was telling Baker the same thing. "The one all-absorbing necessity now," he told the administration in mid-December, "is soldiers with which to beat the enemy in the field, and ships to carry them." If U.S. arms were unable to play a vital role in the fighting in 1918, Bliss warned, there might be no campaign of 1919. Instead of a victory parade for the AEF, Pershing's forces might be incarcerated behind German barbed wire.

The U.S. desire to maintain the identity of its forces and play a decisive role in the defeat of the enemy created division within the anti-German coalition as 1917 came to an end. Frustrated over Pershing's program of building an independent U.S. army, and fearful that Germany might win the war in 1918, the Allies revived the amalgamation question, which the French and British missions in Washington had been forced to drop because of U.S. resistance in April and May. The French and especially the British (who had no U.S. forces in their sector) now made compelling arguments that the only practicable method of getting Americans into combat by the spring and summer (when the

Germans were expected to make a bid for victory) was through "brigading," or amalgamation of U.S. units with French and British divisions.

Amalgamation remained anathema to Chaumont. Pressed by the Allies in December, however, the U.S. administration emphasized to Pershing on 18 December that the identity of U.S. forces was secondary to the utilization of U.S. troops to save the alliance from military defeat. At the same time, Wilson continued to give Pershing total control over the employment of U.S. military power in Western Europe. Pershing alone was responsible for interpreting whether a "critical" military situation existed and determining the manner of U.S. cooperation with the Anglo-French forces.

As events were soon to demonstrate, Pershing was prepared to see the British driven into the sea and Paris conquered before he allowed any military emergency to alter fundamentally his plans to create an independent force as soon as possible with its own zone of operations and strategic goals. When his staff reviewed their operations plans in response to Washington's 18 December note, it emphasized that the U.S. 1919 offensive in Lorraine offered the best opportunity to bring the war to a conclusion. The introduction of U.S. forces piecemeal into battle in 1918, on the other hand, would undermine the gathering of a powerful U.S. strike force. Moreover, if U.S. units smaller than a division cooperated with the British or French, the necessary development of higher U.S. commanders and staffs would be undermined as well.

The British, who had borne the brunt of the fighting during the second half of 1917, were especially anxious to have access to American manpower to keep Haig's forces up to strength. On 9 January, Robertson began direct negotiations with Pershing, trying to persuade him to place a U.S. infantry regiment (or three battalions) with British divisions for training. He used two main arguments. First, maximum use could be made of the scarce available tonnage if the Americans shipped only infantry battalions and machine gun companies instead of full divisions with their artillery, engineers, typists, cooks,

and so on. Second, Americans could come to the rescue of the Allies sooner if they fought as part of mature Allied military organizations, with their experienced and well-organized logistical, artillery, and staff support. None of Pershing's generals had ever commanded even a brigade in action.

Robertson further contended that the Germans, who already had either crippled or defeated Italy, Russia, and France, would do the same to the BEF in 1918 if U.S. assistance was not immediately forthcoming. Pershing was unmoved by these arguments. He was, however, painfully aware that the United States did not have the ships to bring its forces to Europe. Robertson promised to find additional shipping for the transport of brigades (but not complete divisions). Without a substantial increase in British shipping, the AEF would never reach its goal of having 1 million men in Europe during the second half of 1918. Consequently, Pershing gave tentative support to Robertson's plan to transport 150 U.S. battalions of infantry and machine gunners in British bottoms, but he had no intention of allowing these Americans to be introduced into combat under the Union Jack.

Pershing's concession to Robertson could not have come at a worse time for the Wilson administration, which was under attack in Congress in January for the snail-like pace of mobilization. Employing U.S. troops in foreign divisions would offer dramatic proof of the charges that the U.S. war machine was sputtering badly. Wilson warned his military leaders abroad not to allow any shipping negotiations with the British to interfere with the building of an independent AEF.

Fortified by Wilson's suspicions of the British, Pershing backtracked. He told Robertson that he would accept only the transport of American divisions to be placed in the British sector for training. In tangled and heated discussions, Pershing got his way, and the British government reluctantly accepted a plan to transport six divisions instead of 150 battalions in British ships to train with the BEF.

The worrisome question remained of whether the United States could play a military role, independent or otherwise, before it was too late. The War Department's thirty-division program was far from being realized. Nine months after entering the war, the United States had 175,000 troops in France, the vast majority of them unprepared for combat. Only four divisions, in various stages of readiness, had been organized: the First Division (Major General Robert L. Bullard), Second Division (Major General Omar Bundy), Twenty-sixth Division (Major General Clarence R. Edwards), and Forty-second Division (Major General Charles T. Menoher).

Discouraged by his negotiations with Pershing, Robertson informed his government in January that "America's power to help us win the war—that is to help us to defeat the Germans in battle—is a very weak reed to lean upon at present, and will be so for a very long time to come unless she follows up her words with actions much more practical and energetic than any she has yet taken."

THE GERMAN BID FOR VICTORY

The immense cost to attacking armies had discouraged many Allied military and political leaders from thinking big; instead, emphasis was now being placed on the defense until the Americans arrived in great numbers. The U.S. presence in Europe also influenced German strategists, but in a quite different way. Although the Germans had launched only one major offensive (Verdun) in the west during the past two and a half years, their strategy in 1918 was directed toward an all-out offensive to win the war before the AEF became a factor. In 1914, Berlin had failed in its gamble to smash France before Russia could threaten in the east; now the German high command gambled again, committing the country's last reserves in the hope that it could defeat the British and French before the Yanks came to the rescue. General Erich von Ludendorff, the de facto commander of the German army, and the military party rejected any thought of seeking peace negotiations while the military situation favored Ger-

many. Instead, Germany's leaders sought to guarantee their country's hegemony in Europe through victory in the west in 1918.

To succeed where others had failed, the Germans placed their faith in massive reinforcements (nearly a million men) from the moribund eastern front and on innovative tactics that had been developed in successful attacks in Russia at Riga and in Italy at Caporetto. Unlike Haig, who had embraced dazzling distant objectives in Flanders in 1917 without the tactical innovation to achieve them, the Germans placed primary emphasis on new methods to achieve a breakthrough.

These new tactics have been aptly described as infiltration tactics. As opposed to linear tactics with fixed objectives, German troops were trained for a more flexible and responsive form of warfare. To achieve a deep penetration and the disruption of enemy communications, emphasis was placed on surprise; short but violent preliminary bombardments in depth with a mix of high-explosive shells and mustard, chlorine, and phosgene gas; coordination of artillery and advancing infantry; and small-unit actions. Recognizing the dominance of rapid-fire weapons, riflemen were given a subordinate role, that of protecting the machine gun.

Ludendorff's war-winning strategy called for a series of blows against the Allies to achieve victory in the west. Strangely, the ultimate political and military objectives of his attack remain vague. Ludendorff sought to escape trench warfare, but his strategic goals were undefined. Rather, he aimed at shattering the spirit of the enemy, especially the British.

The superiority of German forces on the western front in early 1918 put the anti-German coalition in jeopardy. The British naturally thought of defending their escape and supply route, the English Channel ports; the French gave first priority to the defense of Paris. A unified command, especially the handling of Allied reserves, was more vital in defense than it had been when the Allies had the strategical initiative. In response to the Italian debacle at Caporetto, the Allies at Rapallo, Italy, had created the Supreme War Council (SWC) on 7 November 1917. Located at Versailles, the SWC, consisting of political representatives of the Allies who met periodically and assisted by a body of military advisers in permanent session, represented an attempt to unify Allied war policy. President Wilson and the U.S. military, who believed that the war would be won or lost on the western front, enthusiastically supported the principle of unity of command in Western Europe but withheld full cooperation. Wilson, determined to keep his political distance from the Allies, refused to appoint a permanent political representative, instead allowing Colonel House to represent him on occasion. Bliss was appointed the U.S. permanent military representative at Versailles.

Efforts to give the military representatives at Versailles control of the Allied reserves, however, broke down completely. An executive committee, chaired by French General Ferdinand Foch, was created, but the British and French field commanders argued that they had no spare reserves to delegate to this body. The Americans, they insisted, were the only effective Allied reserve. Pershing, of course, had already stated in unmistakable terms his opposition to using his men as replacements for the reduced French and British divisions. As the Allies squabbled, the Germans methodically advanced their preparations for a massive attack against the British Fifth and Third armies from the Somme to Cambrai.

On 21 March 1918 at 4:40 in the morning, the earth began to vibrate when some six-thousand German big guns unleashed a torrent of steel and poison gas against the British defenses. Under a dense morning fog, the German infantry broke into and through the British defenses of the Fifth Army. Within twenty-four hours, the Germans captured about 140 square miles. The Fifth Army began to disintegrate. On the first day of the German offensive, Haig requested three French divisions as reinforcement, and on the second day requested twenty. The French, however, fearing for the safety of Paris, refused to join the battle.

Elated by his success, Ludendorff attempted to drive a wedge between the British and French armies. Such a rupture would, in all likelihood, spell doom for the Allies. On 26 March, the British and French held a desperate council of war at the small town of Doullens. To provide for a unified response to the German attack, especially in the handling of reserves, Foch was given the authority to coordinate military operations on the western front. Although the Doullens agreement did not cover the AEF, Pershing went to Foch's headquarters on 28 March and made a dramatic pledge of immediate American support: "Infantry, artillery, aviation, all that we have are yours; use them as you wish. More will come, in numbers equal to requirements." A more concrete U.S. commitment to the Allied cause came several days later at the Beauvais Conference on 3 April 1918, when the AEF was officially placed under Foch's command. Pershing, with his course for an independent U.S. force firmly charted, wanted it that way. "I think this resolution should include the American Army," he insisted. "The arrangement is to be in force, as I understand it, from now on, and the American Army will soon be ready to function as such and should be included as an entity like the British and French armies."

The Beauvais Agreement extended Foch's authority to control of inter-Allied strategy on the western front. The field commanders, however, were specifically given the right to appeal to their governments if they believed an order from Foch placed their forces in danger. Bliss, alarmed by the mischief-making potential of this condition, argued unsuccessfully against the right of appeal. Foch's powers after Beauvais should not be exaggerated. He was more persuader in chief than commander in chief. Certainly his position cannot be compared to that of General Dwight D. Eisenhower during World War II. There was no Allied joint chiefs of staff or supreme headquarters for Allied forces to coordinate strategy. Foch relied on his own staff, and future strategy was developed through personal diplomacy with Pershing, General Henri Philippe Pétain (who had replaced Nivelle), and Haig.

Pershing's "all that we have" pledge of 28 March initially had little practical effect. He had neither planes nor artillery of his own, only men. Aware of the seriousness of the situation, he had been prepared to put all four of his divisions in the line as a corps, which would be an important first step toward creating a separate army. General Pétain, however, argued that such an inexperienced force holding its own section of the line would serve as a magnet for the Germans, and he was right. Although the First Division was moved from Lorraine to Picardy, U.S. divisions were not committed to the battle. The only Americans to engage the enemy were two engineer companies, which found themselves in the path of the German advance while engaging in railway work behind the British Fifth Army. The Americans suffered seventy-eight casualties.

Meanwhile, the German advance slowed to a crawl, unable to maintain its momentum across the battle-scarred ground. The brilliant tactical success, a forty-mile advance in eight days, was not matched by a strategic victory as British and French resistance began to stiffen, but the German onslaught took its toll on Allied, especially British, manpower. The BEF lost 38,512 men (more than half of these taken prisoner) on 21 March, and casualties, excluding sick, reached 115,868 by the end of the first week in April. In sharp contrast, American combat deaths after one year in the war equalled 163. On 7 April, Haig reported to his government that "in the absence of reinforcements, which I understand do not exist, . . . the situation will, therefore, become critical unless American troops fit for immediate incorporation in my Divisions arrive in France in the meantime."

The War Office was more emotional in its request for assistance. Following the 21 March attack, the U.S. military attaché in London was told, "For God's sake get your men over!" Faced with the prospect that Germany might triumph on the Continent, the U.S. administration handsomely responded to these appeals. When the British diverted additional shipping through further sacrifices on their home front, Wilson agreed to send 120,000 infantry and machine gunners a month and actually did considerably better than that. The employment of these Americans, however, continued to provoke controversy.

The British and French expected these raw soldiers to be fed into their divisions for training. Pershing, however, skillfully (and not without guile) worked to keep any Americans training with the Allies organized as divisions, which would enable him to develop staff and command. He also sought to keep U.S. units from going into the line on any active front, partly because of the lack of training of many doughboys. In some cases, Americans were being rushed across the Atlantic only days after they had been inducted. Another consideration for Pershing was his fear that U.S. units, once they took their place in the line on an active Allied front, would be difficult to reclaim for the formation of an independent U.S. army.

Ludendorff continued to provide the British and French with their best argument for amalgamation. With its initial drive stalled, the German army shifted its attention to Ypres salient in the north of the British sector. On 9 April, twenty-seven German divisions tore a great gap in the British defenses and pushed forward three and a half miles on the first day. If anything, the British were more anxious than they had been three weeks earlier, because if this German advance carried as far as the one launched on 21 March, the channel ports would be endangered. In desperate fighting the BEF prevented the Germans from capturing their vital arteries, but it was a near thing. While the outcome of this great battle was still uncertain, Lloyd George cabled Washington: "We can do no more than we have done. It rests with America to win or lose the decisive battle of the war." The British insisted that the United States abandon its efforts to create an independent army in order to save the alliance from decisive defeat.

Under intense pressure, Pershing bent—but not by much. Opposed to feeding battalions into the Allied armies, he held out for shipping divisions of infantry and machine gun units, minus their artillery. He was prepared to place temporarily these disembarking divisions with Allied forces for training. Angered by Pershing's continued reluctance to fall in with Al-

WORLD WAR I 917

lied desires for amalgamation, Foch demanded to know at a 1 May meeting of the SWC whether the United States was prepared to see the French driven beyond the Loire. Pershing answered without hesitation, "Yes, I am willing to take the risk. Moreover, the time may come when the American Army will have to stand the brunt of this war, and it is not wise to fritter away our resources in this manner."

DRESS REHEARSAL: CANTIGNY, CHÂTEAU-THIERRY, AND BELLEAU WOOD

The Allies might take issue with Pershing's utilization of American manpower, but they had no complaints about the dramatically increased flow of U.S. troops across the Atlantic. The heightened German menace and increased British assistance in shipping coincided with new leadership for the General Staff in the War Department. In late January, Baker asked Pershing to send his chief of artillery, Peyton C. March, to serve as chief of the General Staff in Washington. March was a tough, no-nonsense soldier who made an immediate impact. The lights literally went on: Before March's arrival, General Staff officers normally did not work on Sunday or at night. March ordered that for the duration of the war the offices of the General Staff would be lit at all hours—and occupied by staff officers long into the evening. His reorganization of the army included the creation of an air service, tank corps, and chemical-warfare service. He attempted to eliminate tension between the regular army, National Guard, and national army (or draftees) by eliminating all distinctions between these forces.

March's most vital contribution to the war effort was increasing the flow of men to Europe. "I am going to get the men to France if they have to swim," he exclaimed. In April the monthly shipment of soldiers to Europe exceeded 100,000 for the first time, the beginning of a massive transport of troops that would

number 1,788,488 while March was wartime chief of the General Staff. The carrying capacity of the transports was increased by putting tiers of bunks all the way to the ceiling; hammocks and slung bunks were placed in passageways and mess halls. They moved to Europe in convoys of packed transports, three men to a bunk, sleeping in shifts. Amazingly, not a single soldier was lost to a submarine attack during the eastward transatlantic voyage. The accelerated U.S. commitment to the western front, with the inevitable snafus because of haste, served to exaggerate the inexperience of the army's leadership. Divisions arrived without essential personnel to make them operational. Cooks and supply clerks might not kill Germans, but they were almost as essential to a modern army as riflemen and artillerymen. An additional problem was that the War Department rushed many raw soldiers across, men who had never fired a rifle or tried on a gas mask, much less experienced hostile fire.

To demonstrate the validity of creating an independent U.S. force over all else, Pershing concentrated his energies on developing the First Division (the Big Red One) into a superior fighting organization. This was no easy task. Most of the U.S. soldiers knew little of modern war or life in the military. On 20 April 1918, the AEF commander had been dismayed when the Twenty-sixth (Yankee) Division, occupying a supposedly quiet section of the front on the Saint-Mihiel salient, suffered 669 casualties when attacked. This engagement at Seicheprey was the largest thus far for the Yanks, and the results raised questions about the competence of American leadership.

Seicheprey encouraged Pershing to redouble his efforts to make the first U.S. offensive of the war a clear success. "Our people today are hanging expectant upon your deeds," he told the officers of the First Division. "Our future part in this conflict depends upon your action. You are going forward and your conduct will be an example for succeeding units of our army." He selected Major General Robert L. Bullard, who had had combat experience in the Philippines, as the commander of the Big Red One.

Seasoned by a winter in the trenches, the First Division was thought to be sound defensively. Given its inexperience in logistics and administration, however, its offensive ability remained in doubt. As April began, the First Division conducted its last exercise in open warfare. The division then marched to the front to join the French First Army. Its objective was Cantigny, a small village some five kilometers west of Montdidier, the site of the deepest penetration of the German 21 March attack.

Lieutenant Colonel George C. Marshall, Jr., an operations officer for the First Division, and Brigadier General Charles P. Summerall, the division's artillery commander, served as the primary planners for the assault, which was conceived as a limited, setpiece battle involving a reinforced U.S. regiment (about four thousand men). This operation was reminiscent of "bite and hold" operations favored by some Allied officers in 1916–1917, as opposed to ambitious attacks aimed at breakthrough and distant objectives.

The planners of the operation made meticulous preparations, building a model Cantigny behind the front and launching mock infantry attacks. Surprise and artillery domination were thought (correctly) to be the formula for success. About 200,000 shells were amassed. A short preliminary bombardment was scheduled to be at its most intense just before the Americans left their trenches. The infantry was taught to advance within fifty to seventy-five yards of the exploding shells of the creeping or rolling barrage as it preceded them across no-man's-land. The planners also emphasized counterbattery fire. No amount of training, of course, could truly prepare the members of the Twenty-eighth Regiment for the hellish conditions of trench warfare that they were about to experience first-hand.

H-hour was 6:40 A.M. on 28 May. Huddled in their jump-off trenches, the doughboys, all freshly shaved, were each equipped with 220 rounds, two hand grenades, one rifle grenade, two water canteens, chewing gum, and emergency rations. Their rifles and bayonets represented their only American-made weapons. The tanks, aircraft, flamethrowers, big guns, and trench mortars were foreign-made. Heartened by the massive artillery support and spurred on by their officers, the men of the Twenty-eighth Regiment easily took Cantigny. Then the major fight began as the Americans faced violent counterattacks and German artillery. The Americans lost fifty men in taking the village, a thousand in holding it.

Pershing was elated by the Cantigny success. The Americans, after repulsing six or seven German counterattacks, now held a village that the French previously had taken and lost twice. He wired the War Department: "It is my firm conviction that our troops are the best in Europe and our staffs the equal of any." The Americans had indeed fought hard and well. They had without question proven their courage in their first major test of wills with the Imperial German Army. Too much should not, however, be made of the first U.S. battle—and victory—of the war. Fourteen months after the United States entered the war, four thousand U.S. soldiers had captured a village in France. Meanwhile, battles of far greater magnitude and importance were taking place elsewhere on the western front in May and June. Much of the French artillery and air support in fact had been withdrawn from Cantigny after the first day to be utilized elsewhere.

One day before the battle for Cantigny began, the Germans launched their third great offensive of 1918. This time the German storm broke upon the French Sixth Army in the Chemin des Dames sector in Champagne. Ludendorff, having dealt two sledgehammer blows in March and April against the BEF, was becoming desperate. His forces had been depleted without decisive effect. Meanwhile, the War Department had sent 117,202 Americans to Europe in April and was in the process of sending 244,207 in May. Ludendorff planned to launch a diversionary attack against the French to weaken the BEF by drawing French reserves southward. Then he would once again seek to defeat the British in Flanders.

In its initial phase, the German attack proved to be the most successful offensive yet on the western front. On the first day, gray-clad troops covered an amazing thirteen miles in one giant leap. The situation quickly became extremely precarious for the Allies as the enemy marched across open country. Within a week the Germans were halfway to Paris, standing on the Marne, near Chateau-Thierry. Panic reigned among Parisians. Bliss requisitioned trucks and prepared to abandon his offices at Versailles if necessary, and Pershing issued secret orders to plan for the evacuation of his headquarters at Chaumont. Fortunately, although this was by no means clear at the time to the Allies, the German advance was grinding to a halt. Mesmerized by his dramatic success, Ludendorff had attempted to exploit the breakthrough with fresh reserves. His troops, supplied by only one railway line, however, were soon running out of supplies. His forty-mile advance served to exhaust his forces, leaving them in an exposed and indefensible salient.

The Supreme War Council met in a crisis atmosphere in Paris on 1 June. Despite the recent U.S. success at Cantigny, the Allied leaders emotionally pressed Pershing to abandon for the immediate future the creation of a separate army, but he proved to be as intractable as ever about amalgamation. When the British prime minister threatened to go over his head to President Wilson, Pershing retorted: "Refer it to the president and be damned. I know what the president will do. He will simply refer it back to me for recommendation and I will make to him the same recommendation as I have made here today." Pershing was, of course, eager to assist the Allies in their crisis, which ultimately threatened the destruction of his forces—but only on his own terms. He ordered forward the two U.S. divisions closest to the battle, the Second and Third, commanded respectively by Bundy and Joseph T. Dickman. Conveyed by trucks the first Americans, two companies of the Seventh Machine Gun Battalion, Third Division, reached the battlefield on 31 May, taking up a position to defend the bridges across the Marne

at Château-Thierry. Infantry began to arrive the next day. The Third Division was soon dug in along a ten-mile front astride the Marne River.

Meanwhile, on 1 June, the Second Division (which included a marine brigade), took up a defensive position on the Metz-Paris highway, west of Château-Thierry. The German offensive had lost its momentum when the Yanks arrived, but this division was still the first unit to hold its ground against the German onslaught. The Americans not only stood against the advance units of Ludendorff's forces, they assumed the offensive. On 6 June, the marines began a twenty-day battle with a twin attack west of Belleau Wood (Hill 142) and the village of Bouresches, including a nearby section of the wood. Hampered by poor artillery support and linear tactics (advancing in waves), the marine brigade suffered heavy losses. The 1,087 casualties represented the bloodiest day in Marine Corps history until Tarawa twenty-five years later. The marines fought their way into Belleau Wood, an attacker's nightmare with its heavy woods, immense boulders, and dense undergrowth. Short of food and water, dirty, under constant gas and artillery attack, the Americans launched repeated attacks to dislodge the Germans. On 26 June the marines finally emerged on the other side of the wood. A terse message arrived at headquarters: "Woods now U.S. Marine Corps entirely."

The marine brigade (Second Division) had won the respect of the Germans as well as a piece of French real estate, later renamed "Bois de la Brigade de Marine," but the cost had been great—5,200 casualties, or more than half of the brigade's strength. The reality of war struck home, not just for the U.S. marines, but for the army brigade (Second Division) that had captured the village of Vaux and for their superior commander who had ordered them into the line—some to their death. Pershing was moved by the sacrifice of his men. Visiting a surgical ward, he stopped by the bed of a young soldier recuperating from an operation. The soldier apologized for not saluting. Pershing, whose reputation as a martinet was well deserved, noticed that the soldier's right arm was missing. "No," he said, gently touching the young man, "It's I that should salute you."

Again, the U.S. role at this stage of the war should not be exaggerated. Of much greater consequence than the capture of the village of Vaux and Belleau Wood was the blunting of the fourth German offensive. The Germans had won three tactical victories in 1918, but at a cost of 600,000 casualties. Ludendorff now attempted to improve his vulnerable position in the Marne salient through an offensive along a twenty-mile front from Montdidier to Noyon. His attack on 9 June resulted in heavy losses and disappointing gains. On 13 June he called off the attack. He was fast running out of time. The arrival of the Americans signaled doom if he could not bring the war to a successful conclusion soon.

A year and two months after declaring war, the United States, at Cantigny, Château-Thierry, and Belleau Wood, was finally entering the fray with tens of thousands more soldiers moving toward the front. Pershing, elated by the success of U.S. forces, believed that future of the war belonged to the AEF. "The Allies are done for," he wrote House on 19 June, "and the only thing that will hold them (especially France) in the war will be the assurance that we have force enough to assume the initiative. To this end we must bend every possible energy, so that we may not only assume the offensive, but do so with sufficient force to end the war next year at the latest."

Believing that the future of the alliance was in his hands, Pershing began maneuvering to collect most of his divisions in one place to form an independent force. Because of his agreement with the British (which had provided him with the necessary tonnage to accelerate the transport of his forces), all of his divisions—except for one coming across in April, May, and early June—ten in all, were stationed behind the British front, where they were fed and equipped by the British. The only exception was the African-American Ninety-second Division. As Lord Milner, the British secretary for war, expressed it to

Pershing, to avoid "a good deal of administrative trouble," the British War Office had asked Pershing and the War Department not to send them black soldiers. Hence, the Ninety-second was temporarily assigned to the French, who, unlike the British, had long employed soldiers such as the Moroccans from their African colonies in the line. When the United States entered the war, W. E. B. Du Bois, a leader of the NAACP, urged blacks to support their country. "If this is our country, then this is our war," he asserted. Almost 400,000 U.S. Afro-Americans participated in World War I "to make the world safe for democracy."

Most blacks who served in France had whites as superior officers and frequently were handed shovels instead of rifles, serving as laborers behind the lines instead of as combat soldiers. The Ninety-second Division, however, played a role in the Meuse-Argonne offensive. Three of its four regiments fought well. The 368th Infantry Regiment did not, falling apart on the battlefield. The racial prejudice of the white officers of this regiment perhaps played the major role in the disintegration of part of this unit in the Argonne Forest. What is certain is that this incident unfairly brought into question the combat effectiveness of black men and their officers. Many blacks won the Croix de Guerre, but no black soldier received the U.S. Medal of Honor. An effort was made to right this wrong in 1991, when President George Bush awarded posthumously the Medal of Honor to corporal Freddie Stowers, a South Carolina farm worker, who was mortally wounded in an assault against a German position on 28 September 1918.

To an even greater extent than that of blacks, the role of women in the war was limited by the prevailing attitudes toward their proper role in society. Still, women had never before participated on so wide a scale in a U.S. conflict. Perhaps as many as a million women were employed in war work, but too frequently their employment proved to be restricted and for only as long as the war lasted. The Women's Committee of the Council of National Defense was created in 1917; women made bandages, served as hostesses at canteens, and provided similar types of volunteer work. Some women went overseas, for the most part as volunteers in France for such service organizations as the YMCA. A handful of women served with the AEF as telephone operators or nurses. The U.S. Navy enlisted eleven thousand women during the war.

Ironically, one of the few occasions when Pershing allowed true amalgamation was in the case of black soldiers. Four black regiments, who arrived without their brigade and divisional organizations and could not be formed as expected into the Ninety-third Division, fought as part of French divisions until the armistice. Pershing, however, was determined that this would be the exception rather than the general rule. Although Americans had thus far fought in small units and in limited engagements, Pershing was now in a hurry to form large military formations.

Pershing had the strong backing of his political superiors in Washington in his attempt to magnify the U.S. role in the war. On 7 July 1917, Baker wrote him a confidential and personal note that stressed two points: "1. I want the Germans beaten, hard and thoroughly—a military victory. 2. I want you to have the honor of doing it." President Wilson was equally determined that U.S. arms play a decisive role in the war. Without a prominent military role, he feared that he would not have the necessary leverage at the peace conference to impose his new world order upon his war partners.

On 10 July, before receiving Baker's personal letter, Pershing met with Foch. He made it clear that he expected soon to have his own army, front, and strategic objectives. Lorraine in the south was Pershing's first choice for a theater, but he was prepared to settle for establishing the nucleus of a U.S. force near the Marne salient, where the German threat was still great and where he already had his best divisions.

To give the AEF the means to victory, he continued to escalate his demands on Washington for men. He now asked for more than a three-fold increase in the thirty division program he had requested at the end of 1917. He pressed the War Department to provide him with the impossible—one hundred divisions in Western Europe by 1919. The Allies, fearing a German victory during the first half of 1918, had also suggested this number, which could mean a force of as many as 5 million men if replacements for casualties and SOS troops were included. This would have meant the creation of a U.S. force the equal of two hundred Allied or German divisions at full strength. With most of the French, British, and German divisions much below their authorized strength, one hundred U.S. divisions would actually be comparable to three hundred or more divisions of the Allies or Germans. Suffice it to say that such an elephantine U.S. force would have trampled underfoot any German force in 1919, but such a massive force was difficult to raise and train and impossible to supply across the "bridge of ships."

March made every effort to give Pershing sufficient manpower for victory. He told the Senate Military Affairs Committee on 7 August that the military stalemate could only be broken through weight of numbers. He also proclaimed in August, "We are going to win the war if it takes every man in the United States." To give meaning to this sentiment, Congress extended the draft age down to eighteen and up to forty-five, although drafting eighteen-year-olds was not popular. The best that March thought that the War Department could actually achieve was an eighty-division program by 1919. Behind these cold numbers and fighting words and actions was an horrific thought. If Pershing's predictions of his manpower needs were proven correct by events, the result promised to be U.S. casualties unmatched by any of the country's prior conflicts.

The War Department's realism on the number of divisions that could be transported and supplied contributed to a growing gulf between the General Staff in Washington and GHQ AEF. Distance, differing perspectives, and personalities explain this friction to a degree, but the conflict also had its roots in an unresolved institutional question. Who was supreme—March as chief of the General Staff or Pershing as commander in chief of the AEF? This power struggle between the War Department and GHQ AEF was never satisfactorily resolved by the secretary of War or the president.

THE AISNE-MARNE COUNTEROFFENSIVE

As Pershing squabbled with March about the size of the AEF, the Germans made their fifth attempt to gain a victor's peace on the battlefields of France and Flanders. If Ludendorff failed this time in gambling his declining manpower for victory, he knew that he would not have another throw of the dice. His plan was to attack east and west of Rheims, hoping to encourage Foch to concentrate Allied strength there to defend Paris. After shifting his reserves north, he would then finish off the British

On 15 July the Germans attacked with fifty-two divisions. Facing them were thirty-six divisions, twenty-three French, two British, two Italian, and nine American (equal to at least eighteen Allied divisions). Forewarned of this attack, the French, taking a chapter from German defensive doctrine, had skillfully prepared defenses in depth with a false front along part of their sector. This time the Germans quickly met their match. The Allied line bent only a little. The U.S. Third Division, serving with the French Sixth Army, was involved in an especially desperate struggle east of Château-Thierry along the Marne. Fighting off the Germans in three directions, front, left, and right, the Yanks held their ground, earning the nickname "Rock of the Marne." The fifth and last German offensive of 1918 ended almost as soon as it began. Ludendorff's offensives had now cost him more than 800,000 casualties. His exhausted and diminished troops lay exposed in vulnerable salients. A chagrined Ludendorff paid Hindenburg a visit. "What must we do?" he asked. "Do? Do?" Hindenburg exploded. "Make peace, you idiot!"

However the war may have looked to the German High Command at this juncture, victory did not appear likely in the near future in Allied cabinet offices and general staffs. It was rare to find a British or French leader who thought that the war could be ended before 1919, and many feared that the stalemate would continue into 1920. Foch, however, had longed to return to the offensive to wrest the strategical initiative from the Germans and regain the moral ascendancy. He got Pershing's enthusiastic support.

Foch's design was to eliminate the Marne salient with counterthrusts along its flanks. The focal point of the attack was the western face of the salient near Soissons. If the heights near Soissons could be secured, Allied artillery could disrupt German rail and highway communications and force a German withdrawal from the salient. The French Tenth Army's XX Corps, which included Pershing's best-trained divisions, the First and the Second, was assigned the task of securing the heights. Both of the U.S. divisions had new commanders: Major General Summerall led the First Division and Harbord commanded the Second.

On 18 July, in great secrecy, the Americans moved forward in darkness to the jump-off trenches just prior to H-hour, 4:35 A.M. Timing was essential because no preliminary bombardment was scheduled. Instead, the attack would open with a rolling barrage, one hundred meters every two minutes, which the infantry had to be in position to follow into the enemy trenches. Some units, at double-quick time, reached their designated positions just minutes before the artillery opened up. At H-hour the Americans and their French comrades surged forward, assisted by almost four hundred French tanks. Facing them were understrength German divisions fighting from hastily and poorly prepared defensive positions. On the first day, the First Division advanced almost three miles, the Second Division some four and one-half miles. During the next three days, the going became much harder as the infantry lost the element of surprise and outdistanced its artillery support. At the end of four days, the two U.S. divisions had advanced from six to seven miles, capturing 143 guns and sixty-five hundred POWs. Other U.S. divisions also participated in the Allied counteroffensive against the Marne salient—the Third, Fourth, Twenty-sixth, Twenty-eighth, Thirty-second, and Forty-second divisions.

The Allied counteroffensive of 18 July–6 August, officially known as the Aisne-Marne Counteroffensive, provided the AEF with its first opportunity at open warfare. The terrain over which the Americans advanced was mostly rolling countryside, dotted with villages and covered with fields of wheat. In sharp contrast to the war-weary French and British, the doughboys were especially impressive in their dash and aggressiveness. Conversely, their hell-for-leather advance cost them dearly. The First Division's Twenty-Sixth Infantry could muster only two hundred effectives out of the three thousand men who went over the top on 18 July. In securing the village of Sergy, the Forty-second (Rainbow) Division suffered catastrophic losses. Douglas MacArthur stumbled over the dead as he walked across the battlefield in darkness. "There must have been at least two thousand of those sprawled bodies. . . . The stench was suffocating. Not a tree was standing. The moans and cries of wounded men sounded everywhere," he later wrote in his *Reminiscences*.

A postbattle evaluation by Pershing's staff revealed tactical weaknesses. The artillery fired by map rather than by direct observation; the coordination of other supporting arms, machine guns, mortars, and 37-mm cannon with infantry was lacking; and the advance, characterized by rigid planning, cost lives through its frontal assaults in waves of infantry and lack of flexibility. As had been demonstrated so often in past attacks on the western front, the rifle and bayonet, no matter how great the élan of the attackers, were no match for artillery and machine guns.

Despite the limits of GHQ AEF's open-warfare doctrine, Pershing had reason to be pleased with the results of the counteroffensive. Eight of his divisions, 270,000 troops, had participated, playing an important role in forcing the Ger-

mans to evacuate the Marne salient. While this battle was progressing, Pershing had met with his fellow commanders in chief and Foch on 24 July. The results of this meeting could hardly have been more satisfactory to the U.S. field commander. The European generals agreed with him that pressure must be maintained on the enemy for the rest of the year, and he secured his own theater of operations with permission to launch an attack to clear a salient in Lorraine, taking its name from the town of Saint-Mihiel. Pershing immediately issued a general order to establish an independent American army.

CREATION OF THE FIRST ARMY AND THE SAINT-MIHIEL OFFENSIVE

The First Army, with Pershing as commander, officially became a reality on 10 August. When his forces had been attached to the French army, he had received his orders from Foch through Pétain. Now, commanding a separate force, he was on equal grounds with Haig and Pétain. Pershing had a right to be proud of the creation of the First Army. In resisting amalgamation, in effect withholding the most viable assistance the United States could give in the near term, he had run the risk that the British and French might be beaten. There had been many anxious weeks, with hundreds of thousands of Parisians fleeing their city and the British contemplating withdrawal of the BEF from Europe, but the alliance had survived the three tactical victories achieved by the German attacks of March, April, and May. The last two German attacks in June and July had been nonstarters, with U.S. soldiers finally beginning to play an important role on the battlefield.

Pershing located First Army headquarters at Lignyen-Barrois, about twenty-five miles southeast of Saint-Mihiel, and began to collect his divisions on and behind the British and French fronts to man an all U.S. front just east of Verdun running south as far as Pont-à-Mousson.

Developments on the battlefield and in inter-Allied strategy, however, threatened to undermine his plans. The BEF hoped to duplicate the Franco-American success in the Marne salient on their own front.

On 8 August two thousand big guns opened fire along a fifteen thousand-yard front in the Amiens salient. In a dense early-morning fog, General Rawlinson's Fourth Army advanced against an outnumbered and poorly entrenched foe. Massed tanks and especially the successful bombardment that neutralized German artillery made this the best day of the war for the BEF. Within twelve hours most objectives had been gained and four hundred guns and twelve thousand German prisoners were taken. "August 8th was the black day of the German Army in the history of the war," Ludendorff later lamented.

Encouraged by his spectacular success at Amiens, Haig began to think that the war might be won in 1918. With considerable justification, he considered the forces he commanded the best army in the anti-German coalition. The French were exhausted after absorbing the latest blows of the German army, and the AEF had yet to prove itself as an independent force. Haig held in contempt the civilian and military authorities in London who—even after his Amiens success—continued to believe that the war might last until 1920. Haig's plan for defeating the German army was an assault against the formidable Hindenburg Line (in reality not a "line" but a series of well-designed redoubts and fortifications in depth) and the rupture of the lateral German rail communications, either through capture or placing them under artillery fire, which would force a German withdrawal.

The BEF commander in chief, however, needed support from the French and Americans to tie down German reserves. Rather than each army attacking separate German salients, he wanted the French and Americans to combine with the BEF, treating the front from Verdun almost to the North Sea as one gigantic salient, attacking it on its flanks or shoulders. The acceptance of Haig's plan would force Pershing to change the direction of his offensive. Instead of eliminating the Saint-Mihiel salient (which would take the AEF sixty miles south from where Haig wanted it to attack), he would have to join the French in a combined attack on the right shoulder of this bulge, driving northwest toward Mézières and Sedan.

Having fallen in with Haig's plan, Foch paid Pershing a visit at the First Army's headquarters on 30 August. Pershing was stunned at this turn of events, which threatened to fragment his forces once again and undermine his ultimate strategic goals. More was at stake than the Saint-Mihiel offensive. The unity of his forces and his long-planned drive in the direction of Metz were imperiled. "But Marshal Foch," he said with feeling, "here on the very day that you turn over a sector to the American army, and almost on the eve of an offensive, you ask me to reduce the operation so that you can take away several of my divisions and assign some to the French Second Army and use others to form an American army to operate on the Aisne in conjunction with the French Fourth Army, leaving me with little to do except hold what will become a quiet sector after the Saint-Mihiel offensive." When Foch bluntly asked him soldier-to-soldier if he wanted to "take part in the battle," Pershing warmly retorted, "Most assuredly, but as an American army and in no other way."

On 2 September, Pershing, Pétain, and Foch effected a compromise. Pershing's counterproposal was accepted. The AEF would launch a limited offensive to reduce the Saint-Mihiel salient, but as soon as this was accomplished, it had to extend its front to the Argonne Forest. With most of the U.S. forces in Europe under his command, Pershing would then cooperate with the converging Allied attacks with a massive attack of his own in late September in the Meuse-Argonne sector.

The timetable and mission that Pershing accepted asked a great deal of his green corps and army staffs. The creation of the U.S. I Corps under Major General Hunter Liggett, which had functioned as a part of the French Sixth Army during the Aisne-Marne counteroffensive, represented the first time since the Civil War that the U.S. Army had employed a corps organization in tactical command of troops. Was it realistic to expect the First Army to reduce the Saint-Mihiel salient, disengage, and then launch an even greater offensive sixty miles to the north in the direction of Sedan and Mézières? Moving the First Army, which would involve mountains of material, a vast force of men, machines, and animals, vital communications, and medical facilities, would normally take months of preparation by even the most experienced military organization. Now it might have to be done in weeks—for the most part with inexperienced staff organizations. Pershing's choice of the Meuse-Argonne area for his offensive has also been questioned. His actions can best be explained by his desire to keep his newly formed army intact.

The First Army now comprised three corps of fourteen divisions, total of 550,000 soldiers. As part of his bargain with Foch about limiting his operations in Lorraine, Pershing requested massive French support to ensure the success of the first operation by an independent U.S. force. He asked for and received the assistance of 110,000 French troops. None of his 3,010 guns or 267 tanks were of American make. Slightly more than 40 percent of the personnel for his tanks and guns were French. Breakdowns in U.S. industrial mobilization and the decision to ship infantry and machine-gun units without their artillery meant that Pershing was almost totally dependent upon the Allies for his firepower.

The AEF also had no combat airplanes of American manufacture. The chief of Air Service, AEF, was Mason M. Patrick, the sixth man to hold that position, but Colonel William "Billy" Mitchell had the greatest influence on the development of American air power. He joined with Major General Sir Hugh Trenchard, the commander of the British Royal Air Force, in stressing the offensive potential of air power. On the eve of the Saint-Mihiel offensive, he commanded the First Army's combat air operations. The 1,481 planes under his command, which included a French air division and British independent bombing squadrons under Trenchard, constituted the largest air strike force yet amassed on the western front. Prior to U.S. entry into the war, neither the army nor Congress had paid much attention to the potential of air power. When the United States entered the war, the army's two flying fields had fifty-five obsolescent airplanes and only a handful of qualified pilots. A war-aroused Congress, attempting to make up for its previous neglect, appropriated millions for what some air advocates called the "winged cavalry." Baker promised "the greatest air fleet ever devised," a pledge the War Department could not fulfill prior to the armistice. The War Department first promised 20,000 airplanes, but the number dropped with each snafu in production, from 17,000 to 15,000 to 2,000. Meanwhile, the U.S. Navy developed its own air arm in Europe. Its Northern Bombing Group, operating from land bases, conducted bombing attacks against German submarine bases. Naval aviators also flew anti-U-boat patrols.

The Army Air Service relied on Americans who had received combat experience prior to U.S. intervention in the war as volunteers in the British Royal Flying Corps or the Lafayette Escadrille (an American avation unit in the French Air Squadron). The most important training base in France, located at Issoudun, had as a member of its training staff Lieutenant Edward V. Rickenbacker, who became America's most famous ace, with twenty-two enemy airplanes and four balloons to his credit.

The Air Service's roles in the war included reconnaissance (including the use of balloons and their defense), bombing communications, the strafing of ground troops, and engaging the enemy for the control of the sky. By the armistice, the Air Service had grown to 20 pursuit squadrons, 18 observation squadrons, and 7 bombing squadrons. The British (97 squadrons) and the French (260 squadrons) played a considerably larger role in the air war. Still, a nucleus had been established for the phenomenal growth that would have taken place if the war had lasted into 1919 or 1920.

The Saint-Mihiel salient, twenty-five miles across and sixteen miles deep, had been formed during the autumn of 1914. Although a quiet sector, the salient posed a threat to Allied lines of communication and served as a barrier to any advance into Lorraine. The First Army had to overcome extensive fortifications in depth and miserable weather. Rain poured down as U.S. soldiers prepared for the offensive. Fortunately, the Germans had only eight and a half second- and third-rate divisions (about seventy-five thousand men) in these trenches. To ensure the success of this limited operation, Pershing employed his best divisions—the First, Second, Fourth, Twenty-sixth, and Forty-second. These veteran divisions were joined by four new divisions—the Fifth, Eighty-second, Eighty-ninth, and Ninetieth. Four French divisions also supported the attack.

In addition to air cover, tanks were given a role in the offensive. Despite continuing rain that made the ground extremely muddy, Brigadier General Samuel D. Rockenbach, AEF chief of Tank Corps, and Lieutenant Colonel George S. Patton, Jr., a tank brigade commander, were optimistic about the effectiveness of tanks. "You are going to have a walkover," Rockenbach promised Pershing. Despite the enthusiasm of advocates of mechanized warfare, however, the 1916–1918 tank was no war-winner, often breaking down on the battlefield.

Artillery was considered vital to success. Some members of Pershing's staff wanted a preliminary bombardment to soften the defenses. In order to gain the element of surprise, other officers favored keeping the big guns silent until the moment of attack. Pershing wavered until almost the last moment, then ordered a preliminary bombardment, four hours on the southern face and seven hours on the western. In addition to demoralizing the enemy, the artillery was expected to destroy the extensive barbed-wire entanglements if the tanks could not do this job for the infantry.

On the eve of the attack there was an air of great anticipation at the headquarters of the First Army. The AEF had made giant strides since its regiment-sized attack against the village of Cantigny in late May. Six carloads of war correspondents, including sixteen Americans, arrived during the evening of 11 September. They met with a U.S. intelligence officer, who,

after using a map and pointer to describe the next day's action, told them: "Gentlemen, it is now midnight; in one hour our artillery begins and at five our infantry starts." The world would soon know whether the AEF was capable of planning and executing a large-scale, independent operation. Secretary of War Baker would not have to await the wire reports; he was present at the front for the debut of the First Army.

Pershing watched the awesome display of the power of artillery from the old Fort Gironville, which afforded him a commanding view of the battlefield from the south. Most of the shells fell on vacant trenches. Faced with overwhelming odds, the Germans had already begun to withdraw from the salient. Except for isolated machine-gun positions, U.S. troops, rifles often slung on their shoulders, advanced without any opposition. Following in the footsteps of the retreating Germans, the Americans made rapid progress. Sergeant Harry J. Adams of the Eighty-ninth Division chased a German into a dugout at Bouillonville, firing his last two shots from his pistol through the door. He then demanded that the German surrender. To his amazement, three hundred Germans, hands raised in surrender, filed through the door. Adams, his revolver still empty, then marched his captives to the rear.

Although local operations continued until 16 September, the salient was reduced and the battle over in about thirty hours. With the loss of only seven thousand casualties, the AEF liberated two hundred square miles of French territory and captured 450 guns and sixteen thousand prisoners. This victory had come with deceptive ease because of the First Army's overwhelming superiority in men and equipment and, even more important, because of its lucky timing. Some characterized the Battle of Saint-Mihiel as "the stroll at Saint-Mihiel" or as "the sector where the Americans relieved the Germans."

For his part, Pershing believed that the battle was one of lost opportunities. "Without doubt an immediate continuation of the advance would have carried us well beyond the Hindenburg line and possibly into Metz," he later wrote. MacArthur, a brigade commander in the Forty-second Division, also argued in his *Reminiscences* that the failure to continue the advance was "one of the great mistakes of the war." The continuation of the advance, of course, would have thrown a monkey wrench into the Meuse-Argonne offensive, but even if Pershing had had the freedom to expand this limited operation into an ambitious attempt to seize Metz and break the Hindenburg Line, it is doubtful that he would have succeeded.

From top to bottom, the First Army was still learning to fight. Much still had to be learned about handling large troop formations, command and control problems abounded, and monumental traffic jams occurred behind the front. Hunter Liggett, the I Corps commander at Saint-Mihiel and later commander of the First Army, was almost certainly correct when he wrote in his account of the war: "The possibility of taking Metz and the rest of it, had the battle been fought on the original plan, existed in my opinion, only on the supposition that our army was a well-oiled, fully coordinated machine, which it was not as yet."

In retrospect, the fact that the First Army existed in September and had won its first battle was just short of miraculous. Even after the United States had been in the war a full year, the military leaders of France and Great Britain believed that it was impossible for the AEF to conduct independent military operations in 1918. On the day the Saint-Mihiel offensive began, 12 September, 13 million Americans registered for the second selective draft. A confident—perhaps too confident—Pershing began to believe that the emergence of the United States as a land power in Europe might mean that none of these Americans would have to fight overseas.

THE MEUSE-ARGONNE OFFENSIVE

Pershing and his staff had no time to enjoy the results of the Saint-Mihiel offensive. Within two weeks, on 26 September, the First Army was expected to engage the Germans sixty miles to the north between the Argonne Forest and the Meuse River. The first hurdles that the First Army had to overcome were the monumental transportation and supply problems. Restricted to three roads in questionable condition leading to the Meuse-Argonne front, the First Army had to replace the French Second Army, which was defending this sector. In approximate terms 600,000 Americans had to move in while some 220,000 Frenchmen moved out. Moreover, the transfer had to take place at night to keep the approaching offensive secret.

Given the responsibility for moving the First Army into position, Colonel George C. Marshall, Jr., who earned the nickname "Wizard" for his work, has rightly received high praise. Nevertheless, there were many breakdowns between paper plans and their execution. A four-mile convoy of as many as one thousand trucks was required to move the personnel of a division. When the division's artillery, food, ammunition, and other baggage were included, transported by thousands of horses as well as by trucks, the movement of a division took up to twenty miles of roadway. Extensive preparation also had to be made to supply the First Army once it engaged the enemy. Almost 300,000 men eventually were assigned directly to its logistical support. Supply depots and a vast and complicated network of road and rails were established to feed the voracious appetite of a modern army in battle—food, fuel, weapons, munitions, medical stores, and other vital supplies. Twelve trains brought some forty thousand tons of ammunition to the front each day.

Another more serious hurdle facing Pershing and his planners was the rugged terrain of woods, steep hills, and ravines that favored the German defenders. Colonel Hugh Drum, the First Army chief of staff, thought that it was the "most ideal defensive terrain" he had ever witnessed. The Germans also had become better than anyone else on the western front in developing elastic defensive systems. They had constructed a sophisticated network of fortifications, which included pill boxes and miles of barbed wire. To reach its distant objective, the vital German rail communications at Sedan-Mézières, the First Army had to advance against a strong defensive position, both natural and man-made, along a narrow front of twenty miles between the Meuse River and the formidable Argonne Forest, coming under artillery fire from the Argonne Hills to the west and the Heights of the Meuse to the east. As Drum later expressed the problem, "There was no elbow room, we had to drive straight through."

The Americans had yet to encounter such formidable fortifications manned by determined defenders. Their narrow front and distant objectives made the goal of winning the war in 1918 an unlikely one unless their initial attack led to a breakthrough and rapid advance. The Anglo-French forces (with U.S. assistance) had won victories during the last half of July and August by attacking the Germans in the salients they had bludgeoned in the Allied front. Beyond the Hindenburg Line, the German army lay exposed with vulnerable flanks to defend. As the Germans retired to the strong defensive position they had held before 21 March, the Allied strategy from September onward focused on violent surprise attacks that led to tactical victories and the growing exhaustion of the German army through attrition. When German resistance stiffened and casualties mounted, however, the British and French would not continue pounding the same section of the front. Instead, they would shift their attention to another part of the line. These attacks were meticulously planned and supported by unprecedented artillery bombardment. In their 28–29 September attack on the Hindenburg Line, for example, the BEF expended 943,847 artillery rounds in one twenty-four hour period. In mid-September, Foch praised Haig and tried to explain this new approach to Lord Milner. "Instead of hammering away at a single point, [the British] made a series of successive attacks, all more or less surprises and all profitable."

Foch's motto was "Tout le monde a la bataille," which could be translated as "Everyone go to it." These simultaneous attacks along most of the front kept the Germans off-balance and prevented them from concentrating their reserves at one or more points. The danger for the AEF was that if its attack bogged down, attracting an increasing number of German reinforcements, it would be unable to switch off to other objectives as the British did during their "Hundred Days' Campaign " of 8 August to 11 November, when the BEF inflicted nine successive defeats upon the German army. On its narrow front the AEF would have nowhere to go but forward, and at a terrible cost in lives.

Operating from the new First Army Headquarters in the town hall of Souilly, Pershing and his staff devised a plan to achieve a breakthrough that emphasized numbers, surprise, and speed. The greatest asset of the AEF was its size and material superiority, with a three-to-one air superiority and an overwhelming advantage in artillery. Nine divisions, organized into three corps, I Corps (Liggett), V Corps (Major General George H. Cameron), and III Corps (Bullard), were crowded along the twenty-mile front. The order of battle from the Meuse River to the Argonne Forest was as follows: the Thirty-third, the Eightieth, the Fourth, the Seventy-ninth, the Thirty-seventh, the Ninety-first, the Thirty-fifth, the Twenty-eighth, and the Seventy-seventh divisions. Facing these nine double-strength U.S. divisions were five understrength German divisions. At the point of attack, with about 100,000 troops in jump-off trenches, the numerical superiority of the First Army was roughly four to one. Overall, the U.S. advantage in men may have been as great as eight to one. To ensure surprise, Americans dressed in French army uniforms inspected the front. Unfortunately, the Germans suspected an attack twenty-four hours before it started and began to bring up reinforcements.

The most questionable assumption of general headquarters concerned the speed of the advance. Perhaps deluded by the easy success at Saint-Mihiel and their great advantage in men and equipment, the planners hoped for deep penetrations on either side of the hogback ridge in the center of the German defenses, which contained the strong point of Montfaucon. Field Order No. 20 envisaged smashing through the first lines of the German defensive system and reaching the most formidable position, the

Kriemhilde Position, part of the Hindenburg Line, by the afternoon of the first day. Drum hoped to breach this line on the next morning, before the anticipated German reinforcements could be brought forward. If the Kriemhilde Position were not taken quickly, Drum worried that the attempted breakthrough would become a slogging battle of attrition.

To succeed in this first and most vital stage of the Meuse-Argonne offensive, the First Army had to advance ten miles the first day, a distance no AEF division had ever covered in a single day. Also, it would almost certainly take a well-trained and -led army with combat experience to achieve such a blitzkrieg. This did not describe the First Army on 26 September. Some of Pershing's best divisions were still at Saint-Mihiel. Only four of the nine divisions in the initial attack had ever been in the line. More than half the troops in the first wave were recent draftees. Some had been rushed to France without receiving even rudimentary training on either side of the Atlantic. The Seventy-seventh, a division that had been in the line, had four thousand replacement troops who had been drafted in July. Some soldiers had never fired a rifle.

On 25 September the opening bombardment began at 11:30 P.M., with nearly four thousand guns raining death upon the Germans in their dugouts. The offensive began the next day at dawn. After initial success, the advancing units began to lose their cohesion in the confusion of the battlefield and in the face of stiffening German resistance. After four days the offensive ground to a halt short of the Kriemhilde Position. The German high command had six fresh divisions at the front by 30 September and five more in reserve. The First Army's original plan of a breakthrough and rapid advance lay in ruins.

The exploits of Corporal Alvin C. York have provided the popular image of Americans at war during this forty-seven-day battle. A lay preacher from the hills of Tennessee, York single-handedly smashed a German machine-gun battalion in the Argonne Forest. He captured 132 Germans and 35 machine guns and may

have killed 25 Germans. When asked by an officer how many Germans he had captured, America's most decorated combat soldier in the war is supposed to have answered: "Jesus, Lieutenant, I ain't had time to count them yet!"

The reality of the battlefield, however, was often quite different. The AEF repeated many of the tactical errors of earlier engagements, with poorly trained doughboys attacking in bunches and being mowed down. Serious breakdowns occurred in the chain of command. Corps headquarters could not even communicate with its divisions. Perhaps the greatest collapse came in logistics. Roads to the front were clogged with monumental traffic jams, the churned-up earth in the battle zone difficult to cross. Artillery, ammunition, food, and even water could not be brought forward; nor could wounded men be evacuated to the rear. Donald Smythe notes in his biography of Pershing (1986): "Whether because of incompetence or inexperience or both, the First Army was wallowing in an unbelievable logistical snarl. It was as if someone had taken the army's intestines out and dumped them all over the table."

On 4–5 October the First Army tried again in attacks that began to resemble the bloody and futile battles of attrition of the Somme and Verdun. The outcome of the battle depended more on the manpower superiority of the AEF than on skill and firepower. The Germans were surprised by the raw courage of the massed infantry attacks and the apparent disregard for the resulting heavy losses. As casualties mounted and his offensive remained mired in the mud, the strain began to tell on Pershing. While driving to the front, he momentarily broke down. His head dropped to his hands, and he repeated his dead wife's name. Pershing's courage and great strength of character got him through this difficult period. He was constantly on the move, visiting his corps and division commanders, pushing his subordinates to drive their men forward.

The continuous fighting prevented GHQ AEF from retraining soldiers. Commanders who displeased Pershing, however, were removed. When Major General Adelbert

Cronkhite of the Eightieth Division hesitated to launch an attack, he was bluntly informed by his corps commander: "Give it up and you're a goner; you'll lose your command in twenty-four hours." Four infantry brigade commanders, three division commanders, and a corps commander were sacked before the battle ended. Pershing also reorganized the AEF into two armies. The First Army had grown to an unwieldy force of 1,031,000 (when 135,000 French soldiers attached to Pershing's command were included). Liggett was appointed commander of the First Army on 16 October. A fat man, Liggett had initially made a poor impression on Pershing because of the latter's emphasis on physical fitness for his officers. Liggett, however, soon proved that that he had "no fat above the neck." His able leadership of the I Corps made him an obvious successor to Pershing as the field commander of the First Army. Bullard commanded the new Second Army, which was activated on 12 October. The Second Army was given the responsibility for operations to the east of the Meuse River, from Fresnes-en-Woevre to the Moselle River, a front of approximately thirty-four miles. Pershing, as Army Group commander, established his headquarters at Ligny-en-Barrois.

On 14 October, the First Army resumed the attack to take the Kriemhilde Position. Although some of Pershing's best divisions spearheaded the attack, the going on the first day was slow and difficult. Three weeks after the Meuse-Argonne offensive had begun, the Thirty-second and Forty-second divisions finally breached the most formidable German defenses. The Thirty-second Division conquered Côte Dame Marie, the key redoubt of the Kriemhilde Position, and the Forty-second Division captured Côte de Chatillon, another vital position.

Although the German army fought a tenacious and skillful defensive battle in the Meuse-Argonne area, it was at the end of its tether by mid-October. The course of the war in Western Europe and elsewhere over the past month had been all Allied. One by one Germany's allies began to drop out of the war. In mid-September, the Allied army in the Balkans shattered the Bulgarian army, forcing that country to sign an armistice before the end of the month. Meanwhile, the Turks were dealt one of the most overwhelming defeats in history at Megiddo and signed an armistice before the end of October, beating Austria-Hungary out of the war by only a few days. As the Central Powers disintegrated, Foch kept unrelenting pressure on the war-weary German army along most of the western front. Germany's generals as well as its politicians knew that they had lost the war. As October began, Berlin appealed to President Wilson for an armistice based on his liberal Fourteen Points. There then ensued a peace dialogue that lasted more than a month, during which time there was uncertainty that Germany would accept armistice terms that reflected its defeat on the field of battle. The chances that they would were greatly increased by the greatest British victory of the war, the breaching of the final defenses of the Hindenburg Line. On October 5, the BEF (with the assistance of a U.S. corps of two divisions) concluded a nine-day drive that had torn a gap in Germany's primary defenses and resulted in the capture of 35,000 prisoners and 380 guns. During its Hundred Days' Campaign, Haig's forces captured a total of 188,700 prisoners and 2,840 guns.

A comparison of the AEF's progress with that of the French and especially the British armies was most unfavorable to Pershing. Many British and French leaders believed that the AEF's limited advance confirmed their frequently expressed view that the creation of an independent American army in 1918 was unwise from a military perspective. Pershing, who had resisted feeding American soldiers into Allied divisions or scattering U.S. divisions along the French and British sectors, became the focal point for biting criticism. Lloyd George characterized the AEF as an "amateur army" suffering enormous casualties because of poor leadership. If anything, the French political leadership was even more critical. Clemenceau commenting on the modest progress made by the AEF after 26 September, wrote Foch: "Nobody can maintain that these fine [American] troops are unusable; they are merely unused." The fierce-tempered premier wanted Pershing's head.

There was some validity to these harsh remarks. When Pershing handed over the First Army to Liggett, it was in some disarray. Immediately behind the front there may have been as many as 100,000 stragglers (Liggett's estimate). On the other hand, the casualties suffered by the AEF during forty-seven days of sustained fighting, approximately 120,000 (25,000 battle deaths) were not unusual for western-front offensives, especially if a breakthrough did not occur quickly. The BEF had suffered almost 60,000 casualties on the first day of the Battle of the Somme (1916), its first monster battle with the German army. During its attacks of August–September 1914, the French army had suffered almost 400,000 casualties. It can be argued that the AEF operationally was at least the equal of the French and British armies when it first engaged the German army in large-scale battles.

There really was no chance in October that President Wilson would accept these Allied criticisms of the performance of the AEF and appoint a new field commander. Pershing, whatever his liabilities as a strategist and tactician, had given strong support to Wilson's revolutionary diplomacy through his creation of an independent army with its own front and strategic objectives. Nevertheless, Pershing's reputation would have suffered if an armistice had been signed on 31 October. With the exception of the easy—some would say misleading—victory at Saint-Mihiel, the AEF had been fought to a standstill by the Germans in September and October. The AEF's greatest contribution to the Allied war-winning offensive had been to tie down German divisions on its front.

On 1 November, Liggett's First Army resumed the offensive. All of his divisions, both in the line and in reserve, were veteran divisions. This time preparations for the attack were carefully made; particular attention was given to the chain of command and the coordination of supporting arms with the infantry. The AEF had come of age, its operational skills forged in the fire of battle. Summerall, whose V Corps would lead the assault against the center of German defenses, visited his battalion commanders in late October. "There is no excuse for failure," he told them. "No man is ever so tired that he cannot take one step forward. The best way to take machine guns is to go and take 'em! Press forward."

At 5:30 A.M. the greatest U.S. force ever sent into battle left its trenches. In its most skillfully executed attack of the war the First Army pressed forward. The V Corps in the center penetrated German defenses almost six miles. The securing of the heights of Barricourt forced a general German withdrawal and assured the success of the operation. During the last week of the offensive, operating on both sides of the Meuse, the AEF advanced twenty-four miles. During its eleven-day advance, the AEF captured more territory than it had during the previous month. The AEF had the Germans—who, without reserves, were unable to establish a new defensive line—on the run. As the German front disintegrated, the Kaiser abdicated and revolution swept across Germany.

THE ARMISTICE AND INTERVENTION IN RUSSIA

At 6:30 A.M. on 11 November, First and Second Army headquarters learned that the Germans had signed an armistice that was to go into effect at 11:00 A.M. In some instances, however, U.S. soldiers continued to kill and be killed until the last minute of the war. Some units never received word of the end of the war, others were ordered forward. What some considered a senseless loss of life prompted a congressional investigation after the war.

Pershing, who had angered Wilson with his opposition to an armistice, believed that the war should have been fought on until unconditional surrender was imposed upon the enemy. "If they had given us another ten days we would have rounded up the entire German army, captured it, humiliated it," he said shortly after the war ended. "The German troops today are marching back into Germany announcing that they have never been defeated. . . . What I dread is that Germany doesn't know that she was licked. Had they given us another week, we'd have *taught* them."

These words were prophetic. Many Germans, with their forces everywhere still on conquered territory in November 1918, came to believe that they had not lost the war. It is extremely doubtful, however, that the Allies could have ended the war through military operations before the end of 1918. Germany was clearly defeated, but all of the armies on the western front were exhausted. The distant advances, which strained logistical systems to the breaking point, the approach of winter, and the heavy casualties combined to prevent an invasion of Germany without a pause to regroup. Logistics alone would have thwarted a continued U.S. advance. The shipping of riflemen and machine gunners had seriously dislocated the supply of the AEF. "We were long on bayonets, and short on stevedores, railroad operating men, engineers and the like," Harbord has written. "It is certain that if the armistice had not come when it did, there would have had to be a suspension of hostilities and movement until the supply and troop movement could be brought back into balance."

With the cannons silent on the western front, the U.S. War Department turned its attention to demobilization, which naturally went much faster than had mobilization, although not fast enough for many homesick soldiers. By June 1919, 2,700,000 of the army's 3,703,273 men had been discharged with a uniform, a pair of shoes, a coat, and a $60 bonus. Soldiers who had served abroad were also allowed to keep a helmet and a gas mask as war mementos. The return home for some soldiers in Western Europe was delayed. As part of the Allied effort to ensure that Germany would sign a peace treaty, U.S. forces occupied a bridgehead on the Rhine at Coblenz. Once peace was formally made, a small occupation force, called the American Forces in Germany, commanded by General Henry T. Allen, remained until January 1923. Other U.S. troops stayed in Europe, some for as long as a year after the armistice, to clean up after the AEF.

The armistice did not mean the end of combat for a few unlucky American soldiers. The collapse of the Romanov dynasty and the eventual triumph of communism in Russia created a confusing and complicated situation for U.S. policymakers. "I have been sweating blood," Wilson wrote to House in July 1918, "over the question what is right and feasible to do in Russia. It goes to pieces like quicksilver under my touch." The Communists, who made themselves the masters of the heart of the old czarist empire, holding such key cities as Moscow and Petrograd (formerly St. Petersburg), signed a peace treaty with the Central Powers in March 1918, the Treaty of Brest-Litovsk. This annexationist treaty gave Germany a dominant position in the east. London and Paris feared that their economic stranglehold over Germany might be broken if Berlin gained control of the wheat fields in the Ukraine and Russia's vast mineral resources. Meanwhile, a civil war erupted between the Communists (the Reds) and anti-Communists (the Whites).

The British and the French pressured a reluctant Wilson to support armed intervention on behalf of the Whites. The motives of the interventionists were varied and are still the subject of heated historical debate. To a considerable degree the advocates of sending soldiers into Russia during the first half of 1918 were motivated more by a fear of Germany (blocking its advance eastward and denying it the resources of Russia) than by fear and hatred of communism. Wilson and his chief military adviser, Chief of the General Staff March, however, remained unconvinced of the strategic arguments advanced in favor of intervention in Russia. They rightly viewed as unrealistic the desperate Anglo-French plan to reestablish the eastern front with a Japanese force sent from Vladivostok along the Trans-Siberian Railway to European Russia. Nonetheless, Wilson eventually acquiesced to a limited U.S. military presence in both north Russia and Siberia.

In August, before the war ended, five thousand U.S. troops landed at Archangel in north Russia, serving under British command, and another nine thousand soldiers, under the command of Major General William S. Graves,

cation, Professionalism, and the Officers Corps of the United States Army, 1881–1918 (1978).

———. "American Military Effectiveness in the First World War." In *Military Effectiveness*, vol. 1: *The First World War*, edited by Allan R. Millett and Williamson Murray (1988).

Prior, Robin, and Trevor Wilson. *Command on the Western Front* (1992).

Rainey, James W. "Ambivalent Warfare: The Tacical Doctrine of the AEF in World War I." *Parameters* 13 (1983): 34–36.

Spector, Ronald. "'You're Not Going to Send Soldiers Over There Are You!': The American Search for an Alternative to the Western Front 1916–1917." *Military Affairs* 36 (1972): 1–4.

Terraine, John. *The Smoke and the Fire: Myth and Anti-Myths of War, 1861–1945* (1980).

———. *White Heat: The New Warfare, 1914–1918* (1982).

Travers, Tim. *The Killing Ground: The British Army, the Western Front, and the Emergence of Modern Warfare, 1900–1918* (1987).

———. *How the War Was Won: Command and Technology in the British Army on the Western Front, 1917–1918* (1992).

Mobilization and Logistics

Chambers, John Whiteclay, II. *To Raise an Army: The Draft Comes to Modern America* (1987).

Clifford, John C. *The Citizen Soldiers: The Plattsburg Training Camp Movement, 1913–1920* (1972).

Finnegan, John P. *Against the Spector of a Dragon: The Campaign for American Military Preparedness, 1914–1917* (1974).

Frothingham, Thomas G. *The American Reinforcement in the World War* (1927).

Gleaves, Albert. *A History of the Transport Service: Adventures and Experiences of United States Transports and Cruisers in the World War* (1921).

Hagood, Johnson. *The Services of Supply: A Memoir of the Great War* (1927).

Hurley, Edward N. *The Bridge to France* (1927).

Huston, James A. *The Sinews of War: Army Logistics, 1775–1953* (1966).

Kreidberg Marvin A., and Merton G. Henry, *History of Military Mobilization in the United States Army 1775–1945* (1955).

U.S. General Staff, War Plans Division, Historical Branch. *Organization of the Services of Supply: American Expeditionary Forces* (1921).

Wilgus, William J. *Transporting the A.E.F. in Western Europe, 1917–1919* (1931).

WORLD WAR II

Ernest F. Fisher

BACKGROUND TO THE WAR

For the United States of America, World War II began with an attack upon its own territory. At 7:55 A.M. on 7 December 1941, Japanese aircraft struck the U.S. naval base at Pearl Harbor, Hawaii. Japanese bombers destroyed or seriously damaged eighteen U.S. warships, including eight battleships. The following day the United States Congress declared war against Japan. Three days later Nazi Germany and Fascist Italy declared war against the United States.

Although twenty-two years had elapsed since Germany signed the Treaty of Versailles in June 1919, the events of December 1941 can be traced directly back to that date. As artillery batteries saluted the signing of the treaty, one historian wrote, ''The First World War was buried and the Second World War conceived . . . not because of its severity, nor because of the lack of wisdom, but because it violated the terms of the Armistice of 11 November 1918.''

In October 1918, the Germans had replied favorably to President Woodrow Wilson's Fourteen Points and requested peace negotiations based upon them. Unfortunately, the Allies failed either to negotiate or to incorporate the Wilsonian peace proposals into the treaty, which enabled a generation of German politicians, among them Adolf Hitler, to reject the Versailles Treaty. Upon this rejection, Hitler was able to build a dictatorship and the Third Reich.

Taking advantage of postwar suffering caused by continuation of the Allied blockade, occupation of the Rhineland, catastrophic inflation, and worldwide depression, the Nazis built up sufficient national resentment of the perceived injustices of the Versailles Treaty to support a rearmament program in defiance of the Allied powers. On 1 September 1939 rearmament culminated in the invasion of Poland by the German armies, despite Anglo-French guarantees of Polish territory. With this act World War II began. Poland vanished under the onslaught of both German and Soviet armies. In 1940 the Netherlands, Belgium, Denmark, and Norway succumbed to German arms, and France surrendered to the Germans on 22 June in the same railway car at Compiègne, France, where the Germans had signed the armistice in November 1918. France was divided between an occupied area, including most of northern France, and a satellite government under Marshal Henri-Philippe Pétain with its capital in the resort town of Vichy. The elimination of France from the alliance left only Great Britain in the ranks of the unconquered enemies of Germany.

Ironically, as Hitler observed in his book *Mein Kampf*, written in 1923 while a prisoner in Landsberg for his participation in the Munich revolt, friendship with Great Britain was a prerequisite for a restored German empire in Europe that would, of necessity, be created upon the ruins of the Soviet Union. Great Britain was now at war with Germany, however, and, despite having been driven from the Continent, seemed determined to carry on the fight against Nazism, as Prime Minister Winston Churchill declared. Great Britain still had formidable resources, as Hitler was aware: seapower and a still viable Anglo-Saxon empire, including Canada, South Africa, India, Australia, New Zealand, and other smaller elements of the empire, all of whom had joined in war against Germany and, with the fall of France, Italy. As British Major General J. F. C. Fuller observed:

> The one enemy was England, as she had been the one enemy of Philip II, Louis XIV, Napoleon, and William II. Yet now in June 1940 the German leader found himself unable to "hit the common center of gravity of the whole war," because the momentum of his strategy of annihilation had been halted at the English Channel—twenty odd miles of water—and how to cross them had not figured in his strategical calculations. While gazing at the map of the British Empire, he [Hitler] had overlooked the Strait of Dover.

Both Churchill and Hitler at first believed that a seaborne invasion of Great Britain was not only possible but likely. From August until mid-October 1940, the Luftwaffe and the Royal Air Force had fought a battle for control of the skies above the channel and England itself. Thanks to the superiority of the British Spitfire fighter over the German Messerschmitt and Sir Robert Watson-Watt's invention of radar, the British retained control of the air. Radar operators along the coast of Great Britain enabled the numerically inferior British fighter command to concentrate its strength where needed and thereby repulse the massive German air fleets. By mid-October the aerial offensive had failed, and Germany faced operations in the Balkans, North Africa, and the Soviet Union, with Great Britain unfallen and its power intact.

With the Italians attempting to expand their dominion in North Africa, and the British clinging desperately to footholds in the eastern Mediterranean, the Germans were drawn inexorably toward the Balkans and eventually into North Africa. Romania, Yugoslavia, Greece, and the island of Crete fell rapidly to German military power. British seapower, however, still controlled the Suez Canal and the Middle East, including Egypt, which denied the Germans the sea-lanes to Persia, Turkey, and southern Russia. Denied power over the eastern Mediterranean, Hitler turned his attention to the Soviet Union, in what turned out to be the critical strategic blunder of World War II. Once Germany invaded the Soviet Union, Hitler was doomed to a vast continental campaign with the Soviets, who were able to more than replace the manpower lost to Great Britain after the fall of France. On 22 June 1941, German troops crossed the Neman River, and the great campaign on the eastern front began. During the first months the Germans drove deep into European Russia, encircling entire armies and capturing thousands of prisoners.

Alarmed by Hitler's apparent success, President Franklin D. Roosevelt, supported by those in the United States who had long urged a policy of aid to Great Britain and intervention in the European war, took steps that eventually involved the United States in war.

U.S. PREPARATION AND PLANNING FOR WAR

Despite the dramatic events taking place in Europe and the Middle East, the attention of U.S. General Staff planners since the 1930s had focused on possible military operations in the Pacific area. Plan Orange (for war against Japan) had received increased attention as the Japanese invaded Manchuria in 1931 and launched a full-scale war with China in 1937. During the same decade, Italy conquered Ethiopia (1935); the Spanish Civil War broke out (1936), in which Italo-German military assistance confronted that from the Soviet Union; and Germany remil-

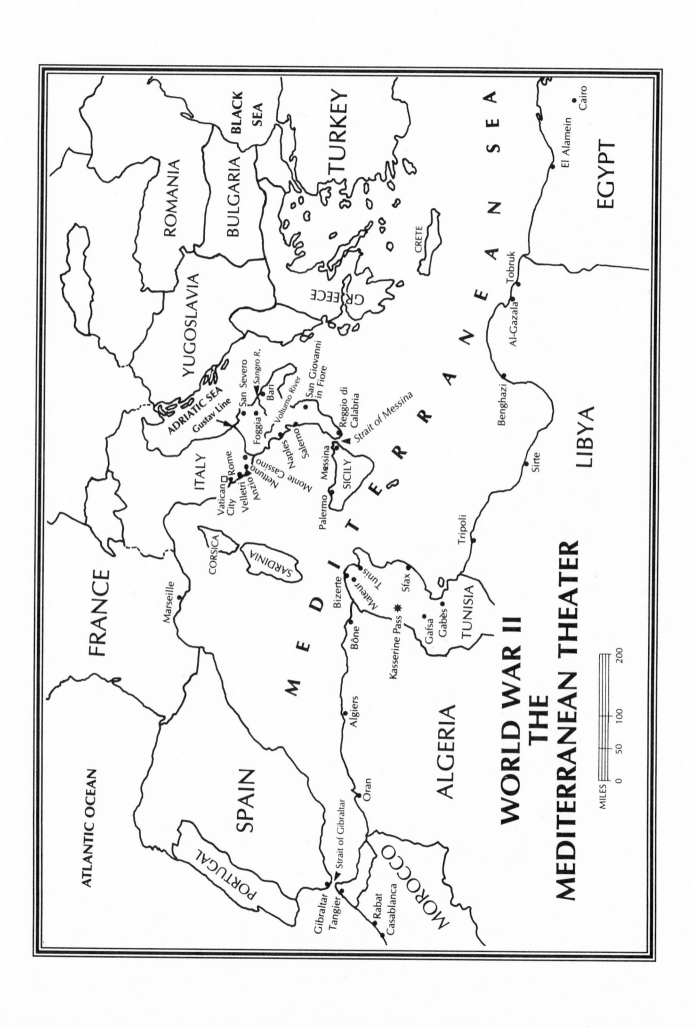

ATLANTIC OCEAN

FRANCE

PORTUGAL

SPAIN

Marseille

Strait of Gibraltar
Gibraltar
Tangier
Rabat
Casablanca
MOROCCO

Oran

Algiers

ALGERIA

CORSICA

SARDINIA

Bône

Bizerte
Mateur
Tunis
TUNISIA
Kasserine Pass
Bône
Gafsa
Gabès
Sfax

Tripoli

LIBYA

Sirte

Benghazi

Al-Gazala
Tobruk

El Alamein
Cairo

EGYPT

M E D I T E R R A N E A N   S E A

ADRIATIC SEA
Gustav Line

ITALY

Vatican
City Rome
Velletri
Anzio
Nettuno
Monte Cassino
Naples
Salerno

San Severo
Sangro R.
Bari
Foggia
Volturno River
San Giovanni
in Fiore
Reggio di
Calabria
Strait of Messina

Palermo
Messina
SICILY

YUGOSLAVIA

ROMANIA

BULGARIA
BLACK
SEA

TURKEY

GREECE

CRETE

WORLD WAR II
THE
MEDITERRANEAN THEATER

MILES

0   50   100   200

itarized the Rhineland. U.S. military planners reexamined Plan Orange with the thought that the United States might become involved eventually in a two-front war. Army and navy staffs developed an uneasy compromise in strategic planning; until it had been determined that the Atlantic flank had been secured, there were to be no offensive operations in the Pacific.

While German armies overran most of Europe, Americans watched with interest but no great concern. Economic depression and a national mood of isolationism had kept both the army and navy limited by modest congressional appropriations—in 1936, less than $578 million for the army and less than $489 million for the navy. The active army numbered fewer than 138,000 men and the navy 96,000. On 5 September 1939, Roosevelt declared U.S. neutrality, according to the provisions of the congressionally endorsed Neutrality Acts of 1936 and 1937, which placed an embargo on arms and munitions to the warring powers. Three days later, the president proclaimed a limited national emergency, under which he authorized small increases in the armed forces—fifty-eight thousand for the navy and seventeen thousand for the army. These increases brought the army up to a strength of 185,000, but none of its units had a full complement of men. In theory, the army had nine infantry divisions, but only three were organized as divisions, and these were at less than one-half strength. All of them lacked sufficient transport for field maneuvers. One mechanized cavalry brigade at half strength was all the armor the army had. The National Guard totaled 199,000 men but lacked enough equipment for its eighteen poorly trained divisions. As for the Army Air Corps, there were only seventeen thousand men organized in sixty-two understrength, ill-equipped squadrons.

Despite the obvious lack of military preparedness, the population of the United States felt reasonably secure behind the shield of the Neutrality Acts. Isolationism, a determination to remain aloof from the distant wars, characterized the nation. The first break in the national mood was dramatized on 10 June 1940 by President Roosevelt during a commencement speech at the University of Virginia, when he declared, upon learning that Italy had attacked France, that the hand that held the dagger had struck. For the first time the president declared publicly his and the nation's full support for the Allied powers: "We will extend to the opponents of force, the material resources of this nation." On 27 August 1940 Congress gave the president authority to call the National Guard and reserves to federal service, and on 16 September approved the Selective Training and Service Act (Burke-Wadsworth Bill). This legislation, however, the nation's first peacetime draft, placed a one-year limit on service, did not permit service outside the United States, and provided for equipment and reserves for 2 million men.

Although both army and navy staffs recommended a purely defensive strategy in the Pacific and mobilization for defense of the Western Hemisphere in the belief that additional aid could no longer save Great Britain from defeat, the president steadfastly refused to accept their evaluation. Instead he directed that presidentially selected observers be sent to London to better determine British chances of survival. They returned predictably convinced that, with U.S. assistance, Great Britain would indeed survive. Accordingly, early in 1941 army and navy staffs agreed that the European theater and aid to Great Britain were to be the first priority if the United States entered the war. A defensive strategy in the Far East would suffice for the present. In March 1941, Congress passed the Lend-Lease Act, urged upon it by Roosevelt, which designated the United States the arsenal of democracy and through which Great Britain, the Soviet Union, and China would be sustained until the United States joined them as a full-fledged ally. Meanwhile, Roosevelt and his British colleagues manipulated public opinion in the United States to support a series of steps that would gradually move the nation toward war. A decisive step in that direction was taken on 18 August 1941, when Congress authorized the extension of service for draftees, following General George C. Marshall's statement that national interests were now emperiled. Even so, the extension passed in the House of Representatives by the narrow vote of 203–202. In the meantime, the administration had slowly created the bureaucracy needed to place the nation on a wartime footing. The Office of Production Management was created in December 1940. To administer military training, General Marshall and Brigadier General Lesley J. McNair established in July 1940 a general headquarters (GHQ) with McNair as chief of staff. In the spring of 1941, Marshall appointed Major General Henry H. Arnold his deputy chief of staff for air. In June 1941, Marshall created the Army Air Forces, with two elements, the Air Corps and the Air Force Combat Command. The latter remained subject to a ground commander.

While the United States continued to organize its armed forces throughout 1941, the war at sea had reached a critical phase. German U-boats, operating in groups known as "wolf packs," were sinking British ships five times faster than their shipyards could replace them. Roosevelt's response was to make lend-lease funds available for building and repairing British merchant ships and convoy escort vessels in U.S. shipyards. The United States also seized sixty-nine Axis and Danish ships then in U.S. ports and turned them over to the British. Certain restrictive sections of the Neutrality Act of 1939 were repealed in November 1941, and the president declared the Red Sea no longer a combat zone from which U.S. ships were barred. U.S. ships could now carry supplies directly to British forces in the Near East.

When the Germans expanded their war zone in the north Atlantic, the U.S. chief of naval operations, Admiral Harold R. Stark, shifted three battleships, an aircraft carrier, four light cruisers, and two squadrons of destroyers from the Pacific to the Atlantic. He also recommended to the president that a line be drawn in the mid-Atlantic beyond which belligerent vessels would be considered intent on possible hostile action. This extended the radius of the "neutrality patrol" formed originally to protect American neutral rights.

The U.S. Coast Guard had patrolled the waters around Iceland and Greenland until early in 1941, then in April the United States, with Danish permission, decided to construct airfields and other defense installations on Greenland and assume its protection until Denmark was liberated. Shortly afterward, army engineers and antiaircraft units landed in Greenland. Iceland also came under U.S. protection, after the British, at the request of Iceland, had stationed troops there. The United States thus moved ever closer to direct involvement in the war. Roosevelt, citing further encounters at sea with U-boats, announced on 27 May 1941 that the war was "approaching the brink of the Western Hemisphere itself" and declared an unlimited national emergency. Concern over possible German incursions into South America was a contributing factor.

Although the president believed Spain and Portugal would be the next German targets, and that the latter's Atlantic islands, the Azores, might fall into Axis hands, the British believed that the Germans were prepared to turn toward the Soviet Union. British intelligence was right, and on 22 June 1941, Germany invaded the Soviet Union. The British promptly assured Moscow of their help. Two days after the invasion, Roosevelt assured the Russians of U.S. assistance by declaring that it would be unnecessary to invoke the Neutrality Act of 1939 against Russia.

Churchill also urged that Roosevelt send marines to Iceland to relieve part of the British garrison there and to provide a useful base for protecting the northern convoy route to Britain and for providing aid to the Soviet Union by way of the arctic port of Archangel. The first U.S. troops were landed in Iceland on 7 July.

In July, Roosevelt directed the secretaries of war and navy to prepare a "victory program." In doing so, the army and navy prepared two divergent concepts of how a war should be fought. The navy planned to exploit the air and sea power of both Great Britain and the United States against Germany and envisioned deploying only about one million men in Europe, preferring to rely on foreign manpower backed by the output of U.S. industry. The army decided that the war should be fought by confronting enemy armies on the ground. Army and air planners estimated that 8,795,000 men would be required—a figure remarkably close to the actual peak strength of 8,291,000 reached during the war. Army planners, however, erred greatly in determining the composition of this force. Instead of a projected 215 ground divisions, the army formed only ninety-one, with far more air and service troops than at first foreseen.

By September, after an abortive encounter on the 4th between the USS *Greer* and a U-boat, the United States had to all intents become a belligerent in the war in the Atlantic. In October two U.S. destroyers were attacked—the *Kearney* was able to limp back into port, but the *Reuben James* was sunk, with more than one hundred of its crew. These incidents persuaded Congress to repeal the remaining restrictions of the Neutrality Act. On 6 December 1941, President Roosevelt decided to produce an atomic bomb, a decision that remained secret until the last months of the war, and across the Potomac work had begun on a new five-sided building (the Pentagon) to house the growing War Department.

As for the Pacific, on 26 July, Roosevelt nationalized the armed forces of the Philippines, placing them under the leadership of General Douglas MacArthur. In addition to the U.S. units under his command, MacArthur counted ten Philippine divisions of doubtful quality—a force totaling about 200,000 men and hardly capable of defeating the battle-hardened Japanese recently deployed from service in China. Confident that their fleet could keep the Americans in place, the Japanese armed forces planned a campaign into the East Indies, where the oil fields of Indonesia could be expected to supply the oil denied them by the U.S. embargo. Japanese strategists did not believe that the United States could vigorously fight and win a war simultaneously on both the Atlantic and Pacific fronts. Despite the misgivings of Japanese Emperor Hirohito, the military commanders remained confident that they could achieve their goals. By November 1941, Roosevelt and his staff had concluded that the Japanese had resolved on war with the United States (U.S. cryptanalysts had broken the Japanese diplomatic code in late 1940), but the question until 7 December 1941 remained when and where.

Although after 7 December 1941 Japan was at war with the United States, Germany for a time demurred, because Japan had attacked the United States without consulting the Nazi government. Hitler had originally preferred to complete the conquest of the Soviet Union before taking on the Americans, but he had promised the Japanese to declare war against the United States even if Japan attacked first. He declared war against the United States on 11 December 1941, as did Italian dictator Benito Mussolini. There was now global war, with the United States, Great Britain, and the Soviet Union arrayed against Germany, Italy, and Japan around the world (although the Soviet Union did not enter the war against Japan until 1945).

Despite two years of gradual buildup, the day following Pearl Harbor found the U.S. Navy with only nine battle-worthy battleships, twenty-nine seaworthy cruisers, and six aircraft carriers. In manpower, the navy numbered about 325,000 men, plus 70,000 in the Marine Corps and 25,000 in the Coast Guard. Although the draft had increased the army to almost 1.75 million men, this was far short of the four million deemed necessary to defend just the Western Hemisphere. At the end of 1940, only one army division was fully trained and equipped for combat, with thirty-seven others in various stages of readiness, but there was not enough shipping to move them overseas. The Army Air Forces contained only 348,535 men, and Japanese operations against Hawaii and the Philippines had reduced the number of aircraft to a low point of 807, of which only 159 were four-engined bombers. The United States moved rapidly to remedy the situation. Aircraft plants employed more than 425,000 workers with a goal of almost three thousand planes off the assembly lines during the first months of 1942.

President Roosevelt reorganized the armed forces command structure. He eliminated the arrangement whereby the commander of the largest of the three navy fleets acted as overall fleet commander. The position of navy commander in chief became a separate post, with

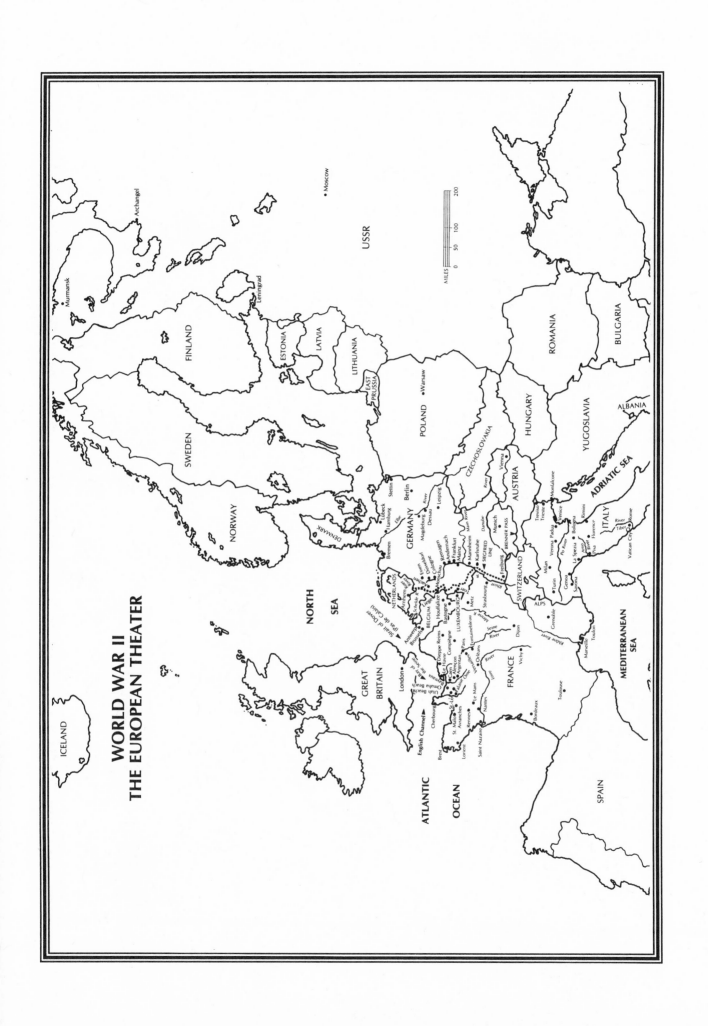

**WORLD WAR II
THE EUROPEAN THEATER**

ICELAND

ATLANTIC

OCEAN

GREAT
BRITAIN

London

English Channel

NORTH
SEA

Strait of Dover
(Pas de Calais)

Cherbourg
Utah Beach
Omaha Beach
St. Lô
St. Malo
Avranches
Mortain Orne
Brest
Lorient
Rennes
Nantes
Saint Nazaire
Le Mans

Brest

Le Havre
Dieppe Reims
Compiègne
Caen
Laon
Argentan
Paris
Alençon
Fontainebleau
Chartres
Orléans

FRANCE

Loire
River

Seine
River

Dijon

Vichy

Bordeaux

Toulouse

SPAIN

MEDITERRANEAN
SEA

Marseille
Toulon

Grenoble

Rhône River

NETHERLANDS
Arnhem
Antwerp
Brussels
BELGIUM
Liège
Houffalize
Bastogne
LUXEMBOURG
Metz
Strasbourg

Essen
Düsseldorf
Cologne
Monschau
Andernach
Remagen
Frankfurt
Mainz
Mannheim
Karlsruhe
SIEGFRIED
LINE
Freiburg

GERMANY

Bremen
Hamburg
Lübeck
Stettin
Berlin
Magdeburg
Dessau
Leipzig

Elbe
River

Main River

Rhine

Rhine River

Danube

Munich
BRENNER PASS

SWITZERLAND

ALPS

ITALY

Milan
Turin
Genoa
Savona
La Spezia
Pisa
Florence
Arno River
Bologna
Po River
Verona Padua
Venice
Rimini
Treviso
Trieste
Montalcone

ADRIATIC SEA

Rome
Vatican City
Tiber River

DENMARK

NORWAY

SWEDEN

FINLAND

Murmansk

Archangel

Leningrad

ESTONIA

LATVIA

LITHUANIA

EAST
PRUSSIA

POLAND

Warsaw

USSR

Moscow

CZECHOSLOVAKIA

AUSTRIA

Vienna

HUNGARY

ROMANIA

BULGARIA

YUGOSLAVIA

ALBANIA

MILES
0 50 100 200

Admiral Ernest J. King, the former Atlantic Fleet commander, the first occupant of the post. The commander in chief had responsibility for plans and operations, while the chief of naval operations (CNO) retained responsibility for logistics, procurement, and housekeeping. The arrangement resembled the relationship between the army chief of staff and the GHQ head. To solve inherent conflicts and ambiguities, in March 1942, Roosevelt put King in both positions, while former CNO Admiral Stark went to Britain as commander of U.S. naval forces in Europe. Roosevelt rounded out his wartime operational command post with General Marshall as army chief of staff and General Arnold as chief of the Army Air Forces. He also enlisted bipartisan support by appointing Republicans Henry L. Stimson as secretary of war and Frank Knox as secretary of the navy. Secretary of State Cordell Hull had only a minor role to play, because Roosevelt preferred to be his own secretary of state. To this inner group was added Harry L. Hopkins, an obscure nonpolitical figure who had resided in the White House since 1940, a crony and confidant of the president.

The War Department completed its reorganization in March 1942 by eliminating the GHQ and putting in its place three separate arms: Army Air Forces, General Arnold; Army Ground Forces, General Lesley J. McNair; and Army Service Forces, General Brehon B. Somervell. Following reorganization of the army high command, provision was made for joint army-navy direction of the war, through the formation of the Joint Chiefs of Staff (JCS), made up of King, Marshall, and Arnold. In the summer of 1942, Fleet Admiral William D. Leahy, as the president's personal chief of staff, was added to the JCS. These four would work with their British opposite numbers—Field Marshal Sir Alan Brooke, chief of the Imperial General Staff; Admiral of the Fleet and First Sea Lord Sir Dudley Pound; and Sir Charles Portal, chief of the Air Staff—to form the Combined Chiefs of Staff (CCS). Since Washington, D.C. was to be the permanent seat of the staff, Churchill appointed Field Marshal Sir John Dill to represent the British chiefs in the intervals between formal conferences.

In addition to the CCS, there were several combined civilian and paramilitary agencies, such as the Munitions Assignment Board, the Shipping Board, and the Production and Resources Board. These enabled the United States and Great Britain to fuse their war efforts in a manner unparalleled in the history of alliances and superior in central planning and direction to those on the Axis side. The Atlantic Charter was signed by Churchill and Roosevelt when they and the CCS met aboard ship in mid-August 1941. The first meeting after the United States entered the war, however, took place in Washington in late December 1941. Designated the Arcadia Conference, it set the pattern for subsequent top-level conferences.

Although there was considerable pressure to concentrate the war effort against Japan, the CCS, Roosevelt, and his advisers remained determined to concentrate on the defeat of Germany and Italy. Washington despaired of holding the Philippines and decided to concentrate on holding open the lines of communication through Hawaii to Australia, which left little shipping available for troop movements across the Atlantic.

Encouraged by recent victories that had carried the British from Egypt into Libya (November 1941–January 1942), Churchill raised the possibility of a British advance westward to the border of Tunisia. Vichy France might then agree to permit the Allies to enter Algeria and Morocco. With the British occupying Tunisia and Algeria, the Americans would have responsibility for Morocco. Roosevelt, eager for successful operations, supported Churchill's idea. His advisers did not, citing a shortage of shipping, and the North African venture was shelved for the time being. Meanwhile, German submarines continued to roam the Atlantic, sinking 506 Allied vessels.

The navy had concentrated its rebuilding program on large battleships, cruisers, and aircraft carriers, leaving little resources for constructing smaller craft, such as destroyers, capable of combating U-boats. Only twenty-three large and forty-two small Coast Guard cutters, plus twenty-nine miscellaneous craft and twenty-two converted trawlers, the latter loaned by the Royal Navy, were available to reinforce against this menace. Despite loud protests from coastal communities, in April 1942 the navy managed to impose stringent restrictions on lighting in cities to make it difficult for enemy submarines to locate targets. Although many antisubmarine measures were devised during the war, the Allies did not check the U-boat menace until the establishment of the convoy system, with sufficient escort craft to protect shipping from Key West, Florida, to Norfolk, Virginia. In May the system was extended northward to join the main convoy routes from the major northern ports. Not a single ship was sunk off the Atlantic coast during the remaining months of 1942. Thus, the submarine was defeated in the Caribbean and U.S. coastal waters. In the north Atlantic the battle against the U-boats went on as they shifted their operations to the transatlantic routes.

As the Japanese broadened their control in the Pacific and East Asia, there was some pressure within the JCS for a shift of emphasis from Europe to the Pacific. Marshall and his chief of war plans, Major General Dwight D. Eisenhower, vigorously opposed this view, and in April 1942, Marshall presented a War Department plan for the invasion of Europe to President Roosevelt. The buildup in Great Britain for this plan was given the code name Bolero, and the invasion itself designated Round Up, which was to be carried out by forty-eight divisions supported by six thousand aircraft. Two-thirds of the divisions and more than 50 percent of the aircraft were to be American. Scheduled for April 1943, the operation might be launched earlier, under the code name Sledgehammer, if the Soviet Union gave indication of collapse. Roosevelt approved the plan immediately and General Marshall left for London to persuade the British staff to accept the plan. Anxious lest their U.S. colleagues shift their efforts to the Far East, the British readily accepted the proposal. At the same time, however, Churchill cautioned Roosevelt against a premature landing in Europe in 1942, but the Americans had assured visiting Soviet Foreign Minister V. M. Molotov that, if necessary, the Allies would open a second front somewhere on the continent in 1942.

Nevertheless, Churchill flew to Moscow to tell Joseph Stalin that the Anglo-American Allies had not enough sea lift to launch an invasion. Stalin indicated that he understood, but this became the basis of a propaganda claim that the Allies planned to allow the Nazis to destroy the USSR.

THE CAMPAIGN IN NORTH AFRICA

In North Africa, British forces had been driven back into Egypt where in May 1941, and by early 1942 there was a threat that the Germans and their Italian allies might reach the Suez Canal, gain control of the Middle East oil fields, and link up with Axis forces occupying the Balkans. This threat was the basis for Churchill's concept of opening another front in North Africa. He faced opposition from General Marshall, who believed the main issue to be rejection of anything that would delay Plan Bolero. In his eyes an Allied operation in North Africa would be expensive and ineffective, and he was so opposed to Churchill's idea that he proposed that the United States concentrate in the Pacific against Japan rather than accept the British plan for operations in North Africa. Roosevelt, however, was willing to accept the British proposal for North Africa, and on the evening of 30 June 1942, he announced his decision for U.S. forces to concentrate on Operation Torch, the code name for an Allied invasion of North Africa, which was to take precedence over all other operations.

The 1940 armistice with the Germans at Compiègne had left the French in control of their North African territories with a lightly equipped 135,000-man army made up mainly of indigenous territorials but with regular French army officers. An air force of some 350 older combat aircraft completed the military picture. What remained of the French navy patrolled the coastal waters of Morocco and Algeria. Although unimpressive, this force was loyal to Pétain, whom the Germans had placed in control of Vichy France. Because of poor relations between the

British and the French, it was agreed that the invasion force should be under the command of an American. The British initially suggested Marshall, with Eisenhower as his deputy. Since late June 1942, Eisenhower had been stationed in London as commander of U.S. forces in the European theater of operations. Roosevelt was heavily dependent upon Marshall for advice and did not want Marshall to leave his side. Consequently, Eisenhower became his and Marshall's choice to command Operation Torch. Eisenhower's deputy, General Mark Wayne Clark, was also his deputy for Torch.

The British insisted upon a landing inside the Mediterranean basin at Oran, Algiers, and Bône. They wanted a landing close enough to Tunisia to enable their armor to strike rapidly overland to Bizerte and Tunis. The Americans wanted to land on the Atlantic coast of Morocco to ensure a line of communications to the United States. The CCS finally agreed that the Americans would land one force on the Atlantic coast to take Casablanca, another on the Mediterranean coast at Oran, and a third at Algiers, followed by British reinforcements landing at eastern Algerian ports to support a drive into Tunisia. Once North Africa had been secured, the Allies were to drive into Libya to strike Axis forces from the rear as the British launched a counteroffensive from Egypt. Thus, the Axis forces would be eliminated from North Africa and the western Mediterranean. This would clear shipping lanes for lend-lease supplies to the Soviet Union. A cross-channel operation planned for 1943 was postponed.

To command the landing of the Western Task Force's thirty-five thousand men on Morocco's Atlantic coast, Eisenhower selected an associate of long standing, Major General George S. Patton, Jr. Patton shared responsibility for the amphibious operation with Rear Admiral Henry Kent Hewitt. The Western Task Force was to sail from East Coast ports in the United States in 107 vessels and to land at three minor ports on the Moroccan coast and then drive five hundred miles to the east to link up with the Center Task Force at Oran, commanded by Major General Lloyd R. Fredendall. The Center Task Force was

to land over the beaches near Oran and then move inland to capture the port. The Eastern Task Force, composed of ten thousand Americans and twenty-three thousand British, was under the command of British Lieutenant General Kenneth A. N. Anderson. Initially, Anderson was to remain at Gibraltar, while U.S. Major General Charles L. Ryder, commander of the Thirty-fourth Infantry Division, led an assault force at Algiers made up mainly of Americans. Both the Center and Eastern task forces were moved from Great Britain in British transports; the naval commander was Admiral Sir Andrew Browne Cunningham. Air support for the Western Task Force was commanded by Brigadier General James H. Doolittle's newly created Twelfth Air Force, with 1,244 U.S. aircraft. The British supplied the Eastern Air Command made up of 454 Royal Air Force planes.

Most landing craft on the Atlantic coast were Higgins boats, thirty-six-foot plywood craft, many without landing ramps, and the men had to clamber over the sides to disembark. A few of the early models of a steel construction LCM (landing craft mechanized), capable of carrying a thirty-ton tank, were also used. For the Mediterranean half of the invasion force, there was a miscellaneous mixture of various craft, some converted to carry tanks, others resembling large lifeboats. (Sophisticated ship-to-shore vessels did not appear until later in the war.)

The major question facing the Anglo-American invasion force was the reaction of the French garrison in Algiers and Morocco. Allied intelligence believed that the French would most likely support General Henri Honoré Giraud, who at that time was residing in unoccupied France but was in contact with General Charles E. Mast, the anti-Vichy chief of staff of the French forces in Algiers who with four civilians comprised the anti-Vichy leadership in Algeria. The senior French official in North Africa, however, was Admiral Jean François Darlan, second in command to Pétain and commander in chief of the French forces in North Africa. The major Allied command problem was how to get Darlan to cooperate with Giraud and Mast. His support was necessary because he controlled

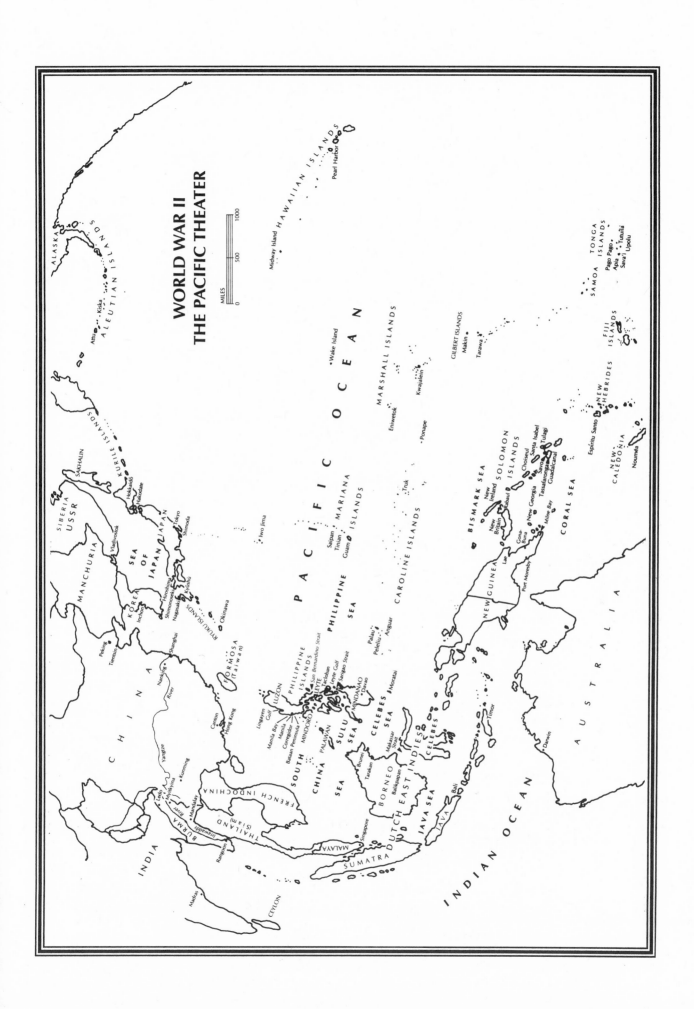

WORLD WAR II
THE PACIFIC THEATER

MILES

0   500   1000

PACIFIC OCEAN

ALASKA

ALEUTIAN ISLANDS

Attu Kiska

Midway Island   HAWAIIAN ISLANDS
Pearl Harbor

SIBERIA

USSR

MANCHURIA

SAKHALIN

KURILE ISLANDS

Hokkaidō
Hakodate

SEA OF JAPAN

Vladivostok

KOREA

Peking
Tientsin

Inchon

Shanghai
Nanking

CHINA

Yangtze River

Canton
Hong Kong

Kunming

Ledo
Myitkyina
Mandalay
Irrawaddy River

BURMA

INDIA

Rangoon

Madras

CEYLON

THAILAND (Siam)

FRENCH INDOCHINA

MALAYA

Singapore

SUMATRA

SOUTH CHINA SEA

JAPAN

Tokyo
Shimoda

Hiroshima
Shimonoseki
Kyūshū
Nagasaki

RYUKYU ISLANDS

Okinawa

FORMOSA (Taiwan)

Iwo Jima

MARIANA ISLANDS
Saipan
Tinian
Guam

PHILIPPINE ISLANDS

Lingayen Gulf
Manila Bay
Manila
Corregidor
Bataan Peninsula

LUZON

MINDORO
San Bernardino Strait
Tacloban
LEYTE
Leyte Gulf
Surigao Strait

PALAWAN

MINDANAO
Davao

PHILIPPINE SEA

Palau
Peleliu

Anguar

MORATAI

Wake Island

MARSHALL ISLANDS

Eniwetok

Kwajalein

Ponape

Truk

CAROLINE ISLANDS

GILBERT ISLANDS

Makin

Tarawa

SAMOA TONGA ISLANDS
Pago Pago
Apia   Tutuila
Savai'i Upolu

FIJI ISLANDS

NEW HEBRIDES

Espíritu Santo

NEW CALEDONIA

Nouméa

BISMARK SEA

New Ireland

New Britain Rabaul

Gona-Buna

Lae

NEW GUINEA

Port Moresby

SOLOMON ISLANDS

Choiseul
Santa Isabel
Savo   Tulagi
New Georgia
Tassafaronga
Guadalcanal
Milne Bay

CORAL SEA

AUSTRALIA

Darwin

BORNEO

Brunei
Tarakan
Balikpapan

SULU SEA

CELEBES SEA

CELEBES

Makassar Strait

DUTCH EAST INDIES

JAVA SEA

JAVA
Bali

Timor

INDIAN OCEAN

what was left of the French fleet. The problem was the subject of a secret meeting between Generals Giraud, Mast, Robert D. Murphy, and Clark, whom Eisenhower had selected to command the army element in Operation Torch.

Clark arrived in a submarine at the meeting place, a seaside villa ninety miles west of Algiers. Murphy, the U.S. intelligence agent in Algiers who hosted the meeting, summoned the others to make plans for Franco-Allied cooperation during the forthcoming invasion. Although the meeting was dispersed by the unexpected arrival of French police, apparently nothing was compromised, thanks to Murphy's skill in reassuring the police. General Clark escaped undetected back to his submarine. Vichy officials had learned nothing, but the Germans remained suspicious that the Allies would strike somewhere in the Mediterranean during 1942. Axis forces, however, were in no position to take protective countermeasures, and as the year drew to a close, the Germans decided that there would be no Allied operation until 1943.

Suddenly, on 23 October the British Eighth Army, commanded by General Sir Bernard L. Montgomery, attacked Field Marshal Erwin Rommel's Italian-German army in the western desert in the vicinity of El Alamein in Egypt. Montgomery's attack was preceded by air and artillery bombardment against Axis supply lines. The Eighth Army attacked across a six-mile front, and on 26 October, Rommel launched a series of violent counterattacks. When the British held their front, on 4 November Rommel ordered his forces to retreat, after losing fifty-nine thousand killed, wounded, and taken prisoner, of whom thirty-four thousand were German. Five hundred tanks, four hundred guns, and thousands of vehicles were also lost. The British losses were 13,500 killed, wounded, and missing and 432 tanks lost. Thus ended the Battle of El Alamein, with a victorious British army in control of the western desert.

The Eighth Army now took up full pursuit against Rommel's skilled withdrawal. Advancing westward across the desert, the British entered Tobruk on 13 November, Al-Gazala on the fourteenth, Benghazi on the twentieth, Sirte on 26 December, and Tripoli, Libya, on 24 January

1943. There was little fighting during the fourteen-hundred-mile advance, but significantly, Rommel gained in strength as he fell back. The Americans, advancing from the west, soon found this out.

During the night of 6 November, Eisenhower, from his headquarters at Gibraltar, ordered his invasion force to land, despite efforts of Giraud, recently arrived from France, to delay the action. Upon learning of the Allied landing on 8 November, Mast and a few hundred men seized control of the telephone service, police headquarters, substations, and Algiers radio, from which they broadcast an appeal in Giraud's name for all French troops to rally in support of the invasion. Mast's men also cut the telephone lines leading to naval headquarters and the big coastal batteries. After placing his superior General Louis Marie Koeltz in protective custody, Mast ordered the main body of French troops, the Algiers Division, to assist the Allied landings. Guides hurried to nearby beaches where they expected the Allied forces to land, while an army detachment seized control of a nearby airfield.

Meanwhile, Murphy hurried to the residence of the French army commander, General Alphonse Juin, to urge him to support the operation. Juin insisted that only Darlan could make this decision. Murphy sent for him, and upon Darlan's arrival, the Admiral found himself a prisoner of Mast's men. Meanwhile, in Morocco General Emile Bethouart had seized control of Rabat, the capital, and awaited the arrival of the invasion force.

Resistance was light almost everywhere except at Oran, where two British cutters ran into heavy fire from French naval units in the harbor. Fire from two French destroyers sank the cutters, killing 307 Allied navy and army men and wounding 350 more. Only forty-seven soldiers landed unhurt and they were quickly captured. Fighting ceased at Oran on 10 November.

Despite sporadic resistance and confusion among both the invasion force and the French defenders, the question of continued resistance was decided in Algiers, Rabat, and Vichy. After some hesitation, Darlan, who had returned to his headquarters in Algiers, decided that this was not just another raid but a major Allied effort. He ordered Juin to cease fire and to arrange for a cessation of hostilities in Algiers. A meeting between Juin and Giraud on 11 November produced an armistice by which Giraud would take command of all French forces in North Africa, with Juin as his deputy.

Thus far the invasion and subsequent combat in Algiers and Morocco had cost the Allies 1,181 men killed and missing, of which 584 were Americans. An additional 891 U.S. soldiers, sailors, and airmen were wounded. British wounded. Political arrangements with Darlan, more than 1,600 men (two-thirds of them naval personnel at Casablanca) and another 1,000 wounded. Political arrangements with Darlan, leaving him in command, enabled Eisenhower's force to gain time and to reach Tunisia, on 15 November, before the Germans and Italians. Nevertheless, the enemy managed to land reinforcements at Bizerte and Tunis.

Operations in North Africa turned into a vast pincers movement, with the British preparing to counterattack Rommel's forces from the east, while from the west, Allied forces under Eisenhower and Clark prepared to advance on Tunisia, the base from which the Axis armies operated, after consolidating their control over Algeria and Morocco.

German reaction to the Allied landings in Algeria and Morocco was to send reinforcements to Tunisia, where they encountered and quickly repulsed French units under General Georges Barre. This was the first French military commitment in North Africa against the Germans. Field Marshall Albert Kesselring, the German commander in chief, south, had poured German and Italian troops into Tunisia to provide depth and maneuvering room for a German beachhead and to check an Allied effort from Algeria. At the same time, he would be able to protect the rear of Rommel's Afrika Korps in Libya and secure Tunisian ports for resupply.

Although Rommel despaired of holding on to North Africa, Hitler ordered him to secure Libya while the newly arrived Axis forces prepared to push westward to drive the Allies from Algeria and to possibly draw Spain into intervention on the Axis side. Both Axis and Allied forces prepared to occupy Tunisia in strength—the Allies to cut off the Germans and the Axis to drive the Allies back into the sea or back into the desert. At first the Axis held on to Tunisia, and the Allies were forced by bad weather to halt their drive.

In mid-February 1943, the Germans, advancing from their Tunisian base against Major General Lloyd R. Fredendall's U.S. Second Corps, recaptured Faïd and Kassarine passes, Gafsa, and Sbeïtla from the hastily assembled Franco-American force that had recently captured them. The next month the newly reconstituted Second Corps, commanded now by Patton, counterattacked eastward to retake Gafsa and to establish supply depots for Montgomery's Eighth Army. After outflanking the Mareth Line, the Eighth Army moved into Tunisia. Meanwhile, U.S. Major General Omar Bradley, Patton's deputy, took over the U.S. Second Corps to enable Patton to concentrate on the forthcoming invasion of Sicily. Bradley now moved northward for a drive along the coast for an advance to Mateur and Bizerte. At the same time, the British broke the Mareth Line and captured Gabès on 30 March and Sfax on 10 April. On 7 May, Bradley captured Bizerte and Montgomery captured Tunis, and Pont du Fahs fell to the French. By 13 May, Axis resistance had ceased, and after General Jürgen von Arnim surrendered 150,000 men, the total number of Axis prisoners numbered 262,000. Additional Axis losses were 30,000 killed and 27,000 wounded. Total U.S. casualties for the North African campaign were 18,558—2,184 killed, 9,437 wounded, and 6,937 missing and prisoners of war. The principal burden of the Allied military effort in North Africa had been borne by the British First and Eighth armies.

THE ITALIAN CAMPAIGN, 1943–1944

In mid-January 1943, while the Axis still occupied Tunisia, Churchill and Roosevelt and their chiefs of staff met at Casablanca in Morocco to plan for an invasion of Sicily following a victory in North Africa. Despite Churchill's preference for an initial landing in Europe, ideally somewhere in the Balkans, the CCS agreed that plans be made for a cross-channel invasion of northern France in 1944. Lack of landing craft and a need to supply the Russians would prevent a cross-channel operation in 1943. Nevertheless, plans were made for an invasion of Sicily in 1943 (Operation Husky). At a press conference in Casablanca on 24 January, Roosevelt announced, with British concurrence, his policy of "unconditional surrender" as a prerequisite for peace with the Axis powers. The Allies were to negotiate on no other terms. The policy was the result of a carefully thought-out effort to reassure the Russians that the western Allies would not make a separate peace with Nazi Germany and use it as a possible bulwark against an advance by the Soviets into Central Europe, leaving them to face the Germans alone. Moreover, the Allies did not want to repeat the mistake of the armistice of 1918 and allow the German military to recreate the myth that their armies had not really been defeated. This time the German generals, not German civilians, would surrender. The demand for unconditional surrender, however, neither promised nor precluded a reasonably generous peace.

Invasion of Sicily.

As long as the Axis powers or nations friendly to them controlled the northern shore of the Mediterranean, the Allies had to make a twelve-thousand-mile detour around the Cape of Good Hope to reach Russia, India, and China. Control of the Mediterranean was the next logical step for the Allies, taken on 10 July 1943 with an amphibious assault on the island of Sicily. As in North Africa, General Eisenhower was in supreme command, with British General Sir Harold R. L. G. Alexander as his deputy commander of Allied ground forces. General Patton's Seventh Army—whose Second Corps, with Bradley in command, landed on Sicily's southern coast—pushed with an armored spearhead northwestward across the island to Palermo. For the first time, U.S. parachute troops of the Eighty-second Airborne Division participated in division strength in combat. After seizing Palermo on 24 July, Bradley moved eastward along the northern coast. Meanwhile, Montgomery's Eighth Army had landed in the southeast and advanced northward along the east coast. After thirty-nine days of combat, the two armies closed the pincers at Messina on 17 August.

Air power, although employed in significant numbers, appears not to have been decisive—a forecast of the later campaign in the Italian peninsula. Unfortunately, Allied naval antiaircraft shot down several troop-carrying craft with their cargo of parachutists from the Eighty-second Airborne. On 19 July, 272 heavy and 249 medium bombers of the U.S. Air Force bombed the San Lorenzo and Littoria railway marshalling yards in Rome and a nearby airfield. Churches and historical monuments had been clearly identified on the maps used by the air crews, and none were damaged. The attack, however, was sufficient to force Mussolini's resignation as premier on 25 July and dissolution of the Fascist party three days later.

During the campaign, however, the Germans, under cover of heavy antiaircraft fire, managed to extricate a considerable portion of their armored and airborne troops across the Strait of Messina to the Italian mainland. The campaign in Sicily cost the Germans 37,000 men and the Italians 137,000, most of whom were prisoners of war. Allied armies lost 31,158 killed, wounded, and missing.

Invasion of Italy.

Following the German army's successful withdrawal across the Strait of Messina despite Allied air and naval superiority, the Canadian and British divisions of Montgomery's Eighth Army also crossed the strait and landed over the beaches near San Giovanni in Fiore and Reggio di Calabria on 3 September 1943, the first Allied foothold on the European continent. Italy accepted the terms of unconditional surrender on 8 September, and the next day Clark's U.S. Fifth Army, consisting of the U.S. Sixth Corps and the British Tenth Corps, came ashore at Salerno on Italy's west coast.

The Eighth Army met little resistance as it raced from the toe to the heel of the Italian boot.

On 13 September, Bari, a major east coast port, had fallen to the British, whose patrols met those from the U.S. Fifth Army forty miles southeast of Salerno. By 16 September, the Allies held a front across the peninsula from the bay of Naples to the Adriatic.

In the Salerno area, however, the Germans, who had expected and prepared for an Allied landing in the vicinity of Genoa, held the high ground, from which they mounted strong defensive operations. Eight German divisions held in the north against a possible Allied landing remained there, but the light divisions stationed in the south were sufficient to limit the two Allied armies to a slow, grinding advance from the line held on 16 September to the so-called winter line of January 1944, which extended from the west coast along the Garigliano and Sangro rivers, across the Liri Valley south of Monte Cassino and the central mountains to the Adriatic. Italian forces, now part of the Allied coalition, forced the Germans from Sardinia on 20 September. On 27 September, Foggia and its vital airfields were captured by the British and Naples fell to Clark's army on 1 October. Kesselring, in command of the German armies in southern Italy since Hitler had made his decision to hold there rather than withdraw to the north, conducted a skillful withdrawal to the Volturno River, then later to the Garigliano and Sangro rivers.

Meanwhile, Allied shipping (300,000 tons) brought forward from North Africa vast quantities of matériel, machine shops, and warehouses to establish an Allied logistical base around Naples. On 1 November 1943 the Fifteenth Strategic Air Force, commanded by General Doolittle, who had led the first air raid against Japan, was activated at the ten airfields around Foggia. From this base Allied bombers could reach into Austria and the Balkans.

On 16 January 1944, General Eisenhower arrived in Great Britain to assume duties as supreme commander of the Allied Expeditionary Forces. His place as supreme Allied commander in the Mediterranean was taken by General Sir Henry Maitland Wilson. Air Marshal Sir Arthur W. Tedder took command of the British air

fleets, and Alexander became commander of Allied armies in Italy. Lieutenant General Sir Oliver Leese took over command of the British Eighth Army from Montgomery, who returned to Great Britain as Eisenhower's deputy. Lieutenant General Ira C. Eaker became commander of the Mediterranean Allied air forces.

Anzio and Cassino. Alexander, with Churchill's encouragement, decided to outflank the admittedly strong German line by landing U.S. General John Lucas' Sixth Corps in the Anzio-Nettuno area, thirty miles south of Rome. Once a beachhead had been established, the Anglo-American forces under Lucas were to capture Rome and cut off Kesselring's armies in the Liri Valley and along the Garigliano. Under the cover of darkness during the night of 17–18 January 1944, the Allies attacked in the south along the winter line. They crossed the river on the left, but the attack ground to a halt before the village of Castelforte, while on the right it failed completely. On 22 January the Sixth Corps, composed of fifty thousand U.S. and British troops, came ashore at Anzio at 2:00 A.M.

The Germans were completely surprised, having expected a landing closer to the Garigliano River. Fortunately for Kesselring, Lucas at first consolidated his beachhead instead of immediately pushing on to the Alban Hills, the high ground overlooking the beachhead south of Rome. The Germans, aware that their lines of communication were not in jeopardy, contained the Sixth Corps flanks and spearhead to build up a strong counterattacking force, which left the Sixth Corps immobilized at Anzio for four months. Along the Garigliano at the mouth of the Liri Valley, the proposed route to Rome, the Allies fought three desperate but fruitless battles for the town of Cassino. Believing the ancient Benedictine abbey overlooking the town to be the key to the enemy's defenses, the Allied command decided to bomb it. On 14 February 1944, Allied aircraft dropped leaflets on the abbey warning the monks and refugees known to be there to leave at once. The following day, 229 bombers dropped 453 tons of bombs on the abbey and destroyed the buildings. Another bombing attack followed on the 16th, but the infantry did not attack until early on the 18th, following a five-hour artillery barrage at the rate of ten thousand rounds per hour. In the meantime, the Germans, who heretofore had remained outside the abbey, moved into the massive ruins to set up defensive positions and forced the Allies to break off their attack on the 19th. The Allies intermittently bombed and shelled the abbey and the town of Cassino for eight days. It was not until 11 May that a second Battle of the Garigliano was launched, but this time Monte Cassino was bypassed, because the Germans evacuated the ruins and withdrew into the Liri Valley.

Operation Diadem. In preparing for the spring offensive, code-named Operation Diadem, that was expected to carry the Allied armies to Rome and beyond, the inhospitable terrain before them left the commanders little choice in their selection of sites for major military operations. The western half of the peninsula, including the Liri Valley and its narrow coastal plain, offered the most favorable terrain and the best possibilities for employing Allied sea power in outflanking operations against enemy defenses. The western coastal plain extended northwestward one hundred miles from the mouth of the Garigliano to San Severo, a small port about twenty miles west of Rome. The Sixth Corps beachhead at Anzio-Nettuno lay in the Pontine Marshes at the foot of the Alban Hills. Crisscrossed with drainage ditches and irrigation canals, the terrain did not offer conditions for employment of armor on a wide front.

From its very inception, Generals Clark and Marshall had opposed the concept of the Anzio beachhead. Churchill and Alexander, however, had envisioned it as a base for a thrust northwest along the axis of Highway 6 into the Alban Hills and on to Rome, while the main Allied forces drove the enemy from the southern front up the Liri Valley into a trap to be formed by the Sixth Corps, now commanded by Lieutenant General Lucian K. Truscott, athwart enemy lines of communication around Rome. The Anzio concept was a British idea carried out in large part by Americans. It had much to do with the later Anglo-American disagreement over the ultimate role of the Allied forces.

Clark saw Truscott's corps as the potential spearhead of a Fifth Army drive on Rome. The Alban Hills and not Highway 6 had become, in Clark's opinion, the road to Rome. He believed that his forces should secure the Alban Hills before attempting to cut off the German Tenth Army's right wing at Valmontone. Alexander, on the other hand, viewed an attack from the beachhead as his most important weapon of opportunity, to be launched when the situation was fluid. If the operation went according to plan, he expected that the Sixth Corps thrust toward Valmontone on Highway 6 would possibly block the withdrawal for a large percentage of the German forces on the southern front. Although he was aware that Clark's views differed sharply from his own, he remained confident that Leese's Eighth Army, after breaking through the Gustav Line in the Liri Valley, would lead the way up Highway 6. Furthermore, the Allied commander believed that the projected French Expeditionary Corps attack (commanded by General Juin) over the Arunci Mountains on the Fifth Army's front would be a secondary and supporting effort to the main operation in the valley.

Instead, when Operation Diadem began on 11 May, the French colonial troops under Juin led the way through the Gustav Line over Monte Majo, the high ground overlooking the valley from the west. To the left of the French Expeditionary Corps, the U.S. Second Corps advanced rapidly across Monte Petrella, the high ground overlooking the narrow coastal plain, on 15 May. With an overall Allied strength of twenty-five divisions as opposed to nineteen enemy divisions, superiority in both air and artillery, sufficient reserves, and the troops rested and ready, the Fifth Army made contact with Truscott's beachhead force by 25 May. Two weeks after the beginning of the offensive and 125 days after the landings at Anzio, the troops from the southern front had joined with those of the beachhead. There remained only for Operation Diadem to break out from the beachhead and for Rome to be captured.

As Truscott prepared the Sixth Corps for the breakout and final drive on Rome, Clark decided on his own initiative to modify the British concept for the landing—a drive on Valmontone and Highway 6 to cut off the enemy withdrawal from the south. From the beginning Clark had believed that there were too many alternate roads leading northward out of the Liri Valley that would enable Kesselring to bypass a trap at Valmontone.

Clark's decision was reinforced by intelligence reports that the German 362d Division had already withdrawn from the vicinity of Cisterna di Latina before the Second Corps' front into a sector between Velletri and Valmontone, and that Kesselring had moved the Hermann Goering Parachute Division into the Valmontone gap. Clark reasoned that even if Truscott managed to reach Valmontone, his lines of communication would be vulnerable to the enemy overlooking it from the Alban Hills. Accordingly, without consulting either Truscott or Alexander, Clark decided to turn the Sixth Corps—the Thirty-fourth and Forty-fifth infantry divisions and the First Armored Division—northwestward, directly into the Alban Hills. Only the Third Infantry Division would continue in the original direction toward Valmontone and Highway 6.

The Thirty-fourth and Forty-fifth divisions attacked on 26 May, while the two British divisions demonstrated west of the Anzio-Albano road in order to hold the Germans to that front. Despite the commitment of the First Armored Division on the 28th, the Germans continued to hold their front. By then Kesselring no longer believed the Third Infantry Division's thrust toward Valmontone to be the axis of the main Allied attack from the beachhead. Only after radio intercepts identified the First Armored Division as being on the Albano-Lanuvio front did he conclude that the offensive toward Valmontone was actually a secondary effort.

This news had come as no surprise to General August von Mackensen, commander of the German Fourteenth Army, who had assumed that the Anzio breakout would move toward his Caesar Line in the Alban Hills. Consequently, von Mackensen was not caught by surprise when, on the night of 30 May, the Sixth Corps turned toward the Alban Hills and halted the offensive.

As discouraging as this repulse was to both Clark and Truscott, a means to crack the line had been found. During the night of 27 May reconnaissance patrols from the Thirty-sixth Division, probing the slopes of Monte Artemisio in the Alban Hills, had discovered a four-mile-wide gap in the Caesar Line, and two regiments began moving through it during the night of 30 May. By the morning of 31 May, the regiments were in firm control of a four-mile-wide sector of the Caesar Line, and von Mackensen's defenses were in danger.

In the meantime, Lieutenant General Geoffrey Keyes's Second Corps had reached Valmontone and Highway 6. The Fifth Army's final drive on Rome was launched on 3 June across the Alban Hills by the Sixth Corps and Second Corps astride Highway 6. It soon developed into a race between the two corps as to which would be the first in Rome. Clark, aware of the imminent cross-channel invasion of Normandy, was anxious to capture the first of the Axis capitals before the world press focused on northwestern France. Faced with an assault on Rome, Kesselring had only two choices—to evacuate Rome or to defend the city street by street and house to house. The latter would be only a modest delaying action and would leave the city in ruins and arouse the condemnation of Christians worldwide.

It was not until late on 3 June, when advance detachments of the U.S. Fifth Army drew within sight of Rome, that Berlin authorized Kesselring to approach the Allies through the Vatican to obtain a joint agreement to declare Rome an open city. Although the Allied command had called upon the civilian populace to rise up and join the battle to oust the Germans from the city, German units were already desperately trying to reach the Tiber River to escape the advancing Americans, who had vowed to spare the city only if the Germans did not resist. As German units fought on in the southern outskirts of the city, Hitler declared that Rome, "because of its status as a place of culture, must not become the scene of combat operations." This order also spared Rome's historic bridges across the Tiber. Operation Diadem, which had begun on 11 May, ended on 4 June with the liberation of Rome.

Although the British Eighth Army had originally been given the major role and a wider front, its casualties in the operation were less than those of the U.S. Fifth Army—11,639, as compared with U.S. losses of 17,931. If the losses of the attached French and British units are added to those of the Fifth Army, however, the disproportion becomes greater—28,566 for the entire Fifth Army, because the Eighth Army figures included Canadian and Polish forces as well as British. Total Allied losses amounted to 40,205 of all categories. For approximately the same period (10 May to 10 June), the two defending German armies had incurred a total of 38,024 casualties. The Allies claimed to have captured 15,606 prisoners.

The feelings of many on the Allied side were perhaps best summed up in the words of a British war correspondent: "Now, at last, the victory had arrived. It was good that it should come, for it had been bravely contested and, in the end, brilliantly achieved. But it had been a long journey, and everyone was very weary. And too many had died."

THE INVASION OF NORMANDY

The Anglo-American forces based in Great Britain had not been idle during the campaigns in North Africa and Italy. During the North African campaign, Allied navies so improved their antisubmarine tactics that by May 1943 U-boat losses rose to 30 to 50 percent of all U-boats at sea. From May onward the famed wolf packs were no longer safe from detection and attack.

Before the end of the North African campaign, owing to the successful antisubmarine campaign, the Allies had transported to Europe and Africa more than two million men and their supplies without losing a loaded troop ship. Meanwhile, the accelerated Allied shipbuilding program had outpaced the German submarine building program. Not only had the war at sea taken a bad turn for the Axis, but the German homeland had come under increasing attack from Allied bombers, with major destruction visited upon cities and industrial centers. By mid-September 1943, one million civilians had been evacuated from Berlin. Europe was awash with bombed-out refugees. The Luftwaffe had lost the war in the air before Allied armies landed in France.

Since late December 1943, Eisenhower and his three senior commanders—Admiral Sir Bertram H. Ramsay, commander of the Allied naval forces; Air Chief Marshal Sir Troffard Leigh-Mallory, commander of the Allied air forces; and Field Marshal Montgomery, commanding general of the Allied land forces—had been planning for the invasion of the Continent. The land forces consisted of the U.S. First Army, including the Eighty-second and 101st Airborne Divisions, under General Bradley; and the Twenty-first Army Group, comprising the First Canadian Army (Lieutenant General H. D. G. Crerar), the British Second Army (Lieutenant General M. C. Dempsey), the Sixth Airborne Division (Lieutenant General F. A. M. Browning), and miscellaneous Allied contingents. On 21 January, Air Chief Tedder was named deputy supreme commander to Eisenhower.

Originally, Allied planners had thought that the initial landing on the Continent (Operation Overlord) might be accomplished with three divisions. This number was eventually deemed insufficient and the force increased to five divisions. D-Day moved from 1 May to 5 June. On 21 January 1944 the changes were agreed to by Eisenhower and his commanders, who also decided upon the Bay of the Seine at Normandy as the landing area. The decision was influenced by the fact that the Cotentin Peninsula provided some protection from the prevailing westerly winds and because destruction of the Seine and Loire bridges would isolate the northwestern quarter of France. Moreover, two large ports, Le Havre and Cherbourg, lay on the flanks. Since the latter lay on the Atlantic tip of the peninsula, once it was overrun, the port would be completely isolated. Frontage on the Bay of the Seine stretched from the town of Quinéville, south of Harfleur, to the estuary of the Orne River. The Americans were to land on the western half, the British on the eastern. The first day's objective was a sixty-mile line from the Orne to the beaches at Sainte-Mère Èglise and Carentan and the towns of Bayeux and Caen, the latter linked by a canal to the channel.

Eisenhower planned first to secure a lodgement area that embraced Caen, Cherbourg, and nearby airfields. Next, the armies were to advance on Brittany with the object of capturing the ports southward to Nantes on the Atlantic coast. The Allies would then turn eastward on the line of the Loire River in the direction of Paris and northward across the Seine River to destroy as many enemy forces as possible. Operation Anvil was to begin simultaneously, with a landing in southern France, followed by an advance up the Rhone Valley to meet the forces under Eisenhower. The landing was to be made by the U.S. Seventh Army under Major General Alexander M. Patch.

Opposing the Allied offensive north of the Loire were two of Germany's most distinguished generals—Field Marshal Karl von Rundstedt, commander in chief of the western front, and Field Marshal Rommel, commander of the armies in France. The two generals held diametrically opposing strategic views. Rundstedt believed German forces to be overextended and favored evacuating France and withdrawing to Germany's frontiers. Nevertheless, he had yielded to Hitler's demand that all of France be defended and agreed that the French Atlantic ports be held to the last man to deny their use to Allied shipping. Rommel planned to engage the Allies on the beaches and

advocated strong garrisons along the coast with nearby reserves. Von Rundstedt was willing to allow the enemy to gain a landing and then counterattack before he had an opportunity to consolidate his beachhead. For this purpose, Von Rundstedt would keep the bulk of the German forces well to the rear of the coasts. These divergent views led, in the words of the British historian Major General J. F. C. Fuller, to a fatal compromise, the worst thing in war.

The Germans kept their infantry forward and the bulk of their armor in the rear, which denied them the benefit of coordination between the two arms when the crisis came. Furthermore, their coastal defenses were linear, in effect a Maginot Line with little depth. There were no secondary defensive positions. The Germans also incorrectly concluded that the Allies would make their main effort in the Pas de Calais area and concentrated their strength there. Allied aerial reconnaissance had revealed this concentration, and the Allied command encouraged the Germans to believe it to be the Allied intent. Eisenhower expected that the deception would pay enormous dividends when the cross-channel offensive began.

To support Operation Overlord, landing craft were drawn from operations in the Mediterranean, which meant that the projected landing on the Mediterranean coast of France could not coincide with the landing in Normandy as planned. A vast naval armada was assembled to cover the landings: 702 warships and twenty-five flotillas of minesweepers, eventually a total of five thousand ships and an additional four thousand ship-to-shore landing craft. All mechanized vehicles and tanks were waterproofed to permit them to be driven through deep water. To permit landings over open beaches, five sheltered harbors, code-named Gooseberries, were formed by sinking sixty blockships and two prefabricated ports, code-named Mulberries, were constructed and towed to sea in sections. An underwater pipeline, known as Pluto, was prepared to carry gasoline to the landing areas. The landings were to be covered by both tactical and strategic air power—the former to provide close air support to the landing forces and the latter to prevent reinforcements of German armor from coming forward. Guns from naval craft offshore were to provide additional support.

General Eisenhower's battle plan, in brief, was as follows: Airborne troops, employing 2,395 aircraft and 867 gliders, were to land at 2:00 A.M.; the aerial bombardment by 2,219 aircraft was to begin at 3:14 A.M. and be augmented at 5:50 A.M. by naval bombardment; the first wave of the five-division landing force, consisting of 4,266 ships and landing craft, were to come ashore at 6:30 A.M. The three airborne divisions—the British Sixth and U.S. Eighty-second and 101st—were to protect the flanks of the assault. Only the first managed to drop precisely on its objective along the estuary of the Orne. The two U.S. divisions were scattered over an area near Carentan that measured twenty-five by fifteen miles.

Prior to the invasion, during one of several Allied training exercises, two German E-boat (torpedo boat) flotillas attacked the convoy, destroying two LSTs (landing ship tanks) and damaging a third. About seven hundred men were lost during the action, reducing the Allied reserve of LSTs to none. The Germans failed to appreciate the potential damage they could inflict on the invasion fleet. Loading of the landing forces began on 30 May, with all on board by 3 June. They were divided into twelve convoys for the crossing of the English Channel, depending on their missions, assembly points, and speed. After several changes in the weather, meteorologists finally forecast a break in unfavorable weather on 4 June. Winds of 25 to 31 knots would moderate, and cloud conditions would permit heavy bombing on the night of 5 June and the morning of 6 June.

Eisenhower and his staff decided to go ahead on schedule, aware both that it was a gamble and of the hazards of delay. On the night of 5 June, five thousand ships and craft of the largest fleet ever assembled set out for the coast of Normandy. Despite several intercepted warnings to the French resistance, the Germans failed to change their state of defense readiness, which had existed throughout the spring.

The six parachute regiments of the two U.S. airborne divisions, together with organic supporting units, some of them seaborne, numbered more than thirteen thousand men. They were carried in 822 transport planes flying from nine airfields. The aircraft began taking off before midnight along routes designed to take them to the drop zones between 1:15 A.M. and 1:30 A.M. over the Cotentin Peninsula. At the same time, the British airborne began landing near Caen, and the main body of the invasion force began landing on the beaches of Normandy. After several hours of confused action by widely scattered units, the U.S. airborne divisions eventually managed to accomplish their missions and make contact with the infantry moving inland from the beaches. D-Day losses among the airborne were 1,259, including 156 known killed and 756 missing, presumed captured or killed.

Beach landing forces were greatly assisted by naval gunfire after H-hour (6:30 A.M.) that neutralized some of the enemy batteries and fortifications, broke up counterattacks, wore down the defenders, and dominated the assault areas. Early success and light casualties on Utah Beach contrasted sharply with difficulties experienced during the first hours at Omaha Beach. For most of the first day, the Germans believed that they had repulsed the Allied landing at Omaha Beach. Heavy seas helped the defenders, swamping considerable equipment before it reached the beach. Mist, mixed with the smoke and dust raised by the naval bombardment, obscured landmarks along the coast. Also, a strong lateral coastal current carried landing craft eastward of their touchdown points.

Most enemy batteries and fortifications were able to continue their fire as soon as the naval bombardment was forced to lift, as some units moved inland from the beach. The resulting heavy losses and disorganization of the first wave of troops had repercussions on each succeeding wave throughout the morning of D-Day. Nevertheless, the Germans were unable to prevent Allied lodgements on both beaches. Rommel's armor, in reserve, was too close to be mobile, being pinned down by naval gunfire and bombing, while Von Rundstedt's was too far away and was prevented from coming forward by Allied strafing and by fuel and ammunition shortages caused by a breakdown in transportation. German reserves did not arrive in time to prevent the establishment of beachheads or in sufficient strength to destroy them, as ordered by Hitler. Moving out from their beachheads, the Allies secured the Cotentin Peninsula by 18 June and captured the port of Cherbourg on 27 June, despite Hitler's orders that it be defended to the last man. The Allies now had a firm grip in Normandy and were prepared to break out from their beachhead.

Although the Allies had secured a major landing in France by the end of June, they were still far behind the original timetable set by the planners. By that time they should have held all of Normandy, but they occupied an area only about one-fifth the size of the province. The question now arose whether a military stalemate had been reached with the possibility of trench warfare similar to that of World War I. To overcome this threat, the Allies ferried additional combat troops to the Continent at the expense of service units. The imbalance between combat and service formations was not serious, because the lines of communication were short, but when the Allies eventually broke out of their relatively modest lodgement area and overran a large area, the small number of service troops might make adequate logistical support difficult.

As had been the case in Italy, local agricultural practices had compartmentalized the terrain, greatly restricting maneuvering and favoring the defense. Centuries-old hedgerows enclosed each plot of land, no matter how small. Half-earth and half-hedge, these fences had a dirt parapet at their base varying in thickness from one to four or more feet and from three to twelve feet high. Hedges of hawthorne, brambles, vines, and trees one to three feet thick and three to fifteen feet tall checked the progress of the infantry. Innumerable wagon trails wound among the hedgerows. Looking like sunken lanes, they formed a labyrinth where the hedgerows overarched the trails. For the next few weeks, this terrain determined the tactics of Allied efforts to break free of the Normandy lodgement.

Perhaps the greatest threat to the Allies, however, was the British failure to secure the port of Caen by 1 July. A vital communications center, Caen was the key to operations eastward to the Seine and southeastward to the Paris-Orléans gap. Although Cherbourg had been captured on 27 June, Montgomery deemed the capture of Caen too difficult to accomplish immediately. Eisenhower, denied access to the favorable terrain east of Caen and to the main approaches to the Seine and Paris, looked to Bradley's First Army for breakout leadership. Thus, in July U.S. troops had the difficult task of launching a major attack on the Cotentin Peninsula through terrain favoring the defense rather than over the more open terrain near Caen where, however, the Germans lay in wait for an Allied offensive.

THE BATTLE OF FRANCE

Despite the lack of a major port in France and frequent periods of bad weather that interrupted the flow of men and matériel through the artificial ports off the Normandy coast, by 25 July the Allies had assembled four armies for a breakout offensive. The Northern Army Group, commanded by Montgomery, consisted of the Canadian First Army under General Crearar and the British Second, commanded by Lieutenant General Sir M. C. Dempsey. The Second was to capture Caen and break into the Seine Valley. General Bradley was in command of the Central Army Group, which included Lieutenant General Courtney H. Hodges' U.S. First Army and (after 1 August) General Patton's Third Army.

On the Allied left wing, the Northern Army Group launched a massive holding attack on 15

July against the stronger enemy forces along the Orne River above Caen. At the same time, the First Army attacked and, under cover of heavy aerial bombardment, broke through at St. Lô (18 July) and Coutances (28 July). The Third Army took advantage of the breakthrough to advance southward by 31 July along the western side of the Cotentin Peninsula through Avranches, thence across the base of the Brittany peninsula through Rennes on 4 August. They reached Le Mans by 9 August and went to Nantes and eastward, up the right bank of the Loire to Angers, where they arrived the next day. The Eighth Corps of the Third Army had the task of over-running Brittany and capturing Saint-Malo, Brest, Lorient, and Saint-Nazaire, all of which was held by seventy-five thousand German troops to deny the Americans use of these ports to support the invasion.

Meanwhile, the Germans under von Rundstedt's successor, Hans Günther von Kluge, saw an opportunity to attempt a counterattack through Avranches and thereby cut off the Third Army, which was supplied through the narrow Avranches corridor. On 7 August the Germans launched a heavy armored counterattack against the Americans and the British and Canadians. These counterattacks continued until 12 August, but the First Army managed to hold open the corridor.

The German defense around Mortain enabled an Allied pincer maneuver to entrap the German Fifth (Panzer) and Seventh armies. Against fierce resistance, the British and Canadians fought their way southeastward to reach Falaise by 17 August. In the meantime, elements of the Third Army turned northward from Le Mans through Alençon. By the evening of 12 August, they had reached the outskirts of Argentan. Despite a severe tank battle with German Panzers desperately seeking to hold open the Falaise-Argentan pocket in order to permit the escape of their Seventh and Fifth armies, which were recalled too late from Mortain, the Allies began to close the pocket on 18 August. Moving from the north and south, the Allies pressed forward rapidly to close the gap near Chambois on 20 August. Two days later the

pocket was eliminated with the capture of 100,000 prisoners and several thousand other casualties. Although many Germans managed to escape to the east, resistance west of the Seine and north of the Loire had collapsed, and the way to Paris lay open.

The Third Army had meanwhile turned eastward to deny the Germans use of lines of communication between the Seine and the Loire. The Twelfth Corps reached Orléans on 17 August; three days later the Americans entered Fontainebleau, outside Paris. By the end of the month these advance units had passed south of Paris and moved east 140 miles to a point within 60 miles of the German frontier. Throughout this advance, fighter-bomber groups of the U.S. Ninth Air Force—attached to the ground force column—flew reconnaissance, bombed, and strafed in close support. The air force also guarded the long open southern flank of the Third Army along the line of the Loire. Allied forces took Versailles to threaten the encirclement of Paris from the south, a signal for an uprising in the city. The ten-thousand-man German garrison ignored Hitler's order to defend Paris or destroy its bridges. On 25 August, General Dietrich von Cholitz surrendered the city and its garrison to General Jacques Le Clerc of the French Second Armored Division.

An important Allied shortfall remained—most French and Belgian ports had not been taken. Brest, Lorient, Saint-Nazaire, and Bordeaux remained in German hands, which prevented the Allied armies from resupplying their forces directly from the United States. The Allies were forced to rely upon the channel ports; Dieppe was captured on 31 August and in use by 7 September, and Le Havre fell on 11 September and was opened as a port on 9 October.

As the Allied armies advanced across France they had a daily requirement of approximately one million gallons of gasoline and needed various vehicles and other supplies to keep the offensive moving. Allied bombers had destroyed so many bridges, however, that the supply problem became critical in September and October. Eisenhower had to decide whether to give supply priority to Patton, who was moving rapidly toward Metz and the Rhine River, or to Montgomery's army group, which had liberated Brussels, Belgium, on 3 September and taken Antwerp the following day. Unfortunately, Montgomery still had to fight for two months to clear the lower Scheldt River in order to open the port of Antwerp to the sea and Allied shipping, and the port was not in operation until 27 November. In the meantime, trucks of the so-called Red Ball Express rolled day and night from the channel ports to forward depots. Pipelines were also laid from channel ports overland in the wake of the advancing armies. Advanced units were supplied frequently by airlift.

In the meantime, Operation Anvil (15 August to 15 September) had opened additional ports in southern France. Supported from the ports of Marseilles and Toulon, the Sixth Army Group, commanded by General Jacob Devers and consisting of General Patch's U.S. Seventh Army and the First French Army, commanded by General J.-M.-G. de Lattre de Tassigny, moved northward toward a planned junction with the U.S. Third Army. After landing on 15 August, the U.S. Seventh Army fanned out eastward, first to take Nice, then northward to take Grenoble on 22 August, and advance up the valley of the Rhone. On Patch's left the First French Army cleared the remaining Mediterranean ports before sending units toward Toulouse and Bordeaux, while other First Army units joined Patch in his advance up the Rhone. The Germans, harassed by French resistance forces, withdrew toward Orléans. On 16 September, about twenty thousand German troops, cut off from their retreat into Germany, surrendered to the Eighty-third Infantry Division southwest of Orléans. The First French Armored Division, attached to the U.S. Seventh Army, on 11 September met with the Second French Armored Division of the U.S. Third Army northwest of Dijon.

The Sixth Army Group continued to be supplied from bases in Italy through Marseilles and Toulon. Eventually fourteen more divisions passed through these ports. With the opening of the main rail lines through Lyons and Dijon connecting the Mediterranean ports with the in-terior, the Southern Army Group was supplied, as well as the Central Army Group until the approaches to Antwerp had been cleared.

As the first summer of an Allied presence on the Continent drew to an end, thirty-eight Allied divisions—twenty American, twelve British, three Canadian, two French, and one Polish—had been landed to liberate Europe from Germany. Awaiting in Great Britain for movement to the Continent were six more U.S. divisions; three of them airborne, of which two were veterans of the Normandy invasion. In addition, the Allies mustered 4,035 operational heavy bombers; 1,720 light, medium, and torpedo bombers; and 5,000 fighter aircraft. There were more than 2,000 transport aircraft in the air transport command. As for the British, they had strained themselves to the limit. They had no more divisions not already fully committed to the fight, and national service (the draft) was calling up men between the ages of sixteen and sixty-five and women between the ages of eighteen and fifty. The Germans, however, had been able to draw upon the labor of other nationalities. In 1944 they also extended the work week to sixty hours and began combing men out of nonessential occupations. German women had not yet been drafted for work.

THE BATTLE FOR GERMANY

German armed forces facing the Allies in the west had paid a heavy price since D-Day. Approximately one million men had been in action. Of these, nearly 500,000 had been lost, 250,000 of which had been captured—135,000 between the breakout at Saint-Lô and the liberation of Paris. Of the fifty German divisions in the field in June, only ten remained as combat-effective units. By the beginning of September the Allies had taken more than 350,000 prisoners. Hitler brought back the elderly von Rundstedt to command what was left of the German armed forces in France. Von Rundstedt was more intent on withdrawing the remnants of his armies to the frontier than on trying to keep French and Belgian territory. The only serious German resistance from September to December was along the waterways controlling the approaches to Antwerp and at Metz and Aachen.

Despite Allied bombing, the Germans were busily producing a jet-propelled fighter aircraft, potentially a serious threat. Another, more immediate threat were the vaunted V-2 heavy rockets, whose production had been increased from three hundred in August to seven hundred per month from September 1944 to March 1945. First launched from sites in the Netherlands on 7 September 1944 against England, they did extensive damage and caused numerous casualties, but in no way did they prove to be decisive war-ending weapons.

After September 1944, the Luftwaffe was hampered greatly by fuel shortages caused partly by the loss of Romanian oil fields and by Allied bombing of synthetic oil plants in Germany. Diesel fuel supplies were always sufficient for the submarine service, but Allied bombing hampered submarine production despite widely scattered prefabrication facilities. Of 290 new boats scheduled between July and December 1944, only 65 were delivered. The number of submarines in service declined from 181 in June 1944 to 140 in December.

The Allies had cleared the enemy from the area north of the Loire and west of the Seine in less than three months, but three more months were needed to close up to the frontiers of the Third Reich. The reasons for this delay in the Allied advance had been chronic logistical problems caused by a shortage of service units and parts. Realizing that without the port of Antwerp it would be impossible to mount a winter campaign, the Allied command decided to allocate to Montgomery's Northern Army Group the supplies and transport needed to establish a bridgehead across the lower Rhine near the city of Arnhem in the Netherlands, then to clear the Scheldt below Antwerp, Belgium, and close up to the lower Rhine. This would eventually open up a vital port for a winter campaign and supply an average of 25,000 tons of military supplies per day.

The Netherlands were filled with natural ob-

stacles—broad streams and low-lying, often flooded, land. It was in this region on 17 September that the First Allied Airborne Army, based in Great Britain, dropped the Eighty-second Airborne Division near Eindhoven west of the Meuse, the 101st Airborne near Nijmegen between the Meuse and the Waal (an arm of the Rhine), and the British First Airborne Division at Arnhem east of the Rhine. Seizing roads and bridges, these units tried to clear the way for ground units that would follow to advance into northwest Germany. Bad weather, however, interfered with airborne resupply and reinforcement, which enabled the Germans to overwhelm the British airhead at Arnhem on 25 September. The Northern Army Group concentrated on clearing the Scheldt (9 October–9 November) so that Antwerp could be employed for resupply. Aachen fell to the U.S. First Army on 21 October, Metz to the Third Army on 22 November, and Strasbourg to the Seventh Army the following day. These advances at last brought the Allied armies up to the Siegfried Line (or Westwall). This defense was most formidable before the Saar but weakest above Karlsruhe and west of Aachen. The defense was costly: By the end of November, German losses since D-Day had risen to 750,000.

THE OFFENSIVE CONTINUES IN ITALY

Following the conquest of Rome on 4 June 1944 by the U.S. Fifth Army, the Allied effort in Italy lost much of its momentum. In June and July, the demands of Operation Anvil had stripped the Fifth Army of much of its strength. Seven of its veteran divisions—the Third, Thirty-sixth, and Forty-fifth infantry divisions, as well as one Algerian and three Moroccan mountain divisions—were withdrawn for operations in southern France. Nevertheless, both the U.S. Fifth and the British Eighth armies steadily pressed their advance toward the northern Apennines and the Po Valley. Their strategic goal was to maintain sufficient pressure against

Kesselring to prevent withdrawal of German units from Italy to reinforce other fronts beyond the Alps. Despite determined enemy resistance along the Arno River, Florence fell to British units under Fifth Army command in early August, Pisa to the Fifth Army on 2 September, and Rimini, on the Adriatic flank of the Po Valley, to the Eighth Army on 21 September. Although this enabled the British to outflank the Po Line, for the balance of 1944 the Germans managed to hold on to much of their transpeninsular Gothic Line south of Bologna until the following spring melted the snows and opened the passes.

In December, Field Marshal Alexander assumed the position of supreme Allied commander in the Mediterranean area. General Clark became commander of the Allied armies in Italy, while General Truscott took command of the U.S. Fifth Army in Italy. At the beginning of 1945, three of the Eighth Army's combat divisions were moved to northern Europe. Another division was shifted to the eastern Mediterranean to take part in operations in Greece, and one remained in reserve. The three Italian combat groups assigned to the Eighth Army were unable to replace these units in terms of quality. The Allied Strategic Air Force, however, remained stronger than the German air force in Italy and continued to assist both in supply and in harassment of the enemy lines of communication.

The Allied spring offensive began on 9 April 1945, and Bologna fell to U.S. and Polish troops on 20 April. From 23 to 25 April, the British crossed the lower Po in force, while the Fifth Army seized the Ligurian naval base of La Spezia. South of the Po, most of the army of General Heinrich von Vietinghoff (Kesselring's successor after he was reassigned to command the western front north of the Alps) had been overrun and much of its equipment destroyed. Beyond the Po during the last week in April, the British Eighth Army swept across the plain to Padua, Venice, and Treviso, and the Fifth Army, after crossing the Po as well, moved on to Verona, Milan, Genoa, and Turin, and onto the approaches to the Brenner Pass and into the foothills of the Alps. Northwest of Trieste, the British contacted Yugoslav partisans at Montfalcone, and the Fifth Army met French forces beyond Savona near the Franco-Italian frontier. In their final sweep, the two Allied armies netted more than 160,000 prisoners. Von Vietinghoff, after protracted negotiations, agreed to surrender his army unconditionally on 2 May 1945.

THE FINAL WEEKS IN THE EAST

While the Allies advanced to the Rhine in the west and to the Alps in Italy, the Soviet army offensive, begun on 23 June 1944, had advanced by August to a line including southeastern Latvia and eastern Lithuania. The Soviets also reached the east bank of the Vistula River opposite Warsaw, Poland, where they deliberately paused while the Germans crushed an uprising in the city on 5 October, and thereby eliminated the remnants of Polish leadership. Meanwhile, on 21 August, the Red Army began another offensive, this time into the Balkans. Romania was the first to capitulate; King Michael surrendered unconditionally to the Russians on 23 August 1944. On 2 September Finland broke relations with Germany and on 10 September signed an armistice with the Soviet Union. The Russians thereby recovered territory lost since 1939, plus a promise from the Finns to pay reparations. Bulgaria, although never at war with the Soviets, had otherwise sided with the Germans. The Soviet Union nevertheless declared war on Bulgaria and occupied it by mid-September. An official armistice between Bulgaria, the Soviet Union, and the western Allies was signed in Moscow on 28 October. About the same time, the Allies announced the results of a conference held 21 August to 7 October 1944 at Dumbarton Oaks near Washington, D.C., to implement the Moscow (October) and Teheran (November) declarations of 1943, which indicated their intention to establish an international organization for maintaining world peace and security.

From positions in Romania and Yugoslavia, Red Army columns bypassed northwestern Hungary to menace Austria from the southeast. The Hungarians managed to delay the Red Army at Budapest, however, until 13 February 1945. Consequently, the Russians were unable to occupy Vienna until 13 April.

THE ARDENNES COUNTEROFFENSIVE

Like the French army command in the first year of the war, in late 1944 Eisenhower placed considerable reliance on the deterring power of the rugged terrain of the Ardennes Forest in Belgium and Luxembourg and the bordering Eifel mountain region. If his confidence was soundly based, he believed that he would be able to maintain the Central Army Group's offensive into the Saarland and thereby enable the Northern Army Group to cross the Rhine below Cologne and lay siege to the Ruhr Valley. Eisenhower backed his decision and his confidence by assigning four divisions, some of them recently arrived in Europe and lacking combat experience, to a front 75 miles wide between Monschau and Trier in the Rhineland.

Allied intelligence officers knew only that a new Panzer army, the Sixth, had been formed in the vicinity of Cologne, but they were uncertain as to its purpose. If it was to be employed in a counterattack, the time and place for such an operation was unknown. Consequently, on 16 December, when the Sixth Panzer Army began to move against the northern flank of the Central Army Group, the Allies were caught by surprise. Hitler and his staff planned to drive a wedge between the Central and Northern Army groups to reach the Meuse River within two days, then to take Namur and Liège and continue on to Brussels and the port of Antwerp within fourteen days. If this offensive succeeded, the Germans planned to deny the Allies the use of Antwerp and trap the Northern Army Group in the Netherlands. Hitler called upon von Rundstedt to command the new offensive.

Von Rundstedt's force included the Sixth Army, commanded by SS General Sepp Dietrich; the Fifth (Wehrmacht) Army on its left; and the reconstituted Seventh Army, which was to hold the salient's southern shoulder against an anticipated counterattack by the Third Army, then facing the western border of the Saar.

Originally planned for 12 December, the offensive was postponed to await a period of bad weather that was expected to limit Allied air power. Four days later, when fog and heavy snow grounded Allied aircraft, von Rundstedt attacked with eight Panzer divisions across a forty-mile-wide front. Caught by surprise, many frontline U.S. units were overwhelmed, and the Germans made rapid progress on the first day, disrupting communications between the northern and southern Allied armies. Therefore, Eisenhower placed Montgomery in command of all forces north of the penetration, including the U.S. First and Ninth armies, while Bradley retained command of the forces to the south. The British Thirtieth Corps had the task of holding the line of the Meuse and the area around Liège.

The Allies managed to halt the Germans four miles east of the Meuse, largely because they held the shoulders of the German offensive and prevented the enemy from widening the base of its penetration. To the north, the Seventh Armored Division of the U.S. Ninth Army held the shoulder at Saint-Vith, and in the south the U.S. 101st Airborne Division rushed forward from a rest area near Reims and held at Bastogne, which had been surrounded by the Germans on 20 December. A change in the weather on 23 December enabled Allied aircraft to harass the stalled enemy columns. By Christmas Day the tide had turned, because the Allies attacked the flanks of the penetration from both north and south. By 2 January, von Rundstedt had decided to withdraw, but he did not receive permission to do so for a week. When the Allied pincers met at Houffalize on 16 January, the Battle of the Ardennes had been won by the Allies and the "bulge" in Allied lines was eliminated.

The failed offensive cost the Germans heavily—220,000 men, half of whom were prisoners;

more than 1,400 tanks and the destruction of assault guns; and 6,000 other vehicles. Allied losses in the Ardennes were 77,000 men—8,000 killed, 48,000 wounded, 21,000 captured or missing, and 733 tanks or tank destroyers destroyed.

Although the Ardennes counteroffensive had delayed the resumption of the principal Allied advance toward the Rhine for about six weeks, it resumed at the end of January 1945 against a greatly diminished Wehrmacht (German armed forces). The Second British Army continued its advance at Sittard and drove ten miles into Germany, as far as the Roer River valley northeast of Aachen. Diversionary thrusts by the enemy southward from the Saar toward northern Alsace and Lorraine were checked. The Colmar pocket in south Alsace on 2 February was also eliminated, which brought the Allies to the west bank of the Rhine from Strasbourg to the Swiss frontier. The territory of the French Republic had now been restored to its 1939 boundaries.

THE LAST YEAR OF WAR IN EUROPE

On 12 January the Russians launched an offensive that would carry them into East Prussia. Tannenberg, site of the great Russian defeat in World War I, fell on 21 January. By the end of the month, the Red Army was in East Prussia and held the east bank of the Oder River from the vicinity of Breslau to near Frankfurt on the Oder, within thirty miles of Berlin. On 20 January, as the American people inaugurated Franklin D. Roosevelt as president for a fourth term, a new provisional national government of Hungary signed an armistice with Russia, Great Britain, and the United States.

British and U.S. strategists were divided over the course to follow for the remainder of the war in 1945. In general, Churchill and his advisers favored a direct thrust, as soon as weather and terrain permitted, across northern Germany to Berlin. They believed that a military conquest of the capital of the Reich would lead to a quick

collapse of the Nazi regime, and, furthermore, that the city would be a valuable pawn in postwar negotiations with the Soviets. Eisenhower believed that such a drive would leave the rest of the western front at a standstill for want of logistical support. Berlin was not, in the U.S. view, worth the price, inasmuch as the Russians were already within easy striking distance of the city. For Eisenhower, the destruction of the German armies as far to the west as possible and the capture of the Ruhr war industries were the primary objectives, followed by an advance across Germany on a broad front.

U.S. Chief of Staff Marshall, at a meeting of the Combined Chiefs of Staff at Malta in January, supported Eisenhower's strategy. His five-step plan was to:

1. Close up to the Rhine, destroying as much as possible of the enemy forces.

2. Cross the Rhine at several points.

3. Send a four-pronged offensive across Germany, north and south of the Ruhr.

4. Advance eastward toward Berlin and via the valley of the Main River toward Leipzig, after meeting east of the Ruhr, to meet the Red Army on or near the upper Elbe.

5. Advance to the upper Danube, then southward to the Brenner Pass and a junction with the U.S. Fifth Army moving northward from Italy, and eastward to a second meeting with the Red Army in Austria and Czechoslovakia.

Decisions, such as zoning boundaries, had already been made in London the previous September and were to be confirmed at a forthcoming conference at Yalta, but Eisenhower deemed these matters as purely political and of little strategic importance.

It was, however, of great importance to Roosevelt to ultimately persuade the Soviet Union to participate actively in the war against Japan as soon as hostilities against Germany had ceased. The president and his advisers believed at this time that the intervention of vast

Russian manpower in the Far East was essential to the defeat of Japan. Neither Okinawa nor Iwo Jima had been taken yet, and the cumulative effect of the Allied war on Japanese shipping was not yet apparent. Costly campaigns in the Philippines and Ryukyus, followed by a costly invasion of the main Japanese islands, loomed large in Allied staff thinking. Furthermore, an expected final campaign on the mainland of China against the self-sufficient Kwantung army was possible only with the assistance of the Soviet Far Eastern Army. Air bases in southeastern Siberia were also needed. These concerns were to dominate Roosevelt's thinking at the Yalta Conference on 4–11 February 1945. Because the Soviet Union was not then at war with Japan, the Yalta agreements were kept secret until the Soviets entered the war in the Far East.

While defining the concept of unconditional surrender, the three conferees claimed supreme authority over defeated Germany, which included disarmament, demilitarization, and dismemberment of the country. Only Churchill expressed doubts as to the wisdom of these policies. The most difficult national and minority problems were deferred until the eventual peace conference. In their final declaration, the three powers, as Chester V. Easum, a distinguished American historian has written, "reaffirmed their faith in the principles of the Atlantic Charter, their pledge, as expressed in the Declaration of the United Nations, and their determination to build, in cooperation with other peace-loving nations, a world order under law, dedicated to peace, security and freedom, and the general well-being of all mankind."

Although post-Yalta criticism of Allied decisions was severe, Roosevelt could not disregard the advice of his military advisers "that virtually no price would be too high to pay for Soviet assistance to speed the day of victory over Japan as well as Germany." Furthermore, he hoped to persuade the Russians to join the United Nations and to obtain their friendship. In his decisions at Yalta, the president undoubtedly had at that time the full support of the American public, who both believed in and desired a continuation of cooperation with the Soviet Union in the postwar period. Roosevelt died (12 April) before the full consequences of the conference were realized, but, in any case, the Russians did not obtain anything of significance at Yalta that their army had not already seized or would soon take.

The Rhineland Campaign. The western Allies had resumed their advance to the Rhine southeast of Nijmegen in the Netherlands on 8 February 1945. The Northern Army Group, including the Canadian First Army, the British Second Army, and the U.S. Ninth Army on the Allied northern wing, at first made slow progress because of the waterlogged terrain of the Roer River valley. The Germans destroyed the floodgates of the Schwammanuel Dam the day before the Allied offensive began. Nevertheless, Kleve fell on 12 February, on 23 February the Ninth Army crossed the Roer, and a week later the Ninth Army, commanded by General William N. Simpson, reached the Rhine opposite Düsseldorf. The U.S. First Army, commanded by General Hodges, also advanced on the southern or right wing, its Seventh Corps reaching Cologne on 5 March. Two days later a small advance unit of the Third Corps, Ninth U.S. Armored Division in the lead, crossed the unexpectedly intact Ludendorff Bridge at Remagen, north of Cologne.

Rapidly expanding their bridgehead from Remagen, the Allies pressed northward toward the Ruhr. In response, the Germans shifted troops northward, thereby thinning out their defenses between Mainz and Mannheim and enabling Patton's Third Army to move easily up to the Rhine in its sector. On 2 March, the Third Army captured Trier and within a week pulled up to the Rhine at Andernach, northwest of Koblenz. Thereafter, it swung southward toward a junction with the U.S. Seventh Army, which on 15 March attacked the Saar salient from the south. During the night of 22–23 March, the Fifth Division of the Third Army crossed the Rhine against slight resistance, establishing a second Allied bridgehead beyond the Rhine.

After intense artillery preparation, Montgomery's Northern Army Group also crossed the Rhine in four places. Some forty thousand airborne troops (parachutists and gliders) assisted in the crossing by dropping beyond enemy defenses along the river. The Ruhr was soon encircled. The British then turned northeastward toward Hamburg and Bremen, and the Canadians swung northward to seal off the Netherlands. The fourth and fifth major crossings of the Rhine were made by the Seventh Army below Mannheim, while the French First Army crossed near Freiburg in the south. After the Allies joined hands along the east bank from Switzerland to the North Sea, they were poised for the final phase of the war—a dash across the remnant of Germany to meet the Red Army along the Elbe. By 25 March the Rhineland campaign had been completed. The Germans had lost about ten thousand men daily, raising their losses since D-Day in the west to about two million men.

By 1 April the Ruhr had been surrounded by the U.S. Ninth Army on the north and by the U.S. First Army from the south. Over the next two weeks the Americans gradually squeezed the encircled garrison, and on 16–18 April the survivors of the garrison, 325,000 men, including thirty general officers, surrendered.

Elements of the U.S. First Army, released from the Ruhr operation, had entered the city of Dessau just west of the Elbe, and on 11 April the Second Armored Division of the U.S. Ninth Army established a small bridgehead east of the Elbe near Magdeburg but withdrew within a few days. Further south, the Eighty-Third Division also crossed the Elbe but also withdrew, inasmuch as earlier Allied agreements had established dividing lines between the Soviet and western Allied occupation zones. The interzonal boundary had been drawn earlier by Eisenhower in direct negotiations with the highest Red Army echelon in order to avoid mistaken confrontation deep within enemy territory.

On 25 April patrols from the U.S. forces and the Red Army met at Torgau, between Dresden and Magdeburg, on the Elbe. German armies north and south were now separated from one another, while the U.S. First and Third armies and the First French Army moved into Czechoslovakia, Austria, and Italy, respectively, and toward junctions with the Soviets, closing up to Vienna, Dresden, Berlin, and Stettin.

Surrender. On 24–25 April, through Swedish Count Folke Bernadotte, Heinrich Himmler, the German minister of the interior, national leader of the SS, and titular commander of the Home Front, sought to arrange for a separate surrender to the United States and Great Britain but insisted upon excluding the Russians. Harry S. Truman, who had succeeded to the presidency following Roosevelt's death, replied through Bernadotte that there could be no partial surrender. German armies in the east must surrender to the Russians at the same time as those in the west. After the Soviets had been informed, negotiations were dropped.

On 30 April, Hitler committed suicide in his command bunker in Berlin. Late on 1 May, Admiral Karl Doenitz, Hitler's successor, announced on Radio Hamburg that Hitler had died "a hero's death at the head of his troops in Berlin." On behalf of the Nazi government, Doenitz once again sought to divide the Allies by saying he would continue to fight the western Allies only insofar as they hindered him in the defense of eastern Germany against bolshevism. This too was rejected, and the following day Stalin announced the fall of Berlin to the Red Army.

Hitler's death released from their oaths those German generals who had sworn fealty to Hitler as long as he lived. The military collapse followed swiftly. In Italy on 29 April, SS General Karl Wolff and von Vietinghoff signed articles of surrender for the remaining one million Germans in Italy. Field Marshal Alexander accepted the final surrender in the presence of U.S. and Russian officers on 2 May at his headquarters in Caserta.

North of the Alps the British Second Army occupied Hamburg on 3 May and Lübeck on 4 May, while Admiral Hans von Friedburg, on behalf of Doenitz, offered to surrender to the western Allies three German armies on the eastern front, in order to avoid surrender to the Russians. Montgomery refused this offer as well. On 4 May, as earlier authorized by Eisenhower, Montgomery accepted the military surrender of all German troops in northwest Germany, the Netherlands, and Denmark. The following day, the German First and Nineteenth armies, composing Army Group B in western Austria, surrendered to General Devers, commanding an Allied Army Group made up of the U.S. Seventh and the French First armies. It was not, however, until early on 7 May at Eisenhower's headquarters in Reims, France, that Admiral Friedburg and Field Marshal Alfred Gustav Jodl signed for all German armed forces an instrument of unconditional surrender. All hostilities were to cease as of midnight on 8 May. Eisenhower ordered the German emissaries to appear at Red Army headquarters in Berlin on 9 May to sign a formal ratification of the surrender instrument of 7 May.

A SUMMING UP

The human costs of the war against Germany were enormous. The German armed forces alone lost in battle about 8 million men killed, captured, or permanently disabled. Allied bombing killed 500,000 German civilians and wounded 700,000 more. Thirty thousand of the original 38,000-man submarine force was lost. Italy, Germany's Axis partner, listed 760,000 military casualties. Of that number, 60,000 had been killed, 500,000 taken prisoner, and 200,000 were missing. From 8 September 1943 to 30 April 1945, as a cobelligerent with the Allies against Germany, Italy lost 48,078 men—17,494 killed, 9,353 wounded, 17,647 missing. The Italian navy lost 3,584 men.

British military losses, including those of the Commonwealth and Empire and those in other theaters of war, exceeded one million. British merchant seamen listed 30,184 of their service dead, 5,264 missing, 4,402 wounded, and 5,556 interned. In Great Britain, there were approximately 150,000 civilian casualties.

Norway, with a population of only 3 million, lost more than 10,000, including 900 members of naval and air forces, and 3,200 merchant seamen. Poland, the first Nazi military target, had 250,000 military casualties, and had a total loss of 5 million persons, including 3 million Jews. An additional 3 million other Jews were systematically killed and millions of others were exiled. Yugoslavia lost 1,685,000 soldiers and civilians, 75 percent of them in battle with the Germans.

The United States sent more than 3 million men to the European theater and employed in combat sixty of the sixty-one combat divisions shipped there; only the Thirteenth Airborne Division was not employed. With the dispatch of these units, there were no ready combat divisions left in the United States. A total of 772,626 battle casualties were incurred in Europe, of which 135,576 were combat deaths. The infantry, comprising 20.5 percent of total armed strength, suffered 70 percent of the casualties, the rate being slightly higher among officers than among enlisted men. Improvements in surgery and medical care, such as plasma, sulfa and penicillin drugs, however, reduced the death rate from wounds to less than half the 1918 rate, returning 58.8 percent of wounded men to duty.

THE OPENING OF WAR IN THE PACIFIC

Unlike the beginning of the war in Europe, in the Pacific, the United States and Great Britain were the direct objects of Japanese aggression. Japan's primary object was to achieve economic and strategic self-sufficiency by conquering what its leaders considered to be their southern resources area—the Malay Peninsula and the East Indies. Before they could embark on this venture, however, they had to eliminate any possible response from U.S. bases at Guam and the Philippines and to neutralize the striking power of the Pacific Fleet based at Pearl Harbor and the British base at Hong Kong. Consequently, the attack on Pearl Harbor on 7 December 1941 coincided with air attacks on Clark

Field near Manila in the Philippines, Hong Kong, and Shanghai, as well as amphibious landings in Thailand and northern Malaya.

Bases for Japanese operations were available in the Pescadores Islands, at Cam Ranh Bay in Indochina, and on Palau, Saipan, and other mandated (former German) islands. Oil and gasoline depots were already in position. On 5 November 1941, Imperial Japanese Navy headquarters notified its combined fleet commanders that war was inevitable. On 21 November all forces were ordered to their rendezvous points. On 1 December the imperial government signaled their commanders that hostilities would begin on 8 December (7 December, Honolulu time).

U.S. forces in the Philippines were caught unprepared at Clark Field, as were the forces at Pearl Harbor. Even though word of the impending air action against Clark Field reached General Douglas MacArthur eight or nine hours before the arrival of the first enemy planes, he chose to ignore it. The Japanese, however, were amazed to find U.S. aircraft at Clark Field lined up in a defensive attitude. The Japanese destroyed the only radar and radio transmitter in the first assault, and half of the heavy bomber strength of the U.S. Army's Far Eastern air force and a third of its fighter force were destroyed the first day. The Japanese quickly overran the Malay Peninsula. In a desperate attempt to intercept a Japanese amphibious force, British Admiral Sir Tom Phillips left Singapore on 8 December with a heavy battle cruiser, the *Repulse,* and a new battleship, the *Prince of Wales,* which had just arrived from European waters. With the fleet were four destroyers but no aircraft carrier and no cruisers. The Japanese attacked the fleet on 10 December. Both battleships were sunk, but two thousand of the nearly three thousand men on board were rescued by the accompanying destroyers. The two commanding officers went down with their ships.

Having gained control of the air, Japanese invasion forces assembled on Formosa (Taiwan) and Palau, moved on 22 December into Lingayen Gulf, southeastern Luzon at Legaspi, and southern Mindanao at Davao. On 10 December,

Thailand had signed a ten-year treaty of alliance with Japan and on 25 January 1942 declared war on the United States and Great Britain. The United States responded on 5 February with a declaration of war against Thailand. Manila and the nearby Cavite naval base fell to the Japanese on 2 January, which enabled the Japanese Third Fleet to return to Formosa to refuel and then to participate in operations against Borneo and the Celebes.

U.S. and Filipino forces withdrew to Bataan Peninsula, across the bay from Manila. General MacArthur, under orders from President Roosevelt, broke through the Japanese blockade by patrol boat and escaped to Australia, which he reached on 17 March. General Jonathan M. Wainwright remained behind to defend Bataan until 9 April and the Manila Bay island fortress of Corregidor until 6 May, when he surrendered the remnants of his forces.

ORGANIZING FOR THE PACIFIC WAR

The U.S. Congress had passed the first War Powers Act on 18 December 1941. Empowered by this legislation, President Roosevelt established the War Production Board to stimulate and coordinate wartime production and appointed Donald M. Nelson as its chairman. The board's first task was to promote synthetic rubber production to make up for the supplies lost to the Japanese. One of the key agencies in waging total war, one of the primary purposes of the board was to deny essential war materials to the enemy by preemptive purchasing and supplying weapons and materials to the Allies and potential allies under the Lend-Lease Act. By 1942 war production in the United States equaled that of Germany, Italy, and Japan combined; in 1943 it increased by 50 percent; and by the end of 1944, production was twice what it had been in 1942.

The War Shipping Administration, established on 7 February, had control over all ocean-going shipping and added more than four thousand newly constructed ships. The United

States also greatly improved its global repair, supply, and refueling facilities and techniques.

Early in 1942, Great Britain and the United States created the Pacific War Council, which included representatives from Australia, New Zealand, the Netherlands East Indies, and India. The Combined Raw Matériels Board was organized in Washington, and the Combined Shipping Adjustment Board was formed in London and Washington. On 5 May the Allied Supply Council was organized in Australia. Thus were created the foundations of what was to be a victorious alliance.

JAPANESE ADVANCES

The Japanese pressed forward from Davao in the Philippines against the Celebes and oil-rich Borneo, using air power from one forward base to another and to support amphibious landings at Tarakan Island, 10–12 January. By 10 February they captured Macassar, on the southwestern tip of the Celebes, which gave them control of the Macassar Strait, then proceeded to Dutch Timor and Bali. The fall of Singapore on 15 February opened the way for an attack on Java from the east and west. Similar conquests were made at Rabaul and Gasmato on New Britain, Kavieng on New Ireland, and Lae on New Guinea.

Throughout this early phase of the war the superiority of Japanese air power was the decisive factor. Dutch, British, and U.S. naval and air forces were heavily outgunned and outnumbered everywhere. The Japanese, notably superior in torpedo tactics and training, also had more dependable torpedoes. Damage to Allied ships and planes was especially serious because replacements were unavailable. Repair facilities, never adequate, rapidly diminished as Japanese air power made base after base untenable. On 19 February, an air attack from four aircraft carriers attached to Admiral Chuichi Nagumo's First Air Fleet, which had begun the war in the Pacific with the attack on Pearl Harbor, destroyed nearly every ship in the harbor at the port of Darwin in northern Australia.

In a final attempt to sink Japanese convoys, in the Battle of the Java Sea, a mixed force of five cruisers and ten destroyers—Dutch, British, Australian, and American—attacked the Japanese on 27 February. Two Allied cruisers and three destroyers were sunk, but no Japanese ships were lost to surface attack. After 1 March, when five more Allied cruisers were sunk while trying to escape from the Java Sea through enemy controlled exits, the Japanese poured into Java. The U.S. cruiser *Marblehead*, crippled in earlier action, escaped from Chirluchop on Java's south coast and reached Ceylon for repairs. Two modern U.S. destroyers, the *Whipple* and the *Parrot*, four old four-stacked destroyers of Division 58, and two U.S. gunboats survived the campaign. The Japanese lost only two destroyers to submarine attack, but none were sunk by Allied surface ships. The major instrument of these victories was Admiral Nagumo's carrier strike force, a combat unit built around a core of six aircraft carriers, two battleships, two heavy cruisers, one light cruiser, and nine destroyers. Without losing a ship or having one damaged by enemy action, it had been the clear victor in operations in the Java Sea and elsewhere.

Nagumo's carriers next ranged westward into the Indian Ocean. In early April their aircraft severely damaged naval installations and shipping in Ceylon and sank a British aircraft carrier, two cruisers, and a corvette in the Indian Ocean. During the week of 2–9 April, twenty-eight Allied merchant ships were lost in waters around India, twenty-three in the Bay of Bengal. During the long run of unbroken success, Nagumo's carrier force was rarely sighted or attacked; only its planes appeared. Its mission completed, in mid-April the fleet returned to Kure in the inland Sea of Japan to refit and to replenish its complement of aircraft and pilots.

BATTLES OF CORAL SEA AND MIDWAY

The first check to the Japanese advances came in the Battle of the Coral Sea (7–8 May). To set up a defense parameter and hold on to what they had seized, the Japanese sent a task force and convoy down from Truk in the mandated Caroline Islands, seized and occupied Tulagi in the Solomons on 3 May, then turned westward across the northern arm of the Coral Sea toward Port Moresby on the southeastern coast of New Guinea. Possession of this port would have given the Japanese control of New Guinea and brought them close to Australia. To intercept them, a U.S. task force built around the aircraft carriers *Lexington* and *Yorktown* entered the Coral Sea from the southeast. Early reconnaissance had been accomplished imperfectly by land-based B-17s. U.S. and Japanese forces sought to locate one another without being discovered by the other.

On the morning of 7 May, U.S. carrier planes discovered and attacked part of the Japanese transport force and sank its escorting light carrier, *Shoho*. The following day, aircraft from each force attacked, each finding its target inadequately protected, with fighter planes away on mission. The *Lexington* was sunk and the *Yorktown* badly damaged, and the destroyer *Sims* and the oiler *Neasho* lost. Two of Nagumo's carriers, *Shokaku* and *Zuikaku*, were heavily damaged, and the destroyer *Kikuzuki* was sunk. The Japanese inflicted more damage than they received, but the principal mission of the Coral Sea operation had been accomplished—halting the southward expansion of the Japanese-dominated area northeast of Australia. The Japanese abandoned the attempt to take Port Moresby by sea, and Milne Bay on the southeastern extremity of New Guinea was occupied by Japanese forces before the end of August.

By June 1942, the Japanese knew that their expansion east and southeastward had reached its limits. Nevertheless, they believed they required outposts to guard against inevitable Allied counterattacks. They planned, therefore, to capture the Fijis, New Caledonia, and possibly even New Zealand in the southwest Pacific, Midway in the central Pacific, and some of the Aleutians in the north Pacific, in order to cut off the United States. Thereafter, they would go onto the defensive and await whether the United States, so heavily involved in a major war in Europe, would make the necessary effort to win back what had been so quickly lost.

The Battle of Midway, a turning point of the war in the Pacific, began at dawn on 4 June 1942. Admiral Isoroku Yamamoto on the super battleship *Yamato* led a force of twelve battleships and six aircraft carriers, including Admiral Nagumo's First Air Fleet, and a full complement of cruisers, destroyers, and supply ships, escorted by submarines and followed by transports carrying an occupation force.

Although the U.S. naval staff, having access to the Japanese code, had anticipated the attack, it could send only three carriers—the *Enterprise, Hornet,* and *Yorktown*—with a complement of cruisers, destroyers, and twenty-nine submarines, commanded by Admirals Raymond A. Spruance, Thomas C. Kinkaid, Frank J. Fletcher, and Charles A. Lockwood. Their strategy was to hold their carriers to the north and northeast of Midway, anticipating a Japanese aerial assault against the islands. While the enemy was so engaged, the Americans planned to launch aircraft to attack the Japanese carriers in the absence of their fighters.

When the Japanese attacked Midway at 6:30 A.M., every U.S. plane capable of leaving the ground was airborne. When the attack ended twenty minutes later, seventeen Midway pilots were missing, but U.S. aircraft and antiaircraft had shot down one-third of the attack force. Meanwhile, the U.S. carrier planes had attacked as planned. By noon they had sunk three enemy carriers, and a fourth, badly damaged, sank the following morning. The cost of this operation was high. The *Enterprise* lost fourteen of its thirty-seven dive-bombers, ten of fourteen torpedo bombers, and a Wildcat fighter plane. The *Hornet* lost all of its torpedo bombers and twelve wildcats and the *Yorktown* all but one of its torpedo bombers, two dive-bombers, and three Wildcats. A second enemy strike launched from other Japanese carriers caught the *Yorktown* with too many of its fighter planes away and so severely damaged it that it had to withdraw from action. On 7 June, while steaming toward Pearl Harbor, the *Yorktown* and its destroyer escort, the *Hammann*, were sunk by an enemy submarine.

Yamamoto withdrew westward, but as he did so two of his damaged cruisers were overtaken by dive-bombers from the *Enterprise* and *Hornet*. The cruiser *Mikama* was sunk, and the *Mogami* withdrew to Japan and remained for two years in drydock undergoing repairs. The Battle of Midway cost the Japanese four of the carriers that had attacked Pearl Harbor, a heavy cruiser, 253 aircraft, and thirty-five hundred men. The United States lost one carrier, a destroyer, 150 aircraft, and 307 men.

Although the carrier strength of the two forces was now numerically equal, Admiral Spruance's striking force had been seriously depleted and his surface complement was not comparable with his opponent's fleet. A Japanese task force of four carriers remained in the north Pacific and would have welcomed a carrier battle with the remaining two of Spruance's fleet. Against such odds, however, Admiral Chester W. Nimitz, commander in chief of the Pacific fleet, recalled Spruance and his fleet from the area.

The Battles of the Coral Sea and Midway confirmed the superiority of naval air warfare. While submarines played important roles, they were not decisive in the battle. Battleships, cruisers, and destroyers did not exchange gunfire, but without them the carriers could not have played their effective roles. Japanese sea power had been halted and forced to retreat. The enemy never regained the initiative, which henceforth remained in American hands.

On 12 June, the Japanese occupied Attu and Kiska in the Aleutians, but, under relentless shelling, the Japanese were gradually forced to withdraw from the Aleutians. They evacuated Kiska, their last outpost, at the end of July 1943, then fell back on their northernmost islands—the Kurils, Karafuto, and Hokkaido.

BATTLES FOR THE SOLOMONS

It was in the Solomon Islands in the western Pacific that the ground arm of the U.S. Navy—the Marine Corps—finally got its opportunity to engage the enemy. The Battle of Guadalcanal, Japan's farthest point of advance in the Solomons, was fought largely by the First U.S. Marine Division. On 7 August, the marines landed east of Lunga Point and quickly seized an unfinished airstrip, which they renamed Henderson Field. Located near the northern coast of the island, Henderson Field was surrounded on the west, south, and east by enemy-held territory and was the center around which fierce fighting raged for six months. Unable to drive the marines from the field with ground forces, the Japanese bombed heavily and frequently.

Rabaul on New Britain, with support from nearby islands, gave the Japanese a logistical advantage over the U.S. Navy, which was operating from faraway bases at Espíritu Santo and Nouméa. This advantage was seen during an engagement at Savo Island, northwest of Guadalcanal, on 9 August with seven enemy cruisers. The battle cost was three U.S. heavy cruisers (*Quincy*, *Vincennes*, and *Astoria*) and one Australian (*Canberra*) and caused major damage to the U.S. heavy cruiser *Chicago*. Allied losses in this engagement were 1,270 killed and 709 wounded. The Japanese lost one cruiser. The accompanying Japanese transports managed to unload their men on Guadalcanal and nearby Tulagi and withdrew unscathed.

The Japanese continued to reinforce their own forces on Guadalcanal. In waters northeast of the island, a U.S. carrier force commanded by Admiral Fletcher attempted to intercept them. On 24 August aircraft from the carrier force attacked the Japanese carrier *Ryujo* far out at sea and sank it, the destroyer *Matsuki*, and a transport, and shot down ninety Japanese planes. The U.S. task force lost twenty aircraft, and the *Enterprise* was slightly damaged by bombs. Two additional Japanese carriers and the U.S. carrier *Saratoga* also took part in the action, with the U.S. carrier *Wasp* in reserve. While serving with the *Hornet* as escort for the Marine Corps Seventh Regiment, which was being sent as reinforcement to Guadalcanal, the *Wasp* was sunk northwest of Espíritu Santo on 15 September. The battleship *North Carolina* and the destroyer *O'Brien* were also damaged by submarine attack. Fortunately, the *Hornet* recovered all but one of the *Wasp's* airborne planes.

WORLD WAR II   973

The *North Carolina* managed to reach Pearl Harbor, where it went into drydock for repairs, but the *O'Brien* sank on 19 October en route to Pearl Harbor. On 18 September the troop transport reached Guadcanal, where within twelve hours it landed four thousand men with their equipment and supplies.

Heavy land and sea battles continued. On 28 September, sixty-two Japanese planes attacked Guadalcanal, and twenty-three bombers and a fighter were shot down without the loss of a single U.S. aircraft. Up to that time, more than two hundred Japanese aircraft had been lost during the battle for Guadalcanal as opposed to thirty-two American. From 16 to 25 October, antiaircraft fire destroyed ten enemy planes, while fighters dispersed 103. U.S. losses for the same period were fourteen.

On 15 October, the U.S. Army Americal Division landed four thousand troops on Guadalcanal to reinforce the four thousand marines landed earlier. By then, Japanese strength on the island had risen to about thirty thousand men. Undeterred by their defeat in the eastern Solomons, the Japanese used fast destroyers at night to continue to reinforce their forces on Guadalcanal. Steaming through what was known to the Americans as "the slot" between New Georgia, Choiseul, and Santa Isabel, the destroyers were referred to as the "Tokyo Express" by U.S. troops.

Early in October, a Japanese task force, composed of four heavy cruisers and a destroyer, headed toward Cape Esperance on Guadalcanal's western extremity. It was surprised and attacked in an engagement on 11–12 October off Javu Island by a U.S. force of four cruisers and five destroyers commanded by Rear Admiral Norman D. Scott. One U.S. destroyer, the *Duncan*, was lost, and the Japanese heavy cruiser *Furutaka* and a destroyer were sunk by gunfire. Two more enemy destroyers were sunk by aircraft from Henderson Field the next day. Nevertheless, the Japanese destroyers managed to land troops and heavy artillery at Tassafaronga, and on 14 October the Japanese shelled the Americans from the sea.

On 24 October, twenty-four Grumman fighters shot down twenty Japanese fighters and a bomber. The following day, marine pilots shot down seventeen enemy fighters and five bombers, but by 26 October, the marines had only twenty-three fighters, sixteen dive-bombers, and one torpedo plane left on Henderson Field. Naval efforts to resupply the marines eventually enabled them to survive the offshore enemy gunfire, mud, mosquitoes, malaria, and food shortages, and to hold the island and begin to roll back the Japanese invasion of the southwest Pacific area.

In the period 25–27 October, the Japanese sent from Truk and Rabaul the largest naval and air fleet they had assembled since Midway. Admiral Nagumo commanded the force, which included four battleships (*Hiei, Kirishima, Kingo,* and *Haruna*), four carriers, and cruisers, destroyers, and submarine scouts in proportion. Meanwhile, two U.S. carrier task forces formed around the *Hornet* and *Enterprise* and moved into the area west of Santa Cruz Island, east of San Cristoval, and southeast of Guadalcanal. On 26 October, Japanese dive-bombers and torpedo bombers from the *Shokaku* and *Zuikaku* took advantage of the absence of the *Hornet's* aircraft away on mission and so badly damaged the ship that it was abandoned and later sunk by U.S. destroyers. The U.S. force also lost seventy-four planes to antiaircraft and the destroyer *Porter* to a submarine in the Battle of Santa Cruz. The *Enterprise*, the battleship *South Dakota*, and the cruiser *San Juan* were damaged, leaving the *Saratoga* the only carrier in the area still fit for action. The Japanese, in turn, lost 100 aircraft and two destroyers, and eight other warships were damaged, including the carrier *Ziuho*, whose flight deck was badly damaged. The *Shokaku* was heavily damaged and knocked out of the war for nine months.

By mid-November 1942, the tide of battle had turned in the Solomons. Deeming destroyers ultimately unsatisfactory to support a force large enough to defeat the Americans on Guadalcanal, the Japanese assembled a fleet of heavy transports with ten thousand replacements and thirty-five hundred elite assault troops. During the night of 12–13 November, near Savo Island, Admirals D. J. Callaghan in the *San Francisco* and Norman Scott in the *At-*

lanta, together with their destroyers, attacked head-on the battleships *Hiei* and *Kirishima* and fifteen destroyers. Although the Japanese guns were loaded, their ammunition was not armor-piercing, unlike their torpedoes.

U.S. cruisers concentrated close-range fire long enough to disable the *Hiei*. The following day, aircraft from Henderson Field so badly damaged the battleship that it was scuttled by its crew. The Japanese also lost two destroyers. Callaghan was killed aboard the *San Francisco*, which incurred major damage, and Scott was killed on the *Atlanta*. The new light antiaircraft cruiser *Juneau*, badly damaged, was torpedoed the next day as it attempted to reach Nouméa with the *Helena* and *San Francisco*. Four U.S. destroyers were also sunk. The next night Japanese cruisers shelled Henderson Field.

On 14 November, Japanese troop transports again approached the island. Eight were sunk, and four were beached at Tassafaronga under attack from marine aircraft operating from Henderson Field and from the *Enterprise*, which, after making emergency repairs, had returned to battle. During the night of 14–15 November, battleships fought one another with radar-directed 16-inch guns. Drawing most of the Japanese fire, the *South Dakota* enabled Admiral Willis A. Lee, in the new battleship *Washington*, to concentrate his fire and sink the *Kirishima* and an accompanying destroyer. The United States lost three more destroyers, the *Benham*, *Preston*, and *Walke*. Although the Japanese had sunk seven U.S. destroyers at a cost of only three of their own, the loss of two veteran battleships and thousands of troops on the transports discouraged the Japanese commanders.

Nevertheless, they attempted once again to reinforce at night with destroyer transports. They were frustrated but at a high price. The cruiser *Northampton* was sunk by torpedoes, and three other cruisers, the *Minneapolis*, *New Orleans*, and *Pensacola*, were severely damaged. In February 1943 the Japanese at last began to evacuate their forces from the island. In the first week of February, twelve thousand to thirteen thousand men were withdrawn. By 9 February, General Patch reported the island cleared of the enemy.

Of the sixty thousand marines and soldiers committed on Guadalcanal, 1,592 were killed in action and many more were incapacitated by wounds and disease. The Japanese had committed thirty-six thousand men, of which one thousand were taken prisoner and nine thousand died of disease. Twelve thousand or so were listed either as killed or missing.

The battles at sea for the Solomons cost the United States and the Japanese twenty-four ships each. Although greatly inconvenienced by the loss of thousands of troops, Japan was more affected by the loss of warships and their crews, which could not be replaced easily. The country was mortally wounded by the severe depletion of land and naval air strength. Moreover, its subsequent defensive efforts were weakened as the result of its losses. It no longer had enough aviation gasoline, training facilities, or time to train and to replace those pilots lost during 1942 in the Indian Ocean, at Midway, in the Coral Sea, and in the Solomons.

SUBMARINE WARFARE

Fortunately, the attack on Pearl Harbor had virtually ignored submarine base and repair facilities, and the U.S. Pacific submarine fleet immediately went on a counterattack. In addition to seventy-three submarines then under construction, the U.S. Navy had fifty-five large and eighteen medium submarines in the Pacific. Japan, which in 1930 had been given treaty right to submarine parity with Great Britain and the United States, had about sixty. As the war continued, the United States increased the number of its fleet of submarines, while Japan only maintained its number of fleet-type submarines and kept an average of forty to forty-five vessels continuously in operation, despite ultimately the almost total destruction of its surface navy. Midget submarines, built for coastal defense, were rarely used.

Neither Japanese nor U.S. submarines had adopted the German snorkel device that enabled the vessels to draw in air for their diesel engines and crews when submerged. Japanese submersibles were faster on the surface but slower when submerged than U.S. vessels, but they were also inferior in radar equipment, radio communications, and electronic search and sound gear that served as underwater eyes and ears. The only advantages the Japanese enjoyed were numerous bases near their operating areas and more reliable torpedoes. Although U.S. torpedoes improved somewhat toward the end of the war, they had many operational faults.

In the first two years of the war, submarines usually operated independently, but in the last years frequently in groups of three. Communication between submarines was always at the risk of betraying one's position, and the boats usually remained silent while on mission. Missions were usually to penetrate enemy defenses, to injure where possible, to operate by stealth, and to strike without warning. Their most important service, however, was cutting the lifelines of Japan by sinking its cargo ships, tankers, and transports. The Japanese, in turn, used their submarines with their fleets of other warships against carriers and cruisers. They were not very effective, however, against U.S. convoys, transports, and naval tankers.

Although Allied submarines sank twenty-five Japanese and five German U-boats in the Pacific, submarines rarely fought their counterparts, but they remained effective throughout the war. The last major U.S. ship lost was the heavy cruiser *Indianapolis*, torpedoed east of Leyte on 29 July 1945 by the Japanese submarine I-58. The last Japanese ships sunk by a U.S. submarine were two coast defense frigates torpedoed in the Sea of Japan on 14 August 1945 by the *Torsk*.

It was merchant shipping, however, that held together the Japanese Empire. At the beginning of the war, Japan had approximately six million tons of merchant shipping. Although three million tons were needed by the civilian economy, more than two-thirds of all available shipping had been allocated immediately to the armed forces. Destruction of this shipping was the U.S. submarine fleet's primary mission. The highest total number of submarine cruising days spent on offensive patrol in operating areas in one month in 1942 by U.S. submersibles was 512 each in November and December; fifty-

five ships were attacked in December, 159 torpedoes expended; in August 1943, 858 days, 105 ships attacked, 387 torpedoes expended; in September, 697 days, 112 ships attacked, 461 torpedoes; in October 1944, 1,306 days, 230 ships, 799 torpedoes; in June 1945, 1,067 days, 147 ships, 522 torpedoes. In July of 1945, the number of targets, military or other, diminished sharply. In August only fifty-nine ships were attacked.

New Japanese ship construction could not keep pace with this loss rate. Starting at 27 percent of losses from all causes in 1942, it reached its peak at 877,392 tons, 49 percent of losses from all causes in the first half of 1944. In the second quarter of 1945, it had fallen to 15 percent. The main islands of Japan were steadily being blockaded. The U.S. Navy paid a price for this success. Of the 288 submarines that saw active duty, 52 (just less than one in five) were lost—a number nearly equal to the number of the larger fleet type available in the Pacific at the beginning of the war. Thirteen percent of the enlisted men, or 3,505 men, and 16 percent of the officers were lost at sea. The Japanese lost 103 submarines and at war's end had only 58 left, many of them unfit for service. Germany lost 801 submarines with thirty thousand men; Italy lost 85 vessels.

THE PACIFIC WAR, 1943–1945

Operations in New Guinea. In July 1942 the Japanese had landed strong forces at Buna, Gona, and Sarnanda on the northeast coast of New Guinea and began to push southward overland toward Port Moresby. During the last week of August, they landed troops at Milne Bay but were driven off in September-October with heavy losses by Australian troops. Australian and U.S. troops of General MacArthur's Southwest Pacific Command, based in Australia, blocked the Japanese overland advance toward Port Moresby and pushed them back toward Buna-Gona.

Lack of adequate overland routes on New Guinea compelled both the Allies and the Japanese to depend almost entirely on air and sea transport. Consequently, on 2–4 March 1943 the Japanese suffered heavy losses in the Battle of the Bismarck Sea, when more than three hundred land-based Australian and U.S. aircraft destroyed eight loaded cargo transports and four destroyers. Although 2,734 Japanese survivors were rescued by Allied destroyers and submarines, more than three thousand went down with their ships.

Although driven from Guadalcanal in February 1943, the Japanese continued to consolidate their airfields and bases to the northwest. The U.S. forces in the south Pacific therefore undertook the conquest of New Georgia. Losses in this operation included the light cruiser *Honolulu* and the destroyer *Gwinn,* as well as damage to the light cruiser *St. Louis.* On 5 August the Americans captured Munda and immediately placed it in operation as a base for future operations. By 9 October, New Georgia was completely occupied. MacArthur's combined forces began a long process of island-hopping and leap-frogging on 30 June along New Guinea's northern coast—a course that eventually carried them back to the Philippines.

Central Pacific, November 1943–November 1944.

Captured by the Japanese in December 1941, Tarawa was the first of the Gilbert Islands to fall to the Second U.S. Marines, on 20–24 November 1943. The battle cost the marines 20 percent casualties among its fifteen thousand combat troops, but of the nearly five-thousand-man Japanese garrison, only 146 were taken prisoner. At the same time, Makin, also of the Gilberts, fell to the Twenty-seventh U.S. Army Division with significantly fewer casualties. Undefended Apamama Island was quickly taken on 21 November by troops landed from a submarine. These operations were all supported by nine hundred carrier-based aircraft. The escort carrier *Liscome Bay* fell victim to a submarine, but the light cruiser *Independence* survived a torpedo attack.

In December 1943, Rabaul, already partially neutralized by carrier-born air strikes, and with the seizure of neighboring islands, was isolated by the capture of Arawe (15 December) and

Cape Gloucester (26 December), in southwestern and northwestern New Britain. After the Japanese withdrew their air strength from Rabaul, U.S. forces seized the Admiralty Islands on 1 March 1944.

From the Gilberts, the Allied offensive moved westward to the Japanese-mandated (formerly German) Marshall Islands. Once again a joint U.S. Army-Marine operation took place. The U.S. Seventh Infantry Division, which on 3 June 1943 had retaken Attu in the Aleutians, and the Fourth Marine Division landed on the Marshalls on 31 January 1944. By 4 February they had completed the conquest of Kwajalein and Majuro, each with atolls offering excellent anchorages.

While U.S. carrier planes raided Truk, Ponape, and the Marianas, the Eniwetok atoll was taken 17–22 February by the U.S. Seventh Division and a marine combat team sailing from Kwajalein. By 25 March all the Admiralty Islands were in U.S. hands, thus neutralizing the Japanese central and southwest Pacific base. In a carrier strike 16–17 February, 200,000 tons of merchant and naval shipping were destroyed. All major Japanese naval vessels abandoned the area and retired either to the Palaus or to their home islands. Except at Brunei Bay on the coast of Borneo and Singapore, the Japanese fleet was back where it had started the war and with far less strength. Moreover, the surviving portion of the Japanese First Air Fleet, found in the Marianas in February 1944, was destroyed.

The Fifth U.S. Marine Amphibious Corps, consisting of the Second and Fourth Marine Divisions, landed on Saipan on 15 June 1944, followed by the Twenty-seventh U.S. Army Division. One month of bitter fighting followed before the enemy garrison was destroyed. From 21 July to 9 August the Seventy-seventh Infantry Division and the Third Marine Division and a Marine Corps brigade fought to conquer Guam, but the conquest of Tinian took only nine days (24 July–1 August). While the fighting went on, engineers prepared runways for the B-29 Superfortresses to use as bases for long-range strategic bombing of Japan. The first major air strike took off on 24 November from

Saipan, which had been declared secure on 9 July.

Japanese efforts to frustrate the operations in the Marianas failed. Three Japanese aircraft carriers and two tankers were sunk, two of the carriers by submarines. One carrier was the veteran *Shakaku*, sunk by the *Cavalla* on the submarine's first patrol. The submarine *Albacore* torpedoed the *Taiho*, Japan's newest and the world's largest (31,000 tons) battleship. Four other carriers, the battleship *Haruna*, and the cruiser *Mayu* were also sunk, which so decimated the Japanese naval air fleet that it was now nearly finished as a factor in the war. The U.S. battleships *Indiana* and *South Dakota* incurred some minor damage in the attack of 19 June.

The first U.S. Marine Corps Division, meanwhile, had landed on Pelelui in the Palau group of the western Carolines on 15 September 1944, and two days later the Eighty-first Infantry Division landed on Angaur, south of Peleliu. Except for a few snipers still hidden in caves, the conquest of both islands was completed on 13 October. On 21 September, Ulithi fell, where the U.S. command established an advance naval base that helped support later operations in the Philippines. As Peleliu fell, the southwest Pacific command's Thirty-first and Thirty-second army divisions seized Morotai, south of Minanao in the Philippines.

Burma-India-China Theater. On 12–25 May 1943, the Anglo-American (Trident) Conference took place in Washington. Generals Joseph W. Stilwell, Claire L. Chennault, and Albert C. Wedemeyer, and a representative from China, argued over differing priorities for the Indo-Burma theater of operations. One of the decisions made was to increase the quantity of aviation gasoline being flown from India into China in order to increase the effectiveness of Allied airpower on mainland China. By January 1945, the Himalayan air route alone was carrying 46,000 tons of gasoline a month.

The Quebec (Quadrant) Conference took place on 11–24 August 1943 to establish the Southeast Asia Command, with Lord Louis Mountbatten as supreme commander with Stilwell as his deputy. He was replaced in the autumn of 1944 by Wedemeyer, who was preferred by Chinese commander Chiang Kai-Shek. The combined Royal and U.S. combat air forces, including the U.S. Tenth, were placed under the command of U.S. General George E. Stratemeyer. On 7 September, MacArthur, having moved his headquarters from Brisbane, Australia, to Hollandia, Indonesia, reorganized his ground forces as the Sixth and Eighth armies under Generals Walter Krueger and Robert L. Eichelberger, respectively.

In February 1944, in the Hukawng Valley in northern Burma, two Chinese divisions, reequipped and trained by General Stilwell in northeastern India, joined Merrill's Marauders, an all-volunteer force of three thousand men commanded by General Frank D. Merrill. On 17 May this combined force captured a Japanese airstrip at Myitkyina and the town on 3 August, while General Orde C. Wingate's British and Indian jungle troops blocked the Irrawaddy Valley. From then on the attempted Japanese invasion of northeastern India was halted, as the Allies steadily drove them from Burma.

The Stilwell Road, a 400-mile military highway from Ledo, India, that joined an existing 717-mile road to Burma from Kunming, China, was completed by 28 January 1945, and the first convoy of trucks carrying war matériel reached China from northeast India. Meanwhile, Japan's sea-lanes to Burma had been cut, while the British captured Mandalay on 21 March and Rangoon on 3 May. Lord Mountbatten estimated that the Burma campaign had cost the Japanese a total of 300,000 casualties, including 97,000 dead.

Until the Marianas base was opened in June 1945, U.S. B-29 Superfortresses flew bombing runs from Chinese bases to Japan. In May 1944 and April 1945, the Japanese launched their last major offensives of these years in a vain effort to make it impossible for the U.S. Air Force in China to join hands with those operating over the Philippines and the Ryukyus. General Stratemeyer's Tenth and Fourteenth air forces operated out of Linchow and Kunming. Living largely off the land, the Japanese continued to occupy most of China's most fruitful areas until ordered by their government to surrender in September 1945.

Philippines Campaign, 1944–1945. As the U.S. Navy closed in on the Philippines in September 1944, Admiral Halsey suggested that the date for the invasion of Leyte Island be advanced to 20 October from 20 December. The CCS, then in conference in Quebec, approved, and troops, already battle-loaded for other objectives, were diverted to join others in the main effort.

In a series of preliminary air strikes on Okinawa, Luzon, and Formosa beginning on 19 June, Task Force 38 encountered the most violent enemy air resistance east of Formosa. In the fiercest battle of the war to date between ship- and land-based aircraft, the Japanese lost 650 planes in the air and on the ground. Their repair shops, facilities, and bases also suffered major damage. During the two-day Battle of the Philippine Sea, Task Force 38 lost 76 aircraft in combat and operational accidents. The Japanese defeat in the battle helped significantly to determine the outcome of the later battles for Leyte Island and Leyte Gulf.

The United States had assembled 53 assault transports, 54 assault cargo ships, 151 tank landing craft, 72 infantry landing craft, 16 rocket launching ships, and 400 assorted amphibious craft to carry the U.S. Sixth Army to Leyte. Planes from 18 escort carriers provided an umbrella for the invasion fleet. Six battleships, with cruisers and destroyers, served as naval escort as the troops came ashore south of Tacloban on 20 October. The Americans needed Leyte as a base for future operations in the Philippines. The Japanese were aware of this and sought to reinforce their garrison through the west coast port of Ormoc. General Tomoyuki Yamashita came down from Manchuria to take charge of the defense of the Philippines. He brought with him one of the finest Japanese divisions from the Kwantung army. By the end of November, U.S. troops had reached Limon on the northern part of the Leyte Island. Ormoc fell on 11 De-

cember, following a landing by the Seventy-seventh Division. Japanese resistance on Leyte ceased by the end of the year.

The Japanese High Command realized that holding the rest of the Philippines was vital for their survival, because if the Americans captured the islands, they could close the China Sea to Japanese shipping and cut off the oil of Sumatra and Borneo. Consequently, the High Command decided to commit their last line of naval defense, their battle fleet, to break up the defensive cordon of the U.S. Third and Seventh battle fleets around the Leyte area.

The U.S. Seventh Fleet, under Admiral Kinkaid, came up from the southwest Pacific with MacArthur, and the Third Fleet under Admiral Halsey came across the central Pacific under the general direction of Admiral Nimitz.

Vice Admiral Takeo Kurita, with a central attack force of four battleships, including the two giants *Musashi* and *Yamato,* eight cruisers, and eleven destroyers, was to push through the Sibuyan Sea and the San Bernardino Strait, then turn southward to Leyte Gulf, where a supporting attack force moving through the Surigao Strait under Admiral Shoji Nishimura was to join him.

During the battle on 23–25 October, Kurita's force lost two heavy cruisers, the *Maya* and the *Atago,* to the U.S. submarines *Dace* and *Darter.* A third cruiser, the *Takao,* was heavily damaged and returned to Brunei Bay with an escort of two destroyers. Kurita transferred with his staff to the *Yamato.* While passing through the Sibuyan Sea on 23 October, Kurita's fleet was attacked by U.S. carrier-based planes, which destroyed the *Musashi.* Kurita flinched but then recovered, continued during the night through the San Bernardino Strait at high speed, and appeared in the morning off Samar. Nishimura's support force was attacked south of Leyte on the night of 24–25. The Japanese lost two battleships, a cruiser, and three destroyers, largely by gunfire, and approximately five thousand men.

Before dawn on 25 October, Kurita escaped through the San Bernardino Strait to attack a weak Seventh Fleet outpost of light escort carriers, destroyers, and a destroyer escort, all that stood between him and his quarry in the Leyte Gulf. He managed to destroy the U.S. carrier *Princeton,* two escort carriers, the *Gambier Bay* and *St. Lô,* and the destroyer escort. Three Japanese heavy cruisers were disabled by aircraft, another by a destroyer's torpedo. The superstructure of the *Yamato* was so badly damaged that the ship was virtually isolated from the rest of Kurita's fleet. Fearing a trap, he reversed his course and again retreated through the San Bernardino Strait.

Carrier- and land-based aircraft harassed the retreating Japanese through 26 October and brought Kurita's losses to three battleships, four carriers, including the *Zuikaku,* ten cruisers, nine destroyers, and a submarine—45 percent of the tonnage committed. The U.S. fleet lost only 2.8 percent of its total tonnage committed to the action.

The conquest of Leyte was completed in December 1944, and the U.S. Seventh Fleet's escort carriers entered the Sulu Sea in support of a two-regiment task force that landed on the south coast of Mindoro. Concerned about this new threat to their South China Sea lifeline, the Japanese had expected their base on Palawan to be the object of the next Allied attack. Consequently, they had only a small garrison on Mindoro, which fell quickly to the U.S. troops that quickly established a base on the island from which to cover an amphibious landing on Luzon. Feints were made to suggest that the next landing would take place on the south coast of Luzon.

In early January 1945, a U.S. Army assault force on transports passed east of Leyte through the Surigao Strait and the Mindanao and Sulu seas. When the landing force turned northward off the west coast of Luzon, it was attacked by land-based Japanese suicide bombers. Despite efforts from the U.S. fast carrier force to close down the Japanese airfields, sixteen ships were hit on 6 January, ten of them incurring serious damage. Nevertheless, sixty-eight thousand U.S. troops landed at Lingayen Gulf on 9 January and a deep beachhead was soon established. Although the Japanese had landed at the same site in 1941, they were apparently surprised by the move.

MacArthur first deployed a cover force to protect the beachhead from strong enemy forces known to be located in the hills to the north and east. He then sent, as the Japanese had done three years before, an armored spearhead southward to Clark Field and Manila. On 29 January a second landing was made at Subic Bay and quickly sealed off the Bataan Peninsula as its base. Two days later, the U.S. Eleventh Airborne Division made an amphibious landing on the west coast at Nasugbu, south of Manila. Within a week the First Cavalry and Eleventh Airborne reached the outskirts of Manila from the north and the south. On 16 February troops landed on Corregidor by parachute and from the sea. Manila was taken on 23 February, and Manila Bay was soon open. More than 4,215 Japanese were killed during the conquest of Corregidor while the United States lost 136 killed, 8 missing, and 513 wounded.

In late February and into March, under the cover of aircraft based on Palawan Island, landings were made against feeble resistance on Panay, Cebu, and Negros. Nevertheless, stubborn and prolonged fighting took place as the enemy retreated into the hilly interior of the islands. Fighting for Mindanao lasted from March until May. At that time in Borneo, Australian and Netherlands East Indies troops took Tarakan Island, Brunei Bay, and adjacent airfields on 10 June and Balikpapan in July.

Resistance continued on Luzon throughout the summer, while U.S. forces steadily expanded their control from Legaspi and Manila, pushing north and northeastward from the central Luzon plain. By 1 July the Cagayan Valley had been cleared. Japanese losses in the Philippines totaled 317,000 killed and 7,236 captured, as opposed to 60,628 U.S. troops killed, wounded, and missing.

With the Philippines in hand, U.S. and Allied forces had virtually cut off the Japanese from the South China Sea. On 11 January a fast U.S.

carrier force had run the strait between Formosa and Luzon, then swept southward along the China coast to Hong Kong and Cam Ranh Bay in Indochina, sinking forty-six ships, including seven large tankers. Seven thousand Japanese aircraft and most of their surface fleet had now been lost. The Allies carried the war into the main islands of Japan through heavy aerial bombardment from bases in the Mariana Islands. Iwo Jima and Okinawa remained to be conquered to enable bombers to operate freely.

Iwo Jima and Okinawa. Iwo Jima, valued for its strategic location—less than eight hundred miles from Tokyo—was the first Japanese possession to be invaded in the war. It had two airfields and was defended by a garrison of more than twenty thousand men under the command of General Tadamishi Kuribayashi. The Third, Fourth, and Fifth marine divisions had trained in the Hawaiian islands for the invasion of Iwo Jima. A fleet of 495 ships carried the assault force of 75,144 men and 36,164 garrison troops to Iwo, supported by seven old battleships, four heavy cruisers, and fifteen destroyers.

On the eve of the invasion, 16–17 February, a fast carrier force of 118 ships, including 8 battleships and 17 aircraft carriers with 1,120 planes, made the first carrier-based raids on the Japanese home islands.

Upon completion of this aerial bombardment, the marines landed on Iwo's southeastern shore on 19 February. Although the bombing had destroyed most surface installations, the island was honeycombed with well-concealed emplacements that had been dug in on the slopes of Mount Suribachi, a volcano that dominated the beach. Other emplacements on a hill at the other end of the beach had also survived. Marines took Mount Suribachi on 23 February, but several weeks of hard fighting followed before the enemy was burned or blasted out. The last Japanese sortie from an emplacement was made on 27 March, ten days after the island had been declared secured.

The defense of Iwo Jima had cost the Japanese an estimated total of 21,304 men, of whom 13,234 were counted and buried by U.S. forces. Two hundred and twelve were taken prisoner. U.S. casualties, not including naval losses, were 4,590 killed, 301 missing, and 15,954 wounded.

The first of the two airfields taken was quickly placed into operation, despite occasional enemy mortar fire from the high ground, saving many lives in emergency bomber landings. A submarine and seaplane lifesaving service was maintained between the island and Japan. A meteorological station was also established, and as long as the war lasted, and for several months thereafter, Iwo was the hub of airborne traffic over the western Pacific.

The U.S. strategic assault forces of the central Pacific next concentrated on forthcoming operations against Okinawa. The largest island in the Ryukyus, Okinawa was large enough to accommodate several large airfields and to serve as a staging area for troops assembled for the invasion of Japan. The island also offered excellent anchorages for naval installations. Most important, it lay athwart Japan's remaining sea and air routes to Asia and the South China Sea and was only 350 miles from the home islands. To prevent interference from the Japanese, carrier aircraft bombed installations in the Inland Sea on 19 and 24 March, then the nearby Kerama Islands were seized on 26 March by the U.S. Seventy-seventh Division to provide an anchorage and seaplane base.

The Okinawan campaign (1 April 1945–21 June 1945), while the last of the Pacific war, was one of the most difficult and costly. The battle for Okinawa was fought by an expeditionary force of 1,213 ships and 451,866 ground troops, covered and supported by a U.S. carrier force of eighty-two ships and a British carrier force of twenty-eight. The latter also bombed Formosa and other Japanese bases. On 1 April the combined ground forces landed with comparative ease on the southwestern coast of Okinawa. Marines and army troops advanced then separated, the marines turning to the north and the army divisions to the south, where they encountered the main enemy resistance in well-prepared positions. Within a week four divisions had landed and Wontan Airfield was prepared for operations. The northern part of the island was secured two weeks later, and the marines joined the army units in a final assault in the south. Despite fire support from battleships and carrier aircraft, organized resistance continued until 21 June.

More than 110,000 Japanese died in defending the island, and approximately 7,500 were taken prisoner. U.S. casualties were 7,213 killed and 31,081 wounded. The U.S. commanding general, Simon Buckner, was killed three days before all resistance collapsed.

At sea, Japan's last battleship, the *Yamato*, a light cruiser, and a destroyer escort were sunk. Suicide aircraft called kamikaze attacked relentlessly, destroying thirty-six ships, twenty-eight by air attack, of which twenty-six were victims of kamikaze. None larger than a destroyer, however, was lost. The Okinawa campaign cost the Japanese navy more than seventy-eight hundred aircraft, of which more than three thousand fell victim to U.S. naval and marine aircraft; 2,655 pilots were lost through operational losses caused by poor pilot training and careless ground crews; and 2,498 sailors went down with the *Yamato*. In addition to ships sunk, U.S. naval losses from 1 April to 1 July were 368 ships damaged, 763 planes lost, 4,907 men killed or missing, and 4,824 wounded. The cost of the battle for Okinawa was high, but a final staging base for the last offensive against the main Japanese islands was won.

On 19 March, 22 June, and 24 July, two thousand carrier-borne aircraft and those based on Okinawa completed the destruction of the Japanese navy in the Inland Sea, and U.S. submarines entered the Sea of Japan to destroy the remaining shipping to the Asiatic mainland. From the new airfields on Okinawa hundreds of heavy bombers and strafing fighter aircraft joined others from the Marianas and Iwo Jima in attacking the main Japanese home islands. Seven times in July and once in August, naval craft bombarded Japanese coastal areas. Two hundred fifty-eight Allied aircraft were destroyed by enemy antiaircraft and 104 in operational mishaps, while 1,386 Japanese planes were destroyed in the air and on the ground,

and 1,980 were lost because of operational mishaps. Throughout July and August 1945, the Allies maintained a complete air and sea blockade of Japan.

Bombing of Japan. Although military resistance on the main islands had been substantially weakened, the Japanese still had five million men in eastern China, Manchuria, and Korea. The Allies had long assumed that large-scale landings on the main islands would be needed, and such landings, it was estimated, would result in one million casualties. Much, therefore, depended upon when the Russians would enter the war against Japan. Against the strategic background, the employment of the atomic bomb appeared as a means to make the Japanese realize the futility of further resistance. Commenting on the decision to bomb Hiroshima and Nagasaki, Secretary of War Henry L. Stimson wrote, "We had developed a weapon of such revolutionary character that its use against the enemy might well be expected to produce exactly the kind of shock on the Japanese ruling oligarchy which we desired, strengthening the position of those who wished peace, and weakening the military party."

The city and military base of Hiroshima was bombed with an atomic bomb on 6 August and the city and naval base Nagasaki with a similar weapon on 9 August. More than 100,000 people died as a result of these two attacks. Approximately the same number had perished in a series of firebomb attacks on Tokyo in 1945. On 8 August, the day before the attack on Nagasaki, the Soviet Union declared war on Japan and rapidly conquered Manchuria, southern Sakhalin, and the Kuril Islands. On 12 August the Red Army entered Korea.

JAPANESE SURRENDER

On 10 August the Japanese government offered to surrender militarily if the prerogative of the emperor as sovereign in Japan could be preserved. The Allies agreed but stated that from the moment of surrender his authority and that of his government were to be subject to the authority of MacArthur. The Potsdam Declaration of 26 July 1945 had already stated the Allied terms for Japan: limitation of Japan's sovereignty to its home islands; Allied occupation; liquidation of war industries; trial and punishment of war criminals; freedom of speech, thought, and religion; and removal of obstacles to the revival and strengthening of democratic tendencies among the population. These terms were similar to those already imposed upon Germany.

At midnight on 14 August 1945, President Truman and Prime Minister Clement Attlee announced that the surrender terms had been accepted by Japan. The next day Emperor Hirohito ordered a cease-fire. On 19 August, representatives of the Japanese armed forces received the instrument of surrender at MacArthur's headquarters. The famed Kwantung Army in Manchuria surrendered to the Red Army on 21 August. On 27 August, U.S. troops took over Atsugi Airfield near Tokyo and began the occupation of Japan.

The instrument of surrender was signed by representatives of the Imperial Japanese government aboard the battleship *Missouri* at anchor in Tokyo Bay on 2 September 1945. Scattered surrenders took place later in the southwest Pacific and in China, culminating in the surrender of Hong Kong on 16 September.

The war cost the Japanese more than five and a half million casualties, of whom more than half a million were civilians. Of Japan's 12 battleships, only one was left; of 22 carriers and escort carriers and 43 cruisers, none was operational; of 165 destroyers, 26 had been heavily damaged; and of 104 submarines, 26 (6 of them German) had survived. Japanese merchant shipping losses exceeded by one-third the tonnage with which Japan had started the war, and replacements by new construction were less than two-fifths of losses; 116,000 had been lost from the merchant marine; twenty-seven thousand were dead or missing.

The United States had sent 1.25 million men to the Pacific. Total casualties amounted to 170,596, of whom 41,322 had been killed.

OCCUPATION OF GERMANY AND JAPAN

With the cessation of hostilities, demobilization of the nation's armed forces proceeded rapidly. One-half of the army's remaining strength remained overseas, however, assigned to the occupation of Germany and Japan. A large force also remained in Korea, with a Soviet force sent into Korea to accept the surrender of Japanese troops stationed there.

At first, the Allied powers, under policies adopted at Yalta and Potsdam, assumed joint sovereign authority over Germany on 5 June 1945. The Allied Control Council, however, was unable to achieve the necessary unanimity. Consequently, each of the occupying powers—the United States, Great Britain, France, and the Soviet Union—developed its own policies and administration for its own zone. The result by September 1949 was a divided Germany, the Federal Republic of Germany comprising the area of the U.S., British, and French zones, and a communist government, the German Democratic Republic, came into existence in the Russian-occupied eastern zone.

Republican federalization of the U.S., British, and French zones was completed with the adoption of a federal constitution by a parliamentary council in Bonn on 8 May 1949. The basic law provided for a federal diet, or Bundestag, whose members would be directly elected for a four-year term, and a federal council of Bundesrat, composed of State of Land governments. The constitution provided that the Bundestag choose a new chancellor by majority vote before it could, by a vote of no confidence, ask the president to dismiss the old one. This resulted in a more stable government than that of the former Weimar (prewar) constitution. U.S. forces continued to occupy Germany until 5 May 1955.

The occupation of Japan, which began on 27 August 1945, developed differently, as a result of President Truman's insistence that the entire country be placed under U.S. control. The Far East Advisory Commission, representing the eleven nations that had fought against Japan, was headquartered in Washington, with a branch in Tokyo. Real power, however, rested with General MacArthur. Unlike Germany, Japan retained its government. By mid-1947, the free election of a new diet and a thorough revision of the nation's constitution began Japan's transformation into a constitutional democracy, with the emperor's role limited to that of a constitutional monarch. The way was thus opened for the ultimate restoration of Japanese sovereignty. A final peace treaty was signed by the United States and Japan on 8 September 1951.

BIBLIOGRAPHY

Grand Strategy

Butler, J. R. M., ed. *History of the Second World War: Grand Strategy*, 6 vols. (1956–1976).

Cline, Ray S. *Washington Command Post: The Operations Division* (1951).

Churchill, Winston. *The Second World War: The Grand Alliance*, 6 vols. (1948–1953).

Conn, Stetson, and Byron Fairchild. *The Framework of Hemisphere Defense* (1960).

Craven, Wesley F., and James L. Cate, eds. *The Army Air Forces in World War II*, 7 vols. (1948–1958).

Fuller, J. F. C. *The Second World War, 1939–1945: A Strategic and Tactical History* (1968).

Green, Constance M., Harry C. Thomson, and Peter C. Roots. *The Ordnance Department: Planning Munitions for War* (1955).

Millett, John D. *The Organization and Role of the Army Service Forces* (1954).

Morison, Samuel E. *United States Naval Operations in World War II*, 15 vols. (1947–1962).

Romanus, Charles F., and Riley Sunderland. *Stilwell's Mission to China* (1953).

The War Against Germany and Italy

Ambrose, Stephen E. *The Supreme Commander: The War Years of General Dwight D. Eisenhower* (1970).

Beckett, Ian F. W. *Great Campaigns of World War II* (1991).

Bennett, Ralph F. *Ultra in the West: The Normandy Campaign of 1944–1945* (1980).

Blumenson, Martin. *Anzio: The Gamble that Failed* (1963).

———. *Breakout and Pursuit* (1964).

Brereton, Lewis Hyde. *The Brereton Diaries* (1946).

Clark, Mark W. *Calculated Risk* (1950).

Cole, Hugh M. *The Lorraine Campaign* (1950).

———. *The Ardennes: The Battle of the Bulge* (1965).

Critchell, Laurence. *Four Stars of Hell: The 501st Parachute Infantry Regiment in World War II* (1947, 1987).

D'Este, Carlo. *World War II in the Mediterranean, 1942–1945* (1990).

Eisenhower, Dwight D. *Crusade in Europe* (1948).

Fisher, Ernest F. *Cassino to the Alps* (1989).

Garland, Albert N., and Howard McGaw Smyth. *Sicily and the Surrender of Italy* (1965).

Gelb, Norman. *Desperate Venture: The Story of Operation Torch, The Allied Invasion of North Africa* (1992).

Gibson, Hugh, ed. *The Ciano Diaries, 1939–1943* (1946).

Goebbels, Joseph. *The Goebbels Diaries* (1983).

Halder, Franz. *Hitler as War Lord* (1950).

Harrison, Gordon. *Cross-Channel Attack* (1951).

Hastings, Max. *Overlord: D-Day and the Battle for Normandy* (1984).

Howe, George F. *Northwest Africa: Seizing the Initiative in the West* (1957).

Kappe, Siegfried, and Charles T. Brusaw. *Soldat: Reflections of a German Soldier, 1936–1949* (1992).

Keegan, John, ed. *Churchill's Generals* (1991).

Kemp, Anthony. *The Unknown Battle: Metz, 1944* (1981).

MacDonald, Charles B. *The Mighty Endeavor: American Armed Forces in the European Theater in World War II* (1969).

———. *The Last Offensive* (1973, 1984).

———. *Company Commander* (1978).

———. *A Time for Trumpets: The Untold Story of the Battle of the Bulge* (1984, 1985).

Merriam, Robert. *Dark December* (1947).

Montgomery, Sir Bernard L. *El Alamein to the Sangro River* (1974).

———. *Normandy to the Baltic* (1974).

Paisley, Melvin. *Ace: Autobiography of a Fighter Pilot, World War II* (1992).

Plivier, Theodor. *Stalingrad*. Translated by Richard and Clara Winston (1983).

Pogue, Forrest C. *The Supreme Command*, 2 vols. (1959).

———. *George C. Marshall*, vols. 2 and 3 (1966, 1973).

Root, Waverly L. *Secret History of the War: Casablanca to Katyn* (1946).

Ruppenthal, Roland G. *Logistical Support of the Armies*, vols. 1 and 2 (1954).

Schlabrendorff, Fabian von. *The Secret War Against Hitler*. Translated by Hilda Simon (1965).

Sears, Stephen W., ed. *Eyewitness to World War II: The Best of American Heritage* (1991).

Smith, Bradley, F., and Elena Agrossi. *Operation Sunrise: The Secret Surrender* (1979).

Stettinius, Edward R. *Roosevelt and the Russians: The Yalta Conference* (1949, 1970).

Trevor-Roper, H. R. *The Last Days of Hitler* (1947).

Weigley, Russell F. *Eisenhower's Lieutenants: The Campaigns of France and Germany, 1944–1945* (1981).

Werth, Alexander. *Russia at War, 1941–1945* (1964).

Wheeler-Bennett, John. *Munich: Prologue to Tragedy* (1948, 1964).

Wilmot, Chester. *The Struggle for Europe* (1952).

Wood, Edward W., Jr. *On Being Wounded* (1991).

Young, Desmond. *Rommel, the Desert Fox* (1951).

The War Against Japan

Baker, Leonard. *Roosevelt and Pearl Harbor: The President in a Time of Crisis* (1970).

Belote, James, and William Belote. *Titans of the Sea: The Development and Operations of Japanese and American Carrier Task Forces During World War II* (1975).

Falk, Stanley. *Bataan: March of Death* (1962).

Feifer, George. *Tennozan: The Battle of Okinawa and the Atomic Bomb* (1992).

Griffith, Samuel B. *The Battle for Guadalcanal* (1979).

James, D. Clayton. *The Years of MacArthur, 1941–1945* (1975).

King, Ernest J. *The U.S. Navy at War, 1941–1945* (1946).

La Forte, Robert S., and Ronald E. Marcello, eds. *Remembering Pearl Harbor* (1991).

Layton, Edwin, with Roger Pineau and John Costello. *And I Was There* (1985).

Leahy, William D. *I Was There* (1950).

Marshall, S. L. A. *Island Victory* (1983).

Miller, John, Jr. *Guadalcanal: The First Offensive* (1949).

Morris, Samuel E. *United States Naval Operations in World War II*, 15 vols. (1947–1962).

Morton, Louis. *The Fall of the Philippines* (1953).

———. *Pacific Command: A Study in Interservice Relations* (1961).

———. *The War in the Pacific, Strategy and Command: The First Two Years* (1962).

Pelz, Stephen. *Race to Pearl Harbor: The Failure of the Second London Naval Conference and the Onset of World War II* (1974).

Prange, Gordon J. *At Dawn We Slept* (1981).

———. *Pearl Harbor: The Verdict of History* (1986).

———. *December 7, 1941: The Day the Japanese Attacked Pearl Harbor* (1987).

———. *God's Samurai: The Lead Pilot at Pearl Harbor* (1990).

Pratt, Fletcher. *The Marines' War* (1946).

Roscoe, Theodore. *United States Submarine Operations in World War II* (1949).

Smith, Robert Ross. *The Approach to the Philippines* (1953).

———. *Triumph in the Philippines* (1963).

Spector, Ronald. *Eagle Against the Sun: The American War with Japan* (1985).

Stimson, Henry L. "The Decision to Use the Atomic Bomb." *Harper's Magazine* (February 1947).

———. "The Nuremberg Trial: Landmark in Law." *Foreign Affairs* (January 1947).

Stockman, James R. *The First Marine Division on Okinawa, 1 April–30 June 1945* (1946).

Toland, John. *The Rising Sun: The Decline and Fall of the Japanese Empire* (1970).

Toynbee, Arnold J. *Civilization on Trial* (1960).

Tregaskis, Richard. *Guadalcanal Diary* (1955).

Van der Vat, Dan. *The Pacific Campaign: World War II and the U.S.-Japanese Naval War, 1941–1945* (1991).

Woodward, C. Van. *The Battle for Leyte Gulf* (1947).

THE COLD WAR

Donald J. Mrozek

The cold war (1945–1990) was conceived in a curious union of victory and fear. Conquest over European and Asian fascism in World War II sent a thrill of accomplishment through the United States, Great Britain, and the Soviet Union, but it also raised deep anxiety over the shape of the future. World War II virtually destroyed two major regional powers—Germany and Japan—each with global aspirations. The removal of their strong military forces, each of which had played a critical role in the balance of power in its respective region, created a vacuum into which the war's most prominent winners might press—or be pulled. The price of victory for Great Britain was so high that it became, at least with respect to British overseas interests and colonies, nearly a Pyrrhic one. Similarly, in France, victory was a word more than a psychological fact, and internal recriminations would long preoccupy the French and limit their role in shaping postwar political structure in Europe, let alone beyond it. The impoverishment of nearly all of Europe, whether its countries had been victim or villain, weakened the economic base needed to sustain influential military force. The economic strength of the United States was one of the few remaining forces capable of extending influence far beyond its national borders, thus providing discipline and structure abroad. The military strength of the Soviet

Union was, or at least seemed to be, another expansive force, extending itself into other countries. The cold war, conceived amid these tensions, was born when anxiety over the consequences of a global war overcame hope for the prospects of a simple peace.

In essence, the cold war supposed the necessity of competition between the political systems and power blocs led by the United States and the Soviet Union, but did not presume the inevitability of full-scale military conflict. In one sense, it was merely the ancient game of regional and world power cast in modern dress, a competition in which political, social, economic, and military power had always been intertwined to some extent. New conditions in the world after 1945, however, did make for a highly distinctive experience. The most important technological development was the invention of nuclear weapons, and the second most important one was the perfection of means to deliver them, notably by long-distance bomber aircraft and then long-range missiles. A key political and cultural problem was that U.S. and Soviet leaders saw one another's political, social, and economic systems not only as dangerous but as evil. This combination of the capacity to inflict swift mass destruction and a largely Manichean vision of world politics made the prospect of global annihilation seem real, and the perception arose among U.S. military and political leaders that they were dealing with problems of a wholly unprecedented nature. In this context, traditional military experience and advice lost status, while civilian strategists became both more numerous and more influential. Saving the United States and its allies from threat and attack in an era when nuclear weapons proliferated became the central task of these new planners and a focal preoccupation of U.S. political leaders.

In grand strategic terms, the cold war was marked by its comprehensiveness of scope, which included the entire world, and by the chilling majesty of its risks, which entailed increasingly the virtual destruction of the earth itself. In this sense, "total war" became a literal possibility and hence a vivid nightmare. In military terms, however, the cold war held curious parallels with warfare in the eighteenth century, when maneuvering sometimes led to battle but just as often served as a substitute. The buildup and deployment of forces was intended to achieve objectives by having the enemy rationally calculate that it would likely be defeated in the event of actual combat, thus affording one victory without fighting an all-out war. Deterring an adversary from an attack also suggested that military power was inseparably intertwined with all other elements of national strength. If war was the continuation of politics by other means, as Carl von Clausewitz has suggested, then politics was also the waging of war by means other than actual armed combat. Short of "hot lead" fired in open battle, the conflict was, therefore, a "cold" war.

Despite the often stated—and often erroneous—notion that Americans have frequently won a war and lost the subsequent peace, U.S. officials gave considerable attention to the shape they wished the future to take even while World War II was still under way. Soviet leaders appear to have done much the same, largely within their own ideological framework. American military planners, obligated to foresee dangers before they had actually materialized, speculated on the identity of future potential adversaries even before the enemies of World

War II had been defeated. Assuming that long-term restraints would be placed on both Germany and Japan, which was the case after 1945, military planners were seemingly left with no plausible enemy other than the Soviet Union. Economic and related foreign policy pressures were to be placed on Great Britain by the United States, aimed at breaking the "imperial preference" system in trade, which gave Commonwealth countries a tariff advantage that made U.S. goods less competitive. No one, however, saw Great Britain as a likely military opponent. Similarly, France and China lacked the economic strength and the political cohesiveness to pose credible military threats. Moreover, China had been a wartime ally and, under the major provisions of the new United Nations organization, was slated to serve as a major power, positively disposed toward Western democratic ideas. This forecast proved unduly sanguine, because Nationalist leader Chiang Kai-shek, favored by the United States, faltered before the Communist forces led by Mao Tse-tung in China's long civil war. The distress and disappointment of U.S. leaders were great when Mao consolidated his victory in mainland China and established the People's Republic of China in 1949. In 1945, however, China could not be—and was not—characterized as a likely threat and potential enemy.

It would be too much to say that the Soviet Union appeared as a potential adversary simply by default, because there were concrete differences in opinion between Harry Truman and Joseph Stalin over the future of the defeated enemies and the liberated peoples as well. It would, however, be too little to ignore how the element of accident—the removal of Germany and Japan, two traditional regional forces from the arena of international power—exaggerated and warped both the roles and images of the United States and the Soviet Union. Unlike Great Britain, whose colonial empire was entering a protracted period of dissolution, the United States retained and, indeed, expanded its informal empire of economic, political, and cultural influence. Unlike France, torn not only by defeat but by half a decade of collaboration with its conquerors, the United States gloried in a newly appreciated sense of itself as purposeful and capable in world affairs. China, a potential world power was treated as an actual one, thanks to Franklin D. Roosevelt's insistence and Stalin's acquiescence, fell back upon itself in its civil war, stripping it of the ability to exert monitoring influence over East Asia, notably Korea and Japan. Meanwhile, the Soviet Union, although physically devastated by German military campaigns and by a horrid occupation, emerged from the war with a measure of unity born of fighting a clear external enemy. Its "internal empire" was thus politically intact and poised to rebuild.

Despite their efforts to generate pro-Soviet sentiment in the United States during World War II, U.S. leaders had never been enthusiastic about the Soviet system or those who ruled it. Before Franklin Roosevelt, presidents had been clearly condemnatory of what the Soviet Union was and of what it did. President Woodrow Wilson had considered the Bolshevik Revolution a betrayal of Russia's chance for liberal democracy, and none of his three Republican successors—Warren Harding, Calvin Coolidge, and Herbert Hoover—chose to seek diplomatic relations with the Soviet Union. The underlying ideological objection of U.S. leaders to the Soviet Communist system never ceased, even when opinions varied about how Soviet ideology was to be countered. Deemed a victim during World War II, after the war the Soviet Union was soon seen not only as a predator but as evil.

In a world sensitized by revelations of the slaughter of millions of European Jews and others by the Nazis, state-sanctioned atrocities and even war itself took on a new aspect. The postulation of a new category of "crimes against humanity," such as at the trials of former Nazi leaders at Nuremberg, meant the insertion of a particular morality into world affairs and into the discourse of power politics. At the same time, the newly established United Nations, aimed at eradicating "the scourge of war" altogether, and condemning all intrusive exercise of force, provided a new forum for the expression of world opinion and cultivated the belief that

ethical concerns must be embodied in the actions of even powerful states. Although the Soviet Union participated in the judgment of the indicted Nazis, it was subject to criticism itself for its own internal state terrorism, which had been an international scandal in the 1930s, and for expansionist military action against Finland and Poland at the start of World War II, bases that resembled the charges leveled against those in the dock.

Shortly after the end of World War II, President Truman and other key U.S. political leaders, as well as foreign leaders, such as Winston Churchill, viewed the Soviet Union as an evil force, advancing a doctrine as malicious and dangerous as nazism. Speaking in Fulton, Missouri, in March 1946 as a former prime minister and with President Truman present, Churchill spoke of an "Iron Curtain" being drawn down through the heart of Europe from north to south, portraying Soviet communism as "a peril to Christian civilization." Political passion increasingly joined religious rhetoric in the condemnation of the Soviet Union, most notably for its actions in Eastern Europe, where it ran roughshod over democratic processes and installed pro-Soviet governments in such countries as Poland, Hungary, Bulgaria, Romania, and Czechoslovakia. The transformation of Eastern Europe into a cordon of Soviet client states was depicted by many Americans not only as a political act but as the advance of "godless communism." Even worse, as an unlimited evil, communism could be expected to seek victims around the world. Such talk made the postwar contention between Eastern and Western blocs not only an exercise in *realpolitik* but an intense moral challenge in which compromise was death and neutrality a sin. Commonly, leaders spoke of unprecedented dangers, unique challenges, and the monstrous evils of the principal adversary, claiming that civilization itself had never been so endangered as it was in the cold war. The intense rhetoric of the cold war and the specific metaphors in which it was cast—with Christian civilization threatened by a communist antichrist—provided a favorable climate for greatly enlarged military spending in peacetime and greatly broadened military action as well.

Seen in the broad context of world history over the centuries rather than as some conceptually peculiar and chronologically isolated moment, the cold war emerged as a seemingly inevitable effort to fill great vacuums of power in different parts of the world. For this reason, the cold war may be said to have started in 1945, fast upon the conclusion of war in Europe and even before the conclusion of the war against Japan.

In July and August 1945, Truman, Churchill, and Stalin met at Potsdam, Germany, to deal with such questions as the political destiny of Germany and its wartime allies and victims, especially in Eastern Europe. The atmosphere of the meeting was less than cordial. For example, Truman had recently cancelled shipments of supplies to the Soviet Union that had been authorized under wartime lend-lease legislation. At the same time, he resisted various Soviet plans for extracting war reparations payments from Germany and other wartime enemies, such as Finland. For his part, Churchill aimed to revitalize Great Britain's battered global empire, an ambition philosophically and politically repugnant to both Stalin and Truman, albeit for fundamentally irreconcilable reasons. He also wished to reassert British interests in Greece and to preclude a future Soviet naval influence through the Dardanelles into the Mediterranean region. Stalin evidently intended to protect the Soviet Union from any prospect of future invasion by creating a buffer zone in Eastern Europe, an undertaking that was to challenge both U.S. and British interests. Therefore, a classic redistribution of power was under way even before Japan, the remaining member of the Axis powers that had not yet surrendered, had been defeated.

During the cold war, both the leaders of the Soviet Union and those of the Western bloc spoke as if their confrontation was without historical precedent. Instead of a unique clash of completely new forces and ideologies, however, the cold war embodied the basic elements of the traditional "balance of power" politics. Stalin himself hinted at this when, in discounting the Vatican's ideas about postwar Europe, he wryly asked how many armed divisions the pope had. Churchill also hinted at this same dynamic when he tried to quantify U.S., British, and Soviet influence in Eastern Europe and the Balkans with percentages that varied from one country to another. Ideology, whether communist or capitalist, was not irrelevant, but underlying shifts in the actual balance of world power were the base on which specific actions depended.

As natural and customary as such a reconfiguration of power was in the aftermath of a great war, it took place in a distinct historical moment whose features lent shape and tone to the cold war and were thus at the heart of the cold war's special identity. For one thing, Great Britain had been weakened badly as a world economic power as early as World War I, and its position eroded even more in World War II. Its economy and infrastructure had sustained great damage during the war, and it would be preoccupied for some two decades before the rebuilding could be called complete.

At the same time, Great Britain's military posture was weaker than it had been in peacetime for centuries. Its ground forces were swiftly returned to typically low peacetime levels on an all-volunteer basis, which was the standard British practice. The Royal Navy had declined in relative strength since the introduction of steel hulls and other technological advancements spawned by the industrial revolution of the nineteenth century. Although the Soviet navy remained small and limited in its capability, the U.S. Navy was the largest, strongest, and most versatile in the world. The Royal Navy had once aspired to a strength equal to that of all other navies combined and to a mission of dominance and control of the seas on a global scale. After World War II, it was not only inferior to that of the United States, it was also most likely insufficient to service Great Britain's far-flung empire, too expensive to increase to meet those needs, and distinctly ill-suited to deal with anticolonialist protest and activism in such places as India. British naval construction had not given priority to carrier task forces, a fact born out of necessity in World War II, thus denying Great Britain much-needed flexibility to deal with its widely distributed imperial interests. The preponderance of its investment in military aircraft had been shot down during the war, and what remained was numerically and in many ways qualitatively inferior to the U.S. Army Air Forces (and, after 1947, to the U.S. Air Force).

The Soviet Union emerged from World War II as the country with by far the largest ground forces, although the numerical weight was not surprising when compared to Russian forces in World War I. On the other hand, Soviet forces were now present in Central Europe, and many Western leaders regarded this as a new problem. From a broader perspective, the Soviet expansion into Eastern Europe was a reassertion of age-old Russian imperial interests in Poland, Romania, Bulgaria, and elsewhere, based partly on the theory of Pan-Slavism, which supposed the unity of all Slavic peoples under Russian leadership. Although some experts on Russian and Soviet history, such as George Kennan, a key enunciator of the U.S. policy of containment of the USSR, understood this, no influential political leaders thought that Russia's long history of intervention in Eastern Europe justified a lasting Soviet military presence or political hegemony in the region.

Where Soviet forces would be deployed and for how long became a contentious issue and, for Western leaders, a highly disturbing one. Soviet participation in the occupation of Germany and Austria placed it far forward of its own boundaries. Although the Soviet Union had built numerous aircraft during the war, their primary purpose had been support of ground forces, making a Soviet bomber force only a potential threat in 1945. The Soviet aircraft industry, however, had proven its mettle in World War II and its potential might be realized rapidly. Soviet naval forces remained minimal by comparison to those of the United States and even to those of Great Britain.

Based on its forces, industrial capacity, economic vitality, scientific establishment, and the number and adaptability of its people, the United States stood at the end of World War II as the greatest and the most immediately capable military power in the world. The obvious superiorities of the United States were concentrated in higher technology rather than in sheer numbers, however, and U.S. military planners were never able to shake off a persistent fear of being outmanned. This fear had deep roots, dating back to such confrontations with American Indians during the colonial era as King Philip's War (1675–1676) and to occasions of manifest local inferiority, such as in the Battle of the Little Big Horn (1876). Taken as a practical matter, however, the great masses of Soviet troops in the heart of Europe inspired a search for means to offset this apparent advantage. Technology seemed to afford the answer. A substantial U.S. air force remained in Britain after World War II under special provisions, and U.S. forces acquired important forward bases for the projection of U.S. military power and its corresponding political influence, such as in Japan after its defeat. U.S. naval forces were not only large but diverse, and they enjoyed versatility as to mission so that they could be used in a wide range of possible conflict situations. These forces enjoyed wartime port visitation rights far from the United States, and they would win similar privileges in the postwar era in Italy, Japan, the Philippines, and elsewhere.

Pressure to return millions of draftees to civilian pursuits rose sharply at the war's end, and demobilization proceeded in due course, causing some inconvenience in the fulfillment of U.S. responsibilities in the occupations of Japan and Germany and in other duties. Nevertheless, the military draft was permitted to lapse and was not restored until 1948, in a time of growing tension with the Soviet Union. Destined to last for a quarter of a century, the selective peacetime conscription of citizens for long-term service in the armed forces violated the long-standing American opposition to a peacetime draft and also broke the long-held fear of a standing army.

At the end of World War II, the espoused political goals of the United States included freedom and self-determination on a global scale, while those of the Soviet Union included the hastening of worldwide revolution. In practice, however, the two superpowers settled into the old habits of spheres of influence, and their military forces and strategies conformed to the characteristics of their respective spheres. In a sense, the cause and effect may have been the other way around, because the force structure of each country dictated what strategy was practical at any given time. The land forces of the Soviet Union significantly outnumbered those of the United States, while U.S. air and sea forces were manifestly superior to those of the Soviet Union. It was a conflict, as Kennan suggested, between a dinosaur and a whale.

The peculiar quality of the distribution of power after World War II was sharpened by the determination to keep Japan and Germany militarily weak. On the face of it, this seemed an obvious solution to many at the time, such as Secretary of the Treasury Henry J. Morgenthau. Yet, even in the early years after the war, some keen observers, such as James V. Forrestal, the first U.S. secretary of defense, cautioned that limiting Japan and Germany to police forces deprived two important regions of counterweights to otherwise potentially dangerous elements. In Central and Eastern Europe, most evidently, Germany and Russia had offset each other for decades. The removal, or artificial control, of these states' military roles would necessitate the quick rigging of new schemes to compensate for them.

The most striking and immediately impressive complicating factor in the distribution of power was the emergence of nuclear weapons. In the early years of the cold war, this awesome and novel development was held solely by the United States, which successfully tested an atomic bomb in the New Mexico desert while Truman, Stalin, and Churchill were meeting at Potsdam. The dreadful scale of its power was evident in the devastation of two Japanese cities, Hiroshima and Nagasaki, soon after Potsdam, each by a single bomb. The novelty extended to how one calculated the relative strength of offense and defense, because the

atomic bomb appeared as a great force multiplier, offsetting manpower and conventional forces by this release of unconventional power.

Truman thought that nuclear weapons would counterbalance Soviet manpower, and Forrestal, who became secretary of defense in 1947, referred to the atomic bomb as "the great equalizer," because few elements in an attacking force would need to penetrate enemy defenses to inflict a total defeat. While losses of 15 percent of an attacking bomber force, for example, were unsustainable with conventional forces and would ensure that the attacker would lose over a protracted period, a penetration rate of 15 percent of an air fleet armed with atomic weapons could probably deliver a knockout punch in a single attack. The enormity of the weapon's effects made it seem an awkwardly attractive necessity for any nation intending to stand as a world power after 1945. Therefore, the Soviet Union accelerated its nuclear research and development program, and Great Britain pressed forward with a separate nuclear weapons program when it was denied shared control of U.S. weapons produced with the help of British scientists. Even though Great Britain was an ally of the United States, the U.S. government first pursued a policy that would have required United Nations control of all atomic weapons with substantial U.S. oversight. When this plan, named for Bernard Baruch, its architect and chief proponent, failed to win Soviet agreement, the U.S. government aimed instead at preventing or at least limiting the proliferation of nuclear-capable nations.

The prospect of a sharp acceleration in the pace of change in military technology was just as awesome as nuclear weapons themselves. First, atomic bombs were not meaningful militarily if kept in depots in the United States, so the enhancement of delivery systems took on great importance. Long-range bombers were crucial, notably the B-29, which was modified for longer range as the B-50, and the B-36, originally designed to permit U.S. strikes against the Nazis if British bases became unavailable during World War II. Second, atomic weapons did not negate traditional principles of war, such as the advantages of speed and surprise. This encouraged the development of jet-powered bombers, first the intermediate-range B-47 and then the long-range, inflight refuelable B-52.

Meanwhile, there was no reason to assume that nuclear weapons had to be delivered by air or used only against industrial or urban targets, and a naval nuclear component, whether from aircraft carriers or submarines, became increasingly a topic of interest. Ground-based missiles also gained importance, although these were initially deemed to be a less realistic option because of the technological limits of bomb technology, where miniaturization of high-yield weapons posed a great challenge. To hold the kind of military superiority widely associated with meaningful defense against a nuclear attack appeared to require armed forces equipped with the most up-to-date and advanced weapons. The rapidity with which new weapons systems would become obsolete made keeping up with advancements in military technology extremely expensive. Obsolescence took on especially threatening implications for the United States, because the technological lead over the Soviet Union that constituted a force multiplier and offset Soviet manpower was ultimately not a long-lasting advantage in hardware but an uncertain and relatively brief advantage in time.

In addition, the swift pace of technological change required new institutional mechanisms for fostering advanced domestic military research and development to ensure that one was not surprised by a weapons breakthrough by an adversary. For example, organized operations research for the U.S. government dates from World War II programs assessing antisubmarine activity. In the immediate years after World War II, the Army Air Forces induced the formation of the civilian RAND Corporation to engage in operations and systems analysis on an ever-widening basis. Also, the federal government proved unwilling to risk relying on the pre–World War II practice of competitively testing weapons systems, such as aircraft, that had been researched and developed at the expense of private companies. Instead, it began to issue contracts covering the costs of more than one

manufacturer during the research and development phases, partly because of the increasing sophistication and hence higher cost of weapons and their development, and also because of the government's wish to preserve a larger military industrial base.

In this and in other ways, the federal government contributed to the expansion and reshaping of the military-industrial complex in the United States, a phenomenon paralleled in the Soviet Union, albeit under a different general economic system, and in Great Britain, although within the limits of its strained postwar economy. The extreme sense of urgency felt among the leaders of the major powers strengthened the habit of classifying official information pertaining to policy, military hardware, and related issues for security purposes. Secrecy had always been an aspect of government, but the extent of security operations and the size of the security establishment both grew markedly after 1945, leading to expanded or even new agencies, most notably the Central Intelligence Agency (CIA).

All of this cost money and many of these new agencies and their procedures represented a challenge to customary political relationships within those countries participating in the hastening arms race. In the United States, while military expenditures were expected to drop from the levels sustained during World War II, the larger military program that seemed in the offing anticipated a higher level of peacetime expenditures for defense than had been sustained in any previous era of peace. This greater expenditure for the military signified that political relationships among the armed forces and between such institutions as Congress, the State Department, and the White House and the armed forces were apt to change. Even during World War II, some members of Congress and factions within the armed forces thought that change in military institutions was needed, but at the request of Secretary of War Henry L. Stimson and others, changes were deferred until after the war was won, lest protracted discussion of military reorganization interfere with the war effort.

Even the most basic political concepts and institutions, such as congressional power to declare war, were challenged. If war was waged swiftly and briefly with nuclear weapons, there might not be time for Congress to declare war. Theoretically, Washington, D.C., itself might be an irradiated ruin before the call had gone out to convene. Was a president to act without the constitutionally mandated act of Congress? And what if the government were decapitated in a nuclear sneak attack, killing not only the president but the entire constitutionally specified line of succession? Who then would lead the counterattack against the enemy? To an unprecedented degree a few changes in military technology were putting a heavy strain upon the fabric of American political beliefs. Similarly, if treachery among the citizenry contributed to an enemy's chances for success, the fabric of civil liberties might be strained, too. In the years after 1945, hypothetical military strategies, such as the projections of future wars by U.S. Defense Department planning staffs, and exaggerated subversive threats tended to be treated as clear and present dangers, actual and immediate, requiring expeditious countermeasures.

Many changes in military and political institutions that appeared in the United States in the years after World War II stemmed from the altered state of military technology, the impulse to fill vacuums of power in key regions of the world, and the sense of urgency derived from the attribution of demonic qualities to the adversary. For example, the advanced state of aviation technology led to the enhanced importance of aviation branches in the governance of the military, and U.S. concern over vacuums of power around the world led to a new structure of overseas bases and a complicated air and sea logistics system to support them. Most changes, however, were necessitated by the perception that the United States would soon be vulnerable to military attack in a way that was novel both qualitatively and quantitatively. With the exception of the War of 1812, the continental United States had been safe from external attack. Once the Soviet Union acquired a capability for penetration of U.S. air space, this security would

end. While the surprise attack at Pearl Harbor was widely perceived as an avoidable lapse, an attack by the Soviet Union could, in theory, succeed even without the incompetence of fools or the collusion of traitors. It was a curious kind of powerlessness to govern its own destiny that seemed to face what was, quite ironically, militarily the most powerful country on earth.

Soon after the first atomic bombs were used against Japan, many U.S. policymakers, such as Forrestal and President Truman himself, concluded that the development of atomic bombs and advanced aircraft to deliver them meant the superiority of offensive systems over defensive ones for far into the future. Specifically, it appeared impossible to guarantee complete protection against a possible nuclear attack by a determined enemy, because the expected damage from even a small fraction of the nuclear weapons sent was enormous and, at the time, conceptually unacceptable. This led swiftly to the belief that deterring such an attack was the only available recourse. Assuring possible attackers that any assault on the United States would bring on a massive and devastating counterstrike, one far more sweeping and effective than their own, emerged as the very heart of strategic defense.

To deter a potential enemy, however, the United States could no longer rely on a gradual buildup of its forces during a time of crisis and before combat began. Because a nuclear attack might come as a surprise and would presumably come quickly and last briefly, a ready defense against an attack was essential. In short, potential force was irrelevant. Only a force actually in being and substantially invulnerable to destruction could provide a sufficient threat. A potential enemy was to be deterred from launching a nuclear attack by the sure fear of massive retaliatory strikes. In the initial strategic conception favored by U.S. leaders, air forces ensured the swiftness of response and nuclear weapons guaranteed that retaliation would be massive.

After 1948, with the passage of the Selective Service Act and the introduction of the peacetime military draft, it was clear that the "force in being" would include a large ground element as well. Persistent pressure within Congress and from special interest groups in industry and elsewhere led to the preservation of a significant naval element in the force in being and, eventually, to its significant expansion. In all, traditional concern over the consequences of maintaining a large standing armed force fell before the urgency of the perceived Soviet threat.

Therefore, air power and atomic weapons were seen as a cause of fear and danger and the means of allaying the fear and countering the danger. This internal tension, if not contradiction, lay at the heart of the psychology of the cold war. Safety appeared to depend on the very weapons that, in the hands of the enemy, would cause one's own ruin. The literally world-shattering power of atomic weapons seemed to many planners to be the only tools adequate to a global strategy.

President Truman also regarded them as the most economical tools, and, throughout the cold war strategic weapons did prove to be cumulatively the least expensive element of force structure and defense as a whole. Containing defense expenditures within limits that the U.S. economy could support indefinitely, however, would have been an exercise in futility and the absurd if the forces sustained at those spending levels had failed to pay for a force sufficient to the military tasks at hand, such as deterrence of a prospective Soviet attack and support of regimes friendly to the United States around the rim of Soviet influence. Truman not only thought a strategy based on air forces and atomic weapons to be economical, he thought it militarily sufficient, a view that would have made no sense outside the narrow framework to which he subscribed of bipolar conflict between the free world and the Communist bloc. The division of the world into two camps and giving controlling power over the Communist bloc to the Soviet Union diminished the autonomy of third-party nations against whom the use of nuclear weapons would have seemed preposterously disproportionate if they were regarded as truly independent. For his part, Truman also believed that all the world was falling

into one camp or the other, and at the end of that process there might be peace or war, depending on the final distribution of postwar power. Within such a scenario, a heavy emphasis on air forces with nuclear weapons fit well.

Deterrence may have appeared to be an active strategy and, in terms of technical implementation, an offensive one, but it actually locked the strategic systems of the United States into a fundamentally reactive posture. The active element of the systems lay in the threat of their use, while actual use itself would have indicated that the nation's general policy of deterrence had failed. The initiative, such as in probes to find where the United States had "drawn a line in the sand" in Greece and elsewhere, lay with the nation's potential adversaries. At the same time, the evidence that deterrence had presumably worked lay in the inactivity of adversaries, which presupposed that they would otherwise have gone on the offensive. Such contrary-to-fact assertions were technically only speculations, and their persuasiveness depended partly on adhering to the most negative interpretation of official statements from the Soviet leadership. For example, when Stalin stated in 1946 that the Soviet people must be ready for a war with the Western nations, Truman and other leaders viewed it as a statement of intent to start one, likening it to a declaration of World War III. When a full-scale war did not develop, the state of relative peace was attributed to the effect of military deterrence.

A striking feature of early cold war strategy was that it was a reaction to fear, or, more specifically, to apprehension. U.S. strategy took into account expected or feasible actions of the adversary, rather than actions already undertaken. Impressed by the devastation that might be caused by a nuclear attack, U.S. strategists relied less on calculations of the adversary's intentions and more on a prediction of its capabilities. Because the consequence of miscalculating intentions might be a defeat from which recovery would be impossible, there was a strong body of opinion, espoused almost uniformly by U.S. military leaders and by such influential congressmen as Carl Vinson, favoring policies based only on material capability. Some, such as Air Force Major General Orvil A. Anderson, even flirted with conducting a preemptive or preventive war against the Soviet Union, depriving them of the military option of attack altogether. In the peculiar context of the immediate postwar world, it seemed to be the only logical alternative to deterrence.

President Truman sharply disciplined open advocates of preventive war within the military, but the option they advocated reveals much about deterrence itself. For example, deterrence presupposed that Soviet leaders were rational and that their logical assessment of likely risks and benefits would cause them to refrain from military adventurism and subversion. In this way, deterrence proved especially compatible with the view that Stalin was masterminding an elaborate conspiracy of global proportions. If the threat were not a conspiracy—that is, a logical design—then it could not be reliably countered by fears of massive retaliation, which required a conventional appreciation of the costs and benefits of actions. Advocates of preventive war, by contrast, refused to rely on the rationality of the enemy in a *reductio ad absurdum* of the contention that the Soviet Union embodied values fundamentally inimical to those of Western civilization, such as respect for human life. In this way, they departed from the traditionally stated purpose of affecting the enemy's will to resist. Preventive war was not about will but about capacity. Deterrence, on the other hand, was concerned about capacity in order to affect will. In this way, deterrence was political as well as military in nature from the very start.

Deterrence was also, in important ways, a highly theoretical strategy, inextricably dependent on the most physically powerful weapons ever created, yet lacking a base in military experience except for the two devastating examples of Hiroshima and Nagasaki. The conviction that atomic weapons had opened a new military world stripped respect away from traditional military knowledge. Atomic weapons also stripped authority from the military leaders who had been the guardians of military lore.

Civilian strategists rapidly rose in importance by articulating theories that took the new weapons into account. A notable example was the academic Bernard Brodie, who promptly grasped the implications of nuclear weapons on the balance of offense and defense. Brodie perceived that a perfect defense against a large nuclear attack could not be assured. Thus, the only fully successful defense was to prevent an attack from being launched in the first place. This strategic emphasis on deterrence, articulated within months after the bombing of Hiroshima, was nevertheless applicable at least until the early 1980s, when President Ronald Reagan reasserted the prospects of a strategic defense. For the remainder of the cold war, other civilian strategists, such as Herman Kahn, explored the theoretical diversity of ways in which a nuclear war might start and might be waged. Kahn exemplified the experts who worked on contract with the U.S. government in "think tanks," such as the RAND Corporation, which was established by the Army Air Forces in 1946, and the Hudson Institute. In such books as *On Thermonuclear War* (1960), Kahn explored dozens of possible nuclear war scenarios other than the all-out "spasm war" that had been the original expectation, thus also contributing the thought that some kinds of nuclear war could be fought and won.

The decline in importance of top-ranking military officers in the formation of strategy did not come about solely because the new class of civilian theorists proved so zealous and energetic. From the birth of the Republic and even from colonial times, Americans had been committed to the principle of the supremacy of the civilian political authority over the military. Effective control of the management of the armed forces had often been delegated for practical purposes to the uniformed officers in the first century and a half of the national experience, but warfare in the twentieth century had blurred the distinction between combatant and noncombatant and between soldier and civilian. Not only did technology emerge that could be indiscriminate in its applications, such as airplanes dropping bombs on cities, but theories also emerged, such as those of Italian military strategist Giulio Douhet, that made cities and their civilian occupants the preferred targets of the military forces. In the twentieth century, too, the concept of total national mobilization was realized on the home front, and if the home territories were truly an arsenal for the nation's war effort, then they were also a relevant target. During the nineteenth and twentieth centuries, moreover, the ratio of civilian to military deaths in war changed markedly, as the proportion of civilians killed rapidly expanded.

In short, military and civilian spheres had been growing more intertwined during the twentieth century, and atomic weapons simply brought the process to fulfillment. If military and civilian spheres were inextricably bound, however, and if the military must not be permitted control over the civilian sphere, then the military could not be allowed substantial autonomy over the military sphere either. This, too, must be an immediate concern of civilian strategists and managers and of the civilian political leaders.

These events help to explain the greater direct participation of the president in military affairs in the cold war era. Under the provisions of the Constitution, the president is commander in chief of the armed forces. Typically, however, presidents in office before the twentieth century involved themselves closely with strategy and the management of the armed forces only during war. James K. Polk and Abraham Lincoln exemplify the activist commander in chief who not only endorsed general plans but followed the details of their implementation. In the twentieth century, such activism became increasingly typical and, eventually, normative. When Truman succeeded to the presidency after the death of Roosevelt, the popular expectation that the president had the right to involve himself in the intimate details of military affairs was widely and well established. Roosevelt's use of military advisers on his own staff had also established the premise that the president could rightly be expected to make military judgments independent of the top-ranking officers of the military services. This premise of presidential

independence was to be a guiding feature of postwar reorganization of the military services, and the persuasiveness of this premise was enhanced by the special threat represented in nuclear weapons and advanced systems for their delivery.

Throughout the cold war era, too, the term "strategic" was increasingly linked with "nuclear," and the terms were often used interchangeably. For many military planners, the next war was envisioned as nuclear, creating a conceptual lacuna in which even a major nonnuclear conflict of a traditional sort might be deemed not a real war at all or, at least, a new kind of war. In time, when war began in Korea in 1950, a traditional and conventional conflict was treated as if it were a historical anomaly, reflecting the compelling sway of the nuclear strategic paradigm. If real war was preconceived as nuclear, then no war had ever been fought that could serve as a referential example for the strategists of 1950.

The heightened sense of peril arising from a global competition in which nuclear weapons were a focusing dimension also contributed to the rise of political bipartisanship in foreign policy in the United States. This political formulation was new to the American scene, at least in peacetime. In the nineteenth century, for example, and even into the twentieth century, there was a presumption that loyalty to the nation required unanimity of opinion about overseas policies. This was true even in time of war. In the War of 1812, the Mexican War, and the Spanish-American War, Americans differed markedly not only as to method but as to the goals of policy. During the twentieth century, however, dissent from the stated policies of the executive branch during wartime became less practicable. In World War II, for example, Democratic President Roosevelt appointed Republicans Frank Knox and Henry Stimson as secretary of the navy and secretary of war, respectively, to build a bipartisan coalition for the U.S. war effort. During the early years of the cold war, Truman also cooperated with important Republicans, such as Senator Arthur Vandenberg of Michigan, who had once been deemed an isolationist, to build a reliable political base for extensive and open-ended U.S. military presence and involvements overseas. To the extent that dissent stopped at the water's edge, the president enjoyed a relative increase in actual power in foreign and military affairs.

The emphasis on global deterrence thus greatly affected American institutions by strengthening the authority of the president, compared to that of Congress, in setting U.S. overseas policy. For two decades, until political dissent against the war in Vietnam broke the bipartisan consensus, Democrats and Republicans in Congress alike assumed a clearly secondary role even in such areas as making war where Congress had a clear constitutional responsibility. It also gave basic shape to U.S. military force structure and greatly affected political and military relations with other countries. A credible threat to a distant enemy presupposed a highly capable offensive force whose weapons were high in yield and whose delivery systems enjoyed great power of penetration. Just as military and civilian spheres seemed to be inextricably linked within the United States, however, so were the interests and the resources of the United States and its allies perceived to be interactive and mutually supportive. The further European economic recovery from World War II progressed, the question of European contributions to regional defense became more relevant. In this way, despite its economic, political, and humanitarian motives, the program for European economic recovery under the Marshall Plan also had significant military implications. The resources of the United States were great but not infinite, and the question of appropriate balance of forces—air, sea, and land within the services, but also U.S. or allied in the free world as a whole—became a regular topic of discussion among allied leaders.

To wage its part in the cold war—or, as President Dwight D. Eisenhower later put it, to "wage peace"—the Truman administration greatly enlarged the military budget in order to fund a substantially greater peacetime defense establishment than had been customary for the United States. Compared to force levels and spending during World War II—$80.5 billion in 1945, for example—the Truman administration cut deeply into the military, but compared to pre–World War II spending, the military was rising to a previously unattained peacetime eminence. The share of the total federal budget devoted to the military was much larger, and the increase in real dollars was impressive. In 1938, for example, excluding veterans' benefits, the military budget amounted to about $1.25 billion. In 1948, it was nearly $12 billion. In 1949, the first budget reflecting the new independent status of the U.S. Air Force, the figure was about $14 billion. In 1953, at the end of the Korean War, the budget surpassed $44 billion, and for the remainder of the 1950s it stayed in the range of $35–$40 billion.

The rate at which the military budget grew far exceeded the growth rate of the entire federal budget. In 1938 the total federal budget was about $6.8 billion, and military spending accounted for about 18.4 percent. In 1948, the total budget was about $33 billion, and the $12 billion in military spending amounted to 36.4 percent. In 1956, when the federal budget ran to $66.5 billion, the military share was 54.1 percent. There are many ways to calculate the economic sustainability of such expenditures. For example, while the 1948 military budget took twice the share of the total federal budget than the 1938 military budget, the gross national product (GNP) had tripled in the same period. Also, while the 1956 military budget took three times more of the federal total than the 1938 budget, the GNP was five times greater. Military spending emerged as a major component of the federal budget and a focal preoccupation of the national leadership.

In 1945, and even as late as the Korean War, it was unclear how much the federal government could afford to spend on a long-term basis to provide for national defense and international security. Peacetime military spending before World War II had rarely approached $1 billion, but after the war the military budget, including supplementals, averaged about $15 billion after World War II obligations had been fulfilled. How much more could be spent without damaging the national economy, such as by contributing to the national debt, inflation, higher interest rates, or the imposition of governmental control of production and prices, was not known. It was a process of trial and error, as well as one of economic forecasting. Although actual U.S. military spending in peacetime rose to all-time highs, fear of overstraining the economy made Truman seek ways to restrain the growth of spending. This gave added impetus to the administration's efforts to restructure the U.S. defense establishment to be better suited for global competition with the Soviet Union.

The desire to save money contributed to calls for unification of the armed forces, but such calls also reflected a wish for coherence within the military so that it could respond promptly and purposefully to the will of the president. The organizational changes wanted by President Truman and such advisers as White House aide Clark Clifford, Secretary of War Robert Patterson, Army Chief of Staff General George C. Marshall, and Assistant Secretary of War for Air Stuart Symington (later the first secretary of the air force) presupposed a shift from a relatively simple notion of defense against specific attacks to a more complex idea of protecting national security. Although traces of this idea can be found in earlier eras, it achieved full force and currency after 1945, especially after the enactment of the National Security Act of 1947. This law created the National Military Establishment, amended to the Department of Defense in 1949, and created the position of secretary of defense. It separated the Army Air Forces from the army and turned them into an independent and coequal air force. In addition, it created the Joint Chiefs of Staff (JCS) and the position of chairman of the JCS.

The principle behind the reorganization was to confine access to the president on military matters to a comparatively few individuals, ultimately, at least in theory, to only the secretary of defense. The prospect of centralized authority led many high-ranking officials to oppose the idea of unification and to weaken its implementation. Secretary of the Navy Forrestal, for example, advocated coordination of the services rather than centralized control, but as the first secretary of defense, he soon learned the weaknesses of his proposals. The history of defense reorganization in the next four decades was basically a quest to replace coordination with greater control.

The restructuring under the act of 1947 did not stop with the uniformed services. The comprehensive vision of what constituted national defense necessitated the creation of the National Security Council (NSC), which to some extent replaced the former meetings of the State, War, and Navy departments during World War II. In addition to the president and secretaries of state and defense, membership on the NSC included agency heads responsible for the national economy and national intelligence, the chairman of the National Security Resources Board (NSRB) and the director of the Central Intelligence Agency (CIA). The creation of the NSRB reflected the view that national strength and security depended on economic vitality, as well as recognizing the dependence of the United States on various critical strategic minerals. The CIA grew out of the wartime Office of Special Services (OSS), and it increasingly put attention on the gathering and assessment of information rather than limiting itself to special covert operations. Even so, the CIA had peculiar significance because it did undertake limited military and paramilitary operations outside traditional U.S. military channels and, consequently, without the customary and constitutionally mandated checks and balances. This legislation also established a niche for the creation of a purely appointed staff dealing with national security policy at the pleasure of the president and without and not subject to the Senate's right to advise and consent to major appointments, such as those of cabinet officers.

While changes in the management of national security were being undertaken within the country, more significant changes were in progress in foreign relations. Notable was the extensive program for the acquisition of overseas military bases initiated by Truman and continued by his successors. The most ironic agreements were those with wartime enemies Italy,

Germany (or at least its western part), and Japan, which became important allies of the United States in the cold war and all of which provided crucial facilities for a forward-basing policy aimed at the Soviet sphere from the Mediterranean and central and northern Europe to northeast Asia. Meanwhile, wartime allies, the Soviet Union and, after 1949, China, were regarded as adversaries. Having been granted independence by the United States in 1946, the Philippines also extended air and naval base rights to the United States.

Perhaps the single most illustrative base agreement was that between the United States and Spain. As late as 1946, the United States denounced the government of Generalissimo Francisco Franco as fascist and totalitarian, and it participated in a United Nations–sponsored recall of ambassadors from Madrid. In 1948, however, Secretary of Defense Forrestal called for U.S. naval bases in Spain, and air force officials sought bases the following year. By 1950 the United States began providing loans and gifts to Franco's regime, and in 1953 a treaty providing for U.S. military bases in Spain was negotiated and approved. Thus, it was clear that old ideological demons had yielded to new ones, and world power politics proved more pertinent in determining practical policy than ideological beliefs.

Antifascism was not the only political belief to be set aside for purposes of pursuing the cold war. Anticolonialism was, too. The most notable example was the shift of U.S. policy toward France in Southeast Asia, where Roosevelt and Truman had opposed the reestablishment of French colonial rule in Vietnam, Laos, and Cambodia. As fear of communism came to outweigh repugnance of colonialism, the United States increased economic and military aid to France, still urging political reform within Southeast Asia but tolerating French intransigence out of fear that the Communists posed an even greater danger. That Vietnamese Communists in particular could seem so threatening reflected the U.S. distress over the Chinese Communist consolidation of power in mainland China and the Truman administration's view

that all unrest in Asia was ultimately keyed to the connivance of Mao's government in Beijing. Seen one way, then, this was a case of resistance to an alien philosophy, as was U.S. cooperation with Spain. Seen another way, however, both were examples of U.S. willingness to accommodate the distasteful political views of its allies out of concern over the power and regional influence of its new adversaries.

In the years after World War II, some military planners, especially within the air force, suggested that there was no military need for overseas bases. Even so, bases could serve a political role, especially if one thought that sufficient military force could be applied from great distances by air and sea forces. U.S. overseas bases could give encouragement to fragile political elements in Western Europe and elsewhere with pro-American sympathies. More significantly—and, as time passed, more durably—the crucial strategic significance of such deployments of U.S. forces overseas included the idea that they served as a tripwire. Let any Americans be killed overseas in an attack launched by an enemy, and the full weight of U.S. military might would be brought to bear upon that enemy from bases in the continental United States. For a strategic theory that was to depend on the threat of massive retaliation, even at the risk of devastation to one's own nation, deployment of U.S. troops at such overseas bases contributed to making nuclear deterrence seem credible.

This array of interlocking policies was designated containment, a term attributed to State Department official George Kennan. In 1946, while serving at the U.S. embassy in Moscow, Kennan, a specialist in Soviet studies, drafted a lengthy memorandum aimed at explaining what he termed "the sources of Soviet conduct." A modified version of Kennan's report was published anonymously in the July 1947 issue of *Foreign Affairs* and, now called the "X article," became a sensation overnight. According to Kennan, the Soviet Union had inherited the deep-seated suspicion of foreigners and their designs that dated back for centuries into Russian history. He likened Soviet energies to a windup toy, and if the United States resisted the momentum of the windup toy, it would gradually spend its energy and fall into stasis. Peace would be at hand, and aggression would have been contained.

The general belief that Soviet power had to be contained within a fixed perimeter existed before Kennan gave his special expression to the concept. His memo was read by several government agencies, whose reaction suggested that Kennan did no more than articulate what was already on the minds of many in Washington rather than persuade them to take a new position. Naval Intelligence, for example, assessed Kennan's analysis for Secretary of the Navy Forrestal, saying that it contained nothing new. It was regarded, however, as an especially lucid presentation of views widely held among high-ranking U.S. officials. Kennan was called back to Washington to lecture at the National War College and then to serve as head of the State Department's Policy Planning Staff, symbolically marking the dominance of containment in U.S. official thinking.

The subtleties of Kennan's version of containment, which he insisted ought not to be narrowly or even fundamentally military, were soon overtaken by the events that the doctrine helped to shape and by other events that the doctrine was used to counter. In the aftermath of World War II, a bitter civil war had emerged in Greece. Although there was an indigenous Communist element in Greece, it was substantially supplied by the Soviet Union through Bulgaria. By 1947 the British government made clear to President Truman that it no longer had the ability to support the anti-Communist government and implied its willingness to accept whatever might happen after the end of their own aid program. On 12 March 1947, Truman spoke before Congress, enunciating as U.S. policy an open-ended commitment to resist attack upon or subversion of any government by Communist factions. The concept of containment, which had been historically particular in its original formulation, was now applied generally to the world as a whole. Truman regarded this as "the turning point in America's foreign policy."

Although the Truman Doctrine has some-times been criticized for its universal extensiveness, it may have created more strain on the United States for the military obligations to which it committed the nation. Given the enfeebled economic condition of Great Britain and the weakness of Europe as a whole, any intervention in Greece to sustain the anti-Communist regime was inevitably destined to be an exclusively U.S. enterprise. Although it had genuine hopes for concerted allied effort against the Communists, the United States, for the most part, had to stay the course on its own. This tension between hopes for concerted effort and coordinated defense and the practical imperatives of resources and timing became a hallmark of Western defense efforts throughout the cold war. What began in 1947 as a recognition that European nations had little within their power to combat communism eventually became a concern that those nations were taking advantage of the U.S. military presence in Europe and also that they lacked political will.

It is striking that no Communist state recognized the "Government of Free Greece" proclaimed by the insurgents. Stalin told Nikos Zachariadis, political leader of the Greek Communists, that armed struggle in Greece should be avoided. Stalin even criticized Josip Broz Tito, the leader of Yugoslavia, for continuing to supply small arms to the Communist rebels from across his southern border with Greece. In fact, Stalin appears to have written off the Greek Communists and, by helping to cut off their supplies, contributed to their demise. If this had been aggression, it was perhaps more in the form of opportunism than ideological compulsion, as suggested by Stalin's recognition of British and U.S. interests in the Mediterranean. What was understood by U.S. military advisers, such as General James Van Fleet, but not given public attention was that the Greek Communists continued to sustain themselves in 1947 and 1948 largely on their own resources, replenishing their numbers from among the Greek peasantry. Not only did they not depend on Soviet aid, but the Greeks actually pursued a program that violated Soviet wishes. Had the indigenous nature of the Greek insurgency received greater attention, the notion that all troubles could be traced to Moscow (or, later, Beijing) would have been discredited and might in turn have impeached the application of containment policy worldwide.

At the same time, however, the pragmatic dimensions of U.S. policy that lay behind the inclusive sweep of the Truman Doctrine are also revealed in this incident and in the curious relationship with Tito and Yugoslavia that grew out of it. Despite Yugoslav support of the Greek Communists even after Stalin had abandoned them, the United States swiftly cooperated with Tito when the Yugoslav leader broke with Stalin in 1948, partly out of frustration over Stalin's behavior toward Greece. Again, the test of cooperation was practical rather than ideological. Tito was surely a Communist, hence deserving of the same hot rhetoric devoted to Stalin, but Tito's defection from the Soviet bloc won him economic and even military support in the west.

Overlapping the U.S. intervention in Greece was one of the early "signature" military operations of the cold war—the conflict between the two superpowers over the status of Germany and particularly over that of Berlin in 1948–1949. The Berlin crisis followed bitter disagreements over both the political and military status of Germany. The United States had never endorsed the extreme if understandable claims of the Soviet Union for war reparations payments from Germany and was thus distressed by the wholesale dismantling of German assets within the zone occupied by Soviet forces. As a part of its de-Nazification policy, the United States was more interested in reconstruction and the rapid introduction of democratic institutions in Germany, aims dating back to the war years when the occupation was being planned. By 1948, U.S. and British officials had come to administer their zones cooperatively, and they eventually persuaded the reluctant French to do the same. The Soviet Union resisted, however, not only for economic reasons but also out of concern over the possible military strength and likely political alignment of a reunited Germany. Seeking to disrupt the creation of a separate

west German state out of the zones occupied by France, Great Britain, and the United States, the Soviet Union imposed a land blockade of the city of Berlin on 23 June 1948, isolating the sectors of the old German capital administered by the three Western nations.

President Truman appears never to have considered acquiescing to the consequences of the Soviet action. At the first cabinet meeting held after the initiation of the blockade, Secretary of Defense Forrestal began to list options, including the withdrawal of Western personnel, but Truman cut him short, indicating that whether to resist the blockade was not the issue but rather how to overcome it. General Lucius D. Clay, the U.S. high commissioner for Germany, recommended shooting through the blockade. Others, relying on the considerable American aviation assets in Europe, urged the creation of an "air bridge" to the city. This latter course became policy, and at the peak of airlift operations, planes brought in thirteen thousand tons of supplies every day, even including such cost-inefficient but crucial material as coal. After a year in which the U.S. air forces proved their ability to sustain West Berlin indefinitely, the Soviet Union ended the blockade on 12 May 1949, but the crisis allowed the issuance of an independent currency and the de facto creation of the state of East Germany. Germany was to remain thus divided until 1990, and in the interval its great military potential was split between the two great power blocs led by the United States and the Soviet Union.

The successful defiance of the Berlin Blockade by the Western allies lent credence to claims that air power gave important new capabilities to those who possessed it. Even more, it appeared that air power could actually substitute for land and sea forces, at least under some circumstances. This notion of substitution played a major role in U.S. strategic thought in the late 1940s and early 1950s, contributing to the rise to dominance of nuclear defense by demonstrating the capabilities of air delivery systems. The relief of Berlin also provided an imaginative precedent for a host of missions proposed or undertaken throughout the cold war that depended on the flexible application of air power, such as the proposed relief of Dien Bien Phu in North Vietnam (1954), the planned support of a Cuban anti-Communist invasion of their home island (1961), and the defense of the fire base at Khe Sanh in South Vietnam (1967–1968).

The success of the Berlin resistance also contributed weight to the argument for establishing a standing alliance among the Western powers, even as the initial Soviet action in staging the blockade suggested the need for such an alliance in the first place. The open split with the Soviet Union over the future of Germany even permitted the inclusion of West Germany into an alliance, provided concerns raised by the French were dealt with.

The alliance that eventually emerged was one of the most extraordinary departures in U.S. security policy in American history. In the North Atlantic Treaty Organization (NATO), the United States assumed the leading role of what was, on the face of it, basically an alliance aimed at the defense of Europe. Equally striking was the fact that the U.S. commitment was not only economic and short-term, for which there were many precedents, but military and open-ended, for which there was none, save perhaps America's agreement with France in 1778. On 4 April 1949, twelve nations signed the treaty—France, Great Britain, Belgium, Luxembourg, the Netherlands, Portugal, Italy, Denmark, Norway, Iceland, Canada, and the United States. By the end of 1949, U.S. officials were also calling for the formation of German military units, possibly to be included in NATO, a possibility that outraged the Soviet Union. Membership in NATO, however, with its profession that attacks on other member states would be treated as an attack on the United States, fit the definition of an "entangling alliance" very well. The description in advance of how the U.S. government would interpret any such hypothetical attack was to make NATO a powerful element in the general scheme of deterrence. By testing the limits of the constitutional provision that the Senate must advise and consent not only to treaties but

to the decision to go to war, NATO also went further than previous U.S. overseas commitments. Moreover, the undertakings were of indefinite duration.

It was by no means clear to all responsible U.S. officials that NATO was even necessary. Kennan, for example, told Secretary of State Dean Acheson that NATO afforded "military defense against an attack no one is planning." John Foster Dulles, later secretary of state to President Eisenhower, claimed in Senate hearings that no "responsible high official, military or civilian," believed that the Soviet Union "plans conquest by open military aggression." Whatever may have been the ultimate rationale for NATO, it had the effect of letting the U.S. government construe its forces as part of an international military structure that provided balance overall, even if U.S. forces were heavily skewed to the strategic side. To fill out the overall force structure of NATO, especially to enable it to meet its requirements for troops, Secretary of State Dulles, beginning in 1953, pressed for West German membership in NATO, which was accomplished in May 1955.

That same month, Soviet officials led in forming the Warsaw Pact, comprising the Soviet Union and its various dependent Eastern European states, which East Germany joined early in 1956. It was not quite the formation of NATO that induced the creation of the Warsaw Pact but NATO's inclusion of West Germany. More than putting a public name on what had already been a private fact, the militarization of Germany—and, at the time, specifically of its two parts—was a genuinely troubling issue, because all the original member states of the Warsaw Pact could regard themselves in one way or another as Germany's recent victims. Still, it is not clear whether the Warsaw Pact may have been, in its early years, meant somewhat as a bargaining chip. Proposals emerged from Eastern Europe, notably from Poland, to dismantle both alliances and create, in essence, a militarily neutral buffer zone through central Europe. At nearly the same moment as Dulles accomplished the inclusion of West Germany within

NATO, the Soviet Union had agreed to withdraw its occupation forces from Austria, and a key provision in the agreement was that the country would remain militarily neutral. The disparity between the Austrian agreement and the dispute over the destiny of Germany could scarcely have been greater.

The pursuit of a strong regional alliance in Western Europe, later followed by similar efforts in the Middle East (CENTO) and Southeast Asia (SEATO), reflected the view that a "division of labor" was desirable in global defense, according to which each member would contribute according to its special abilities. The military forces of the various member states would thus not necessarily be structured proportionately. In NATO, for example, the importance of the U.S. nuclear shield clearly exceeded that of the direct, combat-ready capability of U.S. troop units stationed in Europe. Eisenhower observed that it cost ten times as much for the United States to field an infantryman as it cost Turkey, a new NATO member. At the same time, Turkey lacked the strategic delivery systems and nuclear weapons possessed by the United States. Each state would thus be wise—and most effective—to contribute according to its special strengths.

The kind of force structure envisioned for the United States and the anticipated role international alliances would play in world security grew out of evolving notions of what sort of war the next one, if it occurred, would be. Both popular and military professional literature of the late 1940s abounded with predictions that the next war would be an intense and absorbing third world war in which nuclear weapons would be used promptly and that, because of its brevity, would be fought with whatever forces and weapons were on hand. Later, the notion of an all-out and brief nuclear war acquired the description "spasm war," while the notion of fighting it with what was on hand was called a "come as you are" war. Both notions had tremendous consequence for strategy, force structure, and readiness.

The paradigm of "the next war" is apt to survive for some time even in the face of much

anomalous experience. During the administration of President Eisenhower, for example, many officials appreciated that local and regional military problems, bearing such names as "limited war," "insurgency," and "wars of national liberation," might well be of indigenous origins. The problem was to define a meaningful and effective role for the United States when its force structure and its operational ethos were so heavily oriented toward strategic and even specifically nuclear issues. During the Truman years, one means of accommodation was to conceive of forces as having multiple purposes. Aircraft carriers and other surface vessels, for example, might be capable of a show of force or of a discrete mission in a regional problem, such as when the Seventh Fleet sailed into the straits between Taiwan and the Chinese mainland to secure Chiang Kai-shek at the outset of the Korean War. The fleet might also be used to intervene on behalf of supposedly pro-Western regimes. In 1957, Eisenhower ordered the Sixth Fleet into the eastern Mediterranean to protect Jordan's King Hussein against an attempted overthrow by forces favoring Gamal Abdel Nasser of Egypt, and in 1958 he ordered seven thousand marines to land in Lebanon to shore up the faltering government of Camille Chamoun.

Actual U.S. behavior, therefore, could be flexible, even if rhetoric concerning a single-sourced global conspiracy had to be stretched somewhat to fit the occasion. Indeed, the exploration of this discomforting diversity in the world was a more evidently pressing matter during the Eisenhower years than it had been under President Truman. The force structure and much of the strategic policy with which Eisenhower initially had to work were those of his predecessor, however, and it must be noted that Eisenhower had served Truman as a leading adviser on military and strategic policy until 1952.

Truman's concern over the prospect of a nuclear World War III meant that he did not give nearly so much attention or resources to the development of forces appropriate to undertaking limited and conventional expeditions in widely separated parts of the world. His political policy, as suggested in the Truman Doctrine, was global in scope, but the means available for its implementation were largely strategic in nature. Suitable as this was to the vision of bipolar competition, it was inadequate to the practical demands of regional and local military problems.

The continued importance of the U.S. strategic role was restated in 1950, just months before the North Korean attack that began the Korean War. After an extensive study of the world security situation, the National Security Council concluded that a massive buildup of U.S. and allied forces was essential to counter anticipated Soviet probes against the west long into the future. NSC memorandum 68 (NSC-68), a policy statement intertwining doctrine and strategy, gave an overall vision of world security problems and did not specifically discount the prospect of local military problems of indigenous origin, but it also did not put great priority on them. Given this emphasis on the general strategic picture as well as Truman's understandable preoccupation with problems in Europe and the Middle East, the emergence of war in Korea must be understood as a very special surprise for the Truman administration. Oddly, it was not an entirely unpleasant surprise and the fact that it was not, is itself an illustration of the transitions that had to be made to provide the United States a wider range of military options for the remaining decades of the cold war.

If the Berlin Blockade afforded a chance to test military systems important to the defense of the west, the war in Korea (1950–1953) tested the theory of deterrence itself and probed its nature. The North Korean attack was resisted in a scenario that revealed many problems and tensions in a cold war alliance in which the United States played a dominant role. On the evening of 25 June 1950, while on a visit to Missouri, Truman was informed of the North Korean invasion of South Korea. The president returned to Washington the next day, and soon after his arrival held a meeting on the crisis. The decision to resist the North Korean move was immediate, based less on consultation with other nations that might participate in military action in Korea, whether from NATO or from the United Nations, than on supposition as to how they ought to respond. The task for the U.S. government soon became turning a "U.S. into UN decision," as indicated in notes written by White House aide George Elsey. Thus, U.S. forces were committed prior to any United Nations action and before the U.S. government had obtained comparable commitments from its NATO allies.

The role of the United Nations during this period was itself a curious one. In its initial conception, the United Nations presupposed at least some measure of cooperation among the world's leading powers, represented by the five veto-holding members of the Security Council. The cold war conflict had frustrated that early purpose, and the emergence of two Chinese governments, the Nationalist remnant in Taipei and the triumphant Communist regime in Beijing, complicated the aim even more. Increasingly frustrated at the state of affairs within the United Nations, Truman flirted with seeking to transform the United Nations into a "Free World alliance." Nevertheless, the studied absence of the Soviet delegate from the Security Council vote authorizing the United Nations to use force to repel the North Korean forces permitted the world body to act. Apart from limited efforts at peacekeeping in the Middle East, this marked the first major use of force by the United Nations.

As the war progressed, however, an equitable commitment of forces by various allies within the United Nations was difficult, if not impossible, either to define or to obtain after the United States had already entered the fray. In a sense, the United States lost leverage by sending its own forces so promptly, even if such action was a military necessity. At a minimum, the commitment of U.S. land-based and naval air forces seemed essential to slowing the advance of North Korean units down the peninsula. Once U.S. forces were committed, however, the enterprise had become, practically if not formally, an American war rather than an allied or United Nations one. Thus, instead of seeing their roles in Korea as equal and comparable to that of the United States in support of a poorly armed people against aggression, other combatant nations, such as Great Britain, France, and Turkey, were just as apt to see themselves as helping out the Americans and might do so with no more than token forces. Cooperation with the United States in Korea reciprocated U.S. commitment to Europe in the NATO alliance, and in the case of France, it strengthened the U.S. commitment to support the French effort to hold Indochina against local insurgents. In the event, aside from Korean nationals, the United States provided some 90 percent of the troops fighting against the North Koreans and their allies, the Soviet Union and Communist China.

There were other lessons learned in this conflict. The Korean War was basically a conventional war in both political and military terms and the first significant one fought after the production and deployment of a substantial number of nuclear weapons. The principle of self-restraint and avoidance of first use of nuclear weapons also arose, less as a statement of U.S. policy than as a practical consequence of international political realities. It is not clear that President Truman had any personal distaste for using nuclear weapons in Korea, even though he chose not to do so, but leaders of allied states, such as Clement Atlee of Great Britain, made unmistakable their firm hostility to their use. This issue—when to "go nuclear," how, and under what provocations—became an important theme in discussions of U.S. strategic policy and even tactical military doctrine during the 1950s.

Although the U.S. and UN experience in Korea was often both confused and confusing, the war lent credibility to the sense of threat in other regions, notably in Europe. Difficult though it is to demonstrate concretely, the Korean War appears to have helped in transforming NATO from a paper alliance to a real, working multinational force. Even more, however, Truman believed that the Korean War proved the credibility of U.S. strategic forces and the effectiveness of its policy of deterrence. Truman believed that the Soviet Union was behind the various regional conflicts facing the United

States, including Korea. In the case of Korea, however, this view had some plausibility, because the division of the peninsula into two political entities was essentially an extension of its division into two administrative units during the Soviet and U.S. transitional occupations of North and South respectively. By assuming that his adversary had contemplated an all-out war, Truman saw the war in Korea as it actually developed, limited geographically and fought without nuclear weapons, as a proof that deterrence had succeeded. To the American public, however, the Korean conflict seemed to be a long, drawn-out stalemate, and President Truman's popularity slumped.

Many other Americans failed to see the war as Truman did, but they shared the administration's view that the Korean conflict was a most peculiar sort of war. In some ways, this was so. Rhetorically, for example, the military action in Korea was called a "police action," an awkward and curious choice of terms, but to call it a "limited war" was not the view of Koreans, for whom this civil war abetted by outsiders was as intense an experience as they could manage. Only if one defined "war" as a conflict marked by all-out commitment of the full arsenal and forces of the United States and the Western allies could one construe the Korean War as fundamentally new and atypical. In essence, the reference points were World War II—with its talk of unconditional surrender and a relentless offensive—and the hypothetical nuclear World War III. Yet those might more fairly have been deemed exceptional. The United Nations was committed by its charter to eliminating the "scourge of war" from human experience, which helps to explain the use of rhetorical substitutes for the word "war." Avoiding the use of the word, however, also gave Truman a justification for refraining from calling upon Congress for a declaration of war. This contributed to the broadening of presidential discretion in foreign affairs, even including military action, in the cold war era.

The actual nature of the Korean War merits appreciation, because the Korean War soon became a model both for emulation and avoidance. The slogan that emerged in the presidential campaign of Eisenhower and continued as the Korean conflict came to an end in 1953 was that there must be "no more Koreas," but exactly what did that mean in real military and political terms? What it clearly did not mean was acquiescence to probes or provocations by members of the Communist bloc. One principle important to the new presidential administration of Eisenhower (1953–1961), was to place greater reliance on genuinely allied, cooperative action, achieving agreements for it in advance of committing U.S. troops and thus avoiding the risks and the practical costs of unilateral action. A second major principle was to retain the choice of weapons when an adversary challenged the "free world." Although circumspect on the subject while serving as the supreme allied commander in NATO (1950–1952), Eisenhower later criticized Truman for having limited the U.S. and UN response to the North Korean invasion of South Korea to weapons chosen by the North Korean government in Pyongyang. In fact, this criticism was not completely correct, because early in the war the United States had employed the long-range bombers of its Far East Air Force (FEAF), based in Japan, to destroy North Korean industry and other major facilities useful to a war effort. However indirectly, Eisenhower seemed to be making a point about the deployment of nuclear weapons. For him, there was no sense in denying in advance the use of any weapon in the arsenal.

Curiously, Eisenhower's approach echoed Truman's own manner at the very outset of the cold war when, as Secretary of War Stimson put it, Truman went to the Potsdam Conference (1945) with the wartime allies, notably Stalin, "wearing the atomic bomb ostentatiously on his hip." Given the fact that the United States would not move to accelerated production of atomic bombs until well into 1947, the ostentation was a pretense. The pretense, however, was not so different from that of Eisenhower when he pledged in 1952 that he would, if elected, "go to Korea." Go for what? To observe and to find a resolution of the stalemate, to be

sure. But how? Nuclear weapons had taken their place as the inescapable background static of all undertakings in the early cold war.

Even though this was not the only meaning of "no more Koreas," it was the one that most closely matched the gut feeling of the early and mid-1950s. For many Americans, the Korean War possessed an irony. How was it that so powerful a nation as the United States could be tied up so long by a third-rate military force? Convinced that nuclear weapons could offset manpower and conventional forces, serving as what Forrestal had called the "great equalizer," Americans lapsed into the sense that military power was generic rather than specific.

Limits to violence and to the risk of nuclear war seemed essential, however, clearly so to President Eisenhower. There were several means of holding those limits and trimming those risks. One method was to deploy U.S. forces in Korea on an indefinite basis, thus discouraging a new North Korean attack and providing time for the South Korean regime to grow stronger politically and militarily. Talk of the need for allied cooperation notwithstanding, the Eisenhower administration, like other presidencies, was ultimately willing to commit U.S. forces and prestige on a purely bilateral basis.

Eisenhower was also genuinely interested in improving relations with Soviet leaders, even while pressing for significant strengthening of NATO forces and advancing new weapons programs in the United States, such as new jet-powered bomber forces, intercontinental ballistic missiles (ICBMs) armed with thermonuclear warheads, and nuclear-powered naval vessels and missile-carrying submarines. Eisenhower advocated "people to people" diplomacy for the average citizen, and his interest in "summit diplomacy"—free-ranging talks among the leaders of the world's greatest powers—established one of the devices eventually used as part of the apparatus for developing arms control programs.

Eisenhower also sought ways of making nuclear weapons more "useful." During his presidency, U.S. defense research focused on diversifying the nuclear arsenal, most notably on creating the "clean bomb." Producing low-radiation nuclear weapons would presumably make it easier to use them, especially in European battlefield conditions. Physical destruction would be great and would be produced economically, but the devastated areas could supposedly be reoccupied with relative promptness. Meanwhile, tests in the Nevada desert measured the effects on ground troops of operating near a nuclear explosion and of entering the area of devastation soon after the blast. All such efforts ultimately aimed at enhancing the credibility of the deterrent threat posed by NATO and by the United States. Even though such test programs concentrated on nuclear weapons, it was significant that the more traditionally conceived battlefield was returning to strategic importance. Also, the development of battlefield nuclear weapons eventually forced reexamination within the armed forces, notably the army, of unit organization, tactics, and strategy. This contributed to the doctrine of "flexible response," which embraced a broad spectrum of possible military options from which the United States might choose to react to hostile action. One critical element in flexible response was the concept of limited nuclear warfare, in which atomic weapons would be used in one theater, notably in Europe, without assuming that such a conflict would automatically escalate into global nuclear war. In future wars fought according to flexible response, the choice of weapons would be in the hands of the president of the United States.

Such strategic concepts as flexible response help to explain the real meaning of the statement "no more Koreas." What Eisenhower really opposed was not commitment to "small wars," but Truman's hesitancy over the use of nuclear weapons. Eisenhower and his military aids and advisers insisted that the wronged party had the right to choose the weapons most convenient to its defense. By making various nuclear and nonnuclear options seem more credible, deterrence was further enhanced.

While U.S. military policy included the search for "clean" atomic weapons, coupled with ever more exact targeting and delivery systems, the Soviet Union set about enhancing explosive yield without regard for the "dirt" of radiation. U.S. policy was a sign of its technological superiority over the Soviet Union. A comparatively precise targeting and delivery assured that a weapon yielding perhaps one megaton—the equivalent of one million tons of conventional explosives—could take out the designated enemy site. The inexactness of Soviet targeting and delivery argued in favor of using weapons of much greater megatonnage as insurance against inaccuracy. The larger the crater, the greater the likelihood of destroying the intended target, even if much else in collateral damage went along with it.

The impression that U.S. military policy was dominated by massive retaliation and the spirit of brinksmanship during the Eisenhower years owed something to the image of Dulles. Eisenhower's first secretary of state, Dulles was a fervent and religious man, whose open anticommunism reflected his passionate inner beliefs. As the slogan "better dead than red" won currency as an expression of popular anticommunism, Dulles seemed peculiarly likely to turn the slogan into policy and then, if necessary, into action. If some thought nuclear war disproportionate to the provocations the United States was likely to face, Dulles did not let on that he was among them. Indeed, his vigorous denunciations of communism as utter evil and neutralism as immorality permitted an argument in favor of nuclear war under traditional just war theory. In retrospect, however, it all took on an odd air of doublethink, because this was the same Dulles who in 1950 had doubted the military necessity of NATO. The war in Korea had contributed to his changed views but, still, by himself Dulles remains somewhat puzzling. As part of the Eisenhower administration, however, he was a key player in the elaborate, if not always fully conscious, foreign policy game of "good cop, bad cop."

As always, however, massive retaliation made sense only if the world truly was bipolar, divided neatly into two conflicting camps, with each regional faction taking orders from a central power. Nuclear war, however, could only make sense if there were many discrete levels and kinds of nuclear war, representing many different scenarios. As noted, Eisenhower sought not only to strengthen the U.S. strategic nuclear force but also to develop weapons usable on the battlefield. In this sense, he may be regarded as the presidential parent of tactical nuclear weapons. His advocacy of scaled-down yield and reduced radiation effects for nuclear weapons reflected his perception of the atomic bomb as a realistic part of the U.S. arsenal.

What purpose there might be for such weapons was suggested when, according to French officials, Eisenhower offered France two atomic bombs in 1954 to break the Viet Minh siege against the embattled French outpost at Dien Bien Phu in the far northwest of Vietnam. In the Eisenhower years, it was evident to the government that a policy of massive retaliation did not fit all situations and that it was singularly ill-suited to the anticolonial struggles in Asia and in Africa. Had there been time to train French air crews or a U.S. willingness to use U.S. air crews to deliver atomic bombs in the vicinity of Dien Bien Phu, the selective use of specialized nuclear weapons might have been tested.

The Eisenhower administration did other things to broaden the range of means by which the United States might intervene in widely separated and distinct trouble spots. As judged by the administration's stated aims, its efforts were not unsuccessful. In Guatemala, for example, a CIA operation in June 1954 overturned the reformist government of Jacobo Arbenz Guzmán, aided by the Guatemalan army's refusal to fight in defense of Arbenz's legitimately elected regime. Concerned that Arbenz was leading Guatemala to the political left and troubled by Guatemala's refusal to endorse the March 1953 resolution of the Organization of American States opposing communism, Eisenhower authorized CIA Director Allen Dulles to back exiled Guatemalan Colonel Carlos Castillo Armas with arms and aircraft. Starting with just two hundred men on 18 June 1954, Castillo gathered new volunteers as he advanced toward Guatemala City, but CIA broadcasts exaggerated their

numbers. The Guatemalan army refused to support Arbenz, who ceded power to a provisional government that, in turn, yielded to another short-lived interim regime. After negotiations in which U.S. Ambassador John E. Peurifoy was prominent, Castillo became part of a ruling junta and eventually its head. U.S. air support of Castillo had been a crucial signal to the Guatemalan army to oppose Arbenz.

In the Philippines, on the other hand, the United States provided economic aid and substantial military assistance and advice to aid the government from its independence in 1946, notably through Defense Minister (later president) Ramón Magsaysay, in suppressing the Communist Hukbalahap (Huk) guerrillas. U.S. Air Force Colonel Edward G. Lansdale advocated a mixture of land reform, political rights, and armed resistance against the Huks, depriving them of support among the peasantry and so facilitating the demise of the rebels. In essence, to use the imagery of Mao Tse-tung, Lansdale sought to dry up the "sea of the people" in which the "guerrilla fish" swam, and, albeit temporarily, Magsaysay achieved that aim. It was a test case of counterinsurgency, although the term itself did not enjoy great vogue until the administration of John F. Kennedy (1961–1963).

In other places, however, great losses suffered by the colonial powers during World War II all but destroyed their chances of retaining control against insurgents in the years after the war. Notably, France faced a more intractable problem in the Southeast Asian states of Cambodia, Laos, and Vietnam. French Indochina, as the region had been known for a century, had experienced a generally exploitative colonial rule in which education, health care, and other components of social infrastructure had been neglected. On top of this, the French, who had administered Indochina on behalf of the Japanese during World War II, could expect great difficulty trying to reassert themselves as legitimate rulers of Indochina when the Japanese Empire fell in 1945. French collaboration with the Japanese had helped especially to spark Vietnamese national consciousness and, at the very least, Japan's successes in Southeast Asia in World War II proved that European powers—and presumably the French—could be beaten. By the time the United States became the major active outside influence in the region, from about 1956, the political context in which economic reform and military security would have to be accomplished had been fundamentally and, as it turned out, fatally compromised.

For all the professions of interest in the world as a whole, the preponderance of U.S. and free world forces was concentrated in a very few areas, most notably in NATO Europe. This fact alone necessitated that problems in other parts of the world be viewed in terms of their relationship to Europe and to the North Atlantic community in general. At the time of the Korean War, for example, Truman at first speculated that action on the Korean peninsula might be a diversionary move meant to give the Soviet Union a freer hand in the Middle East and Eastern Europe. Similarly, the change in U.S. policy from opposition to colonialism to support of the French in Indochina owed much to U.S. concern to stabilize a staunchly anti-Communist government in Paris. Time and again, U.S. and Soviet competition for the loyalties of developing nations was assessed for potentially destabilizing implications in Europe.

Hence, events touching upon Europe and the Mediterranean proved most powerful in determining the shape and character of the cold war. After 1953, for example, Korean affairs became an American rather than a NATO issue, and the same was substantially true of the U.S. venture in Vietnam in the 1960s. In fact, despite talk of a unified stance by the Western bloc, there were differences of perspective and of interest among Western nations, notably among Great Britain, France, and the United States. Great Britain and France sought to retain the vestiges of their empires, while the United States genuinely preferred and often promoted political self-determination. U.S. policy aimed at capitalizing on emerging Third World nationalism, provided it could be kept in traditional liberal-democratic political channels. France and Great Britain, however, sought to retain privileged interests, such as ownership and management of the Suez Canal, French domination of Algerian oil, and other practical benefits of empire.

Consequently, U.S. policies occasionally clashed with those of its formal allies. The unity of the Western bloc did not extend beyond opposition to the Soviet Union. Regional issues, such as access to oil, were shaped by national interests that were largely independent of the cold war with the Soviet Union. The tensions within the Western alliance, however, helped to shape the cold war conflict by limiting the measures the Western nations could take against the Eastern bloc.

Therefore, a sequence of events in Europe and the Mediterranean during the 1950s assumes an importance comparable in impact to the Korean War. One event was the Anglo-French conflict in 1956 with Egypt over the ownership of the Suez Canal, into which the Israelis injected themselves, largely in quest of their own national security interests. On 29 October, Israeli forces moved swiftly against Egyptian forces in the Sinai Peninsula, and within days French and British forces occupied the territory along the canal. Eisenhower was displeased at the neocolonialist tone of the operations, and he supported a UN resolution calling for a truce and a cutoff of oil to France and Great Britain, but the president was also angry at not having been consulted about the operation in advance. To the French and British, it was their own affair. To Eisenhower, it was part of the broad fabric of the cold war and a proper issue for consideration under the aegis of the North Atlantic alliance.

The Suez Crisis further exposed the anomalous place of Israel within the cold war. A creation of the United Nations, which authorized its founding in 1948, Israel became a focal point of tension between the superpowers, less because of specific Soviet concerns about Israel itself than because its existence so alienated neighboring Arab states whose anger might be exploited. The creation of Israel did much to help shape Arab consciousness and to give strength to the Arab nationalism and solidarity pursued by Egypt's Nasser. Culturally, the Israel of the

1950s was distinctly an outpost of European ideas and customs in the midst of an equally distinctly Arab region. Militarily, Israel was born in war and put a high percentage of its national income into defense. The country developed a domestic arms industry while also buying arms extensively abroad; it maintained a vigorous intelligence system and engaged in several wars and numerous preemptive strikes against its adversaries. Sympathy for the State of Israel within the United Nations owed a great deal to the revelations of the Holocaust in Europe during World War II, but continuing cooperation between the United States and Israel owed much, too, to U.S. interest in securing free communications in the eastern Mediterranean and free flow of oil from the Middle East. To confuse matters further, Israel was touted as an island of democracy in a sea of autocracy—at a time when U.S. officials wryly referred to the practice of human slavery in Saudi Arabia as an "idiosyncrasy." It is suggestive, therefore, that the U.S. anger over the Suez Crisis was aimed more at France and Britain than at Israel.

The Anglo-French action in Suez also blunted the criticism of the Soviet Union for its invasion of Hungary that same year, when the government of Imre Nagy announced its intention to withdraw from the Warsaw Pact. Secretary of State Dulles had spoken of the need for a rollback of communism and for liberation of the "captive nations," but Soviet Premier Nikita Khrushchev held on to Hungary at a cost of seven thousand Soviet and thirty thousand Hungarian dead. For the United States, the timing could scarcely have been worse. The Soviet action in Hungary began on 31 October 1956, just two days after the start of Israeli operations in the Sinai and immediately before the British and French joined the fight against Egypt. Sandwiched between these aggressive moves by U.S. allies, the Soviet assault on Hungary became less of a political liability for Moscow than might otherwise have been the case.

Despite its earlier calls for rollback of communism, the disquieting calm of the Eisenhower administration in the face of the Soviet attack in Hungary suggested a de facto recognition of

Eastern Europe as a Soviet sphere of influence, although formal acceptance of the notion would have been repugnant to most Americans. Rhetoric aside, the confrontation between NATO and the Warsaw Pact was to be a static one—an indefinite face-off rather than a dynamic series of thrusts and parries. As some Europeans quipped, under Truman there had been "active containment," while under Eisenhower there was "passive liberation." Beneath the superstructure of change, therefore, was the substructural continuity of containment.

The U.S. intervention in Lebanon in 1958 further helped to set the terms of the cold war confrontation. Eisenhower was concerned over the future of the Middle East, particularly with the rise of Arab nationalism. In 1957, he watched the effort by pro-Nasser forces nearly unseat Jordan's King Hussein. In July 1958, the government of Iraq was overthrown in a coup, which was an especially distressing development because Iraq had been the only Arab member of the U.S.–sponsored Baghdad Pact, renamed the Central Treaty Organization (CENTO) when Iraq withdrew. Thus, when Lebanon's President Chamoun sought U.S. intervention in his country, largely to shore up the strength of his political faction against its principal rival, Eisenhower was already primed to accede to the request. On 14 July 1958, Eisenhower ordered U.S. marines into Lebanon to guard against what was termed "indirect aggression." The first marine units to land found tourists and sunbathers on the beaches rather than a hostile force. Fortunately for U.S. interests, Lebanese armed forces refrained from engaging the Americans, and while the situation gradually cooled, the incident suggested the limits of U.S. understanding of the Middle East.

The intervention in Lebanon was premised on the Eisenhower Doctrine, first articulated on 5 January 1957 in a special message to Congress. Eisenhower requested—and later received—a congressional resolution authorizing his use of force to save any friendly Middle Eastern regime from attack by "international communism." The president did not wish the "holy places of the Middle East" to come under the sway of "atheistic materialism," nor did he want two-thirds of the known oil reserves to be "dominated by alien forces hostile to freedom." Although Eisenhower failed to comply with his own professed intention of informing Congress in advance of the use of force, the U.S. action in Lebanon was greeted with almost no question or criticism, thus serving as a milestone in the gradual expansion of presidential power that was a feature of the cold war era.

The emergence of a call for wars of national liberation forced the U.S. government to field questions on whether massive retaliation was a credible threat and hence a real deterrent in all cases. In practice, U.S. policy had proven itself to be relatively flexible for years prior to open debate on the subject in the later 1950s. The intervention in Lebanon proved this, as did the destabilization of the Arbenz government in Guatemala and the war in Korea. Conceivable as a response to a Soviet nuclear attack on the United States, U.S. nuclear retaliation strained belief when applied to anticolonial insurgencies in the "Third World."

What was new at the end of the 1950s was the elevated importance attached to the Third World as deserving of interest and of appropriate policy in its own right. Flexible response was first posed in the mid-1950s to revise strategic and theater nuclear war policies and was advocated prominently by Army Chief of Staff Maxwell Taylor. Flexible response allowed for the possibility of a general nuclear war, but it put greater emphasis on a tactical rather than strategic role for nuclear weapons. Moreover, it gave room for completely nonnuclear options, ranging down to counterinsurgency in conflicts given such terms as "brushfire wars" and "sublimited wars." Clearly, such an approach, if taken as national policy, inferred the need for major realignments of the U.S. military force structure.

How the desire to intervene flexibly in a regional or local conflict could affect force structure, deployments, and strategic thinking was well illustrated in the war in Vietnam, especially from 1956 to 1973. At various times, the war was fought as a counterinsurgency, as a conven-

tional localized ground war, as a quasi-independent air war, as a civil insurrection, as a regional aggression, and as a proxy war within the global cold war context. Each view invited the use of different forces or required the use of weapons and forces in different ways. One extreme example was the use of B-52 strategic bombers in tactical support of ground forces in South Vietnam after 1966. Similarly, the demands of the Vietnam War accelerated development of the combat use of the helicopter gunship, which first seemed key in opposing insurgencies but was soon adapted to planning for possible conventional war in Europe. Although flexible response could provide new options, it also risked fostering confusion.

There were pressures building against the status quo in the cold war from the Soviet side as well. Under Premier Khrushchev, the Soviet Union had developed a significant capability in ICBMs, strengthening Khrushchev's resolve to increase Soviet political influence in areas of long-standing differences, such as Central Europe and in the Third World. From the perspective of public relations, this posed a dilemma for the Eisenhower administration and for the successor Kennedy administration. The need to meet the challenge of insurgency and sublimited war was clear, but the grand posturing of Khrushchev and his claims to superiority in intercontinental missiles seemed to call for rejoinder.

Much of Khrushchev's bluster was simply a matter of personal style, one that contrasted markedly with the reserve of Eisenhower and, later, with the sharply articulated sophistication of Kennedy. Khrushchev's brash manner was more than a personal idiosyncrasy, however, and he knowingly overstated Soviet military capability, hoping to bluff his way into diplomatic leverage that his actual military power did not justify. Although Eisenhower knew that Khrushchev was exaggerating Soviet military strength, he was reluctant to reveal the human and technical intelligence means that gave him evidence that Khrushchev's claims were false. As a result, Khrushchev's bluff contributed to the incorrect view that Soviet military forces and experimental military technology surpassed those of the United States.

Beneath mannerisms, too, lay serious issues, such as the dangers of an escalating arms race, the lethal dangers of atmospheric testing of nuclear weapons, the risks of miscalculation of the intentions of one's adversary, and more. Hoping to resolve such issues, British Prime Minister Harold Macmillan urgently called for a new summit meeting. The major parties agreed—the United States rather as a personal favor to Macmillan—and they were scheduled to meet on 16 May 1960 in Paris.

Shortly before the meeting was to convene, however, on 1 May a U.S. U-2 reconnaissance aircraft was shot down over the Soviet Union. Such overflights had been known to the Soviet leadership for some time. The U.S. government pretended that they were not taking place, and the Soviet Union, for fear of revealing its inability to shoot the aircraft down, had chosen not to complain. By 1960, however, Soviet air-to-ground missile technology had achieved the capability of taking down the high-flying U-2. First doubting that the Soviets could have shot the aircraft down and then believing that its pilot, Francis Gary Powers, would have killed himself, Eisenhower openly described the incident as an accidental straying of the U-2 off course. Unfortunately for Eisenhower—and for Macmillan's hopes for the Paris summit—Powers survived to confess that he had been on a spy mission for the CIA. President Eisenhower's embarrassment at being caught in a lie over the U-2 aerial reconnaissance program was great—made all the more so by Khrushchev's deliberate exploitation of the incident.

The failure of the Paris summit was curiously instructive. Whether he did so consciously or not, Khrushchev chose to capitalize on the political gaffe of Eisenhower, rather than restrain himself and strive for agreement on such issues as development and testing of nuclear weapons. It also suggested that, in the cold war the alleviation of an actual military problem through negotiation might be deemed less advantageous to a nation than the exploitation of the failings of one's adversary for the purposes of public relations. In short, image counted, sometimes it seemed even more than military dangers. Credibility also counted, as if the personal embarrassment of a president caught in a lie might reduce the strategic clout of the nation he represented. In this sense, Khrushchev's belittling of Eisenhower at the Paris summit was a foretaste of his own loss of face during the Cuban Missile Crisis (1962).

Shortly before leaving the presidency in 1961, Eisenhower delivered a "farewell address" to the American people that became his most famous and most enduringly influential speech. In this address, Eisenhower warned Americans to resist the rising influence of university elites and "think tanks," which had enormous impact on government policy despite having no electoral mandate. Above all, however, official and popular attention fastened upon Eisenhower's caution against unwarranted influence from the military–industrial complex. Because of its large place in the economy and its important role as an employer of both civilian workers and military personnel, the military–industrial complex could not escape having widespread impact on American society. Eisenhower saw this as a potential danger to the social, economic, and political system, even if it also seemed to be a necessary cost of waging the cold war. Observant though he was, Eisenhower could offer no concrete solution and no protection, other than lasting public vigilance.

The 1961 farewell address marked a culmination in early cold war thinking. Eisenhower's caution about a military–industrial complex would have been superfluous had it not been for the magnitude of that complex. Eisenhower, who as president had worried over the size of the federal budget in general and the military budget in particular, ironically presided over what was, compared to its share of the federal budget in peacetime years before 1940, the largest peacetime military budget in history. In addition, the increasing complexity and cost of developing new weapons systems had led to a closer intertwining of private contractors and government agencies, as more federal money went into research and development. The armed forces were not only greater in size but more grand in sweep and in mission than in the past.

Eisenhower worried over where it all would lead. He knew that the military forces he left to Kennedy in 1961 enjoyed overwhelming superiority over those of the Soviet Union, but he also knew that Soviet capabilities were growing. Negotiations seemed all the more important, but as his recent experience at Paris suggested, confrontation remained the rule of the day.

When Kennedy succeeded Eisenhower as president in January 1961, he made clear in his inaugural address that he would confront what he saw as a coordinated Communist challenge against the non-Communist periphery of the free world. This made the continuing problems in Southeast Asia, especially in Laos, a major source of concern to Kennedy. Even more galling was the presence of an avowedly Marxist government on the island of Cuba, scarcely seventy miles from the southernmost tip of Florida. The success of the Cuban revolution of 1959, led by Fidel Castro, established a Communist foothold in the Western Hemisphere, and both Eisenhower and Kennedy considered a Communist Cuba to be a violation of the spirit of the Monroe Doctrine and a challenge to the integrity of the Organization of American States. In secret, Eisenhower had authorized the CIA to plan the overthrow of the Castro regime.

In April 1961, Kennedy authorized the implementation of most parts of the CIA plan. He approved a limited invasion of Cuba by about fifteen hundred exiles who had fled their home island during the early phases of its rules under Castro, but Kennedy did not approve air support using U.S. aircraft and crews, a deficiency that contributed to the failure of the plan. Although the invasion had been planned during Eisenhower's tenure, the idea of intervening in a "flexible" way appealed to Kennedy. The landing, at the Bay of Pigs on 17 April, proved disastrous, and the Kennedy administration was soon bartering for the release of prisoners.

Weakened and embarrassed by his failure over the Bay of Pigs incident, Kennedy met with Nikita Khrushchev in Vienna (3–4 June). Evidently, Khrushchev was not impressed. Their key disagreement was over the status of Germany. Khrushchev sought de jure recognition of the boundary between East Germany and West Germany, part of an effort to stem the loss of skilled and educated East Germans to the West. Kennedy feared that any renegotiation of the *modus vivendi* in Germany would open a Pandora's box. Determined to show strength, Kennedy won an immediate multibillion dollar supplement to the military budget, called up reservists, increased draft calls, and otherwise sought to mobilize in the face of what he described as an attempt at the "neutralization of Western Europe." Disregarding the flurry of U.S. activity, on 13 August 1961, Khrushchev ordered the construction of a wall dividing East and West Berlin. For most of three decades, the Berlin Wall was a prominent symbol of the division of Europe in the cold war. Practically, however, it stemmed the exodus of talent through East Berlin that had been a cause of Soviet concern. In essence, Khrushchev had gotten his way.

The Cuban Missile Crisis (October 1962) brought the early phases of the cold war to a frightening culmination in a test of deterrence based on the risk of nuclear conflict. It also reflected the Kennedy administration's belief in crisis management, an approach that contributed to the manner in which the Berlin Crisis had been handled yet also fostered a fixation on one's credibility. The incident also required prompt response of the military to presidential directives, thus reflecting the ever deeper penetration of the president into the management of military operations as the cold war progressed. By establishing a special separate group known as ExCom to manage the crisis, Kennedy did something of an end run around some of the formal and standard mechanisms for defining and executing national security policy.

By early autumn 1962, U-2 reconnaissance aircraft had acquired firm evidence that bases were being built in Cuba for the deployment of Soviet intermediate-range missiles. By deploying a forward threat against targets in the eastern United States before having a sufficient number of intercontinental missiles, Khrushchev sought to leapfrog his own technology to accomplish the same strategic objective. Kennedy viewed such a deployment as a direct violation of the Monroe Doctrine as well as a serious threat to the physical security of the United States. On 22 October 1962, Kennedy informed the Soviet ambassador that he would insist that no missiles be deployed and, as he added in a television broadcast to the American public that same evening, that he would accept the risk of worldwide nuclear war.

Precisely how to persuade the Soviets to reverse their plans, and what methods to use to force the issue, was a subject of intense discussion. The president saw problems with air strikes at targets in Cuba. For one thing, their promptness—customarily seen as a positive attribute—made the decision to use them functionally irreversible. Similarly, for all the talk of precision in the execution of bombing runs, the word "precision" needed political definition. Was bombing "precise" and discriminate if, in destroying missile installations, Soviet technicians were also killed? Would that constitute an escalation in the face-off between the Soviet Union and the United States?

Kennedy thus gravitated toward a naval blockade, aimed at preventing missiles from the Soviet Union from actually reaching Cuba and thus averting the need for a direct attack on Cuban territory. Meanwhile, at sea, the threats raised by a blockade would force the Soviet Union to make yet another decision—whether to attempt to run the blockade—giving it a chance to back away from the challenge or, in the contrary case, raising anew the question of ultimate responsibility for the crisis. Naval blockades have traditionally been regarded as acts of war. Imposing one, therefore, would permit nationals affected by it to condemn the United States for "firing the first shot." Kennedy's solution to this last difficulty was rhetorical. Instead of imposing a blockade, Kennedy specified that it was to be a naval quarantine of the island. Despite specificity as to what cargo was to be interdicted, it amounted to the same thing, but the neologism was politically conven-

ient, permitting friend and foe alike to pretend that the level of challenge was lower than was really the case and to act accordingly.

The widespread tolerance of the Kennedy administration's concept of a naval quarantine was itself a commentary on the nature and state of the cold war at the time—Charles de Gaulle of France, considered Kennedy's actions necessary and statesmanlike, Great Britain's Prime Minister Macmillan loyally supported Kennedy, and there was widespread support in the United Nations, a body presumably dedicated to the preservation of international law. The compelling horror of a possible nuclear war induced nations to give new turns to traditional precepts of international law, affording some latitude to the nuclear-equipped powers by not holding them to the letter of the law. In fact, if not in formal rhetoric, the United States could make a "wartime" commitment without resorting to a full array of wartime measures. In the process, new pages in international law were written de facto. For example, how was it that one country, the Soviet Union, had no right to supply weapons to another, Cuba? How was it, too, that Soviet missiles in Cuba could be called clearly offensive when comparable U.S. missiles based in Turkey and targeted at the Soviet Union were clearly defensive? Both legal and technical argumentation swayed before the power of nuclear armaments. The outcome, however, was that Khrushchev "blinked," offering to remove the missiles in exchange for a U.S. guarantee against an invasion of Cuba. Kennedy agreed on 27 October, and later and much more quietly and in a manner that gave no prestige to the Soviet Union, U.S. missiles were withdrawn from Turkey.

In the Cuban Missile Crisis and other affairs, the Kennedy administration's national security team tended to perceive themselves as engaged in a largely if not wholly new approach to world military problems. They made much of the concept of crisis management, for example, and they relied extensively on new quantitative and conceptual tools in military management. Still, despite the difference in tone that Kennedy hoped to create, his emphasis on "crisis consciousness" in many ways extended the psychology of brinksmanship articulated by Eisenhower and Dulles. Like Eisenhower, Kennedy remained wedded to the pursuit of U.S. strategic superiority over the Soviet Union, which still required a commitment to the use of massive retaliation as the basis for deterrence. Without strategic superiority, what sort of outcome would have been possible in the Cuban Missile Crisis?

The Cuban Missile Crisis, therefore, was one of the most intense moments of the cold war and a culmination and a conclusion of its formative and early phases. The strategy of deterrence based on massive retaliation had been developed, implemented, and terrifyingly tested. The crisis wrought changes in temperament as well as in leadership in the Soviet Union and in the United States. In the Soviet Union, Khrushchev was soon displaced as premier and Communist party chairman, succeeded by Leonid Brezhnev, who set out on a military buildup aimed at achieving strategic military parity with the United States. Meanwhile, while continuing the modernization of its strategic forces in an ultimately vain effort to preserve strategic military superiority, the U.S. government increasingly pursued a capability for flexible response to international challenges. Having come so close to nuclear war encouraged the quest for nonnuclear alternatives. Events after 1962 thus led to a new formulation of the relationship between the superpowers and a new phase of the cold war.

The subsequent history of the cold war was long and tangled, but in the main it recapitulated and then resolved the several major problems that had been set out during its inception and first decades. For example, the quest for nuclear superiority that had been linked to the policy of massive retaliation yielded to a succession of policies that accommodated real, if unwelcome, developments. Under Brezhnev, the Soviet Union built more and larger missiles, modernized and expanded its air forces, and enlarged its naval forces. Despite the Minuteman ICBM deployments in the 1960s and the subsequent fitting of the Minuteman III missiles with

multiple, independently targeted reentry vehicles (MIRVs), the Soviet Union persisted in the arms race until it enjoyed "essential equivalency" with the United States, albeit with a different distribution of weapons.

In this environment, each side was capable of punishing the other so severely in the event of an attack that they were said to have "mutually deterred" one another. After still further developments and deployments, the Soviet Union and the United States were also said to possess the capacity for mutual assured destruction (MAD). These arms buildups, nevertheless, gave added impetus to arms negotiations. From the 1963 treaty that limited nuclear testing through the Strategic Arms Limitation Treaty (SALT I) signed by President Richard Nixon and Leonid Brezhnev in May 1972 to the SALT II treaty signed by Brezhnev and President Jimmy Carter in June 1979, signs emerged that a modus vivendi might be not only necessary but possible. For the Soviet Union, the attainment of parity created a chance for negotiations. For the United States, the ever more evident complexity of the world, perhaps best exemplified by the gradual resumption of U.S. relations with China, beginning in 1969, suggested that much of the conceptual framework of the cold war might be discarded.

Perhaps no single phenomenon so transformed the U.S. perception of world affairs during the cold war era after 1962 as America's long involvement in Vietnam. From its origins in the 1950s and early 1960s, the Vietnam conflict was cast as a battle against China, as a test case in the vast brief of the cold war, and not primarily as an indigenous conflict and civil war. By the late 1960s and most assuredly by 1973, when the United States withdrew from Vietnam, the cold war consensus of bipartisanship within the United States had returned, along with a more traditional spirit of skepticism toward U.S. policies and policymakers. It is telling that the Nixon administration's steps toward normalization of relations with China, at first conceived as the master plan of the Vietnam conflict, were taken during the late throes of that very same war. The U.S. venture in Vietnam took down much of the architecture of cold war thinking along with it.

Tensions arose in many parts of the world in the 1970s, such as in sub-Saharan Africa, southeast Asia, and the Middle East, but U.S. leaders showed increasing sensitivity to the strength of local conditions as the determining force of political and military events, even if it was sometimes too difficult to accept the results that such local conditions by themselves might yield. It appeared that the United States and the Soviet Union were now distinctly third parties in regional conflicts; both were being used as much as they were using others. In 1973, for example, the start of the Yom Kippur War between various Arab states and Israel required neither Americans nor Soviets, but the risk of war between the superpowers rose because of their embroilment in what was, in its inception, the affairs of others. The slow recognition of this phenomenon helped U.S. and Soviet leaders to become more favorable to discussion of complicated regional security issues, the defusing of which would go far toward terminating the cold war.

One region in which a clearly different reality existed by 1990 than had prevailed in 1945 or 1950 was in northeast Asia. As Soviet policy changed under Mikhail Gorbachev, giving more opportunity for institutional change and free expression of ideas, the largely Stalinist regime of Kim Il-sung in North Korea was virtually isolated. South Korea, thriving economically, opened talks with North Korea aimed at eventual reunification of their peninsula. Meanwhile, Japan was being brought toward reexamination of its constitutional prohibition against maintaining an expeditionary military capability, a provision insisted on by the United States as part of the treaty arrangements with Japan executed in 1951 but now questioned by many U.S. leaders. So, too, China was officially acknowledged to be one country, although subtle mechanisms allowed the continuation of a non-Communist government on Taiwan, and it enjoyed its seat on the Security Council in the United Nations as well as diplomatic relations with the world at large. In all, the peculiar and artificial special arrangements concocted after World War II for the administration of east Asian affairs were yielding to relationships that seemed to grow naturally from the economic and social realities of the region.

Europe, however, was the region where perhaps the most significant change had been needed to hasten the end of the cold war. Each side had held to a particularly hard line in central and eastern Europe. The Eisenhower administration had called for a rollback of communism from the Eastern European countries, but Khrushchev had sent troops and tank forces into Budapest to crush the independence-minded Hungarian government when it sought to pull out of the Warsaw Pact in 1956. When the government of Alexander Dubcek in Czechoslovakia pursued a course of reform that smacked too much of intellectual and political diversity, Brezhnev ordered Warsaw Pact forces into the capital city of Prague and throughout the country to reinstitute more repressive policies in August 1968. Worse, Brezhnev articulated his own doctrine, a mirror image of Truman's, claiming the right to intervene anywhere to save a Communist regime from enemies foreign or domestic.

Throughout this period, Europe remained virtually an armed camp, even if its western half and much of its center also enjoyed extraordinary economic vitality. In the late 1970s and throughout the 1980s, special technological efforts to meet the perceived security needs of NATO actually fostered reexamination of many aspects of the policies the technology was designed to implement. The proposal to build and deploy neutron bombs, for example—weapons that would have limited blast effect but had great radiation lethality—forced the issue of whether NATO was to defend people or structures. The deployment of cruise missiles, whose inexpensiveness made it possible to buy them in large numbers and whose low-altitude attack profile made defending against them extremely difficult, raised the ugly prospect of still new realms in the already dizzying arms race. By 1990 the sheer absence of war in Europe for several decades made NATO and the Warsaw Pact seem to be artifacts from a very different age, especially because the large majority of the European population had no first-hand experience of war at all.

Even so, President Ronald Reagan continued to see the Soviet Union as a threat, NATO as a necessity, and the cold war confrontation as a still vital reality. Swept into the presidency in 1980 by a strong majority, Reagan used his political strength effectively to expand and hasten a military buildup that had been started on a more modest basis by Jimmy Carter in the second half of his presidency (1977–1981). In essence, Reagan sought to make clear to Soviet leaders that the United States would not slacken in opposing Soviet efforts to expand its influence. Even more so, the U.S. rearmament program, including the new Peacekeeper ICBM, B-1 and B-2 bombers, and a navy of six hundred ships, would raise the cost of military competition to a level that could not be sustained by the Soviet economy.

While criticizing the Soviet Union as an "evil empire," Reagan also challenged Brezhnev to negotiate a sharp reduction in strategic arms levels. After Brezhnev's death, Constantin Chernenko served briefly, followed by the similarly short-lived rule of Yuri Andropov. Little could be achieved in U.S.-Soviet relations during that unstable period, which nevertheless whetted both the Soviet and the U.S. appetites for renewed efforts at negotiation. This appetite was to be sated when Mikhail Gorbachev came to power. Calling for *perestroika*, a restructuring of Soviet institutions, and *glasnost*, a new openness in Soviet society that seemed to promise the chance for liberal reforms, Gorbachev first warned that the Soviet Union would counter any weapons that the United States chose to deploy. U.S. Secretary of State George Schultz saw this as evidence that the U.S. arms buildup was having the desired effect of forcing the Soviet Union to negotiations, lest the moribund Soviet domestic economy have no prospect for improvement. In essence, *perestroika* seemed inconsistent with a perpetual arms race, and Gorbachev went to great pains to reassure America's NATO allies of his good intentions.

In 1983, Reagan proposed that the United States develop a space-based system to defend against ICBMs carrying nuclear warheads. Officially designated the Strategic Defense Initiative (SDI), the concept was soon given the satirical nickname "Star Wars," after a popular film blending science fiction and myth. Urged upon Reagan by influential scientist Edward Teller, SDI was debated primarily on three grounds. One was its feasibility, which Teller and retired Army Lieutenant General Daniel O. Graham, who promoted SDI under the rubric "High Frontier," insisted was within sight. A second was its effect on the cold war, since critics feared that SDI would open a whole new realm of arms competition. Those who saw space as a sanctuary to be kept free of weapons objected in principle. A third area of debate was SDI's morality, which Reagan, Teller, Graham, and other advocates insisted was unassailable.

The debate over these issues tended to overlook the extraordinary change in strategic conceptualization that Reagan was proposing. Ever since 1945, the primacy of the strategic offensive had been taken as unassailable truth, and preventing the attack by deterrence was the only means of avoiding devastation. Reagan proposed that the technology foreseeable in the 1980s and beyond would restore primacy to the strategic defensive. To the extent that the whole history of the cold war revolved around group risk in an era of inevitable vulnerability to strategic nuclear attack, Reagan was also pointing beyond the horizon of the cold war itself.

For Gorbachev, however, SDI was another threat to the internal reforms that he knew the Soviet Union needed desperately if it were to remain a world power. If a greater arms race over space were to join the existing arms race on the planet's surface, the economy of the Soviet Union would be strained even more severely. Worse, under immediate external pressures from the United States and NATO, Gorbachev would have no breathing room in which to execute internal reforms. The entire arms buildup, then, played a role in making success in strategic arms reduction talks (START) essential.

Reagan and Gorbachev also anticipated aspects of world politics after the cold war when they focused increasingly on regional security issues. A global perspective, which had stereotyped conflict as either part of a centrally organized Communist conspiracy or else a capitalist one, had been part and parcel of cold war thought. Viewing regional problems as having their own dynamics not only pointed beyond bipolar confrontation but also contributed to the eventual joining of the United States and the Soviet Union in common political cause during the Gulf War of 1991.

The relaxation of internal imperial sway over the Warsaw Pact countries by Gorbachev sharply accelerated the pace of change within Eastern Europe, where a succession of political revolutions took place at the end of the 1980s and culminated in 1990. One immediate consequence was the virtual negation of the internal cohesion of the Warsaw Pact as a military force. Effectively deprived of mechanisms of command and forces to control, the pact merely awaited official announcement of its demise toward the end of 1990. Another consequence was the rapid reunification of Germany with the leaders of its eastern and western parts scarcely concealing their comparative disinterest in the fate of NATO and the Warsaw Pact. By late 1990, symbols of the artificial divisions of the cold war such as the Berlin Wall had been torn down, and Germany, the architect of the conflict that had led to the cold war, had itself once again been made whole. Large arsenals and great armed forces remained in many countries and posed many risks, but such phenomena reflected the nature of conventional power politics more than any special ideology-bound conflict. World powers and the world community at large had substantially freed themselves of the clichés of the cold war, and for a while the tormenting union of victory and fear seemed to yield to a moment of accommodation and hope.

The clear end of the cold war came with the clear end of the Soviet Union and hence with the absolute destruction of the bipolar competition that had been under way since 1945. In August 1991 a group of Soviet officials opposed to Gorbachev's internal reforms and external policies as well attempted a coup. Resistance in Moscow formed rapidly, a reflection to some extent of the success of Gorbachev's *glasnost,*

and Boris Yeltsin, president of the Russian Federation and alternately an ally and an opponent of Gorbachev, led the stand against the coup. Gorbachev was soon returned to office, but his power, already depleted as the strains of nationalist sympathy among the Soviet Union's constituent republics increased, continued to decline. By late 1991, little remained of the Soviet Union but a name, and in December 1991 the Chamber of People's Deputies officially voted the Soviet Union out of existence. The cold war was clearly at an end.

The military legacy of the cold war to the succeeding era included still massive arsenals of missiles, warheads, bomber aircraft, sea forces, and other assets, distributed among many of the former Soviet Union's constituent republics, which were now independent states. These arsenals also could be treated as warehouses for arms sales to other nations, whose own local and regional aspirations could no longer be restrained by reference to a global bipolar confrontation or by an authoritarian Communist regime. The political legacy of the cold war included an array of long-suppressed nationalist conflicts within the states of the former Soviet Union and within the Eastern European nations that had been under Soviet sway. The "new world order" foreseen by President George Bush would include many problems that had originated before the cold war era and had survived it.

See also THE DEVELOPMENT OF AN AMERICAN MILITARY PHILOSOPHY; GUNBOAT DIPLOMACY, 1776–1992; THE KOREAN WAR; POLITICAL GOALS AND THE DEVELOPMENT OF MILITARY STRATEGY; THE PRESIDENCY AND THE MILITARY; *and* MILITARY STRATEGY IN THE NUCLEAR AGE.

BIBLIOGRAPHY

Borowski, Harry R. *A Hollow Threat: Strategic Air Power and Containment Before Korea* (1982).

Brodie, Bernard. *Strategy in the Missile Age* (1959).

Campbell, Thomas M. *Masquerade Peace: America's U.N. Policy, 1944–1945* (1973).

Canan, James W. *The Superwarriors: The Fantastic World of Pentagon Superweapons* (1975).

Chang, Gordon H. *Friends and Enemies: The United States, China, and the Soviet Union, 1948–1972* (1990).

Davis, Lynn E. *The Cold War Begins, Soviet-American Conflict over Eastern Europe* (1974).

Dobbs, Charles M. *The Unwanted Symbol: American Foreign Policy, the Cold War, and Korea, 1945–1950* (1981).

Eglin, James Meikle. *Air Defense in the Nuclear Age: The Post-War Development of American and Soviet Strategic Defense Systems* (1988).

Etzold, Thomas H. *Defense or Delusion?: America's Military in the 1980s* (1982).

Gaddis, John Lewis. *Strategies of Containment: A Critical Appraisal of Postwar American Security Policy* (1982).

Gardner, Lloyd C. *Architects of Illusion: Men and Ideas in American Foreign Policy, 1941–1949* (1970).

Halle, Louis J. *The Cold War as History* (1967).

Haynes, Richard F. *The Awesome Power: Harry S. Truman as Commander in Chief* (1973).

Herkin, Gregg. *The Winning Weapon: The Atomic Bomb in the Cold War, 1945–1950* (1980).

Hewes, James E., Jr. *From Root to McNamara: Army Organization and Administration, 1900–1963* (1975).

Kimball, John C. *Europe and North America: An Atlas-Almanac of Allies and Adversaries* (1986).

Kissinger, Henry. *Nuclear Weapons and Foreign Policy* (1957).

Kuniholm, Bruce Robellet. *The Origins of the Cold War in the Near East: Great Power Conflict and Diplomacy in Iran, Turkey, and Greece* (1980).

LaFeber, Walter. *America, Russia, and the Cold War, 1945–1980*, 4th ed. (1980).

Linenthal, Edward Tabor. *Symbolic Defense: The Cultural Significance of the Strategic Defense Initiative* (1989).

Lukacs, John. *A New History of the Cold War*, 3rd ed. (1966).

———. *1945, Year Zero* (1978).

Luttwak, Edward. *The Pentagon and the Art of War: The Question of Military Reform* (1984).

Nincic, Miroslav. *Anatomy of Hostility: The U.S.-Soviet Rivalry in Perspective* (1989).

Russett, Bruce M., and Alfred Stepan, eds. *Military Force and American Society* (1973).

Teller, Edward. *Better a Shield Than a Sword: Perspectives on Defense and Technology* (1987).

Treverton, Gregory F. *The Dollar Drain and American Forces in Germany: Managing the Political Economics of Alliance* (1978).

Wittner, Lawrence S. *Cold War America: From Hiroshima to Watergate* (1975).

———. *American Intervention in Greece, 1943–1949* (1982).

Yergin, Daniel. *Shattered Peace: The Origins of the Cold War and the National Security State* (1977).

York, Herbert. *Making Weapons, Talking Peace: A Physicist's Odyssey from Hiroshima to Geneva* (1987).

THE KOREAN WAR

Billy C. Mossman

On Sunday morning, 25 June 1950, the Communist government of North Korea launched its army in a full-scale offensive against the Republic of Korea to the south. In one sense the invasion marked the beginning of a civil war between segments of a strongly nationalistic people whose country had been divided politically, economically, and geographically in the aftermath of World War II. U.S. officials, however, saw the attack as an eruption in the cold war, the larger sequel to World War II in which, short of open warfare, the United States led efforts to contain attempts by the Soviet Union to extend the reach of its power and Communist ideology. In this view the North Korean attack was a Soviet move, through a puppet state, to bring all of Korea under Communist control. Out of this perception the United States immediately took steps against the venture. Set in motion by the North Korean invasion and the U.S. reaction to it was a multinational war lasting three years.

KOREA AND THE COLD WAR

To much of the world Korea was an unknown place at the time of the North Korean attack. The land had received some notice when the Allied victory over Japan in World War II freed Korea from forty years of Japanese rule. After U.S. and Soviet occupation forces entered the land, most people outside Asia gave scant heed to subsequent events in Korea and, consequently, knew little of the circumstances that set the stage for the North Korean invasion.

Shaped somewhat like the state of Florida, Korea is a peninsula measuring two hundred miles at its widest and reaching some six hundred miles southeastward from the central Asian mainland. Out of a mass of high, jumbled ridges in the far north, the main Taebaek Mountains run the length of the east coast. From this axial spine spur ranges spread southwestward across most of the peninsula. Predominant among these spurs is the Sobaek range in southern Korea, which stands between the drainage basins of the Han River in the north and the Naktong River in the south. The few existing lowlands, dotted by hills and surrounded by mountains, lie mainly along the west coast.

In the north, Korea borders on Manchuria and, for a few miles in the far northeast, on the Soviet Union. To the west the Yellow Sea separates Korea from north-central China. To the east the Sea of Japan stands between the peninsula and the islands of Japan. Less than one hundred fifty miles off the southeastern tip of Korea across the Korea and Tsushima straits lies Kyushu, Japan's southernmost main island.

So located, Korea represented a strategic crossroads to its three stronger neighbors. For China and Russia, it was a dagger pointed at Japan; for Japan, it was a stepping stone to the Asian mainland. Rivalry over control of Korea among these nations ended at the turn of the twentieth century with Japan the victor, first in the Sino-Japanese War (1894–1895), then in the Russo-Japanese War (1904–1905). Japan initially handled Korea as a protectorate, then, in 1910, formally annexed the land as a colony in the Japanese empire. In the course of developing Allied strategy during World War II, President Franklin D. Roosevelt, Great Britain's Prime Minister Winston S. Churchill, and China's Generalissimo Chiang Kai-shek agreed during the Cairo Conference in November 1943 that Japan was to be stripped of all territories it had seized "by violence and greed." Addressing Korea specifically, they declared that "in due course Korea shall become free and independent." Following the surrender of Germany on 8 May 1945, Allied leaders reaffirmed the Declaration of Cairo as they set out terms for the surrender of Japan during the Potsdam Conference in July 1945. The Soviet Union subscribed to the declaration when it entered the war against Japan on 9 August 1945.

At the time of the Potsdam meeting, Allied planning for operations in the Far East rested on estimates that Japan could be defeated in about one year. The end came much sooner. On 6 August 1945, the United States dropped the world's first atomic bomb on the Japanese city of Hiroshima, and three days later—the same day that Soviet forces opened attacks on Japanese troops in Manchuria—delivered a second atomic bomb on the city of Nagasaki. The Japanese sued for peace on 10 August and accepted the Potsdam surrender terms four days later. As planned by U.S. officials, Korea was divided into two occupation zones delineated by the thirty-eighth parallel of north latitude crossing the peninsula at its waist. Soviet troops were to take the Japanese surrender north of the parallel, U.S. forces to the south. Soviet Premier Joseph V. Stalin accepted this plan on 16 August, by which date the Soviet Twenty-fifth Army,

commanded by Colonel General Ivan Chistyakov, already had entered northern Korea. By the end of August, the Soviets interned Japanese military forces and members of the colonial government located in their zone and began transferring many of the captives to labor camps in the Soviet Union.

General Douglas MacArthur was charged by U.S. authorities to handle the occupation of southern Korea as well as all of Japan. He designated the U.S. Army Twenty–fourth Corps, commanded by Lieutenant General John R. Hodge, to accept the Japanese surrender below the thirty-eighth parallel. As commander of U.S. Army forces in Korea, General Hodge led his corps, consisting of the Sixth, Seventh, and Fortieth infantry divisions, into Korea on 8 September. On the following day, he received the surrender of Japanese troops and governmental officials in a ceremony at Seoul, Korea's capital city in the west-central area of the peninsula.

Upon the arrival of Soviet and U.S. forces, the Korean people clamored for full and immediate independence. One group, a Communist-dominated coalition of "people's committees" calling itself the People's Republic, declared itself to be the government of all of Korea. In southern Korea alone, some seventy political and social organizations sprang up, each claiming to be qualified to form a government, but none of these factions possessed a solid constituency or candidates of proven ability and experience. This inadequacy had been anticipated in the Declaration of Cairo, which legislated an independent Korea "in due course." First to be achieved under Allied guidance, at least in the U.S. view, was the regeneration of indigenous leadership, so completely denied by the Japanese, and the redirection and rehabilitation of the Korean economy, which had been geared to serve Japanese requirements and was now in chaos.

According to U.S. officials, the achievement of these goals would be a relatively short-term process. First, Japanese troops in all of Korea would be disarmed and repatriated to Japan, along with Japanese officials and civilians residing in the country. Next there would be a grad-

USSR

MANCHURIA

CHINA

Yalu River

Chongjin

CHINA

Kanggye

UN COMMAND FRONT
25 NOVEMBER 1950

THE
KOREAN WAR
1950-1953

Yalu River

CHINA

NORTH
KOREA

Iwon

SEA

Changjin
Reservoir

OF JAPAN

Chongchon River

Hungnam

PYONGYANG

Yongdok

Wonsan

IRON
TRIANGLE

ARMISTICE LINE
27 JULY 1953

Pyonggang

Imjin R.

Kumhwa
Chorwon

Yangyang

38TH PARALLEL

ONGJIN
PENINSULA

Panmunjom

Kaesong

Kimpo Airfield

Chunchon

Inchon

SEOUL

Suwon
Osan

Han River

T
A
E
B
A
E
K

M
T
S
.

SOUTH
KOREA

YELLOW

S
O
B
A
E
K

M
T
S
.

Yondok

SEA

Kum River

Taejon

N
a
k
t
o
n
g

R
i
v
e
r

Taegu

PUSAN PERIMETER
15 SEPTEMBER 1950

CHIRI
MTS.

Masan

Pusan

STRAIT

KOJE-DO
ISLAND

KOREA

TSUSHIMA

STRAIT

TSUSHIMA

MILES

5 10 20 30 40 50

KYUSHU

JAPAN

ual transfer of governmental functions to Korean officials. Last, U.S. and Soviet forces would withdraw after the Korean people established a united and independent government of their own choosing.

In line with this view, General Hodge spread his divisions throughout southern Korea to disarm and evacuate the Japanese and to maintain order. On 12 September he established the United States Army Military Government in Korea with Major General Archibald V. Arnold, the commander of the Seventh Division, as military governor. General Arnold drew an immediate storm of protest from the Korean people when he retained experienced Japanese in key positions, including zonal police, to bridge the eventual transfer of functions to Korean officials. To the Koreans, retaining the hated Japanese in authority, even temporarily, was unthinkable. Arnold quickly corrected the matter. At top government levels, he replaced the Japanese with U.S. officers, assigning Koreans to them as advisers and apprentices. He also established, under U.S. supervision, the all-Korean Police Bureau. Over time places were nominally reversed. Koreans occupied the positions of authority and Americans assumed the roles of advisers, but the latter continued to exercise decisive influence on government activities.

Late in 1945, U.S. military government officials proposed to establish a South Korean army, navy, and air force, but Washington authorities disapproved any development of full-fledged defense forces lest doing so jeopardize forthcoming negotiations with the Soviet Union on the organization of a provisional government for the whole of Korea. The most allowed was the formation of a constabulary as a police reserve to assist in maintaining internal order, for which there was distinct need, and a coast guard to suppress the smuggling and piracy then prevalent in the coastal waters. Both forces took shape slowly. By December 1946 the constabulary numbered scarcely more than five thousand men, armed with Japanese rifles, a few Japanese machine guns, and a small amount of ammunition for each. Development of the coast guard was handicapped by a pau-

city of experienced Korean seamen and a shortage of ships.

The Soviets established no military government in northern Korea. Initially, they governed through the people's committees that had sprung up. They also brought back large numbers of Korean expatriates who had long resided in the Soviet Union. Under the guidance of a special political detachment from the headquarters of the Soviet army's First Far Eastern Front, the expatriates enlarged and took control of the people's committees. In October 1945, the Soviets placed expatriate Kim Il Sung in control of all Korean Communists, creating the North Korean Labor Party. Four months later, Kim was established as head of a central government called the Interim People's Committee, which was seated in the city of Pyongyang, 120 miles north of Seoul. Thus, behind a facade of native government, the Soviets, in rather short order, communized all of northern Korea.

As had the Americans in the south, the Soviets formed native zonal police. They also organized two groups of military forces, the Border Constabulary and the Peace Preservation Army, drawing their core personnel from experienced Koreans brought back from the Soviet Union and reinforcing these with returning Koreans who had fought the Japanese in China during World War II. Most of the constabulary units eventually took position along the thirty-eighth parallel. The army, which reached a strength of twenty thousand by the end of 1946, trained for combat.

Meanwhile, General Hodge failed in his attempt to negotiate a unification of the economy and a central Korean administration with his counterpart in the north. General Chistyakov restricted movement into and out of northern Korea, limited telephone communications between zones, withdrew a Soviet liaison detachment established earlier in Seoul, and in mid-October 1945 notified Hodge that there would be no negotiations between them until decisions were made and relations established at the top political level. Following his only recourse, Hodge channeled a request to Washington for government action on the matter.

During the Potsdam Conference in July 1945, the Allied leaders had established a council of foreign ministers to guide the progress of post-war settlements, and to develop peace treaties with Italy, Germany, and the latter's European satellites. This process became one of lengthy debate and disagreement, especially between the United States and the Soviet Union. U.S. Secretary of State James F. Byrnes had more success, introducing the question of Korea's unification and eventual independence at a Moscow meeting of the council in December 1945. The ministers agreed that the U.S. and Soviet commands in Korea should establish a joint commission that, in consultation with Korean political and social organizations, would make recommendations for establishing a provisional government for all of Korea. These recommendations were to be submitted for consideration by the governments of the United States, Soviet Union, United Kingdom, and China in the joint development of a trusteeship under which these four powers would guide the provisional government for a maximum of five years.

The prospect of continued foreign control through trusteeship angered almost all Koreans, and most Korean organizations vehemently opposed the measure. Among the major groups only the Communists openly supported the plan. In meetings of the joint commission between January and May 1946, the Soviets insisted that the commission deal exclusively with the Koreans favoring trusteeship. The United States refused because doing so would pave the way for a provisional government dominated by Communists. Persistent Soviet demands to the same end met equally persistent American refusals when the commission reconvened in the spring and summer of 1947. Seeing no possibility that the joint commission could produce a satisfactory government for Korea, the United States submitted the matter to the United Nations for resolution. Addressing the body on 17 September 1947, Secretary of State George C. Marshall stated: "We do not wish to have the inability of two powers to reach agreement delay any further the urgent and rightful claim of the Korean people to independence."

More than the welfare of the Korean people lay behind U.S. efforts to prevent further delay in settling the issue. To begin with, Korea held a minor place among U.S. postwar foreign concerns. In addition to the occupation of Japan, U.S. concerns in Asia focused on China. Stimulated in large part by an abiding commercial and paternal interest developed over decades of trade and missionary work with the Chinese, the United States fostered the establishment of a peaceful, unified China that would help stabilize eastern Asia. Complicating the American effort was the long-standing civil war between the recognized Nationalist Government under Chiang Kai-shek and the Communists under Mao Tse-tung.

Begun in the late 1920s, then largely interrupted when the rival armies turned to fight invading Japanese forces in 1937, the civil war in China resumed soon after Japan's defeat in what amounted to a race for possession of territory that had been occupied by the Japanese. The United States favored and supported Chiang in this contest for control, providing his forces with military supplies and air and sea transportation. In addition, more than fifty thousand U.S. marines were placed in ports and other areas to prevent Mao's forces from occupying them.

At the same time, American diplomats attempted to end the civil war and unify China by promoting the development of a coalition government in which Chiang and his Kuomintang party, then in sole authority, would be dominant, but in which Mao's Communists and other, lesser political elements would have an effective voice. The Soviet Union, whose forces had occupied Manchuria in August 1945, agreed to support the unification of China under Chiang's leadership along the lines proposed by the United States. By late 1947, however, the U.S. diplomatic effort had failed and been discontinued. The civil war by that time centered in Manchuria, where, contrary to their vow to support Chiang, the Soviets had allowed Mao to establish a base of operations.

After confiscating most of Manchuria's well-developed industrial plant as war booty and shipping thousands of Japanese prisoners to Siberia as slave laborers, the Soviet occupation force had withdrawn from the region in the spring of 1946, leaving at Mao's disposal large stockpiles of Japanese military equipment and supplies. The United States continued to provide Chiang with military advisers, matériel, and money, but the outcome of the civil war was now in doubt. There appeared to be no way of ensuring a victory for Chiang short of committing U.S. troops in the conflict, an involvement far greater than could be justified by U.S. interest in China.

In any case, a steep and continuing decline in U.S. military strength precluded large troop commitments anywhere. Immediately after World War II, pressure from an articulate public, Congress, and the troops themselves to "bring the boys home" had led to a rapid, disorderly demobilization. By mid-1947 the strength of the U.S. armed forces dropped from a wartime peak of more than 12 million to just over 1.5 million. At the same time, President Harry S. Truman, out of determination to balance the federal budget and reduce the national debt, had sharply lowered military appropriations.

The sharp manpower losses brought on by the hasty demobilization and budgetary restrictions prompted a close scrutiny of U.S. commitments overseas. By late 1947, U.S. authorities had begun to remove the marines stationed in China and intended to complete their withdrawal in 1948. As for Korea, because the United States had no interest in maintaining bases there, the forty-five thousand ground troops on the peninsula could well be used elsewhere. Until a Korean government had been established, however, these troops could not be withdrawn, a condition that further inspired U.S. action in the United Nations.

On 14 November 1947, over Soviet objections, the United Nations General Assembly established a commission to supervise the election of a legislative body for all of Korea, whose members were then to form a government. The commission consisted of representatives from Australia, Canada, China, El Salvador, France, India, the Philippines, and Syria. The Ukranian

Soviet Socialist Republic was asked to furnish a member, but refused to do so. Soviet authorities responded by declaring the UN project illegal, and when the commission reached Korea in January 1948, blocked its entry into northern Korea. The commission proceeded to arrange an election in the southern zone. While arrangements for the election went forward, authorities in Washington established the basis for U.S. relations with the prospective regime. All occupation forces were to leave Korea by the end of 1948. During that time General Hodge was to enlarge the South Korean constabulary to fifty thousand, equip it with U.S. gear, and train it for border defense and internal security. After the troop withdrawal, the United States would provide both economic and military aid to the new nation and establish a diplomatic mission. Above all, as set out in a formal policy statement prepared by the National Security Council and approved by President Truman in April 1948, the United States was not to become "so irrevocably involved in the Korean situation that an action taken by any faction in Korea or by any other power in Korea could be considered a *causus belli* for the United States." The continuing low state of the military forces and increased tensions in Europe served to deepen U.S. resolve to avoid commitment in Korea or indeed anywhere on the Asian mainland.

In southern Korea the election was set to take place on 10 May 1948. Few South Koreans relished the prospect of a government whose authority reached only to the thirty-eighth parallel, and many political factions urged a boycott of the election. Pressing hardest for a boycott were the Communists, now organized as the South Korean Labor Party and affiliated with the labor party in the north. Despite the resulting propaganda, demonstrations, riots, and raids on voting places, the election established a national assembly of two hundred representatives for the twenty million people living in the south. One hundred seats were left vacant for representatives of the nine million people in the north, but appeals to the northerners to elect representatives and join in establishing a government proved fruitless. In July the assembly developed a constitution and elected as president Syngman Rhee, the assembly chairman and longtime champion of Korean independence. With the inauguration of Rhee, the government of the Republic of Korea (ROK) was established on 15 August 1948.

The Soviets reacted by creating a Communist government in the north. On 25 August northern Korea elected the Supreme People's Council from candidates chosen by the Interim People's Committee. On 9 September 1948, the council proclaimed the establishment of the Democratic People's Republic of Korea, with Kim Il Sung as premier. Thus, by the autumn of 1948, the thirty-eighth parallel represented a confirmed border between two hostile governments. Both claimed jurisdiction over all of Korea, and their leaders, Kim and Rhee, each vowed to reunite the land under his authority.

By the end of 1948, the Soviets withdrew all their troops from North Korea except for military advisers, who remained with the North Korean armed forces. Under Soviet supervision the Border Constabulary and, as it was now called, the North Korean People's Army (NKPA) grew substantially in the following year. Thousands of conscripts were gathered at training centers, Koreans who had served with Chinese Communist forces were brought home and inducted, and increasing numbers of men were sent to the Soviet Union for training in tank warfare and as pilots and aircraft mechanics. Tanks, heavy artillery, and aircraft began to arrive from the Soviet Union.

In South Korea the U.S. military government ended, and Special Representative John J. Muccio arrived on 26 August to establish a diplomatic mission. Under plans calling for the departure of all U.S. troops from Korea by the end of 1948, the first troops left in September. U.S. advisers meanwhile continued to train the South Korean constabulary and coast guard. As U.S. forces began to withdraw, some constabulary units took station along the thirty-eighth parallel, where a third of each unit occupied strongpoints opposite North Korean border troops while the remainder engaged in training well away from the parallel. Other constabulary units trained in areas farther south and worked with the national police in maintaining internal security.

As the withdrawal continued, Rhee appealed to President Truman for the retention of a U.S. force in Korea. Fearful of a North Korean invasion, shaken by recent rebellions incited by Communist groups within two regiments of the constabulary, and disturbed by increasing disorder and guerrilla raids in much of the countryside, Rhee wanted U.S. troops to remain until his own forces had grown stronger. The most serious internal threat came from the South Korean Labor Party, which, although driven underground after its attempt to prevent the May election, remained a functioning organization firmly allied with the Communist regime in the north. With a membership exceeding 100,000, the party maintained cells in all provinces; in most counties, cities, and large towns; and in some constabulary units. The party organization also included about five thousand armed guerrillas, a force that was growing as those trained at a special school in North Korea worked their way south through the Taebaek Mountains. Almost all the guerrillas were concentrated in three mountain areas, some in the Taebaeks along the east coast, others in the Sobaeks near the center of South Korea, most in the Chiri Mountains in the southwest. Their raids were launched mainly against farms, villages, and police installations in and around their mountain bases and were designed to create doubt among the people that the Rhee government could protect them. Outside the guerrilla areas, party members provoked riots and strikes, committed widespread robbery and arson, and disrupted commercial communications. Emulating the Communist line being broadcast from North Korea, party propaganda blamed the government for all the troubles besetting the people, promised the redress of grievances, and called for a peninsula-wide election of a new legislature.

In response to the appeal from President Rhee, U.S. authorities kept troops in Korea beyond the planned withdrawal date. After a full review, however, and some modification of policy toward the new republic, all the forces were removed by the end of June 1949. By then General Douglas MacArthur, commander in chief of the Far East Command, was relieved of all responsibilities in Korea except for providing supplies to the military advisers and for evacuating U.S. personnel in an emergency. Designated as the United States Military Advisory Group to the Republic of Korea (KMAG), the advisers became part of the military section of the U.S. diplomatic mission, now raised to embassy level under Ambassador Muccio. The role of the advisers was to assist in developing a considerably larger constabulary and coast guard—since renamed the army and navy by the ROK government—and a small air force. Still, the air group was to receive no combat aircraft, the navy no ships of the line, and the army no tanks, heavy artillery, or other heavy equipment. As had been decided in 1948, the ROK military establishment was to be designed only for maintaining internal order and border security. The United States would supply matériel to sustain the enlarged forces and further economic aid to promote national stability, but it remained the U.S. goal to minimize involvement in Korea.

Because of further budget cuts, the withdrawal of troops from Korea scarcely improved the posture of U.S. armed forces. The ceiling placed on military expenditures for the fiscal year beginning 1 July 1949 not only would erase manpower increases allowed in 1948 but would compel further reductions in the army and navy. In effect, the continuing budgetary limitations largely restricted the defense of the United States and any NATO commitment to air power and the atomic bomb. For any circumstance in which use of the bomb would be excessive or otherwise inappropriate, military resources were decidedly limited.

During the last half of 1949, two events jarred U.S. leaders into new lines of action. The first was the explosion of an atomic bomb over Siberia by the Soviet Union. The loss of the atomic monopoly drew recommendations from Truman's advisers for a major expansion of conventional military power. Defense Department planners began to translate the recommenda-

tions into forces and costs, but whether President Truman would raise military appropriations to allow expansion remained in question, still unanswered by the time of North Korea's breach of the thirty-eighth parallel in June 1950. The second event was a Communist victory in China. With most of the Chinese mainland in his grasp by 1 October, Mao Tse-tung proclaimed establishment of the People's Republic. As Chiang Kai-shek, the Nationalist Government, and remnants of Chiang's armed forces withdrew offshore to Taiwan (Formosa) by the end of the year, Mao also claimed sovereignty over the island and vowed to capture it. At that point the United States applied its policy of containment to Asia. In January 1950, Secretary of State Dean G. Acheson announced that the United States would defend by force a line running south from the Aleutian Islands through Japan and the Ryukyu Islands to the Philippines. Both Taiwan and South Korea lay outside this perimeter. Amid harsh protests from the China Lobby, an American group of Chiang supporters and anti-Communists in and out of government, President Truman declared that U.S. armed forces would not help defend Taiwan and that Chiang would receive no more military supplies. South Korea, on the other hand, would continue to receive both economic and military aid. Otherwise, as Secretary Acheson stated with respect to areas outside the U.S. defense perimeter, "should an attack occur . . . initial reliance must be on the people attacked to resist it and then upon the commitments of the entire civilized world under the Charter of the United Nations."

From the time of Secretary Acheson's announcement until the invasion five months later, South Korea's ability to resist an attack from the north was a question given mixed answers by U.S. officials in Seoul, Tokyo, and Washington. In June they placed the strength of the NKPA near sixty-six thousand men, which made up, at most, six infantry divisions and an armored brigade equipped with sixty-five tanks. The north's border constabulary was rated as essentially a paramilitary police force and its navy as an insignificant collection of torpedo boats and patrol craft. Its air force, however, they considered a worthy group of one hundred fighters and seventy attack bombers. In judging the south's ability to withstand an attack, their main concern was the north's possession of tanks, combat aircraft, and medium and heavy artillery, while the South Koreans had no similar equipment.

The South Korean army (ROKA) totaled ninety-five thousand men in eight divisions, only half of which were at full strength, and six battalions of light artillery. Four divisions and a regiment stood along the thirty-eighth parallel. Remaining forces, some in the Seoul area but most farther south operating against guerrillas, constituted a reserve for counterattacks or reinforcement under long-established plans for defending the border. Despite the north's edge in armor, artillery, and air support, KMAG officials believed that the ROKA was otherwise superior and therefore could repel any invasion. Central Intelligence Agency analysts predicted that the NKPA superiority in tanks, artillery, and aircraft gave its armed forces the capability of attaining limited objectives, including the capture of Seoul, but doubted that they could overrun all of South Korea. Ambassador Muccio, on the other hand, stated flatly on 6 June, that the NKPA tanks, artillery, and planes would provide its forces with the margin of victory in any full-scale invasion of the republic.

Whatever their opinions on the relative military strength of North Korea, U.S. diplomatic and intelligence officials repeatedly reported during the first half of 1950 that South Korea was not in imminent danger of invasion. They forecast a continuance of the northern regime's efforts to undermine the Rhee government through propaganda, political pressure, and guerrilla raids, which had intensified after the last U.S. troops withdrew in mid-1949. North Korean border troops launched hundreds of forays into ROK territory. South Korean forces at the parallel held their ground, and even responded in kind, but the border clashes nevertheless further strained the southern republic. U.S. authorities concluded that the North Koreans saw promise of unifying Korea under their

control by such efforts and thus would continue that course rather than resort to open warfare.

The U.S. estimates of North Korea's armed strength were close to the mark for its navy and air force but not for its ground strength. A concerted buildup during the first months of 1950 increased the NKPA by June to eight infantry divisions with full complements of light, medium, and heavy artillery; two divisions at half strength; an armored brigade with 120 Russian T-34 medium tanks; a separate armored regiment with thirty tanks; a separate infantry regiment; and a regiment of reconnaissance troops mounted on motorcycles. Also ready for field operations were the staffs and support elements of the Army Front Headquarters and two corps. These forces numbered almost 117,000 and, together with five infantry-trained constabulary brigades, placed the total North Korean ground strength at more than 135,000. Except for the South Korean navy, which equaled its northern counterpart, ROK armed forces were clearly outmatched in both numbers and guns.

The U.S. prediction of North Korean intentions was also wrong. On 15 June the North Korean high command had begun moving forces toward the thirty-eighth parallel, and by the evening of 24 June more than ninety thousand troops were deployed along their lines of departure for attack. Remarkably, their deployment was neither seen nor sensed from the south, providing the NKPA assault forces the added advantage of surprise when they struck the next morning.

INVASION

In deploying the invasion force, General Chai Ung Jun, commander in chief of the NKPA, distributed two corps across the breadth of the peninsula. In the west, the First Corps, with the First, Third, Fourth, and Sixth divisions and the 105th Armored Brigade was to clear the isolated Ongjin Peninsula on the far west coast and, in its main effort, converge on Seoul. The Second Corps was to launch secondary attacks in the center of the peninsula and along the east coast. In the central zone the Second and Seventh divisions with a regiment of tanks were to strike toward the towns of Chunchon and Hongchon. On the east coast the Fifth Division, 766th Independent Infantry Regiment, Twelfth Motorcycle Regiment, and a band of one thousand guerrillas were to combine an overland attack with amphibious landings well south of the thirty-eighth parallel. In every zone of attack, axial roads led to Pusan, South Korea's principal port at the southeastern tip of the peninsula, whose seizure was the final North Korean objective.

Behind early morning artillery and mortar barrages on 25 June, NKPA forces scored gains everywhere in their initial attacks. In support of the First Corps, North Korean fighter planes sporadically strafed Seoul and the nearby airfield at Kimpo. Although taken by surprise, the South Korean border garrisons fought stout delaying actions and brought the North Koreans to a full halt in two areas, along the Imjin River northwest of Seoul and at Chunchon. Major General Chae Byong Dok, the ROKA chief of staff, began moving the bulk of his reserve divisions north to reinforce the defense of Seoul. Of these divisions, the Second was to join the Seventh in counterattacks on the morning of the 26th against the greatest threat to the capital. Positioned due north of the city, this threat was posed by the North Korean Third and Fourth divisions and the bulk of the 105th Armored Brigade.

The Seventh Division launched its counterattack, but the Second arrived too late and the attempt failed. By evening of the 26th the North Koreans advanced within twenty miles of Seoul against what became increasingly uncoordinated defensive efforts by units of the South Korean Capital, Second, Third, Fifth, and Seventh divisions. Elsewhere, the Seventeenth Regiment of the Capital Division, after losing its forwardmost battalion on the Onjin Peninsula, had withdrawn by sea to the port of Inchon west of Seoul to assist in defending the capital area. On the east coast the Eighth Division had fallen back twenty miles and was preparing to withdraw inland to escape being trapped be-

tween the North Koreans advancing from the north and those that had come in by sea to the south. Northwest of Seoul the First Division maintained positions along the Imjin River but was in danger of being outflanked by the North Koreans driving on the capital from the north. In the central sector the Sixth Division still held Chunchon but the NKPA Second Corps commander was reinforcing his attack to take the town. South Korean ammunition stores were dwindling fast, although a resupply requested of General MacArthur by KMAG officials on the 25th, was en route by sea from Japan. Even so, with almost all South Korean forces now committed, it was becoming clear that they could do no more than slow the North Koreans.

As this picture developed, Ambassador Muccio ordered all dependents of U.S. government and military officials out of Korea. By 29 June about two thousand people were safely evacuated by sea and air to Japan, including other Americans, foreign nationals, and some KMAG officials.

INTERVENTION

The first reports from Seoul to Washington of multiple border attacks came from a United Press International representative; next the military attaché at the U.S. embassy, which also alerted General MacArthur's headquarters; and a cable from Ambassador Muccio, which stated that the North Korean attacks constituted "an all-out offensive against the Republic of Korea." Secretary of State Acheson immediately notified President Truman at his home in Independence, Missouri, and, with the president's approval, arranged a meeting of the United Nations Security Council to consider the North Korean aggression as a threat to world peace. The council immediately passed a resolution proposed by the U.S. representative, which demanded an immediate cessation of hostilities and a withdrawal of all North Korean forces to the thirty-eighth parallel. The resolution also called on all UN members "to render every assistance to the United Nations in the execution of this resolution." The swift action of the council was facilitated by the absence of the Soviet delegate, who had boycotted meetings since January 1950, when the council refused to replace the Chinese Nationalist representative with a Communist. Shortly after passage of the resolution, Acheson cabled Moscow, requesting that Soviet officials use their influence to persuade North Korean authorities to withdraw their forces. The Soviets replied that their government "adheres to the principle of the impermissibility of interference by foreign powers in the internal affairs of Korea."

That same evening, President Truman directed General MacArthur to continue supplying South Korean forces and determine how best to assist them further. The president also ordered the Seventh Fleet from Philippine and Ryukyu waters to Japan. The next day, in a broad interpretation of the UN request for support of the Security Council's resolution, Truman placed MacArthur in charge of all U.S. military activities in Korea and authorized him to use the planes and ships of his Far East air and naval forces against North Korean targets south of the thirty-eighth parallel. He also redirected part of the Seventh Fleet to Taiwan, where, by controlling the waters between the Chinese Communists on the mainland and the Nationalists on the island, naval air and surface forces could discourage either one from attacking the other and so prevent a widening of hostilities.

The U.S. commitment of forces reversed the earlier policy against fighting in Korea, but President Truman, convinced that the North Korean attack was an eruption in the cold war rather than an extension of a local dispute, concluded that the United States had to contest the invasion lest inaction invite armed aggression elsewhere.

North Korean authorities ignored the UN call for withdrawal. Attacking on all fronts on 27 June, General Chai's forces gained ground everywhere except at Chunchon. As the main force neared Seoul, which it reached at midnight, members of the ROK government, army headquarters, KMAG, and embassies left the capital, accompanied and followed by crowds of citizens and soldiers streaming over three railroad bridges and a highway bridge spanning the Han River at the south edge of the city. Previously prepared for demolition as the final feature of withdrawal should Seoul have to be surrendered, the bridges were ordered blown up by a panicky South Korean official long before the bulk of the city's defenders were pushed out of position at the northern outskirts. As the North Koreans drove through the city on the 28th, retreating South Korean troops, in growing disarray, abandoned nearly all their trucks, supplies, and heavy weapons and swam the Han or crossed on boats and rafts.

While the North Koreans regrouped after capturing Seoul, South Korean commanders struggled to reassemble forces in defenses at Inchon, the Kimpo airfield, and along the Han directly below and east of the capital. Further east, the Sixth Division lost Chunchon on the 28th, but withdrew in good order to positions fifteen miles south. The Eighth Division moved inland from the east coast to come alongside the Sixth, while a regiment of the Third Division took over defense of the coastal road. The ROKA estimated that it had so far lost almost half its men and more than half its weapons and equipment.

On 27 June the UN Security Council asked all UN members to provide military assistance to help South Korea repel the invasion. President Truman's first response was to extend U.S. air and naval attacks into North Korea and to allow ground troops to protect and operate the port of Pusan. After observing the ROKA weak defenses along the Han River, General MacArthur recommended that a U.S. infantry regiment be deployed in the Seoul area at once and that this force be enlarged to two divisions. Truman's reply on 30 June allowed MacArthur to commit all ground units available to him.

Infantry units in the Far East Command included the First Cavalry; Seventh, Twenty-fourth, and Twenty-fifth divisions under Lieutenant General Walton H. Walker's Eighth Army in Japan; and the Twenty-ninth Regimental Combat Team on Okinawa in the Ryukyus. The post–World War II reductions had affected all of them; each regiment except one had only two of the normal three battalions, most artillery battalions had just two of the normal three firing batteries, organic armor was generally lacking, and weapons and equipment on hand were largely worn leftovers from World War II. Nevertheless, MacArthur believed that two of his divisions, strengthened from other units at hand, could halt the North Koreans.

SOUTH TO THE NAKTONG

MacArthur would have no opportunity to deploy forces in the Seoul area because by the time he received approval to commit ground units, the main NKPA force had moved over the Han River. Crossing west of Seoul, the Sixth Division captured Kimpo Airfield and Inchon, while the Third and Fourth divisions crossed directly below the capital into its suburb, Yongdungpo. Pausing while engineers repaired a railroad bridge so that tanks could join the attack, the Fourth Division then pressed forward astride the main road and rail line that followed a gentle southeastward course all the way to Pusan. The division reached Suwon, twenty miles south of Seoul, on 4 July. With the secondary attacks at the center of the peninsula and down the east coast keeping pace, North Korean forces had now advanced some fifty miles into South Korea.

MacArthur still expected to stop the North Koreans with two divisions and, once done, intended to defeat them by sea-landing a third division behind them in concert with a counterattack from the south. In opening operations, however, the speed of the North Korean drive compelled him to trade space for time. His first order went to Major General William F. Dean's Twenty-fourth Division encamped in southwestern Japan nearest to Korea. Dean's division was to fight a delaying action against the main North Korean attack while MacArthur strengthened and shipped the Twenty-fifth Division to complete the blocking force and prepare the First Cavalry Division for the amphibious landing. General Dean was to begin with an "arro-

gant display of strength," as MacArthur called it, by airlifting an infantry task force to the peninsula and deploying it as far north as possible. As task force members expressed it, the North Koreans might "turn around and go back when they found out who they were fighting."

When finally organized, Task Force Smith, named after its commander, Lieutenant Colonel Charles B. Smith, included two rifle companies and supporting units of the Twenty-first Infantry, plus a five-piece battery of the Fifty-second Field Artillery Battalion. The 540-man force took position near Osan, ten miles south of Suwon, before dawn on 5 July. Coming out of Suwon in a heavy rain, the North Korean Fourth Division attacked the Americans around 8:30 A.M. In the ensuing battle the North Koreans lost four tanks, forty-two men killed, and eighty-five wounded. The U.S. force suffered larger losses. It lacked antitank mines, its recoilless rifles and 2.36-inch rocket launchers could not penetrate the armor of the T-34s, and its artillery had only a few rounds of antitank ammunition that did prove effective. The rain cancelled air support, communications broke down, and, in any case, the task force was too small to prevent North Korean infantry from flowing around its flanks. By midafternoon Task Force Smith was in retreat with more than 150 casualties and the loss of all equipment save small arms.

Although given air support, delaying actions fought by larger forces of the Twenty-fourth Division over the next week had similar results. By 13 July the division was pressed back on Taejon, sixty miles south of Osan, where it took position along the Kum River above the town against the approach of the NKPA Third and Fourth divisions and 105th Armored Brigade. In central Korea, where the North Koreans had added the Fifteen Division to their attack, South Korean forces had backed off slowly. By 13 July they were defending three road corridors through the Sobaek Mountains. With the North Korean advance along the east coast still keeping pace, General Chai's forces now had overrun half of South Korea.

As General Dean's division and ROKA forces fell back, General MacArthur realized that he had far underestimated the NKPA. Putting aside his plan for an amphibious landing, he directed the First Cavalry Division to join the delaying action and requested substantial reinforcement from the United States, mainly in ground troops but also in air strength. His requests far exceeded the numbers and readiness of forces in the United States, but by mid-July, Washington officials began a concerted buildup from forces available to strengthen MacArthur's command.

Meanwhile, fifty-three of the fifty-nine UN members signified support of the Security Council's 27 June resolution and twenty-nine made specific offers of assistance. As it became clear that the United States would be the major contributor of forces by far, the Security Council on 7 July asked the United States to form a field command into which all forces would be integrated. The evolving command structure placed President Truman in the role of executive agent for the UN Security Council, although he had no obligation to clear his decisions with that agency. Assisting him were the National Security Council and Joint Chiefs of Staff, which helped develop the strategic concepts of operations in Korea. In the strictly military channel, the joint chiefs issued instructions to the unified command in the field through its army member, General J. Lawton Collins. The unified command, designated the Unified Nations Command, was formally established on 24 July under General MacArthur, who superimposed its headquarters over that of his Far East Command in Tokyo.

Forces and facilities eventually assembled within the unified command came from twenty UN members and one nonmember nation (Italy). The United States, Great Britain, Australia, New Zealand, Canada, Turkey, Greece, France, Belgium, Luxembourg, the Netherlands, Thailand, the Philippines, Colombia, and Ethiopia furnished ground combat troops. The United States, Sweden, Norway, and Italy provided field hospitals and India an ambulance unit. Ground-based air units, including combat and transport formations, came from the United States, Australia, Great Britain, South Africa,

Canada, Belgium, Greece, and Thailand. Naval forces, including carrier-based aircraft and hospital ships, arrived from the United States, Great Britain, Australia, New Zealand, Canada, Colombia, France, the Netherlands, Thailand, and Denmark.

As forces arrived in Korea, MacArthur assigned air units to the Far East Air Forces, commanded by Lieutenant General George E. Stratemeyer, who, in turn, placed them with his Fifth Air Force and Combat Cargo Command. With its ninety-nine B-29s, Stratemeyer's Bomber Command remained an entirely American-manned force. Incoming naval units joined Naval Forces, Far East, under Vice Admiral C. Turner Joy. All of them, along with the South Korean navy, eventually became part of a force blockading the Korean coast. General MacArthur assigned all ground units to the Eighth Army, which established headquarters in Korea on 13 July. Shortly after taking command of U.S. ground troops then on the peninsula, General Walker also assumed control of the ROKA at the offer of President Rhee.

As the United Nations Command was taking shape, the Twenty-fifth and First Cavalry divisions, strengthened by forces taken from the Seventh Division, entered Korea between 10 and 22 July. By then the battle for Taejon had opened. New 3.5-inch rocket launchers hurriedly airlifted from the United States proved effective against the T-34 tanks, but the Twenty-fourth Division lost Taejon after the NKPA Third and Fourth divisions established bridgeheads over the Kum River and encircled and then penetrated the town. In running enemy roadblocks during the withdrawal from Taejon, General Dean took a wrong turn and was captured a month later as he attempted to reach U.S. lines through mountains to the south. On 22 July the First Cavalry Division relieved the much-reduced Twenty-fourth Division in positions about twenty miles southeast of Taejon, and the Twenty-fifth Division backed up ROKA forces being steadily pushed back in the Sobaek Mountains passes. General MacArthur had meanwhile ordered two battalions of the Twenty-ninth Infantry from Okinawa to Korea, which reached the peninsula and reinforced the Twenty-fourth Division just as General Walker was obliged to recommit the damaged unit in the face of enlarged North Korean attacks.

In continuing their advance the North Koreans added two divisions, the Thirteenth and Eighth, the latter newly created by expanding a border constabulary brigade. Two divisions of the main force opened an enveloping maneuver, the Fourth moving fifty miles south out of Taejon and then pivoting east through undefended ground, the Sixth marching down the west coast to the tip of the peninsula and then turning east toward Pusan over the south coast road. Walker sent the Twenty-fourth Division back into the line to oppose these threats.

By 24 July, UN air forces had won control of the air, destroying almost all North Korean planes in the process and, with good effect, began concentrating attacks on the advancing North Koreans and their lengthening supply lines. In a single engagement naval warships had decimated the small North Korean navy, blockaded both coasts to prevent any movement of enemy troops or supplies by water, and were delivering punishing gunfire on the North Koreans moving down the east coast. Nevertheless, U.S. and ROKA forces steadily gave way and by 1 August held only a small portion of southeastern Korea.

Pressed by General MacArthur to stop further withdrawals, General Walker ordered a stand along a 150-mile line running from the south coast town of Chindong-ni, thirty miles west of Pusan, north to a bend above the city of Taegu, then east to the coastal town of Yongdok, ninety miles north of Pusan. By 4 August, Walker placed his three U.S. divisions along the western segment of the line, basing most of their positions behind the Naktong River, and set ROKA forces, recently reorganized into two corps and five divisions, along the northern stretch.

The North Koreans raised additional units by converting constabulary brigades and conscripting large numbers of recruits, many from overrun regions of South Korea. During the six weeks of the Battle of the Pusan Perimeter (6

August–15 September), they committed thirteen infantry divisions, an armored division, and two tank regiments against Walker's line. The additional strength, however, failed to compensate for fifty-eight thousand trained men and the many tanks lost during their advance to the new line. Lieutenant General Kim Chaek, head of the North Korean Army Front Headquarters and now in charge of operations, also failed to mass his forces for a single decisive penetration. Instead, he dissipated his strength by attacking at several points along the Eighth Army line.

General Walker's defense hinged on shuttling his scarce reserves to block a gap, reinforce a position, or counterattack wherever needed. Timing was the key. With air support all along the front and naval gunfire support at the eastern anchor of the line, Walker's responses successfully contained enemy penetrations and inflicted telling losses that steadily drew off North Korean offensive power. His own strength meanwhile was growing. By mid-September he had more than five hundred medium tanks, and troop replacements came in a steady flow. Additional units also arrived, among them the Fifth Regimental Combat Team from Hawaii, the Second Infantry Division and First Provisional Marine Brigade from the United States, and the British Twenty-seventh Infantry Brigade from Hong Kong. As NKPA forces weakened, the Eighth Army acquired the men and means for offensive action.

ENVELOPMENT, BREAKOUT, AND PURSUIT

Meanwhile, General MacArthur returned to his concept of an amphibious landing behind the North Koreans combined with an overland attack from the south. He favored Inchon as the landing site because the landing force would have to move only twenty-five miles inland to recapture Seoul and cut the principal North Korean supply routes. Enemy troops retiring before the Eighth Army attack would be cut off by the amphibious force or be compelled to make a difficult withdrawal through the eastern mountains.

In shaping a landing force, MacArthur formed the headquarters of the Tenth Corps from members of his own staff, naming his chief of staff, Major General Edward M. Almond, as commander. The Seventh Division was rebuilt with incoming replacements and more than eight thousand ROKA recruits. He also acquired the bulk of the First Marine Division from the United States, which he filled out with the marines in the Pusan Perimeter. The Tenth Corps, operating as a separate force under MacArthur's direct command, swept into Inchon on 15 September against light resistance and pushed inland over the next two weeks. One arm struck south and seized Suwon, while the bulk of the corps cleared Kimpo Airfield, crossed the Han River, and fought through Seoul. In a dramatic ceremony, General MacArthur returned the capital city to President Rhee on 29 September.

General Walker's Eighth Army attacked out of the Pusan Perimeter on 16 September. For a week his forces could make only scant gains, but on 23 September the North Koreans broke in retreat. Reorganized into four corps—two American and two South Korean—the Eighth Army rolled forward in pursuit, linking with the Tenth Corps near Suwon on 26 September. Approximately thirty thousand NKPA troops escaped above the thirty-eighth parallel through the eastern mountains while several thousand hid out in South Korea, most of them in the Chiri Mountains, to fight as guerrillas. By the end of September the NKPA no longer existed as an organized force anywhere in the southern republic.

NORTH TOWARD THE YALU

Up to this point, President Truman had frequently described the U.S.-led operations in Korea as a "police action," a euphemism for war that produced both criticism and amusement, but he was reaching for perspective. Determined to halt the North Korean aggression, he was equally determined to limit hostilities to the peninsula and to avoid taking steps that might prompt Soviet or Chinese intervention. Thus, a case could be made for halting ground operations at the thirty-eighth parallel. In reestablishing the border, General MacArthur's forces had met the UN call for assistance in repelling the attack on South Korea, but failure to destroy the NKPA forces that had escaped above the parallel and the thousands more in northern training camps could leave South Korea at risk of another invasion. A complete victory, which appeared within easy grasp, also could set the scene for reunifying Korea under UN supervision. There had been warnings from Communist China against the entry of the United Nations Command into North Korea, but these were considered diplomatic blackmail rather than genuine threats to enter the war. On 27 September, President Truman authorized General MacArthur to send his forces north.

MacArthur's subsequent plan called for the Eighth Army to advance overland with its main attack aimed at Pyongyang, the North Korean capital, in the west, while the Tenth Corps made another amphibious landing, this time to capture Wonsan, North Korea's major seaport on the east coast. Earlier, General Walker, General Almond, and most of MacArthur's principal staff officers had assumed that MacArthur would assign the Tenth Corps to the Eighth Army after the two commands joined forces in the Seoul area. Doing so would follow the military principal that ground operations can be conducted most effectively under a single field commander. MacArthur, however, believed that Walker would have trouble controlling widely separated forces in the rough terrain of North Korea, where lateral communications were difficult, and maintained the Tenth Corps as a separate force. MacArthur reasoned that the Eighth Army and Tenth Corps, coordinated and supported from Japan, especially after gaining the Wonsan port facilities, could operate separately without impairing the effectiveness of either.

On the east coast, the ROKA First Corps crossed the parallel on 1 October, and the ROKA Second Corps entered central North Korea on the 6th. The next day the UN General Assembly voted for the restoration of peace and security throughout Korea, thereby giving tacit approval to MacArthur's attack. On 2 October, Communist China's foreign minister, Chou Enlai, had passed word through diplomatic channels that if any forces other than those of South Korea crossed the parallel, China would enter the war, but this warning was dismissed. The U.S. First Corps crossed the parallel in the west on 9 October in an attack toward Pyongyang.

Two weeks later, the Eighth Army was deep in North Korea. In the west the U.S. First Corps cleared Pyongyang on the 19th. On the following day, the U.S. 187th Airborne Regimental Combat Team, which had arrived at Kimpo Airfield from the United States in late September, parachuted at two sites twenty-five miles beyond Pyongyang in an effort to trap North Korean government officials leaving the capital. These officials, however, had moved out of Pyongyang on 12 October and eventually established a new seat of government in the town of Kanggye, deep in the north-central mountains. The airborne landing nevertheless helped ease the advance. On 24 October, the First Corps reached the Chongchon River within sixty-five miles of Korea's Yalu River border with Manchuria, while the ROKA Second Corps veered northwest to come alongside. On the east coast on 10 October the ROKA First Corps captured Wonsan and over the next two weeks reached the town of Iwon, another hundred miles north. Meanwhile, under KMAG tutelage, the ROKA had formed three new divisions, for a total of eight, and activated the Third Corps. For the time being, the new corps and two of the new divisions operated in South Korea against bypassed enemy troops and guerrillas.

In the hope of ending operations before the onset of winter, General MacArthur ordered his ground commanders on 24 October to clear the remainder of North Korea as rapidly as possible. In the west the Eighth Army sent several freewheeling columns toward the Yalu. In the

east the separate Tenth Corps came in by sea at Wonsan and Iwon and took control of the ROKA First Corps, sending columns up the coast and inland toward the Yalu River and the huge Changjin Reservoir atop the Taebaek Mountains. The forces on both coasts advanced easily, and reconnaissance troops of an interior South Korean column in the Eighth Army zone reached the Yalu.

Almost everywhere else the columns encountered stout resistance, and on 25 October discovered that they were being opposed by Chinese. Initially, General MacArthur's intelligence officer, Major General Charles A. Willoughby, and MacArthur himself discounted the appearance of Chinese troops in Korea as clear evidence that China had intervened in the war. As stated by General Willoughby on 28 October: "It would appear that the auspicious time for such intervention had long since passed; it is difficult to believe that such a move, if planned, would have been postponed to a time when remnant North Korean forces have been reduced to a low point of effectiveness." On 6 November, however, after receiving further intelligence reports from the field, MacArthur charged China with having "committed one of the most offensive acts of international lawlessness . . . by moving without any notice . . . Communist forces across the Yalu River into North Korea," and with massing possible reinforcements behind the sanctuary of the Manchurian border.

In the east, Chinese forces delayed General Almond's advance toward the Changjin Reservoir. In the west, stronger attacks compelled General Walker to pull the Eighth Army back to the Chongchon River. In the air, Chinese pilots flying into Korea from Manchurian airfields challenged UN air forces with Russian-built MIG-15 jets. The MIGs were more maneuverable than the F-80 jets flown by Americans, but the Chinese pilots were less skilled and, more often than not, either disengaged or were shot out of the sky. Meanwhile, on the ground, the Chinese abruptly broke contact on 6 November.

As announced by the North Korean government and the Chinese ministry of foreign affairs on 7 and 11 November, all Chinese forces in

Korea were "volunteers," an obvious ploy to reduce reprisals because of China's intervention, primarily to mitigate the American response. In fact, the forces constituted regular units of the People's Liberation Army led by its deputy commander, Peng Teh-huai, and were in Korea by government order. By 6 November intelligence agencies estimated these forces at three divisions in the Eighth Army sector and two divisions in the Tenth Corps area—altogether about fifty thousand men. In light of this estimate and with no sightings of additional troops entering Korea by aerial observers, General MacArthur believed that future Chinese operations would be defensive only and would not be strong enough to block a reinforced UN Command advance. Given assurances by Mac-Arthur that his forces could defeat the Chinese and that his air power could prevent any substantial reinforcement from crossing the Yalu, U.S. authorities allowed him to resume his attack toward the border. There was, MacArthur said, no other way to obtain "an accurate measure of enemy strength."

MacArthur opened air attacks on Yalu River bridges on 8 November, restricting the bombing to the overwater spans on the Korean side of the river so as to not violate Manchurian territory. In northeastern Korea the Tenth Corps, now strengthened by the arrival of the Third Infantry Division from the United States, resumed its advance on the 11th. Along the east coast, South Korean units reached the city of Chongjin, about sixty-five miles short of Korea's border with the Soviet Union. Inland, the U.S. Seventh Division forces reached the Yalu on 26 November, and on the corps' west flank, U.S. marines and other Seventh Division units occupied the Changjin Reservoir area. Westward, the Eighth Army, strengthened by the U.S. Ninth Corps with the Second and Twenty-fifth divisions and a newly arrived brigade from Turkey, attacked on 24 November. Other new arrivals in the Eighth Army included the British Twenty-ninth Brigade and infantry battalions from the Philippines, Netherlands, Thailand, and Australia. Except for the last, which joined the British Twenty-seventh Brigade, these troops remained

in reserve. Two more new divisions also raised the ROKA's total to ten.

For two days, General Walker's forces met little opposition as they drove west and north astride the Chongchon River. During the night of the 25th, however, strong Chinese attacks struck Walker's center and right, and on the 27th hit General Almond's units at the Changjin Reservoir. Continued assaults on the 28th began to carry the Chinese through the inland flank forces of both the Eighth Army and Tenth Corps. General MacArthur now had a truer measure of Chinese strength. The Thirteenth Army Group with six armies of eighteen divisions stood opposite the Eighth Army, and the Ninth Army Group with three armies of twelve divisions opposed the Tenth Corps in the Changjin Reservoir area. Altogether some 300,000 Chinese were in Korea. As General MacArthur reported to Washington on the 28th, the UN Command faced "an entirely new war."

THE NEW WAR

On 29 November, MacArthur instructed General Walker to withdraw as necessary to escape being enveloped by Chinese troops pushing deep through his eastern sector. General Almond was ordered to pull Tenth Corps forces into a beachhead around the port of Hungnam, north of Wonsan. In the Eighth Army's withdrawal from the Chongchon, a strong roadblock, set by Chinese attempting to envelop Walker's forces from the east, caught and severely punished the U.S. Second Division, last away from the river. Thereafter, at each report of approaching enemy forces, Walker ordered another withdrawal before any solid contact could be made. By 15 December the Eighth Army was completely out of contact with the Chinese and was back at the thirty-eighth parallel. There Walker began to develop coast-to-coast defenses.

In the withdrawal of the Tenth Corps to Hungnam, General Almond's central and rightmost forces had little difficulty reaching the port, but the First Marine Division and Seventh

Division forces retiring from the Changjin Reservoir had to fight a costly battle through the Chinese rimming a long stretch of the road leading to the coast. By the time these forces reached Hungnam, General MacArthur had ordered the Tenth Corps to withdraw by sea and proceed to South Korea where, at last, it was to become part of the Eighth Army. With little interference from enemy forces, the last of General Almond's forces left Hungnam on Christmas Eve. Under additional orders from MacArthur, the ROKA First Corps went ashore not far below the thirty-eighth parallel and took up east coast positions along the new Eighth Army front. The remainder of the Tenth Corps proceeded to Pusan and then into assembly areas nearby.

On 23 December, General Walker was killed in a motor vehicle accident while traveling north from Seoul to the front. Lieutenant General Matthew B. Ridgway was hurriedly flown in from Washington to take command of the Eighth Army. Earlier, in routine anticipation of casualties, General MacArthur had obtained chief of staff General Collins' agreement that Walker's replacement, should one be needed, would be General Ridgway. Ridgway's experience and strong leadership as commander of an airborne division and an airborne corps during World War II had MacArthur's high respect, and his service as the deputy chief of staff for operations and administration on the Department of Army staff, which had involved visits to MacArthur's headquarters, had kept him well informed of operations in Korea.

During his initial inspection of the front, General Ridgway found dispirited troops, the result of the hard Chinese attacks and successive withdrawals. He also found the defense line thin in the central and eastern sectors, manned only by the ROKA Third, Second, and First Corps. Having slowly followed the Eighth Army's withdrawal out of North Korea, the Chinese Thirteenth Army Group meanwhile was massing on the front of the U.S. First and Ninth corps in the west, while the NKPA Fifth and Second corps with twelve reconstituted divi-

sions were concentrating in the east-central region.

Ridgway's first tactical move was to place the U.S. Second Division, still damaged but now reinforced by infantry battalions from the Netherlands and France, in a central position where it could oppose any North Korean penetration of the South Korean front. At the same time, he pressed General Almond to quicken preparation of the Tenth Corps, whose forces needed refurbishing before moving into the line. Judging that an enemy attack was likely before he could fully strengthen his defenses, Ridgway also ordered his western forces to organize a bridgehead above Seoul to cover a withdrawal over the Han River, should that become necessary.

Enemy forces opened attacks on New Years' Eve. As expected, the Chinese made the main effort toward Seoul while the North Koreans pressed south in the central and eastern sectors. As the offensive gained momentum, General Ridgway withdrew his western forces to the Seoul bridgehead, pulled the rest of the Eighth Army to positions roughly on line to the east, and strengthened the central sector with the Tenth Corps. Unable to hold the bridgehead, Ridgway ordered his forces back to a line across the peninsula anchored in the west at a point forty miles south of Seoul. The last troops left the capital on 4 January 1951, just as the Chinese entered the city from the north. Only light Chinese forces pushed south of the city and attacks in the west diminished. In the east-central sector, however, NKPA forces infiltrated South Korean lines and reached within a hundred miles of Pusan before they were defeated by Tenth Corps troops striking from the west and the First Marine Division blocking in the south.

By mid-January enemy pressure subsided all along the new Eighth Army line. As the front quieted, reconnaissance patrols searching north encountered only screening forces, and intelligence sources reported that most enemy units had withdrawn to refit. It became clear to General Ridgway that enemy forces operated under the limitations of a primitive logistical system.

The Chinese troops in particular could conduct offensive operations for only a week or two before having to pause for replacements and new supplies, a pattern Ridgway intended to exploit. In coming Eighth Army operations ground gains and losses would have only incidental importance. Primarily, Ridgway's forces were to inflict maximum casualties on the enemy with minimum losses to themselves. "To do this," he instructed, "we must wage a war of maneuver—slashing at the enemy when he withdraws and fighting delaying actions when he attacks."

While Ridgway was certain his forces could achieve that objective, General MacArthur was far less optimistic. He had notified Washington earlier that the Chinese could drive the Eighth Army out of Korea unless it received major reinforcement. At the time, there was still only a slim reserve of combat units in the United States. National Guard divisions had been brought into federal service but only two of these, the Fortieth and Forty-fifth, were scheduled for the Far East—for duty in Japan, not Korea. The main concern in Washington was the possibility that the Chinese entry into Korea was only one part of a Soviet move toward global war, a concern great enough to lead President Truman to declare a state of national emergency on 15 December. Washington officials, for their part, considered Korea no place to become involved in a major war. For all these reasons, the U.S. Joint Chiefs of Staff (JCS) notified MacArthur that a major buildup of his forces was out of the question. MacArthur was to stay in Korea if he could but should the Chinese drive the Eighth Army back to a line along and eastward from the Kum River, the JCS would order a withdrawal to Japan.

Opposing the reasoning in Washington, MacArthur urged four retaliatory measures against the Chinese—blockade the China coast, destroy China's war industries through naval and air attacks, reinforce the troops in Korea with Chinese Nationalist forces, and allow diversionary operations by Nationalist forces against the China mainland. Although these proposals for escalation received serious study

in Washington, they were discarded in favor of confining the fighting to Korea. Next, the issue of withdrawal from Korea was settled after General Collins visited Korea and saw that the Eighth Army was improving under Ridgway's leadership. He became as confident as Ridgway that the Chinese would be unable to drive the Eighth Army off the peninsula. "As of now," General Collins announced on 15 January, "we are going to stay and fight."

Ten days later, Ridgway opened a cautious offensive, beginning with attacks in the west and gradually widening them to the east. With naval gunfire support on both flanks and ample air support all along the front, the Eighth Army advanced methodically, wiping out each pocket of resistance before moving farther north. Enemy forces fought back vigorously and in February struck back in the central region. During that counterattack, the Twenty-third Regiment of the U.S. Second Division successfully defended the town of Chipyong-ni against a much larger Chinese force, a victory that symbolized to Ridgway the Eighth Army's recovery of its fighting spirit. After defeating the enemy's February effort, the Eighth Army again advanced steadily, reentered Seoul in mid-March, and by the first day of spring stood just below the thirty-eighth parallel. In the meantime, infantry battalions from Greece, Canada, and Belgium, including a detachment from Luxembourg, and an artillery battalion from New Zealand joined Ridgway's forces.

More Chinese forces also had entered Korea, the Nineteenth Army Group in February and the Third Army Group in March. The additions raised the Chinese total to four army groups, fourteen armies, and forty-two divisions. As sensed by intelligence agencies, the Chinese reinforcement was part of preparations for a new offensive. Aiming to spoil these preparations, Ridgway opened an attack on 5 April in which he pointed the main effort toward the Iron Triangle, a centrally located road and rail complex bounded by the towns of Pyongyang in the north and Chorwon and Kumhwa in the south. A unique center of communications, the complex was of obvious importance to the enemy high command's ability to move troops and supplies within the forward areas and to coordinate operations laterally. Ridgway's first concern was to occupy ground that would serve both as a base for continuing the attack toward the complex and as a defensive position. The ground he selected, Line Kansas, followed the Imjin River in the west, extended two to six miles north of the thirty-eighth parallel across the approaches to the Iron Triangle, then reached a depth of ten miles above the parallel before falling off southeastward to the town of Yangyang on the coast. On 11 April, as the Eighth Army closed on Line Kansas, Ridgway sent his central forces toward Line Wyoming, which traced the prominent heights commanding the Chorwon-Kumhwa base of the Iron Triangle. Evidence of an imminent enemy offensive mounted as these troops advanced, and as a precaution, on 12 April Ridgway issued plans for delaying actions to be fought when and if the enemy attacked.

Plans being written in Washington in March might well have kept the Eighth Army from moving above the thirty-eighth parallel. Since the Chinese intervention, the United States and other members of the UN coalition had gradually come to accept what they had not been ready for the past autumn—the clearance of enemy troops from South Korea as a suitable final result of their efforts. On 20 March the JCS notified General MacArthur of a forthcoming announcement by President Truman expressing his willingness to negotiate with the Chinese and North Koreans to make "satisfactory arrangements for concluding the fighting." The announcement would be issued "before any advance with major forces north of the thirty-eighth parallel." Before the president's announcement could be made, however, MacArthur issued his own offer to enemy commanders. More an ultimatum than an offer to discuss an end to the fighting, MacArthur placed the United Nations Command in the role of victor. "The enemy . . . must by now be painfully aware," MacArthur said in part, "that a decision of the United Nations to depart from

its tolerant effort to contain the war to the area of Korea, through an expansion of our military operations to its coastal areas and interior bases, would doom Red China to the risk of imminent military collapse." President Truman considered the statement at cross-purposes with the one he planned to issue and so cancelled his own. Hoping the enemy might sue for an armistice if kept under pressure, he permitted the question of crossing the thirty-eighth parallel to be settled on the basis of tactical considerations, and thus it became Ridgway's decision.

On 5 April, Joseph W. Martin, Republican leader in the House of Representatives, read to the House MacArthur's response to a request for comments on Martin's proposal to use Nationalist Chinese forces to open a second front. MacArthur said he believed in "meeting force with maximum counterforce," and that the use of Nationalist forces fitted that belief. He added that there could be "no substitute for victory" in Korea. President Truman could not accept MacArthur's open challenge of national policy and concluded that MacArthur was "unable to give his wholehearted support to the policies of the United States government and of the United Nations in matters pertaining to his official duties." MacArthur was recalled on 11 April and General Ridgway was named his successor. MacArthur returned to the United States to receive the plaudits of a nation shocked by the relief of one of its military heroes. He defended his own views against those of the Truman administration before Congress and the American public. The controversy endured for many months, but the American people eventually accepted the fact that, whatever the merit of MacArthur's arguments, the president as commander in chief had a right to relieve him.

Before transferring to general headquarters in Tokyo, General Ridgway turned over the Eighth Army to Lieutenant General James A. Van Fleet on 14 April. Van Fleet was the personal choice of army Chief of Staff Collins, who considered him to be cast in the same leadership mold as Ridgway. Van Fleet had achieved wide acclaim as head of the U.S. military assistance group sent to Greece in 1948, where he was the mainstay in guiding Greek forces to victory over the Communist-led insurgency. As General Van Fleet assumed command, the Eighth Army was consolidating positions along Line Kansas while its west-central forces moved toward Line Wyoming. Until 21 April the units making the Wyoming advance and patrols searching elsewhere above Line Kansas encountered few Chinese or North Koreans and aerial observers sighted no enemy forces massing near the front. All this changed on the night of the 21st, when patrols ran into strong enemy positions; at daybreak on the 22nd, aerial reconnaissance disclosed the forward movement of large enemy formations from rear assembly areas. By evening Chinese and North Korean assault forces were massed at the front. Around 8:00 P.M. they launched their opening attacks.

The main objective of the enemy offensive was Seoul, whose capture Peng Teh-huai reportedly promised to Mao Tse-tung as a May Day gift. Peng planned to converge on the city with the newly arrived Nineteenth and Third Army groups from the northwest and north and the Ninth Army Group, now restored after losing heavily at the Changjin Reservoir, from the northeast. These three groups constituted a force of 270,000 men. Peng's plan included auxilliary attacks along each flank of the main effort—the NKPA First Corps on the west and the somewhat worn Thirteenth Army Group on the east. In what would be essentially a separate effort, the NKPA Third and Fifth corps were to attack in the east-central region.

Under an umbrella of strong support from both ground- and carrier-based aircraft and helped by 8-inch naval gunfire along the west flank, the Eighth Army fought hard defensive battles as it withdrew twenty to thirty miles through successive delaying positions. By 30 April, Van Fleet's forces had contained Peng's advance along a line reaching northeastward from positions a few miles above Seoul. Enormous casualties compelled Peng to pull his forces well to the north for refurbishing.

The high enemy losses notwithstanding, Van Fleet cautioned his forces that the Chinese and North Koreans had the men to attack again as hard as before or harder. He ordered the full length of the Eighth Army line fortified, counterattack plans developed, and provisions made for delivering lavish artillery fire wherever Peng's forces might attack. Although local advances to improve the line and deep patrolling produced little meaningful contact with the enemy, the composite of reports from aerial observers, agents, civilians, prisoners, and other intelligence sources made clear that some major Chinese units were shifting eastward from the area above Seoul. Expecting, therefore, that the enemy's next principal effort would come either in the west as before or on the central front, Van Fleet shifted forces to place most of his strength in those sectors.

Actually, Peng had shifted five armies of the Third and Ninth groups into the east-central area, where they and the NKPA Fifth Corps struck south during the evening of 16 May. Apparently realizing that his superior numbers of men could defeat an enemy superior in other respects only if the latter's superiority was not too great, Peng chose to attack through some of the most difficult ground on the front. Rugged ridges and a sparse road net would reduce to some degree the UN Command's advantage of superior mobility, firepower, and air power. His strategy nevertheless failed. Adjusting units to place more troops in the path of Peng's advance while his forces laid down tremendous amounts of artillery fire, Van Fleet halted the attack by 20 May after enemy forces had penetrated thirty miles. He immediately ordered the entire Eighth Army forward in counterattack. The Chinese and North Koreans resisted wherever their escape routes and supply installations were threatened, but elsewhere Van Fleet's forces advanced with almost surprising ease. By 31 May they were just short of Line Kansas, and on 1 June Van Fleet sent forces toward Line Wyoming. By mid-June the Eighth Army occupied both Line Kansas and the Wyoming bulge.

Because the Kansas-Wyoming line traced ground suitable for a strong defense, Washington decided to hold that line and wait for a bid for armistice negotiations from the Chinese and North Koreans. In line with this decision, General Van Fleet began to fortify his positions. Enemy forces used the respite from attack to recoup heavy losses and to develop their own defenses. The fighting lapsed into patrolling and small local clashes.

THE STATIC WAR

In an effort to encourage an offer to negotiate an armistice, Secretary of State Acheson enlisted the help of George F. Kennan, a State Department official with a solid background in U.S.-Soviet relations. On 31 May, Kennan met with Yakov A. Malik, Soviet delegate to the United Nations, to make sure that the Soviets were clearly aware of the U.S. desire for a cease-fire and to obtain Moscow's views and suggestions. At a second meeting on 5 June, Malik told Kennan that the Soviet government wanted a peaceful solution in Korea but could not appropriately take part in negotiations. His personal advice was that U.S. authorities should approach their Chinese and North Korean counterparts. In a speech broadcast on the United Nations "Price of Peace" program on 23 June, Malik, after blaming the United States for the war, announced that the Soviet Union believed the conflict could be settled. As a first step, he said, the belligerents should start discussions to arrange a cease-fire and an armistice that provided for the mutual withdrawal of forces from the thirty-eighth parallel. After China endorsed Malik's proposal over Peking radio on 26 June, President Truman authorized General Ridgway to arrange armistice talks with enemy commanders. Through an exchange of radio messages and a meeting of liaison officers, both sides agreed to begin negotiations on 10 July at the town of Kaesong in western no-man's-land, which would be designated a neutral area. General Ridgway appointed Admiral Joy to head a delegation that included four other officers of general or flag rank. The five-man Communist delegation was led by General Nam Il, chief of staff of the NKPA, but from the beginning, he

appeared to be dominated by the ranking Chinese member, Hsieh Fang.

At the first conference the two delegations agreed that hostilities would continue until an armistice was signed. In a little more than two weeks of negotiations, they established the points to be settled: fixing a military demarcation line; organizing a supervisory body to carry out the terms of an armistice; arranging the disposition of prisoners of war; and developing recommendations to the governments of countries involved in the war. On the first point, negotiations to fix a military demarcation line, there was a complete impasse. General Nam insisted that the thirty-eighth parallel be the dividing line, while Admiral Joy, acting on instructions from Washington, pointed out that the parallel had no military significance and proposed that the division be located along the line of contact between opposing forces. After accusing the UN Command of dropping a napalm bomb in the conference area, a fraudulent charge, the Communist delegation broke off negotiations on 22 August.

At that juncture, General Van Fleet opened limited attacks, hoping that the pressure would help persuade enemy authorities to resume the armistice talks and drive enemy forces off positions that favored attacks on Line Kansas. UN Command naval surface forces also applied pressure by keeping enemy shore installations under bombardment, and air forces concentrated attacks on major road and rail lines, troops, vehicles, and supply dumps in enemy rear areas and on Pyongyang, which was again the seat of North Korean government. In air-to-air combat, the fighting was concentrated in the far northwest between the Chongchon and Yalu rivers, an area that became known as MIG Alley.

As Van Fleet began his attacks, the Eighth Army was strengthened by infantry battalions from Ethiopia and Colombia and the Canadian Twenty-fifth Infantry Brigade, which absorbed the Canadian battalion already in Korea. In July all British Commonwealth units were consolidated to form the First Commonwealth Division. Chinese forces had been reinforced by two armies from the Twentieth Army Group. On both sides these recent arrivals would be the last ground units to enter the war.

In east-central Korea, Van Fleet sent forces toward terrain objectives five to seven miles above Line Kansas, among them places given the names Punchbowl, Bloody Ridge, and Heartbreak Ridge. Forces struck in the west on a wide front to secure a line three to four miles north. All objectives were taken by the last week of October. At that point the Comunist delegation agreed to return to the armistice conference table.

Negotiations resumed on 25 October, but this time, at General Ridgway's insistence, in Panmunjom, a small settlement seven miles southeast of Kaesong. Hopes for an early armistice grew on 27 November, when the two delegations agreed that the line of demarcation would be the existing line of contact, provided an armistice agreement was reached within thirty days. Hence, while both sides awaited the outcome of negotiations, the fighting during the remainder of 1951 tapered off to patrol clashes, raids, and small battles for possession of outposts. Discord over several issues, including the exchange of prisoners of war, prevented an armistice agreement within the stipulated thirty days. The prisoner of war quarrel heightened in January 1952, after UN Command delegates proposed to give captives a choice in repatriation proceedings, maintaining that those prisoners who did not wish to return to their homelands should be free to choose their own destinations. The Communist delegates protested vigorously. While the argument continued, both sides tacitly extended the 27 November provisions for a line of demarcation, which had the effect of holding battle action to the pattern of the thirty-day waiting period.

By May 1952 the two delegations worked out all armistice matters except the prisoner repatriation issue, on which they were completely deadlocked. On 7 May, inmates of United Nations Command Prison Camp Number 1 on Koje-do, an island off the southern coast, on orders smuggled to them from North Korea, enticed the camp commander, Brigadier General Francis T. Dodd, to a compound gate, pulled him inside, and held him captive. The strategy, which became clear in subsequent prisoner demands, was to trade General Dodd's life for admission of inhumane treatment of captives, including alleged cruelties during the screenings of prisoners, during which large numbers of them declared their wishes not to be repatriated. The obvious objective was to discredit the repatriation stand taken by Admiral Joy's delegation. A new camp commander, Brigadier General Charles F. Colson, obtained Dodd's release but in the process signed a damaging statement admitting that "there have been instances of bloodshed where many prisoners of war have been killed and wounded by UN Forces." There was no change in the UN Command stand on repatriation, but the statement was widely exploited by the Communists at Panmunjom and elsewhere for its propaganda value.

During the Koje-do affair, General Ridgway received orders placing him in command of NATO forces in Europe. General Mark W. Clark became the new commander in the Far East on 12 May, with one less responsibility than MacArthur and Ridgway had carried. On 28 April a peace treaty with Japan had gone into effect, restoring Japan's sovereignty and ending the occupation. Faced immediately with the Koje-do matter, General Clark repudiated General Colson's statement. Moving swiftly, he placed Brigadier General Haydon L. Boatner in charge of the camp with instructions to move prisoners into smaller, more manageable compounds and to institute other measures that would eliminate the likelihood of another uprising. General Boatner completed the task on 10 June.

On 22 May, Major General William K. Harrison replaced Admiral Joy as chief delegate at Panmunjom, where arguments continued over repatriation. Meanwhile, action at the front held to a pattern of artillery duals, patrols, ambushes, raids, and bitter battles for outposts on oddly shaped land masses such as Sniper Ridge, Old Baldy, The Hook, T-Bone, and Pork Chop Hill. On the Eighth Army front, the National Guard Fortieth and Forty-fifth divisions had replaced the First Cavalry and Twenty-fourth divisions, which returned to Japan. Although costly fighting continued, the lines remained substantially unchanged at the end of 1952. In October the armistice conference went into an indefinite recess with the repatriation issue still unresolved.

There had been a great deal of popular discontent over the war in Korea among the American people, especially with the lack of progress toward an armistice. During the presidential campaign in 1952, Dwight D. Eisenhower pledged to "go to Korea," implying that if elected he would end the war quickly. Consequently, when the president-elect visited Korea in early December, there was some expectation of a dramatic change in the conduct of the war. General Clark even set out detailed estimates of measures needed to win a military victory. Eisenhower, however, like Truman before him, preferred to seek an armistice. Still, he let Communist authorities know that if satisfactory progress toward an armistice were not forthcoming, "we intended to move decisively without inhibition in our use of weapons, and would no longer be responsible for confining hostilities to the Korean peninsula." Immediately after taking office, he made sure these words reached Moscow, Peking, and Pyongyang.

In the hope of prompting a resumption of armistice negotiations, in February 1953 General Clark proposed to his enemy counterparts that the two sides exchange sick and wounded prisoners. His offer was ignored and by spring there was still no break in the deadlock at Panmunjom. At the front, where in February Lieutenant General Maxwell D. Taylor had replaced General Van Fleet as Eighth Army commander, the battle action continued in the mold of the previous year.

The break finally came near the end of March 1953, about three weeks after the death of Joseph Stalin, when enemy armistice delegates

not only replied favorably to General Clark's proposal on the exchange of sick and wounded captives, but also suggested that this exchange perhaps could "lead to the smooth settlement of the entire question of prisoners of war." The armistice conference resumed in April and an exchange of sick and wounded prisoners was carried out that same month (Operation Little Switch). Enemy authorities returned 684 ailing prisoners, of whom 149 were American, while the UN Command returned 6,670 captives. The prisoner repatriation problem was finally settled by mid-June with an agreement offering each side an opportunity to persuade those captives refusing return to their homelands to change their minds.

The pace of battle meanwhile quickened in May when sizable Chinese forces attacked several outposts guarding the Eighth Army's main line in the west. A larger battle opened in the central sector on 10 June, when three Chinese divisions drove two miles through South Korean positions before being contained. Because the terms of an armistice by then were all but complete, that engagement could have been the last of the war. On 18 June, however, President Rhee, who had steadfastly objected to any armistice that left Korea divided, ordered the release of North Korean prisoners who had refused repatriation. Within a few days about twenty-seven thousand North Korean captives were allowed to escape and disappeared among a cooperative South Korean populace. Because the prisoners had been guarded by South Korean troops, UN Command officials disclaimed responsibility for the break, but enemy armistice delegates denounced the action as a serious breach of faith. Another month of negotiations was required to repair the damage done by Rhee's attempt to disrupt the conclusion of the proceedings.

During the delay, enemy forces attacked on 13 July, driving a wedge eight miles deep in the Eighth Army's central sector. General Taylor deployed units to contain the attack and then sent them forward in counterattack. On 20 July he halted the attack force because the armistice delegations finally reached accord and needed only to work out a few details. Taylor's order ended the last major battle of the war.

After a week of dealing with administrative details, the senior delegates, Generals Harrison and Nam, signed the military armistice agreement at Panmunjom at 10 A.M. on 27 July. Shortly afterward, General Clark, Kim Il Sung, and Peng Teh-huai affixed their signatures at their respective headquarters. As agreed, all fighting stopped twelve hours after the first signing, at 10 P.M., 27 July 1953. By the terms of the armistice, the line of demarcation between North Korea and South Korea approximated the front line as it existed at the final hour. Three days after the signing, each opposing force withdrew two kilometers from the line to establish a demilitarized zone that was not to be trespassed. The new border differed only slightly from the prewar division of the country, slanting from a point on the west coast fifteen miles below the thirty-eighth parallel northeastward to an east coast anchor forty miles above the parallel.

Over the thirty-seven months of fighting, the total United Nations Command losses in dead and wounded numbered 385,274. The estimate of enemy dead and wounded was 1,467,000, of which 945,000 were Chinese and 522,000 North Koreans. South Korea had suffered 58,127 dead and 175,743 wounded, United Nations members other than the United States 3,194 dead and 11,297 wounded, and the United States 33,629 dead and 103,284 wounded. After the return of American prisoners in the repatriation proceedings, more than 8,100 men remained unaccounted for. Officially written off as "presumed dead," their true fate remains unknown.

To oversee enforcement of armistice terms and negotiate any violations, the Military Armistice Commission, composed of an equal number of officers from each side, was established, with Panmunjom as its meeting site. Assisting this body was the Neutral Nations Supervisory Commission, whose members were from Sweden, Switzerland, Czechoslovakia, and Poland. Representatives of these same countries, with

India furnishing an umpire and custodial forces, formed the Neutral Nations Repatriation Commission to handle the disposition of prisoners refusing repatriation. Also, a provision of the armistice agreement recommended that the belligerent governments convene a political conference to negotiate a final settlement of Korea's future.

All prisoners wishing to be repatriated were exchanged by 6 September. UN Command authorities delivered 75,823 captives, of whom 70,183 were Chinese and 5,640 North Koreans. Returned from the north were 12,773 prisoners, of whom 7,862 were South Koreans, 3,597 Americans, and 1,314 from other countries. From these returnees came accounts of brutal treatment in enemy prison camps and of an extensive Communist indoctrination program, of brainwashing techniques designed to produce prisoner collaboration. Of several hundred American returnees investigated on charges of collaborating with the enemy, only fourteen were tried and, of these, eleven were convicted.

The transfer of nonrepatriates to the Neutral Nations Repatriation Commission came next. Few prisoners changed their minds when officials from both sides tried to convince former members of their commands to return. Of 22,604 Chinese and North Koreans delivered to the Repatriation Commission, 14,247 Chinese and 7,674 North Koreans returned to UN Command control. Most of the Chinese eventually were shipped to Taiwan. Of 325 South Koreans, twenty-three Americans, and one Britisher brought to the commission, just twelve changed their minds. Almost all of the twenty-one Americans who stayed with the Communists eventually returned to the United States. Because these men had already been dishonorably discharged from military service, no further action was taken against them. After releasing the last of the nonrepatriates, the Repatriation Commission dissolved itself on 1 February 1954.

The scene then shifted to Geneva, Switzerland, where the political conference recommended in the armistice agreement convened on 26 April. From the beginning there was a complete deadlock. Representatives of UN Command member countries wanted to reunify Korea through elections supervised by the United Nations; the Communist delegates refused to recognize UN authority to deal with the matter. The talks ended on 15 June 1954 with Korea still divided and with opposing forces still facing each other across the demilitarized zone.

Although the armistice agreement and the Geneva impasse left Korea divided essentially along the prewar line, the war had far more consequence than merely to restore its *status quo ante bellum*. In South Korea the ROKA, under an able chief of staff, Major General Chung Il Kwon, and with KMAG guidance, had grown into a well-developed and experienced force of sixteen divisions. Scheduled to raise four more divisions, it was a force that North Korea's resources would be strained to match. To further discourage any future North Korean aggression, substantial U.S. army combat troops were to remain in Korea. In addition, sixteen nations who had contributed forces to the UN Command, including the United States, declared on the day the armistice agreement was signed that they would resist any renewal of armed attack and that if Communist aggression reoccurred, "in all probability, it would not be possible to confine hostilities within the frontiers of Korea," a warning aimed not just at North Korea, but also at China.

The conflict also had a transforming impact on the course of international relations in both Asia and Europe. For the Communist East, the major result was the emerging of China as a great power. A steady improvement in the Chinese army and air force during the war gave China a more powerful military posture at war's end. Despite vast losses, its performance in Korea won China respect as a nation to be reckoned with not only in Asian but in world affairs. For Western nations, a primary result was a decided strengthening of the NATO alliance. Greece and Turkey were now members and, whereas before the war the total forces available to the organization included just twelve divisions, four hundred aircraft, and a small navy,

by the end of the Korean War, NATO had grown to fifty-two divisions, four thousand aircraft, and substantial naval units.

As a direct consequence of the war, there was also a multiplication of U.S. political, economic, and military ties with non-Communist nations throughout the western Pacific. Between 1951 and 1953, the United States negotiated bilateral security ties with Korea, Japan, Taiwan, the Philippines, Australia, and New Zealand. The Communist armed aggression in Korea also inspired the United States to hedge a repetition in Southeast Asia, principally in Indochina. In 1954 it promoted and joined the Southeast Asia Treaty Organization (SEATO), a defense alliance whose members included Great Britain, France, Australia, New Zealand, Pakistan, Thailand, and the Philippines, and whose defense area included Laos, Cambodia, and South Vietnam.

The war also prompted a marked rise in U.S. military strength. By war's end, U.S. armed forces had increased by two million. The army alone numbered more than a million and a half and had twenty divisions, twice the prewar number. There would be a substantial postwar reduction of forces but no drastic dismantling as had followed World War II. The cold war obviously would continue and U.S. authorities intended that the United States would maintain ready forces fully capable of supporting the U.S. strategy of containment. In the process there would be added emphasis on nuclear power. The air force would increase its strategic bombing capability, the navy would concentrate on developing nuclear missiles that could be launched from submarines and other ships, and the army would seek to perfect tactical nuclear weapons. In January 1954, Secretary of State John Foster Dulles announced that in the future the United States would "depend primarily upon a great capacity to retaliate instantly, by means and at places of our choosing," a policy to become known as "massive retaliation" during Dwight Eisenhower's presidency. Indeed, the Korean War was a landmark in the rise of the United States as a superpower.

BIBLIOGRAPHY

Acheson, Dean. *Present at the Creation: My Years in the State Department* (1969).

Alexander, Bevin. *Korea: The First War We Lost* (1986).

Appleman, Roy E. *South to the Naktong, North to the Yalu: June–November 1950* (1961).

Barclay, C. N. *The First Commonwealth Division: The Story of British Commonwealth Land Forces in Korea, 1950–1953* (1954).

Biderman, Albert D. *The March to Calumny: The Story of American POW's in the Korean War* (1962).

Blair, Clay. *The Forgotten War: America in Korea, 1950–1953* (1987).

Bohlen, Charles E. *Witness to History, 1929–1969* (1973).

Bradley, Omar, N., and Clay Blair. *A General's Life: An Autobiography* (1983).

Cagle, Malcolm W., and Frank A. Manson. *The Sea War in Korea* (1957).

Cho, Soon Sung. *Korea in World Politics, 1940–1950: An Evaluation of American Responsibility* (1967).

Clark, Mark W. *From the Danube to the Yalu* (1954).

Collins, J. Lawton. *War in Peacetime: The History and Lessons of Korea* (1969).

Cowdry, Albert E. *The Medics' War* (1987).

Dean, William F. *General Dean's Story* (1954).

Deane, Philip. *I Was a Captive in Korea* (1953).

Eisenhower, Dwight D. *Mandate for Change: The White House Years, 1953–1956* (1963).

Farrar-Hockley, Anthony. *The Edge of the Sword* (1954).

Field, James A., Jr. *United States Naval Operations, Korea* (1962).

Futrell, Robert F. *United States Air Forces in Korea, 1950–1953* (1961).

George, Alexander L. *The Chinese Communist Army in Action* (1967).

Gittings, John. *The Role of the Chinese Army* (1967).

Goldberg, Alfred, ed. *A History of the United States Air Force, 1907–1957* (1957).

Goodrich, Leland M. *Korea: A Study of U.S. Policy in the United Nations* (1956).

Goulden, Joseph R. *Korea: The Untold Story of the War* (1982).

Griffith, Samuel B., II. *The Chinese People's Liberation Army* (1967).

Gugeler, Russell A. *Combat Actions in Korea* (1954).

Heinl, Robert D., Jr. *Victory at High Tide: The Seoul-Inchon Campaign* (1968).

Heller, Francis H., ed. *The Korean War: A 25-Year Perspective* (1977).

Hermes, Walter F. *Truce Tent and Fighting Front* (1966).

Higgins, Trumball. *Korea and the Fall of MacArthur: A Precis of Limited War* (1960).

James, D. Clayton. *The Years of MacArthur, Triumph and Disaster, 1945–1964* (1985).

Joy, C. Turner. *How Communists Negotiate* (1955).

Kinkead, Eugene. *In Every War but One* (1959).

Leckie, Robert. *Conflict: The History of the Korean War, 1950–1953* (1962).

MacArthur, Douglas. *Reminiscences* (1964).

McCune, George M., and Arthur L. Gray, Jr. *Korea Today* (1950).

Marshall, S. L. A. *The River and the Gauntlet* (1953).

———. *Pork Chop Hill: The American Fighting Man in Action, Korea, Spring 1953* (1956).

Meade, Edward Grant. *American Military Government in Korea* (1951).

Montross, Lynn, et al. *U.S. Marine Corps Operations in Korea, 1950–1953*, 5 vols. (1954–1972).

Mossman, Billy C. *Ebb and Flow: November 1950–July 1951* (1990).

Office of the Chief of Military History, Department of the Army, *Korea 1950* (1952).

———. *Korea 1951–1953* (1956).

Rees, David. *Korea: The Limited War* (1964).

Ridgway, Matthew B. *The Korean War* (1967).

Sawyer, Robert K. *Military Advisers in Korea: KMAG in Peace and War* (1962).

Schnabel, James F. *U.S. Army in the Korean War: Policy and Directions: The First Year* (1972).

Sebald, William. *With MacArthur in Japan: A Personal History of the Occupation* (1965)

Simmons, Robert R. *The Strained Alliance: Peking, P'y'ongyang, Moscow and the Politics of the Korean Civil War* (1975).

Taylor, Maxwell D. *The Uncertain Trumpet* (1960).

Truman, Harry S. *Memoirs: Years of Trial and Hope*, vol. 2 (1955).

Vatcher, William H., Jr. *Panmunjom: The Story of the Korean Military Armistice Negotiations* (1958).

Weigley, Russell F. *History of the United States Army* (1967).

Whiting, Allen S. *China Crosses the Yalu* (1960).

Wood, Herbert Fairlie. *Strange Battleground: The Operations in Korea and their Effects on the Defence Policy of Canada* (1966).

THE VIETNAM ERA

Richard A. Hunt

The tragic involvement of the United States in Vietnam began with little fanfare. Most Americans knew nothing of the limited contact U.S. servicemen had with Vietnamese anti-Japanese resistance fighters during World War II or paid much attention when President Harry S. Truman decided to aid the attempt by the French government to restore colonial rule after the war. That ignorance ended in the 1960s. Throughout the decade Vietnam was on nearly everyone's mind as the U.S. military commitment inexorably grew into a costly, inconclusive war that, before it ended in 1975, tore apart the American body politic. The Vietnam War raised questions about the fitness of the U.S. military and the role of military power in a political struggle. It also opened debate about priorities—whether domestic problems of poverty and racial discrimination had a higher claim on the purse and conscience of the nation than the expenditure of lives and money in an overseas crusade to preserve South Vietnam. A sideshow in World War II, the Vietnam War arguably became the dominant issue in U.S. history from the mid-1960s to the mid-1970s and divided the United States as no other conflict had since the Civil War.

The decisions of U.S. presidents and military leaders on how and when to fight directly influenced the course of the war. Throughout its involvement in Vietnam, the United States fought a limited war for limited objectives. The goal was not the destruction or surrender of its foe, North Vietnam, or the conquest of its territory, but the preservation of the U.S. ally, South Vietnam, as a sovereign, non-Communist nation. Successive administrations, hoping to keep costs at acceptable levels, placed limits on how the military employed air, sea, and ground power. To preserve its ally and deter its foe required the U.S. government to develop a sophisticated political/military strategy that precisely formulated ends and means and dealt with all aspects of the threat. That task proved difficult, as conventional military measures to defeat enemy forces could work at cross-purposes with political efforts to help the Saigon government establish a solid base of support. Differences arose between civilian and military leaders over priorities and procedures. The need to balance the political and military components of strategy for a limited war proved to be a vexing issue throughout the period of direct U.S. involvement.

BACKGROUND TO A U.S. WAR

The U.S. commitment to Vietnam evolved from the abortive attempt by France to retain its colonial holdings in Southeast Asia. Ambivalence characterized U.S. policy toward Indochina during World War II. On the one hand, the United States reassured France that it would get back its former possessions. On the other, President Franklin D. Roosevelt personally advocated independence for Indochina, and members of the Office of Strategic Services (OSS) fought alongside the League for the Independence of Vietnam—the Vietminh guerrillas—against the Japanese. Ultimately, military strategy and British intransigence on colonial policy determined U.S. policy. Concentrating its forces against Japan, the United States agreed that the British and Chinese would divide Indochina for purposes of occupation. With British cooperation, French military forces returned to Vietnam in September 1945.

After World War II, most European powers relinquished their Asian empires. The French were the exception. Great Britain granted independence to India, Pakistan, Burma, Ceylon, and Malaya, and Holland gave up control of Indonesia. The French opposed Vietnamese independence and sought to reassert dominion over Vietnam. France rejected the claim of the Vietminh to rule Vietnam. Under their leader, Ho Chi Minh, who was both an ardent nationalist and the leader of the Indochinese Communist party, the Vietminh in 1945 had sought to replace departing Japanese occupation forces, establishing in Hanoi the Democratic Republic of Vietnam (DRV). French authorities returned to Hanoi in March 1946, following an accord in which Ho acceded to their return in exchange for limited recognition of the DRV. In April the United States acknowledged French control. Relations between the French and the Vietminh quickly deteriorated, and in late 1946 war broke out. The Vietminh fought to end colonial rule and establish an independent Vietnam.

The involvement of the United States in Vietnam grew steadily. In 1950, in an international climate characterized by open hostilities in Korea and worldwide confrontation between Communist and non-Communist powers, President Truman began to increase military supplies to the French through the newly formed U.S. Military Assistance Advisory Group (MAAG), Indo-china. Headquartered in Saigon, the MAAG grew from 65 men in 1950 to 342 in 1954. Linking the war against the Vietminh to the worldwide struggle to contain Communist expansion, the United States late in 1950 committed more than $133 million in aid to Indochina and ordered immediate delivery of large quantities of arms and ammunition, naval vessels, aircraft, and military vehicles. By 1952 the amount of aid exceeded $300 million.

The French had plenty of equipment, but they used it unwisely, trying to defeat the Vietminh in large battles. They neglected the village war, failing to protect the Vietnamese people from Vietminh guerrillas and political operatives. The decisive battle in 1954 at Dien Bien Phu, a remote village in the northwest, which led to the withdrawal of France, epitomized the folly of their strategy. Hoping to lure the Vietminh into a set-piece battle, French forces occupied Dien Bien Phu, a site far removed from coastal supply bases. Vietminh forces surrounded and slowly strangled the garrison. Antiaircraft fire made it difficult for the French to bring in supplies by air. General Paul Ely, French chief of staff, arrived in Washington on 20 March 1954 to ask for direct U.S. military intervention. Admiral Arthur Radford, chairman of the Joint Chiefs of Staff (JCS), proposed an air attack against Vietminh positions. President Dwight D. Eisenhower declined to provide air support or send U.S. forces to save the French. A bleak intelligence estimate, the difficulty of obtaining congressional support, and the warning of Army Chief of Staff General Matthew Ridgway and others who feared that the use of U.S. ground forces in an Asian land war would severely strain the army dissuaded Eisenhower from unilateral intervention.

Dien Bien Phu fell in May 1954 while the fate of Indochina was being negotiated in Geneva, Switzerland. Faced with political divisions at home, soaring war costs, and a decisive military defeat, the French ceded control of Indochina. The Geneva Accords of 1954 established Vietnam as an independent but divided country. Two newly recognized, distrustful regimes warily eyed each other across a common border, the

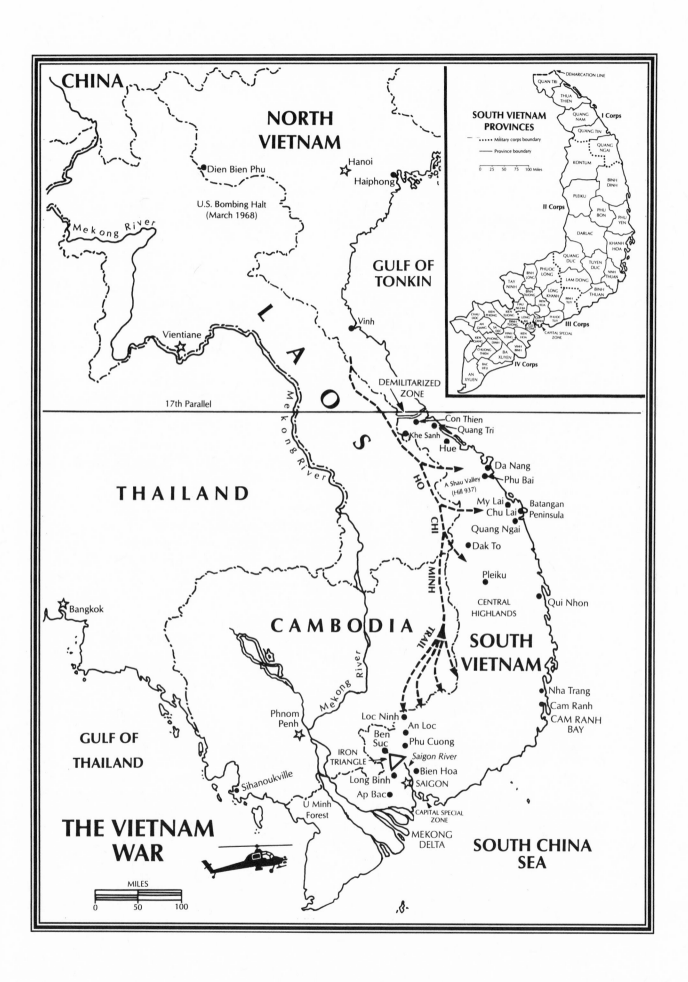

CHINA

NORTH
VIETNAM

● Dien Bien Phu

Hanoi ☆
Haiphong ●

Mekong River

U.S. Bombing Halt
(March 1968)

GULF OF
TONKIN

Vientiane ☆

● Vinh

17th Parallel

THAILAND

Mekong River

L
A
O
S

DEMILITARIZED
ZONE

Con Thien ●
Khe Sanh ● Quang Tri
Hue ●

Da Nang ●
A Shau Valley ● Phu Bai
(Hill 937)

My Lai ● Batangan
Chu Lai ● Peninsula

Quang Ngai ●

● Dak To

Pleiku ●

CENTRAL
HIGHLANDS

● Qui Nhon

H
O

C
H
I

M
I
N
H

☆ Bangkok

CAMBODIA

Mekong River

T
R
A
I
L

SOUTH
VIETNAM

Phnom
Penh ☆

● Nha Trang
● Cam Ranh
CAM RANH
BAY

Loc Ninh ●

GULF OF

THAILAND

● Sihanoukville

IRON
TRIANGLE

Ben
Suc ●

An Loc ●
● Phu Cuong

Saigon River

Long Binh ●
Ap Bac ●

● Bien Hoa
☆ SAIGON

U Minh
Forest

CAPITAL SPECIAL
ZONE

THE VIETNAM
WAR

MEKONG
DELTA

SOUTH CHINA
SEA

MILES

0   50   100

SOUTH VIETNAM
PROVINCES

DEMARCATION LINE

QUAN TRI
THUA
THIEN

QUANG NAM   I Corps

QUANG TIN

QUANG
NGAI

····· Military corps boundary
—— Province boundary

0 25 50 75 100 Miles

KONTUM

BINH
DINH

PLEIKU

II Corps

PHU
BON   PHU
YEN

DARLAC

KHANH
HOA

QUANG
DUC
PHUOC
LONG   TUYEN
DUC   NINH
THUAN

BINH
LONG   LAM DONG   BINH
THUAN

TAY
NINH   BINH
DUONG   LONG
KHANH

CHAU
DOC   PHUOC
TUY   III Corps

AN
GIANG   CAPITAL SPECIAL
ZONE

KIEN
PHONG

KIEN
GIANG   CHUONG
THIEN

BA
XUYEN

BAC
LIEU   IV Corps

AN
XUYEN

seventeenth parallel. The Democratic Republic of Vietnam, the Communist regime in the north invoking Vietnamese nationalism, sought to unite Vietnam under its banner. The non-Communist State of Vietnam in the south was determined to resist unification under the Communists. Neither the United States nor South Vietnam signed the accords.

Following the withdrawal of France from Indochina in 1955, the Eisenhower administration, which, like its predecessor, was fearful of Communist expansion in Indochina, enlarged the U.S. role in Vietnam. The administration decided to give military aid directly to the newly formed South Vietnamese government in Saigon, headed by Ngo Dinh Diem, a Roman Catholic of mandarin background. Eisenhower also set up a collective defense organization, the Southeast Asia Treaty Organization, to provide for regional security.

To preserve its independence, the Diem regime needed to establish itself as the sole legitimate political authority in South Vietnam in place of the Vietminh and the departing French colonists, no easy task for a new political entity that lacked a unifying national identity. Regional, ethnic, and religious antagonism afflicted South Vietnam from its creation as a separate nation. Sizable ethnic minorities, principally Chinese, ethnic Cambodians (Khmers), and mountain tribes, called montagnards, living in the central highlands lived uneasily with the Vietnamese. Between 1954 and 1956, thousands of Roman Catholics fearing persecution left the north and settled in South Vietnam. The Catholic émigrés, a minority in a predominantly Buddhist country, filled many critical military and political leadership posts in the south as colonial authorities withdrew. Many Diem supporters, having cooperated with the French, had questionable credentials as nationalists. Most émigrés from the north had little knowledge of the problems that burdened the peasants. Opposition from the Communists as well as from the armed sects—the Cao Dai, the Hoa Hao, and the Binh Xuyen—made the early survival of the Diem regime uncertain. In 1954 the government of South Vietnam con-

trolled only the cities and large towns. To govern, Diem had to extend his rule to the villages, where the bulk of the people lived, and gain their support. Pacification, the effort to provide security and improve economic conditions in the countryside, was thus a key government program from the inception of the government of South Vietnam.

By 1956, Diem had taken some promising steps toward building a political base. He had disarmed the sects and installed loyal province and district chiefs, establishing a degree of political stability many thought unattainable when he took power, and his government enacted a land reform statute in 1956. In consolidating his rule, however, Diem also turned against his political opponents and remnants of the Vietminh, many of whom were anti-Communist nationalists. As Diem became more authoritarian, a growing number of the politically disaffected joined the insurgent movement.

In Hanoi, Ho Chi Minh's Indochinese Communist party (renamed the Dang Lao Dong Vietnam or the Vietnam Workers Party) governed North Vietnam and led the battle for unification. The party issued guidance to the Vietminh cadres remaining in the south and trained in the techniques of revolutionary warfare some ninety thousand southern-based Vietminh who had moved north following the partition of the country. They later returned south and merged with the stay-behind cadres to form a new insurgent force, commonly known as the Vietcong.

In 1956 the Vietcong started building a political organization and forming local military units in Quang Ngai province, the U Minh forest, and the heavily populated farming regions around Saigon and in the Mekong River delta. The former Vietminh leaders rebuilt their base camps in the unsettled jungles close to the capital—War Zones C and D and the Iron Triangle, a base area with headquarters directing military and political activity around the capital. The key base area, War Zone D, forested and difficult to penetrate, was close to the Cambodian border but accessible to the lower delta and the central highlands. These remote bases allowed the nascent guerrilla forces to develop and operate in secret. By the following year, Vietcong forces numbered thirty-seven armed companies and began small-scale guerrilla operations. Vietcong strength grew from roughly five thousand at the beginning of 1959 to about 100,000 by the end of 1964. The growth resulted from the return of the Vietminh trained in the north, recruiting within South Vietnam, and the infiltration of native North Vietnamese soldiers into South Vietnam as replacements and reinforcements.

Over time, Vietcong forces encompassed part-time hamlet and village guerrillas and full-time professional soldiers. Guerrillas gathered intelligence, propagandized, and recruited, and kept government officials away. The presence of guerrillas allowed the political cadres that comprised the infrastructure, or secret government, to impose taxes and run the village. Local force units consisted of full-time soldiers, who usually attacked isolated, weakly defended outposts or vulnerable government forces. Main force units, larger and more heavily armed, were formed into battalions, regiments, and even divisions. Each unit included a three-man political cell to impose party policy and military discipline. A political officer assigned missions to Vietcong units, often specifying which South Vietnamese unit to attack.

In the early years of his rule, the harsh attacks by Diem on the Vietcong movement, which relied on police sweeps, detention, and operations by the Army of the Republic of Vietnam, known as ARVN, put the Communists on the defensive. By 1957, Diem had so weakened the movement that its leaders feared for its survival. In 1959, Hanoi decided that it had to resume the armed struggle and began sending supplies and manpower southward. Under the new strategy, the insurgents stepped up attacks on villages and government outposts, aiming to undermine Saigon's ability to govern the countryside. Several hundred government officials were assassinated. The party enlarged the political struggle. To organize and lead the opposition to Diem's rule, in December 1960 Hanoi created the National Liberation Front of South Vietnam. Through a combined military and po-

litical struggle they hoped to hasten the disintegration of the Saigon government and gain adherents to their movement from the ranks of dissatisfied Vietnamese. Throughout 1959, the insurgency grew, forcing Saigon to move people into protected settlements, so-called *agrovilles*, from villages vulnerable to Communist political action.

MORE AID FOR VIETNAM

The burgeoning guerrilla war found the MAAG and ARVN ill-prepared to mount effective opposition. In the late 1950s, the United States, fearing another invasion of South Korea by a Communist army, viewed the regular forces of North Vietnam as the most significant threat to South Vietnam. Consequently, the MAAG, which had grown to 740 men by 1956, trained the South Vietnamese military to stop a conventional invading force. The MAAG emphasized the operations of large tactical military formations—regiments, divisions, and corps—and the gathering of conventional military order of battle information. U.S. funds covered some of the costs of Vietnamese military pay and allowances, training, construction, and medical services. The MAAG fixation on the threat of an invasion by conventional forces caused it to slight counterinsurgency doctrine, intelligence, and training. An insurgency, or a war of national liberation, as the Communists termed it, was as much a contest for political legitimacy as it was an armed struggle. Most army advisers assigned to Vietnam in the late 1950s and early 1960s were inadequately trained to help their counterparts deal with the political and social dimensions of insurgency. In a civil conflict between warring Vietnamese groups, the advisers were political and cultural outsiders. To quell the insurgency would require both the defeat of the guerrillas and the successful engagement of popular support for the government cause.

That the United States underestimated the danger from Communist guerrilla forces or political cadres was apparent in the counterinsurgency plan that Admiral Harry Felt, commander in chief of Pacific forces (CINCPAC), began to develop in March 1960. The plan emphasized preparations for conventional war and financed an increase of 20,000 men in the South Vietnamese army, bringing total strength to 170,000. It also supported a modest expansion of the paramilitary forces charged with providing local security to 68,000. Those security forces were already less well-trained and less well-armed than the ARVN. It was assumed that the Saigon government would make political reforms on its own to enhance its popular support.

After President John F. Kennedy took office in 1961, he tried to change the direction of national security policy. Eschewing what his administration considered to be the rigidity of the Eisenhower New Look policy of relying on massive retaliation to protect U.S. national interests, Kennedy advocated flexible response, training, structuring, and equipping forces to fight across the spectrum of conflict from limited guerrilla campaigns to full-scale nuclear war. The new strategic framework was also intended to help his administration better handle insurgencies, such as the one in South Vietnam, which Soviet Premier Nikita Khrushchev had pledged to support. Kennedy believed it important to stop the Communists in South Vietnam, which he called "the cornerstone of the Free World in Southeast Asia." His administration hoped to sharpen the focus on counterinsurgency. U.S. Army Special Forces featured prominently in counterinsurgency thinking.

In the early 1960s, the U.S. Army did not embrace counterinsurgency as fervently as civilian disciples of the doctrine in the administration. Army Chief of Staff General George Decker allegedly told Kennedy that "any good soldier can handle guerrillas." Like much of the army staff, Decker was unenthusiastic about special training for insurgent warfare. He favored the development of "balanced" U.S. Army forces that could meet a range of threats rather than specialists trained in one kind of warfare. The army did little to alter its force structure to meet the requirements of counterinsurgency, which called for a simpler form of combat, lighter weaponry, and constant small-

unit patrolling. The army simply added the counterinsurgency mission to combat divisions that were organized, trained, and equipped to fight as conventional units. Like the ARVN, U.S. divisions were better prepared to engage regular than irregular forces.

Even ostensible counterinsurgency measures gradually took on a conventional cast. In 1961, the Special Forces took over responsibility for advising the Civilian Irregular Defense Groups (CIDGs), a village self-defense and development program. Composed of montagnard tribesmen, the CIDGs soon were involved in border surveillance and control as well as village defense. Located in the sparsely populated provinces of the highlands, the camps and the Special Forces were far removed from the populous Mekong Delta and coastal regions, which were the primary targets of the Vietcong insurgency. Relatively isolated, the CIDG camps were also vulnerable to enemy attack, and by 1965, as the military situation worsened, many CIDG units changed their role and began to launch quasi-conventional operations.

By October 1961, Kennedy had to help the South Vietnamese counter growing Vietcong attacks and increases in enemy forces. Mounting political discontent with Diem inside South Vietnam promised to complicate U.S. initiatives to help Saigon. Any U.S. assistance that strengthened Diem's hand might also allow him to become more authoritarian. Kennedy sent a high-level delegation headed by General Maxwell Taylor, the president's military representative, and Walt Rostow, a White House adviser, on a fact-finding mission to Saigon. They discovered the plight of the Diem government to be more desperate than anticipated and recommended that the president send eight thousand troops and three companies of helicopters to Vietnam. Absent from their report was any consideration of how to invigorate Diem's fragile political base in the villages, which some members of the delegation feared made the regime vulnerable over the long term.

Kennedy ordered two helicopter companies to Vietnam and decided to assign U.S. Army advisers to South Vietnamese regiments, battalions, and provinces. He believed that the gradual dispersion of advisers to smaller Vietnamese units in the field would more directly help improve South Vietnamese military performance and give the U.S. command a new source of influence. The introduction of advisers to field units was a major change that Diem had resisted, in hopes of minimizing U.S. involvement in his affairs. Fewer than one hundred U.S. Army advisers had worked with the Vietnamese before, mostly at the command level and in ARVN training centers; it was hoped that their advice would filter down to units in the countryside. By early 1962, the army had stationed close to nine hundred advisers in Vietnam and had begun to train officers and non-commissioned officers (NCOs) at the Special Warfare Center at Fort Bragg, North Carolina. By early 1965, the army posted officers in all South Vietnamese corps and division headquarters, thirty-one regiments, three brigades, ninety-three battalions, forty-four provinces, and numerous districts.

Advising was an extremely difficult assignment. An adviser helped plan operations and train forces and served as a conduit between the U.S. command and the South Vietnamese, reporting to his superiors on local conditions and attempting to get his counterpart to heed his advice. He also tried to ensure that his South Vietnamese counterpart used U.S. funds and materials honestly and productively. In practice, the adviser could exercise little leverage over South Vietnamese officials, who might be senior in rank, age, and experience. The adviser had no authority to issue direct orders. Instead, his superiors encouraged him to work to establish rapport with his counterpart. It usually took an American several months to begin to understand the local military situation and the nuances of South Vietnamese military and civilian politics. Unfortunately, short tours of duty for advisers made it difficult to build rapport or develop more than a superficial acquaintance with the local scene. A military adviser would also need to coordinate his activities with those of the province representative, a civilian official of the Agency for International Development

(AID), who administered U.S. support of non-military programs, such as police training and economic development.

Army advisers were well-represented in nearly every aspect of South Vietnamese military activity, except territorial security, a critical element of pacification. Only 100 to 150 of 1,820 U.S. Army advisers were assigned to pacification-related duties at the end of June 1964. This figure represented something of an improvement; before 1963 only five advisers assisted the territorial security forces. Despite Kennedy's interest in stemming wars of national liberation, U.S. assistance from the counterinsurgency plan to the 1964 buildup of advisers concentrated on conventional forces.

To help ARVN cope with the Vietcong, Kennedy continually sent helicopters to Vietnam. First used to support ARVN corps and divisions, they soon became indispensable in carrying out other functions. The UH-1, or Huey, which was introduced in the early 1960s, transported men and supplies, reconnoitered, evacuated wounded, and provided command and control for ground operations. Advisers instructed ARVN in special air assault tactics that took advantage of the speed, mobility, and lift of the craft. Exercises in 1963 and 1964, encouraged by Defense Secretary Robert McNamara, validated new uses for helicopters. Armaments—first machine guns and later rockets—were added to suppress antiaircraft fire, "soften" landing zones, and furnish fire support to ground soldiers.

The Kennedy administration witnessed a dramatic growth in U.S. resources invested in the preservation of South Vietnam. Military strength went from fewer than eight hundred in the last year of the Eisenhower administration to about twenty-three thousand by the end of 1964. The army accounted for the bulk of these numbers, fifteen thousand, of whom about two thousand were advisers. In 1962 a provisional Special Forces Group was formed in Vietnam. Air force strength reached six thousand; the navy, 1,150; and the marines, 850. With a growing military presence in South Vietnam, the United States obviously committed its prestige.

Less obvious at the time was how difficult it would be to withdraw or compel the Saigon regime to make basic reforms.

Changes in the command structure accompanied the growth in military personnel. In February 1962, the JCS established the United States Military Assistance Command, Vietnam (MACV), to oversee the U.S. military effort. The MACV commander, army General Paul Harkins, was the senior U.S. military official in Vietnam. Responsible for U.S. military policy, operations, and assistance, Harkins reported to Admiral Felt, CINCPAC, in Hawaii, but because of the growing interest in Vietnam he also enjoyed direct access to military and civilian leaders in Washington. Harkins was authorized to discuss military operations and assistance with President Diem and other Vietnamese leaders. Under Harkins, MACV also came to assume direction of the advisory effort from the MAAG, which was formally disestablished in 1964. In addition to managing the advisory effort, MACV commanded army support units. The U.S. Army Support Group, Vietnam, provided administrative and logistical support for army units. Harkins' responsibility also extended to U.S. forces in Thailand, where he exercised the same authority he did as commander of MACV.

The creation of MACV raised new organizational issues. After MACV was set up, the Pacific Air Forces Command (PACAF), which was part of the Pacific Command in Hawaii, established the Second Advanced Squadron in Vietnam. Originally formed as an air component command, the squadron evolved into the air component command headquarters. A separate naval component was thought unnecessary when MACV was established. The Naval Section of the MAAG and the Headquarters Support Activity, Saigon, a small navy logistical office under MACV, was assigned to develop a viable Vietnamese naval force. Some army officers pressed for a separate army component commander, but the air force opposed the idea, arguing that an army command already existed under MACV. In their view, Harkins favored the army in resolving joint issues, such as the

respective aviation roles of the services. Interservice disagreements over command of aircraft continued through the war.

FUTILE EFFORTS

While Kennedy was president, the Diem government devised the Strategic Hamlet Program to defeat the Vietcong in the countryside. Launched late in 1961 by Diem and his brother, Ngo Dinh Nhu, the program sought to create thousands of new, fortified settlements that would isolate people from the Vietcong. The new residents, who frequently were moved from their homes involuntarily, were responsible for hamlet construction and defense. ARVN and paramilitary units provided security during construction. The government planned to carry out social, political, and economic reforms in the hamlets to preempt Vietcong promises of land ownership and economic improvement. The program directly imperiled insurgent ties with the rural population, which was the movement's base of support.

By 1963 the program met determined resistance from the Vietcong, who concentrated on its destruction. In too many instances, inhabitants had scant security from insurgent raids, and Vietcong agents easily entered hamlets, levying taxes and obtaining fresh recruits. With increased Communist pressure, rural security dropped. In late November 1963, Harkins, a constant purveyor of good news, reported that no strategic hamlets were under the control of the Vietcong, but the situation deteriorated dramatically. A U.S. and South Vietnamese survey undertaken in July 1964 judged that only thirty of the 219 strategic hamlets completed in Long An province, for example, still remained under government control.

Grandiose plans led to overexpansion, creating far more hamlets than Saigon's military forces could protect or its cadre administer. Too many strategic hamlets had been built too hastily. MACV was justifiably skeptical about how many viable hamlets existed, because the central government exerted strong pressure to show gains, and official reports from the field were generally unreliable. Some hamlets existed only on paper, lacking credible defenses and social programs. Many peasants resented the often harsh living conditions. Promised reforms did not materialize and the program failed to realize its potential.

Not all U.S. officials approved of the strategic hamlets. The head of the MAAG between September 1960 and July 1962, Lieutenant General Lionel McGarr, objected because the program downgraded the activities of conventional military forces. In his mind, defended hamlets connoted a defensive posture of ground forces tied down in static positions.

The MAAG effort to build ARVN as a competent fighting force, however, was having little success. New weapons and U.S. technical advice failed to compensate for deficient ARVN leadership and planning, unimaginative operations, and unwillingness at times to engage the foe. The widely publicized and embarrassing defeat of government forces at the village of Ap Bac in January 1963 pointedly demonstrated the skill of Vietcong forces in negating ARVN advantages in firepower and mobility. The defeat was an ominous sign that the Vietcong could challenge ARVN units of equal strength and step up the intensity of the fighting. If Ap Bac emboldened the Vietcong, it made ARVN more tentative. Government forces generally refrained from night operations and resorted to large sweeps that avoided known enemy base areas.

By the summer of 1963, Diem was in serious trouble. The war was going badly and the main pacification effort, strategic hamlets, was being subverted by the Vietcong and vitiated by the ham-handed management of the regime. When Buddhists mounted protests against the government in the summer, Diem used military force to suppress them, further weakening his political support. Some of his generals concluded that South Vietnam would go down to defeat if he remained in power. With U.S. encouragement, a group of ARVN generals overthrew Diem on 1 November. His ouster and murder

prefaced a period not of reform but of political turmoil.

In the aftermath of the coup, no leader was able to unite the South Vietnamese political factions vying for power and reverse the losing trend of the war. The vestiges of central government authority in the countryside began to disappear. The new government replaced thirty-five of forty-one province chiefs, most of whom had been Diem loyalists. Almost all military commands changed hands. Vietcong forces took advantage, increasing their control over rural areas. By March 1964, Washington estimated that 40 percent of South Vietnamese territory was under Communist control. Leaders in Hanoi moved to intensify the armed struggle by training North Vietnamese army units possibly to intervene and by sending conscripts (replacements for the original members of the Vietminh) down the Ho Chi Minh trail, a complex network of trails and roads from North Vietnam through Laos and Cambodia to South Vietnam.

DIRECT U.S. INTERVENTION

The disintegration of the South Vietnamese government and armed forces and the undeniable enemy gains caused the United States to seek new ways to bolster its ally. The restricted U.S. role of providing advice and support had failed to strengthen its ally and had no impact in deterring the Communists. Lyndon B. Johnson, who became president in November 1963 upon the assassination of Kennedy, explored a number of options for limited military action before eventually authorizing direct intervention. He gradually escalated the commitment of U.S. armed forces, hoping with each step to deter North Vietnam and bolster South Vietnam. As one of his first initiatives, he approved OPLAN 34A, authorizing U.S. support for South Vietnamese covert operations against North Vietnam. It was hoped that the plan, which was implemented in February 1964, would increase military pressure on North Vietnam and signify U.S. support for the Saigon regime.

In effect, OPLAN 34A served as the preamble for a new statement of policy, National Security Action Memorandum (NSAM) 288 of March 1964, calling for an enlarged U.S. effort. Washington's new objective was to seek an independent, non-Communist South Vietnam that was free to accept outside assistance to maintain its security. This objective, which advanced no U.S. claims on South Vietnam, came to justify whatever steps were needed to prevent a Communist victory. As part of NSAM 288, the JCS developed a program of air attacks against military and industrial targets in North Vietnam. Air force planners and such presidential advisers as Rostow assumed that because the Vietcong relied heavily on backing from North Vietnam, harming the north would induce Hanoi to curtail its support. The bombing plan was temporarily shelved because the administration regarded the government of General Nguyen Khanh, then ruling Saigon, as so weak and unstable that it might collapse before the bombing could have any effect. Punishing North Vietnam by bombing was at the least an indirect, if not enigmatic, way to implement the policy of developing an independent, sovereign nation in the south. The bombing could in no way render the Saigon government more effective. The bombing also failed to acknowledge the self-sufficiency of a Vietcong movement that could carry out an insurgency with indigenous resources.

Pacification, the objectives of which were tantamount to the NSAM 288 goal of an independent non-Communist state, received comparatively less emphasis under the new policy. The ill-fated *Hop Tac* plan, an effort to secure the area around Saigon, became part of the NSAM. Poorly supported by ARVN, *Hop Tac* was a major disappointment, failing to improve security or shift the balance of power in the countryside around the capital. Alongside the planning for a bombing campaign and the initiation of covert operations (intelligence overflights, commando raids, and the infiltration of guerrilla units into North Vietnam), the new pacification plan was a minor step.

Johnson's graduated pressure had little effect. North Vietnam showed no inclination to back down and responded defiantly to U.S. warnings. In August, North Vietnamese torpedo boats attacked U.S. Navy destroyers engaged in electronic eavesdropping in the Gulf of Tonkin off the coast of North Vietnam. The episode was sufficient reason for President Johnson to approve retaliatory air strikes. Aircraft from the U.S. Navy carriers *Ticonderoga* and *Constellation*, stationed in the South China Sea, bombed North Vietnamese torpedo boat bases and oil storage dumps, destroying twenty-five boats and damaging the oil storage facility at Vinh. The president also used the incident to secure passage on 7 August, with only two dissenting votes, of a congressional resolution authorizing him to take "all necessary measures" to repel any armed attacks and prevent further aggression. It was analogous to a formal declaration of war and allowed Johnson to consider additional military efforts in Vietnam without prior congressional approval.

The Tonkin Gulf Resolution also filled domestic political needs. It demonstrated that the nation was united. The show of force and appeal for national support permitted Johnson to disarm his Republican challenger, Senator Barry Goldwater, who had vigorously urged escalation of the war, but this apparent domestic benefit carried a hidden cost. In arguing for the resolution, the administration misled Congress and the public, portraying the attacks as deliberate and unprovoked aggression. The decision not to disclose the program of covert actions that the destroyers were carrying out later harmed the administration.

The retaliatory raids and the threat of further reprisals seemed to spur the Communists on rather than dissuade them. In November 1964 the Vietcong shelled the U.S. air base at Bienhoa, killing four men. Later in the year, regular North Vietnamese Army (NVA) units began to move south and were poised to enter the central highlands. In February 1965, enemy forces struck U.S. installations in the highlands, first attacking an advisory compound in Pleiku and then sabotaging quarters in Qui Nhon.

The administration again looked to bombing to show U.S. resolve, promptly mounting retaliatory raids on military targets in North Vietnam. Individual raids gave way to a sustained bombing campaign of increasingly intense strikes against military and industrial targets in North Vietnam that began on 13 February 1965. Code named Rolling Thunder, the campaign was designed to harm the enemy and boost South Vietnamese morale by demonstrating the commitment of the United States to the defense of its ally. A parallel air war, identified as Operation Barrel Roll, had begun on a limited scale in December against military targets in the Laotian panhandle. From the beginning, Rolling Thunder proved controversial. It was viewed by the White House as a campaign for political objectives, and the president and his top civilian advisers established controls on bombing targets and the frequency of attacks, much to the annoyance of the military. The president's top civilian advisers—McGeorge Bundy, Rostow, McNamara and his deputy John McNaughton, and William Bundy, an assistant secretary of state—subscribed to the theory of limited war, and Rolling Thunder was carried out under its tenets. The underlying notion was to limit the U.S. military response to avoid a wider war or the involvement of other Communist powers, but to use enough force, coupled with the threat of greater punishment, to induce Hanoi to seek terms. The administration viewed bombing as a means of communicating resolve. Only Undersecretary of State George Ball vigorously objected to the bombing, and by late March 1965 other advisers had lost faith in its sufficiency and doubted that Rolling Thunder alone would quickly achieve the goal of deterring North Vietnam from fighting. At this time, the White House began to contemplate the use of U.S. ground forces in Vietnam as the primary way to win.

Even as some in the administration came to question the bombing, Rolling Thunder galvanized elements of the U.S. populace. Antiwar and radical political groups, which had started to coalesce at the beginning of the bombing, made it the focal point of their outcry. An Easter march against the war drew about twenty thousand mostly young persons to Washington. Teach-ins, protest lectures on the war, started at the University of Michigan in May 1965 and by the end of the school year had been held in more than 120 schools. At this point, public opinion polls indicated that most Americans supported the president and looked on the demonstrations as radical troublemaking.

Throughout the spring the Vietcong continued to disrupt pacification, making gains in the central coastal provinces and resisting government efforts in the delta and provinces around Saigon. The Communists pressed for a major military victory over the ARVN, attacking border posts and highland camps and hoping to draw government units away from populated areas. Strengthened by several NVA regiments that infiltrated into South Vietnam, Vietcong forces were decisively winning the war in most of the country. ARVN losses in the summer were the equivalent of nearly a battalion a week. By inflicting a series of defeats on government forces already suffering serious losses from casualties and desertions, the Communists hoped to force the Saigon government into negotiating a political settlement and the withdrawal of U.S. forces.

President Johnson did not wish to become embroiled in an Asian land war that would divert funds from his ambitious social and economic reform program, the Great Society, and he wanted to avoid a confrontation with Hanoi's Communist allies, Russia and China. He nevertheless realized he had to do more than bomb North Vietnam to prevent the almost certain defeat of South Vietnam. His desire to avoid a wider war and his concern with saving Vietnam persuaded him to commit a small number of ground forces. On 8 March 1965 the Third Battalion, Ninth Marine Regiment, and the First Battalion, Third Marine Regiment, landed on the beaches north of Danang, where the Americans had a sprawling air base. The mission was to protect the facility, but the force was barely adequate to do so. More marines followed, and the president modified their mission to allow them to conduct offensive operations close to their bases. To protect U.S. installations near the capital, Johnson sent the first army combat unit to South Vietnam and, to support the growing military presence, authorized the army to begin deploying twenty-five thousand logistical troops, the main body of the First Logistical Command. By May, U.S. military strength in Vietnam passed fifty thousand. Presidential caution about the domestic and international consequences of widening the war led to the incremental deployment of ground troops rather than sending at one time the number of soldiers necessary to preserve South Vietnam.

The president indicated he would go only so far in pursuing the war. The combat units he sent were regulars, and he had turned down a recommendation by McNamara to mobilize National Guard or reserve units, expecting the gradual escalation of the air and ground war to induce Hanoi to negotiate. His decision, however, had a serious impact on how the army, the only service that had to rely on the draft to fill its ranks, would sustain the buildup and manage its role in the war. The Department of the Army and the Continental Army Command in their contingency planning had assumed that a partial call-up of the reserves would offset the deployment of forces to Vietnam. Johnson's decision rendered these plans useless. To meet the need for additional combat forces, preserve the training base, and develop a pool of replacements for Vietnam, the army had to increase its active strength over a three-year period, relying on draft calls, volunteers, and the reassignment of experienced soldiers from units in Europe and South Korea. Combat units were pulled out of the strategic reserve, essentially a contingency force, and sent to Vietnam to help meet MACV force requirements. Significantly, no reserve units were called up to fill their places. At bottom, the decision against a call-up of reserve forces implied a lack of political will to support the national objective in Vietnam. The president decided to wage war in Vietnam and fight poverty at home, but he limited the military commitment in hopes of being able to win without compromising his domestic agenda.

The decision not to call up the reserves also required the army to organize additional combat units. In the second half of 1965, it activated three light infantry brigades, reactivated the Ninth Division (the first army division activated, organized, equipped, and trained for de-

ployment to a combat theater in two decades), and alerted the Fourth and Twenty-fifth divisions for deployment. By the end of 1966, military strength in Vietnam reached 385,000 and the next year almost 490,000. Army personnel accounted for almost two-thirds of the total.

The arrival of North Vietnamese and U.S. combat forces in South Vietnam in the summer of 1965 transformed the nature of the war. It was no longer just a struggle to defeat Vietcong insurgents. A war between North Vietnamese conventional forces that had entered South Vietnam and U.S. ground forces, the main force war, was superimposed on the continuing political struggle for the countryside. The deployment of growing numbers of ground troops also represented the relative downgrading of pressure against North Vietnam in favor of more intensive activity in South Vietnam. Operation Rolling Thunder eventually assumed a secondary role, its main value as a bargaining chip to get Hanoi to begin talks. President Johnson periodically halted the bombing over the years to entice Ho's government into serious negotiations.

With the growth in military strength, the army tried to establish the U.S. Army, Vietnam (USARV) as the component command responsible for army operations, but General William Westmoreland, who had become MACV commander in June 1964, opposed this idea and prevailed. He remained unified commander of MACV as well as commander of USARV. USARV served exclusively in a logistical and administrative capacity but in the course of the buildup managed a massive support base. Westmoreland also established several army corps-level headquarters, called field forces, to oversee ground operations in various regions of Vietnam. Westmoreland perceived the conflict in the south as essentially a ground war, with air power playing a supporting role. Consequently, he resisted requests from the other services for high-level representation on the MACV staff. Throughout his tenure, indeed throughout the existence of MACV, the army dominated MACV headquarters in numbers of personnel and control of key slots.

Unity of command proved unachievable in other areas. Westmoreland had no command authority over South Vietnamese troops or of those of other countries—Korea, Australia, New Zealand, and Thailand—contributing combatants to defend Vietnam. He executed compacts with commanders of each national force (including the South Vietnamese) that ensured cooperation but fell short of giving him actual command over allied forces. The MACV commander did not have authority over the operations of other U.S. agencies, such as the Central Intelligence Agency (CIA), that in effect were running their own war in Vietnam.

Westmoreland viewed air power as a key weapon in supporting his effort to defeat enemy forces, but he exercised limited operational control of the air war. Much of the U.S. air and naval operations, including Rolling Thunder, fell outside his authority and were carried out by forces under the overall command of Admiral Ulysses Grant Sharp, CINCPAC, with the White House playing a role in target selection. Interservice rivalry stood in the way of establishing a single commander for the air war. The respective air and naval components of the Pacific Command, PACAF and PACFLT, directed the efforts of their respective services at Rolling Thunder. Navy and air force units divided North Vietnam into separate zones for aerial attacks, and navy and air force units vied for the highest sortie rate. Under PACAF, the Seventh Air Force located in Vietnam and an echelon of the Thirteenth Air Force operating from Thailand shared control. The Seventh Air Force served two masters, providing planes for Rolling Thunder under CINCPAC and supporting allied ground operations under General Westmoreland. Under the overall control of PACFLT, the commander of the Seventh Fleet mounted the naval portion of Rolling Thunder, tactical reconnaissance operations in North Vietnam and Laos, and ground support in South Vietnam. The large Marine Air Wing flew its missions under the operational control of III Marine Amphibious Force (III MAF), a corps-type headquarters at Danang. To further complicate the situation, the B-52 force, upon which

MACV relied to break up enemy troop concentrations and strike base areas in South Vietnam, remained under the operational control of the Strategic Air Command, although MACV designated the targets.

Prosecuting the war suffered from divided command in another area—where military and pacification operations intersected. After the military intervention, the conduct of military operations and U.S. support of pacification were handled separately, with MACV tending to military issues and the civilian agencies tending to support pacification. In a war fought for the political goal of establishing a viable nation in South Vietnam, the failure to unify the political and military aspects of the struggle, as the Communists had, was a serious flaw. The patchwork of command arrangements, the division of the war into civil and military spheres, contributed to the absence of a unified strategy and the pursuit of parochial service interests. Westmoreland, the senior military officer in South Vietnam, lacked authority to devise an overall strategy or coordinate all military aspects of the war.

In addition, Westmoreland faced severe constraints in using the forces under his command. In the spring of 1965, although Johnson issued no directives to General Westmoreland on how U.S. troops should operate to sustain the independence of South Vietnam, he did limit options by prohibiting ground operations against Communist sanctuaries in Laos and Cambodia. He banned U.S. conventional ground operations inside North Vietnam, despite that country's role as a de facto belligerent. Restrictions on ground and air operations and the prospect of receiving more U.S. troops were the framework within which Westmoreland planned his ground strategy.

Westmoreland believed that the Communists had decided to start the climactic third stage of guerrilla warfare (mobile warfare by battalions, regiments, and divisions). As evidence he pointed to the North Vietnamese Army units coming into South Vietnam and the Vietcong strengthening of forces from village guerrillas to main force regiments. Because he could not pursue enemy units into their cross-border sanctu-aries, Westmoreland hoped to find and destroy enemy formations inside South Vietnam before they could endanger population centers. Accordingly, he decided to station U.S. Army forces in base camps and firebases away from population centers and near probable infiltration routes so they could more readily engage enemy forces in remote areas. The mobility and firepower of the army made such a deployment feasible. Hueys, which arrived with the newly activated First Cavalry Division in the fall of 1965, provided air transport for combat troops and allowed U.S. commanders to concentrate quickly soldiers in scattered bases against an enemy unit.

Westmoreland devised a three-phase concept of operations in which pacification had a distinctly subordinate role. His plan called first for averting the defeat of South Vietnam by using forty-four U.S. battalions (army and Marine Corps units), his initial increment of soldiers, primarily to clear logistical base areas and protect military installations for the arrival of subsequent units. Because he felt that the threat posed by North Vietnamese and Vietcong main force units was severe, he did not include support of ongoing pacification efforts in the first phase. His primary concern was to contain the enemy's spring-summer offensive of 1965 with the relatively small number of U.S. troops on hand. The offensive in the central highlands, led by at least three NVA regiments, overran border camps, besieged district towns, and, Westmoreland feared, threatened to cut the nation in two. In the second phase, beginning in 1966, Westmoreland expected, with the twenty-four additional battalions that would then be at his disposal, to go on the offensive and "resume and expand pacification operations" in priority areas—the capital region, certain delta provinces, most of I Corps, and Binh Dinh and Phu Yen provinces in II Corps. In the final phase, he envisioned victory at some unspecified time after 1968. By that point, the incremental attrition of enemy strength would make the war so costly the enemy would seek a negotiated settlement, an underlying rationale identical with that of the air campaign.

Not everyone agreed with Westmoreland's approach. Another school of thought believed that U.S. ground forces should focus on population security and pacification, concentrating their efforts in coastal enclaves around key urban centers and bases. U.S. forces would provide security so that the Vietnamese could expand pacified areas. This concept, reflecting the pattern of initial deployments, proved short-lived as more U.S. and regular North Vietnamese forces entered South Vietnam. At the end of July 1965, President Johnson announced plans to increase U.S. military strength in South Vietnam to 175,000 by the end of the year. By late summer, enemy combat strength reached an estimated 221,000, including fifty-five NVA battalions and 105 Vietcong battalions. Given the superior firepower and mobility of U.S. ground forces, Westmoreland rejected what he regarded as the defensive strategy of using U.S. soldiers to protect populated enclaves, a strategy suggested by Army Chief of Staff General Harold K. Johnson and embraced by Taylor, whom the president had named U.S. ambassador to Vietnam. Westmoreland regarded the enclave theory as "an inglorious, static use of U.S. forces in overpopulated areas" that would leave them positioned in vulnerable beachheads and allow the enemy to hold the initiative on the battlefield.

As part of his concept of operations, Westmoreland agreed with the South Vietnamese command that U.S. forces would concentrate on fighting the main force war against the NVA, while ARVN, which was disintegrating as a fighting force, would fix their efforts on the Vietcong. He focused on pursuing the enemy away from population centers, even though throughout the spring and summer guerrilla units seriously threatened the inhabited areas of the countryside. In large parts of the country, government control was restricted largely to areas surrounding district and province capitals and the major roads and waterways during daylight.

Not all U.S. forces subscribed to Westmoreland's emphasis on search-and-destroy and attrition. Stationed in I Corps, U.S. Marine Corps units under Lieutenant General Lewis Walt, III

MAF commander, concentrated on providing security for the densely populated hamlets in their area of operations, which, Westmoreland complained, left the enemy free to recruit in areas the marines had not yet entered and to operate in nearby hills with impunity. Walt saw little advantage in having marines seek out enemy forces in remote areas when the real target of the war was political—control of the population. Marine Corps operations represented a clear alternative to Westmoreland's strategy and were frequently praised by critics of the so-called big-unit war.

GROUND OPERATIONS UNDER WESTMORELAND

South Vietnam's high command divided the nation into four corps (I, II, III, and IV) largely for purposes of organizing and controlling military operations. Westmoreland followed Vietnamese precedent and deployed his forces within existing corps boundaries, appointing an army or Marine Corps general as the senior U.S. military official in each. The corps consisted of several provinces, and owing to varying terrain, proximity to North Vietnam, population density, and the enemy strength and force structure, the nature of the ground war was different in each corps.

In III Corps, Westmoreland concentrated on the defense of Saigon, deploying his forces where they could protect the approaches and infiltration routes to the city. The first army unit in Vietnam, the 173d Airborne Brigade, deployed from Okinawa. It was initially assigned to protect the air base at Bien-hoa, northeast of the capital, and in June 1965 began operations in War Zone D. The First Infantry Division secured base camps north of Saigon and helped South Vietnamese forces clear the Chu Chi area of Hau Nghia province, which was west of the capital. After the spring of 1966, the Twenty-fifth Infantry and the Fourth Infantry divisions assisted in the defense of Saigon, completing an arc of U.S. deployments around the capital.

During the buildup of U.S. ground forces, most operations were devoted to base and area security and to clearing and rebuilding roads. In road-clearing operations, the army improvised a new technique, Rome plows (bulldozers with a modified sharpened front), to remove vegetation alongside roads that might provide cover for ambushes. Over time the army also used chemical defoliants to kill trees and plants along canals and to destroy crops and the natural cover in enemy-held areas. In Operation Ranch Hand the air force conducted aerial spraying of herbicides on South Vietnam jungles and mangrove forests between 1961 and 1971.

By the summer of 1966, Westmoreland believed his forces were strong and large enough to begin the second phase of his strategy, offensive operations to search out and destroy enemy main force units. Operation Attleboro represented this transition. It began in September, when the 196th Infantry Brigade and a brigade from the Fourth Division moved into Tay Ninh province against War Zone C, and grew into a multidivision battle. Despite the large U.S. force involved, most combat occurred at night at the platoon and company level. As the U.S. contingent swelled, the opposing Ninth Vietcong Division avoided contact and withdrew across the Cambodian border to fight again. The reaction of the Vietcong under fire was not unusual. The enemy preferred to mount small-scale attacks on isolated outposts containing few troops or poorly defended settlements, having little interest in allowing the Americans with their superior firepower to decimate them in a set piece battle. The enemy approach to combat was the perfect antidote to Westmoreland's strategy of attrition.

The U.S. Army launched another major operation, Cedar Falls, in January 1967. This time the target was the Iron Triangle, the base area near the capital. Westmoreland hoped to uproot enemy forces and dismantle the Vietcong infrastructure, which, in effect, governed many villages and hamlets. Operation Cedar Falls was a multidivision assault. Although sparsely populated, the Iron Triangle was strategically situated between the cross-border sanctuaries in Cambodia on one side and the population and rice crops of the capital region and delta on the other.

Expecting organized defense to come from the vicinity of Ben Suc, a settlement of about three thousand people thirty miles northwest of the capital on the Saigon River, Major General William E. DePuy, commander of the First Infantry Division, wanted to seize and evacuate the village before the Iron Triangle itself was encircled. That would allow him to use the division's firepower while minimizing the risk of inflicting civilian casualties. Relocating and assisting the villagers was the responsibility of South Vietnamese provincial officials and the Office of Civil Operations (OCO), a U.S. organization under Deputy Ambassador William Porter.

Fearing that Communist agents in the government and armed forces might compromise Operation Cedar Falls, the Americans closely held their plans. They informed South Vietnamese paramilitary forces, the ARVN Fifth Division commander, the U.S. civilian province representative, and the Binh Duong province chief after the operation was under way. The province chief had no time to plan for relocating refugees, even though it was his responsibility. John Paul Vann, director of OCO in III Corps and the only official of his agency to participate in the early planning, was expressly forbidden to coordinate with South Vietnamese authorities or to stockpile supplies at the site of the refugee center in the town of Phu Cuong in advance of the operation. Not surprisingly, the evacuation of Ben Suc was delayed. It took the province chief two days to obtain enough boats to move some twenty-eight hundred people, their personal belongings, and livestock. Then, the village was razed.

Attentive primarily to the enemy threat, military planners overlooked the political problems associated with the involuntary relocation of South Vietnamese civilians from their homes. Many of the new refugees complained about being removed from their land and put into poorly prepared camps that offered them little chance of earning a living. The necessity from the military perspective of having to relocate civilians, many of whom were already unsympathetic or even hostile to the government, gained no support for Saigon. Concerns over security exacerbated relations between civilian AID officials and the First Division. General DePuy wanted to run the refugee relocation and assistance effort, because he was convinced that Vann's agency and the South Vietnamese would be unable to handle the operation. Strained relations between the U.S. military and the Saigon government were an inauspicious outcome of Operation Cedar Falls. South Vietnamese authorities apparently had no voice in the decision to destroy and evacuate several villages—actions that clearly denigrated government sovereignty. The U.S. press publicized the relocation as a brutish action.

Besides the cost in adverse publicity, friction between U.S. civil and military agencies, and strained relations with the South Vietnamese government and people, Cedar Falls failed to achieve lasting military or political control of the Iron Triangle. According to Brigadier General (later general and chief of staff of the army) Bernard W. Rogers, assistant commander of the First Division, neither the South Vietnamese nor the Americans had sufficient forces to continue to operate in the Iron Triangle or prevent the enemy from returning.

The operation was significant for another reason—it clearly illustrated Westmoreland's operational priorities. Although he frequently preached about the importance of army operations in support of pacification, he devoted his energies to operations like Cedar Falls and not to clearing and holding the small hamlets and villages around Saigon. Despite the steady growth of U.S. personnel in 1965 and 1966, Westmoreland still lacked sufficient forces to conduct search-and-destroy missions and to provide security for Vietnamese settlements.

Operation Fairfax, a joint operation to improve security around Saigon, began about the time of Cedar Falls. U.S. units paired off with South Vietnamese Rangers in a year-long operation that ended in December 1967. Even though the operation lasted more than twelve months and combined military and police forces against the Vietcong, it failed to eliminate the infrastructure in the districts adjacent to the capital.

This lack of success was evidence to U.S. and Vietnamese pacification officials of the need to devise a special program that joined Vietnamese police forces and intelligence agencies in an integrated effort to attack the Communist underground government.

In a war fought for political control, IV Corps, located south of Saigon, was critical. This heavily populated area contained the most fertile rice lands of the Mekong River delta. There the conflict was largely between the Vietcong and South Vietnamese regular and paramilitary forces. Besides army and navy advisory teams, only one major U.S. Army unit, the Second Brigade of the Ninth Division, was assigned to the delta, but it carried out an innovative campaign with the U.S. Navy reminiscent of river operations by Union forces in the western theater of the Civil War. Riverine operations sought to dislodge Vietcong forces, protect food-producing areas, and stem the movement of enemy supplies. The Vietcong used the thousands of miles of interconnecting inland waterways as their chief routes for transporting men and equipment. To patrol and fight in the marshlands and rice paddies, the Second Brigade was quartered on navy barracks ships, which transported infantry and artillery units to battle and provided fire support from monitors, heavily armed and armored river craft.

The Second Brigade began operations in May 1967. The riverine force proved its value by being able to move rapidly through difficult terrain to relieve beleaguered villages and pursue enemy forces. The force effectively integrated the capabilities of army and navy units and carried out wide-ranging operations into previously inaccessible or remote Vietcong territory. Mounting artillery on barges substantially increased effectiveness. Such mobility and fire support improved the security of the waterways for South Vietnamese citizens.

Riverine operations in the delta's waterways complemented the navy's task forces of Operations Game Warden and Market Time. Market Time had the mission of patrolling coastal areas to prevent the resupply of Vietcong forces by sea. Game Warden sought to interdict enemy lines of communication and assist government forces in repelling attacks on river outposts of the Regional and Popular Forces (RF/PF), Vietnamese paramilitary units that were responsible for providing local security.

II Corps, geographically the largest corps in Vietnam, posed a unique challenge for Westmoreland. The MACV commander had to stem the 1965 Communist offensive in the sparsely settled central highlands, which he feared was intended to cut South Vietnam in two, and also to protect the heavily populated coastal areas where the ports and logistical bases that supported the U.S. buildup were located. To deal with both contingencies, the First Cavalry Division, with more than four hundred helicopters, established its main base at An Khe, halfway between Qui Nhon and the highland city of Pleiku, allowing it to keep the main east-west road open and operate in the highlands or the coastal plain. In addition to the First Cavalry, South Korean forces and other U.S. units were deployed to II Corps in 1965 and 1966. Some of these units, along with the South Vietnamese forces, provided area security for the ports and supply facilities at Cam Ranh Bay, Nha Trang, and Qui Nhon.

In the fall of 1965, three battalions of the First Cavalry ran into elements of two NVA regiments in a series of engagements in the Ia Drang Valley, a mountainous region in the western part of Pleiku province. At Landing Zone X-Ray, a surrounded U.S. unit had to call on all available firepower—helicopter gunships, artillery bombardment, bombing and strafing by tactical aircraft, and heavy ordnance dropped by B-52 bombers flying from Guam— to hold off repeated NVA assaults. This fight cost six hundred enemy and seventy-nine American deaths.

Acclaimed as a major victory, Ia Drang was a costly and questionable success. The enemy did not leave the valley. At Landing Zone X-Ray and Landing Zone Albany, the enemy assaulted vulnerable U.S. units, which were saved by massive air and artillery support. This support required incredible logistical efforts to bring in fuel, spare parts, air support crews, pilots, and aircraft. The division's logistical resources proved insufficient. Prolonged operations consumed more fuel and ammunition than helicopters could supply, and air force tactical aircraft were pressed into resupply missions; divisional helicopters suffered from heavy use, heat, and humidity. Following the Ia Drang fighting, frequent North Vietnamese attacks on remote Special Forces camps signaled the enemy's intention to continue to infiltrate forces and fight in the highlands. Westmoreland felt compelled to deploy forces near the border in an effort to keep enemy main forces as far as possible from heavily populated areas.

It was part of Hanoi's strategy to keep U.S. forces off balance by posing simultaneous threats in the highlands and the coastal plain. The threat in the highlands siphoned friendly forces from supporting pacification programs in the more populous regions. Whenever guerrilla or local forces were endangered, Hanoi tried to draw U.S. units from the capital region in III Corps and the II Corps coastal plain to the less populous zones along the border. Ground operations took on an all too familiar pattern. Airmobile assaults, often in the wake of Arc Light air strikes of B-52 bombers flown from bases on Guam to bomb Vietcong bases, resulted in episodic contact with the Vietcong and withdrawal after a few days of extensive patrolling of enemy territory. Enemy forces generally chose when to stand and fight.

In I Corps, U.S. Marine forces operated under a different philosophy than army troops in II and III Corps. In their initial operations, the marines sought to provide security for the area around the air bases at Phu Bai, Chu Lai, and Da Nang. They gradually expanded the tactical area of operations within which they attempted to weed out the Vietcong. In the fall of 1965, the marines sought to protect the rice harvest in the agricultural areas south of Da Nang. The goal of Operation Golden Fleece was to keep the crop out of Vietcong hands and allow farmers to sell their rice on the local market. The operation targeted anyone trying to interfere with the harvest and protected farmers from Vietcong levies but did not provide continuous security.

The marines set up the Combined Action Platoon (CAP) program to do just that. A noteworthy innovation begun in August 1965, a CAP consisted of a marine rifle squad, a navy medical corpsman, and a Popular Forces (PF) platoon. The CAP would settle in a village, typically consisting of five hamlets spread out over four square kilometers and containing thirty-five hundred people, and help to protect the settlement from Vietcong raids. Although the number of CAPs grew, there were never enough to cover all the villages in I Corps, and, partly owing to Westmoreland's opposition, CAPs were not tried in other parts of Vietnam. Unfortunately, the program often induced a sense of dependency in the PF platoon, resulting in only transitory improvements. After a marine squad left a village, security usually deteriorated. In many cases, PF platoons had come to depend on outside assistance and frequently proved unable to cope with the local Vietcong on their own.

As the marines recognized, sustained local security was the critical component of pacification, providing a shield for the government cadre that carried out programs to improve conditions in poor villages that lacked schools, adequate sanitation, and water supply. If the government could not protect its people, it had little chance over the long term of holding their political support. Without effective security provided by paramilitary or regular forces, the Vietcong could assassinate or kidnap local officials, levy taxes, spread propaganda, and obtain recruits. In the absence of security, reforms and social welfare programs would prove ephemeral.

Westmoreland was critical of marine operations because of their relatively static deployment and primary focus on pacification. Rather than have them protect villages and rice harvests, he wanted the marines to deploy as mobile units actively seeking out Vietcong formations over a broad area. The marines objected to Westmoreland's determination to fight guerrillas by staging decisive battles, reflecting from the outset the strong disagreement within the military over his attrition strategy.

HELP FOR THE "OTHER WAR"

Despite the promise of innovations such as the CAP program and the humanitarian and medical projects of military civil affairs teams, the pacification program was in trouble. The Vietcong continued to consolidate their rule in the absence of an effective national pacification program. Although the Johnson administration called pacification the "other war," it regarded the political struggle as more than an adjunct to the fighting. Westmoreland's concept of operations and the tendency of U.S. forces to fight the war for the Vietnamese worried policymakers, who feared that pacification was being pushed deeper into the shadows as more U.S. soldiers arrived in South Vietnam. The White House was convinced that military actions alone could not accomplish the stated goal, expressed in NSAM 288, of developing an autonomous South Vietnam that could defend itself.

The imbalance between the "other war" and an expanding military conflict was troubling. Even at the start of the buildup in 1965, money for military assistance (hardware, gear and clothing, and ammunition for the Vietnamese), a total of $318 million, already outstripped economic aid of $290 million, and the amount spent for military assistance excluded the cost of U.S. military operations. As policymakers pondered how to improve pacification, they came over time to consider directly involving MACV, because it had the largest logistical structure and the most personnel in Vietnam. In practical terms this meant formally recognizing that offensive operations by U.S. units to destroy the Vietcong were "but a part of the total pacification program," as one army officer described it.

The eclipse of pacification by the burgeoning ground war was only one aspect of pacification's troubles. U.S. support of the program was poorly organized. Although the ambassador was in charge of the country team and thus the nominal manager of U.S. support, the representatives of the separate agencies largely went their own way, taking direction from their respective headquarters in Washington. The ab-

sence of strong centralized management led to duplication of effort in the field and poor coordination among responsible U.S. agencies. It proved close to impossible to forge a pacification plan with common goals.

The efforts of civilian and military advisers in the provinces also were not coordinated. There was no clear delineation of military and nonmilitary responsibilities, and procedures to reconcile overlapping programs or conflicting priorities were inadequate. Advisers were not empowered to take charge. Without a single advisory coordinator at the province level, it was hard to develop a concerted policy on ways to influence South Vietnamese officials. Under their guidance, South Vietnamese cadre teams, police, and territorial forces carried out the economic and security programs that comprised pacification. Difficulty in coordinating civil and military programs extended to the district level. In the provinces and districts, two separate U.S. hierarchies—civilian and military—supported different aspects of pacification and advised the Vietnamese. With the relative neglect by the U.S. Army, poorly organized support, ineffective South Vietnamese management of its various programs, and a strong adversary in the Vietcong, pacification had little chance against a well-organized and entrenched Communist movement that controlled significant parts of the countryside.

A number of developments made reform of pacification possible. Growing numbers of U.S. Army forces, which exceeded 180,000 by the end of 1965, made unlikely the military defeat of South Vietnam. With that threat removed, the administration could seek to remedy pacification. The Saigon government itself, long vitiated by factional fighting, attained a measure of stability under the military rule of Premier Nguyen Cao Ky and Chief of State Nguyen Van Thieu, who came to power in June 1965. Thus, there was hope of establishing a program to bring security to the countryside on a secure political foundation.

The program's stagnation concerned President Johnson, who became directly involved in making reforms. At the Honolulu Conference with South Vietnamese leaders in February 1966, he sought to redress the imbalance of U.S. strategy, which he felt was skewed to military solutions, and the managerial weaknesses of U.S. nonmilitary programs. The conference resulted in two noteworthy appointments that the president hoped would lead to more effective use of U.S. resources for pacification. Johnson named Robert W. Komer, a member of the White House staff, as special assistant to the president for Vietnam, with a mandate to provide a Washington focal point for the other war. He was authorized to work directly with the secretaries of state, defense, and agriculture and the heads of AID and the CIA. He also had authority to direct, coordinate, and supervise the nonmilitary programs making up the other war and had direct access to the president, a privilege which enormously strengthened Komer's hand. On paper at least, the appointment of Komer remedied the absence of a single manager. The second appointment occurred in Saigon. The president placed Ambassador William Porter, deputy to Ambassador Henry Cabot Lodge, in charge of U.S. nonmilitary programs and assigned him the task of weaving together the civil and military strands of the pacification effort.

The two appointments foretold other organizational changes. In the fall of 1966, Ambassador Lodge tried an experimental "single manager" approach to pacification in Long An, a III Corps province directly south of Saigon. He appointed the province representative, U.S. Army Colonel Samuel Wilson, as leader of the entire provincial advisory team. The ambassador expected all civilian and military advisers to respond to Wilson's directions and the U.S. Army battalion commanders to consult with him on combat operations. Significantly, Wilson could call upon the assistance of U.S. Army battalions in the province to provide security and logistical support.

The single-manager experiment helped persuade President Johnson of the desirability of military involvement in pacification, an option vigorously advocated by Komer. In 1967 the president acted, putting Westmoreland in charge of all aspects of pacification. Johnson then appointed a single manager to serve as Westmoreland's deputy for U.S. support of pacification throughout South Vietnam. His decision made Westmoreland responsible for ensuring that pacification received adequate logistical and engineering support and that newly drafted plans eliminated overlapping and redundant military and civil efforts.

Johnson's decision may be regarded as part of an administration effort to modify the ground strategy. In the spring of 1967, Westmoreland had requested 200,000 more troops to undertake ground operations in Laos to cut infiltration from the Ho Chi Minh trail. Civilian advisers in the White House and Pentagon, who had lost faith in Westmoreland's attrition strategy, opposed the request, arguing that the enemy could bring in more forces and offset any U.S. reinforcements. Fearing that additional soldiers in Vietnam might result in Americans taking over even more aspects of the war and higher casualties, the president chose to enhance support of pacification and improve the South Vietnamese armed forces.

A new agency, Civil Operations and Revolutionary (later Rural) Development Support (CORDS), was created within MACV to carry out the president's decision. Headed by Komer, who was given the rank of ambassador, CORDS was composed of both civilian and military (primarily army) personnel. Its key feature was the appointment of a single manager (either a military officer or a civilian official) for pacification support at each echelon—Saigon, corps, province, or district. The organization combined army officers and civilians from the State Department, AID, the U.S. Information Agency, the Department of Agriculture, and the intelligence agencies in such a way that civilians commanded army officers and officers civilians. Komer more than doubled the number of advisers who were assigned to CORDS from twenty-three hundred in 1967 to more than fifty-two hundred in 1968. About 95 percent of the military advisers assigned to CORDS came from the army. In addition, Komer had army civil affairs companies in Vietnam put under the operational control of CORDS. The new organization took on responsibility for many of the pacification programs formerly run by Ambassador Porter, such as Revolutionary Development Cadre (a CIA-run training program to develop a Vietnamese cadre to counteract Vietcong influence in the villages), refugees, police, and the *chieu hoi* ("open arms") program to encourage defections from the Vietcong. CORDS simplified command and control of U.S. support of pacification, even if divided control persisted in other areas, such as the air war, and the main force war and pacification remained as separate and sometimes conflicting efforts.

During the early 1960s, Washington policymakers had debated whether programs to win political allegiance or programs to protect people deserved precedence. CORDS settled that argument on pragmatic grounds, concluding that security was a prerequisite for development programs, although it worked to open roads and waterways in areas considered secure. It undertook two new major initiatives in 1967 to improve security. The first was the Phoenix program, which was designed to eliminate the Vietcong infrastructure by capturing key members. The program was supposed to collate current information on Vietcong leaders and cadre from U.S. and Vietnamese intelligence agencies so the Vietnamese authorities could arrest, interrogate, and try suspects and jail those convicted. Phoenix attempted to redress a fundamental weakness of earlier pacification efforts—the absence of a systematic effort designed specifically to dismantle the underground leadership that controlled guerrilla operations and provided political leadership in Communist-controlled areas. Despite pressure from the Americans, Thieu did not immediately put this program into operation.

In addition to devising a new program for attacking the infrastructure, Komer also worked to upgrade the combat effectiveness of the RF/PF. RF companies were lightly armed infantry forces that operated within a district or province; PF platoons were assigned to a specific village for local security. Komer won approval for a significant increase in the size of the RF/PF

(they grew from 300,000 to more than 500,000 between 1967 and 1970), developed better training programs, and was successful in replacing the hand-me-down weapons of the territorials with new M-16s and other modern light weapons so the guerrillas would not outgun them in firefights.

By establishing a single-manager system for pacification, CORDS essentially solved the interrelated problems of poor interagency coordination and overlapping programs. By making more U.S. military assets available for the other war, logistical and security support had greatly improved. It would take longer, however, to achieve a comprehensive pacification strategy that integrated military operations with pacification campaigns and that counteracted all aspects of the Vietcong threat from guerrilla raids on villages to political subversion.

BEFORE THE STORM

During 1967, U.S. leaders in Saigon felt that the tide of battle was against the Communists. Allied military power had reached formidable levels, with 278 maneuver battalions, twenty-eight tactical fighter squadrons, three thousand helicopters, and twelve hundred monthly B-52 sorties available for combat. U.S. military strength reached 486,000 men during the year. Ground forces were well-armed, well-supplied, and well-trained. South Vietnamese armed forces also had increased in size during 1967. By the end of the year the total strength of the South Vietnamese military reached 643,000—an increase of 129,000 (about 25 percent) since the end of 1964.

The allies could point to evidence that the ground campaign had weakened the enemy. Thanks to their firepower and mobility, allied forces had mounted large operations inside formerly inviolate bases within South Vietnam and kept steady pressure on enemy units. These forays into base areas, which housed supplies, hospitals, headquarters, training centers, and rest areas, took the initiative from the Vietcong and made it more difficult for main forces to support guerrilla operations near populated areas. Operations like Cedar Falls convinced the Communist leadership that they could no longer use main force units near populated areas, forcing enemy units into increased reliance on the border sanctuaries. Even though body count statistics were notoriously inflated and need to be regarded skeptically, the enemy suffered a heavy cumulative casualty toll. Estimated enemy combat deaths went from seventeen thousand in 1964 to eighty-eight thousand in 1967. The Vietcong also had to contend with understrength units and recruiting difficulties in the delta. They suffered losses not merely from battlefield casualties but also from desertion, disease, and defections—more than twenty-seven thousand soldiers and political cadre in 1967—to the government. As the percentage of North Vietnamese fillers in Vietcong units grew, Westmoreland estimated that by the end of 1967 half the enemy combat battalions in the south came from the North Vietnamese army. Vietcong tax revenues were also lower, because allied military operations had opened more roads to commerce, making it more difficult to tax goods in transit. Most important, captured enemy documents indicated a decline since 1965 in Vietcong-controlled population. An enemy cadre's notebook seized in January 1967 during Operation Cedar Falls estimated that the number of people living in areas under Vietcong authority had fallen by more than one million between mid-1965 and mid-1966. A loss of anything near that magnitude represented a significant reduction of the Communist manpower base.

In addition, prospects for pacification looked promising. Westmoreland had incorporated the notion of increased military support of pacification by U.S. forces into the 1967 Combined Campaign Plan. CORDS possessed more funds, personnel, and equipment and by sheer mass of resources seemed to be better equipped than its predecessor to wear down the insurgents. The South Vietnamese presidential and legislative elections of 1967 carried out under a new constitution promised an end, Washington hoped, to political instability and constituted the first step

toward a broad-based popular government. Thieu, an ARVN general, was elected president but did not receive a clear majority in a race against several rival candidates.

Restoration of elected government and continued allied military victories on the battlefield failed to assuage the American public's impatience with the war. In September 1967, an opinion poll showed for the first time that more Americans opposed than supported the war. Opposition was linked to U.S. casualties, which mounted the longer the war lasted. The number of Americans killed, wounded, or missing grew to eighty thousand in 1967. Draft calls began to rise, causing many young men to regard the war not as an abstraction but as an event affecting them personally. The president's request for a surtax to help pay for the war also proved unpopular. The ranks of those against the war began to include professionals and businessmen. To the argument voiced on college campuses that the war was immoral was added the damning verdict that the U.S. military effort was leading not to victory but to an inconclusive struggle at a higher level of cost in dollars and lives. Some questioned the worthiness of the cause, finding no compelling national interest at stake that justified defending a military regime halfway around the world against what many at the time concluded to be an independent nationalist movement, the Vietcong.

The president had little success in rallying opinion. A Gallup poll of June 1967 concluded that half of the Americans interviewed had no idea why the United States was fighting in Vietnam. Some mainstream newspapers began to express doubts about the war, feeling that misleading government claims about progress had created a credibility gap and that the president could no longer count on unquestioning support from Congress.

Dismayed that press and television accounts gave little sense of U.S. and Vietnamese progress in the war, President Johnson launched a public relations campaign to counteract what Rostow called the "stalemate doctrine." His reasons were largely political. During the coming year, Johnson was expected to seek reelection, and the campaign for the highest office could become a referendum on Vietnam. An antiwar wing took root in the Democratic party, and Senator Eugene McCarthy of Minnesota, a Democrat, decided in November to challenge the president for his party's nomination. As part of an effort to disprove the notion that the country was bogged down in a futile war, the president had Westmoreland and Ellsworth Bunker, ambassador to Saigon, return to Washington in November. They spoke before Congress and tried to reassure the public and the legislature that the allies were winning the war. These public reassurances would have unforeseen consequences in the months to come.

THE TET OFFENSIVE

In the latter part of 1967, the Johnson administration publicly expressed confidence about its prosecution of the war. At the same time, the Communists reappraised their strategy, aware that the sheer weight of U.S. arms was grinding down their military forces and weakening their ability to control the population. General Vo Nguyen Giap, head of North Vietnam's military forces, feared U.S. forces might invade North Vietnam, Laos, or Cambodia. The loss of these sanctuaries would be catastrophic to the Communist cause. The bombing was also a cause for alarm. The sortie rate over North Vietnam had risen from 2,401 in June 1965 to an average of eight thousand to nine thousand per month in late 1966 and early 1967, causing mounting destruction of roads, bridges, petroleum, oil, lubricant (POL) facilities, and heavy industry and unintended and incidental damage to homes, schools, office buildings, and other structures near military targets. In February 1967, the U.S. Navy began to mine internal waterways and coastal estuaries in North Vietnam below the twentieth parallel. Hanoi worried that the National Liberation Front (NLF), under increasing military pressure, might attempt to settle with the Saigon government.

If the leadership in Hanoi acknowledged its military vulnerabilities, it also knew the political weaknesses of its foe and hoped to exploit them. The Buddhist antigovernment protests of 1966, the so-called Struggle Movement, which Ky ended by dispatching one thousand Vietnamese marines to Da Nang, had revealed deep divisions in South Vietnam, and internecine intrigues continued among political factions in Saigon. Popular resentment of corruption and the lack of a strong popular base for the central government also helped persuade the Communists that enough people in South Vietnam were disaffected and could be induced to overthrow the Thieu government. Hanoi also believed that the South Vietnamese army was a political and military liability to the Saigon government. It was poorly led and equipped and split into factions. Morale was low and units lacked a strong commitment to the regime. Assessing its position, Hanoi decided to embark upon a new strategy to end the war. It would mount a general offensive throughout South Vietnam during the Tet holiday season coupled with a popular political uprising against the "puppet" government. By focusing attacks on South Vietnamese units and facilities, Hanoi sought to undermine the will and morale of the Saigon forces, subvert confidence in the ability of the government to provide security, further weaken support for the war in the United States, and force a political accommodation. Ho's government also took comfort in the antiwar movement within the United States, correlating the loss of political support with the traffic in coffins.

In December intelligence officers detected massive enemy troop movements throughout the country and along infiltration routes. Vietcong main forces moved toward Saigon, Da Nang, Hue (the former imperial capital of Vietnam), and a number of provincial capitals; the evidence pointed to an impending offensive. In mid-January 1968, two NVA divisions massed for an attack on the marine base at Khe Sanh, located in the northwest corner of South Vietnam, not far from Laos. The garrison at Khe Sanh could serve as a base for a potential corps-size operation into Laos to cut the Ho Chi Minh trail. Enemy attacks on Khe Sanh, beginning at the end of 1967, riveted the attention of Westmoreland, the president, and much of the press. Many commentators regarded Khe Sanh as Giap's play for a repetition of Dien Bien Phu. President Johnson insisted that the outpost be held, and the media carried daily reports of the action. To defend the outpost, B-52s carried out some of the heaviest air raids of the war, eventually dropping more than 100,000 tons of explosives on a five-square-mile battlefield.

The siege of Khe Sanh may have been part of a long-standing attempt to lure U.S. forces to the border regions. In the spring of 1967, heightened activity (artillery barrages and infiltrating NVA units) along the northern border drew marine units from southern I Corps to the demilitarized zone (DMZ). Army units from II and III Corps, making up Task Force Oregon, replaced the marines. (The task force was later reorganized as the Twenty-third Infantry Division, also known as American, the only army division to be formed in South Vietnam.) In September, the North Vietnamese regulars attacked the marine base at Con Thien just south of the DMZ. Supported by air power, naval gunfire, and artillery, the marines beat back the assault. In II Corps, North Vietnamese attacked the CIDG camp at Dak To in November 1967. Westmoreland sent the Fourth Infantry Division and the 173d Airborne Brigade into the central highlands to reinforce the garrison.

The battle for Dak To, the longest and most violent in the highlands since the struggle for Ia Drang in 1965, was only won by grueling infantry assaults supported by artillery fire and B-52 air strikes. Elsewhere, U.S. forces confronted the enemy along the border. North Vietnamese forces moved against Loc Ninh and Song Be, district capitals in III Corps. Westmoreland sent reinforcements to drive back the enemy units, leaving U.S. forces dispersed. By the end of 1967, the First Infantry Division was concentrated near the Cambodian border and the Twenty-fifth Division had returned to War Zone C. The border battles opened the way for the Tet offensive by inducing Westmoreland into withdrawing forces from populated areas.

While the enemy increased pressure against Khe Sanh, a force of eighty-five thousand men, mostly Vietcong units, reinforced with recruits and part-time guerrillas, prepared for the offensive. Arms, munitions, and trained bands of fighters were infiltrated into Saigon and other towns, mostly without being detected. Although the U.S. command had warnings of an impending attack and pulled some army units, such as the Twenty-fifth Infantry Division, closer to the capital, U.S. and Vietnamese forces were largely unprepared for what was to happen.

On 31 January fighting erupted throughout South Vietnam. Vietcong forces attacked thirty-six of forty-four provincial capitals and sixty-four of 242 district capitals, as well as five of South Vietnam's major cities, among them Saigon and Hue. The government moved a number of its ARVN and RF/PF units out of the countryside to defend beleaguered cities. Without security forces to protect them, the government pulled some Revolutionary Development (RD) cadre teams, which brought government economic and political programs to rural areas, from their assigned villages. The withdrawal of local security forces and cadre teams represented a setback for the pacification program.

Many Americans were involved in the fighting during Tet—advisers to ARVN units, isolated detachments, troops that intercepted enemy units, air force pilots, helicopter crews, and military police. Except at airfields used jointly by Americans and Vietnamese, such as that at Bien-hoa, the only major strike against a U.S. installation was made by a Vietcong regiment at the perimeter of the massive Long Binh compound. The 199th Infantry Brigade under Colonel Frederic Davison defeated the invading regiment. Davison's later promotion made him the first black general officer in the army since World War II. In most cities and towns, U.S. and South Vietnamese forces repelled the attacks and regained control after a few days of fighting. The exception was Hue, where it took U.S. Army and Marine Corps units and South Vietnamese forces three weeks of house-to-house fighting to drive out North Vietnamese regulars. Civilians rallied around the Thieu government, ignoring Communist calls for a general uprising.

With a strong push from CORDS, the government quickly embarked on a plan to rebuild war-ravaged cities and resettle families made homeless by the offensive. U.S. agencies provided funds and relief supplies, and army engineer and navy Seabee units helped rebuild damaged roads, bridges, and neighborhoods. President Thieu approved a number of measures over which his government had long temporized—general mobilization, an armed militia, and full implementation of the Phoenix program, the U.S. plan to attack the Vietcong infrastructure. The government finally issued operational guidance to the Vietnamese agencies involved in Phoenix and set up intelligence operations and coordination centers in the provinces and districts. The Police Special Branch, the National Police Field Forces, and the Provincial Reconnaissance Units (PRU) exercised the principal operational role. The PRUs were CIA-financed and CIA-controlled elite Vietnamese commando squads. The goal of the Phoenix program to capture known members of the infrastructure often proved difficult. Some suspects were killed resisting arrest, others died in the course of firefights, and an unknown number of others were likely eliminated in contravention of the program's regulations. The government's decision to promulgate standard operating procedures signified its readiness to attack the infrastructure. The Phoenix program would prove to be the one that the Communists most feared, because it targeted the control center of their organization in South Vietnam, and would also prove to be the most controversial program as well.

After the initial shock wore off, MACV realized that the offensive offered an opportunity. In targeting the cities, the Vietcong had suffered a major military defeat, losing thousands of seasoned fighters and veteran political cadres, seriously weakening their insurgent base. By March, Westmoreland concluded that the worst was over and urged his commanders to go on the offensive. The Tet offensive had hit the province and district towns, bypassing the rural villages. Komer judged that the government could make relatively easy gains in pacification simply by returning RF/PF units and the RD cadre teams to the countryside. In his estimation, the enemy was too weak to resist.

Tet Hits Home. On the battlefield, the Tet offensive turned out to be a bloody setback for the Vietcong, but the drama of the initial assaults on the U.S. embassy in Saigon and the other cities overwhelmed the media, creating an image of allied defeat. The offensive deeply shocked Americans, who witnessed on television the skirmish for the embassy in Saigon and heard respected newscasters conclude that the war could not be won. Coming after repeated claims of progress, the Tet attacks severely damaged the credibility of Johnson's war policy and Westmoreland's affirmations of success in wearing down the enemy. By early 1968 support for Johnson's war policy was already weak on Capitol Hill and fading in the press. Campus protests against the war and the draft were spreading and increasing in intensity. Tet hit Johnson when he was vulnerable and the country uneasy.

The request by the military for an additional 206,000 troops, which was leaked to the press in February, was the psychological knockout punch. Nearly half a million U.S. troops were already in Vietnam, and the call for such a large increase reinforced the erroneous, as it would turn out, public perception of a military defeat. Most of the additional forces were intended to reconstitute the U.S. strategic reserve that had been depleted by the Vietnam buildup. Westmoreland had asked for his share of the 206,000 additional soldiers not to stave off defeat but to operate inside Laos and cut the Ho Chi Minh trail.

By early 1968, the manpower requirements of the war had already attenuated the capability to meet other contingencies. More combat units for Vietnam meant that the army could deploy fewer forces to Europe or South Korea, where Communist forces posed an imposing and immediate threat. The army had already diverted units from Germany to Vietnam. The air force was using bombers from the Strategic Air Command in the Pacific to provide tactical support. Heightened international tensions following chronic crises in the Mideast and the seizure of the USS *Pueblo* by North Korea prior to the Tet offensive underscored the potential danger of further weakening forces deployed overseas and of not reconstituting the strategic reserve. In addition, the administration had to call on army units to quell civil disturbances in Newark and Detroit in 1967. Riots by blacks protesting racial discrimination and the lack of economic opportunity intensified antiwar sentiment, evoking calls for the administration to end the war so that more resources would be available to solve domestic problems. An antiwar march on the Pentagon in October 1967 also required the mobilization of federal troops.

Mounting demands on dwindling military resources, the shock of the Tet offensive, and growing public clamor against the war forced the Johnson administration in February and March to reassess its commitment to Vietnam. The new secretary of defense, Clark Clifford, took the lead, objecting to a strategy that devoured more and more resources in pursuit of an elusive victory in the indefinte future. The president decided to limit the U.S. commitment. As in 1967, Johnson vetoed a major infusion of soldiers, only sending two army brigades and calling up a small number of reserves, about forty thousand men, for service in Vietnam and South Korea. His decision clearly implied that the ARVN would have to shoulder a larger part of the fighting. Johnson also decided not to seek reelection, hoping his withdrawal would facilitate a settlement, and curtailed air strikes against North Vietnam. His moves led to the opening of peace talks in Paris between the United States, South Vietnam, North Vietnam, and the Vietcong.

Although Americans opposed to the war generally viewed Johnson's withdrawal and the start of talks as hopeful signs, other domestic crises intensified antiwar sentiment. On 4 April, civil rights leader Dr. Martin Luther King, Jr., was assassinated, a tragic event that provoked rioting in black neighborhoods in many cities. Federal troops were mobilized and National Guard units were called out to restore order in Washington, Chicago, and Baltimore. In all, major disturbances erupted in 125 cities in twenty-nine states. The murder of the nation's most influential black civil rights leader was particularly appalling to those who believed social programs had been sacrificed to help pay for the growing costs of an unpopular war. King had spoken out against the fighting, claiming that a disproportionate number of blacks were dying in the conflict.

THE ACCELERATED PACIFICATION CAMPAIGN

The Tet offensive raised sharp questions about the shortcomings of the South Vietnamese government and military. With increased U.S. casualties and heightened skepticism about progress, the criticism that the Saigon regime was corrupt, undemocratic, and unwilling to defend itself took on added virulence. Public sympathy for the goal of preserving South Vietnam noticeably declined. U.S. leaders in Vietnam—Komer, Ambassador Bunker, Westmoreland and his deputy General Creighton Abrams—realized that public alienation was likely to grow unless the government and ARVN were able to accomplish more on their own behalf. They concluded that demonstrable progress against the enemy was the only possible way to convince the American electorate that the war would not be lost or end in a stalemate. Restoring credibility, they hoped, would regenerate support at home.

The Americans made repeated efforts to galvanize the South Vietnamese in the spring. Westmoreland proposed that the commanders of the allied forces and General Vien, chief of the Joint General Staff, undertake a general counteroffensive before the enemy could recover. Komer wanted Thieu to send South Vietnamese territorial forces back to the villages from which they had withdrawn in February.

He reasoned that if the government could quickly increase its hold on the countryside, it would limit Communist access to the rural population, promote the expansion of pacification programs into new areas, and strengthen Saigon's position at the bargaining table. A counteroffensive would also put the government in a stronger position in rural areas in case of a cease-fire that would fix opposing forces in the areas they controlled. Cautious by nature and lacking a strong political base, Thieu was fearful throughout 1968 of a repetition of Tet. He resisted Komer's calls for a counteroffensive until he was certain that the last wave of the enemy's 1968 offensive, which occurred in August, had failed. Only in October did he agree to carry out a counteroffensive.

Called the Accelerated Pacification Campaign (APC), the counteroffensive was a three-month crash effort that began on 1 November 1968. Its primary goal was to improve security in a thousand contested hamlets. The APC employed no new concepts of pacification but brought together all civil and military programs in a tightly integrated effort. It coordinated the upgrading of hamlet security by South Vietnamese paramilitary forces, police, and cadre teams with the other programs comprising pacification as well as with operations by U.S. and South Vietnamese ground forces. What was unprecedented was the degree of military involvement. The APC represented the first time that the military campaign was subordinated to the objectives of the pacification program. U.S. Army and Marine Corps operations provided a shield for government cadres and territorial forces. According to Pentagon statistics, an estimated 50 percent of U.S. ground operations during the APC supported pacification. The efforts of U.S. ground forces were concentrated for the first time on the struggle for control of the people. For most forces, the APC was a period of small unit actions—ambushes, surveillance, and mobile spoiling attacks.

General Abrams, who replaced Westmoreland in July, exhorted his commanders to support the campaign, which, in his view, would help establish a rural political base for the South Vietnamese government. If the RF/PF and the police could keep the Vietcong out of the villages and prevent them from assassinating government officials, thus allowing South Vietnamese villagers to manage their own affairs, then, Abrams believed, the government would stand for something.

In quantitative terms, the results of the APC were significant. By the end of the campaign, according to official statistics, more than eleven hundred contested hamlets had been brought under some degree of government control, and MACV estimated that Vietcong control had dropped from about 17 to 12 percent of the rural population. Nearly all newly secured hamlets had popularly elected or appointed officials, an important step toward establishing responsive local government. More than eight thousand Vietcong had defected and some seven thousand members of the infrastructure had been killed or captured.

Prior to the campaign, no pacification effort had significantly raised the degree of government control of the countryside. The success of the APC was attributable to the centralization of pacification support under the military, the development of an integrated military/pacification plan that set objectives for the Americans and South Vietnamese, the insistence of General Abrams on army and Marine Corps participation, and a severely weakened insurgent force. The campaign set the stage for the expansion of pacification in succeeding years.

Its success, however, was at best qualified. While it achieved its immediate statistical goals, it failed to realize its larger purpose of erasing public doubts about the war. The campaign's premise, that evidence of progress would dispel public skepticism, resembled the supposition behind President Johnson's effort to rebut the stalemate doctrine. That premise was flawed. After years of exposure to official claims of progress, the jolt of the Tet offensive decisively altered public perceptions of the war. Much of the public and media in the aftermath of the enemy attacks had come almost reflexively to dismiss official claims without consideration of their merits. The APC, like other aspects of the war, had relied on statistics to measure progress, and by 1968 the numbers emanating from MACV and the Pentagon had little popular credibility. Moreover, Thieu's slow start in launching the campaign, about nine months after the Tet offensive, hardly contributed to the image of a bold, resilient Saigon government. The APC, which began with the U.S. presidential election and ended with the inauguration of a new president, was little noticed in the larger debate over Vietnam. The campaign ended on 31 January 1969, twelve months after the start of the Tet offensive.

NIXON AND VIETNAMIZATION

The administration of Richard M. Nixon continued the policy of seeking an independent, non-Communist Vietnam but found its pursuit of that goal severely circumscribed. Nixon was elected president by a narrow margin in 1969 in part because he claimed to have a plan to end the war. He faced a restive population tired of a stalemate achieved at a high cost in casualties and dollars. He did not want to abandon Vietnam, but he realized that political pressure in the United States compelled him to pull out forces. His stragegy became known as what his secretary of defense, Melvin Laird, called "Vietnamization," or turning over the war to the South Vietnamese.

Initiated in the spring of 1969, Vietnamization had three interrelated components: gradual withdrawal of U.S. troops from South Vietnam; the buildup of South Vietnamese military capabilities (better equipment and weapons as well as greater numbers); and the assumption of greater combat responsibility by the South Vietnamese. In general, Vietnamization bought time for South Vietnam to prepare itself for the day when it would have to fight the war on its own. Vietnamization was part of the so-called Nixon Doctrine, the administration's basic foreign policy. Hoping to avoid U.S. involvement in limited wars unless the national interest was

at stake, Nixon called on the country's allies to bear more of the burden of their own defense.

Ostensibly, U.S. troop withdrawals would be measured. The pace would be tied to success in pacification, improvements in South Vietnamese armed forces, and progress in the Paris peace talks. The departure of the first units from Vietnam in July 1969 increased domestic political pressure for additional redeployments, and it became impossible to slow, let alone reverse, the withdrawals whether or not the military situation warranted reductions in fighting strength. Antiwar moratoriums of 15 October and 15 November drew large and emotional crowds across the nation. Secretary of Defense Laird, a former congressman, believed that the political fate of the administration was tied to the withdrawals and became a catalyst within the administration for the steady, one-sided redeployment of forces. The pullout of U.S. troops was not contingent on the reciprocal departure of North Vietnamese forces.

ABRAMS IN COMMAND: ONE WAR

During the Nixon years, U.S. forces operated in an environment beset with contradictions. Early in his administration, the president decided that maintaining the greatest possible military pressure on the enemy would best serve U.S. negotiators, forcing the enemy to make concessions, but other presidential policies created difficulties for the MACV commander. Like President Johnson, Nixon held that Communist sanctuaries in Laos, Cambodia, and North Vietnam were off-limits to U.S. Army and Marine Corps ground forces, although small cross-border raids and reconnaissance patrols continued. The Nixon administration also wanted to keep U.S. casualties as low as possible. The political need to do so and the continuing ban on invading the sanctuaries limited General Abrams' military options.

By mid-1969, Abrams had to plan for the withdrawal of U.S. forces while carrying out military operations and keeping pressure on the enemy. Although he faithfully carried out Nixon's policy, he believed it unwise to remove U.S. troops precipitously before ARVN had matured as a fighting force. The need to scale down combat forces was a severe limitation in conducting the war not faced by his predecessor. The number of U.S. ground, air, and naval forces steadily declined, from 536,000 at the end of 1968 to 158,000 at the end of 1971. By the end of 1972 only 24,000 remained. Over the same period, Vietnamese force levels increased from about 850,000 to more than one million. Huge quantities of the newest weapons, including M-16 rifles, M-60 machine guns, M-79 grenade launchers, mortars, and howitzers, plus ships, planes, helicopters, and vehicles, were turned over to the Vietnamese as U.S. troops left the country.

Vietnamization made the advisory effort increasingly important. Abrams sought advisers who could work with the Vietnamese in the related areas of pacification and upgrading South Vietnamese armed forces. In light of the planned U.S. withdrawal, advisers from all branches of military service had to think in terms of working themselves out of a job. Management support programs were critical. Assistance was most needed in the areas of command and control, personnel, logistics, training, communications-electronics, intelligence, and local self-defense. Army and marine advisers had to prepare the Vietnamese to operate and maintain weapons, helicopters, and computers on their own. Air force advisers had to prepare pilots to fly and mechanics to maintain a large number of aircraft. The Vietnamese air force had to integrate many types of aircraft into their logistical system and take over several large air bases vacated by the U.S. Air Force. Likewise, U.S. Navy advisers needed to ready Vietnamese naval personnel to operate and maintain complex equipment. Specific problem areas such as overhaul scheduling, supply and parts requisition, and repair capabilities required attention. Unfortunately, Vietnamization also dictated the swift decline of the advisory structure. MACV staff advisory strength, province and district

pacification advisers, combat assistance teams at the battalion and regimental level, and personnel assigned to Vietnamese training centers sharply declined through 1971 and 1972. The U.S. Air Force and naval advisory groups, mostly technical personnel, remained strong until the final departure.

According to some accounts, Abrams had been long dissatisfied with Westmoreland's attrition strategy. To Abrams, all aspects of the struggle comprised "one war," adopting a phrase Ambassador Bunker had used in 1967 to describe his approach to the war. In his view, the pacification program was equal in importance to military operations against enemy main forces. He wanted the war of the battalions fused with the struggle to pacify the countryside.

Soon after assuming command of MACV, Abrams began to devise a framework for ground operations that would link them more directly to the ultimate goal of building a viable government and society in South Vietnam. He wanted to emphasize small-unit operations, extensive patrolling, and ambushes to reduce the enemy base of support among the population. A related objective was to wear down the enemy logistics system, crippling their ability to mount offensive operations and sustain their guerrilla forces. These steps represented more a change in emphasis than a radical break with the past. Abrams chose to focus on the Vietcong threat to Saigon's control of the countryside rather than the main forces of the enemy and to use U.S. forces to protect critical populated areas (especially the capital) so that the government could extend its hegemony to contested areas. In the summer and fall of 1968, Abrams redeployed three powerful units—the First Cavalry Division, the 101st Airborne Division, and the Third Brigade of the Eighty-second Airborne Division—from the northern provinces to the Saigon area.

The redeployments proved significant. In February 1969, the enemy launched another offensive during Tet. In contrast to the Tet attacks of the previous year, the Communists focused on U.S. forces and installations, hoping to inflict heavy casualties. Vietcong main and local forces supported by the North Vietnamese Army struck more than a hundred targets, but allied forces, aware of enemy intentions, repulsed all attacks, at a cost of more than eleven hundred Americans killed. The enemy was unable to hold any major objectives. Communist forces shelled Saigon but, unlike the previous year, failed to enter the city. The First Cavalry and the First and Twenty-fifth U.S. Infantry Divisions stopped the movement toward the capital of the First North Vietnamese Division and the Fifth Vietcong Division.

Not as intense as the offensive of the previous year, Tet 1969 further weakened the Vietcong and North Vietnamese, who suffered heavy personnel losses on top of the serious casualties of the previous months. Between October 1968 and 22 February 1969, enemy battle deaths, according to MACV data, averaged twenty-five hundred per week; between November and January defections averaged around 650 and infrastructure losses about 500 weekly. Unable to sustain continued heavy erosion of manpower, the enemy decided to forgo large countrywide assaults against strong allied positions and primarily emphasized sporadic, small-unit actions designed to reduce casualties. Communist attacks by units of battalion size and larger, for example, fell after the peak year of 1968, while the number of attacks by enemy units smaller than a battalion remained fairly constant. Tet 1969 was the last major enemy effort for several years.

After Tet 1969, it was easier for Abrams to focus on promoting population security because the Vietcong were weaker and main force units had tended to remain in sanctuaries for extended periods and avoid contact after Tet 1968. Moreover, the enemy was unable to operate as freely as before because allied ground operations had disrupted the enemy logistics system inside South Vietnam. Abrams consequently had less reason to stress the big-unit war, although like Westmoreland he still had to be prepared to cope with the entire spectrum of the Communist threat, from the assaults of North Vietnamese divisions and regiments to

guerrilla attacks and terrorism. Abrams' preferences were clear, but he had to allow subordinate commanders flexibility to meet local contingencies. His guidance did not result in a universal change in the nature of ground operations.

ONE WAR: PACIFICATION

Between 1969 and 1972, the Americans and South Vietnamese continued the strategy used successfully in the Accelerated Pacification Campaign of moving territorial forces into contested or enemy-controlled hamlets. Security in the countryside steadily improved, as measured by official statistics and the movement of allied forces into previously contested or enemy-held villages. During this period, the Thieu government took steps to open the South Vietnamese political system to broader participation and to give more people an interest in supporting the Saigon government. The number of villages with elected local governments grew, and, through the Land to the Tiller Law, sweeping land reform legislation enacted in March 1970, unprecedented numbers of Vietnamese became landowners. By 1973 the government issued titles to more than a million hectares of redistributed land. Land tenancy fell and the new group of landowners were better off economically. These developments sparked optimism in CORDS, even if critics assailed the credibility of the official numbers and some officials in Washington doubted the ability of the South Vietnamese to translate the gains of these halcyon days into lasting political and security improvements.

Because the ultimate political goal of pacification, frequently expressed at the time as "winning hearts and minds," was largely intangible, it proved difficult to reach a clear verdict on what was accomplished by pacification. Improvements in rural economic conditions and limited local rule were no guarantee of popular allegiance. Moreover, the Thieu government proved inconsistent about building a democratic government. The 1971 election was a public relations disaster. Although Thieu won, the campaign procedures seemed designed to eliminate rivals from the race. Some candidates boycotted the election, which confirmed the view of critics that the regime was authoritarian, lacked genuine political support, and sought to emasculate the anti-Communist opposition. Before and after reelection, Thieu suppressed political dissent and curtailed press freedoms and village elections.

In extending its writ in the countryside, Saigon depended on the sheer size of its growing military forces to protect the people living in areas under its control. Under Vietnamization, the RF/PF would take on the former role of ARVN in area security and the militia would become responsible for village and hamlet defense. To accommodate the added role, RF/PF grew in size until by 1971 they accounted for roughly half the South Vietnamese force structure of 1.1 million men.

As South Vietnamese territorial forces grew, their ability remained open to question. According to its own criteria (the Territorial Forces Evaluation System), CORDS deemed more than half the RF/PF units in the country in March 1971 to be unsatisfactory. The standards used for this evaluation took into account the number of men present for duty, the quality of their training and equipment, and their performance in the field. The large number of units rated as unsatisfactory in 1971 made it problematical that the RF/PF could sustain a high level of security over the long term and assume the role of ARVN.

The sheer size of the Saigon defense establishment, seemingly a sign of strength, was also a source of weakness. The government could not maintain more than a million men in its armed forces without continued, massive material support from the United States. That fact posed a serious problem for the Thieu regime, because in 1971 and 1972 the level of U.S. assistance began to decline, and the American political will to sustain the war had begun to wane even earlier. More than the war effort was dependent on U.S. funds and equipment. Economic and social programs for the peasantry also required continued U.S. support.

The effect of pacification on the Vietcong appeared clear in some respects. Between 1967 and 1971, more than 145,000 Vietcong or North Vietnamese defected to the government under the *chieu hoi* amnesty program. About 60 percent of the defectors were from military units, contributing to the difficulty the Communists had in stopping pacification cadres and territorial forces from gaining access to contested and enemy-controlled villages. The effect of the Phoenix program was harder to gauge. Although the infrastructure dropped from an estimated eight-five thousand in 1967 to sixty-six thousand in October 1971, much of that loss was suffered in the course of routine combat operations, not through the police arrest or capture of suspects. Most of those captured or sentenced under Phoenix were low-ranking officials and not hard-core leaders, suggesting that the party retained the nucleus for regenerating itself.

Phoenix suffered from a mismatch of U.S. managerial philosophy and South Vietnamese interests. Coordination of South Vietnamese intelligence and police units against the nerve center of their adversary was sensible by U.S. standards. For bureaucratic and political reasons, however, CORDS found it difficult to get the individual Vietnamese agencies to cooperate, share information, and contribute qualified personnel to a combined anti-infrastructure effort.

The program was flawed in other respects. A quota system was established to monitor results but led to false reporting. Among other problems were arbitrary sentencing and detention procedures, a shortage of detention facilities, bribery, political accommodation between government officials and the Vietcong, and the occasional use of the program to silence political opponents. Without question, the program's objective was essential to the defeat of the Communists, who with good reason feared its effects. Phoenix proved to be a two-edged sword. Although the program weakened the enemy, its negative image stemming from abuses and allegations of torture and assassination forced South Vietnamese and U.S. officials to prove that they were not engaged in crimes. Such adverse publicity did nothing to rekindle support for the war in the United States and only added to public disenchantment.

ONE WAR: GROUND OPERATIONS

During the period of Vietnamization many ground operations focused on support of pacification. Their underlying objective was to clear enemy forces from populated areas, providing an opportunity for the South Vietnamese government to strengthen itself without interference from its adversary. Small engagements for control of villages, mostly initiated by enemy forces, constituted the overwhelming majority of combat actions. Despite the prevalence of small operations, large-scale conventional fighting and the major bombing campaigns captured public attention. Ground operations, especially the large publicized ones, had significant political ramifications. Were they too costly in lives at a time of withdrawal? Major campaigns could also be regarded as tests of Vietnamization. Did they demonstrate growing military competence on the part of ARVN?

In view of the proximity of the Ho Chi Minh trail and the DMZ, it proved difficult in I Corps to ignore the big-unit war. The scene of heavy fighting, nearly 30 percent of friendly combat fatalities throughout the war occurred there. Throughout 1969, U.S. Army and Marine Corps units, ARVN, and South Korean troops drove deep into established enemy bases, inflicting heavy losses on main force units, seizing supplies, and destroying fortifications. The North Vietnamese and Vietcong were still able to mount attacks, especially in northern I Corps, but supply shortages and allied military pressure forced them to revert to harassing tactics, and the number of engagements with major enemy units steadily declined. Despite setbacks, Communist forces continued to contest the pac-

ification program, especially as U.S. forces began to leave. Even in operations that directly supported pacification, it was hard to discern long-term gains.

Meade River, a Marine Corps operation lasting from September 1968 to January 1969, was launched to pacify the Dien Ban district in the eastern part of Quang Nam province. Long under enemy domination, Dien Ban had a heavy concentration of North Vietnamese forces and served as a staging area for numerous attacks against Da Nang and the provincial capital. Operation Meade River sought to clear the Vietcong from villages and hamlets so that cadre teams could restore local government and administer social and economic programs. The operation employed six U.S. Marine Corps battalions, three battalions of the Fifty-first ARVN regiment, and one battalion of South Korean marines to sweep the target area. In addition, National Police units and elements of the Special Police Branch were also involved, interrogating civilians and identifying members of the guerrillas. The operation opened with a U.S. Marine heliborne assault from ships of the U.S. Navy's Amphibious Task Force 76 and swept enemy forces from the area. Abrams and William Colby, who replaced Komer as head of CORDS, saw Operation Meade River as an example of the effective use of tactical units in support of pacification, but at the end of the operation security remained problematic. Continuous U.S. Marine patrolling, the use of free fire zones, sensors, and scanners were all needed to prevent the enemy from massing forces to attack isolated PF outposts in the district. Vietcong agents still circulated freely among the people and carried out assassinations. Meade River left unanswered questions about the permanence of any gains after the withdrawal of U.S. ground forces. A weakened but still viable Vietcong remained.

By June 1971, all Marine Corps units had left Quang Nam province, leaving the army's 196th Light Infantry Brigade as the remaining U.S. ground unit. The brigade had only brief firefights with small enemy detachments and suffered most of its casualties from booby traps.

Guerrillas and local force units kept up a steady campaign of terrorism and small attacks by fire on South Vietnamese positions, eroding security. Security also declined in the neighboring provinces of Quang Tin and Quang Ngai.

Other I Corps operations seemed to set back progress toward the goal of building support for the government. Operation Russell Beach/Bold Mariner, which took place in the Vietcong stronghold of the Batangan Peninsula on the coastal plain of Quang Ngai province, was indistinguishable from those conducted during the days of the big-unit war under Westmoreland. Reversing a trend toward the more sparing use of force in inhabited areas, the operation was marked by practices that had characterized earlier sweeps, like Cedar Falls, through enemy-controlled populated areas. Its object was to further pacification, but it resulted in heavy property destruction and made refugees of area inhabitants. This occurred despite MACV policy, dating from the middle of 1968, of minimizing damage to homes and crops and making inhabited villages secure rather than moving people into secure zones or camps.

The coastal plain was an unforgiving area. Sweeps by U.S., South Vietnamese, and Korean forces in 1967 and 1968 had failed to clear out the Vietcong. The infamous My Lai massacre of South Vietnamese civilians occurred in this area in March 1968. A year after My Lai, allied forces still had made little headway against the Vietcong. Enemy forces attacked U.S. units, launched rocket attacks on the province capital, Quang Ngai city, and protected the infrastructure.

Operation Russell Beach/Bold Mariner began in January 1969 when two U.S. Marine Corps battalion landing teams stationed with the Seventh Fleet landed on the Batangan Peninsula. On the same day, the southern boundary was sealed off by Task Force Cooksey, composed of units from the U.S. Twenty-third Division; the Fifth Battalion, Forty-sixth Infantry Regiment; and the Fourth Battalion, Third Infantry Regiment. The U.S. battalions and two battalions of ARVN infantry forced the enemy toward the sea, killing more than two hundred and capturing more than one hundred. More than two hundred persons were identified as Vietcong cadre. The allied sweep displaced close to twelve thousand people, more than 40 percent of the population. They were evacuated by helicopter from their villages. Because their homes had been destroyed, the refugees were forced to live in camps. Poor security delayed resettlement. It was not until 1971 that the environment had improved enough to permit all refugees to leave the camps and rebuild their homes.

The marines considered Russell Beach/Bold Mariner a successful invasion of an enemy sanctuary, and the province adviser called it a symbol of the successful expansion of government control, but these judgments proved premature. Allied forces had temporarily occupied, but not eliminated, a Communist stronghold. Vietcong forces in the area continued to levy taxes and abduct local officials. The relocations bestowed no political advantage on the government. It was unlikely that the experience of the refugees, many of whom were already sympathetic to the Communists, kindled any allegiance to the Saigon government. Rather than a successful pacification operation, Russell Beach was a misguided failure.

Unwilling to cede control of the remote, mountainous western part of I Corps, the enemy built up logistic bases in the A Shau Valley near the Laotian border after the 1968 Tet offensive. Some U.S. ground operations in this area were little different than those conducted under Westmoreland's command. On 11 May 1969, a battalion of the 101st Division climbing a hill literally collided with the waiting Twenty-ninth North Vietnamese regiment. The division fought to capture Hamburger Hill (Hill 937), a remote mountain distant from any population centers. Supported by artillery and air strikes, the Americans had to root out the enemy regiment, engaging in hand-to-hand combat as they cleared out one entrenched position after another. After ten days of fighting, the 101st captured the hill, sacrificing seventy dead and 372 wounded. The costly operation achieved no lasting gains. The division abandoned the hill a few days later allowing the enemy to return and reestablish bases. To many the battle seemed to be a pointless use of men and equipment that did nothing to bring the allies closer to military victory. Critics regarded the engagement as epitomizing the futility of attrition, and Washington quietly reminded Abrams to hold down casualties. The 101st Division departed from the A Shau Valley in June. By the summer of 1970, strong pressure from NVA units forced abandonment of two outlying fire support bases, an ominous sign that Communist forces still sought to dominate the valleys leading to the coastal plain. Enemy moves forced the 101st Division and the marines to protect the coastal city of Hue until they left Vietnam in 1971, ironically as if it were an enclave.

Until redeployment, army units in the highlands of II Corps carried out several types of missions. They guarded the borders, protected population centers, and kept major roads open. Special Forces detachments were stationed in remote areas to detect the movement of enemy units across the border. A few Special Forces personnel and CIA personnel conducted clandestine operations outside Vietnam. Detachments also served as reinforcement and reaction forces for CIDG camps, called mobile strike (MIKE) forces. Composed of ethnic minorities under U.S. leadership, these units were better armed and trained than normal CIDG elements. Because of their proximity to infiltration routes and enemy strongholds, Special Forces camps continued to be lucrative targets for enemy attacks. The Fifth Special Forces Group left Vietnam in March 1971, by which time all CIDG units had been converted to Regional Force units or had been absorbed by the South Vietnamese Rangers.

The pacification effort received special attention in the II Corps province of Binh Dinh, where the Vietcong movement was deeply entrenched. In this critical province, however, even exemplary support of pacification failed to eradicate doubts about the ability of the central government to control the Vietcong over the long term. In furtherance of the one-war concept of Abrams, the 173d Airborne Brigade carried out Operation Washington Green, working closely with the South Vietnamese, to deny logistical support to local Vietcong units and keep them away from hamlets. The operation emphasized the continuous deployment of U.S. and South Vietnamese forces in hamlets long dominated by the Vietcong. It was an opportune time to strike. The operation began in April 1969, after the enemy main forces had pulled back to the Que Son mountains in the west to rest and refit, and generally avoided engagements with allied forces. When Washington Green formally ended in December, the 173d had disrupted enemy organization and restricted access to hamlets in the area of operation. The operation's methods were held up for emulation. Unfortunately for the South Vietnamese, the benefits were also short-lived. The infrastructure in this province had earlier bounced back after losses suffered during the Tet offensive of 1968 and did so again. The Vietcong began in early 1970 to step up their recruiting and proselytizing in order to build strength for the day when U.S. troops would be gone. The infrastructure in Binh Dinh began growing in 1971, jumping from nine thousand in September to about fifteen thousand in October. It was no surprise that security declined. Looked at over the long term, Washington Green offered little reason for optimism. Considered a model operation, it had achieved noteworthy gains, but the Vietcong, as determined as ever, were able to recoup their losses.

In III and IV Corps, U.S. units were involved in joint training operations with the South Vietnamese to protect the Cambodian border and the land and river approaches to Saigon. Over time, helping provide security became the predominant role for U.S. forces in this populous area. As in I Corps, the exceptions stand out. The operations of the Ninth Division during the first half of 1969 more closely resembled the war of attrition than they conformed to a pacification-oriented strategy.

The Ninth was the only U.S. division to mount ground operations in the fertile, populous Mekong delta. MACV sent the unit there originally because of poor ARVN performance and because another U.S. unit, the Twenty-fifth

Division, had complied a good pacification re-cord in the deltalike provinces of Long An and Hau Nghia. The Twenty-fifth employed special rules of engagement to help prevent noncom-batant casualties in highly populated areas. Op-eration Speedy Express, conducted from De-cember 1968 to June 1969, concentrated on attacking the Vietcong in Dinh Tuong, Kien Hoa, and Go Cong provinces in the upper delta. The division's commander, Major General Ju-lian Ewell, insisted on measuring performance with statistics, such as the body counts, which by this point in the war had earned a measure of public scorn. Because his approach was to wear down enemy forces by unrelenting military pressure, a favorable body count was proof of success. Relying on the relatively free use of air strikes, artillery, and helicopter gunships in the densely populated provinces, the Ninth Divi-sion claimed to kill 10,883 enemy while suffer-ing only 267 combat deaths. The results of Speedy Express were hard to take at face value, especially when the division captured fewer than eight hundred enemy weapons. According to some accounts, it was likely that many non-combatants—Vietcong supporters and innocent bystanders—were killed in addition to enemy personnel bearing arms. It was also likely that operational statistics were inflated to satisfy the quest for high kill ratios. Operation Speedy Ex-press left behind a weakened foe and a great deal of devastation. The Ninth Division had provided a security umbrella and thus aided pacification, but any positive effect was counter-balanced by civilian casualties. At the end of the operation, security in Dinh Tuong and Kien Hoa, long-time enemy strongholds, remained disappointing.

Vietnamization began first in IV Corps when two brigades of the U.S. Army Ninth Division left Vietnam in July 1969. Their departure ended the innovative riverine operations with the U.S. Navy and made the ARVN Seventh Division re-sponsible for securing the southern approaches to Saigon. The Seventh, which had fought a de-fensive war, virtually collapsed under an inef-fective commander after the departure of the U.S. division.

After the Fourth Division withdrew at the end of 1970, the remaining army combat units in III Corps—the First Cavalry Division, Twenty-fifth Infantry Division, and the Eleventh Ar-mored Cavalry Regiment—concentrated on the defense of Saigon. Elements of the First and Twenty-fifth Divisions and other units also guarded the Cambodian border to cut enemy supply trails into the capital area. In the heavily populated lowlands, U.S. forces conducted search-and-destroy operations to ferret out en-emy supplies and push guerrillas away from vil-lages, but the sanctuaries in Cambodia re-mained a serious concern for Abrams, because they allowed the Communists to sustain opera-tions by North Vietnamese and Vietcong units.

Cross-Border Operations: Cambodia.
With most U.S. combat units slated to leave Vietnam by the end of 1971, time was critical for the success of pacification and Vietnamization. Neither could thrive if the enemy could attack villages or challenge Saigon's forces from well-established cross-border sanctuaries, which provided haven and served as logistic bases. In March 1969, Nixon ordered intensive bombing attacks against North Vietnamese positions in Cambodia, an action that the Joint Chiefs of Staff had advocated for years, to curtail the North Vietnamese capacity to mount an offen-sive. Nixon also wanted to demonstrate that he would take measures avoided by Johnson, hop-ing the intensified military pressure would in-duce the Communists to settle on his terms. Over the next fifteen months, more than 100,000 tons of bombs were dropped on Cambo-dia in Operation Menu, which the administra-tion concealed from the American public and from much of the government and military. The secrecy of the bombing mocked congressional oversight of the war and put the military in the position of deliberately concealing the existence of a major operation. In addition to its political liabilities, the bombing did not destroy the Cambodian bases. Their existence, which the neutralist leader of Cambodia, Prince Norodom Sihanouk, tolerated, posed a continuing threat to South Vietnam. The overthrow of the prince

by a pro-American clique under Prime Minister Lon Nol gave Nixon the opening for a ground assault on the Cambodian sanctuaries. Lon Nol closed the port of Sihanoukville to Communist shipping, sought U.S. aid, and was amenable to military action against the sanctuaries. In authorizing units of the First Cavalry Division, the Twenty-fifth Infantry Division, and the Eleventh Armored Cavalry Regiment to enter Cambodia in May 1970, Nixon expected to buy time for Vietnamization by destroying enemy supply bases and headquarters. He also hoped to prop up the feeble regime of Lon Nol.

Although the cross-border operation caused heavy losses of Communist manpower, weapons, ammunition, and supplies, the reaction in the United States was cataclysmic. The surprise expansion of the war during a period of withdrawal enraged those opposed to the war and provoked violent demonstrations on campuses across the nation. Students at Kent State University in Ohio and Jackson State College in Mississippi were killed in confrontations with National Guardsmen and police. More than 100,000 protesters gathered in Washington, D.C., in early May to protest the incursion and the killings at Kent State. An outraged Senate revoked the Tonkin Gulf Resolution of 1964 by an overwhelming vote. The Cambodian incursion, as the Pentagon termed it, was a major event in the alienation of the public. The later disclosure of the secret bombing campaign contributed to the erosion of credibility in the administration's Vietnam policy and the loss of public support.

Cross-Border Operations: Lam Son 719.

With the closing of Sihanoukville, the destruction of supply caches in Cambodia, and the effectiveness of Operations Market Garden and Game Warden, the Ho Chi Minh trail was the only available way for Hanoi to supply its forces in the south. Years of bombing the trail in Laos—Operation Commando Hunt, which used sensors to identify targets for U.S. gunships—had diminished but never completely halted the movement of supplies. Abrams believed a ground operation inside Laos to sever

the trail physically could give Vietnamization another breathing spell. The Cooper-Church amendment, however, passed by Congress after the Cambodian incursion, prohibited U.S. ground forces or advisers from entering Laos or Cambodia. The U.S. role in any cross-border operation would thus be limited to strikes by airplane and helicopter pilots flying over Laos; artillery units firing from inside South Vietnam; logistic, combat, and engineering support for the South Vietnamese; and maintenance of fixed-wing aircraft and helicopters. ARVN would have to enter Laos on its own. Operation Lam Son 719, to sever the trail in Laos, began in February 1971. Compromised by security leaks, it was in trouble from the outset. ARVN units stalled inside Laos when they encountered strong resistance from North Vietnamese infantry, armor, and artillery. Thieu, fearing the loss of some of his elite troops, ordered his forces to withdraw. South Vietnamese units hastily pulled out while under heavy counterattack from North Vietnamese combined arms fire, leaving behind many dead and wounded. Although Thieu's concerns about excessive casualties hindered the operation, the performance of ARVN demonstrated the inadequacy of its leadership. Lam Son ended with renewed questions about the ability of the ARVN to stand by itself; it was an ominous test of Vietnamization.

The Americans contributed to the failings of Operation Lam Son 719. Planning was hasty and too closely held, allowing ARVN little time to train, and the ARVN military intelligence office had no part in the planning. The Americans kept their command post about eight miles from that of ARVN, complicating allied coordination. In addition, the U.S. Seventh Air Force and the U.S. XXIV Corps, the ground force headquarters, disagreed over the concept of air support and which headquarters should control assault and support operations. As it turned out, the Americans supported a major operation with inadequate planning, deficient coordination with ARVN, and major service differences over the concept and execution of the operation. At the bottom of these deficiencies lay a lack of unity of command. Nobody took charge of the operation and nobody coordinated it. In Operation Lam Son the allies paid a price for the long-unresolved issues of command and control.

THE EASTER OFFENSIVE, 1972

Operation Lam Son 719 had convinced the North Vietnamese that ARVN was vulnerable to attacks by tanks and heavy artillery. In May 1971, the political bureau in North Vietnam, hoping in the coming year to win the war militarily and hasten a negotiated settlement, elected to launch a major offensive against South Vietnamese forces. Hanoi timed the offensive to begin after U.S. ground combat elements had left the country. The Communist leadership expected that the Saigon government would have to redeploy large numbers of its forces to battle the invading divisions. In turn, the diversion of units would weaken local security, permitting Vietcong and North Vietnamese forces to return to their former strongholds and regain sources of manpower and supply.

On 30 March 1972, Hanoi launched the so-called Easter Offensive, a massive invasion by twenty North Vietnamese Army divisions. Making extensive use of armor and artillery fire, the NVA attacked across three fronts—the DMZ, the central highlands, and the III Corps border area west of Saigon. The enemy made dramatic gains on all three fronts. The task of stopping the ground offensive fell almost completely on South Vietnamese army and territorial forces. Total U.S. military strength had fallen to ninety-five thousand, of which only six thousand were combat troops. By March 1972, the air force had withdrawn most of its planes, leaving only seventy-six fighter and attack aircraft in Vietnam. Only two navy carriers, the *Hancock* and the *Coral Sea*, with a total of 180 aircraft, were stationed off the coast of Vietnam. Only eighty-three B-52s operated in theater.

In April, Nixon augmented U.S. Navy and Air Force personnel in Southeast Asia in an effort to halt the offensive. Air force fighter and

attack planes soon totaled 409, and 171 B-52s were available at the end of May. The navy brought four additional carriers, one heavy cruiser, five cruisers, and forty-four destroyers to the South China Sea. With the added aircraft, there was a jump in the number of sorties that B-52s and fighter and attack planes flew against the invading divisions. In large measure, U.S. airpower was responsible for stopping the advance of the NVA in the northernmost province of Quang Tri, the central highlands, and the III Corps town of An Loc. The inexperience of the North Vietnamese Army in maneuvering tanks and infantry slowed their advance and made their forces more vulnerable to air strikes.

In addition, Nixon ordered the bombing of targets in North Vietnam, codenamed Linebacker. Between May and October 1972, air force and navy pilots struck the cities of Vinh, Haiphong, and Hanoi with fighter-bombers and B-52s. North Vietnam had been a refuge from U.S. bombing since November 1968, when President Johnson had ended the Rolling Thunder program. Compared to Rolling Thunder, which largely served to restrict the movement of men and supplies from the north to support the guerrilla war in the south, the Linebacker bombing campaign proved more effective. It was directed at stopping a conventional military offensive that required large amounts of fuel, supplies, and ammunition. More sustained bomb tonnage was dropped between May and October than in any other comparable period. The bombing damaged lines of communications, destroyed oil storage facilities and a significant percentage of North Vietnam's power-generating capacity, and wrecked the ability of North Vietnam to conduct conventional offensive war. Nixon also ordered the navy to mine Haiphong harbor, closing off sea traffic to the country's primary port. His resolve in bringing air and naval power to bear provided the margin of victory.

As a test of Vietnamization, the Easter Offensive was as discomfiting as Operation Lam Son 719. In addition to the inability of ARVN to stop invaders, territorial forces and militia proved no match for large conventional units. Pacification ceased when the North Vietnamese Army entered an area. The need to stop an invasion forced the government to spread its forces thinly, reducing the protection provided to the rural populace. The absence of U.S. units and advisers meant that the South Vietnamese had to deal with the Communists in provinces where they were traditionally strong and government control weak. In addition, North Vietnamese forces entered the delta between 1969 and 1973, compensating for Vietcong losses and reviving the insurgency. After the 1972 offensive, the Communists were in a strong position to continue the struggle to unify Vietnam under their banner.

The fighting of 1972 failed to break the stalemate. Although U.S. bombing and the South Vietnamese army had stopped North Vietnamese forces at heavy cost, Hanoi retained significant forces in the south. Both sides turned to negotiations, but when talks bogged down in the fall of 1972, Nixon resumed the air war, bombing North Vietnam in December in order to force Hanoi to conclude a treaty. The JCS conducted this air campaign without the restrictions on targets, sorties, and tonnage routinely imposed by the Johnson administration. The bombing was intensive and devastating. From 18 December to 29 December, B-52s and fighter bombers dropped more than twenty thousand tons of bombs, exceeding the tonnage that fell during 1969–1971. The so-called Christmas bombing (Linebacker II) destroyed Hanoi's airport, major bus and train stations, and North Vietnam's largest hospital, but at a considerable toll. Fifteen B-52s were lost to intense antiaircraft fire. Nixon's bombing provoked a fresh outcry on the part of congressional critics and war protesters. Many who had accepted the spring bombing as necessary to stop a blatant invasion questioned the necessity of the harsh Christmas attacks. Nixon's approval rating dropped to 39 percent.

In early 1973, the United States, North Vietnam, South Vietnam, and the Vietcong signed a peace agreement that promised a cease-fire and national reconciliation. Hanoi dropped an earlier demand for the removal of Thieu, but the

United States agreed that Hanoi could keep its troops in the south, a concession that directly contributed to the final defeat of South Vietnam. Under the agreement, MACV was dissolved and remaining U.S. forces were withdrawn. U.S. military advisers, still the backbone of the ARVN command structure, were completely pulled out, although Nixon secretly promised Thieu he would take steps, such as bombing and continued matériel support, to preserve the independence of South Vietnam.

THE END OF A WAR

The defeat of South Vietnam in 1975 after a major invasion by North Vietnamese ground, armor, and artillery forces was a bitter end to a long struggle by the United States to preserve the sovereignty of South Vietnam. Ranging from advice and support for all components of South Vietnamese armed forces to direct participation in air, ground, and sea combat, which eventually involved nearly three million U.S. servicemen, the effort failed to prevent Hanoi from unifying Vietnam. The decisive defeat of Saigon tended to obscure the inability of the U.S. military undertaking to compensate for the regime's political shortcomings. For nearly two decades, from the hopeful days of Diem's rule to the ignominious collapse of Thieu's government, no South Vietnamese leader or group had succeeded in mobilizing that nation's political, social, and economic resources to build a base of support. The final role of the U.S. military was to use its helicopters to evacuate U.S., Vietnamese, and Cambodian citizens to the waiting ships of the Seventh Fleet as the capitals of Saigon and Phnompenh fell in April 1975.

In assessing the defeat, the shortcomings of U.S. policy and strategy stand out in sharp relief. Political limitations on the conduct of the war obviously hampered the armed services. Restrictions on bombing, prohibitions against ground operations inside North Vietnam and the cross-border sanctuaries, and the application of graduated military pressure under the doctrine of limited war made it more difficult to wage war in Southeast Asia. The lack of a realizable, positive political/military objective, such as the defeat of North Vietnamese forces, was a more crucial failing. The U.S. goal expressed in NSAM 288 of seeking an independent South Vietnam was difficult to conceptualize in a military strategy that would be carried out on behalf of an ally. The chosen means of fighting were ill-suited to realize the U.S. objective. Bombing infiltration routes and industrial targets in North Vietnam might halt a conventional invasion but could not force Vietcong guerrillas to cease fighting. They enjoyed indigenous logistic and political support and sources of manpower inside South Vietnam. Search-and-destroy operations were all too frequently exercises in futility. The enemy, whenever possible, refused to stand and fight and tried to avoid being trapped and destroyed by superior allied firepower. U.S. generals conducted untold sweeps in a largely unavailing effort to find, fix, and destroy enemy units. The Americans operated again and again in the same areas and made infrequent contact with the enemy. Repeated fruitless operations built up frustration. Continuous sweeps also meant that U.S. forces were not well-deployed to provide sustained local security against Vietcong guerrillas and infrastructure. Enemy forces initiated most engagements throughout the period of U.S. involvement, choosing as a rule to strike U.S. and South Vietnamese forces where they appeared vulnerable or where the Communists could enhance their control in the countryside.

With the establishment of CORDS, the Accelerated Pacification Campaign, and Abrams' one-war approach, allied strategy was more sharply focused. This change, however, came too late to make a difference. By the time the APC demonstrated the potential of a comprehensive pacification program in defeating the insurgency, support for the war had sharply fallen and Nixon had decided to disengage from Vietnam.

The success or failure of pacification and Vietnamization ultimately rested on the ability of the government and armed forces of South Vietnam. Lacking authority to manage Vietnamese programs or command Vietnamese units, advisers had limited ability to influence their counterparts, let alone have them removed for incompetence or corruption. The goal of an independent, sovereign South Vietnam precluded the Americans from taking control of the war effort at the local or national level. Even with the advantages of Vietnamization—better weapons, equipment, and training and greater numbers—South Vietnamese forces on their own proved incapable of standing up to the North Vietnamese. Leadership remained politicized and weak. Government cadres generally lacked the fervor their adversary routinely displayed and inspired no outpouring of political enthusiasm in the countryside for the corrupt, authoritarian Thieu regime. It may not be too harsh to conclude that Vietnamization, which denied Abrams the chance to obtain military victory, served primarily to prolong the stalemate long enough for the Americans to depart.

THE IMPACT OF VIETNAM

The U.S. military paid dearly in a futile undertaking to preserve South Vietnam, suffering more than fifty-eight thousand deaths. Young, low-ranking enlisted men, of whom 13 percent were black, made up the majority of the fatalities. With the relative infrequency of large set-piece battles, it was not surprising that most soldiers died from small-arms fire. In a war of numerous small-unit actions, it was also no surprise that a significant proportion of the deaths, 30 percent, resulted from mines, booby traps, and grenades. Artillery, rockets, and bombs were responsible for only a small share of total casualties.

Save for the unprecedented medical care that the armed services provided in South Vietnam, the death toll would have been higher. The expert emergency care given by battlefield medics at great personal risk was the first link in the medical treatment system. Medical helicopters quickly evacuated the wounded to nearby army, Marine Corps, and navy hospitals and hospital ships, where they were relatively secure from attack. With access to up-to-date technology and sufficient supplies of drugs and whole blood, military doctors and nurses were able to save the lives of innumerable servicemen with the kinds of wounds that had proved fatal in earlier wars.

Exposure to herbicides that were sprayed to destroy crops and foliage in Communist-held areas harmed U.S. soldiers and sailors as well as Vietnamese. In many cases, the servicemen's suffering commenced after they returned home, because not all wounds were physical. Some who served in Vietnam suffered adverse psychological effects from combat, including post-traumatic stress syndrome, and required counseling and psychiatric help long after they returned to civilian life.

American prisoners of war endured long and harsh captivity at the hands of the Vietcong and North Vietnamese. Search-and-rescue missions saved some downed pilots and crews from capture, but not all were so fortunate. Air force and navy pilots were shot down by MIGs and surface-to-air missiles while bombing North Vietnam. Soldiers and helicopter pilots were captured in the south. POWs remained imprisoned, chiefly in Hanoi, until the cease-fire of 1973. Because war had not been formally declared, Hanoi chose not to observe the Geneva Conventions on the treatment of POWs. Most prisoners were physically and psychologically tortured by their captors, who extracted "confessions" of war crimes as part of a propaganda effort to weaken political support for U.S. policy.

The final reckoning of the human cost of the war may never be complete. More than a decade after the end of the war, about twenty-three hundred Americans remained unaccounted for. South Vietnamese military deaths exceeded 200,000, while war-related civilian deaths were close to half a million. Many others were wounded, maimed, or harmed by herbicides. Accurate estimates of enemy military casualties are especially difficult because of imprecise body counts, verification problems, and the uncertainty of distinguishing between civilians and combatants. Still, close to one million Vietcong and North Vietnamese soldiers probably perished in combat through 1975.

The costs of the war to the U.S. military were more than battle casualties. Defeat in Vietnam tarnished the image of the military and called its competence into question. Doubts centered on the air and ground strategy, the necessity and effectiveness of the bombing campaigns, and the soundness of the military's advice to its ally. Critics questioned the military's understanding of the nature of the war and the caliber of those in uniform.

The presence of less than ideally trained and disciplined soldiers in dangerous areas long sympathetic to the Communist cause led to tragic results on the coastal plain of southern I Corps. For years French forces had labored unsuccessfully to subdue insurgents in this area, which they termed "Street without Joy." The Americans had no better success. Operations against enemy units were slow, dangerous exercises in which snipers, mines, and booby traps caused most U.S. casualties. The line between combatants and civilians was blurred, especially in this area of Vietnam, where, as in other areas where the population sympathized with the Vietcong, old men, women, and children planted mines and booby traps. Operating in such a climate often raised anxiety and frustration to the breaking point. Self-protection became primary. In the hamlet of My Lai, soldiers of the U.S. Twenty-third Infantry Division killed about two hundred civilians in the spring of 1968. The incident came to light in 1969, prompting a major investigation, the dismissal of the commanding general of the division and other army officers, and the trial and conviction of one officer of war crimes.

The My Lai incident might have occurred in any other army unit in the late 1960s and early 1970s. The withdrawal of U.S. soldiers by a government and nation eager to escape the war and the lack of a clear military purpose in continuing to risk U.S. lives in an unpopular cause contributed to weakened discipline. Troop withdrawals and the emphasis on negotiated peace signified to servicemen that the United States was engaged in a no-win war. Criticism of the war and low public regard for the military services also served to degrade discipline and morale and contributed to a growing disenchantment with the war among soldiers in the field.

During the latter stages of its involvement in Vietnam, the U.S. Army, perhaps more than the other services, seemed to be coming apart. Although personnel problems afflicted all branches of the armed forces, the army, which had come to depend on draftees to fill its ranks, seemed to epitomize the array of serious problems besetting the military in Vietnam. Because of the policy of granting educational deferments to college students, draftees tended to be from less well-educated and lower socioeconomic groups. One-year tours in Vietnam exacerbated personnel turbulence and shortages of qualified leaders and technicians. The long inconclusive war and failures of leadership also contributed to the erosion of morale and discipline. The number of drug offenders in Vietnam jumped nearly sevenfold between 1970 and 1971, even as the number of U.S. troops in Vietnam fell. Drug use became so serious that mandatory drug testing of military personnel in Vietnam was imposed in 1971. As the fighting wound down, there was an increase in incidents of "fragging," attempts by enlisted personnel to scare or kill their commanding officers. Desertions and AWOLs in all services also climbed. The number of general and special courts-martial increased in 1970 and 1971, as did the most serious military offenses—insubordination, mutiny, and refusal to perform a lawful order. Racial tensions, mirroring those in U.S. society, also became a serious problem with troops stationed in support units, especially after the riots of the late 1960s and the assassination of Martin Luther King.

Although a generation of officers, including many of the future leaders of the armed services, gained combat experience in Vietnam, many regretted that the reputation of the military had been besmirched in a crusade that only marginally involved the national interest. The military had won battles on land, sea, and air yet lost the war. How to avert the mistakes of Vietnam became the central issue for the services as they examined doctrine and strategy after the war.

The end of the draft in 1972 and the transition to an all-volunteer army in 1973—a direct consequence of the war—meant that the nation would be unlikely to fight another major conflict with the flawed personnel policies of Vietnam. No longer would the draft and deferment system create "winners and losers" among the population of young adults. The all-volunteer military would be composed of persons who wanted to serve. Reliance on volunteers also meant that future administrations would have to mobilize reserve forces and in so doing tap the national will in fighting wars.

The War Powers Act of 1973 also made it unlikely that the Vietnam War would be repeated. The legislation required the president to inform Congress within forty-eight hours of the deployment of U.S. forces abroad and obligated him to withdraw them in sixty days in the absence of an explicit congressional endorsement. The act was intended to prevent a president from committing armed forces, as Lyndon Johnson had, in prolonged conflict without a formal declaration of war. The trauma of defeat manifested itself as a universal and deep-rooted desire to avoid another Vietnam.

BIBLIOGRAPHY

Reference Works

Olson, James S., ed. *Dictionary of the Vietnam War* (1988).

South Vietnam: U.S.-Communist Confrontation in Southeast Asia, 7 vols. (1973).

Summers, Harry G. *Vietnam War Almanac* (1985).

U.S. Pacific Command. *Report on the War in Vietnam (as of 30 June 1968), Sec. I: Report on Air and Naval Campaigns against North Vietnam and Pacific Command-wide Support of the War, June 1964–July 1968,* by U.S. Grant Sharp; Sec II: *Report on Operations in South Vietnam, January 1964–June 1968,* by W. C. Westmoreland (1969).

General Accounts

Andrews, Bruce. *Public Constraint and American Policy in Vietnam* (1976).

Baskir, Lawrence, and William A. Strauss. *Chance and Circumstance: The Draft, the War, and the Vietnam Generation* (1978).

Berman, Larry. *Planning a Tragedy: The Americanization of the War in Vietnam* (1982).

———. *Lyndon Johnson's War: The Road to Stalemate in Vietnam* (1989).

Blaufarb, Douglas S. *The Counterinsurgency Era: U.S. Doctrine and Performance, 1950 to the Present* (1977).

Braestrup, Peter. *Vietnam as History: Ten Years After the Paris Peace Accords* (1984).

Charlton, Michael, and Anthony Moncrieff. *Many Reasons Why: The American Involvement in Vietnam* (1978).

Colby, William, and James McCargar. *Lost Victory: A Firsthand Account of America's Sixteen-Year Involvement in Vietnam* (1989).

Cooper, Chester. *The Lost Crusade: America in Vietnam* (1970).

Davidson, Phillip B. *Vietnam at War: The History, 1946–1975* (1988).

DeBenedetti, Charles. *An American Ordeal: The Antiwar Movement of the Vietnam Era* (1990).

Ellsburg, Daniel. *Papers on the War* (1972).

Gelb, Leslie, and Richard Betts. *The Irony of Vietnam: The System Worked* (1979).

Herring, George. *America's Longest War: the United States and Vietnam, 1950–1975* (1979).

Herrington, Stuart. *Silence Was a Weapon: The Vietnam War in the Villages* (1982).

Johnson, Lyndon. *The Vantage Point: Perspectives of the Presidency, 1963–1969* (1971).

Karnow, Stanley. *Vietnam: A History* (1984).

Kinnard, Douglas. *The War Managers* (1977).

Kolko, Gabriel. *Anatomy of a War: Vietnam, the United States, and the Modern Historical Experience* (1985).

Kissinger, Henry. *White House Years* (1974).

———. *Years of Upheaval* (1982).

Komer, Robert. *Bureaucracy at War: U.S. Performance in the Vietnam Conflict* (1986).

Lewy, Guenter. *America in Vietnam* (1978).

McGarvey, Patrick J., ed. *Visions of Victory: Selected Vietnamese Communist Military Writings, 1964–1968* (1969).

Mueller, John. *War, Presidents, and Public Opinion* (1973).

Nixon, Richard. *RN: The Memoirs of Richard Nixon* (1978).

Pike, Douglas. *Viet Cong: The Organization and Techniques of the National Liberation Front of South Vietnam* (1966).

Schandler, Herbert. *The Unmaking of a President: Lyndon Johnson and Vietnam* (1977).

Shawcross, William. *Sideshow: Kissinger, Nixon, and the Destruction of Cambodia* (1979).

Summers, Harry G., Jr. *On Strategy: A Critical Analysis of the Vietnam War* (1982).

Thompson, Robert. *Defeating Communist Insurgency: The Lessons of Malaya and Vietnam* (1966).

Turley, William. *The Second Indochina War: A Short Political and Military History* (1986).

Vogelsang, Sandy. *The Long Dark of the American Soul: The American Intellectual Left and the Vietnam War* (1974).

Ground, Air, and Naval Operations

Andrews, William. *The Village War: Vietnamese Communist Revolutionary Activities in Dinh Tuong Province, 1960–1964* (1973).

Bergerud, Eric. *The Dynamics of Defeat: The Vietnam War in Hau Nghia Province* (1991).

Bonds, Ray, ed. *The Vietnam War: The Illustrated History of the Conflict in Southeast Asia* (1983).

Braestrup, Peter. *Big Story: How the American Press and Television Reported and Interpreted the Crisis of Tet 1968 in Vietnam and Washington* (1977).

Chandler, Robert. *War of Ideas: The U.S. Propaganda Campaign in Vietnam* (1981).

Clarke, Jeffrey. *Advice and Support: The Final Years, 1965–1973* (1988).

Clodfelter, Mark. *The Limits of Air Power: The American Bombing of North Vietnam* (1989).

Coleman, J. *Pleiku* (1988).

Cooper, Chester. *The American Experience with Pacification in Vietnam* (1972).

Cosmas, Graham, and Terrence Murray. *U.S. Marines in Vietnam, 1970–1971* (1986).

Croziat, Victor. *The Brown Water Navy: The River and Coastal War in Indochina and Vietnam, 1948–1972* (1984).

Demma, Vincent. "The U.S. Army in Vietnam." In *American Military History*, edited by William Stofft (1989).

Dorland, Peter, and James Nanney. *Dust Off: Army Aeromedical Evacuation in Vietnam* (1982).

Duiker, William. *The Communist Road to Power* (1981).

Hay, John. *Vietnam Studies: Tactical and Materiel Innovations* (1974).

Hooper, Edwin, Dean Allard, and Oscar Fitzgerald. *The United States Navy and the Vietnam Conflict* (1976).

Kelly, Francis. *U.S. Army Special Forces, 1961–1971* (1973).

Krepinevich, Andrew. *The Army and Vietnam* (1986).

Marolda, Edward, and Oscar Fitzgerald. *The United States Navy and the Vietnam Conflict*, Vol. 2 (1986).

Marolda, Edward, and G. Wesley Pryce III. *A Short History of the United States Navy and the Southeast Asian Conflict, 1950–1975* (1984).

McChristian, Joseph. *The Role of Military Intelligence, 1965–1967* (1975).

Meyerson, Harvey. *Vinh Long* (1970).

Meyerson, Joel. *Images of a Lengthy War* (1986).

Morrocco, John. *Rain of Fire: Air War, 1969–1973* (1985).

Palmer, Bruce. *The 25-Year War: America's Military Role in Vietnam* (1984).

Palmer, Dave. *Summons of the Trumpet: A History of the Vietnam War from a Military Man's Viewpoint* (1984).

Rogers, Bernard. *Cedar Falls–Junction City: A Turning Point* (1974).

Schlight, John. *The War in South Vietnam: The Years of the Offensive, 1965–1968* (1988).

Scoville, Thomas. *Reorganizing for Pacification Support* (1982).

Sheehan, Neil. *A Bright Shining Lie: John Paul Vann and America in Vietnam* (1988).

Shulimson, Jack. *U.S. Marines in Vietnam, 1965* (1978).

———. *U.S. Marines in Vietnam, 1966* (1982).

Spector, Ronald. *Advice and Support: The Early Years* (1983).

Stanton, Shelby. *The Rise and Fall of an American Army: U.S. Ground Forces in Vietnam, 1965–1973* (1985).

Thayer, Thomas. *War Without Fronts: The American Experience in Vietnam* (1985).

Thompson, James. *Rolling Thunder: Understanding Policy and Program Failure* (1980).

Thompson, W. Scott, and Donaldson D. Frizzell, eds. *The Lesson of Vietnam* (1977).

Turley, G. *The Easter Offensive, Vietnam 1972* (1985).

Tilford, Earl. *Search and Rescue in Southeast Asia, 1961–1975* (1981).

Walt, Lewis. *Strange War, Strange Strategy: A General's Report on Vietnam* (1970).

Westmoreland, William. *A Soldier Reports* (1976).

Zaffiri, Samuel. *Hamburger Hill* (1988).

GUNBOAT DIPLOMACY, 1776–1992

Richard W. Turk

The term "gunboat diplomacy" may be defined as the use of warships in peacetime to further a nation's diplomatic and political aims. The focus of this essay, however, is not exclusively on gunboat diplomacy or even on the United States Navy. Instead, its concern is with the potential or actual use of military force in nonwar contexts. In continental North America, it may involve militia, volunteer forces, or regular army units on the frontier in a peacekeeping role. It also may involve naval units anywhere on the world's oceans, protecting commerce, ensuring the safety of American nationals whose lives or property may be threatened, and furthering the nation's interests abroad, however they are defined. It may involve the use of military force to "preserve domestic tranquillity," to police occupied territory, or to combat unrest or insurrection abroad.

NOTE: For early frontier Indian-fighting, see map on page 597. For Cuba and Puerto Rico, see also map on page 833. For interventions in the Pacific Ocean, see maps on pages 837 and 959.

THE EARLY NATIONAL PERIOD, 1783–1815

The end of the American Revolution understandably brought about a reduction in the military establishment. Both the Continental army (1784) and the Continental navy (1785) were largely dissolved, but even before the war's end, national leaders had begun to grapple with the problem of national security. The solution seemed deceptively simple. With Great Britain on the verge of admitting defeat, and with weak Spanish forces to the south and west unable to menace the Confederation, there was no need for a standing army. Downplaying the degree to which Spanish and French military assistance had contributed to the British defeat, national leaders assumed that the country could, as it had once before, create its own military establishment should any European power again threaten invasion. Reliance could be placed on state-raised and state-funded militia forces, which posed no threat to American liberties. As with most simple solutions, it also turned out to be wrong, although this would not be immediately apparent.

Requests to Congress for military assistance from the states of Pennsylvania and New York in the spring of 1783 prompted the formation of a congressional committee to grapple with the issue of security. As chair of the committee, Alexander Hamilton wrote to George Washington, the commander of the Continental army, for his advice. Washington, consulting first with his subordinates, worked their recommendations into a proposal titled "Sentiments on a Peace Establishment." Assuming that the government must occupy and police the trans-Allegheny region, Washington urged the establishment of a national army, a uniform nationally controlled militia force, federal arsenals, and the establishment of an institution for the study of war and military skills.

The army, as Washington envisioned it, would consist of four infantry regiments and one artillery regiment—more than twenty-six hundred officers and men. One detachment would guard the New England frontier and the Lake Champlain–Hudson River corridor; a second would be stationed along the Great Lakes frontier (Fort Oswego, Fort Niagara, Fort Detroit, Fort Michilimackinac); a third would occupy various posts in the Ohio River valley; and the fourth would patrol the frontier in the Carolinas and Georgia. Washington's proposal, revised but not significantly changed by Hamilton's committee, was rejected by Congress, which on 3 June 1784 established the seven hundred-man First American Regiment, comprised of militia from the states of Connecticut, New York, New Jersey, and Pennsylvania, under the command of Lieutenant Colonel Josiah Harmar. Its inadequacies soon were made manifest.

The occupation and control of the trans-Allegheny region was contingent upon relations with the Indian nations resident there. Those relations were not good. An expedition launched against the Shawnees in 1774 by the colony of Virginia, although successful, had been followed by Indian raids against the Kentucky territory settlements in 1777 and 1778. These in turn were a factor in the George Rogers Clark expedition that captured the British posts at Kaskaskia, Cahokia, and Vincennes. Raids along the northern frontier in 1778 at Wyoming Valley, German Flats, and Cherry Valley prompted a retaliatory expedition in 1779 against the Iroquois. In addition, British aid and support to dissident native American tribes did not end after the revolutionary war. Great Britain's refusal to evacuate the posts held along the line of the Great Lakes and the Saint Lawrence River emboldened Indian resistance. The refusal to evacuate was based on American noncompliance with portions of the Treaty of Paris of 1783 and facilitated British control of the fur trade.

From 1784 to 1789 a series of military posts were established along the Ohio River and its tributaries. The garrisons—companies of the First American Regiment—were to provide escorts to those sent to treat with the Indians, evict squatters, and defend land surveyors and settlers. It was an impossible task. In 1786, Congress voted to increase the size of the army to 2,040, ostensibly to deal with the Indians but in reality to confront the menace of Daniel Shays's Rebellion (August 1786–February 1787) in Massachusetts. In the event, only two artillery companies assembled, and the rebellion was put down by Massachusetts militia.

Based on recent experience, therefore, delegates to the Constitutional Convention in Philadelphia in 1787 could agree that the government's ability to enforce its will had been insufficient. There was some hesitation that any augmentation of military power, be it in terms of an army or a navy, to defend the nation against enemies foreign or domestic, carried the risk of oppression of both states' rights and individual citizens' rights. Thus, the Constitution gave Congress the power to "provide and maintain a navy" and "raise and support armies," levying taxes for these purposes. The Department of War was created in August 1789, the First American Regiment was adopted as a nucleus for a regular force, and four more companies were added within six months, bringing the total force to 1,216 officers and men. They were soon needed in the Ohio Valley.

The tribes that inhabited the Wabash, Maumee, and Sandusky valleys had never recognized any American right to their lands either by virtue of conquest or treaty cession. Westerners—4,200 whites in the Northwest Territory, another 1,820 west of the Mississippi in Spanish territory, and more than 61,000 in Kentucky—felt neglected and ignored by the federal government. They believed that the army detachments were inadequate and that peace on the frontier was unobtainable unless expeditions were undertaken against Indian settlements to destroy both them and their inhabitants. Federal leaders, who were predominantly easterners, preferred negotiation to war. Wars were costly, and the regular military establishment was insufficient to defeat the Indians, who could bring into the field from fifteen hundred to twenty-five hundred warriors. Furthermore, the militia was unreliable. The Washington administration, preferring peace, began to descend the slope to war. In the fall of 1789, Congress approved a measure authorizing the mobilization of a frontier militia, which allowed the president to wage war without applying to Congress. These preparations, in turn, threatened the success of a negotiated settlement; to the Indians, a punitive expedition, or even the threat of one, seemed little short of total war.

Kentuckians not only viewed the national government's Indian policy as misguided, but believed that the army's presence was designed to prevent them from mounting their own expeditions against the tribes north of the Ohio. To disregard Kentucky's concerns risked the establishment of a separate government, possibly allied with Spanish Louisiana. Finally, there also was the matter of the land companies: both Harmar (now a general) and Arthur St. Clair, governor of the Northwest Territory, were Ohio Company shareholders.

Early in June 1790, Secretary of War Henry Knox ordered an expedition against the Indians. In fact, a two-pronged expedition was planned: the western arm, consisting of three hundred militia and the garrison of Fort Knox (Vincennes, Indiana), under the command of Major John F. Hamtramck, would proceed up the Wabash; the eastern arm, consisting of twelve hundred Kentucky and Pennsylvania militia and three hundred regulars, commanded by General Harmar, would leave Fort Washington (Cincinnati) for the Maumee. The columns would be mutually supporting. After dealing with any opposition, a military garrison would be established on the upper Maumee, designed in part to sever the Indians from their British suppliers. The plan did not work out that way. The western prong of the expedition turned back before reaching its objective. Harmar's eastern prong destroyed some Indian settlements, but two detachments were ambushed, and by early November the force was back at Fort Washington, minus two hundred men.

The failure of Knox's expedition was attributed partly to Harmar, but even more to the inept performance of the militia. With the Indians emboldened rather than cowed, the administration would try again with a larger force composed of regulars. The only portion of the government's plans that were successful were negotiations with the Iroquois and the conclusion of a treaty with the Cherokees. Hostilities thus remained limited to the northwestern Ohio tribes.

Whatever could go wrong with the buildup of forces did in 1791. St. Clair's force of regulars, militia, and levies was an army in name only when it headed north in October. Five weeks later, on 4 November, a predawn attack by one thousand Indians led to the destruction of St. Clair's force, which suffered a 60 percent casualty rate—632 deaths and more than 300 wounded out of a force of 1,400. After this disaster the army was increased the following year from two regiments to five (more than five thousand men), reorganized into four legions of twelve hundred men each and comprised of infantry, cavalry, and artillery. There also was a new army commander, Major General Anthony Wayne. Before resorting to force, however, President Washington attempted to negotiate a settlement.

These diplomatic efforts, undertaken seriously in 1792 to assuage public opinion, and somewhat less so in 1793, amounted to very little. The Indian tribes wanted the removal of all whites north of the Ohio. The British, hoping for the establishment of an Indian buffer state between Upper and Lower Canada and the United States, supported the Indians in their refusal. Wayne, kept apprised of the state of negotiations, would have undertaken a campaign in 1793 were it not for the lateness of the season and illness among his forces. The establishment of a British fort at the Maumee Rapids (Toledo, Ohio) was the final straw. Wayne's campaign began in the early summer of 1794.

During the winter Wayne established Fort Recovery at the site of St. Clair's 1791 defeat. In June 1794 its garrison beat off a two-day assault by the Indians. On 28 July, Wayne's force (two thousand regulars and fifteen hundred Kentucky volunteers) left Fort Greenville and proceeded northward, establishing Fort Defiance at the junction of the Auglaize and Maumee rivers, then proceeded down the Maumee. The Battle of Fallen Timbers was fought 20 August 1794. It was a decisive Indian defeat, which, coupled with the failure of the British to continue previous levels of support, led to the Treaty of Greenville the next year. Most of the future state of Ohio was ceded to the United States and the British decided to evacuate the frontier posts they had held since 1783.

The Washington administration not only had to deal with the Indians along the Northwest frontier but also with domestic unrest sparked by an excise tax on whiskey. The so-called Whiskey Rebellion of 1794 came at an awkward time for President Washington, as the regular forces were fully committed on the frontier. Deciding that the need to preserve "domestic tranquillity" was overriding, the government called upon state militia. Ultimately a force of 12,500 was assembled to move against the rebels in the southwestern portion of Pennsylvania. The rebellion collapsed and the government appeared vindicated. In another sense, it succeeded too well.

The coalescing opposition to the Federalists in the Fourth Congress proposed a 60 percent reduction in the army. Legislation passed in 1796 provided for a force of two thousand men in four regiments of eight companies each, a thousand-man contingent of artillerists and engineers, and a small cavalry force. Even more important, this act marked the true establishment of a permanent peacetime army, in a form that was to exist well into the nineteenth century. The army's primary mission became the manning of frontier posts, overseeing Indian-white contacts, and keeping settlers out of Indian territory—in short, serving as a frontier constabulary to maintain peace along the nation's borders.

The country possessed maritime frontiers as well as those on land. As colonists and part of the British empire, merchants and shipowners could look to the Royal Navy for protection. Naturally, the winning of independence saw the loss of this protection, felt most keenly in the eastern Atlantic and the Mediterranean. For the North African states of Morocco, Algiers, Tunis, and Tripoli, U.S. shipping vessels were easy prey. In 1783 six vessels fell to Moroccan and Algerian corsairs, and the toll continued in succeeding years. Options seemed few; the last Continental navy vessel was sold in 1785. With force unavailable, negotiation appeared the only alternative. A fifty-year treaty of amity and friendship was signed with Morocco in 1786. The situation improved only briefly.

The outbreak of war between the European powers in 1793 was followed by a British-inspired settlement between Portugal and Algiers, which allowed Algerian vessels into the Atlantic to harass neutral commerce. Eleven American vessels were captured that year, their crews held hostage. In January 1794 a House committee recommended the construction of four forty-four-gun and two twenty-four-gun vessels, and Congress approved the program on 27 March, with the proviso that it would be suspended if an agreement could be reached with Algiers. A September 1795 treaty with the Dey of Algiers provided for a payment of $21,600 annually in tribute in the form of naval stores, and the "gift" of a thirty-six-gun frigate (actually delivered to Algiers in 1798). Less costly settlements were reached with Tripoli in 1796 and Tunis in 1797.

Meanwhile, the improvement in relations with Great Britain signified by Senate ratification of Jay's Treaty in 1795 was followed swiftly by a deterioration in U.S. relations with France. The French viewed Jay's Treaty as a virtual Anglo-American alliance, and in retaliation began to seize American shipping. In 1797 President John Adams sent a commission to France to resolve differences between the two nations, but when faced with the prospect of a bribe to even begin negotiations, the commissioners balked. The subsequent uproar in the United States against France led to the Quasi-War (1798–1800). Congress appropriated funds to send three of the six frigates authorized in 1794 to sea and to build the remaining approved vessels. In 1798 it created a separate Department of the Navy, and authorized the reestablishment of the Marine Corps to provide ship's guards and when necessary to serve in shore landing parties. The end of the Quasi-War and the election of Thomas Jefferson as president in 1800 led to a significant reduction in naval strength. At this point, however, the Pasha of Tripoli declared war on the United States (May 1801).

Commodore Richard Dale, the first of a series of naval commanders in the Mediterranean, succeeded in immobilizing two Tripolitan vessels at Gibraltar. His forces also blockaded Tripoli for a time, but lacking authority to negotiate, Dale returned to the United States in April 1802. His successor, Commodore Richard Morris, did have authority to negotiate, but what he could offer was far from what was sought by the Tripolitan ruler. Morris himself was captured by the Bey of Tunis and had to be ransomed, an incident that led to his dismissal from the navy.

Commodore Edward Preble, who arrived in the Mediterranean in September 1803, enjoyed better fortune. He possessed both sufficient naval strength—four frigates and five sloops—and the will to use it. Learning that the emperor of Morocco had authorized attacks on U.S. merchantmen, Preble took his squadron to Tangier and forced the emperor to abide by the terms of the 1787 treaty. Meanwhile, unfortunately, the frigate *Philadelphia*, commanded by William

Bainbridge, ran aground in the harbor of Tripoli, 31 October 1803, and its entire crew of 307 was taken prisoner. The following year, during a series of attacks launched by Preble against Tripoli, a contingent of volunteers under Lieutenant Stephen Decatur burned the captured *Philadelphia* (16 February). Negotiations were less successful; Preble was succeeded as naval commander by Samuel Barron.

Barron accomplished little, but General William Eaton, agent to the Barbary states, more than compensated for him. Leading a motley force of some 450 men westward from Egypt in March 1805, he succeeded in capturing the port of Derna. This assault posed a potential threat to Tripoli itself, but the hostages remained at risk. An agreement ending the conflict was signed 3 June 1805. U.S. merchantmen were to be immune from attack, and the United States was to be granted most-favored-nation treatment for its vessels. On the other hand, Derna had to be evacuated, the captives ransomed for $60,000, and payment of tribute resumed. John Rodgers, who succeeded Barron shortly before the conclusion of the agreement, overawed the Bey of Tunis into making a separate settlement later that year, and might well have had sufficient strength to capture Tripoli itself had he been given the opportunity. American commerce was free to sail the Mediterranean once more, although the Barbary states would be heard from in the future.

The regular army's primary role of peacekeeping along the frontiers of the United States had remained unchanged following the Treaty of Greenville in 1795. During Jefferson's second term in office, it became a domestic peacekeeping force, detachments being called upon to help enforce the embargo on trade with Great Britain passed in 1807, particularly along the Canadian boundary. The deterioration in relations with Great Britain, combined with renewed unrest among the Indians in the Northwest, led to an expedition mounted by the governor of Indiana Territory, William Henry Harrison, in 1811. This expedition grew out of opposition to the 1809 Treaty of Fort Wayne and was led by the Shawnee chief Tecumseh. Taking advantage of

Tecumseh's absence from the area, Harrison moved against a Shawnee concentration on the upper Wabash with a force of one thousand men comprised of regular infantry, militia, and volunteers. The Indians attacked Harrison's force on 7 November 1811 but were repulsed after severe fighting. The Battle of Tippecanoe resolved nothing; discovery of British-supplied equipment nearby angered settlers and frontiersmen and brought closer a renewed struggle for control of both the Northwest and the Southwest—a struggle that would resume during the War of 1812.

A projected invasion of Upper Canada across the Detroit River in 1812 did not go well. In rapid succession that year, a British force captured Fort Michilimackinac, the garrison of Fort Dearborn (Chicago) was massacred as it retreated after evacuating the post, and General William Hull surrendered both his army and Detroit. An attempt to retrieve the situation during the winter of 1812–1813 miscarried as a portion of Harrison's relieving force was cut to pieces at the Battle of Frenchtown on the River Raisin. Much of the Northwest Territory thus passed from American control for the duration of the conflict. Oliver Hazard Perry's victory at the Battle of Lake Erie, 10 September 1813, led to the retreat of British forces from Detroit. Pursued by the Americans, they were brought to bay and defeated at the Battle of the Thames on 5 October. Tecumseh's death in this engagement was to break up the coalition of Northwest tribes.

In the Southwest an uprising of a portion of the Creek nation (the Upper Creek or Red Sticks) occurred in 1813. The massacre of the garrison of Fort Mims near Mobile, Alabama, on 30 August was followed by the raising of a force of twenty-five hundred Kentucky and Tennessee volunteers, led by Andrew Jackson. The Creek were defeated in the engagements of Tallishatchee and Talladega later that same year, and on 27 March 1814 the Battle of Horseshoe Bend effectively ended the conflict. Some of the Creek fled to Spanish East Florida, in retreat but hardly defeated.

The War of 1812 also led to renewed depredations against U.S. shipping by the Barbary states. In 1815 the U.S. Navy had the opportunity to retaliate. A squadron led by Commodore Stephen Decatur captured the Algerian frigate *Mashuda* off the coast of Spain on 17 June, and two days later took the *Estedio*. On 28 June, off the port of Algiers, Decatur compelled the dey to pay an indemnity for seized vessels and to renounce future demands for tribute. Tripoli and Tunis, which had permitted British warships to seize U.S. vessels in their harbors during the War of 1812, were also forced to pay indemnities. An Anglo-Dutch expedition against Algiers in 1816 ended the Barbary threat for good. The conclusion of the Napoleonic wars marked an end to the era when warfare in Europe more often than not had meant warfare in North America and the Caribbean. The United States was to remain aloof from European conflicts for the next century, allowing its armed forces to concentrate on the role of maintaining peace on both the land and maritime frontiers.

INDIAN REMOVAL AND THE BEGINNING OF EXPANSION, 1815–1861

The army was able to slip rather easily back into its constabulary role, extending or reestablishing the authority of the federal government, controlling Indian-white and Indian-Indian relations, and, on occasion, dealing with domestic disorder. Military posts were established in the upper Great Lakes area along the principal water routes from the Great Lakes to the Mississippi and less quickly on the western tributaries of that river. In the former instance, a primary purpose of the army was to control the routes by which British goods from Upper Canada could reach the northwestern tribes. An 1816 congressional prohibition against foreign traders helped to accomplish this. Except for a near uprising among the Winnebago in southern

Minnesota Territory in 1827, the Northwest remained quiet. Not so the Southeast.

Spanish Florida was inhabited by Indians of the Muskhogean family, who, although sharing the Creek culture, were called Seminole—"wild people"—because they had broken away from the Georgia and Alabama Creek towns and migrated southward. Following Andrew Jackson's victory over the Red Stick Creeks in 1814, their numbers were augmented when about one thousand warriors and their families moved into Florida. The problems caused by their arrival were exacerbated by the presence of free blacks who had also chosen to settle near the Seminole. Spain lacked a strong military presence in Florida, and there were frequent raids and counterraids across the border. The destruction of Negro Fort on the Apalachicola River in 1816 was followed by an assault on the Seminole village of Fowltown in Georgia, which inaugurated the First Seminole War. In March 1818, Andrew Jackson led a force of five hundred regulars, one thousand militia, and two thousand Creek warriors across the Florida border against the Seminole, decisively weakening their power and forcing them further southward. Jackson went on to capture St. Marks and Pensacola from the Spanish, and the expedition contributed to the Spanish decision to transfer Florida to the United States in 1821. Two years later, with the Treaty of Moultrie Creek, the Seminole relinquished their territorial claims in northern Florida in return for reservation lands in the south central part of the state.

Peace on both the northern and southern frontiers brought with it congressional demands for a reduction in the size of the army. A 50 percent cut was effected in 1821, bringing the army to approximately six thousand officers and men, and was the last such reduction incurred by the antebellum army. On the eve of war with Mexico in 1846, its strength had risen to 8,349; in 1861 the total stood at 16,367.

Enforcement of trade and intercourse laws regulating relations with the Indians brought the army, more often than not, into conflict with white traders and settlers. The sympathies of military personnel often lay with the Indians, particularly as efforts at law enforcement often brought lawsuits from outraged traders whose supplies of liquor were confiscated, or from white settlers whose title to Indian lands was none too clear. The Indian Removal Act, to transplant eastern Indians west of the Mississippi, was passed in 1830, and removal reached its peak during Jackson's presidency (1833–1841) and inevitably led to army involvement as well. In some instances, such as with the Choctaw and Chickasaw, removal was accomplished without incident. In others there was resistance, as with the Creek (1836) and the Sac and Fox (Black Hawk War of 1832).

The removal issue lay at the heart of the Second Seminole War (1835–1842), which, like the Vietnam War in the twentieth century, was both protracted and unpopular because it was indecisive. It ultimately involved army, navy, and Marine Corps forces, caused 1,466 deaths in the army alone, and cost the government $30 million to $40 million. A series of commanders tried, usually without success, to force the elusive Seminole to stand and fight. The presence of so great a portion of the army in Florida also proved an embarrassment to the government when two rebellions occurred in Canada along the border in 1837–1838. The absence of available troops to calm the tempers of Americans who sided with the Canadian rebels threatened to widen the conflict. This crisis in Anglo-American relations eventually subsided. It also was fortunate that the trans-Mississippi area remained peaceful, although in 1845 the annexation of Texas would bring the United States closer to its conflict with Mexico (1846–1848).

The navy, like the army, had a responsibility to protect American citizens. In the latter case, this occurred within U.S. territory; in the former, it could occur anywhere on the globe. The expansion of overseas trade and commerce after the War of 1812 was accompanied—except in northern European waters—by a naval presence, which is best illustrated by the proliferation of squadrons based abroad. The earliest such squadron, the Mediterranean, was formally established in 1815. The Latin American Wars of Independence (1808–1829) provided a backdrop for the establishment of the West Indian Squadron (1822), the Pacific Squadron (1818), and the Brazil Squadron (1826). Last to appear were the East Indian (1835) and African (1843) squadrons.

Protection of U.S. commerce and those engaged in it was a complex endeavor. Naval officers could be involved in dealing with foreign officials and on occasion were called upon to negotiate commercial treaties. Officers might also be required to rescue American nationals afloat or ashore whose possessions or lives were threatened. These threats could be met with the actual or potential use of force.

In time of peace, any interference with U.S. trade afloat or ashore was considered an act of piracy, and the perpetrators were dealt with accordingly. In time of war, as was the case during the Latin American Wars of Independence, each of the contending parties attempted to ensure that its forces received necessary food, equipment, and military reinforcements while denying these same resources to the opposition. Denial took the form of a naval blockade of ports controlled by the opposition and the capture of all vessels trading with the enemy. These captures were made occasionally by naval vessels but more often by privateers licensed for the purpose. The U.S. government's desire to protect the right of its citizens to trade freely required naval officers enforcing this right to make certain that declared blockades actually were in existence and that they could effectively determine the nature of the seized property. Trading in goods of direct military applicability was considered contraband; all other goods were immune. Naval officers were often required to make decisions or take action without reference to the State or Navy departments in Washington, D.C. This was the case until the expansion of the Atlantic cable network late in the nineteenth century.

West Indian Squadron.

The Caribbean became positively unsafe for U.S. merchant shipping as both the Spanish government and insur-

gent regimes in Venezuela and Colombia issued privateering licenses in carload lots in 1817. Not only did these vessels prey on any weaker ship, but the situation was worsened by the existence of pirates living ashore in uninhabited regions of the Caribbean, particularly portions of Cuba and Puerto Rico. These buccaneers would dash to sea in small craft, snap up their victims, and dispose of the loot ashore, often with the connivance of local officials. In 1819, Congress empowered the navy to convoy U.S.-flag vessels and to capture any pirate vessel interfering with commerce, which was easier said than done. The formation of the West Indian Squadron in 1822 helped. Under the command, successively, of James Biddle (1822–1823), David Porter (1823–1824), and Lewis Warrington (1825–1826), the threat of piracy was finally eliminated, but the tide did not begin to turn until the squadron's vessels were downsized to beat the pirates at their own game, and Spanish authorities in Cuba and Puerto Rico extended permission for the pursuit of pirates ashore. The cooperation of the Royal Navy also helped.

Pacific Squadron.

Life was equally difficult for successive naval commanders off the west coast of South America. The Spanish navy lacked sufficient ships to effectively blockade rebel Chilean ports, but U.S. vessels that chanced to be in any of these ports when a Spanish warship appeared were liable to seizure. The Chileans made strenuous efforts to establish a navy, and in due course succeeded in wresting control of the eastern Pacific from the Spanish.

In November 1819, Chilean Admiral Thomas Cochrane was sent in a cutting-out expedition to seize the Spanish frigate *Esmerelda* in the harbor of Callao, Peru. Spanish forces ashore, assuming U.S. naval complicity in the assault, fired upon the USS *Macedonian*. The vessel's tender, sent ashore for supplies, was also fired upon; two crewmen were killed and six were wounded. An American schooner, the *Rampart*, also came under fire and was abandoned by its crew. For a time it appeared that Americans ashore and in the nearby capital of Lima were in danger from loyalist mobs. Captain John

Downes of the *Macedonian* entered a vigorous protest with the Spanish viceroy, who released the *Rampart* and promised to conduct a thorough investigation of the entire episode. The triumph of the insurgents in Peru and Bolivia made the task of U.S. naval officers much easier as the wars in Latin America drew to a close.

Mexico's proximity to the United States and its continuing political and social instability after independence from Spain was achieved in 1821 seemed to presage a significant level of involvement by the U.S. Navy. Such involvement as did take place occurred following the independence of Texas (1836), when Mexican efforts to institute a blockade of the Texas coast were vitiated by the navy's recognition of Texan belligerence. U.S. warships frequently escorted merchant vessels through the blockade. The seizure of the Mexican warship *General Urrea* by Commander William Mervine for having illegally detained two American merchantmen created a brief war scare in both countries.

The actions in October 1842 of Commodore Thomas ap Catesby Jones caused even greater damage to Mexican-American relations. Jones, the commander of the Pacific Squadron, received information from the U.S. consul in Mazatlán that led him to believe that war between the two countries was imminent. He also had to deal with the reported sale of the province of California to Great Britain and the mysterious departure of British and French warships stationed in the eastern Pacific. With the *United States* and the *Cyane*, Jones sailed to Monterey, capital of Alta California. Hearing nothing that might cause him to change his intended course of action, Jones demanded the surrender of the port and took possession of Alta California in the name of the United States. Two days later, as information came to light proving that war was not imminent, he restored Monterey to the Mexican authorities and sailed away. He was recalled as squadron commander but was subject to no further disciplinary action at the government's hands.

South Atlantic Squadron.

Brazil established its independence from Portugal in 1822 without undue violence, but soon after came into conflict with Argentina over the Banda Oriental (Uruguay). Brazil, which enjoyed command of the sea during much of its 1825–1828 war, established a blockade of the Rio de la Plata that affected American merchant shipping. Captain Jesse D. Elliott (*Cyane*) and Commodore Biddle (*Macedonian*) were involved in separate episodes, the former insisting that foreign shipping must have prior notification of the blockade, and the latter successfully protesting against the requirement that U.S. vessels purchase bonds from the Brazilian government. The bonds would be forfeit should such ships attempt to run the blockade. In December 1828, Commander Daniel Turner with the *Erie* cut out the Argentine privateer *Federal* in the harbor of Swedish St. Bartholomew. The Swedish authorities had refused Turner's demand for the *Federal*'s surrender because of the seizure of a U.S. vessel bound for Brazil. The seizure occurred after the end of the Argentine-Brazil conflict, a fact known to the privateer's captain. Some years later, Turner, back on the South Atlantic station, seized a U.S.-owned slave ship, the *Porpoise*, for violation of U.S. laws. In this instance his action was repudiated and apologies made to the Brazilian government.

A major crisis in U.S.-Argentine relations erupted in 1831–1832. The governor of the Falkland Islands seized several U.S. merchantmen that, he claimed, had engaged in illegal sealing among the islands. Their cargoes were seized and the crews imprisoned. Protests to mainland authorities proved unavailing. Commander Silas Duncan (*Lexington*), arriving off Puerto Soledad late in December 1831, forced the surrender of the port, dismantled its guns, liberated the captive American crewmen, and broke up the Argentine settlement there. The Argentine government subsequently severed diplomatic relations with the United States. Duncan's action was upheld by his government, even though he had exceeded his orders. The British government, which also claimed the Falklands, seized them soon after the *Lexington* departed, in part to preempt a possible takeover by the U.S. government.

Juan Manuel Rosas, president of Argentina, imposed an intermittent blockade of Uruguayan ports between 1843 and 1852. The governments of France and Great Britain opposed this action, and Rosas, hoping to enlist the sympathy and support of the United States, refrained from interfering with U.S. merchant vessels. In September 1844 a warship of the Uruguayan rebel movement that Rosas supported was pursuing a fishing vessel. In the course of its pursuit, a nearby U.S. merchantman was struck accidently by gunfire. Assuming the complicity of Argentine vessels on blockade duty, Captain Philip Voorhees (*Congress*) captured them all in rapid succession, which resulted in the raising of the blockade on Montevideo. Voorhees, however, was under orders to observe strict neutrality between the contending parties. Although he subsequently freed the Argentine warships, he made a bad situation worse by announcing his refusal to recognize a reimposed Argentine blockade. Voorhees's actions were overruled by Commodore Daniel Turner of the Brazilian squadron. Voorhees himself was recalled and court-martialed, but rather than being dismissed from the service, he received a five-year suspension of duty.

Improbably, in 1859 the U.S. government dispatched a major naval expedition to the Rio de la Plata. Under the command of Commodore William B. Shubrick, it consisted of nineteen warships, mounting an aggregate two hundred guns, and comprising twenty-five hundred officers and men. This expedition came about because of a variety of disputes with the Paraguayan dictator Carlos Antonio López. Equally capable was the American adventurer and former naval officer Edward A. Hopkins, who tried to throw his weight around; navy Lieutenant Thomas Jefferson Page, who in the course of exploring the rivers of the Paraguay-Paraná system exceeded his authority; and Lieutenant William N. Jeffries, whose vessel, the *Water Witch*, was fired upon by a Paraguayan fort after ignoring repeated requests to withdraw. Matters were amicably resolved, thanks largely to the efforts of commissioner James B. Bowlin, and U.S. merchant vessels were permitted to ply

Paraguayan rivers. It was not the threat of force that gave López pause—most of the vessels of Shubrick's force could not ascend the river any distance—but rather the prospect of a U.S. blockade of the Rio de la Plata disposed all sides to conciliation.

West Indian Squadron.

Growing interest in the acquisition of Cuba (President James K. Polk unsuccessfully offered Spain $100 million for it in 1848), particularly in the southern states, involved the navy in thwarting several filibustering episodes. Three such expeditions, led by a Cuban exile, Narciso López, were mounted from U.S. territory against Cuba. The first, in 1849, was broken up before it got started by order of President Zachary Taylor. The following year, López and five hundred American followers tried again. Leaving New Orleans in three vessels, they sailed to an island off the Yucatán peninsula, boarded one of the vessels, the *Creole*, and managed to elude patroling American and Spanish warships and land 18 May 1850 at Cárdenas, east of Havana. After clashing with Spanish troops, the filibusters reembarked and headed for Key West, Florida, hotly pursued by the Spanish warship *Pizarro*. Arriving just ahead of their pursuer, they avoided capture and possible execution because Lieutenant John Rodgers, commanding the USS *Petrel*, insisted that although the *Creole* and its crew had been guilty of piracy, he could not allow the seizure of vessel or crew in a U.S. port. Acquitted by a U.S. court, López and four hundred followers tried once again in 1851. Going ashore at Bahia Honda on 11 August, one detachment moved inland while the other remained to guard the expedition's supplies. The first group was attacked by converging Spanish forces, and all of López' force was captured. The leaders were subsequently executed in Havana.

The navy was heavily involved in events in Nicaragua soon after. Nicaragua represented one of the two routes across the Central American isthmus—Panama was the other—utilized by those preferring a sea route to the California goldfields. New Yorker Cornelius Vanderbilt and other investors had established the Acces-

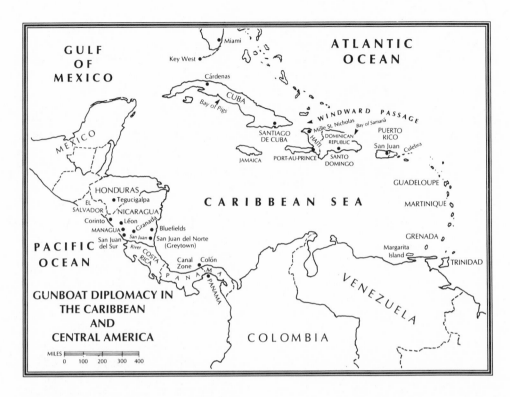

GUNBOAT DIPLOMACY IN
THE CARIBBEAN
AND
CENTRAL AMERICA

sory Transit Company (ATC), with a major terminus at San Juan del Norte. This port near the mouth of the San Juan River, also called Greytown, lay within the British protectorate of Mosquitia. Greytown had been named a free port, with the right to levy its own harbor duties on goods landed there. Vanderbilt's refusal to pay duties in 1851 led to his ship being fired upon by a British warship. Refused harbor, the ship was compelled to return to the United States. Because the U.S. government did not recognize the protectorate, this episode had ominous overtones of a major crisis in Anglo-American relations. That it did not become so (despite the dispatch of U.S. warships to Greytown) was due to the efforts of the British naval commander in the Caribbean who repudiated the actions of his subordinate in firing upon Vanderbilt's vessel in the first place.

Two years later, some Greytown inhabitants sought to dismantle some ATC property at nearby Punta Arenas, but were stopped by Captain George N. Hollins in command of the *Cyane*. This was merely a curtain-raiser to an

even more serious episode in 1854, triggered by the murder of a Greytown native by the captain of one of Vanderbilt's ships and the attempted arrest of a former U.S. consul who intervened on the captain's behalf. Word of this incident prompted the dispatch of the *Cyane* to Greytown once more; Hollins was ordered to uphold the authority of the United States and to show that its nationals could not be subject to arrest with impunity. Arriving on 11 July 1854, Hollins learned from a U.S. commercial agent for Central America that the inhabitants would not pay for destruction of ATC property nor apologize for the assault on the former consul. Hollins formally demanded restitution; if it was not forthcoming, he declared he would bombard the town the next day. He was as good as his word. His actions ultimately were upheld by the U.S. government in the face of a vigorous British protest on the ground that although he had stretched his orders, he had not exceeded them.

This was not the navy's last involvement in Nicaragua. In 1856 the country was taken over by filibusterer William Walker, who erred by cancelling the ATC's concession and becoming dependent for supplies upon rivals of Commodore Vanderbilt. The commodore struck back, helping to form a coalition of other Central American states against Walker and interdicting supplies and reinforcements ordered from New York. U.S. Navy Commander Charles H. Davis was sent to the Pacific coast of Central America with orders to protect American citizens and their property. Arriving at San Juan del Sur in February 1857, he was soon in contact with Walker. Davis was instrumental in working out an agreement between the beleaguered Walker and opposing Costa Rican forces, whereby Walker agreed to leave the country, unharmed, in return for surrendering his weapons.

Walker had no sooner returned to the United States than he planned another expedition to Nicaragua, which sailed from Mobile, Alabama, in mid-November 1857, landing near Greytown despite the presence of a U.S. warship. On 6 December, Commodore Hiram Paulding appeared off Greytown and leveled the guns of the *Wabash, Saratoga,* and *Fulton* at Walker's camp; a landing party cordoned it off. Walker was captured and once again he and his men returned to the United States. Paulding received a reprimand and a brief suspension from duty for having exceeded his authority by seizing Walker in Nicaraguan territory.

The navy also became involved in two brief episodes in Panama at this time. The first intervention followed the so-called Watermelon Riot of April 1856; the second followed an outburst of unrest in September 1860. Naval forces went ashore at Panama City on both occasions to maintain or to restore order. Other occasions would arise for similar displays of force on the isthmus during the next half century.

East Indian Squadron.

Across the Pacific, China posed a different set of problems. Commercial relations had begun in the eighteenth century through the southern port of Canton— the only one where westerners were permitted. The first U.S. naval vessel did not visit Chinese waters until 1819; the de facto establishment of the East Indian Squadron in 1835 signified a more regular naval presence, but formal relations between the United States and China had to await the Treaty of Wanghia in 1844. Ratifications were exchanged in 1846. Aside, however, from operations to suppress piracy along the south China coast, no U.S. warship used force or intervened ashore until the 1850s, during the internal convulsions brought on by the Taiping Rebellion, which began in 1849, and the Arrow War (1856–1858), in which Great Britain and France went to war against China.

The city of Shanghai had been occupied by Taiping rebels in the spring of 1854, and imperial troops attempted its recapture. When a U.S.-owned vessel was halted by imperial troops and its crew taken into custody, Commander John Kelly (USS *Plymouth*) compelled their return. Kelly and the *Plymouth*'s crew also took part on 4 April 1854 in an assault with British forces against imperial troops camped outside the city. Two years later, with the Arrow War under way, imperial forces in the barrier forts below Canton fired on two U.S. merchantmen. Unable to obtain assurances from Chinese authorities that similar incidents would not occur again, Commodore James Armstrong ordered Commander Andrew H. Foote, the new commander of the *Plymouth,* and the *Levant* into action. In an operation lasting from 16 to 22 November 1856, Foote's forces, at a cost of seven dead and twenty-nine wounded, successfully stormed four major forts and captured nearly two hundred guns from imperial troops. Armstrong refused to be drawn into the Sino-British conflict, having finally received assurances that U.S. vessels would not be harassed again.

Commodore Josiah Tattnall was less restrained three years later. Tattnall, in a chartered Chinese steamer, observed an Anglo-French assault on the Taku forts on 25 June 1859. The British commander, Admiral James Hope, had three flagships shot from under him; Tattnall had himself rowed to the fourth and, despite admonitions from the U.S. minister, John E. Ward, not to become involved, utilized his steamer to tow British reinforcements into range. He also authorized his men to man the guns on the fourth British flagship and later that day took ashore a British landing party that failed to storm the Great South Fort. Tattnall escaped a court-martial, probably because of the favorable British governmental reaction to his doings. Anglo-American relations were well served, even if Sino-American relations suffered.

Contacts with Japan were even more limited than those with China. It was not until 1846 that a U.S. warship visited Japanese waters, when Commodore Biddle entered Edo (Tokyo) Bay with the USS *Columbus* and *Vincennes* to inquire whether or not Japanese ports might be opened to American shipping. The Japanese refused, and Biddle sailed away. Three years later, Commander James Glynn (USS *Preble*) succeeded in obtaining the release of some U.S. sailors at Nagasaki. Neither experience promised much success to Commodore Matthew C. Perry on his expedition to "open" Japan to U.S. commerce. On his first visit in July 1853, the Japanese agreed to accept a letter from President Millard Fillmore outlining trade proposals. Perry returned to Edo Bay in February 1854, remaining in Japanese waters until late June. The Treaty of Kanagawa, signed on 31 March, provided that shipwrecked U.S. sailors would be cared for, and also authorized the opening of two ports—Hakodate and Shimoda—to American vessels for supplies and provisions.

The East Indian Squadron, as its name implied, had a greater area of responsibility than China and Japan. The Indian Ocean, Southeast Asia, and the Dutch East Indies also lay within its sphere. When the Malayan inhabitants of Kuala Batu, in northwestern Sumatra, seized and plundered a Salem, Massachusetts, vessel engaged in the pepper trade in 1831, the Jackson administration dispatched Captain John Downes to obtain an apology and redress. Downes, not stopping to negotiate, sent ashore a force of 282 sailors and marines, captured four forts, and killed nearly a hundred Malays. Although publicly defended by the administration, Downes was privately castigated for failing to enter into negotiations with the local inhabitants before resorting to force. His naval career was ruined.

Commodore George C. Read was dispatched on a commerce-protecting mission in 1838 with orders to stop in Sumatra to see if the Malays had been truly pacified. Learning in Ceylon of the plunder of another U.S. vessel, he arrived off Kuala Batu on 22 December 1838. Having requested and failed to receive either the guilty parties or restitution for the goods seized, he bombarded Kuala Batu on 25 December and nearby Muki 1 January 1839. Unlike Downes, Read followed his instructions. Neither officer's action, however, permanently altered Malay behavior.

Pacific Squadron. A growing U.S. presence in the Kingdom of Hawaii led to the appearance of the navy, the first warship arriving in 1826. Later that year Commander Thomas ap Catesby Jones of the USS *Peacock* negotiated an agreement with the Hawaiian monarchy that provided for peace between the two nations and granted most-favored-nation status to merchants of both countries. Although the treaty was never ratified, it nevertheless was observed by both countries for many years until superseded by an 1849 trade pact. The growing U.S. commercial presence, which achieved predominance by midcentury, neither foreshadowed annexation by the United States nor precluded it by other powers. When in 1843 a British naval officer unilaterally annexed the kingdom, Commodore Lawrence Kearny of the USS *Constellation* protested the action, which was soon nullified by the British admiral commanding the Pacific Squadron. The following year the governments of France, Great Britain, and the United States agreed to the continued independence of the islands.

A significant U.S. naval presence among the islands of Polynesia and Melanesia, south of the equator, dates from the time of the Charles Wilkes Exploring Expedition of 1838–1842. Agreements signed with Samoa and Fiji chiefs to protect the persons and property of Americans, although praiseworthy, could not be enforced. Less praiseworthy were punitive expeditions in 1840–1841 in Samoa, Fiji, and the Gilbert Islands, when the destruction of villages (and their inhabitants) by the U.S. Navy often exceeded the crimes committed. In 1855, Commander Edward B. Boutwell aboard the USS *John Adams* extorted an agreement from a Fiji chief recognizing vastly inflated U.S. claims for property damage. A second treaty inflicted upon Chief Thakombau in 1858 led him to offer Fiji to the British government if it would agree to assumption of the debt. The offer was refused; it was not until 1874 that Fiji was passed to British rule.

Mediterranean Squadron.

There was proportionately less need for the protection of persons and property by the navy in European waters than in other portions of the globe, but on occasion a naval presence could be useful. One such instance occurred in 1832, when U.S. naval vessels at Naples in the Kingdom of the Two Sicilies lent weight to efforts to reach agreement on spoliation claims stemming from the Napoleonic wars. In the aftermath of the revolutions of 1848 in Hungary, Germany, France, and Italy, there was much showing of the flag, particularly in the Italian peninsula. These operations lessened as peace was restored.

The Hungarian uprising of 1848 against Austria, crushed the following year by a massive Russian intervention, incited considerable sympathy for the Hungarian revolutionaries by the American public. Lajos Kossuth and Martin Koszta, two revolutionaries who had fled to the Ottoman Empire, were offered passage by the United States minister to Turkey in an American warship. Captain John C. Long refused to compromise American neutrality, however, by permitting Kossuth to disembark at Marseilles when France refused him permission to transit the country. Kossuth eventually made his way to the United States, where he received a tumultuous welcome. Austro-American relations plunged accordingly.

A potentially more serious incident arose in 1853 when Koszta was abducted and confined aboard an Austrian warship in the harbor of Smyrna (İzmir) in Turkey. Commander Duncan N. Ingraham demanded Koszta's release and was refused. On 2 July 1853, he issued an ultimatum stating that he would release Koszta himself, using force if necessary. The Austrian captain finally agreed, and Ingraham's actions were upheld despite the fact that Koszta was not an American citizen.

African Squadron.

In 1824 the West Indian Squadron had West Africa added to its area of responsibility. The dispatch of individual vessels from time to time had done little to deter a thriving trade in slaves there, nor were British vessels on that station able to stop ships flying the U.S. flag. The Webster-Ashburton Treaty of 1842 provided for the establishment of a West African Squadron and promised a more effective assault against the slavers. Successive commodores, however, were hampered by orders to further U.S. commerce to West Africa as a first order of business. In addition, many U.S. warships were too deep draft to effectively interdict the inshore traffic. In 1862 an Anglo-American treaty gave the British navy the right to search U.S.-flag vessels suspected of carrying slaves.

Between 1815 and 1862, therefore, the navy's overseas squadrons increased from one to six, establishing a presence in most of the globe's oceans.

The Civil War.

In similar fashion, the army moved westward, from the upper Great Lakes–Mississippi region in 1817 to the fringe of the Great Plains, Texas, and, in the 1840s and 1850s, to the Southwest, California, and the Pacific Northwest. Within these larger maritime and territorial spheres, both services continued to perform increasingly traditional roles—protecting American settlers, traders, and nationals abroad; supporting trade and commercial expansion; and, on occasion (as in Kansas and Utah territories), responding to breakdowns in civil authority. The Civil War interrupted these operations as officers and men of the army returned to the East and vessels on foreign stations were called home. The Civil War did not, however, cause any fundamental change in the peacetime missions of either service.

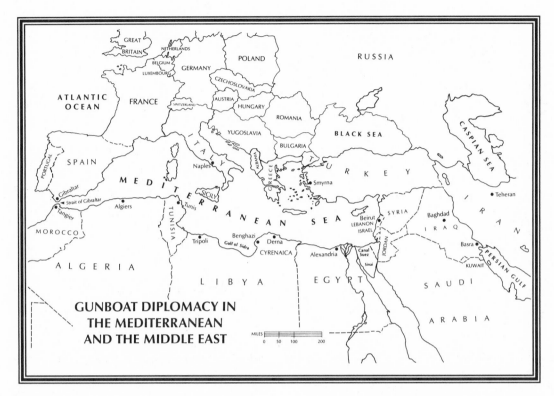

Naval vessels from the disbanded overseas squadrons served on the Union blockade of the Atlantic and Gulf coasts or were employed to hunt down commerce raiders. The army's pacification of the trans-Mississippi and Far West perforce ended, but its role was taken up by settlers and militia. The conflict between North and South did not end Indian-white conflict, only the regular army's dominant role in such fighting. In some locales, regular forces were committed, such as the upper Mississippi region in 1863 and 1864.

RECONSTRUCTION AND THE BEGINNINGS OF IMPERIALISM, 1865–1885

The war's end in 1865 led to the shrinkage of both services to peacetime levels and a resumption of traditional peacekeeping roles. The navy's overseas squadrons were reconstituted, and the army resumed its role of frontier con-

stabulary. Thus for both services the thirty-eight-year interval between the end of the Civil War and the outbreak of the Spanish-American War bore many similarities with the antebellum era. There were differences as well, particularly with the army.

The presence along the Texas-Mexican frontier of a force of fifty-two thousand troops under the command of General Philip Sheridan in June 1865 was especially helpful to the efforts of Andrew Johnson's administration to keep the civil war in Mexico from spreading northward. Their presence also led to the withdrawal of French forces from Mexico—a withdrawal that occurred within two years.

Another peacekeeping mission—more precisely, the maintenance of law and order in the South—proved less easy to accomplish. On average, one-third of the army was stationed in the military districts of the South from 1865 to 1869, and although the percentage fluctuated over the remaining years of Reconstruction, it never went below 13 percent. Neither the experiences of the Mexican War nor its service in the

South during the Civil War had prepared the army for this postwar duty.

Nor did its antebellum experiences of peace-keeping prove helpful in its policing of labor disputes in 1877 and 1894. To many, the railroad strike of 1877 in Pittsburgh and West Virginia and the boycott by the American Railway Union of the Pullman Palace Car Company, which affected the western railroads in 1894, proved as distasteful as their duties during Reconstruction.

Peacekeeping and pacification in the West also had its low points. As had been true of the antebellum army, both officers and troops often showed greater sympathy toward the Indians than their civilian counterparts. Respect for the foe, however, was combined with a determination to force the Indians onto reservations and to keep them there, although the task was frequently unpleasant. The disappearance of the frontier in the 1890s and the simultaneous disappearance of the army's principal constabulary role potentially represented the greatest challenge to its continued existence since its establishment in the 1780s. If one purpose of the army in peacetime is to prepare for war, the question in the 1890s was, war against whom? The answer, surprisingly, was the Spanish empire.

The end of the Civil War enabled the navy to resume the squadron dispositions of the antebellum era. From 1865 to 1885 the occasions on which naval force was used or threatened were few; most occurred in the Caribbean or the Pacific Ocean and east Asia. Naval interest in obtaining a coaling station in the Caribbean indirectly contributed to an instance of "big stick" diplomacy. Efforts by the Johnson administration to acquire a lease of the Bay of Samaná in the Dominican Republic in 1868 having been unsuccessful, the incoming administration of Ulysses S. Grant raised its sights by concluding a treaty in 1869, which, if it had been approved, would have led to the annexation of the Dominican Republic. Opposition to the treaty surfaced both in the Dominican Republic and adjacent Haiti. The toppling of a pro-treaty Haitian president and his replacement by an opponent of

annexation led Grant to order a massing of U.S. warships at Port-au-Prince in 1870. Admiral Charles H. Poor informed the Haitian regime that "any interference or attack therefore by vessels under the Haytien or any other Flag upon Dominicans . . . will be considered an act of hostility to the Flag of the United States, and will provoke hostility in return." In the short run, this declaration had the desired effect, but in the long run contributed to the failure of the treaty in the U.S. Senate.

Two years before, a rebellion broke out in Cuba against Spanish rule, which was to smolder for ten years. As would be the case in the 1890s, success for the insurrectionists was dependent in large part upon the attitude of the U.S. government. Secretary of State Hamilton Fish convinced President Grant that it would be unwise to recognize the belligerency of the rebels. This decision notwithstanding, the Spanish desire to halt the flow of arms and supplies from sympathizers in the United States to the rebels led to two incidents involving the U.S. Navy. The first, in 1869, followed the deaths of two Americans whose ship had been comandeered by Cuban rebels who landed the vessel near Santiago. Admiral Henry H. Hoff, commander of the North Atlantic Squadron, entered into discussions with Spanish authorities in Santiago in July 1869 and received assurances that such incidents would not reoccur.

There was in fact a much more serious recurrence four years later. The *Virginius*, a rebel vessel that had long been a thorn in the side of the Cuban authorities, was captured by a Spanish gunboat and taken into Santiago on 31 October 1873. Fifty-three passengers and crew, many of them Americans, were executed. A British naval officer stopped further retribution by threatening to bombard the town. His threat was echoed several days later by Commander William B. Cushing. The threat of war between Spain and the United States was averted, although not before a substantial concentration of warships was effected at Key West.

Such naval interventions as occurred in East Asian waters in this time period involved protection of merchant vessels and sailors. In 1863 the closure of the Shimonoseki Strait between the Japanese islands of Kyūshū and Honshū was followed in June and July by the firing upon an American steamship by the Choshu clan. Commander David McDougal and the USS *Wyoming* seriously damaged several Choshu vessels and bombarded shore batteries in retaliation, without however succeeding in reopening the strait to commercial use. In September a chartered American warship participated in an international seventeen-vessel assault on Shimonoseki and its forts on 5–6 September, which reopened the strait.

The misadventures of two U.S. merchantmen also led in due course to naval intervention. In 1866 the *General Sherman* ascended the Taedong River in Korea. Trapped in the river by the falling water level, the vessel fired upon a group of Koreans ashore. The local governor responded by ordering the ship and its crew destroyed. Efforts to investigate the affair in 1867 and 1868 proved abortive. Another two years passed before further efforts were made to obtain satisfaction for the destruction of the *General Sherman*, enter into arrangements with the Korean authorities for treatment of shipwrecked sailors, and perhaps conclude a trade treaty. To this end, in the spring of 1871 a fleet commanded by Rear Admiral John Rodgers, consisting of a frigate, two corvettes, and two gunboats (eighty-five guns, 1,240 men), assembled off Inchon. Korean forts on Kanghwa Island opened fire on the gunboats on 1 June. The fire was returned. An ultimatum demanding an apology was ignored, and Rodgers dispatched a landing force against the forts on 10–11 June. This operation was successful in capturing the positions but brought the Korean government no closer to agreement over a trade treaty. In early July the squadron left Korean waters and returned to China.

In March 1867 the American bark *Rover* was driven ashore on the southern tip of Formosa by a storm. The crew managed to get ashore but were killed by local tribesmen (Koaluts). The Asiatic Squadron commander, Admiral Henry H. Bell, ordered to investigate the deaths, took the bit in his teeth and sent a landing party ashore to punish the Koaluts. He, too, was unsuccessful. Later efforts mounted by the U.S. consul at Amoy, China, resulted in a treaty protecting shipwrecked seamen and, not long after, the extension of Chinese control over the area.

Elsewhere in the Pacific that same year, Captain Fabius Stanley aboard the USS *Tuscarora* threatened to bombard the capital of Fiji if the king failed to sign a treaty recognizing his indebtedness to several U.S. merchants. A final settlement was made two years later, and the islands were annexed to Great Britain in 1874. That same year, a joint Anglo-American force went ashore in Honolulu, Hawaii, to break up an attack on the courthouse by followers of a disappointed candidate for the Hawaiian throne.

The European Squadron's area of responsibility in the post–Civil War era included North Africa and western Africa as far south as Portuguese Angola. In 1875 the U.S. consul in Tripoli, Michel Vidal, managed to antagonize the pasha by his opposition to slavery and his outspoken advocacy of an expanded American commercial and naval presence in the province of Cyrenaica. A minor incident involving a Turkish sailor reached an impasse and led Vidal to ask the State Department for naval protection. The USS *Congress* (Captain Earl English), later joined by the *Hartford*, was dispatched to "exact ample reparations." The appearance of the vessels excited local opinion and resulted in the landing of a company of marines with a Gatling gun. Captain English presented what amounted to an ultimatum to the pasha by ordering both vessels to anchor with their guns trained on the shore fortifications. The pasha blinked first, going to the consulate in full uniform to abase himself. The episode did nothing for American prestige either in North Africa or Europe.

A somewhat better performance occurred in Alexandria, Egypt, in 1882. Growing foreign influence and Egyptian nationalism combined to produce riots that resulted in the death of a number of Europeans and rumors of anti-Christian massacres. Rear Admiral James W. A. Nicholson (USS *Lancaster*) commanded the European Squadron, which also included the *Galena, Nip-*

sic, and *Quinnebaug.* All four vessels converged on Alexandria, providing refuge to Americans and other foreign nationals. Nicholson received word on 9 July that the British intended to bombard the forts, which they did on 11–12 July, prompting Egyptian forces to evacuate both the forts and the city. Portions of Alexandria were set on fire and looting was widespread. Acting in response to a request from the U.S. consul, Nicholson sent ashore a landing party of 150 sailors and marines commanded by Lieutenant Commander Caspar F. Goodrich on 14 July. As contingents from other nations went ashore in subsequent days, the U.S. presence gradually was reduced. On 22 July the *Lancaster* and *Nipsic* sailed for Villefranche, France, leaving the other two vessels at Alexandria.

1885–1898

The apparently random, ad hoc interventions that had characterized the navy throughout much of its existence were about to change. The protection of shipwrecked sailors or American nationals threatened by a variety of perils abroad would become more and more the protection or furtherance of U.S. national interests abroad. Some Americans were beginning to look outward, in the process discovering that the European powers were moving to extend their control of Africa, Asia, the Middle East, and perhaps even Latin America—both economically and politically. Technological change in warship design and capability not only threatened to shrink the moats guarding the United States from overseas foes but to render obsolete the traditional reliance on coastal defenses and commerce raiding in time of war. Change began within the navy early in the decade of the 1880s, and the pace of change would accelerate throughout the remainder of the nineteenth century.

Continued concern over U.S. control of Central American isthmian transit routes is a case in point. Interest in the 1840s and 1850s had focused on Nicaragua and Panama. In the former

instance, the signing of the Clayton-Bulwer Treaty of 1850 provided for joint Anglo-American control of a Nicaraguan canal. In the latter case the Bidlack-Mallarino Treaty with Colombia provided U.S. nationals freedom of transit of the isthmus on equal terms with Colombian nationals. For its part, the government of the United States undertook to guarantee the neutrality of the isthmus and ensure that freedom of transit was not interrupted. On a number of occasions, and always at the invitation of Colombian authorities, naval forces were employed ashore or afloat in times of domestic unrest or revolution, as in 1865, 1873, and 1879. The beginning of the Ferdinand de Lesseps Panama Canal venture in 1881 was answered by a U.S. governmental pronouncement that its policy was a canal under U.S. control. In 1884 the Frelinghuysen-Zavala Treaty with Nicaragua provided for a U.S.-controlled canal, but the Senate refused to approve it. Matters rested there when revolution in Colombia in 1885 was followed by interruption of isthmian transit and much destruction of property.

A cable dated 1 April 1885 from the U.S. consul in Colón, Panama, reported the burning of much of the town and threats of death to American nationals on the isthmus. The administration of Grover Cleveland authorized a full-scale intervention. At its height it comprised six vessels from the North Atlantic Squadron and two from the Pacific Squadron. Between them they put ashore a landing force of four hundred men—the largest number actually employed in an amphibious operation abroad between the Mexican War and the Spanish-American conflict. Rear Admiral James E. Jouett, the expedition's commander, was instructed to restore freedom of transit, protect American lives and property, but to "interfere in no respect" with Colombian authority. By late April the worst was over, and the landing force was withdrawn. Pressure for a permanent naval presence on or near the isthmus was rejected by Secretary of the Navy William C. Whitney, and normal operations were resumed by vessels of both squadrons, although care was taken to keep at least one naval ship at Colón and Panama City as frequently as possible.

Trouble of a different sort and in a different quarter greeted the Republican administration of President Benjamin Harrison in 1889. The governments of Great Britain, Germany, and the United States had supported commercial and strategic interests developed by their nationals in Samoa in the southwest Pacific. By 1880 all had concluded treaties with Samoan rulers; all desired coaling stations. These conflicting interests and aspirations had led to the dispatch of naval forces to the islands. In early March rumors of a clash between German and U.S. naval units were followed by a report from Rear Admiral L. A. Kimberly, commander of the Pacific Squadron, that a hurricane sweeping through the islands had destroyed or driven ashore three German warships, the *Eber*, *Adler*, and *Olga*, and three U.S. vessels, the *Trenton*, *Vandalia*, and *Nipsic*. Only HMS *Calliope* had been able to steam out to sea. Secretary of the Navy Benjamin F. Tracy concluded, not inaccurately, that the United States had almost no warships "worthy of the name" in the Pacific Ocean. Much might be made of this in encouraging Congress to loosen the purse strings for further construction of warships; in the meantime, the Samoan situation was resolved—or at any rate placed on hold—by an agreement between the contending nations to establish a tripartite rule of Samoa, an arrangement that would last until 1899.

President Harrison in his inaugural address had called for an expansion of the navy and the acquisition of overseas bases for its use. The search for bases would assume growing urgency and lead to the use or threatened use of force both in the Western Hemisphere and the Pacific Ocean. The Môle Saint Nicolas affair was an example. The overthrow of the president of Haiti in 1888 led to a scramble for power among the generals who had deposed him. One, François Legitime, was elected president and recognized as such by the governments of France and Great Britain. Another, Florvil Hyppolite, sought and received assistance from the U.S.

government, promising in return both commercial concessions and the lease of Môle Saint Nicolas on the Windward Passage to the navy. This latter promise was withdrawn, but Hyppolite's triumph in August 1889 raised expectations in Washington. Rear Admiral Bancroft Gherardi, commander of the North Atlantic Squadron, noting the strategic value of the island of Hispaniola, urged continued support of the Hyppolite regime "by the display of a naval force" at frequent intervals. In due course, the government might obtain possession of the desired base.

The granting of commercial privileges to the Clyde West India Steamship line in 1890 prompted William P. Clyde (a close friend of Secretary of the Navy Tracy) to request the Haitian government to grant use of Môle Saint Nicolas exclusively to his company—and the U.S. Navy. The request was refused by the Hyppolite regime but Admiral Gherardi, appointed as a special agent to negotiate the lease of Môle, tried again early the following year. Despite the presence at Port-au-Prince of his vessels and the navy's Squadron of Evolution, commanded by Rear Admiral John G. Walker, Gherardi failed to secure a lease for Môle. In the final analysis, the U.S. government was unwilling to seize Môle itself or to force the Haitian government to cede it. Lacking an enemy in the Caribbean at the time, there was no imperative either to acquire Caribbean bases or to deny their acquisition by a potential foe.

At this point events in Chile distracted the attention of the administration. In January 1891, civil war broke out between supporters of President José Manuel Balmaceda and his congressionalist opponents. Although proclaiming neutrality, the United States government continued to recognize the Balmaceda regime for a time, and raised the ire of the opposition by granting asylum to Balmacedistas in the U.S. embassy and aboard naval vessels in Valparaiso roadstead. The USS *Baltimore*, commanded by Captain Winfield S. Schley, carried a number of refugees to Peru in September, and against the wishes of the insurgents had also been involved in a cable-laying operation off Iquique. The pursuit and seizure of the insurgent vessel *Itata*, accused of having violated U.S. neutrality laws, earlier that summer also created a climate of opinion hostile toward the navy.

In any event, the triumph of the congressionalist faction and its recognition by the United States government early in the fall should have quieted matters but did not. Sailors from the *Baltimore*, which had remained at Valparaiso, were granted liberty on 16 October. A subsequent riot ashore by a Chilean mob left two American sailors dead and led to a full-blown crisis in U.S.-Chilean relations. The U.S. government subsequently demanded both an apology and reparations from the Chilean regime. The USS *Yorktown* (Commander Robley D. Evans) remained at Valparaiso through most of December 1891 and January 1892, figuratively daring the Chileans to do their worst. Perhaps fortunately, the *Yorktown* had sailed for Callao when a U.S. ultimatum arrived late in January 1892. The Chilean government apologized for the incident, paid $75,000 to the injured and survivors of the dead sailors, and war was averted.

In the Pacific, long-standing interest in the Hawaiian Islands led the Harrison administration in 1890 to propose the establishment of a U.S. protectorate over the islands. A feature of the proposal would have made the 1887 cession of Pearl Harbor to the navy both permanent and exclusive. The failure of the protectorate and the ending of commercial reciprocity led to a revolution in January 1893 by pro-American interests, which overthrew the government of Queen Liliuokalani. A timely landing of marines from the USS *Boston*, commanded by Captain Charles G. Wiltse, to protect U.S. property helped to consolidate the new regime's power. A treaty of annexation was concluded and submitted to the U.S. Senate in mid-February. Democratic opposition prevented its prompt ratification, and it was later withdrawn by the administration of Grover Cleveland. Hawaiian annexation did not occur for another five years.

A revolution in Brazil against the government of Floriano Peixoto late in 1893 claimed the attention of the Cleveland administration and Secretary of State Walter Q. Gresham. The insurgents, with tacit support from some of the European powers, were opposed to a recently concluded commercial reciprocity treaty with the United States. Gresham evolved a policy that required a U.S. naval presence at Rio de Janeiro, which necessitated denying the insurgents belligerency status (which would render an insurgent blockade of Rio illegal), thus frustrating their attempt to blockade Rio and impose a ban on imported goods, thereby starving the Peixoto regime of customs revenues. Gresham replaced two U.S. naval commanders who had pursued a policy of strict neutrality between the Brazilian government and the insurgents. A third, Rear Admiral Andrew E. K. Benham, aligned his South Atlantic Squadron forces behind Gresham's policy. Matters came to a head late in January 1894, when an insurgent vessel fired a blank across the bows of a U.S. merchant ship being escorted to its berth by the USS *Detroit*. The *Detroit* replied with a live shell into the side of the insurgent craft, warning that if they fired on merchant ships again they would be sunk. Further efforts by the insurgents to obtain belligerency status were denied by the U.S. government; this time the European nations followed the American lead. By April the insurrection had collapsed.

That same year the Nicaraguan government moved to establish its control over the Mosquito Indians who inhabited the Caribbean coast. The area had been a British protectorate since the 1850s, although within the past decade an increasing U.S. economic interest, attributable to the development of banana plantations, had become apparent. The British reaction to the Nicaraguan move was to dispatch a naval force to Bluefields and disarm the Nicaraguans. Gresham used the occasion to force the British to relinquish control of the protectorate (formal Nicaraguan sovereignty was recognized in December 1894) and at the same time ensure that President José Santos Zelaya would not infringe upon U.S. rights in the Mosquito reservation or disturb the Maritime Canal Company concession. Both policies ultimately were successful. A

July uprising by the Mosquito authorities against Nicaraguan rule resulted in the landing of U.S. forces to restore order, an episode that marked the beginning of the British retreat in the Caribbean.

The first Venezuelan Crisis (1895–1896)—perhaps an exercise in gunboat diplomacy without the gunboats—was simultaneous with another one in Mediterranean waters. Turkish repression of Armenian nationalism, and the threat to sympathetic American missionaries and their property in the interior, led to an increased naval presence in the eastern Mediterranean from 1894 to 1897. This U.S. presence in Ottoman ports proved unable to aid the missionaries materially and was unsuccessful in obtaining redress for destroyed property. The only successful episode of gunboat diplomacy in the Mediterranean at this time occurred at Tangiers in 1897 when a naval presence reinforced the U.S. consul's demand for an apology and an indemnity growing out of the robbery of a servant of a naturalized American.

A crisis materialized in the Caribbean rather than the Mediterranean. A renewal of the Cuban rebellion against Spanish rule in 1895 overshadowed for a time a growing U.S.-German antagonism. This state of affairs had developed in 1897 with two episodes of German gunboat diplomacy in areas traditionally of interest to the United States. The first incident followed the murder of two German missionaries by Boxers in China, precipitating Germany's seizure of Kiaochow on the Shantung Peninsula. An insult by Haitian officials to a German merchant, Emil Luders, provided the occasion for the second when Germany threatened a bombardment of Port-au-Prince if an apology and indemnity were not forthcoming. Japanese-American relations also were briefly strained that same year by Japanese protests over the proposed U.S. annexation of Hawaii. Finally, if the dispatch of the USS *Maine* to Havana in January 1898 can be considered a form of gunboat diplomacy, it surely was one with unintended consequences. The vessel's destruction on 15 February was arguably the greatest single step on the road to war with Spain.

FROM WAR WITH SPAIN TO WORLD WAR I, 1898–1918

The Spanish-American War, undertaken to free Cuba from Spanish rule, had a number of unexpected consequences. High on the list was the decision to acquire the Philippines from Spain for $20 million. The other provisions of the Treaty of Paris of 10 December 1898 were clear-cut and understandable. The island of Guam in the Marianas, which surrendered to Captain Henry Glass of the USS *Charleston* 20 June 1898, was extracted from Spain for use as a coaling station and cable terminus. Puerto Rico, occupied in the latter stages of the war, was also retained by the United States. This acquisition, along with the right to establish a base or bases in Cuba through the Platt Amendment of 1901, significantly improved the navy's strategic position in the Caribbean on the approaches of the Central American isthmus. Independently of the war, but not coincidentally, Hawaii was acquired 7 July 1898 by a joint congressional resolution of annexation.

As for the Philippines, the Asiatic Squadron, commanded by George Dewey, had been given the task of eliminating Spanish naval forces there. Once this was accomplished in early May 1898, an expeditionary force arrived to capture Manila and its environs. Once the United States gained control of the capital, the Philippines might be used as another bargaining chip in subsequent negotiations with Spain. It soon became apparent, however, that whatever the ultimate fate of the islands, independence was not a viable option. If the United States did not retain them, other powers—in particular Germany—would arrive. In retrospect, it is clear that insufficient consideration was given to the aspirations of the Filipinos themselves. The insurrection that had begun in 1896 against Spanish rule now spilled over into an assault on U.S. occupation forces.

Fighting began 4 February 1899, two days before the U.S. Senate approved the Treaty of Paris. The subsequent exercise in peacekeeping (or conquest) was to involve a substantial commitment both by the army and the navy. By the summer of 1900, seventy-thousand troops (approximately three quarters of the army) were in the Philippines. The six naval vessels on the Asiatic station in 1898 increased to thirty in 1899, thirty-five in 1900, and fifty-two in 1901. The conflict, officially declared at an end by President Theodore Roosevelt in July 1902, cost the United States between $400 million and $600 million, 4,234 dead, and 2,818 wounded. Estimates of Filipino casualties run to 20,000 military deaths and perhaps 200,000 civilians. The naval side of the Philippine Insurrection included transporting and supplying U.S. troops, maintaining patrols throughout insular waters to sever insurgent communications, and intercepting the import of arms.

South of the Philippines trouble arose in another quarter. The death of the Samoan king in August 1898 led to the appearance of rival candidates for the throne, one backed by the governments of Great Britain and the United States, the other by Germany. A revolt by the German-supported candidate, Mataafa, broke out early in 1899, prompting the dispatch of the cruiser *Philadelphia*, commanded by Rear Admiral Albert Kautz, to Apia. When the ultimatum to the insurgents to return to their homes was ignored, the *Philadelphia* and two British cruisers bombarded the hinterland 15 March. A subsequent Anglo-American landing party was ambushed on 1 April by Mataafa's forces and lost eight men. At the suggestion of the German government, a tripartite commission was established to restore peace. Admiral Kautz left Samoan waters on 21 May. The commissioners recommended to their governments that Samoa should be ruled by one power. The accord worked out gave Upolu and Savai'i to Germany, Tutuila (with the harbor of Pago Pago) to the United States, and the Tonga Islands and most of the German Solomon Islands to Great Britain. The acquisition of Tutuila, along with uninhabited Wake Island that same year, rounded out U.S. acquisitions in the Pacific.

The significant military presence in the Philippines enabled the U.S. government to respond more forcefully to events in China than would otherwise have been the case. The Ch'ing dynasty, beset by internal foes and the imperial powers, attempted to capitalize on growing antiforeign sentiment within the kingdom to bolster its declining authority. The rise of the antiforeign secret society known as the Righteous Hand, or Boxers, particularly in north China, and increasing attacks on foreign interests prompted the ministers of the foreign powers in China to request an armed demonstration and an expanded military presence in the legation compound in Peking. Matters came to a head in the spring of 1900. At the request of U.S. Minister Edwin H. Conger, the USS *Newark*, flagship of Rear Admiral Louis Kempff, was ordered to Taku at the mouth of the Pei-ho River on 17 May. The vessel landed a force of fifty marines and sixty sailors on 29 May, and two days later, the marines proceeded to Peking by rail with a multinational contingent. They were subsequently involved in the defense of the legation compound during the fifty-five-day siege from 17 June to 14 August.

By 3 June no fewer than twenty foreign warships were off the mouth of the Pei-ho. The shallow-draft monitor *Monocacy*, commanded by Captain Frederick W. Wise, was ordered north from Shanghai. The severing of the Tientsin-Peking railway on 6 June prompted the formation of an international contingent that departed for Peking on 10–11 June. Bowman H. McCalla, captain of the *Newark*, commanded the Americans in the party. The *Monocacy* arrived 15 June and anchored in the Pei-ho above the Taku forts. When the demand for their surrender was refused, the imperial garrison opened fire on gunboats in the river 17 June. Although it did not return the fire, the *Monocacy* was forced to shift its anchorage. Chinese forces also attacked the foreign quarter of Tientsin, and Admiral Kempff received orders to act in unison with the other foreign contingents. Additional forces were ordered north from the Philippines, including the USS *Nashville* and the USS *Oregon*, as well as the Ninth Infantry Regiment (with other units to follow). The force that had set out from Tientsin on 10–11 June had been unable to reach Peking and was required to fight its way back downriver to Tientsin, which had been secured on 23 June.

While a larger force was being assembled, the siege of the legation quarter in Peking continued. On 8 July, Rear Admiral George C. Remey, commander of the Asiatic Squadron, arrived in the USS *Brooklyn*. The international relief expedition of fourteen thousand (including twenty-five hundred Americans commanded by Brigadier General Adna R. Chaffee) departed Tientsin for Peking on 5 August, arriving nine days later to lift the siege. Restoration of order in north China permitted a gradual reduction of U.S. naval and army forces during the fall.

The aftermath of the Spanish-American War proceeded much more smoothly in the Western Hemisphere than in Asia. The occupations of both Cuba and Puerto Rico proceeded without incident, and the Treaty of Paris provided for the annexation of the latter colony. The status of Cuba remained to be settled. Although the Teller Amendment of 1898 had forbidden the annexation of Cuba, it was by no means certain that U.S. occupation of the island would not result sooner or later in something very much like it. Events in the Philippines were to make the administration of William McKinley reluctant to risk something comparable occurring in Cuba. At the same time, certain broader needs vis-à-vis Cuba had to be met. The resulting Platt Amendment, which evolved early in 1901, was ultimately approved without change by the Cuban constitutional convention and the U.S. Senate. The amendment prohibited an independent Cuban government from making treaties with foreign governments that could impair its political or financial independence. The United States would have the right to naval bases in Cuba, and Cuba had to grant the United States "the right to intervene for the preservation of Cuban independence." Cuba thus became a U.S. protectorate, and the right of intervention was to be tested sooner than the U.S. government expected or wished.

Control of Cuba through the Platt Amendment and the acquisition of Puerto Rico—both fruits of the Spanish-American conflict—made U.S. hegemony feasible in the Caribbean. At the same time, it was becoming clear that the U.S. government was about to undertake construction of the long-deferred isthmian canal. The second Hay-Pauncefote Treaty (November 1901) removed fears that Great Britain, the only nation then deemed capable of blocking a canal controlled and fortified by the United States, might actually do so. British acquiescence in U.S. hegemony in the region was accompanied by a growing concern on the part of both naval and civilian policymakers that Germany was able and willing to contest such control. Political instability and the appearance of financial irresponsibility on the part of some of the nations in the area, added to the perceived threat of German intervention, led to the second Venezuelan crisis (1902–1903), the taking of Panama in November 1903, and an expanded U.S. presence in the Dominican Republic.

The Venezuelan crisis could be said to have begun in 1901, when Lieutenant Commander Nathan Sargent reported that the German gunboat *Vineta* had been making hydrographic surveys of the harbors on Margarita Island. It was clear to Sargent that the German government wanted a coaling station there, because German naval leaders had earlier "made a pretext of hydrographic work to lay their plans for obtaining Kiaochow [in 1897]." His report caused considerable unease in Washington. Sargent was recalled for consultation with Navy Department officials and Secretary of State John Hay, Secretary of War Elihu Root, and Senator Henry Cabot Lodge. Despite subsequent denials by the German government, the damage had been done. The appearance in contemporary U.S. naval war plans of Margarita Island as the probable location of a German base in the Caribbean unquestionably stems from this incident.

The refusal of Venezuela's President Cipriano Castro to make payment on bonds worth more than $12.5 million finally exhausted the patience of Germany and Great Britain—never very great in any case when dealing with the Latin American republics. In his first annual message to Congress, President Theodore Roosevelt had declared that the Monroe Doctrine did "not guarantee any state against punishment if it misconducts itself, provided that punishment does not take the form of acquisition of territory by any non-American power." The German government, receiving—as was thought—a green light, decided to initiate a blockade of Venezuelan ports and seizure of gunboats to compel Castro to settle the outstanding debt. The British government, and later the Italian government, joined in the action. Castro asked the United States to arbitrate. In due course, the matter was submitted to the Permanent Court of International Justice at The Hague.

Years later, Roosevelt claimed that German reluctance to arbitrate had caused him to assemble the U.S. battle fleet at Culebra, a small island off the coast of Puerto Rico, for maneuvers. He further claimed to have informed the German ambassador that he would send the U.S. fleet into Venezuelan waters unless Germany agreed to arbitration. In fact, the fleet was sent to Culebra in mid-October 1902, long before the crisis erupted in December, to test some of the conclusions reached during the 1901 summer course at the Naval War College. The planning for these maneuvers had begun months earlier, and in this sense it was purely fortuitous that the U.S. warships were in the Caribbean. Naval officers with the fleet were aware that their presence might well strengthen Roosevelt's hand, preserve peace, and render U.S. diplomacy effective. The broader significance of this episode of muscle-flexing, whether or not an ultimatum was presented to Germany, was that it led to a hardening of naval and civilian attitudes towards the Kaiser's restive global ambitions.

The Venezuelan crisis, in turn, deepened official Washington's already profound apprehension that some European power might intervene in the Isthmus of Panama. Both in 1901 and in 1902, U.S. naval forces were dispatched to the isthmus, and forces landed in order to preserve the freedom of transit of the isthmus (guaranteed to American nationals under the terms of the Bidlack-Mallarino Treaty of 1846). American sailors had gone ashore on many previous occasions, but invariably only after the Colombian government expressly requested assistance in combating local disturbances. On these last two occasions, however, U.S. intervention either occurred before the Colombian authorities requested it or went well beyond the degree of assistance envisioned by Bogotá. At one stage U.S. naval officers denied Colombian forces the use of the Panama railroad until overruled by the U.S. State Department. Reports from these same officers reveal a hardening of attitude to the chronic disturbances on the isthmus. Their major concern was that instability would lead to intervention by other powers in an area of great strategic importance to the United States.

Roosevelt shared the apprehension. From the beginning of his administration, he moved to eliminate residual British influence in Central America and to obtain exclusive U.S. rights to build and fortify a canal. Convinced of the superiority of the Panama route, he directed Secretary of State Hay to conclude an agreement with Colombia. The resulting Hay-Herrán Treaty of 22 January 1903 involved the cession of canal rights to the United States for $10 million. The Colombian legislature insisted on a higher payment (presumably a portion of the $40 million the United States had agreed to pay the New Panama Canal Company for its assets), Roosevelt balked, and from mid-1903 on there was growing talk of the possibility of an uprising on the isthmus that would obtain U.S. support.

Well before the actual insurrection of 3 November 1903, the Navy Department (at Roosevelt's instruction) ordered ships in the Pacific and the Atlantic to steam southward to within easy range of the isthmus. On the eve of the revolution, the cruiser *Nashville* was dispatched from Jamaica to Colón, on the Caribbean side of Panama, with orders to prevent Colombian government troops from suppressing the insurrection. Those instructions miscarried, but the *Nashville* nonetheless arrived in time to lend moral support to the revolutionaries as they resourcefully kidnapped and bribed the senior Colombian officers. At noon on 4 November— the day after the revolution began—Secretary of

State Hay bestowed formal recognition on the newly sovereign republic of Panama. A growing U.S. naval and military presence prevented Colombia from reversing the province's secession.

The ink was scarcely dry on the Hay-Bunau-Varilla Treaty of 18 November 1903, by which the United States acquired virtual sovereignty over Panamanian territory sufficient for construction of the canal, when the United States government moved to close another gap in the Caribbean defense perimeter. The object was the Dominican Republic. In this instance the initiative lay with the State and Navy departments, because Roosevelt, stung by public criticism of his role in the Panama affair, was reluctant to intervene. His hand, however, was forced to some extent by Assistant Secretary of State Francis B. Loomis and Rear Admiral Henry Clay Taylor. Furthermore, when The Hague, deliberating on the Venezuelan claims case, decided that the powers participating in the blockade—Great Britain, Germany, and Italy—were entitled to preferential treatment, an uncomfortable impetus to European intervention in the affairs of other Caribbean states was established.

The navy's General Board was convinced that German merchants were financing one of the insurgent groups active in the Dominican Republic. As a countermeasure, the board urged a course of action that would bring the Dominican Republic under U.S. control. A board memo stated that it would be easy "to develop a request for some sort of occupation by the United States, and this would virtually secure to us control of this most important strategic point in the Caribbean." In conjunction with the army, the navy also began to develop plans for the preemptive seizure of Hispaniola should the United States become involved in war with a European power.

U.S. Minister William F. Powell and Dominican President Carlos Morales drew up a request for a U.S. guarantee of Dominican independence and for military and financial aid against the insurgents, which was presented in February 1904. Roosevelt dispatched several General Board members, accompanied by Loomis, to investigate conditions in the Dominican Republic. On his return, Loomis reported that the country was "approaching—indeed, if it has not already reached—a state of anarchy." After noting that Morales wished to turn the customshouses over to U.S. officials as well as to give the navy a long-term lease of Samaná Bay, he suggested that the status quo could be maintained for the time being by maintaining a strong naval patrol in Dominican waters.

Rear Admiral Taylor recommended that the customshouses be taken over and administered by the U.S. government for at least three years. "It is quite possible," Taylor intoned, "that three years of enforced public order would make the whole country self-governing to the extent Cuba is now." A protectorate along Platt Amendment lines was never far from the mind of Loomis or Taylor. President Roosevelt proposed another solution. The Roosevelt Corollary to the Monroe Doctrine, first enunciated publicly in late May 1904, served notice that the United States was prepared to act as "an international police power" in the Caribbean. Roosevelt's avowed purpose was to forestall European intervention. "If we are willing to let Germany or England act as the policemen of the Caribbean," Roosevelt stated succinctly, "then we can afford not to intervene when gross wrongdoing occurs. But if we intend to say 'Hands off' to the powers of Europe, sooner or later we must keep order ourselves."

Despite continued professed reluctance to intervene, the Roosevelt administration was driven by the logic of the corollary and continued unrest in the Dominican Republic to propose a customs receivership, provided by an agreement of 8 February 1905. Despite difficulties in implementation, the agreement initiated a period of U.S. involvement in Dominican affairs that was to culminate a decade later in a full-fledged protectorate.

Cuba, despite the existence of the Platt Amendment, was finally a subject of military intervention in 1906. Trouble began the preceeding year, when the incumbent president, Tomás Estrada Palma, threw in with the Moderate faction against the Liberals headed by José

Miguel Gomez. When the Moderates fraudulently controlled a September election, the Liberals boycotted the December presidential contest and planned a rebellion. The Liberals hoped that the United States would be forced to intervene and in due course oversee fair elections—elections that the Liberals felt they would be sure to win. The uprising occurred in August 1906. At the request of U.S. Consul General Frank Steinhart, warships were sent to Havana and Cienfuegos.

The Roosevelt administration, reluctant to intervene, was slow to realize that both factions were counting on U.S. intervention to uphold their respective positions. Estrada Palma, rather than compromise with the opposition, resigned in September, and Secretary of War William Howard Taft ordered the marines ashore on 29 September. The second occupation of Cuba lasted only until January 1909. There were to be no further interventions in the Caribbean–Central American region during the remainder of Roosevelt's presidency.

Although the intervention by European powers in Latin American affairs had led to the promulgation of the Roosevelt Corollary, the United States itself was not above resorting to similar interference elsewhere. In 1899, and again in 1901, Tangier was visited by U.S. warships whose captains were instructed to deliver an ultimatum to the authorities ashore where debts owed American nationals were unpaid. In both instances the Moroccan authorities paid up, and the ships' guns remained silent.

In 1903 the Roosevelt administration was involved in an episode at the other end of the Mediterranean. Receiving word on 27 August that the U.S. vice-consul in Beirut, Lebanon, had been killed (it turned out that he had not), Roosevelt ordered several vessels of the European Squadron, commanded by Rear Admiral Charles S. Cotton, to Beirut. The ships arrived 3 August, and three days later rioting broke out in the city between Christians and Muslims. Requests from some of the local representatives of the European powers that a landing force be put ashore were turned down by Admiral Cotton. Calm ashore returned, but the fleet's continued presence there was utilized in an unsuccessful attempt to obtain a settlement of certain other U.S. claims against the Ottoman government. The warships left Beirut 1 February 1904.

The kidnapping of a naturalized U.S. citizen, Ion Perdicaris, by the Moroccan chieftan Ahmed ibn-Muhammed Raisuli on 18 May 1904 from his summer villa near Tangier not only provoked much discussion in the press concerning his release or recapture, but permitted the Roosevelt administration to flex its naval muscles. In the aftermath of Caribbean maneuvers, the South Atlantic Squadron, the European Squadron, and the battleships of the North Atlantic fleet all headed for European waters. The South Atlantic Squadron (Rear Admiral French E. Chadwick) and subsequently the European Squadron (Rear Admiral Theodore Jewell) were diverted to Tangier. The battleships (Rear Admiral Albert S. Barker) were in nearby Gibraltar. The 22 June cable from Secretary of State Hay to the U.S. consul-general in Tangier, Samuel Gummere, stated (for public consumption): "We want Perdicaris alive or Raisuli dead." No forces from the squadrons at Tangier went ashore, however, and when Perdicaris was released the ships departed. One by-product of the U.S. naval presence in the Mediterranean was the agreement on 12 August of the Ottoman government to many long-standing U.S. demands (such as proper treatment of missionaries and their property), coincidentally, just as the European Squadron arrived for a visit in Smyrna.

Amid the changes occurring in east Asia during Roosevelt's presidency, those brought about by the Russo-Japanese War of 1904–1905 were perhaps the most sweeping. Japan's goal was to make the island nation the foremost military power in the region and one with which the United States would have to reckon. Both Japan and China were to serve notice that the old relationships of dominant Western powers and subservient Asian states no longer would apply. China declared a boycott of U.S. goods entering through the treaty ports in late 1905, in part a protest against U.S. exclusion of Chinese laborers, which prompted an expanded U.S. naval presence in Asian ports. Roosevelt also authorized the preparation of an expeditionary force from the Philippines should the need arise. The waning of the boycott in 1906 obviated the use of military forces in China.

Similar discrimination against Japanese immigrants on the U.S. West Coast, such as segregation of Japanese schoolchildren in San Francisco, led to a momentary crisis in U.S.-Japanese relations in 1907. Its peaceful resolution through the "Gentlemen's Agreement" was followed by the decision to send the U.S. battleships from the Atlantic coast to the Pacific, and subsequently across the Pacific on what has become known as the cruise of the Great White Fleet. At first glance what appears as an exercise in gunboat diplomacy against Japan in fact was nothing of the kind. Far from threatening Japan, the cruise was designed to test the capability of moving the battleship fleet to the Pacific should the need arise. The success of the cruise in this respect was demonstrated when the fleet, which departed Hampton Roads, Virginia, in mid-December 1907, arrived at San Francisco in May 1908 on the first leg of the voyage.

Trouble, meanwhile, was brewing closer to home in the Caribbean, an area of traditional concern. The Taft administration had long been unhappy with Nicaragua's President Zelaya. In October 1909 a revolt broke out against Zelaya, centered upon the Caribbean port of Bluefields. The leader of the rebellion, Juan J. Estrada, received substantial financial support and encouragement from the local American community, which hoped to see Central America become independent of Nicaraguan control. Zelaya erred in ordering the execution of two American soldiers-of-fortune serving with the Estrada forces, thereby giving the Taft administration the opportunity to sever diplomatic relations on 1 December. Zelaya resigned two weeks later, turning the presidency over to José Madriz. The rebellion continued, and the United States refused to recognize Madriz's regime. A naval buildup began in Nicaraguan waters—the *Des Moines, Marietta, Tacoma,* and *Prairie* stationed on the Caribbean coast and the *Albany, Yorktown, Vicksburg,* and *Princeton* on the Pacific

coast. Overall command of naval and marine forces rested with Rear Admiral William W. Kimball. He was ordered not to land any forces without authorization from Washington and (following Madriz's accession) to observe "strict neutrality" between the factions.

Kimball found himself in difficulty with the State Department for his apparent sympathies for Madriz and the Liberal faction. A major setback for the Estrada forces in late December led the admiral to recommend the recognition of the Madriz regime. His advice was ignored. Rather than relieving Kimball from command, as he requested, the naval units under his authority were withdrawn for other duty, and on 7 April 1910, the Nicaraguan Expeditionary Squadron was formally disbanded. Madriz now dispatched an expedition against Bluefields, whose capture effectively ended the rebellion.

Bluefields was invested by land and blockaded from the sea by the *Maximo Jerez.* At this point, Commander William W. Gilmer (USS *Paducah*) on his own initiative informed the belligerents that he would permit no fighting in the city, presumably to protect the lives and property of foreign nationals, but also clearly in favor of the Estrada contingent. Both the Navy Department and State Department tried unsuccessfully to find a precedent for Gilmer's action but supported the commander in any event. Gilmer was instructed to ignore the *Maximo Jerez's* blockade of Bluefields on the grounds that it had violated U.S. neutrality statutes by claiming falsely that it was not going to undertake military operations when it sailed earlier from New Orleans. Gilmore was also instructed to ignore the capture of the Bluefields customshouse because the town itself remained under Estrada's control. Madriz' forces, baffled, retreated westward. Conservative opponents of the regime fomented new uprisings against the Liberal government, and on 20 August, Madriz resigned and followed Zelaya into exile.

The course of events in Nicaragua over the next two years substantiated the dictum that whatever can go wrong, will. The Estrada regime was in a perilous position from the beginning, having to fend off charges of subserviency to the United States, infighting among its leaders, and the continued hostility of the Liberal opposition. Attempting to curb his rivals, Estrada was ousted from power in May 1911, and succeeded by Vice President Adolfo Díaz. The Knox-Castrillo Convention, concluded in June 1911, provided that Nicaragua would receive a $15 million loan from a consortium of New York banks, repayment to be secured by customs revenues. The U.S. Senate failed to act on the treaty, and a stop-gap loan of $1.5 million was first rejected then approved by the Nicaraguan assembly, but the government's financial woes continued. With ever more stringent conditions being imposed by the bankers, Nicaraguans feared the country had been sold out to Wall Street interests. A visit by Secretary of State Philander Knox in the spring of 1912 did little to resolve the issues. Díaz, fearing an uprising by the Liberals, moved to arrest his political opponent, but the attempt backfired, and a new rebellion was launched with widespread Liberal support.

With Managua surrounded and bombarded by rebel forces, the U.S. minister, George T. Weitzel, successfully pressed Díaz to request U.S. forces in order to protect the lives and property of foreign nationals. An initial detachment of 100 sailors and marines arrived in Managua in mid-August, followed soon after by an additional 350 marines commanded by Major Smedley D. Butler. The rebels subsequently occupied both Granada and León, severing railroad communications between Corinto and Managua. Two additional marine battalions arrived on 4 September and entrained for Managua. Overall command of forces in Nicaragua, now approximately twelve hundred strong, was assumed by Rear Admiral William H. H. Southerland. Acting Secretary of State Huntington Wilson, comparing the situation in Nicaragua to the Boxer Rebellion in China in 1900, wanted army forces from the Panama garrison sent to Nicaragua, but was opposed by Secretary of War Henry Stimson, who believed the commitment of the army would have an adverse impact on world and regional opinion. Stimson also believed that the unrest in Nicaragua was less crucial to the United States than the revolution in Mexico. In any event, the orders to the Tenth Infantry were cancelled.

Admiral Southerland had hoped to quell the rebellion by denying the rebels the use of the railway to move troops and munitions, and in this respect largely succeeded. Secretary Wilson, fearing that Southerland was carrying neutrality to an extreme (government forces also had been denied railway use), prevailed upon Taft to revise the admiral's orders. Southerland also was told to clear the remaining forces, led by Liberal General Benjamin Zeledon, from their position near Masaya. Butler's assault force of three battalions stormed Coyotepe Hill on 4 October, routing Zeledon's force. León, a Liberal stronghold, was occupied by another marine battalion. With the exception of minor skirmishing in northern towns, the rebellion was over. The largest commitment up to that time of U.S. forces overseas in peacetime— 2,350 sailors and marines—was withdrawn, except for a legation guard of one hundred marines. Díaz remained in power, at some cost to Nicaraguan autonomy.

The change of administrations in Washington in 1913, contrary to expectation, brought about little change in policy in the Caribbean–Central American region. No less than his predecessors, Woodrow Wilson desired stability in Latin America and in order to achieve it was prepared to countenance intervention in a variety of forms. The outbreak of revolution in Mexico in 1910 threatened substantial U.S. interests that had developed during the lengthy rule of Porfirio Díaz. The subsequent overthrow of popularly elected President Francisco Madero by one of his generals, Victoriano Huerta, in 1913 led Wilson to refuse to recognize the Huerta administration and to lift a U.S. arms embargo so that the Constitutionalist opposition could more easily obtain weapons. Wilson also undertook to build up a U.S. naval presence off the Gulf and Pacific coasts of Mexico.

The navy's presence off Veracruz and Tampico in Mexico created the possibility of an incident, as the Constitutionalist forces moved to invest the port of Tampico and its nearby oil fields. On 9 April 1914, a party of sailors from the USS *Dolphin* was apprehended and detained by Federalist forces as they were removing supplies of gasoline from a warehouse. Their release, together with an apology for their detention, soon followed, but Rear Admiral Henry T. Mayo, on his own authority, demanded a more formal apology and a salute of the U.S. flag. His demand was upheld by Wilson and Secretary of State William Jennings Bryan. The refusal of Huerto to acquiesce created the condition for a more significant military riposte, which occurred some miles up the Pánuco River, at nearby Veracruz. Orders to land sailors and marines from the force off Veracruz, commanded by Rear Admiral Frank F. Fletcher, went out from Washington 20 April. Contrary to expectations, the occupation of the town was not unopposed. It took two days—21 and 22 April—to complete occupation in the face of sporadic opposition and sniper fire. Within four days nearly twenty-four hundred marines and four hundred sailors were ashore, later joined by a brigade of army troops under the command of General Frederick Funston. At a cost of nineteen dead and forty-seven wounded, U.S. forces secured Veracruz. It soon became apparent that this would not be followed by a march on Mexico City, as had happened during the war with Mexico in the previous century. Huerta resigned and fled the country in July, but U.S. forces were not withdrawn until late November.

Trouble was also brewing on the strategically important island of Hispaniola. The customs receivership established by the Roosevelt administration in the Dominican Republic had briefly achieved economic and political stability. The assassination of President Rámon Cáceres in 1911, however, brought about renewed instability that invited foreign intervention. The U.S. stake in the Banque Nationale d'Haiti had also failed to lead to political stability—rather the reverse. Government succeeded government as efforts by the Wilson administration to bring about the election of a president it could support served only to undermine the Haitian leaders negotiating with the administration. Inter-

vention by the United States seemed—not only in retrospect—increasingly probable. The fact that it occurred first in Haiti rather than the Dominican Republic was largely a matter of accident.

As Europe was sliding into war in July 1914, the U.S. government offered to support Haitian President Oreste Zamor in return for the establishment of a customs receivership similar to that in place in the Dominican Republic. Zamor temporized, and by the time he agreed it was too late for his regime. U.S. Marines sent to Port-au-Prince remained aboard ship. His successor, Davilmar Theodore, agreed to a similar arrangement, but opposition to the negotiations in the national assembly forced him to withdraw it. His government was replaced by yet another, led by Vilbrun Guillaume Sam. In return for protection against foes both internal and external and U.S. supervision of the country's finances, Sam and his regime were offered recognition and support by American commissioners in May 1915. This proposal also was rejected.

An uprising in the north was followed by one in the capital itself. A number of political prisoners were executed, which led to Sam's taking refuge in the French legation. Admiral William B. Caperton (USS *Washington*), who had been off the north coast of Haiti, was ordered to Port-au-Prince to protect foreign life and property, but arrived too late to save Sam, who was taken from the legation by a mob and torn to pieces. A landing force of sailors and marines took control of Port-au-Prince on 28 July 1915. Reinforcements dispatched to Caperton enabled the Americans to extend their control to other ports. The Haitian national assembly chose as president Philippe Sudre Dartiguenave, who had promised to cooperate with the U.S. authorities. A treaty, signed in mid-September and ratified later that year, provided for U.S. control of customs and government finance, a national constabulary trained and officered by Americans, and automatic extension of the agreement should either side request it after ten years.

The task of pacification fell to the First Marine Brigade, commanded by Colonel L. W. T.

Waller, and Major Butler. The opposition was led by Ronsalvo Bobo, drawing upon *caco* (guerrilla) bands of peasants in the northern mountains. A combination of selective offers of amnesty, the buying up of weapons, and assaults against the most militant groups gradually had its effect. In mid-November 1915 an operation led by Major Butler killed fifty-one Haitians in Fort Rivière. By 1916 dwindling opposition allowed the marines to settle into routine occupation duties.

Meanwhile, conditions in the neighboring Dominican Republic were leading the United States closer to direct intervention as well. The election of Juan Isidro Jiménez as president in 1914 might have led to the long-sought-for stability had the United States not insisted upon Jiménez's agreement to a series of controls that would have established a protectorate in fact as well as name. The minister of war, Desiderio Arias, went into open opposition against Jiménez in the spring of 1916. U.S. Marines went ashore, Jiménez resigned the presidency, and Admiral Caperton, who arrived 12 May at the capital of Santo Domingo, sent additional forces ashore to operate against Arias' forces. The capital was occupied on 13 May without opposition while Caperton called for more reinforcements, some of which were sent from Haiti, and began to occupy Dominican port towns. A campaign was mounted against Arias' forces in the Cibao Valley in the north, and succeeded against slight opposition in forcing their surrender by early July. Unable to find any Dominican leader willing to cooperate with the occupying forces, the State Department finally opted for direct military rule. In late November, Rear Admiral Harry S. Knapp was appointed military governor. The task of suppressing opposition and confiscating weapons was given to the Second Marine Brigade under Colonel Joseph Pendleton. By the fall of 1917, pacification on Hispaniola seemed well in hand.

In fact, it was not. A fresh *caco* uprising began in Haiti in 1918 and was not suppressed until 1920. In the Dominican Republic resistance flared in the eastern provinces at the same time and was not ended until 1922. These low-grade conflicts brought about changes in U.S. occupation policy in both countries, sparked by accounts of mistreatment and on occasion unauthorized executions of prisoners and civilians. A special Senate committee concluded that the initial interventions, although justified, had been characterized by poor administration. Preparations were made to bring the occupation of the Dominican Republic to a close; that of Haiti would continue for more than another decade. There would be a reduced marine presence in both countries, with the Haitian *gendarmerie* and Dominican *Guardia Naçional* taking on increasing responsibilities for peacekeeping.

Both in 1912 and 1917, uprisings in eastern Cuba (principally Oriente province) led to the commitment of U.S. marines. Their role was restricted to guarding U.S. property in the disaffected areas, thus permitting the Cuban government to concentrate on suppressing the dissidents. Admiral Caperton, who had taken charge of the initial occupations of the Dominican Republic and Haiti, believed it was time the United States tightened its grasp on the "wavering republics" of the Caribbean. The grasp had indeed been tightened; whether it was for good or ill remained to be seen. The United States was on the verge of entry into the First World War. All that could be foreseen at the time was that the world would be changed for both victors and vanquished.

BETWEEN THE WORLD WARS, 1919–1939

One of the consequences of World War I was the breakup of empires: Imperial Russia, Austria-Hungary, and the Ottoman Turkish empire. In Russia, convulsed by revolution as was Mexico, the U.S. government found itself committing military forces. In northwestern Russia, centering upon the ports of Murmansk and Archangel, approximately five thousand U.S. troops were sent in March 1918, ostensibly to protect U.S. and Allied supplies. These forces were withdrawn in June 1919.

The northern expedition was simplicity itself compared to the Siberian Expedition (1918–1920), centered on the port of Vladivostok. It was variously characterized as aiding Czechoslovakian forces along the trans-Siberian railway, protecting Allied and U.S. supplies, preserving order as various factions struggled for control of the maritime region, and keeping an eye on Japan, who had interests of its own in the region. The decision to send ten thousand troops from the Philippines early in August 1918, under the command of Major General William S. Graves, was based on an amalgam of all of these reasons. Following the armistice with Germany of 11 November 1918, the continued presence of U.S. forces in Vladivostok was increasingly viewed as supporting the regime of Admiral A. V. Kolchak's White forces against the Bolsheviks. The subsequent collapse of Kolchak the following year and the eastward advance of Bolshevik forces led to the decision to withdraw U.S. troops, which was completed by 1 April 1920. Thereafter the navy maintained a watching brief (continued observation) on the Japanese, who themselves finally withdrew in the fall of 1922.

Naval forces also appeared in the Black Sea. In May 1920, U.S. naval and relief personnel were withdrawn from the Caucasus region. A larger operation, consequent upon the collapse of Bolshevik opposition in southern Russia, was mounted in the Crimea in November that same year. From late 1921 to late 1922, naval vessels delivered supplies to various Russian Black Sea ports under the auspices of an arrangement worked out by the American Near East Relief Administration.

Rear Admiral Mark L. Bristol, senior naval officer in the Near East and subsequently U.S. high commissioner to Turkey, opposed the breakup of the Ottoman Empire and, in particular, the idea that the United States acquire a mandate in the area under League of Nations auspices. Turkish nationalists continued to oppose Allied designs in Anatolia, that is, the establishment of an Armenian state, and the Greek occupation of Smyrna, which came to an end in the fall of 1922 when Turkish forces re-captured the area. Several U.S. destroyers under the command of Captain Arthur J. Hepburn were dispatched to the area to protect U.S. lives and property and became involved in the subsequent evacuation of more than 250,000 people from the area. Following the conclusion of a treaty between Turkey and the Allied powers in 1923, U.S. naval forces left Turkish waters and Bristol's command dissolved the following year.

In China the position of the western powers also was steadily eroded. The outbreak of revolution against the Ch'ing dynasty in 1911, followed not long after by the outbreak of World War I, ushered in a lengthy period of instability in the country that, in some degree, was to last for nearly forty years. The U.S. Open Door policy of maintaining and supporting the administrative entity and territorial integrity of China complicated any straightforward attempt to protect U.S. lives and property. The U.S. presence was buttressed by the Legation Guard in Peking (initially soldiers but after 1905 comprised of marines), a battalion of the Fifteenth Infantry at Tientsin, and elements of the Asiatic fleet. During the interwar years the United States also maintained a fleet of river gunboats based at Shanghai that patrolled the Yangtze River and its main tributaries. In contrast to the Mexican revolution, which at its most chaotic never threatened the essential unity of the state, the overthrow of the Ch'ing dynasty led to a dissolution of central authority. North of the Yangtze competing warlords ruled, while south of the Yangtze the Chinese Nationalist Party (Kuomintang) gradually consolidated its position, and in the mid-1920's began to move northward.

Nationalist forces reached the Yangtze Valley in 1926. In September of that year, British naval forces ran into an ambush at Wanhsien in which they were roughly handled. Nor was it at all unusual for foreign-owned vessels—private or military—to be fired upon from shore.

In March 1927 matters came to a head. In Shanghai defeated warlord forces attempted to flee into the International Settlement on 21–24 March but were repulsed. U.S. marines came ashore to help man the defenses but were not involved in hostile action. At the same time, in

Nanking, Nationalist forces entered the city and local mobs, in some cases aided by the soldiery, attacked foreign nationals. To protect one group of refugees ashore, the U.S. destroyers *Noa* and *Preston* opened fire to drive back the threatening soldiery. This was the most serious episode involving American nationals, because much of the antiforeign sentiment in the Yangtze Valley and in the south around Canton had been aimed at the British.

In response to the apparently deteriorating situation, reinforcements of marines and naval vessels were sent to China in the early part of 1927. A buildup of forces occurred in the Peking-Tientsin area in north China in late 1927, although most were withdrawn the following year as the Nationalists succeeded in establishing control of the region. Rear Admiral Bristol, commander of the Asiatic fleet from September 1927 to September 1929, recognized that the days of traditional gunboat diplomacy were numbered. If the need arose, American lives and property could best be preserved by evacuation rather than by force. Foreign concessionary areas, including those controlled by Americans, were increasingly reverting to Chinese control.

Perhaps more ominously, the Fourth Marine Regiment witnessed clashes between Japanese and Chinese forces in Shanghai in 1932. Five years later the Sino-Japanese War began. The Fourth Marines was reinforced by the Sixth, although the latter subsequently was withdrawn. The Fourth remained in Shanghai until its withdrawal in November 1941 to Corregidor in the Philippines. For the five hundred members of the regiment stationed in Peking and Tientsin, the withdrawal decision came too late. They were captured by the Japanese after Pearl Harbor and became prisoners of war for the duration.

The interwar years also brought change to the Caribbean and Central America. In Honduras, local U.S. interests supported the Conservative presidential candidate, Tiburcio Carías Andino, against his Liberal opponent, Rafael Lopez Gutiérrez, in the October 1923 election. Carías declared himself the winner, but the elec-

tion was thrown into the national assembly. As the U.S. government withdrew its recognition of the Liberal regime, supporters of the respective candidates looted and shelled the capital of Tegucigalpa. Sailors and marines from the USS *Milwaukee* occupied the city. In the spring of 1924, a State Department representative, Sumner Welles, arrived to negotiate between the two factions. The Conservative candidate, Carías, finally withdrew from the contest after Welles persuaded United Fruit, a U.S. company, to halt loans to his faction.

In Nicaragua, the marine legation guard had been withdrawn in August 1925. In April of the following year, Emiliano Chamorro Vargas forced out of office the incumbent president and vice president. The United States, however, refused to recognize Chamorro as president; the Liberal opposition rose in revolt, assaulting Bluefields and seizing funds from the town's banks. These incidents prompted a landing by U.S. marines in Bluefields in early May. An American-sponsored conference between the contending groups settled little, although Chamorro did resign the presidency. The Nicaraguan assembly chose Adolfo Díaz as his successor. Juan Secasa, the deposed vice president, rose in open revolt against Díaz with the backing of the Mexican government. In December, marines again were sent ashore. An arms embargo was declared to stop the importation of weapons by the Liberals. The U.S. government, which in the meantime had recognized Díaz, landed 160 marines at Corinto from the USS *Galveston* in February 1927. These forces proceeded to Managua. Admiral Julian Latimer declared the Corinto-Managua railroad a neutral zone. In April 1927, Henry Stimson was appointed as a special mediator. The subsequent Convention of Tipitapa granted amnesty to the Liberals. Díaz for his part agreed to step down after the 1928 elections, which were to be supervised by the U.S. government.

Most Liberals ceased their hostilities; one, Augusto César Sandino, did not. General Logan Feland, marine Commander in Nicaragua, assigned Nicaraguan constabulary forces to track down Sandino's guerrilla bands. These efforts were not entirely successful. By January 1928 reinforcements had brought the number of marines in the country to fifteen hundred. The election was won by the Liberal candidate, José Maria Moncada. In 1929, U.S. marine forces, having reached a peak of five thousand, were gradually withdrawn. Sandino, who had been in Mexico for a time, returned to Nicaragua in May. Again, Nicaraguan forces, with marine assistance, unsuccessfully attempted to bring him to bay. The insurrection continued, with Sandino's forces eluding capture and, in the spring of 1931, attacking Standard Fruit interests in the eastern lowlands. Stimson, now secretary of state, opposed further marine reinforcements. In the election of 1932, Juan Secasa became president, and the remaining marines were withdrawn the following year. Sandino entered Managua in February 1934 to discuss the disarmament of the last of his forces. A plot engineered by Anastasio Somoza, commander of the *Guardia Nacional*, resulted in the capture and execution of Sandino. Somoza would emerge as the ruling force in Nicaragua, and he and his family would remain in control until 1979.

THE EARLY COLD WAR, 1945–1960

The end of World War II in 1945 continued what some have called "the American century." The strength of its military, the possession of the atomic bomb, and an industrial capacity unravaged by war gave the United States the power, seemingly, to exert its influence anywhere on the globe. As had been the case after earlier wars, however, a massive demobilization, which affected all the services, soon reduced the capacity of the United States to intervene even if the will to do so had existed. The apparent threat posed by the Soviet Union, soon to harden into the cold war, was perceived initially as applying particularly to Europe. The threat was met initially with nuclear deterrence, economic aid to the Western European countries, and the North Atlantic Treaty Organization (NATO), established in 1949.

Another legacy of the war, although one not immediately perceived, was the decisive weakening of the will to empire of the European powers. The first effects were felt in east and south Asia. Burma, India, Malaya, the Netherlands East Indies, and the Philippines all achieved independence in the 1940s. France, attempting to retain control of Indochina, found itself involved in a guerrilla war with the Viet Minh. The U.S. government provided economic aid and, on occasion, military advisers. As long as the U.S. Navy controlled the Pacific, and Japan remained occupied and pacified, what happened elsewhere in Asia evoked little concern in Washington. The sole exception was China.

Fifty-five thousand marines from the Third Amphibious Corps were sent into northern China (Hopeh and Shantung provinces) in September-October 1945 to assist in the surrender and repatriation of Japanese troops and help maintain order. The first part of the mission was completed by mid-1946. The second portion became increasingly difficult outside the cities, as China slid into civil war between the Nationalist and Communist forces. Occasional clashes between marines and Communist irregulars resulted in casualties to both sides. By early 1947 the remnant of the marine forces, now numbering five thousand and designated Fleet Marine Force Western Pacific, was based at Tsingtao. As they had done in the 1920s, the marines helped evacuate American nationals caught in the conflict from north China and the Yangtze Valley. By 1949 the last marines left China.

The U.S. naval presence in east Asian waters was also significantly reduced. By 1950 the Seventh Fleet consisted of one heavy cruiser, eight destroyers, four submarines, and one aircraft carrier. The Naval Forces Far East Command, operating from Japanese ports, was even more modest.

In the Mediterranean there was also a slow awakening to new responsibilities. The British government told the administration of Harry S. Truman in 1947 that it would have to withdraw its forces from Greece. The near-simultaneous threat to Turkey from the Soviet Union over a revision of the Montreaux Convention governing passage of the Bosporus and Dardanelles not only gave rise to the Truman Doctrine but saw the establishment of a U.S. naval presence in the Mediterranean—the Sixth Fleet. Economic aid and military advisers were sent to the Greek government. This aid, coupled the following year with the withdrawal of Yugoslav aid to the Greek Communist insurgents, helped to bring victory to government forces. A U.S. naval presence in the Mediterranean seemed also sufficient to deter Soviet adventurism. For the near term, perhaps it did. In the long term, however, the Middle East would become an area of constant concern, as the United States assumed Great Britain's traditional role in the "great game" of blocking Soviet access to the Mediterranean, the Persian Gulf, and the Indian Ocean.

The relatively modest commitment of U.S. forces overseas was to change with the end of the U.S. nuclear monopoly in 1949, the establishment of NATO, and above all with the North Korean invasion of South Korea in June 1950, signaling not only an expansion of the cold war to Asia, but, during the presidency of Dwight D. Eisenhower (1953–1961) to the Middle East, Africa, and Latin America.

Containment of communism in the Middle East took the form of supporting milder forms of nationalism in the area and simultaneously seeking to keep the Soviet Union from the region through the alliance of 1955 called the Baghdad Pact, consisting of Great Britain, Turkey, Iraq, Iran and Pakistan. The pact was one element that was to lead to the Suez Crisis the following year. In 1956, Egyptian President Gamal Abdel Nasser denounced the Baghdad Pact and sought to strengthen Egypt militarily. Failing to obtain aid from the West, he successfully sought it from the Communist bloc. His subsequent decision to recognize the People's Republic of China proved to be the last straw for U.S. Secretary of State John Foster Dulles, who in July abruptly reversed the decision to provide economic aid for the Egyptian Aswan High Dam project. Nasser, in turn, nationalized the

Suez Canal, thereby bringing Great Britain, France, and Israel to a decision to attack Egypt.

The Israeli invasion of the Sinai Peninsula on 29 October 1956 was followed just days later by an Anglo-French invasion to "separate" the combatants and maintain freedom of transit of the canal. The U.S. Sixth Fleet was ordered to assist in the evacuation of U.S. citizens from the war zone. A marine battalion landing team went ashore at Alexandria on 1–2 November and assisted in the evacuation of more than fifteen hundred U.S. and other foreign nationals. Pressure by the U.S. government halted the Anglo-French invasion and ultimately led to the evacuation of allied forces from Egypt. In the aftermath of the crisis was the realization by Great Britain and France that their governments could no longer act without U.S. approval in the Middle East. The crisis also did not signal the end of Soviet involvement in the region.

In an effort to reassure the member states of the Baghdad Pact that the United States was committed to their security and integrity, the Eisenhower administration promulgated the Eisenhower doctrine, put forth in a special address to Congress on 5 January 1957 and which declared the Middle East vital to U.S. national interests. Even more important, Congress was requested to authorize the dispatch of military and economic aid to any country desiring it, plus the dispatch of military forces should they be necessary to prevent political subversion or to counter foreign invasion. Both the Senate and the House of Representatives passed the necessary legislation in March. The presence of the Sixth Fleet in the eastern Mediterranean enabled Jordan's King Hussein to weather a crisis that same year, but could not prevent the union of Syria and Egypt into the United Arab Republic early in 1958.

Civil war erupted in Lebanon in May 1958 between Christian and Muslim elements, leading to a strengthening of marines within the Sixth Fleet and contingency plans to put ashore two battalion landing teams in that country. The overthrow of the pro-Western Iraqi government on 14 July led to the decision by the Eisenhower administration to land forces in Lebanon lest

Lebanon's government, too, be overthrown. Three marine battalion landing teams went ashore 15–16 July, secured control of the Beirut airport, and established a defensive perimeter around it. U.S. Army forces were flown in from Germany, landing on 19 July. At the end of the buildup phase on 5 August, nearly fifteen thousand personnel were in place. Although in the early stages the marines were subject to some harassing rifle fire, no casualties were incurred. A political settlement that called for the election of the Lebanese army commander, General Fuad Shehab, to the presidency enabled the withdrawal of U.S. forces to begin on 14 September 1958. The last military personnel left on 25 October. Clearly, U.S. military power could be projected into states along or near the Mediterranean littoral. Whether they could be committed without risk was yet to be determined.

Meanwhile, in the Caribbean, the United States had first isolated then destabilized the government of Guatemala. The president, Jacobo Arbenz Guzmán, was deemed to be Communist-leaning; his decision to purchase weapons from the Communist bloc helped to seal his fate in 1954. A U.S.-sponsored insurgency led by Carlos Castillo Armas and the defection of key Guatemalan military personnel led to the overthrow of Arbenz. No U.S. forces were involved; the closest the United States came to military intervention was the transfer of two P-51 aircraft via a third country to Castillo Armas' insurgents.

In Panama, late in 1959, U.S. Army personnel stationed in the Canal Zone were called to the zonal borders to prevent the entrance of Panamanians determined to fly their country's flag in the zone as a symbol of ultimate sovereignty. The incoming administration of John F. Kennedy would test whether U.S. military power could be threatened or actually committed hemispherically at little or no cost. It seemed, initially, that it could.

The downfall of the Fulgencio Batista regime in Cuba in 1959 and the triumph of Fidel Castro was at first greeted with rejoicing or at least with equanimity. Disquieting signs soon appeared that this revolution promised to be different. Castro's predilection to export his revolution to other Caribbean countries, plus his inability or unwillingness to reach a modus vivendi with the United States that might compromise Cuban nationalism began a downward spiral that neither side could halt. The nationalization of the Cuban sugar industry in the fall of 1960 was followed by the severance of diplomatic relations by the United States on 4 January 1961.

THE 1960s

Vice President Richard M. Nixon had recommended as early as April 1959 that Cuban exiles be organized to overthrow Castro. President Eisenhower formally ordered such an operation in mid-March 1960. It was this plan, run by the Central Intelligence Agency, that was inherited by the incoming Kennedy administration. Kennedy, having charged Eisenhower with "losing" Cuba, was almost obliged to let the plan proceed. Essentially the CIA called for a conventional military operation, in which air cover was a key component. Kennedy specified there were to be no Americans involved in the actual landing. On the eve of the operation, he ordered the CIA's Richard Bissell to keep U.S. air support to a minimum.

On 15 April 1961, a raid was staged by several B-26 bombers on Cuban airfields. It failed in its attempt to knock out or cripple the Cuban air force. The invasion fleet carrying Brigade 2506, consisting of 1,453 men, had sailed from Puerto Cabezas, Nicaragua, and was off the southern Cuban coast in the early hours of 17 April. Landings were made at Playa Largo and Playa Giron in the Bay of Pigs (Cochinos Bay), and the brigade pushed inland against slight resistance. Cuban air attacks against the vessels that morning sunk one craft and knocked out nine others. Belatedly, a dozen B-26s arrived to provide air cover but five of them were shot down. The loss of the invasion force's supply and communication network, and the absence of any wide-scale uprising on the part of the Cubans themselves made failure a virtual certainty. The surviving

1,179 captives of Brigade 2506 were released by Castro in the fall of 1962 in exchange for $53 million in medical supplies and food.

The Guatemalan experience of 1954 had misguided the planning of the 1961 venture. Even worse, Soviet Premier Nikita Khrushchev drew certain conclusions regarding Kennedy's performance in the entire affair, which were to lead to a much more serious crisis in U.S.-Soviet relations eighteen months later. The Monroe Doctrine was seriously weakened by Castro's survival, and the United States incurred considerable obloquy both in the Western Hemisphere and elsewhere for having intervened in Cuba while simultaneously proclaiming the principle of nonintervention.

The Kennedy administration, for its part, saw the failure to commit U.S. forces as one of the reasons for the Bay of Pigs fiasco, and the Joint Chiefs of Staff were ordered to prepare for a direct intervention in Cuba should one be ordered. The planning involved all four services, and exercises undertaken in 1961 and 1962 in the Caribbean tested the readiness of some units. The threat of invasion in turn prompted a step-up in Soviet military aid to the Cuban government, although it does not by itself explain the decision to introduce intermediate range ballistic missiles and nuclear-capable medium bombers into Cuba. Given overwhelming U.S. preponderance in reliable nuclear weapon delivery systems at the time, no "quick fix" was possible for the Soviets. If Khrushchev believed Kennedy was prepared to acquiesce in the presence of missiles in Cuba, he seriously miscalculated. Not only would operational missiles pose a threat to U.S. cities, their presence would seriously threaten the administration's authority, hemispheric hegemony, and leadership of the NATO alliance.

In the course of forty-eight hours (20–22 October), U.S. armed forces went to a war footing that was both impressive and unprecedented since World War II. Troops from the Second Marine Expeditionary Force would have led the way ashore on beaches west of Havana had an invasion been ordered. One hundred thousand army troops, including armored and airborne

units, would have been committed to the assault. The navy, for its part, not only was prepared to provide air cover for the invasion from the nuclear carriers Enterprise and Independence, but also the blockading ("quarantine") force to halt further importation of missiles into Cuba. The blockade went into effect on 24 October, and achieved its goals. On 28 October, Kennedy was informed by Khrushchev he was prepared to dismantle the missiles already in Cuba and return them to the Soviet Union. Khrushchev fell from power eighteen months later. The Soviet government nevertheless embarked on a massive program to strengthen both its nuclear capabilities and its navy, so that it would never, as one Soviet diplomat succinctly put it, be caught like that again. The United States decided that economic sanctions and hemispheric isolation would be sufficient against Cuba, but if not, the U.S. government was prepared to live with the Castro regime, so long as it was not duplicated elsewhere in the Caribbean.

The U.S. fear of Castro-inspired regimes contributed to right-wing military coups in Guatemala, Honduras, and the Dominican Republic in 1963. In the Dominican Republic, the democratically elected regime of Juan Bosch was overthrown. Bosch went into exile, but pro-Bosch elements, including some in the military, agitated for his return. This all came to a head when the regime of Donald Reid Cabral was toppled 25–26 April 1965 by pro-Bosch forces. The following day right-wing military forces under General Elias Wessin y Wessin attacked the Constitutionalist forces in Santo Domingo but were unable to crush them, which in turn led to U.S. military intervention. Marines from the USS Boxer went ashore early on 28 April and established a perimeter west of the city around the Hotel Embajador. Ostensibly this step was undertaken to protect and evacuate foreign nationals caught in the fighting. In fact, however, in a critical meeting of top U.S. officials in Washington on 29 April, it was decided that the intervention was to be a massive one; U.S. prestige was at stake. There would be no Castro-style regime in the Dominican Republic. An airlift of troops began into the San Isidro airport, and in the space of two weeks force levels were raised to more than twenty thousand. Support of the venture from the Organization of American States (OAS) and of the Johnson Doctrine (equated in some circles with the Roosevelt Corollary to the Monroe Doctrine) was less than fulsome. Much energy was expended in the search for a regime acceptable to the U.S. government. U.S. troops eventually withdrew in September 1966.

Other areas saw U.S. military interventions between 1961 and 1969. Army and marine forces were introduced into Thailand, March 1961, at the height of the Laotian crisis that year but were withdrawn by July. In November 1964, Belgian paratroopers were dropped from U.S. aircraft to rescue foreign nationals in the Congo trapped by rebel forces. Earlier that same year, army forces in the Canal Zone again were called upon to disperse Panamanian rioters. The U.S. Sixth Fleet stood by during the 1967 Arab-Israeli war although not, as in 1956, without casualties. On 5 June the USS *Liberty*, an electronic surveillance vessel, was attacked by Israeli warplanes and torpedo boats, resulting in 34 killed and 171 wounded. Overshadowing all these episodes was the growing U.S. presence in Vietnam, which reached its peak in 1968 and was to diminish slowly during the presidencies of Richard Nixon and Gerald Ford.

THE 1970s

It is surprising how few interventions involving U.S. forces occurred from 1969 to 1977. Seizure of the container ship *Mayaguez* in Cambodian waters by Khmer Rouge forces in May 1975 prompted a military operation mounted to retrieve the vessel and rescue its crew. The ship was retrieved on 15 May, but marine forces lifted by helicopter onto Koh Tang Island suffered severe casualties (fourteen dead or missing, forty-one wounded) in the effort to rescue the crew. They were later released unharmed into U.S. custody. This episode aside, the temper of the years of Nixon's and Gerald Ford's administration was anticipated in the 1969

Nixon Doctrine, which declared that the United States would continue to honor its commitments to the NATO alliance, Japan, and South Korea. Elsewhere, and particularly in Asia, Africa, and Latin America, the United States would perhaps provide air support, economic and technical aid, and weaponry—but the burden of resisting insurrection or outside aggression would fall upon the nations in which it was occurring. No longer the world's policeman, the United States would rely more and more on regional surrogates, such as South Vietnam, Israel, Iran, and Brazil, to keep order. Covert operations had also fallen from favor. The destabilization of the Salvatore Allende regime in Chile and its subsequent overthrow in 1973 by the Chilean military provoked such an outcry that Congress was prompted to pass legislation the following year severely limiting covert action. The decision by Congress to refuse further funding to support insurgency in Angola the following year led to the triumph of the Popular Movement for the Liberation of Angola in 1976. In neither the Jordanian crisis of 1970 nor the Yom Kippur War of 1973 did the United States intervene. The presence of the Sixth Fleet in both instances, however, was a deterrent to a widening of hostilities.

Jimmy Carter became president in 1977 determined to make changes in U.S. foreign policy as practiced during the Nixon-Ford years. U.S. defense budgets would be pared; forces abroad would be reduced; economic and military aid to right-wing regimes would be cut; and there would be no more Vietnams and no more Chiles. This new *weltanschauung* (world view) helped to produce an historic settlement in the Middle East; the 1977 Camp David Accords brought peace between Egypt and Israel, and, as part of a United Nations peacekeeping detachment, U.S. forces into the Sinai region. The accords also contributed to the U.S.-Panamanian agreements that same year abrogating the Hay-Bunau-Varilla Treaty of 1903 and granting Panama increased revenues and greater administrative authority within the Canal Zone. The United States retained the right to defend the "neutrality" of the canal, and could intervene unilaterally should service through the canal be interrupted. The long rule of the Somoza family in Nicaragua ended in 1979 without interference from the United States.

On the other hand, one of the regional pillars of the United States in the Middle East toppled in 1979—the government of the shah of Iran. The successor regime was dominated by fundamentalist Iranian clerics led by the Ayatollah Khomeini. The decision later that year to permit the shah to receive medical attention in the United States was followed within weeks by the seizure of the U.S. embassy in Teheran by militants on 4 November. U.S. embassy personnel were held hostage. Late in November, President Carter ordered two carrier battle groups (the *Midway* and the *Kitty Hawk*) into the Indian Ocean. The *Kitty Hawk* and its escorts were relieved by the *Nimitz* in January 1980. Negotiations for the release of the hostages were unsuccessful, and in March the president decided to undertake a rescue mission.

The plan, dubbed Operation Eagle Claw, was devised by Air Force General David Jones, chairman of the Joint Chiefs of Staff. The two-day operation called for a nighttime rendezvous at a site (Desert One) two hundred miles southeast of Teheran. Six C-130 Hercules transports carrying the multiservice Delta Force commandos, fuel, and equipment would fly from an Egyptian airfield and be met by eight navy RH-53 Sea Stallion helicopters from the *Nimitz*. The refueled helicopters would take the assault team to a location closer to Teheran (Desert Two) and take cover until the second night. The commandos would proceed by commandeered vehicles to the embassy compound and the Iranian Foreign Ministry building, free the hostages, then proceed to a nearby stadium, from which they would be transported by helicopter to an airfield south of Teheran, occupied that same evening by a U.S. military transport group. All personnel would then be flown out to safety.

The operation, which began on 24 April 1980, was unsuccessful. Two of the eight helicopters turned back en route to Desert One. A third developed a problem in its hydraulic system. Colonel Charles Beckwith, the commander of the operation, recommended that the mission be terminated at that point. President Carter concurred. During takeoff one of the remaining helicopters struck a C-130, and eight crewmen were killed. Abandoning the helicopters, the assault force flew out in the transports. The embassy hostages were ultimately released on 20 January 1981, after 444 days in captivity, in a deal brokered by Algerian government representatives. To add to the Carter administration's woes in this part of the world, the Soviet Union sent troops into Afghanistan in December 1979, and Iraq's Saddam Hussein attacked Iran in September 1980, beginning a conflict that would drag on for eight years and involve the United States naval forces in the Persian Gulf before it ended. Carter lost his bid for reelection in 1980 to Ronald Reagan in part because of his presumed weaknesses in the international realm.

THE REAGAN-BUSH YEARS, 1981–1993

Reagan came into office committed to strengthening the U.S. military, aiding foreign governments combating communism, and undermining those regimes (as in Angola and, closer to home, in Nicaragua) that were too leftist for comfort. He proclaimed that the United States was back, free of its post-Vietnam syndrome. The administration's resolve would be severely tested in Lebanon, which had gained the unenviable reputation as the snakepit of the Middle East.

Israeli forces moved into Lebanon in June 1982, driving northward to Beirut. Late in August, eight hundred U.S. marines went ashore, the Thirty-second Marine Amphibious Unit (MAU), but were withdrawn fifteen days later. The marines returned that fall as part of a multinational force to safeguard civilians and foreign nationals, with the task of protecting the Beirut international airport and its environs. The position of the Twenty-fourth MAU, 1,250 strong, which replaced the Thirty-second MAU in early November, was increasingly tenuous.

Forbidden to fire unless directly fired upon and subject to sniper fire and artillery fire from the hills to the east, they were perceived as being in league with Lebanese Christian forces. Neither return fire by their own artillery, naval gunfire (including at one point the big guns of the battleship *New Jersey*), nor naval air assault seemed to help. In mid-April 1983 the bombing of the U.S. embassy in Beirut resulted in more than sixty deaths (including seventeen Americans). On 23 October an explosives-laden truck was driven into the marine headquarters building and detonated, killing 241 of the 300 marines asleep there. On 26 February 1984 the marines were withdrawn from Lebanon and the following month the U.S. government announced its formal withdrawal from the multinational police force.

Even before the Lebanese venture, the U.S. military had encountered problems elsewhere in the Mediterranean. The ruler of Libya, Colonel Muammar Khadhaffi, claimed the Gulf of Sidra as part of Libya's territorial waters. During maneuvers by the Sixth Fleet in the gulf in August, two Libyan jets were shot down by naval fighters. Libya, as well as Syria and Iran, was seen as responsible for a number of terrorist-related acts in the Middle East and elsewhere during the 1980s. In 1982 the U.S. government embargoed Libyan oil. In January 1986 all trade with Libya was banned, and in March a further clash with naval forces in the Gulf of Sidra left two Libyan patrol boats sunk. Libyan shore missile batteries and radar installations also were attacked. In April the bombing of a West Berlin discotheque resulted in the death of a U.S. serviceman. This, too, was laid at Khadhaffi's door and resulted in an assault days later on Benghazi and Tripoli by carrier- and land-based planes. As an exercise in extreme power quickly applied and quickly withdrawn, it proved highly successful.

The Iran-Iraq conflict that had begun in 1980 also involved the U.S. military. With the war stalemated on the ground, Iraq turned increasingly to attacks on Iranian oil installations and the tankers using them. The Iranians replied in kind. The U.S. Navy became responsible for en-suring the safe passage of U.S.-flag or flag-of-convenience tankers through the Persian Gulf and the Strait of Hormuz. On 17 May 1987 the guided-missile frigate *Stark* was hit by two Exocet missiles fired from an Iraqi F-1 Mirage fighter. The attack was in error, but the vessel's commander was criticized for failing to take action (arming its own surface-to-air missiles), even though it had been warned that the approaching fighter's radar was locked on to the ship. On 14 April 1988 the frigate *Samuel B. Roberts* was badly damaged by a mine. Just days later A-6 Intruder attack bombers sank an Iranian frigate. The navy's mission was broadened to protect all friendly, neutral, and innocent shipping. In June 1988, two Iranian oil platforms utilized as bases for harassment of shipping were attacked and destroyed by naval and marine forces. On 3 July the Aegis missile cruiser *Vincennes*, during a clash with Iranian speedboats, mistakenly shot down an Iranian airliner, killing all 290 aboard.

During Ronald Reagan's presidency, the U.S. military did not intervene in Cuba, El Salvador, or Nicaragua. In the latter two cases, it proved to be a near-run thing. The triumph of the Sandinistas in 1979 and the outbreak of an insurrectionary movement in neighboring El Salvador the following year prompted the Reagan administration to send military aid and advisers to the El Salvador regime, and to undertake a policy of supporting *contra* opposition to the Nicaraguan government. This near-obsession with leftist forces in Central America supported by Cuba and the Soviet Union also figured in the 25–27 October 1983 invasion of Grenada. Since 1979, Grenada had been ruled by an avowed Marxist, Maurice Bishop. His overthrow by an even more radical faction in 1983, it was feared, would lead to even closer ties to Cuba. The extension of the island's airport by Cuban laborers also seemed suspicious. American nationals living there were thought to be at risk as hostages. Finally, the overthrow of the coup's leaders would send a strong message to the Cubans and the Sandinistas (not to mention those responsible for the bombing of the marine headquarters building in Lebanon days before). The invasion force of Operation Urgent Fury consisted of a marine amphibious battalion, two army Ranger battalions backed by fighter-bombers from the USS *Independence,* air force C-130 gunships, five M60 tanks and other armored fighting vehicles, helicopters, and two Eighty-second Airborne battalions flown in 26 October as reinforcements. It took three days to secure the island despite minimal Cuban-Grenadian resistance. At a cost of $75.5 million, it was shown that gunboat diplomacy still could succeed. U.S. forces were withdrawn in mid-December.

Panama strongman Manuel Antonio Noriega was a thorn in the side of both the Reagan and George Bush administrations. Allegations of corruption in 1987 by a former aide led to increasing calls for Noriega's resignation by Panamanians. U.S. foreign aid to Panama ceased early in 1988, and two Florida grand juries indicted Noriega for his involvement in the drug trade and for permitting the laundering of drug money by Panamanian banks, among other charges. Refusing all threats and blandishments, Noriega overturned an internationally supervised election in May 1989. Several months later he easily foiled a plot by elements of the Panamanian Defense Force to unseat him. Claiming that a state of war existed between Panama and the United States, Noriega remained impervious to all forms of economic coercion by the Bush administration. Clashes between Panamanian forces and U.S. military personnel in the zone claimed the life of one marine. Contingency planning for an invasion of Panama, begun early in 1989, turned into the real thing. Operation Just Cause, launched early on 20 December 1989, involved 22,500 troops from the United States and the 13,500 in the Canal Zone. Panama City itself was devastated, 24 U.S. servicemen were killed, and more than 300 Panamanians also died. Noriega ultimately surrendered to the U.S. forces and was remanded to a jail in Florida. The invasion forces were withdrawn early in February 1990.

Six months later another invasion occurred, not in Latin America, but at the head of the Persian Gulf. Iraq's Saddam Hussein invaded and occupied Kuwait, ostensibly to restore to his country one of its lost provinces. Fearing a subsequent invasion and occupation of Saudi Arabia, President Bush ordered in more than 500,000 combat troops, several carrier task forces, and a number of air squadrons to help defend Saudi territory. Bush also orchestrated an international economic boycott of Iraq. The U.S. military contingent of Operation Desert Shield was in time joined by forces of other nations, including Great Britain, France, Egypt, and Syria. With the backing or neutrality of the international community, and the authority of the U.S. Senate to resort to military action, the allies went over to the offensive—Operation Desert Storm—in mid-January 1991. Following some days of air operations and missile attacks, General Norman Schwarzkopf's forces distracted Iraqi forces in Kuwait with a feigned seaborne assault near Kuwait City, sending instead his armored forces on a sweep west and north behind the prepared Iraqi defensive positions. In four days the Iraqi army was routed and Kuwait liberated.

To the extent that the cold war formed the backdrop to a number of U.S. interventions in the post–World War II era, the ending of the cold war and the breakup of the Soviet Union into its constituent parts presaged a new order indeed—although not precisely in the form envisioned by President Bush.

During the first century of its existence, the United States committed forces in peacetime with both a continental and a maritime dimension. The latter approached most closely gunboat diplomacy in its classic form, defined as the use of naval vessels to protect American lives and property abroad. The disappearance of the western frontier in the late nineteenth century ended the continental dimension, while the commitment of forces abroad increasingly was undertaken in furtherance of perceived national interests, such as the security of the Central American isthmian canal and the maritime approaches to it. The greatest incidence of force geographically occurred in the Western Hemisphere, east Asia, and the Pacific during the last decade of the nineteenth century and the first three decades of the twentieth. In the second half of the twentieth century, U.S. interests became global, encompassing not only the western Atlantic and the Pacific littoral but the Mediterranean and Indian oceans as well. Where forces have been committed, they increasingly have involved all of the armed services. Ideally, when military force is to be used during peacetime, the objective should be clear, the mission limited in scope and time, and the force itself proportionate to its task. More often than not, the reality has corresponded to the ideal.

See also COALITION WARFARE; THE COLD WAR; THE EARLY NATIONAL PERIOD: 1783–1812; EXPANSION AND THE PLAINS INDIAN WARS; THE AMERICAN MILITARY AS AN INSTRUMENT OF POWER; RECONSTRUCTION AND AMERICAN IMPERIALISM; THE SPANISH-AMERICAN WAR AND ITS AFTERMATH; UNCONVENTIONAL WARFARE; THE VIETNAM ERA; *and* THE WAR OF 1812 AND POSTWAR EXPANSION.

BIBLIOGRAPHY

General Works

Asprey, Robert B. *War in the Shadows: The Guerrilla in History*, 2 vols. (1975).

Blechman, Barry, and Stephen S. Kaplan. *Force Without War* (1978).

Cable, James. *Gunboat Diplomacy* (1971).

Dupuy, R. E., and Trevor N. Dupuy. *Military Heritage of America* (1956).

Hagan, Kenneth J. *This People's Navy: The Making of American Sea Power* (1991).

Hagan, Kenneth J., ed. *In Peace and War: Interpretations of American Naval History, 1775–1984*, 2nd ed. (1984).

Hagan, Kenneth J., and William R. Roberts, eds. *Against All Enemies: Interpretations of American Military History from Colonial Times to the Present* (1986).

Hassler, Warren W. *With Shield and Sword: American Military Affairs: Colonial Times to the Present* (1982).

Heinl, Robert D. *Soldiers of the Sea: The United States Marine Corps, 1775–1962* (1962).

Howarth, Stephen. *To Shining Sea: A History of the United States Navy, 1775–1991* (1991).

Hoyt, Edwin P. *America's Wars and Military Excursions* (1987).

Millett, Allan R. *Semper Fidelis: The History of the United States Marine Corps* (1980).

Millett, Allan R., and Peter Maslowski. *For the Common Defense: A Military History of the United States of America* (1984).

Morris, James M. *America's Armed Forces: A History* (1991).

Perrett, Geoffrey. *A Country Made by War: From the Revolution to Vietnam* (1989).

Stern, Ellen P., ed. *The Limits of Military Intervention* (1977).

Weigley, Russell F. *History of the United States Army* (1967).

———. *The American Way of War: A History of the United States Military Strategy and Policy* (1973).

1783–1815

Bird, Harrison. *War for the West, 1790–1813* (1971).

Bradford, James C. *Command Under Sail: Makers of the American Naval Tradition, 1775–1850* (1985).

Coakley, Robert W. *The Role of Federal Military Forces in Domestic Disturbances, 1789–1878* (1989).

Coffman, Edward M. *The Old Army: A Portrait of the American Army in Peacetime, 1784–1898* (1986).

Field, James A., Jr. *America and the Mediterranean World, 1776–1882* (1969).

Fowler, W. M., Jr. *Jack Tars and Commodores: The American Navy, 1783–1815* (1984).

Guthman, William H. *March to Massacre* (1975).

Kohn, Richard H. *Eagle and Sword: The Federalists and the Creation of the Military Establishment in America, 1783–1802* (1975).

Long, David F. *Nothing too Daring: A Biography of Commodore David Porter, 1780–1843* (1970).

———. *Ready to Hazard: A Biography of Commodore William Bainbridge, 1774–1833* (1981).

———. *Sailor-Diplomat: A Biography of Commodore James Biddle, 1783–1848* (1983).

———. *Gold Braid and Foreign Relations: Diplomatic Activities of U.S. Naval Officers, 1798–1883* (1988).

Mahon, John K. *The American Militia: Decade of Decision, 1789–1800* (1960).

McKee, Christopher. *Edward Preble: A Naval Biography, 1761–1807* (1972).

Prucha, Francis P. *The Sword of the Republic: The United States Army on the Frontier, 1783–1840* (1969).

Remini, Robert V. *Andrew Jackson and the Course of American Empire* (1977).

Sword, Wiley. *President Washington's Indian War: The Struggle for the Old Northwest, 1790–1795* (1985).

Szatmary, David. *Shays' Rebellion: The Making of an Agrarian Insurrection* (1980).

Tucker, Glenn. *Dawn Like Thunder: The Barbary War and the Birth of the U.S. Navy* (1963).

1815–1861

Billingsley, E. B. *In Defense of Neutral Rights: The United States Navy and the Wars of Independence in Chile and Peru* (1967).

Bradford, James C., ed. *Captains of the Old Steam Navy: Makers of the American Naval Tradition, 1840–1880* (1986).

Buker, George E. *Swamp Sailors: Riverine Warfare in the Everglades, 1835–1842* (1975).

Eby, Cecil D. *"That Disgraceful Affair": The Black Hawk War* (1973).

Henson, Curtis T. *Commissioners and Commodores: The East India Squadron and American Diplomacy in China* (1982).

Johnson, Robert E. *Thence Round Cape Horn: The Story of the United States Naval Forces on the Pacific Station, 1818–1923* (1963).

————. *Rear Admiral John Rodgers, 1812–1882* (1967).

————. *Far China Station: The U.S. Navy in Asian Waters, 1800–1895* (1979).

Mahon, John K. *History of the Second Seminole War, 1835–1842* (1967).

Morison, Samuel Eliot. *"Old Bruin": Commodore Matthew C. Perry, 1794–1858* (1967).

Prucha, Francis P. *Broadax and Bayonet: The Role of the United States Army in the Development of the Northwest, 1815–1860* (1953).

Satz, Ronald N. *American Indian Policy in the Jacksonian Era* (1975).

Utley, Robert M. *Frontiersmen in Blue: The United States Army and the Indian, 1846–1865* (1967).

Wheeler, Richard. *In Pirate Waters* (1969).

1865–1898

Barrow, Clayton R., Jr., ed. *America Spreads Her Sails: U.S. Sea Power in the Nineteenth Century* (1973).

Bradford, James C., ed. *Admirals of the Steel Navy: Makers of the American Naval Tradition, 1880–1930* (1990).

Bradford, Richard H. *The Virginius Affair* (1980).

Coletta, Paolo E. *A Survey of U.S. Naval Affairs, 1865–1917* (1987).

Cooling, Benjamin Franklin. *Benjamin Franklin Tracy: Father of the American Fighting Navy* (1973).

Cooper, Jerry M. *The Army and Civil Disorder: Federal Military Intervention in American Labor Disputes, 1877–1900* (1980).

Drake, Frederick C. *The Empire of the Seas: A Biography of Rear Admiral Robert Wilson Shufeldt, USN* (1984).

Goldberg, Joyce S. *The "Baltimore" Affair* (1986).

Grenville, John A. S., and George B. Young. *Politics, Strategy, and American Diplomacy* (1966).

Hagan, Kenneth J. *American Gunboat Diplomacy and the Old Navy, 1877–1889* (1973).

Herwig, Holger H. *Politics of Frustration: The United States in German Naval Planning, 1889–1941* (1976).

Herrick, Walter R., Jr. *The American Naval Revolution* (1966).

LaFeber, Walter. *The New Empire* (1963).

Offut, Milton. *Protection of Citizens Abroad by the Armed Forces of the United States* (1928).

Plesur, Milton. *America's Outward Thrust* (1971).

Sefton, James E. *The United States Army and Reconstruction, 1865–1877* (1967).

Still, William N., Jr. *American Sea Power in the Old World: The United States Navy in European and Near Eastern Waters, 1865–1917* (1980).

Utley, Robert M. *Frontier Regulars: The United States Army and the Indian, 1866–1891* (1973).

1898–1917

Braisted, William R. *The United States Navy in the Pacific, 1897–1909* (1958).

————. *The United States Navy in the Pacific, 1909–1922* (1971).

Challener, Richard D. *Admirals, Generals, and American Foreign Policy, 1898–1914* (1973).

Collin, Richard H. *Theodore Roosevelt's Caribbean: The Panama Canal, the Monroe Doctrine, and the Latin American Context* (1990).

Gates, John M. *Schoolbooks and Krags: The U.S. Army in the Philippines, 1898–1902* (1973).

Healy, David F. *The United States in Cuba, 1898–1902: Generals, Politicians, and the Search for Policy* (1963).

———. *Gunboat Diplomacy in the Wilson Era: The U.S. Navy in Haiti, 1915–1916* (1976).

———. *Drive to Hegemony: The United States in the Caribbean, 1889–1917* (1988).

Karnow, Stanley. *In Our Image: America's Empire in the Philippines* (1989).

Langley, Lester D. *The United States and the Caribbean in the Twentieth Century*, rev. ed. (1985).

Linn, Brian M. *The U.S. Army and Counterinsurgency in the Philippine War, 1899–1902* (1989).

Miller, Stuart C. *"Benevolent Assimilation": The American Conquest of the Philippines, 1899–1903* (1982).

Millett, Allan R. *The Politics of Intervention: The Military Occupation of Cuba, 1906–1909* (1968).

Munro, Dana Gardner. *Intervention and Dollar Diplomacy in the Caribbean, 1900–1921* (1964).

Musicant, Ivan. *The Banana Wars: A History of the United States Military Intervention in Latin America from the Spanish-American War to the Invasion of Panama* (1990).

Quirk, Robert E. *An Affair of Honor: Woodrow Wilson and the Occupation of Veracruz* (1962).

Reckner, James R. *Teddy Roosevelt's Great White Fleet* (1988).

Roth, Russell. *Muddy Glory: America's "Indian Wars" in the Philippines, 1899–1935* (1981).

Sweetman, Jack. *The Landing at Veracruz: 1914* (1968).

Welch, Richard E., Jr. *Response to Imperialism: The United States and the Philippine-American War, 1899–1902* (1979).

1919–1941

Lester H. Brune. *The Origins of American National Security Policy: Sea Power, Air Power, and Foreign Policy, 1900–1941* (1981).

Cole, Bernard D. *Gunboats and Marines: The United States Navy in China, 1925–1928* (1986).

Goldhurst, Richard. *The Midnight War: The American Intervention in Russia, 1918–1920* (1978).

Kennan, George F. *The Decision to Intervene* (1956–1958).

Macaulay, Neill. *The Sandino Affair* (1967).

Offner, Arnold A. *The Origins of the Second World War: American Foreign Policy and the Second World War: American Foreign Policy and World Politics, 1917–1941* (1975).

Unterberger, Betty Miller. *America's Siberian Expedition, 1918–1920* (1956).

Wheeler, Gerald E. *Prelude to Pearl Harbor: The United States Navy and the Far East, 1921–1931* (1963).

1945–1993

Allison, Graham T. *The Essence of Decision: Explaining the Cuban Missile Crisis* (1971).

Bryson, Thomas A. *Tars, Turks, and Tankers: The Role of the United States Navy in the Middle East, 1800–1979* (1980).

Cable, James. *Gunboat Diplomacy, 1919–1979: Political Applications of Limited Naval Force* (1981).

Cottrell, Alvin J. *Sea Power and Strategy in the Indian Ocean* (1981).

Etzold, Thomas H. *Defense or Delusion? America's Military in the 1980s* (1982).

Hammel, Eric M. *The Root: The Marines in Beirut: August 1982–February 1984* (1985).

Hosmer, Stephen T. *Constraints on U.S. Strategy in Third World Conflicts* (1987).

Howe, Jonathan T. *Multicrises: Sea Power and Global Politics in the Missile Age* (1971).

Johnson, Haynes B. *The Bay of Pigs* (1964).

Karsh, Efraim, et al. *The Iran-Iraq War: Impact and Implications* (1989).

Kupchan, Charles. *The Persian Gulf and the West: The Dilemmas of Security* (1987).

Lowenthal, Abraham F. *The Dominican Intervention* (1972).

Neff, Donald. *Warriors at Suez: Eisenhower Takes America into the Middle East* (1981).

Paul, Roland A. *American Military Commitments Abroad* (1973).

Ryan, Paul B. *The Iranian Rescue Mission: Why It Failed* (1985).

DISSENT IN WARTIME AMERICA

John E. Jessup

Americans do not usually accept thoughts about the military or about war with equanimity. Many believe that there is not now and has never been a need for the violence usually associated with war and the military when they are used to settle the nation's arguments. Many more people believe that it was only during the Vietnam era that citizens took to the streets to exercise their First Amendment rights to voice their opposition to what was considered an unjust war. Nothing is farther from the truth. Indeed, American history is replete with examples of vociferous, often violent, dissent by significant segments of the population that opposed one or another of the country's military adventures. Even in times of crisis or war, when the survival of the nation has been at stake, Americans have often refused to toe the line and raised their voices and their fists in anger against the government.

Dissent is a part of the American tradition, much the same as war and the military are, and citizens have used their right, to paraphrase historian Henry Steele Commager, to exercise their freedom to inquire, investigate, and voice dissent as an imperative necessity. "Freedom," Commager wrote in 1954, "is not a luxury that we can indulge in when at last we have security and prosperity and enlightenment; it is, rather, antecedent to all of these, for without it we can have neither security nor prosperity nor enlight-

enment." Commager believed that nonconformity always leads to attack by broad official or nonofficial elements, and that these attacks have deep, far-reaching implications. His reference was indirectly aimed at the paranoic investigations of Senator Joseph McCarthy into Communist activities in the United States, but it applies equally to all dissent and to all dissenters.

By definition, dissent is a differing in thought or opinion from the generally accepted norm or, in the case of war or the military, from national policy. Supreme Court Chief Justice Charles Evans Hughes called dissent "an appeal to the brooding spirit of the law, to the intelligence of a future day." Dissenters refuse to accept policies with which they disagree and often demonstrate their dissatisfaction through anger, public discord, and strife. This does not make the dissenter the enemy—too often it has—but rather indicates that a spirit of freedom exists in the United States and that it is an individual's right to express dissatisfaction with a policy or act of government. In the context of the subject of war and the military, the exercise of this freedom in America has meant that the people have demanded an inescapable logic to convince them that the military is indispensable or that war is the inevitable solution. Unless these criteria are met, antiwar and antimilitary dissent can and should be the expected result.

British statesman Edmund Burke wrote in *On Moving His Resolutions for Conciliation with America* (1775): "All protestantism, even the most cold and passive, is a form of dissent. But the religion most prevalent in our northern colonies [New England] is a refinement of the principle of resistance: it is the dissidence of dissent." Burke was convinced that England had been wrong in its exercise of power over the American colonies. As a result, he considered that not only was dissent apparent among the colonials, but dissidence and insurrection in the colonies most directly affected the legalistic and intransigent laws passed by Parliament for their regulation. Burke's influence was diffused by other considerations, but much that he wrote and said was relevant in the contemporary world, and his words were absorbed by those who helped shape the future of America.

There have been all types and levels of dissent in America, and Americans have felt innately obliged to voice opposition to much that has been suggested or provided. Welfare has been too little or too much, taxes have been too high or too encompassing, politicians have been statesmen or scoundrels, the military has been the nation's savior or an unnecessary luxury that should be cut from the budget. The spectrum of dissent covers all of the real and imagined ills of American society. Nowhere is this more apparent than in issues dealing with war and the military.

The opposition to U.S. involvement in Southeast Asia in the 1960s and 1970s was the most vocal dissent toward U.S. military policy in the twentieth century. Although violence was a part of the anti-Vietnam War phenomenon, it was certainly not the most violent, nor was its rhetoric the most damning. There has been significant dissent during every American war, except possibly World War II. In much of the dissident commentary from past wars there is an ironic similarity to charges leveled against the national military policy of the United States during the Vietnam conflict, a struggle that many Americans believe was stopped by the dissent itself.

THE REVOLUTIONARY WAR PERIOD

During the Vietnam War, many Americans were dismayed to learn that a significant percentage of South Vietnamese worked against their country's struggle for freedom from communism or remained neutral or uninvolved and took no part in the events that surrounded them. Much was said about the halfhearted determination on the part of the Vietnamese people in repelling invasion, an attitude used by both sides in the United States to prove the correctness of their causes. If the situation in South Vietnam is compared, however, to that of the American population before and during the American Revolution, a different relationship may be perceived.

Before the outbreak of the revolutionary war, the signs of dissidence were a direct corollary of the Americanization of earlier English resentment against the Crown and the military for what were perceived as excesses of authority and the use of power. This resentment manifested itself in the Boston Massacre of 1770, which was likened to the excesses of Oliver Cromwell in Ireland in the mid-seventeenth century, and in the more subtle dissent of the First Continental Congress when it accused General Thomas Gage, British commander in chief of North America, of having been granted authority over all "the civil governments in America."

The population of two to three million colonists was divided only slightly in favor of the rebellion, with the remainder staunchly loyal to the Crown or neutral and unconcerned about who won what. Many of those loyal to England found themselves tarred, feathered, and driven out of town. Some were beaten mercilessly and others were killed; homes and property were destroyed by the rebels, the same men who fought to ensure dignity through independence. Captain William Lynch's overzealous use of the rope in dealing with Loyalists he discovered in Virginia gave rise to the term "lynch law."

THE WAR OF 1812

During the Vietnam era, the term "hawk" took on the same meaning as when it was first used, to designate those who advocated war with England in 1812, particularly those who wanted to use the opportunity to annex Canada and Florida. Regionalism played an important part in the determination of who supported the war and who did not. New England, the commercial hub of the country, was vehemently opposed to the war even though it was their shipping and their seamen that were being harassed by the British. Their opposition stemmed from the knowledge that a war would ruin trade, and trade was the backbone of commerce. They saw to it that less than $3 million of the $80 million raised by the federal government to prosecute the war came from the New England states. The northern border states of New York, Vermont, and New Hampshire defied President Thomas Jefferson's embargo of 1807 and the war itself by continuing to supply foodstuffs and other goods, such as potash and whiskey, to Canada.

In October 1814, the Massachusetts legislature called for a convention of New England Federalists to consider revising the U.S. Constitution and even leaving the Union. After meeting in secret from 15 December to 5 January 1815 in Hartford, Connecticut, the convention agreed that secession was justified only as a last resort. This was a far cry from Hamiltonian federalism, but the power of the Hartford Convention was dissipated by the signing of the Treaty of Ghent on 24 December and the victory at the Battle of New Orleans on 8 January. The only real outcome of this expression of dissidence was the sounding of the death knell for the Federalist party and the quieting for a while of any talk of states' rights.

Southerners and westerners cared little about trade and New England's problems: their eyes were focused on the Northwest and Florida and the expected riches that would accrue from the acquisition of those regions. Some trade questions arose in the South, however, when Spanish control of the delta below New Orleans blocked downriver commerce. The concerns of the West and the South were viewed in the East as dissidence resulting from local trade problems that overshadowed love of flag and country.

In sharpening this focus, the perfidy of Napoleon Bonaparte in his dealings with President James Madison, a relatively naive man who could not see the trap laid by France to force the United States into a war with Great Britain, was overlooked. Great Britain, because it possessed Canada, and its ally, Spain, which owned Florida, became the chief targets of the War Hawks, those people bent on war and who were quite often savage toward those who were not. A Baltimore newspaper was closed by mob violence for remarks critical of Madison and the war. When other citizens objected to the violence and spoke for freedom of the press, they too were attacked, including a revolutionary war general who was beaten to death, and Henry Lee, father of Robert E. Lee and also a well-known officer, who was so badly injured that he lay near death for two months and spent several more months in convalescence.

THE MEXICAN WAR AND ITS AFTERMATH

> It is a mean and infamous war we are fighting. It is a big boy fighting a little one, and that little one feeble and sick. What makes it worse is, the little boy is in the right, and the big boy is in the wrong, and tells solemn lies to make his side seem right.

These words are from a sermon given by the Massachusetts theologian Theodore Parker and referred to U.S. involvement in the war with Mexico (1846–1848). Parker's opposition echoed that of most of New England, where the Whig party openly criticized national policy. Massachusetts officially declared the U.S. military moves a war of conquest. At the same time, abolitionists everywhere viewed the war as nothing more than a means of adding more slave states to the Union and said so loudly and often.

For Henry Clay, the American political leader known as the Great Pacificator, the struggle with Mexico was easily classified: "This is no war of defense, but one of unnecessary and of offensive aggression. It is Mexico that is defending her firesides, her castles and altars, not we." Clay had been defeated by James K. Polk in the 1844 presidential election and had hedged against the annexation of Texas. The majority of the country supported Manifest Destiny—the notion that the United States was destined to rule the continent from sea to sea. Whether the average citizen understood Manifest Destiny or not, the concepts that drove the doctrine made Mexican provocations in disputed territory on the Texas side of the Rio Grande all that more dramatic. Dissent, on the other hand, was both widespread and outspoken from those who saw other issues besides Manifest Destiny as being involved. Numerous newspapers worked actively to hinder the war effort. Many northern intellectuals, especially in New England, saw the war as a device for destroying the delicate balance that had been achieved by the Missouri Compromise of 1820–1821. Ralph Waldo Emerson wrote that "The United States will conquer Mexico, but . . . Mexico will poison us." Henry David Thoreau also objected to the war and refused to pay taxes that might be used to support its goals. James Russell Lowell, a poet and abolitionist, satirized the war in his *Biglow Papers* as an attempt to extend the area of slavery. John Greenleaf Whittier, also a New England poet and abolitionist, voiced his displeasure with the war by composing a battle hymn for Mexico, using a Spanish pseudonym to conceal his identity.

Not all of the notable dissent of the Mexican War period came from intellectuals; some who fought in the war did so against their convictions. Ulysses S. Grant, a relatively junior officer who landed at Veracruz with General Winfield Scott and marched with him into Mexico City, later wrote: "For myself, I was bitterly opposed . . . and to this day regard the war . . .

as one of the most unjust ever waged by a stronger against a weaker nation." Other military personnel expressed their dissatisfaction by deserting. Nearly 10 percent of the available strength of the U.S. forces never made it into Mexico because they had already left the ranks. A number of them joined the Mexican army and fought on the side of the enemy in such units as the San Patricio Battalion, a Mexican regular army unit made up largely of U.S. deserters.

Dissent culminated after the war, when Illinois Representative Abraham Lincoln openly challenged President Polk by demanding to be shown the spot on U.S. soil where the American blood was spilled that precipitated the fighting. The House of Representatives had passed a resolution charging the president with unnecessary and unconstitutional exercise of power in starting the war, but this condemnation was offset by the fact that Congress had consistently voted appropriations for the prosecution of the war.

Another form of dissent arose in Congress in the aftermath of the conflict that was political, even though it was directly associated with the military and the prosecution of the war. This dissent was generated by President Polk's relief of General Scott for what some saw as political reasons rather than a matter of Scott's conduct in the field. Senator Daniel Webster questioned the president's action after Scott's brilliant campaign in Mexico and his honorable and humane treatment of the vanquished enemy.

Scott had been relieved in January 1848 to face a court of inquiry about his conduct of the campaign, criticisms that most likely were circulated by two of Scott's generals, Gideon Pillow and William Jenkins Worth. Scott was soon exonerated and received a promotion to brevet lieutenant general, the first such use of that rank since it was bestowed on George Washington.

Webster, like Clay and John Calhoun, had opposed the war from the beginning and had lost a son in the fighting, as had Clay. When Webster sided with Clay in the Compromise of 1850, he was roundly denounced by the antislavery forces. Webster's dissent against the war and his opposition to Polk's action against Scott were as political as they were righteous. Webster aspired to the presidency and Scott's relief was an ideal method to gain a little more public attention. Webster's plan failed as the great expanse of new territory gained by the Treaty of Guadalupe-Hidalgo so greatly increased the potential of the nation that the public appeared not to want to hear the plight of soldiers, even one of Scott's stature.

Scott's well-known political ambitions, which directly opposed and nettled Polk, and his party did as much to cause his downfall at that moment as did anything that occurred within his command. The dissent that was produced in the long run affected the entire military structure, however, and it is therefore worth noting. That the dissent over the war did not develop into a more serious affair and have a greater effect on the prosecution of the war was due largely to the fact that the war ended too soon and without any great calamity or defeat that might have engendered a more violent reaction from the opposition. The war lasted only eighteen months, and the U.S. forces seldom incurred a reverse. One victory followed upon another, and when there is a clear victory, Americans have seldom complained too much or too loudly.

THE CIVIL WAR

The United States entered into the Civil War in a state of almost total divisiveness. Sectionalism transcended anything seen before or after. The East distrusted Republican President Lincoln and was jealous of the West. The population of the Ohio Valley states, largely of southern origin, were antiabolitionist in their views and felt the South was being unfairly coerced by northern economic interests. The South distrusted the North, which, they claimed, sought to destroy its traditional way of life.

The issues that caused the war were complex and profound, but the burning question was that of slavery. Emerson wrote: "If you put a chain around the neck of a slave, the other end

fastens itself around your own." Blacks, on the other hand, "had no rights which the white man was bound to respect," wrote Chief Justice Roger B. Taney in the majority opinion in *Dred Scott* v. *Sanford* (1857). Abolitionists rose in fury at the decision, which fundamentally denied citizenship to slaves and any semblance of protection against the law. The Dred Scott decision became the political issue of the period and without question helped elect many antislavery Republicans to Congress in 1858. The prestige of the Supreme Court was diminished to its lowest point.

In 1856, Robert E. Lee, then a colonel in the U.S. Second Cavalry, wrote to his wife, Mary Custis Lee, at Arlington, Virginia: "In this enlightened age there are few, I believe, but what will acknowledge that slavery as an institution is a moral and political evil in any country." After President Lincoln's election and South Carolina's ordinance of secession in 1860, Lee still hoped that "the wisdom and patriotism of the country" as a whole would prevail, and that he could continue to serve the nation "inaugurated by the blood and wisdom of our patriot fathers." He had apparently already made up his mind to leave the army before Scott called him to Washington in February 1861. Despite Scott's appeals and Lincoln's offer to give him command of the northern armies, he resigned on 20 April and returned to Virginia. His retirement was short-lived, and he took command of the Virginia Confederate forces on 23 April.

When Lincoln went to war, it was not to end slavery but to preserve the Union. Therefore, many abolitionists initially did not support the war, and all hoped that it would be over after a few brief skirmishes. As the war dragged on, however, and the death toll mounted, the enthusiasm of those who had initially supported the war dimmed. Only after Lincoln signed the Emancipation Proclamation on 1 January 1863 did more abolitionists give their wholehearted support to the war effort.

Throughout the war, the border slave states of Delaware, Maryland, Kentucky, and Missouri remained in the Union, although the loyalties of their citizens were sharply divided. The same was true in Washington, D.C. In California, which was as sparsely settled as most of the West, southern sympathies ran high. In the northern cities and in the rural Midwest, the poor and Irish and German immigrants were bitterly opposed to the notion of emancipation because they saw the freed slaves as a challenge to their own jobs.

The technological advance of the telegraph made it possible for newspaper reporters to become critical armchair strategists, though few possessed the necessary background to do so. Military secrets were often revealed and the reports of journalists often discredited the government and defamed military commanders. Newsmen who were vehemently opposed to the war used their papers to express one-sided and perfidious statements and clamored for a compromise peace that would have left the nation in chaos. In 1864, antiwar sentiment was so strong that the defeatist and pacifist wing of the Democratic party known as the Copperheads had become strong enough to dictate that a peace plank be included in the party platform.

The dissidence became vociferous as President Lincoln took steps to prosecute the war—proclaiming a blockade of the southern states in April 1861, increasing the size of the regular army in March 1863, and suspending the right of habeas corpus. The nation's first genuine conscription law, the Enrollment Act of 3 March 1863, became one of the chief focal points of dissent because of its unequal treatment of individuals who faced the call. The Confederacy had already established an equally inequitable draft law on 16 April 1862. In the North, officers charged with enrolling citizens for the draft were often beaten and several were killed or crippled. To avoid the draft, many fled the country, some to the Confederacy and others to Canada, which favored the southern side in the war.

Many men amassed small fortunes as "bounty-jumpers," by enlisting, collecting the bounty, and deserting, only to enlist again somewhere else. The wealthy paid $300 to avoid service or bought substitutes to serve in their stead—an American tradition by that time—

and others bought false exemptions. Although many derelictions can be charged to cowardice or lack of conviction, a good number of cases were directly related to dissidence. Entrepreneurs published pamphlets telling their readers how to avoid the draft, while others sold bogus draft-exemption insurance.

The Enrollment Act also resulted in open rioting in several cities. On 13 July 1863, a riot began in New York City that focused on the draft and on the fact that the Emancipation Proclamation would glut the market with cheap, black labor. New York had been basically sympathetic toward the Confederacy, if not for the right reasons. When the first drawing of names produced a disproportionate number of poor Irish immigrants, mobs assembled, and rioting spread through the city. The city's black population became one of the principal targets of the predominantly lower-class Irish rioters; many were beaten, a few were hanged from lampposts, and others were simply killed on sight. What had started as an antidraft protest had turned into a race riot of the worst sort. Tens of thousands of rioters rampaged through the city, terrorizing the populace and looting and burning at will. The rioting culminated—and the government reacted—when a black orphanage was burned down, killing a number of occupants. Thirteen regiments of militia and federal troops, some fresh from the battlefield at Gettysburg, were rushed into the city on 15 July. Their presence did little to abate the rioting, and on several occasions mobs attacked formations of troops. Order was restored only after the troops turned cannon loaded with canister and grapeshot on the rioters. When the rioting ended, an estimated twelve hundred were dead. Property damage ran as high as $1.5 million. Few of the ills illuminated during the course of the riot had been corrected. The drawing of names resumed on 19 August and freed slaves still constituted a threat in the minds of the poor whites in the city.

Within the military, the war was not uniformly popular. General Ulysses S. Grant estimated that only one out of every eight bounties paid produced one effective soldier, most of the others being lost through desertion. At the end of the war, Union desertions numbered more than two hundred thousand. Some criticized the military courts-martial system for not meting out harsher punishments for deserters, but Lincoln responding by stating that "you cannot order men shot by dozens or twenties. People won't stand for it, and they ought not to stand for it."

A number of Union army mutinies took place during the war. One regiment of the New York Volunteers refused to march into Virginia, but when the mutineers were surrounded by a reinforced battalion of regulars, their ardor diminished rapidly and the incident was closed. The act was reminiscent of the refusal in 1860 of the predominantly Irish Sixty-ninth Regiment of New York militia to march in a parade in honor of the Prince of Wales. The reaction carried over into the Civil War, with many Irish joining the Union cause for the specific purpose of gaining skills to aid in fighting England. In another incident, when the enlisted men of the Second Rhode Island Cavalry refused transfer orders, two of the mutiny's leaders were summarily executed in front of the assembled troops. The ardor of those who witnessed the executions faded and order was quickly restored.

THE SPANISH-AMERICAN WAR AND PHILIPPINE INSURRECTION

The War with Spain in 1898 ended so quickly that there was little time for dissent to develop. The very nature of the conflict, greatly aided by the lurid and often totally fabricated newspaper accounts of the plight of the Cuban people, also acted as a damper on dissent during the combat phase of the war. Sober afterthought proved the predicament of the Cubans to be real and that sensationalist "yellow journalism" had played a more than passing role in marshalling the American people to what was in and of itself a just cause.

The aftermath of the fighting in the last Spanish colonial bastion, the Philippine Islands, proved to be another matter. The guerrilla campaign that followed the annexation of the Philippines in 1899 engendered more vocal dissent than any previous war in American history. In remarks made in 1902, for example, Senator George F. Hoar commented on U.S. operations aimed at suppressing the Filipino insurrectionists:

> We converted a war of glory to a war of shame. We vulgarized the American flag. We introduced perfidy into the practice of war. We inflicted torture on unarmed men to extort confession. We put children to death. . . . We devastated provinces. We baffled the aspirations of a people for liberty.

After the Treaty of Paris, which ended the Spanish-American War and ceded Guam, Puerto Rico, and the Philippines to the United States in exchange for $20 million, the way was open for more sensational headlines, and a rift developed in the U.S. Senate between imperialists and antiimperialists. After the Senate ratified the treaty in February 1899, congressional dissenters formed the Anti-Imperialist League, which soon had chapters in most cities and claimed a membership of thirty thousand, with an additional 500,000 contributors.

Andrew Carnegie, the millionaire steel tycoon and a member of the Anti-Imperialist League, was one of their largest contributors and one of their most ardent spokesmen. Carnegie offered to purchase Filipino independence by reimbursing U.S. payment. His offer fell on deaf ears, and, after the Senate ratified the purchase, Carnegie wrote one of the senators: "It is a matter of congratulations that you have about finished your work of civilizing the Filipinos. It is thought that about 8,000 of them have been completely civilized and sent to heaven. I hope you like it." What Carnegie was referring to, of course, was the inordinately high casualty rates suffered by the Filipinos who fought with primitive weapons and bamboo shields against trained U.S. troops.

Once the Filipinos realized the hard fact that they had simply replaced a Spanish master with an American one, open rebellion raged throughout the island chain. It took three years and more than $175 million to show the native population that the United States meant to establish hegemony over their homeland. Americans read newspaper accounts of the atrocities committed by the rebels and by the Americans. As one senator stated, "I do not believe when Jesus Christ said to his disciples 'Go ye into all the world and preach the gospel to every creature,' that He meant to say, 'Go ye into all the world and shoot the gospel into every creature.'" Another critic described the claim by the administration of President William F. McKinley that the Philippines had never been promised independence as "the most incredible, unbelievable piece of sneak-thief turpitude a nation ever practiced." Samuel Clemens (Mark Twain) declared, "For a flag for the Philippine Province, it is easily managed. We can just have our usual flag, with the white stripes pained black, and the stars replaced by the skull and crossbones." Nearly 100,000 U.S. troops were involved in some phase of the insurrection between 1899 and 1902, and the war did not begin to wind down until the capture of the Filipino leader Emilio Aguinaldo in March 1901.

The years of peace between the end of the Philippine Insurrection and the outbreak of World War I were punctuated with dissent against the military policies of the United States. In April 1914, under the pretext that the arrest of U.S. service personnel in Tampico, Mexico, by followers of General Victoriano Huerta's government, constituted an attack on the American flag, President Woodrow Wilson authorized the landing of troops on Mexican soil. By the end of April, eight thousand soldiers and marines occupied Tampico and Veracruz. The fact that the U.S. servicemen had already been released with an expression of regret from Mexico did not matter in official circles in Washington, where the ouster of Huerta was the political objective, which was accomplished in July. One critic of this action, Joseph Lincoln Steffens, whom Theodore Roosevelt called a muckraker,

wrote, "We Americans can't seem to get it that you can't commit rape a little." Steffans would later subscribe to Communist theory, but his comments about Mexico, which were not written until 1931, reflected the feelings of many throughout the country that the U.S. intervention in Mexico was wrong.

WORLD WAR I

The United States became directly involved in World War I only after the conflict had raged in Europe for three years. President Wilson had urged that the United States remain "impartial in thought as well as in action." His position on the war had helped in his successful reelection bid in 1916, and the slogan "He kept us out of war" did much to ensure the victory. Wilson's position and leadership, however, could not prevent the slow drift toward war that began with the sinking of the liner *Lusitania* by a German submarine on 7 May 1915. This act, more than any other, helped illustrate the basic difference between German and British blockade policies, that is, that Germany went to unrestricted warfare and Great Britain did not, and aided in the erosion of support for Germany, which had been quite strong in the United States early in the struggle. A strong war party developed that was centered around northeastern shipping interests. This group wanted an immediate declaration of war against Germany, which they believed was the surest means of sweeping the sea-lanes of German submarines and raiders, ensuring that commerce could continue without interruption. A split in popular opinion soon emerged, however, pitting those favoring a strong preparedness program against those who urged continuation of a strictly neutral stance.

Antimilitary and antiwar elements joined together to form the American Union Against Militarism, which found strong and articulate support in William Jennings Bryan, an outspoken opponent of the U.S. campaign in the Philippines and secretary of state (1913–1915) with pacifist convictions. Bryan resigned as secretary of state when Wilson sent strong diplomatic notes to Germany demanding an apology for the sinking of the *Lusitania* and the abandonment of unrestricted submarine warfare.

The high point of the antiwar debate came during the period between 3 February 1917, when the U.S. broke diplomatic relations with Germany, and 6 April, when Congress declared war. This was a time of intense antiwar activity aimed at changing the course of U.S. foreign policy. The American Union Against Militarism published a national appeal for peace and the Socialist party held many antiwar rallies. Bryan delivered speech after speech across the country advocating neutrality. David Starr Jordan, former president of Stanford University, became the leader of the academic community's antiwar element and devoted most of the remainder of his life to the cause of peace, associating himself with the World Peace Foundation. After war was declared, however, Jordan and Bryan both volunteered their services to the president, with Jordan delivering a number of prowar speeches that stressed Wilsonian ideals.

Resistance also came from the Congress, where sectionalism caused a group of six western and five southern senators to conduct a five-day filibuster in March 1917 against passage of a bill aimed toward arming U.S. merchant vessels. Wilson called these senators "a little group of willful men." One of those senators, Robert M. La Follette of Wisconsin, and Senator George Norris of Nebraska declared that the country was being dragged into the war by financial interests that would profit by arms sales to the Allies. They further demanded that Congress, instead of allowing Wilson to take the country into war without the consent of the people, hold a national referendum on war or peace. The attempt to delay what already appeared inevitable failed, and the United States declared war on Germany.

Most of the opposition to the war quickly disappeared, in large part because of the lofty ideals espoused on 8 January 1918 by Wilson in his Fourteen Points address to Congress. The opposition that did remain focused on the controversial Selective Service Act and worked to

defeat its passage, although it was enacted on 18 May 1917. Led by the Socialist party, dissent against the draft law took the form of hundreds of leaflets, distributed in New York, Chicago, and other cities, that decried the horrors of war. One read in part:

> Into your homes the recruiting officers are coming. They will take your sons. . . . They will be shipped . . . by the hundreds of thousands to the bloody quagmire of Europe. Into that seething, heaving swamp of torn flesh and floating entrails they will be plunged . . . screaming as they go. Agonies of torture will rend their flesh from their sinews, will crack their bones and dissolve their lungs. . . . Black death will be a guest at every American fireside.

Socialist-led dissent turned from rhetoric to violence in Boston in the summer of 1917, when about eight thousand marchers against the war were attacked by a group of off-duty soldiers and sailors formed into an impromptu unit led by an officer. The parade was effectively broken up by the servicemen and many of the marchers were badly beaten. In another incident, an antiwar Socialist was stripped and covered with molasses and feathers and marched through the town of New Brunswick, New Jersey, for refusing to speak at a patriotic rally at Rutgers University.

A California group called the American Patriots Association published and sold a pamphlet informing its readers on how to dodge the draft. Whether antiwar dissent or profit was the primary purpose of the association is unknown. In New York and several other cities, there is little doubt that the mass meetings held on the eve of the draft were sincere efforts to thwart its purpose. The *Industrial Worker*, a labor union newspaper, published a piece of doggerel in 1917 whose message is clear:

> *I love my flag, I do, I do*
> *Which floats upon the breeze.*
> *I also love my arms and legs*
> *And neck and nose and knees.*
> *One little shell might spoil them all*
> *Or give them such a twist*
> *They would be of no use to me.*
> *I guess I won't enlist.*

Dozens of people were killed in pitched battles between rural and mountain community citizens and local authorities over draft registrations. In one incident, later called the Green Corn Rebellion, poor tenant farmers and sharecroppers in three Oklahoma counties, under the leadership of labor union organizers, planned to destroy bridges and telegraph lines in order to isolate their area and prevent draft registration. They also planned to march on Washington, gathering recruits as they went, in order to confront President Wilson. There was even talk of seizing the government. The protestors intended to subsist on green roasting corn. A posse of local law enforcement officers moved in when they learned of the farmers' plans.

There were more than 363,000 draft evaders in World War I. Certainly not all of this number can be attributed to dissent against the war, but some cited antiwar sentiment as their reason for deserting. Another four thousand refused to serve in combat, claiming conscientious objection, many even refusing to line up to be counted or fed during their processing into the very status they sought. Many refused to bathe, to wash their clothes, or to submit to medical examinations and vaccinations, despite an extremely virulent influenza epidemic that gripped the nation in the summer of 1918.

THE PERIOD BETWEEN THE WORLD WARS

Although the antiwar movement was strong during World War I, it was completely submerged beneath the lofty ideals that the majority of the U.S. population saw as the justification for the sacrifices. "The world must be made safe for democracy," Wilson said in his 2 April 1917 address before Congress. "Civilization itself seems to be in the balance, but right is more precious than peace." The nation joined in the crusade. When the kind of peace that had been fought for did not materialize and when U.S. entry into the League of Nations was scuttled because of partisan politics, the nation became

disillusioned, and a new wave of antiwar sentiment swept across the country. The 1920s and 1930s, when the nation was at peace, witnessed a greater display of antimilitarism than at any other time in U.S. history. The novels *All Quiet on the Western Front* (1929) by Erich Maria Remarque and *Three Soldiers* (1921) by John Dos Passos became the written essence of the futility of war and the blunderings and stupidity of military institutions and the governments that control them. Other media picked up the same themes, perhaps most memorably in the fade-out of a French soldier's hand grasping barbed wire in the film adaptation of Remarque's novel.

In 1929, Ernest Hemingway wrote in *A Farewell to Arms*:

> I was always embarrassed by the words sacred, glorious and sacrifice and the expression in vain. We had heard them, standing in the rain almost out of earshot, so that only the shouted words came through, and had read them, on proclamations that were slapped up by billposters over other proclamations . . . and had seen nothing sacred, and things that were glorious had no glory and the sacrifices were like the stockyards at Chicago if nothing was done with the meat except bury it.

Newspaper revelations inundated the country about atrocities (some real, some imagined) that accompanied the fighting in World War I—prisoners of war used for bayonet practice or pushed ahead of advancing troops to clear minefields, the suffering of civilians near the battlelines, the victims of gas. The raw brutality of war in the modern age became indelibly stamped on the American psyche, and by the late 1930s, there was fundamental agreement among the citizenry that the United States should never again be drawn into a war to save the British or French. The Republican party added a nonintervention plank to its 1928 platform: "The Republican party maintains the traditional American policy of noninterference in the political affairs of other nations. This government has definitely refused membership in the League of Nations and to assume any obligations under the covenant of the League."

Congress paid attention to the upsurge of antiwar emotion and severely limited military appropriations. Liberal educators and pacifists focused on removing Reserve Officer Training Corps (ROTC) programs from state-supported campuses. Their goal was the total abolition of military training at any American college. Students joined in the activity by forming the Veterans of Future Wars, vowing they would refuse to fight if the United States ever again became involved in war. In 1936, New York Congressman Vito Marcantonio said: "I protest against the militarism [of the ROTC]. Keep on in this fashion and the day is not far off when the youth of this nation will be forced to goose-step over the campus with right arm aloft shouting 'Heil, Doktor!'"

Between 1921 and 1936, isolationists demanded avoidance of war and military alliances with the major powers. Congress responded by keeping military strength at an absolute minimum. Walter Lippmann, columnist for the *New York Herald Tribune*, wrote on 17 May 1934, "As long as Europe prepares for war, America must prepare for neutrality." Others, such as the humorist Will Rogers, expressed a different view:

> We Americans are the only nation in the world that waits until we get into a war before we start getting ready for it. Pacifists say, "If you are ready for war, you will have one." I bet there has not been a man insulted Jack Dempsey since he has been champion."

The United States and fourteen other nations entered into the Kellogg-Briand Pact (also called the Pact of Paris), 27 August 1928, which renounced war as an instrument of national policy. Inspired by the U.S. movement to outlaw war, it was subsequently ratified by sixty-three nations. The United States, fearing foreign entanglements, added a number of modifications, and the pact lost much of its original purpose. One U.S. codicil was the right to self-defense. In 1929 the War Plans Division informed the army chief of staff that about all the nation could do was defend itself. Thus, for the moment, the political and military strategies of the country were the same—fight only if attacked within the forty-eight contiguous states. Even so, the isolationist movement continued to gather strength, and the U.S. military received even greater cuts in appropriations, which soon put into question the ability of the United States even to defend itself.

In 1933, the United States was ranked seventeenth as a world military power. The army was still equipped with World War I–vintage arms and equipment, including worthless tanks. Tactically, all units of the army were below authorized strength, and the onset of the Great Depression only further cut into military appropriations. Isolationist and budget-cutting policies stayed in effect until 1936, when sufficient evidence was amassed that the world was on the brink of war, and that the desire for peace had been shattered by Adolf Hitler's renunciation of the Treaty of Versailles, the occupation of the demilitarized Rhineland, and the rearmament of Germany. The activities of Italy and Japan were no less worrisome and, in combination with German aggression, led to a need for U.S. action aimed at improving national defense.

The U.S. rejection of the League of Nations had weakened the prestige and power of that organization to a point where its efforts to prevent Japanese aggression in Manchuria and the Italian annexation of Ethiopia fell far short of the hopes of its original sponsors. The United States instead attempted to singlehandedly secure peace as the world's "good neighbor," an ineffective policy put forth by President Franklin D. Roosevelt in March 1933. As the threat of war in Europe increased, a State Department committee was formed in 1934 to consider drafting a policy that might preserve the neutrality of the United States. Beginning in September, Senator Gerald P. Nye of North Dakota disclosed in publicized Senate hearings that bankers and the munitions industry had made tremendous profits from the sale of arms to the Allies in World War I, reviving the belief that the nation had been led into war in 1917 by unscrupulous Wall Street bankers and arms makers. That same year the National Council on Limitation of

Armaments claimed a membership in the millions and had as its goal the abolition of arms-making as a means of halting war. In December 1937 a constitutional amendment was proposed by Representative Louis Ludlow requiring a national referendum before Congress could declare war except when American soil was involved. The vote to place the Ludlow amendment before the House of Representatives failed by only twenty-one votes.

In August 1935, following the outbreak of war between Italy and Ethiopia, Congress passed a neutrality act directing the president, after he declared a state of war existed, to place an embargo on the shipment of arms to all belligerents. The neutrality act passed in February 1936 prohibited the extension of loans and credits to all belligerent countries except Western Hemisphere republics at war with non-hemisphere nations. The Neutrality Act of 1937 extended the embargo on the shipment of arms, but added a "cash and carry" proviso that would allow belligerents to buy raw materials from the United States as long as no U.S. ships were involved in their transport. As the situation continued to deteriorate in Europe and the likelihood of war increased, there was a somewhat halfhearted congressional loosening of the pursestrings for the needs of the armed services. Larger military appropriations followed, but there was little respite from the widespread antiwar sentiment that pervaded the country and that would remain in place until 1941. In 1939, newspaper publisher William Randolph Hearst instructed his editors, "Be neutral. Be American."

Although American public opinion was strongly set in favor of peace, President Roosevelt launched a limited preparedness program in 1939 that was designed to offset the technological advances in aviation that had given rise to the possibility that an Old World power could establish secret air bases in the Western Hemisphere and lay waste to the Panama Canal, the key to the U.S. naval defenses. The developments in aircraft, it was thought at the time, could endanger the concept of oceanic security that the United States had long embraced, and that had been one of the chief arguments of those who opposed a large army.

Following the German invasion of Poland on 1 September 1939, President Roosevelt proclaimed a limited emergency and increased the size of the armed forces. Congress passed the Neutrality Act of 1939, which repealed the arms embargo and allowed the United States to supply desperately needed munitions to Great Britain and France. This single action helped U.S. industry prepare for what was to come. After Poland fell, however, the six-month lull in the European war that followed led to a slackening of interest in preparedness.

Even after Denmark, Norway, Belgium, Holland, and France fell in quick order from April to June 1940 to the tactics of the Nazi blitzkrieg, many Americans hoped that Hitler could be defeated by no greater effort than extending material aid to the Allies. Up to that time the principal opposition to U.S. involvement in Europe came from the America First Committee, founded in July 1940 by R. Douglas Stuart, a Yale University law student. The committee claimed such notable members as Midwest executive Robert E. Wood, its first national chairman; Senators Nye, Burton K. Wheeler, and John T. Flynn; automaker Henry Ford; historian Charles A. Beard; and aviator Charles A. Lindberg, who also openly praised the Germans. This noninterventionist organization, which sought to halt aid to the Allies, was branded a front organization for the Central Powers and was accused, probably incorrectly, of harboring Nazi sympathizers. Although the committee was unsuccessful in its fight against the Lend-Lease Act of 1941 and the use of U.S. warships on convoy duty in the Atlantic before December 1941, its strength was sufficiently impressive to restrain Roosevelt from moving toward intervention. When Japan attacked the United States on 7 December 1941, the America First Committee quickly disbanded and urged its members to support the war effort.

During the same period, the Committee to defend America by Aiding the Allies gained some prominence. It came into being in mid-May 1940 with the sole purpose of keeping the

United States out of the fighting by supplying the Allies with the means for prosecuting a successful war. The committee never gained the level of support it intended for itself because the country was already carrying out much of what the group had wanted to do.

Isolationism remained strong until the very end of the prewar period. The Selective Service and Training Act, the first conscription law in peacetime history, was passed in September 1940, its proponents arguing that it was a defensive measure designed to protect the Western Hemisphere. To paraphrase Lippmann, the U.S. contribution to the war was to be the navy, the air force, and manufacturing. Even so, a prohibition was added to the conscription act that prevented draftees from being sent overseas. Throughout the summer of 1941, servicemen and other citizens bombarded Congress with petitions calling for an end to the draft, and when the act came up for renewal in August, it passed the House of Representatives by a single vote, 203–202. Just three months before Pearl Harbor, other elements, both in and out of uniform, called for mass desertions if the draft was continued. The key word became OHIO—"Over the Hill in October" (a reference to the selection of the first draft numbers in October 1940).

In fact, the pace of preparedness had been slowing, and by autumn 1941 plans were afoot to begin the demobilization of the National Guard, which had been federalized in August 1940, and to allow U.S. troop units to remain short of certain items of essential equipment so that those items might be shipped to the Allies. Four days before Pearl Harbor, the *Chicago Tribune* and its affiliated newspapers published the text of the Victory Program, the secret plan Roosevelt had ordered the army to draw up as a strategic military hedge against the possibility that the Soviet Union might collapse under the German military onslaught. When the plan's option of sending a U.S. expeditionary force into Africa to reinforce the British was denied by George C. Marshall, the army chief of staff, the *Tribune* called him a liar.

The unconcerned approach of the American people could be especially noted in the general national apathy toward German U-boat attacks on the U.S. destroyers *Greer* in September and *Kearney* in October. Only the apparent ambivalence of the American people allowed Nazi submarine attacks, some within sight of the U.S. shoreline and a serious threat to security, to take place without a greater public outcry.

WORLD WAR II

At approximately three o'clock on the afternoon of Sunday, 7 December, Senator Nye was giving an antiwar speech at a rally in Pittsburgh sponsored by the America First Committee. When an aide rushed to the rostrum and handed him a note stating that the Japanese were attacking Pearl Harbor, he refused to believe it and continued with his speech.

The sneak attack by the Japanese ultimately silenced antiwar dissent in the most effective way possible and brought the American people together in a common cause to an extent unparalleled in U.S. history. There were, of course, those who still protested the violence of war, but they generally kept their own counsel, as antiwar or antimilitary comments generally resulted in fights. Draft dodgers met similar reactions and faced not only criminal charges but the wrath of an aroused citizenry. Japanese-Americans were harassed and often beaten by their neighbors. Chinese-Americans in New York City wore signs that read "I'm Chinese" around their necks.

On 8 December the army recruiting office in New York City was inundated by volunteers, many of whom had been staunch advocates of remaining aloof from the war just two days earlier. Although much of the flag-waving that accompanied U.S. entry into World War I was missing in 1941, a more serious and determined nation undertook the task of again making the world safe for democracy. Typical soldiers entered service willingly, even some with the same disdain for war and its military institutions as their fathers had in 1917.

As soon as victory was achieved in 1945, a clamor arose from the American public and from around the world, wherever U.S. servicemen were stationed, to bring the boys home. Organized campaigns were started to pressure Congress and the president to accomplish that task. In the Pacific, thousands of letters were sent to Congress expressing the comment "no boats, no votes." Similar demonstrations of frustration with what was deemed to be a snail's-pace return of troops took place in Europe and the United States. Full-page ads were taken out in U.S. newspapers demanding the immediate return and discharge of all servicemen. One angry group of army personnel confronted General Dwight D. Eisenhower in his office and demanded an explanation for the lack of adequate shipping to carry the troops home. Other criticism centered on the officer-enlisted man relationship and the "officer caste system." Subsequent boards of inquiry found many of the complaints justified, and corrective action was taken to ensure a more even treatment of all military personnel in the future.

Demobilization was not completed until 30 June 1947, when the last nonvolunteer was released from active duty. In the meantime, both General Eisenhower in Europe and General Douglas MacArthur in the Pacific reported that their forces could operate in an emergency at only 50 percent of wartime efficiency and for no more than thirty days. Thus, "Bringing the boys home" meant a concomitant reduction in overall combat effectiveness. Public pressure and fiscal restrictions had forced a situation where the rate of demobilization had little or no relationship to planning for the future security of the United States. At the end of fiscal year 1946, the strength of the armed forces stood at 1,889,690, or 6,133,614 less than the strength on 1 September 1945, the day before V-J Day. This meant that 843 men and women were mustered out of service every hour of every day during that 303-day period. By June 1947, the armed forces were a shadow of their wartime capabilities, and Congress then let the Selective Service Act expire.

THE KOREAN WAR

In June 1950, Soviet-backed North Korean forces invaded South Korea. The American people gave President Harry S. Truman immediate and widespread support in his decision to intervene, believing it would be a short conflict, under United Nations control, and such campaigns usually meant few troops, and regulars at that. As the prospect of a quick and easy victory faded, however, the American public, while remaining strongly anti-Communist, raised subtle questions of method and expediency, as opposed to those of morality and pacifism, which had been the primary issues in past wars. After Communist China entered the war in November 1950, when North Korea appeared near defeat, no one seemed to know exactly what they wanted—the use of nuclear weapons, a full-scale attack on China, war with the Soviet Union, a negotiated settlement, or withdrawal from Korea.

As for the U.S. military, the low morale at the beginning of the Korean War improved noticeably as the fighting progressed. The overall spirit of the troops was not diminished despite World War II–issue equipment and ammunition, the disastrous retreat forced on the Americans by the Chinese intervention, the self-defeating rules of engagement imposed from Washington, and the inept command structure placed on the field forces by MacArthur.

Public frustration over the conflict in Korea peaked when Truman relieved General MacArthur of command in April 1951. The removal of MacArthur, architect of victory in the Pacific in World War II, was viewed as heresy by many Americans who did not understand that he had exceeded his orders and authority and the aims of the United States and the United Nations. Tumultuous crowds greeted MacArthur after his return to the United States, and he addressed Congress in what many considered a direct affront to the president.

Ironically, MacArthur would have expanded the war by attacking the Chinese mainland.

Had the original mission of freeing South Korea been carried out, and had MacArthur held at the thirty-eighth parallel, the war would probably have ended in victory in 1950. Instead, the war lasted three more years, cost thousands more casualties, and ended in a stalemate.

As the war wore on, the criticism did, too. Senator Robert Taft of Ohio, the chief spokesman for the neoisolationist movement, demanded the withdrawal of all U.S. troops. Those opposing the continuation of the war began calling the Korean conflict "Mr. Truman's War," echoing critics who called the War of 1812 "Mr. Madison's War." Members of the opposition Republican party accused the president of sending troops into Korea for the principal purpose of having them defeated and said that the administration had denied these troops proper air support and naval blockade. They later erroneously claimed that Truman had given away a sure victory by bargaining with the enemy. The Republican presidential candidate in 1952, Eisenhower, announced his intention of going to Korea if elected, the connotation being that he would end the war. After a visit to Korea as president-elect, however, he came away convinced that Truman's handling of the situation had been sound, which effectively ended much of the Communist enemy propaganda aimed at widening a schism in the United States over the war.

There were few antiwar demonstrations in the United States and little organized resistance to the draft, although there were some desertions and draft dodging. Some later claimed that the war was fought by the underprivileged, because college students were generally exempted from service while they remained in school. Truman countered that notion by stating, "It was a police action, a limited war, whatever you want to call it, to stop aggression and to prevent a big war. And that's all it ever was." Members of the administration also found fault with Korea, not so much because of the conflict, but with the country itself. Secretary of State Dean Acheson was later quoted as saying, "If the best minds in the world had set out to find us the worst possible location to fight a war, the unanimous choice would have to have been Korea."

What turned out to be the most serious manifestation of dissent during the war were the so-called turncoats, American prisoners of war who defected to the enemy. It has been estimated that approximately 13 percent of the U.S. prisoners of war held by the North Koreans and Chinese collaborated in one form or another. Twenty-three Americans even refused repatriation when the prisoner exchanges were arranged, although two recanted shortly afterward and returned to the United States. A number of Chinese and North Korean prisoners also refused to go back to their homelands, but the specter of U.S. servicemen betraying their country was a bitter pill. General Mark Clark, the UN commander, was quoted in *U.S. News and World Report* in August 1955: "There were heroes in those prison camps, great heroes. There were but a few rats."

Two decades later, Americans equated Korea with Vietnam. Both were lumped together as failures because neither was won. In Korea, political limitations were placed on the forces in the field; "fighting with one hand tied behind its back" was a common expression. Critics of the Korean War also looked back at World War II as the proper model for U.S. military conduct. Military leaders and citizens criticized what appeared to be the direct interference of political leaders in the details of military operations with a resultant failure to achieve victory.

Max Hastings wrote in *The Korean War:*

> Korea merits close consideration as a dress rehearsal for the subsequent disaster in Vietnam. So many of the ingredients of the Indochina tragedy were already visible a decade or two earlier in Korea: The political difficulty of sustaining an unpopular and autocratic regime; the problems of creating a credible local army in a corrupt society; the fateful cost of underestimating the power of an Asian Communist party. For all the undoubted benefits of air superiority and close support, Korea vividly displayed the difficulties of using air power effectively against a primitive

economy, a peasant army. The war also demonstrated the problem of deploying a highly mechanized Western army in a broken country against a lightly equipped foe.

THE VIETNAM ERA

The Vietnam era was one of the most trying times in America's history, and the war was unpopular from the beginning. Erstwhile allies warned the United States against becoming embroiled in a conflict on the Asian mainland, but to no avail. By 1948, the policy of containment of communism had become the pervasive strategy in U.S. foreign affairs. In 1950, commitment to the struggle in Southeast Asia began when the United States, along with Great Britain, gave de jure recognition to the government of Vietnam. For the next twenty-three years, the United States poured its wealth and manpower into fighting a limited war for the status quo against a tenth-rate Asian power that was fighting a relentless war for total victory.

On 8 March 1965, the first U.S. ground troops were committed to Vietnam and there was immediate objection to the war. Objections came from a sizable, highly vocal, and often violent segment of U.S. citizenry. The Vietnam War polarized the country and set groups of people against each other in ways not seen since the Civil War. Antiwar demonstrations paralyzed the nation's capital and forced the employment of regular army troops to clear the streets. Campus administration buildings were occupied by student groups. In May 1970 poorly led and harried National Guardsmen inexcusably opened fire on rampaging students at Kent State University in Ohio, killing four people. Selective Service offices were ransacked and burned. Open defiance of the law was preached and practiced before television cameras, from pulpits, on street corners, and in the halls of government. Disaffection set in that bordered on insurrection and a loss of faith in the country.

J. William Fulbright, writing in the *New York Times* in 1985, said, "The biggest lesson I learned from Vietnam is not to trust [United States] government statements. I had no idea until then that you could not rely on [them]." This naive statement by one of the leading senatorial opponents of the war points out one of the principal lessons of dissent. Much of the frustration that appeared was because of the fact that what the government told the American people differed considerably from what they were able to see on the nightly television news. The modern age of communications gave the U.S. populace a ringside seat to the war. War came into the living rooms of every American, and what was shown was not pleasing.

Historian Charles Fair wrote in *From the Jaws of Victory* (1971): "From the historian's standpoint, the significant feature of Vietnam is not that the methods we have used there are immoral; it is that they have not worked." Indeed, what people saw on the nightly news was the massive military capability of the United States being dashed against an anonymous enemy in the seemingly impenetrable wilderness of Vietnam; the largely ineffective but dramatic napalm attacks on what were, but were hardly ever reported as being, North Vietnamese sanctuary villages; and the equally dramatic summary execution of a Vietcong guerrilla leader in Saigon by a senior police official. The overall attitude of the government was expressed by German-born political scientist Hans J. Morgenthau: "No general was going to admit that the U.S. couldn't win this lousy war against a couple of hundred thousand peasants in pajamas."

As the U.S. government struggled with the war, the populace was voicing its opposition. Author Graham Greene was quoted as saying, "The conflict in Vietnam can only be resolved by the complete and unconditional withdrawal of American troops." Jules Feiffer, another author, stated, "Lyndon Johnson should go on nationwide TV and say to the American people, 'Ah have goofed,' thus ending the only real aggression in Vietnam: our own." Others prophesied a dire outcome. Doctor Benjamin Spock, a leader in the antiwar movement, wrote, "To win in Vietnam, we will have to exterminate a nation." More realistically, in 1968 the *Wall*

Street Journal editorialized, "We, the American people, should be getting ready to accept, if they have not already, the prospect that the whole Vietnam effort is doomed." That same year, at the height of U.S. military involvement in Vietnam, *Time* magazine echoed the sound of doom: "Victory in Vietnam—or even a favorable settlement—may simply be beyond the grasp of the world's greatest power." As military operations in Vietnam floundered, and as Washington bureaucrats bickered and postured, dissent grew and assumed new dimensions. Antiwar groups sprang up in every sector, the "American Advertising Committee to Unsell the War" being but one of many.

The aftermath of the war in Southeast Asia was as unpalatable as the war itself. "Vietnam is still with us," said Henry A. Kissinger, the architect of the peace plan that finally ended the fighting. "It has created doubts about American judgment, about American credibility, about American power—not only at home, but throughout the world. It has poisoned our domestic debate. So we paid an exorbitant price for the decisions that were made in good faith and for good purposes." In his farewell address as secretary of defense in 1987, Caspar Weinberger completed the epitaph of Vietnam: "The decade of neglect [the 1970s] was fed, really, by the most insidious idea—that somehow American power was immoral. We began doubting the war in Vietnam, and we ended up doubting ourselves."

AMERICA STRUGGLES TO REGAIN ITS PRESTIGE, 1973–1993

U.S. involvement in Vietnam ended in 1973. The conclusion of a war usually begins a period of soul-searching and, quite often, recrimination. The failure of the Vietnam War should have given the United States insight into the way future conflicts should be conducted, but the defeat was sufficiently ambiguous to deny

any such profit. Since the end of U.S. involvement in Southeast Asia, there has ben an ongoing struggle by antiwar groups to prevent any more Vietnams and any further proliferation of nuclear weapons.

From the mid-1970s through the 1980s, there were protests at missile plants, nuclear submarine facilities, and nuclear production facilities, and attacks on military recruiting stations and ROTC offices added to the general picture of a much smaller antiwar, antimilitary movement than openly existed in peacetime in the past.

Military operations involving U.S. forces after Vietnam—Lebanon, Grenada, Panama, and the Persian Gulf—were each accompanied by antiwar, antimilitary sentiment. The bombing of the marine barracks at the U.S. Embassy in Beirut on 23 October 1983 was a command error of the worst sort. At the same time, it was a terrorist victory that claimed the lives of 241 marines. The scene was repeated a few minutes later at the headquarters of the French peacekeeping forces in Lebanon. That kamikaze-style attack cost the French fifty-nine dead and fifteen injured. A third terrorist attack was carried out by Israeli forces at Tyre.

Senator Ernest F. Bollings was quoted on 26 December as saying, "If they've been put there to fight, there are too few. If they've been put there to be killed, there are too many." Questions were heard from around the world about the role of the multinational force that had been placed in Lebanon. Most of the criticism heard in the United States dealt with the political decisions made by the nation's leadership and not against the military, but the reflection on the military could not be misunderstood. The inept leadership of senior officers charged with the responsibility of securing the embassy in Beirut raised questions about the overall capabilities of the armed forces, at a time when the Soviet Union still constituted a major threat to world peace.

On 25 October 1983, just two days after the bombing in Beirut, U.S. military forces carried out a tactical landing on the Caribbean island of Grenada and restored order to what was quickly becoming a Cuban-dominated stronghold. The landings came about as the result of a series of events that began during the administration of President Jimmy Carter and culminated with the murder of Prime Minister Maurice Bishop by radical Communists in the third week of October. Within two days of the initial landings, the island was free of Cuban and Grenadian forces opposition. The U.S. press raised the first howls of protest because they had been effectively barred from accompanying U.S. forces during the assault. The second measure of dissent came from Congress, which voiced its displeasure over what they saw as a flagrant violation of the War Powers Act of 1973, which requires congressional approval of such troop deployments within sixty days of commitment. The fact that the entire operation took less than sixty hours was somehow overlooked.

The secrecy that surrounded the Grenada invasion was considered by many to have been un-American. Television news anchor Dan Rather fumed about First Amendment rights on the air, while some of the more intrepid newsmen found themselves under U.S. naval guns when their chartered boat was ordered to turn around and return to the mainland of the United States. Within the inner circles of the White House, as a hedge against a slip to the media, press spokesman John Speaks had been effectively kept out of the group who knew of the plan for the invasion. He commented in 1988: "The Grenada affair did teach me one valuable lesson about dealing with people like [Vice Admiral John] Poindexter. In the future, if I asked a question like "Are you invading Grenada today?' and the answer came back, 'Preposterous!' I would have to follow up with, 'Then are you invading Grenada tomorrow?'"

The success of the Grenada invasion helped relegate Lebanon to the back pages for a while and provided an outlet for many Americans who prefer a quick, relatively clean victory. The invasion of Panama on 19 December 1989 created another situation altogether. U.S. forces, including some of the most sophisticated troop units and equipment in the U.S. arsenal, including Stealth aircraft, were employed in an opera-

tion the seeming main purpose of which was the removal of Panamanian dictator Manuel Noriega, the leader of the most strategically important Central American nation. Reaction was immediate and covered the gamut of response from praise to consternation from all corners of the nation. The United States lost men (twenty-three servicemen killed, 322 wounded, plus three U.S. civilians killed and one wounded) and prestige in an operation that gained little in the way of advantage. The subsequent surrender of Noriega and his removal to the United States and his subsequent trial raised more questions among Americans, specifically about Noriega's association with the Central Intelligence Agency and how much monetary support he had been given over the years.

When Iraq invaded Kuwait on 2–3 August 1990, the United States, along with a number of other countries, responded by sending forces into Saudi Arabia, another Middle East country seen as Iraqi dictator Saddam Hussein's next target. The military buildup, called Operation Desert Shield, was sanctioned by the United Nations. Congress debated the issue and gave it their approval. There was immediate dissent among the American populace, who wondered over the real issues involved. Was it to stop aggression or was it to protect Kuwait's oil production? Congress posed some legitimate questions that the administration of President George Bush was forced to answer in such a way as to satisfy not only the politicians but the American people as well.

The stunning victory following the offensive carried out in Operation Desert Storm did not quiet the dissent that came from all sides. Granted the dissent was not as vociferous as was seen earlier in American history, it still asked searching questions that ranged from those about meddling in Middle East affairs to why the coalition forces had not finished the job by capturing Baghdad and Saddam Hussein. Americans were mesmerized by the instantaneous television coverage that produced dramatic highlights of modern war. The press was not so pleased, however, with the security measures that precluded their roaming freely during the buildup and offensive phases of the operation. The nation was even less thrilled when, a year after the operation, the Patriot missile was exposed as being less accurate and effective than it had been portrayed and it learned that pertinent facts had been omitted from the daily press briefings. While much of the information had been withheld for security reasons, there was sufficient evidence to support the claim of press manipulation.

One of the early public criticisms during the opening phase of the Gulf War of 1991 was precipitated by the apparent lack of interest on the part of President Bush, who apparently refused to interrupt his vacation and return to the seat of government to oversee the American response to the ongoing situation. As one citizen put it, "He had a nice time playing golf and speedboating. . . . Maybe if our leader played his Gulf game as assiduously as his golf game, we wouldn't be trapped in the rough." In a letter to the editors of *Newsweek* magazine (24 September 1990), another reader commented from the other side of the issue about the U.S. role in the Gulf War, "We seem to have become a nation of sheep and to have lost our ability to think for ourselves. If our primary response is that we are too concerned with our own lives to get involved, then our democracy will undoubtedly cease to function." The letter ended with a quote from the Bible: "For whatever a man soweth, that shall he reap."

By November 1990, the fourth month of Desert Storm, dissent began to take a more strident tone. Hecklers taunted the president as he spoke at a Republican rally. "No war for oil" was shouted and the taunters were quickly ejected from the hall. One citizen commented, "If the confrontation with Iraq becomes a war for resources, it could be our most futile action since we burned Vietnamese villages in order to save them." Another wrote, "The United States has shown contempt for the Arab people for decades and only cares about protecting 'its' oil and diverting attention from the economic decline at home." Polls indicated a substantial drop in support for the president's strategy in the Middle East and his position was linked to

the situation in Israel, where the government steadfastly refused to alter its position on the Palestinian question and on the issue of the occupied territories. Events in the Middle East from 1990 to 1993 did not improve the situation. Saddam Hussein remained a threat to the security of the region and his obstinate refusal to cooperate with the United Nations and campaign against the Kurds and other groups in his own country led to uncertainty for the future.

Whatever events come to pass, the level of dissent in the United States will be proportionate to the success or failure of the troops in the field. A quick victory anywhere is almost certain to quiet much of the opposition, especially that of Congress. Heavy casualties or military setbacks will eventuate louder, more shrill dissent that might take the violent form seen during the Vietnam conflict. History has shown that when wars are not won and won big, frustration sets in and the American people take to the streets. Nagging doubts about America's purpose in the Middle East and about Korea and Vietnam set the stage for dissent in any future military adventures that might be undertaken by the United States.

The initial euphoria that surrounded the U.S. show of strength in the Gulf War is akin to the attitudes of Washingtonians who traveled down the Warrenton Pike to Manassas in July 1861 to watch the First Battle of Bull Run, where they expected to see the Confederacy routed. The battle did not turn out the way it was expected to, and four long years of fighting was required to reestablish the Union. The war in Iraq turned out better and was won quickly, and with a minimum of friendly casualties. Any military operation in the future will seemingly have to meet the same standard.

Congress will probably continue its assertion of the right to debate U.S. involvement in conflicts and, after sufficient press coverage and media events, will attempt to make the correct decisions. Not everyone is so hopeful that this will happen. As Secretary of Defense Richard Cheney said during the debate on Iraq, "There are 535 of them [Congressmen], and they all want to be secretary of defense." One price of freedom and democracy, thankfully, is that not everyone will agree on all issues and how they should be settled.

BIBLIOGRAPHY

A Dissenter's Guide to Foreign Policy (1968).

The Dissenters: America's Voices of Opposition (1993).

The Dissenters: Voices from Contemporary America (1986).

Distrust of Authority: An Anthology on Dissent (1981).

Allmand, C. T., ed., *Society at War: The Experience of England and France During the Hundred Years' War* (1973).

Anderson, M. S. *Europe in the Eighteenth Century, 1713–1783* (1961).

Aron, Raymond. *The Century of Total War* (1955).

Aston, Sir G. *The Study of War* (1927).

Bailey, Thomas A. *A Diplomatic History of the American People* (1955).

Bailyn, Bernard. *The Peopling of British North America: An Introduction* (1986).

————. *Voyagers to the West: A Passage in the Peopling of America on the Eve of the Revolution* (1986).

Bancroft, George. *History of the United States of America from the Discovery of the Continent* 10 vols. (1834–1875).

Barrett, Donald J. *The Military and Society* (1972).

Bernardo, C. Joseph, and Eugene H. Bacon, *American Military Policy: Its Development Since 1775* (1955).

Blainey, Geoffrey. *The Causes of War* (1973).

Bolton, Charles Knowles. *Portraits of the Founders* (1926, repr. 1976).

Coakley, Robert W., and Stetson Conn, *The War of the American Revolution* (1975).

Colin, J. *The Transformation of War* (1912).

Commager, Henry Steele. *Freedom, Loyalty, Dissent* (1954).

Corbett, Michael. *Political Tolerance in America: Freedom and Equality in Public Attitudes* (1982).

Cousins, Norman. *Who Speaks for Man?* (1953).

Cunliffe, Marcus. *Soldiers and Civilians: The Martial Spirit in America, 1775–1865* (1968).

Doyle, J. A. *The English in America: Virginia, Maryland and the Carolinas* (1882, repr. 1969).

Drew, Dennis M., and Donald M. Snow, *The Eagle's Talons: The American Experience at War* (1988).

Dyer, Gwynne. *War* (1985).

Ekirch, Arthur A. *The Civilian and the Military* (1956).

Falls, Cyril. *The Place of War in History* (1947).

Furnas, J. C. *The Americans: A Social History of the United States* (1969).

Fiske, John. *The Critical Period of American History* (1899, repr. 1916).

Gewehr, Wesley G., et al., eds. *American Civilization* (1957).

Hastings, Max. *The Korean War* (1987).

Henkin, Louis. *How Nations Behave: Law and Foreign Policy* (1970).

Herring, George C. *America's Longest War: The United States in Vietnam, 1950–1975*, 2nd ed. (1986).

Hoyt, Edwin P. *America's Wars and Military Excursions* (1987).

Jameson, J. F. *The American Revolution Considered as a Social Movement* (1926).

Jeffreys-Jones, Rhodri. *Violence and Reform in American History* (1978).

Jessup, John E. *A Chronology of Conflict and Resolution, 1945–1985* (1989).

Jones, Archer. *The Art of War in the Western World* (1987).

Kane, Frank. *Voices of Dissent: Positive Good or Disruptive Evil?* (1976).

Key, Ellen. *War, Peace, and the Future* (1916).

Kessler, Lauren. *The Dissident Press: Alternative Journalism in American History* (1984).

Lancaster, Bruce. *The American Revolution* (1985).

Lens, Sidney. *Radicalism in America: Freedom and Equality in Public Attitudes* (1969).

Liston, Robert A. *Dissent in America* (1971).

Lubasz, Heinz. *The Development of the Modern State* (1964).

Marcus, Robert D., and David Burner, eds., *America Since 1945*, 5th ed. (1991).

Matloff, Maurice. "The American Approach to War, 1919–1945." *The Theory and Practice of War*, Michael Howard, ed. (1966).

Mecklin, John M. *The Story of American Dissent* (1934).

Miller, Albert J. *Confrontation, Conflict, and Dissent: A Bibliography of a Decade of Controversy, 1960–1970* (1972).

Millett, Allan R., and Peter Maslowski. *For the Common Defense: A Military History of the United States of America* (1984).

Millis, Walter. *The Martial Spirit* (1931).

———. *Arms and Men: A Study in American Military History* (1956).

Miroff, Bruce. *Icons of Democracy: American Leaders as Heroes, Aristocrats, Dissenters, and Democrats* (1993).

Morison, Samuel Eliot, et al. *Dissent in Three American Wars* (1970).

Naylor, David T. *Dissent and Protest*, (1974).

Nunn, Clyde Z., et al. *Tolerance for Nonconformity* (1978).

Ogg, David. *Europe in the Seventeenth Century*, 8th ed. (1962).

Paine, Thomas. *The Age of Reason* (1794).

Paret, Peter. "The History of War," *Daedalus* 100 (Spring 1971): 376–396.

Patterson, Thomas G., ed. *Major Problems in American Foreign Policy: Documents and Essays*, vol. 1 (1978).

Phillips, Ulrich B. *Life and Labor in the Old South* (1963).

Ravitch, Diane, ed. *The American Reader: Words That Moved a Nation* (1990).

Rousseau, Jean-Jacques. *Du contrat social* (1762).

Shafritz, Jay M. *Words on War: Military Quotations from Ancient Times to the Present* (1990).

Shy, John. "The American Military Experience: History and Learning." *Journal of Interdisciplinary History* 1 (Winter 1971): 202–228.

———. *A People Numerous and Armed: Reflections on the Military Struggle for American Independence* (1976).

Swope, George. *Dissent: The Dynamic of Democracy* (1972).

Tocqueville, Alexis de. *De la démocratie en Amérique* (1835).

Upton, Emory. *The Military Policy of the United States* (1917).

Vagts, Alfred. *A History of Militarism*, rev. ed. (1959).

Weigley, Russell F. *The American Way of War* (1973).

Weiss, Ann E. *We Will Be Heard: Dissent in the United States* (1972).

PART 5

☆

MILITARY ARTS AND SCIENCES

INTRODUCTION

— ☆ —

Phillip B. Davidson, Jr.

THE TERM "MILITARY ARTS AND SCIENCES" HAS NO PRECISE or universally accepted definition. A useful meaning of the term may be obtained, however, by breaking it into its component parts. The word "military" pertains to the armed forces of a nation state. The term "military art" refers to the practice of war as opposed to the theoretical science of war. The word "art" stresses the creativity with which a military leader fashions his strategy and operations to the realities of the conflict.

Military sciences must be defined in two separate ways. First, the advances of the natural and applied sciences, such as physics, aerodynamics, electronics, and medicine, have exercised a dominant, sometimes overwhelming, influence on the military policy and armed conflicts of nations. Examples abound—the breech-loading rifle, the steamship, the telegraph, the airplane, radio, radar, nuclear devices, "smart" bombs, and, particularly, medical advances in the care of the wounded. As the applied sciences have advanced and the scope of warfare has broadened, specialties within the military field, such as personnel management, intelligence, communications, and logistics, have themselves become esoteric disciplines.

Beyond the manifest influence of the physical sciences on the American military, there is another use of the term "military science" that is more abstract and controversial. This usage revolves around the proposition that there is a military science, that is, a systematized body of knowledge or principles that govern the effective use of armed force in war. Many military practitioners, philosophers, and institutions have held, or now hold, that such a science exists. Numbered among the famous practitioners are Napoleon, French Marshal Ferdinand Foch, and Mao Tse-tung. Some of the military philosophers are Carl von Clausewitz, Henri de Jomini (both analysts of the Napoleonic wars), and the most prolific writers on strategy in the twentieth century, the Englishmen B. H. Liddell Hart and General J. F. C. Fuller. Military institutions also espouse the proposition that there are immutable principles of war. Since 1921 the United States Army has endorsed a list of one-word principles of war that the army maintains are the fundamental truths governing the prosecution of war. The United

States Air Force has a different set of principles, as do both the French and British armies.

There is a general reluctance to accept the validity of any list of principles of war. The lists vary widely, each thereby refuting the others. Some lists (the U.S. Army and Air Force are examples) have been changed with the passage of time, destroying any claim to the immutability of the principles. Even the U.S. Army admonishes that the principles of war should be applied selectively, depending on the situation. Historians point out that about as many battles, campaigns, and wars have been won by violating the principles as by following them.

The truth is that war is too complex to be reduced to any simple formulae. What is actually required is merely the highest common sense. First, military leaders must have the ability to see the situation as it actually is and as it changes during the conflict and the ability to select the correct objectives. Leaders also must have the perception to deduce the strengths and weaknesses of both sides and the decisiveness to seize and hold the initiative in order to exploit their strengths against enemy weaknesses while nullifying the enemy's strengths and their own vulnerabilities. Last, a flexible mind that can adapt quickly to the inevitable changes and surprises endemic in war is essential.

In addition to defining "military arts and sciences," this introduction must compartmentalize the American military experience into periods of historical similarity. Five such historical eras have been selected. In each of the selected eras, a specific idea, concept, or circumstance dominated that period. The first era, 1607–1815, saw the struggle of Americans to survive, both as colonies and as a new and vulnerable nation. The second period, 1816–1865, was dominated by the two issues of expansion and slavery, culminating in the Civil War. The third era encompasses 1866–1920 and featured the expansion and rise of the United States as a world power. In the fourth segment, 1921–1945, the United States became the dominant superpower in the world. The fifth era, from 1945 to the present, features the nuclear age with a new set of complexities, varying from the doctrines of mutual assured nuclear destruction to limited war.

Certain themes have endured throughout American military history. The first is that the nation has fought its wars in accordance with the national life-style of each era. For example, during the American Revolution the Continental army and the American militia, both composed largely of untrained merchants, farmers, and backwoodsmen, fought generally as semiguerrillas, eschewing the rigid parade-ground formations of European armies. In the fifth era of U.S. history, the U.S. forces in the Persian Gulf War of 1991 waged a high-tech, completely mechanized conflict, reflecting the American life-style of the late twentieth century. As a corollary to this theme, one should note that domestic politics have often played a crucial, sometimes preponderant, role in the formulation of both national and military strategy. The several U.S. strategies in the Vietnam War, for example, were devised almost entirely for their effect on domestic politics and American public opinion, rather than for their direct impact on that conflict.

There also has been a continuing debate throughout American history as to the structure of the nation's armed forces. In the immediate post–revolutionary war period, the debate centered on whether the nation should be defended by a professional, standing army or by militia alone. The argument later became what proportion of the force structure should be full-time professionals and what proportion should be drawn from the reserve forces in time of war. From the American Revolution to the Gulf War, there have been serious controversies concerning the manning, training, employment, and call-up of the militia and reserves.

The third recurring theme is the peculiar dichotomy with which Americans have viewed the use of armed might. On one hand they have been quick to resort to military power. Over more than two hundred years of history, the United States has engaged in ten major wars, put down two insurrections (Shays's and Whiskey), launched several incursions into the territory of its Latin American neighbors, and waged countless campaigns against the native American Indians. On the other hand, American participation in its wars (with the exception of the Spanish-American War and the two world wars) has been opposed by significant elements within the United States, and the nation has consistently manifested an incapacity to sustain a long, bloody, inconclusive war.

There is another aspect of this particular theme worthy of note. Americans view war as an aberration—something to be concluded quickly with a rapid return to peacetime pursuits. The United States has traditionally demanded that the armed forces that have fought a major war be promptly demobilized and defense expenditures drastically reduced, regardless of the threat to national interests. As a result, in every conflict from the revolutionary war to the Korean conflict the United States entered those wars woefully unprepared.

1607–1815: THE STRUGGLE FOR SURVIVAL

This era, one of inherent danger to the early European settlers, may be broken into three periods. First, from 1607 to 1689 the colonists fought a brutal war against native Americans. The period from 1689 to 1775 saw a more conventional type of warfare, as France and England battled for hegemony in America. The third period, 1776–1815, included the American Revolution and the War of 1812, by which the fledgling United States first won and then confirmed its independence.

The New World to which the earliest settlers came was a perilous place. While the English, French, Spanish, and even Dutch colonies were rivals, and sometimes combatants, the greatest menace came from the Indians among whom they settled. While the Indians had neither political cohesion nor a coordinated strategy to meet the threat of the colonists, they were formidable foes. They fought a guerrilla conflict with war parties that operated without any coordination. Their favorite tactics were ambushes and raids, followed by a rapid departure into the forest. They refused to fight a defensive battle, if it could be avoided.

The English colonists, the dominant group, faced the Indian threat without military support from the British Crown. In response to the Indian menace, the colonists devised the first American military policy—an organization and a strategy. The organization was the militia. These part-time soldiers, organized into units of various sizes by locality and colony, were well-suited to the intermittent and dispersed warfare waged by the Indians.

Colonial strategy had two prongs. First, the colonists, exploiting the traditional enmity between the tribes, used Indian allies, augmented by native scouts and informers, to gather intelligence on the hostile tribes. Using the intelligence thus gained, the colonists ignored the elusive war parties and instead waged a relentless offensive against Indian villages and food supplies. Colonists ruthlessly killed women and children and destroyed property and livelihoods. For both sides the battle was a total war for survival and the colonists won.

Of the four wars transplanted from Europe to America between 1689 and 1763 only one had any lasting impact, the French and Indian War (1756–1763), which established British hegemony over vast areas of North America. For American military history the indirect consequences of the colonial wars between the French and British were important. In the first place, American officers obtained valuable combat experience, during which they gained a high opinion of themselves and a dismal view of the British professionals, both unjustified. Conversely, the British held both American officers and their militia troops in the utmost contempt. Second, with one or two exceptions (for example, Louisbourg in 1745), the colonial militia proved inadequate to the demands of offensive campaigns. Third, the colonial wars forced the separate American colonies into a closer union, particularly in defense matters. In addition, British practices, such as billeting troops in American homes, seizing private property, and stationing large numbers of British troops in American towns, strained the colonial ties of loyalty and subservience to the Crown.

The American Revolution was a pivotal event in history, launching, as it did, a world superpower. Historians continue to be confounded about how this revolution succeeded. After the war, George Washington, bemused by his own success, attributed it to "Divine Providence." He may well have been right, because it took a combination of fortuitous events for the American colonies to gain their independence. The transcending feature of this war is that the English lost it. In the final analysis, the British means were simply not sufficient to subjugate the rebellious American colonies. The global war in which England was engaged against France, Spain, and Holland precluded the necessary concentration of effort against the Americans to achieve victory. The British logistic problems alone were monstrous. They had to recruit an army in Europe, move it three thousand miles, and supply it in a vast, primitive, and hostile country.

Other deficiencies undermined the British effort in North America. In England, the war became a severe financial burden, and the Whig party continuously opposed the American conflict and sabotaged it in Parliament. In the early years, this opposition carried over into the indifferent conduct of operations by the British commander, Sir William Howe, a devoted Whig. Even after he was replaced, the British effort floundered for lack of clear objectives and adequate coordination of military effort. Last, the British made no effort to utilize the American Loyalists, approximately one-quarter of the population. In a war that was as least as much political as military, this was a monumental oversight, because it forfeited the one real chance the British had to keep the American colonies.

The Americans, more by intuition and circumstances than by considered thought, brilliantly exploited their strengths against British weaknesses. They blended military, political, and psychological operations. They protracted the war and succeeded in keeping an army-in-being as a constant threat. They fought a total war against the limited war waged by the British and creatively combined guerrilla warfare (particularly in the South) with conventional war. The Americans also seized the initiative by using their external ally, France, to execute the coup de grace at Yorktown. By the combination of these events, they convinced the British that the gain (holding the colonies) was not worth the foreseeable cost in lives, treasure, and time. The United States faced a similar predicament some two centuries later in Vietnam.

The revolutionary war was marked by some of the themes running throughout American history. The Americans were grossly unprepared for the war and disbanded their forces immediately thereafter. For the first time, there appeared significant opposition to a war (the Loyalists) and the incapacity of the Americans to sustain a long, bloody, inconclusive war. Washington himself thought that a determined British effort in 1780 would have caused the collapse of the Revolution because of American war weariness. The argument of the value of the militia versus a professional standing army surfaced again in the Revolution. The American militiamen proved once again unfit for extended campaigns far from their homes, but they fought well near their own firesides. It was the Continental army, however, aided by the French, that closed the war at Yorktown.

The period between the Revolution and the War of 1812 is the dark age of the American military. In 1784, Congress reduced the Continental army to eighty caretakers with no officer above the rank of captain. The navy was disbanded. As a result of the demobilization of the forces, the United States entered the War of 1812 almost totally unprepared.

The military infirmities following the Revolution were offset, however, by substantial progress in other areas. The U.S. Constitution established a central government with the power to raise armed forces. The clauses of that document set up the army, navy, and militia, the foundation of future military power. In 1803 the United States acquired a vast territory with the Louisiana Purchase from France. In many ways, however, the most far-reaching development of this period was the founding in 1802 of the United States Military Academy at West Point, New York, which was the first step toward the professionalization of the American military, although the academy was to be starved for resources and ignored until 1815.

The War of 1812 can be dismissed as a farce. The alleged causes of the war were insubstantial and the results ambiguous. The United States Navy performed well, but the conduct of the ground forces was often disgraceful. The militia reconfirmed the experience gained in the colonial wars and the Revolution that it was unsuited for anything except the repulse of intermittent Indian raids. The New England states strenuously opposed the war and even refused to commit their militia to the common defense.

Two advantages did result from this comfortless experience. First, the war destroyed the idea that the nation could be defended by the militia alone, although the militia concept in varying form lasted through the Spanish-American War of 1898. Second, the bungling American military leadership in the ground conflict convinced the U.S. government and the American people that war could not be waged by amateurs. As a result, West Point was given the resources and prominence to produce the trained military leaders and the engineers needed by the westward-moving nation.

Americans survived the first two centuries of their existence by outlasting the Indians, the Spanish, the French, and the British. They survived not by any martial precocity or ardor but mostly from many fortunate events, most of them unearned and unplanned.

1815–1865: THE ERA OF EXPANSION AND SLAVERY

The years 1815–1865 were marked by two transcending circumstances within the United States—territorial expansion and the conflict over slavery. Following the War of 1812, the U.S. Army was reduced to some ten thousand men. This force had to eject the Spaniards from Florida—which it did—and suppress the guerrilla warfare of Indians, whose raids ranged from Florida to the Canadian border. The navy fared better. Seven ships-of-the-line were constructed in the 1820s and were used principally to suppress the Barbary pirates and other corsairs. These developments and campaigns became a sideshow, however, with the advent of the Mexican War in 1846.

The Mexican War was an imperial war of American aggression. President James Polk had two clearly defined objectives—extend the southern border of Texas from the Nueces River to the Rio Grande and annex California and the great Southwest. Domestic politics played a major part in these objectives. Polk and the Democrats had just won an election by advocating territorial expansion, and the slave states hoped to expand slavery into the acquired territory.

The United States won the Mexican War quickly with relatively few battle casualties. Zachary Taylor seized the disputed territory down to the Rio Grande, while Stephen W. Kearny took New Mexico and Arizona with a small force. In California, American colonists, the U.S. Navy, and a group under John C. Frémont seized that state. When Mexico refused to acquiesce to these annexations, Polk had General Winfield Scott land in Mexico at Veracruz, move inland, and take Mexico City, ending the war.

Several factors contributed to the victory over Mexico. Polk was a superb war president. He was served by competent commanders in Scott, Taylor, and Kearny, and graduates of West Point gave the junior officer corps a professionalism theretofore lacking. As usual, there was significant domestic opposition to the war, principally in New England, but people as far apart ideologically and politically as John C. Calhoun and Abraham Lincoln opposed the war for political or moral reasons. This opposition, however, had little chance to erode the support for this short, relatively bloodless, and successful war, which brought Texas, New Mexico, California, Utah, Nevada, Arizona, and parts of Colorado and Wyoming into the United States. The nation now stretched from "sea to shining sea," and it had fulfilled the dreams of its founders as to its Manifest Destiny.

In May 1844, Samuel Morse transmitted the first message over the telegraph: "What has God wrought?" The military should have asked the same question, because the telegraph and other technological developments were revolutionizing war. The steamboat and the railroad, which had been in existence since the early 1800s, came of age. Naval strategy and tactics underwent radical changes as steam and iron replaced sail and wood, while the railroad revolutionized the movement and supply of huge forces. Perhaps the most important military change was the emergence in quantity of the rifle, a vast improvement over the musket in reliability, range, and lethality. This weapon upset the previous balance between the offense and defense in favor of the latter, a factor that would prove critical in the Civil War.

In 1861 no American leader, North or South, wanted civil war, yet it came on with the steady march of inevitability. With the outbreak of war in April 1861, the comparison of strengths and weaknesses drastically favored the Union. The first Union strength lay in its manpower superiority, 20 to 23 million people opposed to the Confederacy's 6 million (plus 3.5 million slaves). The North's industrial and matériel advantages were equally great. Control of the seas, another strength, allowed the North to blockade the South, preventing foreign aid from reaching the Confederacy and strangling its commerce with Europe. It also gave the Union an advantage in riverine warfare, a significant advantage in view of the navigable rivers leading into the heart of the Confederacy.

The first Union weakness was the opposition to the war in the North. The Democrats covertly opposed the war for partisan political reasons; others objected on moral grounds, judging the North to be a wanton aggressor. The second Union weakness lay in the tremendous logistical support required for the huge Union forces. Railroads were sparse and vulnerable to easy destruction. Eventually, millions of tons of supplies had to be hauled over primitive roads by horses and wagons.

Outmanned and outgunned, the strengths of the Confederacy were intangible but nevertheless potent. First, most of the outstanding officers of the "old army" were Southerners, and they followed their states into the Confederacy. Second, the war was supported fervently by the entire white population of the South. Third, geography and the dispositions of the opposing forces gave the South the advantage of interior lines, as opposed to the Union's possession of exterior lines. When exploited, these interior lines allowed the Confederacy to shift forces within its defensive circumference from one front to another either to bolster threatened areas or to mount an offensive.

The South, of course, had serious weaknesses. The North's strengths in men and resources constituted the major southern weaknesses, but there were others. The nature of the Confederate cause, its weaknesses in men and matériel, and its geography forced it onto the defensive, and it could not be strong everywhere. Thus, it could not fight a passive perimeter defense, because the Union with its manpower and matériel advantage would break through somewhere or simply crumple the whole defensive periphery.

These circumstances dictated the opposing strategies. Initially, Lincoln adopted a concept proposed by the venerable Winfield Scott. Scott's concept envisioned blockading the ports of the Confederacy and gaining control of the Mississippi River throughout its length. It came to be called, derisively, the Anaconda Plan, since it would "squeeze" the South into negotiations for reentry into the Union without undue bloodshed or destruction. It was a strategy of limited means to gain limited ends, but the bloody battles and other events of 1862 revealed the inadequacy of Scott's strategy. By mid-1862 it was evident that both sides were faced with a total war. Thereafter, the aim of northern strategy was to crush the South. The Union campaign plan for the western theater sought to exploit the South's vulnerabilities because of the configuration of its rivers and the Union's naval and riverine superiority. First, the Mississippi River would be cleared and controlled, isolating Texas, Louisiana, Arkansas, and the Indian Territory. Second, the North would drive down the Tennessee River to Chattanooga, a road and rail center, then to Atlanta, Georgia, the jewel of the South, cutting off Mississippi, Alabama, and part of Georgia from the rest of the Confederacy.

Meanwhile, in the East, other Union forces would bear in from Ohio and western Virginia toward Richmond. Finally, the proximity of the two capitals and their symbolic value dictated that a major effort would be made by both sides in northern Virginia and adjoining areas, where the seizure of the enemy capital or the destruction of one of its major armies would have a cataclysmic effect on national morale and international relations. This entire strategy, both east and west, required the North to seize and hold the strategic initiative.

The objective of the South's grand strategy was to convince the people of the North that the restoration of the Union and the emancipation of the slaves would not be worth the blood, treasure, and time required to do so. This political objective, however, posed tremendous difficulties for General Robert E. Lee, the chief Confederate strategist. Because the South could not opt for a passive defense, Lee's solution was to conduct an offensive-defensive operation by which the South, using its position on interior lines, would concentrate a superior force against one of the Union armies and destroy it. Lee believed that such a blow would shatter the wavering will of the North to continue the war. This strategy required the South to seize and hold the strategic initiative, at least intermittently. To understand the Civil War, one must grasp that it was a contest for the strategic initiative.

In the western theater, the South, largely through inept command, surrendered the strategic initiative early to the North. The Confederacy did undertake some tactical initiatives from time to time (the battles of Shiloh, Nashville, and Atlanta are the major examples), which usually came off badly. As a result, the fortunes of the Union in time prospered in the west, and it was able to carry out its strategy of carving up the Confederacy in that theater.

The real battle for the strategic initiative took place in the Virginia-Maryland-Pennsylvania theater. When the Union had the initiative in the early years of the war, it attempted to capture Richmond. These efforts, hesitant and fumbling, were thwarted by Lee and his Army of Northern Virginia. In riposte, Lee would concentrate his forces, seize the strategic initiative, and attempt to inflict a catastrophic defeat on the Union Army of the Potomac.

The first of these Confederate ripostes began with Thomas J. "Stonewall" Jackson's Shenandoah Valley Campaign of 1862. This brilliant operation ejected the Union forces from the valley, threatened Washington, D.C., and diverted an entire army corps from General George B. McClellan, who was advancing on Richmond. Lee quickly brought Jackson's force to the Richmond area and struck McClellan with this reinforcement. The offensive freed Richmond but did not destroy McClellan's army, which was Lee's objective.

Lee next launched an offensive into Maryland, hoping again to destroy the Army of the Potomac. He failed again at Antietam, and in some desperation, he initiated the Gettysburg campaign in 1863 with disastrous results. The Gettysburg campaign completed the destruction of the strategic offensive capability of the Army of Northern Virginia. Lee's offensives from the first valley campaign to Gettysburg had killed off the flower of his army, a shocking sixty-two thousand men. Even his victories (Second Bull Run and Chancellorsville) cost him twenty-two thousand more casualties. One of the Confederacy's great strengths, its superior corps of officers and soldiers, had been consumed on these battlefields.

Lee never won his climactic victory, and many historians aver that he never could have won such a victory. The Army of the Potomac was too large and too far-flung to be destroyed in one battle. Even more important, the new infantry weapon, the rifle, had made the cost of offensive warfare excessive, particularly for the side with limited manpower—the fatal flaw of Lee's strategy.

In March 1864, Ulysses S. Grant became general in chief of the U.S. Army. He envisioned two strategic objectives to win the war. The first was to deny the Confederacy the ability to use its interior lines to transfer troops within and between theaters, which the South had done throughout the war. To do so, Grant ordered all Union forces to attack relentlessly, thereby seizing the initiative and pinning southern troops in place. Second, Grant determined to exploit a growing vulnerability of the South, its difficulties in supplying its forces, particularly those in the eastern theater. Accordingly, he directed all Union forces to destroy crops and livestock, particularly in the breadbasket areas of Georgia, Tennessee, and the Shenandoah Valley. Coupled with this tactic, Grant ordered raids, sometimes in corps strength, to destroy the railroads supporting Confederate forces.

Acting on these strategies, Grant promptly seized the initiative in the East. He fastened onto Lee's army, employing his superior manpower to exhaust the Army of Northern Virginia. Under his direction, General William T. Sherman moved to Atlanta and then to the sea, and with the surrender of General Joseph E. Johnston's Confederate forces on 14 April 1865, the war ended.

Sherman's final campaign through Georgia and the Carolinas brought a new dimension to American warfare—calculated barbarism. His announced aim was not only to destroy the resources supporting the Confederate war effort but also to shatter the will of the noncombatants in his path to continue their support of the conflict. This new dimension of American warfare led directly into the modern era.

1865–1920: EXPANSION AND RISE OF THE UNITED STATES AS A WORLD POWER

This third era can be divided into three periods: the winning of the West, 1865–1890; the Spanish-American War, 1898; and the events leading up to and through World War I.

In 1865, as in previous years, the United States hastily demobilized the magnificent army and navy that had won the Civil War, leaving a small regular army of thirty-six thousand men to carry out occupation duties in the South and to protect the burgeoning movement of settlers into the western frontier, a flood that brought white settlers into direct confrontation with the western Indians. It has often been said that the military, particularly the U.S. Army, has no corporate memory, and its campaigns against the western Indians confirm this defect. What made this memory lapse more inexcusable was the fact that the Indians had not changed essentially since 1607. They still fought each other, had no political cohesion or overall strategy, and operated almost always as guerrillas in isolated war parties. What had changed was that the Indians now had horses and guns, which increased their mobility and firepower.

At first the army tried to combat Indian guerrilla tactics by establishing a string of small isolated forts along the line of the frontier, but that arrangement failed. Generals Sherman and Philip H. Sheridan, who conducted the campaigns against the Indians, soon fell back on the strategy that had worked two centuries earlier—the use of friendly Indian scouts and even

Indian combat units and the initiation of a relentless campaign against the villages and livelihood of the Indians, particularly during the winter. This strategy, ruthless and often barbaric, eventually succeeded, and by 1890 the West had been won.

Another important movement was taking place in the army and navy—the growth of professionalism. Under the aegis of Sherman and Admiral Stephen B. Luce, and spurred by the studies of army Lieutenant Colonel Emory Upton and the navy's Alfred T. Mahan, officers began the serious study of war as a profession. Professional publications appeared, and advanced service schools were established—the Infantry and Cavalry School at Fort Leavenworth, Kansas, in 1881, and the Naval War College in 1884. Under Upton's urging, civilian and military leaders began to study seriously the need for a professional standing army of substantial size.

The period from 1890 to 1907 encompassed the Spanish-American War and the Philippine Insurrection. The Spanish-American conflict was one of those "splendid, little wars" that Americans relish—short, almost bloodless, and victorious. It was won essentially by the victories of the navy at Manila Bay in the Philippines and Santiago, Cuba. The ground campaigns, such as they were, were poorly conducted, and nonbattle deaths outnumbered those from battle by a fourteen-to-one ratio. By the Treaty of Paris, Spain granted Cuba its independence, ceded Puerto Rico and Guam to the United States, and sold the Philippines to the United States for $20 million.

When the United States took control of the Philippines, it inherited a native insurgency. Initial U.S. efforts to put down the uprising by conventional military methods failed. In 1901, President William McKinley made William Howard Taft the civil governor of the Philippines with control of the military. Taft began a pacification program that included land reform, a civil affairs effort, and an educational program, and he replaced the U.S. troops with a Filipino constabulary. By 1902 the insurgency was over, but sporadic guerrilla warfare continued until 1907.

Even before the Philippine Insurrection was overcome, U.S. forces found themselves exposed to the inevitable frustrations inherent in coalition warfare. In 1900 the Boxers, a Chinese xenophobic society, attempted by violence to drive all foreigners from China. They besieged and attacked the foreign legations compound in Peking. To lift this siege several European nations plus Russia, Japan, and the United States organized a relief force under a complex system of joint command. Although the coalition force eventually relieved the legations, the expedition was beset throughout by jealousies, bickering, and disunity of effort.

This experience was more than offset by the construction of the Panama Canal, completed in 1914. It was the United States armed services, particularly the army, that eliminated the tropical diseases by building modern sewage and water systems, coupled with an aggressive health-care campaign. This accomplishment allowed the army engineers under Lieutenant Colonel G. W. Goethals to complete this monumental construction project.

Shortly thereafter, the army had another "little war" on its hands, against the Mexican Francisco "Pancho" Villa. In March 1916 Villa attacked Columbus, New Mexico, killing eight soldiers and ten civilians. President

Woodrow Wilson launched the Punitive Expedition into Mexico, under Brigadier General John J. Pershing, to punish Villa. The expedition failed for a number of reasons—the restrictions imposed by Wilson, the harsh terrain, a hostile population, and the army's lack of proper training and equipment to do the job. There appeared, however, some noteworthy innovations—a truck company, machine-gun companies, a field radio unit, and eight JN-4 aircraft (the Flying Jennies).

When the United States entered World War I in 1917, it was wretchedly unprepared, as usual. The army lacked a modern rifle in sufficient numbers and an effective artillery piece. There was not one organized infantry division, and its General Staff included only nineteen officers. The air arm had fifty-five aircraft, of which fifty-one were obsolete and four were obsolescent. The navy was in better condition but had too many battleships and not enough destroyers and transports, which were critical in moving a vast army across the Atlantic, which was teeming with German U-boats.

The situation dictated that U.S. participation be principally on the western front, a line of trenches stretching from the North Sea to Switzerland. By 1917, the conflict had become a war of attrition that had bled the combatants white, particularly the French and British. The British were exhausted and the French faced mutiny. With the entry of the Americans in 1917, the strategical problem on the western front came down to the factor of time. Could the Americans with their millions of fresh soldiers participate effectively on the western front before the Germans overpowered France and Great Britain? This threat was intensified in late 1917, when Russia collapsed on the eastern front, freeing a huge German force for operations to the west.

The Allied problem of time was aggravated by two factors. First, there was the sheer immensity of the task of mobilizing, training, equipping, transporting, and employing millions of Americans in Europe. The second factor was a prolonged debate among the Allies over what came to be called "amalgamation." Desperate about time and lack of manpower, the British and French wanted U.S. soldiers sent as individual replacements (or in small replacement units) to be absorbed into existing French and British units. The Americans resisted this, insisting that their troops be employed in large units under the U.S. flag. The Americans won the debate, but, as a result, made their presence felt only during the last six months of the war.

In effect, for the Americans, World War I was a short, victorious war, a significant fact because the support of the war never wavered despite the fact that U.S. casualties reached 203,000 wounded and 53,000 killed. The army, after a few false starts, performed well, and the navy did yeoman service in its convoy and antisubmarine campaigns. The army air service did not contribute significantly to the Allied victory, but its advancement in aircraft and tactics gave encouragement to its future. Above all, the United States had shown that it had the manpower, the industrial resources, the skilled leaders, and the will to be a great power. It had come of age in the global arena.

1921–1945: THE DOMINANT SUPERPOWER

As was customary, the United States promptly demobilized the huge armed forces of World War I. The army, including the Army Air Corps, shrunk to a force of about 130,000. The navy, titularly the first line of defense, fared better. Although the U.S. ship inventory was cut by the Washington Naval Conference of 1921–1922 and the London Conference of 1930, the navy emerged with a viable and modern fleet, including two aircraft carriers and a submarine force.

The 1920s and 1930s were times of professional ferment. The navy air arm came into being, and the army created an embryo armored force. Both the army and the navy developed and expanded their professional educational systems, while new and radical concepts appeared in the service journals. Nowhere was the ferment as intense and radical as in the struggle regarding the future of the air arm of the army. In the immediate post–World War I period, the air power enthusiasts, led by Brigadier General William "Billy" Mitchell, believed that air power alone would win future wars. In view of this conviction, Mitchell demanded that the air arm be established as a separate service on a par with the army and navy. In 1926 his extravagant charges against the Navy and War departments of "criminal negligence and almost treasonable administration" brought about his court-martial and subsequent resignation. His many disciples carried on the battle, however, with unabated vigor.

In 1933 the army became a key part of a new experiment—the Civilian Conservation Corps (CCC). This New Deal agency was created to provide relief for unemployed young men. The CCC devoted itself mainly to reforestation but also worked on projects of soil erosion and fire prevention. The CCC was organized into quasi-military camps under the command of army officers. The CCC was the most widely accepted of all the New Deal agencies and was terminated in 1942 as World War II brought on the draft and full employment.

When World War II erupted in Europe in September 1939, the United States was, as usual, unprepared. By the time of U.S. entry into the war in 1941, however, significant steps had been taken to mobilize the immense manpower and industrial potential of the nation. After the United States entered the war, the first strategic decision was to decide which enemy, Japan or Germany, should be given Allied priority of effort. Germany's successes in 1942 in Russia and North Africa dictated that the Nazis, the most dangerous foe, should be defeated first.

The second major strategic decision flowed from the first—how to defeat Adolf Hitler. The British and the Americans split on this issue. The British advocated a strategy relying on blockade, bombing, subversion, and propaganda with ground military operations limited only to the periphery of Nazi-controlled territory. The Americans espoused the Grant-like strategy of landing on the Continent and smashing the Germans between the western Allies and the Soviets. The American view was adopted in 1944, largely because the preponderance of the western effort would be American, and because Stalin strongly supported the cross-channel attack.

Whereas the war in Europe was an air-land battle, the Pacific conflict was a maritime war. Although not clearly realized at the time, the war was decided by the navy's victory at Midway, where the Japanese lost four carriers and the strategic initiative in the Pacific. This victory and others, plus the early breaking of the Japanese strategic communications code, permitted General Douglas MacArthur to advance by island-hopping from Australia to the Philippines, as did Admiral Chester Nimitz from Hawaii to Okinawa. They were preparing a joint assault on the Japanese island of Kyushu, when the atomic bombs were dropped on Japan, ending the Pacific war.

World War II saw great innovations—huge armored forces in Europe, strategic bombing campaigns in both theaters, the elevation of the carrier to predominance in naval warfare, the effectiveness of U.S. submarines against the Japanese, the development of a massive amphibious capability, and, above, all, the advent of nuclear weapons.

THE NUCLEAR ERA

When the post–World War II great powers gained nuclear weapons, war between them as the final arbiter of international conflict became unthinkable. No nation could determine how to use nuclear devices without bringing about its own destruction. As a result, a different kind of warfare emerged—surrogate conflict—in which the great powers opposed each other through pawns in local wars, regional revolutions, wars of national liberation, terrorist attacks, and military assistance to the combatants, including use of U.S. forces.

The postwar expansionist policies of communism and the Soviet Union and the containment posture of the United States soon brought the two superpowers into the first major U.S. surrogate conflict—the Korean War. As in most wars, the outline of the Korean conflict was dictated by the flow back and forth of the strategic initiative. The North Koreans gained it on 25 June 1950, by the initial surprise attack that opened the war. They held the initiative and pushed the United Nations forces back into the Pusan Perimeter. On 15 September, MacArthur's landing at Inchon reversed the flow and virtually destroyed the North Korean army. The UN forces kept the initiative, advancing boldly into North Korea. The Chinese army struck the UN forces a devastating blow in late November 1951, seized the initiative, and drove them back to the vicinity of the thirty-eighth parallel, the prewar boundary. From then until the final armistice in 1953, the initiative flowed back and forth in a series of alternating offensives. As the war wore on inconclusively and as U.S. casualties increased, American support for the war waned.

The Korean War was notable for three events. First, it saw the racial integration of the armed forces, a social breakthrough of deep significance. Second, it saw the controversy between MacArthur and President Harry

Truman over how the war should be conducted. Actually, it was not a confrontation as much as it was an ethical and constitutional question about the actions a major theater commander may take when he fervently believes that the war policy of the president is inimical to the security of the nation. Unfortunately for future commanders, this fundamental question was carefully avoided by both disputants and remains unanswered. Third, most Americans initially saw the outcome of the Korean War as a defeat or, at best, a tie, the first abhorred and the second scorned. It was not until after the American defeat in Vietnam that the nation saw the Korean War for what it really was—a limited victory.

The U.S. objective toward South Vietnam as stated in National Security Action Memorandum No. 288, dated 17 March 1964, was "a free, independent, non-Communist South Vietnam," an objective the United States failed to achieve. It was the first defeat the United States had suffered, and a unique one, because Americans won every battle on, over, and around Vietnam. One of the principal causes of this disaster was that President Lyndon Johnson never established clear, tangible objectives. As a result, neither the president nor his top military and civilian advisers could establish a viable political or military strategy. Second, Johnson's limited war policy, his restrictions of U.S. ground forces to the territorial limits of South Vietnam, and his restrained use of air power in the north surrendered the strategic initiative to the North Vietnamese. The enemy determined the type of war, its intensity, and its duration by moving back and forth from its border sanctuaries. This allowed them to protract the war, which was their strength and one of the historical weaknesses of the United States.

The war also was grossly mismanaged, not only in Washington but down to the field units. Unity of effort was missing throughout the chain of command. Johnson micromanaged some aspects of the war and refused to even consider the major issues that only the president can decide. Johnson fought the war as a secondary adjunct to his domestic political objectives, including his Great Society Program. He refused to do what had to be done to win the war (call up the reserves, put the nation on a war footing, raise taxes, and, above all, use all of the nation's military might), because he believed to do so would forfeit his political objectives. As a result of these deficiencies in the conduct of the war, the American people in traditional fashion refused to support another long, bloody, inconclusive war. By 1969, with support for the war eroding fast, President Richard Nixon could only disengage U.S. forces from Vietnam and hope for a decent interval before South Vietnam succumbed to North Vietnamese aggression. The Vietnam war was an American tragedy and a monument to the way not to fight a war.

The defeat in Vietnam and the subsequent fumbling in Grenada and Panama were redeemed by the victory of U.S. and coalition forces in the Persian Gulf War of 1991. They won that war by conducting it in a fashion precisely opposite to that of the Vietnam conflict. President George Bush played his role as commander in chief to perfection. The military, unrestrained by civilian micromanagement or limited war theories, struck hard and relentlessly in the air and on the ground. The result was a prototype of war, American-style—short, relatively bloodless, high-tech, and victorious. Reserve forces were called up in large numbers and contributed immensely to the victory. To professionals, the war is noteworthy in that for the first time air power alone might have brought off the victory. The land campaign, however, precluded the proof or disproof of this theory cherished by air power enthusiasts.

The real question posed by the Gulf War is this: Was that conflict a one-time aberration, or is it the first of a series of similar conflicts with which U.S. military forces must cope? The answer will shape U.S. military policy well into the twenty-first century. Regardless of the answer to the question, the historical themes of American military history will persist. The future wars of the nation will be fought as the country lives with a healthy (or unhealthy) input from domestic politics. If one of these conflicts becomes bloody, long, and inconclusive, eventually domestic support for it will be eroded. The United States will probably enter any future war more or less unprepared, and there will be a controversy over the use, training, and call-up of the reserves.

The nation's leaders who are called on to fight future wars will do so, as they have in the past, in a highly pragmatic fashion. It is hoped that they will determine the realities of the situation, set clear, tangible objectives, use strength against weakness, seize and hold the initiative, and conduct unified operations with mental flexibility. If there is a military science of warfare, it is that any conflict situation presented requires the same approach to solution as any other problem. Military art is only how well a leader does it.

BIBLIOGRAPHY

Asprey, Robert B. *War in the Shadows*, 2 vols. (1975).

Association of the United States Army, *The U.S. Army in Operation Desert Storm* (1991).

Borowski, Harry R., ed. *The Harmon Memorial Lectures in Military History, 1959–1987* (1988).

Coakley, Robert W., and Stetson Conn. *The War of the American Revolution* (1975).

Davidson, Phillip B. *Vietnam at War: The History, 1946–1975* (1988).

———. *Secrets of the Vietnam War* (1990).

Liddell Hart, B. H. *Strategy* (1954; rev. ed., 1967).

Huntington, Samuel P. *The Soldier and the State* (1957).

Jessup, John E., and Robert W. Coakley, eds. *A Guide to the Study and Use of Military History* (1979).

Millis, Walter. *Arms and Men* (1956).

Millett, Allen R., and Peter Maslowski, *For the Common Defense: A Military History of the United States of America* (1984).

Paret, Peter, ed. *Makers of Modern Strategy: From Machiavelli to the Nuclear Age* (1986).

Stamps, T. Dodson, and Vincent J. Esposito, eds. *A Short History of World War I* (1950).

Steele, Matthew Forney. *American Campaigns* (1909).

Stokesbury, James L. *A Short History of the American Revolution* (1991).

Weigley, Russell F. *The American Way of War: A History of United States Military Strategy and Policy* (1973).

Weigley, Russell F., ed., *New Dimensions in Military History* (1975).

U.S. Department of the Army, *FM 100-5, Operations* (1986).

U.S. Department of Defense, *Conduct of the Persian Gulf Conflict: An Interim Report to Congress* (1991).

Utley, Robert M. *The Indian Frontier of the American West: 1846–1890* (1984).

DECISION-MAKING

Raymond E. Bell, Jr., and Cynthia C. Bell

Much has changed in the conduct of warfare in America since men first took up arms in the name of protecting their homes and country. What has not changed, however, is the basic process of making decisions in the conduct of military operations. Military decision-making can be described as consisting of a cycle of sensing a situation, understanding it, deciding what is to be done, and then executing the decision. Although military decision-making fundamentally is a matter of common sense, increasingly commanders have had to act rapidly in order to co-opt the decision-making of opponents, often called getting inside the opponent's decision-making cycle.

Successful decision-makers develop a sixth sense derived from present and past experience. They rely on their own reconnaissance and on reports and recommendations of subordinates. If they rely exclusively on what they themselves see and hear, they may not be able to get the entire picture. Inborn prejudice may cause them to exclude or dismiss pertinent factors. Rash commanders who have "instant" decision-making power can easily find themselves in a critical situation if their judgments are too selective. Lieutenant Colonel George Armstrong Custer's decision at the Battle of Little Big Horn in 1876 could well have been colored by his underestimation of the capabilities of his Indian opponents.

Commanders who cannot choose competent subordinates or who have them foisted on them are in danger of having to make decisions based on incorrect or incomplete data. Many commanders have lost battles because they relied too heavily on the reports of subordinates who either could not report accurately what they had experienced or made up false reports to conceal their inability to gain the proper information.

In the past there was often a paucity of information; today there is a surfeit, and it is difficult to separate what is important or significant from that which is trivial. Modern decision-making is complicated by a multitude of means of gaining, processing, analyzing, and disseminating accurate information, especially with the use of computers.

Understanding a "situation" requires integrating reports that have been received or information garnered; eliminating that which is inaccurate; asking for additional information when required; and organizing the assemblage in a coherent manner. Throughout history, the more concisely a mission has been expressed, the easier it has been to execute. A long, imprecise rendering of a mission statement leads to immediate confusion and inevitably to sloppy execution. Understanding the enemy has become more and more difficult over time because the means of deception—electronic, audiovisual, and other—have grown extremely complicated and effective.

Antidotes to an enemy's schemes to conceal defensive or offensive preparations from friendly forces include such procedures as electronic eavesdropping, satellite imagery, aerial photography, human spying, and map reconnaissance. Essential to successful interpretation, however, is the experienced intelligence officer, who can sift through all the material and develop a viable and coherent picture of the enemy's place on the battlefield.

Terrain often dictates how a mission is to be carried out. In some cases what appears the least likely approach may be the most appropriate, because the enemy can be taken unaware. The best approach is frequently the one on which the enemy, having done its own analysis of the situation, places its major defenses or over which it attacks. In the defense, an enemy would welcome an attack made over terrain that it has carefully prepared.

The word "troops" means not only the friendly forces available to accomplish the mission but the logistical support required to carry out the commander's decision. In many cases the decision may be completely predicated on having the correct amount and type of material on hand and the consumable supplies needed to support the operation.

Time is also a key decision-making ingredient because it gives form to accomplishing a mission and can determine how to achieve surprise. If the normal method of operation is to attack at dawn, the enemy may be so accustomed to seeing action at that time that it will let its guard down at other times. A night attack or one launched at dusk or when the sun is in the eyes of the enemy might be in order.

At all command levels, there is a scheme known as troop-leading procedures. These procedures are followed at all echelons from squad to field army, with variations as appropriate. Using the company level as one of these echelons, a commander might arrive at a decision in the following manner. First, the mission is received from the battalion commander, who is at the next higher echelon in the chain of command. The mission is a concise statement of what the battalion commander wants accomplished. It may be either in writing or given orally. In the case of the company that is at a relatively low echelon, it is normally given orally. Second, the company commander issues a warning order that alerts the forces to get ready for an operation. Third, the company commander begins to estimate the situation and considers a tentative plan based on explicit orders from the next higher echelon—in this case, the battalion. Fourth, the commander may now have to set the unit in motion in the direction of the objective so that it is in position to execute the mission based on the orders the commander will issue. If the company is close to the area in which it will see action, such movement may not be necessary.

Fifth, the company commander attempts, as appropriate, to make a ground reconnaissance. Where this is difficult a map reconnaissance is conducted. Sixth, based on the reconnaissance, the commander completes the plan and integrates the results with other information received, which includes that from the battalion's operation order, to make a decision. Seventh, the commander issues a decision in the form of explicit orders. Such orders are concise and follow a format, usually the five-paragraph field order, the standard format for issuing action orders to subordinates that any soldier can understand.

THE COLONIAL PERIOD

The settlement of the New World and the establishment of an American nationality has had a significant impact on the entire world in a relatively short time. Immigrants came from all strata of society and included castoffs, indentured servants, and slaves. Most developed a self-reliance that enabled them to endure the hardships of a vast, largely unexplored continent. It is not surprising then that colonial soldiers were inclined to be independent and highly individualistic and resented discipline and the restrictions of military life. They often were suspicious of committing themselves unconditionally, and once committed, they discharged their responsibilities as quickly as possible in order to return to civilian pursuits.

As to terrain, bays and harbors gave shelter along the eastern shore of the continent, and broad rivers made it easy to penetrate a considerable distance into the interior. The land was mostly undeveloped and sparsely populated, which presented difficulties in troop supply and transport and greatly hampered the decision-making process. Neither formal battles in the open nor stylized sieges were the norm, due as much to the haphazard and ill-coordinated manner in which the loosely associated colonial governments operated as to the tactics of the period and the American terrain.

Military decisions were not solely the domain of a commander or high-ranking official. Instead, individuals often made decisions by seizing the initiative in the heat of crisis, especially when the threat was local, as in the case of defending against attacks by native Americans. A colonial governor, who was appointed either by the king or the proprietor of the territory, was normally the first person in the decision-making chain of command. Some type of advisory council might assist him and often there was a representative assembly in the colony consisting of prominent people. Each colony had a militia organization, usually made up of able-bodied males from ages sixteen to sixty. In addition, the governor might have small detachments of royal troops he could call on as well as volunteer organizations that performed specialized functions, such as mounted escorts and serving artillery pieces.

Royal governors or the colonial assembly appointed general officers and regimental colonels, and the men in the militia companies generally elected their own officers. Decisions to appoint commanders were based more on popularity than on ability. Because commanders were not necessarily chosen on the basis of military merit, they did not always meet the criteria

considered vital to the achievement of military success—that is, to regard properly the welfare of the men, accurately analyze military problems, make decisions, and execute them effectively. Thus, the quality of military decision-makers varied greatly.

Colonial decision-making was also uniquely affected by the Indians, whose tactics maximized surprise and stealth. The Indians performed accurate and detailed reconnaissance before launching an attack, deployed scouts, and adopted open battle formations. They employed natural cover and concealment in a way that was little appreciated in European military circles. Colonial governments found that organized units of professional soldiers often were not effective. Instead, the government mustered bodies of armed citizens led by experienced civilians. In these cases success depended more on individual initiative and courage than on strict discipline and control. Decision-making was informal and unstructured, with leaders adopting highly individualistic styles.

During uprisings of colonials, such as that of Nathaniel Bacon in Virginia in 1676, decision-making was hardly formalized. It took the French and Indian War (1756–1763) for rudimentary methodology to emerge. British intervention allowed Americans to observe how the British army conducted operations. British contempt for the methods of the native American enemy led to at least one military disaster. In 1755, General Edward Braddock violated the principles of security and maneuver, which the colonials had learned from the Indians. He also failed to give credence to the counsel of his military advisers, especially that of aide-de-camp Lieutenant Colonel George Washington, who was accompanying him on a campaign against the French and Indians at Fort Duquesne.

Washington tried to warn Braddock that his column required outguards and proper security and encouraged him to adopt an open battle formation. Braddock had little experience in dealing with situations other than those normally found on a European battlefield, where units lined up opposite each other and fired from a few paces away. He had difficulty understanding a mindset that allowed for fighting from behind rocks and trees. His ability to make decisions appropriate to the American battle-field was too stultified, and he lost the battle and his life. As a result of this disaster, the British learned the desirability of organizing and employing light infantry formations.

THE REVOLUTIONARY WAR

Washington was appointed commander in chief of the Continental army on 15 June 1775. Washington was an untested military leader but a capable individual. He faced the challenge of attempting to form an army from a group of highly individualistic men who were prone to reject all discipline. As principal military decision-maker, he headed an organization that was structured on the British model. Brigadier and major generals led large tactical units. Officers bearing the title of general but not necessarily holding that rank headed administrative departments for legal affairs, personnel administration, food and clothing procurement, and hospital service. A quartermaster general was responsible for transportation and delivery of supplies, arranging the camp, regulating marches, and establishing order of battle. An adjutant general issued orders in the name of the commander and handled other administrative duties. These principal staff officers provided valuable input into the decision-making process but sometimes followed their own agendas, which did not help make for harmonious relationships among principal military players in the Revolution.

Washington sometimes formed a council of war for operations and strategy. Although he was a strong leader, he was not averse to taking the advice of subordinates. His principal commanders formed the select group when he felt it necessary to call such a council. Washington and his subordinates did not have formalized staffs but informally gathered individuals around themselves whom they trusted. Aides-de-camp wrote and delivered orders, messages, and reports and took care of routine headquar-

ters work. They also served as the eyes and ears of commanders.

Many of the obstacles confronted by colonial American leaders had not changed when Washington took command. Units were generally poorly organized, untrained, and undisciplined. Men were enlisted for short periods of time, usually not more than a year, and their interest lay more in tilling the land and taking care of family than in fighting for independence. Communication still relied on messengers who moved on foot, horse, or boat. Roads were of poor quality.

During the first years of the Revolution, decisions by Washington and his subordinate commanders were often based on factors other than strategic considerations. Instead, they were often based on whether or not to act before more of their men deserted camp or how much longer their supplies would last. The physical and psychological state of Washington's men were often considerations when deciding whether or not to take the field of battle. At times Washington found himself deploying his men before morale had completely dissipated or before total exhaustion had set in. He had the added burden of dealing with a Continental Congress that often had its own agenda. Sometimes he had to take extreme measures to gain even minimal support from that body of highly individualistic men. Interference in the prosecution of the war by the Committee on War and other politicians was frequent and extended down to tactical decision-making. The time of day, terrain, and weather were also major factors that influenced decisions. Unfamiliar territory hampered the progress of units, and inclement weather could cause attacks to be aborted because of wet powder.

What may be remembered best about the revolutionary war was the need for a strong, central direction in prosecuting the war and that the individual colonies had to give way to incipient national interests. It became evident that even though men would rise to a cause, it was a difficult task to create and fight an effective British army. To keep men enlisted for the duration of the war was practically impossible, and as a result, considerable time had to be spent on administrative tasks, both of which had an adverse effect on decision-making.

Although leaders like Washington learned the need for the proper procurement of food and clothing, reliable intelligence, and proper training and organization, their grasp of effective decision-making was sketchy at best. Without an established methodology, decision-making was as individualistic as the character of the American soldier.

THE WAR OF 1812

The War of 1812 was not noteworthy for its military achievements or for the competency of military leadership. In addition, since the revolutionary war, there had been no significant technological advances that had a serious impact on decision-making. Communications were still rudimentary, and the transmission of orders, plans, and reports still depended on foot, horse, or waterborne means. Indeed, had it been possible to communicate more effectively over long distances, such battles as that at New Orleans in 1815 may never have been fought, because a peace treaty had already been signed when the battle began.

Decision-making in the first years of the War of 1812 was marked by poor reconnaissance, hesitancy, indecisiveness, and confusion, because of incompetence and the age, inexperience, and indolence of the commanders. The actions of Brigadier General William Hull at Detroit against a combined British and Indian force exemplified the situation that existed at the beginning of the war. Hull had been considered a dashing officer in the Revolution but had become timid and overcautious as the result of age and infirmities. In attempting to take Fort Malden, some twenty miles south of Detroit, he overestimated the size of the enemy and launched a series of minor and inconclusive attacks, then retreated to the fort. There he awaited an attack on his position by a British force and their Indian allies. He surrendered his force to the British without firing a shot when they arrived.

On the other hand, the navy generally performed with distinction. It took effective control of Lake Erie when Commander Oliver Hazard Perry fought and defeated the British fleet on 10 September 1813. Decision-making was characterized by boldness and imagination in the face of situations that did not lend themselves easily to guidance from higher authorities.

Toward the end of the war the situation improved as younger, more competent army commanders came to the fore, among them Andrew Jackson, whose direction at New Orleans in 1815 enabled the Americans to win a major if strategically insignificant battle. Jackson had demonstrated expertise in October 1813, when he prepared an expedition to punish the Creek Indians for the August massacre of more than five hundred settlers at Fort Mims, Alabama, after which he would push on to Mobile. From there he would capture Pensacola, Florida, eliminating the influence of Spain in the region. As part of this expedition, Jackson made expert use of spies to learn the numbers of and disposition of his enemies. He carefully selected white men and half-breeds whose homes were in the woods and who were thoroughly familiar with the area to carry out such missions. Thus, he was able to base his plans on up-to-date information and cross-check its accuracy with different sources.

The War of 1812 hardly added to the development of decision-making, but it did show that success could be gained by those who carefully gathered information, properly evaluated it, looked at various courses of action, and formulated effective plans.

THE MEXICAN WAR, 1846–1848

Unlike the early stages of the War of 1812, the principal U.S. generals in the Mexican War proved to be competent, effective leaders. The regular army, which composed a significant percentage of the fighting force, was also better trained and disciplined. The impact of the U.S. Military Academy at West Point was also beginning to be felt, especially among engineers who performed much of the required reconnaissance. The war was characterized by operations exclusively outside the borders of the then United States. Communications were strained because of the long distances involved. Although the railroad was not yet available, the telegraph was in use between Washington, Philadelphia, and New York. The Mexican War resulted in much territory being added to the fledgling nation, including the annexation of Texas. Battles were fought over terrain unfamiliar to the Americans, and it was in this war that such officers as Robert E. Lee and George B. McClellan made important contributions, not only in providing information as to where to build roads but in outmaneuvering the enemy.

General Winfield Scott established decision-making procedures that exploited the capabilities of his staff of professional army officers. He was seldom surprised and was able to defeat his foe because he had superior knowledge of the enemy's capabilities and limitations. General Zachary Taylor effectively employed a small staff and used councils of war, still a familiar decision-making body, but only in an advisory capacity.

The most serious decision-making difficulties were not found in the realm of combat operations. Rather, the authorities in Washington actively tried to interfere with General Scott's conduct of the campaign. Because Scott was considered a potential presidential candidate, this interference was sometimes intense. To make matters worse, the ability of ships to carry dispatches and orders swiftly made it impossible for Scott to ignore completely Washington's meddling. Scott, however, overcame the effects of improper, confusing, and misguided directives by acting as he saw fit in the pursuit of victory.

THE CIVIL WAR

The armies that had taken the field prior to the Civil War were insignificant when compared to those that fought each other from 1861 to 1865. The decision-making methodology that had worked well in the Mexican War was inadequate to direct the large forces of the North and South, but there were no radical changes in the way commanders at all echelons operated, and no uniform way evolved of arriving at a decision. Individual commanders continued to dictate strategy.

At first, inexperience on both sides resulted in poor decisions. Where the more professional officers made up the various staffs, especially at higher echelons, the units were more likely to be successful. The South benefited from those West Point graduates who decided to fight for the Confederacy. Such generals as Lee and Ulysses S. Grant made use of company-grade experience from the war with Mexico.

Lee carried the lessons for the need for proper reconnaissance forward into his generalship. General J. E. B. Stuart served as Lee's "eyes and ears" during most of the war, and much of Lee's success can be attributed to the quality of information delivered by Stuart. At the Battle of Gettysburg in July 1863, however, Stuart failed to provide Lee adequate support, and Lee's understanding of the battlefield was not as complete as it should have been, resulting in a Union victory.

Union forces also suffered because of inadequate means of information gathering and poor use of cavalry, which initially operated in small groups as headquarters guard or on provost duty. Toward the end of the war, cavalry was more properly employed, and Union leaders received better and more complete information from those performing reconnaissance. Technology was the biggest new factor in decision-making in the Civil War. Railroads and the telegraph allowed decisions to be made and executed more quickly and accurately. Spies were often able to travel deep into enemy territory and bring back detailed reports using the railroads. The telegraph lacked the security that messengers riding the railroads provided because lines could be easily tapped. Both the railroad and telegraph had a significant drawback, however, from the point of view of the field commander. Authorities in the central government were able to exert much tighter control over the activity of commanders; the latter, in turn, often felt their initiative stifled and were forced to consider who in the capital was trying to interfere by providing additional or corrective guidance.

On the battlefield, more rudimentary decision-making means were augmented. Signal or wigwag flags were widely used to apprise commanders of the appearance of enemy troops and to transmit orders to subordinate units. At night, wigwag torches were employed. Balloons were also introduced, enabling commanders to have large segments kept under observation, thus avoiding surprise.

Still, the Civil War ended with little changed in the format and methodology of decision-making. Councils of war were perhaps more frequent because of the extent of the scope of operations; despite new technology, it was still hard for one commander to "see" the battlefield.

THE SPANISH-AMERICAN WAR

Like the Mexican War, the Spanish-American War of 1898 was fought outside the continental limits of the United States, part of it on the other side of the world, which necessitated coordination among the army, navy, and civilian authorities to an unprecedented degree. Logistically, the war was marked by a level of incompetence exceeded only by the enemy's poor performance.

Of the two services, the navy performed more efficiently. It had evolved through the latter part of the nineteenth century into a first-class fighting force and was equipped with the latest fighting ships. It had, however, no real adversary against which to test its mettle, the Spanish fleet being poor in quality. The army, once it got into place to fight, acquitted itself well, both in Cuba and in the Philippines. Getting to the battle area was a different matter. Moving expeditionary forces from the United States to Cuba should have taken eight hours

but often took that many days. Men, horses, supplies, and equipment were loaded on ships with no consideration as to how they might have to be unloaded. Soldiers were inadequately equipped and armed against the enemy and nature. The fact that an effective army got to Cuba at all was something of a miracle.

Chaos also reigned at the highest levels of government. Conflicts between Secretary of War Russell Alger and Lieutenant General Nelson A. Miles, the commanding general, resulted in instances of countermanding orders. Decision-making was flawed by the lack of a general staff and clear lines of authority. Nevertheless, in the army the need for uniformity in the issuance of orders had been recognized well before the war with Spain. In 1887, for example, at the School of Application for Infantry and Cavalry at Fort Leavenworth, Kansas, instructors lectured on the proper format for issuing orders and making estimates of the battlefield. Their efforts had not permeated sufficiently to the field, however, to be employed effectively by all units.

The lessons of the war were not lost on authorities. The time had arrived when a methodology was established that permitted not only the effective employment of large bodies of troops but their adequate support over long distances. When the United States entered World War I, the U.S. Army was finally prepared to direct their operations according to a proven methodology.

INTO THE TWENTIETH CENTURY

The turn of the century was a watershed for military decision-making in the U.S. military establishment. The experiences of the Spanish-American War made it very clear that there were major deficiencies in intelligence gathering, organization for war, logistical and operational planning, and the conduct of amphibious warfare.

Had the Spanish not been as inept as they were in conducting operations in 1898, Americans could well have seen a much more costly outcome. As it was, the need for a change in the approach to fighting a war was one of the more significant outcomes, resulting in the formation of the General Board of the Navy in 1900 and, in 1903, the General Staff of the army and the Joint Army-Navy Board, the first interservice planning body. In addition to being a major step in developing general principles and plans for the defense of the United States and its possessions in the Western Hemisphere, the establishment of these bodies also led to a more formalized system for making decisions, especially in the army, which hitherto had relied on the personal styles of its leaders.

The prime mover in this area was Secretary of War Elihu Root (1899–1904). After studying the experiences of the Spanish-American War, he set out to rectify what he perceived as the major deficiencies. He sought to streamline the chain of command so that the formulation of army policy remained under civil authority but that command in strictly military matters belonged to the army. This meant that command and operations in the field as well as administration and fiscal matters all came under the purview of the newly established position of chief of staff.

Root first had to break the traditional power hold of the bureau chiefs in their respective areas of competence. Legislation to permit Root's proposed changes by the U.S. Congress did not alone suffice to allow him to accomplish removing this powerful block to reform. It took years to get bureau chiefs to give up their long-established power bases and correct the negative impact they had on the decision-making process.

Nevertheless, the groundwork was put in place for integrated decision-making as opposed to the commander in the field being forced to negotiate for what was needed with the bureau chiefs, who provided goods and services based on their perceptions of requirements. This basic reform was to prove very important during the First World War in moving and fighting large masses of men.

The General Staff was brought together for the purpose of full-time policymaking and preparation of military plans. Its establishment also provided an avenue for streamlining decision-making, because it provided a focal point to bring together all matters pertaining to a decision. Operational plans could now be developed with input from the intelligence community, logistics experts, and administrators of personal matters in a methodical way that allowed for proper integration of pertinent factors and helped preclude the omission of significant facts.

One of the results of the organization of the General Staff was the promulgation of the Field Service Regulations (1905), which provided guidelines for making decisions by setting forth operating procedures that recurred routinely and that, if not standardized, detracted from the consideration of more important matters. Again, standardization was to prove important during World War I, when, because of the enormous scope of military effort, it became necessary to cut through the myriad matters dealing with administration, logistics, plans, and operations and reach the core of complicated situations requiring delicate and careful attention.

The establishment of the Navy Board complemented and enhanced the modernization of the navy. The U.S. Navy had not counted for much during the nineteenth century; it was the British fleet that provided a realistic screen of protection. In the American Civil War there was a temporary growth, but this was followed by a long period of relative stagnation. In the 1890s reconstruction of the navy gained momentum, especially after the publication of Alfred Thayer Mahan's *The Influence of Sea Power Upon History, 1660–1783* in 1890. By 1898 the character of the navy had changed from a small number of commerce raiders to a fleet of modern battleships.

Americans thought of the navy primarily in terms of being able to keep an enemy from sacking and pillaging the ports and shorelines of the United States. Considering the length of the coasts and the many ports, large and small, upon which commerce depended, this concern was understandable. There was, however, no real feel by the U.S. naval establishment for the concept of projection of power, that is, extending the influence of the United States abroad by sending ships and troops to foreign waters and countries.

The war with Spain was a historic milestone for the maturing of U.S. naval thought. Theodore Roosevelt, as secretary of the navy, pushed for the building of a large fleet capable of power projection as envisaged by Mahan. By 1905, Congress had authorized the building of ten additional first-class battleships, plus armored cruisers and other ships, making the U.S. Navy a power with which to be reckoned. Then, in the next few years, four more capital ships and twenty destroyers were added that further enhanced the navy's capability and prestige.

With the modernization of the fleet, the days of the captain standing at the ship's wheel and directing combat operations while making ship movement decisions came to an end. Electronic communications, beginning with radios, both within a ship and between ships, became more sophisticated and reliable. At the same time, command and control of vessels became more complicated, because enclosing the fighting ship in steel tended to isolate the decision-making components within the vessel.

In addition, the command and control centers became the tactical decision-making nerve centers of ships and needed to be protected against destruction if the ship was to survive in combat. A captain on the bridge was important because the basic decisions were still made there, but the command and control center became an extension of the captain. Captains came to depend more and more on the information generated by the centers, especially when maneuvering within large groups of ships.

WORLD WAR I

U.S. battleships spent most of the First World War in the Atlantic coast ports and were not major naval players. Instead, submarines assumed the role, similar to the commerce raiders of the nineteenth century. The submarine could act effectively as a lone killer until a viable anti-submarine strategy was devised and the losses

to submarine warfare declined. Submarine commanders had to be decision-makers of the first order, and personal style was the key to effective employment of submarines. The command position in the submarine, usually at the periscope, placed a captain in intimate contact with all those who reacted to the orders that resulted from his decisions.

While technology had a strong effect on decision-making techniques in the navy, the language employed by ship captains and admirals, which had been used for centuries, remained basically the same. Technology, however, made it possible to translate the decisions of captains into action more swiftly.

As for the army, when the United States entered World War I in 1917, it lacked experienced staffs for directing large-scale operations in the field. Commanders could not look to a tested and formalized organization adequately designed to assist in decision-making. Americans, however, did have the opportunity to study foreign approaches to the problem. General John J. Pershing had sufficient time to observe British and French staff arrangements and to organize his staff systematically for combat operations. By the time U.S. troops were deployed to France and grouped into army corps, he had a system in place that provided a logical procedure for making decisions. His staff was organized in such a way that the commander was provided with information and assessments needed to render necessary decisions. Using primarily the French model, Pershing organized the General Headquarters American Expeditionary Forces (GHAEF) staff at Chaumont in France into three major divisions—a general staff, a services staff, and an administrative staff. The general staff, in turn, was divided into five sections. The G-1 Section was in charge of administration and organization in the command; G-2 was the intelligence section; operations were in the G-3 section; G-4 had "coordination," which meant responsibility for supply or logistics; and G-5 was charged with training.

As the system began to operate, standardization at different levels of command was ordered and achieved, and staff sections became part of the organizations from battalion to corps. Today, brigades and battalions have a standardized staff organization of four sections, designated S-1 for administration, S-2 for intelligence, S-3 for plans and operations, and S-4 for supply or logistics. Divisions and corps have the same scheme (designated as "G" sections) and an additional section for civil-military affairs, the G-5 section. The highest level staffs have a more detailed and extensive numbering system but generally follow the same format.

Pershing's services staff consisted of such specialized sections as chemical (gas) warfare, engineer operations, and signal communications. The sections provided input to the general staff, which then integrated it into the overall considerations presented to the commander. Thus, if defense against chemical attack was required, the gas service officer might provide technical assistance to the G-2 on how to identify enemy gas units or to the G-4 on the expected rate of expenditure of gas masks per division.

The third division, the administration staff, consisted of the adjutant general, inspector general, and judge advocate sections. By far the largest of all sections, the adjutant general's section consisted of more than thirteen hundred men.

All three staff divisions were coordinated by a chief of staff. A chief of staff was to be found on the division and corps staffs as well. Although he was a primary adviser to the commander on any of the staffs, he was really responsible for seeing that appropriate staff members provided the commander with the information required to render a complete and clear decision.

The result of the system that Pershing put in place provided standardization and uniformity in staff organization and operations throughout the AEF. It made possible the effective employment of troops on the battlefield. Even more far-reaching was the fact that the system has endured, although in modified form. Pershing may have made his greatest military contribution in establishing a viable framework for making decisions that is flexible enough to accommodate the most complex of challenges.

Pershing's experience in decision-making is also noteworthy from the perspective of operating for the first time with the large forces of other nations. During the 1900 Boxer Rebellion in China, a small U.S. force acted in conjunction with several European armies, but not for a long period and not under conditions that placed unusual stress on the accomplishment of the mission. Pershing had to work with the French and British military. Each had different perspectives on how the AEF could best be employed; the French and British wanted to break up U.S. forces and scatter the components among the Allies. Suggestions were made that Americans could best be employed as replacements for depleted allied units. Although some U.S. units, such as the 369th Infantry Regiment, which fought under French command, served with foreign forces, Pershing resisted the attempts to break up the army and was successful in having a sector set aside where U.S. formations could function in accomplishing a particular mission. Initially this was in the St.-Mihiel salient, where it was possible to mass U.S. forces along a relatively quiet and insignificant front, and the Americans gained confidence from obliterating the salient.

Pershing's dealings with the Allies required that his decision-making be compatible with theirs to the extent that a united front was presented to the Germans. This did not preclude, however, having to deal with the prejudices and peculiarities of the Allies, whose staff organizations had been in place longer than that of the American forces. Pershing persevered and was effective in bringing the Americans into the fight and making them part of a winning team.

World War I also saw the genesis of the air arm of the U.S. armed forces. At first only the army had airplanes, but the navy soon saw the utility of aircraft. Both services saw two primary uses for an aerial capability—the use of aircraft as another set of eyes for a commander and to destroy enemy targets.

Balloons had been employed in the Civil War for observation of the enemy, but the information gained was not used in a systematic way for the development of intelligence that might assist commanders in making decisions. The employment of aerial observation was a hit-and-miss proposition that added minimally to the prosecution of the war. In World War I, however, balloons were used extensively for the direction of artillery fire and convoy escort at sea.

Airplanes were first used by the army's Signal Corps before World War I, but early in the war it became obvious that aircraft could best be employed as part of an independent branch of the army. In May 1918, the air arm was separated from the Signal Corps, and it became the Air Service in 1920.

The appeal of a separate air force was great, but from the perspective of ground and naval decision-makers, it was less than desirable. As history has shown, the air arm's independence has often proven to be a hindrance to integrated decision-making. The priorities of air commanders have sometimes been markedly different from those of the army ground commanders. The commanders on the ground complained that the priority to accomplish requirements for providing information to the ground commander was too often downgraded by air commanders who deemed it more important to fly other types of missions.

While World War I brought about the emergence of aerial reconnaissance as a significant aid to the surface force decision-maker, it also brought forth a challenge for aerial decision-makers in dealing with the destruction of the enemy. This challenge consisted essentially of two parts—air-to-air combat and air-to-ground bombing. The first posed fewer problems. The second required deliberate decision-making to be effective.

The aerial decision-maker was the pilot or individual who fired the aircraft's guns or dropped the bombs. For fighter aircraft, the guns' firer and pilot were generally the same individual, although early aircraft had gunners who fired toward the rear of the aircraft, because the technology of firing through the propeller had not been fully developed at the beginning of the war.

Initially there was no communication between aircraft. Pilots relied on reflexes to keep out of harm's way and could not depend on fellow pilots to provide early warnings of being tracked by an enemy and of imminent danger. Decision-making by a pilot became akin to that of the submarine commander. For both, the advent of increased sophistication in communication meant more time to make well-reasoned decisions.

Bombing in World War I by aircraft was notoriously ineffective because the instruments required for the accurate placing of bombs on targets had not yet been invented. Bombing aircraft, even the German airships that bombed London, were hardly more than nuisances. As it developed, the most important aspect of air-to-ground bombing was target selection, which started with a reconnaissance or map and aerial photography study. Early in the war, pilots and observers were the primary sources of information, but soon aerial photography proved effective.

With the reports and photographs, the air mission commander strove for a good sense of the target area. He had to understand the nature of the target and gain knowledge of the threat to his attacking aircraft. For example, he might discover airfields close to the target area that could pose a threat. In addition, he sought to locate antiaircraft positions to be avoided when the target was attacked.

Another consideration was the need to analyze targets in light of the attack resources available. If the target was, for example, a railroad yard where rail cars loaded with military matériel was located, the air commander might have decided to make a maximum effort against it, using as many aircraft as could be put in the sky. On the other hand, the elements of the target might have been so spread out that only selective bombing by the best pilots could have achieved the desired results.

THE INTERWAR YEARS

In 1921 the War Department published its first listing of principles of war that commanders could use in making decisions. Published in War Department Training Regulations No. 10-5, they are the principles of the objective, the offensive, mass, economy of force, movement, surprise, security, simplicity, and cooperation. The principles have undergone some modification since 1921 but have remained essentially the same. By 1953, for example, the principle of movement had become the principle of maneuver, and the principle of cooperation became the principle of unity of command.

The codification of basic tenets of successful battlefield operations has been instrumental in helping commanders deal with the increased complexities of war when making decisions. The list also serves as a check. For example, is the decision a straightforward one that leaves little margin for error? Or is it complicated and involved, and are subordinates likely to become confused? Has the commander's decision been translated into one that even the most tired and frustrated subordinate commander can comprehend and execute faithfully and accurately? Ideally, the principle of simplicity will always be applied.

The formalization of the staff system during World War I and the subsequent codification of the principles of war were necessary measures for commanders to keep up with the technological developments in the art of war and to make logical and appropriate decisions. Between World War I and World War II, communication became more and more sophisticated, allowing the receipt and processing of information to be performed more quickly and efficiently. Electronic detection means gave decision-makers more tools to develop information. Code-breakers, for example, provided accurate and damaging intelligence.

At the same time, standardized procedures that allowed for a uniform methodology for arriving at accurate decisions were taught and practiced in the service schools. One way of practicing procedures to solve problems and make decisions was war gaming, which the navy had begun in the latter part of the nineteenth century. Besides using its North Atlantic Squadron to test maneuvers and new schemes, the navy used model ships on indoor grids at the Naval War College in Newport, Rhode Island. Such war games allowed for concentration on decision-making in the maneuvering of ships

at much less expense than sending ships to sea. Squadrons and flotillas could exercise at small cost, and it was possible to stop the action at any point to conduct critiques. The navy also exercised its roles in war plans so that when World War II began, there was a great deal of experience to draw on for the conduct of battle operations.

The Germans were the leaders in European war gaming (*kriegspiel*) at the beginning of the twentieth century, and they developed it to a high art. *Kriegspiel* was employed in the German General Staff College on a continuing basis; they also developed operational plans based on the results of the games, combined actually riding over the contested terrain and map exercises, and wrote extensive after-action reports. Orders written during the exercises were carefully filed for possible future use in actual battles.

Tools developed by the Germans for their war games became important for the U.S. Army because of its reduction in size after World War I. This smaller force consisted of a large ratio of officers to enlisted men. Approximately three times the number of officers needed to work with troops in the active army were retained for the purpose of providing regular army officers to the reserve components, especially the National Guard. The officers had to be trained, and the military school system was expanded to accommodate them.

The Army War College and the Command and General Staff College at Fort Leavenworth, Kansas, provided army officers with the opportunity to command and maneuver troops on paper. Map exercises became a major means of instruction. Scenarios were posed that required students to deal with brigades and divisions in such maneuvers as the attack and defense. Troop-leading procedures were followed step by step to ensure understanding of the correct methodology for estimating situations and then making decisions that were promulgated in orders following set formats.

One such procedure developed by the army was the estimate of the situation, which is now used as a primary decision-making tool. It provides the commander with a means to systematically address and assess how to accomplish a mission by looking at different alternatives and choosing the best one available. The estimate is a five-step procedure, starting with the statement of the mission, which is generally received from a higher headquarters and specifies what is supposed to be accomplished but not how to do so. It is usually a straightforward statement that focuses on basic elements. A mission statement might read as follows: "The First Battalion, Thirty-second Infantry, will attack and secure Hill 304 at 0530 on 15 October." Thus, the parameters are set for the decision-making process. The second step is the paragraph concerned with the situation and courses of action. Intelligence personnel provide information on the weather, terrain, and enemy capabilities. Logistics personnel provide input on the state of supply, identifying limiting factors that might adversely affect the operation. Operations personnel provide information that allows for a comparison of the enemy and friendly situation. Planners look at different courses of action in order to give commanders a number of options. All this information becomes the basis for the third part of the estimate, the analysis of opposing courses of action.

In this third part, the commander and the staff look at each of the enemy's courses of action in comparison to each of their own. In the example given, the enemy can withdraw before the attack begins and bombard the position when the friendly force takes the position, or it can defend the position, reinforcing it with additional forces. Courses of action that are not viable are discarded, and the most probable ones become the center of focus. Each course of action is examined against each of the most probable enemy courses of action. A decision is not reached at this point, because the idea is to better understand the most logical solution to accomplishing the mission.

In the fourth step, each of the commander's own courses of action are compared. The advantages and disadvantages of each are discussed and analyzed. By this time the different courses of action have been narrowed down to possibly two or three. By looking at the advantages and disadvantages of each, a commander has a clear idea of which is the best and is able to, as a fifth step, make a decision.

The estimate of the situation fits into the troop-leading procedure at the point where a tentative plan based on orders from the next higher echelon is made and continues through the steps of conducting a reconnaissance and then completing the plan. This becomes the basis for a decision, which is rendered in the form of an operations order.

The operations order had its genesis early in American military history but it was formally standardized just before the beginning of the twentieth century. Field orders (as opposed to special and general orders, which are administrative pronouncements) direct the execution of battle plans. The five-paragraph format followed in World War I was:

1. Description of the enemy's position and location of friendly troops on either flank.

2. The announcement of the mission.

3. The troops to be employed, starting with the artillery support, followed by the maneuver force of infantry. (Special troops like engineers were tasked in subparagraphs after the maneuver units.)

4. Administration or logistics. (The assignment of ambulance companies, for example, may be found here.)

5. The location of headquarters.

An example of an order following this format was the one that directed the Second Division of the AEF to occupy a defensive sector, which was issued on 3 June 1918 at 8:00 P.M. in the vicinity of Montreuil-aux-Lions as Field Orders #7.

The basic format for announcing the decision to conduct an operation has seen no fundamental changes since World War II. There have been expansions and modifications, but the format has stood the test of time and battle. The field order is the operations order, a standard part of the troop-leading procedures. The same format is followed at all echelons, and the order is given orally or in writing. At squad level the order is given orally as concisely as possible. At the higher echelons it is published in great detail, with annexes and appendices, both of which elaborate on information given in the basic order, but even in its most complex form, it is possible to extract pertinent information quickly and accurately. The first paragraph is the situation and has information that is essential for subordinate units to understand. It generally has three parts—enemy forces, friendly forces, and attachments and detachments to the task organization. The second paragraph is a concise statement of the task to be accomplished and its purpose. The third paragraph is termed "execution." It is here where subordinate units are told what their part in the task is; what the course of action to be followed is; and outlines the intentions of the commander. (Subparagraphs give a brief summary of the overall course of action intended by the commander; specific tasks relating to each element of the action; and coordinating instructions, which apply to two or more of the participating units or to the organization as a whole.) The fourth paragraph is concerned with logistics and administration. The fifth paragraph contains command and signal matters. Signal operating instructions are specified that provide such information as radio channels and call signs for radio transmissions. (A subparagraph gives the location of the command post and when it opens for operations.)

WORLD WAR II

The U.S. military establishment may not have been ready to fight World War II when it began, but from the perspective of having a decision-making apparatus in place, it did not take long for the services to get the apparatus started. The interwar years of schooling in the navy and the army were soon to bear fruit. Officers at the higher echelons may not have had practice in deploying large formations, but their theoretical background was sound. The Naval War College, the Army War College, the Industrial War College in Washington, D.C., and the army's Command and General Staff College had produced a generation of officers well versed in decision-making procedures. There was little change in format, although technology proved to be a renewed stimulus.

Electronic means of intercepting communications made it possible for American cryptologists to break Japanese operational codes using a system called MAGIC. In addition, there was the code-breaking device known as ULTRA, the use of which materially helped the Allies defeat Germany by allowing key leaders to gain high-level enemy information in a timely manner. Intelligence production reached a zenith during this war, and it made possible many important decisions that resulted in the unconditional surrender of Germany and Japan.

Between the wars radar was invented and sonar improved, which made target determination a great deal more positive and decision-making more efficient and accurate. Nevertheless, new aspects of decision-making presented themselves in aerial bombing and combined (inter-Allied) operations, where the British and Americans closely coordinated their operations. Operation Torch, the Anglo-American invasion of North Africa in 1942, is an excellent example not only of military decision-making but of how the heads of two governments interacted with each other and their own military establishments.

The close coordination of the Americans and the British proved an interesting challenge because of subtle differences in terminology. Both countries wrote their operations orders in the five-paragraph format, but the paragraph headings were, respectively, situation, mission, execution, administration and logistics, and command and signal; and information, intention, method, administrative arrangements, and intercommunication.

On the highest levels of cooperation, Operation Torch brought into contention how the Americans and British wanted to fight the war. There was a theory that the British preferred the indirect approach, or chipping away at the periphery of the German conquests, as opposed to the Americans, whose instincts were to go right to the source of the problem. The decision to invade North Africa first instead of mounting an assault on the European continent has been judged to represent a concession by the Americans to the British approach, but there were more than just military considerations involved in making this decision.

President Franklin D. Roosevelt and Prime Minister Winston Churchill had to contend with Soviet pressure to open a second front in Europe as soon as possible. It was felt that the ultimate military decision had to support the political goal of providing the necessary assistance to the Soviets. It was feared that the Soviets would do what the Russians did in World War I—make a separate peace, resulting in a victory for the Axis powers.

At the same time, there was political pressure on the leaders at home. In the United States in 1942, the public demanded action against both Japan and Germany. There was also a crusade to save the Soviet Union from fascism that could not be ignored. The British public, at the same time, was disenchanted with the way the war was being run.

British military leaders did not hold Americans in high esteem. General Sir Alan Brooke, chief of the British General Staff, for example, denigrated the strategic ability of U.S. General George C. Marshall, army chief of staff, but political and military pressures worked together to produce a plan for the invasion of North Africa. It was not the preferred plan, which was to invade the continent (Operation Sledgehammer). Instead, Roosevelt advanced Operation Torch. He and Churchill agreed to this course of action over the protests of the military, which favored continued delay until an invasion of the continent could be launched.

Although Roosevelt understood the American people's desire for action in the Pacific and defeat of the Germans, he knew that political and military factors limited him to concentrating on the defeat of Germany first. He sensed that he had to do something relatively quickly,

which meant a military action soon, and he knew that it had to be with British concurrence. He also knew that a massive buildup would be required to launch a meaningful invasion of the European continent.

In considering his options, he took into account the opinions of his military advisers, General Marshall and Admiral Ernest J. King, chief of naval operations. Marshall wanted Sledgehammer but was overruled. King wanted more attention paid to the Pacific, but Roosevelt stuck to the Germany-first policy. The responsibility for the decision thus rested squarely on Roosevelt's shoulders.

There were politics involved in the decision-making in aerial bombardment as well. They tended to be muted, however, by the momentum to invade the continent at a minimum cost in casualties to the ground troops. In fact, the air power advocates proposed that they could win the war through aerial bombardment alone. One of the earliest advocates of air power, the Italian Giulio Douhet, said that the most difficult and delicate task in aerial warfare was the selection of the proper targets. The strategists of the Army Air Forces (AAF) agreed, and in August 1941, even before the United States entered the war, the Air War Plans Division set forth basic doctrine on priority of targets to be bombed in a strategic campaign. The guidelines required modification as military and political factors were brought to bear.

The AAF attempted to make a determination as to the relationship of air power to the national purpose. It was assumed that the defeat of Germany first was to be the basic premise. The leadership of the AAF felt that the most efficient way to defeat Germany was to destroy its industrial capacity, but they also recognized that they would not be able to sell this idea to the army chief of staff or to Secretary of War Henry L. Stimson. They finessed the situation by issuing a statement that supported the overall strategy of invading the continent if efforts to bomb Germany into submission did not succeed.

The AAF leadership sensed that trying to buck Marshall and Stimson would be counterproductive to achieving a significant place for aerial bombardment in the defeat of Germany. They understood that there was a need for such a campaign but that it had to be launched in the proper context. If they could prove that the bombardment was effective, then they could push for an even larger role in the defeat of the Third Reich. The decision made was to emphasize the proper targeting for destroying the German industrial complex.

The immediate objective of overriding importance was the destruction of the German Luftwaffe. The fighter defenses had to be defeated before the bombing of key targets could begin, which required going after those plants that were crucial to the production of aircraft, including eighteen airplane assembly plants, six aluminum plants, and six magnesium plants. Three other systems were targeted to be hit once the Luftwaffe was neutralized, including fifty electric-power generating plants and switching stations. The transportation system of forty-seven marshalling yards, bridges, and locks was also targeted, as were the synthetic petroleum production facilities, consisting of twenty-seven installations. The AAF estimated that more than thirty-eight hundred heavy and medium bombers would require six months to accomplish the task. The bomber force would act independently of other Allied forces and essentially ignore the presence of the enemy. The AAF would concentrate on determining targets through the process of scientific analysis.

These decisions were made on the basis of projected results, because there were no data available that could be used to forecast the effectiveness of a massive air effort. Aerial photography had been in use for many years, but its resolution still left something to be desired in making detailed analyses of targets and bomb damage. In addition, the antiaircraft artillery and fighter defense systems in Germany made it hazardous for low-flying aircraft to penetrate enemy air space until relatively late in the war, by which time the campaign was about over. Because it was difficult to sense, and thus understand, how effective the air campaign was on a continuing basis, targeting had a tendency

to go amiss. The Americans chose to bomb during the day because they felt that they could get more accurate results. They specifically targeted those installations and systems listed, doing their best to avoid hitting civilian targets. The British, on the other hand, bombed at night and were less concerned about hitting civilian populated areas. The results of the AAF campaign could not be accurately assessed. This failure to determine the exact amount of damage frustrated the AAF decision-makers in assessing how effective their raids were, which resulted in repeated costly raids on many targets. The degree to which the AAF bombing campaign was successful is still debated, but it is generally agreed that the decision to ignore German anti-aircraft fire and fighter aircraft was incorrect. AAF bomber losses were staggering at times, as the Flying Fortress and Liberator bombers tried to tough it out alone. When the long-range P-51 Mustang became available, it was possible to escort the bombers to the targets, but initially it was felt the bombers could protect themselves.

By March 1944 the AAF had made the decision to go over to the traditional military strategy of courting battle with the enemy's main force in order to destroy it. Although the decision to conduct a campaign of aerial attrition came late in the war, it proved to be conclusive because, although German aircraft production rose, it was impossible to replace the lost pilots.

In retrospect, it appears that the decision to go after the German aviation production facilities was a mistake. After the war it was discovered that many such installations were placed underground and were immune to aerial bombardment. On the other hand, had there been an initial concentration on petroleum facilities and their complementary chemical production works, the Luftwaffe could have been grounded much sooner. In addition, the assessment of the fragility of the German rail system lent itself to easy disruption, and it was found that the Ruhr Valley could have been isolated from the rest of Germany, helping to cripple the German war effort.

After World War II, the atomic bomb introduced the question of how to achieve deterrence in light of the enormous destructive power of the weapon. In simplistic terms, the AAF—soon to be the United States Air Force—saw the atomic bomb as just a larger bang, because it changed little in the way planes would be used in war. The strategic bomber, indeed, became even more important, which meant a role for a larger air force. For the army and navy, the bomb meant more destructive firepower, with the added implications of nuclear radiation and other secondary effects. The major change, however, was to be found in control. The use of the weapon became dependent on presidential prerogative.

The contribution of the military to presidential decision-making was the ability to gather and assess information from hostile sources, which enabled him to act. Strategic reconnaissance became extremely important, and was practiced by all services. The purpose was to provide the president as much reaction time as possible to make the decision. The second major contribution of the military was the stepped-up effort to improve communications so that the president could react quickly. Bringing sophisticated communications on line through cooperation with the civilian community made it possible to greatly accelerate the ability to transmit information, especially when satellite communications became a reality.

The successes enjoyed in gathering and transmitting information made strategic deterrence a reality. Fear of employing the atomic bomb was based as much on the accuracy and speed of response as it was on the destructive power of the weapon. The use of nuclear weapons except as an aberration is now largely deterred by the U.S. ability to react to a potential threat and defeat it in other ways.

THE KOREAN WAR AND THE COLD WAR

The Korean conflict (1950–1953) for the air force was an exercise in frustration. The North Koreans and Chinese often successfully thwarted the United Nations air effort using the most simple means, and as the ground situation became stabilized, they established an effective antiaircraft defense system. For the navy there were only two significant actions, both amphibious. The first was on 15 September 1950, when U.S. and South Korean soldiers and marines went ashore at Inchon in South Korea, and the other was the evacuation from Wonsan in North Korea later that winter. For the army, after the rout of the North Koreans from South Korea, the war became pedestrian, approximating in many instances more the defensive action in World War I than in World War II.

Korea was fought with World War II–vintage weapons, equipment, and decision-making methodology. The decision to land troops at Inchon was made by General Douglas MacArthur, who had established a notable reputation in World War II for his island-jumping campaigns in the southwest Pacific, bypassing Japanese strongpoints until he reached the Philippines. To some degree, MacArthur faced the same kind of enemy situation in Korea as he had in the southwest Pacific. Most of the North Korean army was concentrated around the Pusan perimeter, with only minimal forces elsewhere. They were poised to crush the perimeter, but UN resistance held the North Koreans and, in effect, fixed them in place. (The same situation had existed in World War II with the Japanese, who had limited sea lift and were fully committed to certain islands because they could not shift forces. MacArthur recognized this and chose his objectives with care, deciding to take those that were weakly held but that proved to be stepping stones to the Philippines.)

MacArthur and his staff applied this same logic to landing at Inchon. If he could get a large enough force near the enemy's rear, he felt he had an excellent chance of destroying it by attacking from two directions. There was, however, a risk in landing at Inchon that made such an attempt a significant challenge. Inchon is the port city for Seoul, the capital of South Korea. Located on the west coast of the peninsula, it is set behind a narrow channel and extensive mud flats. The difference between high and low tide exceeds thirty feet. When the landing force went ashore on 15 September, the tides were right, and MacArthur had skilled intelligence, weather, and naval personnel who accurately informed him of his options. The North Korean army was caught completely by surprise and streamed north in retreat.

While the Korean conflict turned into a stalemate, the cold war continued unabated. The hydrogen bomb was developed and deployed. The North Atlantic Treaty Organization (NATO) and the Warsaw Pact Organization built up nuclear arsenals and positioned conventional forces against each other across the waist of Germany. For almost forty-five years, enormous forces faced each other in Central Europe, poised to strike or defend as the situation demanded.

The nuclear deterrence established early on held. The cold war ended in the early 1990s when the Soviet empire collapsed with hardly a shot being fired between the East and the West. Although the sophistication of the weaponry was extremely high, it was the decision-making apparatus that held its use in check. Whichever side moved first to deploy nuclear weapons was sure to receive punishment in kind in return.

While the superpowers were building nuclear arsenals, other countries sought to extend their hegemony by means other than nuclear attack. Thus, the Communists in North Vietnam sought to rule the entire country, but not in such a way as to lay themselves open to annihilation by nuclear weapons.

VIETNAM AND AIRLAND BATTLE

The war in Vietnam was the last one Americans fought using the technology and methodology of World War II. The weaponry also was essentially the same, although aerial bombs that could see and home in on enemy targets appeared on the scene. It was, however, still the age of gunfire from battleships, aircraft strikes using "dumb" bombs, and tanks employing 90-mm cannon. Decision-making was pushed down to the lowest echelons. Sergeants on extended patrols had to make difficult decisions in the face of an enemy who knew his jungle area of operations and could disappear into it. Junior officers leading attacks on enemy positions often had to coordinate different kinds of artillery, mortar, and aerial bombardment to support such decisions as bringing down fire close to their own positions.

Generals vented their frustrations by trying to command many echelons below their normal level of influence and often made decisions better left to captains and majors. Starting with the president of the United States, who personally chose the targets of B-52 bombers, people in positions of great responsibility were reluctant to delegate authority. Instead of gaining flexibility, the system became hidebound and stilted. Disillusionment set in after the 1968 Tet Offensive because it seemed to the American people that their leadership had lost control of the ability to gain projected results. Clearly the battle was not to be won if the most powerful members of the leadership appeared impotent.

Toward the end of the Vietnam War, the U.S. armed forces were in a state of disarray. The system analysis approach that Secretary of Defense Robert McNamara had tried to introduce stymied, rather than enhanced, the ability of the soldier to win on the battlefield. It enabled decision-making power to be withheld from the battlefield and concentrated in Washington. Sophisticated communications means inhibited decision-making by allowing the Washington power elite to procrastinate or change recommendations coming from the field according to their own preconceived ideas.

The decision as to which forces were to leave Vietnam first in 1969 came out of Washington in direct contradiction to the recommendations of General Creighton Abrams, the commander of U.S. forces in Vietnam. An astute officer, Abrams developed his own plan and rationale for how the forces were to be drawn down. Not only could he accurately sense the situation, he understood the factors with which he was dealing. He knew he was taking a risk in making his proposal to bring the entire Third Marine Division off the Demilitarized Zone (DMZ) at one time as the opening move for the withdrawal of forces, but his rationale was sound. He wanted to show the North Vietnamese that the United States had enough confidence in its achievements in pacifying the countryside that it could take the risk of denuding the DMZ of its major protective force. The plan appeared riskier than it actually was, because Abrams had taken the precaution of planning to reintroduce a large force along the DMZ again if necessary. At the same time, he had assessed the situation in South Vietnam's northernmost province as being the most secure in Vietnam.

The plans that went to Washington, however, were not the ones President Richard Nixon took with him in June 1969 to a meeting with President Nguyen Van Thieu of South Vietnam on the island of Midway. The plans were neither bold nor particularly noteworthy. They called for bringing three brigades out from three scattered locations in South Vietnam. The picture painted by this plan was one of the United States leaving Vietnam with its tail between its legs. The North Vietnamese and their counterparts in South Vietnam were now confident that all they had to do was wait. The Americans unwittingly admitted defeat by signaling that they wanted to leave as expeditiously as possible without further challenging the efficacy of their Vietnamese opponents. In 1972, B-52 bombers stopped the North Vietnamese drive south, but this was a short interlude, because a cease-fire went into effect in January 1973.

While the Americans were struggling in the jungles of Vietnam, undermanned and demoralized units led by inexperienced junior officers stood on the border in Germany, while intermittent fighting along the DMZ in Korea required a combat-ready posture.

The failure to call up the reserve components, another presidential decision typical of where the weight of the military decision-making process lay in the 1960s, stymied efforts to enhance the military's combat posture. The United States also saw no lessening of the Soviet threat in Europe. Fortunately, the continuing umbrella of

nuclear deterrence made an invasion unattractive.

Then, in the late 1970s, the army began tightening standards. Having placed the all-volunteer force on a firm footing, it started to develop the concept called AirLand Battle doctrine. Essentially, the doctrine embraced modern technology, especially the advanced electronics that were becoming available. It became possible to fight the enemy "smarter" rather than with more forces. Decision-making did not change, but its accuracy and speed were greatly enhanced. The idea was to get inside the enemy decision-making process and cripple it before the enemy could react. Getting inside meant that a commander could make a more accurate decision sooner than his opponent and execute it in such a manner as to stymie a countermove. To do so required that a commander be able to "see" the battlefield better than his opponent, which, in turn, meant that there had to be close integration of the air arm into any ground battle scheme. Destruction of the enemy had to begin well before it arrived on the battlefield. When, or if, the foe arrived, it was expected that it would arrive in such a condition as to be easily defeated, even though it had started out in a superior force posture.

Maneuver on the battlefield, enhanced by sophisticated look-and-see devices and extralethal firepower means, was to make up for any deficiency in numbers of troops and weapons systems. Thus, the decision-maker had to rely on being swifter than the opponent in reaching decisions. At the same time, it was necessary to decentralize decision-making. Leaders at all echelons had to be prepared to operate in consonance with overall plans even if they were out of communication with their higher headquarters. Thus, the concept "power down" became an important adjunct to the AirLand Battle.

Unfortunately, during Operation Desert One in 1980, the aborted mission to rescue U.S. hostages in Iran, the ambiguous joint task force command structure and the high command's bungling of the planning resulted in a humiliating disgrace for the armed services and the decision-making process. The failure of the operation represented the nadir of the military's reputation.

THE GRENADA AND PANAMA OPERATIONS

The administration of President Ronald Reagan helped restore military prestige by reacting quickly and convincingly to a perceived threat to regional stability when the government of Grenada was overthrown in 1983 by a Cuban-supported faction. Grenada's strategic value in terms of its location in the Caribbean was insignificant. On the other hand, the Cubans were helping to build a major airfield to handle large jet aircraft, enhancing the island's military importance. The major threat, however, was a perception that aggressive communism was spreading. After failure of the United States to intervene in Afghanistan, this perceived Communist expansion was unacceptable. The president took into consideration the fact that there were Americans in a medical school on the island who were conceivably in some danger. The marine barracks in Beirut, Lebanon, had also recently been blown up, and the president was not averse to using his military power to achieve small but significant success.

The decision to invade Grenada caught the U.S. armed forces off guard. There were no plans for such an operation, and there were not even adequate maps upon which to base the most rudimentary reconnaissance. The operation could have been limited to naval and marine forces using amphibious and helicopter elements, but the inclination was to attack with the maximum force and with the participation of all the armed services. Adding to the difficulty was the fact that the army and navy had not conducted joint amphibious operations since the Inchon landing in Korea in 1950.

When the Grenada situation confronted U.S. decision-makers, they were presented with the dilemma of having to react quickly and effectively. They turned to readily available forces, which meant U.S. marines afloat in the vicinity of the island with their limited **ground** and air mobility and army forces on **alert at** Fort Bragg, the Eighty-second Airborne Division. In addition, there were two battalions of army rangers and special operations forces available, including navy sea-air-land forces (SEALS), highly specialized assault and reconnaissance units that could be delivered by small boat or air.

Such decisions were relatively straightforward. Clearly, the island was too small for large mechanized forces, and the terrain did not lend itself to their deployment. Although the Grenadan army had motorized equipment on the island, the marine expeditionary unit (MEU), with its platoon of tanks and the armor protection of its amphibious vehicles, seemed to be adequate for providing the required force. Forces that could not land and fight immediately could not be employed. The army's new light divisions, for example, which cannot sustain themselves without additional logistical support from outside sources, were not adequate. Conventional infantry divisions could not be moved fast enough to be employed effectively.

The key decision-makers were naval personnel who had limited experience with extensive ground operations and army forces. Therefore, Major General Norman Schwarzkopf, who commanded the army's Twenty-fourth Infantry Division (Mechanized), which played no role in the operation, was attached to the naval staff to assist in planning the operation. Time constraints forced planning to be based largely on assumptions. It was necessary to err on the side of conservative estimates. Decision-makers also employed the tool known as METT-T (Mission, Enemy, Terrain, Troops, Time available).

In applying METT-T, decision-makers had to base their plans on limited knowledge of the enemy and terrain using specialized types of forces. The decisions made reflected such conditions. The marines with their amphibious capability were to land on the northern part of the island. The intention evidently was that there should be no conflict with operations on the southern part of the island. In the south, navy special operations units would seize key objectives before an airborne assault was launched by rangers, who were to attack government buildings and command and control facilities. Rangers would parachute onto and seize the airfield. Once the field was cleared, soldiers from the Eighty-second Airborne Division would be either landed or parachuted to clean up the southern end of the island.

As it turned out, the operation went relatively smoothly, although capturing the airfield proved troublesome because the Cubans placed construction equipment on it to block its sudden seizure. In addition, at least one SEAL team was lost before it could land; another was caught in a government building and had to be rescued by paratroopers. Because information about the island was so limited, the decision-makers had sensed that backup forces might be necessary, especially in the south, where much of the population lived. As a result, more of the Eighty-second Airborne was deployed (along with elements of the Eighteenth Airborne Corps) than was at first thought to be required.

The sophistication of communications should have been such that decision-makers could be kept up to date on what was happening during the operation, but because the army, navy, and air force do not have a common communications system complications arose. A classic example of inadequate communications was the soldier in Grenada who used a telephone to call long-distance over the local system to the United States to get needed support. This lack of commonality in communication could have been detrimental in trying to get inside the enemy's decision-making cycle if the enemy had been anything more than police and militia.

The result of the operation was a foregone conclusion, but it did point up the need to decision-makers that more and better information was required and the communications capability had to be improved. The basics of decision-making, however, were again validated and served as guideposts in Panama in 1989 and the Gulf War of 1991.

Lessons learned from Grenada were applied to the operation in Panama, another short-notice endeavor, but prior planning had been accomplished and it was primarily a one-service operation conducted by the army. The air force tried out its Stealth fighter, and the Marine Corps proved the adequacy of the new light armored vehicle (LAV). U.S. Southern Command, of which the army was the principal component, had the advantage of already being situated in the potential area of operations and having troops on hand from all services. These troops included army light infantry units, military police, LAVs, and mechanized forces. In addition, troops had been maneuvering around Panama for some time, and points critical to controlling the countryside had been identified through reconnaissance. It was also possible to make contingency plans and to practice them under the guise of training exercises.

The most elusive element for the planners and decision-makers was the enemy. President Manuel Noriega, whose removal from power was the invasion's primary purpose, seldom remained long in one place. He constantly provoked the U.S. military stationed in Panama, and he continually tested President George Bush's patience by inciting incidents. Sooner or later Noriega was going to make a wrong move, and the United States was determined to be ready to react.

The plan to eliminate Noriega was simple in concept but detailed in execution. The central idea was to paralyze the effectiveness of the Panamanian armed forces and capture its leaders. Identifying the location of the leaders was the first challenge. Easier to accomplish was deciding how to stop the Panamanian forces from reacting to Noriega's orders. Key force installations were well known to the United States because there had been close contact with units and their members for many years. As special types of U.S. units were introduced into Panama under the guise of bolstering U.S. security or training in the area, they were fitted into the plans. It was therefore possible to tailor units to accomplish specific tasks. The requirement for surprise was to be achieved by the parachuting into Panama of large forces, such as elements of the Eighty-second Airborne and the rangers. Targets were laid out and reconnoitered well in advance.

When President Bush decided to remove Noriega, the U.S. armed forces were generally ready, but the prime targets were initially able to escape. The operation was a military success but a potential civil-military disaster. No attempt appears to have been made to determine post-invasion requirements until after the operation was under way. Once soldiers were on the ground they became more policemen than fighters, and they were not trained for this task. To a lesser extent this same problem recurred in the Gulf War.

THE GULF WAR OF 1991

One of the best examples of U.S. military decision-making is the success of the combined and unified forces in the Gulf War of 1991 against Iraq in retaliation for its invasion of Kuwait the previous year. One of the greatest advantages the allies had was that forces originally targeted against the Warsaw Pact could be shifted to Saudi Arabia for employment against Iraq in a relatively short period of time. It was possible to pick up an armor heavy corps, consisting primarily of two armored divisions, in Germany and place it in Saudi Arabia, where its capability could be brought to bear effectively. In addition, mechanized and armored units in the United States that were destined for deployment to the northern plain of Germany were available. Although it took them longer to reach the area of operations, their AirLand Battle orientation made their effective use possible in a short period of time.

As to other available forces, the ability to move large heavy formations to the Middle East was a key factor in the success of the operation. Syrian, Egyptian, British, and French mechanized units all made significant contributions, although the Syrians and Egyptians were hampered by lack of transportation, the British and French did not have enough troops, and the French had the added difficulty of not being able to deploy draftees, which meant that the Sixth Light Armored Division had to be organized from a number of different units, to include those from the French marine corps. Only the United States was able to marshal and move the necessary large force to Saudi Arabia. As it was, the capability was strained, and ship and aircraft had to be called to active service from the reserve components.

For decision-makers, Gulf War planning was eased by the relative homogeneity of the force. There was just the right mix of U.S. and allied forces to allow for the imposition of U.S.-style decision-making to ensure success. In addition, the large U.S. Marine Corps contingent engaged in ground combat had no problems with the decision-making process that was employed. Experience in Vietnam, Korea, and World War II made it possible for army and marine units to operate effectively in unified ground operations.

The Gulf War was the ideal opportunity to test the precepts of AirLand Battle. At the same time, in the combat phases, both the air force and the navy were required to play roles that were more supportive than primary. They were, nevertheless, important players, and their successful integration was essential to winning the war. General Schwarzkopf, overall commander of UN forces, could not have asked for a better situation when it came to downplaying interservice rivalry. The Strategic Air Command employed its B-52s in a tactical role. The air force also had the opportunity to test its Stealth technology and precision bombing techniques on a large scale. The "target-rich" environment made it possible to validate the tenets of the air force in conducting the AirLand Battle to the fullest. At the same time, the resistance from the Iraqi air force was insignificant, so the combined air forces were able to focus on servicing the battlefield and not worry about maintaining air supremacy.

From the initial interdiction of vessels carrying goods to Iraq to the launching of Tomahawk missiles, the navy exercised almost every aspect of its operational art. The marines fought on land but honed their amphibious doctrine as well. The enemy, in the form of the Iraqi army primarily, afforded an excellent opportunity to try out decision-making techniques that might have been used by the Soviet Union. Iraqi tactics and equipment had Soviet origins, so this was a test of how Western allies might have done against the Soviets.

The Gulf War was not a straightforward military operation, although unlike Vietnam, the politicians stayed out of the conduct of military operations. President Bush left the military decision-making to the military. He employed the chain of command skillfully, using his diplomatic, political, and military advisers in supportive roles, which enabled General Schwarzkopf to concentrate on victory.

With firm civilian leadership support, the military leadership was able to make effective decisions. U.S. Central Command was given complete jurisdiction over the conduct of operations, although advice was freely given by the Joint Chiefs of Staff. The unity of command thus achieved made it possible to overcome many of the minor problems that presented themselves and that could have crippled the operation. The principal problem was that there was no completely predeveloped plan in place for dealing with the challenge presented by the Iraqis. U.S. Central Command had only started to take a look at the threat posed by Iraq to Saudi Arabia and Kuwait in the summer of 1990. In previous years the focus had been on Iran and its possible invasion by the Soviet Union. Indeed, Iraq was a de facto ally in the eyes of planners. Iraq's President Saddam Hussein used this fact in calculating his move into Kuwait, and although it has been denied, the United States certainly appeared to be looking the other way prior to the Iraqi invasion.

Once the Iraqis were discouraged from further adventures by the imposition of an embargo and the deployment of U.S. light forces,

the decision-makers had the luxury of determining when and where to attack. The navy and the army had rehearsed plans for blockading ports and for swift imposition of forces. The experience in escorting Kuwaiti tankers in the gulf in previous years gave the navy a good feel for operations in the area. The army had conducted a swift and successful operation in Panama a short time before. Its standard operating procedures for insertions had already received a good scrubdown. The real test for the military decision-makers came when it was determined that the Iraqis would have to be driven out of Kuwait by force. By this time, however, the options available were fairly obvious. There was the possibility of conducting a limited ground operation out of northern Saudi Arabia against Kuwait in combination with an amphibious assault. This was a course of action for which the Iraqis specially positioned their forces. There was also the option of making a feint from the sea and making a power move right into Kuwait from directly across the Saudi-Kuwaiti border. The Iraqis were positioned to counteract this option as well. Finally, there was the option of conducting an amphibious feint or assault while conducting a shallow sweeping operation around Kuwait through Iraq. The Iraqis also considered this option and therefore posted their best troops, the Republican Guard, in such a position as to be able to maneuver against the threat.

General Schwarzkopf and his staff assumed that the Iraqis were expecting the principal action would take place in Kuwait and that international pressure would keep any fighting localized in that country and not in Iraq. Based on satellite photography, the allies began to sense that the Iraqis, by placing several divisions along the coast and fortifying it, felt an amphibious attack was probable. The Iraqis knew from television news broadcasts by CNN that there was a large amount of allied battle shipping in the area. It was obvious to Saddam Hussein that the U.S. Navy would play a larger role than just blockading the ports. A number of news stories were written about the amphibious exercises and aircraft carrier activities, conveying the impression that an assault from the gulf was a likelihood.

As time went on, Schwarzkopf determined that a wide flanking maneuver was a preferable course of action, especially if he could achieve surprise. If it were possible to pinch off the bulk of the Iraqi army in Kuwait, he could destroy it by surrounding it and forcing it against the sea. He knew he had to take into account the contributions that the air force and navy could make, and he understood the Iraqi fear of naval assault from the Persian Gulf. He also understood that the Iraqi air arm would be little match for that of the allies. The question was how all this could be put to the advantage of the allies.

He understood that if the enemy could not see well, he could probably get inside its decision-making cycle and tear Saddam Hussein's forces apart. He recognized that neutralization of the enemy's ability to see by paralyzing its "visual" elements through air power was a key as well to a successful operation. The core of the challenge was to get the Iraqis out of Kuwait with the least amount of damage to the country and the most destruction to the Iraqi war machine.

The final decision was to execute a broad turning movement with Arab allies attacking through the south border of Kuwait and the British, French, and Americans making a sweep into Iraq, pinning the Iraqis against the gulf. To fix Iraqi attention on the waters of the gulf, a feint was to be mounted by amphibious forces. Preceding the ground operation, the air forces were to destroy the Iraqi capability to make war as much as possible and to whittle down the numerical odds facing the allies. The wide sweep through Iraq was to be a swift surprise move once the Iraqi ability to see the battlefield was seriously degraded.

As a corollary, the enemy was to be demoralized as much as possible before a ground assault was launched. If it were possible to convince Saddam Hussein to withdraw without having to launch a ground attack, all the better. As a result, a psychological attack was to be launched against Iraqis in the trenches. They were to be subjected to bombing, which would break their morale, make them pliant and ready to surrender, or kill them.

Once the decision was executed, the course of the war went as planned, although Schwarzkopf and Bush clashed over when to stop the fighting. Nevertheless, Kuwait was liberated with a minimum of friendly casualties in a combined and unified operation that was unique in U.S. military history.

INTO THE FUTURE

As the twenty-first century approaches, military decision-making is at a crossroad. The electronic battlefield is a reality, as demonstrated by the Gulf War. The Aegis cruiser, the Tomahawk missile, and the global positioning satellite are all part of the new and available technology. All have proved themselves in battle. Although these systems answered a good many questions about their effectiveness when tested, they also raised new questions, including how the decision-making process will be conducted in combat in the future and how responsive will it be to technology.

The crossroad was reached when the Soviet Union ceased to exist in 1990. Until that time there was a definitive potential foe. NATO existed expressly to stop a Soviet invasion of Western Europe. The Soviets had actual or potential clients in such countries as North Korea, Cuba, North Vietnam, and Ethiopia, against which at least some allied resources were oriented. Military decision-makers could therefore focus their efforts in a coherent manner.

Because the Soviets had developed sophisticated weapons systems that were targeted primarily against the West, it was necessary for decision-makers to place a great deal of reliance on technology. Advances in sophistication of weapons systems and the means to control and employ them became critical. The ability of the United States and its allies to get inside the enemy decision-making cycle was therefore seen as the primary means of overcoming a significant deficiency in the amount of armaments possessed by the Soviets.

A Soviet-style invasion now appears nonexistent, so the question is, who is the primary potential enemy? The Commonwealth of Independent States has evidently taken itself out of the running for being an enemy of the West even though they possess a potent capability. Many of the former Soviet clients have also removed themselves from consideration as potential foes. Ethiopia and Nicaragua appear to be in this category. On the other hand, North Korea, China, and Cuba remain committed to Communist totalitarian regimes, and Iraq, Iran, and Libya are still opportunistic. None of these potential foes, however, possesses the capability of defeating the United States or a UN coalition by engaging in the sophisticated kind of combat the Soviets were once able to pursue. This poses a problem for such military decision-makers who have been working, for example, in the field of large-scale nuclear weapons, and there is a good chance the requirement for them will be sharply diminished.

In the 1990s, the United States military establishment invested considerable resources in special operations forces, because it sees low-intensity conflict as being the major challenge in the future. A primary thrust of this investment is to gain the capability to deter and combat threats to the United States and its allies that do not involve high-technology weapons systems. The military, for example, has joined the war against drugs. Information gathering is essential to blocking drug traffic, and every source for obtaining information must be exploited. At the same time that a high level of sophistication is required for detecting the movement of drugs, every bit of human intelligence is also required.

A dichotomy exists therefore about which track to follow. On the one hand there is the high technology track, in which decision-making is heavily augmented by satellite communications, high resolution imagery, and automatic response by sophisticated weapons systems to certain types of threat stimuli. On the other hand, there is the track that is almost a reversion to colonial days, where individuals had to make decisions based on information at hand or that was otherwise readily available. The former track could take decision-makers to the Middle East, the latter, to South America, but no one knows for certain which of any directions will be the most important.

In summary, from colonial times to the present, decision-making by American military personnel has been marked by increasing levels of sophistication with improvements in the ability to communicate and gather information, but basic procedures have changed little. Instead, a codification has taken place that enables commanders and staff officers to direct masses of troops as well as sergeants to direct their squads effectively on the battlefield. The system of sensing, understanding, and deciding has not been altered, nor does it appear that it will in the future.

See also COALITION WARFARE; COMMUNICATIONS; INTELLIGENCE; INTEROPERABILITY; LOGISTICS; MILITARY STRATEGY IN THE NUCLEAR AGE; OPERATIONS RESEARCH; PSYCHOLOGICAL OPERATIONS; *and* THE DEVELOPMENT OF OPERATIONAL ART.

BIBLIOGRAPHY

Allen, Robert S. *Lucky Forward* (1947).

Atkeson, E.B. *The Final Argument of Kings* (1988).

Ayer, Fred, Jr. *Before the Colors Fade* (1964).

Bradley, Omar N., and Clay Blair. *A General's Life: An Autobiography* (1983).

Callahan, North. *Henry Knox, General Washington's General* (1958).

Combined Arms and Services Staff School. *Quantitative Skills* (1983).

Cushman, John H. *Organization and Operational Employment of Air/Land Forces* (1984).

Davis, Burke. *The Billy Mitchell Affair* (1967).

DeSeversky, Alexander P. *Victory Through Air Power* (1942).

Dolan, Raymond. *Crisis Decision-making* (1989).

Dupuy, R. Ernest, and Trevor N. Dupuy. *Brave Men and Great Captains* (1959).

Earle, Edward Mead, ed. *Makers of Modern Strategy: From Machiavelli to Hitler* (1943).

Eisenhower, Dwight D. *Crusade in Europe* (1948).

Ellis, O. O., and E. B. Garey. *The Plattsburg Manual* (1917).

Freeman, Douglas Southall. *R. E. Lee*, 4 vols. (1934).

———. *Lee's Lieutenants*, 3 vols. (1944).

Frisbee, John L., ed. *Makers of the United States Air Force* (1987).

Fuller, John F. C. *The Generalship of Ulysses S. Grant* (1929).

Ganoe, William Addleman. *The History of the United States Army*, rev. ed. (1942).

Gavin, James M. *On to Berlin* (1978).

Goldhurst, Richard. *Pipe Clay and Drill: John J. Pershing, The Classic American Soldier* (1977).

Grant, Ulysses S. *Personal Memoirs* (1885–1886).

Greenfield, Kent Roberts. *American Strategy in World War II, A Reconsideration* (1963).

Greenfield, Kent Roberts, ed. *Command Decisions* (1959).

Hagan, Kenneth J. *This People's Navy: The Making of American Sea Power* (1991).

Heichal, Gabriella. *Decision Making During Crisis* (1984).

Henry, Robert S. *The Story of the Mexican War* (1950).

Hewes, James E. *From Root to McNamara* (1975).

James, Marquis. *Andrew Jackson* (1933).

Jessup, Philip C. *Elihu Root* (1938).

Johnson, W. Fletcher. *Life of Wm. Tecumseh Sherman* (1891).

MacArthur, Douglas. *Reminiscences* (1964).

Marshall, S. L. A. *Men Against Fire* (1947).

Matloff, Maurice, and Edwin Snell. *Strategic Planning for Coalition Warfare, 1941–1942* (1959).

Military Service Publishing Company. *Tactics and Techniques of Cavalry* (1935).

———. *Tactics and Techniques of Infantry*, vol. 2 (1953).

Millis, Walter. *Arms and Men: A Study in American Military History* (1956).

Morison, Samuel Eliot. *John Paul Jones* (1959).

Mosley, Leonard. *Marshall: A Hero for Our Times* (1982).

Nye, Roger H. *The Challenge of Command: Reading for Military Excellence* (1986).

Paret, Peter, ed. *Makers of Modern Strategy: From Machiavelli to the Nuclear Age* (1986).

Patton, George S. *War as I Knew It* (1947).

Pershing, John J. *My Experiences in the World War* (1931).

Pogue, Forrest C. *George C. Marshall: Ordeal and Hope, 1939–1942* (1969).

Prince, Howard T., II, ed. *Leadership in Organizations* (1988).

Ryan, Cornelius. *A Bridge Too Far* (1974).

Shaara, Michael. *The Killer Angels* (1974).

Taylor, Maxwell D. *The Uncertain Trumpet* (1960).

Truscott, Lucian K., Jr., *The Twilight of the U.S. Cavalry: Life in the Old Army, 1917–1922* (1989).

Tuchman, Barbara W. *Stillwell and the American Experience in China 1911–1945* (1970).

U.S. Department of the Army. *Military Operations of the American Expeditionary Forces* (1948).

———. *American Military History, 1607–1953* (1956).

U.S. War Department. *Handbook on the British Army TM 30-410* (1943).

U.S. War Department, Office of the Chief of Staff. *Field Service Regulations United States Army 1905* (1905).

———. *Field Service Regulations United States Army 1910* (1910).

Van Creveld, Martin. *Command in War* (1985).

Watts, Barry D. *The Foundations of U.S. Air Doctrine: The Problem of Friction in War* (1984).

Wedemeyer, Albert C. *Wedemeyer Reports!* (1958).

Weigley, Russell F. *The American Way of War: A History of United States Military Strategy and Policy* (1973).

Wellard, James. *General George S. Patton, Jr.* (1946).

Westmoreland, William C. *A Soldier Reports* (1976).

Woodward, Bob. *The Commanders* (1991).

OPERATIONS

Clayton R. Newell

Military operations generally refer to those activities involved with the application of or threat of application of military force in support of national policy. In addition to combat operations, U.S. military services conduct a wide variety of other activities, including training, logistical, administrative, peacekeeping, humanitarian, and nation-building operations. Today, virtually all of these activities involve forces from more than one of the armed services. Although the army, navy, Marine Corps, air force, and Coast Guard each conduct operations unique to their service, they also conduct joint operations with one or more of the other services. Joint operations have taken on greater importance as warfare has grown more complex, with air, land, and sea forces supporting each other throughout the world.

The military forces of the United States have routinely conducted operations with the armed forces of other countries. Operations conducted with allied forces are known as combined operations, which can be conducted on the land, in the air, on the sea, or in any combination of joint operations. Joint and combined operations are the most difficult activities to plan and execute because of the many organizational differences of the various services and armed forces involved and how they conduct operations. The historical experience, geographical location, and sociological influence of a nation all contribute to the way its armed forces plan and conduct

operations. U.S. military operations, like those of any other country, reflect the characteristics of the nation. Likewise, the evolution of U.S. military operations has been influenced by and contributed to the development of the character of the United States. Among other influences, two centuries of technological and socioeconomic change have affected operations dramatically.

MILITARY OBJECTIVES

Military operations require specialized forces, weapons, and equipment. Although there was a time when it was fairly obvious that the army conducted operations on land and the navy operated at sea, the versatility of modern armed forces blurs that distinction. While the army is the dominant land force, it also maintains a sizable fleet of helicopters; the navy has a formidable number of high-performance aircraft and missiles that can hit targets hundreds of miles inland; the air force can change the face of battle on the ground; and the Marine Corps can go to sea with the navy, fight on land alongside the army or by itself, and provide its own aerial fire support.

Even with the wide variety of forces, weapons, and equipment used, all operations share one fundamental characteristic. Regardless of their size, they are always directed toward the attainment of specific goals, or objectives, that should be clearly designated and realistically attainable. Directing military operations toward specific objectives provides unambiguous standards by which to measure their success or failure, and it provides a solid basis for planning and allocating forces.

In basic terms, successful military operations lead to the attainment of designated objectives, while unsuccessful ones do not. It may appear that determining the success or failure of military operations in terms of whether or not they attained the designated objective is simple, but in reality it is not. Operations are generally conducted against an opponent who has a different objective in mind. An attacking force, for example, usually wants to destroy the forces opposing it or gain control of something the opponent is protecting, while the defenders want to prevent that outcome. Operations that result in battle are almost always chaotic and frequently result in something less than complete success or utter failure. In fact, even a failed operation can contribute to future success by wearing down an opponent. Lack of success in an operation may be the result of having no clearly defined objective on which to base the planning and conduct of operations in the first place, or it may be impossible for an operation to attain the specified objective for a variety of reasons, including inadequate forces, poor preparation, and stronger than anticipated enemy resistance.

A clear statement of the objective is the essential first step for planning and conducting operations, regardless of the size of the military forces involved. Military objectives can be either strategic or tactical. The fundamental difference between strategic and tactical objectives is not necessarily size but their relation to national policy goals. Attaining a strategic military objective will make a specific and positive contribution toward attaining a U.S. national policy goal, whereas attaining a tactical objective does not. There may, however, be circumstances in which tactical and strategic objectives coincide with one another.

Examples of strategic military objectives are occupation of disputed territory, defeat of an opposing force, and destruction of an opponent's military or industrial capabilities. A widespread or long war may entail the attainment of a succession of strategic military objectives, whereas a small or short war may well have only a single strategic objective. In World War II, the Allied strategic objective was the unconditional surrender of the members of the Tripartite Pact—Germany, Italy, and Japan. Because of the global nature of the war and the large forces deployed by each side, however, the final goal was not achieved until the Allies met a lengthy series of intermediate strategic objectives, each of which contributed to the ultimate unconditional surrender of all Tripartite forces. Individual members of the opposing coalitions conducted military operations to attain strategic objectives in various combinations against each other. The Allies agreed on the ultimate strategic objective of unconditional surrender of all opposition, but that could not happen until members of the alliance attained specific strategic objectives. In the war against Germany and Italy, for example, intermediate strategic objectives included defeating German forces in North Africa, followed by invasion and occupation of Sicily and the rest of Italy, and finally, invasion of the continent of Europe. Each of those strategic objectives required attainment of many tactical objectives.

A tactical objective is generally one of many steps a military force must take to attain a strategic objective. Although a tactical objective may be smaller than a strategic objective, its attainment may involve large force. During World War II, the Allied island-hopping campaign in the Pacific required attainment of a series of tactical objectives by amphibious assaults, many of which involved significant air, land, and sea forces.

Occasionally, the tactical and strategic objectives of a particular operation are practically synonymous, as in the U.S. military operation conducted against Libya in 1986. Simultaneous bombing raids were conducted on a group of tactical targets by air force and navy bombers to attain the strategic objective of demonstrating to the Libyan government that the United States had the will and the capability to retaliate against state-sponsored terrorism. This strategic objective supported the national policy of the United States, which condemns all types of terrorism. By successfully bombing selected targets simultaneously, the United States achieved its strategic objective in a swift and relatively small military operation.

In wars that lead to decisive success for one side, there generally is a systematic attainment of the tactical objectives, which constitutes a campaign. Campaigns consist of one or more battles, while one or more campaigns comprise a war. It is possible for a war to consist of only one campaign in which there is only one battle, as in Libya in 1986, but that situation is the exception. Battles and campaigns have different objectives. A battle has a tactical objective; a campaign has a strategic objective. The planning to attain a military objective, either tactical or strategic, begins with the commander's concept of the operation. The concept of the operation is a short statement of how he expects to use the military forces available to attain the assigned objective. Regardless of the size of the forces involved, the commander's concept of the operation should be clear and concise; it is the focus of how the battle or campaign will be conducted. Experienced commanders understand that their plans will rarely be executed exactly as envisioned. The concept of operations, however, provides guidelines that keep the conduct of operations from straying too far from the intended objective, even if operations do not precisely conform to the original plan. If the concept of the operation cannot be simply stated, it may be too complicated. In conducting military operations, simple plans generally work best.

LEVELS OF WAR

Although there are only two types of military objectives, there are three broad divisions of war in U.S. military doctrine—strategy, tactics, and operational art. Strategy constitutes the plans by which military forces are used to support national policy, while tactics is the actual handling of military forces in combat. Between tactics, where military forces fight battles to attain tactical objectives, and strategy, where national leaders develop the objectives of war that will support national policy, lies the area of operational art. Senior military commanders and their staffs use operational art to plan and conduct the campaigns that will attain strategic objectives by coordinating the efforts of forces from all of the services.

Strategy involves waging war with whatever pressure the nation can bring to bear on the enemy, including diplomacy, economics, and technology. Tactics consist of fighting battles, usually with the forces of a single service, although in modern warfare air and ground forces frequently work together. Operational art is planning and conducting campaigns using forces from two or more of the services and employs the tactical capabilities of the military services to attain designated strategic goals through a series of battles in a campaign.

Campaigns. Ideally, throughout the history of U.S. military operations, campaigns would always have been thought out and planned thoroughly beforehand and then conducted to reach a specific strategic objective. Unfortunately, there have been times when battles apparently just happened, with tactical results that contributed little or nothing to the overall war effort. Even when individual battles are successful, they will make little or no contribution to attaining a strategic objective unless they are planned and conducted within the framework of a campaign. The U.S. experiences in World War II and Vietnam provide contrasts in effective campaign planning.

In World War II, U.S. campaigns generally resulted in the attainment of a series of tactical objectives that led to a strategic objective. The attainment of strategic objectives then led to conclusion of the war on Allied terms. The strategic objective of clearing North Africa of German and Italian forces in 1942 was attained after a series of battles that began with three amphibious assaults from the Mediterranean Sea and

Atlantic Ocean, which had the tactical objective of securing ports for Allied use. The North African campaign culminated in the capture of German and Italian forces in 1943. During the campaign the success of each battle drew the Allies closer to the desired strategic objective.

In contrast to the U.S. conduct of operations in World War II, there is very little evidence of any campaign in Vietnam attaining a series of tactical objectives that led to a strategic objective that, in turn, contributed to the conclusion of the war. The battles in Vietnam, although conducted with great skill and usually successful in attaining their tactical objectives, did not have the cumulative effect of attaining a strategic objective that supported U.S. national policy. There was apparently little or no campaign planning to guide the tactical successes to strategic objectives. Part of the difficulty was simply that, in retrospect, there is little evidence of there having been a clearly identified and militarily attainable strategic objective on which to base any coherent planning.

In World War II the civilian leadership, in consultation with the senior military leadership, set strategic military goals that supported national and Allied policy. In Vietnam, however, the civilian leadership generally set strategic goals that were not militarily attainable, rarely consulted with the senior military leadership on strategic questions, and routinely interfered with the tactical conduct of the war. The campaign planning that came to characterize joint operations in World War II did not occur in Vietnam because there were no clearly defined strategic goals through a series of battles in a campaign.

Campaigns are one way the United States remembers its military past. Individual participants in specific campaigns receive medals or ribbons, and military organizations are authorized to attach embroidered strips of cloth, generally referred to as streamers, to their distinctive flags, based on participations in campaigns, which are designated as such after the event. These designated campaigns, however, may or may not coincide with a specific series of battles that concluded in the attainment of a specific

strategic objective. Frequently, campaigns are but a convenient method of measuring time periods in a lengthy war. The campaign designations in Vietnam, for example, simply break the war into different periods of activities and have little or no relation to the attainment of strategic objectives. In World War II, although campaigns were indeed made up of a series of battles that led to the attainment of a strategic objective, the designated campaigns were also measurements of time. The administrative and historical designation of campaigns is not necessarily how the participants planned and conducted these operations. War has a way of changing even the best-laid campaign plans, and history can be misleading as it organizes the record of events and gives the appearance of order in war.

Joint and Combined Operations.

Military operations planned and conducted by modern forces vary widely in size and scope. They may involve only small forces from just one of the services, or they may be large, complex operations with participation from all the services and military forces from allied countries. U.S. air, land, and sea forces routinely work together to plan and conduct joint operations that cover thousands of square miles of the earth's surface, extend thousands of feet into the atmosphere, plunge hundreds of fathoms under the oceans, and even penetrate into the earth's crust on land. These joint operations are frequently also combined operations. Like joint operations, combined operations range from small teams to vast armadas. Each operation has within it a wide variety of smaller operations, all of which contribute to the goal.

U.S. campaigns since World War II have almost always been joint operations. Planning and conducting joint campaigns is the essence of operational art. Although operational art has its origins in continental warfare in eighteenth-century Europe, it is a relatively new concept in the U.S. military experience. The concept is generally more readily accepted by the army and Marine Corps than by the air force or navy, because the air force and the navy are both capable of attaining strategic goals by themselves. They properly see strategy and tactics as the two most important divisions of war, because in many cases they can use their tactics to directly attain strategic goals. The army and Marine Corps, however, require the support of the air force and navy to attain strategic goals and are therefore more likely to see operational art as a critical element of planning and conducting war. Operational art coordinates interservice operations, while the individual services concentrate on developing the tactics they will use in conducting the battles in the campaign.

Since World War I, the United States has not had to conduct a military campaign on its own or contiguous land. The last land campaign on the North American continent involving U.S. forces was the Mexican Border Campaign in 1916, just before the United States entered World War I. The United States prefers to conduct military operations outside its borders, and the army and Marine Corps require sea and air transportation to reach theaters of operations throughout the world and to sustain those operations. Because the navy and the air force provide that strategic transportation, simply moving large land forces is inherently a joint operation. During amphibious operations or operations close to the sea, the army and Marine Corps require fire support from the navy, and the army routinely requires aerial fire support from the air force during operations against an enemy that itself has air power. Traditionally, the close relationship between the navy and the Marine Corps makes joint operations involving those two services relatively easy. Likewise, the historical relationship between the army and the air force (which were once the same service) makes joint operations involving close air support relatively simple. Indeed, between the navy and the Marine Corps and between the army and the air force there are some elements of joint operations that are more tactical than operational art.

Unlike the army and Marine Corps, the air force and the navy can attain strategic goals without necessarily conducting joint operations. At sea the navy frequently operates inde-

pendently of the other services to attain strategic goals, and the air force can use tactical bombing techniques to attain strategic goals. The close relationship between tactical and strategic operations can be seen in the employment of nuclear weapons. Both the air force and the navy have strategic nuclear weapons that they can employ using tactical operations. The air force has long-range bombers and intercontinental ballistic missiles with multiple warheads, while the navy has submarines that carry long-range missiles with nuclear warheads. Both services also have variations of the cruise missile to deliver nuclear warheads far into the interior of an opponent's homeland. Although these nuclear weapons are strategic, the techniques and procedures available to launch them are tactical.

While the navy and air force capability to attain strategic goals independently will contribute to winning wars, rarely will these two services be able to win wars alone. Historically, wars have not been won until ground forces have defeated enemy ground forces or occupied disputed territory. Because ground forces generally depend on support from both the air and sea, the army and Marine Corps tend to place more emphasis on operational art than the navy or the air force.

SERVICE CULTURES AND OPERATIONAL ART

Each service has a unique culture—a body of knowledge and experience combined with a specific pattern of education and behavior that determines how its officers acquire and transmit information among themselves. Officers serving on a joint staff have generally spent many years mastering their specialty and absorbing their service culture. When joint staffs plan and conduct the joint operations that constitute operational art, the different cultures interact with one another at both a personal and institutional level.

The army, specializing in land power, is designed to conduct long-term operations. Its two hundred years of experience has led the army to believe that it is the service that wins wars. It takes time for the army to move long distances, and although it depends on the air force and navy for movement between theaters of operations, the army's force structure includes logistic support for other services. It provides ground transportation for air force ordnance, for example. Army officers learn to cooperate out of necessity; they must rely on others for support and understand that they will be expected to provide support in return.

The navy specializes in sea power and conducts both long- and short-term operations. Its ships move across the sea independently of the other services, but it can take considerable time for them to cover long distances. The navy's capability to move by itself and its history of independent operations ranging from the Barbary Wars in the nineteenth century to blockading Iraq in 1990–1991 can make its officers by nature less cooperative than the army.

The air force is the youngest service and has the most faith in technology. It conducts its operations over long distances, frequently very rapidly. Air force officers have a shorter institutional memory to absorb, so they are frequently more responsive to new ideas. They can be the most independent of all services, believing that air power alone has the power to win wars.

The Marine Corps, a force that combines air, land, and sea power as a matter of course, embodies joint operations. Marines specialize in amphibious operations; they understand the value of cooperation because they must be prepared to rely on the navy for transportation and naval firepower support, the air force for aerial firepower support, and the army for logistical support in extended operations.

The different cultures may be self-evident to an impartial observer, but they do affect the way the services relate to one another. Since 1986, with the implementation of the Goldwater–Nichols Act, the services have made a concerted effort to improve the planning and conduct of joint operations. Each service accepts students from other branches of the armed forces into its staff and war colleges, which serves to educate officers about the similarities and differences in their cultures. Ironically, the different viewpoints officers bring to a joint staff can be both strengths and weaknesses for a joint commander. Wise commanders will blend the different backgrounds into a unified team, taking advantage of the varied points of view on a subject, even as they overcome the rivalries.

The U.S. military experience provides examples of excellent cooperation in joint operations as well as examples of abject failure when the services simply refused to get along with one another in a joint campaign. The armed forces recognize the need to master joint operations, but there is simply no way to eliminate all so-called service rivalry. Indeed, some rivalry is healthy and necessary to maintain an innovative and viable military force. The organization of the military establishment of the United States, however, emphasizes service cooperation in conducting joint operations.

ORGANIZATION OF THE U.S. ARMED FORCES

Although American armed forces have been planning and conducting joint operations since before the revolutionary war, it was not until after World War II that the defense establishment was organized to facilitate joint operations. The creation of the position of secretary of defense in 1947 and the establishment of the Department of Defense in 1949 provided both the foundation and requirement for planning and conducting joint operations at the highest levels of command.

The senior military body in the United States is the Joint Chiefs of Staff (JCS), an agency that traces it origins to World War II. Shortly after the Japanese attack on Pearl Harbor in December 1941, President Franklin D. Roosevelt and Prime Minister Winston Churchill established the Combined Chiefs of Staff to provide strategic direction for the Anglo-American war effort. The British Chiefs of Staff Committee had been in existence for some time, but there was no U.S. counterpart. In response to the requirement to coordinate the war effort with the British at the highest military levels, the United

States established the JCS in 1942, which functioned throughout the war without official legislative or presidential definition. The first JCS consisted of Admiral William D. Leahy, the president's special military adviser, with the title of chief of staff to the commander in chief of the army and navy; General George C. Marshall, chief of staff of the army; Admiral Ernest J. King, chief of naval operations and commander in chief of the navy; and General Harold H. Arnold, deputy chief of staff for air and chief of the Army Air Corps. From its establishment to the end of the war, the JCS was the primary agent for coordinating the activities of the army and navy. It became an official agency with the passage of the National Security Act of 1947.

The National Security Act organized the armed forces of the United States into a number of unified commands, with forces from all the services, throughout the world, with emphasis on those areas of vital national interests. The Unified Command Plan (UCP) concentrated U.S. forces in areas that required occupation forces, and immediately after World War II, U.S. national interests focused on Europe and the Pacific. The UCP has since modified the size, composition, and areas of the unified commands in consonance with changes in U.S. national interests. The UCP is flexible. Although some of the unified commands, such as the U.S. Pacific Command (USPACOM) and the U.S. European Command (USEUCOM), have remained virtually unchanged since their creation after World War II, others, for example the U.S. Central Command (USCENTCOM), the headquarters that planned and conducted the Gulf War of 1991, reflect changes in U.S. national interests. USCENTCOM began as the Rapid Deployment Joint Task Force (RDJTF), part of President Jimmy Carter's recognition in 1979 of the Middle East as an area of vital U.S. interest. In 1983 the RDJTF became USCENTCOM when President Ronald Reagan's administration reorganized it as a unified command. Although the names and boundaries change periodically, the concept of designating areas of the world with a single commander of U.S. armed forces remains the basis of the organization for war. At the head of each of these vast areas of the world, known as theaters, is a commander in chief (CINC) who plans and conducts joint operations, which include forces from all of the services. It is these CINCs who command U.S. military forces in time of war, planning and conducting joint and combined campaigns to attain strategic goals. They practice operational art as they coordinate the capabilities of the services to attain the strategic objectives of their campaigns.

The CINCs are responsible to the National Command Authority (NCA)—the president and the secretary of defense—and not to the chiefs of each particular service. Removing the CINC from the service chain of command reduces the chance of service parochialism in planning and conducting operations. The CINC is as close to a true joint officer as a career army, navy, air force, or Marine Corps officer can become. His staff, composed of officers from all the services, is a joint staff that plans and conducts joint operations under his direction. Immediately subordinate to the CINC are component commanders from each service who plan and conduct tactical operations in accordance with the theater campaign plan. The component commands are service-oriented, but their commanders report directly to the CINC, not the service chief, as they plan and conduct operations.

Each of the services has a military chief: chief of staff of the army, chief of naval operations, commandant of the Marine Corps, chief of staff of the air force, and the commandant of the Coast Guard. Each of these chiefs organizes, equips, and trains forces from his service. The forces are then provided in response to an assessment by the CINCs of what forces will be needed to attain the assigned strategic objective.

DEVELOPMENT OF U.S. MILITARY STAFFS

Since the revolutionary war, American military operations have grown from relatively simple affairs planned and controlled by a commander with little or no assistance into vast, complex activities requiring large, highly organized staffs. The U.S. experience of planning and conducting operations coincides with the development and maturation of the military staff system. The function of a staff is to assist a commander by gathering information, preparing detailed plans, translating a commander's decisions into orders, and transmitting instructions to subordinate elements of the command. The staff monitors the myriad activities of military operations, bringing to the attention of a commander matters that require action on his part. It also plans ahead by preparing plans for future operations.

The staff doctrine of the United States developed slowly. From the beginnings of the American military, there has been a great reliance on militia forces to conduct any necessary military operations. Historically, after a war the United States has usually rapidly reduced its military forces to an absolute minimum. This traditional reduction came about in part because it has been an article of faith in American society that the citizen-soldier is as capable of conducting military operations as regular forces with only a little training, and in part because of the traditional American fear that a large standing military force might unduly influence the government. The result has been that the armed forces have generally been unprepared for war, and competence in planning and conducting operations had to be learned by trial and error. When the leadership finally mastered planning and conducting operations, the war was usually over. The trained forces then went back to being civilians, leaving the lessons they had learned by experience to be lost until they had to be relearned under fire by a new generation when it went to war.

In the eighteenth century, battles rarely lasted longer than a day, and the forces were controlled by a commander who could see the entire battlefield. The situation was generally the same at sea, where the fleet simply sailed in a column behind its admiral to do ship-to-ship battle with the opposing fleet. During the nineteenth century, as military forces in Europe

grew in size and complexity, commanders required staffs to assist them in planning and conducting larger and larger battles, campaigns, and wars. While the United States did keep abreast of the development of staffs in European armies and navies, the relatively small standing armed forces and the general lack of interest in participating in international affairs, except as they affected U.S. national interests, precluded development of effective military staffs.

Even the impetus of the American Civil War was not enough to stir much interest in developing military staff doctrine in the United States. It was not until the United States attempted to field forces in the Spanish-American War in 1898 that it became apparent that the army and navy were incapable of dealing effectively with the increasing complexities of planning and conducting operations. As a result of that unfortunate experience, the Joint Army and Navy Board was formed in 1903 as a continuing body that could plan joint operations and resolve problems of common concern. The heads of both services and their chief planners sat on the board, but because they had no authority to enforce its decisions, the board was largely ineffectual and had little or no impact on the conduct of World War I. After the war the services attempted to revitalize the board in 1919, but it continued to suffer from a lack of authority. Its 1935 publication, *Joint Action Board of the Army and Navy*, a guide for joint operations, had no influence in the conduct of World War II, and the board was formally disbanded in 1947 with the establishment of the JCS as a permanent agency.

By the time the United States entered World War I, however, the planning and conduct of operations at all levels of war was so complex that large, well-trained staffs were essential to commanders. Although the joint boards did not survive the rigors of war, the model for today's joint staffs originated in World War I and has since flourished. In 1903, Secretary of War Elihu Root established a small general staff for the army, headed by a chief of staff. That staff provided the nucleus for coordinating the movement of men and matériel to Europe after the United States declared war on Germany in April 1917, but there was no established staff organization for forces in the field. Compounding the problem, the relationship between the army chief of staff, General Peyton C. March, and the commander of the American Expeditionary Forces (AEF), General John J. Pershing, was far from clear. As chief of staff, March had technical authority over Pershing, but the commander of the AEF had gone to Europe with almost total authority to do the job there as he saw fit. Pershing was resistant to any interference from March, and the AEF headquarters staff was organized with little consultation with March.

The AEF general staff was modeled after the French system, with a chief of staff and five sections, each headed by an assistant chief of staff: G-1 (personnel), G-2 (intelligence), G-3 (operations), G-4 (supply), and G-5 (training). This model, which was adopted and refined by the U.S. Army and Marine Corps, has evolved into the joint staff now in use by U.S. forces. The organization and increased size of the joint staff reflects some of the complexities in warfare since World War I. The six sections of the joint staff are J-1 (personnel), J-2 (intelligence), J-3 (operations), J-4 (logistics), J-5 (plans and policy), and J-6 (command, control, and communications systems).

OPERATIONS EDUCATION

The U.S. armed forces maintain an extensive education system to ensure that the officers who command joint forces and serve on joint staffs understand how to plan and conduct effective military operations. Each of the services trains its junior officers to plan and conduct the tactical operations for which it is responsible. There is usually very little interservice training at this level of schooling.

After about ten years of active service, officers attend a staff college, where they learn how to plan and conduct larger tactical operations and receive an introduction to joint operations. Each service has a staff college that focuses on

its unique operations, and selected officers have the opportunity to attend staff colleges from a service other than their own. The highest level of the U.S. officer education system is the senior service school or war college, where the focus is on planning and conducting joint and combined operations. The army, navy, and air force each operates its own war college, although a significant number of officers attend the war college of another service. There is also the National Defense University, which draws its faculty and students from all of the services. The CINCs and the joint staffs of the unified commands are usually selected from the pool of officers who have had a joint education and have experience planning and conducting joint operations.

TECHNOLOGY AND U.S. OPERATIONS

As the planning and conduct of military operations has grown more complex, commanders and their staffs at all levels of command have relied more heavily on technology. Technology provides more powerful weapons, increases mobility, and improves communications for planning and conducting operations, all of which have an impact on the organization of military forces for combat. By increasing the capabilities of armed forces to wage war, technology has also required the development and maintenance of complex support organizations. Military forces were once predominately groups of soldiers and sailors in which every member of the force, including the commander, took part in the fighting, unlike modern armed forces, where participants in the fighting are usually in the minority. Like planning and conducting campaigns, the so-called tooth-to-tail ratio, which roughly compares the number of warriors (the teeth) to the number of personnel required to support them in combat (the tail), has changed dramatically in two hundred years of military operations.

Warfare has seen the steady development of large, highly technological military forces, while, at the same time, American society has become more concerned with individual development and human life. This combination of powerful armed forces and a high regard for the lives of its service personnel has produced an American style of operations that emphasizes the use of firepower in planning and conducting operations.

In their most basic form, military operations are a combination of maneuver and firepower. Even the most complex modern joint operation is essentially coordinating firepower and maneuver. U.S. military operations generally feature a tremendous amount of firepower, including aerial bombing, in the hope of forcing an enemy to capitulate with little or no loss of American lives. Although with one notable exception, the atomic bombing of Japan in World War II, firepower alone has not been sufficient to end a war in the American experience, U.S. military operations still center on delivering massive amounts of firepower on the objective.

Industrial Capacity. During the Civil War, Confederate General Nathan B. Forrest offered the advice that the key to success in war was to "get there first with the most men." With its prodigious industrial capacity in World War II, the United States adhered to that principle as it equipped millions of men in both its own forces and those of the Allies with the latest weapons and equipment, which eventually overwhelmed the Axis powers. Germany opened the war in Europe with an unprecedented combination of maneuver on the ground and firepower from the air, known as blitzkrieg, or "lightning war." The Japanese combined air and naval power to overpower isolated U.S. and British garrisons in a sweeping campaign to gain control of the Pacific. While Germany and Japan started the war in the European and Pacific theaters of operations with maneuver, the United States was eventually able to counter with a preponderance of mass, using its industrial capacity to force an unconditional surrender.

Forrest's simple principle provides an example of the danger of oversimplifying military operations. In World War II an overwhelming number of soldiers attained the Allied goal of unconditional surrender through a series of battles and campaigns designed to attain the desired strategic objectives. In Vietnam, however, sending the "most men" was no help, because there was apparently little planning above the tactical level of military operations. On the surface, being first with the most appears to be a sure recipe for success in battle, but as the U.S. experience in Vietnam demonstrates, it is not a panacea. Tactical victories without a campaign plan that has a strategic objective will often be irrelevant. The concept of overwhelming the enemy with concentrated combat power backed by a giant industrial capacity, however, will continue to be fundamental to the success of U.S operations as long as it is applied with a firm idea of how it will lead to strategic goals.

In the twentieth century, successful U.S. military operations can generally be traced back to vast industrial and technological capabilities. The United States became the "arsenal of democracy" during World War II because its vast industrial capability, untouched by the chaos of war, could produce huge quantities of almost anything the Allies needed in their quest for the strategic goal of unconditional surrender, including the ultimate technological triumph of the atomic bomb. Even in the Vietnam War, which was not successful from the strategic perspective, U.S. military forces were able to attain tactical victories almost at will by using unprecedented aerial mobility and firepower to overwhelm the enemy. In the Gulf War in 1991, the four-day ground war was set up by a massive joint aerial bombardment that destroyed the weapons, equipment, and morale of the Iraqi forces.

THE PRINCIPLES OF WAR

During the eighteenth century, as the foundations for the American military heritage were laid, the systematic study of war became popular in Europe. The Age of Enlightenment demanded a scientific explanation of many activities, including war. Military theorists studied the history of warfare, searching for a scientific formula for planning and conducting operations. Some theorists became convinced that generals who understood mathematics and knew the topography of theaters of operations would be able to plan military operations with precision and to conduct successful campaigns with little or no bloodshed. The theoretical conduct of war became like a game of chess, where the maneuvering of armies would attain the desired objectives with little use of firepower. Although this theoretical view of war fit very nicely into the eighteenth-century practice of conducting war, in which European monarchs were reluctant to commit their small, expensive armies to combat, battles, once joined, remained chaotic.

The introduction at the end of the eighteenth century of the Napoleonic method of war with mass armies ended rather abruptly the quaint idea of winning wars without battles. Napoleonic warfare was made possible by establishing a nation in arms where all manpower was made available for military operations. There was a growing industrial capability to equip large armies with the weapons and impedimenta of war. During the nineteenth century, war became more scientific, as technology and industry developed more destructive weapons and provided commanders with the capability to assemble and move armies rapidly and to communicate over long distances. Innovations such as steam power, railroads, and the telegraph, initially developed for civilian use, quickly found a place in planning and conducting military operations in both Europe and the United States.

While military operations developed a greater reliance on the ability of science and technology to provide weapons and matériel, military theoreticians continued to articulate the fundamental principles of war. There had long been a belief that somewhere in the accumulated experience of war there were a few simple truths that could guide commanders to success on the battlefield. As early as 500 B.C., the Chinese military philosopher Suntzu set down his

thirteen principles of war, and in the nineteenth century, ideas blossomed from a variety of European military writers, such as Baron Henri Jomini and Carl von Clausewitz, whose works continue to influence military doctrine.

Principles of war have become a fact of life in planning and conducting modern military operations, but they must be used with caution. Rarely do any two lists match precisely, and despite the use of the term, the principles are not absolute. Indeed, one aspect of using the principles of war to analyze or plan military operations is to examine exceptions to the rule. The principles on any list are interrelated, and it is entirely possible that adhering to one principle necessitates violating another. Analysis of almost every military operation provides examples of how one principle or another was followed or ignored. Rarely will planners or commanders use a list of principles as a checklist to develop a concept of operations. The principles are less fundamental truths than considerations to bear in mind when planning and conducting operations.

Regardless of the source or the form, a list of principles or considerations can be a useful method of analyzing military operations. The principles can be used to study and generally compare the planning and conduct of military operations from different periods in history. In the United States the services vary in their interest in principles of war. The army, for example, has specifically incorporated a list into its operations doctrine, while the navy rarely refers to principles of war, which is in consonance with how most navies and armies of the world view the principles of war. Historically, it is army officers rather than navy officers who tend to ponder principles of war.

The list of principles found in the army's Field Manual 100–1, *The Army*, has remained generally the same since it first appeared in the 1920s. Although other services may use different versions, the army list is instructive because it is part of its published doctrine. The nine principles therein and accompanying explanatory phrases are listed in the following table.

U.S. Army Principles of War

Objective	Direct every military operation towards a clearly defined, decisive, and attainable objective.
Offensive	Seize, retain, and exploit the initiative.
Mass	Concentrate combat power at the decisive place and time.
Economy of Force	Allocate minimum essential combat power to secondary efforts.
Maneuver	Place the enemy in a position of disadvantage through the flexible application of combat power.
Unity of Command	For every objective, ensure unity of effort under one responsible commander.
Security	Never permit the enemy to acquire an unexpected advantage.
Surprise	Strike the enemy at a time or place, or in a manner, for which he is unprepared.
Simplicity	Prepare clear, uncomplicated plans and clear, concise orders to ensure thorough understanding.

Even with the short explanations given, the army principles of war are a bit cryptic and of limited use without further explanation.

Objective. Although the army implies that there is no particular order in which it has listed the nine principles, common sense dictates that one should know what it is one wants to do before beginning. The principle of the objective, therefore, becomes the logical first consideration for planning and conducting military operations. Having once clearly determined the objective, the other eight principles form a checklist against which military planners and commanders can consider how to plan and conduct appropriate military operations.

Offensive. In order for any military operation to be successful, the forces involved will generally have to conduct some sort of offensive action. Remaining in a defensive posture rarely allows military forces to attain anything, and the principle of the offensive reflects that basic truth. The situation facing a military force, however, is not always conducive for going on the offensive. At the beginning of the Korean War,

for example, U.S. military forces had no choice but to remain on the defensive. In a classic example of this principle's admonition to seize the initiative, General Douglas MacArthur, against almost all conventional wisdom, conducted an offensive operation against the North Korean rear at Inchon that dramatically changed the complexion of the Korean War. Within a matter of weeks the North Koreans were forced from an offensive posture into a desperate defense. While MacArthur's determination to take the initiative in Korea did force the North Koreans onto the defensive, his continued offensive pressure led to the Chinese intervention that put the United Nations forces into their own desperate defense. The war in Korea might have had a rather different result had MacArthur halted the offensive after attaining the strategic objective of forcing the North Korean People's Army out of South Korea. MacArthur's preoccupation with the principle of the offensive caused him to neglect proper consideration of the principle of the objective.

Mass. The principle of mass has been prominent in U.S. operations since the Civil War, when the industrial capacity of the North eventually overwhelmed the agrarian South. While it may appear obvious that concentrating combat power is an appropriate method of conducting operations, it is important to select the decisive time and place to apply that power. When MacArthur launched the invasion into Inchon he did not have much mass, but he did select a decisive time and place. On the other hand, when General George McClellan advanced on Richmond during the Peninsular Campaign in 1862, he had the mass, but because he could not determine a decisive time or place, he was unable to attain the desired strategic objective, the capture of the Confederate capital.

Economy of Force.

The principle of economy of force is a corollary of mass. Concentrating combat power in one place generally requires that another place be designated as a secondary effort that may have to conduct operations with less than desirable combat power. This principle is also related to the offensive, because concentrating combat power for offensive operations in one place generally means conducting defensive operations in another. Although economy of force operations are necessary to concentrate combat power and conduct offensive operations, they do entail some risk. In World War II, during the advance across Europe in late 1944, General Dwight D. Eisenhower elected to make the Ardennes region of Belgium and Luxembourg an economy-of-force sector of the Allied line. The U.S. divisions holding that sector of the line did not have the capability to concentrate much combat power, because the Allies were preparing for offensive operations in other areas. When the Germans, using the principle of mass, along with apparently better intelligence, concentrated superior combat power on that point, they came very close to attaining their strategic objective of splitting the U.S. and British forces. An economy-of-force operation on one side is a potential decisive point against which the other side can mass combat power.

Maneuver.

Maneuver and firepower are basic elements of conducting military operations, and the principles of maneuver and mass should be considered together, because in a practical sense mass means firepower. Maneuver is how military commanders concentrate combat power in consonance with the principle of mass. While operations are a balance of mass and maneuver, one or the other will predominate, depending on the style and capabilities of a particular military force. U.S. military operations tend to favor mass over maneuver. Since the Civil War, using industrial and technological capabilities to concentrate combat power through firepower has been characteristic of U.S. military operations. During the liberation of Kuwait in 1991, U.S. forces maneuvered ground forces to trap the retreating Iraqi army, but that maneuver came only after the most concentrated aerial bombardment in military history. The massed aerial combat power provided the key to the rapid success of the ground maneuver.

Unity of Command.

In the history of U.S. operations, unity of command has frequently been sought but rarely achieved. Unity of command is especially difficult when conducting joint operations with two or more of the services. U.S. forces adhered to the principle of unity of command in the liberation of Kuwait. In compliance with the Unified Command Plan, Army General Norman Schwarzkopf was the commander in chief of U.S. forces from all services, but that example is an exception to the general rule. While it makes eminent good sense to strive for unity of command or at least unity of effort in planning and conducting military operations, it is difficult to attain that goal.

Successful military commanders tend to be very strong personalities and frequently show something less than great enthusiasm for serving as a subordinate to a commander from another service. During World War II, the army and the navy expended considerable effort arguing with each other about how to coordinate the efforts of the southwest and central Pacific theaters, an effort that could not help but detract somewhat from the objective of defeating the Japanese. As often as not, unity of command in the history of U.S. military operations has translated to unity of effort.

Security and Surprise. Security and surprise, like mass and maneuver, are principles that should be considered together. The principle of security cautions not to let the enemy acquire an unexpected advantage, and the principle of surprise advises to strike the enemy when or where he is unprepared. By considering them together, it becomes apparent that there must be a lapse of security on one side for the other to gain surprise. In the broadest sense both security and surprise cover the acquisition of intelligence information about enemy capabilities.

Security includes gathering information to ascertain enemy capabilities in order to gain surprise or avoid being surprised; it also involves denying intelligence information to the enemy so that he will not acquire an unexpected advantage. The U.S. forces in the Ardennes in 1944, for example, were surprised because they allowed the Germans to acquire an unexpected advantage by failing to ascertain German capabilities. The Japanese surprised U.S. forces at Pearl Harbor in 1941 in part because intelligence information that could have led to a determination of enemy capabilities was not noticed in the message traffic. For example, in the days immediately preceding the bombing at Pearl Harbor, British intelligence had predicted a Japanese attack on either Malaya or Hawaii, but the messages exchanged between the United States and Great Britain during that period numbered in the thousands. Only after the attack did it become clear that the British analysis was credible.

Simplicity. With the conduct of operations becoming ever more complex as new technology floods the battlefield, the principle of simplicity assumes great importance. In the Gulf War of 1991, U.S. forces had the most complex military force ever assembled in terms of weapons and equipment, but General Schwarzkopf's concept of operations was fairly simple. The campaign began by pounding the Iraqi army for weeks with firepower from the air, then ground forces simply cut the lines of communications and escape. It was a simple campaign plan executed with precision, even though the operations that contributed to the success of the campaign were themselves complex. Many of those operations, however, were made relatively simple in their execution because the forces conducting them had been given adequate time and opportunity to prepare and rehearse before going into combat. Part of the success of the campaign was selecting the decisive time when U.S. forces were ready to fight and Iraqi forces were not.

THEATERS OF OPERATIONS

A theater of operations encompasses those areas of land, sea, and air in which campaigns are conducted. Under the Unified Command Plan, a theater CINC plans and conducts the campaigns that will attain strategic goals. Because the theater CINC commands forces provided by all the services, he must plan and conduct operations from a joint perspective. The service that provides the CINC is generally determined by whether the theater of operations is continental or maritime.

A continental theater is primarily land and features ground and air operations, while a maritime theater includes considerable areas of sea, requiring naval forces for operations. In World War II the European theater of operations was a continental theater, and the battles in the Pacific took place in a maritime theater. In Europe, the CINC, General Eisenhower, was an army or ground officer in large part because the theater was continental. In the Pacific there were actually two theaters of operations—the southwest Pacific area, commanded by General Douglas MacArthur, an army officer, and the central Pacific area, commanded by Admiral Chester Nimitz, a navy officer. Both of the Pacific theaters of operations were maritime and demanded the coordination of considerable air, land, and sea forces. The decision to establish two theaters in the Pacific had more to do with personalities and service rivalry than with operational logic. In 1942, MacArthur was the army's choice to hold the high command in the Pacific; he was well-known to the American public, had the president's confidence, and was considered something of an expert on the Far East. The navy, however, wanted Nimitz, then a virtually unknown figure, to be the commander in chief, and it certainly was not willing to turn command of its Pacific fleet over to an army officer, no matter how prestigious he might be. The result was the two-theater compromise.

Lines of Communications. Within a theater of operations, whether maritime or continental, the CINC will maintain a line of communication (LOC)—the physical air, land, and sea routes that connect operating forces in the field or at sea with their base of operations and along which move supplies, personnel, and equipment. A line of communications may also be referred to as a line of operations. One of the first jobs within a theater is to establish a base of operations that can support the campaign. When the theater of operations is not contiguous with the United States, the theater CINC will need lines of communications into the theaters. The United States, with its worldwide national interests, requires sea lines of communications (SLOCs) to move the weapons and equipment necessary for ground forces to the theaters of operations and air lines of communication (ALOCs) to respond rapidly. An ALOC provides a rapid method of moving military forces. While it cannot entirely support a large, sustained buildup of forces for a campaign in a distant theater of operations, it does provide for rapid movement of troops. By the latter stages of the Vietnam War, ALOCs were carrying most of the personnel between the United States and Southeast Asia. During the 1990 buildup of U.S. forces in the Middle East, the ALOC was an essential element of the deployment. The first

forces into the theater moved entirely by air and nearly all personnel moved by air.

Movement of U.S. military forces into theaters of operations and the support of major campaigns, such as the Gulf War of 1991, will generally be a combination of ALOCs and SLOCs; personnel are transported by air, while heavy weapons, equipment, ammunition, food, and POL (petroleum, oil, and lubricants) move by sea. Smaller campaigns, where time is short, such as the invasions of Grenada and Panama, however, may be supported primarily by ALOCs.

TYPES OF OPERATIONS

Regardless of the theater, there are two basic military operations, offensive and defensive, either of which may include special operations. Within a theater of operations, a CINC conducts offensive operations, defensive operations, or some combination of the two. In a long war, one theater might be designated a defensive theater or economy-of-force operation, in order to concentrate combat power to conduct offensive operations. Even in a defensive theater, however, the CINC will try to conduct offensive operations to seize, retain, and exploit the initiative. Differentiating between offensive and defensive operations often depends on the level of war. In World War II, for example, the Pacific theaters of operations were initially designated as defensive theaters, while the United States focused its offensive attention and massed its combat power to defeat Germany and Italy in Europe.

In a theater that is conducting a strategic offensive, however, some elements of the military force may be conducting defensive operations. Although both MacArthur and Nimitz were on the strategic defensive, they sought to conduct offensive tactical operations by concentrating whatever combat power they could muster. The forces conducting the defensive or economy-of-force operations will generally be relatively small in comparison to the enemy, thereby allowing for a larger offensive force. In the Korean War, when MacArthur, the theater CINC, was assembling the amphibious force to mass the available combat power that would maneuver to conduct offensive operations against the North Koreans at Inchon, the forces in the Pusan perimeter were conducting an economy-of-force defensive operation. The success of the offensive operations in Korea also depended in large part on surprise.

The U.S. armed forces have an operations terminology that facilitates communications within and among the services. Some of the terminology may be more closely associated with one service than another, but understanding modern warfare requires at least some familiarity with a wide variety of operations. The terms used in planning and conducting operations include both theoretical concepts and practical definitions.

In modern warfare many types of operations, whether single service or joint, have developed common designations that in a word or short phrase convey specific meanings for planners and commanders. While each of these different types of operations requires experts to do the detailed planning and then execute the plans, the short term is useful to joint planners who must coordinate the tactical capabilities of the different services into an overall campaign plan to attain the desired strategic objective. Although some specialized operations may involve only one service, they must still be coordinated into the CINC's joint campaign plan for the theater of operations.

Sea Operations. The navy conducts a variety of operations on its own at sea, but those operations must be coordinated into the joint campaign plan, because they may require forces that will not be available for other uses. If, for example, there is a threat to sea lines of communications, the navy may have to dedicate forces to convoy operations, forces that would then not be available to support amphibious operations. Even though the convoy operation may be an implied navy responsibility, it has an impact on how the theater CINC plans and conducts the joint campaign.

Some of the operations that the navy generally conducts using only its own forces and equipment, but that can contribute significantly to the success or failure of any campaign in which they are required, include antisubmarine warfare (ASW), antiair warfare (AAW), and surface warfare (SW). ASW conducts operations against enemy submarines and includes air, surface, and subsurface forces working together; AAW includes operations to protect the navy's surface forces from enemy air attack and to project aerial firepower at sea and inland; and SW features operations against enemy surface forces. Each of these types of operations require specially equipped and trained navy forces, and each one is a navy responsibility to plan and conduct. The navy may conduct a combination of operations to ensure the security of the SLOCs, secure an area for amphibious operations, or provide fire support to land forces in support of maritime or continental campaigns. Generally, theater CINCs do not become directly involved in naval operations, which are the responsibility of the navy component commander to plan and conduct within the framework of the theater campaign plan.

Air Operations. Like the navy, the air force is responsible for planning and conducting a variety of specialized operations in support of a theater campaign. Air force operations include close air support (CAS), air interdiction (AI), battlefield air interdiction (BAI), and air superiority. In a maritime theater of operations, the air power available from the navy and the Marine Corps also will be a factor in such operations.

Although it is conceivable for a joint force to conduct all of these air operations at the same time, it is generally considered essential to conduct air superiority operations before conducting other types of air, land, or sea operations. The goal of air superiority operations is to gain control of the airspace in the theater. Before gaining control of all of the theater airspace, it may be necessary to attain local air superiority so that ground operations can begin. Local air superiority means friendly air forces can maintain temporary control of the airspace over a specific part of the theater. Implied in local air superiority is the enemy's continued ability to challenge control of the air, which can limit the ability to conduct other friendly air operations in support of ground or sea forces. An early objective in U.S. campaigns is gaining air superiority over the entire theater of operations. Theater air superiority allows friendly aircraft to conduct other air operations with little or no threat from enemy aircraft.

Close air support operations provide aerial fire support to ground forces involved in close combat with the enemy. It is a method of concentrating combat power. The air force generally conducts CAS operations in support of the army, while the Marine Corps has the capability to provide CAS for its own ground forces. In joint operations, however, CAS aircraft from the air force, navy, or Marine Corps can support both army and marine ground forces. Because the aircraft best suited for CAS operations are designed specifically for the needs of the ground forces, they are generally unsuited for other types of operations and are particularly vulnerable to enemy air attack. CAS operations, therefore, rarely begin before the theater CINC can be assured of at least local air superiority over the areas where ground operations will be conducted.

Air interdiction and battlefield air interdiction operations are closely related to each other and to air superiority and CAS operations. They also can include aircraft from the air force, navy, and the Marine Corps. AI operations focus on destroying forces, matériel, and installations deep behind enemy forces in the theater. Examples of AI targets are airfields, bridges on lines of communications, and ammunition stockpiles. BAI operations concentrate on targets immediately to the rear of enemy front-line forces. BAI targets include such things as reserve formations of enemy ground forces and command facilities. While the differences between AI and BAI may be subtle, neither can really begin until there is at least local air superiority because, like CAS aircraft, the bombers used for those operations can be vulnerable to enemy air attack.

Ideally, air superiority operations will gain complete control of the theater airspace early in the campaign, which will then allow the conduct of AI, BAI, and CAS in support of ground forces. The theater CINC determines how much of the available air power will be devoted to each type of air operation based on recommendations from the air component commander. Generally the air force component commander plans and conducts air operations to support the theater campaign plan, but the Marine Corps and navy also participate when they have aircraft involved.

Thus far in the history of warfare, no campaign has been successful until ground forces have actually occupied the area in question. Like air and sea forces, U.S. ground forces can conduct a variety of operations. To gain entry into a theater of operations ground forces can conduct airborne, air assault, or amphibious operations in conjunction with air and sea forces.

Air-Land Operations. In airborne operations ground forces enter the battlefield by parachute. Close coordination between the services is required in airborne operations. The air force is responsible for providing the transport aircraft that deliver ground forces to the objective area, and the army usually provides specially trained and equipped ground forces that parachute from the air to the ground, although the Marine Corps also has some airborne qualified forces. Airborne operations are used for such things as capturing a critical objective behind enemy lines (for example, a bridge, command post, or dam); securing an airfield in order to land additional forces, equipment, and supplies; and demoralizing enemy forces by disrupting their rear-area activities. Although airborne forces are equipped with a variety of weapons with which to defend their airhead, they do require timely reinforcement, because they are not trained to engage in combat for extended periods of time. By necessity, airborne forces must have weapons and equipment that can be carried inside aircraft, survive a parachute drop, and then operate on the ground with a high degree of reliability. Airborne operations rely largely on surprise to strike the enemy in an unexpected manner. They are usually conducted as part of a larger operation so that the relatively lightly equipped airborne forces, once on the ground, can be reinforced for sustained battle. While airborne operations can result in surprising the enemy, there is also the possibility that they will sustain large losses either because the air-drop does not go well or because they cannot be reinforced.

Air assault operations, like airborne operations, consist of delivering ground forces to the battlefield by air. In air assault operations, however, the mode of transportation is generally the helicopter, although fixed-wing aircraft from the air force can also be used, as in Grenada in 1983. Transport helicopters, escorted and supported by armed helicopters, carry the ground forces into battle.

Although there are similarities between airborne and air assault operations, there are also significant differences. In airborne operations, personnel and equipment are dropped by parachute from fixed-wing aircraft at an altitude between five hundred and one thousand feet above the ground; in air assault operations, forces are carried in helicopters or fixed-wing aircraft, which land briefly to discharge their loads on or close to the ground. An air assault operation may closely follow an airborne operation that secures an airfield so that it can be used by fixed-wing aircraft. Both airborne and air assault forces are limited in the size and amount of weapons, equipment, and supplies they can carry into battle. As in airborne operations, air assault forces require timely reinforcement by forces equipped with heavier weapons for extended operations. Both the army and the Marine Corps can conduct air assault operations using their own helicopters. Air superiority is essential before air assault and airborne operations can be conducted. Because of their extremely high vulnerability to aerial firepower, the theater CINC will want some reasonable assurance that air superiority can be maintained until the airborne and air assault forces on the ground can be reinforced.

Sea-Land Operations. Amphibious operations, which feature projection of land power from the sea onto a potentially hostile enemy, are a Marine Corps speciality, although the army also trains for them. Traditional amphibious operations consist of landing ground forces from ships onto a beach by small landing craft, although amphibious forces can use both surface and aerial transportation to effect the rapid buildup of forces on the shore. Amphibious operations seek to gain a beachhead and then conduct a rapid buildup of forces on the shore. They are joint operations that include air, land, and sea forces. The navy is always involved, the Marine Corps is usually involved, and the army and air force may also participate. Amphibious operations may be an end in themselves, as they were in the Pacific in World War II, when they were used to capture islands; they may be just the beginning of a campaign, as in the invasion of Normandy, which gave Allied forces a foothold on the European continent in World War II; or they may be a phase in a campaign, as the Inchon invasion was in the Korean War.

A characteristic of the airhead established by an airborne operation and the beachhead established by an amphibious operation is their vulnerability to nuclear and chemical attack. Both operations depend on air superiority over the airhead or beachhead for their success, and both require extensive joint cooperation between the involved services.

Land Operations. In the course of a campaign, ground forces, however they arrive on the battlefield, may attack or defend in a variety of operations on land featuring combined arms operations, which consist of the integrated use of the different weapons and support systems available to ground forces. Almost any ground operation on a modern battlefield is a combined arms operation and will usually include some form of infantry (mechanized, airborne, air assault, or light), armor (tanks), field and air defense artillery, engineers, reconnaissance elements, attack helicopters, and logistical support elements. Both the army and the Marine Corps conduct combined arms operations on land, although the army has a wider variety of forces with which to work.

Special Operations.

Special operations, also known as unconventional operations, consist of activities carried out by highly specialized, well-trained, and inconspicuous forces drawn from all the services. The theater CINC may use special operations forces to obtain intelligence information, conduct raids, or perform reconnaissance missions. Special operations are usually covert, and their contribution to the success of a campaign is usually not made public until well after the event, if then.

U.S. military forces are prepared to conduct a wide variety of operations around the world. Ironically, most of the planning and training for these operations is conducted in the hope of never having to execute them in combat. Perhaps the most successful military operation is the one that attains its objective simply by threatening its use, but to make that threat credible the military must be demonstrably proficient in strategy, tactics, and operational art.

See also COALITION WARFARE; DECISION-MAKING; THE DEVELOPMENT OF OPERATIONAL ART; INTEROPERABILITY; POLITICAL OBJECTIVES AND THE DEVELOPMENT OF MILITARY STRATEGY; PSYCHOLOGICAL OPERATIONS; *and* UNCONVENTIONAL WARFARE.

BIBLIOGRAPHY

Adams, Dwight, and Clayton R. Newell. "Operational Art in the Joint and Combined Arenas." *Parameters* (June 1988).

Atkinson, Edward B. "The Operational Level of War." *Military Review* (March 1987).

Bolt, William J., and David Jablonsky. "Tactics and the Operational Level of War." *Military Review* (February 1987).

Cable, James. "The Diffusion of Maritime Power." *International Relations* (November 1982).

Dixon, James H., and Associates. *Military Planning and Operations: The Joint Perspective* (1985).

Furlong, Raymond B. "*On War*, Political Objectives, and Military Strategy." *Parameters* (December 1983).

Greenfield, Kent Roberts, ed. *Command Decisions* (1960).

Hewes, James E., Jr. *From Root to McNamara: Army Organization and Administration, 1900–1963* (1975).

Hittle, James D. *The Military Staff: Its History and Development*, 3d ed. (1961).

House, Jonathan M. *Toward Combined Arms Warfare: A Survey of 20th-Century Tactics, Doctrine, and Organization* (1984).

Hughes, Wayne P., Jr. *Fleet Tactics: Theory and Practice* (1986).

Huston, James A. *The Sinews of War: Army Logistics, 1775–1953* (1966).

Jablonsky, David. "Strategy and the Operational Level of War." *Parameters* (Spring 1987).

Leonhard, Robert. *The Art of Maneuver: Maneuver-Warfare Theory and AirLand Battle* (1991).

Lind, William S. *Maneuver Warfare Handbook* (1985).

Luttwak, Edward N. *Strategy: The Logic of War and Peace* (1987).

Mahan, Alfred Thayer. *The Influence of Sea Power Upon History, 1660–1783* (1890).

Matloff, Maurice. *The Theory and Practice of War* (1966).

Mendel, William W., and Floyd T. Banks. *Campaign Planning* (1988).

Military Review (September 1990), entire issue.

Millis, Walter, ed. *American Military Thought* (1956).

Nenninger, Timothy K. *The Leavenworth Schools and the Old Army* (1978).

Newell, Clayton R. *The Framework of Operational Warfare* (1991).

Turner, Stansfield. "The Formulation of Military Strategy." In *The Art and Practice of Military Strategy*, edited by George Edward Thibault (1984).

Upton, Emory. *The Military Policy of the United States* (1917).

Watts, Barry D. *The Foundations of U.S. Air Doctrine: The Problems of Friction in War* (1984).

THE DEVELOPMENT OF OPERATIONAL ART

Clayton R. Newell

The American armed forces have been shaped by the wars they have fought, and an American style of operations has evolved, influenced, but not dominated, by military thinking in Europe. During two centuries American armed forces have grown from part-time militia forces held in contempt by the regular armies of Europe to one of the dominant world military powers. Today, officers from all over the world come to the United States to learn the American style of operational art.

Since 1775 the United States has participated in ten major wars: the American Revolution, the War of 1812, the Civil War, the Spanish-American War, the Mexican War, World War I, World War II, Korea, Vietnam, and the Gulf War of 1991. In between those wars, U.S. armed forces have conducted a wide variety of military operations around the world, including the Quasi-War with France, wars with the Barbary states in the Mediterranean, a lengthy series of wars with American Indians, the Philippine Insurrection, the Boxer Rebellion, stability operations in Lebanon, and the invasions of Grenada and Panama. Those accumulated experiences have all contributed to how the U.S. armed forces plan and conduct military operations.

The evolution of American operational art be-

gan even before the armed forces as we now know them came into existence. While the revolutionary war generally marks the beginning of an organized national military force in the United States, the foundations of an American style of operations were established during the colonial period, before there was any serious thought of an independent United States.

COLONIAL OPERATIONS

American land operations had their genesis in the wars waged between France and Great Britain in the seventeenth century, as they attempted to increase their colonial holdings in North America. When conflicts between European powers spread to their colonies in America, the wars usually had different names. The War of the League of Augsburg (1689–1697), for example, was known in America as King William's War. During that war an expeditionary force of Massachusetts troops led by Sir William Phips, a successful merchant, conducted operations against French colonies in Canada. Such operations, generally planned and conducted by European officers based in North America, frequently involved militia forces from the colonies, and officers in the militia thereby gained practical military experience. Since then American officers have continued to emphasize the practical application of conducting operations rather than developing military theory. By the same token, the fundamentals of planning and conducting land operations in America have been products of European military thought and science modified to suit American circumstances.

Throughout the seventeenth century, as American colonists were struggling against the wilderness and the Indians, European monarchs conducted a wave of small wars for personal or dynastic gains. Armies were small but costly to maintain, because the available manpower pool was relatively small when compared to the population at large. Most able-bodied men were needed to feed the population, and because agriculture was manpower intensive, little of that manpower could be spared for the army. Large armies meant less production in the fields. Even if there had been no constraints on manpower, the minimal industrial capability of the period could not adequately equip a large army. Commanders in the field, responsible to their monarchs for the armies, were loath to actually fight unless virtually certain of success, and war became an elaborate series of maneuvers in which each side attempted to avoid battle until the circumstances were in its favor.

At the beginning of the eighteenth century, infantry formations in Europe were linear rather than massed and were designed for maximum firepower, because the most common characteristic of the standard infantry weapon, the flintlock, was inaccuracy. The usual fighting formation was a line of infantry three deep. Infantrymen were rigidly drilled to reload as fast as possible and fire their weapons in an area to the front. There was no aimed fire; the weapons could not hit a target consistently. The goal was a high volume of fire at ranges between fifty and one hundred yards. Opposing infantry formations literally tried to blast holes into the formations of their opponents. Battles were generally mirror images of infantry formations facing each other across an open field.

The advent of mobile field artillery increased the firepower available on the battlefield. The development of the science of ballistics and improved metallurgical techniques in the eighteenth century produced smaller and lighter artillery pieces that could accompany an army on the march. With improved mobility, field artillery became a weapon that could be used against the linear infantry formations. Although the American environment required some changes in European tactics, firepower soon became characteristic of American military operations and continues to be a fundamental element of operations.

American land operations developed during a period of rapid and constant change in warfare, which differed from the European emphasis on stability. By the eighteenth century, American colonists were learning to conduct land operations against an opponent who did not adhere to the rules of European warfare. The native American style of operations emphasized stealth and surprise, and their battles were a melee of individual combat with no disciplined formations or easily identifiable uniforms to distinguish friend from foe. Colonists learned from the Indians as both friend and enemy. In 1753, Major George Washington of Virginia included Indians among his forces when he carried a message to French authorities to inform them that they were encroaching on English territory. In May 1754, Washington, now a lieutenant colonel, fought and won his first battle near Fort Duquesne at the confluence of the Allegheny and Monongahela rivers, and his biggest difficulty was keeping his Indian allies from killing their French prisoners. When the French regrouped shortly thereafter, Washington was forced to lead his men out of the hastily constructed Fort Necessity, and during the retreat found themselves driving off hostile Indians. In this type of operation, individual initiative counted more than rigid discipline, and initiative remains a highly regarded attribute in U.S. military forces.

American colonists followed military developments in Europe through their contacts with elements of the French and British armies stationed in the colonies and by the immigration of military officers from other European armies. American military operations on land, however, influenced by terrain and opponents, developed differently from those in Europe. While seventeenth-century monarchs watched their armies perform military minuets, the American colonists learned to fight Indians. Compared to European experience at the beginning of the eighteenth century, military operations in the colonies were unconventional. While eighteenth-century European nation-states maintained professional armies that conducted land operations against each other using the same tactics and weapons, the colonies relied on militia forces to protect them from Indian raids. Although they varied from colony to colony, militia forces generally employed light infantry tactics learned from their Indian opponents. Whereas European armies maintained rigid battle lines with massive volumes of firepower from inaccurate weapons, Americans used open skirmish lines and aimed fire by individuals. Perhaps the most famous irregular forces of this period are Major Robert Rogers' Rangers, which conducted scores of raids and assaults in 1757–1760, during the French and Indian War. Rangers still symbolize the best light infantry forces in the army today.

The colonial solution to the manpower problem was a part-time military called to arms when needed. The concept of maintaining military forces only when necessary has had a continuing influence on American operations. The militia tradition of friends and neighbors banding together in battle had made American officers sensitive to unnecessarily wasting lives. It has become characteristic of American military operations to use firepower to preserve as many American lives as possible. Even with the relatively large professional military forces the United States maintains now, there is still considerable reliance on reserve and National Guard forces, modern descendants of the colonial militia.

Although the colonies developed their own militias for protection, France and Great Britain at various times maintained elements of their professional armies in the New World, although the British forces were generally very small

units. On occasion the colonial militias would join these professional soldiers in combined operations. These shared experiences produced differences that had a significant effect on the early development of American land operations. On the one hand, colonial officers gained experience with trained and disciplined military forces, which provided a foundation for building the Continental army. On the other hand, the British, schooled in the disciplined European type of land operations, developed a disdain for what they perceived as the ragged operations of the colonial militias.

In comparison with the wars fought in Europe, land operations in colonial America were small affairs with the various militias rarely venturing outside their own colony. The goals and the means of these operations were limited and the militia could not afford to stay away from home too long. Because there was little in the way of multicolony military operations, each colonial militia developed its own doctrine for planning and conducting operations. Although the colonies did not have a common doctrine for conducting land operations, they did share the same experience of conducting their military operations on terrain that was strategically larger but tactically more congested than that in Europe. European armies were not used to routinely moving long distances without resupply, and they were generally unfamiliar with the closely wooded terrain over which the small land battles in America were generally fought.

THE REVOLUTIONARY WAR

At the beginning of the American Revolution, colonists relied on the militia, which fought part-time and maintained the home front the rest of the time. Militia forces had the advantage of understanding local terrain, but a lack of cooperation and common doctrine was evident when forces from different colonies gathered together to face the relatively large, disciplined British forces. The early skirmishes between colonial militias and British regulars, however, tended to strengthen the American belief that they would not need a professional army.

One of the first encounters of American militia against British regulars was the Battle of Bunker Hill, fought in Boston on Breed's Hill in June 1775. The British officers elected to march their regiments uphill in a frontal assault against a fortified defensive position, rather than conduct a flanking movement to the rear of the colonials. British officers perhaps hoped the frontal assault would demonstrate to the part-time soldiers behind hastily constructed barriers the power of professional infantry, but the Americans had begun to learn how to successfully conduct operations against the British. They now knew that at the Battle of Lexington in April most of the militia had fired too soon against the British regulars. At Bunker Hill, with the traditionally attributed admonition "Don't fire until you see the whites of their eyes," the American militia, firing from fortified positions, relied on the massed firepower of muskets, augmented with aimed fire from a few rifles, against the advancing British. The British won the battle, but by fighting from defensive positions, the militia had been successful in preserving American lives to fight another day.

During the revolutionary war, the British army had difficulty adapting its European view of war to the American terrain and the colonial tactics. For their part, the Americans eventually recognized the shortcomings of the militia and created the Continental army. Under the leadership of George Washington, the army developed a modified version of European linear tactics for its infantry. Americans used irregular formations as a matter of course, although Baron Friedrich von Steuben, a Prussian immigrant who had learned his tactics as a junior officer in Europe, drilled the Continentals in European formations. The result was a looser sort of formation that combined the European tradition with the colonial experience and was revolutionary in the general evolution of warfare. The American infantry, although schooled and disciplined to some degree, took advantage of available cover and used aimed fire rather than the massed fire common to the British.

In the latter half of the eighteenth century a new infantry weapon, the rifle, began to make its presence known on the battlefield. Originally a sporting weapon, the rifle had a grooved barrel that imparted a twist to the bullet, giving it greater range and accuracy than the smoothbore musket. Although the rifle became popular with American forces, the majority carried muskets into combat, because the technology did not exist to mass-produce the more sophisticated rifles. The number of skilled marksmen who were able to pick out and hit individuals was generally fewer than put forth by American legend, but there were enough to appall the British, who were used to a more gentlemanly style of operations. American marksmanship with the rifle, although widely scattered in the Continental army, eventually led to a change in the tactics of most armies from the massed fire of muskets to the aimed fire of rifles.

New technology was frequently recognized earlier in America because the colonists were used to getting along with what was available, while the British relied on their European experience in warfare. American forces tended to carry less and move faster than the heavier laden British, who carried all of the impedimenta of European operations. The ability to travel light helped American forces against the British, but traveling light is not a characteristic that has endured in U.S. military operations. The penchant for taking advantage of technology has made the U.S. military one of the heaviest in the world. Today, U.S. forces face the same sort of difficulties the British did in the revolutionary war. U.S. forces now require extensive logistical and technical support to conduct operations against even the most rudimentary opponent, a situation that sometimes puts the better-equipped force at something of a disadvantage.

Although American forces were generally lighter than the British, during the course of the revolutionary war, the Continental army developed some of the characteristics of European armies. The light infantry that developed from operations against the Indians was an American innovation in warfare. With the emphasis on firepower, however, light infantry became something of a stepchild, useful for some chores but not fully integrated into the Continental army, a position it still holds in the U.S. Army.

Unlike military operations on land, colonial naval operations were almost nonexistent. Although the American colonies produced seamen as proficient as any in the world, they had relied on the British navy for protection of trade. The colonies developed an unequaled sailing tradition, but they had no naval tradition. America in the eighteenth century was, and still is for that matter, essentially a maritime nation that relied on the sea lanes to maintain trade with the rest of the world. Although the American Revolution was successful as a result of continental operations, it required cooperation from the sea. Recognizing that it simply could not afford to build a navy that could challenge the British at sea, in 1775 the Continental Congress authorized the building of four frigates to conduct raiding operations on British commerce, but to avoid general engagements with the British fleet. Congress also authorized privateers to operate against British commerce, and during the Revolution some six hundred merchant ships were taken by American privateers. The strategy of attacking enemy merchant shipping while avoiding set battles with fleets of larger warships established the strategy of U.S. naval operations for the next hundred years. American naval operations until the late nineteenth century were generally single engagements, one ship pitted against another, with the larger having the advantage. The U.S. Navy remained small and coastal until the twentieth century, although it did conduct some transatlantic expeditions.

The British fleet, however, remained a potential problem for land operations during the Revolution, because it could transport land forces along the coast faster than American forces could move on land. In the absence of an American navy capable of joint operations with the Continental army, the French navy was instrumental in the decisive campaign against the British forces in Virginia.

In 1781 the British army was divided between New York and Virginia and depended on the Royal Navy operating in the Chesapeake Bay and along the Atlantic coast for maintaining a line of communications between the two forces. Between the British forces was a combined American and French army. Washington, commanding the Continental army, and Comte de Rochambeau, in command of the French troops, developed a campaign plan that would mass their combat power against the divided British. In coordination with the French fleet, the bulk of the American and French land forces moved from New York to Virginia. A small number of American troops remained in New York to contain the British while Washington concentrated his combat power against the British in Virginia. In the meantime, the British had moved into a fortified position at Yorktown in Virginia. The British had hoped to reinforce or withdraw from this port city with the help of the British navy at a time of their choosing. With the French fleet blocking British lines of communication through the Chesapeake Bay, however, Washington laid siege to Yorktown and forced a British surrender. This successful joint and combined operation decided the war in the American's favor.

POST-REVOLUTIONARY PERIOD

Although the revolutionary war was fought and decided primarily on land, the decisive Yorktown campaign depended on joint land and sea operations. U.S. operations have almost always had both a continental and a maritime flavor. Since the founding of the nation, however, there has been a rivalry between the army and the navy, as each argued that their contribution to the security of the country was paramount. During the first one hundred years of their existence, the army and navy conducted few joint operations, each service operating in its respective medium, and until the end of the nineteenth century, the national policy of the United States was to shun interaction with the rest of the world and avoid entangling alliances. The navy, therefore, concentrated on raiding the shipping of enemies and protecting coastal waters in time of war. Although the navy conducted small operations far removed from the United States to ensure the freedom of American merchantmen, its mission was not to control the sea. The strategy remained one of avoiding fleet engagements.

The end of the revolutionary war saw the dissolution of most of the Continental army, and the desire to get troops back home as soon as the fighting is over has remained a characteristic American attitude. The regular army remained small when at peace, but became swollen with militia or volunteer forces when at war. The wartime experience gained in conducting military operations, however, although retained by individual officers, was lost to the army as an institution. Planning and conducting operations depended on the ability of senior army officers in the field, and that ability varied greatly.

When U.S. reaction to the Napoleonic wars led to the War of 1812, the army was supposed to invade and capture Canada while the navy swept British commerce from the seas. Although both services met with some success, neither accomplished its objective. The army suffered from poor senior leadership and conflicts between the regulars and the militia; the navy initially did well with its successful commerce raiding and blockade running, but in the end, the small number of U.S. ships could not cope with the British fleet. Despite the results, both services benefited from larger peacetime spending as a result of the war. In 1815, Congress tripled the size of the army to ten thousand, authorized nine ships of the line and twelve heavy frigates for the navy in 1816, and initiated a long-range program to fortify the U.S. coast.

During the nineteenth century, there were no large land forces in either Mexico or Canada, so there was no great concern for protection against a surprise invasion. While this enabled the United States to maintain only a small regular army, it also meant that the army had no incentive to develop any theoretical basis for conducting operations. Studying the art and science of war was left to European armies. U.S. military policy would simply be the augmentation during war of the small regular army with militia and volunteer forces.

The navy's situation was not all that different from that of the army. It was not until after the Barbary pirates posed an economic threat to American merchant shipping in the Mediterranean that Congress authorized the construction of six new frigates. In what has become an American tradition of equipping its fighting forces with the latest technology available, the first ships authorized for the new navy were the finest in the world, but their operations were not much changed from those conducted during the Revolution—commerce protection and raiding on the high seas and coastal patrols near U.S. shores. The United States, although ready to provide protection to commerce, was not yet capable of putting together a fleet to challenge the European sea powers in major fleet operations.

THE MEXICAN WAR

For the most part, during the first half of the nineteenth century the army and the navy each went their own way planning and conducting small operations, although there were times that required their mutual cooperation and support. One such time was during the Mexican War, when General Winfield Scott conducted an ambitious campaign to capture Mexico City in 1847. The campaign began with a joint operation to land Scott's ten thousand troops at Veracruz after a naval bombardment. The amphibious operation, which put almost nine thousand army troops ashore in the initial landings on 9 March, was a remarkable performance, although a storm that blew up a few days later slowed the landing of the artillery, horses, and supplies. Once ashore, Scott called on U.S. firepower to reduce the fortress at Veracruz before assaulting it. He began the bombardment with seven 10-inch mortars on 22 May, added six naval guns contributed by the navy on 24 May, and accepted the Mexican capitulation on 27 May, all with fewer than one hundred U.S. casualties. Having reduced the fortress, Scott deliberately cut the line of communications to Veracruz and moved overland to the strategic objective of the campaign, Mexico City. It took six months to finally capture the city (13–14 September), but capturing Mexico City effectively ended the war.

The joint campaign demonstrated that the army and navy could work together. Both services learned much from the Mexican War, and the experience influenced how they would conduct operations in the next war. For the navy, the steamboat proved itself useful in coastal operations along the Mexican shoreline, and operations on inland rivers provided valuable experience for officers who would soon be conducting operations along America's greatest rivers. The army's faith in firepower to save American lives had been validated at Veracruz, and the war gave junior officers experience in planning and conducting large operations.

THE CIVIL WAR

Before the Civil War, with the exception of the Mexican War, the army had only conducted small land operations. The officer corps of the regular army, however, had learned European theories on conducting a new style of warfare—the Napoleonic style of conducting large land operations—as cadets at the United States Military Academy, established at West Point in 1802. The academy produced most of the generals who conducted active operations during the Civil War. In the sixty major battles of the Civil War, fifty-five had West Point graduates on both the Union and Confederate sides and the remaining five had an academy graduate commanding on at least one side. Dennis Hart Mahan, professor of military art and engineering at the academy, was a dedicated teacher and inspired apostle of Napoleon and impressed the importance of Napoleon's method of conducting land operations on the cadets. Mahan's teaching was probably the greatest single influence on how army commanders on both sides planned and conducted operations during the Civil War.

The Influence of Napoleonic Warfare.
Napoleon inspired the rise in Europe of theoretical literature on war in the early nineteenth century. His approach to war was to crush the main body of the opposing army, believing that strategy would end a campaign quickly and decisively in his favor. Napoleon perfected military innovations of the French Revolution, such as using skirmishers to move ahead of assault forces and standardizing the column as the infantry attack formation. He developed well-organized armies by enhancing the divisional structure established in 1794 and making the corps a permanent part of the French army in 1804. He also took advantage of the fruits of technology, in the form of improved artillery with increased firepower and greater mobility. With almost unlimited manpower and increased firepower to pour into his operations, Napoleon revolutionized the conduct of war.

One of the most prominent military theorists in the nineteenth century was Baron Henri de Jomini, a Swiss officer who had served with Napoleon. Jomini was a product of the Age of Enlightenment, when intellectuals sought to find logical explanations for virtually everything. His goal was to define the fundamental principles of war, which he felt were timeless and unchanging. The basic tenet of his theory of war was to bring superior forces to bear on an enemy's inferior force; he emphasized the importance of lines of communications to the point of making geometry an essential element of strategy; and he stressed that offensive operations were absolutely essential to attain victory. Jomini explained strategy as the art of directing masses of forces within the theater of operations for offensive operations. Mahan taught this theory of strategy at West Point, using Napoleon's campaigns as interpreted by Jomini.

Defensive Operations.
During the Civil War, commanders on both sides emulated the Napoleonic style of operations as they conducted offensive campaigns, hoping to fight the big, decisive battle that would end the war. They did not recognize, however, that offensive

operations were very costly. Relying on what they learned of Napoleonic operations, artillery became an essential element of conducting operations, but by the middle of the nineteenth century, artillery could no longer dominate the battlefield. Napoleon had massed his artillery beyond the range of infantry weapons and battered formations with relative ease. Once the enemy infantry formations had been broken by artillery fire, the French infantry would breach the gap and rout the opponent.

By the Civil War, however, technology had provided the infantry with the capability to retaliate. In 1855 the army received a new standard shoulder arm, the .58 caliber rifle with improved range and accuracy. The range was considerably longer than the old smoothbores against which Napoleon had used his artillery so effectively. The longer range and more accurate rifles forced the artillery to be placed back so far that it lost much of its effectiveness against infantry in defensive positions. The new rifles also meant that infantry assaults had to face a higher rate of fire from defenders. The defense also grew stronger as commanders learned the value of field fortifications to protect their troops from both artillery and rifle fire. Frontal assaults against dug-in infantry became very expensive in terms of lives.

Technology influenced Civil War operations in more ways than increased firepower. Ironically, as increased firepower favored tactical defensive operations, other technological innovations encouraged offensive strategic operations. The railroad, although not developed primarily for military operations, allowed commanders to rapidly concentrate combat power at decisive points, and the telegraph provided them with the capability to coordinate operations across long distances. With the railroad and telegraph, commanders could conduct rapid strategic offensive operations, but the dominance of firepower at the tactical level of war caused the elegantly planned campaigns to end in bloody battles. The battles cost manpower, but in addition to technology's direct contributions to military operations, it was also making more manpower available because the U.S. economy was

moving from being primarily agrarian to increasingly industrial. Fewer farmers were able to supply more food, making more men available for the armies. The shift to an industrial economy also meant that military operations were less influenced by seasonal campaigning because troops did not have to return home for the harvest season.

Most of the operations during the Civil War were land campaigns, but the navy played an essential role. As with the opposing armies, the officers from both navies came from a common heritage in which command of the sea was not the strategic goal. When the war began, neither the Union nor the Confederacy had a fleet that could challenge for control of the sea and neither attempted to build one. The primarily agrarian South did not have the industrial capability to build such a fleet, and the industrial North did not need one if no one challenged its shipping. Whereas the army commanders relied on Napoleonic warfare, the senior naval leaders on both sides drew on the lessons of the War of 1812 and the Mexican War in preparing to conduct naval operations. The Mexican War had demonstrated the value of blockades and amphibious operations, while the War of 1812 left a legacy of commerce raiders capable of thwarting even the most dedicated blockaders.

The Vicksburg Campaign. In April 1862, after capturing New Orleans, the Union navy moved up the Mississippi River to wrest control of that river from the Confederacy. At Vicksburg, Mississippi, a fortified city on the banks of the river, the navy met southern resistance and fell back to New Orleans. In June, reinforced by U.S. naval forces operating from Memphis, north of Vicksburg, the navy tried again. After shelling the fortress for most of July and fighting some minor skirmishes, Union army forces accompanying the navy determined they had insufficient strength to attempt a landing and the northern forces retired once again.

In March 1863 the Union forces again set out to capture Vicksburg and gain control of the Mississippi River. This time the naval activities were coordinated with the movements of large army forces against Vicksburg by land. The navy ferried General Ulysses S. Grant's army from the western side of the river to the eastern side, where he laid siege to the city from its landward side while the navy conducted operations along the river line. The navy provided three essential elements in support of Grant's siege operations—troop transport, logistical support, and fire support—all of which were part of the joint operations of the Mexican War and all of which would be characteristic of future U.S. joint operations. Vicksburg surrendered on 4 July 1863, which split the Confederacy and placed the Mississippi under Union control.

The Gettysburg Campaign.
As the joint operations in Vicksburg brought Union success in the west, the decisive campaign in the east reached its culminating point at Gettysburg, Pennsylvania. By June 1863 the situation facing the Confederacy was bleak. Vicksburg was on the verge of falling to Grant, and Union troops were capturing southern seaports in a series of amphibious operations. The South was slowly being surrounded despite the efforts of Confederate General Robert E. Lee. Like most of the senior generals in the war, Lee was a West Point graduate and had been exposed to the teachings of Mahan and the writings of Jomini. Lee believed it would take an offensive campaign into the North to win the war for the South. Because remaining on the defensive meant giving up the initiative, Lee and the Army of Northern Virginia in early June began moving north into Maryland in the hope of inflicting a decisive defeat on the Army of the Potomac, the primary Union force in the eastern theater. Lee also had other objectives in mind for the move north; Confederate forces were running out of horses and chronic logistics shortages in the South had left his troops sorely wanting. Maryland and Pennsylvania had horses, food, forage, and clothing.

In a campaign reminiscent of Scott's offensive campaign to capture Mexico City, Lee cut his lines of communication and supply with Virginia as he moved north, requiring his army to live off the land. Perhaps he remembered his service as a lieutenant of engineers under Scott in 1847, or perhaps the support system in the South could not have helped him anyway. In addition to cutting his lines of communication and supply, Lee also lost track of the Army of the Potomac because his cavalry was off on a ride around the Union army. With little or no idea of the location of the nearest Union forces, he moved north into Pennsylvania, unaware that the Army of the Potomac, under a new commander, General George G. Meade, was already moving north. On 1 July the two armies blundered into one another at Gettysburg. Although both commanders were seeking battle, neither planned to fight it in Gettysburg. Meade elected to conduct a conservative defensive operation against Lee's repeated attacks. The defensive positions held for three days, until the exhausted Army of Northern Virginia surrendered the field, its strategic offensive campaign to end the war blunted on the Union's tactical defensive.

Grant's Strategy.
After the Confederate setbacks at Vicksburg and Gettysburg, the Union had the upper hand. Although the North had more manpower because of its larger population and could field superior firepower by virtue of its industrial capability, the Union needed a commander who understood that war had changed since Napoleon. No longer would one decisive battle be enough to end a war against a determined nation in arms. War had to be prosecuted using firepower to relentlessly wear down the opponent in annihilation operations. Grant learned that lesson in the western theater of operations when he forced the surrender of Vicksburg.

Assuming command of all Union armies in March 1864, Grant quickly set about coordinating army operations in all theaters toward the strategic goal of destroying the South's capability to wage war. After Lee's brief foray into Maryland and Pennsylvania, Union armies, in consonance with Grant's strategic concept of operations, moved relentlessly against the South. Meade's operations in May around Richmond, Virginia, under the direct supervision of Grant and General William T. Sherman's march to the sea in November were both campaigns designed to destroy the South's ability to wage war and erode its will power. The Civil War was a preview of wars to come, in which armies would no longer fight battles in relative isolation from the population at large, and civilians would bear as much of the suffering of war as the front-line troops. Ironically, while U.S. officers had learned and attempted to apply their lessons of European military theory in the Civil War, European officers did not recognize that defensive tactics had far outstripped the capabilities of an offensive strategy. They would learn that hard lesson for themselves in World War I.

POST–CIVIL WAR PERIOD

The Civil War included a number of theaters of operations and eventually involved a considerable portion of the population of the United States. It was a landmark event in the history of U.S. military operations, and its operations continue to be studied at staff and war colleges in the United States and abroad. At the end of the war in 1865, however, there was a popular belief that the United States had seen the last of war, because there were no enemies strong enough to attack it on land and Great Britain had become more friend than foe on the high seas. The American tradition of warriors returning home as soon after war as possible was already strong and popular. Proponents of large standing military forces were unable to convince Congress of their necessity. The army returned to conducting small operations against Indians and the navy saw its fleet reduced year by year.

In the period immediately after the Civil War, both the navy and the army were considerably reduced. In something of an intellectual backlash, however, the wave of pacifism that swept over the United States as people tried to put the war behind them enhanced the sense of duty within the military. The small officer corps turned inward, believing that the profession of arms had a calling to be ready even if the public did not want to think about it. In the late nineteenth century, both the army and the navy developed a new outlook for conducting their operations. The army began a program of indoctrinating its officers in the conduct of operations by establishing a series of schools for teaching tactics, and the navy produced one of the few great U.S. military theorists, Alfred Thayer Mahan, son of Dennis Mahan, who had influenced Civil War strategy through his teaching at West Point.

Development of Sea Power. Alfred Thayer Mahan was one of the first faculty members of the Naval War College, where he lectured and wrote on sea power. When his theories of how sea power influenced history were published in 1890, they were widely praised and enthusiastically received by the navy. His thesis was that there were general, but universally applicable, principles that governed war at sea. Mahan has been characterized as the Jomini of the sea, which is not surprising because his father had also been an ardent student of Jomini at West Point. His influence changed the fundamental approach to naval strategy. For the first time since its founding, the U.S. Navy looked toward developing a fleet capable of sea control. Mahan argued that commerce raiding, the essence of one hundred years of U.S. naval strategy, could not by itself win a war. In his view, there had to be a fleet action for navies to win wars.

Mahan's sea power theories were published at a time when the United States was booming and for the first time could afford to build a large blue-water navy capable of conducting fleet actions and challenging for control of the sea. Steam power and armor plate had changed the way tactical naval operations were conducted, and Mahan's theories would change the way the United States conducted strategic naval operations. During the Civil War, the historic battle between the Union *Monitor* and the Confederate *Merrimack* in March 1862 provided a glimpse into the future. Although steam-powered ships had seen useful service in both the

Mexican War and the Civil War, there was a sentimental return to sail in the navy. The development of steam power and iron hulls during the Civil War, however, finally made it clear that sailing ships were soon to be a thing of the past. With steam power, ships were not at the mercy of the wind, and iron hulls could stand up to the improvements in firepower. The benefits of technology, however, were not without a price. Steam provided freedom of maneuver, but it forced the United States to become more involved in the world as it sought to find coaling stations around the world to maintain its growing fleet.

The Army Officer Corps. While the navy developed its new approach to strategy, the army developed a new approach to preparing its officer corps for war. Taking its cue from the development of military staffs, which assisted commanders in controlling the growing complexities of war, army schools were established for engineers, the Signal Corps, and the Hospital Corps, as well as combined schools for the infantry and cavalry and for the field artillery and cavalry. The most influential of the schools established by the army in the latter half of the nineteenth century was at Fort Leavenworth, Kansas, in 1881. Known by a variety of names throughout its history, it is now the army's Command and General Staff College. From the graduation of its first class, so-called Leavenworth men have shaped the army's operational art.

One of Fort Leavenworth's most enduring accomplishments is the format in which the unified commands of the United States prepare and publish operations plans and orders. The five paragraphs of situation, mission, execution, logistics, and command and control are a direct descendant of the format developed by one of the first instructors at Fort Leavenworth, Captain Eben Swift. Like so much of the development of U.S. operations doctrine, the five-paragraph format was inspired by a European model, in this instance the German Field Orders of 1890. Swift was also instrumental in introducing the idea of war games, in which officers could anticipate problems and simulate planning and conducting future operations. The war games concept continues to be used by all services, in the form of computer simulations.

THE SPANISH-AMERICAN WAR

Much of the incentive for the work done at Fort Leavenworth came from the experience of the army and navy in the Spanish-American War. Although the war with Spain in 1898 was a relatively small war that presented few hardships to the United States, it was also probably the low point in the capability of the armed forces to conduct joint operations. The army and the navy, rather than searching for ways to cooperate, seemingly went to great lengths to make things as difficult as possible for each other during their joint campaign to capture Santiago de Cuba.

When the U.S. battleship *Maine* exploded in Havana harbor on 15 February 1898, the army bureaucracy was not up to the challenge of waging war against Spain. There were plenty of men available when war was declared, but very few officers were capable of planning and coordinating the operations necessary to make good use of the available forces. Reacting to war fever, Congress authorized thousands of National Guard troops to be called to active duty. The bulk of the army's fighting was confined to Cuba, and the army forces there generally acquitted themselves well. There was some concern over the performance of some of the National Guard regiments on active duty for the war, but there were as many exemplary performances as there were deficiencies. The real failures in the war centered on the joint operations that moved the army's forces from the United States to Cuba.

The port of embarkation selected for the Santiago de Cuba campaign was Tampa, Florida, because of its proximity to Cuba. The difficulties that accompanied the selection were exacerbated by constant quibbling between Secretary of War

Russell Alexander Alger and the commanding general of the army, Major General Nelson A. Miles, neither of whom ever took charge of the army's expansion or appointed anyone to be responsible for the activities of the port. Unfortunately, Florida's transportation system was not as well developed as those in other parts of the United States and simply getting the troops, weapons, and supplies to the docks would have been a problem even under the best of circumstances. The port of Tampa had only one rail line and one pier. Through this ill-equipped port, seventeen thousand army troops had to be loaded onto thirty-eight ships for the trip to Cuba. While the administration wavered in its decision to initiate the campaign, planners in Tampa developed a schedule that would get the troops to the ships in some sort of order. The commander of army forces, General William Shafter, disregarded the schedule, however, and announced on 7 June that the ships would depart the next day with whatever units were loaded. The resultant rush to the port was exacerbated by the rumor (which turned out to be true) that the navy had not provided enough shipping for all army forces. Chaos reigned as regiments vied with one another to get aboard ships. Although most of them made it on board before the deadline, they ended up sitting on the transports for a week before sailing on 14 June.

The Santiago Campaign. The debarkation in Cuba was no improvement over the performance in Tampa. The landing site, chosen for its seemingly advantageous line of communications to Santiago de Cuba, had virtually no facilities for landing cargo, and once landed the cargo reflected the disarray with which it had been loaded in Tampa. It soon became apparent that while the landing area might be close to Santiago, the roads between the city and the port were inadequate at best. The result was a line of communications and supply from the United States to the theater of operations that could barely keep minimal supplies flowing. Despite great quantities of matériel available in Florida as a result of the increased wartime pro-

duction, the U.S. troops in Cuba were short of almost everything.

Transportation, or more accurately, the lack of transportation, was a big problem during operations of the Santiago campaign. Many of the problems could have been resolved had there been an organized planning staff to examine the deficiencies of port facilities in Tampa and in Cuba. Transportation continues to play a major role in planning and conducting both strategic and tactical U.S. operations and has been identified as the single most important factor in the logistical support of military operations. The best that can probably be said for the comic opera performance of joint operations in the Spanish-American War is that they were conducted against an essentially ineffective enemy. The subsequent outcry when the inept planning became public knowledge, however, did stimulate changes in the services and led to the development of military staffs.

In sharp contrast to the ineptness of the joint operations in Cuba, the navy demonstrated its mastery of steam power and iron hulls, in the short, decisive Battle of Manila Bay. Leaving Hong Kong on 25 April 1898, Commodore George Dewey, commanding the U.S. Asiatic Squadron of four cruisers and a number of supporting vessels, arrived at the entrance to Manila Bay under cover of darkness on 30 April. The battle opened the next morning when Dewey told Captain Charles V. Gridley aboard the flagship *Olympia,* "You may fire when you are ready, Gridley." In less than seven hours, the Spanish commander surrendered, and the U.S. Navy had become a force to be reckoned with in the Pacific.

INTO THE TWENTIETH CENTURY

When Elihu Root became secretary of war in 1899, he was determined to get the army intellectually ready for modern warfare, with education his highest priority. Within the army, doctrine became the watchword. Military thinking looked toward larger armies, which required indoctrination of the officer corps in a common concept of planning and conducting operations. Doctrine became more than principles of war as espoused by the Mahans. The goal of doctrine was to provide solutions to common situations on the battlefield. The German general staff, sometimes referred to as the brain of that nation's army, led the way in establishing doctrinal solutions to tactical problems, and other countries tried to emulate their methods. In the United States, however, there was a concern that a strong general staff might challenge the authority of the secretary of war.

Root was able to establish a general staff for the army in 1902, but Congress made sure it would remain clearly subordinate to the secretary of war. Although a mere shadow of the general staffs common to European armies, Root had managed to create an element of the army that could devote itself to planning for wartime operations, a change from the peacetime-oriented bureaus of the army that had demonstrated their inability to cope with the complexities of the Spanish-American War. For the first time in its history, at least part of the army was able to think about how to conduct operations in the next war rather than simply waiting for them to happen.

While Root established the Army War College and army General Staff, the navy was also looking to the future. Like the army, the navy was profoundly changed by the Spanish-American War, but where the army saw a lack of staff officers, the navy saw the validation of Mahan's theories of naval strategy. Since the American Revolution, the navy had deliberately avoided fleet operations against an opponent, preferring a strategy of commerce raiding and coastal defense. With the victory over the Spanish and acquisition of port facilities in the Pacific and Cuba, the navy made a fundamental shift in strategy and set as its goal control of the seas through decisive fleet battles. As the nineteenth century drew to a close, the capital ship of navies was the battleship, and with the end of the Spanish-American War, the U.S. Navy was ready to build a fleet of battleships that could command the seas. By 1905 there were twenty-eight U.S. battleships either at sea or under construction. Command of the seas would guide U.S. naval strategy for the rest of the century.

During the nineteenth century, the Atlantic Ocean was both the sea line of communications that linked the United States and Europe and a barrier that prevented any European power from easily conducting continental operations against the United States. By the end of the century, the United States had spanned the North American continent and defending the long Pacific coastline required the navy to maintain two fleets, one that could conduct operations in the Atlantic and Caribbean and one in the Pacific. The Spanish-American War, with naval operations in both oceans, demonstrated the difficulties of concentrating combat power quickly and effectively. During that war the battleship *Oregon* sailed thirteen thousand miles from Seattle on the Pacific coast, around South America, and arrived at Hampton Roads, Virginia, on the Atlantic in sixty-eight days. Although it arrived fit to fight and attained a place in naval folklore, it also demonstrated the need for fleets in both oceans and a better way to consolidate combat power. The requirement to mass combat power was a driving force behind construction of the Panama Canal. Although there were economic advantages to be gained from a canal across the isthmus between the Atlantic and Pacific oceans, the more important factor for the United States, with its newly acquired imperial view of the world, was the ability to quickly move naval power from one coast to the other.

One of the results of the Spanish-American War was the development of naval bases in the Caribbean and the Pacific, as the navy reaped the benefits of a Congress eager to provide protection for America's growing empire. The sea lines of communications now reached across both the Atlantic and the Pacific, requiring the navy to contemplate a two-ocean war.

When the twentieth century opened, Great Britain and France were the dominant naval powers in the world, with the U.S. Navy number three but growing. The United States, however, was not the only nation building a navy to control the seas. Germany had aspirations over the Atlantic, and Japan saw domination of the Pacific as its destiny. Although it was not clear yet, the future of the United States rested, in large part, on the ability of the navy to conduct global operations. In the absence of a clearly defined strategic objective beyond building a fleet second to none, the navy turned most of its attentions to building the best possible ships, and the navy's desire to have the latest technology on its ships has been a major factor in planning and conducting operations at sea.

WORLD WAR I

Although the Spanish-American War ended with the United States acquiring overseas colonies, it did not end the traditional American desire to avoid international entanglements. When World War I began in Europe in 1914, the United States preferred to remain on the sidelines as a spectator. It was soon apparent, however, that a nation with the global interests of the United States could not simply stand by and watch the countries of Europe destroy each other. The United States, although it had gained possessions in the Caribbean and the Pacific, still looked to Europe as its primary area of interest. Reluctant though the nation might be to enter the war, the army and the navy, having initiated changes stimulated by the results of the Spanish-American War, were up to the challenge when it came.

During World War I the United States faced the problem of raising large land forces and transporting them overseas to fight in a theater of operations far from its support base. Although the army had sent forces to Cuba and had been fighting guerrillas in the Philippines for some time, the numbers of troops involved in those operations were minuscule when compared to the appetite of the western front in Europe. U.S. forces were heartily welcomed in Europe when the United States joined the war in 1917 as an ally of France and Great Britain against Germany. From the outset, however, it was apparent that there were fundamental dif-

ferences in doctrine. The armies of France and Great Britain, having been fighting for three years when the United States entered the war, were prepared to take whatever troops and units the U.S. Army could provide and integrate them into their operations. The U.S. Army, for its part, with its concern for officer education, its school system, and its General Staff, had been following the conduct of operations on the continent since the beginning of the war in 1914. U.S. officers, however, were not ready simply to accept the experiences of the French and British. From the very first, General John J. Pershing, commander of the American Expeditionary Forces, insisted that U.S. forces would fight only under American commanders using American doctrine to conduct operations.

By 1917 the French and British had settled in to fight a war of attrition with the Germans. The opposing systems of trench works spanned the continent from the English Channel to Switzerland. On both sides generals and their staffs were struggling to reconcile their belief that wars were won by offensive operations with the reality that for three years every major attack by either side had been broken on the defensive trench works. Strategic offensive operations were simply unable to overcome the tactical defensive. Technology had multiplied the firepower of the defense with the machine gun and barbed wire. In the eighteenth century, firepower was the product of a disciplined infantry line; in the nineteenth century, it was the result of riflemen firing from breastworks; and in the twentieth century, it was the machine gun spewing forth hundreds of rounds per minute.

Offensive tactics in the meantime had changed little in two hundred years; attackers were still expected to advance en masse to overwhelm the defenders. Technology had improved the firepower, the industrial revolution had provided an almost endless supply of munitions, and the general staffs had calculated the tactics so that each side could spend days pulverizing its opponents before asking the infantry to once again advance against the trenches. Ironically, the vast amounts of artillery fire probably made it more difficult for the infantry to advance rapidly because of the craters, mud, and debris it produced. In addition, the defenders could leave their firing positions for the protection of deep bunkers during the artillery barrages fired at the beginning of an attack. Because the barrages had to be lifted before the attackers could assault the trenches, the defenders could wait until the artillery attacks stopped, quickly reoccupy their firing positions, and be ready to fend off the attackers.

During the Civil War, Americans had learned at high cost the power of the tactical defense; Europeans were still not convinced three years into World War I. Both sides had repeatedly launched strategic offensive operations involving millions of men only to see them dissolve in the smoke and mud of the western front, and the only thought the French and British had when Pershing arrived was that they now had a renewed supply of manpower to throw against the German trenches. Pershing, however, with an American's high regard for human life, would have none of it. He believed that there had to be a way to break the stalemate on the western front. His first battle, however, was to maintain American freedom of action. Although some U.S. units were placed under French command, Pershing labored throughout the war to avoid having U.S. forces placed under the command of Europeans. Pershing's insistence on independent command in World War I continues to be one of the most enduring characteristics of U.S. combined military operations. Since World War I, rarely, and then only under extraordinary circumstances, have U.S. forces from any service been commanded by foreign officers for any length of time.

Finding a way to overcome the tactical defenses of the enemy and regaining the initiative was quite another matter. Pershing insisted that U.S. troops be trained for a war of movement. He also demanded that rifle marksmanship and bayonet skills be fundamental elements of infantry training and that soldiers not be allowed to become too comfortable with the protection offered by the trenches. Pershing's vision was open warfare, where the traditional U.S. strengths of marksmanship and individual ini-

tiative would prevail over the massed fire of the machine gun. To this end, he insisted that the U.S. Army in Europe be trained in a doctrine of open warfare.

During the course of the war, both sides had observed the European tradition of winter quarters and spring campaigns. During the winter of 1917–1918, in order to defeat the tactical defense, the German army had trained their best units as shock units. They dispensed with the days of artillery fire that preceded an attack and instead fired their artillery for shorter periods of time, using a mixture of gas and high explosive shells designed to drive defenders into the trenches and to break up the barbed wire for the shock troops. The concept was not merely to smash through the trench lines with masses of troops, but to penetrate them with infiltrators who would then strike in the rear, disrupting the organization of the defense and leaving it vulnerable to the infantry forces that followed to exploit the confusion. In the first attack of the spring 1918 campaign, the Germans advanced to a point forty miles behind British lines in France, an unheard of accomplishment in the days of trench warfare. Without knowing it, the Germans had vindicated Pershing's insistence on training for open warfare.

Even as the success of their tactical offensive overcame the stalemated front, the German strategy failed to split the Allies. The Allied forces, although surprised, reacted with a unity of effort that surprised the Germans. Acting in concert with the French and British armies, the the U.S. Army counterattacked in force. Although the operations did not become as open as Pershing might have liked, the U.S. training program had prepared the forces well. The trench war ended with the introduction of the new German tactical offensive doctrine in which maneuver overcame firepower, but the war itself ended with the disintegration of the German army.

Although German tactical operations were initially successful against the Allies, another infusion of technological innovation was needed to overcome the inherent strength of the tactical defense. World War I was fought on land mainly by armies composed of infantry whose primary method of mobility was walking. The machines that would dominate the future of warfare made their debut at the close of the war. On land the internal combustion engine that powered tanks and trucks revolutionized tactical mobility, much as railroads had changed strategic mobility in the nineteenth century. The tank-truck team first saw combat in World War I, but it would dominate land warfare in World War II.

World War I also opened the new dimension of air warfare. The army initially saw the airplane as the eyes of the ground forces, seeking out and reporting the locations of enemy formations. The fragile nature of early heavier-than-air machines was one argument that there could not be a realistic combat role for them, and the planes were assigned to the Signal Corps. World War I, however, pushed aerial technology, and Europeans were soon routinely using airplanes in combat. When the United States entered the war, air operations were already a part of warfare. Although the United States relied on the Europeans for all of their airplanes, the army produced an outspoken advocate of air power whose ideas and actions laid the foundation for the future of U.S. air operations.

William "Billy" Mitchell was a Signal Corps officer who went to France in 1917 to study French aviation and eventually flew combat missions. Mitchell experimented with his ideas of using massed aerial firepower in 1918 as chief of Air Services in the U.S. First Army in France. For Mitchell the more glamorous air-to-air duels involving entire squadrons of fighter planes were simply taking the attrition warfare of the trenches out of the mud and into the sky. He advocated massive bombing to stun the enemy and make the job of ground forces a bit easier, an idea in keeping with the American view of using firepower whenever possible to preserve lives. At the end of the war his vision was victory through air power, a radical idea in 1918, but air operations have come to be an essential element of the way U.S. military forces conduct modern warfare. Mitchell became an outspoken

advocate of air power in the years between the world wars, his confidence in its technical capabilities constantly growing.

Unlike Mahan, whose strategic ideas of naval warfare were accepted quickly and enthusiastically by the navy and the American public, Mitchell had to wage a constant campaign for air power. His enthusiasm, including widely publicized magazine articles and a series of demonstrations of successfully finding and bombing ships at sea eventually earned him a court-martial. Although the guilty verdict did force him out of uniform, it did not erase his vision of the future of aerial firepower.

When the United States entered World War I in 1917, the navy, despite its commitment to a strategy of sea control, was not quite ready for battle. Under the stimulus of the Battle of Jutland between the British Home Fleet and the German High Seas Fleet in 1916, Congress authorized the largest expansion in the history of the U.S. Navy. Although the battle itself was inconclusive, it was enough to convince U.S. planners that the United States needed a navy that could hold its own with that of any other power. The 1916 congressional action was intended not so much to build a navy for the immediate war in Europe but for the future. German actions, however, forced the navy to move faster than originally anticipated. In an effort to cut the sea line of communication between the United States and Europe, submarine warfare against shipping in the Atlantic became the centerpiece of German naval strategy. Mahan's theories of sea control had to be put aside temporarily while the U.S. Navy prepared to challenge Germany's updated version of commerce raiding by attacking from beneath the sea. Preparation for the decisive battle between fleets took a back seat to defeating the German U-boats in the Atlantic. Between convoy operations conducted in conjunction with the British and an accelerated building program of specially designed submarine chasers, the destroyers, the navy was successful in ending the German bid to cut the lifeline between the United States and Europe. Although it could not have been known at the time, U.S. operations on land, in the air, and at sea were as much an introduction to World War II as they were an end to the Great War.

THE INTERWAR PERIOD

At the end of what the world hoped would be the war to end all wars, the United States brought home the forces it had deployed to Europe, reduced the size of its army and navy, and attempted to withdraw from all international intercourse except that which directly affected its national interests. There was little interest in maintaining an army of any size and certainly no thought of more massive overseas deployments. The experience of the war, however, was not altogether lost within the army. As chief of staff of the army (1921–1924), Pershing established the War Plans Board and made it responsible for operations planning. For the first time, the General Staff was given responsibility to look beyond peacetime activities. In World War I, the General Staff had confined itself to building the army in the United States, leaving war planning and operations to the Army Expeditionary Forces in Europe. With the establishment of the War Plans Board, however, the General Staff planted the seed that would grow into the command center for planning and coordinating the worldwide operations conducted by the army in World War II.

World War I saw little in the way of U.S. joint operations. The army conducted its operations well inland, beyond the range of naval support, and the navy was preoccupied with submarine chasing. The army did rely on the navy for logistical support, because men and matériel had to travel across the Atlantic in escorted convoys. Recognition of the army's logistical dependence on the navy rekindled interest in the Army-Navy Joint Board. The board had been established in 1903 to engender interservice cooperation after the debacles of the Spanish-American War, but interest in joint operations had waned during World War I. Between the world wars, however, the board became a planning agency for operations involving both the army and the navy. During the 1920s and 1930s, it prepared a series of contingency war plans against specific countries, each plan identified by a different color. In addition to the joint planning with the navy on the color plans, the army's General Staff devoted much of its planning efforts to mobilization, an activity with which it had gained considerable experience in World War I. The complexities of trying to rapidly increase the size of the army in World War I had made a much greater impression on the General Staff than operations planning because raising and training units had been its center of interest during the war.

The years between the world wars brought dramatic improvements and refinements in technology that demanded changes in tactical and strategic operations from U.S. air, land, and sea forces. While the United States sought peace, there were growing signs of war in Europe and Asia. At the beginning of the 1930s, Germany began rearming in defiance of the Treaty of Versailles, which had ended World War I, and Japan invaded northern China. By the late 1930s, the United States was beginning to realize that war might begin in Europe and Asia. The military services turned to the members of the Joint Board who developed the Rainbow Plans. Where the color plans considered only one country per plan, the Rainbow series postulated operations pitting the United States against a variety of coalitions. One of these plans, Rainbow 5, formed the basis for strategic operations in World War II.

While planning proceeded for strategic operations, the air, land, and sea forces of the army and navy made changes in their tactical operations. Advocates of air power fought for a separate air service, independent of the army and the navy, but on the eve of World War II, most of America's air forces remained within the army. The navy had its own air arm, but even though aircraft carriers had made their appearance, the battleship remained the capital ship for sea control.

WORLD WAR II

World War II was a series of concurrent, related wars with a variety of opponents for the United States. Although the United States and its allies, primarily Great Britain, were fighting Japan, Germany, and Italy, the theaters of operations were so large that no one country was able to make the major effort in every theater. The United States eventually made major contributions in the Mediterranean and European theaters; provided forces in the Middle East and China, Burma, and India theaters; and conducted operations almost single-handedly in the Pacific. The nature of the various theaters influenced the types of strategic operations conducted by U.S. forces, but regaining the offensive in the Pacific and Europe were initial objectives that required major joint operations involving air, land, and sea forces. By late 1942, after having been at war on paper for almost a year, U.S. forces finally were able to mass enough combat power to conduct offensive operations in the Mediterranean and the Pacific.

Although joint operations were the key to victory in World War II, service cooperation was frequently the result of a shotgun marriage in which neither party was particularly comfortable. There were only two services in World War II, the army and the navy, which included the Marine Corps, a force specializing in amphibious warfare for the navy, but capable of conducting land operations in conjunction with the army. Both the army and navy were oriented to conducting traditional surface operations, and the air power that was taking them into a third dimension did not yet constitute a separate service. The senior leadership of both the army and navy, lacking experience with air power, were reluctant to expend scarce resources on something they did not understand. The Army Air Corps, and later the Army Air Forces, predecessor of the U.S. Air Force, was still tied to the ground forces, although it spent part of its energies during the war becoming an equal partner rather than a subordinate of the army ground forces. Naval air power was both carrier- and shore-based and included marine and navy aviators. From its carriers, the navy could project the power of the fleet hundreds of miles in all directions, and by flying from land bases it could conduct antisubmarine operations to protect friendly shorelines and convoys far out to sea. The Marine Corps, flying its own aircraft, provided close air support to its ground forces during amphibious operations in the Pacific.

At the beginning of World War II, air power had yet to establish a place for itself with either the army or the navy. Airmen wanted to exploit the capabilities of air power by conducting independent operations, but senior commanders from both services had gained their experience in war conducting surface operations, and they were not eager to relinquish control of their aviators. Although the integration of air power into sea and land operations led U.S. armed forces into joint operations involving air, land, and sea forces, service differences remained. During the war in the Pacific, the navy concentrated on air-sea operation using the aircraft carriers while the marines integrated their air and ground forces under a single commander. The Army Air Corps designed its own system of supporting ground forces, based on the British model developed during their experience in North Africa, and perfected the techniques of daylight bombing as part of the concept of strategic bombing in Europe.

Between World War I, when air power made its wartime debut, and the beginning of World War II, when the German blitzkrieg style of operations demonstrated the potential of aerial firepower working in close support of ground forces, the U.S. Army did little to develop air-ground operations. In 1941 the Army Air Corps provided a few bombers to support the British in Egypt in their campaign against the German and Italian armies, and U.S. officers were impressed by the British procedures for coordinating air-ground operations. The British use of co-equal headquarters for air and ground forces was a system that appealed to the Army Air Corps because it argued very nicely for a separate air service. Today's close air-support operations conducted by the U.S. Air Force in support of ground forces trace their origins directly to the lessons of the desert war in North Africa. While Army Air Corps officers were learning how to support land operations in North Africa, the marines, with their own aircraft and pilots, kept air and ground forces under a single commander. Like the air force, the marines continue to use the same basic system for air-ground operations.

When the Japanese Imperial Navy struck its crippling blow against the U.S. Navy at Pearl Harbor in December 1941, it inadvertently advanced U.S. naval aviation in importance. The Japanese attack, a classic example of both tactical and strategic surprise, caught the battleships of the U.S. Pacific fleet lined up at Pearl Harbor and destroyed or severely damaged nearly all of it. As it happened, none of the aircraft carriers was in the harbor at the time of the attack. With the Pacific battleship fleet all but gone, and the example of Japan's remarkable success with carrier-launched air power before them, the aircraft carrier leapt forward as a candidate for the position of capital ship of the navy.

At the Battle of Midway in June 1942, the navy executed air-sea operations perfectly, sinking four Japanese carriers in the first naval battle fought without the capital ships of either fleet seeing each other. Midway established the aircraft carrier as the dominant ship in the U.S. Navy, and because flight operations required a very close relationship between ship and plane, there was never any real question of naval aviation becoming a separate service or even part of a separate air service. The navy perfected joint air-sea operations in World War II, and they continue to be the centerpiece of modern carrier battle groups, which can project air power over vast areas of sea and land.

One of the more prosaic but vital operations perfected by the navy in World War II was the use of logistical support groups. These groups, composed of fast cargo ships of various types and oceangoing repair facilities, relieved the battle fleets of having to periodically steam to land bases. In the far reaches of the Pacific, combatants could find themselves unavailable for combat for weeks or even months moving to and from ports for repairs and resupply, but the logistics groups were able to keep the fleets at sea by adding support ships to the fighting task forces. The concept of logistics groups at sea continues to be a fundamental element of U.S. naval operations.

In World War II the navy was able to conduct strategic operations to attain sea control in consonance with Mahan's theories, but the commerce-raiding experience of the navy's first hundred years appeared again, in the use of submarine warfare. In the Pacific, U.S. submarines crippled Japanese commerce by concentrating on the merchant fleet vital to importing raw materials to the island nation, while in the Atlantic, the U.S. Navy worked with the British navy, conducting escort operations to safeguard the Allied ships carrying men and matériel to Europe against the German wolf packs of U-boats. The submarine, like the airplane, tank, and aircraft carrier, came into its own in World War II and continues to be a vital part of U.S. operations.

In 1942, U.S. air, land, and sea forces worked together for the first time in the war as the Marine Corps landed on Guadalcanal in the Solomon Islands in August. Air, land, and sea operations went on for six months before the campaign ended with the island cleared of all Japanese forces. The lessons learned in this joint campaign were applied throughout the Pacific theater of operations and air-land-sea operations became the key to success in that theater. As the war progressed in the Pacific, both army and marine ground forces conducted amphibious operations in coordination with each other, and air power came from both ground-based Army Air Corps squadrons and navy aircraft carriers. While the tactical forces from each of the services mastered the complexities of air-land-sea operations, interservice rivalry on the strategic level continued throughout the war in the Pacific.

The rivalry between the army and the navy led to two separate theaters of operations in the Pacific war, one commanded by an army general, Douglas MacArthur, the other by a navy admiral, Chester Nimitz. Each of these theater commanders reported to the Joint Chiefs of Staff, created in February 1942, which was trying to coordinate the global war effort and the need for forces and equipment. Although joint operations were mastered at the tactical level of war, the seeds of discontent germinated among the air, land, and sea forces at the strategic level and would burst forth when the war was over.

Three months after the campaign to secure Guadalcanal began, U.S. and British forces began joint and combined air-land-sea operations in North Africa to regain the offensive against the occupying German and Italian forces. In the Mediterranean theater of operations, as in the Pacific, the tactical forces mastered joint operations. Unlike the Pacific, however, once the ground forces were landed, the navy had less of a direct role in the operations. In both the Mediterranean and European theaters of operations, the ground forces of the army had to move inland to attain the strategic objectives, and they relied on the Army Air Corps for aerial fire support. After the initial air-land-sea operations that characterized the amphibious assaults into North Africa, Sicily, Italy, and northern and southern France, operations in the Mediterranean and European theaters of operations were conducted primarily by air and land forces.

As much as anything else, industrial capability allowed the United States to develop and field the military forces that won World War II. The military operations that U.S. forces planned and conducted during the course of the war would simply have not been possible without the so-called arsenal of democracy in the United States, which produced a seemingly endless stream of items, from the airplanes that dominated the skies to the infantrymen's boots that marched along the ground.

By 1945, the U.S. armed forces were capable

of worldwide joint air-land-sea operations. Although U.S. forces continued their reliance on tactical firepower, the war was one of vast strategic maneuvers. The War Plans Board and the Joint Army-Navy Board had developed into a joint staff that planned and conducted operations around the world. A remarkable feature of strategic operations in World War II was the intimate cooperation in combined operations achieved by British and U.S. forces. From the Combined Chiefs of Staff to the combined and joint theater staffs, Anglo-American military planning was completely integrated. The Combined Chiefs of Staff consisted of the British Imperial General Staff and the U.S. Joint Chiefs of Staff, which was composed of a chairman, the chief of staff of the army, the chief of naval operations, and the chief of the Army Air Forces.

Tactical operations in World War II confirmed the desirability of the U.S. penchant to rely on firepower on the battlefield, but technology also produced an awesome capability for strategic firepower. By the end of the war, air power had gone far beyond simply supporting surfaces in tactical operations; it had the capability to deliver strategic firepower in massive doses to targets deep in the enemy rear areas. The three basic air operations were delineated in World War II. Close air support evolved from direct support of ground forces, air interdiction from long-range strategic bombing, and air superiority from the need to command the air. Strategic firepower grew from the advances in long-range bombing techniques developed by the United States and Great Britain—the vision Mitchell had in the 1930s. By the end of the war in Europe, U.S. and British bombers in raids consisting of hundreds of planes conducted strategic bombing operations against the industrial heartland of Germany. In the Pacific, the use of strategic firepower revolutionized warfare. The atomic bomb ended the war against Japan in a blinding flash. Warfare entered a new age, and the massive air-land-sea operations that had led the Allies to victory appeared for the moment to be things of the past.

At the end of World War II, the United States had one of the most formidable military forces in the world. The armed forces of the United States had mastered air, ground, and sea operations in a wide variety of geographical locations and climates around the world. U.S. military forces could plan and conduct joint and combined operations quickly and effectively, and its only real potential challenger appeared to be the Soviet Union. The Soviets, however, were limited for all intents and purposes to conducting continental operations, while the United States had the capability to project its massive military power anywhere in the world. The United States also had the atomic bomb, and in 1945 it was widely believed that the U.S. nuclear monopoly would last a good long while.

THE POST-WORLD WAR II PERIOD

With the end of the war, the United States rapidly dismantled its armed forces, which had become its tradition. This time, however, as the dominant power in the world, the nation determined to maintain something of a permanent armed force. War and the world had become too complex for a world power to remain without some semblance of a professional armed force. In recognition of this, the 1947 National Security Act created the National Military Establishment (NME). That act designated a secretary of national defense, made the Air Force a separate service, and gave each of the service secretaries cabinet rank. A 1949 amendment renamed the NME the Department of Defense and removed the cabinet rank of the service secretaries, leaving the secretary of defense in that role. The 1947 act also established the concept of unified commands wherein forces from two or more services would be commanded by a single commander in chief (CINC). The Unified Command Plan (UCP) divided most of the world into large areas wherein a unified CINC would have responsibility for the operations of U.S. armed forces. The unified command CINCs were to be responsible for conducting joint operations, with the services providing the necessary

forces. The services, however, retained control of the money that raised, trained, and equipped their forces, and they tended to set aside concerns for joint operations as they jockeyed for position to gain what they believed was their fair share of a much-reduced defense budget. Each of the services sought to demonstrate how their particular operational specialty was key to the defense needs of the United States, and the joint operations that had made victory possible in World War II were soon forgotten.

Atomic weapons had a tremendous influence on how U.S. forces planned and conducted operations in the years immediately following World War II. There was widespread belief that with the mass destruction capability of the atomic bomb, large-scale surface operations on land and sea were a thing of the past. The newly independent U.S. Air Force, with its long-range bombing capability, proclaimed itself the premier armed force for conducting war in the nuclear age. Proponents of the atomic bomb argued that the other services would be auxiliaries to the air force, supporting its bombers. The army and navy struggled to maintain their force structure in the face of budget constraints and the air force's parochial view of the future. That future, however, changed with two unexpected events. In 1949 the Soviet Union detonated an atomic bomb, and in 1950 North Korea launched a surprise invasion of South Korea. The former event ended the U.S. monopoly on nuclear weapons and raised the specter of atomic war with the Soviets, and U.S. and United Nations intervention in the latter required large land and sea operations in and around Korea. The two events led to increased defense spending in the United States but did not necessarily improve service cooperation on joint operations.

THE KOREAN WAR

In June 1950 the forces of North Korea took advantage of what they thought was a distracted United States and invaded South Korea, which had been occupied by U.S. forces since the end of World War II. When the United States decided to respond with military force, it discovered that there was not much available. The initial U.S. response was a piecemeal commitment of air, land, and sea forces in a desperate attempt to stem the North Korean invasion before it occupied the entire peninsula. In the midst of frantically putting together an effective force, General MacArthur, commander of U.S. forces in the Far East and commander in chief of the United Nations Command in Korea, put together a bold plan for a joint and combined air-land-sea operation that would cut the North Korean army off from its sources of support. The plan to invade Inchon was not well-received either by MacArthur's own staff or the Joint Chiefs of Staff. By dint of his powerful personality, however, he was able to gain approval for the joint operation. The success of the amphibious landing at Inchon on 15 September temporarily revitalized interservice cooperation, but MacArthur's campaign plan was flawed, and what began as a brilliant victory drew the Chinese into the war in late October, bogging it down into long stalemate.

MacArthur had failed to identify an appropriate strategic objective for his Inchon campaign that would support U.S. policy in Korea. In his desire to capture Seoul, he concentrated most of X Corps against the capital city and ignored the road networks leading north, allowing thirty thousand North Korean troops to escape across the thirty-eighth parallel, the border between North Korea and South Korea. The announced policy of the U.S. and UN intervention had been to restore the border, but the forces that escaped into the north posed a continued threat to South Korea. The failure to cut the routes into North Korea in order to eliminate continued invasion threats led to a decision for UN forces to move north until the Chinese entered the war in massive numbers. Although the evacuation of X Corps, consisting of both army and marine forces, from the Hungnam perimeter shortly after the Chinese intervention was an excellent example of a major air-land-sea operation, the ground war that followed left little room for

joint operations except for air-land operations between the air force and the army, where the tactical techniques of close air support developed in World War II became institutionalized.

The joint operations in Korea were planned and conducted by officers with World War II experience. They simply looked back a few years and drew on their operational art experiences in Europe or in the Pacific. At the tactical level within the services, officers were either veterans of World War II or were newly indoctrinated in the conduct of tactical operations. The fighting in Korea (1950–1953) did not last long enough for many officers to move from the tactical level to the operational or strategic levels of war. As a result, the services ended the Korean War with a wealth of experience in conducting wartime tactical operations, but the officers who knew and understood how to plan and conduct joint operations were on the verge of retirement.

THE POST-KOREAN WAR PERIOD

War weariness soon put Korean lessons aside, and once again the services were more interested in budget battles than they were in operational art. By the 1960s the senior military leadership of the services, even though many had planned and conducted operations in Korea and World War II, had practical experience only at the tactical level of war. Officers who had been lieutenants or captains in World War II were majors or colonels in Korea, but their view of operations in that war remained tactical; the flag officers, generals and admirals, who had planned and conducted the joint operations in Korea were on the retirement rolls when the United States began its long, agonizing war in Vietnam. There was little or no joint cooperation, and each service concentrated on what it did best to convince Congress that it deserved a larger share of the dwindling defense budget.

After the Korean War, the air force debated the future of manned bombers for conducting strategic operations. Technology was making missiles more powerful and more accurate at an astonishing rate, raising the possibility of delivering firepower great distances without risk to pilots. The Strategic Air Command (SAC), formed in 1946, continues to plan for both manned and unmanned delivery of nuclear weapons with intercontinental ballistic missiles and bombers.

The Tactical Air Force was created at the same time that SAC was formed. Now known as the Tactical Air Command (TAC), it provides support to ground forces. In many respects TAC and SAC are two separate air forces, so different in capabilities that their operations are generally coordinated by the theater CINC with his joint staff. While TAC works closely and routinely with ground forces to conduct tactical operations, SAC conducts strategic missions and has the capability to attain strategic objectives without conducting joint operations.

Although the Unified Command Plan divided the world into theaters of operations, each with a CINC who would plan and conduct joint operations in wartime, the services retained responsibility for establishing and promulgating tactical doctrine. There was little or no joint-operations training and the services rarely cooperated on joint exercises. The Joint Chiefs of Staff were organized so that they gave their military advice as a group, which meant that their advice was generally what one would expect from a committee—not very meaningful—there was no real incentive for the interservice cooperation required for effective operational art.

THE VIETNAM WAR

The war in Vietnam (1965–1973) was a tactical war. The wartime experience of the senior military leadership was nearly all tactical, and the senior civilian leadership had little or no experience in conducting a war or setting realistic strategic objectives. The services concentrated on developing and implementing their tactical doctrine, and they trained their forces to conduct tactical operations without much consideration for the activities of the other services or for the type of war they were fighting. The emphasis on tactics was encouraged because the military objectives of the war were vague at best, constantly changing at worst. Because the military had no readily apparent strategic objective on which to base campaign planning, as they had in World War II and Korea, they planned and conducted tactical operations in Vietnam. While the tactical operations were generally well planned and executed, with no strategic objective to guide campaign planning, battles simply became ends unto themselves. Instead of each battle making a contribution in a campaign leading to attainment of a strategic objective, battles in Vietnam were frequently fought simply for the sake of being fought. Lack of clearly defined strategic objectives also deprived the national leadership of the ability to demonstrate progress in the war. In World War II and Korea, progress, or the lack thereof, was relatively easy to measure following operations on a map.

The army concentrated on its tactical doctrine to the exclusion of almost everything else. It referred to its World War II experience to develop and refine the mechanized and armored operations that had been impossible to conduct in the hills and valleys of Korea. When it found itself in the jungles of Vietnam, an area no more conducive to mechanized operations than Korea, it had to return again to dismounted infantry, although this time the helicopter gave it greater tactical mobility. The army built another air force with helicopters for transportation and firepower.

On the ground, technology gave the infantry increased firepower with individual automatic weapons, and operations relied on high volumes of fire rather than the American tradition of aimed fire. In some respects, the army found itself in a position similar to the British in the American Revolution. Modern, heavily equipped forces faced light infantry using different tactics in unfamiliar terrain. The U.S. Army in Vietnam did no better than the British in America.

THE POST-VIETNAM PERIOD

After eight years of fighting battles with no readily apparent strategic results in Vietnam, the United States brought its military forces home. The services tried to put the experience behind them as defense budgets and troop morale fell. Emphasis on planning and conducting operations remained at the tactical level. In an era of warfare that demanded joint operations, the services continued to concentrate on tactical operations to the virtual exclusion of interservice cooperation. In an effort to cleanse themselves of Vietnam, the services returned to what they thought they had done right in World War II, which in many military and civilian minds was the last good war. In so doing, however, they missed the fundamental element of success in that war—joint operations and operational art.

Coming out of Vietnam, the army again turned to the plains of Europe for developing its doctrine for tactical operations. The 1973 Arab-Israeli War came along at just the right time to convince the army that armored tactics were indeed the correct thing on which to concentrate. While extolling the tactical operations of the Israeli army, however, the U.S. army failed to recognize that success in the 1973 war was the result of coordinated air-ground joint operations conducted by Israeli Defense Forces. As a result, army doctrine continued to have a distinctly tactical focus until the 1980s.

While the army turned to tactics after Vietnam, the navy embraced strategy. With the aircraft carrier as queen of the fleet and capable of air-sea operations and nuclear submarines carrying nuclear missiles to strike strategic objectives, the navy saw no need for joint operations, especially when it also had its own land force, the Marine Corps. The navy controlled the sea, steaming anywhere in international waters it chose, and as technology gave it longer-range weapons, it began to assume a new role—power projection far inland not only with ballistic missiles aboard submarines but with carrier-launched planes and cruise missiles. With its maritime strategy, the navy is the service least inclined to joint operations. At sea it needs little

or no support from other services. Near shore, however, or in congested waters, the navy must operate in concert with other services. It was not until the 1980s that well-coordinated joint operations along the lines of the cooperation attained in World War II became a reality.

DEVELOPMENT OF JOINT OPERATIONS

In 1980 a joint operation involving the army, navy, marines, and air force fell apart in the Iranian desert while attempting to rescue American hostages following the takeover of the U.S. embassy in Teheran. Although the debacle in the desert apparently stimulated Congress to look into how the services planned and coordinated joint operations, the failure of the attempted rescue was not entirely the fault of the participants. The bulk of the responsibility for the failure of the mission lay with President Jimmy Carter and his advisers, including the Joint Chiefs of Staff, for exercising poor judgment in not providing clear guidance and not allowing time for proper planning and coordination of an extraordinarily complex joint operation.

In the mid-1980s, Congress examined how the services trained and educated officers and concluded that there was inadequate emphasis on joint operations. The Goldwater-Nichols Department of Defense Reorganization Act of 1986 prompted the services to renew interest in what has been termed "jointness," one aspect of which is joint operations. The act also designated the chairman of the Joint Chiefs of Staff, rather than the collective body of service chiefs, to be the senior military adviser to the president; it streamlined the chain of command between the Unified Command CINCs and the president; and it gave the CINCs a role in the budget process. These actions reduced the participation of the service chiefs in operational matters, making it somewhat easier for the CINCs to plan and conduct joint operations without being vetoed by individual members of the Joint Chiefs of Staff. Staff and war colleges from all services developed curricula that supported joint operations. On a more personal note for many officers, the Goldwater-Nichols legislation tried to improve planning and conducting joint operations by making promotion to flag grades (admiral in the navy, general in the other services) contingent on having served in a joint assignment. Prior to this requirement, the services tended not to place their most promising officers in joint assignments, preferring to keep them focused on service interests. Almost overnight, joint assignments went from being bad news to highly desirable positions for aspiring officers of all the services.

In 1983, U.S. forces conducted a joint operation in Grenada that attained its assigned strategic objectives of rescuing the medical students detained on the island and freeing the government from Cuban dominance. Although the joint operation was declared a success by President Ronald Reagan and the services, a number of congressional and civilian defense experts criticized its poor planning, coordination, and communications. In 1986, in a joint air force–navy bombing operation against Libya in retaliation for terrorism activities against U.S. military facilities, the services demonstrated that interservice cooperation was not only possible but desirable. In 1989 the army, navy, marines, and air force cooperated in a joint operation in Panama in which the strategic objective was the apprehension of that country's dictator, Manuel Noriega. The objective was attained and the problems that occurred in the Grenada operation appeared largely corrected. As the 1980s drew to a close, although joint operations were becoming the norm rather than the exception for U.S. forces, it remained to be seen if the services were capable of anything more ambitious than what were essentially raids requiring only relatively small forces cooperating for a short time against a much smaller opponent.

By the time Iraq invaded Kuwait in 1990, the U.S. military had demonstrated its capability to conduct effective joint operations to the satisfaction of President George Bush, and he had enough confidence to "draw a line in the sand"

and announce his intention to use force if necessary to stop Iraq from moving into Saudi Arabia. Sending military forces into Saudi Arabia to back up his rhetoric, President Bush established the strategic objective of forcing the Iraqi army out of Kuwait and then let the CINC (General Norman Schwarzkopf) plan and conduct the campaign. The result was a dramatic demonstration of U.S. technology. The campaign opened with six weeks of aerial bombardment, confirming that firepower remains the foundation of U.S. military operations. Aircraft from all the services and coalition partners conducted aerial operations throughout Iraq and Kuwait in preparation for land operations. When the ground forces launched their assault, the result was an unexpectedly easy hundred-hour war that ended with the Iraqi army racing out of Kuwait to avoid complete destruction by the advancing ground and air forces. The Gulf War of 1991 was a remarkable demonstration of U.S. operational art.

U.S. military doctrine for planning and conducting operations is generally applicable worldwide, but it leaves room for local adaptation and individual initiative, a characteristic reminiscent of the colonial experience of learning to fight an unconventional force on unfamiliar terrain. The U.S. desire to use technology to best advantage stems from the early use of the rifle while European armies were still armed with smoothbore muskets and in the eighteenth-century mandate of Congress to provide the navy with the best possible ships. The military's concern for preserving its manpower by using firepower and fortifications whenever possible stems from the earliest militia concerns about friends and neighbors fighting alongside each other in the ranks. In most of America's wars, firepower has been preferred over ground assaults; the Civil War is the prime exception and that experience so impressed U.S. leaders that they have never since underestimated the value of superior firepower. The navy has had a strategy of sea control for more than one hundred years, but it maintains the capability for the commerce raiding that marked its first century of existence. In

World War II, commerce raiding by submarines and sea control with large carrier-fleet operations took place side by side in the Pacific.

The colonial militia's desire to get the fighting over with and go home can still be seen in America's consistent desire to reduce its military forces at the end of a war and send its service personnel home as soon as possible. By the same token, the professional force that President Bush so confidently ordered into the Persian Gulf could not have conducted its spectacular operations without calling on significant numbers of reserve and National Guard forces. In two hundred years of planning and conducting operations, U.S. military forces have developed a unique style of operational art that reflects the character of American society and the country's location in the world. The traditional American desire to get a job done as quickly as possible and then go home, coupled with a secure homeland flanked by wide oceans, has produced a military force oriented toward deploying from secure bases, fighting away from home, winning a quick and decisive victory, and returning to a grateful population. It may not always happen that way, but that is the expected pattern.

See also AMERICAN PERSPECTIVES OF WAR; COALITION WARFARE; GUNBOAT DIPLOMACY: 1776–1992; OPERATIONS; THE PROFESSION OF ARMS IN AMERICA; *and* UNCONVENTIONAL WARFARE.

BIBLIOGRAPHY

Abrahamson, James L. *American Arms for a New Century: The Making of Great Military Power* (1981).

Dupuy, R. Ernest, and Trevor N. Dupuy. *Military Heritage of America* (1956).

———. *The Encyclopedia of Military History from 3500 B.C. to the Present* (1970).

Eccles, Henry E. *Military Concepts and Philosophy* (1965).

Freiberg, Aaron L. "A History of the U.S. Strategic 'Doctrine'—1945 to 1980." *Journal of Strategic Studies* (December 1980).

Futrell, Robert F. *Ideas, Concepts, Doctrine: A History of Basic Thinking in the United States Air Force, 1907–1964*, 2 vols. (1971).

Hassler, Warren W., Jr. *With Shield and Sword: American Military Affairs, Colonial Times to the Present* (1982).

Heller, Charles E., and William A. Stoft, eds. *America's First Battles: 1776–1965* (1986).

Holder, L. D. "A New Day for Operational Art." *Army* (March 1985).

Hoyt, Edwin P. *America's Wars and Military Excursions* (1988).

Hurley, Alfred F. *Billy Mitchell: Crusader for Air Power* (1964).

Huston, James A. *The Sinews of War: Army Logistics, 1775–1953* (1966).

Katzenbach, Edward L., Jr. "The Horse Cavalry in the Twentieth Century." *Public Policy* (1958).

Kohn, Richard H. *Eagle and Sword: The Federalists and the Creation of the Military Establishment in America, 1783–1802* (1975).

Komer, Robert W. "Maritime Strategy versus Coalition Defense." *Foreign Affairs* 60 (Summer 1982).

Korb, Lawrence J. *The Joint Chiefs of Staff: The First Twenty-Five Years* (1976).

Leckie, Robert. *The Wars of America*, rev. ed. (1981).

Matloff, Maurice, ed. *American Military History* (1969).

Millett, Allan R., and Peter Maslowski. *For the Common Defense: A Military History of the United States of America* (1984).

Newell, Clayton R. "Balancing the Ends, Ways, and Means." *Army* (August 1986).

Palmer, Michael A. *Origins of the Maritime Strategy: The Development of American Naval Strategy, 1945–1955* (1990).

Perret, Geoffrey. *A Country Made by War: The Story of America's Rise to Power* (1989).

Potter, E. B. *The United States and World Sea Power* (1971).

Sprout, Margaret Tuttle. "Mahan: Evangelist of Sea Power." In *Makers of Modern Strategy: Military Thought from Machiavelli to Hitler*, edited by Edward M. Earle (1943).

Waltz, Kenneth N. "A Strategy for the Rapid Deployment Force." *International Security* (Spring 1981).

Warner, Edward. "Douhet, Mitchell, Seversky: Theories of Air Warfare." In *Makers of Modern Strategy: Military Thought from Machiavelli to Hitler*, edited by Edward M. Earle (1943).

Weigley, Russell F. *The American Way of War: A History of United States Military Strategy and Policy* (1973).

Williams, T. Harry. *The History of American Wars from 1745 to 1918* (1981).

LOGISTICS

Daniel R. Beaver

It has always amazed me that the system worked at all, and the fact that it works rather well is a tribute to the inborn capacity of teamwork in the average American.

SECRETARY OF DEFENSE ROBERT A. LOVETT, 1952

The study of logistics investigates the general management and coordination of military supply and includes the examination of the acquisition, transportation, and distribution of supplies to the military forces in the service of the United States. In peace it explores the nature of the bureaucratic apparatus and procedures necessary for the routine support of the armed forces. In war it analyzes the assembly of the sinews of war to achieve success in battle. The study of logistics also deals with the issues of command and control; how people, often in inappropriately constructed organizations, managed to make those organizations function effectively; and chronicles the efforts of logisticians—those in the military involved in supplying, equipping, and maintaining their comrades in the field. Last, it examines all of these issues within the context of modernizing American organization life as a whole. While the navy and air force are referred to, this essay focuses on logistics in the War Department and the army as a central platform from which to examine the broader American experience.

American logisticians have always faced peculiar problems of time, space, and scale. In the eighteenth and nineteenth centuries, they operated continentally, and in the twentieth they supported vast forces over multiple theaters around the globe. Before 1815 they compiled a record ranging from bare sufficiency to outright failure. After the War of 1812, however, their performance improved. Americans successfully mobilized, supplied, and supported substantial forces over long distances during the War with Mexico of 1846–1848. During the Civil War, 1861–1865, the federal government constructed innovative organizations that brought extensive informal coordination of state and federal authorities, developed effective army-navy cooperation, and established important connections between the public and private sectors of the economy. The campaigns in the Caribbean and the Philippines at the end of the century required long-range logistical support. Little in the nineteenth-century experience, however, prepared the nation for the massive coalition wars of material of the twentieth century.

Since 1914 the United States has fought two total wars and two limited wars and conducted numerous short campaigns, the most substantial of which was the Gulf War of 1991 against Iraqi forces. World War I and the Korean War were conducted with very little preliminary planning and preparation. World War II and the Vietnam War brought many logistical misapprehensions and misplaced priorities. Even the Gulf War was in a certain sense a lucky accident, proving inadvertently to be the kind of short, violent campaign Americans were prepared to undertake logistically. Since 1815, however, given sufficient time and continued public support, Americans have demonstrated admirable organizational abilities to raise, supply, and sustain effective military forces over vast distances.

THE EARLY NINETEENTH-CENTURY LOGISTICAL SYSTEM

The original American logistical system had its roots in seventeenth- and eighteenth-century colonial politics and administrative practices. Its components were powered by wind, water, and muscle and were controlled through an often labyrinthine bureaucracy whose motivating forces in many cases were connections, personal greed, and family advantage. The system did not rely heavily on material, and the greatest expenditures were on food for the troops and fodder for the animals. Road networks were thin and poorly surfaced; heavy equipment and bulky supplies were moved by rivers and, later, canals. Armies traveled at from three to five miles an hour and deployed weapons whose lethal range was under three hundred yards.

Serious shortcomings were revealed during the American Revolution, when civilian contractors, freighters, and teamsters proved unreliable, and the ill-equipped army often starved in the midst of plenty. Hampered from the outset by inadequate land transportation to support a sustained conventional conflict, the Continental army staggered from crisis to crisis and never solved its logistical problems. In the 1790s, after supply and logistical failures during the early campaigns against the Shawnee Indians in the Old Northwest, Congress introduced

a number of reforms and in 1794 established two national arsenals of production at Springfield, Massachusetts, and Harpers Ferry, Virginia, to supplement or possibly even replace private small-arms manufacturers and suppliers—but the essence of the original system remained. Control of supply rested with a civilian purveyor general of supplies, who was accountable to the secretary of the Treasury, not the secretary of war. American officials of the day still considered a public office a species of property to be exploited for personal or family advantage, and their contracting and purchasing methods meant corruption and mismanagement in logistics, general supply, and procurement.

Logistical disaster stalked the army during the War of 1812, and postwar congressional investigations revealed dishonesty of unsurpassed magnitude and inefficiency bordering on treason. Difficulties with private suppliers ranged from cynical exploitation of the government by fraudulent contract merchants to Eli Whitney's failure to reach an effective financial resolution of his 1812 musket contract with the War Department. Primitive transportation and communications accounted for much of the failure of supply, but the investigations also highlighted the poor performance of those who should have taken such difficulties into account. The result was a reorganization of the War Department that responded simultaneously to wartime failure and to the challenges of revolutions in transportation, industry, and technology that were reshaping governments in Europe and America. The reorganization also reflected peacetime military missions and the ambitions of bureaucrats. The process through which new industrial-energy sources, tools, and methods were integrated has been labeled military modernization.

Before 1840 the American organizational landscape was relatively stable. There was little institutional innovation in private American business. Organization was characterized by either single entrepreneurship or simple partnerships whose members exercised personal control of the enterprise. After 1840 the industrial system expanded organizationally and technologically. Mechanization of production was a critical factor in the process. Although the steam engine appeared toward the end of the eighteenth century, water still powered industry at the midpoint of the nineteenth century. The process of technological change—substituting machines for hand labor, applying new sources of energy, and transforming, molding, and reshaping materials—had been expanding slowly for more than a century, and the pace of change had only begun to accelerate at the opening of the Civil War in 1861. The transportation and communication revolutions drove the process forward. Steam railroads and the electric telegraph increased the speed of business and presented an organizational challenge to businessmen. Technology increased the speed of production, communication, and transportation of goods to market. For the first time, materials and products moved on land faster than the pace of a walking horse, and communication by telegraph made news immediately available. It took a carefully monitored and controlled enterprise to maximize the potential returns from such a revolution, and to meet this need the nineteenth-century corporation emerged, with its sophisticated division of labor and a hierarchy of salaried, accountable managers to superintend its various units.

The armed forces made substantial contributions to antebellum modernization, providing private business and industry with managerial and technological experts. The U.S. Military Academy at West Point was one of only three engineering schools in the country in 1835, and many of its graduates left the army after 1837 to become prominent civilian engineers, factory managers, and business executives. Talented former soldiers in industry and transportation closely linked the army to the emerging new industrial society, while ordnance technicians introduced "armory practice"—the machine-production of small arms with interchangeable parts—into the Harpers Ferry and Springfield arsenals and encouraged the "American system" of manufacturing. Soldier-technicians explored, surveyed, planned, and helped construct a network of roads, canals, and railroads that drew the national economy together; they also cleared snags, bypassed rapids, and improved the channels on the Ohio and Mississippi rivers. Substantial coastal fortifications along the Atlantic and Gulf coasts were erected before 1850, requiring extensive interbureau cooperation that forged connections with local construction firms—connections that in turn linked the army to the prosperity of East Coast and Gulf Coast cities. Similar work after 1850 around San Francisco and Puget Sound resulted in contracts for supplies and construction with rising West Coast entrepreneurs. Coastal garrisons established connections with local commission merchants and construction firms, which, like those around the inland and western forts, contributed to the prosperity of local economies. West of the Mississippi, the frontier army relied on civilian freighters and contractors for transportation and supply from St. Louis to Leavenworth and the outlying posts.

Aware of the strategic implications of steam technology, army topographical engineers surveyed the roads and spied out the routes that became the paths of the great transcontinental railroads. In 1839, General Edwin P. Gaines argued that a broad national strategy dictated that steam power, especially railroad communication, would help develop the vast territories west of the Mississippi River, increase the national wealth, and improve the national defense.

The nineteenth-century War Department was a complex, multipurpose institution. Its chief architect was Secretary of War John C. Calhoun. Appointed to the post on 10 October 1817, the South Carolina nationalist aspired to the administrative mantle of Alexander Hamilton. Calhoun was convinced that the major reason for the failures of the War Department during the War of 1812 was inadequate executive management and leadership. His administration replaced ineffective aspects of the existing system with procedures that would enhance command, control, and departmental accountability. The central thrust of War Department policy was toward public control of supply and logistics. Although the Ordnance Bureau, with its arsenals of production and storage, had been in existence since the 1790s, and there had been a chief of ordnance since 1812, Secretary Calhoun expanded and reinvigorated the office. Despite the fact that it remained for a time part of the artillery, it was Calhoun who began the process that brought a separate ordnance establishment into being in 1832. Calhoun reorganized the Offices of Commissary General and Quartermaster General and urged replacement of civilian-contract teamsters and suppliers with military personnel. He pressed for public production of military clothing and equipment. The experience of war, he claimed, had shown that the most significant supply and logistical functions should be completely militarized and that the army should live on its own.

Jacksonian politicians were opposed to the idea and declared that an exclusively federal supply system would create a bureaucratic monster. They claimed that a national monopoly of military supply was as much a threat to liberty as a central bank. Such a system would also eliminate private manufacturers with local and regional congressional connections from the business opportunities associated with army contracts. Lobbies and special interests blocked such efforts in the House and Senate Appropriations and Military Affairs committees and on the floors of Congress. A "mixed system" of supply, neither a free market nor a public monopoly, appeared to be the only solution. Therefore, during the years before the Civil War, logisticians depended on civilian freighting and transport concerns and detached details of officers and enlisted men in the field. War Department supply experts and weapons technicians worked, not always harmoniously, with a relatively small number of private mercantile houses and arms manufacturers who made up, with the public armories and depots of manufacture, a small national-security sector of the American economy.

Modernization changed the ways soldiers thought of themselves, their connections with each other, and with society, creating a system in which the definition of soldier as warrior was challenged by one of soldier as logistician and manager. For most of the nineteenth century, the federal army never exceeded twenty-five thousand officers and men. Combat units comprised a tiny constabulary organized into regiments but scattered in penny-packets along the coast and frontier. The commanding general of the army represented the old warrior tradition, which stressed honor, duty, obedience to orders, courage, a single hierarchical chain of command, and leadership by example in battle. The warriors scorned noncombatants. For them, the only purpose of an army was achieved in the field. Officers in the combat branches, asserting their special training and virtue, sought exclusive command of the army and a controlling voice in supply, weapons selection, and logistics.

Soldiers of the staff in the technical and supply bureaus were parts of the new technological and managerial leadership of the nineteenth century. They designed and made the guns, procured the supplies, transported the army, and, in their depots and armories, coped with the problems of the early industrial era. Accepted as peers by the civilian entrepreneurial, intellectual, and academic communities, they sought professional legitimacy in the War Department and confirmation from the line that they were also soldiers of the Republic. Children of the age of iron and steam, they seldom sought command, but they did demand consultation. The system encouraged cohesion and stability but also fostered separatism between line and staff, increased jurisdictional conflicts, and discouraged habits of mind that could have made regular cooperation easy. As in any traditional community or extended family, soldiers knew each other's good points and weaknesses and, if occasion demanded, could exploit one or both.

The growing pace of technological innovation required sophisticated organizations to incorporate ideas and weapons, so the nineteenth-century board system linked inventors, technicians, producers, and the combat soldiers who used the weapons and equipment. Committees of officers selected and tested new technology, but the real power rested with bureau technicians who controlled the boards that conducted experimental tests, selected the weapons, and turned them over to the line for prolonged field testing. With so many interests involved, the army was conservative in adopting new inventions, and ordnance officers tended to favor production over innovation. Nevertheless, the United States was in the forefront of small-arms technology, and Americans, not Prussians, were the first to adopt a breech-loading musket, the Hall, and the first to issue breech-loading carbines to the cavalry.

The Navy Department, originally part of the War Department, was established in 1798. Although its first public ships, six frigates, were contracted for in 1794, the building program soon fell afoul of party conflicts between small-navy Republicans, who favored a fleet of cruisers, if any at all, to show the flag in peacetime and engage in commerce raiding, and big-navy Federalists, who supported a large, balanced fleet to contest the sea lanes in wartime. Under the administration of Thomas Jefferson, the country got neither. Supported by a mixture of public and private building facilities and operating from logistical bases along the East Coast, it was barely sufficient to deal with the Barbary pirates, and, despite a few single-ship victories during the War of 1812, it proved ineffective against the forces of a first-class power. Privateers rather than national vessels inflicted most of the damage on British commerce while the few public vessels available were quickly bottled up by the blockade.

After the war the conflict between big-navy and small-navy proponents was joined again. A large building program for a balanced fleet was voted by Congress in 1815, but it was never implemented. Under the Jacksonians, small-navy forces prevailed. Indeed, until 1885, with the exception of the Civil War, U.S. naval policy supported a modest long-range cruiser fleet to show the flag and conduct a wartime *guerre de course*. The Board of Naval Commissioners, established in 1815 to give the secretary of the navy a group of professional advisers, soon proved ineffective in handling the management

problems of the department. In 1842, Secretary of the Navy Abel P. Upshur reorganized Navy Department logistics along lines similar to those that had been developed in the War Department. The Board of Naval Commissioners was abolished and its duties assigned to five bureaus: docks and yards; construction, equipment and repair; provisions and clothing; ordnance and hydrography; and medicine and surgery.

The Navy Department was profoundly effected by the industrial revolution. As tidal changes from sail to steam, from wood to steel, and from shot to explosive shell in ordnance revolutionized war at sea, professional conflicts arose between sailors who had the same view of their craft as their counterparts in the army combat arms. The naval "warrior aristocrats" were led by the chief of the Bureau of Navigation (1862) and the naval technocrats were championed by chief of engineers (1862). The technocrats, supported by special interests in Congress and in the seaboard states where their construction facilities were located wielded tremendous power. They controlled the construction of ships and guns and, as a result, a substantial part of the naval budget. In this naval bureaucratic landscape of separate spheres and parallel paths similar to those that prevailed in the War Department, the sailors sought for control and the technocrats struggled for recognition.

The army and the navy reflected the society they served. Although they were national institutions, the structure of power in the military establishment, like the structure of power in the nation, was decentralized and obstinately—at times frustratingly—plural. Although the army was organized and administered through geographic divisions and departments, during the first half of the century, effective military administration was inhibited by the slow pace of transportation and communication, which encouraged localism and regionalism. Command and management involved politically appointed civilians and career officers. The civilians came and went, but military appointments were permanent. Promotion was by seniority within the separate regiments and bureaus, and, until the

Civil War, there was no military retirement system. Army and navy personnel lived and worked separately. Each group considered its own bureau or branch an independent domain and interagency communication a privilege, not a requirement. They had separate hierarchical structures, but they could and did interact. When matters arose that transcended a single organization or involved outsiders, they could cross interior and exterior administrative barriers with ease. They were not isolated from each other or from the civilian communities with which they worked on many occasions. They operated through boards and councils, informal consultation, and personal contact. In an era of small, independent businessmen, loosely connected communities, and prickly personalities whose reactions were dominated by the values of voluntary cooperation, the language of command, if it were to be heeded, was couched in comradely and conciliatory terms. Connections were personal. Even inside the separate branches and bureaus, careful consultation preceded the appearance of regulations and general orders.

With no powerful enemies within striking distance of the United States, there was time to prepare the military forces for war against any conceivable foreign threat. The nation relied in emergencies on the state militia and United States Volunteers. Militiamen initially supplied their own food, clothing, arms, and equipment, and as late as 1850 in some states, they reported for active service equipped at their own expense. Clothing, arms, and equipment were not standardized. Although the Militia Act of 1808 provided federal money for small arms and ordnance, state officials often purchased locally produced weapons. In war the states created multiple parallel supply-and-logistical agencies, which complicated terribly the work of national supply authorities. The whole cumbersome system has been called one of separate spheres and parallel paths. Expanded and matured, it served the administration of Abraham Lincoln successfully and lasted with some modifications through the Spanish-American War.

The nineteenth-century logistical system received its first real test during war with Mexico and offered a splendid contrast to the failures of the War of 1812. The Mexican War was not a big war. Neither Zachary Taylor in northern Mexico nor Winfield Scott in his campaign from Veracruz to Mexico City commanded more than fifteen thousand men. Traditional mobilization practices still held. Regular troops deployed forward, and the volunteer militia that reinforced them supplied their own issue of uniforms and equipment or secured them from state arsenals and depots. The War Department took responsibility for their maintenance only after they were mustered into national service. President James Polk directed the war through his official cabinet, the military members of which acted as an informal war council. After Scott left Washington for Veracruz, Polk coordinated policy and logistics and set the strategy of the combined forces in action against the Mexicans. He personally consulted Quartermaster General Thomas Sidney Jesup and pressed him to speed supplies to the depots established on the Rio Grande, at Tampico, and at Veracruz. Below the Rio Grande, both road and river systems were thin and often nonexistent. The field forces lived off the land when they were actively campaigning, securing food, fodder, and many of their transport animals and wagons by seizure and local requisitioning. General Scott even managed to reclothe his troops in Mexico City by seizing cloth and hiring Mexican seamstresses to cut and stitch new uniforms for his ragged troops.

In part the effective support given the armies in Mexico reflected the maturation of the national transportation and communication infrastructure. Supplies and equipment moved overland from the northeastern arsenals and depots, then down the Hudson to New York, then by sea to the main supply and logistical base at New Orleans. Troops and more supplies moved from Ohio River cities down the Mississippi to the Louisiana port. Steam speeded the process, but it took people who knew how to use the new production and transportation technology effectively to make the system work. The Ordnance and Quartermaster bureaus produced much of the clothing, equipment, and munitions in government factories. Logistical momentum was forward from armories, arsenals, and clothing depots in the United States toward the battle. Distances were great, and time, space, and the absence of uniformed support personnel plagued the supply men and logisticians. Without ships of its own, the War Department contracted with civilian owners. Often cargo ships and troop transports were late or did not arrive at all, or their captains refused to go in harm's way. Civilian-contract teamsters who handled the wagon and mule trains were often unreliable, and troops detailed to supply and logistical duties cut into the modest forces available for combat. As the armed forces moved beyond the sea and river ports into the Mexican hinterland, all the age-old problems of supply and reequipment appeared, but there were no starving times as there had been in the past. Troops were moved, clothed, and fed; they were rarely short of arms or ammunition. At the end of the war, complaints by President Polk and Generals Scott and Taylor that they had been badly served were ill-founded. Under difficult conditions, and with relatively new and untried technologies, War Department supply agencies had performed their missions effectively.

THE CIVIL WAR AND ITS AFTERMATH

The Civil War marked the greatest triumph of the nineteenth-century logistical system. In 1861 American society was still agriculturally oriented, and industry and commerce were in the industrial revolution's first organizational stages. Except for the railroads and the commercial telegraph companies, business organizations were still relatively small. Iron and textile factories engaged work forces of fewer than a hundred people. Agriculture was in transition from labor-intensive production to more mechanized forms. There was no national system to generate and control credit. The country had

not yet recovered completely from the Panic of 1857, and there was excess industrial capacity available to meet initial demands for clothing and equipment. Strategic transportation and communication had already been revolutionized by the railroad, steamboat, and telegraph. Facilities were available to manufacture locomotives, freight cars, and steamboats rapidly. Tactical logistics and communication, however, dependent on animal and human power, moved at the speed of eighteenth-century armies. Complex industrial and manufacturing processes had not yet become important elements in national mobilization. Although small arms and ammunition were in mass production with some interchangeable parts, improved artillery was still two decades in the future. Some progress had been made in metallurgy, but scientific testing was in its infancy and empirical and practical methods were the rule. In 1861, casting an artillery tube was a simple process and field guns could be provided in quantity in a matter of a few months. Wagons were relatively simple to build. The textile industry was the most advanced technologically and could provide clothing for very large forces in a relatively short time. Ammunition expenditures were large by Napoleonic standards but small by twentieth-century measurements. Armies still consumed more food and fodder than ammunition.

The Lincoln administration found it unnecessary to create a command economy or to build a complex bureaucracy to coordinate the industrial war effort. The required raw materials were a small portion of total national resources and formal production priorities were unnecessary. Most of the problems were met by informal adjustment of market variables. Indirect government encouragement through tariff protection and attractive contracting arrangements were, in most cases, sufficient to increase production. The unwillingness of the government to advance credit to new, innovative businesses, however, concentrated orders in the hands of large, established firms.

For the first year of the war, the supply bureaus depended on civilian and foreign sources for war material, subsistence, and animals. Initially, there was competition with state officials for arms and equipment, but within eighteen months, in one of the great transfers of authority in the nineteenth century, the War Department assumed control of the supply and equipment of all Union forces. The biggest problem was expanding the public arsenals and tooling up. Once that had occurred, the Ordnance, Quartermaster, and Subsistence bureaus, working in a simple yet mature nineteenth-century organizational mode, produced a significant proportion of military supplies, arms, and equipment. Only in land and water transport and wire communication did federal authorities rely on a central logistical command system. The government regulated the railroads in the public interest and on occasion ran them to expedite the shipment of troops and supplies. It ran its own steamship lines and railroads in the active military zones. It administered its own riverboat and telegraph lines. The armies fought primarily east of the Mississippi River, and the major campaigns, especially in the West, were fought along the railroads and waterways that led directly into the heart of the Confederacy.

During the war the Union army expanded from 16,000 men organized in 10 infantry regiments, 3 cavalry regiments, and 2 artillery regiments to 1,696 infantry regiments, 272 cavalry regiments, and 78 artillery regiments. By the end of the war, northern factories had produced 1.7 million small arms and had maintained an army of 446,000 men and 221,000 animals in the field. The Springfield Arsenal alone produced 200,000 small arms a year, while foundries cast 7,892 cannon of all calibers. By January 1863, Union depots could provide full uniforms, reserve supplies, and equipment for 100,000 troops. The Commissary Bureau provided so much food that a French observer claimed that waste alone could have fed another 300,000 men. The logistical thrust was forward, and when Quartermaster General Montgomery Meigs rode the lead ship to resupply the troops of General William Tecumseh Sherman at Charleston in 1864, he symbolized the vigor of the Union effort.

The war brought expansion of naval adminis-

tration as well. Creation of the posts of chief of navigation and chief of engineers brought recognition to representatives of the two basic roles of the fleet—fighting plus construction and logistics. The technocrats won temporary recognition as they exploited the new naval technology to produce armored, shell-firing monitors to secure the river lines and enforce the blockade. The industrial base of the country proved sufficient to support massive efforts by both the army and the navy. Supported from East Coast ports, the navy maintained the blockade with increasing efficiency as the war went on.

Secretary of War Simon D. Cameron has been blamed for the alleged failures of the early mobilization period, whereas little attention has been given to the important successes of the bureaus under his leadership. The first year of the war was replete with venality, corruption, and administrative shortfalls characteristic of rapidly expanding institutions. Cameron was addicted to aiding his Pennsylvania political cronies, and he did lack a certain administrative vigor. During the first two years of the war, the War Department command system revealed all the problems that had surfaced during the Mexican War. Scott was too old to exercise command, and George B. McClellan was made commanding general and took the field with the Army of the Potomac. Reform was difficult. Cameron was too absorbed in mobilization to attack the problems, and it was not until Edwin M. Stanton took office in January 1862 that attempts were made to clarify lines of command and communication. With action on multiple fronts, a vacuum grew in Washington that Stanton filled with the War Board headed by Major General Ethan Allen Hitchcock. The board exercised a general overview of the conflict until it became a special staff council in 1864 coordinated by Henry W. Halleck, after Ulysses S. Grant became commanding general. Aside from the council, there was only informal interagency cooperation, and no effort was made to coordinate institutionally the public and private sectors, with the exception of contractual and political manipulations involved in contract negotiations.

As supply and logistical demands grew, the Ordnance, Quartermaster, and Commissary bureaus added appropriate procurement divisions and commissioned experienced private businessmen to meet the growing challenge. Under Quartermaster Meigs, logistical support of the Union forces was much more decentralized than most historians have indicated. Meigs divided the North into two major supply regions. Western armies drew supplies from sources west of the Allegheny Mountains; eastern armies drew from the industrial base east of the mountains. Because of the concentration of the small-arms industry in the Connecticut Valley and upper New York State, that region became the source of small arms for the entire army. Supplies were shipped by rail and water in bulk and stored at general depots from Washington to Nashville. The manufacturing of cannon moved beyond Pittsburgh to Cincinnati, where Miles Greenwood established in 1862 the first cannon foundry in Ohio. Uniform manufacture expanded at Philadelphia and moved to "Union halls" from Cincinnati to Jeffersonville, Indiana, where the widows and dependents of Union soldiers toiled to supply the army. Communications to the battle line, however, were still plagued by contract teamsters who were often unreliable, and the combat effectiveness of the armies deteriorated when troops were detailed to perform supply and logistical duties.

The system worked through informal cooperation between the Ordnance and Quartermaster bureaus, department commanders, and local business leaders. Manufacturing and river transportation were arranged by chambers of commerce and boards of trade in the various western cities, and railroad transportation was coordinated by Assistant Secretary of War Thomas Scott. By early 1863 the Union army was no longer dependent in any significant way on foreign sources for arms, clothing, and equipment. Under the prodding of the humorless, single-minded Stanton and his efficient subordinates, the bureaus completed their expansion and located sufficient resources in the burgeoning home economy to support the war effort without formal economic controls. Despite the complaints of soldiers who wanted to expand the public sector and militarize the entire system except for food and fodder, the mixed system of procurement and supply gave good results. Agricultural mechanization increased geometrically. Arms suppliers multiplied. Clothing stocks expanded until, by 1863, the government could replace equipment from its own expanded clothing manufactories.

By the beginning of 1863, federal forces were beyond want. Indeed, the War Department returned to its traditional practice of requiring sealed competitive bids on army contracts. On 3 July 1863, after the Battle of Gettysburg, War Department supply agencies had already replaced the total ammunition requirements of the Army of the Potomac, and supply depots held reserve clothing and equipment sufficient to reequip Major General George G. Meade's entire army. The bureaucracy creaked, groaned, expanded, and met the military requirements of the Union.

The introduction of new technology, however, made slow headway. Army boards often deadlocked when attempting to introduce new or innovative weapons. For example, with good single-shot breech-loading rifles available, the Union army fought the Civil War with obsolescent muzzleloaders. The small-arms boards, which met continuously during the war, were "Towers of Babel." Some field soldiers demanded breechloaders immediately. Others said they were still unreliable and advised that no changes be made during the war. Inventors wanted to introduce entirely new repeating weapons. The Ordnance Bureau was production-oriented, and Chief of Ordnance James W. Ripley, who knew from experience in the Mexican War the problems of building a new weapon and its ammunition with existing manufacturing technology, feared being caught short. He resisted the new weapon until a reserve of standard weapons was secured. Even his successors, George D. Ramsay (appointed September 1863) and Alexander B. Dyer (appointed September 1864), wanted to wait until it was possible to equip the entire army at one time, so that ammunition supply would not be complicated. Ramsay awarded small contracts for breechloaders to reveal production problems and let ammunition contracts to build up an initial supply. Dyer finally shifted the main production effort to breechloaders, but by that time the war was almost over.

The Confederate government had to be organized from the ground up. From the first moments, it faced a war of scarcity. The South's industrial base was modest, and the Confederacy suffered throughout the war from a shortage of machine tools. Too much land had gone into cotton production and too little into foodstuffs; ironically, within a short time the Confederates faced a shortage of corn and hogs in a region where the land and the weather were most favorable to their production. The textile industry was small, and there was little hope to expand it. Outside the active military forces, there was only a small pool of managerial talent. Without the luxury of finite demands and infinite supplies, Southerners turned by necessity to a command economy.

It was to the credit of Confederate bureaucrats that the rebel army did not suffer any more than it did from shortages of arms and ammunition. With the aid of foreign imports and captured equipment, southern enterprise provided 600,000 small arms and managed to feed, clothe, and arm a force roughly two-thirds the size of the Union army. At the beginning of the war, demand was beyond supply, and the internal economy had to be converted, by force if necessary, to ordnance and supply production. There was nothing except the French revolutionary model to serve as a precedent. The Virginia maximum price for food was consciously modeled on the "Revolutionary Maximum of 1793." What was required, however, was the total coordination of the economy, which would allow supplies to be allocated from theater to theater and between soldiers and civilians from some central point. This was beyond Confederate capacity. The government had the powers of national confiscation and commandeering, but these flew in the face of the belief in local autonomy, which was among the reasons the southern states had given for secession from the Union in the first place.

With political power decentralized, state authorities were both a help and a hindrance in pursuing the war effort. They were coordinated only with the greatest difficulty, and there was not enough time for new institutions to grow. Southerners were unable to coordinate their railroads and establish priorities of production between rolling stock, engines, rails, guns, and ammunition. It was invasion, however, that ultimately wore them down. Moving along the rail and water lines, destroying what they could as they went, advancing Union armies raided deeply, cut off the Confederates from necessary supplies, and ruined their transportation network. When Robert E. Lee surrendered his virtually naked and shoeless starving army at Appomattox, there were supplies of grain, meat, and clothing in Georgia depots that could not be delivered. The Confederacy had the material resources for a long war, but, given southern ideological commitments, it could not rapidly develop administrative tools to make the best use of them in the war that it was forced to fight.

After the war there was another dramatic expansion of the American organizational landscape. Although small-scale business and agriculture remained characteristic of the economy, the number of businesses with capital in excess of $5 million that produced for national and international markets grew substantially. The national rail network approached completion. Capital and credit were available—some self-generated, some from abroad, and some provided through the new national banking system. The growing urban marketplace encouraged great new merchandising firms to compete with local merchants through mail-order houses and nationally controlled local outlets. By the mid-1880s it was clear that neither traditional single entrepreneurship nor simple partnerships could cope with such vast industrial development. It was also clear that some form of organization had to be created that combined centralized policymaking with decentralized management. During the early 1890s, the solution was found in the integrated and diversified corporation—a "new American system" of large-scale enterprise that challenged still-viable nineteenth-century networks of small producers. Advocates called it progress. Critics called it an abomination that turned living communities into artificial machines—factories with interchangeable parts, human and material—adrift in time and space.

For fifteen years the armed forces basked complacently in the reflected light of the great victories of the Civil War. No outside threat encouraged change. Military innovation could occur only with the cooperation of powerful, often antagonistic, groups, some within the military establishment and many entirely beyond the War Department or the army. Issues of command and control and communication that had defined the debate within the military establishment for almost a hundred years became part of an emerging argument involving two apparently irreconcilable concepts of organizational efficiency—one corporate and hierarchical and one community-centered and cooperative. The antebellum compromise had achieved bureaucratic control and coordination by harmonizing relationships among staff and line organizations in the same ways they might be handled in an extended family. The system fed on improvisation, negotiation, connection, and consultation. Imprecise and unscientific as they were, such traditional familial and community-powered organizations had armed, fed, clothed, equipped, and transported the armies of the Republic to victory.

The system of separate spheres and parallel paths remained. The combat arms, with their hierarchical structures and self-conscious professionalism, continued to define "soldier" narrowly, as one possessing only the expertise of the warrior, and were committed to the heroic tradition of battlefield command. With their civilian and congressional allies, such military men argued that the only task of the army was to fight and that War Department organizations were mere supporting agencies.

The technicians, administrators, and supply specialists in the bureaus, with their own powerful congressional and civilian lobbies, continued to insist that they should be treated as equals. They associated themselves as much with engineers, factory managers, merchants, lawyers, doctors, and administrators in civilian life as with the combat soldiers with whom they served. Proud of their expert knowledge and often dictatorial in their own organizations, they resented their ambiguous place in the military system. They did not quarrel with the line's view of the function of an army, but they resisted all efforts to be brought under the sole authority of the combat arms. They wanted to be consulted on broad issues of military affairs and were comfortable with the informal system of boards and councils that had been developed earlier in the era. They ran their affairs with their usual efficiency. Technicians and supply experts in the War Department seldom atrophied intellectually or allowed their organizations to deteriorate. As they saw it, the system was adequate to the needs of the day and there was no compelling reason to change. Interbureau relations followed the old practice of informal horizontal communication and consultation through ad hoc boards that, in theory, still offered an opportunity for designers, producers, and users to cooperate in adapting new technology to the needs of the various branches of the army. Power was diffused through the equipment-acquisition system, in which decisions were reached through consultation, cooperation, and consensus.

For fifteen years, whatever criticism occurred was only part of the traditional struggle of the line to assert command and control over the staff, and of the latter to achieve military respectability and recognition as soldiers of the Republic. Affairs seemed to continue much as before the Civil War. Officers of the line fought with Indians and bureau chiefs, kept their legislative fences mended with influential friends, and fretted over promotion; the supply and technical bureaus worked and tested, jousted with the line over petty matters of administration, kept their legislative fences mended, and fretted over promotion.

The Ordnance Department was still the largest public manufacturer in the United States and also one of the most politically unpopular. It resembled a traditional family guild. In 1872, as part of the postwar reform movement to rationalize army administration, design, and procurement, the department was assigned all infantry, cavalry, and artillery accoutrements except clothing and boots. The patron-client relationship with the small national-security sector of the economy continued. The department still built its own artillery carriages and contracted for tubes and powder with private manufacturers. Rigorous inspection standards ensured the quality of iron work from old associates, such as the West Point Foundry, the South Boston Iron Works, and the Allegheny Iron Company. Ordnance technicians still chose and built small arms and offered modest contracts to favored private firms, such as the Colt Firearms Company, to maintain an industrial mobilization capacity and to compile records to judge the efficiency of emergency contractors. Cordiality declined, however, as lack of appropriations brought few government orders for guns to the iron industry, and cutthroat competition in the small-arms field led to efforts by private producers to eliminate public competition. Paradoxically, after 1885, at a time when historians have claimed the country was most committed to private entrepreneurship, the Ordnance Department began to develop its own facilities to make the new steel artillery tubes and began a running feud with private small-arms and artillery producers that sputtered until the Spanish-American War.

The quartermaster general had vast stores of clothing and equipment on hand. There had been little planning for demobilization after the Civil War, and even after the sale of army clothing on the open market, enough remained that no appropriations for uniforms for the reduced force were needed for almost five years. The bureau sold horses, mules, and wagons at public auction, and almost a decade had passed before it exhausted wartime surpluses of wagons

and accoutrements. Although the textile industry expanded dramatically after the Civil War, and the modest needs of the army made it a relatively unimportant consumer in peacetime, occasional purchases of 100,000 yards of material through publicly advertised contract bidding still caught the attention of the industry. Small but continuous contact with civilian producers and middlemen gave the bureau an effective list of suppliers to call upon in an emergency.

For Quartermaster General Meigs, the mixed system provided flexibility. Sometimes he favored public production, sometimes private contracting. He and his successors continued manufacturing operations on a reduced scale. The permanent Equipment Board, composed exclusively of quartermaster officers, began meeting regularly in 1883 to receive recommendations from the field and give consistency to development and procurement programs. In 1889, Quartermaster General Samuel Holabird made a significant contribution when he published the first complete quartermaster's specification book, providing guidelines for private bidders and strict instructions to quartermaster inspectors who accepted the products.

By 1895 the U.S. military included some of the most experienced transportation experts in the world. In 1884, Tasker H. Bliss, then a young lieutenant, published one of his first articles in *Ordnance Notes*, entitled "Strategical Value of the Inland Canal Navigation of the United States." In it he argued that on the basis of interior lines, defense of the eastern sea frontier, the northeastern lake frontier, and the southern sea frontier was intimately connected with improving river and canal transportation in the United States. Quartermaster General Holabird was a careful student of logistics and published several serious essays on army transportation. In 1895, Captain Henry G. Sharpe of the Subsistence Office published a prizewinning article, "The Art of Supplying Armies in the Field as Exemplified During the Civil War," in the *Journal of the Military Service Institution*, which contained a careful analysis of the uses of railroads during the conflict. The military understood the importance of rail and water transportation, but there was concern about the capacity of the Quartermaster Bureau at its current strength to use it effectively. In a report to the quartermaster general in 1884, Colonel C. G. Sawtelle advised that a transportation corps be created. He wrote:

> The history of all wars, modern and ancient, proves that army is the weakest whose transportation facilities are the most inefficient. A well-equipped and organized transportation service is a necessary adjunct to every army in the field, and its absence, or even its presence with ignorant or inexperienced officers in charge, has resulted in more disasters and defeats and unsuccessful marches and campaigns than perhaps any other cause.

He went on to point out that the Quartermaster Bureau was adept at moving relatively small bodies of troops—it could handle twenty-five thousand well-trained regulars and their equipment—but in a great emergency, he concluded, "our country would be found sadly deficient in this most important requisite to successful military operations."

THE WAR WITH SPAIN

The United States met the crisis of the Spanish-American War in 1898 with nineteenth-century bureaucratic tools. A war council was established, but there were no formal, institutional ways to coordinate the war effort. Planning started very late and the army always reacted to events. In March 1898, War Department planners headed by General Nelson A. Miles recommended that the regular army concentrate near the Gulf Coast and carry out a reconnaissance in force during the summer to establish contact with the Cuban patriotic army. They would use the malarial rainy season to mobilize, equip, and train a modest force of volunteers to invade Cuba, then conquer Havana during the good weather in the fall. Seizure of Havana would bring the collapse of the rest of the Spanish Ca-

ribbean empire. The army, however, could not withstand the powerful private and congressional groups that wanted to play their own parts in the war and demanded immediate action. Control slipped quickly from the War Department's grasp. Volunteers were raised far faster than desired. By June, almost a quarter of a million men were headed for training camps and clamoring for equipment.

President William McKinley, under great political pressure, called for immediate movement against the Spaniards. An experienced volunteer officer from the Civil War, McKinley forced the pace and adopted an indirect strategy. He ordered attacks on the periphery of Spanish power in the Caribbean and the Pacific rather than a potentially costly assault against Havana. The president, who from personal experience abhorred battle, defined U.S. objectives closely and sought peace with Spain at the earliest possible moment. Like Polk and Lincoln, he convened a war council to direct the conflict. Secretary of War Russell Alger, like Stanton, coordinated the war effort through an ad hoc War Department council of bureau chiefs and administrators and worked through the president's council with Secretary of the Navy John D. Long. The war was waged on three fronts—Cuba, Puerto Rico, and the Philippines—and required close coordination of the army and navy if operations were to be effective. As Winfield Scott and George McClellan had done, however, the commanding general abdicated the role of coordinator and took the field. Unlike Grant, Miles had no Henry Halleck in Washington to act as his agent to control the army and coordinate the campaign. Adjutant General Henry C. Corbin undertook that task, gained the ear of the president and the secretary of war, and, in the process, further undermined the already shaky authority of Miles in the army and in the government.

Among the soldier-technicians in the War Department, Civil War organizational models also proved adequate. Mobilization moved at a quicker pace than in 1861. The scale of battle did not require mass mobilization, industrial conversion, or assignment of production priorities among a number of competing agencies, and there was no need for a command economy. Chief of Signals General Adolphus Greely had no trouble obtaining wire and communications equipment rapidly. General William R. Shafter, in command of the expeditionary force to Cuba, may have had no use for telegraphers, but President McKinley and Secretary Alger did. There was no need to seize the national telegraph or telephone lines. Greely cooperated with private firms to connect Washington with the coasts by multiple telegraph and telephone lines, and in his report for 1898 proclaimed that strategic war communication had come of age.

The public sector carried the weight of arms and equipment production. The Ordnance Department expanded small-arms and ammunition production at Springfield and at Frankford, Pennsylvania, and bought or made personal equipment for more than a quarter of a million men at the arsenal in Rock Island, Illinois. Speedy production was paramount and orders were placed regionally by arsenal commanders and the contracts were approved in Washington. Shortages occurred because the army was thrown into battle more quickly than anticipated by the planners. Reserve supplies were out of balance. There were more artillery tubes than carriages and more tubes and carriages than shell and smokeless powder. Even the most experienced civilian contractors could not deliver small arms or artillery of government pattern in less than six months. The arms that were delivered during the war came from government arsenals, and the war ended abruptly before supply could be synchronized.

In September 1898 the Ordnance Board, headed by Major Stanhope Blunt of the Rock Island Arsenal, interviewed regular army combat officers at Camp Wikoff on Long Island, New York. The board concluded that, aside from shortages of smokeless powder and artillery ammunition, the initial scarcity of modern rifles, and some other minor failures, the department's performance had been adequate. When Chief of Ordnance Daniel Flagler reviewed the lessons of the war, he concluded that the Civil War experience had been re-

peated. The nation had no war reserve of modern arms. State troops had arrived poorly equipped. It would have been better, he wrote, to have them leave all their material behind, as the Civil War volunteers finally did, and be supplied by federal authorities with whatever was available. Flagler recommended that the federal rifle-producing capacity be increased by equipping the Rock Island plant and that a war reserve of at least 100,000 rifles be accumulated quickly after each equipment change and that production continue to replace losses. He also recommended that field and siege artillery with carriages, a three-month supply of artillery ammunition, and a portion of the harness required for an army of 500,000 men should be put in reserve for an emergency.

Commissary General Charles P. Eagan oversupplied the army with food, and at the end of the summer of 1898 supplies were deteriorating in the depots and camps. Quartermaster General Marshall I. Luddington managed to clothe, feed, equip, and shelter, after a fashion, more than a quarter of a million men in three months. He decentralized purchasing, and departmental quartermasters contracted regionally for clothing and expanded production at the facilities in San Francisco, Philadelphia, and Jeffersonville, Indiana. The first deliveries of tent canvas, uniform cloth, and boots were substandard, and wagons were always in short supply, but nothing like the clothing scandals of the early Civil War occurred. The performance was in part the result of the improved state of the U.S. textile industry and in part the result of superb quartermaster inspectors and Holabird's list of standard specifications.

With few ocean vessels of its own, and dependent on civilian contractors, the Quartermaster Bureau supported three major overseas expeditions in six months. Only the hastily organized expedition to Cuba stumbled. There were great difficulties with railroad shipping priorities during May and June and terrible congestion on the single track line to Tampa, Florida. Transports intended to house troops for a few days had to support them for more than a week, and in June 1898 civilian captains refused to risk their vessels off Daiquirí. The Puerto Rican campaign, however, was well-supported, and the Quartermaster Bureau built a base at San Francisco to move well-equipped U.S. forces to the Philippines safely and rapidly. In his report for 1898, Luddington recommended that stronger legislation be enacted to control the railroads in wartime in the public interest and that a quartermaster war reserve for 500,000 men be created and kept current by annual issues to troops and National Guardsmen.

The age of imperialism had already marked a sea change in American naval policy, as Alfred Thayer Mahan and his disciples sought and won their fight for a revolutionary big-navy policy of victory through sea power. The need to construct a great fleet in peacetime had brought large budgets and substantial expenditures to improve shore facilities and create overseas logistical bases. Naval technocrats benefited the most from the introduction in the late nineteenth century of steel, armor plated warships armed with improved weapons, powered by new propulsion systems, and linked by new methods of communication. Creation of the Office of the Chief of Naval Ordnance in the mid-1880s gave the department an independent gun factory in Washington to rival the army's new plant at Watervliet, New York. Money for the new fleet began to flow after 1885 and shipbuilding in private and public yards doubled. The effects were shown in the Spanish-American War. Sailing from Hong Kong, Admiral George Dewey annihilated a Spanish fleet at Manila Bay in the Philippines on 1 May 1898. Two months later another American fleet, supported effectively from expanded East Coast and Gulf Coast bases disposed of Spanish naval forces at Santiago, Cuba, and secured the Caribbean for American arms. Not one vessel involved had been laid down before 1885. For the new navy it was "a splendid little war."

For most of the twentieth century, the historiography of the Spanish-American War reflected the views of disgruntled line soldiers, such as General Miles, or modernizers and progressive reformers inside and outside the army who shaped the military legislation in the years fol-lowing that war. The temporary congestion at Tampa; the filthy, disease-ridden mobilization camps of the U.S. Volunteers; the August "skedaddle" of the Fifth Corps from Cuba to Montauk Point, Long Island, pursued by yellow fever and malaria; and the sensational postwar charges by Miles against Commissary General Eagan all contributed to the view that the war was a colossal botch. After months of postwar testimony, however, the Dodge Commission praised the army for accomplishing a "herculean" task despite general unpreparedness. The Dodge Report was not a whitewash. It cataloged well-known shortcomings in the U.S. military establishment and catalyzed the movement toward army reorganization. Its final conclusions suggested that in conducting the supply and logistical parts of the short war against Spain, the nineteenth-century system had reached the limits of its capacity.

THE PROGRESSIVE ERA, 1900–1916

During the years before the First World War, reform forces, only a few of which were located exclusively in military circles, brought increased administrative vigor into the War Department. Like the legislation after the War of 1812, the legislation of 1903 that established the General Staff was part of an incremental trend toward organizational modernization of national institutions and not an isolated event caused by the military difficulties of the Spanish-American War. Progressive reformers in the War Department and the army, in accordance with the contemporary organizational and managerial wisdom, created the corporate General Staff system.

Secretary of War Elihu Root (1899–1903) understood the need for reform. He formalized the nineteenth-century system and, with the creation of the Army War College, added a much-needed planning capability to the War Department. He also recognized the significance of the previous arrangement of separate spheres and parallel paths and continued to allow the bureau chiefs direct access to his office. In his view the new system was not a rejection of nineteenth-century practices and traditions but rather a modification of existing institutions, one that retained the best elements of the past. The army chief of staff would be first among equals in the military and the official conduit through which the president and the secretary of war communicated with the army as an institution. Merging the best of the old with the best of the new, it was hoped, would eliminate dependence on personality, integrate the old board and council system, accelerate decision-making, reduce paperwork, and harmonize relations within the military establishment, with Congress, and with the enlarged national-security sector of the economy. Armed with methods perfected through the new science of industrial management, the War Department would become a contemporary organization—scientific, professional, predictable, efficient, and impersonal.

During the Progressive Era, the army expanded, reorganized, and secured a continental defense mission. Mobilization planning began, and state forces, now formally titled the National Guard, were integrated into the national military establishment. The War Department finally assumed responsibility for standardizing its organization and issuing its arms and equipment. By 1910 federal authorities could equip and field a combined force of 500,000 men in three months. The War Department reorganized its technical and supply agencies and linked them more closely with the combat branches of the army. The technical bureaus improved coastal defenses, designed and built new artillery and small arms, and accumulated a small emergency reserve. Significant experimentation began with motorcars and trucks, wireless communication, and aircraft of all kinds. Cooperation with the line improved and new weapons were deployed quickly and effectively.

Between 1903 and 1916 much of the supply and logistical support system was finally militarized, and the War Department, at least in peace, controlled many of its own assets. Army engineers showed their expertise in managing big construction on the Panama Canal (1904–1914). The Quartermaster and Commissary bureaus were combined and, under a new chief, Henry Sharpe, routinely moved and maintained troops over long distances in Panama and the Philippines. The new Quartermaster Corps, created in 1912 after almost a century of agitation, began to move from animal-drawn transport to internal-combustion technology. The Signal Corps laid the Pacific cable and built a telegraph line to Alaska. Indeed, the new chief signal officer, George Squier, and his assistants in the signal laboratory were in the forefront of the communications revolution of the day and carefully examined the new technology of the airplane.

By 1916 the army had modern armaments, and a board chaired by Brigadier General Charles Treat recommended that its artillery component be increased. Chief of Ordnance William Crozier, who had introduced systematic consultation with the line in weapons development, reequipped and reorganized the arsenals and depots, and made them models of contemporary management, asserted that he was ready to supply modern guns within two years if money was available. Congress promised to appropriate money to provide a future war reserve for a million men. Although other legislation allowed the construction of government nitrate and armor-plate plants, a munitions production board, headed by Brigadier General Francis Kernan, counseled that the long-term interests of the army and the nation were best served by continuing the traditional mixed system, building ordnance in peace in the federal arsenals, distributing a few peacetime contracts to private industry to keep a warm mobilization base, and relying on an expanded private sector for support in wartime.

The continuing technological revolution at sea made the navy a glamorous "high-tech" service before 1914. Readiness rather than mobilization was the concern of progressive naval strategists and logisticians and the continuing bureaucratic battles, which ranged from conflicts over ship design, involving the new dreadnoughts, to struggles over gunnery control and wireless telegraphy, exacerbated the traditional conflicts between sailors and technicians. Public and private shipyards bulged with work and prospered as the United States built big ships not only for itself but also for foreign powers. The shift from coal- to oil-burning ships, which began shortly before the outbreak of the First World War, required that the entire fleet be overhauled in the near future. Meanwhile, bases on the East and West coasts were modernized and some work was undertaken to improve logistical conditions in Hawaii and the Philippines. Completion of the Panama Canal in 1914 solved the basic problems of fleet strength and deployment that had plagued planners since the mid-1880's.

The European war spurred progressive naval reform. Creation of the Office of Chief of Naval Operations in 1915 marked an improvement in control similar to that effected by the creation of the War Department General Staff in 1903. In 1916, the Navy Appropriations Act, passed as part of the preparedness campaign, provided for, over a period of five years, expanded arsenals, docks, and yards, improved logistical support at sea, and a combat fleet "second to none."

All the changes in national policy were consolidated in the National Defense Act of 1916, the first comprehensive military legislation in one hundred years. It was a compromise that modified traditional institutions in the light of current world conditions. The result of almost three decades of incremental reform and military modernization, the act was not intended to be an instrument through which the nation would conduct a major war on the European continent. The administration of President Woodrow Wilson controlled the debate. Only fringe groups, such as doctrinaire line officers, corporate extremists, anticorporate populists, and antimilitary ideologues, advocated further changes. The Naval Appropriations Act expanded the fleet to unprecedented size, and the Shipping Act brought merchant-marine policy under central guidance and created the Emergency Fleet Corporation to construct govern-

ment vessels in government yards. The Adamson Act of the same year established the eight-hour work day on the nation's railroads and confirmed the power of the federal government to control the lines in an emergency; the Federal Aid Road Act of 1916 inaugurated the study of an all-weather road network to meet the strategic needs of the country. A new organization, the Council of National Defense (CND), supported by an advisory commission of expert engineers and administrators, would provide coordination between the military and the private economy in the future.

The legislation passed in 1916 marked the end of a decade and a half of organizational turbulence in the War Department. The army's national security mission was clear. The War College had developed plans to defend the coast of the United States, the Western Hemisphere, and the Philippines. The General Staff, however, still lacked the power to do anything other than advise and coordinate. Leonard Wood, in his attempt to resurrect the power of the commanding general during his struggle with Adjutant General Frederick C. Ainsworth in 1912, had alienated the bureau chiefs and key members of Congress and set managerial modernization back a decade. In 1916 the bureau chiefs retained their political power in the War Department and continued to control the design and production of weapons and equipment.

In November 1916, General Treat labeled existing conditions most unsatisfactory. The chiefs of the supply and logistical bureaus, he claimed, were cantankerous and jealous of their prerogatives. Every dispute or attempt to coordinate activities between the bureau chiefs required a third party, and the secretary of war was constantly asked to referee conflicts between them and the chief of staff. Everything took so much time and involved so many people in so much detail that there was no time left for the important tasks of planning and organization. There had been no general reassignment of procurement functions since 1872, and the division of responsibilities at times bordered on the ludicrous. Blankets, hardware, and wagons were purchased by five separate bureaus. Ordnance bought web equipment for the combat arms, but the medical service bought its own special web accoutrements. Five bureaus bought trucks to different specifications. There were no formal mechanisms to prevent competition with other services or among the army procurement bureaus in an emergency. In 1916, however, that did not seem a problem. It seemed all conceivable issues had been discussed and, within the limits of political realities, soldiers and civilians had hammered out orderly and rational military policy for the United States in an age of industrialized war. Progressive reformers believed they had suitably modified the nineteenth-century military system to meet the demands of a more formal, corporate age. When the United States went to war in April 1917, however, the army was too light, and the navy had too many heavy ships and too few destroyers and antisubmarine craft. The United States had built the wrong forces for the war it was about to fight.

WORLD WAR I

The First World War tested the reformed logistics system and the results were uneven. It was not the war the army was prepared to fight, and what the Wilson administration conceived in April 1917 as a carefully controlled limited intervention became, by the spring of 1918, a battle in which the country was prepared to commit an independent American army of at least eighty divisions to northern France. Strategically, U.S. logisticians could move troops, supplies, and equipment no faster than a transatlantic cargo ship or a French freight train could carry them. Tactically, they could operate only at a pace set by primitive, unreliable trucks, animal transport, and tired doughboys. Between June 1917 and June 1919, however, despite those great handicaps and a year earlier than anyone thought possible, they deployed forty-two divisions—more than 2 million men—to France, supported them after a fashion in battle, and moved them home again.

The Navy Department did not face the massive problems of mobilization and transportation that faced the War Department. Those battleships and cruisers that went to Europe were amalgamated with the British fleet and were supplied from British bases. The Americans also established fifteen overseas bases to fight the German U-boats and protect troop convoys on their way to France. The navy launched a crash program to build a fleet of several hundred submarine chasers. The wooden fleet composed of small 110-foot ships powered by gasoline engines and built by private contractors was successfully developed, and more than half the vessels laid down were deployed during the war. The steel "Eagle Boats" built by the Ford Motor Company were badly designed and few ever joined the fleet. Of the 285 new destroyers authorized, few actually entered the battle.

Market forces that had proved sufficient to channel resources into federal programs during the Civil War proved inadequate in the face of the enormous military demands of World War I, and the public and private sectors of the economy had to be coordinated in ways previously thought undesirable. Although the new Advisory Commission of the CND was of some assistance, the army was reluctant to cooperate with civilian war agencies, and the war opened with unacknowledged ignorance about the nation's economic and organizational capacity. The original Thirty Division Program approved in the summer of 1917 was well within the nation's capacity, but the 1919 Eighty Division Project posed problems of quantity and quality not previously encountered by Americans. Driven by unrealistic intelligence reports and national pride, the U.S. government built an army twice the size it needed to meet the emergency. No one in the War Department, the emergency war boards, or the rest of the executive branch raised any questions about the 1919 program, itself; they only questioned the capacity of the nation to carry it out. It was not until the summer of 1918 that Congress and a few leaders in the automobile and housing industries voiced any concern at all. Then, initiatives considered daring in the spring of 1917 proved inadequate, and President Wilson began reluctantly to move toward a command economy. The armistice of

11 November 1918 ended hostilities before the logistics crisis became apparent to the public, and Americans who were not closely involved convinced themselves that the war effort had been a remarkable success for traditional American organizational methods.

Planning for the American Expeditionary Forces (AEF) began on the basis of the 1915–1916 mobilization program, which called for a force of a million men composed of the regular army, the National Guard, and a body of United States Volunteers. During April 1917 the administration abandoned the volunteer principle in favor of immediate conscription. On 3 May 1917, during the visit of the first interallied missions, President Wilson directed that a small U.S. force be sent to France immediately. A few weeks later, Major General John J. Pershing, after stripping the War Department and the army of many of its best younger officers, led an advanced headquarters to Europe. In early June 1917, the War College proposed a scheme to place a million troops in France by the end of 1918, but General Bliss preferred to wait for advice from U.S. officers who had actually seen the situation in France. In early July 1917, a War Department planning group led by Colonel Chauncey Baker reached Paris and began conversations with members of Pershing's staff on the organization and scale of an American force. On the basis of the group's recommendations, the combat elements of the army were completely reorganized. The Thirty Division Program, with its supporting Service of the Rear Project, was received in Washington at the end of September 1917.

In March 1917, War Department bureau chiefs had enlarged their organizations and began to place contracts for the initial supply of the expanded army. The path from program to production and distribution posed far fewer obstacles for Quartermaster General Sharpe than for Chief of Ordnance Crozier or the chief signal officer, George Squier. Sharpe faced no compelling questions of doctrine and design and had substantial uncommitted civilian plants at his disposal. All he needed, even to handle camp construction, was a target number and a mobilization schedule. Crozier faced complex design and production problems unknown in the quartermaster's office. Squier, whose Signal Corps was responsible for aircraft selection as well as communications equipment for the first year of the war, had little trouble with signal equipment, but lacked a doctrinal framework upon which to base decisions on aircraft. He had little domestic capacity to produce engines and airframes of a quality and quantity equal to the wartime challenge.

Each bureau developed different relationships with the emergency civilian war managers with whom they had to deal. Sharpe, who had to house, clothe, and feed the troops, simply procured large amounts of extant materials from technologically mature industries. A certain amount of conversion was required, but after a relatively short time, the capacity of existing plants was equal to any challenge. Following plans formulated the previous year, in March 1917 the quartermaster general began to clothe and equip the first million men. Although existing stocks had been drawn down by the demands of the Punitive Expedition to Mexico in 1916, the Philadelphia and Jeffersonville depots could fill minimum requirements for the regular army within three months. Much of the annual wool clip had already been bought by the Allies, and the Quartermaster Bureau placed emergency orders for nonstandard textiles to meet the immediate needs of the drafted troops who would arrive in camp in September 1917. At the start Sharpe relied on cotton summer uniforms and hoped the situation would improve before winter issues were necessary. The bureau secured thousands of horses and mules and let contracts for motorcars and trucks of various makes. Bureau technicians designed a standard military truck and presented it to the automobile industry for bid. They placed massive orders for wagons, animal harness, tentage, and food.

Full tables of organization and equipment were not ready before 3 May 1917 and had to be extensively revised during August and September, after the arrival of recommendations from France. When the first elements of the AEF went abroad, their equipment was shipped to the East Coast by the Transportation Division of the Quartermaster Bureau, but in August 1917, General Bliss, in one of the first transfers of operating power from a bureau to the General Staff, organized the Embarkation Service, which put command of each port of embarkation under an officer directly responsible to the chief of staff.

Between 2 April and 15 October 1917, the Ordnance Department laid down the initial U.S. munitions program. The U.S. Army was very light by European wartime standards. In 1917 it still followed its traditional practice and traded weight for flexibility and mobility in the sparsely populated, arid, and poorly connected country in which it expected to fight. Since 1901, General Crozier had warned three different administrations that it would require at least two years to equip a large force with artillery in an emergency. Now he believed that, as long as U.S. forces were not to go abroad before the end of 1918, he could supply them with an adequate mobile artillery from U.S. sources. Any earlier deployment would make other arrangements necessary. The government arsenals at Watertown, Massachusetts, and Watervliet, New York, would have to be enlarged. The two private concerns capable of producing artillery, Bethlehem Steel and Midvale Steel, would have to be cleared of Allied orders. In fact, the relatively small, private national-defense sector was preempted by the Allies for at least three months, and little could be gained by commandeering their plants and interrupting the flow of material to forces already in battle. Support facilities would have to be expanded. Storage and warehousing were inadequate, and the railroads had already had trouble the previous year in moving foodstuffs to the East Coast. There was no reason to believe things would be any better in 1917.

In May 1917, after the arrival of the Allied war missions in the United States, General Crozier met with French representatives and secured promises that their plants would provide artillery for the anticipated U.S. reinforcement. The War Department–AEF program devised in July increased field artillery requirements by a third and called for large numbers of heavy and super-heavy guns and howitzers for corps and army artillery parks. Uneasiness about the supply situation had already been reflected in General Bliss's June order to Crozier to continue the production of modified U.S. artillery and in Pershing's warning, which arrived in mid-July, that France was not so rich in supplies as the French had claimed. Production, not innovation, became the prime directive of the war.

The critical element was shipping. In May 1917, Chief of Staff Bliss told Secretary of War Newton D. Baker that shipping would be the key to successful U.S. military participation in the war. In addition, unless more tonnage became available, the country was involved in a work of extreme folly. During the summer the War Department was hampered by both the navy and the Allies. The navy refused to convoy troop ships loaded below Chesapeake Bay, and the Allies requested that a number of U.S. vessels be released for their use. In September, Baker and Navy Secretary Josephus Daniels called upon the recently appointed chairman of the United States Shipping Board, Edward N. Hurley, to secure every ship possible to support the Thirty Division Program. Knowing that construction would not bear fruit for at least a year, Hurley seized all German vessels interned in U.S. ports and commandeered all U.S. vessels over twenty-five hundred tons for war work. In November 1917, he helped form the War Board for New York Port to cooperate with the Army Embarkation Service. In mid-October, however, Hurley had to inform the War Department that there was insufficient tonnage available for the army unless it could be taken from essential commercial-trade routes. In October 1917, however, U.S. officials were still optimistic. The Thirty Division Program seemed well within U.S. capacity, and, if nothing changed, it could be carried out within the next year.

Conditions quickly deteriorated, however. In November the successful Bolshevik seizure of power in Russia, the Italian collapse at Caporetto, and the failure of the British offensive in Flanders signaled a period of extreme danger for the Allied cause. At home the mobilization organization almost collapsed during the late fall and winter of 1917–1918. Rail transportation ground to a halt and ocean shipping proved inadequate to meet demands. The railroad business was seasonal, and the lines suffered from car and locomotive shortages at peak movement periods. It also suffered from industry-wide attitudes and federal regulations that favored competition and made equipment-pooling and interline cooperation difficult, if not illegal. In 1916 the lines east of Pittsburgh were congested, and storage facilities proved inadequate to handle the American harvest and Allied war orders. In the spring of 1917, the CND authorized the voluntary Railroad War Board, composed of the chief executive officers of the major trunk lines, to coordinate the movement of troops and building materials to the mobilization camps. They accomplished the tasks, but cars that ordinarily would have carried fuel to eastern industries and seaports were transferred to other work, and freight accumulated at ports of embarkation faster than the available ocean tonnage could carry it to Europe.

The most severe weather in years struck the United States. Rivers and canals froze. Autumn gales slowed the passage of both cargo and troop ships in the North Atlantic, while trainloads of military supplies continued to pour into the northeastern ports from which the army was scheduled to embark. Ships could not find berthing facilities in New York Harbor, and the congestion made it impossible to provision ships ready to sail. In the heavily industrialized East only enough coke remained by mid-December to keep the blast furnaces going for a few more weeks.

On 28 December 1917, President Wilson seized the railroads and turned operations over to Secretary of the Treasury William G. McAdoo, who became director general of the United States Railroad Administration. In January 1918 transportation and industrial conditions became so bad that McAdoo, in order to clear the rail lines east of the Appalachians, embargoed the movement of nonwar materials, and Fuel Director Harry Garfield ordered manufacturing plants not engaged in vital war work to operate on a limited basis for two weeks and for subsequent Mondays until March. The crisis precipitated three months of tumultuous political debate, and the deliberate pace of U.S. mobilization came to an end.

Both the vastly expanded civilian national security sector of the economy and Congress advanced their own solutions to the crisis. Since April 1917, the CND had spawned emergency agencies, including the War Industries Board (WIB). The new scientific industrial managers were confident that rationalization and standardization of the industrial process, the cornerstone of the "new American system," would unite technicians and experts to direct whole societies. Many civilian industrial managers demanded that all procurement be turned over to the business community and that an organization outside the War Department's control—modeled, perhaps, on the British Ministry of Munitions—be erected to secure business efficiency in support of the war effort. Nothing lived up to its promise. Existing management theory had little to offer leaders who were trying to organize and train millions of people, procure a variety of high-quality products in massive amounts from multiple, widely distributed sources, bring people and products together, and transport them all over a three-thousand-mile communication line on a reliable schedule. Many established industrialists called for the appointment of a "czar," preferably an old-fashioned captain of American industry, who would get the job done on his own terms.

Congress, slow to react at first, had by mid-autumn 1917 passed legislation creating a food directorate, a fuel directorate, and a war trade directorate. With the passage of the Emergency Revenue Act of October 1917, Congress opened the way for large-scale innovation in government support for industrial expansion. It acquiesced in executive seizure of the telegraph, telephone, and railroad systems in December 1917. Finally, in spring 1918, the administration turned from conventional peacetime practices to face imaginatively the organizational requirements of a war effort that had quadrupled in less than a year. In March 1918, President Wilson strengthened the WIB by delegating to Bernard M. Baruch, a loyal supporter and Wall Street speculator, the power to coordinate the demands of the various war agencies on the American economy. Even then, as Secretary of War Baker recalled, Baruch was more a conciliator and facilitator than a dictator, and his potential power was only beginning to be felt at the end of the war. The Overman Act of May 1918, drafted in the War Department, gave President Wilson power unheard of since the Civil War to reorganize the executive branch, and the administration moved toward a command economy, but the councils, emergency boards, and executive directorates that were constructed revealed more of the informal approach of the traditional American system than desired by many of the new industrial management experts. If the war had continued, further concentration of executive power would have been necessary, but the organizational direction President Wilson and his advisers might have taken remains obscure.

Meanwhile, army supply and logistical agencies expanded and reorganized relentlessly. Jurisdictional conflicts, many of which went back to the previous century, brought ambitious men opportunities to advance their branch of service or their part of the War Department bureaucracy. Commitment to the war effort, however, and a common desire to keep control of events in the hands of the army ultimately transcended branch and bureau parochialism. During the summer and autumn of 1917, the staff and the bureaus launched a consultative movement to meet the challenge. In the winter of 1917–1918 the coordinating power of the General Staff was increased and the vital importance of bureau cooperation recognized through the creation of a War Department War Council in which all interests were represented. The council period ended, however, when Peyton C. March returned from France. Contrary to his memoir, March found a dynamic cooperative organization that he transformed into a structured directorate dominated by the chief of staff. By means

of the reorganizations that culminated in General Order 80 of 26 August 1918, March attempted to make line control permanent and create an operational role for the General Staff. At the armistice, the War Department was certainly not a well-oiled machine. Some functions were located in the General Staff, others were retained by the bureaus. The end of the fighting prevented resolution of those outstanding questions.

If there was an "organizer of victory" during World War I, it was George W. Goethals, whose Purchase, Storage and Traffic Division (PS and T) of the General Staff controlled supply and logistics in the United States from ports of embarkation to ports of debarkation in England and France. Necessity dictated, or so Goethals asserted, that the vast army supply system be brought under central direction, and by the end of hostilities, he had concentrated command and control of supply and logistics in the General Staff. The PS and T was conceived as having its most important relationship with the Operations Division of the General Staff and the supply bureaus. A protégé of Goethals, Hugh Johnson, was director of purchase and supply. Johnson received the program from the Operations Division and transmitted it to the supply bureaus for calculation of requirements and procurement of equipment. The bureau chiefs, it was hoped, would gain a common interpretation of the military program and move in a coordinated way toward the common objective. The General Staff could control the process without rousing the enmity of the bureau chiefs or destroying utterly the traditional purchasing practices of the army. As army programs came increasingly to shape the business life of the country, Goethals himself served as the military representative on the WIB, while Johnson handled routine matters of requirements, clearance, and production.

In late May and early June, Goethals began to shift procurement of standard articles to the Quartermaster Corps, although the purchase of technical items remained in the hands of the regular bureaus. In July he recommended that a central agency be formed to procure all standard articles of army supply and exercise direct control over movement and storage in the United States and shipment abroad. Goethals would thus assume full responsibility for the supply program, and all the bureaus would be absorbed into the PS and T. Goethals encountered considerable opposition from the bureau chiefs, who considered it an insult to tradition and a blow to their not-inconsiderable accomplishments thus far in the war. When Chief of Staff March approved General Order 80 in late August 1918, it was a victory for Goethals. Transfer of functions began in late September 1918 and the major part of the project was completed by the armistice. The traditional bureaus virtually disappeared, replaced by a centralized supply and logistical directorate within the General Staff. Goethals and his new organization struck a severe blow at the doctrine of separate spheres and parallel paths, but even at the armistice, continued bureau resistance to the PS and T showed that the old debate remained unresolved.

In the meantime, the war crisis abroad grew more serious. As the Germans advanced on every front in the winter of 1917 and the spring of 1918, the U.S. program exploded first to sixty divisions in April and then to eighty divisions in July, creating intractable transportation and cargo problems. Consolidation of inland traffic, the Embarkation Service, and troop and cargo shipping in Goethals' office eased some pressure. Expansion of the Shipping Control Committee of Hurley's Shipping Board to include the entire country in early 1918 improved the allocation of U.S. tonnage, but nothing could succeed unless the U.S. program could be stabilized. General Pershing and the AEF had to be brought under War Department control, and cooperation with the Allies had to be expanded to secure more French and British equipment and shipping.

During World War I, there were two American armies, one in France and one in the United States. From the beginning, General Pershing insisted that he must control the entire U.S. military effort from the field of battle. With only one active front, there was little difficulty until March became chief of staff and the war program tripled in the summer of 1918. Devices then had to be developed to return control to Washington, or the army in France would become a bottomless pit, devouring all the treasure the nation could send and demanding more. The contest between March and Pershing was more reminiscent of the nineteenth-century War Department than a twentieth-century boardroom, and March was neither an Ethan Allen Hitchcock nor a Henry Halleck. He insisted that there was only one military chain of command, and it came from his headquarters in Washington. At the end of the war, however, it was still not at all clear that the AEF accepted a subordinate role.

When Pershing sailed for France in May 1917, he carried orders from Secretary Baker that he believed gave him supreme command of the U.S. war effort. In July 1917, shortly after he established his headquarters at Chaumont, Pershing anticipated that the Thirty Division Program then taking shape would create enormous supply problems and place a great strain on available shipping. He knew that every pound of material that could be purchased in Europe would reduce his dependence on transatlantic shipping. Early relations with French bureaucrats were frustrating, and Pershing soon found that the assistance promised in Washington was difficult to secure in France.

From the start the U.S. command in France competed with the War Department and strove to bring its agencies in Washington under AEF control. In mid-July, Pershing organized his staff functionally along the French "G" system and placed the chiefs of his supply and logistical agencies under his personal command. Bureau chiefs in the United States, however, treated him as a mere field commander, he complained, contracted for equipment in Europe without informing his headquarters, and issued directives to their people in Chaumont along their own chains of command. At the end of August, Pershing ordered all communication between the War Department and bureau chiefs in France to pass through the appropriate sections of his headquarters.

The AEF commander also established a single purchasing control agency. An old friend, Charles G. Dawes, had arrived in France in July, and Pershing ordered him to bring together all the purchasing bureaus in the AEF, approve all purchases made in Europe, procure the transport necessary to bring them to the front, and establish liaison with Allied authorities. As general purchasing agent for the AEF, Dawes consolidated interbureau ordering to gain the lowest prices and attract the attention of the greatest European wholesalers. He also handled all transfers of equipment from the Allies to the AEF. Although he did no direct buying, he approved the orders of the AEF bureaus and had veto power over inappropriate contracts. The Chicago banker had more power in the fall of 1917 than any single War Department administrator except possibly Secretary Baker. By the end of the war, Dawes had overseen the purchase of more than ten million tons of supplies for the AEF, three million tons more than were shipped from the United States.

In August 1917, Pershing established a line of communications (LOC) under Major General Robert M. Blatchford, to control supply depots and land transportation from the French ports to the line of battle. For the first time, in part as a result of the military reforms of the Progressive Era, troops were assigned permanently to organized supply and logistical units. By the end of the war an organized force of more than half a million men supported Pershing's army in battle. The AEF, however, often treated officers and enlisted men assigned to such duties with contempt. They were considered second-class soldiers, not real fighting men.

Command changed twice in two months before Major General Francis Kernan took over in November 1917. Although he had some difficulty with French port and rail facilities, conditions seemed controllable until the winter crisis of 1917–1918 created a logistical traffic jam extending back to the United States. Troops and supplies from home poured in as Goethals ex-

panded and improved port operations and shipped supplies in bulk under automatic supply programs to stock depots in France with at least forty-five days of reserves. The PS and T chief ordered divisions embarking for France to take only their uniforms and small arms and to draw organic equipment on the other side. He demanded that U.S. shipping be supplemented with all British, French, and Dutch tonnage available.

AEF equipment and supply cables oscillated wildly week by week and the situation in France became increasingly difficult. Construction lagged on port facilities and inland bases while depots and the French railroads lacked the capacity to support the U.S. program. French port facilities were so congested that more ships would simply make the situation worse. If troops and supplies could not clear the ports, more shipping would be locked up waiting to unload and the Atlantic ferry would grind to a halt. All the ships in the world would not help if Pershing's supply and logistical situation continued to deteriorate.

In early February 1918, Pershing assembled a board chaired by Major General Johnson Hagood that recommended the supply and logistics functions be separated from the General Staff and reorganized with a separate staff in Tours and Paris. On 13 February 1918 the LOC was abolished, the supply and logistical functions of the AEF were reorganized, and a new Service of Supply (SOS) was created under General Kernan's command. As general purchasing agent, Dawes became the link between the SOS and the French and British supply systems. In April 1918, Pershing urged that all Allied and U.S. supplies in France be pooled and advised General Ferdinand Foch, the Allied armies' supreme commander, that the U.S. Army favored what would become the Inter-Allied Board of Military Supply. Predictably, however, Foch insisted that the questions of tonnage and supply pooling were intimately connected with battlefield command and should be under the control of his headquarters. At the first meeting of the board, on 28 June 1918, measures were taken to place in common use, so far as possible, all the

Allied and U.S. supply depots, permanent warehouses, depots of ammunition, engineer depots, and regulating stations.

Meanwhile, after the March offensive was contained, Pershing's staff, on the advice of General Foch and without consulting Washington, developed a plan to increase the size of the AEF to one hundred divisions, or 4 million men, by the end of 1919. Even after the AEF became aware of the War Department Eighty Division Project in July 1918, they refused to accept it. Dawes went on placing orders in Europe without consulting Washington, and contradictory cables continued to flow from Chaumont. Representatives of the AEF insisted they were in command and, as the only people who understood the situation, they should be instantly obeyed. By implication, and often by direct assertion, they insisted they were the equals and possibly the superiors of representatives of the War Department and other government agencies. This was the situation when the British began to call for restriction of General Pershing's authority and the transfer of logistical, supply, and diplomatic functions into hands other than those of the AEF.

General March saw in the British suggestion an opportunity to bring supply and logistics from home to the front under War Department control. The chief of staff recommended that Goethals place a subordinate—possibly Purchase and Supply Director Hugh Johnson—in charge in Washington while Goethals himself went to France, where he would take over supply matters from Kernan. When Pershing heard of the plan, he exploded. He had rejected Goethals for service in France earlier in the war and was adamant that all theater military activity remain under his own control. To meet March's criticism, he unjustly relieved Kernan and appointed James G. Harbord as commanding general of the SOS. Things seemed to improve under Harbord, but in November 1918 the supply and logistics issue was still unresolved.

Interallied cooperation was driven by battlefield events. As the military situation darkened in 1917 and early 1918, cooperation grew. As the situation improved during the last summer and

autumn of the war, cooperation deteriorated. Although there was never sufficient U.S. leverage to move control of the war from London and Paris to Washington, President Wilson was able to bring the Allies to accept the United States as an equal partner in the war against Germany. In the process, U.S. soldiers and their civilian leaders participated in an unparalleled effort to integrate the logistical and military resources of the Allies into an international command economy.

The process began in mid-October 1917 when the first U.S. mission, headed by the president's personal emissary, Edward M. House, sailed for Europe to attend the Supreme War Council, which had just been established to coordinate entente strategy. Wilson had told House to insist upon unity of plan and control between all the Allies and the United States. As the European powers soon discovered, however, Wilson meant that unity of plan and control should be accepted only if it forwarded U.S. interests. Americans were suspicious of the Allies, and representatives of the Treasury, the War Trade Board, and the Food Administration analyzed Allied requests coolly, maintaining the distance from their Allied associates in the war that had been so marked during the previous summer.

To the Supreme War Council, the function of the United States was to supply money, raw materials, and manpower. Allied artillery production capacity exceeded demand, and even after resupplying the Italians, French and British arms factories could provide all necessary field, medium, and heavy artillery to the AEF. Ocean tonnage remained the controlling factor. Submarine sinkings, despite the introduction of convoys, were still outrunning new ship construction, and it was recommended that the United States supply British yards with as much ship and boiler plate as possible to maintain British production. In addition, the Americans were urged to increase the shipbuilding program from six to nine million deadweight tons.

The conferees proposed that a functional approach be taken to production of tanks, aircraft, artillery, and ammunition. The Italians would build aircraft engines, the British and

French would build airframes, and the United States would furnish the raw materials. The Americans and British agreed to build heavy tanks jointly. The Americans would provide engines and drive trains while the British furnished frames, armor, and guns. The French would produce light tanks. The Allies would continue to supply the AEF with artillery, and American sources would furnish semifinished castings and forgings. It was anticipated that ammunition expenditure would outrun supply in late 1918, and the council recommended that the United States increase its production and delivery of smokeless powder, shells, and fuses.

In essence, the Allies recommended that the Franco-American agreement of June 1917 be extended into 1919. After the calls for cooperation and the pledges of support were over, after all the formal recommendations of the council were approved, Bainbridge Colby of the Shipping Board asserted that inveterate jealousy, traditional mistrust, acute self-interest, domestic politics, and irreconcilable slants of racial and national bias would conspire to baffle effective interallied coordination.

During the spring crisis, intense negotiations resulted in the creation of a number of interallied economic and supply committees to establish priorities, allocate resources, and coordinate a joint war program for 1919 and 1920. As the various councils and committees were formed, a stream of cables from abroad reached Washington urging closer cooperation, but it was midsummer before the Americans agreed to send a full mission. It was not a coincidence that the mission's departure, in late July 1918, coincided with the crisis of logistical command with the AEF. Headed by Assistant Secretary of War Edward R. Stettinius, the mission had orders, first, to assure sufficient cargo and troop tonnage for the American army that was pouring into France; second, to secure reliable information from the associated powers about their future requirements, so that the Wilson administration could plan its 1919 program; and third, to bring the supply and logistical activities of the AEF under War Department control. Warm re-

lations did not always prevail. Stettinius had trouble with the AEF. He would not share information with his own colleagues and the WIB. Leland Summers of the WIB later commented that it was harder to get information from the War Department than from the Allies. The British were recalcitrant on shipping, and from the American point of view, it seemed they could no longer be depended on for anything.

Cooperation improved, however, when Secretary Baker arrived in early September. The secretary met with British shipping authorities and, after initial conversations had failed to bring forth a shipping agreement, asked the president to allow him to meet all the British objections. While awaiting Wilson's reply, Baker continued his conferences with Pershing and his staff and attended sessions of the new Munitions Council and the Maritime Council. The problem with these bodies was that everyone was reluctant to reveal production capacity and import and export programs. Self-interest dictated that postwar economic and commercial positions be protected. On 2 October 1918, Secretary Baker announced that President Wilson had ordered that the U.S. mission should fully disclose all its programs, and the way was cleared, or so it seemed, for an interallied shipping agreement for 1919.

Meanwhile, Baker talked with Pershing about the Eighty Division Project. Baker apparently thought his stubborn general agreed with him and wrote Pershing that the British had agreed to provide the shipping to put the 1919 program in place. Then Foch made a startling disclosure. He had demanded one hundred U.S. divisions in the spring of 1918. He had made the same request in July and August, but in the midst of the September negotiations he suddenly told Baker, to the latter's stupefaction, that he needed no more troops and that the war would be won with the U.S. divisions that were already in France.

In October interallied affairs seemed to make great progress. Four boards for shipping, munitions, food, and finance were created to sit permanently in Paris to supervise pooling of supplies and to prevent duplication of effort. On 26

September the AEF launched the greatest ground offensive in American history. On 6 October, Baker cabled the president, informing him that the American attack was progressing and that the shipping situation was cleared up as well. As the German army collapsed, however, the agreements so carefully fabricated during the summer and early fall unraveled. The British refused to turn over any more shipping to the Americans, and when the Americans asked for an explanation, the British replied that they were withholding more ships because they believed that the Americans still had excess shipping in their civilian import-export trades. The reply brought on a heated debate in the United States between the War Department, the Shipping Board, the WIB, and the War Trade Board that was still sputtering when the armistice was signed.

Throughout the war the Wilson administration was reluctant to make changes that might modify in unforeseeable ways traditional American social and governmental roles. The president had refused earlier to centralize supply in a separate ministry of munitions. The army, navy, State Department, Treasury, Food Administration, Railroad Administration, WIB, War Trade Board, and Shipping Board conducted the war through temporary joint committees in which each decision had to be negotiated. The War Department, with its fear of losing logistical and procurement control to the emergency agencies and its suspicion of the business community, shared responsibility with the president for the absence of a central coordinating and planning agency. If the conflict had continued, the army might have been forced to submit its unrealistic programs to systematic scrutiny by an independent agency of some kind. In 1919, Baruch and the WIB might have become something more than traffic managers. The CND might possibly have been revitalized with representatives of the emergency boards included in its membership and its Advisory Commission turned into a permanent staff. President Wilson's war cabinet had potential as well. Very much a nineteenth-century council, it included the heads of the emergency agencies, the secretary of state, and representatives from the War and Navy departments. It might have brought all the actors together as a kind of national security council with its own staff.

At the armistice, the U.S. supply and logistical effort was still in organizational disarray. Aside from small arms, U.S. weapons production programs never reached fruition. The tank and aircraft programs were failures. On 11 November 1918, the army camps were filled with newly drafted, influenza-racked soldiers. Supply and procurement programs were piled on one another. Warehouses and docks were crammed with equipment and rotting subsistence, plants were filled with half-finished artillery, and depots and arsenals were loaded with millions of pounds of deteriorating powder and ammunition. In Europe the army fought with French and British airplanes, guns, and tanks, and at home U.S. industry imported foreign military technology on a vast scale. Hugh Johnson stated later that in October 1918 shipping was failing and U.S. authorities were filling the vessels they had with "junk"—incomplete artillery, unfinished trucks, machine guns without tripods—just to fill the holds, knowing full well that they would never be able to ship the other parts. "It is my firm conviction" he said, "supported by accurate information and by the opinions of other men, that had the war continued two months longer there would have been a serious disaster in the supply of our army. . . . I think it was the finger of God that saved this government from the most terrible cataclysm that ever overtook the nation."

THE INTERWAR YEARS

During the years between the world wars, the ideas of the new corporate order defined the American organizational landscape. The new ideology supported expanded corporate organization, and the trade-association movement of the 1920s brought business leaders to perceive the nation as an economic unit controlled through voluntary cooperation. In the 1930s, New Dealers experimented with national planning and brought into government people who were comfortable thinking about American society as an organized entity rather than an association of localities and regions.

The ability of the United States to support and conduct industrialized war at long range also improved. Continued mechanization and the introduction of new automated machinery improved industrial productivity. The Transportation Act of 1920 made it possible to operate the railroad network as a unified system in an emergency without nationalizing the lines. The wartime Shipping Board continued to function until 1936, retaining at least the legal power to mobilize shipping in a national emergency, then was replaced by the United States Maritime Commission, a regulatory agency that also was charged with directly subsidizing new construction. Despite the Great Depression, the industrial base expanded 50 percent between 1920 and 1939. According to Industrial War College statisticians, in 1937 the United States accounted for more than 50 percent of world manufacturing capacity and built 75 percent of all the motor vehicles in the world. Indeed, more Americans were employed in manufacturing and servicing motor vehicles and producing spare parts than in any other industry in the country.

By 1940 the United States had the logistical infrastructure, the experienced managerial talent, and the industrial potential to undertake a major war effort. As Brehon B. Somervell, commanding general of the Army Service Forces, wrote at the end of World War II: "When Hitler put his war on wheels, he drove it right straight down our alley."

In the War Department and the army, however, loyalties, antagonisms, habits of mind, and routines similar to those of the days of John C. Calhoun still played significant roles. For a time it seemed logisticians had achieved an equal place in the military hierarchy. "Logistics," declared a staff text in 1926, "cannot be separated from tactics and strategy. It is a major factor in the execution of strategic and tactical conceptions, so inextricably interwoven that it is a part of each." In reality, however, the techni-

cians were still held in low esteem. Combat soldiers still gave their colleagues engaged in supply and logistics only perfunctory recognition and treated them as they might expert civilian advisers rather than as fellow soldiers actively engaged in military affairs. Warriors still demanded full command. Technicians insisted on consultation. Private entrepreneurs still sought profit and influence. They remained separate and often antagonistic groups, defined by their own ambitions and values. When war came there would be no single corporate, hierarchical direction of the national supply and logistical effort. Nineteenth-century perspectives would be supplemented by complex, less formal, corporate military-industrial connections. In 1940 attitudes from the era of separate spheres and parallel paths still played their historical roles in the army and the War Department.

The navy retained its traditional attitudes as well. Restrained by the provisions of the Washington Treaty system, which established a ten-year building holiday for capital ships and fixed the 5:5:3 tonnage ratios for the U.S., British, and Japanese fleets, and plagued by reduced appropriations, it made only a few additions before the Great Depression. It was not until the New Deal and, especially, after passage of the Vinson-Trammell Act in 1934 that the U.S. fleet secured authorization to build up to full treaty strength and improve its production and logistical support facilities. Traditional policies were followed and some vessels were built in public yards and others built by private contractors based in competitive bidding. It was not until 1940 that negotiation contracts replaced competition in naval construction contracts.

Four popular myths generated by World War I shaped military policy between 1919 and the 1941 Japanese attack on Pearl Harbor. The first was that the war had changed nothing and traditional U.S. foreign policies and assumptions about national defense remained viable. Peace was the rule and war was an aberration. Despite wartime failures, time and space worked to American advantage and there would always be time to mobilize and build a war machine after war began. The second myth was that U.S. industrial institutions had proved themselves in the war and further adjustments of industrial-military relations were unnecessary. The third was that, aside from inadequate War Department support for the AEF, the modified nineteenth-century supply and logistical system as embodied in the National Defense Act of 1916 had worked admirably, and the AEF had proved U.S. military institutions superior to Prussian militarism. The fourth myth was that a self-serving alliance of American military men and "merchants of death"—industrial arms makers and financiers—had maneuvered the United States into World War I and used the conflict to advance their own career or financial interests. In the future, it was claimed, these death merchants hoped to change traditional military-industrial arrangements and turn American society into what political scientist Harold Lasswell in 1941 labeled a "garrison state."

During the debates over the National Defense Act of 1920, modernizers and progressive reformers demanded that any remaining parts of the nineteenth-century system be abolished, replaced by a model corporate "American war machine" capable of commanding and managing the total resources of society in the service of the state. These reformers were labeled warmongers by opponents who insisted that the war had not been a harbinger of the future. Other critics preferred traditional council, consultation modes of cooperation and supported no changes in military policy at all. The modernizers and progressives antagonized every interest group in the country, and no one believed world conditions had changed so completely that extreme reconstruction was required. Thus, the 1920 National Defense Act was a compromise, merely amending the one passed four years earlier.

The new legislation modestly expanded command and control of the army under the chief of staff, who became responsible for general military planning. In an effort to separate the business side of war from the conduct of operations, responsibility for procurement planning and industrial mobilization was placed in the office of the assistant secretary of war. Coordination between the line and the technical and supply bureaus was improved. A section of the National Defense Act of 1920 encouraged the assignment of young officers to universities for advanced study, and in 1923 the Army Industrial College was established with a view toward improving communication among the military, corporate, and academic communities. Some nineteenth-century traditions remained. A war council like the one abolished by General March in the spring of 1918 reappeared in the 1920 legislation. A short time later the joint Army-Navy Munitions Board was created to reinforce the older joint war-planning board and to coordinate industrial production and procurement.

The Harbord Board, which implemented the new legislation in 1921, created a complex division of labor between the supply division of the General Staff (G-4), which set requirements; the supply and logistical bureaus, which designed, tested, and issued equipment; and the office of the assistant secretary of war, which handled the business aspects of military procurement. There were problems with implementing the legislation within the War Department bureaucracy, and return of control over supply and logistics to the bureaus posed unacknowledged problems of scale for the future. Overall, however, the Harbord system was a vast improvement over prewar practices. Coordination was achieved through a system of interbranch technical committees, which included members of the issuing agency, all concerned bureau and combat arms, and the office of the chief of staff. In each case there were provisions to add representatives from the industrial sector when appropriate. A War Department coordinating committee resolved differences that could not be ironed out formally inside the committee structure or informally between the chief of staff and the assistant secretary of war. Significantly, the war council never met.

The formal technical committee system met the complaints about lack of consultation that had long been voiced by the using arms and services, who were now responsible for designating types of equipment, priority of development, adoption, and issue. Coordination was still time-consuming and fraught with administrative pitfalls, but consumers, designers, and producers were certainly more closely linked than they had been before 1917. Although procurement still rested with the individual supply bureaus, the assistant secretary's office cleared all purchases. All requests for new or improved equipment went first to the appropriate bureau technical committee. If the request was considered worth pursuing by the technical committee, it was referred to the chief of staff for a statement of need. Upon favorable action by the chief of staff, the item was placed on the design-and-development list of the branch of service responsible for its issue to the army. Under the close scrutiny of the branch technical committee, it moved from design to development to field testing. Representatives from concerned industries were formally consulted regarding the feasibility of production. If the reports were favorable, a recommendation for adoption as standard equipment went forward from the issuing branch of the secretary of war, who placed it on the War Department procurement priority list pending availability of funds. A War Department technical committee resolved any differences that could not be ironed out in the bureau committees or informally between the chief of staff and the assistant secretary of war. Among greatest successes of the interwar technical committee system was the development of the standardized multidrive army motor-transport fleet, including the deuce-and-a-half truck.

The Army Industrial College strengthened communication with the industrial sector. Under the direct authority of the assistant secretary of war, it introduced top business leaders and army officers to the production and procurement problems they might encounter in an emergency. An important organizational connection, the college was the first institution of its kind in the world and offered a unique opportunity for full-time study and investigation of the basic industrial, economic, political, and administrative aspects of harnessing national resources in modern war.

During the interwar era, an innovation of a quite different sort with tremendous significance for the future occurred when the Army Air Corps, created from the Air Service in 1926, developed its unique system of research, development, and procurement. Historically, both the army and the navy secured their arms and equipment from a mixed system of public and private production facilities. Aside from the short-lived Naval Aircraft Factory, a public-private mix of producers never developed for aircraft. In an understandable effort to encourage civil aviation, the authors of the national defense legislation of the early 1920s decreed that no public aircraft production plants would be created and that even research, design, and development of military aircraft would be carried out primarily by private industry. Because so many of the aircraft industry's top executives during the interwar era were former military airmen, a close, even symbiotic, relationship grew up between the Air Corps and civilian aviation executives. It was not until the early 1930s, when the feasibility of civilian air transportation was established, that there was sufficient outside demand for aircraft to free producers from their sole reliance on military orders. Contracts were not always awarded on a competitive basis, but were spread around, as they had been during the nineteenth century. During World War II, the Army Air Force developed its own independent system. The design, development, and procurement policy for the aircraft industry, with its broad interpersonal connections and its unique, semiintegrated public-private corporate structure, that had grown during the early 1920s became a harbinger, after the partial deconstruction of the national arms production establishment of the Department of Defense in the early 1960s, of a new industrial-government organization in the national security sector of the economy.

In 1930, General Charles P. Summerall, the retiring chief of staff, warned that the failure to consolidate command and control of supply and logistics in the General Staff would bring difficulties in a future emergency similar to those encountered in 1917–1918. There was a need for more effective institutions to coordinate military strategy, supply, and logistics, but General Summerall could see only one way to achieve his purpose. Like his predecessors, he insisted on a single hierarchical command system with supply and logistics under an assistant chief of staff. Until the mid-1930s, formal strategic planning, procurement, and logistics remained separate, despite the efforts of the Army-Navy Munitions Board. Mobilization planning did not take into account the resources that were likely to be available, and there was little thought given to the connections between military requirements and material resources. It was not until Malin Craig became chief of staff in 1935 that any attempt was made to link strategy and resources. The Protective Mobilization Plan (PMP) of 1937, undertaken at his request, was the first to take into account the industrial capacity of the nation.

Interwar army and navy planners assumed that the United States would fight its next war without allies and without the logistical support so fortuitously available in 1917. Fighting within a coalition in 1917–1918 had been an unpleasant experience. The logistical and supply failures that left American soldiers at the mercy of the British and French created an abhorrence of interallied cooperation that endured into the first years of World War II. The isolationist political environment of the 1920s and 1930s also affected the military. The curriculum of the Industrial College devoted much time to industrial mobilization and material acquisition, but it gave no attention to interallied cooperation. The Rainbow Plans, for waging war against different nations and developed by the Joint Board before 1938, concentrated on colonial defense, defense of the continental United States, and defense of the Western Hemisphere. That was the situation in September 1939 when George C. Marshall succeeded Craig as chief of staff and war broke out in Europe.

The M-Day (Mobilization Day) plans assumed that the United States would enter any future conflict in a traditional manner—a period of tension would be followed by a declaration of war by Congress. Mobilization plans would then be put into play as they had been in 1917.

The military had learned the importance of lead time in tooling up for production and filling the supply lines, and asserted that the nation could not hope to field large, efficient, well-equipped forces for eighteen months after hostilities began.

Modest rearmament programs were in place by 1939. The administration of Franklin D. Roosevelt ordered partial mobilization in the summer of 1940, and in the months that followed, the National Guard was mobilized and the first peacetime draft in American history went into effect. Although Allied munitions orders in 1939 and 1940 spurred industrial mobilization, it was the big navy, army, and Air Corps orders placed during the fall and winter of 1940–1941 that provided industry time to tool up and begin quantity production. The lend-lease initiative of 1940–1941 transferred large quantities of arms and equipment to the British, Russians, and Chinese. On 7 December 1941, army combat forces in the United States were organized into twenty-seven infantry divisions, five armored divisions, two cavalry divisions, and about two hundred incomplete air squadrons, few of whom were available for overseas deployment in the near future because of equipment and shipping shortages. A big naval building program was in progress, but new combat vessels would not begin to join the fleet for at least six months. During the eighteen months before the Pearl Harbor attack, the initial mobilization processes were completed. By early 1942 the United States was in far better supply and logistical condition than it had been at the end of the eighteen frenzied months of World War I.

WORLD WAR II

The Second World War was fought on a grand scale over great distances. By early 1945 the United States was supporting 12 million soldiers, sailors, marines, and airmen in seven active military theaters over supply lines stretching more than ten thousand miles in a global enterprise unprecedented in military history. Mobilization was in some ways easier than it was in World War I. There was much greater slack in the U.S. economy than there had been in 1917, and it was easier to pull 12 million people out of the work force in the first two years of World War II than it had been to secure 4 million in 1917–1918. During the interwar years the industrial base had been expanded and dispersed to the Midwest and the Far West. The eighteen months of lead time before Pearl Harbor, during which the country began to build, in President Roosevelt's words, the "arsenal of democracy," made it possible to absorb the vast new orders that poured out of Washington.

The war production programs followed traditional patterns. As in World War I, the military expanded its own arsenals, depots, and construction yards and constructed new nationally owned facilities on a vast scale (government owned–government operated plants called GO-GOs). They also followed World War I precedent by constructing new plants, especially in the aircraft industry, and contracting them out to established reliable private producers to operate (government owned–contractor operated plants called GOCOs). Expanded government arsenals, new government factories (such as the Detroit Tank Plant), and the giant industrial corporations accounted for more than 70 percent of the production, but as the war went on, small producers were brought into the process as subcontractors. By late 1943, production of most items of military equipment had reached such levels that government officials actually cut back procurement programs for 1944.

At the end of the war the United States bestrode the world like an economic colossus. Its industries had expanded more than 300 percent and supplied an army of 8 million people organized into ninety divisions, a navy of 4 million people and 2,000 ships, an air force of 4 million people and 100,000 airplanes, and a half million marines organized in six divisions. The merchant marine had received more than 10 million tons of new shipping. The United States supplied the British, French, Russians, and Chinese with the equipment for two thousand divisions and an air force equal to that the Americans placed in the field and, at the same time,

doubled the standard of living of the average American.

The multifront nature of the war made it possible to efficiently employ U.S. and Canadian rail facilities, seaports on the Atlantic, Pacific, and Gulf coasts, and ocean transport. By mid-1943 the military—supplied by depots linked to ports of embarkation and regulated by the Traffic Control Division of the Office of the Chief of Transportation in cooperation with the Office of Defense Transportation—was delivering troops and material smoothly across the continent to ports of embarkation for Europe and the Pacific without the terrible bottlenecks and congestion that characterized the North Atlantic coast during World War I. The roads were not nationalized, and, aside from the brief moment in late 1943 when the army temporarily seized the railroads to prevent a threatened strike, they operated during the conflict under private ownership. Air transport was a new factor in World War II, and in terms of total tonnage delivered, was insignificant, but for the quick movement of small units and small amounts of specialized equipment the Air Transport Command began to come into its own. The difficult task of flying supplies across "the hump" (the Satsung Range) into China received the most public attention, but the total tonnage carried with great effort over three years could have been matched by one convoy of thirty-five liberty ships.

To an even greater degree than in World War I, the issue ultimately came down to ships. Sea transport in all its varied forms was the most important single element in logistics and supply. The various services controlled some of their own sea transport, but the allocation of ocean tonnage rested with an independent body, the War Shipping Administration. There was better coordination than in World War I, when connections between the Emergency Fleet Corporation and the Shipping Board left much to be desired. Supported by the Maritime Commission, whose building program delivered more than 18 million tons of new shipping (mostly mass-produced, prefabricated liberty ships), and the War Shipping Administration, which allocated most of the existing tonnage and new construction to the services on the basis of need, the services secured sufficient cargo and troop tonnage to meet their requirements. The only real shortages that developed after 1943 were in oceangoing landing craft, leading Prime Minister Winston Churchill to remark, in a cable to General George C. Marshall in 1944, "How is it that the plans of two great empires like Britain and the United States should be so hamstrung and limited by a hundred or two of these particular vessels will never be understood by history." Shortfalls in ocean transport would occur, but they would be the result of a slow turnaround rate caused by inadequate docking, unloading, and storage at ports in Europe, as well as undeveloped harbors in the Pacific that often made it necessary to use cargo vessels for storage. Still, by the end of 1943, sealift, in the form of new construction and priority allocations or pooled resources, had converged with prodigious home production to place U.S. military forces beyond the reach of want.

As in World War I, the Americans fought as part of a coalition, and their effort lacked the cohesiveness of one conducted under a single national authority. As early as the fall of 1940, U.S. armories and arsenals were stripped bare to send arms and equipment to the British. After lend-lease became official policy in the spring of 1941, the Chinese and, later, the Russians joined the line of supplicants for U.S. supplies. In 1943 and 1944, the United States completely reequipped the Free French army. Thus, international relations, including difficult and incongruous ones with Soviet Russia and China, compelled continuous reconciliation of often competing national interests.

Although a "Germany first" strategy shaped the U.S. war effort, there was considerable maneuvering for men and supplies between commanders in Europe and those in the Pacific until late 1943. In fact, U.S. forces in the two theaters were roughly equivalent until the final commitments to Operation Overlord (the landing at Normandy) were made. A literal partnership developed between the United States and Great Britain, and the two countries moved much more quickly than in World War I to combine their resources for the fight. By the end of 1942, the partners had created an organization that linked committees representing each country's military and emergency war boards into a coordinated North Atlantic enterprise. In part, the effort reflected the special relationship between Roosevelt and Churchill, but it also emerged from a common understanding of the demands of total war on a global scale. Strategic control rested with the two leaders, who met with the Combined Chiefs of Staff in Washington.

Combined committees representing all facets of the joint war effort studied conditions and prepared reports for consideration. "Localitis," the inability of theater commanders to see beyond their own needs, was always a problem, and issues of strategic priority were resolved by joint U.S. services and combined Anglo-American planning and logistical staffs in Washington. The British and Americans pooled shipping and made every effort to utilize production facilities efficiently wherever they existed. So-called reverse lend-lease from the British Commonwealth made it possible for U.S. troops to secure training facilities and much of their food, clothing, housing, and transportation abroad, thus saving precious shipping from home. Ultimately, the two countries equipped their own forces, partially equipped those of the Russians, and fully supported the Chinese and the French.

After the Japanese attack on Pearl Harbor, it was clear to Marshall that a major reorganization of the army was necessary to control the massive war effort upon which the nation was about to embark. Only such a crisis could have paved the way for passage of the War Powers Act of 18 December 1941, which in turn made possible the most complete reorganization of U.S. supply and logistics since World War I. Marshall understood that command required effective consultation as well as hierarchy and systematic organization. As army chief of staff at the Washington command post, as a member of the joint and combined staff, and as adviser to the president, he revealed both decisiveness and a sensitivity to others that led his biographer, Forrest Pogue, to proclaim him "the organizer of victory."

The Marshall reorganization secured effective executive control over the War Department and the army. It rationalized military organization along contemporary business lines by creating the Army Ground Forces (AGF), Army Air Forces (AAF), and Army Service Forces (ASF). Strategic decision-making was concentrated in a section of Marshall's office designated the Operations Division (OPD) in March 1942. A short time later, the OPD was linked with the overseas theaters of operations, the joint and combined chiefs of staff, and civilian war agencies to become the Army Management Staff. The Marshall reorganization separated routine operations of the supply and logistics services from the General Staff, while policy and strategic logistical decisions remained with the Logistics Group of the OPD. Former Assistant Chief of Staff for Supply (G-4) Brehon Somervell, a dynamic engineer officer who had broad experience with civilians as well as soldiers, became commanding general of the Services of Supply (SOS), later renamed the Army Service Forces (ASF). Supply and logistics support became Somervell's responsibility.

Traditional conflicts between the fighting men and the technical and logistical staffs plagued the new organization. The army, navy, and air force quarreled continuously about allocating resources. Although strategy and logistics were inextricably intertwined, General Somervell always complained that the ASF was not consulted by the OPD until the basic military planning had already been completed. Civilian agencies, including the U.S. Maritime Commission and the War Shipping Board, allocated shipping to the various military services. The War Production Board (WPB), headed by Donald Nelson, was also influential in shaping the war effort. In mid-1942, during a dispute with Nelson, General Lucius Clay, Somervell's director of material, spoke for the military technicians when he asserted that modern warfare was largely a matter of logistics and that control of military procurement and production was a part of the strategy governing the use of U.S. armed forces.

The only precedent for the ASF was the Purchase, Storage, and Traffic Division of the General Staff during World War I. The Marshall reorganization concentrated virtually all supply functions in the United States in the ASF. Somervell's main missions were industrial mobilization and supply planning for overseas operations. Ultimately, the ASF included the Supply and Material Division, which was a key planning link between the army technical services, the Allies, and the U.S. business community; the Plans and Operations Division, which handled overseas theater requirements; a series of service commands in the United States; the Office of the Chief of Transportation; and the usual administrative support organizations. The Control Division developed and employed the most current industrial management techniques to direct the various operations for which the ASF was responsible.

General Somervell, who had none of Marshall's tact or understanding of people in organizations, strove to control the mobilization of the entire national economy. If unrestrained, he would have created a single supply agency to handle the war effort. He most certainly aimed to create a single service of supply with equal institutional status in the War Department. The chief of the ASF showed little concern for civilian needs and fought the WPB over critical priorities. The old struggles between warriors and technicians brought him into conflict with Undersecretary of War Robert Patterson, the Logistical Committee of the OPD, and the WSB when Somervell insisted that military strategy was dependent on finite supply and logistical realities.

Four times before the war ended Somervell proposed that all supply missions assigned to the General Staff and the technical bureaus and services be relocated in a separate supply system similar to the one created by General Goethals in World War I. He further suggested that overseas supply agencies be reorganized along lines similar to the ASF in the United States and with commanders in the same relation to theater commanders as General Somervell was to General Marshall. Finally, Somervell advised that the chief of such a separate staff for supply and business should be consulted on all aspects of strategic planning and report directly to the chief of staff. "The commander of the logistical agency," Somervell wrote, "must be recognized as the adviser to and staff officer for the chief of staff on logistical matters" and should be accountable for all "administrative and supply activities, procedures, and systems." The changes that Somervell proposed were so radical and comprehensive that, had they been implemented, they would have created a new service affecting every agency in the army, the navy, and the air force.

Somervell's aggressive empire-building reinforced opinions among many top military and civilian leaders that he was brilliant but unwise. His first plan was blocked by the OPD in April 1943. The next was vetoed by Secretary of War Stimson, who remembered the destruction wrought by General Wood and General Ainsworth three decades earlier. The third was sidetracked by Undersecretary of War Patterson in the interest of interservice harmony, and the last was simply buried in the ASF files when the war ended. Somervell was right in his fashion, but it would be another twenty years before a functional command structure for supply and logistics would be introduced into the armed forces, and even then it would not be as a separate service branch.

Home-front civil-military and intermilitary conflicts ultimately were resolved by President Roosevelt, who, like Wilson, had no intention of militarizing the economy of the country or allowing the military inappropriately to dominate national policy. During the pre–Pearl Harbor period, however, when the country became the "arsenal of democracy," and after substantial U.S. land, sea, and air forces were committed to battle in 1942, the government was again driven toward a command economy. With the appointment in October 1942 of former Supreme Court Justice James F. Byrnes as director of economic stabilization and, later, director of the Office of War Mobilization (OWM), the president took control.

In November 1942 a system similar to the commodity control committees of the earlier WIB, the Controlled Materials Plan (CMP) was created. By mid-1943 the CMP had brought the Army Supply Program (ASP) into line with the demands of the other services and with the civilian sector of the economy. Throughout the war the military retained control of its own procurement but had to adjust its requirements to those of others through the Requirements Committee of the WPB, which established priority and rationed a select list of scarce materials to the military. The military in turn allocated such raw material on a priority basis to its contractors. Thus, in a peculiar American response to crisis, control of national wartime logistics was not exercised through a simple, corporate, hierarchical command-and-control system. Strategy, force structures, logistics, procurement, production, and shipping were controlled by separate agencies. They coordinated their efforts through a set of connections within a number of horizontal organizations and negotiated their needs through a complex consultative system. The authority to adjust differences and to make the political decisions that emerged from the interplay of those diverse forces rested in the hands of the president of the United States.

Calculation of force structures and requirements were at the heart of the U.S. war effort. The ill-conceived, overambitious eighty division plan of July 1918 remained an unlearned lesson for military planners during the first eighteen months of World War II. As in 1918, the objective seemed to be to secure as much of everything as possible and sort matters out later. The Victory Program of November 1941, which included 215 divisions, 61 of which were armored, was based on what seemed to be available rather than on what was strategically necessary to win a possible war. On 6 January 1942, President Roosevelt went before Congress to request a huge production program to provide 60,000 airplanes in 1942 and 125,000 in 1943. He asked for 45,000 tanks in 1942 and 75,000 in 1943. The list went on: 35,000 antiaircraft guns, 14,000 antitank guns, 500,000 machine guns, 720,000 tons of bombs, and thousands of tons of merchant ships and warships. Roosevelt challenged the country to think big and plan big, but the multitheater, multiservice, and multinational nature of the war made it necessary to assign priorities of production and delivery.

In mid-1942 the WPB announced that the war program was beyond the productive capacity of the country and thus launched the "feasibility debate" between civilians and the military. The civilians were right. In September 1942, in the interest of a balanced war effort, parts of the effort had to be cut back. In late 1942 the army was reduced to one hundred combat divisions and, in mid-1943, to its final strength of ninety combat divisions, including one dismounted cavalry division, sixteen armored divisions, five airborne divisions, and one rather incongruous mountain division. In late 1942 the new ASP, which took all the material factors into account, was introduced. Revised semiannually, the ASP became the basic statement of requirements and procurement policy for the war. In 1944, a more comprehensive and detailed approach was introduced in the Supply Control System (SCS), which attempted more precisely to tailor military procurement to demand on a monthly basis.

World War II was an industrial enterprise. U.S. and British forces were fully mechanized and motorized and operated on an industrial model of warfare that marked the maturation of the military industrial revolution that had begun one hundred years earlier. World War I technicians had been challenged to design, test, produce, and field new equipment and to develop fighting doctrine, and they had not done well; during World War II they did much better. Effective systems of production, control, and development defined under the rubric "operational research" were pioneered by the British; these systems united research and development, doctrine, design production, and deployment into mutually supporting communication loops. War certainly was no longer simply a business for soldiers, but neither was it one for

civilians. The demands of the battlefront integrated all societal resources into a war of machines. It was lucky for the Allies that the Germans never understood the importance of long-range research and development. The German high command decreed that material not immediately useful was not to be developed. Adolf Hitler and his entourage distrusted intellectuals and scientists and never organized German research and development facilities.

In the United States, affairs were different. Vannevar Bush headed the Office of Scientific Research and Development (OSRD), ably assisted by such scientists as James B. Conant and Karl Compton. Bush, whose office was in the executive branch and separate from the military services, sat on all the key boards and committees and coordinated the whole. After January 1942 he was a critical member of all the various military research-and-development divisions. Control over research and development in the army rested with Somervell's ASF, but the AAF and the Office of the Chief of Naval Operations had their own organizations, making it difficult for Bush's office to coordinate the total effort. Conflicts over weapons development and doctrine were chronic among administrators, engineers, designers, and soldiers in the field. The results were mixed. Technicians were still production-oriented and resisted innovations if they might interrupt the flow of arms and equipment. The bazooka and the proximity fuse were successful innovations. The heavy-tank program left much to be desired.

By far the greatest success was the Manhattan Project, which became the model for the Apollo space program of the 1960s. On 2 August 1939, Albert Einstein, at the behest of fellow physicists Enrico Fermi, Edward Teller, and others, wrote President Roosevelt to warn him that the German government was working on a nuclear bomb. Einstein advised the president to undertake a crash program to build such a device first. With enthusiastic encouragement from the OSRD, the U.S. government created the Manhattan District of the Corps of Engineers under General Leslie R. Groves and J. Robert Oppenheimer. The Manhattan Project was always a separate program. Although assigned to the Corps of Engineers and officially part of the ASF, Groves reported directly to Secretary Stimson through Chief of Staff Marshall. The best scientists in the country worked as a team at the University of Chicago, where they created the first controlled chain reaction. Concurrently, Groves created production facilities at Oak Ridge, Tennessee, where producers could take advantage of TVA (Tennessee Valley Authority) electric power, and at Hanford, Washington, on the Columbia River. The practical work of building and testing the prototype weapon took place at the Los Alamos Scientific Laboratory in New Mexico. The secret project, carried forward under the "black budget," cost billions of dollars and employed thousands of people to build the device, which was successfully exploded on 16 July 1945 at Alamogordo Air Base in New Mexico. Secretary Stimson called it the greatest achievement of the combined efforts of science, industry, and the military in all history.

General Somervell might have preferred that the organization of all overseas supply and logistical agencies should parallel those in the United States, but no one in Washington ever proposed, as Secretary Baker had suggested in July 1918, that their commanders should report to the chief of Army Service Forces at home. The Pershing precedent of 1918—that the commander in the field must command his own supply and logistical service—was far too firmly fixed to be changed. Control from Washington to the battle line might have succeeded in a one-front war, but it would never have worked in a global, multitheater war such as World War II. Separate theaters of operations were established in Europe, under General Dwight D. Eisenhower; in the Mediterranean, under British Field Marshal Sir Harold Alexander; in the Persian Gulf Service Command, a special creation with the mission of speeding supplies to the Soviets, under U.S. Brigadier General Donald H. Connolly; in the China-Burma-India theater under Lord Louis Mountbattan; and in the central Pacific, the south Pacific, and the southwest Pacific. All the theaters except the Pacific were joint, unified U.S.-British commands, each with a British or U.S. supreme commander. The Pacific was an exception to the rule in that there was never a single supreme commander. There, where the navy's Admiral Chester W. Nimitz and the army's General Douglas MacArthur ruled, the Basic Logistical Plan (BLP) of May 1943, with its joint Army-Navy Logistical Board, established theater priorities for the shipment of supplies across thousands of miles of open sea, atolls, and island chains, from the West Coast to Hawaii, the central Pacific, Australia, and the Aleutians.

At first the supply problem was one of quantity. Goods of all kinds from the United States, organized under various classifications according to type, filled every available bottom under a system of automatic supply. Then, in 1943, as men, equipment, and munitions built up and the mere accumulation of materials was no longer the central issue, the system was modified into a more sophisticated, semiautomatic one based on periodic requisitions from theater commanders linked first to the ASP and later to the improved SCS. In an increasing tide in late 1942 and 1943 and 1944, men and materials moved to designated ports of embarkation on the East, Gulf, and West coasts. The New York Port of Embarkation supplied the European theater of operations and the Mediterranean while Boston supplied the North Atlantic. Charleston, South Carolina, was responsible for the Caribbean, Central Africa, Middle East, and Persian Gulf. New Orleans handled Latin America and the South Atlantic. San Francisco supplied the central, south, and southwest Pacific, and Los Angeles handled the China-Burma-India theater. Seattle floated men and munitions to Alaska and the northern Pacific.

Wartime logistics and supply absorbed soldiers and sailors like a sponge. Time, space, and scale dictated that the SOS at home and theater-support organizations abroad required up to 80 percent of the available uniformed personnel to support the other 20 percent in battle. The derisive label "blue-star commando" still stigmatized logisticians. In 1944, after nearly three years of distinguished work as director of material in the ASF, General Clay made a plaintive request to General Somervell: "Can I go to war, *now?*" Supply men and logisticians still harbored doubts about their status.

Between December 1941 and August 1945, the U.S. Army sent more than 7 million men and women to theaters of operations more than six thousand miles from home and twelve thousand miles from each other, and supported them with 126.7 billion tons of supplies and equipment. In the European theater alone, U.S. forces received 47.6 billion tons of supplies, six times the amount sent to the AEF in World War I. U.S. theater commanders put in their requests for men, supplies, and equipment, and priority between theaters was set by the Logistical Group of the OPD in Washington, which made its decisions on the basis of Allied strategic objectives. The technical services controlled the types of supplies and equipment to be shipped. Except in the Pacific, supplies from the United States came under the control of a unified theater supply and logistics command as soon as they entered port for off-loading.

The North African campaign, along with Sicily, Italy, and the early campaigns in the southwest and central Pacific, were training schools to prepare supply men for the logistical climax of the war. In the great campaigns that began in June 1944, Allied forces landed at Normandy on the French coast and, at the same time, marines and army troops went ashore at Saipan, Tinian, and Guam in the Mariana Islands in the Pacific. On 6 June 1944 the initial wave of more than 200,000 Allied troops landed on five separate beaches on the Normandy coast. They were supported by five thousand ships and thousands of airplanes and carried initial supplies of all classes for eight days. Within three months, U.S. forces in France grew to 1.25 million men. On 15 June 1944, 125,000 Americans, supported by a fleet of 535 transports and warships, landed on Saipan. They had staged from the forward base of Eniwetok, a thousand miles away, but their main support came from Hawaii, thirty-six hundred miles from the invasion beaches. In mid-April 1945, Americans crossed the Elbe River to finish the war with Germany

as other Americans went ashore at Okinawa on the other side of the globe in what became the last great battle in the war against Japan. Hugh Johnson, who had decried the U.S. logistical effort during World War I, would have been hard put to find fault with the performance. During World War II, the United States became the chief supplier of weapons and equipment and the arsenal of all the forces.

THE COLD WAR, KOREA, AND VIETNAM

By 1945 the United States had gained, at small cost, a preponderance of global power. Between 1944 and 1964, fifty-three nations, primarily in Africa and Asia, gained independence. The United States was drawn into Africa by the departure of European imperialists and into the Middle East by a need for oil as well as by the creation of the State of Israel. In the eighteen months after the end of World War II, it became clear that the multistate military system characteristic of the world before 1940 was temporarily destroyed, and vacuums existed in Europe and Asia that prevented U.S. withdrawal to a traditional stance. The United States moved to contain the Soviets in Europe, and the cold war became a part of American life. In 1949 the North Atlantic Treaty Organization (NATO) was formed, marking the end of 150 years of independent U.S. foreign policy. Between 1950 and 1953, with the collapse of Nationalist China and the North Korean invasion of South Korea, the cold war became warm and global. Military, economic, and ideological confrontations swept from the thirty-eighth parallel across Southeast Asia to the Middle East and Turkey and along the Balkan flank to the Elbe River and the Fulda Gap in Germany. For the next three decades all situations were forced into a simple matrix of cold-war ideology.

The New Deal and World War II had transformed American society, and the continuing postwar revolution in the U.S. organizational landscape made it possible to shape a powerful response to the new cold war conditions. The gross national product exploded. In 1946 it was $320 billion. In 1960 it reached $503 billion. In 1980 the trillion-dollar mark was passed, and in 1991 the total production of goods and services in the country reached an estimated $6.5 trillion. Organizational and transportation expansion brought railroads, airlines, and a great network of national interstate highways to link the country together. A cybernetics and robotic revolution transformed industrial production and a communications revolution of equal power made possible the transfer of vast amounts of information instantaneously over great distances. Even after world recovery in the 1960s and 1970s and the movement of the U.S. economy into a postindustrial era, the national industrial, transportation, and communications infrastructure could support forces of unparalleled power.

Traditional U.S. national security policy was inappropriate for the new era. Commitment to containment of communism replaced the belief in the separation of war and peace with conceptions of prolonged struggle and continuous tension. A potentially hostile power of great strength was in direct contact with the United States, thanks to new technology that had forged weapons of unprecedented range and strategic power. For the first time, the United States was vulnerable to initial attack. Containment was not a doctrine of total war. Nuclear arsenals and intercontinental nuclear delivery systems made general war politically and socially unacceptable and economically counterproductive. Diplomacy and military power had to be linked in order to deter war and advance U.S. interests. War between the great powers would mark the failure of policy, not simply its transfer to the arbitrament of arms. Americans had to correlate national economic power, conventional military power, strategic nuclear forces, and diplomacy as parts of an integrated policy applied over time in an environment of great tension.

A single national command authority was imperative, and there were precedents in President Wilson's War Council of 1918 and in President Roosevelt's policy-coordinating committees. Some critics claimed that such an organization could be created with a stroke of the executive pen. The idea of a single defense department had been pressed by management experts and administrative reformers since William F. Willoughby introduced the notion during debates over the National Defense Act of 1916. Politically experienced people, however, such as President Harry S. Truman, knew that any immediate comprehensive solution was impossible. The National Security Act of 1947 created the National Military Establishment under a secretary of defense. It continued the wartime staff organization but provided for neither a chairman of the Joint Chiefs of Staff nor an independent planning staff. With the formation of the National Security Council (NSC), it established machinery to coordinate military power and foreign policy. It was there that planning document NSC-68 was drafted—a document that would, with modifications, shape the U.S. response to the Soviet Union for the next forty years.

Paradoxically, the legislation added a third service, as air force leaders achieved their dream of independence from the army and navy. It was not until 1950 that the National Security Act was amended to broaden the powers of the secretary of defense and to provide for a chairman and a separate staff for the Joint Chiefs of Staff. The legislation removed the service secretaries from the cabinet and empowered the NSC to coordinate foreign policy, military policy, and national economic power at the highest levels. In 1953 the administration of Dwight D. Eisenhower institutionalized the NSC and further strengthened the Office of the Secretary of Defense. When Charles E. Wilson proved an ineffective leader, President Eisenhower became his own secretary of defense. Incessant interservice bickering and accompanying difficulties over force levels, new roles, and missions, which had erupted in 1947 and seemed never to abate, drove the president to distraction. Finally he intervened personally, remarking that he ought to abolish the entire military establishment and create combined task forces under the Department of Defense. "Wouldn't that be wonderful," he concluded. The problem, as he saw it, was that the secretary of defense needed even more power, and commanders in the field needed better direction and coordination. He believed separate ground, sea, and air forces were operationally obsolete and that campaigns would be fought in the future with all the services acting as a single concentrated force. Thus, the basic function of the secretary of defense and the Joint Chiefs of Staff was to create such a force. The unified theater commands of World War II were an example of what must be done, but they had not gone far enough.

At the end of World War II, General Somervell recommended retaining the Army Service Forces but abolishing the supply and technical bureaus and incorporating their functions into a permanent ASF organization. On the advice of a board headed by General Alexander Patch and, after his death, by General William H. Simpson, the functional ASF model was rejected. In the army reorganization of 1946, the ASF was abolished, but General Staff direction over logistics was strengthened by transferring the Logistical Group from the OPD to the new director of service, supply, and procurement (SS&P), who reported directly to the undersecretary of war for procurement and industrial affairs. The supply and technical bureaus were retained under their own chiefs, but, together with the chief of the new Transportation Corps, they reported to the director of SS&P on general policy matters. In 1948 the director of SS&P became director of logistics in the General Staff.

Between 1946 and 1950 air and sea transportation was consolidated into three unified agencies, the Military Air Transport Command (MAT) and the Military Sea Transport Service (MST), while coordination with civilian carriers came under the Military Traffic Service (MTS). In one of the most important postwar developments within the logistical community, the jerry-built SOS units of the past were abandoned and logistical support services organized as formally as infantry units were established. Logistical commands combining technical and administrative services could be deployed

quickly to support the forces in the field. Many experts thought the technical services under a strong director of logistics could work effectively. There were others, including influential civilians, who believed the ASF should never have been abolished and that a complete reorganization of the old bureaus should be undertaken, placing supply, procurement, and research and development in separate functional divisions under one agency.

Until 1953 mobilization planning was dominated by memories of the two world wars. It was assumed that a war with the Soviet Union would require massive economic mobilization, deployment of armed forces of millions, and years of bloody effort to secure a satisfactory outcome. Between 1953 and 1970, however, conditions changed dramatically. As newer, more powerful long-range weapons entered the inventories of all the superpowers, and as delivery times were reduced from months to days and from days to hours, it became clear that wars would be concluded in a matter of days or weeks and that the era of mass mobilization and the armed horde was ending. Military experts were saying that if war came it was going to be "Come as you are and go with what you've got." Although the global scale of operations consumed more U.S. supply and logistical personnel than those required by armies operating closer to home, the U.S. peacetime forces in fixed positions abroad posed few supply and logistical problems. After 1970, prepositioned weapons and equipment that could be issued to troops transported to the theater by air made a modest quick surge in combat capacity at least feasible. Air transport, however, could not move masses of heavy equipment and, despite containerization and new roll-on, roll-off cargo ships, tanks and heavy artillery moved by sea at the same pace as in World War II.

Neither the Korean War nor the Vietnam War posed the difficulties that logisticians had encountered in the world wars. With large forces being supported by an enormous industrial base, such conflicts required only partial mobilization. Both were single-theater operations conducted from stable supply and logistical bases. They generated relatively low levels of demand for people and material over long periods of time. Their outcomes were never affected by supply and logistics. The Korean conflict was fought until its last year with World War II supplies and equipment. An "ammunition crisis" in 1952 caught the eye of a vigilant press, but that was the exception rather than the rule. In both conflicts the new air and sea transportation systems worked relatively well. Ironically, however, the nature of both wars made the rational deployment of the new logistical commands impossible, and the supply bases for both endeavors were "built on the fly" by harried logisticians trying to keep up with changing politics and escalating force levels. Operations so far from home ate up personnel, and complaints in both Korea and Vietnam concerned the number of Pusan or Saigon commandos, organizational unresponsiveness, excess paperwork, waste, corruption, and oversupply.

Continuous threats from powerful adversaries placed the traditional system under great stress. Logisticians no longer had the lead time to build prototypes; experiment, produce, and test equipment; build stockpiles of supplies; and construct the means to move them to the battle after war began. To support the expanded regular forces, with their greater supply and logistical needs, equipment had to be developed, tested, produced, deployed, improved, and integrated continuously. Weapons and equipment acquisition programs suffered from delays and frightening cost overruns, which elicited continuous criticism from Congress and the public. The army design, development, and deployment systems had always been characterized by difficult conflicts between the using arms and the technical services. The acceptance of the primacy of the using arms, a reform in the interwar era, became a hindrance in the postwar environment.

In part this hindrance came from attempts to improve existing weapons too dramatically. In part it was also the result of the introduction of entirely new, partially tested designs on the cutting edge of technology. It also came from unclear combat doctrine, which led to frequent changes of specifications. It also came from resistance to complex, innovative weapons from the production-oriented technical services. It took more than twenty years to secure a new infantry rifle and the same amount of time to field a new battle tank and armored fighting vehicle. The notorious Divisional Air Defense Vehicle (DIVAD), which began as a simple follow-on weapon, suffered for years from changes in specifications and arguments over capability until it was mercifully cancelled in 1984. In addition, the traditional peacetime dependence on public design, development, and production facilities supported by a small private national security sector simply was no longer adequate. Since the 1920s the air force had depended on the private rather than the public sector for such services, and U.S. corporate industrialists and their congressional allies opposed continued public production, arguing that the vast expansion of government-owned plants would move the country toward a command economy and the very state socialism at home that the nation opposed abroad.

In 1958 the Eisenhower administration had pushed through Congress more amendments to the National Security Act of 1947, creating unified and specified multiservice commands with direct channels of command from the Joint Chiefs of Staff, the secretary of defense, and the president. The reform program was carried forward, and the full potential of the Office of Secretary of Defense was revealed under Robert McNamara, who, supported by his own independent staff, brought management tools from corporate America into the Department of Defense. McNamara strengthened the unified and specified commands. Combat forces were functionally organized into strategic forces, general-purpose forces, and counterinsurgency forces, and the size of the force and the nature of its equipment was quantified under a systems-analysis approach that handled particular defense issues as parts of a total process. Called management by objective (MBO) and supported by a sophisticated planning, programming, and budgeting system (PPBS), it purported to reduce issues of defense decision-making to scientifically definable alternatives. Future secretaries of defense might use different approaches or be more deferential to the military, but, for better or worse, the organization within which they worked was marked substantially by McNamara and his staff, known as the "Whiz Kids." During his years in office (1961–1968), two decades of reorganization and reform came to fruition, and the contemporary Department of Defense emerged.

The cold war created the opportunity to settle century-old rivalries between combat soldiers, technicians, logisticians, and private-arms suppliers. The operations research methods introduced during World War II and the new systems-analysis approach being pioneered in Secretary McNamara's office seemed to offer solutions. The answer was to separate design and doctrinal development from production and break the hold of army technicians on the introduction of new equipment. Ending an era, McNamara introduced the air force model of design, development, and procurement. The Defense Department closed most of the publicly owned arsenals of production and retired or transferred their personnel to other operations. The technical and supply bureaus were abolished and their functions incorporated into the formal system of unified and specified commands that theoretically linked the procurement and deployment of supplies and equipment with the newest technology, training, and doctrine. The Army Material Command (AMC) designed, improved, procured, and supplied weapons. The Combat Developments Command (CDC) planned army organization, tactics, and doctrine. The Defense Supply Agency (DSA) controlled items of common issue to all the services. A further organizational change in 1975 created the Material Development and Readiness Command (MDRC) and placed even more emphasis on research and development. To oversee the production of particularly complex or difficult weapons, the new command adopted the innovative approach pioneered by General Groves and the Manhattan Project and appointed individual project managers.

By the late 1980s, although still plagued by some design inadequacies and high development costs, the system seemed to be working and revolutionary weapons were entering the army inventory in substantial numbers. It was a victory for the combat soldiers and the private sector, but it left a legacy of bitterness that never completely disappeared among the logisticians and technicians whose proud organizations had been eliminated.

In 1960 President Eisenhower had expressed concern that the unprecedented expansion of U.S. military power would, over time, create a "military-industrial complex"—an arms lobby that might exercise inappropriate influence in American politics. The elimination of most public production capacity during the 1960s brought even closer connections with civilian weapons manufacturers. Private corporations in the expanding national security sector were legally shareholder-owned businesses and contributed managerial and technical expertise to the arms-making enterprise. The plants were often public property with machinery supplied by the federal government and depended for their prosperity almost exclusively on government contracts. Just how these ambiguous private-public enterprises fit into a competitive, free-market economic system became a matter for public debate. During the Vietnam era and into the 1970s, criticism of the powerful economic connections between arms producers, their military clients (many of whom joined their firms after retirement), and other elements in the expanded national security sector grew into the widely held belief that the country was in the grip of a conspiracy to make it a "warfare state"—just as such critics as Harold Lasswell had predicted a generation earlier. That such charges were, for the most part, no more verifiable than they had been before did little to diminish their public persuasive power.

AFTER THE COLD WAR

In 1991 the Berlin Wall was down, the Warsaw Pact was no more, and across the globe whatever challenges existed to national survival were not liable, or so it seemed, to military solutions. As the twentieth century neared its close, some observers claimed the vision of the modernizers and progressive reformers had come to pass. The U.S. military had become a giant machine—a modern, integrated system like many other modern corporate institutions. Its enlisted people were interchangeable machine tenders, noncommissioned officers were foremen, and officers were managers of violence, with the entire system run by a civil-military board of directors.

At first glance the Department of Defense of the 1990s, with its functional, interservice control organizations, its closed circle of quasi-public industrial suppliers, and its unified and specified commands to orchestrate the nation's land, sea, and air power, appeared to support such a description. History, however, often confounds analysis. To their dismay, many Department of Defense officials rediscovered that to be effective, an organization had to be consultative as well as hierarchical. The U.S. military establishment, with all its myriad historical parts, still retained a persistent institutional life, purpose, and body of received truths of its own beyond contemporary managerial modes, and preserved many organizational attitudes from the days of Calhoun.

Very little ever really seemed to go away. Inventors and developers still wanted to explore the limits of the possible. Field soldiers still wanted the best supplies and weapons for their missions. Suppliers, technicians, and logisticians still wanted quantity and quality. Ambitious officers still sought advancement. Congressmen still wanted influence. Businessmen still maximized profits. All the old dilemmas remained, and the many irreconcilable imperatives could only be endured, and at times, with luck and commitment, temporarily transcended. The perpetual dissonance between warriors and logisticians from the days of Grant, Sherman, and Pershing was still reflected in the words of a colonel of armor in the Gulf War of 1991: "Logisticians can go to war with us any time they want, so long as they remember who's driving the bus."

See also COALITION WARFARE; COMMUNICATIONS; DECISION-MAKING; ENGINEERING AND SCIENCE; INDUSTRIAL MOBILIZATION AND DEMOBILIZATION; IN-TEROPERABILITY; THE MILITARY-INDUSTRIAL COMPLEX; MOBILIZATION AND DEMOBILIZATION OF MANPOWER; *and* RESEARCH AND TECHNOLOGY.

BIBLIOGRAPHY

The Historical Context

Black, Cyril E. *The Dynamics of Modernization: A Study in Contemporary History* (1966).

Burns, James MacGregor. *The Deadlock of Democracy: Four Party Politics in America* (1963).

Chandler, Alfred D. *Strategy and Structure: Chapters in the History of Industrial Enterprise* (1962).

———. *The Visible Hand: The Managerial Revolution in American Business* (1977).

Hawley, Ellis W. *The Great War and the Search for a Modern Order: A History of the American People and Their Institutions 1917–1933* (1979).

Lynn, John A., ed. *Feeding Mars: Logistics in Western Warfare from the Middle Ages to the Present* (1993).

McNeill, William H. *The Pursuit of Power: Technology, Armed Force, and Society Since A.D. 1000* (1982).

Millis, Walter. *Arms and Men: A Study of American Military History* (1956).

Mumford, Lewis. *Technics and Civilization* (1934).

Nef, John U. *War and Human Progress: An Essay on the Rise of Industrial Civilization* (1950).

Shrader, Charles R. *U.S. Military Logistics, 1607–1991: A Research Guide* (1992).

Wiebe, Robert H. *The Search for Order* (1967).

———. *The Opening of American Society: From the Adoption of the Constitution to the Eve of Disunion* (1984).

Command and Control

Abrahamson, James L. *America Arms for a New Century* (1981).

Bauer, K. Jack. *The Mexican War, 1846–1848* (1974).

Beaver, Daniel R. *Newton D. Baker and the American War Effort, 1917–1919* (1966).

Blum, Alfred A. "Birth and Death of the M Day Plan." In *American Civil-Military Decisions,* edited by Harold Stein (1963).

Borklund, Carl W. *Men of the Pentagon: From Forrestal to McNamara* (1966).

Brodie, Bernard. *Strategy in the Missile Age* (1959).

Brown, Harold. *Thinking About National Security: Defense and Foreign Policy in a Dangerous World* (1983).

Burk, Kathleen. *Britain, America, and the Sinews of War, 1914–1918* (1985).

Coffman, Edward M. *The Hilt of the Sword: The Career of Peyton C. March* (1966).

———. *The War to End All Wars: The American MIlitary Experience in World War I* (1968).

Cosmas, Graham A. *An Army For Empire: The United States Army in the Spanish American War* (1971).

———. "Military Reorganization After the Spanish-American War: The Army Reorganization of 1898–1899." *Military Affairs* 35 (February 1971).

Dallek, Robert. *Franklin D. Roosevelt and American Foreign Policy, 1932–1945* (1979).

Ferrell, Robert H. *Woodrow Wilson and the World War, 1917–1921* (1985).

Freidel, Frank Burt. *The Splendid Little War* (1958).

Gaddis, John Lewis. *The Long Peace: Inquiries into the History of the Cold War* (1987).

Greenfield, Kent Roberts. *Command Decisions* (1960).

Hammond, Paul Y. *Organizing for Defense: The American Military Establishment in the Twentieth Century* (1961).

Hewes, James E. *From Root to McNamara: Army Organization and Administration, 1900–1963* (1975).

Higginbotham, Don. *The War of American Independence: Military Attitudes, Policies, and Practice, 1763–1789* (1971).

Hyman, Harold M. *Stanton, The Life of Lincoln's Secretary of War* (1962).

Jacobs, James R. *The Beginnings of the United States Army, 1783–1812* (1947).

Karsten, Peter. "Armed Progressives: The Military Reorganizes for the American Century." In *Building the Organizational Society*, edited by Jerry Isreal (1972).

Kaufman, Burton. *Efficiency and Expansion* (1974).

Kinnard, Douglas. *The War Managers* (1977).

———. *The Secretary of Defense* (1980).

Kohn, Richard H. *Eagle and Sword: The Federalists and the Creation of the Military Establishment in America, 1783–1803* (1975).

Larrabee, Eric. *Commander in Chief: Franklin Delano Roosevelt, His Lieutenants, and Their War* (1987).

Mahon, John K. *History of the Militia and National Guard* (1983).

Meneely, Alexander H. *The United States War Department, 1861: A Study in Mobilization and Administration* (1928).

Millis, Walter. *Road to War: America, 1914–1917* (1935).

Nevins, Allan. *The War for the Union*, 4 vols. (1959–1971).

Parrini, Carl P. *Heir to Empire: United States Economic Diplomacy, 1916–1923* (1969).

Pogue, Forrest. *George C. Marshall: Ordeal and Hope, 1939–1942* (1965).

———. *George C. Marshall: Organizer of Victory, 1943–1945* (1975).

Raymond, Jack. *Power at the Pentagon* (1964).

Schnabel, James F., et al. *The History of the Joint Chiefs of Staff: The Joint Chiefs and National Policy*, 5 vols. (1979).

Schratz, Paul R., ed. *Evolution of the American Military Establishment Since World War II* (1978).

Shannon, Fred D. *Organization and Administration of the Union Army, 1861–1865*, 2 vols. (1928).

Smythe, Donald. *Pershing, General of the Armies* (1986).

Trask, David F. *The United States in the Supreme War Council* (1961).

———. *Captains and Cabinets: Anglo-American Naval Relations, 1917–1918* (1972).

———. *The War with Spain in 1898* (1981).

Ward, Harry M. *The Department of War, 1781–1795* (1962).

Watson, Mark. *Chief of Staff: Pre-War Plans and Preparations* (1950).

White, Leonard D. *The Federalists: A Study in Administrative History, 1789–1801* (1948).

———. *The Jeffersonians: A Study in Administrative History, 1801–1829* (1951).

———. *The Jacksonians: A Study in Administrative History, 1829–1861* (1954).

Williams, T. Harry. *Lincoln and His Generals* (1952).

Wiltse, Charles M. *John C. Calhoun*, 3 vols. (1944–1951).

Logistics, Supply, Technology, and Industrial Cooperation

Adams, Gordon. *The Iron Triangle: The Politics of Defense Contracting* (1981).

Aitken, Hugh G. H. *Taylorism at Watertown Arsenal: Scientific Management in Action* (1960).

Albion, Robert G., and Robert H. Connery. *Forrestal and the Navy* (1962).

Armstrong, David. *Bullets and Bureaucrats: The Machine Gun and the United States Army, 1861–1916* (1982).

Art, Robert J. *The TFX Decision: McNamara and the Military* (1968).

Baldwin, Ralph B. *The Deadly Fuze: Secret Weapon of World War II* (1980).

Baxter, James P. *The Introduction of the Ironclad Warship* (1933).

———. *Scientists Against Time* (1946).

Beaver, Daniel R., ed. *Some Pathways in Twentieth Century History* (1969).

———. "Politics and Policy: The War Department Motorization and Standardization Program, 1920–1940." *Military Affairs* (October 1983).

Beringer, Richard E., et al. *Why the South Lost the Civil War* (1986).

Bidwell, Sheldon, and Dominick Graham. *Firepower: British Army Weapons and Theories of War, 1904–1945* (1982).

Black, Robert C., III. *The Railroads of the Confederacy* (1952).

Bowler, R. Arthur. *Logistics and the Failure of the British Army in America, 1775–1783* (1975).

Brodie, Bernard. *Sea Power in the Machine Age* (1941).

Brodie, Bernard, and Fawn Brodie. *From Crossbow to H Bomb*, rev. ed. (1973).

Bruce, Robert V. *Lincoln and the Tools of War* (1956).

Carse, Robert. *The Long Haul: The United States Merchant Service in World War II* (1965).

Carter, Worrall R. *Beans, Bullets, and Black Oil: The Story of Fleet Logistics Afloat in the Pacific During World War II* (1953).

Clark, Victor Selden. *History of American Manufactures in the United States* (1929).

Coffman, Edward M. *The Old Army: A Portrait of the American Army in Peacetime, 1784–1898* (1986).

Cook, Chris. *The Warfare State* (1964).

Cooling, B. Franklin, ed. *War, Business, and American Society: Historical Perspectives on the Military-Industrial Complex* (1977).

———. *Grey Steel and Blue Water Navy: The Formative Years of America's Military-Industrial Complex, 1881–1917* (1979).

Corcoran, Thomas. "Did the Civil War Retard Industrialization?" In *The Economic Impact of the Civil War*, edited by Ralph Adreano (1967).

———. *Frontiers of Change: Early Industrialization in America* (1981).

Coulam, Robert F. *Illusions of Choice: The F-111 and the Problem of Weapons Acquisitions Reform* (1977).

Cromwell, Giles. *The Virginia Manufactory of Arms* (1975).

Crowell, Benedict, and Robert F. Wilson. *How America Went to War*, 5 vols. (1921).

Crozier, William. *Ordnance and the World War* (1920).

Cuff, Robert D. *The War Industries Board: Business-Government Relations During World War I* (1973).

Davis, Carl L. *Arming the Union: Small Arms in the Civil War* (1974).

Dawes, Charles G. *A Journal of the Great War*, 2 vols. (1921).

Dew, Charles B. *Ironmaker to the Confederacy: Joseph R. Anderson and the Tredager Iron Works* (1965).

Deyrup, Felicia J. *Arms Makers of the Connecticut Valley: A Regional Study of the Economic Development of the Small Arms Industry, 1798–1870* (1948).

Dupree, A. Hunter. *Science in the Federal Government: A History of Policies and Activities* (1986).

Ellis, John. *The Social History of the Machine Gun* (1975).

Ezell, Edward C. *The Great Rifle Controversy: The Search for the Ultimate Infantry Weapon from World War II Through Vietnam and Beyond* (1984).

Finnegan, John P. *Against the Specter of a Dragon: The Campaign for American Military Preparedness, 1914–1917* (1974).

Frothingham, Thomas. *The American Reinforcement* (1927).

Fuller, Claud E. *The Breechloader in the Service, 1816–1917* (1933).

Fuller, J. F. C. *Armaments and History* (1945).

Furer, Julius A. *Administrative History of the Navy Department in World War II* (1959).

Gansler, Jacques S. *The Defense Industry* (1980).

Gleaves, Albert. *A History of the Transport Service* (1921).

Goetzmann, William H. *Army Exploration in the American West, 1803–1863* (1959).

Goff, Richard D. *Confederate Supply* (1969).

Gough, Terrence J. *U.S. Army Mobilization and Logistics in the Korean War: A Research Approach* (1987).

Hagood, Johnson. *The Services of Supply: A Memoir of the Great War* (1927).

Hattaway, Herman, and Archer Jones. *How the North Won: A Military History of the Civil War* (1983).

Hawke, David Freeman. *Nuts and Bolts of the Past: A History of American Technology, 1776–1860* (1988).

Headrick, Daniel R. *The Tools of Empire: Technology and European Imperialism in the Nineteenth Century* (1981).

Hewlett, Richard G., and Oscar E. Anderson, Jr. *The New World, 1939–1946* (1962).

Hill, Forest G. *Roads, Rails, and Waterways: The Army Engineers and Early Transportation* (1957).

Hitch, Charles J. *Decision Making for Defense* (1965).

Hines, Walter. *War History of American Railroads* (1928).

Hoffman, George. "A Yankee Inventor and the Military Establishment: The Cristie Tank Controversy." *Military Affairs* (February 1975).

Holley, Irving B. *Ideas and Weapons: Exploitation of the Aerial Weapon by the United States During World War I* (1953).

———. *Buying Aircraft: Material Procurement for the Army Air Forces* (1964).

Hounshell, David A. *From the American System to Mass Production, 1800–1932: The Development of Manufacturing Technology in the United States* (1984).

Hunter, Louis C. *Steamboats on the Western Waters: An Economic and Technological History* (1949).

Hurley, Edward N. *The Bridge to France* (1927).

Huston, James A. *The Sinews of War: Army Logistics 1775–1953* (1966).

Kennedy, David. *Over Here: The First World War and American Society* (1980).

Koistinen, Paul A. C. "The Industrial Complex in Historical Perspective: The Interwar Years." *Journal of American History* 55 (March 1970).

Kreidberg, Marvin A., and Morton G. Henry. *History of Military Mobilization in the United States Army, 1775–1945* (1955).

Lane, Frederick. *Ships for Victory: A History of Shipbuilding Under the U.S. Maritime Commission in World War II* (1951).

Leighton, Richard M., and Robert W. Coakley. *Global Logistics and Strategy*, 2 vols. (1955, 1968).

Lord, Francis A. *Lincoln's Railroad Man: Herman Haupt* (1969).

Melman, Seymour. *The Permanent War Economy* (1974).

Miller, Darlis A. *Soldiers and Settlers* (1989).

Morison, Elting E. *Men, Machines, and Modern Times* (1966).

Nelson, Donald M. *Arsenal of Democracy* (1946).

North, Douglas C., and Robert Paul Thomas, eds. *The Growth of the American Economy to 1860* (1968).

Ohl, John K. *General Supply: General Brehon Sommervell and the American War Effort* (1993).

Peck, Taylor. *Round-Shot to Rockets: A History of the Washington Navy Yard and the U.S. Naval Gun Factory* (1949).

Polenberg, Richard. *War and Society: The United States, 1941–1945* (1972).

Prucha, Francis Paul. *Broadax and Bayonet: The Role of the United States Army in the Development of the Northwest, 1815–1860* (1953).

Pursell, Carroll. "Science Agencies in World War II: The OSRD and Its Challengers." In *The Sciences in the American Context: New Perspectives*, edited by Nathan Reingold (1979).

Risch, Erna. *The Quartermaster Corps: Organization, Supply, and Services*, 2 vols. (1953–1955).

———. *Quartermaster Support of the Army: A History of the Corps, 1775–1939* (1962).

———. *Supplying Washington's Army* (1981).

Roland, Alex. "Science and War." In *History Writing on American Science: Perspectives and Prospects*, edited by Sally Gregory Kohlstedt and Margaret W. Rossiter (1985).

Rosen, Steven, ed. *Testing the Theory of the Military Industrial Complex* (1973).

Sanders, Ralph. *The Politics of Defense Analysis* (1973).

Singer, Charles, et al, eds. *A History of Technology*, 5 vols. (1954–1958).

Shy, John. *A People Numerous and Armed* (1976).

Smith, R. Elberton. *The War Department: The Army and Economic Mobilization* (1959).

Smith, Gene E. *Lucius Clay: An American Life* (1990).

Smith, Merritt Roe. *The Harpers Ferry Armory and the New Technology: The Challenge of Change* (1977).

———. *Military Enterprise and Technological Change* (1985).

Sprout, Harold, and Margaret Sprout. *Toward a New Order of Sea Power: American Naval Policy and the World Scene, 1918–1922* (1943).

———. *The Rise of American Naval Power, 1776–1918*, rev. ed. (1967).

Stewart, Irvin. *Organizing Scientific Research for War* (1948).

Thompson, Harry C., Constance Green, and Peter C. Roots. *The Ordnance Department: Planning Munitions for War* (1955).

Turner, George Edgar. *Victory Rode the Rails: The Strategic Place of the Railroads in the Civil War* (1953).

Van Creveld, Martin. *Supplying War: Logistics from Wallenstein to Patton* (1977).

———. *Command in War* (1985).

———. *Technology and War from 2000 B.C. to the Present* (1989).

Vandiver, Frank E. *Ploughshares into Swords: Josiah Gorgas and Confederate Ordnance* (1952).

Weigley, Russell F. *Quartermaster General of the Union Army: A Biography of Montgomery C. Meigs* (1959).

Wilgus, William J. *Transporting the AEF in Western Europe* (1931).

Yoshpe, B. "Economic Mobilization Between the Wars." *Military Affairs* 15 (Winter 1951).

Syrett, David. *Shipping and the American War, 1775–1783* (1970).

Zimmerman, Phyllis. *The Neck of the Bottle: George W. Goethals and the Reorganization of the U.S. Army, 1917–1918* (1992).

INTELLIGENCE

Ray S. Cline

The American experience with intelligence activities and agencies is neither as recent in origin as many believe nor merely the product of forty years of cold war conflict. Instead, that experience reaches back before the founding of the Republic. It is exemplified by George Washington's long-standing interest in and concern with intelligence enterprises, which ensured the survival of the colonies and their joining together to become the United States of America.

To be sure, the American intelligence experience has been episodic in nature, never truly professional until after the beginning of World War II, and not very well understood, even today. Nevertheless, the nation's varied intelligence services are now designed to collect accurate, reliable information about existing and potential dangers to American national security interests at home and abroad.

That information, designated intelligence when it is provided exclusively to government authorities, has been and remains indispensable to sound decision-making on military and foreign policy during times of peace and war. When the collective efforts of the U.S. intelligence agencies, now known as the intelligence community, have failed or have been ignored by American leaders, difficulties, and sometimes disasters, have been the result. The attack on Pearl Harbor, a catastrophic failure of intelligence, is not an isolated example, although it is

the best known. The cry of "intelligence failure" that was heard in the aftermath of that Pacific disaster is, in fact, a very old one. Invariably, however, that accusation seldom grapples with the real issues and problems involved in the collection, analysis, and reporting of national intelligence to constitutional authority in a timely manner.

Since the American Revolution, U.S. presidents in their role as chief executive and commander in chief of the armed forces have attempted to learn as much as possible about enemies, potential and actual, particularly in time of war or impending war.

CAMEO: THE PERSIAN GULF CRISIS, 1990–1991

Before describing the long and painful evolution of a modern central coordinating intelligence machine, it is useful to examine the role of intelligence operations in the Persian Gulf crisis of 1990–1991. The first test of conventional arms since the inconclusive Korean War and the dismal experience of the Vietnam War occurred when the United States and its allies decided to liberate Kuwait from Iraqi military occupation.

The dramatic victory in the desert, in which coalition forces literally tore apart a huge entrenched army in an air battle of one hundred days and a ground battle of four days, has blinded many to a vitally important lesson: this military triumph, with its high-technology air and missile attacks that virtually immobilized the Iraqi army, was almost entirely dependent on the information obtained by intelligence sources. These sources pinpointed most of the enemy's military installations, facilities, and armed forces in Iraq and Kuwait, allowing military objectives to be targeted with extraordinary specificity for the first time in the history of warfare.

The greatest achievement of the U.S. intelligence community during the Persian Gulf campaign was its comprehensive coverage of the entire Middle East through orbiting satellite vehicles. These satellites continue to collect imagery that is digitally communicated at great speed to ground stations where the photographic data can be produced in hard-copy and video displays. But that was not all. When cloud cover obscured the satellite photography, radar imaging that produced less detailed but highly useful resolution carried out the mission. In short, the forces of Saddam Hussein were under constant surveillance whatever the weather.

Adding to this avalanche of data were the signals intercepted by high-altitude satellite vehicles and military ground stations. These stations garnered electronic intelligence (ELINT) from the Iraqi armed forces that betrayed the location of military installations, including command, control, and communications centers. When the codes were broken, if they could be broken, more information could be extracted from the intercepted communications signals, including the exact structure of and the precise links that existed between military units, as well as what they were saying in comparatively simple military field unit communications.

U.S. and coalition forces in the gulf also collected tactical military intelligence on the battlefield, where units conducted reconnaissance missions and submitted after-action reports. These reports added another dimension to the allies' knowledge of Iraqi forces, capabilities, and intentions. Finally, espionage penetrations

of Iraq and Kuwait were collected principally by the Central Intelligence Agency (CIA) but often through interservice contacts with Middle East intelligence agencies (Israel and allied Arab states). These penetrations added crucial details about the disposition of Iraqi military units.

Information based on human sources (HUMINT) was and remains important in the aftermath of the Gulf War. Knowing the future plans and remaining capabilities of the Iraqi leadership and its forces is important, even vital, because even the most detailed imagery cannot tell U.S. officials what is going on inside the minds of Saddam Hussein and his entourage or their successors.

Although the conflict over Kuwait began 2 August 1990, much of the relevant intelligence on the Iraqi military had been collected years earlier by the CIA and its military companion, the Defense Intelligence Agency (DIA). That early collection came about primarily because of the U.S. intelligence community's concern over military equipment supplied to Saddam Hussein by the Soviet Union and over French, German, South African, and Brazilian weapons that had reached Baghdad's polyglot army during the Iraq-Iran War.

That such information was vital to the allies' victory can be demonstrated by one example. The U.S. Patriot missile, which protected Saudi Arabia and kept Israel from entering the war by downing (for the most part) incoming Iraqi SCUD missiles, was the result of intelligence gathered early enough to allow the military to create a countercapability.

The high-technology intelligence collection effort was complemented by battlefield military reconnaissance carried out by small units of special forces. These long-range patrols spent days and nights clandestinely probing Iraqi strengths and weaknesses. They mapped out minefields, discovered crucial details about the Iraqi defense lines and bunkers, and determined the accuracy of enemy artillery fire.

As in all conflicts, however, intelligence was not perfect. The most serious failure was underestimating the number of Iraqi mobile SCUD launchers by a factor of at least five. The failure was important because it allowed Baghdad to fire more missiles at Israel, raising the chances that Israel would enter the war, possibly destroying the Euro-American and Arab coalition arrayed against Iraq.

The second major failing, according to the critics, was the inability to read correctly Saddam Hussein's intentions toward Kuwait until only a few days before the 2 August invasion, when the CIA and DIA, on the basis of Baghdad's military preparations and deployments, became certain Iraq would attack the emirate. Inability to discover intent is, of course, largely a matter of human source intelligence, the most difficult information to acquire in a strictly run police state such as Iraq. Espionage is always difficult to manage and nearly always requires a long period of time and investment of effort to penetrate the upper-echelon strategic thinking of a dictatorship.

The Gulf War of 1991 thus vividly demonstrates how crucial intelligence is to military success. The central intelligence system providing for the coordination of all intelligence activities under the authority of the director of central intelligence requires a mature national intelligence mechanism of which the military services and the theater commands are part. How this mechanism came about historically is the story that needs to be spelled out.

AMERICAN INTELLIGENCE IN THE EIGHTEENTH CENTURY

The American central intelligence system evolved over a long period of time and, notwithstanding many false starts and a few halts along the way, was the result of the not uncommon American view that intelligence is needed only in wartime. It is essential, therefore, to understand how recent and how belated the formation of the modern intelligence apparatus was and how long it took.

The Colonial Period. American intelligence contributed to the vital task of ensuring national survival even before the nation achieved its independence. At the center of this early effort fittingly was George Washington, who may also be called—among his other many achievements—the father of the American intelligence community. (It is ironic that only two presidents have worked as professional intelligence officers—Washington and George Bush—who served more than two centuries apart.)

Washington's experience in the collection of critical information began early as a young officer in the Virginia militia when the commonwealth was still an English colony. Washington's "case officer" was the acting governor, Robert Dinwiddie, a remarkably perspicacious man and a political leader whose instincts and judgment directed the intelligence mission—in retrospect, wisely so.

As governor of the largest and most important colony in the early 1760s, Dinwiddie greatly feared that French control of Canada and military infiltration into the Ohio and Mississippi valleys would confine the thirteen English colonies forever to the small strip of coastal plain east of the Alleghenies. In Dinwiddie's grimly prophetic words, the French and their Indian allies "would cramp them into perpetual littleness . . . while remaining in helpless wardship."

Like many other farsighted strategic thinkers, Dinwiddie was not believed—especially by the House of Burgesses, the colonial legislature, where his requests for increased defense spending in the Ohio Valley were rejected. The legislators—or at least some of them—understood the danger but did not wish to pay to meet it, at least at first. In utter frustration Dinwiddie wrote: "They had rather the French should conquer them than give up their privileges. Truly, . . . I think they give their senses a long holiday."

Frustration and failure, however, did not paralyze Dinwiddie entirely. To complement his approach to the legislators, the royal governor decided to authorize a clandestine intelligence collection mission led by the very young Washington. Posing as a surveyor and acting as a personal envoy of Governor Dinwiddie, the twenty-one-year-old major and adjutant general of the Virginia militia volunteered to explore the vast territories of the Ohio west of the Alleghenies (all claimed by the British Crown). His goal was to determine the size and location, as well as to sound out the intentions, of the recently arrived French military forces and to ascertain the number and identity of France's Indian allies and win them over (through bribery) if possible.

It was, to say the least, a hazardous mission threatened by suspicious French officials and filled with hairbreadth escapes from Indians, who had little use for English-speaking strangers. Washington, however, managed to pull it off, keeping a journal during the mission, which lasted for the better part of three months in the winter of 1753–1754—the first example of a strategic reconnaissance mission in American history.

Intelligence During the American Revolution.
Washington's experience with intelligence prior to the French and Indian War (which ended in an Anglo-American victory in 1763) would serve him in good stead as commander in chief of the Continental army during its struggle for American independence against the British twenty years later. Washington, in fact, during the Revolution was his own G-2 (intelligence officer). The American commander personally supervised the collection and analysis of information on British forces, both their capabilities and their intentions.

Washington also understood that because his forces were militarily inferior to the British (and remained so until victory at Yorktown), the American cause could never rely on bigger battalions but required better intelligence in order to survive and, finally, to prevail. Nevertheless, early patriot attempts at espionage, the short career of Nathan Hale being the prime example, were the work of amateurs, many of them brave, some talented; others not so.

Washington's chief needs were tactical. How strong were local British forces? What were their intentions? To answer these questions, he was able to set up separate (in fact, competing) spy networks in key cities, such as New York and Philadelphia. On occasions, whole families (among them the Darraghs of Philadelphia, who were Quakers and thus as pacifists had perfect cover) were employed to ferret out the information for the undermanned and undergunned Continental forces.

The networks were only part of Washington's bag of intelligence tricks. As historian Nathan Miller (1989) has observed:

> Spies, double agents, counterintelligence, covert operations, disinformation, propaganda, and codes and ciphers were all part of [Washington's] astonishingly contemporary tradecraft. He personally recruited agents, issued them instructions, and analyzed and acted upon their reports. Although this system added to his burdens as commander in chief, it made certain that—unlike later periods in the nation's history—intelligence received the prompt attention of those in authority.

On several occasions Washington's timely acting upon information provided—usually at great risk—saved the forces of the infant Republic from complete destruction. Once Washington's successful planting of false intelligence led the British General Sir William Howe to believe that the badly battered Continental army camped in the wilds of New Jersey was triple its actual size and in fine fettle, and thus immune to attack.

Washington did not run the only American intelligence system during the War for Independence. The Continental Congress and its Secret Committee contributed as well. Like the nation's commander, the committee was heavily involved in all phases of intelligence work. As Miller has observed: "The committee employed secret agents, conducted covert operations, engaged in gunrunning, originated codes and ciphers, established a courier system that included dispatch vessels, funded propaganda activities, and provided 'gratuities' for foreign officials whose influence it thought worth buying." Sometimes Congress and the commander in chief worked at cross-purposes in carrying out intelligence operations, and sometimes the inadequacies of the Congress in the intelligence field were glaringly apparent. For one thing, members of Congress were prone to talk too much about secret activity.

American intelligence was not confined to the New World. In fact, the fledgling Republic had a variety of agents in the major European capitals making their case for independence. Propaganda—the swaying of public opinion—was, of course, practiced, as was bribery of European officials thought useful and sympathetic to the cause. The objective, of course, was not only sympathy but actual support, and the greatest effort was made in France.

The Americans knew perfectly well the French abhorrence of the British, particularly after France's defeat in a series of worldwide conflicts known in the colonies as the French and Indian War. As a consequence, the Continental Congress dispatched its best-known and most influential citizen to Europe, Benjamin Franklin, who lobbied for years at the French court for assistance, which began to flow after the American victory at Saratoga in 1777. The aid (which would later include troops and ships) at first took the shape of a classic covert operation. The cautious Louis XVI, having been counseled (correctly) that another direct war with Great Britain might lead to political catastrophe, ordered French arms and ammunition to be transferred to Washington's armies through cut-outs—dummy companies that gave the king plausible deniability. It worked.

The totality of the American intelligence effort is, in retrospect, astonishing. Using nearly all the tools of the craft known in the eighteenth century, the revolutionaries, Washington in particular, fought a war as best they could—through irregular means and with heavy reliance on intelligence as the main resource for defeating the British. Their efforts and success are even more surprising because there was scant time to learn the trade, and they faced an adversary who was no stranger to intelligence. Indeed, the British Secret Service was extremely active and successful, particularly in the use of double agents who had access to, among other things, at least some of Franklin's operations in Paris.

The nation's founders were thoroughly aware of the importance of intelligence after independence was achieved in 1783. They also knew through bitter experience that the newborn United States had almost no intelligence capability after the war concluded, a perhaps fatal flaw for the weak, young Republic.

The Early National Years. What remained of the Continental forces was reduced to practically nothing. The nation's intelligence capability—setting a thoroughly American precedent—was largely disbanded under the new government set up under the Articles of Confederation. Scouting and mapping conducted by a tiny U.S. Army was all that was left. To make matters worse, the British never resigned themselves to losing the American colonies and maintained an extensive intelligence network based in, but hardly confined to, Canada.

The failure of the Articles, of course, inspired the effort to remake the Republic's basic institutions, among them the intelligence-gathering apparatus, at the Constitutional Convention of 1787. The importance of intelligence was made plain by John Jay, who had run counterintelligence operations in New York State. He argued in *Federalist Papers* No. 64 that intelligence collection would be enhanced if it were under the direction of the president rather than the Senate, much less "a larger popular assembly." Under the president, the security of the information and the informants was likely to be better. It was a view strongly shared by another *Federalist Papers* author, Alexander Hamilton, who also had a low regard for any legislative body's ability to keep a secret.

The drafters of the Constitution wisely abandoned the wartime and unworkable two-tier system of separate presidential and congressional intelligence networks and instead placed intelligence matters largely under the control of the president in his capacity as commander in chief. (One reason for doing so was the universal assumption that the trusted and experienced General Washington would be the nation's first chief executive.)

As president, Washington continued to play the intelligence role he had enjoyed as commander of the Continental forces. He wedded his presidential office with that of, in effect, the Republic's first director of intelligence—something that his successors would do with greater or lesser success for generations. Washington insisted on (and received from Congress) a secret fund, a "Contingent Fund of Foreign Intercourse," that would eventually absorb 12 percent of the federal budget, dwarfing the percentage of the federal budget allocated to the CIA during the cold war.

By Washington's third year in office, a secret fund of $1 million was made available to the president, and larger sums were made available to later presidents. Well into the twentieth century, they would have relatively ample and unvouchered sums from the discretionary Secret Service Fund. Thus, by law and tradition, presidents had ample money for "secret" activity that helped Dinwiddie's "strangled colonies" evolve into a powerful nation continent.

INTELLIGENCE IN THE NINETEENTH CENTURY

The presidential fund and its operations were hardly without flaws and failures. In the war of 1812, America's military reverses were matched only by the government's conspicuous lack of intelligence successes. Perhaps the most significant of these failures was a near-total ignorance of Canada and British military capabilities and intentions. The government lacked maps of the border region, which helps account for the utter fiasco of America's attempt to annex its northern neighbor.

The conduct of the Mexican War (1846–1848) was at best a mixed success when it came to the use of intelligence. The War Department, for example, had no capability to collect and analyze information, and maps of the Southwest were lacking or could not be retrieved because of a chaotic filing system. The actual conqueror of Mexico, General Winfield Scott, knew that

intelligence was vital if he was to enter Mexico City. He had formed a reconnaissance company made up of Mexican irregulars—a euphemistic term for bandits and smugglers—the kind of people the more fastidious General Zachary Taylor had refused to employ. As a result of the irregulars' contributions, Scott's march from Veracruz to the Mexican capital and his seizure of the city were made considerably easier and cost far less in human life.

The United States enjoyed other intelligence successes before the Civil War, although even these would take their share of strange bounces. The expedition of Captain Meriwether Lewis and Lieutenant William Clark of the U.S. Army (1804–1806) was planned as an almost wholly intelligence collection mission for President Thomas Jefferson. An echo of Washington's earlier trip to the West, Lewis and Clark's venture was to determine the size and location of Spanish and British military forces, as well as to locate possible sites for future American fortifications.

The covert nature of the mission is evident from the president's further instruction to conceal their identities and the purpose of their expedition. Lewis and Clark's cover story was that they were searching for the Northwest Passage, which would give eastern shore–based American commerce a shorter trip to the teeming markets of Asia. Only Spain's sudden transfer of the Louisiana territories to France and the quick U.S. acquisition (1803) of one million square miles of territory from a cash-starved Napoleon transformed the proposed intelligence mission to a successful and open voyage of exploration by Lewis and Clark. They managed to enter uninvited then British-held territory in the present-day Northwest region of the United States.

The Civil War. A review of American intelligence efforts throughout the nineteenth century reveals, on the whole, a rather unimpressive performance. The Civil War (1861–1865), in particular, vividly demonstrates the American penchant for inventing nearly out of whole cloth an intelligence system that begins as something close to hopeless amateurism and ends with a measure of professional capability—all of which is virtually abandoned once peace is achieved.

At the beginning of the conflict, neither the Union nor the Confederacy had an organized system of intelligence permitting the collection of even basic military information. Before the First Battle of Bull Run in July 1861, both North and South were abysmally ignorant of the other's capabilities. Nevertheless, and not surprisingly, the South which had fewer resources—in both personnel and matériel—moved more quickly in this field in order to compensate and to overcome its other weaknesses.

The core of southern intelligence assets came from Virginia, whose governor, John Letcher, foresaw the need for such an operation and therefore created an intelligence service, including a spy network in Washington and a special operations capability that among other things ran guns to secession-minded Marylanders. As the Confederacy's most populous state, Virginia would thus prove invaluable throughout the war.

The Confederacy was also helped by the fact that its president, Jefferson Davis, was already familiar with all phases of intelligence and its requirements. As a soldier in the Mexican War and as secretary of war in the Franklin Pierce administration, Davis had firsthand experience with American intelligence deficiencies in the prewar era and moved rapidly to overcome them in his capacity as president of the Confederacy. At the close of the war, there were signs that Davis understood the necessity of centralizing intelligence and was planning legislation to carry this task to completion—the first attempt to do so by any American government and not successfully done until after World War II.

Quite possibly the best-known, if hardly the most successful, Union intelligence operator was Chicago detective Allan Pinkerton, whose great claim to fame was protecting Abraham Lincoln on his way from Illinois to his presidential inauguration in March 1861. Pinkerton's capabilities at counterintelligence—tracking down southern spies, especially in Washington—was his other great contribution to the Union's intelligence effort. He was also able to slip northern agents into Richmond, the capital of the Confederacy. Counterintelligence work suited Pinkerton because of his own background and experience, and he played a leading role in the investigation and arrest of Rose Greenhow, the South's best-known spy in Washington.

Pinkerton's efforts at positive intelligence, particularly its analysis, were considerably less apparent. Working for the cautious General George McClellan, commander of the Army of the Potomac in 1862, Pinkerton consistently exaggerated southern military strength, often doubling the size of Lee's forces—a strategic misjudgment that made McClellan even less willing to confront the enemy, which greatly frustrated President Lincoln. Pinkerton's importance in Union intelligence ended with McClellan's career.

Lincoln, however, was no Davis when it came to overseeing intelligence operations. Although Lincoln followed the war news carefully and was thoroughly involved in the making of military decisions, there is little evidence that the president immersed himself in intelligence matters as did his counterpart in Richmond. This may help explain in part the rampant confusion among the North's various intelligence arms, especially in the first three years of the war. The rivalry between at least two secret services was so intense that each one's agents were known to have arrested agents from the other service.

The North remained woefully lacking for positive intelligence until the Bureau of Military Intelligence was formed in 1863 under the leadership of Colonel George H. Sharpe, who can best be called an inspired amateur. Nevertheless, by war's end, Sharpe's bureau had become a formidable collector of military intelligence. In addition, Sharpe's lavish use of balloons (something the Confederacy also employed, but not as much) was a technical innovation that marked the beginning of aerial reconnaissance.

Despite steady improvements in intelligence gathering throughout the war, however, neither the North nor the South ever really put together a thoroughly professional intelligence system that could collect and analyze information, while at the same time running carefully crafted special operations. Indeed, in some ways their work remained totally that of amateurs. For example, the Union and the Confederacy employed relatively simple codes and ciphers that were easily read by both sides. Anything put on paper and intercepted would be known almost instantly to the other, and this remained the case until the surrender at Appomattox. However deficient the collective American intelligence effort was during the Civil War, that effort came to an end with the South's surrender. The nation, absorbed in the task of internal rebuilding, virtually forgot the need to obtain and analyze intelligence, and its limited intelligence capability withered.

The Post–Civil War Years. The most notable intelligence advances in the years after the Civil War were the founding of the Office of Naval Intelligence (ONI) in 1882, paralleled by the beginning of the construction of the modern U.S. Navy, and the establishment of the army's Bureau of Military Intelligence (later the Military Information Division, or MID) three years later. Army attachés were subsequently posted to all the major European capitals.

Thus, the Spanish-American War of 1898 did not catch the U.S. armed forces completely without an intelligence capability. There was, however, much anxiety at the time over the exact location of the Spanish Atlantic fleet, of which U.S. officials were entirely unaware—a grim foreshadowing of what would happen forty-three years later with a different adversary in another ocean. Still, the navy managed to assemble networks of informants on Spanish capabilities in Europe, Asia, and the Caribbean. These networks, characteristically, were abandoned shortly after the war. The army went even further. It abolished its intelligence arm altogether in 1908 by turning it over to the Army War College, where it became a document and map library for officers interested in research.

TWENTIETH-CENTURY INTELLIGENCE TO WORLD WAR II

Lack of foresight left the United States ill-prepared for the swirling and dangerous currents of the twentieth century. On the eve of U.S. involvement in World War I, the United States had almost no intelligence capability. Its naval and army attaché service, for example, had been cut to the bone. A close cooperative relationship developed, however, between the British intelligence services and the U.S. Army's revived intelligence department, the MID, which had limited capabilities. As would happen during the early stages of World War II, the British taught the basics of the intelligence craft to the inexperienced and ill-equipped Americans.

The primitiveness of U.S. intelligence capabilities at the beginning of World War I is vividly demonstrated by the fact that the Germans were able to read the U.S. War Department's code with little difficulty. The discovery of that fact not only prompted a more serious effort at codes and ciphers but inspired the first serious effort at codebreaking, or cryptographic analysis. On 20 May 1919, Herbert Yardley, a State Department code clerk, founded the Black Chamber, a secret organization funded jointly by the State and War departments. He engaged fifty cipher experts, who deciphered Japanese messages in 1921–1922. Japan's complex codes were especially important because decrypting them gave U.S. diplomats knowledge of the Japanese fallback position during the Washington Naval Conference talks of 1921. U.S. officials knew that Tokyo's representatives would not leave the negotiating table—despite threats to do so—if the United States and Great Britain insisted on a 10:10:6 ratio for capital ships. Despite this major success, and with President Herbert Hoover's concurrence, the State Department withdrew its funding of the Black Chamber eight years later.

The U.S. penchant for unilateral disarmament in the intelligence field is well illustrated by the fate of the Black Chamber. In this particular case, the reason for the dismemberment of the decoding operation was not only budgetary but also moral. President Hoover's secretary of state, Henry M. Stimson believed that breaking codes—reading other people's mail—was morally objectionable.

Cryptanalysis, however, did go on. In 1930 army intelligence picked up the pieces and formed a new service within the Signal Corps, although Yardley himself went into retirement and wrote a best-selling book, *The American Black Chamber* (1931), about his life's work—to the vast discomfort of U.S. officials, Stimson in particular, and to the delight and consternation of foreign governments. Yardley's work was soon translated into a number of languages, including Japanese.

From an intelligence perspective, Yardley's book was a disaster. Many foreign leaders had simply assumed their codes and ciphers were immune to primitive and low-cost American snooping. After the former code clerk's revelations, however, foreign intelligence services quickly adopted new codes and, more important, stimulated the development of entirely new systems of encryption, making decoding vastly more difficult.

As a result of all these reverses, the United States was in an extraordinarily poor position when it came to even the rudiments of intelligence. What had been painfully learned and acquired during World War I and in the 1920s deteriorated and atrophied in what seemed to be peacetime to isolationist America.

The nation's fragmented and ineffective intelligence operation disturbed President Franklin D. Roosevelt, and in June 1939 he signed a classified executive order that attempted to resolve the endless battling for turf. Intelligence operations would be divided between the Federal Bureau of Investigation (FBI), the army's MID, and the navy's ONI. Roosevelt also authorized the FBI—at J. Edgar Hoover's insistence—to track German and Italian agents in Latin America. Some successes were scored. Not surprisingly, most of them occurred in the realm of code-breaking. Thanks to the War Department and the navy, the United States was not totally bereft of intelligence, even if it did not act upon that information in timely fashion.

Much of the new money appropriated for the prewar U.S. intelligence community in the late 1930s was wisely spent on a chain of radio intercept stations that recorded the coded messages foreign governments were communicating to their military and intelligence forces.

The War Department's super-secret Signal Intelligence Service (SIS), under the direction of the brilliant but erratic William F. Friedman, was especially busy. Friedman set a pattern at the SIS that the future U.S. intelligence community would follow. America's premier codebreaker, Friedman recruited a band of scholars—mathematicians, logicians, and experts in linguistics—to assist him in the work. Friedman's greatest achievement—one that remains a world-class intelligence coup—was breaking the Japanese Foreign Office's Purple Code. That code, like the German Enigma, depended upon a machine to generate nearly infinite and ever-changing codes and ciphers (although the principal of construction of the two was quite different). By the summer of 1940, a few months after France fell to the Germans, the Friedman team had been able to reproduce (roughly) the Purple machine after a mind-numbing effort at reconstruction.

While Friedman labored over the exotic Purple Code, U.S. Navy cryptanalysts for once coordinated their work with the army by concentrating on other codes while helping build additional Purple machines. Even more useful, the navy built intercept stations in the Pacific and provided the raw Japanese traffic to Friedman's scholarly codebreakers. Their end product, decrypted diplomatic messages, became collectively known as MAGIC—and magic it surely was, because the Japanese continued to believe throughout the entire war that their codes were invulnerable and invincible. Not surprisingly, the MAGIC product was a closely held secret, with only a handful of top officials knowing its contents.

Prewar MAGIC had other problems. Nowhere, for example, in the federal government was the product systematically analyzed. Instead, a few top officials saw the messages without being provided any context, leaving them to puzzle out the significance, if any, of each message. Consequently, no patterns, other than the ones inferred by the individual consumer, were detected. Worse, even Roosevelt did not retain any copies of the MAGIC material. Neither the army nor the navy trusted Roosevelt's civilian advisers, Harry Hopkins in particular. Although utmost security precautions were appropriate to prevent the secret getting around that the United States had broken the German and Japanese codes and ciphers, it would also have been appropriate to tell the president and his closest advisers the in-depth meaning of the material they were being provided. It was strictly a matter of eyes-only for the president and a few key policy advisers, but once they had seen the intercepted messages, the messages would then disappear into a military archival black hole. The lack of systematic analysis of the meaning of these transmissions was a failure that left decision-makers unable to exploit this rich intelligence material.

WORLD WAR II: A NEW INTELLIGENCE ERA

Despite the government's successes in codebreaking, President Roosevelt knew it was not enough as the country edged closer to war. William J. Donovan, a staunch Republican lawyer with a taste for adventure and called "Wild Bill," was also a friend and admirer of the president. He waited impatiently in the wings to play a role in U.S. intelligence, and eventually had a key role in creating the concept of centralized intelligence tasks and procedures.

Donovan, a World War I hero, had long urged the creation of a new clandestine service that would be prepared to battle the Germans when the time came. He had been encouraged by the British, whose intelligence services had already briefed him on their activities through the British representative in the United States, William Stephenson. Donovan's notion of a superagency predictably drew the fire of nearly every intelligence arm of the U.S. government. Hoover and the FBI were adamantly opposed, as were navy and army intelligence. The latter was led by General George V. Strong of the MID, who nearly made a career of opposition to Donovan and his ideas on centralizing intelligence.

Roosevelt, however, had other ideas. With the German armies sweeping onto the broad Russian plains in the early summer of 1941, the president on 11 July created the innocuous sounding Office of the Coordinator of Information (COI), with Wild Bill Donovan as its chief. The COI was not much at first, only a bureaucratic orphan, but Donovan was no shrinking violet. He knew the president was determined to be prepared for war when it came to intelligence—at least as much as Congress and the public would allow.

Donovan's first (and correct) priority was recruiting the brains of the new organization; the brawn would come later. He drew on America's elite schools, an idea borrowed from the British. Scholars from Harvard and Yale Universities and Williams College, to mention only a few, were recruited to go about the business of forming America's first-ever strategic analysis capability, a wedding of spies and scholars.

According to historian Miller, the speed of the buildup was astonishing. The COI staff mushroomed to more than six hundred people and occupied space all over Washington, and in New York as well. "And that was merely the beginning," according to Miller. "Donovan was aiming at a staff of 1,300 and a $14 million budget."

The COI was not popular with the entrenched powers outside the White House, and Donovan would lose his share of early battles. The COI (and its successor) was kept out of Latin America by Hoover, and Donovan also lost control of his foreign radio propaganda service, which became the Office of War Information (OWI).

Nevertheless, the COI and its follow-on, the Office of Strategic Services (OSS), created in June 1942, laid the foundation for a modern intelligence collection and analysis system for use in peacetime as well as in war. The central driving objective was to ensure that the United States would never again be caught by surprise as it was by the August 1939 Soviet-German rapprochement, which led to the occupation of Poland and the outbreak of war in Europe, as well as, of course, by the extraordinary disaster of Pearl Harbor in December 1941. Not only did intelligence have to be collected, it needed to flow to one focal point where it could be analyzed and then given to proper civilian and military authorities for use in making well-considered decisions. The concept of central intelligence was, in short, the legacy of hostilities in Europe and the attack on Pearl Harbor.

The Beginnings of a Centralized Intelligence Service.

Creating a centralized intelligence system was an enormous achievement. Nevertheless, it drew much criticism from conservatives and liberals alike who argued (and still argue) against the need for such a system, especially in times of peace.

When Germany invaded hapless Poland in 1939, the U.S. armed forces numbered 190,000 in both the army and the navy. The defense budget was less than $2 billion, most of which was spent on capital ships and warplanes that still could not match those of any of the major powers, including technologically primitive Japan.

The intelligence community consisted of barely more than a thousand people, 750 of them low-paid technicians involved in radio interception, the single success of the U.S. prewar intelligence effort. The army's MID in 1939, for example, had twenty-two officers. That number expanded to five hundred by the time of Pearl Harbor, but few of the new men had much basic intelligence experience. The navy's ONI was only marginally better off. Most naval officers avoided intelligence duty, preferring sea duty, which led to more rapid promotion. As a result, by mid-1941 the navy, the favored service in terms of both budget and high-level attention, had 150 officers and civilian analysts attached to naval intelligence, the bulk of them in Washington, D.C. Compounding the problems, the ONI had three chiefs in 1941, none of whom was eager to serve in that post. Like the army's leaden MID, the ONI concentrated on counterintelligence, that is, the prevention of sabotage to its ships and facilities. It was expressly forbidden to engage in any overall analysis of naval threats to U.S. security.

The paucity of numbers performing even basic intelligence duties in prewar America was matched by the equally important lack of an integrated central system of intelligence collection and analysis. Moreover, there was no sense of common mission, and each unit went its own separate way in near-total ignorance of what the others were doing. As a result, positive intelligence capability added up to very little in 1939, except in codebreaking—and even that was not properly exploited.

The FBI, according to Hoover, had been in the counterespionage business since 1936 and thus claimed *primus inter parus*, although its budget for such activity was absurdly small—$50,000 in 1938. Hoover asked Roosevelt for permission to create a special intelligence service that could conduct operations worldwide. Instead, Hoover's FBI got Latin America, the navy was given the Pacific, and the army was assigned the rest of the world, including the Panama Canal.

The military services did make one feeble prewar effort at coordination. The seed was the Joint Army-Navy Board, which had existed in limbo for years. Roosevelt ordered it to life in 1939, but for two years it remained a committee making interservice recommendations on munitions procurement and aviation development, rather than a general staff in being.

Nevertheless, by October 1941, General George C. Marshall, chief of staff of the army, and Admiral Harold R. Stark, chief of naval operations, ordered the establishment of the Joint Intelligence Committee (JIC) to serve as a central intelligence group serving the Joint Board. What the senior officers envisioned—a meshing of the best of the MID and the ONI—did not happen, however. For weeks, Army G-2 and naval intelligence wrangled over procedures and office space; and as a result, the first JIC meeting, a sterile affair, took place four days before Japanese bombs and torpedoes fell on the U.S. Pacific fleet, anchored peacefully off Ford's Island, Pearl Harbor.

As for the State Department, its foreign service officers were poorly prepared to act as any kind of intelligence arm. In fact, the department had no clandestine collection capability whatsoever. There was one exception. In November 1940, while Great Britain was barely surviving the German aerial onslaught, the department formed the Division of Foreign Activity Correlation. It was a polysyllabic term for a small intelligence section, consisting of eighteen people in 1943, that simply collected information on foreign leaders from any source at hand.

Overall, it was an amateur system that depended entirely on the judgment of the foreign service officers, who varied wildly in quality. A few were outstanding, for example, George Kennan and Charles "Chip" Bohlen. None of them thought of themselves as professional intelligence officers—that would have been unseemly. That such a separate profession should exist within the sacred temple grounds of diplomacy was viewed by many as profane. It comes then as no surprise that departmental diplomatic reports were often limited and that senior officials in Washington were better informed if they read those few of America's newspapers that took any interest in foreign affairs or listened to the new breed of radio correspondents who were now broadcasting from major European capitals.

Related to the work of such foreign correspondents as Edward R. Murrow, Harry K. Smith, and William Shirer was a single, wholly new intelligence service that had been created even before Donovan's COI. The Federal Broadcast Monitoring Service had been established in February 1941 by the Federal Communications Commission at the request of the State Department. This agency, later called the Federal Broadcasting Information Service (FBIS), moni-

tored, translated, and distributed texts of significant foreign broadcasts and newspaper and journal articles. Within a year, the fledgling agency coordinated its worldwide work with the British BBC, which performed a similar service. During the war, the monitoring service became a joint Anglo-American enterprise, with the governments literally dividing the world and publishing a joint document. Although controversial in prewar, see-no-evil, isolationist America, the FBIS remains the longest running intelligence operation in existence.

The U.S. intelligence community as it existed in 1939 was fragmented. It lacked a common data base and provided no centralized evaluation of foreign events. Top U.S. officials were frustrated or merely left in the dark as the world went to war.

The Coordinator of Information and the Office of Strategic Services.
To remedy an untenable situation, Roosevelt, after several false starts and half-starts, created the COI in July 1941. The presidential directive was recorded in the *Federal Register* of 11 July 1941, making the COI a legal reality. It created the position of Coordinator of Information who had the authority:

> To collect and analyze all information and data which may bear upon national security; to correlate such information and data, and to make such information available and data available to the President and to such departments and officials of the Government as the President may determine; and to carry out, when requested by the President, such supplementary activities as may facilitate the securing of information important for national security not now available to the Government.

The directive's key words—"collect," "analyze," and "correlate"—were to be the core of the modern U.S. intelligence system. The order also set the stage for an "all-source" intelligence that would come from "open" (published) sources, diplomatic reports, military reporting by attachés, espionage, and behind-the-lines intelligence. After a long turf battle, the COI and

OSS were denied access to intercepted signals and codebreaking data, but otherwise they were, at one level or another, getting most of the information needed for systematic analysis of foreign situations.

The concept of an all-encompassing intelligence agency would animate Donovan. As written, the directive outlined the critical role of central evaluation and analysis along with the need for coordination among the government's disparate intelligence arms. "Supplementary activities," in addition, became an intended euphemism for covert actions. The drafters of the order also invented the term "national security" and used it for the first time in a presidential document. More important for the successor organizations, the OSS and the Central Intelligence Agency (CIA), Roosevelt's directive gave the COI independence from any cabinet-rank department. On the other hand, it did not give Coordinator Donovan the ability to issue orders to other agencies.

Despite Donovan's penchant for foreign travel and his disdain for managerial humdrum, he placed high priority on personally recruiting academic talent. Within a few months, Donovan had assembled an astonishing group with wide-ranging foreign expertise that completely outclassed the staff at the hidebound State Department. The scholars (eventually there would be two thousand of them) worked immediately from the all-source framework of research and analysis. The bulk of their work, especially at first, was done in the Library of Congress (LOC), whose doors were open to the COI thanks to Donovan's friendship with LOC librarian Archibald MacLeish.

The Research and Analysis Division of the COI soon was issuing a steady stream of secret reports on a wide variety of subjects. Because Germany was perceived to be the main enemy, it is not surprising that that nation would be the focus of the effort. William Langer, a Harvard professor of history and a distinguished expert on nineteenth-century Germany, became chief of research.

The work of the COI, however, did not impress everyone. The State Department in partic-

ular resisted the idea that systematic research was vital for good policymaking. Nevertheless, Sumner Welles, then undersecretary of state, reached an agreement with Donovan in August 1941 conceding to the COI the responsibility for the clandestine collection of economic and related data overseas. Moreover, the COI would supply reports and studies on foreign countries of interest to the department—but not in Latin America, where Hoover insisted on the FBI's preeminence, as did Nelson Rockefeller, then the coordinator of inter-American affairs, a satrapy only loosely controlled by the State Department.

It took several months of arduous negotiations by Donovan and skillful manipulation of the civilian secretaries of the navy and war—Frank Knox and Stimson, respectively—before the COI coordinator got what he wanted—the privilege of monopolizing clandestine intelligence collection.

Donovan's target was French North Africa. The Vichy regime still maintained control of the area in 1940 and 1941, and, before its entry into the war, the United States maintained diplomatic relations with unoccupied France. Donovan placed twelve of his agents in North Africa in June 1941 under diplomatic cover. For the first time in the twentieth century at least, Americans, posing as vice consuls, were gathering information as best they could, using the time-honored methods of the spy. The information gathered, incidentally, was shared with the British, who had no access to the area. Indeed, the intelligence provided was largely in response to British tasking.

For the most part, the U.S. Army and U.S. Navy welcomed the flow of intelligence from North Africa, but State Department officials were deeply uneasy about the use of the department as a cover for espionage. Foreign service officers not in the know also bitterly complained about the new vice consuls' seeming lack of interest in their work, as well as their questionable professional backgrounds. The success of the North African mission, however, gave Donovan the clout to win permanently the right to oversee clandestine intelligence collection. This right was something that the COI's successors, the OSS and then the CIA, would zealously preserve.

Donovan had now taken control of the two principal intelligence activities—clandestine collection and intelligence analysis. His hard-won victories in the Washington turf war were preserved in Roosevelt's military order dated 13 June 1942, which created the Office of Strategic Services. Collecting and analyzing strategic information were to be functions of the OSS, as was the planning and operation of "special services."

It was only a beginning, but Donovan laid down a foundation that has been preserved ever since. In a March 1942 memorandum, Donovan told the president that it was necessary to convert his agency into a quasi-military organization reporting to the Joint Chiefs of Staff (JCS), as well as to the president. In saying this, Donovan was simply reflecting wartime reality. Everything would be directed to the war effort whether anyone liked it or not, and Donovan's new intelligence outfit was obliged to conform. The U.S. intelligence community, like all other functions associated with the war effort, simply plunged ahead, expanding rapidly without regard to the costs. From a few hundred staffers at the COI, laboring in a ragtag warren of separate offices, the wartime Office of Strategic Services grew to no fewer than thirteen thousand people by the end of the war.

The unknowns it faced were largely the result of Donovan's enthusiasm for irregular warfare. The OSS would not only research, analyze, and steal information, it would blow things up as well. Even before the war, Donovan had had very much in mind irregular paramilitary operations behind enemy lines. Great Britain's Special Operations Executive (SOE) served as the model. Pearl Harbor reinforced Donovan's belief that his agency could be effective (and useful to the JCS) only if it had a paramilitary arm. This idea also suited Donovan's penchant for action, to the chagrin of his analysts, because, although Donovan constantly bragged about his "professors," he had less and less time for them.

Despite the sometimes sloppy, sometimes chaotic nature of the operation, the Office of Strategic Services and its military counterparts at their height became the working model for the U.S. postwar intelligence community, which was shaped with the help of many of the old hands on the basis of what they had learned and experienced firsthand during World War II. For the most part, the OSS worked closely with the military organizations deployed in combat theaters, sharing intelligence.

The OSS had two major branches—intelligence and special operations. The broad area of intelligence, the first major branch or analytic arm, had five component parts. The oldest and "senior" service was research and analysis which itself was divided into several parts. R&A, with its two thousand scholars and analysts, turned out often lengthy economic and political reports on countries of interest to the researchers, if not always to the officials they were supposed to be serving.

Within R&A's jurisdiction fell current intelligence (CI) with a small staff of editors who goaded the R&A professors to write shorter, snappier pieces each day on recent trends and developments, summaries that CI personnel thought needed to be seen by the president or the JCS. In addition, CI contributed to a weekly summary prepared by the military's Joint Intelligence Command (JIC)—the nearest thing to an interagency intelligence report ever done to that date. This summary gave busy top officials a sense of proportion as well as of the flow of events in a world at war. The greatest deficiency of analysis in the OSS was that R&A was never a true all-source information unit. Not only did the State Department keep its secrets, but others did, too. Signals intelligence, for example, was never a part of either OSS or JIC reporting. This failure was the single most serious, in fact, crucial, limitation of all OSS intelligence reporting.

Nor was that the end of the problem. Even the OSS's own clandestine secret intelligence (SI), the second branch of intelligence, proved remarkably uncommunicative when it came to sharing with other divisions information it had obtained around the world, some of it from special operations (SO) groups working behind enemy lines.

Occasionally, the SI material was genuinely sensational. Its reporting on the various plots against the life of Adolph Hitler, including the July 1944 attempt, was passed along to Washington and London. (Incidentally, the Fuhrer knew nothing about the plot until the assassination effort actually occurred and only by accident failed to kill him because he happened to move away from the briefcase satchel charge placed at his side.) Much of the SI information came from the OSS/SI's listening post in Berne, Switzerland, which was presided over by Allen Dulles. One of his agents, Hans Gisevius, a German intelligence official, saw virtually everything produced by the Third Reich's many and often competing intelligence services. Gisevius, a devout Christian and an ardent anti-Nazi, risked his life to pass along the most important of these documents and proved once again that one well-situated and dedicated agent in place is worth a thousand routine spies. By 1944 the SI net had spread around the world, and its agent handlers, supported by plenty of money, had little difficulty in recruiting foreigners. It was, by far, the largest U.S. espionage network ever to operate abroad.

The third branch of OSS intelligence was X-2, the deliberately mysteriously named counterintelligence/counterespionage arm of Donovan's empire. The heart of X-2 was a basic namecheck file of dossiers on all persons who had been reported by anyone to be involved in espionage. Accumulated with the help of British and other friendly agencies, the card files would be inherited by the OSS's successors and later converted into computer bank information.

Continuity and comprehensiveness is the mark of useful counterintelligence data. Gathering these data was and still is labor-intensive, which is why seven hundred employees were hired for X-2, including James Jesus Angleton, who became, in his long career in the OSS and the CIA, America's best-known, if not best-loved, counterintelligence officer.

A fourth element that figured prominently in the OSS's organization chart was the Foreign Nationalities Branch, an OSS innovation in the intelligence field that was continued under the CIA. The Foreign Nationalities Branch oversaw the overt collection of useful data about foreign areas provided voluntarily by Americans and foreigners who had firsthand knowledge of the area and intelligence subject that OSS officials wanted to know more about. The only guarantee given these sources was a commitment to protect their anonymity. Thus, journalists, businesspeople, academics, and travelers often became prime sources of information. The Foreign Nationalities Branch and its product, often overlooked by intelligence historians, in fact was an invaluable source of information that would have been otherwise difficult or impossible to obtain, especially in wartime in the occupied areas.

The fifth and final division of the intelligence analytic arm was the support unit censorship and documents (C&D), but cover and documents is a more precise two-word description of its activities. C&D was a technical services department. It provided the forged papers and all other identifying material needed by agents for their cover in denied areas. C&D also supplied disguises, concealed electronic listening devices, and even laboratory analysis of poisons that might be used by agents in extreme danger or that could be used by enemy intelligence agencies against Americans. It worked closely with the Office of Research and Development, which produced surreptitious weapons for subversive warfare and self-protection by agents.

The OSS's special operations (SO) division, the second major branch of the service, was the action arm to which Donovan gave his personal attention throughout the war. The SO was intended to be a near-exact duplicate of the British SOE. Indeed, the SO's personnel were trained by the British organization in the earliest part of U.S. involvement in the war. Special operations teams, for the most part, were small, often three to five men (and sometimes women). Invariably they parachuted into hostile territory at night and established contact with local partisan forces while maintaining secret radio communications with U.S. support bases and OSS headquarters. Their principal job was to arrange drops of military supplies for the arms-starved guerrilla units.

A spin-off of the SO was formed at the end of 1944. This new service, the Operational Group Command (OG), trained and deployed commando groups of thirty to forty men who fought alongside resistance forces in Europe. The OGs were especially important in Italy and France as German forces retreated back into Germany. Their use in actual combat, rather than in liaison and supply, distinguished the OGs from the SO teams; their specialty was the sabotage of German transport.

The elite of the SOs were the joint British-American JEDBURGH teams that parachuted into occupied Europe. The "Jeds," which were the personal pride of Donovan, usually included a French agent. They carried out the most difficult and dangerous of the European missions. The best-known survivor of the Jed drops—there were not many—was William Colby (later director of central intelligence), who after being in France later took an OG into Norway in March of 1945.

Liberating Europe was a big task, but the SO teams and the OGs were fairly small, totaling about fifteen hundred. They soon established, however, a reputation for dash, vigor, and courage, accomplishing perhaps their most difficult mission of all—winning the respect of the regular U.S. armed forces. Indeed, their contribution helped create the best-known part of the OSS legend, which—for all its romantic distortion—made it possible for the U.S. intelligence tradition to be continued after the war.

The most enduring achievement of all this clandestine activity, however, was the right to have independent coded communications connecting headquarters, secure from the enemy as well as from other U.S. agencies, with all its field units. Not all covert operations were successful; it is in the nature of such actions that they are risky and difficult to pull off. A good number of operations, particularly in the Balkans and in Eastern Europe, were bloody fail-

ures. Repeated OSS missions into Czechoslovakia to help the partisans in that country were near-total failures and cost many lives. These operations were, according to one history of the OSS, "ill-conceived and poorly planned" (Hymoff, 1986).

In China, matters were not much better. The OSS—and other services, the navy in particular—were always at dagger's point with their Nationalist Chinese counterparts. Obtaining objective information and analysis proved impossible. The seventeen-man Dixie Mission, a joint American political-military observer group that established liaison with the Chinese Communists in Yenan, was also a failure. The five-man OSS detachment and its work within the Dixie Mission, according to its leader, Colonel David Barrett, remained a mystery even to him. Next to nothing was learned of the Chinese Communist leadership or its intentions.

Overall, the OSS left behind it a myriad of problems as well as successes. Clearly the public legacy greatly exaggerated the benefits of covert paramilitary operations and encouraged the kind of confidence in such operations that led later presidents into disasters, such as President John F. Kennedy and the Bay of Pigs operation (1961). The most lasting legacy of the OSS, however, was Donovan's belief that intellectually well-prepared men and women could carry out valuable research and analysis that, in turn, would provide information that was relevant to policy.

Although Donovan wanted his agency to live on after the war as a central intelligence service, it was not to be. Other officials reasoned that the coming of peace meant the United States no longer needed an intelligence action arm. The need for intelligence was simply overlooked or minimized. As a consequence, President Harry Truman, who had no experience with intelligence, abolished the OSS on 1 October 1945. A critical factor in the president's quick decision was the Bureau of the Budget and its head, Harold D. Smith, who recommended the immediate disbanding of the OSS. The tidy Smith had long resented Donovan's casual approach to funding and personnel. The disappearance of the OSS thus also represented the revenge of the accountants.

The OSS clandestine services were abolished and its assets absorbed by the army's newly formed Strategic Services Unit (SSU). The SI and X-2, as well as the rapidly demobilizing OSS paramilitary branches, disappeared into the SSU, where they survived but were administratively left in limbo. Despite Donovan's warning to President Roosevelt that "this talent should not be dispersed," it was in fact dispersed. The army absorbed the operational elements of the OSS with a view to closing them down.

The research and analysis branch was assigned to the State Department, which did not really want it or know what to do with it for a long time, and relatively few scholars from the OSS actually stayed on. The State Department in its own quiet way took a while before reorganizing and expanding the OSS unit into the present-day Bureau of Intelligence and Research (INR).

Although Donovan failed to preserve a peacetime OSS, he had, at Roosevelt's request, outlined what a peacetime intelligence service might look like in a memorandum dated November 1944. This proposal was the culmination of Donovan's wartime experience, and three years later it became the blueprint for the new Central Intelligence Agency, created under the National Security Act of 1947.

Donovan recommended the new service be established in the Executive Office of the President and headed by a director appointed by the president. No longer dependent on the military or any cabinet officer, the new chief of intelligence would be authorized "to call upon Departments and agencies of the Government to furnish appropriate specialists for such supervisory and functional functions . . . as may be required." The director, as conceived by Donovan, could also direct departments and agencies to make available—with the president's consent—any intelligence material requested. America's diverse and separate intelli-

gence services would no longer squirrel away information and leave it unshared with a central service.

The unnamed agency would also coordinate the functions of all the government's intelligence agencies and integrate the nation's intelligence efforts. The collection of intelligence would be done either directly by the new agency or through the existing services. Final evaluation of all intelligence would be done by the new unit, which would also carry out "other functions" relating to intelligence as the president directed—in other words, clandestine collecting and covert activities. Donovan also made clear that the new service would have "no police or law enforcement functions, either at home or abroad," a recommendation that forestalled objections from the ever-vigilant FBI and prevented comparisons with the Soviet secret police, the NKVD/KGB.

Donovan was prescient, but, after the death of Roosevelt in April 1945, he was in no position to get his wishes, and he was not helped by his rivals. Roosevelt had sent Donovan's memorandum to the JCS and the State Department for their comments, and the general bureaucratic reaction was one hostile to the idea of a new agency with direct responsibility to the president and a strong coordinating role. The JCS and State reactions, however, were gentlemanly compared to that of the FBI's Hoover, who still harbored hopes that the bureau would become America's postwar worldwide intelligence agency. His bitter opposition to Donovan's idea was a foregone conclusion, but his leaking of Donovan's plan in February 1945 to Walter Trohan, a journalist at the *Chicago Tribune*, was an underhanded political move to torpedo the idea of central intelligence. In a series of articles, Trohan blasted the postwar agency as a New Deal superspy organization that would "pry into the lives of citizens at home," a veritable American Gestapo.

The public reaction caused Roosevelt to shelve the plan for several critical months. A week before his death, however, the president asked Donovan to obtain agreement within the wartime intelligence community on the establishment of a central intelligence service. Donovan failed. With Roosevelt's death, the hope for a genuine central intelligence service was postponed for two critical years.

BETWEEN THE OSS AND THE CIA

Although the OSS was abolished in 1945, a complete intelligence vacuum did not develop. As President Harry Truman became familiar with his global responsibilities and realized the futility of his naive hope that the State Department would handle peacetime foreign intelligence, he began to change his mind about the need for an intelligence operation in peacetime. By late 1945 it had become apparent that a return to the prewar fumbling was not at all desirable. Still, the various services retained their fierce independence and jealously guarded their intelligence perks and privileges. Nevertheless, it was not entirely business as usual.

The U.S. Navy, for one, put forward a postwar intelligence plan seeking a central entity powerful enough to prevent any other agency (the army's G-2, in particular) from dominating every other service (especially the ONI) but weak enough to present no threat to the navy's control of its own affairs. Merger of existing intelligence services in one command was out of the question for the navy, which argued that each department required intelligence peculiar to itself. The navy's notion of a central intelligence service also included the novel suggestion that it should report to a new institution—the National Security Council.

After further refinements by the JCS and its Joint Intelligence Staff, the JCS sent a recommendation to the President in January 1946 that led to the creation of an entirely new intelligence service to be jointly funded and staffed by the departments of state, war, and navy. Called the Central Intelligence Group, the CIG was to be supervised by the new National Intelligence Authority (NIA), composed of the secretaries of war, state, and the navy, plus the president's personal representative. The NIA was in effect a proto-National Security Council (the NSC itself would be created a little more than a year later), but the NIA lacked the president's direct authority, leaving the cabinet mandarins more interested in protecting their own services than in managing the CIG.

The CIG resembled the old COI, minus Donovan, and merely continued the American penchant for reinventing the intelligence wheel. Like the COI, the CIG staff was drawn from the other services, primarily the military, and it was supposed to be small, originally limited to eighty officers. Unlike the COI appropriations, however, CIG funds were to come entirely from other departments. The CIG was also expected to reassemble the OSS analysts, who would, in turn, process intelligence supplied by the other agencies and forward the information to the president.

The CIG lacked both stature and independence in other ways. For example, the group's chiefs were never civilian, but in fact the positions on the NIA became short-term military assignments for flag-rank officers. The top slot, director of the NIA, was to be rotated, in JCS fashion, among the services. Rear Admiral Sidney Souers, a trusted confidant of President Truman, was the first director of the CIG, but he stayed only six months and then moved into the White House to become Truman's adviser on intelligence and national security.

The next man to get the nod was air force Lieutenant General Hoyt Vandenberg, an ambitious officer with good political connections; his uncle was Senator Arthur Vandenberg, one of the architects of U.S. postwar bipartisan foreign policy. The new NIA director's chief purpose, like that of Donovan before him, was to expand the total personnel strength, which he successfully did in short order. Vandenberg created a COI/OSS-style research and analysis division, called the Office of Reports and Estimates (ORE), which after August 1946 began to put out a current intelligence daily summary for the president. The CIG, however, did not and could not coordinate either intelligence activities or intelligence judgments. It was only one more player in the intelligence field and a competitor for the ear of the president and other top officials.

Attempting to coordinate efforts among the many competing services was an interminable process of which no one was in charge. Consensus was the exception, never the rule. Thus, the prewar chaos in intelligence services was almost perfectly replicated in 1946; the lessons of Pearl Harbor had not yet thoroughly sunk in.

In the area of clandestine operations, the busy Vandenberg managed to retrieve some of the old OSS assets from the army and its barely functioning Strategic Services Unit. These assets were redesignated the CIG's Office of Special Operations (OSO), consisting of espionage and counterespionage units. Even more than the OSS, however, the OSO was kept strictly compartmentalized within the CIG and isolated from the rest of the intelligence community. This left the ORE analysts, among others, largely in the dark when it came to getting access to secret intelligence.

By the middle of 1946, despite tight budgets and the absence of a real sense of alarm, the CIG had nevertheless expanded to eighteen hundred men and women, a third of whom were overseas attached to the OSO. Another four hundred were assigned to special operations in Washington, six hundred were on administrative and support staffs, leaving only two hundred for analysis and reporting. Still, it was a big improvement over the paltry numbers originally intended by President Truman and his penny-pinching Bureau of the Budget.

By the spring of 1947, the CIG, despite having overcome some obstacles, was still a disorganized assembly of parts, not a functioning intelligence machine at all, much less a central intelligence service. Fortunately, the presidential directive that created the CIG was about to be replaced with congressional legislation, an unprecedented move in the U.S. intelligence experience. The legislation would be an attempt to establish at least the foundation of the nation's first system of central intelligence.

The big change in intelligence thinking in 1947, however, did not happen in a vacuum. Two factors were especially important. First, congressional investigations of Pearl Harbor conducted after the war finally brought home to the American public the serious, nearly fatal flaws in U.S. intelligence capability prior to the beginning of World War II. That shock of recognition was compounded by a rapidly deteriorating international situation. Although the Axis powers had been blown into dust and rubble, the Soviet Union was increasingly recognized as an untrustworthy ally and dangerous to boot.

THE NATIONAL SECURITY ACT AND THE CENTRAL INTELLIGENCE AGENCY

A thoroughly concerned President Truman and Congress (which he would later deride as do-nothing) forged one piece of extraordinary legislation, the National Security Act, that created America's modern national security system. Signed into law in July 1947, it was the most ambitious and far-reaching reconstruction of the U.S. armed forces and intelligence services since the writing of the Constitution one hundred and sixty years earlier.

Ironically, the new intelligence service came about as a by-product of a much broader debate that ended in the reorganization of the armed forces and their relationship to civilian authorities. The separate War and Navy departments were abolished and replaced with a single Department of Defense. The military heads would be brought together under the Joint Chiefs of Staff, who in turn would report directly on military policy to the newly created National Security Council. The NSC, unlike the weak NIA, was chaired by the president, with the secretaries of state and defense acting as his key policy advisers. Above all, it was recognized that peacetime problems could not be dealt with by a separate department of peace and an isolated department of war with a president free now and then to pull policy rabbits out of a hat. Rather, the basic issues of national security were to be discussed collectively and taken for the intertwined political, economic, military, and intelligence problems they really were.

U.S. intelligence would directly benefit from this new approach. The Central Intelligence Agency and its presidentially appointed director, according to the National Security Act, would, along with the JCS, report directly to the president and the NSC. Donovan's dream of an intelligence chief having direct access to the president had finally been realized. The U.S. intelligence service no longer would be a mere handmaiden of the JCS or any cabinet agency. Donovan's full agenda, as outlined in his 1944 memorandum to President Roosevelt, to all intents and purposes became part of the legislation.

The CIA would collect, correlate, and evaluate all intelligence relating to the national security. Furthermore, the agency would have the responsibility of disseminating intelligence within the U.S. government. Although the words "espionage," "counterespionage," and "covert action" do not appear in the law, these activities are hinted at in Aesopian language; "additional services" and "such other functions and duties related to intelligence affecting the national security" are prize examples. The latter, in fact, became the elastic clause that was later cited as the agency's authority to conduct covert intelligence operations.

Equally important, the CIA and its director were given special leverage with the other intelligence services. In effect, intelligence gathered by the latter would be "open" to the director of central intelligence (DCI), which meant the DCI was to have access to all intelligence matters relating to national security, including military and signals intelligence, something that the OSS had never been given a right to see. It was a major step toward an all-source central intelligence service. In short, the new CIA was not to be a supplicant pleading for information from the older services. Instead, the agency would be a central coordinator and a central evaluator of

all intelligence, with direct access to the president and the NSC.

Donovan's recommendation that the new agency have no police or law enforcement powers was also incorporated into the legislation. Truman himself insisted on this, because of his belief that the American people would never accept anything that smacked of a secret police. One matter not dealt with by Donovan was wisely included in the National Security Act. Facing up to the general mediocrity of CIG officials, the new law gave the DCI the power to fire employees when "necessary or advisable in the interests of the United States," thus avoiding the usual civil service procedures that make federal employees virtually permanent fixtures regardless of the effort they put forth. Although the CIA generally followed civil service procedures, it had the right to remove employees from the rolls, particularly if they constituted a security problem. Dismissals were handled with discretion and tact, but the privilege to fire as well as to hire marked the intelligence service as a sensitive and important element of the government.

Despite the new charter, the fledgling CIA had plenty of problems in establishing itself along the lines envisioned by Congress and the president. For one thing, it had a weak director, Rear Admiral Roscoe Hillenkoeter, who had little clout with the other services, congressional legislation notwithstanding. In fact, Hillenkoeter cut such a small figure that he was not present at President Truman's NSC meeting in which the U.S. response to North Korea's attack on South Korea in June 1950 was weighed and measured. At the same time, Hillenkoeter's support staff was not much better equipped than the admiral. The agency's employees, largely taken over from the CIG, were still the same mediocrities on loan from other agencies. Because the new service had no track record, able men and women were not flocking to join it in large numbers.

Intelligence collection and analysis, in short, were proceeding with no great initial improvements over CIG operations. The CIA Office of

Reports and Estimates dutifully wrote papers that were largely ignored by policymakers. The early reports and estimates were too long in the making, too noncommittal as a result, and nearly always blanketed with dissenting notes from the other services, leaving the reader puzzled or annoyed.

There was another, even bigger problem. The new agency, while struggling in its infancy, was handed major responsibilities in the field of covert action. Responsibility for covert action was unmentioned in the CIA's charter, but events in Europe soon forced U.S. officials to react with measures short of war—although many feared that war might come when the Soviets acquired a deployable nuclear weapon. Two events in particular raised the tocsin in Washington. First came the Czech coup in February 1948, in which a minority Communist party seized power under the protective umbrella of the Red Army. Second were the Italian elections in April 1948, which many feared would be won by a thoroughly Stalinist Italian Communist party.

Despite the earlier Soviet threats to Iran, Greece, and Turkey and Stalin's success in swallowing much of Eastern Europe outright, the Czech coup, particularly the murder of democratic Foreign Minister Jan Masaryk in March 1948, shocked U.S. officials more than any other event since the end of the war. The brutal seizure of power in Prague, despite promises by the Soviets not to do so, snapped the last link of trust in anything Soviet authorities would say or do.

At roughly the same time, the Truman administration began to worry about the future of Italy, a strategically located Western Europe country, which faced its first set of postwar elections two months after the Czech coup. A Communist victory at the ballot box might well lead, it was believed, to a seizure of permanent and absolute power. Italy had been a concern of U.S. officials since late 1947 and was the subject of the NCS's first report (NSC 1/1) to the president. Other reports would follow until a plan of action was formulated shortly after the Czech coup. Various overt measures were carried out,

such as military assistance to Italy's feeble armed forces and economic aid, including large shipments of wheat, for a wrecked economy.

The covert measures that the newly organized CIA somewhat reluctantly took on included contributing secret financial and technical assistance to the Christian Democrats and other non-Communist parties. Efforts were also made to split off the Socialists from their common-front alliance with the Communist party of Italy. In addition, under a new NSC directive (NSC 4 and its top secret annex, NSC 4/A), the director of central intelligence was instructed to carry out psychological warfare designed to counteract Stalin's extensive propaganda operations in Western Europe.

NSC 4/A, in fact, was the first official charter for covert activity by any U.S. agency since the end of World War II. To carry out the orders, the Special Procedures Group was set up within the CIA Office of Special Operations (OSO). The Christian Democrat victory in the April elections was viewed by U.S. officials as a success for the covert political strategy. Consequently, Kennan, then director of the policy planning staff in the Department of State, and others recommended the formal creation of a permanent covert political action capability. This capability was acquired by the CIA in June 1948 under the authority of NSC 10/2.

The approved covert activities clearly were intended to include paramilitary operations, as well as economic and political warfare. A covert staff, soon named the Office of Policy Coordination (OPC), was added to the CIA organization chart to replace the ad hoc Special Procedures Group. It would be kept completely separate from the clandestine collectors in the OSO, much less the analysts in the ORE. Just as the OSS paramilitary and secret intelligence units had been compartmentalized, so were those in the CIA.

The formal add-on of the OPC covert arm, however, was no victory for any would-be empire builder within the CIA. Although the OPC budget would be part of that of the CIA, its instructions would come from State and Defense, bypassing completely the agency's director. It was, to be sure, an unusual way of doing business and violated the spirit, if not the letter, of the National Security Act of 1947. To the drafters of NSC 10/2, however, it appeared less odd for the simple reason that they believed covert action would be called for only on occasion. Nevertheless, this haphazard arrangement (which worked surprisingly well) remained in place until October 1950, when a new DCI, four-star General Walter Bedell Smith, was appointed.

One reason that the system worked at all was that guidance from the State and Defense departments on covert operations was very general in nature, allowing the OPC a freedom of action of which its director, Frank Wisner, the former OSS station chief in Romania, took full advantage. The success of the early programs, however, was one more two-edged sword. The fledgling CIA received much of the credit for the success—which it only partially deserved—but that success would tempt later policymakers to overuse and to misuse the instrument of covert action. Failure in these later cases was also cheerfully passed on to the agency by the nation's political leaders, although covert action was always a presidential prerogative, because the CIA had no authority to make policy decisions but only advised on covert action. Only the president could decide.

Overall, however, during its first three years of life, the CIA came nowhere near being the central intelligence service envisioned by its founders, congressional and executive. It is one thing to write a charter; it is another to carry it out. Despite some successes in the covert field—thanks to the press of foreign events—the young CIA was a far cry from what Donovan and others had hoped it would be. Its failures also did not go unnoticed. A 1948 NSC study blasted the agency for drafting intelligence estimates that were loosely coordinated within the intelligence community. The Hoover Commission (1947–1949), established to study the growth of government during World War II, repeated virtually the whole of the NSC criticisms, but bureaucracy prevailed, and skillful coordinated analytical intelligence lagged.

THE KOREAN WAR AND THE CIA UNDER GENERAL SMITH

The single event that radically transformed the rather bleak picture at the CIA was the outbreak of the Korean War on 25 June 1950. This bloody conventional struggle that went on for three years transformed the entire U.S. national security system. Defense spending, after hitting immediate postwar lows, rose dramatically, from about $15 billion to $50 billion in a single year, 1950, and the United States constructed its first powerful peacetime armed forces in history.

These profound changes were matched in the intelligence community as well. Like Pearl Harbor, the North Korean aggression revealed the deficiencies in the U.S. intelligence system, especially the new CIA and the agency's limited relationship with senior policymaking officials. The agency's ORE analysts had written some warnings about the possibility of a North Korean attack, but they had not been nearly emphatic enough to capture the NSC audience's attention.

Fortunately, the agency was spared endless scapegoating in 1950—an otherwise favorite Washington practice after defeat and disaster—and a constructive approach was used instead. The first positive step was Truman's replacement of the hapless Hillenkoeter with the hard-driving General Walter Bedell Smith.

General Smith had spent his lifetime in the army, beginning as an enlisted man in World War I. In World War II he became secretary of the General Staff under General George Marshall and then went to London in 1942 as Dwight Eisenhower's chief of staff. "Beetle" Smith became a take-charge, no-nonsense director who knew the arcane world of intelligence and could not be bullied or finessed by either intelligence or policymaking bureaucrats. For the first time since the days of Wild Bill

Donovan, central intelligence was in the hands of a man with vision and determination who also had the prestige and clout that are persuasive to military commanders, foreign service officers, and members of Congress alike. Smith also had the vitally needed confidence of President Truman and, of course, Eisenhower, who became president in 1953.

General Smith moved quickly to convert a paper charter into a reality, sometimes using unorthodox means à la Donovan. Shortly before Smith's arrival, CIA analysts finally achieved complete access to military signals intelligence, making the analytical branch at last an all-source unit. This was the single most significant step taken after the war to ensure that compartmentalization of signals intelligence would not pave the way for another Pearl Harbor. Still, it took nearly a decade after that disaster to put it in place.

As for General Smith, he moved quickly to tighten up the agency's loose organizational structure and to improve its leverage over the other services. Until the advent of "Beetle" Smith, what coordination did take place was under the aegis of the Intelligence Advisory Committee (IAC), which was, to say the least, a tenuous connection with the other services. For the most part, the various agencies in time-honored fashion used the IAC to prevent estimates from surfacing that conflicted with individual departmental policies. The first estimate on the future of communism in the Soviet Union, of utmost priority in those days, for example, was two years in the making.

All of this began to change, however, with Smith's arrival. Smith first picked good men for the key jobs; in some cases, as with William Langer, they were people who had worked for Donovan. Smith also had Langer organize the Office of National Estimates as the highest analytical and estimative body in the CIA. The office originally amounted to an elite group of about twenty-five senior analysts and never included more than one hundred staffers. To maintain coherence, however, the Office of National Estimates was folded within a renamed

general analytical branch, the Directorate of Intelligence, headed by the deputy director for intelligence (DDI). This directorate was staffed with the most experienced officers capable of taking on the onerous duty of calculating options and probabilities in foreign conflicts, real or hypothetical.

Smith demanded as a first priority that all intelligence activities be tightly coordinated and based on all sources of information. Furthermore, he insisted that all reports and estimates be reviewed by a panel of impartial experts, called the Board of National Estimates. More important to the morale of the previously neglected CIA analysts, Smith read their product closely, paying particular attention to the national intelligence estimates (NIEs), which are still the best-known analytical product of the U.S. intelligence community. The new DCI also made sure the NIEs were presented to Truman before the president received negative briefings from other agencies—a common practice until the arrival of General Smith. If other services objected to the CIA's judgments, the objections were noted in the NIE in a footnote, a practice that is still in use.

Smith moved quickly in the area of covert activities as well. Unlike his predecessor, the new DCI refused to be cut out of the chain of command. Smith's method for regaining control of the OPC was a study in simplicity: he simply announced that it would be so, and it was. State and Defense could issue guidance, he decided, but only through the director of central intelligence.

Two more years elapsed, however, before Smith took Dulles' advice and integrated clandestine collection with covert activity, putting them both under the deputy director for plans (DDP), namely Dulles himself, in the newly created Directorate of Plans. It took time for these two activities and operators to be truly merged, and the process was not completed until Dulles became DCI in 1953 after Eisenhower's election to the presidency and Smith transferred to the State Department. The benefits of employing common tradecraft procedures to ensure secrecy was helpful for both the espionage experts and the political activists, even while specific projects remained tightly compartmentalized.

What General Smith did until his retirement from the CIA was nothing less than to found the U.S. intelligence system in much its present form. The Korean War, however, was what made it happen. As in any war, the demand for intelligence increased exponentially, and so did budgets. As a result, by war's end the CIA had taken on something like its modern size.

DIRECTORS DULLES AND McCONE: GROWTH TO MATURITY

The Directorate of Intelligence grew to three thousand and the Office of Policy Coordination from three hundred to nearly three thousand by 1953, with more than three thousand additional personnel serving overseas. The CIA total strength reached ten thousand by the time President Eisenhower and Dulles took office in January and February 1953 respectively. The CIA staff personnel strength would peak at eighteen thousand a few years later.

The Dulles Years. During the tenure of Dulles, the first career intelligence officer to become DCI, the CIA solidified its position as the nation's central intelligence service. Nearly every branch of the agency grew in size and professionalism, including the director's first love, covert and clandestine operations (a passion Dulles shared with his old chief, General Donovan). To Dulles' credit, there was in these "mature" years a considerable number of achievements, and the CIA acquired from the media an image of success, glamour, and mystery. Although exaggerated, that image also made recruitment of highly talented people possible and improved enormously contact with friendly foreign services.

In Europe the CIA organized and financed Radio Liberty and Radio Free Europe, turning a ragtag propaganda and information service aimed at the Soviet Union and Eastern Europe into a thoroughly professional operation that endured into the 1990s under different, completely overt, management. The CIA also quietly assisted non-Communist European intellectuals through such forums as the Congress of Cultural Freedom, thus giving them opportunities to express their views in respectable journals.

After the Korean War, most CIA covert actions were small-scale efforts plainly authorized by various NSC directives and overseen by a succession of NSC committees. They were largely aimed at influencing and activating local political groups to build their own parties, organize free labor unions, and establish independent, antitotalitarian media. Paramilitary actions, however, were not completely neglected. During the Korean War, the CIA was authorized—in fact, urged by the NSC—to create networks of agents, including fleets of aircraft and small boats, to support paramilitary efforts. The overriding objective was to undercut Chinese fighting ability on the Korean peninsula and to prevent the consolidation of Communist control on the China mainland.

During the Eisenhower years, however, the covert side of CIA activities quickly achieved a mystique it did not really deserve, thanks in part to publicized U.S. successes in Iran (1953) and Guatemala (1954). Although the CIA contribution in each of these cases was relatively small, its power and influence were to grow in the telling, including the revisionist accounts that deplored the idea of any CIA intervention anywhere in the world, particularly in the struggling countries of Africa, Asia, Latin America, and the Middle East. These covert operations were justified at the time, but romantic misconceptions about the role and capabilities of the agency in overthrowing governments gave rise to expectations of easy political victories. These unrealistic expectations would have disastrous consequences; later covert operations in this period, especially the larger ones, such as the 1961 Bay of Pigs invasion, were embarrassing failures.

The Bay of Pigs was an attempt to oust the Cuban dictator Fidel Castro, an avowed Communist. Planned initially in the last year of the Eisenhower administration, the operation was a clear example of paramilitary exercises attempting more than can be done with a relatively small group of men, no matter how well-trained and motivated. The upshot of the Bay of Pigs, aside from acute U.S. embarrassment, was Castro's elimination of all opposition to him on the island. It also paved the way for Castro's hoped-for alliance with the Soviet Union by branding his Cuban revolution "socialist."

The Bay of Pigs failure had serious intelligence overtones as well. Such a large undertaking, for example, strained beyond any credibility the doctrine of plausible deniability on the part of the United States government. Moreover, the senior analyst in the CIA, the DDI, was never officially consulted about the pros and cons of the operation. All estimates of success were generated by the operators under the DDP, a thoroughly unsound procedure that was nevertheless accepted by the inexperienced Kennedy administration. Moreover, the original concept of covert infiltration of Cuban forces in a mountain redoubt area gradually changed into a plan for a frontal military assault in an unlikely area far from the mountains. Neither the CIA nor the JCS, however, recognized that a military invasion would need U.S. combat support if it met with opposition. Kennedy seemed to believe that plausible deniability of U.S. support for the operation meant that no military aid could be given.

Meanwhile, despite Dulles' personal preference for classical cloak-and-dagger, he did support the development of the intelligence community's analytical product under CIA direction. In fact, the national estimates process improved steadily. Dulles had no intention of letting his substantial research and analysis component wither away, leaving the State and Defense departments to carry out these chores.

Dulles also insisted that the agency continue to provide accurate current intelligence analysis, combining the latest political, economic, military, and scientific research. He did so be-

cause, for the most part, neither State nor Defense provided that kind of comprehensive intelligence capability, focusing on the departmental rather than the national process. As a result, the Directorate of Intelligence also expanded, taking on more and more difficult jobs. The heart of the Office of Current Intelligence was the Sino-Soviet research analysts; this division in the 1950s probably had more genuine Soviet and Chinese experts than could be found anywhere else in the world.

The greatest accomplishment of the Eisenhower era in intelligence collection, however, was the harnessing of high technology, particularly advanced photoreconnaissance, for that purpose. The modern age in intelligence collection began with the flights of U-2 reconnaissance planes over the Soviet Union, starting in 1956. An ungainly bird, the U-2 flew higher than any craft at the time and took photographs in exquisite detail. The avalanche of information from these photos opened up the secretive Soviet Union as never before. It was interpreted by special trained analysts, photo interpreters, whose numbers within the CIA grew from twenty in the early 1950s to more than two thousand by the end of the decade. The camera could not tell U.S. officials everything—it said nothing about the intentions of Soviet leaders, for example—but it immeasurably expanded the once scant knowledge the CIA and other services had of Soviet military capabilities. By the time a Soviet surface-to-air missile (SA-2) managed to shoot down a U-2 in May 1960, the agency already had under way a superior replacement for the plane, photoreconnaissance satellites that were immune to unfriendly ground fire.

By the end of Eisenhower's second term, the CIA and the other U.S. intelligence services had reached a point of maturity never before seen in U.S. history. Collection, analysis, and covert action were coordinated through a civilian agency that had direct access to the president and his national security decision-making system. The agency and the greater intelligence community were not, however, without their flaws. Furthermore, much of what had been accomplished depended on a dedicated staff that learned its craft in the hard school of World War II but that was now too old for aggressive field operations.

McCone Takes Over. The fallout from the Bay of Pigs—the agency's first great failure as well as that of the Kennedy administration—caused some changes. Kennedy did not suffer failure lightly and considered a radical reorganization, if not the dissolution, of the CIA. Second thoughts, however, prevailed, and after a decent interval Dulles was allowed to retire. He was replaced by a civilian businessman, John McCone, who had gained substantial experience in the air force and as chairman of the Atomic Energy Commission.

Unlike Dulles, McCone was less fascinated with the clandestine and covert; he hated being called a spymaster. Consequently, he put less emphasis on covert operations, although he did manage several major programs in this field, including the massive paramilitary undertaking to create a secret Laotian army to cope with North Vietnamese infiltration of South Vietnam. Overall, however, McCone spent the bulk of his time on intelligence analysis, for which his keen, skeptical intellect was well-suited. McCone was particularly fascinated with technical collection programs, especially the possibilities of photo-reconnaissance, the details of which he quickly learned. Fortunately, McCone also believed his frequent personal contact with and briefing of the president was his first priority. McCone is the only CIA director to have believed this, and it was a shrewd judgment that did much to preserve the agency in the dark days after the Bay of Pigs.

McCone deserves much credit for the CIA's comeback in the fall of 1962, when aerial photographs taken from U-2s detected Soviet nuclear armed medium-range rockets in Cuba. The picture-taking, however, was only the best-known element of a large, CIA-led interagency effort, beginning in the summer of 1962, to discover what kind of weapons the Soviets were sending to their new ally in the Caribbean. Debate had raged for months within the intelligence com-

munity, with most CIA analysts expressing profound skepticism that the Soviets would station nuclear missiles off their own soil for the first time. That was the judgment contained in the national intelligence estimate published less than a month before the discovery of the weapons at San Cristobal. It was also a judgment not shared by the shrewd McCone, who was convinced that would be precisely the move Soviet Premier Nikita Krushchev would make.

Linked to this strategically important intelligence coup was, in fact, another. In addition to information yielded by high-technology aerial reconnaissance, the CIA also had the old-fashioned work of an agent-in-place, Colonel Oleg Penkovsky of the Soviet Union. Penkovsky was a walk-in, that is, a volunteer who freely gave to the British and the Americans an extraordinary array of information about Soviet military technology. Much of it revealed how far behind the Soviets really were, an invaluable insight when it came time for U.S. officials to call Krushchev's bluff in Cuba. Penkovsky, however, was caught and arrested the day of President Kennedy's speech disclosing the presence of missiles in Cuba. Several months later, the Soviet army colonel was executed.

In retrospect, the reformed CIA under McCone during the Kennedy administration was probably the U.S. intelligence community's high-water mark in prestige and capability. The well-publicized handling of the Cuban Missile Crisis gave an unusual credibility to the CIA performance.

THE TIME OF TROUBLES: VIETNAM AND ITS AFTERMATH

For a variety of reasons, the CIA went into a decline during the presidency of Lyndon Johnson, mainly because of the mismanagement of the Vietnam War. The time of troubles was prolonged by the Watergate scandal during Richard Nixon's administration and when Jimmy Carter subsequently took office in 1977 with a very clear bias against intelligence services. The fortunes of the intelligence community did not improve until the presidency of Ronald Reagan, and even then the legacy of suspicion continued to haunt the CIA and other intelligence services.

The Loss of Influence Under Johnson and Nixon.

President Johnson had comparatively little interest in the products of the intelligence community. It was simply not his style to listen patiently to staff recommendations or to read intelligence reports carefully. Johnson preferred to talk matters over with a few of his intimates and then make decisions, often strategically fuzzy.

The CIA's work meanwhile, grew less and less congenial to the president for another reason. In contrast to Robert McNamara's Defense Department, the CIA provided Johnson with pessimistic estimates about the likelihood of winning a guerrilla war in Vietnam using conventional military power. Furthermore, the CIA station chief in Saigon, fully supported by McCone, had strongly opposed a State Department–supported coup against South Vietnamese President Ngo Dinh Diem, a coup that shattered that country's political stability in 1963 when Diem and his brother Ngo Dinh Nhu were murdered by the Vietnamese army shortly before Kennedy's assassination. The effects of disagreements between the CIA and the State and Defense departments could be felt long into the presidency of Johnson and, indeed, throughout the 1970s.

As the Indochina war wore on with no end in sight, Johnson restricted his circle of advisers even further, and during his last years in office, the intelligence community had virtually no place at the table, literally and figuratively. A clear sign of Johnson's cavalier attitude toward the CIA was the selection of retired Vice Admiral William Raborn to replace McCone as DCI in 1965. Raborn, a decent and intelligent man, had no experience in foreign affairs, much less in intelligence. Moreover, as a sailor, Raborn was inclined to take orders from his commander in chief without ever presenting him with the unpalatable evidence coming from the DCI's own empire of analysts and operators. In fairness to Raborn, his replacement a year later, Richard Helms, did not have much better luck in getting through to the White House, either in the Johnson or the Nixon era. Although Helms was the second career intelligence officer to become DCI, he, like his predecessors, was viewed from the White House as merely an efficient executor of orders by secret methods and nothing more.

This view did not change under the equally secretive Richard Nixon. Analytical intelligence was routinely dismissed by the White House unless it fit standing policy. Nixon's national security adviser, Henry Kissinger, epitomized this attitude. As a result, the national estimates function fell into comparative neglect, and the Office of National Estimates itself was abolished. The entire interagency intelligence bureaucracy was also emasculated as more and more crucial intelligence was closely held by the inner Nixon-Kissinger circle.

When intelligence was used by Johnson or Nixon, it was often misused; President Johnson's exploitation of the shaky evidence that led to passage in Congress of the Tonkin Gulf Resolution (1964) and his decision to intervene in the Dominican Republic in May 1965 are prime examples. The one lasting achievement of the Dominican episode—the creation of the agency-wide, all-sources Operations Center that kept and still keeps top officials informed of important breaking events twenty-four hours a day—went totally unnoticed.

Another set of questions that would become grist for the antiintelligence mill after 1965 was the agency's connection with assassination attempts against foreign leaders, the most prominent being Fidel Castro. It is clear that a few U.S. intelligence officials believed they had been given the go-ahead to eliminate the Cuban dictator. By 1960 various schemes had been hatched, including some using bizarre techniques, but none were successful. It is also not completely clear how serious many of these attempts were. Nevertheless, the assassination revelations badly hurt the U.S. intelligence community, the CIA in particular, which would be compared to a rogue elephant in 1976 by an investigative Senate select committee. Although the intelligence planners dealing with Cuba thought they had approval from above, there was no clear accountability or chain of command; at least, none was recorded.

The failure in Vietnam also affected the CIA, especially its covert capabilities. As frustration increased over the length of the war, CIA covert involvement grew correspondingly in a desperate search for quick fixes. Enormous sums were spent on covert and counterintelligence programs. Meanwhile, the sheer scale of effort and the overall militarization of that effort frustrated nearly every undertaking. Whenever, for example, the CIA developed a promising operation involving a hundred Vietnamese, invariably the U.S. Command wanted to take it over, increase the size tenfold, and radically alter a man-to-man effort into a battalion-size, totally non-Asian campaign. These efforts became another part of the litany of complaints against the CIA by its critics; worse, professionally, the running of an army got in the way of the original task—intelligence collection.

The intelligence community also suffered from the fallout of the Watergate scandal. In fact, Helms was abruptly replaced as DCI after the 1972 election because he had refused to go along with President Nixon's effort to use the agency as a shield for the White House's complicity in the Watergate operation. Helms's replacement was James Schlesinger, a relative novice at intelligence. Schlesinger served in the job only a few months, but in that time he made some major changes and mistakes that did further damage to U.S. intelligence.

First, Schlesinger summarily fired some two thousand employees, an act that brought morale at the much-battered CIA to a new low. The mass dismissals added to the impression that something had gone very wrong at the agency—rather than at the White House. Second, the new DCI subordinated an overt collection system to the clandestine services. Specifically, no longer would contacts with U.S. citizens and friendly foreigners, the counterpart of the OSS's old Foreign Nationalities Division, be a relatively benign one. Instead, the agency mistakenly acquired a cloak-and-dagger image that imperiled a source of information that had been successfully used for thirty years.

The third Schlesinger decision was to abolish the Office of National Estimates, a move that served no purpose other than tightening the Nixon White House's control over intelligence estimates, the vital underpinning of policy decisions. Although the ONE would later be replaced with an elite group of National Intelligence Officers (NIOs), men and women who commanded special expertise in a region or aspect of national intelligence, the NIOs would not serve as a collegial body in the way ONE did and, therefore, no longer issued consensus reports.

The intelligence community's trouble scarcely ended with the resignation of Nixon in 1974. As part of the post-Watergate catharsis, the new DCI, William Colby, finished a review of all of the CIA's operations over the past years in search of irregular or legally questionable actions. Eventually, a list of 683 possible violations of directives or laws were reported. The compilation, which became known as the "Family Jewels," was forwarded to the congressional oversight committees, where the report was promptly leaked in dribs and drabs to friendly reporters. Having been beaten on the Watergate story by the *Washington Post*, the *New York Times* was especially aggressive in reporting stories about CIA abuses, invariably described as massive, over the years. The impression that the CIA had gone out of control was largely based on CIA domestic activities that either fell into a gray area or, on occasion, were in fact illegal and in violation of the law and the agency's 1947 charter. Most, but not all, of these activities were a direct result of orders issued by the Johnson and Nixon administrations.

Among these questionable operations was the surveillance of domestic groups opposed to the Vietnam War. Presidents Johnson and Nixon believed that American radicals not only were in touch with foreign governments but also were being financed by them. Each president pressured both the FBI and the CIA to turn up evidence of such links. Although the objective was legitimate, some of the methods used were not, and it is clear that the White House did not care much which means were employed.

The sum total of these activities hardly appears to have been massive or to have turned the agency, much less the entire intelligence community, into the American Gestapo once feared by President Truman. Great damage had been done, however, and by the mid-1970s the questionable and illegal activity threatened to injure, perhaps fatally, the entire U.S. intelligence effort at a time when Soviet expansion in the Leonid Brezhnev years was approaching historic highs.

The CIA in the Ford and Carter Administrations.

To revive confidence in U.S. intelligence, President Gerald Ford, who succeeded Nixon in August 1974, carried out some reforms of the intelligence community through Executive Order 11905, reforms designed to strengthen the director of central intelligence and improve his access to the president. The order also forbade any employee of the U.S. government to "engage in, or conspire to engage in political assassination." Under the Ford administration, morale slowly improved, especially during the year (1976–1977) when George Bush served as DCI.

The mood changed once again with the presidency of Jimmy Carter. Carter had campaigned against Republican "disgraces," which included vague references to the iniquities of the CIA. He was highly suspicious of intelligence activity, particularly if it was clandestine or covert or had any domestic component. Like Ford, Carter would issue an executive order (12036), this one establishing even more restrictions on U.S. intelligence activities. That presidential attitude coincided with the appointment of a DCI, Stansfield Turner, who remained an active duty naval officer and had less rapport with the agency's personnel than any previous director. These factors combined to make for difficult years for professional intelligence officers. To make matters worse, two hundred clandestine staff officers were abruptly retired. This policy was cou-

pled with the abolition of an additional six hundred jobs in the covert action and espionage field. As a consequence, by the late 1970s the total number of CIA employees had decreased by more than a third from the agency's peak years, and the budget had also shrunk in terms of constant dollars.

The American penchant for seeing world problems through a strictly domestic lens eventually would change once more. With the Soviet Union active in Africa and Afghanistan and a manifestly unfriendly regime in Iran, even President Carter began to complain about the lack of quality intelligence reporting and his inability to do anything about, for example, liberating American hostages held in Teheran, Iran. The new atmosphere, however, did not mean a return to the old ways of doing things, even after the Reagan sweep of 1980. That was especially true in the area of congressional oversight of U.S. intelligence activities.

Congress had always exercised some control over the intelligence services, primarily through the budget, although presidents from Washington on always had access to secret and unvouchered funds, that is to say, money that could be spent free of congressional control. The structural informality of this procedure was largely retained in the first thirty years of the CIA's existence. Until the mid-1970s, Congress, by and large, stayed away from involving itself in the murky business of overseeing intelligence.

The working arrangement involved simply the CIA and its senior briefers keeping a small number of senior senators and representatives informed of major programs, including covert activities. There were no hearings as such; the meetings were informal and behind closed doors. The secrets were not leaked. The net effect of this modus operandi was that a small group in Congress assigned to the intelligence subcommittees reassured members of the parent committees in general terms that the CIA programs were legitimate and would not prove embarrassing to Congress. If the special CIA appropriations subcommittees gave their sanction, intelligence funding was then hidden in the Department of Defense budget. This procedure gave the CIA and the intelligence programs an exceptionally privileged position in the legislative process. Moreover, the members of Congress in the 1950s and 1960s did not see themselves as exercising anything more than the general legislative responsibility for intelligence activities that accrued to Congress through its power over the budget.

The system worked well as long as the main outlines of U.S. foreign and intelligence policy enjoyed bipartisan support in Congress and in the nation. That consensus, of course, had cracked during the Vietnam War and was left shattered by the Watergate scandal and its aftermath. Bitter, partisan warfare, always a feature of domestic politics, spread to foreign policy on many fronts, not just Vietnam, all of which deeply touched the intelligence community.

In 1975 and 1976, Senate and House special investigating committees delved into the alleged and real sins and failings of the intelligence community, the CIA in particular. In addition to the issues that had already been long discussed, new scandals were unearthed. Heading the list was Chile. The congressional investigating committees cleared the agency of assisting a Chilean military coup that ended with the murder of President Salvador Allende Gossens in 1973. This exoneration made no difference in the end. Congressional oversight of intelligence activities became much tighter after the Chile episode than in the past.

In the beginning eight committees of Congress had virtual veto power over clandestine and covert activities. Agency reporting to the committees often leaked to the news media. As a result, virtually no covert activity occurred in the second half of the 1970s. Needless to say, this was a unilateral American abstinence, not reciprocated by the Soviet Union or Cuba.

By 1980, however, it became apparent even to the intelligence-wary Carter administration that this state of affairs could not continue. Having suffered reverses in Angola, the Horn of Africa, and Afghanistan, not to mention Iran, the White House had learned the damaging political effect of looking ineffectual in foreign affairs. An excessively controlled and shackled intelligence community was part of the problem.

The Intelligence Reform Act of 1980 undid some of the damage inflicted in the 1970s. For one thing, it mandated reporting only to two select committees, rather than to eight separate bodies, and it exempted certain categories of intelligence data from Freedom of Information Act (FOIA) inquiry. The new legislation also made it a crime to disclose the identities of intelligence agents, a favorite sport of some U.S. magazines. As for covert action, the president's approval—called a presidential finding—required only notification to the two select committees. Normally, the oversight committees were to be told prior to initiation of any secret action, but in "extraordinary circumstances" doing so merely "in timely fashion" was permitted.

REAGAN AND THE RESURGENCE OF THE CIA

Along with the new and somewhat improved atmosphere concerning intelligence came a new presidency. This fact made a huge difference. President Ronald Reagan and the Republican party were determined to rebuild the intelligence capabilities of the United States, along with the economy and the defense establishment. It was unusual but not surprising that a former director of central intelligence, George Bush, became vice president under Reagan.

Reagan's choice for director of central intelligence fit the new mood almost exactly. William Casey was a pioneer intelligence professional, having served in Donovan's OSS as London station chief presiding over agent operations penetrating Nazi Germany. Casey later served in a variety of government posts, but he spent the bulk of his career in law and in business. Because of his own intelligence background, Casey preferred action and the direct approach to strategic risk-taking, both in business and government, as had Donovan and, only to a slightly lesser extent, Dulles.

Casey was also a thoroughly political person, and he became an intimate part of the Reagan campaign for the presidency. Indeed, Casey's tightfisted financial management of that campaign after the New Hampshire primary convinced Reagan that Casey had kept the campaign from stalling altogether in the later primaries. As a result, Casey had a close personal relationship with the president, probably unique in the history of presidents and directors of central intelligence, certainly since the Eisenhower era.

Casey used the president's backing to rebuild the agency. More money and jobs were approved. Morale improved as Casey vigorously defended professional intelligence officers, and the CIA's various divisions were all strengthened. He also insisted that the Directorate of Operations and Directorate of Intelligence cooperate closely, something that had not always been the case.

Casey, who had begun his career in clandestine activity, moved quickly to revitalize both the analytical and the clandestine services after his initial and intensive study of the CIA's problems that included personal trips to nearly all the overseas stations. The result was that the United States was soon back in the covert action field after having ceded it for more than five years to the Soviet KGB. With considerable effort and money, Casey's CIA helped equip Afghan mujahedeen in an ultimately successful effort to force the Soviet Union to withdraw from Afghanistan. This policy had the enthusiastic support of Congress. In Angola, a smaller program supporting pro-Western guerrillas turned up the pressure on the Cuban presence, forcing Castro's troops to begin leaving at the end of the decade.

All the news was not good for the intelligence community. Casey himself was a vulnerable target because of his political connections and his high-profile Republican views. The bad news reached a head with the Iran-Contra affair, which became public knowledge in November 1986. Members of the NSC were using money earned from covert arms sales to Iran to finance rebel activities against the Sandinista government in Nicaragua, which was supported clandestinely by Cuba and the Soviet Union. The

problem was that Congress had earlier suspended U.S. aid to the anti-Sandinista guerrillas through the Boland Amendments (1984), promoted by the House Permanent Select Committee on Intelligence. Although the CIA was thus prohibited by Congress from aiding the Contras and did not do so, the funneling of aid through the National Security Council staff in the White House was a hazardous enterprise and eventually came unstuck as the Iran-Contra stories leaked.

The Reagan administration and the intelligence community survived more than a year of investigation more or less intact, but damage was done to morale. The larger questions of defining congressional oversight and the president's prerogatives as commander in chief were also left unanswered. Congress assumed that its power to oversee intelligence entitled it to dominate the inquiry and to reveal all data that normally would have been kept secret. Another result of the investigation, was a much-lower-profile DCI. Casey's successor was the former director of the FBI, Judge William Webster, whose chief asset was the trust he enjoyed on Capitol Hill.

Iran-Contra also dashed hopes that partisan politics would never again intrude into the intelligence field. In fact, the affair vividly demonstrated that the U.S. experience in intelligence would always include a heavy dose of political controversy. It also demonstrated that a foreign policy establishment bitterly divided between a Republican White House and a Democratic-controlled Congress would inevitably involve the intelligence community, whether the latter liked it or not.

THE INTELLIGENCE COMMUNITY IN THE 1990s

The modern national intelligence community is a crucial part of the strategic decision-making process and evidently will always be part of the cyclical ups and downs of congressional, media, and public support of intelligence programs. The intelligence mission has been sustained by all presidents, even though sometimes erratically, ever since Pearl Harbor.

Despite the ups and downs of the last third of the twentieth century, the U.S. intelligence community has taken on an air of permanence even as the cold war faded and new challenges replace the old bipolar struggle. The various member agencies of the intelligence community advise and report to the DCI through their representatives on the specialized committees that deal with all aspects of intelligence work. The umbrella committee, the community's equivalent of the National Security Council, is the National Foreign Intelligence Board. The board is chaired by the DCI and includes the heads of the community's various agencies, including the military intelligence services.

The DCI also presides over the NSC's Inter-Agency Group on intelligence matters. This working committee hammers out the nation's intelligence requirements and priorities and links these to available resources. The Inter-Agency Group also acts as a central review committee, weighing the product for quality, responsiveness, and relevance to policy requirements.

The director of central intelligence, as the coordinator of the intelligence community, is also the president's primary adviser on all national intelligence matters. In NSC meetings attended by cabinet-rank officials, invariably the DCI or a deputy begins with an overall intelligence estimate of the issue or issues to be discussed. In addition to that responsibility, the DCI also takes the lead in developing the National Foreign Intelligence Program budget. The greatest power the director has in shaping the intelligence product is the power to direct all intelligence collection tasking for the various elements within the intelligence community.

In the exacting task of community coordinator, the DCI is supported by the intelligence community staff, which coordinates the collection activities of all agencies in order to minimize overlap and duplication. The staff also ensures that major and often quickly developing intelligence targets are adequately covered. On

a humbler but highly practical plane, the community staff makes certain that intelligence is disseminated properly and that the "consumer" is satisfied with the product—its quality as well as its timeliness.

In addition to coordinating the intelligence community as a whole, the director of central intelligence and the CIA have the primary responsibility for the clandestine collection of intelligence and for conducting counterintelligence abroad. The agency also has the chief responsibility for developing and exploiting new technology for intelligence purposes through its Directorate of Science and Technology, a creation of McCone.

The CIA also takes the lead in producing military, political, economic, biographic, and scientific and technical intelligence to meet the needs of U.S. officials, often on a crash basis. Receiving the highest priority are the Special National Intelligence Estimates, or SNIEs, which provide the president and his closest advisers the best intelligence available from all sources on special and pressing problems. The SNIEs draw on the accumulated data bank prepared for the NIEs, the systematic estimates of probable developments in the major countries of the world. About fifty comprehensive NIEs on key international issues are produced annually.

Although the Central Intelligence Agency is dominant, it does not have a monopoly on intelligence collection and analysis. Moreover, unless the director is particularly aggressive, managing this complex apparatus can prove difficult. An added problem is that the largest share of the budget has gone to the military intelligence services, which have always been less responsive to the DCI than the civilian community. The FBI also often limits its contributions on domestic counterintelligence targets because the FBI jealously protects its own sources and methods and has law enforcement duties, which the CIA does not.

The CIA does not even enjoy a monopoly position in civilian intelligence. The Department of State, for example, retains a major role in intelligence. Much of what the State Department's foreign service does is to collect intelligence from the field. Every day hundreds of cables pour into Washington from hundreds of diplomatic posts established by the United States around the world. Primarily political and economic in nature, the most critical of that reporting is folded into the secretary of state's evening report to the president.

The best intelligence from the field is of little use, however, if it cannot be quickly and safely reported to Washington. Communication facilities in U.S. embassies around the world provide the critical link through the use of secure ciphers. The worldwide CRITICOM (Critical Communications) Net includes separate State and CIA communications channels through which priority messages can reach the desks of senior officials in a matter of minutes.

In addition, the State Department retains the Bureau of Intelligence and Research (INR) whose founding core of intelligence experts was taken from the disbanded Office of Strategic Services. Its best-known publication is the Morning Summary prepared for the secretary of state and distributed to other senior officials. The summary, which is classified, is the INR's counterpart to the CIA's National Intelligence Daily (the NID). Like the Morning Summary, the bulk of the INR's work is research and analysis. It has no independent collection capability and therefore relies mainly on embassy and consulate reporting, as well as on raw intelligence provided by other agencies and departments. The INR also coordinates State's dealings with other intelligence agencies and participates in the communitywide preparation of National Intelligence Estimates.

Also within the intelligence community charter is the mission of the FBI, the investigative arm of the Department of Justice. The bureau's chief intelligence activity has been counterintelligence carried on within the United States. Bureau personnel are also attached to U.S. embassies as legal attachés for liaison duties involving investigative and security matters. Domestic counterintelligence embraces detection, penetration, and neutralization of espionage, sabotage, and terrorism aimed at the United States by foreign intelligence services and groups. That work is carried out by the FBI's domestic intelligence unit.

Since the 1980s the FBI has cooperated more fully with the CIA, and both services have liaison officers permanently stationed at each other's headquarters. This close contact is especially important in coordinating foreign and domestic counterintelligence operations. Interagency cooperation is especially close in counterterrorism and counternarcotics intelligence.

The Treasury Department is also an active member of the intelligence community, which it formally joined in November 1971 at a time of international monetary instability. Treasury's primary responsibility remains the open collection of foreign financial and monetary intelligence. Treasury also produces analyses to support the secretary of the Treasury in the production of national intelligence for the president and other senior officials, especially those at the Department of State.

The Department of Energy, created in 1977, and its predecessor, the Atomic Energy Commission, also have had an important intelligence function affecting the strategic security of the United States. Both the DOE and AEC openly collected all political, economic, and especially technical information dealing with foreign energy matters, ranging from nuclear power to petroleum production. The DOE and especially the AEC in earlier years also had primary responsibility for estimating the atomic weapons capabilities of all the nuclear powers, most prominently the Soviet Union before its collapse in 1991. DOE and AEC personnel also have analyzed detected radioactive particles in the atmosphere since 1948 for evidence of nuclear weapons testing. When atmosphere tests were abandoned for the most part by the nuclear powers, the DOE and AEC continued to monitor test explosions underneath the earth's surface. The DOE analyzes all test-ban proposals for feasibility and thus remains an active member of the arms control community.

Complementing these civilian agencies are the old-line and more traditional military intelligence services. Until the early 1960s, they competed with each other, often providing intelligence that confirmed their particular service's need for a larger budget. Much of that rivalry took place at intelligence community meetings, where civilian officials became frustrated over the incessant quarreling. One bitter dispute in particular marked the late 1950s and ultimately changed the character of the military intelligence community. It sprang from the air force's insistence that the Soviets were outstripping the United States in the production of intercontinental ballistic missiles.

The air force was the most tenacious service in propounding a "missile gap." The resulting ongoing bureaucratic warfare led to a high-level investigation of the intelligence community to correct these and other problems. Consequently, the study recommended the removal of the military intelligence services from the United States Intelligence Board (USIB) and the creation of the Defense Intelligence Agency (DIA), which would replace the services at community meetings. The idea attracted the incoming Kennedy administration and especially Secretary of Defense McNamara. Dulles, as DCI, was beginning to have second thoughts. It was true that he had wearied of the incessant service arguing, but, Dulles concluded, eliminating the services from a direct role in the intelligence community meant that the new DIA could forge a false consensus before passing on estimates to the CIA, leaving the latter without all the facts and opinions it needed to form its own final judgment. Dulles' objections were overridden in the wake of the Bay of Pigs disaster, and President Kennedy ordered the creation of the DIA, which he hoped would better coordinate the military side of intelligence.

The Modern Military Intelligence Structure.
The Defense Intelligence Agency, created in October 1961, was supposed to act as an umbrella organization over the military intelligence services. It retained that status, at least on paper, into the 1990s. The DIA reports to the secretary of defense and the Joint Chiefs of Staff, and it, rather than the individual services, provides the foreign intelligence and counterintelligence requirement for the secretary of defense, the Joint Chiefs of Staff, and the unified and specified commands. It also prepares the order of battle estimates that calculate the size and deployment of enemy forces.

Originally, the DIA was supposed to ride herd on the diverse and competitive military intelligence community. In reality, it has not worked out that way. In cases of dispute among the military intelligence services or between a service and the DIA on, for example, military jurisdictional questions, the DIA does not have the final say. Its director can only appeal to the Joint Chiefs of Staff for a decision. Furthermore, each military intelligence service has the right to report directly to the JCS without any DIA filter. Furthermore, the service representatives continue to sit at community intelligence meetings as observers, and they reserve the right to footnote their dissenting views in the National Intelligence Estimates.

The DIA, therefore, never succeeded in replacing the various services, and it has had mixed success in controlling the almost infinite number of army, navy, and air force intelligence units that have proliferated over the years and that have never been seriously interested in central guidance from either the CIA or the DIA. Nevertheless, the DIA has managed to act as a coordinator, if not a controller, of the military intelligence services and is their representative at intelligence community meetings. The DIA also manages the Defense Attaché System, which assigns military attachés to U.S. embassies, although again the various services nominate the actual personnel.

Like the Central Intelligence Agency, the DIA is a collector and analyst of every conceivable military topic, from weapons being produced by foreign powers to estimates on the battle-readiness of foreign armed forces, friendly and otherwise. Like the CIA and the State Department's INR, the DIA produces daily, weekly, and monthly intelligence summaries. The CIA's Directorate of Intelligence, the INR, and the DIA employ the top analysts and estimates experts. The overlapping and competitive structure ensures that every idea is examined carefully and resolved at the national level.

What are the composition and roles of the military intelligence services? In a military order of battle, the command structure from field army through corps, division, regiment, and battalion, in fact every size of force, has a G-2 component.

There are now four basic military intelligence units that are major players in the U.S. intelligence game. The oldest service, the army's G-2, has fought a long battle for survival. It competed with the wartime OSS, it lost its air intelligence arm when a separate air force was created in 1947, and it lost more ground when the DIA was set up in 1961. Despite these setbacks, G-2 continues to provide the technical intelligence on the ground forces of foreign countries. Its attachés in U.S. embassies, including an elite corps of foreign area officers (FAOs), provide additional data and contact with their opposite numbers in the countries to which they are assigned. Thus, G-2 continues to collect worldwide and to disseminate intelligence relevant to all of the army's responsibilities. All of its reports are sent to the army chief of staff, with the emphasis on raw reports rather than finished evaluations. G-2 also has a counterintelligence capability in the Counter Intelligence Corps, as well as responsibility for developing and managing tactical intelligence systems and equipment.

U.S. naval intelligence has had an easier time of it than its army counterpart, but the Office of Naval Intelligence remains the smallest of the military intelligence services, with about two thousand men and women. The ONI fulfills the same broad tasks for the U.S. Navy that G-2 does for the army, including both intelligence collection, especially on foreign naval forces, and counterintelligence. Formerly the ONI's most critical assignment was the tracking of Soviet submarines carrying nuclear warheads. With the end of the cold war, its major responsibility became patrolling the oceans' sea lanes for the safety of U.S. shipping. It depends on the navy's own satellite reconnaissance, supplemented by the ultrasensitive array of sound-sensing devices planted on ocean floors or carried on surface ships or submarines. The ONI also has the more mundane task of compiling detailed reports on beaches and ports.

Complementing but separate from naval intelligence is the intelligence arm of the Marine Corps. Its specific mission is to provide timely information for marine tactical commanders, primarily in amphibious operations.

The newest intelligence service is the young but aggressive air force's A-2. It is also the largest of the intelligence services collecting and analyzing information relevant to its missions. The air force has also put together the most technically proficient service, which has remained so by, among other things, retaining control of the U.S. reconnaissance satellites launched from Vandenberg Air Force Base in California. The bargain made by DCI McCone in the early 1960s created a national intelligence entity in which, the CIA joined with the air force to develop an overhead reconnaissance mechanism combining CIA analytical skills and air force technology. This system, seldom identified, has existed since 1961 and was one of the showpieces of the Gulf War of 1991. The most strategic mission of A-2 is estimating ICBM capabilities of the Commonwealth of Independent States (CIS). This is a task that directly feeds into all CIS-U.S. strategic weapons negotiations. The Foreign Technology Division of A-2 is the leading source of technical analysis for all foreign aircraft and missiles. The Air Force also compiles human intelligence, which it carries out through its attaché system.

All of the military services report to their chiefs of staff, who also receive intelligence from their military commands around the world. Understandably, these reports vary in quality and quantity. Army intelligence coming from Western Europe on the Soviet threat, for example, was long recognized as a superior product—it had to be—far better than other theater operations. The tactical military intelligence units are preoccupied primarily with training until and unless they get into combat operations. Their main job is to absorb national intelligence data for use when needed.

An outstanding example of the complexity of theater military intelligence is Europe. As intelligence expert Lyman Kirkpatrick (1973) explained it:

> The Commander-in-Chief (CINC) of the U.S. Army, Europe, has his own intelligence staff, as does the CINC of the U.S. Air Force, Europe. These headquarters report to CINCEUR, who also has an intelligence staff and who reports directly to the Joint Chiefs of Staff. At the risk of confusing but to be quite correct and further illustrate the complexity, the CINC, U.S. Army, Europe, also reports to the Chief of Staff of the U.S. Army in Washington, to whom he looks for personnel, equipment, etc., although he is under the field command of CINCEUR.

In fact, the complexity issue has not gone away. In March 1991 the Senate Select Committee on Intelligence began a year of hearings designed to reduce this complexity, as well as what it called "duplication, waste, and poor performance" within the intelligence community. Although the committee considered several organizational changes obvious from the Desert Shield–Desert Storm experience, it took no comprehensive action. The other major concern of the Senate panel was the growing division between the national intelligence community headed by the CIA and the tactical military intelligence bureaucracy that belonged to the theater commands of the armed forces. As a result, some members of Congress feared, the United States no longer has a truly centralized intelligence service. During its hearings, the Senate Select Committee concluded that Congress should take a role in fashioning and maintaining an intelligence structure that would strengthen the links between the CIA and the theater commands. Its immediate action was to approve the nomination of Vice Admiral William Studeman as deputy director of the CIA. The committee agreed that the admiral, with thirty years in military intelligence, including serving as director of naval intelligence and director of the National Security Agency, would

bring together the civilian and military intelligence communities.

Photoreconnaissance played a major role in the Gulf War. A great deal was theater tactical military reconnaissance, employed after theater forces were deployed. Of course, the strategic coverage provided by satellite vehicles in the national system needed to be integrated with the tactical field forces. Through the extraordinary proliferation of computerized display screens in all field units, the combined national and theater intelligence effort became truly a new kind of wizard war.

Supervising this enormous worldwide effort is the still-secret air force element that works closely with the CIA to manage overhead reconnaissance but that seldom appears on any organizational charts. The actual work of image and photo interpretation is carried out by the National Photo Intelligence Center (NPIC), originally created by the CIA but now run jointly by the DIA and CIA. Hundreds of photo interpreters monitor their target areas each day and disseminate the product in countless target folders that give field units precise knowledge of what they are up against.

As with many advances in intelligence, the jump to the use of more sophisticated techniques was not a simple matter of mindless technological accretion. It came about as a result of the drive and vision of Arthur Lundahl, whose role was comparable to that of Herbert Yardley of signals intercept fame. Lundahl was a photo interpreter in World War II and was put back to work within the CIA's DDI in 1953. He became chief of a twenty-member unit, which he built in a decade into a staff of twelve hundred at NPIC. Even more important, Lundahl worked with the U.S. private sector to obtain the very best in cameras, lenses, and special films for the required high-level photography. The U-2 photoreconnaissance plane, one of his greatest achievements, proved itself in targeting the Soviet Union, Cuba, and, later, China.

After 1960 the cutting edge of photographic intelligence technology was no longer the U-2 but the orbiting satellite. Thanks to rapid advances in technology, by the 1990s satellites deep in earth orbit could detect objects less than a foot in length, and priority pictures could be transmitted directly to ground stations for analysis by photo interpreters.

Along with ELINT (electronic communications) and COMINT (communication intercepts), photographic sensors form the "national technical means" that both superpowers employ to verify arms control agreements while charting the signatories' deployments of military equipment. Nevertheless, satellites can be blinded, at least temporarily. Pictures cannot be taken through heavy clouds, smoke, or dust storms (as the Iran-Iraq and Persian Gulf wars have proven). Nor can satellite cameras get inside buildings and shelters where weapons may be stored. Nearly everything else, however, is fair game for the camera. There are few analytical problems that do not start with the skilled interpreters and analysts of the NPIC. If the U.S. intelligence community had accomplished nothing else since World War II except to develop modern overhead reconnaissance imagery, it would easily have justified its cost to the nation.

Nevertheless, the most successful and longest-running component of the intelligence community is so-called communications intelligence. It is a direct and lineal descendent of Yardley's Black Chamber, and its historical accomplishments include the breaking and exploiting of the Japanese and German codes.

After World War II, the military services maintained their separate capabilities, despite pressure to unify them. A major step toward that unification came about in 1949, when the Defense Department created the Armed Forces Security Agency (AFSA). Three years later, and as a by-product of the Korean War, the AFSA was reorganized as the National Security Agency by a secret presidential order. The NSA became the centralized communications service reporting to the secretary of defense through the deputy director of defense research and engineering but not directly to the Joint Chiefs of Staff. Because the NSA was established as a national intelligence entity, not just a military service, it is obliged to work closely with the CIA and it also participates in the work of the National Foreign Intelligence Board.

Nevertheless, each armed service's communications unit, for example, the Army Security Agency, the Naval Security Group, and the air forces' Security Service, has managed to retain its own capability for tactical communications intelligence gathering through its own field units. Their intelligence, however, is reported to the NSA and thus to the entire intelligence community, where the data are correlated with all other relevant information. The system is truly integrated and serves the national community well, in addition to serving theater units and regional commanders.

As a result of the 1952 reform, the NSA is the nation's premier codebreaking and code-making service. Its work has historically been aimed principally at Soviet-bloc and other Communist countries, but not exclusively. Breaking codes of friendly countries has always been done and has always been controversial (as Yardley proved), but the rule is simple. Codebreaking is not done simply on a strategic life-or-death basis. Reading someone's mail can also be helpful when it comes to diplomatic negotiations on something as mundane, but increasingly important, as a commercial treaty.

The NSA's codebreaking mission in this highly computerized era is, however, not nearly as dramatic as the decrypting of the Japanese Purple Code. In fact, modern high-level ciphers are usually difficult to break into, leaving U.S. and foreign analysts with something less than MAGIC in their hands. Nevertheless, mechanical and human errors sometimes reveal messages meant to be hidden. Moreover, traffic analysis of the senders and receivers often reveals much about the structure and activity of the armed forces involved. Thus, even if the texts cannot be read, NSA analysts can reconstruct radio networks that parallel military organization and deployment.

During actual conflict, as in the 1991 Gulf War, NSA monitors have had great success in reading the military communications traffic, for the simple, battle-tested reason that combat units use less complex codes and ciphers to meet the needs of a rapidly changing battlefield. In these cases, signals intercepts become one of the richest sources of intelligence about the size and deployment of the available enemy forces.

The NSA also is heavily involved in another aspect of what Winston Churchill called the Wizard War. This is the special area of ELINT, or electronic intelligence. ELINT is possible because most modern military weapons and equipment emit electronic signals—blips and bleeps—all of which can be recorded by sensitive monitors. ELINT yields an enormous harvest of information about the rapidly changing technical specifications of each weapon system. ELINT also can provide an overall electronic order of battle describing the deployment of radar, electronic countermeasures designed to jam U.S. ELINT capabilities, and even enemy counter-countermeasures.

Greatly supplementing earthbound tactical ELINT machines are NSA satellites capable of recording earth-generated signals. In addition to following battlefield signals, ELINT satellites also monitor the strategic bleeps emitted by missile launches, especially test vehicles, which transmit to their headquarters through telemetry vital data on their performances. Unless encrypted, that information is also available to satellite eavesdroppers, which both the NSA and the CIA use to detect new research and development trends within the missile-firing nation's military establishment. Not surprisingly, therefore, ELINT satellites are the most complex and expensive in the entire arsenal of modern intelligence collection.

It is also no surprise that the NSA is the most secretive of U.S. intelligence services. Budgets are classified, as is the exact number of agency employees. Its main headquarters is surrounded by three fences, and armed guards patrol the building and the grounds on an around-the-clock basis. Moreover, NSA directors have always been military officers who keep an extremely low profile, unlike any number of directors of central intelligence who have come into the light of publicity. Unlike the CIA, there is no NSA press office to serve inquiring reporters.

The NSA has had major security breaches, however, particularly in the early 1960s. Partly in reaction, Congress passed legislation giving the NSA director the right to dismiss employees without showing cause—a power that the DCI had from the beginning.

Despite the NSA's penchant for secrecy, something is known of NSA structure. For example, the NSA has three important divisions. One is the Office of Production, which has been assigned the job of breaking codes and ciphers of foreign countries. That effort is mounted by a small band of senior cryptanalysts who number no more than several hundred. Second is the Office of Communications Security, which produces U.S. codes and devises ways to protect them. Finally, the Office of Research and Development designs new communications equipment and carries out long-term research on cryptanalysis.

The NSA, aside from its headquarters in Fort Meade, Maryland (completed in 1957), has a sprawling empire (including deployed units in the military services) of two thousand intercept "positions" on land and sea and in the air and outer space. They are concentrated, however, on the eastern periphery of the CIS, in Russia, Ukraine, Kazakhstan, and Byelarus. Many of them are deployed in signals intercept satellite vehicles orbiting the earth or placed in geostationary orbit at a particularly advantageous collection point. These extraordinarily sensitive facilities and vehicles are meant to pick up almost any communication or electronic signal emitted from these four states of the former Soviet Union. These signals complement the photographic imagery obtained by satellite and airplane. Together they give the U.S. intelligence community the clearest idea of military and industrial activity in the area. They were extensively used during the Gulf War.

The NSA has the largest budget (much larger than that of the CIA) and the greatest number of personnel in the U.S. intelligence community. The NSA, in fact, was called during the cold war the largest intelligence service in the free world and is technologically the most advanced. This is an advantage that is not likely to be overcome by any nation, thanks to U.S. superiority in computer technology and its application to cryptanalysis.

The NSA's great cost reflects two facts of communications intelligence: first, the high-technology equipment used is expensive; second, despite the number of machines used, cryptanalysis remains labor-intensive. In a world where intelligence collection and counter-intelligence have become increasingly advanced technologically and thus increasingly expensive, neither the NSA nor the rest of the U.S. intelligence community has much choice in the matter.

How the Military Forces Use Intelligence.
The goal of the modern U.S. intelligence system is to provide a globally integrated two-way flow of relevant information. It moves from the individual military unit in the field through the layers of intelligence services until it reaches the top level in Washington. Finished intelligence then flows down to the relevant theater commands and field units in the shortest time possible. It is a daunting assignment, but the United States, after two centuries of trial and error, has managed this task better than any other nation in history as demonstrated by the intelligence contribution to the overwhelming military victory in the Gulf War.

The two-way flow begins at the tactical unit or strategic force level, where the intelligence sections of every command strive to have up-to-date and reliable information on any possible enemy order of battle. The information must also include technical intelligence about weapons characteristics, as well as about the capabilities and vulnerabilities of all support facilities, such as transportation and communications equipment, and at least the main features of the terrain of potential battlefields.

All this data goes up the chain of command, as well as directly back to Washington and the U.S. intelligence community. In Washington, all sources and all services are melded into one combined evaluation process from which, it is hoped, emerges the overall picture confronting the U.S. military machine. From this national picture, the various military services, along with the Joint Chiefs of Staff and the Office of the Secretary of Defense, abstract the intelligence relevant to their missions and build an intelligence data base for their own use in operational planning. This information is also sent to the joint theater commands and to service headquarters around the world. The theater command staffs sort out the intelligence relevant to the units under them and pass it along to the field. Thus, there is a constant flow of finished intelligence from the intelligence community to the front line for the purpose of aiding combat unit readiness.

The president of the United States, in his capacity as commander in chief of the armed forces, is nominally the recipient of all military and military-related intelligence that affects his very broad strategic responsibilities. It is the president's prerogative to share or compartmentalize the intelligence and to change the direction of intelligence collection if he feels it is not adequate for his responsibilities.

Meanwhile, at every command level, there is an intense demand for reliable intelligence upon which strategic planning can be based, forces can be trained and deployed, and combat readiness can be maintained. Whereas reporting goes up the various chains of command, strategic intelligence mainly goes down after it has been coordinated, evaluated, and aggregated at the top level of each part of the intelligence community in Washington. The national intelligence system is the key to integration and coordination of the total military data base.

In peacetime, these tasks must be done smoothly if the intelligence community is to function properly in the heat of war. Moreover, the abrupt change from peace to war, as the United States learned once again during the Persian Gulf crisis, may not be detected until overt military action occurs. As in the Israeli-Arab Yom Kippur War of October 1973, the tip-off for imminent hostilities can come through a peripheral event, in this case the abrupt withdrawal of Soviet advisers from Egypt and Syria. The CIA at the time also circulated some very sensitive clandestine reports on Syrian and Egyptian war plans for an attack on Israel. Unfortunately, the data were dismissed by almost all military intelligence analysts as contrary to their estimates of Arab intentions. Oddly enough, only the State Department's INR put on the record that the Egyptian military forces might attack the Sinai, but these warnings were largely disregarded.

Thus, the flow of globally integrated intelligence does not necessarily mean U.S. policymakers always know what is going on or act upon the information they receive. No intelligence system, no matter how expensive or sophisticated, can guarantee successful prediction of events. Its job is to pull together the best guesses possible in answering the hardest questions and to present the various options as probability estimates. These informed guesses are made not because they are always exactly right (sometimes they are not even close), but because the estimates are as objective and accurate as the evidence allows. Thus, the mathematical-chance calculations are likely to be better than seat-of-the-pants intuition.

The American experience in intelligence has been the struggle to do these apparently simple tasks, but it has taken more than two centuries to create the most effective—although definitely not flawless—integrated intelligence system ever created. It is this advanced national intelligence machine that gives U.S. military forces, American diplomats, and the nation's political leaders a potential edge in every area of the world in peace or war.

See also DECISION-MAKING; LOGISTICS; OPERATIONS RESEARCH; POLITICAL GOALS AND THE DEVELOPMENT OF MILITARY STRATEGY; PSYCHOLOGICAL OPERATIONS; *and* U.S. MILITARY STRATEGY IN THE NUCLEAR AGE.

BIBLIOGRAPHY

General Works

Cline, Ray S. *Secrets, Spies, and Scholars: Blueprint of the Essential CIA* (1976).

———. *The CIA: Reality Versus Myth* (1982).

Colby, William, and Peter Forbath. *Honorable Men: My Life in the CIA* (1978).

Constantinides, George C. *Intelligence and Espionage: An Analytical Bibliography* (1983).

Defense Intelligence School. *Bibliography of Intelligence Literature: A Critical and Annotated Bibliography of Open-Source Intelligence Literature*, 7th ed. Edited by Robert P. Palmer (1981).

Dulles, Allen W. *The Craft of Intelligence* (1963).

Godson, Roy, ed. *Intelligence Requirements for the 1980s: Analysis and Estimates* (1980).

———. *Intelligence Requirements for the 1980s: Elements of Intelligence* (1983).

Harris, William R. *Intelligence and National Security: A Bibliography with Selected Annotations* (1968).

Hilsman, Roger. *Strategic Intelligence and National Decisions* (1956).

Kent, Sherman. *Strategic Intelligence for American World Policy* (1965).

Maurer, Alfred C., Marion D. Tunstall, and James M. Keagle, eds. *Intelligence: Policy and Process* (1985).

Miller, Nathan. *Spying for America: The Hidden History of U.S. Intelligence* (1989).

Pettee, George S. *The Future of American Secret Intelligence* (1946).

Rowan, Richard Wilmer. *The Story of Secret Service* (1937).

U.S. Army Security Agency. *The Origin and Development of the Army Security Agency, 1917–1947* (1978).

Colonial and Revolutionary War Eras

Augur, Helen. *The Secret War of Independence* (1955).

Bakeless, John E. *Turncoats, Traitors, and Heros* (1959).

Central Intelligence Agency. *Intelligence in the War of Independence* (1976).

Colonial Williamsburg Foundation. *The Journal of Major George Washington* (1982).

Currey, Cecil B. *Code Number 72/Ben Franklin: Patriot or Spy* (1972).

Parkman, Francis. *Montcalm and Wolfe* (1884).

Pennypacker, Morton. *General Washington's Spies on Long Island and in New York* (1939).

Rossiter, Clinton, ed. *The Federalist Papers* (1961).

Sellers, Charles Coleman. *Patience Wright: American Artist and Spy in George III's London* (1976).

Civil War to World War I

Bakeless, John E. *Spies of the Confederacy* (1970).

Bates, David H. *Lincoln in the Telegraph Office: Recollections of the U.S. Military Telegraph Corps During the Civil War* (1907).

Dorwart, Jeffrey M. *The Office of Naval Intelligence: The Birth of America's First Intelligence Agency, 1865–1918* (1979).

Friedman, William F., and Charles J. Mendelsohn. *The Zimmerman Telegram of January 16, 1917 and Its Cryptographic Background* (1976).

Lester, Richard I. *Confederate Finance and Purchasing in Great Britain* (1975).

Stern, Philip Van Doren. *Secret Missions of the Civil War: First-Hand Accounts by Men and Women Who Risked Their Lives in Underground Activities for the North and the South* (1959).

Tidwell, William A., James O. Hall, and David Winfred Gaddy. *Come Retribution: The Confederate Secret Service and the Assassination of Lincoln* (1988).

Tuchman, Barbara W. *The Zimmerman Telegram* (1958).

Van Deman, Ralph Henry. *Memoirs of Major General R. H. Van Deman*, 3 vols. (1950–1956).

Zacharias, Ellis M. *Secret Missions: The Story of an Intelligence Officer* (1946).

World War II

Alsop, Stewart, and Thomas Braden. *Sub Rosa: The OSS and American Espionage* (1964).

Cave Brown, Anthony, ed. *The Secret War Report of the OSS* (1976).

Ford, Corey. *Donovan of OSS* (1970).

Hymoff, Edward. *The OSS in World War II* (1986).

Koch, Oscar W., and Robert G. Hays. *G-2: Intelligence for Patton* (1971).

MacCloskey, Monro. *Secret Air Missions* (1966).

Smith, Richard Harris. *OSS: The Secret History of America's First Central Intelligence Agency* (1972).

Smith, Truman. *Air Intelligence Activities: Office of the Military Attaché, American Embassy, Berlin, Germany: August 1935–April 1939* (1954–1956).

Stevenson, William. *A Man Called Intrepid: The Secret War* (1976).

Strong, Kenneth. *Intelligence at the Top: The Recollections of an Intelligence Officer* (1968).

U.S. Counter Intelligence Corps School. *History and Mission of the Counter Intelligence Corps in World War II* (1951).

U.S. Department of Defense. *The "Magic" Background of Pearl Harbor*, 8 vols. (1978).

U.S. War Department, Strategic Services Unit. *War Report of the OSS*, 2 vols. (1976).

Wohlstetter, Roberta. *Pearl Harbor: Warning and Decision* (1962).

The Modern Intelligence Community

Bonds, Ray, ed. *The U.S. War Machine: An Illustrated Encyclopedia of American Military Equipment and Strategy* (1978).

De Silva, Peer. *Sub Rosa: The CIA and the Uses of Intelligence* (1978).

Karalekas, Anne. *History of the Central Intelligence Agency* (1977).

Kirkpatrick, Lyman B., Jr. *The Real CIA* (1968).

———. *The U.S. Intelligence Community: Foreign Policy and Domestic Activities* (1973).

McChristian, Joseph A. *The Role of Military Intelligence, 1965–1967* (1974).

Martin, David C. *Wilderness of Mirrors* (1980).

Meyer, Cord. *Facing Reality: From World Federalism to the CIA* (1980).

Meyer, Karl E., and Tad Szulc. *The Cuban Invasion: The Chronicle of a Disaster* (1962).

Phillips, David Atlee. *The Night Watch* (1977).

Powe, Marc B., and Edward E. Wilson. *The Evolution of American Military Intelligence* (1973).

Powers, Thomas. *The Man Who Kept the Secrets: Richard Helms and the CIA* (1979).

Ransom, Harry Howe. *The Intelligence Establishment* (1970).

Rositzke, Harry. *The CIA's Secret Operations: Espionage, Counterespionage, and Covert Action* (1977).

Troy, Thomas F. *Donovan and the CIA: A History of the Establishment of the Central Intelligence Agency* (1981).

Wise, David, and Thomas B. Ross. *The Invisible Government* (1964).

Technical Intelligence

Brookes, Andrew J. *Photo Reconnaissance* (1975).

Burrows, William E. *Deep Black: Space Espionage and National Security* (1986).

Clark, Ronald W. *The Man Who Broke Purple: The Life of Colonel William F. Friedman* (1977).

Jones, Reginald Victor. *The Wizard War: British Scientific Intelligence, 1939–1945* (1978).

Kahn, David. *The Codebreakers: The Story of Secret Writing* (1967).

Klass, Philip J. *Secret Sentries in Space* (1971).

Moore, Dan Tyler, and Martha Waller. *Cloak and Cipher* (1962).

Paine, Lauran. *The Technology of Espionage* (1978).

Powers, Francis Gary, and Curt Gentry. *Operation Overflight: The U-2 Spy Pilot Tells His Story for the First Time* (1970).

Pratt, Fletcher. *Secret and Urgent: The Story of Codes and Ciphers* (1939).

Shulman, David. *An Annotated Bibliography of Cryptography* (1976).

Streetly, Martin. *Confound and Destroy: 100 Group and the Bomber Support Campaign* (1978).

Taylor, John W. R., and David Mondey. *Spies in the Sky* (1972).

U.S. Army, Security Agency. *The History of Codes and Ciphers in the United States Prior to World War I* (1978).

———. *The History of Codes and Ciphers in the United States During World War I* (1979).

Yardley, Herbert O. *The American Black Chamber* (1931).

PERSONNEL MANAGEMENT

David R. Segal

MANPOWER POLICY

The history of American military manpower policy has been marked by major discrepancies between principle and reality. The militia principle, adopted from the British and put into law in the Uniform Militia Act of 1792, asserted the responsibility of citizens to serve in the military, a principle frequently enunciated by George Washington. Although universal service thus became an ideal, neither the forces that resulted from mobilization of the militia nor the volunteer forces that served on the frontier were broadly representative of society but rather depended on recruits from the lower social strata. Many of the inequities of the militia derived from their control by the states.

From the colonial period through the Civil War (1861–1865), as the United States evolved as a nation, attempts to draft military personnel were no more equitable and produced popular opposition and domestic unrest. The first federal draft, instituted during the Civil War, did establish the right of the federal government directly to induct men into military service, but, as in earlier conflicts, the draft was not a major source of manpower in the Civil War. Rather, the war was fought primarily by volunteers.

The Dick Act of 1903, which sought to establish effective federal control of the armed forces through repeal of the Militia Act of 1792, re-pealed the principle of a universal military obligation as well. World War I was the first war in which the United States actually depended on a draft for military manpower. Although that draft was an equitable one, the postwar National Defense Act of 1920 reaffirmed the nation's reliance on voluntary recruitment in peacetime, despite the fact that the nation had assumed a new international role.

Conscription was reinstituted in World War II. Again, with a major mobilization, the draft was generally equitable. In the absence of support for universal military training or universal service during the postwar years, conscription was continued with only one fourteen-month lapse and elicited relatively little opposition during periods of major mobilization or periods when virtually nobody was drafted. On the other hand, during periods when large numbers, but not majorities, of the eligible population were drafted, such as during the Vietnam War, opposition on the basis of inequity grew.

The experience of the all-volunteer force, particularly in the early 1970s and early 1980s, demonstrated that under conditions of high unemployment, with military compensation at levels comparable to civilian pay, and with a nation willing to invest resources in recruiting, sufficient people with desired levels of education and mental aptitude can be recruited to staff the force.

The 1991 war in the Persian Gulf demonstrated the ability of the force to execute a large-scale deployment—more than 600,000 personnel—and to execute a modern conventional war. It also demonstrated the dependence of that force on its mobilization base—the reserves—and that with women comprising more than 10 percent of the force, any statutory and regulatory exclusions of military women from combat roles does not prevent their being captured, wounded, or killed.

The Colonial and Revolutionary War Periods. America's early military traditions, which were inherited from the British, included both a favorable predisposition toward militia organization and a distrust of centralized standing peacetime forces. As British subjects, the North American colonists carried with them the lessons learned from the excesses of King James II's seventeenth-century standing army, which had been used to suppress the freedom of the English. Threatened by both American Indians and rival colonial powers, the colonists developed a militia force of citizen-soldiers.

As the colonies became more secure and as threats from the Indians faded, the militia system deteriorated in much the same way that conscription would deteriorate two centuries later—through a system of deferments and exemptions that moved away from the principle of universal obligation and that spread the burden of military service in an increasingly inequitable fashion.

The common militia during the colonial period was in theory composed of all able-bodied free white men. It was to serve as the mobilization base of the colonies, with the volunteer militia providing the long-term military nucleus. A considerable proportion of the citizenry, however, was exempted from militia service by more than two hundred militia laws. The Massachusetts Militia Act of 1647, for example, exempted officers, fellows, and students of Harvard College; church elders and deacons; schoolmasters, physicians, and surgeons; captains of ships of more than twenty tons; fishermen who were employed year-round; people who had physical problems; members of the general court; and people who were excused from service by the courts. The burden of service was increasingly lifted from the shoulders of the wealthy and placed upon the shoulders of the poor.

When the volunteer militia failed to produce a sufficiently large force to meet a threat and when legislative calls for additional volunteers failed to expand the force sufficiently, men were drafted from the common militia. Such drafts increased the inequity of the distribution of the burden of service, resulting in desertions and draft riots. Both of these forms of opposition were to become commonplace in America during periods of military draft.

During the revolutionary war, the colonies temporarily had to centralize control over the militias and to resort to conscription to raise the Continental army. The conscription process, however, was left to the states, which continued past inequities, causing draft riots. After the victory of the Continental army over the British in 1783, George Washington urged Congress to accept the principle "that every Citizen who enjoys the protection of a free government, owes . . . his personal services to the defense of it."

On the basis of this principle of universal national military obligation, Washington recommended the establishment of a small peacetime army, backed by a national militia, which would consist of citizens from eighteen to fifty years of age and who would be equipped and trained at federal expense. Congress ruled against General Washington, declared that standing armies in times of peace were inconsistent with the principle of republican government, and discharged the Continental army, except for "twenty-five privates to guard the stores at Fort Pitt and fifty-five to guard the stores at West Point, with a proportionate number of officers," none of whom were to be above the rank of captain.

From the Early Republic to the Spanish-American War. The victory of the Antifederalists in preventing the formation of a national military institution did not eliminate the need for an armed force. Although hostilities against the British had ended, the new nation still had a western frontier to protect. On 3 June 1784, the day after it had dismissed the Continental army, Congress requested that the states of Connecticut, New Jersey, New York, and Pennsylvania recruit a total of seven hundred militiamen for a year of service on the frontier. One year later, the term of frontier service was extended to three years, and the militiamen were replaced by regular soldiers. The First American Regiment, operating under the dual authority of the states, which supplied its officers and enlisted men, and the Congress, which provided its authorization, was plagued by problems of morale, drunkenness, and desertion; it proved to be ineffective even in the protection of its own garrisons. The Constitutional Convention, convened in Philadelphia in 1787, ultimately had to deal with the issue of whether responsibility for the maintenance of an armed force would reside with the states or with the central government.

The resolution reached by the convention was a compromise. The new government was given the power to "raise and support armies," with a two-year limit on appropriations; to "provide and maintain a navy"; and to "make rules for the regulation of the land and naval forces." The right of the states to control their militias, which were to be the nation's major land force in the event of a crisis, was also confirmed. The navy, which was not subject to a two-year limit on appropriations, would be the major defense of the isolated nation against foreign powers. The small voluntary national army would protect the frontiers and handle any encroachment by colonial powers or problems with native Americans, and the militias would help maintain internal order, reinforce the regulars on the frontier when necessary, and provide a mobilization base for the national army in case of emergency. With few exceptions, white male able-bodied citizens between the ages of eighteen and forty-five were liable for militia service.

Failures of the state militias in the Whiskey Rebellion (1794) and in the Indian wars led the leaders of the Federalist party to continue to press for a national militia or a standing army, but these proposals were just as firmly opposed by the Jeffersonian Republicans. At the end of the eighteenth century, the United States balanced local and national interests by maintaining an expanded national army, the mobilization base for which still belonged to the states.

Events across the Atlantic helped shape the evolution of American military manpower policy. The success of the French Revolution (1789–1799) and the establishment of the *levée en masse* by the Committee of Public Safety tied citizenship to military participation for all French men, women, and children, who were required to provide support for the army if they did not themselves serve. The *levée* demonstrated to Americans, Federalist and Jeffersonian Republican alike, the potential ugliness of a national militia, and it frightened the Americans by its military successes over professional European soldiers.

Relations between the United States and France deteriorated during the 1790s, and in the face of skirmishes on the high seas and abrasive diplomatic relations, Congress expanded the navy, established a separate Navy Department, and in 1798 passed both the Provisional Army Act, which provided for the recruitment and training of a ten-thousand-man reserve force, and the New Army Act, which added twelve regiments and more than ten thousand volunteer soldiers to the regular army. Both acts were designed to remove responsibility for national security from the state militias and to give it instead to the central government. The Republicans anticipated that this all-volunteer force would be recruited from the lowest strata of society, men who, motivated solely by pecuniary concerns, would be unlikely to fight for the principles of the Republic. At the beginning of the nineteenth century, with Napoleon's ascent to power in France having removed the threat from that quarter, and with the election of Thomas Jefferson to the presidency, the initiatives of the Federalists to establish a strong national army were reversed.

In his inaugural address (1801), Jefferson emphasized his belief that state militias should be the major defensive force of the nation, and in his first message to Congress, he requested and received a reduction in the size of the regular army to about thirty-three hundred soldiers. With a major war being waged between Great Britain and France, Jefferson maintained a position of neutrality, using his forces to prepare to defend the U.S. coastline and to explore, organize, and protect the western frontier.

Maintaining neutrality, however, became increasingly difficult. In 1807 the British warship *Leopard* attacked and defeated the U.S. frigate *Chesapeake* off the Virginia coast and impressed several members of its crew. Jefferson, although continuing to seek neutrality, called for an increase in the size of the army, and in 1808, Congress made the organization and arming of the militia a federal responsibility. James Madison, elected in 1808 as the fourth president, inherited a nation committed to neutrality and to a militia-based military organization.

The impressment of American seamen and British interference with U.S. shipping continued. To respond to these provocations and to take advantage of what it perceived to be opportunities to expand into British Canada and Spanish Florida, the United States declared war against Great Britain in June 1812. The British had only a few thousand troops in Canada, and there was virtually no Spanish garrison in Florida, but the United States was not in a better posture significantly than its rivals to wage a land war. At the time war was declared, there were fewer than seven thousand regular U.S. troops, scattered over scores of posts. The state-based militia was theoretically large, numbering in the hundreds of thousands but was poorly equipped and trained.

Congress sought to improve the American posture by creating an expanded regular (albeit temporary) force, recruited through economic incentives and supplemented by militia. The new regiments, commanded by veterans of the Revolution and manned by a combination of regular soldiers from previously existing units, new regulars recruited for this war, volunteers, and militiamen, did not fare well against the British professional soldiers in Canada. It fell to the navy, at Lake Erie and Lake Champlain, to prevent the British from bringing the campaign south.

With the defeat of Napoleon in 1814, the Brit-

ish could make a larger investment in the war in North America. The British advance down Lake Champlain proved the efficacy of the U.S. Navy but also once again demonstrated the weakness of the state-based militia system. With the British at Plattsburgh, New York, the governor of Vermont sought to withdraw his militia from the battle, noting that the Vermont militia was constitutionally required to "repel invaders," but that an invasion of New York did not constitute an invasion of Vermont.

With the British drive south halted and a British attack on Baltimore, Maryland, repelled by forces at Fort McHenry, both sides sought peace, and a treaty was signed in December 1814. News of the treaty did not travel rapidly enough, however, to prevent General Sir Edward Pakenham from marching his ranks of professional British soldiers toward the entrenched citizen-soldiers, regular soldiers, and pirate-soldiers commanded by Andrew Jackson at New Orleans during the second week of January 1815. The relative losses—the British, advancing in ranks, lost one-third of their force, and the Americans, firing from cover, lost seven soldiers—probably tell more about maneuver formations than about the relative merits of professional and citizen armed forces, and the difficulties experienced by Jackson in controlling his militia after the battle added to the accumulating evidence of the weakness of the militia system.

If the War of 1812 indicated a weakness in the militia system, the Mexican War (1846–1848) pointed to the desperate nature of the situation. The militia did not do well in the Indian wars of the 1830s, being poorly armed, poorly trained, and convinced that they were obligated to only three-month tours of service. In the 1840s, Joel R. Poinsett, President Martin Van Buren's secretary of war, attempted to reform the militia but met with no greater success than his predecessors.

Texas had declared independence from Mexico in 1836, and after the massacres at Goliad and the Alamo, the likelihood increased of a war with Mexico. In 1844, president John Tyler submitted to the Senate a treaty to annex Texas. When James Knox Polk was elected president that fall, the nation seemed committed to a war with Mexico. The annexation of Texas was accomplished in the summer of 1845, and General Zachary Taylor, with roughly fifteen hundred regular troops, was sent to Corpus Christi. Reinforcements such as the nation could afford were sent to him, but at the end of the year, he had fewer than four thousand troops. In April 1846, the Mexican army crossed the Rio Grande and a week later destroyed one of Taylor's outposts.

Having previously been authorized to mobilize the militia, Taylor called for five thousand militia from Louisiana and Texas. He in fact got ten thousand, but they arrived too late for the early battles of the war and, committed to only three-month terms of federal service, left too early to participate in the Mexican War. In any case, the militia was protected by law from being required to fight on foreign soil. Thus, the militia played a negligible role in the war.

The Mexican War was fought for the most part by volunteers who, although nominally federal troops, fought in units raised by the states and commanded by officers appointed by the governors. By statute, the volunteers were to serve for one year or for the duration of the war, which President Polk interpreted as a term of service not to exceed one year. Thus, like militia units, these regular regiments were likely to dissolve at key points in the campaign as their tours of duty expired. The U.S. victory over Mexico cannot be credited to the militia system. Rather, just as the War of 1812 demonstrated the efficacy of the navy, the Mexican War demonstrated the importance of a professional officer corps. The senior commanders in Mexico had learned their trade in the War of 1812 and in the Indian wars, and the company and junior field grade officers were the graduates of the U.S. Military Academy at West Point, New York, created in 1802 by Jefferson. Nevertheless, as in the case of the War of 1812, the military victory convinced the nation, erroneously, that the state militia organization, based upon the principle of obligatory service, was sufficient for its needs.

The Mexican War had caused the mobilization of 104,000 U.S. soldiers, primarily volunteers. In keeping with the mobilization model, after the war the volunteers were sent home, and the regular army was reduced to about ten thousand soldiers. The militia model, which supported the rights of the states over those of the central government, continued to serve as the basis for the land forces. Ironically, it was the issue of states' rights that was to lead to the attempted dissolution of the Union and to the first national military draft in U.S. history.

Tensions between the northern and southern states, largely over the issue of slavery, built throughout the 1850s. The election in 1860 of Abraham Lincoln as president was the catalyst to crisis, and in December 1860 South Carolina declared itself a separate and independent state. Six other Deep South states followed suit, and in February 1861 the seven formed the Confederate States of America. Lincoln was willing to concede much on the issue of slavery, but he was not willing to concede the right of secession. Although he attempted a peaceful resolution of the crisis, the Confederacy fired on Fort Sumter at Charleston, South Carolina, harbor on the morning of 12 April.

Technological advances in communication, transportation, and weaponry increased both the rate and the scale of mobilization compared to what had been experienced in conflicts past. Congress sought to mobilize an army of 500,000 soldiers, and the Confederacy sought a force of 400,000. In the course of the war, the two armies mobilized almost 2.5 million men, with the Confederate army being 261,000 strong at its peak, and the Union army 622,000.

The militia organization of the Union forces in 1861 and the fact that the president had to seek mobilization through the states, calling militiamen to serve three-month tours of federal service, forced the border states to choose sides, and the South benefited from this situation. The greater part of the regular army remained loyal to the Union, having been recruited primarily in the North. In order to raise the manpower it needed, the Confederacy enacted conscription one year and four days after Fort Sumter was fired upon. Eleven months later, the Union's Enrollment Act of 1863 established the first federal conscription and lengthened the term of service for conscripts to three years. The military was responsible for most of the administration of the draft. Enrollment officers sought people out in their homes, but people could provide substitutes or purchase their way out of military service.

Conscription was neither equitable nor popular in either the North or the South. Both systems favored the rich. In the North, draft liability could be commuted for a $300 fee, and in the South, owners of slaves were exempted. More important, although the Confederacy had adopted a more centralized manpower system than the Union, the southern states, having seceded on the basis of states' rights, were unwilling to yield even to Jefferson Davis, the president of the Confederacy, a principle they had refused to yield to Abraham Lincoln. The governors of the Confederate states exempted tens of thousands of men from draft liability.

Opposition to the draft was more violent in the North. The commutation provision led to complaints that poor men's blood was going to be spilled in rich men's interests. Opposition to the draft in the North had important racial undercurrents as well, with anticonscription forces blaming the war on blacks. When the first federal draft lottery got under way in New York City in July 1863, the provost marshall's office was stormed by an angry mob and burned to the ground. About fifty-thousand people rioted for four days, in one of the largest acts of collective violence yet experienced in the United States. A great deal of property was destroyed, and roughly a thousand people were injured. It took six regiments of Union troops, returning from the Battle of Gettysburg, to restore order. Additional rioting took place in Massachusetts, Ohio, New Hampshire, and Vermont.

Interestingly, although the draft was a major issue, it was not directly a major source of military manpower in the Civil War, which, like America's previous military engagements, was fought primarily by volunteers. Only about 6 percent of the soldiers who served in the Union army were federal draftees. The draft did, of course, provide an incentive to enlist, beyond the bounties and bonuses that were offered to

volunteers, and yielded America's first draft-motivated volunteers. It also produced substitutes, who served in the place of those draftees who could afford to purchase their way out of service. Most important, it established, at least symbolically, the right of the federal government to induct men into national military service without the intervention of the militia.

General Robert E. Lee's forces surrendered at Appomattox Courthouse in 1865, and in the year after the Grand Army of the Republic marched triumphantly down Pennsylvania Avenue in Washington, D.C., hundreds of thousands of volunteers were mustered out of the federal service, leaving a regular army of six cavalry regiments, five artillery regiments, and nineteen infantry regiments. The veterans of the Union army were to become a major political force in the development of benefit programs that eventually became America's first old-age insurance system.

General George A. Custer lost most of his regiment of cavalry in battle against the Sioux at Little Big Horn in 1876, and in 1877 federal troops were called in to control striking railroad workers who had the sympathies of local militia, but there were no large-scale military engagements in the 1880s. Although the states recognized the shortcomings of militia organization, neither was there a strong move to establish a large federal army. When the Spanish-American War (1898) began, the army consisted of about twenty-eight thousand soldiers scattered around the country.

President William McKinley called for 125,000 volunteers in April 1898, and National Guard units, expanded by recent and untrained volunteers, answered the call, as they did the following month, when Congress authorized an additional 75,000 troops. Of the 200,000 to 300,000 troops that served in the war, the great majority were volunteers from the militia. Two-thirds of the troops never had to leave the United States, and conscription was never considered. Very few men were killed. After the war the volunteer force was demobilized, leaving the remaining federal forces in a garrison posture. As a result of the war, however, the garrisons now included strategic locations outside the continental United States.

At the dawning of the twentieth century an interesting foundation had been laid, in terms of both principle and organization, for the military manpower debate that was to follow. There was general agreement with the principle espoused in the 1790s by Washington regarding the responsibility of citizens to contribute to the common defense. The doctrine of states' rights still required that this contribution come primarily through participation in the militia, although the Militia Act of 1792 was ultimately to be a casualty of the Spanish-American War.

The country's military leaders also recognized that in the absence of a large peacetime standing army, mobilization of the militia for war was neither as smooth nor as socially representative as the principles of militia organization suggested it should be. During the Civil War, the United States had attempted, for the first time, a national draft; this effort had violated the principle of equity, and it had produced riots. All of the nation's wars had been fought for the most part by volunteers, many of whom served no longer than three months and most of whom expected to return home at the end of hostilities, and the country had committed itself to continuing overseas responsibilities.

This was the situation in 1899 when Elihu Root was asked by President McKinley to become secretary of war. Root understood the organizational problems facing the military establishment. In an attempt to deal with them, he brought to the military many of the principles of scientific management that were then being developed in American industry. Part of his organizational reform was intended to provide the federal government with a military force not controlled by the states. This change was accomplished by the Dick Act (1903), which repealed the Militia Act of 1792 and gave the federal government much firmer control over the National Guard, making it both a training ground for volunteer soldiers and the nation's first-line military reserve, at the cost of sacrificing "all but the ghost of the universal military obligation" (Millis, 1956).

The World Wars. In 1910 on the European continent, massive armies were being raised on the basis of universal military obligation, although Great Britain still clung to the principle of voluntary service. The United States attempted to assume a posture of neutrality and mediation in the evolving conflict in Europe and after the outbreak of war in 1914. This stance, however, became increasingly difficult to maintain after the sinking by Germany of the British passenger ship *Lusitania* in May 1915. President Woodrow Wilson and the Democratic party attempted to avoid expanding U.S. military forces, but the Republicans increasingly preached preparedness. The Republicans justified their position by pointing to the need to be able to repel an invading European army, however, not to intervene in the European war.

In moving toward the goal of preparedness, Congress in June 1916 passed the National Defense Act, which established a four-component land force, consisting of an expanded peacetime regular army of 175,000 troops; the National Guard, which carried an obligation for federal service; a reserve force, consisting of men completing their active duty enlistments with the regular army and officers from reserve officer training programs in colleges; and a volunteer army, to be raised in time of war. The efficacy of the act was tested during the summer of 1916, when virtually the entire National Guard was federalized in support of General John J. Pershing's Punitive Expedition into Mexico in pursuit of Francisco "Pancho" Villa. The guard was unable to bring itself to full wartime strength through voluntary enlistments, the guardsmen who were mobilized in many cases made it clear that when they had enlisted in the National Guard, they had not considered the possibility of a real mobilization. The Mexican experience demonstrated that voluntarism would not bring either the regular army or the National Guard to full wartime strength.

President Wilson tried to keep the United States out of the European war, but he also told his defense secretaries to prepare for the expansion of the armed forces. In April 1917 the United States declared war on Germany in the wake of German torpedoing of U.S. ships. Within three months of the declaration of war, more than 300,000 men volunteered for the regular army and the militia, and more than 100,000 joined the navy.

One day after war was declared, the president presented a selective service bill to Congress. The bill, which was signed into law on 18 May, established civilian boards to administer the registration of young adult males. While the weaponry of 1917 required larger armies than had participated in the wars of the nineteenth century, technologies of communication and transportation allowed the luxury of a mobilization that, by contemporary standards, would be regarded as leisurely. The first registration was held on 5 June, and about 9.5 million young men registered immediately. During the course of the war, about 24 million Americans registered. The first lottery drawing to establish order of induction was held on 20 July, and the first inductions took place almost four months after the declaration of war.

Enlistments in the army and in the National Guard decreased after the implementation of the draft, dropping from about 100,000 a month to about 25,000 a month. There was a surge in December 1917 to 141,000, just before voluntary enlistments in the army and in the militia were prohibited among draft-eligible men in order to make manpower management less cumbersome. (Volunteers had more service options than did conscripts.) In July 1918, draft-eligible men aged twenty-one to thirty were prohibited from enlisting in the navy or marines. The following month, all male voluntary enlistments were prohibited.

By the end of 1917, half a million young men had been inducted. During the course of the war, nearly 3 million men were inducted, roughly two-thirds of the U.S. armed forces. About 300,000 people evaded the draft, with prosecution being pursued through the civilian court system. Substitutes and commutation fees were not permitted in this draft, but about 145,000 students under the age of twenty-one were allowed to defer service by enrollment in the Army Student Training Corps (ASTC) for

three years. When the lower age limit for the draft was reduced to eighteen, the period of deferment was reduced to nine months. The first students were activated in October 1918, but an armistice was signed in November 1918 and all trainees were demobilized by the end of the year. The draft was allowed to lapse at the end of the war, establishing precedents, not only for a national draft and for student deferments from that draft, but also for those deferments to expand into exemptions from service.

From the end of 1919 until 1940, the United States had an all-volunteer armed force. Congress considered a system of universal military training, but a nation that believed it had won the war to end all wars did not see a military manpower policy that would guarantee a large mobilization base as a pressing issue. The National Defense Act of 1920 reaffirmed the reliance of the armed forces and of the nation on voluntary recruitment. The Joint Army and Navy Selective Service Committee was convened in 1926, setting the stage for a conscription system, but no action was taken. In 1936, Major Lewis B. Hershey was assigned to the joint committee.

In the early 1930s, in the face of the Great Depression and with hostilities erupting in Asia, Europe, and Africa, the United States responded as it had prior to World War I—with a retreat into neutrality. In September 1939, as World War II began, however, President Franklin D. Roosevelt proclaimed a limited national emergency and authorized immediate increases in the armed forces. By that time, the Joint Selective Service Committee had developed a proposed conscription law. In early June 1940, Roosevelt requested authority to call the National Guard into federal service. Late that month, France fell to Germany. Neither the president nor the War Department seemed to want to initiate conscription, but a pro-draft movement among private citizens brought the Selective Service Act before Congress. Once again the nation had the luxury of time to mobilize for war, because two years passed between the declaration of limited national emergency and the declaration of war. More than a year before the declaration of war, local Selective Service System boards were being appointed, men were being registered, and lotteries and inductions had started.

In late August 1940, the president was authorized to federalize the National Guard, and the Selective Training and Service Act was passed by Congress in September. The act called for registration of all males aged twenty-one to thirty-five. In the first registration in 1940, more than 16 million men registered, and induction began in November. Men were called into service for a training period of a year or less, with service beyond the Western Hemisphere being limited to U.S. territories and possessions.

Congress had initially limited the number of draftees to 900,000 serving at any one time, but the limitations on number, time, and location of service were subsequently modified to meet the needs of the war. By the time the United States entered the war in December 1941, about a million men had been inducted. Between November 1940 and November 1946, nearly 50 million men registered, and more than 10 million were inducted. The Selective Service System provided more than two-thirds of America's military manpower during World War II.

The Cold War and Korea. President Harry S. Truman recognized that new technologies of warfare and transportation and the evident hostility of the Soviet Union would preclude complete demobilization after the war. Truman was not a proponent of conscription and preferred a small voluntary active force supported by a mobilization system rooted in universal military training (UMT). In 1945 he attempted to obtain approval for a universal military training plan, requiring all physically qualified males to receive a year of compulsory military training when they reached the age of eighteen. He was unable to generate consensus on the need for or the efficacy of such a program, however. Critics argued that a short period of military training followed by return to civilian life would not really prepare young men for war; that to the extent the system worked it would be most successful in producing ground combat soldiers, al-

though the wars of the future would be decided by air power and atomic weapons; and that UMT did not address the only pressing military manpower problems of the day—the provision of occupation forces for Europe, Japan, and Korea. Truman shifted from arguments based on military manpower needs to those based on citizenship responsibility and opportunities for self-improvement, which moved the debate to the philosophical choice between liberty and equality as basic national values. Congress and the nation opted for individual liberty.

Induction authority under the 1940 Selective Service Act was to expire on 15 May 1945, but the army believed that an extension of conscription was necessary to maintain a force in being, and Congress extended the draft for a year. In the wake of the 1946 Soviet invasion of Iran— the first crisis of the cold war—the 1940 draft was further extended, to March 1947. In late 1946, Truman initiated a second campaign to adopt a program of universal military training, but again Congress did not act. Although Truman was committed to maintaining a peacetime force in being, he recommended that the Selective Service Act be allowed to lapse and Congress concurred. Congress did establish the Office of Selective Service Records, with now-General Hershey as its director, and retained a nucleus of selective service personnel in case the system had to be recovered from its standby status for a mobilization. From April 1947 to June 1948, however, the armed services were to rely wholly on volunteer recruitment.

During the postwar period, relations between East and West became increasingly hostile. Dangerous conditions existed in Palestine, Greece, Italy, Korea, and China, any of which, it was feared, might precipitate major military problems. The navy and the air force—newly evolved from the Army Air Corps—were maintaining their authorized strength, or close to it, through voluntary recruitment, but the ground combat forces—the army and the Marine Corps—were experiencing significant manpower shortages. In an unstable international environment, and with combat forces below strength, the Communist coup in Czechoslovakia in February 1948 proved to be the catalyst for a change in policy. At the time that this last central European democracy was drawn into the Soviet bloc, the United States had roughly 1.6 million active duty military personnel, including a quarter of a million occupation troops in Europe who were not equipped, organized, or trained to go into combat.

Three weeks after the coup in Czechoslovakia, President Truman again asked for a system of universal military training, as well as for reenactment of selective service, which was seen as a short-range program to strengthen all the services, rather than just the army, because World War II had demonstrated the increased importance of air power. Universal military training was meant to eliminate the need for draftees in the long run by enriching the reserve pool, but, in contrast to selective service, the UMT mobilization base was intended primarily for the army and was opposed by the air force, which many saw as the most important service.

In June 1948 a new selective service law, to be in effect for two years, was passed, and General Hershey was again appointed director of the Selective Service System to oversee America's first peacetime draft. An active duty force of 2 million men was authorized. All men between the ages of eighteen and twenty-one were required to register, with selections to be made by local draft boards. Students could defer induction, and the president was given the authority to defer persons whose activity was deemed to be in the national interest.

The existence of a draft encouraged voluntary service, and in the wake of the act, enlistments increased. Only a few thousand men were actually inducted, and in June 1950, as the act was about to expire, there had been no inductions for about eighteen months. The Truman administration had requested a three-year extension of the existing law, a request that the House of Representatives was not happy with, in view of the fact that the law had not been used in a year and a half. Although there was concern about the fact that in 1949 the Soviet Union had broken the U.S. monopoly on nuclear weapons, many people felt that air power, rather than a mobilization base for a land army, would provide the most effective counterforce to the Soviet threat.

In the debate on extension of the Selective Service Act, questions were also raised about the authority of the president to begin inductions without congressional authority. Both houses of Congress passed bills limiting the president's authority to induct young men. A conference committee met on 22 June to resolve differences between the House and Senate bills. Then, on 25 June, the armies of North Korea crossed the thirty-eighth parallel into South Korea. The conference committee quickly recommended, and Congress passed, a one-year extension of the Selective Service Act.

Young men were drafted to fill the divisions that the United States contributed to the United Nations force that was sent to Korea. In 1951 the Universal Military Training and Service Act extended the president's induction authority until 1955, granted him authority to recall reservists, and expanded the manpower pool by lowering the induction age from nineteen to eighteen, lengthening the term of service, and canceling deferments for married men without children. Although the feasibility of universal military training was to be studied, Congress did not approve putting UMT into effect.

President Truman had continued to regard selective service as a transitional measure until universal military training could improve the nation's mobilization posture. When UMT failed to win passage, however, selective service had to be institutionalized. During the Korean War, more than a million and a half young men were inducted through selective service. In 1955 the Universal Military Training and Service Act was extended to 1959. In addition, the mobilization base was enriched through the Reserve Forces Act of 1955, which provided a means of adding men with critical skills to the reserves.

The administration of Dwight Eisenhower furthered the institutionalization of selective service. Although Eisenhower believed more strongly in air power as the key deterrent than did Truman, he also favored a large standing army. Universal military training and volunteer service were both regarded as too expensive to serve as the nation's chief way of meeting its perceived manpower needs. The Reserve Forces Act, however, continued to strengthen the mobilization base, and the threat of conscription produced large numbers of draft-motivated volunteers who enlisted in order to get their choice of service and time period, rather than leaving themselves at the mercy of local draft boards.

As voluntary enlistments increased, inductions under the Selective Service System dropped from more than a third of accessions in the mid-1950s to fewer than 10 percent in the early 1960s. As fewer draftees were needed, the Selective Service System sought to expand the categories of young men who would not be called, in order to justify the relatively few selections that were made. At the end of the Korean War in 1953, fathers and men over twenty-six were deferred. During the postwar period, occupational deferments were eased, largely through the channeling program, which was intended to encourage people with scientific, engineering, and mathematical aptitudes to seek education and employment that would enrich the nation's ability to design and produce weapons. Ultimately, even marriage became a justification for deferment.

Although conscription was sufficiently accepted to be renewed periodically and routinely without much debate, it was recognized that the deferment system produced continuing inequities. The system was maintained not because it produced draftees, who were relatively few, but because it stimulated enlistments for all the services, in particular bringing high-aptitude young men both into the enlisted ranks and into officer training programs, and because it supported the reserve forces. Ironically, it could fulfill these nonconscription functions only as long as the few conscription decisions that were made were perceived to meet some minimal criterion of equity.

The equity of the deferment system came under increasing pressure as the baby-boom generation came of age for military eligibility. Although occupational deferments had been made increasingly liberal, by the early 1960s it was clear that there would be more young men who would not qualify for any of the liberal deferment categories than the services could use. In late 1963 the Selective Service System began to defer all married men, which conceptually gave them a tool for handling the increased pool of potential manpower but which increased the marriage rate and raised renewed questions in the media and Congress about the equity of the system. Senator Barry Goldwater, who was seeking the Republican nomination for the presidency, announced in early 1964 that he intended to end the draft, and, in response, President Lyndon Johnson ordered the Defense Department to study the draft. Had it not been for the Vietnam War, conscription might have been phased out in the United States a decade earlier than it was.

The Vietnam War. The Department of Defense study projected that by the early 1970s, a peacetime all-volunteer force would be feasible. By the spring of 1965, however, when Defense Secretary Robert McNamara expected to act on the department's recommendations, the nation's involvement in Vietnam had intensified, and draft calls, which had been low in the early 1960s, had increased, as had opposition to the draft. The opposition was manifested in a variety of ways, including sit-ins at Selective Service System offices, burning of draft cards, demonstrations on college campuses, and weddings arranged to take advantage of marital deferments. Reactions to the opposition to the draft were also varied. Legislation prescribed severe penalties for draft-card burning; draft resisters were prosecuted; the Justice Department investigated antidraft groups for Communist involvement; General Hershey ordered local draft boards to reclassify antidraft demonstrators 1-A (immediately available for the draft); and President Johnson ordered an end to deferments for married men.

Pressure for reform of the system was widespread. Secretary McNamara spoke in favor of civilian alternatives to the draft, and former Defense Secretary Thomas Gates spoke in favor of a more broadly based national service system. A national lottery was proposed to alleviate the inequities of decentralized conscription decisions made by local draft boards; this proposal was strongly opposed by General Hershey. Public support for conscription decreased markedly, with a large majority eventually coming to favor a change in the system.

The pattern of bias that existed in the Vietnam-era conscription process was a complex one. The poor were overrepresented among draftees. Advanced technology had led to higher standards for induction, however, and large numbers of young men were judged to have less than the minimum required level of mental aptitude and were found not qualified for service; from 1950 to 1965, for example, almost as many young men were rejected on mental as on physical grounds. Because mental aptitude tends to be correlated with socioeconomic status, many poor young men were found unqualified. In sum, the poor were more likely to be found unqualified for service, but among those found qualified, the poor were more likely to be drafted than were men of higher social status. Blacks were overrepresented in the draft through this process, not because they were black, but because they were poor. Predictable consequences followed. Once people from lower socioeconomic backgrounds were drafted, they were more likely to be channeled into the ground combat forces than into branches requiring technical aptitudes. They were therefore also more likely to be wounded or killed than were persons of higher socioeconomic status. Again, blacks were overrepresented in these strata and because of socioeconomic rather than racial discrimination were overrepresented among casualties.

The Vietnam War came in the wake of the civil rights movement, and the War on Poverty in the United States, and conscription seemed to discriminate against those whom these efforts had been meant to help—the poor and the black. By 1966 there were widespread student demonstrations against the draft and its inequities.

In the summer of 1966, President Johnson appointed the National Advisory Commission on Selective Service (the Marshall Commission, named for its chair, Burke Marshall), which was to consider ways to reform the existing system and to make recommendations prior to the expiration or renewal of the existing legislation in June 1967. Ultimately, both the Marshall Commission and the president endorsed a continuation of the draft, but their positions differed markedly in tone. The commission was critical of the concept of a volunteer force, fearing that it would be too expensive, would lack flexibility, and would become a mercenary force. The president, on the other hand, stated a preference for an all-volunteer force, and although he pragmatically saw a need to extend the draft, he sought major reforms of the conscription system, including the development of a national lottery, elimination of student deferments, and reduction of the autonomy granted local boards in making deferment decisions.

Congress rejected all substantive reform proposals and passed the Military Selective Service Act of 1967, extending the draft for four years. Although Congress refused to eliminate student deferments completely, men would now lose their eligibility for such deferments after reaching age twenty-four or after four years of study, whichever occurred first. This change denied young men the opportunity to avoid military service through long-term student status.

The failure of the Johnson administration and Congress to reform the Selective Service System in the face of high draft calls and continuing opposition to the draft probably contributed significantly to the draft becoming a major issue in the 1968 presidential campaign and ultimately to the end of the draft and the advent of the all-volunteer force.

In 1968 deferments for all graduate study except medicine and allied fields were ended. The channeling system was being wound down. During the 1968 presidential election campaign, the Republican nominee, Richard Nixon, promised to end the draft once the Vietnam War was over. Within three months of his inauguration, against the advice of Secretary of Defense Melvin Laird, he appointed the President's

Commission on an All-Volunteer Armed Force. The commission was chaired by former Secretary of Defense Gates, who had been an advocate of national service. Among the members of the commission were two former supreme allied commanders in Europe, retired Generals Alfred Gruenther and Lauris Norstad.

There was considerable disagreement among the members of the Gates Commission, with Generals Gruenther and Norstad in particular skeptical about a voluntary military force. Chairman Gates, however, was able to get unanimous agreement from the commission members to the principle that an all-volunteer force supported by a standby draft was preferable to a mixed force of conscripts and volunteers and to the proposal that entry-level military pay be raised. These principles became the first part of the commission's report, the part that was most widely read and that most influenced the policy debate. The dissent and disagreement were confined to later sections of the report. A stronger sense of unanimity was reflected in the report than actually characterized the commission.

The issues addressed by the Gates Commission focused primarily on economic concerns. Would the United States be able to afford an all-volunteer armed force? The commission concluded that an all-volunteer force was feasible. Critics claimed that an all-volunteer force would weaken patriotism, would attract primarily the economically disadvantaged segments of society, and would therefore attenuate the relationship between the soldier and the military, and between the U.S. armed forces and civilian society. In the absence of a sense of citizen duty to serve, employment in the military would lack personal meaning for the serviceperson, and the nexus between civilians and the military would be similarly impersonal, particularly in those strata of society whose young adults elected not to serve. The commission considered these objections but decided that the composition of the force would not be fundamentally changed by ending conscription, nor would the relationship between armed forces and society be significantly altered.

In 1969, with the war in Asia being turned increasingly over to Vietnamese military personnel, draft calls were drastically reduced. Much of the discretionary power of local Selective Service System boards was eliminated by the establishment of a national draft lottery. The first drawing was held in December 1969 and the first inductions were made the following month. The lottery assigned selective service registrants priorities on the basis of their birth dates. The reductions in student deferments and the introduction of a lottery increased the likelihood that males from higher socioeconomic backgrounds would be drafted. At the same time, the reduction in categorical deferments meant that only a small proportion of those liable for service would be called. This raised anew the issue of equity unless one assumes, as the administration appears to have done, that randomness is equivalent to equity.

The years 1970 and 1971 were years of debate. In a message to Congress in April 1970, President Nixon stated as his objective the elimination of draft calls and outlined a series of military pay increases and other steps designed to reach that objective. He addressed Congress again in January 1971, when he proposed further steps to move toward an all-volunteer force but also requested an extension of the draft. The issue of draft extension was debated vigorously, but in September 1971, the final two-year extension of the draft was passed, along with a major increase in entry-level military pay. The 1972 defense appropriation, also passed in 1971, provided the funds for the all-volunteer force. Draft calls were low during the two-year extension of selective service, and in January 1973, six months earlier than required by Congress, Secretary of Defense Laird announced the end of peacetime conscription.

The All-Volunteer Force. The blueprint that the Gates Commission had set out for the all-volunteer force was rooted in economic behavior. It assumed that by making entry-level military compensation competitive with civilian wages, sufficient numbers of high-quality personnel would be attracted to military service, that the racial composition of the force would not be significantly altered, and that the people brought into the military could be molded into an effective fighting force. In 1973 the U.S. economy was in trouble. Youth unemployment was high. Entry-level military pay was roughly competitive with civilian wages, thanks to increases in the last years of conscription. In the absence of employment alternatives, the all-volunteer force appeared to be an immediate success. With unemployment particularly high among young black males, and with women increasingly coming to regard the military as a mobility channel thanks to the women's movement, the armed forces were able to bring in a sufficient number of people. Contrary to the expectations of the Gates Commission, however, the social composition of the force did change. It became increasingly dependent on the poor, blacks, and, to a lesser extent, women.

The Gates Commission's projections of personnel quality and quantity had been based on the assumption that entry-level military pay would be competitive with entry-level civilian pay. Military pay had been tied to general-schedule federal civil service pay; a series of caps on federal civil service pay in the 1970s led to a violation of this assumption. By the end of the decade, entry-level military pay had begun to lag behind what high school graduates were earning upon entry into the full-time employed civilian labor force and, indeed, behind the federal minimum wage. The second phase of the all-volunteer force (1976–1980) was less successful than the first (1973–1975). The pay of first-term junior enlisted personnel, which had been 115 percent of the federal minimum wage in 1972, had fallen to 84 percent by 1979. The services, which had been achieving more than 100 percent of their recruiting objectives in the middle of the decade, were achieving only 93 percent in 1979, a shortfall of more than twenty thousand recruits.

One would have expected the recruits attracted to the military to decline in quality as well as in quantity. The research done by and for the Office of the Secretary of Defense, however, suggested that this had not been the case—that the social composition of the military had not changed with the advent of an all-volunteer force and that indeed the level of mental functioning of the force had improved.

Soldiers in the field, and particularly those responsible for training new personnel, however, maintained throughout the decade of the 1970s that there had in fact been a real decline in personnel quality. By the end of the decade, it became impossible to deny that there were indeed important personnel problems tied to compensation and to the fact that a new personnel selection test that had been implemented in 1976 had been miscalibrated, leading to an unintentional decrease in quality of recruits. In addition, the recruiting successes at the beginning of the all-volunteer force, which occurred in years of high unemployment, were followed by reductions in funding for recruitment. Between 1973 and 1976—years in which the age-eligible population was increasing, and so was youth unemployment—funding for recruiting was cut back and the purchasing power of the average enlistee declined. Then, in 1976, the GI Bill ended. Not surprisingly, recruiting became more difficult. As noted, the recruiting picture was confounded by an error made in a new selection and classification test introduced in 1976. In that year, the Department of Defense specified the Armed Services Vocational Aptitude Battery (ASVAB) as the single selection test to replace the various test batteries then in use by the various services. In order to maintain consistency over time, the scores of recruits on four subtests in the battery were combined into an Armed Forces Qualification Test (AFQT) score and calibrated to previous selection tests so that, for the period beginning with World War II, the meaning of the percentile score would be standardized.

A major error was made in the calibration of the 1976 AFQT to earlier selection tests, however, inflating the scores of enlistees at the lower end of the mental aptitude distribution. The error was discovered and corrected in 1980. In 1976, when the services believed that they had admitted only about 5 percent Category IV (the lowest acceptable mental category) personnel, accessions were in fact nearly 30 percent Category IV. In 1980, when accessions were thought to be about 6 percent Category IV, the actual figure was closer to 32 percent.

Going into the decade of the 1980s, with upward adjustments having been made in military compensation, educational benefits having been expanded, young unemployment having increased, and the norming of the AFQT having been corrected, recruiting efforts produced the desired quantity and quality of recruits. If the all-volunteer force is to be judged on the basis of number of people in the active force and their average level of mental ability, the force in the early 1980s—years that constitute a third phase in the history of the all-volunteer force—would have to be defined a success.

Using sociodemographic representativeness as a yardstick against which to measure the force would temper that optimistic assessment. Although in the late 1980s and early 1990s the all-volunteer force drew at least its fair share of noncollege-bound youth from the upper working class and the lower middle class, over the years it has become increasingly dependent on racial and ethnic minorities. Throughout the early 1980s, the military attracted a decreasing number of recruits from the higher socioeconomic groups and from among those of greater mental ability.

During the first decade of the all-volunteer force, the greatest decrease in strength came in the reserves. This occurred at a time when the military was developing a total force policy, leaving itself increasingly dependent on the reserve components if the United States were to go to war. President Ronald Reagan's military manpower task force reported in late 1982 that the army's individual ready reserve (IRR), which is the most important source of pretrained manpower in an emergency, was short by 180,000 men in 1981. It projected that the shortage would be 240,000 troops by 1988 and that the shortfall would be in enlisted personnel with combat skills. The task force also judged the all-volunteer force to be a success.

The all-volunteer force did improve in the late 1980s, with the implementation of a new GI Bill. Enlistment rates were uncoupled from youth unemployment, and there was increased accession of college-oriented youth. Dependence on the reserves also increased. In 1989, for the first time since World War II, reservists in units became a majority of the total army force. The U.S. Army National Guard became the eleventh largest army in the world, and the Air Guard the seventh largest air force. Active army combat divisions became dependent on "round out" brigades from the reserves to be brought to full strength. The Gulf War of 1991, which involved the call-up of more reservists than any event since World War II, demonstrated that, although reserves in combat support roles functioned well in wartime, reserve combat brigades were not as combat-ready as the divisions they were to round out. In addition, many reservists, having joined for extra income or educational benefits, were surprised to learn that their job might involve going to war.

Selective Service Registration. The mobilization problems that continue to characterize the all-volunteer force have been recognized from the outset. Although conscription ended in 1973, selective service continued to register young men until 1975, when President Gerald Ford put it in "deep standby," to be resurrected in an emergency. In 1976 the Defense Manpower Commission called for a resumption of peacetime registration.

In 1978 the Defense Department conducted a mobilization exercise, called Nifty Nugget, to determine whether the reserves could be called up in an emergency. The worst fears of the mobilization planners were realized: They gave a practice war and virtually nobody came. Analyses of Nifty Nugget by the Joint Chiefs of Staff, the Congressional Budget Office, and the General Accounting Office all agreed that at that time the mobilization mission could not be fulfilled.

In December 1979 the Soviet Union invaded Afghanistan, and the following month, President Jimmy Carter announced in his State of the Union Address his intention to reinstate draft registration. The president had the authority to order registration but was dependent on Congress for the funds to do so. The issue of registration for a potential draft was no less controversial in January 1980 than it had been at other times in American history. Congress did not authorize funds until June, and the first registration took place in July. Four months later, Ronald Reagan, who had taken a position against registration in the course of his election campaign, was elected president.

For a year, in the face of ambiguity about policy, compliance with registration requirements was low, and no attempt was made to prosecute noncompliers. On 1 July 1981, however, President Reagan established the Military Manpower Task Force under the chairmanship of the secretary of defense. In January 1982 he announced that, on the basis of the report of the task force, he would continue registration and that, after a grace period, noncompliers would be prosecuted. Draft law in the early 1990s required young men to register within thirty days of their eighteenth birthday.

During late 1981 and early 1982, compliance was elicited primarily through publicity reminding young men of the legal requirements of registration. Actual enforcement of the law was "passive," limited to nonregistrants who were reported by others or who brought themselves to the attention of the authorities. In December 1981, Congress authorized a more active enforcement program. In addition, attempts were made to link citizenship rights to the obligation to register. New York State, for example, denied state employment to nonregistrants. Beginning in July 1983, registration compliance was required of students who sought federal education loans, grants, or employment assistance. This requirement was one of the most controversial aspects of the system.

Compliance with the registration system seemed comparable to the experience of earlier Selective Service System registrations: More than 93 percent of those required to register eventually did so, although many did not do so within the time interval required by law. Although the rate of compliance appeared high, it made literally hundreds of thousands of young men criminals because of their noncompliance. The registration system was not without its critics. It did not involve classification and, in a highly mobile society, a large proportion of its address file became outdated each year.

BENEFITS POLICIES

In the early years of the American Republic, under the militia model of military organization, military benefits were available only to those who sacrificed the most—the injured, who received disability benefits, and dependents of those who died, who were eligible for survivors' benefits. These benefits were broadened in the post–Civil War period to provide for those who had served but had not been injured and for dependents and survivors. After World War II, a much broader benefit program was made available to veterans under the first GI Bill of Rights.

In the era of the all-volunteer force, with an increasing percentage of military personnel being married and indications that the happiness of service families affects both personnel retention and performance, the defense establishment has attempted to increase family benefits. There is a basis in equity for such programs: Family members share with military personnel many of the disadvantages of service.

Disability and Survivors' Benefits. The United States has historically granted pension benefits to soldiers mobilized during times of conflict. Because the numbers of people involved in conflicts were relatively small and because benefits were restricted to those who had actually served in combat or had service-related disabilities, the benefit programs prior to the Civil War were themselves small. In 1840 fewer than 4 percent of Americans over the age of sixty were receiving federal military pensions. The programs that had been established were firmly rooted in a principle of compensation for sacrifices made in defense of the state. The Civil War, involving a massive mobilization and the first national draft in U.S. history, redefined the role of the state as a provider of benefits for veterans and their survivors.

The Civil War pension system, established in 1862, was initially consistent with the principle of benefits earned through sacrifice and was intended to provide compensation only to soldiers who had been permanently disabled as a direct consequence of service in the Union army and to the widows and children of Union soldiers who had died as a result of injury or illness sustained during military service.

Initial disbursements under the program were modest and remained fairly stable during the decade of the 1870s. The size of the Civil War mobilization, however, had produced a generation of veterans who were not entitled to pensions under the death or disability criterion but who constituted a significant proportion of the electorate. Both political parties in the Union sought to woo voters with more readily available benefits, and in 1879 disbursements increased markedly when the Arrears of Pension Act authorized lump-sum payments of accumulated benefits to soldiers who registered belatedly to receive pension benefits. A special-interest group, the Grand Army of the Republic, mobilized the veteran population and pressed for further liberalization, and the veterans' vote strongly influenced the outcome of the congressional and presidential elections of 1888.

In 1890 a new Civil War pension law extended benefits to veterans who had served at least ninety days in the Union army or navy during the war, had been honorably discharged, and had subsequently become disabled, without a requirement that the disability be service-related (although disabilities due to a veteran's "own vicious habits" were disqualified). In 1906 attainment of the age of sixty-two was legislatively defined as a disability within the intent of the pension law. The criteria for receipt of benefits were thus made less stringent, and disability entitlement became an old-age insurance system for almost 760,000 former soldiers. The 1906 legislation also provided for a more broadly based survivors' benefits program, which expanded as the number of vet-

erans was reduced by mortality. The cost of the precedent set by broadening the definition of disability is being felt most severely a century after the legislation, as the veterans of the massive mobilization for World War II and the smaller mobilization for the Korean War, who tend to live longer than did Civil War veterans, increasingly reach retirement age and begin to experience its associated health problems.

In 1890, when the provision that disability be service-related was deleted from the law, only about 10 percent of Union veterans had reached the age of sixty-five. Most were middle-aged. By 1891, however, the Bureau of Pensions had grown to become the largest executive agency in the world, with more than six thousand employees, and by 1893, pensions made up 42 percent of all federal expenditures. At the beginning of the twentieth century, most Union veterans were in their sixties or older, and there were nearly a million veterans and survivors on the pension lists. In 1913, although the number of veterans was declining because of deaths, pension outlays were still climbing, and about two-thirds of native white males aged sixty-five or older living outside the South were drawing federal veterans' benefits.

This early massive social insurance program had relatively little impact on the most disadvantaged segments of the American population. Blacks, although accounting for about thirty-eight thousand Union fatalities, had been excluded from military service for most of the war, accounted for only 10 percent of the Union army at the end of the war, and were not major beneficiaries of the pension system. The recipients of Civil War veterans pensions were disproportionately northern white rural landowners or members of the urban middle class.

In the twentieth century, the military pension system grew to be a major federal expenditure and was the subject of frequent policy debates. The system as it applies to new military personnel was changed in the mid-1980s. Career military personnel are eligible to retire after twenty years of active duty and, with few exceptions, must retire with no more than thirty years of active duty. Because career military personnel tend to enter service between eighteen and twenty-two years of age, they retire at a point that would be mid-career in most civilian occupations, that is, in their late forties. This system provides an incentive for people to leave active duty rather than remain and builds into the federal budget a large expenditure for "retired pay," compensation for not being on active military duty.

Expenditures for retirement pay, which fluctuated between 1 and 2 percent of the defense budget between 1947 and 1962 (in current dollars) and which did not exceed 4 percent until 1971, reached almost 10 percent of defense expenditures in the early 1980s. At the beginning of the 1990s, they constituted more than 6 percent of the defense budget, the percentage decline since early in the 1980s reflecting not a decrease in absolute retirement costs but rather an absolute increase in other military expenditures, primarily in budget elements other than personnel costs. During the 1980s, costs for active duty personnel declined from more than 40 percent of the defense budget to less than 20 percent, despite the maintenance of a large peacetime force in being, as expenditures were shifted away from people and toward military hardware.

The changes in the military retirement system that went into effect in the 1980s may in the long run help to bring its increasing costs under control. In the interest of honoring commitments to personnel on active duty before the change, however, the plan contained a "grandfather clause," allowing personnel already in the military to retire under the former system. Major savings, therefore, will not be realized for almost four decades, because military personnel who entered the service prior to the change and remain for at least twenty years will begin drawing benefits under the old system when they retire and will continue to draw those benefits until they die.

In addition to debate on the cost of the military retirement system, the 1980s saw the emergence of divorced military spouses as an interest group that demanded access to their former spouses' military retirement pay as part of divorce settlements on the grounds that they had shared the hardships of military life. As the percentage of military personnel who are married increases and as divorce becomes more common, former spouses' access to military benefits will continue to be a legal and political issue and will highlight the general trend of extension of benefits to those who have not directly served. Indeed, in 1982 the Uniformed Services Former Spouses Protection Act extended medical care and commissary and exchange privileges to unremarried former spouses divorced after 1 February 1983.

Housing and Medical Benefits for Dependents.

Prior to World War I, army and navy officers were either assigned to quarters or given an allowance for quarters, but family size was not a determinant of quarters assignments or allowances. An officer's civilian dependents of course lived in officers' quarters, but there was no assumption that they were entitled to living space. They simply occupied a portion of the officer's quarters, along with the officer's possessions. Unlike officers, very few enlisted personnel prior to the twentieth century were married and did not need family housing.

Formal legislation establishing the basis for quarters allowances for army officers was passed in 1878 and for navy officers in 1899, but in neither case was family size considered a basis for determining the allowance. The benefit of housing for a military officer did not formally extend to his family, and family size was not a criterion when the first legislation authorizing quarters allowances for enlisted personnel was passed in 1915. As had been the case with the pension system, women became the recipients of benefits only through their association with men who served in the military.

Family size was first recognized as a basis for quarters allowances in a temporary World War I measure passed on 16 April 1918. This act recognized that dependents, as well as members of the military, have specific needs for space and shelter. The provisions of the 1918 act were extended by later legislation until the early 1940s.

In 1940 allowances recognizing family size and need were authorized for the top three enlisted grades. The Pay Readjustment Act of 1942 changed the basis for fixing housing allowances from the number of rooms for which personnel were eligible to a combination of pay grade and family status. The current system of rental allowances, developed in 1949, extended family housing allowances to all personnel at the rank of sergeant or above, with allowances for lower ranking personnel being made at a "without dependent" level. That exemption was relaxed during the Korean conflict through the Dependents' Assistance Act of 1950. Several subsequent readjustments have been made in an attempt to ensure that military personnel and their dependents are provided with housing roughly equivalent to what they would have if they were all civilians. This has led to increased expenditures for family housing, although the defense establishment still falls far short of providing on-post housing for all military families, and location of families off-post has implications for military cohesion.

Prior to World War II, enlisted personnel tended not to be married, but the proportion of married personnel increased steadily after the war, except for a brief decline during the Vietnam War. The proportion of enlisted personnel who were married was 33 percent in 1953, 48 percent in 1960, and was approaching 60 percent by the late 1970s. In the 1980s military personnel married at younger ages than their civilian peers. Expenditures for family housing were less than .01 percent of the defense budget during the 1950s, increased to nearly 1 percent in the 1960s, and were slightly above 1 percent in the 1970s and 1980s. Responsibility for the continued housing needs of servicepeople was built into the first GI Bill of Rights, and the Veterans Administration's home loan guarantee program is the second most widely used benefit (after educational benefits) among U.S. veterans, with about one-third of veterans participating.

The increase in the number of military families produced requirements for family medical benefits as well as for improved housing. Historically, medical care was provided to military dependents on a space-available basis, and availability varied greatly by time and place.

Provision of medical care to dependents was officially authorized during World War II, but still on a space-available basis, and during the war nearly all space was dedicated to the treatment of active-duty personnel.

It was not until 1956 that the Dependents' Medical Care Act provided the first statutory basis for provision of medical care to military dependents, as well as to retirees, retirees' dependents, and retirees' survivors. The act authorized the secretary of defense to contract with civilian sources for the provision of health and medical care to military dependents. Ten years later the Military Medical Benefits Act established the CHAMPUS program—basically a medicare program for the civilian dependents of military personnel—and in 1971 the program was expanded to include certain surviving dependents of servicepersons. It has been revised periodically since then, and the military has been experimenting with other ways of providing for the health care needs of military family members.

The GI Bill. Just as the Civil War demobilization produced a major broadening of the constituency for federal benefits, so did the Servicemen's Readjustment Act of 1944, which defined the benefits associated with the post–World War II demobilization, to become the major basis of welfare expenditures for nearly two decades. Faced with the demobilization of millions of men who would flood the labor force of a recently repaired economy, who would be junior in terms of job seniority and educational attainment to their peers who had not served in the armed forces during the war, and who might resent being economically disadvantaged because they had served their country, the United States in 1944 established a massive program of education and training for veterans at government expense; government guaranteed loans for homes, farms, and businesses; a system of job counseling and placement; and medical care benefits that have served as the basis for the largest hospital system in the world.

The number of veterans aged sixty-five and

over was about 2.9 million in 1980 and about 5 million in 1985. It reached about 7.2 million in 1990, when more than half of American men aged sixty-five and over were veterans. The nation will have to determine the degree to which it will continue to provide medical care to veterans whose ailments may not be related to their military service—but it will have to do so in the face of an increasingly powerful veterans' lobby.

The educational benefit program did achieve its short-term objectives. Nearly 8 million World War II veterans—more than half the total eligible population—received training under this first GI Bill, reducing pressure on the employment system and improving the veterans' competitive position in the labor force. The Veterans' Readjustment Assistance Act for Korean War veterans was passed in 1952, and more than 2 million veterans—about 43 percent of the eligible population—participated in training programs with its support. In 1966 a third act was passed, to cover personnel who had served at least 180 days during the post-Korea cold war period and who had received honorable discharges.

The 1966 act was the first GI Bill explicitly intended primarily to provide benefits for veterans who did not serve during wartime, although it ultimately covered veterans of the Vietnam War. More than a million veterans of the cold war period—about 46 percent of the eligible population—were trained under the third GI Bill, as were nearly 7 million Vietnam-era veterans—a record 72 percent of the eligible population. The Vietnam-era veterans, however, did not profit as much compared to their peers who did not serve as did their predecessors, in part because of changes in the availability of educational benefits not related to military service.

Research comparing veterans with their peers who did not serve in the military has demonstrated that, prior to the Vietnam War period, veterans received higher levels of education than their nonveteran peers, with much of the difference credited to GI Bill educational benefits. These differences, in turn, were reflected

in differences in income in the civilian labor market.

Some economists have suggested that military service has a negative impact on subsequent earnings because military service delays or interrupts a civilian career, which is precisely the kind of effect that the framers of the first GI Bill sought to avoid, and the evidence suggests that they were in the main successful during the pre-Vietnam period. A series of studies has shown that veterans from the World War II and Korean War periods earned more than their nonveteran counterparts, other things being equal, and that these positive effects were greatest for groups that have been disadvantaged in the civilian labor market: blacks, Hispanics, and women. Thus, military service can be thought of as contributing to the subsequent welfare of veterans in general and of veterans who are members of disadvantaged groups in particular.

The picture changes with regard to Vietnam veterans. Vietnam veterans have had the highest rate of utilization of GI Bill educational benefits of all veteran groups. More than 72 percent of Vietnam-era veterans utilized their educational benefits, compared to 50 percent or less of earlier veteran groups. Moreover, a far greater percentage of Vietnam veterans used their GI Bill benefits specifically for college educations, rather than for other kinds of training, than did earlier veterans. More than 45 percent of Vietnam-era veterans used their benefits for college, compared to 15 percent of World War II veterans, 22 percent of Korean War veterans, and 24 percent of post–Korean War veterans. Vietnam-era veterans, although better educated than veterans of earlier wars, nonetheless achieved lower levels of education than did their peers who did not serve and thus did not achieve an advantaged position in the civilian labor force. Their educational benefits did not offset the costs of their absence from civilian careers during military service.

GI Bill educational benefits were discontinued during the first decade of the all-volunteer force, because a volunteer force was presumed to impose a lesser degree of sacrifice on those who served than had conscription and because noncontributory educational benefits were not seen as a cost-effective recruitment incentive. With the escalating cost of higher education, the widespread availability of educational assistance programs not tied to service, the decrease in the size of the military age–eligible cohort, and the desire of the services to recruit personnel with greater mental ability to operate increasingly sophisticated weapons, a new GI Bill was established in 1985, not to reward personnel who had served, but rather to induce civilian youths to serve.

RACE, GENDER, AND SEXUAL ORIENTATION POLICIES

The Racial Integration of the Armed Forces. African-American soldiers have participated in every war in which the United States has been engaged, but in every one up until the Korean Conflict, they have been denied status equal to that of their white peers through segregation, subjection to quotas, and exclusion from combat specialties and officers' commissions. Some five thousand blacks fought on the side of the colonists in the Revolution, participating in the early battles, including Lexington, Concord, and Bunker Hill. Their use, however, was a source of controversy. Some colonial leaders felt it morally wrong to ask slaves and former slaves to share in the burden of defense, whereas white supremacists felt that blacks were inferior and untrustworthy. Bowing to political pressure, in 1775, George Washington prohibited the enlistment of additional black soldiers. An estimated twenty-thousand blacks, primarily slaves in the southern colonies, served with the British as scouts, soldiers, and supply handlers, hoping that their service would lead to their emancipation. In an effort to reduce such "defections" and to help solve the problem of manpower shortages, the Continental Congress allowed free black soldiers to reenlist, and most states allowed the use of black substitutes to fill militia draft quotas. After the war, however, blacks were excluded by policy from the federal forces and the state militias.

Policies are one thing and manpower needs in wartime quite another. Benjamin Stoddert, the first secretary of the navy, had excluded blacks from the navy and the Marine Corps. Nevertheless, blacks served in the Quasi-War against France from 1798 to 1800, and several thousand blacks served in the War of 1812, where they constituted about one-sixth of the navy's enlisted personnel and were integrated into all ratings. Blacks were, however, more effectively excluded from the ground forces. At the end of the war, when manpower requirements were reduced, the exclusionary policies were enforced in the navy as well.

At the onset of the Civil War, President Lincoln initially excluded blacks from service in the Union army, both to maintain the loyalty of the border states and to emphasize that the issue over which the war was being fought was the maintenance of the Union, not the abolition of slavery. Despite that policy, the navy, ever mindful of its manpower needs, authorized black enlistments in September 1861. Similar manpower pressures were felt by the ground forces, and by mid-1862 some Union generals were raising black regiments despite Lincoln's policy.

The Emancipation Proclamation in 1863 provided for the enlistment of blacks, and the states began to establish black units. More than 185,000 blacks were recruited and organized by the Bureau of Colored Troops. About 10 percent of the Union army and a quarter of the navy was composed of blacks. If one includes black volunteers serving in independent and state units, then almost 390,000 blacks served with the Union forces. Almost 10 percent of the blacks who served—more than 38,000—were killed, a fatality rate almost one and a half times that of white troops.

The Confederacy, as might be expected, was slower than the Union to explore the use of black troops. It was not until early 1865 that the Confederacy authorized the enlistment of "slave soldiers" and a few companies of black soldiers were organized. General Lee surrendered in early April of that year, however, and none of these units saw combat.

After the Civil War, the U.S. Army established six black units, to consist of 12,500 soldiers: the Ninth and Tenth cavalries and the Thirty-eighth, Thirty-ninth, Fortieth, and Forty-first infantries. Because of a shortage of funds, the infantry units were subsequently reduced to two. The four remaining units accounted for about 10 percent of the army's personnel. The segregated structure guaranteed that, except in an emergency, black and white soldiers would not serve together. The navy, by contrast, continued to allow blacks to serve on an integrated basis in the enlisted ranks, most commonly in the lowest of them.

Black soldiers fought in the Indian wars. In the Spanish-American War, the Ninth and Tenth cavalries participated in the charge up San Juan Hill, and black sailors distinguished themselves in the Battles of Manila and Santiago de Cuba. The presence of black troops in predominantly white towns, particularly in the South, produced tensions, which peaked in the early twentieth century and were reflected most dramatically by the so-called Brownsville Riot.

Black soldiers arrived at Fort Brown, Texas, in July 1906. The bars in nearby Brownsville either were segregated or excluded blacks completely. One night in mid-August, a group of black men rioted in the streets of Brownsville, discharging firearms into buildings, killing a bartender, and wounding the chief of police. An investigation concluded that soldiers from Fort Brown had been involved but failed to identify any specific individuals. The investigating officer recommended, and the army's inspector general concurred, that unless the guilty parties came forward, all enlisted personnel in the black battalion be dishonorably discharged.

President Theodore Roosevelt, who had praised the performance of black soldiers under his command in the Spanish-American War, ordered the dishonorable discharge—without benefit of court-martial—of 167 black soldiers, or three full companies. Some of these soldiers had as many as twenty-six years of service, and six of them had been awarded the Medal of Honor. They were denied pay, allowances, pension, benefits, and access to civilian federal employment. Although fourteen were readmitted to military service after a year, it was not until 1972 that the army ruled the investigation had been biased and changed the records of the 167 soldiers to reflect honorable discharges, but with no award of back pay or allowances. In 1973, Congress awarded the last survivor of the Brownsville group a pension of $25,000 and medical benefits.

The participation of African-Americans in the U.S. military, and racial tensions involving black soldiers, continued in the pre–World War I period. During the Mexican Punitive Expedition of 1916–1917, General Pershing used the Tenth Cavalry as a major part of his operation in pursuit of Pancho Villa. Also in 1917, however, after a fight between white policemen in Houston, Texas, and black soldiers of the Twenty-fourth Infantry over the alleged abuse of a black woman, more than a hundred soldiers from the regiment mutinied against their officers, armed themselves, marched downtown, and continued the battle. Many policemen, citizens, and soldiers were killed or wounded. More than a hundred black soldiers were indicted and convicted, thirteen were speedily executed, six were later hanged, and sixty-three were sentenced to life imprisonment. The rest were dishonorably discharged and sentenced to prison terms ranging up to fifteen years.

In the navy, official policy was still to allow blacks to enlist for all ratings and to serve with integrated crews. The unofficial practice, however, was segregation, and in 1919 the navy instituted a formal segregationist policy for the first time in its history. The ten thousand blacks who served in the navy during World War I were almost all messmen, stewards, or coal handlers in the "black gangs" of the engine rooms. The Marine Corps recruited no blacks.

The army continued its segregationist policies. Leaders in the black community had begun to suggest that blacks might earn citizenship rights in American society by helping defeat the German kaiser, and blacks were represented in the army roughly in proportion to their percentage in the general population—about 10 percent. The great majority—more than 80 percent of the 200,000 black soldiers who served in France—were assigned to menial noncombat roles. Blacks made up only one-thirtieth of the combat strength but were one-third of the military labor force.

After the war, the navy ceased recruiting African-Americans and instead filled the ranks of the messmen's and stewards' branch with Philippine nationals—a practice that persisted until 1932, after which blacks were again recruited as messmen. The army remained segregated, set an official quota that would keep the representation of blacks at no more than their representation in society (this quota was in fact never approached in the interwar years), kept the officers corps predominantly white, and excluded blacks from the Air Corps. At the beginning of World War II, as a result of these policies, blacks served in the navy only as stewards and messmen, were absent from the Air Corps, and were under a quota in the army, where they served in segregated units and in menial jobs (even the black combat regiments were assigned primarily support roles, such as the construction of fortifications) and were virtually excluded from the officers corps. On the eve of Pearl Harbor, blacks accounted for 5.6 percent of the army. There were five black officers, three of them chaplains.

The Selective Training and Service Act of 1940 specified that the selection of draftees and volunteers for military service not be influenced by race or color. Also in 1940, the War Department adopted a policy to increase black accessions to be roughly proportional to their representation in the general population, to establish black units in all branches of the army, and to admit blacks to officer candidate schools so that they could serve as pilots in black aviation units. The services were given discretion in determining enlistment standards, however, and the War Department policy insisted on racial segregation at the regimental level in order to maintain troop morale. Because the navy had sufficient numbers of volunteers to eliminate the need for draftees, it was able to continue enlisting blacks only as messmen.

In 1942 the navy liberalized its regulations,

opening additional shore billets to blacks. Training continued to be racially segregated, however, and blacks went to sea only as messmen and stewards. No African-American officers were commissioned in the navy. The Marine Corps also began recruiting blacks for the first time in 1942, to serve in segregated battalions occupying islands in the Pacific that had been captured from the Japanese by white units. The following year, under pressure to meet the goal of proportionality, the navy recognized that it would have to open sea billets to blacks and experimented with ways of sending blacks to sea, including assigning all-black crews to two antisubmarine vessels. It was not until 1945 that the navy integrated basic training and allowed African-Americans to serve as members of integrated crews on noncombat ships.

The army also resisted the principle of proportional representation. Segregation was presumed to be necessary for the maintenance of cohesion, and segregation required separate training facilities, as well as efforts not to locate black units in places where their presence would offend a white host community.

Racial problems notwithstanding, more than a million blacks served in the armed forces in World War II, making up nearly 8 percent of the force. More served proportionally in the army than in the other branches, and most continued to serve in menial jobs. Seventy-eight percent of the blacks in the army were in the service branches—primarily quartermaster and transportation corps—compared to 40 percent of the whites. By contrast, less than 10 percent of the blacks, and more than 30 percent of the whites, were in the combat arms.

In the fall of 1944, an army board (the Gillem Board) was established to determine how better use might be made of African-American soldiers within the army's segregated structure. That December, shortages of white infantrymen as replacements for line units forced the army to increase its utilization of blacks as combat soldiers.

A call for a limited number of black noncombat soldiers to volunteer for service as infantrymen to fight "shoulder to shoulder" with white soldiers and share the privilege of defeating the enemy produced more than forty-five hundred volunteers in two months. Of these, nearly three thousand were retrained as infantrymen and assigned, in all-black platoons, to serve in previously all-white divisions. The Gillem Board, which issued its report in 1945, found that these black troops had performed well in the context of white divisional units. The report was critical of the performance of the all-black Ninety-second Division, which had been criticized in World War I as well; however, these performance problems were eventually attributed to poor planning and preparation on the part of the army and to the assignment to black units of inferior white officers, who themselves resented the assignment. The Gillem Board recommended increased opportunities for blacks in the military, continuation of racial segregation at the small-unit level but incorporation of black platoons, companies, and battalions into larger white units, and the implementation of a quota system to keep the army at no more than 10 percent black.

In July 1948, three months before the presidential election, President Truman issued Executive Order No. 9981, declaring a policy of "equality of treatment and opportunity in the military." This order did not end segregation in the military. It did state a policy and establish the President's Committee on Equality of Treatment and Opportunity (the Fahey Board) to work with the secretaries of defense and of the services to implement the policy. A review of service policies by the Fahey Board in 1949 found that the navy had been integrating crews since 1946 (although placing a ceiling of 10 percent black representation on any one ship); that the Marine Corps, although maintaining segregated units, had integrated basic training; and that the new air force, unconstrained by traditional notions of military manpower, was in favor of integrating its personnel, ending racial quotas, and making personnel decisions on the basis of ability alone. Only the army remained in favor of segregation. At the time, 40 percent of the occupational specialties and 80 percent of

the army's schools were still closed to black soldiers.

The army believed that the conclusions of the Gillem Board and of a subsequent study by the Board to Study the Utilization of Negro Manpower (the Chamberlin Board) demanded segregation in the interest of cohesion and military effectiveness, because the army remained convinced that most whites did not associate with blacks and that most blacks did not have the skills required for the army's more technical occupations. The Fahey Board proposed that if skills rather than race were the issue, then the army should establish quotas on the basis of achievement, rather than race.

The army agreed to experiment with an achievement-based system, thus becoming the last service to accept integration. It did so on the basis of an informal agreement with President Truman that if a system based on equality of treatment and opportunity produced a racially disproportionate force, racial quotas could be reestablished. When the Korean War broke out in the summer of 1950, however, although officer candidate schools had been integrated, neither the army's enlisted training bases nor its operational units had been integrated.

The mobilization for the police action in Korea accomplished what the executive order had not. By 1951, one-quarter of the army's recruits were black, and the black training units could not absorb the number of troops. As black infantrymen completed their training, they were assigned where they were needed most—to fill vacancies in previously all-white line infantry units. Thus was the army integrated—not without opposition from some senior commanders. By the end of the war, more than 90 percent of the blacks in the army were in integrated units. The air force and the Marine Corps had also eliminated segregated units. In late 1954 the Defense Department officially announced that all-black units had been abolished in the armed forces.

Despite the integration of the forces, African-Americans remained underrepresented in the service relative to their proportion in the civilian population. In 1964 the President's Committee on Equal Opportunity in the Armed Forces (the Gesell Committee) found that blacks were concentrated in the lower pay grades, that the reserves and the National Guard were still segregated or integrated only to a token degree, and that discriminatory practices still existed on military installations and in their host civilian communities.

The underrepresentation of blacks in the military was dramatically reversed by the widening conflict—and expanded U.S. involvement—in Vietnam. For the first time in the twentieth century, rather than being underrepresented or excluded from combat, blacks were more likely than whites to be drafted, to be sent to Vietnam, to serve in high-risk combat units, and to be killed or wounded in action. In the early 1960s, with blacks accounting for slightly more than 10 percent of the population aged nineteen to twenty-one, they accounted for a quarter of the casualties in Vietnam.

Racial tensions grew within all the services, manifested most dramatically by race riots among soldiers in the United States and Germany in the late 1960s, among prisoners in a military stockade in Vietnam in 1968, among marines at Camp Lejeune in North Carolina and Kaneohe Naval Air Station in Hawaii during the summer of 1969, at Travis Air Force Base in Texas during the spring of 1971, and on the aircraft carriers *Kitty Hawk* and *Constellation* in October and November 1972. Racial tension was clearly a problem for the military as it entered the all-volunteer-force era.

The Gates Commission, appointed by Nixon to study the feasibility of an all-volunteer force (AVF), had projected that the racial composition of such a force would not be substantially different from that of the conscription-era army. In the early years of the AVF, however, more than a quarter of new recruits were black—double the proportion in 1970—and in some years, as many as a third of new recruits in the army have been African-American. Black soldiers have also been more likely to seek reenlistment, further increasing their overrepresentation. In December 1987, 30 percent of the enlisted soldiers in the army were black, as were 22 percent of enlisted personnel across all services. Blacks remained underrepresented in the officer ranks in all services (6.6 percent), with the army having the largest representation of black officers (around 10 percent) and the navy the smallest (about 3 percent).

The response of the services and of the Department of Defense to racial tensions was a management response. In 1971, in the wake of racial disturbances, the Defense Race Relations Institute was established at Patrick Air Force Base, Florida, with the goal of changing behavior through educational programs. As racial discrimination decreased in the armed forces and as problems concerning the integration of women into the military came to the fore, the mission of the institute was broadened, and it became the Defense Equal Opportunity Management Institute (DEOMI).

The Integration of Women. If African-Americans are the overrepresented minority in the U.S. armed forces, then women are the underrepresented majority. Constituting slightly more than half the military-age civilian population, women constitute slightly more than one-tenth of U.S. armed forces personnel. The same barriers that have historically been raised against black participation in the military have been raised against female participation as well. Women have at various times been completely excluded, allowed to serve only in auxiliary units, administratively segregated in their own branches, restricted by quotas, allowed to serve only in limited occupational specialties, restricted from command positions and access to senior officer ranks, and excluded from combat specialties (although not necessarily from combat areas). Women still have not been integrated to the extent that blacks have, although they have served in all of the nation's wars. Clearly, the parallel between the integration of blacks and women is not a perfect one.

Women did not serve officially as members of the U.S. armed forces until the twentieth century, but some small number did manage to serve as soldiers by posing as men as early as the Revolution. This pattern persisted throughout the nineteenth century. Women served as nurses during the Civil War, and during the Spanish-American War, faced with a typhoid epidemic, the army recruited more than fifteen hundred female nurses, who served as civilians employed under contract, not as military personnel. Dr. Anita Newcomb McGee, who had supervised the nurses during the Spanish-American War, was asked to serve as acting assistant surgeon in charge of the Nurse Corps Division and to draft legislation to give nurses quasi-military status. In 1901, Congress established the Army Nurse Corps as an auxiliary unit. Nurses were not entitled to military rank, pay, or retirement and veterans' benefits. In 1908 the Navy Nurse Corps was established under the same conditions.

The navy had been the first service to integrate racially, and it led the way toward the incorporation of women as well, at least temporarily, in the pre–World War I years. Secretary of the Navy Josephus Daniels, anticipating the nation's forthcoming involvement in the world war and recognizing a shortage of personnel in those administrative specialties into which women were beginning to move in the civilian labor force—clerical workers, typists, stenographers, and telephone operators—authorized the enlistment of women in these specialties in the Naval Reserve as yeomen (F) early in 1917. Yeomen were required to be assigned to a ship, but women were prohibited from shipboard duty. The problem was solved by assigning all yeomen (F)s to a navy tugboat buried in the mud in the Potomac River.

A year after the establishment of the yeomen (F) classification, the Marine Corps authorized the recruitment of Marines (F). In the course of World War I, about thirteen thousand women served in these roles, and some eventually moved out of clerical duties and into more traditionally male domains, such as draftsmen, recruiters, and translators. The War Department continued its prohibition against enlisted women in the army.

Women did of course continue to serve as nurses. Twenty thousand served in the Army Nurse Corps, half of them overseas. Another fourteen hundred served in the Navy Nurse Corps. Thus, approximately thirty-four thousand women served in uniform in World War I, and many were highly decorated. The War Department had been under increasing pressure, including requests from commanders in the field, to bring female enlisted personnel into the army and had capitulated to the point of allowing female civilian employees onto army posts—provided that they were of "mature age and high moral character"—but with the end of the war, the pressure was dissipated. The female auxiliaries to the navy and the Marine Corps were demobilized.

Late in 1940 conscription was reestablished, and women's patriotic organizations lobbied for the right to be part of the mobilization effort. Representative Elizabeth Nourse Rogers of Massachusetts, who had been concerned that the women who had served—and suffered—in World War I had not received veteran's benefits because they had not had regular military status, announced her intention to introduce legislation to gain regular military status for them. General George C. Marshall asked Rogers to introduce a plan for a women's auxiliary in lieu of her proposal for full military status, which she did in May 1941. Later that year, the army asked the navy to support a proposal to establish women's auxiliaries for both services. The navy demurred and in fact tried to dissuade the army from supporting a women's corps for itself. Rogers' bill languished in congressional committees for a year.

Pearl Harbor was attacked in December 1941, and with the need for mobilization, Rogers' bill establishing the Women's Auxiliary Army Corps (WAAC) was reported out of committee and passed in May 1942. The navy also found itself facing a personnel shortage, and two months later Congress passed legislation establishing the Navy Women's Reserve, whose members, identified as WAVES (Women Accepted for Volunteer Emergency Service), had full reserve military status rather than status as auxiliaries, and the Marine Corps Women's Reserve. That winter, the Coast Guard Women's Reserve was established.

The auxiliary status of the WAAC was a problem from the outset. Its members were not part of the army, did not get the same pay as men doing the same job, and did not get military benefits, protection, or rank. The army's women's auxiliary suffered in the recruiting market compared to the women's reserve branches of the other services. By February 1943 the WAAC was failing to reach its recruitment goals, and, shortly after its first anniversary, it was converted by legislation to the Women's Army Corps (WAC) with full military status.

Thanks to the establishment of these reserve branches, women were eligible for commissions. Although they were no longer auxiliaries, however, neither were they equal to their male counterparts. They were in gender-segregated reserve branches whose very existence was under statutory limitations. They were not trained for combat but rather were intended to free men for combat. There were limitations in how high they could rise in the rank structure. The women's units also were subject to quotas, although these proved to be unrealistic—unrealistically low at the outset and unrealistically high later on. When the WAAC was founded, for example, it had been projected to peak at twenty-five thousand recruits in its second year, but commanders in the field requested a total of eighty thousand WAACs, and strength projections were raised, first to sixty-three thousand and later to 1.5 million.

Ultimately, about 350,000 women served in the armed forces during World War II, most in traditionally female fields such as administrative and clerical jobs, health care, and communications. As had been the case in World War I, however, some moved into more masculine domains, such as parachute riggers, aircraft mechanics, and gunnery instructors. Several hundred women who did not get full military status and benefits during the war served as Women's Airforce Service Pilots (WASPs) and ferried military aircraft to overseas theaters. During the war, military women served in all combat the-aters. There were more than eight thousand WACs in Europe on V-E Day, and more than five thousand served in the Pacific.

The army excluded women from jobs involving great physical strength, long training, working in "improper" environments, or supervising men and from combat, although in late 1942 the army experimented with gender-integrated crews for antiaircraft guns on the East Coast of the continental United States. The women proved effective, and the Anti-Aircraft Artillery requested increased assignment of WACs. The threat of aerial attack on the East Coast decreased, however, and noncombat jobs were found for the women in the army. Despite the constraints, the army identified more than a million personnel slots that could be occupied by women.

The navy opened all specialties to women. At first, however, WAVES could not be assigned outside the continental United States; although they were later allowed to serve in U.S. territories, geographical constraints limited their utilization. These constraints did not apply to nurses. Thirty-seven military nurses became Japanese prisoners of war at Corregidor and five others were captured on Guam.

At the end of the war, the U.S. military demobilized from a force of more than 12 million personnel in 1945 to about 1.5 million in 1948. The number of women in the service declined from 266,000 to about 14,000 during this period, influenced in part by an awareness on the part of the women that the statutory authorization for the WAC was scheduled to expire in 1948. Conscription lapsed in 1947, however, and, faced with declining male enlistments, the recently unified Department of Defense sought continued authorization to utilize women in the military in order to avoid personnel shortfalls.

The Women's Armed Services Integration Act, passed in 1948, provided regular status for women in the military. It established a ceiling for enlisted women of 2 percent of total enlisted strength and a ceiling for female officers of 10 percent of female enlisted strength. This latter ceiling did not include nurses, who were regarded differently from other women in the military. The act required women to be eighteen years of age to enlist (males could enlist at seventeen), required them to have written parental consent up to the age of twenty-one (males needed such consent only if they were under eighteen), restricted the ranks to which women officers could rise, and restricted women's dependents benefits unless they could demonstrate they were the primary breadwinners in their families. It assigned all army women who were not nurses or medical specialists to the Women's Army Corps. (Women were not organizationally segregated in the other services in the same way.) It established a separate promotion system for women, and it explicitly excluded women from service aboard combat aircraft and aboard navy ships other than hospital ships and transports (but did not exclude women by statute from participation in ground combat).

The Communist coup in Czechoslovakia and the Soviet blockade of Berlin led to the passage of a new Selective Service Act shortly after the Women's Armed Services Integration Act was passed. With the reinstitution of conscription, the dependence of the services on female personnel decreased. During the two decades after the passage of the 1948 integration act, the representation of women in the military, including nurses, never exceeded 1.5 percent.

When the Korean War erupted in 1950, the primary military manpower pool was the small Depression-era generation. The Defense Department sought to mobilize sources of personnel that were underutilized in peacetime—notably women. Within a year, Congress had (temporarily) lifted the 2 percent limit on female enlisted strength. There had been only 22,000 women in the services when the war broke out, including 7,000 nurses. The Defense Department sought to increase the number to 112,000, only 16,000 of whom would be nurses. For a variety of reasons, the recruitment campaign to meet this goal failed. The number of women in service did more than double, to a peak of almost 49,000 late in 1952, but it never even reached the 2 percent limit that had been suspended.

The turbulence of the 1960s in the United States led to policy changes regarding military personnel. In 1966 the Defense Department created a task force on the utilization of women in the services, and in 1967, acting partly on the recommendations of that task force, several provisions in the 1948 act were changed. Women for the first time were allowed to be promoted up to the permanent rank of colonel and to be appointed as flag-rank officers. The 2 percent limit on female enlisted strength was removed. Gender differences in retirement benefits were eliminated. The Defense Department announced an immediate increase of sixty-five hundred women in the armed forces.

Unlike the mobilizations for the two world wars, the mobilization for the Vietnam War did not lead to a major expansion of women in the military. Service policy was to keep women—except nurses—out of combat zones. Although between five thousand and six thousand nurses and female medical specialists served in Vietnam, the total number of other military women in the theater was less than fifteen hundred, including about five hundred WACs, about six hundred WAFs (more than half of them officers), and thirty-six women marines.

The 1967 legislation did not create gender equality of service conditions any more effectively than Executive Order 9981 had ended racial segregation. It left intact separate promotion systems in all services except the air force, which had only one system from the outset. It left women in the army in a segregated corps. It did not redress unequal treatment of dependents of male and female military personnel. It continued to exclude women from the service academies.

Although the Gates Commission had not anticipated an increase in military women as a consequence of the end of conscription, the all-volunteer force saw a quadrupling of the utilization of women in the U.S. armed forces. At the end of fiscal year (FY) 1973—the year the AVF was born—there were about forty-three thousand enlisted women on active duty—about 2.2 percent of the total enlisted force. By the end of FY 1975, there were ninety-five thousand enlisted women on active duty, about 5.3 percent of the force. In December 1987, 10.3 percent of active duty military personnel were women, ranging from 12.6 percent in the air force to 4.8 percent in the Marine Corps. Women made up 10.5 percent of the officer corps and 10.2 percent of the enlisted force.

The expansion in the number of women in the services was accompanied by important organizational changes. The major source of officer accessions, the Reserve Officers Training Corps (ROTC), was opened to women in 1970 by the air force, and in 1972 by the army and the navy. In June 1970 the army promoted two women—the chief of the Army Nurse Corps and the director of the Women's Army Corps—to the rank of brigadier general, and the following year, the other services followed the army's lead. Under congressional mandate, women were admitted to the service academies in 1976. In 1978 the Women's Army Corps was abolished, and army women were integrated into the other branches. By 1980 there were twenty-two thousand female commissioned officers in the U.S. armed forces. In December 1987, there were more than thirty-one thousand.

There were concurrent increases in the occupational roles in which women were allowed to serve. Women in uniform had traditionally not only been excluded from combat roles but had been concentrated in fields that, in the civilian labor force, were defined as appropriate for their gender—health care, clerical, and communications. During World War II, women had served in tasks that had previously been defined as male. At the end of the war, however, the traditional gender role restrictions were once again enforced. In 1972 fewer than 10 percent of enlisted women were in jobs that were not traditionally female. By 1976 the percentage of enlisted women in nontraditional jobs had quadrupled, to 40 percent, and by 1980, 55 percent of all enlisted women were in jobs that had not traditionally been done by women.

The statutory exclusion of women from combat has been lifted. The exclusion of navy women from warships, allowed in the 1948 integration act, was continued under 10 U.S. Code 6015 until, in 1978, Federal District Court Judge John J. Sirica ruled that the navy could not use this statute as the sole basis for excluding women from duty aboard ship, thereby constraining their career opportunities as navy personnel. The navy, which had been seeking greater flexibility in the assignment of women than was then allowed by law, did not appeal the ruling and has been assigning increased numbers of women to shipboard duty. In 1993, Congress repealed the exclusion of women from combat ships.

Women in the air force were similarly constrained by 10 U.S. Code 8549 from serving on aircraft engaged in combat missions, but there are no parallel statutory constraints on the potential utilization of women in ground combat operations by the army. The army does maintain a combat exclusion policy for women, based in part on the presumed intent of Congress in passing combat exclusion legislation affecting the other services, on assumptions regarding the negative impact that gender integration would have on unit cohesion, and on the subsequent ability of units to perform their missions, on the difficulty of clearly differentiating between combat and noncombat in land warfare, on assumptions about the ability of women to do the job, and on assumptions about the logistical problems of providing for feminine hygiene and toilet facilities in the field. The primary reason for the army's policy, however, is its continuing adherence to traditional notions of military service and of appropriate roles for women.

In the early 1980s, the Women in the Army Policy Review was conducted, the major focus of which was to evaluate the utilization of women in army jobs in light of the physical requirements of those jobs and the location of those jobs in relation to combat. The review recommended the use of gender-free strength tests based upon validated job requirements in the assignment of personnel. It also recommended that twenty-three military occupational specialties previously opened to women be closed on the basis of the proximity of those jobs to actual combat operations in the event of war. More than twelve hundred women were serving in those specialties at the time they were defined inappropriate for women (thirteen of these specialties were subsequently reopened to women).

When the United States sent forces to the Caribbean island of Grenada in 1983 to rescue American medical students, the army, with an ambiguous combat exclusion policy, shuttled women assigned to support units in the Eighteenth Airborne Corps back and forth between the island and Fort Bragg, North Carolina, while it tried to figure out whether they could be on the island. In the same conflict, the air force landed aircraft that had women as flight crew members at Point Salinas Airport while it was under fire, in apparent violation of statute, noting that it could not remove the women without hurting effectiveness.

Six years later, in December 1989, about eight hundred women soldiers participated in the invasion of Panama, and between one hundred and two hundred were near enemy fire. The meaninglessness of the combat exclusion policy was demonstrated by the experience of women aviators whose helicopters took hostile fire while they were flying male soldiers into combat zones, of women truck drivers who for hours, under sniper fire, drove male troops into combat areas, and of a woman military police captain whose company was engaged in a firefight with Panamanian Defense Forces.

The role of American military women in combat operations became even more apparent during the 1991 Gulf War against Iraq. More than thirty-three thousand women served in this campaign as pilots or as crew members of military aircraft, directing artillery, driving vehicles, supervising enemy prisoners of war, and serving on support ships and in construction and port facilities units, as well as fulfilling medical and administrative functions.

Women were among the casualties of the war. Thirteen were killed. Two women were prisoners of war of the Iraqis and both received the Purple Heart award for combat injuries sustained. The experience of the Gulf War led to renewed debate on combat exclusion policies.

In the wake of that conflict, Congress passed an amendment to the 1992 Defense Appropriation Bill removing the statutory exclusion of women from combat aviation and calling for a presidential commission to review the combat exclusion statutes. The commission recommended the continued exclusion of women from combat, but in April 1993 Secretary of Defense Les Aspin approved the training and assignment of women to combat aviation in all services.

Sexual Orientation. If racial integration was a fundamental personnel management issue in the 1950s and 1960s and gender integration was a major issue in the 1970s and 1980s, the practice of screening military personnel on the basis of sexual preference replaced those issues in the 1990s. The removal in the military of exclusions, quotas, and segregation based on gender and race reflected broader societal changes. Similarly, extension of greater legal and citizenship rights to homosexuals and lesbians in the United States portends continued debate on their appropriate role in the armed forces.

The issue of sexual preference in the military came to the fore in World War II when service policies defined homosexual tendencies as incompatible with military service, and recruiters and examination stations screened out admitted homosexuals even as significant numbers of gay men and women avoided the screen and were drafted or joined the armed forces. Estimates of how many served vary widely.

The expansion in the number of women in the services was a special cause for concern, in part because of a widely held belief that women, and particularly those who chose to serve in the military, were more likely than were men who volunteered for military service to be homosexual. This belief was aggravated by a widespread slander campaign that suggested that the Women's Army Corps was filled with lesbians and prostitutes.

Of those homosexuals who avoided the screen, some were identified and given "blue" discharges (conditions other than honorable) from service for "undesirable habits or traits of character." This category, which also included frequent AWOL, alcohol or drug abuse, theft, or serious abuse of army discipline, accounted for about 8 percent of the approximately 470,000 separations from the army of male soldiers for ineffectiveness between 1945 and 1947. The official army and navy histories state that homosexuality among women was not a problem; an army study concluded that lesbianism was less common in the military than in civilian life. The Marine Corps separated twenty-one women (out of about twenty-three thousand women marines) for lesbianism.

Other homosexuals who avoided the screen—probably the great majority—were undetected or ignored. Regulations were vague with regard to both the nature of the offense of homosexuality and the reasons for regarding it as an offense. In many cases, homosexual preferences were overlooked if the individuals involved did not act on them. That is, the problem was regarded as one of sexual behavior rather than sexual preference, and the behaviors that were involved were generally illegal among heterosexual couples as well. In general, military commanders tended to ignore homosexuality unless it was brought to their attention by criminal acts or indiscretion. Once brought to the leadership's attention, homosexuality was treated as either a major disciplinary infraction or a psychiatric problem.

One of the major effects of the World War II mobilization was that it brought together significant numbers of gay men and women from rural areas and taught them that they were not alone in their preferences. In an important sense, the mobilization provided a basis for the gay rights movement, although that movement has not reached the magnitude or the influence of the civil rights movement or the women's movement. More generally, the mobilization contributed to movement away from traditional sexual attitudes and behavior patterns in the United States.

The pattern established during the war extended into the cold war period. Identified homosexuals were screened from service, but many who evaded the screen and went undetected performed satisfactory service and were discharged honorably. Through the 1950s and into the 1960s, homosexuality was still largely unacceptable in the United States, and homosexuals in the service did not so identify themselves in large numbers. Those who were brought to the attention of military authorities were generally discharged.

During the Vietnam War, the use of homosexuality as a reason for not being drafted was a more visible issue than was the treatment of homosexuality within the military. Since the advent of the all-volunteer force, however, with military service increasingly being defined as an employment opportunity, with somewhat greater tolerance for alternative life-styles emerging in the country, with larger numbers of homosexuals publicly admitting their preferences, and with the gay rights movement achieving some success, discrimination on the basis of sexual preference within the military—as in other areas of American society—has become an issue. In addition, as increasing numbers of homosexuals in the military have become public about their preferences, attention has shifted from sexual behavior to sexual orientation. For example, in a widely publicized case in 1975, when an air force sergeant with fourteen years of satisfactory service and excellent performance ratings advised his superiors that he was a homosexual, he was discharged because of unsuitability.

The courts have generally upheld the right of the armed forces to bar the recruitment of gay men and women and to separate homosexuals and lesbians from service if they are detected. In this legal context, most separations after detection do not involve judicial action. Of 4,316 men and women discharged for homosexuality between 1984 and 1987, only two had been court-martialed, but there has been judicial movement in the other direction. In 1991, for example, the Ninth Circuit Court of Appeals in California reinstated the lawsuit of a former army reserve captain who was discharged in 1986 because she was a lesbian. The perception that military women are more likely to be homosexual than military men persists. During the first three quarters of fiscal year 1991, 168 soldiers were discharged for homosexuality. Sixty of them—more than a third of the total—were women, more than twice as many as would be expected on the basis of the gender distribution of the service.

One of the major justifications for the exclusionary policy is that homosexuals might be subject to blackmail and thus pose a security risk. If, however, homosexuality were not grounds for separation, the problem of potential blackmail would disappear. Indeed, a 1988 study conducted by the Defense Personnel Security Research and Education Center and released not by the Defense Department but by a homosexual member of Congress who has been an advocate for gays in the military found the security risk argument unwarranted. During the administration of George Bush, Defense Secretary Richard Cheney, while he chose not to seek a change in the policy, noted that the security argument did not hold up and acknowledged that the policy was discriminatory because it was not based on performance and was painful to many gay servicemen and women who served well.

As the 1980s began, progress toward greater tolerance of alternative sexual preferences within the military was interrupted by the AIDS epidemic and a perception that AIDS was a homosexual disease that would threaten the supply of blood for battlefield transfusions in a deployed army. (That supply is the blood of other soldiers.) With the rate of heterosexual transmission of AIDS increasing rapidly and with all military personnel being tested regularly for the disease, that argument will lose its force.

In early 1993, President Bill Clinton announced his intention to lift the ban on homosexuals in the armed forces, but was opposed by both military and congressional leaders. After five months of study and hearings, a compromise policy was formulated, whereby the services would neither ask personnel about their sexual orientation nor seek them out, but homosexuals had to be secretive about their orientations.

Perhaps the most dramatic reflection of changing sexual mores in America is the number of colleges and universities that are taking positions against discrimination on the basis of sexual preference. The consequences of these policies include banning from campuses organizations and activities that discriminate. These could well include the Reserve Officer Training Corps, which is the major source of officer accessions in the United States, as well as all military recruiters. At the same time, increasing legislation against gender discrimination in the workplace might well be applied to the military by the courts in the future.

See also MINORITIES IN THE ARMED FORCES; MOBILIZATION AND DEMOBILIZATION OF MANPOWER; PERSONNEL MOTIVATION; SEXUAL ORIENTATION AND THE MILITARY; SOCIALIZATION OF THE ARMED FORCES; *and* WOMEN IN THE ARMED FORCES.

BIBLIOGRAPHY

Manpower Policy

Anderson, Martin, ed. *Registration and the Draft* (1982).

Bachman, Jerald G., John D. Blair, and David R. Segal. *The All-Volunteer Force* (1977).

Baldwin, Robert H., and Thomas V. Daula. "The Cost of High Quality Recruits." *Armed Forces and Society* 11 (1984).

Berryman, Sue E. *Who Serves: The Persistent Myth of the Underclass Army* (1988).

Bowman, William, Roger Little, and G. Thomas Sicilia, eds. *The All-Volunteer Force After a Decade* (1986).

Chambers, John Whiteclay, II. *To Raise an Army* (1987).

Clifford, J. Garry, and Samuel R. Spencer, Jr. *The First Peacetime Draft* (1986).

Cress, Lawrence Delbert. *Citizens in Arms* (1982).

Curry, G. David. *Sunshine Patriots* (1985).

Dale, Charles, and Curtis Gilroy. "Determinants of Enlistments." *Armed Forces and Society* 10 (1984).

Danzig, Richard, and Peter Szanton. *National Service* (1986).

Davis, James W., Jr., and Kenneth M. Dolbeare. *Little Groups of Neighbors* (1968).

Faris, John H. "Economic and Noneconomic Factors of Personnel Recruitment and Retention in the AVF." *Armed Forces and Society* 10 (1984).

Fligstein, Neil D. "Who Served in the Military, 1940–73." *Armed Forces and Society* 6 (1980).

Fullinwider, Robert K., ed. *Conscripts and Volunteers* (1983).

Gerhardt, James M. *The Draft and Public Policy* (1971).

Gold, Philip. *Evasions: The American Way of Military Service* (1985).

Goodpaster, Andrew J., Lloyd H. Elliot, and J. Allan Hovey, Jr. *Toward a Consensus on Military Service* (1982).

Gilroy, Curtis L., ed. *Army Manpower Economics* (1986).

Hale, Robert F. "Congressional Perspectives on Defense Manpower Issues." *Armed Forces and Society* 11 (1985).

Hansen, W. L., and B. A. Weisbrod. "Economics of the Military Draft." *Quarterly Journal of Economics* 31 (1967).

Janowitz, Morris. "Toward an All-Volunteer Military." *The Public Interest* 27 (1972).

———. "The All-Volunteer Military as a 'Sociopolitical' Problem." *Social Problems* 22 (1975).

Janowitz, Morris, and Charles C. Moskos. "Five Years of the All-Volunteer Force." *Armed Forces and Society* 5 (1979).

Little, Roger W., ed. *Selective Service and American Society* (1969).

Marmion, Harry A. *The Case Against a Volunteer Army* (1971).

Millis, Walter. *Arms and Men: A Study in American Military History* (1956).

Moskos, Charles C. *The American Enlisted Man* (1970).

Oi, Walter Y. "The Economics of the Draft." *American Economic Review* 57 (1967).

Puscheck, Herbert C. "Selective Service Registration: Success or Failure?" *Armed Forces and Society* 13 (1983).

Segal, David R. *Recruiting for Uncle Sam* (1989).

Segal, David R., and H. Wallace Sinaiko, eds. *Life in the Rank and File* (1986).

Tax, Sol, ed. *The Draft: A Handbook of Facts and Alternatives* (1967).

Scowcroft, Brent, ed. *Military Service in the United States* (1982).

Benefit Policies

Beck, Bernard. "The Military as a Welfare Institution." In *Public Opinion and the American Military*, edited by Charles C. Moskos (1971).

Bowen, Gary L., and Dennis K. Orthner, eds. *The Organization Family* (1989).

Cohen, Jere, David R. Segal, and Lloyd V. Temme. "The Educational Cost of Military Service in the 1960s." *Journal of Political and Military Sociology* 14 (1986).

Segal, David R., and Jerald G. Bachman. "The Military as an Educational and Training Institution." *Youth and Society* 10 (1978).

Segal, Mady W. "The Military and the Family as Greedy Institutions." *Armed Forces and Society* 1 (1986).

Stanley, Jay, Mady W. Segal, and Charlotte Jean Laughton. "Grass Roots Family Action and Military Policy Responses." *Marriage and Family Review* 3–4 (1990).

Villemez, Wayne J., and John D. Kasarda. "Veteran Status and Socioeconomic Attainment." *Armed Forces and Society* 2 (1976).

Race, Gender, and Sexual Orientation

Berube, Allan. "Marching to a Different Drummer: Lesbian and Gay GIs in World War II." In *Powers of Desire: The Politics of Sexuality*, edited by Ann Snitow, Christine Stansell, and Sharon Thompson (1983).

Binkin, Martin, and Shirley J. Bach. *Women and the Military* (1977).

Binkin, Martin, Mark J. Eitelberg, Alvin J. Schexnider, and Marvin M. Smith. *Blacks and the Military* (1982).

Bogart, Leo, ed. *Social Research and the Desegregation of the U.S. Army* (1969).

Brinkerhoff, John R. "Homosexuals in the Armed Forces." *Defense Analysis* 5 (1989).

Campbell, D'Ann. *Women at War with America* (1984).

Dalfiume, Richard M. *Desegregation of the U.S. Armed Forces* (1969).

De Pauw, Linda Grant. "Women in Combat: The Revolutionary War Experience." *Armed Forces and Society* 7 (1981).

Devilbiss, M. C. "Gender Integration and Unit Deployment." *Armed Forces and Society* 11 (1985).

Fletcher, Marvin. *The Black Soldier and Officer in the United States Army, 1891–1917* (1974).

Foner, Jack D. *Blacks and the Military in American History* (1974).

Goldman, Nancy Loring, ed. *Female Soldiers—Combatants or Noncombatants?* (1982).

Holm, Jeanne. *Women in the Military* (1982).

Hope, Richard O. *Racial Strife in the U.S. Military* (1979).

Moskos, Charles C. "The American Dilemma in Uniform: Race in the Armed Forces." *Annals of the American Academy of Political and Social Science* 406 (1973).

Quarles, Benjamin. *The Negro in the American Revolution* (1961).

Segal, Mady W., and David R. Segal. "Social Change and the Participation of Women in the American Military." *Research in Social Movements, Conflicts and Change* 5 (1983).

Snyder, William, and Kenneth L. Nyberg. "Gays and the Military: An Emerging Policy Issue." *Journal of Political and Military Sociology* 8 (1980).

Williams, Colin J., and Martin S. Weinberg. *Homosexuals and the Military* (1971).

RESEARCH AND TECHNOLOGY

Barton C. Hacker

Conventional military history takes its shape from wars and battles. Attention focused instead on hardware, especially those primary weapons that mainly determine the character of warfare in any given period, does not greatly disturb that basic structure but does alter its contours. What follows is neither a catalog of weapons nor a celebration of the march of invention. Rather, this account attempts to use technological change as an aid to fuller historical understanding.

Recognizing the crucial role technology has played in American military history does not mean claiming that weapons alone decided events. Technological innovation was never more than one factor among many, although a vital one. In colonial America, for example, the fact that battle held quite different meanings for transplanted Europeans and for native Americans mattered no less than did disparities in the tools of war available to each side. This remained equally true at deeper levels. As military technology shaped the social order, so social institutions, interests, and values shaped technological change. Military-technological criteria suggest that American military history can best be divided into three major periods: preindustrial, industrial, and postindustrial.

Preindustrial European military technology transplanted to America exhibited certain per-

sistent traits throughout the period from the Spanish conquest through the early nineteenth century. Soldiering during this era is perhaps best understood as a preindustrial craft, jealously guarding the tools of its trade and slow to accept innovation. Although still glacial by later standards, Western military technological change had nevertheless already begun to outpace that of contemporary non-Western cultures. The Western edge, however, with a few notable exceptions, remained modest before the nineteenth century.

If soldiering was a craft in early modern Europe, weapons were the tools of the trade. They required individual expertise to wield effectively and individual experience to improve. Practical innovations in weaponry were mainly incremental, coming from the actual users filtered through other craftsmen, because weapon-making also rested on craft traditions. Like other preindustrial technologies, it improved by rule-of-thumb, cut-and-try methods. Nothing resembling organized research existed, although individual practitioners doubtless sometimes experimented with new processes or designs.

Accordingly, the pace of technological change in weaponry, as in all other preindustrial technologies, was slow. Putting it another way, troops carried much the same weapons from one decade to the next, or even from one century to the next. That left plenty of time for tacticians to devise, via the same cut-and-try approaches that marked weapon development, appropriate means of using arms and combining them effectively.

The military technology of the industrial period, from the 1840s through the 1940s, displayed certain broad trends. On land it comprised a single military-technological cycle that reached its climax in World War II. New materials and new techniques produced a series of linked innovations in small arms and guns that vastly expanded their ranges, rates of fire, and accuracy. Successful frontal attack, never easy, became all but impossible. When huge armies and restricted terrain eliminated flanks, as on the western front in World War I, stalemate ensued, to be broken only when new tactics and new machines, especially tanks and aircraft, restored movement to the battlefield.

Innovation no less radical transformed war at sea. Accelerating technological change transmuted the classic sailing man-of-war, expensive but effective, into an exorbitantly costly armored behemoth that, despite its heavy guns, may well have been obsolete before it ever saw combat. In any event, concurrent improvements in mines and torpedoes did much to deny freedom of the seas to capital ships that proved all too vulnerable to attack below the water line and, later, even more so to attack from the air. In the mid-twentieth century, the twilight of the industrial age, aircraft carriers and submarines ruled the waves.

Military-technological change in the second half of the twentieth century includes certain striking features that seem to have no real parallel in past experience. Military technology has bifurcated along tactical and strategic lines. Although sharing certain common features—notably the vital role of electronics and computers in almost every aspect of military activity—tactical and strategic technologies have followed largely independent paths, one continuing the traditional focus of military-technological research on battlefield weapons periodically tested in combat, the other elaborating the

inherently untestable dream of war-winning weapons seemingly embodied in nuclear-armed missiles.

A constant military problem has been how to prevail in the field against comparably equipped armies. During the modern period, perhaps especially in the United States, one way out of the impasse often seemed to be technological innovation—that is, eliminating "comparably equipped" from the equation. This was the dream of decisive secret weapons that the Manhattan Project and the development of the atomic bomb seemed to confirm. Directed research and development promised a constant edge to the nation able to sustain so costly an effort.

MILITARY TECHNOLOGY IN EARLY AMERICA

Technologically speaking, the early modern period—corresponding roughly to the colonial period of American history—comprised two major eras in land warfare. These eras can be defined in terms of their predominant weapons as that of pike and shot and of flintlock and bayonet, with the dividing line falling late in the seventeenth century.

The pike-and-shot cycle in Europe culminated in the Thirty Years War (1618–1648), when a century or more of trial and error at last produced the tactics and organization that fully accommodated the main infantry weapons—pike, arquebus, field gun, and armored horse—and allowed generalship to decide the outcome of battle between comparably equipped forces. By the late eighteenth century, the tactics and organization suited to armies equipped with flintlock and bayonet had been fully worked out, and Napoleonic warfare stands as the culmination of a military-technological cycle that saw the power of decision once again restored to battle.

The perfected tactics of flintlock and bayonet provided the larger setting, at least in part, for the two wars with England that first achieved, then confirmed, American independence—the revolutionary war and the War of 1812. Neither in Europe nor in America did technological innovation significantly alter the course of war. Anglo-American conflict between 1775 and 1815 spanned a time that may be characterized as a military-technological plateau.

Conquest and Settlement. Within particular military culture areas, such as Western Europe or the Eastern Woodlands of North America, military technology was likely to achieve and maintain rough parity. Across culture areas, however, technological advantages might be decisive, as shown by European horses, steel, and guns in the New World. The uncontested supremacy of European ships and guns were the foundation of European conquest in America, although other aspects of Western military technology also contributed significantly. At sea the gun-carrying sailing vessel remained the master military-technological system of the early modern era, right up to the mid-nineteenth century. It also remained a Western monopoly throughout the period.

During the era of pike and shot, conflicts between European forces in America were few and far between. Military interaction chiefly pitted Europeans against native Americans, with victory ordinarily crowning the most advanced arms, but better arms told only part of the story. For one thing, the technological gap tended to narrow as native Americans adapted European military technologies to their own purposes, but European settlers also came to enjoy other advantages over their indigenous rivals, most notably manpower. Chiefly because of devastation wrought by Old World diseases in virgin New World populations, European Americans acquired a growing edge in numbers.

International rivalries reflected in the New World dominated events during the flintlock-and-bayonet era. American conflicts increasingly resembled those in Europe—that is, fought between forces more or less evenly matched in technological terms—despite some novelties stemming from the mutual interaction of native Americans and European Americans.

Although European Americans continued to enjoy some degree of technological advantage, their decisive edge increasingly became weight of numbers. Native American populations suffered wave after wave of disease, as likely to precede as to follow the westward movement of settlers, always debilitating and too often fatal, while the population of European origin grew steadily.

Technology and Independence. For the most part, America fought Great Britain with the standard weapons of the age. The basic firearm in America, as throughout the Western world, in the late eighteenth century was the flintlock musket, the perfected product of more than a century's evolution. Although individual weapons varied in length, weight, and bore, each was a single-shot smoothbore muzzleloader firing a heavy lead ball—fifteen to the pound was one standard recipe—about two-thirds inch in diameter. Individual paper cartridges held ball and gunpowder, the soldier tearing them open to load, which made for speedy firing. Trained troops could get off three to four shots a minute, or two volleys against a normal charge. To receive the charge, the soldier fitted a socket bayonet over its muzzle and converted the musket into a surrogate pike; this was the key late seventeenth century innovation that rendered the pike superfluous.

Rifles hold a special place in the folklore of the American Revolution. Well-known since the fifteenth century as a way to improve range and accuracy, rifling suffered a major military drawback. It demanded a tight-fitting bullet, which the soldier had to ram down the barrel of his muzzleloader, a task far harder and slower than loading smoothbore muzzleloaders. In the right circumstances, however, such as those that prevailed along the western colonial frontier in the early eighteenth century, the rifle's advantages could outweigh its shortcomings. Pennsylvania gunsmiths transformed the stubby, large-bore Jaeger rifle they knew from central Europe into the first distinctively American contribution to firearms technology, the legendary Pennsylvania-Kentucky rifle with its long barrel and relatively small bore. Despite the glamour attached to the weapon then and now, it was not particularly effective in battle. For military purposes, the rifle's drawbacks restricted it to an essentially auxiliary role until well into the nineteenth century.

Although without impact on the course of the war, one novelty allowed the fledgling United States to stake an early claim on the technology of undersea warfare. Creatively adapting European ideas, David Bushnell designed and built a submersible one-man boat to attack British warships from below. He intended the muscle-powered *Turtle* to approach an enemy vessel unseen and to attach a mine to its hull beneath the water line. Initially using his own funds, then partly subsidized by the Connecticut legislature—a pattern that would be repeated more than once in later American history—he completed building his boat in 1775. A year later he had his first target, the sixty-four-gun *Eagle* moored in New York harbor. On the night of 6 September 1776, the Bushnell-trained sergeant manning *Turtle* on its first sortie got as far as the *Eagle*'s hull, but when his auger failed to pierce its bottom he could not attach the mine. Two later attempts achieved even less. Although the *Turtle* undertook no more missions, it was not forgotten, and the dream of undersea warfare stayed alive.

Early Naval Innovation.

Like the revolutionary war, the War of 1812 saw the United States display technological novelties at sea. The most novel and least successful came from Robert Fulton. Long before he achieved fame by promoting commercial steamships, he designed and built a muscle-powered submarine for Napoleon. Launched in 1801, the *Nautilus* used ballast tanks to submerge—it had enough air to sustain a four-man crew for three hours—and a horizontal rudder to maintain depth. Despite successful trials, Fulton's boat proved ineffective in combat, and he had no better luck trying to sell his idea in England. He did, however, persuade the U.S. Congress to fund an even more ambitious project, a steam-powered vessel with a hundred-man crew. It remained untried when its inventor died in 1815.

Fulton also pioneered steam warships, launching the world's first in 1815. Fast, well-armed, nearly impervious to existing ordinance, the *Demologos* (also known as *Fulton I*) completed its trial runs only after the War of 1812 had ended and so never entered service. Unseaworthy and intended strictly for harbor defense, it inspired little enthusiasm among naval officers. Many years passed before steam warships again appeared on the scene.

Another naval innovation, this one the result of improving tradition rather than promoting radical change, enjoyed greater success. The Naval Act of 1794 produced three storied frigates, the *Constitution* and *United States*, each forty-four guns, and the thirty-six-gun *Constellation*, all launched in 1797. They outgunned the British frigates they fought in the War of 1812 and outsailed the men-of-war that might have overwhelmed them. Although none of this much affected the outcome of the war, their exploits did help create an American naval tradition. Sail-powered warships, however, were nearing the end of the line. The future belonged to steam, even if few yet recognized the fact.

The American System.

Interchangeable parts manufacturing or the uniformity system, America's first major contribution to military-technological innovation, was a step removed from the field of battle. Its evolution spanned America's transition from a preindustrial to an industrial economy.

The technique had French roots, like many aspects of military institutional development in the young American Republic. The first firearms manufactured at the new Springfield Armory, for instance, simply copied a French model. Uniformity cannot be so firmly pinned down. Beginning in 1763, Jean-Baptiste Vacquette de Gribeauval tried to create standard guns and gear for the French artillery. His reforms provided the mobile field guns that became the basis of Napoleonic tactics. Gribeauval also promoted the work of Honoré Blanc, who from the mid-1780s sought to produce in French armories small arms with uniform parts. Developed further in U.S. Army arsenals during the first half of the nineteenth century, this approach decisively reshaped the organization and equipment of armies as the so-called American system of manufactures.

Although Eli Whitney was a key figure in this development, the reason is not, as most textbooks have it, his invention of a way to make muskets with interchangeable parts. In fact, he added nothing of technological moment to techniques that Gribeauval and Blanc had pioneered in France during the 1770s and 1780s, which Whitney learned about from Thomas Jefferson, but he did become an ardent promoter of the uniformity system. Whitney's greatest contributions involved organizing an enterprise and publicizing a still novel approach to arms making.

A more direct, if less well-known, source of French technological ideas was Louis de Tousard, a graduate of the French artillery school at Strasbourg seconded to the American army during the revolutionary war. Returning to the United States in 1793, he became a key figure in creating the U.S. Military Academy at West Point, New York. His three-volume *American Artillerist's Companion,* a standard text at West Point for years after its 1809 publication, strongly promoted the principles of uniformity and regularity pioneered by Gribeauval.

Neither Whitney nor Tousard played major roles in converting ideas to practice. Others actually created the uniformity system during the 1820s and 1830s. Two contractors, Simeon North and John H. Hall, worked closely with army managers, notably Roswell Lee at the Springfield Armory in Massachusetts, to perfect the required technology, which included specialized machinery and precision measurement. The U.S. Model 1842 musket, Springfield designed and manufactured, was the first weapon produced in quantity with interchangeable parts.

MILITARY TECHNOLOGY IN TRANSITION, 1840–1865

The United States entered the first stages of the nineteenth-century military-technological revolution by the 1830s. Change that was far more rapid than had ever prevailed under preindustrial conditions became the rule. More telling, the rate of change increased. As time between idea and product grew shorter, the pace of meaningful military-technological change accelerated. Craft traditions gave way to factory production, random invention to planned innovation, hit-or-miss improvement to organized research and development.

Military education dramatically expanded and improved, both for officers and for enlisted men. Gunnery and engineering, in particular, became subjects of higher education for officers, helping not only to promote greater professionalism but also to foster a remarkable degree of inventiveness. Through much of the nineteenth century, a surprisingly large share of innovations came from graduates of West Point and the U.S. Naval Academy at Annapolis, Maryland. Technical courses for lower ranks provided basic training in operating and maintaining ever more complex weapons and equipment.

During the middle third of the nineteenth century, military technology began to undergo far-reaching alteration. Practical rifled firearms dramatically transformed land combat. At sea, steam power and armor worked a no less dramatic transformation, marking the first stages of the nineteenth-century naval revolution. Occurring in the midst of these changes, the American Civil War was notably transitional. Commanders looked to the past for tactics and organization, even as battle itself presaged the growing mechanization of war.

Toward Modern Small Arms. The Springfield Armory's Model 1842 smoothbore musket replaced the flintlock with the new percussion caplock. Caplocks eliminated the external ignition that made flintlocks prone to misfire; a sharp blow from the hammer detonated an unstable chemical, the flame passing through a sealed port to ignite the powder in the chamber. Percussion ignition greatly enhanced reliability. When allied with a practical rifling system, as it soon was, it helped radically transform small arms.

One stopgap answer to the rifling problem came to fruition in the 1840s, the handiwork of Captain Claude-Étienne Minié building on earlier work by another French army inventor, Gustav Delvigne. The key idea was a bullet small enough to slip easily down the barrel, then deformed to grip the rifling. Delvigne proposed tapping the ball with a ramrod to deform the bullet, but Minié devised a more elegant solution—the self-expanding bullet. Exploding powder expanded the bullet's hollow base, spreading the lead to fill the barrel and grip the rifling.

The U.S. Model 1855 rifle-musket incorporated this system, plus an improved percussion system. Earlier model smoothbores were also converted to rifles, and percussion-rifled muzzleloaders became the mainstay of Civil War infantry. Far more accurate and dependable than their predecessors, they also outranged the smoothbore gun that still formed the backbone of army artillery. When the technical framework for the tactics that defined Napoleonic warfare ceased to exist, consequences were written in blood on every Civil War battlefield.

Breech-loading was the next crucial step. Like rifling, it had both a long history and a serious military drawback—gas escaping from the breech. Breech-loading weapons entered service well before metal cartridges finally solved the problem for good. John Hall, who helped perfect the American system, also invented the best flintlock breechloader, which saw limited use in the U.S. Army from 1819. The link was not accidental. Hall received not only a contract specifying royalties on his musket but also a job at the Harpers Ferry Armory, West Virginia, where he helped advance the uniformity system while working to improve his design.

A clever solution to the problem of leaking gas allowed Hall's protégé, Christian Sharps, to devise the Sharps Model 1859, the last word in percussion breechloaders. Although Sharps rifles saw wide service, rifled muskets dominated the battlefields of the Civil War. Only after the war and the development of practical metal cartridges did breech-loading fully replace muzzle-loading.

Ordnance in Transition.

Ordnance in Transition. Attempts to apply rifling to guns through the mid-nineteenth century met less success. Metal barrels too often burst under the strain of explosions confined by tight-fitting projectiles, unless firing reduced powder charges. Unfortunately, smaller charges meant lesser impact and limited effectiveness, even for the best rifled artillery of the mid-nineteenth century. West Point graduate Thomas J. Rodman developed a new founding process and introduced a reasonably satisfactory three-inch rifled gun, but the most widely used rifled field gun in the Civil War was the work of another West Point graduate, Robert P. Parrott.

Although rifled ordnance had begun to assume growing importance on mid-century battlefields, improved smoothbore guns firing shells and shrapnel as well as solid shot played the larger role into the 1860s. Outstanding among these weapons was the twelve-pounder field gun of 1857, called the "Napoleon." Named after the chief author of the improved design, Napoleon III, who had devoted extensive study to artillery of all kinds, it may have been the best muzzle-loading smoothbore cast-metal field gun ever made. It was also the last. In a pattern familiar to historians of technology, an obsolescent technology achieved its finest expression just before its demise.

Naval ordnance likewise remained predominantly smoothbore but enjoyed the first notable advances in two centuries. Stimulated by Henri-Joseph Paixhans, a French artillery officer, and especially by his *Nouvelle force maritime* (1822), European navies began to adopt explosive shells of improved design in the 1830s. Eventually, the United States followed suit. Because shells were hollow, they could be larger than solid shot of comparable weight. Paixhans also advocated standardization for naval guns, another innovation soon under way.

A Swedish-American naval officer and inventor, John A. B. Dahlgren, learned how to raise the caliber of shell guns from eight to eleven inches, and Rodman's new founding process made guns with calibers up to twenty inches feasible. Explosive shells ended the day of steam warships propelled by paddle wheel. Improved naval guns also promoted the use of armor on ships.

The Naval Revolution Begins.

After Fulton's turn-of-the-century experimental steam warship failed, the U.S. Navy abandoned steam for decades. Abroad, steam warships remained minor, specialized fleet adjuncts. Steam power afloat posed several intractable problems in the early nineteenth century. Machinery remained bulky and inefficient; installed above the water line to push paddle wheels, it also remained far too exposed for a warship, especially when shell guns appeared. Paddle boxes meant fewer guns, thus lesser weight of broadside. Fuel demands that sharply constrained cruising radius only made matters worse.

In a single stroke, screw propulsion seemed to resolve most of the problem. One of the first three U.S. Navy vessels mounting shell guns, the ten-gun sloop *Princeton*, launched in 1843, was also the world's first warship driven by a stern-mounted screw propeller. Designed by transplanted Swedish engineer John Ericsson, who also oversaw building, the 400-horsepower engine turned a six-bladed screw that gave the *Princeton* a top speed of thirteen knots.

The extreme vulnerability of wooden ships to shell guns also promoted the next major changes in naval architecture—iron hulls and armor plate. The United States was once again a pioneer, when Congress in 1842 authorized construction of an all-iron armorclad war steamer. Like the *Demologos*, an essentially private venture that the navy endorsed only reluctantly, the so-called Stevens Battery (after its builders) suffered from bureaucratic delays and rapidly changing technology. Ordnance growing in power outstripped efforts to armor the ship against penetration by shot or shell. Never completed, it eventually went for scrap.

When the Civil War began in 1861, the Union navy had eighteen relatively modern steam-powered, screw-propelled, wooden warships. Iron hulls and armor had yet to enter regular service. Although steam proved indispensable to the Union blockade of the Confederacy, iron and armor were not. The burden of blockade fell on wooden ships, which were built at a furious pace. Armorclads played only an auxiliary role, although an important one, dictated in part by the South's reliance on makeshift armorclads to defend its ports.

Armor Afloat.

The Confederacy had a cadre of Annapolis-trained officers but began the war without ships. It also lacked factories for armor plate and marine engines, hampering naval defense throughout the war, but Confederate efforts to rectify the imbalance produced the war's most famous naval action and its best-known military innovation. Despite (or perhaps because of) its indecisive outcome, the March 1862 clash in Hampton Roads between the Confederate *Virginia* (better known as the *Merrimack*, the name of the ship upon whose hull it had been constructed) and the Union *Monitor* marked a historic moment. As the first meeting between steam-driven, ironclad warships, it dramatized the revolutionary developments in naval technology when under way.

Of the two, the *Monitor* was by far the most novel, another product of the inventive Ericsson. Nearly everything about it was new and untried, but it became the namesake for an entire class of warships that persisted for decades. Ericsson himself made the detailed drawings that guided the workmen. Riveted on the *Monitor*'s 124-foot hull was a raft-like deck 172 feet long and 41.5 feet at its widest, with 4.5-inch iron armor on its sides, 1 inch on its deck. Most distinctive was the 140-ton turret amidships, a cylinder 9 feet high and 20 feet across encased in 8-inch armor. Revolving on a spindle cogged to an auxiliary steam engine, the turret could swing two 11-inch Dahlgren guns through a full 360 degrees, a field of fire unblocked by masts, rigging, or other sailing-vessel paraphernalia. The *Monitor* relied entirely on its engines, also of Ericsson's design, two decades before most warships gave up their auxiliary sails.

The *Virginia*, in contrast, was built on the remains of a standard wooden hull, armor merely draped over a wooden casemate housing two pivoted seven-inch rifles, along with three nine-

inch Dahlgren smoothbores and two six-inch rifles on each broadside. It also carried a heavy
iron wedge fixed to the bow as a ram, largely
useless because the rebuilt engines could manage only four knots. Heavily damaged in the
battle, the *Virginia* required extensive repairs,
then had to be destroyed when Union forces
seized Norfolk, Virginia.

Unsolved design problems largely precluded
either side from using ocean-going ironclads.
Notoriously unseaworthy, these ships remained restricted to protected coastal waters.
Such shortcomings mattered little on western
rivers, where steamboats had multiplied before
the war. Fitted with iron plate and guns, they
became armored gunboats, valuable adjuncts to
army operations that supported the Union conquest of the Mississippi.

Civil War Technology and Research.
The transitional nature of the Civil War has
tended to obscure its place in military history.
Occurring in the midst of far-reaching changes,
it straddled two ages as the last great preindustrial war and the first major war of the industrial
era. The complex interrelationship among war,
science, technology, and industry so characteristic of the modern age scarcely existed then,
even in embryo. Industrialization had only begun, not yet run its course, when North and
South went to war.

In time the progressive and rapid improvement of old, as well as the introduction of new,
weapons would become core factors in military
planning and operations, but that took decades.
Engineering and industry had yet to master the
skills that allowed speedy development of warlike invention or improved weapons and their
prompt mass production. Although that ability
had scarcely emerged before World War I and
was not fully realized until World War II, its
prospect could be glimpsed even in the 1860s.

Despite numerous portents of things to
come, mostly technological, there survived
enough of the old—mainly tactics and organization—to leave room for effective generalship. In
this respect the Civil War very much looked
back toward Napoleonic warfare, which had

seen the triumph of mass armies but which belonged technologically to the past more than the
future. From this angle, the Civil War might
well be termed the last war of the old era.

At the same time, the war stimulated changes
that were profoundly to affect the future of military-technological innovation. Explored as a
source of new weapons, applied research
achieved little success. Unimpressive as the
results were in the actual course of the Civil
War, the idea, however, triumphed. Memory
tended to invest the efforts of the National
Academy of Sciences with more success than
they had actually earned. When the United
States once again entered a major war, such efforts were promptly resumed.

The military-technological innovations that
began to transform warfare by the mid-nineteenth century still followed the age-old path
from lone inventor through cut-and-try development. Team research was an invention of the
later nineteenth century, and then only in industry; organized military research took several
decades longer. Nothing new significantly affected the course of the Civil War. The likeliest
explanation is that industrial capacity had not
yet reached the point where an innovation
could be quickly and efficiently placed in large-
scale production so as to equip very large armies. That limitation would change decisively in
the next half-century.

MILITARY-TECHNOLOGICAL
REVOLUTION, 1865–1915

With the end of the Civil War, the innovative
role played by U.S. armed forces in military-
technological development through much of the
nineteenth century declined, perhaps because
the military became less receptive to innovation,
perhaps because the military simply no longer
enjoyed levels of funding that allowed it to
sponsor research and development. Individual
American inventors and entrepreneurs continued to spin off ideas and proposals but found
their warmest welcome in Europe. From the

end of the Civil War until well into the twentieth century, the United States remained largely a borrower of weaponry developed abroad.

Despite significant improvements in military technology, the most striking feature of the late nineteenth and early twentieth centuries was an extraordinary expansion of productive capacity. Industrialized states could produce so much in so little time with so few workers that armed forces no longer seemed able to enforce decision. When armies upon armies could be raised, equipped, and maintained, war became nothing so much as a giant siege operation. The paradox of military-technological change in the late nineteenth and early twentieth centuries can be stated simply: Sources of change remained chiefly empirical, but rates of change continued to accelerate. Vast as the accumulation of technical knowledge had become, it remained normally the product of hit-or-miss accident by craftsmen or tinkerers, laboriously augmented over many years, unevenly developed, and slow to spread.

Something more novel loomed on the horizon, however, a kind of systematic empiricism that waxed as the nineteenth century advanced. Nonmilitary sources of military-technological innovation and improvement gained importance, especially when the invention of the industrial research laboratory in the late nineteenth century laid the groundwork for still more rapid and far-reaching innovation. The full effects of that change, however, would not be felt until well into the twentieth century.

Perfecting Small Arms. Military small arms continued their revolutionary changes in the late nineteenth century. Breech-loading, fixed ammunition, magazines, and smokeless powder all achieved practical form in rapid succession and transformed the rifled musket of the 1860s into the modern rifle by the 1890s. Several forms of fixed ammunition incorporating primer, charge, and bullet in a metal cartridge were devised in the middle years of the nineteenth century. Such ammunition solved the chief problem of breechloaders, leaking gas, since the metal casing served as an effective obturating agent. With improved manufacturing techniques and metal cartridges, arms makers could meet military needs for cheap, plentiful, and reliable breechloaders.

Once metal cartridges and breech-loading became standard, magazine rifles quickly replaced single-shot arms. The centuries-old concept of multiple-shot weapons sprang from obvious advantages to soldiers who could fire several times without reloading. Efforts to turn concept into practical weapon, however, demanded breechloading. Metal cartridges not only solved that problem, their easy handling quickly led to magazines and other repeating mechanisms.

Repeating rifles, Christopher M. Spencer's by far the most important, saw Civil War service. Patented in 1860, Spencer's rifle reached full production by 1863. A lever action moved rimfire cartridges into the chamber from the seven-shot tubular magazine in the stock of the rifle. Technically the most advanced repeating rifle of its time, it became the standard arm of the Union cavalry by war's end. No rifle, however, gained wide use; rifles were more a portent of things to come than a decisive influence on the war itself.

Two innovations completed the transformation of infantry small arms—metal-jacketed bullets and smokeless powder. The work of Swiss army Major Edward A. Rubin resulted in the first successful metal-jacketed bullet in the early 1880s. French chemist Paul M. E. Vielle invented smokeless powder in 1886 when he plasticized nitrocellulose with ether and alcohol. Smokeless powder suitable for firearms had two major consequences: First, it reduced to mere traces the formerly dense cloud of smoke that betrayed the soldier's position and obscured his vision, and second, and more important, its relatively slow-burning qualities yielded much higher muzzle velocities without matching increases in internal pressure. Because metal jackets prevented rifling from stripping or heat from melting the soft lead bullet, this innovation likewise contributed to sharp increases in internal velocity.

Beginning with the French Lebel in 1886, new small-bore rifles combined these changes to produce radically higher velocities, flatter trajectories, and increased range. When the U.S. Army in 1892 decided to replace the twenty-year-old single-shot Springfield with a new .30-caliber magazine rifle firing smokeless cartridges, it turned to the Danish Krag-Jörgensen. It was not until 1903 that the United States designed and produced its own magazine rifle, the bolt-action Springfield, which remained in service until the eve of World War II.

Multiplying Fire. Even as the individual weapons of soldiers achieved new levels of efficiency, new weapons tended to reduce their significance. Machine guns and quick-firing artillery dominated the second stage of industrial war. The machine gun had numerous forerunners, none of them truly ancestral. Early attempts to achieve rapid fire relied on multiple barrels. In this form the idea can be traced to the earliest years of gunpowder weapons. Workable systems, however, did not appear until the second half of the nineteenth century, when reliable fixed ammunition became available.

Richard J. Gatling patented the most successful of all multiple-barrel guns in 1862. Civil War models used copper rim-fire cartridges, gravity feed, and six rotating barrels. In the course of its long career, the Gatling gun underwent numerous modifications, but its essential feature always remained the crank-controlled revolution of several rifled barrels about a central axis, each barrel firing as it came into contact with the breech mechanism. It remained the only authorized machine gun in U.S. service until 1904.

The French mitrailleuse reversed the method: Cranking successively discharged the cartridges in twenty-five fixed barrels in a wrought-iron casing. Its salient shortcoming was its comparatively great weight. In fact, because they required horse-drawn carriages, the French army regarded mitrailleuses as artillery pieces. Consequently misused as light guns rather than in close support of infantry, they forfeited their potential impact during the Franco-Prussian War by being employed at excessive ranges.

The first true machine gun—that is, a weapon automatically self-actuated rather than externally powered—resulted from the work of Hiram S. Maxim, an American expatriate in London. Between 1883 and 1885 he patented virtually every imaginable method for automatic fire. His basic patent, dating from 1884, covered a recoil-operated lock breech system applied to machine guns. The formerly wasted power of the gun's recoil loaded, fired, and ejected belt-fed cartridges continuously as long as the trigger was depressed. Maxim's basic design was so well-conceived that it remained virtually unchanged throughout its long career.

At its inaugural demonstration in 1885, Maxim's first model fired more than six hundred rounds per minute through its single barrel. Enclosing the barrel in a water-cooling jacket dispersed the excessive heat generated by firing so many bullets so rapidly. Relatively lightweight because it dispensed with multiple barrels, the gun also used a tripod rather than the wheels of multiple-barrel systems. Machine guns became much harder to confuse with field artillery.

By 1897 several armies had adopted Maxim guns, but doctrine for their effective combat use lagged behind the proliferation of automatic weapons after Maxim's breakthrough. Although the machine gun was essentially an American invention and the models most widely used in World War I and after all bore American names—Maxim, Hotchkiss, Lewis, Browning—U.S. forces clung to the Gatling gun until the turn of the century. The U.S. Army did not adopt Maxim guns until 1904 or acquire machine guns in any great numbers until World War I.

Quick-Firing Guns. The same advances in fixed ammunition, smokeless powder, and metallurgy that revolutionized small arms transformed artillery. Controlling recoil was the last step in perfecting the field gun; such control allowed the gun to remain on target and greatly increase its rate of accurate fire.

The French Model 1897 75mm gun, the storied "Seventy-five," was the first and most successful design. Hydraulic braking absorbed the recoil, and compressed air pushed the barrel forward to its original position. Because the carriage remained fixed, laying and firing the gun became a continuous operation, rather than a process to be repeated from the beginning after each shot. Another benefit of the fixed carriage was that it could mount a shield, thus offering the crew some protection against small-arms fire.

Nickel-steel barrels good for six thousand rounds, interrupted-screw breeches that combined easy manipulation with great reliability, brass-cased fixed ammunition, shells filled with high explosive rather than black powder, and flat trajectories yielded by smokeless powder all joined to make the French Seventy-five an incomparable field gun. A trained crew could fire as many as thirty well-aimed shots a minute with devastating effect. Larger guns were correspondingly slower but also longer-ranged.

By the turn of the century, the eclipse of artillery by small arms that had so colored the Civil War was over. Quick-firing field guns allied with machine guns, not small arms, swept the fields of World War I. In this as in so many other areas of military technology at the turn of the century, U.S. forces lagged behind European. While other European nations promptly followed the French example, U.S. guns still fired black powder in the Spanish-American War (1898). Only after the War Department's postwar reorganization did the U.S. Army acquire a near equivalent to the French Seventy-five, the Model 1902 three-inch field gun. That U.S. forces adopted the French weapon in World War I owed more to American production shortcomings than to any significant defect in the homegrown gun.

The Naval-Industrial Complex.

The decades preceding World War I saw a technological arms race. Navalism was at its center, and the United States, remote from Old World frictions, became an eager participant. In fact, an American naval officer furnished the race's ideological underpinnings. Alfred Thayer Mahan's *The Influence of Sea Power upon History, 1660–1783* (1890) wrapped navies, commerce, colonies, and national power into a neat package that ex-

cited imaginations throughout the Western world and beyond. It came at a time when naval technology was in the throes of revolutionary change. Wooden sailing warships had long since become obsolete as steam replaced sail and iron replaced wood, the whole encased in ever-thicker armor. As masts and sails vanished, guns moved from the fixed broadside to rotating turrets and breech-loading rifles replaced muzzle-loading smoothbores. In the second half of the nineteenth century, European navies competed in building ships with increasingly thicker armor and larger guns.

In contrast to its often pioneering role in early nineteenth-century naval innovation, the United States lagged behind Europe after the Civil War. Only late in the 1880s did the U.S. Navy reenter the naval era that it had helped inaugurate in the Civil War. Coincidentally, Mahan's *Influence of Sea Power* appeared in the same year the U.S. Navy launched its first modern warship, an armored cruiser, and received congressional authorization for its first three battleships. When launched in 1893, they became the first U.S. warships to compare with contemporary European designs—fast, heavily armed, and belted with eighteen-inch armor. Although also of doubtful seaworthiness and range, they acquitted themselves handsomely in their one trial by fire, the Spanish-American War.

To a degree quite unmatched in earlier periods, armament-making became an entrepreneurial activity in the late nineteenth century. Western armed forces increasingly relied on industrial research for technical innovation, development, and production. In the United States a new naval-industrial complex provided research as well as hardware. American entrepreneurs had never been shy about seeking military contracts but had seldom enjoyed much luck except during wartime. As the earlier experiences of Whitney, Hall, and North suggest, the armed forces preferred to rely on their own resources.

The army's arsenal system survived largely intact through the early twentieth century, but the navy forged an alliance with the steel industry toward the end of the nineteenth century.

When Congress in 1883 approved building the navy's first steel ships and decreed in 1886 that only domestic materials might be used, it created the first really large and lucrative market for peacetime military industry. The all-steel navy program of the 1880s and 1890s marked a fateful step along the way to transforming the relationship between armed forces and industry.

As the twentieth century opened, the navies of the world were undergoing another, even more far-reaching transformation than the one that had marked the late nineteenth century. The Royal Navy soon provided perhaps the most potent symbol of the new navalism with the 1906 launching of the *Dreadnought*, leading to an even more intense naval armaments race. Enormously fast and heavily armed, battleships and battle cruisers epitomized early twentieth-century military might.

"Dreadnought," like "battleship," became a common noun, and the British design was promptly emulated throughout the industrialized world. Two U.S. big-gun battleships had been authorized by Congress in early 1905, but the *South Carolina* and *Michigan* were not laid down until late 1906. By then, in an extraordinary feat of construction, the *Dreadnought* had already been launched. The two U.S. vessels were not completed until late 1909, as were the more powerful battleships *Delaware* and *North Dakota*, which had actually been laid down a year after *South Carolina* and *Michigan*. Battleship-building in the United States continued at a fevered pace for the next decade and a half.

Torpedoes and Submarines. Impressive as such figures might be, dreadnoughts were also the end of the line for capital ships whose power resided in their guns. The first challenge to their supremacy already existed in the form of torpedoes. "Mine" and "torpedo," synonymous terms for stationary or free-floating explosive devices through much of the nineteenth century, achieved their first substantial success in the Civil War. They did not emerge as potentially decisive factors in naval warfare until they acquired the means of propelling themselves through the water.

Expatriate British engineer and Austrian factory manager Robert Whitehead devised the modern self-propelled torpedo in the 1860s, developing the ideas of the Austrian naval officer Johann Luppis. Unimpressive in its early trials—erratic and inaccurate, with a speed well under ten knots and a range of only a few hundred yards—it nevertheless promised much. Hydrostatic depth regulation proved to be the crucial innovation. The so-called Whitehead torpedo incorporated an ingenious mechanism that allowed it to maintain constant depth, which meant it could run deep enough to avoid being deflected by surface waves but not too deep to pass under its target.

Speed and range improved steadily, as did accuracy when gyroscopic rudder control (an American invention) appeared in the mid-1880s. Although Whitehead torpedoes attained thirty-knot speeds and five-hundred-yard effective ranges by the turn of the century, the technology clearly had not reached its limits. Initially, the promise of self-propelled torpedoes stimulated the development of torpedo boats, then of torpedo-boat destroyers that usurped their function, but self-propelled torpedoes also provided the first really effective armament for submarine boats.

The turn of the century saw the introduction of the first practical submarines. Combined with the self-propelled torpedo, a centuries-old dream seemed on the verge of realization. Submersible boats, like torpedoes, had some effect in the Civil War, but like the torpedo, the modern version of the submarine awaited the end of the century. The last third of the nineteenth century saw much work on such vessels, especially in France. When the modern submarine appeared at the very end of the century, however, it was largely the work of American inventor John P. Holland, with a strong assist from his longtime competitor, Simon Lake.

Holland won the U.S. Navy's first submarine contract in 1895, but the navy insisted on steam for surface propulsion, and the vessel became a much delayed failure. Undaunted, Holland built his own design, using internal combustion for surface travel and electric batteries for submerged power. The navy liked the result, and the vessel bearing Holland's name entered service in 1900.

The *Holland*'s dual propulsion system featured a 120-horsepower gasoline engine giving it a surface speed of eight knots and a range of fifteen hundred miles; with storage batteries driving a 150-horsepower electric motor, it could make the same speed underwater for fifty miles. Horizontal rudder and ballast tanks controlled diving, submerged travel, and surfacing. *Holland* carried two reloads for its bow torpedo tube and two fixed pneumatic guns intended to hurl so-called "aerial torpedoes," or dynamite shells. Diminutive by later standards, or even compared to most of its contemporaries—ten feet across, fifty-three feet long, displacing seventy-five tons—the *Holland* was nonetheless the true prototype of the modern submarine.

Like the torpedoes that became their main weapons, the first submarines left plenty of room for technical improvement. As had happened with many other military-technological innovations during the preceding century, further development of the basic design moved more quickly abroad, and the United States soon found itself outclassed. Although submarines were much enlarged and refined over the next half-century, they retained intact the basic features of Holland, at least until the advent of nuclear-powered submarines in the 1950s.

INDUSTRIAL WAR, 1915–1918

In the decades before World War I (1914–1918), military and naval technologies had greatly changed. Repeating rifles, quick-firing field artillery, and machine guns multiplied fire and extended the killing zone. To the older support technologies of telegraph and steam were added telephone and wireless, oil and gasoline, and other innovations that had only begun to make themselves felt in military affairs, but were already exerting enormous effects. Equally dizzying changes marked naval technology. So rapid was the pace of change toward century's end that the ships of one decade seemed almost worthless in the next. Indeed, some ships may

well have been obsolescent even as they came down the ways.

Radical innovations in military and naval technology before World War I had scarcely passed unnoticed, but judging their likely impact was beyond most contemporary imaginations, military and civilian alike. Innovations in military technology still came primarily from nonmilitary sources, making the flood of new and improved arms hard to control or direct. Military planners did not so much ignore problems as misjudge their magnitude. Whatever the reasons, the result was catastrophe almost beyond comprehension.

World War I was the first great industrial war. Manufacturing and logistics mattered more than all other aspects of war-making. The Allied and Central Powers alike reorganized themselves to manufacture death. The new weapons demanded ammunition in staggering quantities, but meeting that demand was only the first crisis. Huge armies required supplies of every kind on a formerly unimagined scale. The terms "war economy" and "home front" entered the lexicon for the conversion of industrial capacity, the reorientation of civic life, and the concentration of all resources toward fighting total war. Managing the armies and keeping them supplied exhausted military art and science. Industrial engineering displaced generalship, and attrition became the recipe for victory.

Stalemate on the Ground. World attention focused on the deadlock that quickly emerged on the western front, where the United States would later intervene. Battle ceased being a decisive meeting of moving forces as mechanized firepower drove troops to ground. Maneuver vanished in trenches, and operations took on the guise of a gigantic siege, or a network of interrelated sieges. Like all sieges, war on the western front locked the foes into close contact and highlighted the work of gunners and engineers. Strategy for much of the war seemed to mean little more than augmenting gunfire; tactics centered on the attack and defense of ever more elaborate fieldworks. Huge armies, in essence, fought continuously. The so-called battles along trench lines from the Swiss frontier to the North Sea were merely more intense episodes in largely uninterrupted combat. Several thousand casualties accrued every day even when neither side was mounting a major offensive.

Firepower created the deadlock, but the failure of other technologies frustrated attempts to break the impasse. Transportation and communication shortcomings may have been the most critical. Bombardment regularly opened the way for infantry to seize forward enemy positions, but when troops advanced, they left behind easy links to artillery and reinforcements. Railroads terminated behind the lines; motorized transport carried some material forward, but men and mules provided most carriage. Beyond the trenches were only the troops themselves to convey supplies across broken and trackless ground. Reinforcements similarly had to make their way on foot, exhausting much of their strength before ever reaching the enemy.

Timing—how to obtain artillery support, supplies, or fresh troops when and where needed—often became a major problem. There was simply no easy, reliable way to maintain contact across no-man's-land. Telegraph or telephone depended on wires too easily broken when strung at ground level behind moving forces; for fixed positions the wire could be buried, but even then was often disrupted by artillery barrage. With portable wireless gear unavailable until the final year of the war, only ancient and inadequate techniques existed, but visual signals were almost worthless and runners or animal couriers too slow and uncertain. Artillery support thus became problematic, as did calls for reinforcement. Defenders falling back on their lines of communication could almost always react more quickly than attackers leaving theirs behind.

As befitted a scientific-industrial age, efforts to break the deadlock called on technology. Technical fixes, however, enjoyed only limited success. Stalemate derived in part from still changing military technology, but even more from the vastly improved artillery and machine guns developed in the decade or two before war began, and perhaps most of all from the enormous productive capacity that made it possible to equip, maintain, and restore huge armies. The apparent role of novel technology in creating the stalemate of World War I suggested to many the promise of searching for technological solutions to the stalemate.

World War I has sometimes been called a chemist's war, because several of its most prominent and promptly exploited innovations were chemical—notably toxic gases, artificial nitrates, and mass-produced explosives. Among these novelties, only gas directly affected the battlefield. Initial success notwithstanding, however, gas yielded no decision. Although trenches offered scant protection against gas, masks and better training largely controlled the danger. Extensive use during the war, even creation of separate forces such as the U.S. Army Chemical Warfare Service in 1918, meant no more than the briefest flurry of postwar interest in the future of gas warfare.

Trucks and Tanks. It was quite otherwise with a range of mechanical innovations based on the internal combustion engine, a late nineteenth-century product that laid the groundwork for large-scale changes in the conduct of war. Mechanics, not chemists, had the future in hand. Development along three lines significantly, if not decisively, affected the course of World War I, while holding out still greater promise of future use: motorized transport, armored vehicles, and armed aircraft.

By 1910 the United States had become the world's leading automobile maker. Despite having enormous resources to draw on, U.S. armed forces were slow to recognize motorization's potential. Several European nations had substantial motor-car industries, however, and their armed forces had taken steps toward turning motorized vehicles to military advantage. Motor transport especially began to influence logistics significantly, although it hardly displaced animal-drawn transport.

When World War I began, trucks were rare; the United States registered scarcely ten thousand in 1910, at the same time car registrations neared half a million. The flood of Allied war orders spurred massive industrial growth. Financed by government money, U.S. truck production leaped from just under twenty-five thousand in 1914 to well over two hundred thousand in 1918, with important consequences for the U.S. economy. Standardization and reliability of engines, transmissions, and body designs tested in the harsh school of the western front soared.

Motorized transport, much as it contributed to supplying the front lines, could not solve the battlefield stalemate. Various experiments with armored cars proved equally marginal. Wheeled vehicles could not traverse the shell-torn ground that impeded all movement. The answer appeared in the form of the tank, the British code name that track-laying, gun-carrying, armored vehicles have since retained. Tanks allowed self-propelled guns to keep up with advancing infantry, tracks took them across broken ground, and armor protected them from machine guns.

Conceived as siege machines, a technological fix for the problem of breaking through defenses too strong for men alone, tanks promised more than they could yet deliver. Relatively slow, thin-skinned, short-ranged, lightly armed, and fragile, the machines of the Great War could not always achieve even their intended purpose, limited though it was. Although aborted by the armistice, the Allied Plan 1919 called for an attack by massed tanks of new design, able to speed to the enemy's rear and paralyze the defense, while fleets of airplanes carried the assault from above.

Powered Flight in War.

Like tanks, flying machines evoked visions of a different kind of war. The airplane was little more than a decade old when the war began, but rapid progress had followed the success of the Wright brothers. Reconnaissance from the air quickly became a vital aspect of war-making. Air combat promptly followed, and a technological race for air superiority brought still more rapid improvement.

Constantly improving aircraft and weapons periodically shifted technological advantage from one side to the other, with direct effects on the war in progress. Technological innovation is not alone decisive; new weapons require new doctrine, tactics, and organization. This has always been true, but in the modern era the pace of change has so increased that the time available has decreased from centuries and decades to years and months.

Airplanes went to war in 1914 as general-purpose flying machines without weapons, able to fly no faster than seventy miles per hour and to remain aloft no longer than an hour. By 1918 both top speed and endurance for the single-place fighter had doubled, and planes now sported twin machine guns synchronized to fire through their propellers. Fighters had become but one of several specialized types of aircraft, which also included ground attack machines, light bombers, and huge multiengined long-range heavy bombers, such as Germany's Gotha.

Tactically, attacks on ground forces from the air produced only modest results during the war. Aerial bombing of factories and civilians, on the other hand, showed real promise. Despite limited numbers of machines, German attacks on London, first with zeppelins and then with heavy bombers, spread panic and disrupted the city's work. The raids, however, at intervals of many days or weeks by twenty bombers, each carrying but half a ton of bombs, could not achieve decisive results, even though the potential of such attacks using far larger numbers of much more powerful aircraft seemed clear to many. Plan 1919 included massive long-range bombing attacks on German cities as well as mass tank attacks.

War at Sea.

The primary exemplars of the prewar arms race, the great fleets of Great Britain and Germany, achieved little at sea. Powerful though they might be, dreadnoughts proved all too vulnerable to mines and torpedoes. While one may argue that the mere existence of the British fleet sufficed to maintain command of the sea and thus the blockade against German commerce, the fact also remains that the ships themselves could rarely venture from their protected anchorages.

Submarines, on the other hand, although little regarded in prewar thought, achieved notable success against other warships by launching torpedoes while submerged. Like so many products of technology geared to military purpose, the submarine in its early years relied more on promise than accomplishment. During the decade and a half before World War I, submarines acquired diesel engines, periscopes, and wireless gear. They also grew bigger, faster, and more seaworthy. Improvement never stopped, but submersible warships that had attained eminently practical form just before the outbreak of world war provided a stage to display their newfound prowess.

Even the largest submarine could carry few weapons the size of torpedoes and none could remain long underwater. The submarines of World War I, indeed of World War II, were not true underwater vessels. Properly speaking, they were diving boats, surfaced most of the time but able to hide beneath the waves for a while. Far slower underwater than afloat, submerged submarines could only lie in wait rather than actively seek their prey. They had little choice against surface warships far more heavily armed and armored than any submarine could be; stealth provided their chief defense.

This was not so against their preferred prey. Unarmed merchant ships could be hunted on the surface and attacked with quick-firing deck guns; valuable torpedoes need not be expended on such targets. Submarines did best raiding commerce, not attacking other warships. A handful of German U-boats came close to applying the kind of blockade against Great Britain that the huge Royal Navy imposed on Germany. Technology provided no ready answer to this threat, although organization did. Undersea warfare was thwarted by the convoy system. Despite their quite limited capabilities and ultimate defeat, however, submarines had proved by far the most effective warships of World War I, and the technology of undersea warfare would only improve.

American War Research. Well before joining the war, the United States had begun acting on the hope of military-technological breakthroughs. Efforts to organize military invention and technological innovation to warlike ends, however, met only limited success. Among the first, and least rewarding, was the Naval Consulting Board, created in 1915. With Thomas A. Edison serving as chairman, a distinguished panel of working engineers and inventors screened proffered inventions for practicality and value, among other tasks. Individual inventors, however, proved to have no better grasp of the scientific-technical needs of modern warfare than did most officers; few of the suggested ideas even merited discussion.

Although building on a more solid base, the National Advisory Committee for Aeronautics (NACA) still failed to contribute much to the war effort. Established by Congress in 1915, NACA served a larger purpose than its name implied. Besides advising on aeronautical policy, it also directed the Langley Aeronautical Laboratory, an aeronautical engineering research laboratory derived from turn-of-the-century experimental work at the Smithsonian Institution in Washington. Already a going, if small-scale, concern at the Smithsonian, the laboratory needed room to expand and, after the war, moved to Langley, Virginia, and new facilities.

Far more broadly based than NACA or the Naval Consulting Board, the revitalized National Academy of Sciences (NAS) seemed the likeliest choice to centralize war research. The NAS was remembered, inaccurately, as having successfully performed such a function in the Civil War. Although the academy's true role had been quite limited, that memory inspired action. In 1916 the academy formed the National Research Council (NRC), with members from government, academic, and industrial research. The NRC sought to promote long-term basic research as well as immediately relevant war work.

Early in 1917 the Council of National Defense made NRC its research department, assigning the Naval Consulting Board solely to evaluating inventions, but no one had yet devised means for shifting military funds to civilian research. Scientists and technologists were conscripted for specific projects, leaving little scope either for a balanced program or for detached judgment.

Scientific mobilization in World War I may have gone more smoothly than it had in the past, but it was likewise only beginning to achieve results when the war ended. Technologically, the United States remained on the sidelines. Ambitious plans to arm and equip the American Expeditionary Forces from U.S. sources proved unattainable. American industry was still gearing up when the war ended, and U.S. forces fought chiefly with French ordnance and flew French and British aircraft.

Technology Demobilized.

World War I imposed extraordinary economic and social demands. Every state reorganized people and resources to sustain its home front, cope with shortages, maintain production, and keep supplies flowing to the war fronts. Bureaucratic management formerly limited to individual businesses or government agencies now applied to the entire state and displaced free-market capitalism at the center of war economies. Technology and science took their places among the activities the state sought to control, with varying success. In the United States these trends were less marked than in other active belligerents only because of the country's late entry into the war.

Relatively little of the wartime research system survived the armistice. Although well begun by the standards of former wars, it also followed past patterns in ending promptly with the war. Reliant heavily on scientists in uniform, direct military research shared the fate of the armed forces. Armistice brought abrupt cuts in military funding and rapid demobilization.

The Naval Consulting Board expired but not without issue. In 1916 the board had persuaded Congress that the navy needed a research laboratory and secured the funding required to begin building, primarily because of the academic links the navy had been forging since the turn of the century. Internal squabbling over a site, as well as other pressing concerns, deflected the effort for a time; the Naval Research Laboratory remained in limbo until 1923. Once established, its research program progressed from small beginnings, most notably during the interwar period in work on radar.

The National Research Council survived the war but lost whatever function in military research it may have had. It did, however, acquire the congressional mandate it had lacked during the war and maintained significant links with the scientific community. Ultimately, NRC would again assume a larger role in the conduct of U.S. research, but during and after World War II.

Of all World War I technology agencies, only NACA flourished much beyond the war's immediate aftermath. Conducting basic and applied research for military and civilian clients at the Langley Aeronautical Laboratory, it pioneered most interwar advances in aeronautical technology, notably cantilevered wings, cowlings, and metal skins. When World War II began, the best fighters were streamlined all-metal monoplanes armed with wing-mounted machine guns. Virtually every feature of these airplanes derived from NACA research.

FROM WAR TO WAR, 1921–1940

The armed forces had begun to recognize in the late nineteenth century the possibility of directed innovation—that is, the possibility that weapons or weapon systems could be designed and built not merely to meet military needs but to realize military desires. That insight became firmly lodged only after the end of World War I and triumphed only after World War II.

Institutional promises of technological breakthroughs from directed research resided in a flourishing NACA and an expanding Naval Research Laboratory during the interwar period. Both provided concrete evidence of how directed innovation might be organized and its benefits reaped. In sharp contrast to World War I, the United States entered World War II as a leader in aeronautical design and development. No less important when the United States entered the war, NACA also became the model for organizing U.S. war research.

Visions of Air Power. Between the wars, new doctrines of air power and military mechanization provided the framework for rethinking operations, tactics, and organization. Accommodating newly available technologies derived from directed research was only one problem. Advocates of military mechanization and air power played a key role in furthering the idea that this relationship could be reversed, that military desires, from tactical to strategic, might be achieved with machines and weapons designed and built to promote military visions of future war. They constantly stressed the future promise of technology over its current manifestations.

Uniquely among the technologies of World War I, aircraft and tanks inspired long-range thinking. Actual wartime experience served more to spur reflection than to provide concrete examples. Visionaries nevertheless invoked the power of modern science and technology to create future bombers vastly more powerful than the frail machines that then existed. Modern heavily armed bombers of great range and large capacity, procured in large enough numbers, could win the next war. The production of munitions had reached a level in World War I that seemed to render battlefields all but irrelevant to the outcome; factories and workers suddenly emerged as prime military targets. After seizing command of the air with its aerial fighting forces, a nation might destroy a foe's factories from the air and deprive its armed forces of the wherewithal to fight on. Rendered defenseless, the enemy might thus be defeated on the home front rather than the battlefield. Air power would simply bypass the stalemate on the ground, and victory would follow inevitably— once the appropriate strategic bombing aircraft became available. It was a long time coming,

and the results were not everything the prewar visionaries might have wished.

Implementing such a doctrine demanded a new kind of airplane, but the prototype of a strategic bomber did not actually fly until 1935. The Boeing XB-17, called the Flying Fortress, united defensive armor and machine guns, large bomb capacity, long range, and great speed. It also could take advantage of the highly accurate Norden bombsight introduced in 1931 to carry the attack deep into an enemy's homeland. In 1939, as the air force accepted deliveries of its first B-17s, a second heavy bomber, the Consolidated B-24 Liberator, made its maiden flight, with first deliveries the following year. Both bombers saw extensive service in World War II but fell short of realizing the hopes of air power advocates.

Armored Doctrine. In fact, quite different uses of aircraft shaped the war to come— fighters and bombers designed to provide close tactical and operational support for sea and ground forces. Developing the machines for such cooperation formed a central theme in interwar research and development. Two areas in particular deserve attention—the decisive contribution of ground-attack aircraft to the spectacular successes of armored forces in World War II and the radically new role of aircraft in sea warfare as a result of the development of aircraft carriers.

Tanks no less than aircraft inspired potent visions, although less strategic than tactical or operational. Like the doctrine of strategic bombing, the doctrine of mechanized (or armored) warfare invoked the power of modern science to produce the required machines. Its earliest proponents were British, and the British army conducted the first armored exercises in the late 1920s and early 1930s. Although the British army seemed to lose enthusiasm for the new techniques, its example inspired widespread emulation, notably in Germany, where it contributed significantly to rebuilding and reequipping the Wehrmacht.

Armored doctrine also aroused resistance. Opponents included officers romantically attached to the horse and others whose motives might be suspect, but they also numbered those who raised well-reasoned objections. Mechanized forces would be costly to provide, hard to maintain, prone to rapid obsolescence, and difficult to supply. Only the experience of war clinched the argument by showing conclusively that such obstacles could be overcome, adequately if not always easily.

From the beginning, the message of mechanized war won converts in the United States as elsewhere. The Tank Corps formed in World War I lasted only until 1920. Vehicles dispersed in small packets among the infantry, to say nothing of sharply limited funds, allowed little scope for tactical or organizational innovation, although an experimental mechanized force on the British model underwent trials in 1928. Little money meant no production. Research and development focused on prototypes and components, a policy that paid handsome dividends when mass production began in 1940.

American tank designs stressed simplicity, reliability, and standardization. None equaled the best German tanks but they were quick to build and easy to maintain. Available in the thousands, lavishly supplied, and skillfully directed, they proved able to win victory after victory even over armored forces equipped with tanks that individually outmatched them. They also enjoyed the inestimable advantage of superb tactical air support.

Aircraft at Sea. Aircraft also decisively reshaped war at sea. Although the Royal Navy pioneered aircraft carriers, this warship reached its fullest development in the navies of Japan and the United States. The vast stretches of the Pacific Ocean confronted both nations with operational and logistic problems to which seaborne aircraft seemed at least part of the solution. Although both nations devoted the larger share of their naval appropriations during the interwar years to traditional battleships, both also made real progress on aircraft carriers.

A converted collier commissioned in 1922 as USS *Langley* became the navy's first experimental aircraft carrier. Its successful testing led the navy to convert two battle cruisers, disallowed under the Washington Naval Treaty of 1921, into aircraft carriers. Commissioned in 1927, the *Lexington* and *Saratoga* were colossal ships, 888 feet long and 106 feet across, with displacements of 33,000 tons and 1,900-man crews. They also were the fastest capital ships afloat, with 180,000 horsepower driving them at top speeds exceeding 33 knots. The first U.S. purpose-built aircraft carrier, the *Ranger*, commissioned in 1934, was lighter and slower and proved an altogether less successful design, although it could accommodate a large number of aircraft. It was not until 1937 that a third heavy carrier joined the fleet. The *Yorktown* was an 800-foot, 20,000-ton ship with a top speed of 34 knots and able to operate eighty aircraft. Within three years it was followed by two similar ships, the *Enterprise* and *Hornet,* and another light carrier, the *Wasp.*

The first U.S. airplane specifically designed for carrier-based operations entered service aboard the *Langley* the same year it was commissioned. Built by Curtiss from a Bureau of Aeronautics design, the NAF TS-1 was a single-seat biplane fighter built of wood and fabric and armed with a single .30-inch Browning machine gun synchronized to fire through the propeller. Other fighters followed, notably the series of Boeing biplanes from 1927 to 1937, as well as more specialized aircraft, such as the Martin T3M torpedo bomber and scout, which entered service aboard the *Langley* and *Lexington* in 1927, and the Curtiss and Martin dive-bombers, which began arriving in the early 1930s.

Aircraft performance improved steadily during the interwar period, with a large assist from NACA research. Improvement had less to do with radical innovation than with steady refinement of engineering practice, reflected in engines of growing power, closer attention to streamlining and reduced drag, variable-pitch propellers, and wing flaps. Civilian aircraft actually led the way, but by 1937 the navy was beginning to receive its first monoplanes designed for carrier-borne operations: Douglas torpedo planes in 1937, Douglas dive-bombers in 1940, and Grumman fighters in 1940.

Amphibious Warfare Defined. Carrier-based aircraft also contributed to a remarkable reversal of prospects for success in making opposed landings on hostile shores, aided by such innovations as bombardment rockets and amphibious vehicles. In World War I, the British attempt to invade Gallipoli from the sea was a costly fiasco. Between the wars, the U.S. Marine Corps studied the problems of seaborne assault under fire, developed a suitable doctrine, and acquired the specialized vehicles required; in World War II, U.S. forces succeeded in dozens of such operations, culminating in the extraordinary invasion of Europe in 1944. This success depended on the Allies winning complete local air control, but good tactics and machines on the surface were no less indispensable.

Amphibious doctrine, like armored doctrine, outran the machines it required. Throughout the 1930s the Marine Corps sought something better than ships boats to land troops and matériel on hostile beaches. Disappointed in its own experiments, the corps found outside help; the day of the lone inventor had not entirely passed.

Andrew J. Higgins of New Orleans tried to interest the navy in his "Eureka" boat as early as 1926, although it took another twelve years to persuade the skeptics. Designed for use in bayou waters, the Eureka featured shallow draft, protected propeller, and a broad, flat bow that made it easy to beach and refloat. It needed only a retractable bow ramp to become the navy's landing craft vehicle personnel (LCVP), the boat that brought marines ashore under fire for the next three decades. Higgins also contributed to the development of the larger landing craft needed to bring heavy equipment ashore, designing the fifty-foot landing craft mechanized (LCM) that became another mainstay of amphibious landings.

A third major landing craft was also derived from a civilian inventor. Retired engineer Donald Roebling devised an amphibious tractor for rescue work in the Florida Everglades or after hurricanes. Propelled by its tracks both ashore and afloat, drawing less than three feet of water, seaworthy and close to unsinkable, the lightweight "Alligator" became the subject of a *Life* magazine story in 1940, which brought it to the attention of the military. Its obvious potential led to its prompt adoption as landing vehicle tracked (LVT). Variously modified and armed, it became a crucial factor in amphibious operations during World War II and long after.

Toward a New Kind of War Research. World War II saw science harnessed to war and institutions established to direct technological innovation toward desired ends. The problem of turning ideas into hardware, if not entirely solved, at least appeared entirely practical. The National Defense Research Committee (NDRC) and the Office of Scientific Research and Development (OSRD) provided the basic framework for applied military-technological research in World War II, and universities became major participants in war-related technologically oriented research.

Both sides of the new military-scientific partnership mattered. Military institutions able to recognize the value of research and willing to support it formed only one side. By no means a minor issue, military resistance to scientific weaponeering seemed quite rational given past failures. Experience would soon show, however, that a stream of useful new devices from the laboratory would tend to overcome most qualms.

The other side of the partnership, organizing researchers for the job, posed equally crucial questions. Finding scientists and technologists willing and even eager to do war research presented little problem. Every American war had produced them, and they appeared quickly after 1939 at merely the prospect of war with Nazi Germany. What made the United States different on the eve of its entry into World War II was the organization of proper means to convert offers of help into directed research leading to engineering development of actual weapons. In short, the United States in 1940 and 1941 learned how to harness research to military needs effectively.

The key was directed team research. In contrast to the chemist's war of 1914–1918, World

War II has been called a physicist's war. It might better be termed a physicist's and engineer's war. Lines between scientific research and engineering development, the juncture of applied physics and science-based engineering in the service of technological innovation, never easy to draw precisely in the best of circumstances, blurred beyond definition under wartime pressure. Persistent images of lonely scientists or heroic inventors notwithstanding, team research had been gaining importance since the late nineteenth century.

Evaluating proffered inventions had been the main role of science in the Civil War. World War I produced a rough parity between the invention-rating Naval Consulting Board and the research-promoting National Research Council. In World War II the task of dealing with unsolicited inventions was relegated to a corner in the Commerce Department, while research took center stage. The result has profoundly shaped relations between American research and military institutions ever since.

The NDRC and OSRD improved or developed an extraordinary array of weapons and other products and processes useful to fighting World War II. Radar and proximity fuses topped the list of those that most decisively affected the war's course, but there were many others, ranging from operational analysis to blood plasma. What made the World War II experience unique was the speed of innovation. By 1940 the United States possessed an unmatched combination of resources in science, engineering, technology, and industry. Properly organized and directed, such resources could turn ideas into weapons quickly and massively enough to alter the course of war in progress. No other nation in World War II equaled the United States across the entire spectrum of research applied effectively to war, primarily because of the work of the NDRC and OSRD.

Creating Research Institutions. Credit for conceiving NDRC belongs chiefly to Vannevar Bush. Fresh from doctoral study in electrical engineering at the Massachusetts Institute of Technology (MIT) and Harvard, he had worked

for the navy on submarine detection in 1917. Back at MIT after the war, Bush proved himself an outstanding teacher, researcher, and administrator. In 1939 he became president of the Carnegie Institution of Washington and also became chairman of NACA. Bush thus found himself at the heart of America's scientific establishment when war erupted in Europe, just months after news of the discovery of nuclear fission in a German laboratory. Well aware of German technical and scientific prowess, Bush and his colleagues feared the prospect of a uniquely powerful bomb in Nazi hands. Science and technology would clearly play a major role in the coming war, into which the United States would almost certainly be drawn.

Bush set himself to mobilizing scientific and technological research. Experience in World War I had persuaded him that the military technical services were too narrow to imagine genuinely new weapons; they could at best improve what they already had. The civilian side had not done much better. The screening of inventions by bodies such as the Naval Consulting Board was a relic of nineteenth-century thinking. Although a better idea, the National Research Council was also badly designed. As a privately funded organization, it lacked both the authority and the budget to impose any real direction on American science. In Bush's eyes, NACA offered a much more promising model for what in June 1940 became NDRC. Rather than building new research facilities from scratch, NDRC adopted NACA's method of letting research contracts for selected problems with well-established academic and industrial organizations. Bush kept administration control of NDRC but left technical decision-making to five research divisions: armor and ordnance, chemistry and explosives, communications and transportation, instruments and controls, and patents and inventions.

Although it would discuss service needs, NDRC would not simply accept assignments from the armed forces. Military utility and unlimited money merely defined the framework. In accord with Bush's vision, the choice of specific research problems remained in expert hands, which left the crucial decisions to science—recognizing what technical possibilities inhered in science and judging which prospects to pursue with the talent and resources available. The constant goal was weapons useful in the current crisis, the focus on applied research of immediate utility. Relying chiefly on academic research facilities, NDRC left industrial and military research groups to pursue their own ends. Industry would be gearing up for an enormous production effort, to which it would have to devote all its resources; military research would presumably continue to stress improving weapons already in use.

By mid-1941, NDRC was reaching its functional limits, and Bush devised a larger organization to include development as well as research. The Office of Scientific Research and Development (OSRD) subsumed NDRC into an advisory role, joined by a new committee for research in military medicine. The five divisions of NDRC expanded to eighteen, supported by panels on applied mathematics and applied psychology that worked with any division needing help in those areas. In contrast to NDRC's support through presidential contingency funds, OSRD enjoyed a line item in the federal budget; assured funds allowed the fruits of research to be developed into working prototypes for production. Perhaps most amazing, the entire structure was in place and operating effectively half a year before the United States became an active belligerent. The next four years would see the spectacular consequences.

MECHANIZED WARFARE, 1940–1945

Finding efficient means for turning research into weapons across the full spectrum of modern warfare was the crucial problem that the United States largely solved in organizing for World War II. Instead of relying on makeshift expedients, as it always had before, the nation enjoyed a well-considered and effective system for making research useful to the war effort.

Nor were consequences limited to the war itself. Arrangements made to exploit research during World War II permanently transformed relations between American military, technological, and scientific institutions. Academic and industrial laboratories largely dependent on government funding became major sources of military-technological innovation during the twentieth century. Some aspects of this new order emerged during the nation's brief plunge into World War I, but World War II marked its coming of age.

Innovative technologies nevertheless played important and even vital roles in World War II, but their source may have mattered even more than their actual contributions. Applied research in government-funded laboratories produced an endless stream of weapons and techniques that proved not only novel but useful and effective. Such impressive success, in sharp contrast to the futility of such efforts in the past, seemed to promise that directed innovation through applied research might become truly decisive in future war.

For centuries, trial and error had chiefly guided technological innovation, although applied science and systematic research began to achieve impressive results late in the nineteenth century. By the mid-twentieth century, the balance had been reversed. Trial and error persisted, but reasoned approaches to technological innovation could produce weapons to order. Just as engineering was becoming more systematic and mathematical, science was tending toward greater practicality. Military technology proliferated as applied science became ever less distinct from scientific engineering.

Radar and the Rise of Automation. Electronics became the focus of OSRD support, with the Radiation Laboratory at MIT its chief research center. Applications of many kinds dramatically improved techniques of integrating combat arms, controlling battle, and destroying the foe, but radar (radio detection and ranging) was most important. Radar was known in principle to all the major powers by the 1920s. By 1938 the U.S. Navy had installed a prototype operational system on the battleship *New York*, but in 1940 the real contest between radar measures and countermeasures began during the Battle of Britain.

The United States soon followed Great Britain's lead and, thanks to OSRD and the Radiation Laboratory, made rapid progress. At British urging and aided by the British-invented magnetron, the United States specialized in microwave radar. The Radiation Laboratory produced 150 systems during the war to serve purposes as varied as detecting enemy planes and ships, directing guns, aiding navigation, controlling operations, locating targets, and warning of attack.

Proximity fuses were another OSRD product that mattered, begun well before the United States was formally at war. The idea was simple: Put a tiny radar set in the nose of a bomb or shell to measure precisely when it reached a specified distance from the target; the explosive could then be reliably detonated at the set distance. When NDRC opened in mid-1940, the navy proposed work on radar-fused shells as a likely counter to enemy air attack. In August, NDRC's first research contract went to the Carnegie Institution for preliminary studies. A prototype fuse for five-inch shells was ready the month after the attack on Pearl Harbor. The Applied Physics Laboratory of Johns Hopkins University then completed development.

Production was under way by fall 1942, and the new fuses, called VT (for variable time) as a security precaution, began reaching the navy before the year ended. The new shells proved to be at least three times as effective as their closest competitor, shells fused to explode at a preset time, and as much as fifty times better than shells fused to explode on contact. Proximity fuses also enhanced the performance of other explosive devices, such as torpedoes, depth charges, and rockets.

Extraordinarily successful in its own right, the VT fuse, as a sensor in a complex computer-controlled firing system, also marked a large step toward automation. World War II forged the modern military-computer linkage. Analog computers, mechanical and electromechanical, had deep roots in the practical demands of compiling such products of tedious calculation as actuarial, navigational, and (by World War I) artillery firing tables. During World War II antiaircraft fire control promoted automation with still greater demands.

Although analog computers provided most wartime firing tables, the task also promoted further development of electronic digital computers, a much speedier alternative that was highly successful in breaking enemy codes since the beginning of the war. Computer-generated firing tables programmed into gun directors, also analog computers, dramatically enhanced the accuracy of VT-fused shells. In the final step, target-locating radar connected to gun directors rendered human judgment, or even participation, largely superfluous.

Computers and radar stimulated thinking about system organization, first in Great Britain, then in the United States. Operations analysis was one result. The effective use of radar raised technical questions related to the equipment itself, in the first instance, but quickly led to other questions about organization and strategy. Systematic and quantitative approaches to problems of military tactics and strategy offered the exciting prospect of war made truly scientific. The relatively narrow focus of the war years involved NDRC and OSRD in such problems as hunting submarines and dropping bombs accurately. The OSRD Applied Mathematics Panel played an especially prominent role in these studies. Valuable as they were, the further development of operations analysis after the war would prove even more significant.

Fighting a Machine War. However novel laboratory products may have affected the course of war, it was improved and refined older weapons and tactics that most directly decided the outcome. Better guns, tanks, aircraft, and ships made the difference. Mechanization did not eliminate masses of men and guns. Artillery still caused most of the casualties, and tanks without foot soldiers and guns could achieve little. Properly combined, however, and linked by field radio, balanced forces of armor, infantry, and artillery could in fact play their role. Capable of swift battlefield movement, they restored to ground forces the potential for successful offensive action.

Although much of prewar mechanized theory revealed itself wrong in detail, the larger vision of mechanized warfare proved valid: Nothing resembling the large-scale, long-term trench warfare of 1914–1918 recurred. Like the Thirty Years War and the Napoleonic wars, World War II came at the end of a long military-technological cycle. The climax of the mechanical era made World War II a war of maneuver by restoring to commanders their ability to direct the course of battle to decisive conclusion.

The promise of mechanical war could be fulfilled, however, only with the cooperation of air forces. Without air support, armored forces lost much of their impact; against an enemy superior in the air, they could scarcely function at all. In the final analysis, Allied victories became possible only because Allied air forces could achieve air superiority. Skies swept clean of enemy aircraft meant that Allied ground forces could move without fear of attack from the air, as their foes could not.

Rocket Development.

Tactical bombing in support of ground forces achieved notable success throughout the war, interdiction of enemy supply lines perhaps even more than direct attacks on enemy forces. No less successful were Allied long-range patrol aircraft equipped with radar and bombs or depth charges in defeating the German submarine threat in the Atlantic. It was the tactical and operational use of aircraft that mattered most during World War II. The importance of air superiority became all the greater as aircraft armament improved, notably with the development of effective air-to-ground rockets.

Although the best-known rocket program in World War II was German—it produced the huge liquid-fueled, surface-to-surface V2—NDRC and OSRD also pursued an active, if far less grandiose, program. Tactically and operationally oriented, the U.S. program may have exerted greater effects on the course of World War II than the more spectacular German effort.

Especially effective against armored forces and fortifications, unguided solid-fuel, rocket-propelled missiles became a major weapon in close air support and interdiction.

Rockets had been known for centuries and had enjoyed periods of considerable military use. Their great advantage was lack of recoil, which gave them the promise of powerful explosives that could be fired from aircraft, light surface vehicles, or even human shoulders. Unfortunately, they were also notoriously inaccurate, chiefly because solid propellants had never reached an adequate level of strength, uniformity, and consistency. In 1940 these shortcomings no longer seemed insurmountable, and by spring 1941, with help from British researchers, who had begun work even earlier, NDRC had several rocket weapons under development.

Perhaps the best-known of the rocket weapons to attain operational status was the bazooka, a tube-launched 2.36-inch fin-stabilized rocket fitted with an armor-piercing charge that allowed an individual infantryman to engage a tank. Standardized by early summer 1942, the bazooka was in the hands of troops before the end of the year. Other early projects included shipboard rocket-launched antisubmarine depth charges (Mousetrap) and barrage rockets with a thousand-yard range that could be launched from landing craft.

The focus of work in 1943 shifted to air-launched rockets, which quickly proved effective against surfaced submarines and other unarmored vessels. Armor-piercing rockets took longer, but the 5-inch high-velocity aircraft rocket (HVAR) reached combat units by July 1944. Launched from low-flying P-47s and Typhoon fighter-bombers at 1,375 feet per second, the 6-foot, 140-pound HVARs devastated German armor trying to contain the Allies in Normandy or to counterattack advancing Allied forces.

The Air War.

Teamed with other machines or systems, airplanes transformed the conduct of war on land and at sea from the heart of Eurasia to the far reaches of the Pacific. During World War II, aircraft carriers replaced battleships at the center of naval warfare. Although surface engagements by no means vanished, they became essentially sideshows. Great actions were fought between fleets hundreds of miles apart; aircraft alone decided the outcome, no warship on the sea's surface ever glimpsing an enemy vessel. Aircraft flying from carriers largely dictated the course of events, especially in the Pacific war between the United States and Japan.

Flying from five heavy carriers and the *Wasp* (the *Langley* had long since been retired and the *Ranger* remained in the Atlantic), these aircraft formed the backbone of the U.S. Pacific fleet in the first year of World War II, holding the line, although just barely, until joined by carriers of the new *Essex* class. Conceived in 1939, these 27,000-ton vessels could attain speeds of thirty-two knots and operate ninety aircraft. The first of the class was commissioned on the last day of 1942; more important, it was followed by twenty-three more before the war ended, a rate of production that Japanese industry could not hope to match. Japanese forces also could not match the improved aircraft in growing numbers flying from the new carriers.

In many respects, World War II in the air came closest to war dictated by laboratory research. Major scientific-technical advances, from radar to atomic bombs, addressed one aspect or another of the air war or defense against air attack, but there was more. Fortune seemed to favor closely the side flying the latest model airplane or deploying the most recent radar measure or countermeasure. In contrast to the theorists of armored warfare, however, the prophets of strategic bombing misread the future in almost every respect. Even apart from its moral implications, air attack on enemy industry and population proved far harder to mount, more costly to maintain, and less productive of results than had been anticipated.

Consistent success by fighter planes against heavy bombers emerged as a major factor in strategic bombing failures. It was not until the long-range P-51 (Mustang) began to escort U.S. bombers that aerial attack by B-17s and B-24s could be carried home to Germany. Another factor was the surprising inaccuracy of high-altitude bombing, which meant that destroying a target required bombers in much larger numbers. It was only after a costly war of attrition, when Axis defensive aircraft and guns had become too few to counter the still growing and now strongly escorted bomber fleets made possible by an American productive capacity untouched by war, that attack from the air approached its promised power. At that point, the availability of atomic bombs introduced an entirely new factor. Explosives of such power seemed to restore plausibility to strategic bombing doctrine. Modest forces armed with nuclear weapons might well inflict the kind of damage that would end a war soon after it began.

Developing the Bomb. By 1945 the military-scientific project that produced nuclear weapons had become the paradigm of research in the service of war. It stands as a remarkable accomplishment, technological as well as scientific. The initial discovery of nuclear fission became public early in 1939. That it came from a German laboratory troubled several refugee scientists in the United States almost at once and took on ominous implications with the outbreak of war later that year. Fear of a Nazi bomb drove British and American nuclear research and development, although in fact the German project made little progress toward production of a viable atomic bomb.

With a large assist from NDRC and OSRD, what became known as the Manhattan Project was fully under way by fall 1941. American research had followed the normal pattern of NDRC-sponsored work; like so many other crucial weapon projects, it began well before the United States formally entered the war. Shortly after NDRC was formed in mid-1940, it took over the small, year-old nuclear research program conducted chiefly by academic teams via contracts with selected universities.

The first question was whether the fissionable isotope of uranium, U-235, could be separated from uranium ore, of which 99.3 percent was nonfissionable U-238. A year's research suggested two reasonably promising large-scale methods of obtaining U-235—gaseous diffusion and electromagnetic separation. The discovery that U-238 bombarded with neutrons could be converted into a new fissionable element, plutonium, offered a third method—chemical separation. Scientific work consolidated under OSRD auspices at the University of Chicago proved on 2 December 1942 that a chain reaction could be sustained and that reactor-produced plutonium could be used for a bomb.

Success had been anticipated, or at least seemed likely enough by mid-1942 to justify a major effort. In view of the project's vastly increased scope as it shifted from research and development to engineering, procurement, construction, and production, OSRD began turning the project over to the newly formed Manhattan Engineer District, U.S. Army Corps of Engineers, and the scale of effort skyrocketed. In three years the Manhattan Project designed, built, and operated an industrial plant that rivaled in scale the entire prewar U.S. automobile industry.

As part of a crash program, work on the bomb received top priority. Providing fissionable material was only part of the problem. Designing, developing, and proving a bomb under intense time pressure was something else. The task fell to the laboratory created for that purpose at Los Alamos, New Mexico, operated under contract by the University of California. Theoretical and experimental physicists joined forces with chemists, engineers, and technicians to convert a recently discovered physical phenomenon into a militarily useful weapon. Officially, work at Los Alamos began 15 April 1943; twenty-eight months later a single U-235 bomb had destroyed Hiroshima, a plutonium bomb had leveled Nagasaki, and Japan had surrendered.

MILITARY RESEARCH INSTITUTIONALIZED, 1945–1951

In the decade and a half after World War II, the United States erected a vast, if piecemeal, institutional structure for turning research to military purpose. The intensifying cold war between West and East spurred this effort, but hot war in Korea was the key to recasting American research. Time brought difficult questions about the assumptions underpinning that structure and about its consequences not only for military and scientific institutions themselves but also for American polity, economy, and society.

Since 1945 military technology has become almost entirely the product of directed research. Institutionalized research began haltingly, largely because of postwar cutbacks in military funding, and research money remained tight until the early 1950s. Bolstering research and development across the board was a major goal of the post-1951 buildup triggered by the Korean War (1950–1953). Defense Department budgets remained at permanently higher, and rising, levels even when fighting in Korea ended. Military agencies and the Atomic Energy Commission (AEC) accounted for 70 percent of U.S. research and development funding by the early 1950s, as well as more than 90 percent of federal funds allotted to campus research.

Permanent Technological Revolution.
Since the early nineteenth century, armed forces had faced a flood of new and improved weapons. Although some reflected military initiatives, most came from independent inventors. New weapons demanded new tactics and organization, although of just what kind was seldom obvious. Extraordinary increases in firepower ashore and afloat outmoded traditional offensive tactics and operations, setting the stage for stalemate and the frustration of command.

In World War II further technical and tactical innovation bore fruit, yielding opportunities for generalship comparable to the Napoleonic wars. Mechanized armed forces wedded to the tactics of infiltration restored maneuver to battle and decisiveness to war. Striking differences in the course and outcome of the two world wars reflected the success of interwar efforts to harness research to military needs. The United States was not a leader in all these developments before the war, but neither was it the laggard it had once been, and in war research, it soon emerged a pacesetter.

From 1940 on, the United States devised new forms for mobilizing research that succeeded beyond expectations. Science, technology, engineering, and military institutions emerged from World War II utterly transformed. The reluctant military innovators of the late nineteenth century had become enthusiastic seekers of novel technology by the late twentieth. Perhaps more significant, they began finding money to support research and development, as well as testing and procurement, required by new weapons. Old claims that properly funded research might produce war-winning weapons had generally proved to be will-o'-the-wisps, seeming near but rarely quite within reach. In the United States during World War II, that claim seemed at last to have been validated.

World War II reversed military attitudes toward research. Useful, even decisive, innovations flowing from wartime laboratories, both military and civilian, persuaded practical officers and officials that the prewar visionaries had been right. Research and development clearly would play major roles in future wars fought by machines instead of men. It was not so clear what kind of research would develop or who would be responsible for choosing among the alternatives.

Influence flowed both ways. War touched technologists and scientists as well as politicians and officers. Not only had researchers enjoyed virtually unlimited resources, a state of affairs many were eager to see sustained, they also found themselves attracted to military-funded research in unprecedented numbers. Institutions emerged after World War II to convert wartime arrangements into permanent features of American government and society. Permanent technological revolution became U.S. military policy.

Basic Research Versus Applied. U.S. armed forces emerged from World War II with an array of research and development skills and organizations. All of them tended to focus on applied science, development engineering, and hardware related to the needs of their specific branch or bureau. Many ended with the war, but some survived, although not always in the same form. Military funds had also supported several laboratories with close university ties in addition to those linked to the Manhattan Project, among them the Applied Physics Laboratory at Johns Hopkins University and the Jet Propulsion Laboratory at the California Institute of Technology. Many aspects of postwar science policy—a term that always includes technology policy and often very little science—bore the hallmarks of wartime experience.

Explicitly designed as a war measure, OSRD ceased operations when the war ended, although its formal termination by presidential order came only in 1947. Its reputation and influence long survived its official demise, however. OSRD remained a model for the effective linking of research and government, even in areas seemingly remote from military concerns. Much of postwar America's research bore the stamp of the OSRD model and example. Curiously enough, military research did not, with one notable exception in the Office of Naval Research (ONR). Created in 1946, ONR promptly began to divert funds from canceled procurement contracts into research. Like OSRD, the navy office adopted the research contract as its primary funding device, but it accepted the inherent value of basic research and found money for a wide range of projects without insisting they show direct links to naval needs.

Technologically oriented applied research had actually dominated the wartime effort. Producing better machines was not, however, the only purpose that united research and military concerns during World War II. The postwar world offered wider prospects for military uses of research, as Bush, the OSRD wartime director, had testified. Other scientists also argued persuasively for the value of basic research.

Discussion usually centered on the promise of science but really meant technology, the products of applied research and engineering. Military research funding totaled some $10 billion between 1945 and 1965. A 1966 study concluded that more than 90 percent of the work had been purely technological, aimed at the incremental improvement of existing technologies, and most of the remainder could best be described as applied or mission-oriented research. Basic science was virtually irrelevant.

Although a later study contradicted this finding, the issue has never been fully resolved. Government support of basic research nevertheless declined. Largely because of the Vietnam War, the armed forces became noticeably less willing to support basic research by the end of the 1960s, an inclination strongly reinforced by congressional action. Controversy about science tarnished by military funds sharply increased in step with protests against the Vietnam War. In 1969 the so-called Mansfield Amendment prohibited military funding for research not directly related to military needs. Consequences were relatively minor. A Pentagon review of outstanding contracts found that only 4 percent could not meet the standard of military relevance.

The Strategic Atom.

Its extraordinary success had promptly made the Manhattan Project a symbol of the power of research to transform society and a gauge against which to measure other organizations. It became a paradigm for the military organization of applied research. Extravagant dreams of science-based superweapons seemed to have been realized, but the new age held promise as well as threat. Successful military-science cooperation raised hopes of larger social benefits, of problems conquered, and of other dreams realized. Profound consequences flowed from both deed and symbol. The future of nuclear energy headed the postwar science policy agenda, and Congress singled out this area for special treatment. Nuclear policy was linked too closely to national security for routine handling; in the postwar United States the bomb was the very symbol of science and technology as military resource. Ultimately, Congress opted for civilian control, but the Atomic Energy Act of 1946 mixed civilian and military authority in ambiguous fashion.

The Atomic Energy Commission created by the act comprised five presidentially appointed civilian commissioners, one serving as chairman but all of whom made policy. The larger organization included a headquarters staff of several divisions to oversee all military and civilian aspects of nuclear research and development, procurement, production, and use. Although the 1946 act mandated a civilian commission, it also imposed a strong military presence. The Division of Military Application became the largest in AEC headquarters, its director by law a general or flag officer and its staff drawn from the uniformed services. Military influence reached much further. Former officers provided a disproportionately large share of AEC officials, both at headquarters and in the field. Developing and testing nuclear weapons remained one of AEC's central functions throughout its career, a burden its successors have retained.

Following OSRD precedent, the AEC directed its funding through contracts for both basic and applied research. Operating contracts also proved most useful. Formal agreements with universities enabled the AEC to support and expand a network of national laboratories, beginning with those at Argonne, Illinois; Oak Ridge, Tennessee; and Los Alamos. Industrial firms received contracts to manage production facilities, such as Hanford, Washington, and Sandia, New Mexico. Contracting for both research and operations remained the hallmark of the AEC and its successors.

The Manhattan Engineer District was dissolved in 1946, and most of its assets, facilities, and workers were transferred to the AEC. Military members of the wartime project became in 1947 the nucleus of a new combined agency, the Armed Forces Special Weapons Project (AFSWP). Augmenting its rosters from all branches of the armed forces, this new agency worked closely with the AEC to develop and test nuclear weapons. The AFSWP later became the Defense Atomic Support Agency and since 1971 has been known as the Defense Nuclear Agency.

New Technology and Old in Korea.

The North Korean invasion of South Korea in 1950 quickly brought United States intervention under United Nations auspices. Although largely fought with World War II weapons and tactics, including updated tanks and piston-engine aircraft, the combined effect of limited ends and restrictive terrain eventually imposed something very much like the trench warfare of World War I on war in Korea. In two notable respects, however, Korea differed sharply from the earlier conflict—the widespread use of jet aircraft and of helicopters.

Jet aircraft first flew in combat near the end of World War II, although in numbers too small to affect the course of events. The most successful operational turbojet-powered aircraft in the air late in the war was the German ME-262. Advanced features such as swept wings and automatic leading-edge slats, when brought back to the United States after the war, helped designers at North American Aviation dramatically increase performance of the F-86 Sabre then under development.

Entering the race to develop jet aircraft late, the United States demonstrated the airworthiness of three models but had only one in production before World War II ended, which became the Lockheed F-80 Shooting Star, the main fighter of air force squadrons in the Far East when war in Korea began. The F-80s were soon joined by Republic F-84 Thunderjets and F-86, both developed during the late 1940s. Piston-engine ground-attack aircraft saw significant combat in Korea, but jet aircraft assumed the major burden. F-84s armed with HVARs took over the main ground-support role, while F-86s fought Soviet-made MIG-15s for control of the skies over the peninsula, the first aerial combat between jet aircraft.

Although navy piston-engine aircraft played a larger role in Korea than their air force counterparts, the navy had also begun flying jets from its carriers. Transitional aircraft such as the Ryan Fireball, a hybrid with both piston and jet engines, and the McDonnell Phantom, the new company's first design adopted for quantity production and the navy's first all-jet fighter, allowed navy personnel to experiment with carrier operations in the late 1940s.

Helicopters, like jets, had seen minor service in World War II but became a major factor in Korea. Rotary-wing aircraft promised enormous benefits in their ability to rise and descend vertically, but they also presented enormous technical problems. Russian émigré Igor Sikorsky was finally able to persuade U.S. military observers in 1939 that helicopters could be of practical use, when he successfully demonstrated his model V-300. Small numbers of the first production models entered service late in World War II; the army used them for liaison and observation, the navy for reconnaissance and air/sea rescue.

Sikorsky, joined by Bell and Hiller, became the major helicopter suppliers for the army and navy in Korea. Primarily used in medical evacuation and rescue work, but also more experimentally in spotting for artillery, for moving troops, and even for raiding, they became a ubiquitous presence on Korean battlefields. They also inspired early thinking about what later came to be termed air mobility. In 1952 the army formed twelve helicopter battalions on paper, even though the required troop-carrying machines did not yet exist. Technology and tactics gestated together in the mid-1950s, leading to major changes in combat operations when the United States again went to war a decade later. In the interim, the leading edge of military technological research lay in the direction of strategic warfare.

Delivering the Bomb. The fission bombs dropped on Japan weighed five tons. Each of them rode to its target in a Boeing B-29 Superfortress. The only airplane large and powerful enough for the job, the B-29 was the culmination of the long-range, four-engine strategic bomber through which prewar theorists had hoped to realize their dreams of air power. In the war's waning months, fleets of such bombers did in fact devastate Japanese industry, as their predecessors had German. In many eyes air power doctrine appeared to have been vindicated, although neither as quickly nor as easily as its advocates had supposed. Atomic bombs confirmed to many the war-winning potential of strategic bombing.

Early in 1946, the Strategic Air Command

MILITARY ARTS AND SCIENCES

(SAC) became one of the three major combat commands into which the U.S. Army Air Forces was divided, and it remained intact the following year when the air force attained equal status with the army and the navy under the Department of Defense. Technologically, SAC faced a decade of transition, symbolized by the Convair B-36 with its six piston and four jet engines. Designed to carry ten thousand pounds of bombs over a range of ten thousand miles, it could accommodate a maximum payload of eighty-four thousand pounds. During the late 1940s and early 1950s, it filled the strategic bomber gap between the obsolescent piston-engine B-29 and the first all-jet heavy bomber, the Boeing B-52 Stratofortress.

Relegated to medium-bomber status by the giant B-36, the B-29 and its upgraded version, the B-50, remained by far the most numerous of SAC bombers through the early 1950s. SAC deployed its first all-jet bomber, the North American B-45 Tornado, in the late 1940s. Essentially a conventional bomber fitted with jet engines, it served chiefly in its reconnaissance version. It was not until 1953 that SAC began to receive a jet bomber that could fill the strategic role, although only because developing the techniques and equipment for inflight refueling had been given high priority. Without such aid, the Boeing B-47 Stratojet had only a fifteen-hundred-mile radius of action, but its deployment marked the end of the line for piston-engine bombers. In 1955, B-52s began to reach operational units and in successive modifications have remained SAC's main strategic bomber ever since.

Carrier-based naval aircraft joined the nuclear club soon after World War II ended. Two piston-engine attack bombers entered service in the late 1940s—the Douglas BT2D Skyraider, late models of which were modified to carry tactical nuclear weapons, and the twin-engine North American AJ Savage, designed specifically as a nuclear-strike aircraft. The navy's first jet-powered nuclear strike bomber was the Douglas A3D Skywarrior. Design work began just after World War II for what proved to be the largest and heaviest airplane ever proposed for routine carrier use. The Skywarrior went through several versions; the first was delivered in 1953 and the definitive A3D arrived in 1957. It had an operational radius of more than one thousand miles with a twelve-thousand-pound payload.

STRATEGIC TECHNOLOGIES ASCENDANT, 1952–1965

Whether or not fission bombs ended the war against Japan, nuclear weapons exerted their greatest impact on the future, an impact more relevant to institutional development than to the conduct of war. Institutional changes, however, matter no less than shifts in tactics, doctrine, or operational philosophies. The combination of nuclear weapons and long-range guided missiles has dominated strategic planning and military policymaking in the postwar world, although nuclear weapons have not been used in war since 1945. Although the kind of war for which such weapons exist has never been fought, the technology has undergone continuous development without respect to practical experience.

H-Bomb Development. Military budgets dropped steeply after World War II. Relying on its monopoly of nuclear weapons and following long-standing precedents for postwar demobilization, the United States canceled most wartime contracts and sharply reduced its armed forces. Euphoria engendered by victory proved short-lived, however, giving way to an intensifying cold war with the Soviet Union. Coming sooner than many expected, the 1949 Soviet success in testing its own nuclear weapon brought a quick response from the United States, a crash program to develop hydrogen bombs. The outbreak of war in Korea just a few months later underscored this decision and brought soaring military budgets. Prosecuting the war absorbed relatively little new money; the higher budgets went instead to enlarge the nuclear weapons stockpile and to support expanded military-technological research of many kinds.

Thermonuclear weapons exploited the explosive fission of heavy elements to ignite the fusion of light elements, in theory multiplying explosive power virtually without limit. Conventional bombs in World War II could destroy a few hundred square yards, the fission bombs dropped on Japan a few square miles. Conceivably, destruction of such limited areas might fall within the scope of military planning based on the concept of war as a rational political tool. Not so hydrogen bombs. Devastation across hundreds of square miles, a scale more nearly appropriate to force of nature than human agency, seemed to render military experience largely irrelevant.

By the late 1950s, the theory of nuclear warfare and deterrence had become almost exclusively the province of civilian experts. Development, however, proceeded apace. Nuclear tests at Eniwetok in the Pacific in 1951 and 1952 showed that fusion could be achieved. Although the air force sought and obtained a so-called emergency capability weapon by mid-1953, the prospective twenty-five-ton monster, more than five feet across and eighteen feet long, could be carried only by a specially modified B-36. Operation Castle early in 1954 proved actual bomb designs. Rapid progress in making smaller and lighter thermonuclear weapons opened up the first real opportunities for services other than the air force to join the nuclear club. Carrier-based aircraft would become available as delivery systems, as would land- and sea-based rocket-powered missiles.

Sputnik's Impact. The United States faced a military-scientific crisis after the Soviet Union launched the first artificial satellite on 4 October 1957 and a second one month later, this one with a dog as passenger. Two Sputniks in a month shook the casual confidence many Americans placed in their country's scientific and technological prowess. One direct consequence was the creation of a new federal science agency, the National Aeronautics and Space Administration (NASA).

NASA incorporated the old NACA and a number of military rocket and space projects.

Like its predecessor, it had its own laboratories but also relied on academic and industrial contractors for much of its research and development. Unlike NACA, NASA became heavily involved in engineering development. The structuring of the new space agency raised questions about civilian versus military control of research. The outcome was an ostensibly civilian agency with large military participation; all of NASA's early launch vehicles, for example, were modified missiles.

After Sputnik, obtaining top-quality science and technology advice for the president again became a high priority. A new post, special assistant for science and technology, was established in the White House and was promptly filled by MIT President James R. Killian, Jr., marking the first time a U.S. president enjoyed the services of a full-time science adviser. At the same time, the Science Advisory Committee, created in 1951 in the Office of Defense Mobilization, moved to the White House as the President's Science Advisory Committee. Given a voice at the highest levels of government, science flourished over the next decade. The decision reflected still widespread beliefs about science as a source of military technology and concerns about using it properly in the national interest. Much of the advice sought concerned nuclear weapons and missile development.

Pentagon reorganization in 1958 replaced the largely advisory assistant secretary of defense for research and development (established in a 1953 defense reorganization) with a director of defense research and engineering who enjoyed direct authority to approve, reject, or modify all defense research projects. Reorganization also created an Advanced Research Projects Agency (ARPA, later the Defense Advanced Research Projects Agency, or DARPA) to act promptly on special projects, especially in the areas of space and missile defense.

Successful research symbolized by the Manhattan Project could not easily be separated from the fear generated by nuclear weapons. Radioactive fallout from nuclear weapons testing inspired a wave of protest during the 1950s, but qualms about science and technology, especially as linked to military imperatives, spread much more widely. President Dwight Eisenhower's 1961 farewell address articulated some of these concerns. His warning against the military-industrial complex was only part of the message. He also warned against the twin dangers arising from science too closely entwined with government: the possibility that academic research might suffer from excessive dependence upon federal support and that government policymaking might be surrendered to a scientific-technological elite.

Strategic Missiles.

Soviet satellites were more than merely a blow to American pride. They also posed a clear, if not explicit, military threat. Boosters powerful enough to lift a payload to space might just as easily loft a nuclear bomb across oceans, and guidance systems able to place a satellite in orbit might well be capable of putting a warhead on target. A surprise missile attack could destroy SAC's manned bombers, upon which the United States relied to carry nuclear weapons to the enemy. Without bombers the nation would be left unable to retaliate. Motivated in part by such concerns, the United States soon began to deploy its own missile force.

That such missile programs were well under way at the crucial moment, however, had little to do with SAC vulnerability. Stimulated by an exciting new technology, the army, navy, and air force were at work on guided ballistic missiles by the early 1950s. German technologists brought to the United States after World War II by Project Paperclip gave American rocket research a major boost. Although work soon moved beyond the German wartime achievements, intermediate and long-range ballistic missile programs proceeded with little urgency and many question marks.

Intercontinental ballistic missiles (ICBMs), in particular, posed formidable technical problems: Nuclear warheads, the most plausible payload, seemed too heavy, guidance systems too inaccurate, for the state of the art in the early 1950s. That changed as rockets and guidance systems improved, but the key breakthroughs

came in nuclear weapons design. More efficient warheads meant lighter payloads, while the vastly greater power of thermonuclear explosions relaxed demands on guidance by the mid-1950s. These developments had several consequences.

In 1956 the army lost to the air force its longer-range missile programs and concentrated thereafter on short-range rockets for tactical nuclear weapons. Acquiring control of all long-range land-based missiles, the air force promptly accelerated its ICBM programs, Atlas and Titan, as well as Thor, the intermediate-range ballistic missile (IRBM). Activation of the first operational Atlas squadron at Vandenberg Air Force Base, California, followed in April 1958; seven months later an Atlas missile completed its full-range operational test flight, hitting a target area more than six thousand miles away. Both the single-stage Atlas and the two-stage Titan used cryogenic propellants, making them slow to launch and vulnerable to attack.

By the mid-1950s research had overturned the belief that solid propellants were inherently unreliable; researchers also found chemically energetic combinations of liquid fuel and oxidizer that did not require temperatures near absolute zero. Purse strings loosened by orbiting Sputniks allowed development of second-generation ICBMs—the solid-propellant Minuteman and the Titan II with storable liquid propellants—without slowing Atlas or Titan. Both missiles could be protected in hardened underground silos ready for immediate launching. Successful operational test flights during 1962 brought them into the American arsenal. By 1967, SAC had added a strategic missile force of one thousand Minutemen and fifty-four Titan IIs to augment its fleet of jet-propelled B-52 bombers with intercontinental range.

Nuclear Power at Sea.

Nuclear-tipped missiles also found their way to sea, but nuclear power came first. When World War II ended, the navy had no approved nuclear weapons role. Turning instead to nuclear propulsion, it found a redoubtable champion in a then-obscure naval engineering officer, Hyman G. Rickover. The key problem involved choosing a reactor design at a time when very little was known about reactors. Relying on sound engineering judgment, Rickover made a long series of decisions that worked. He promised to have a nuclear-powered submarine in the water by 1955, and he did.

When the *Nautilus* was launched in January 1954, it was the world's first nuclear-powered ship. Its power plant, a compact boiling-water reactor, could drive the ship either on the surface or underwater at better than twenty knots. More important, the *Nautilus* was the first true submarine; on its mid-1955 shakedown cruise it eclipsed every record for running submerged. In making the underwater passage from Connecticut to Puerto Rico in eighty-four hours, it averaged sixteen knots over a distance of thirteen hundred miles. No submersible boat had ever traveled a tenth as far continuously submerged, nor had any sustained so high a speed underwater for more than an hour. The *Nautilus* did even better later, averaging more than twenty knots on a fourteen-hundred-mile voyage from Key West, Florida, to New London, Connecticut. Impressive as such figures were, they were soon surpassed as nuclear reactors became the standard power plant for all U.S. submarines.

Nuclear reactors came to power surface vessels, although more slowly and ultimately less completely than submarines. Their advantages were simply less compelling on the surface—endurance far greater than conventionally powered ships barely outbalanced the far greater costs. Keels of the first nuclear-powered surface vessels were laid in the late 1950s—the guided-missile cruiser *Long Beach* in 1957, the aircraft carrier *Enterprise* in 1958, and the guided-missile frigate *Bainbridge* in 1959—but years elapsed before others joined them.

By the mid-1980s, the U.S. Navy had ninety-five nuclear-propelled attack and thirty-seven missile submarines in commission, but only nine cruisers and four aircraft carriers. Although diesel-powered submarines by the late 1950s had achieved levels of performance far beyond World War II standards, the U.S. Navy decided to build no more; all future attack submarines would be nuclear-powered, as were the submarines adopted for the Polaris Fleet Ballistic Missile (FBM) system. Nuclear-propelled vessels, in contrast, remain a small portion of the surface fleet.

Sea-Launched Strategic Missiles. The navy had pursued its own missile programs, starting with Bumblebee in 1944 and leading eventually to the Talos and Terrier systems based on short-range rockets designed as surface-to-air missiles (SAMs). System deployment began in the early 1950s, with the first SAM-armed cruisers commissioned in mid-decade. These missiles carried conventional warheads, but the navy also sought to deploy nuclear-armed cruise missiles, such as Regulus.

Cruise missile development began shortly after World War II with Loon, an American version of the German V-1. Like Loon, Regulus was a subsonic jet-propelled aircraft. Operational in 1954 but not deployed until 1956, Regulus had only the briefest of careers. It was overtaken by the offspring of Germany's other major wartime missile, the V-2 rocket. By the mid-1950s it began to look technically feasible to put nuclear warheads on medium- to long-range guided missiles capable of shipboard launching. Coincidentally, the first nuclear-powered submarine had just put to sea.

In 1955 the navy formed the Special Projects Office to solve the problems of launching IRBMs from ships and so create a sea-based nuclear deterrent. Promised a warhead small and light enough to fit within a nine-hundred-pound payload by the new nuclear weapons research laboratory at Livermore, California, the navy designed the solid-propellant Polaris, a fifteen-ton missile, twenty-eight feet long and five feet across, that could toss such a payload fifteen hundred miles. Polaris, like Minuteman, benefited from funds more freely available after Sputnik. Development began in 1956 as an extraordinarily successful crash program. The first submerged launch of a Polaris missile came in 1960. By the end of that year, the first Polaris submarine, the *George Washington,* was on patrol. The last of forty-one such vessels, each with sixteen missiles, went to sea in 1967, the same year Minuteman deployment was completed.

Armed with missiles it could launch while submerged, a nuclear-powered submarine seemed an almost invulnerable deterrent. Submarine and missile together became the Polaris FBM system, which was succeeded in due course by Poseidon and then by Trident FBMs as both missiles and submarines continued to develop. Technology pursued largely for its own sake had completed what the nuclear theorists now dubbed the deterrent triad: three distinct forces—manned bombers, land-based missiles, and submarines—armed with nuclear weapons, each independently capable of inflicting unacceptable damage in retaliation against attack.

From SAGE to Missile Defense.

Although most analysts judged defense against nuclear attack impossible, explosive growth of microelectronics since World War II, particularly computing, has repeatedly seemed to put that eminently desirable goal within reach. Immediate postwar computer research and development depended chiefly on military funding. It was a pattern repeated at every critical stage in the history of computers, as exemplified in the career of the transistor and later in the development of integrated circuits. Military money has again and again bridged the gap between laboratory breakthrough and commercial viability.

Initially, costly and unpredictable computers attracted little commercial interest. Military support did not demand quick returns. Despite wartime successes and indirect benefits flowing from such scientific uses as analyzing the dynamics of nuclear explosions, the huge and fragile machines of the 1940s and early 1950s were hardly suitable for weapons systems. Automation, however, like mechanization a generation earlier, caught military imaginations. Faith in the longer-term prospects for enormously enhanced command and control mattered more than the failure-prone and hard-to-use machines immediately available.

By the 1950s such prospects appeared promising enough for large-scale application. Continental air defense provided the problem. The answer was a centralized command and control system termed SAGE (semi-automatic ground environment). Enormous mainframe computers would process data from a vast network of distant radar stations, then direct interceptors against attacking bombers. Simply building the system—including seventy-eight radar stations on the shores of the Arctic Ocean to form the DEW (Distant Early Warning) Line, as well as forty-six four-story air-conditioned concrete structures, each housing one of the 175-ton SAGE computers—was a fifteen-year feat of engineering.

Integrating the system proved an even greater challenge in an era of rapid technological change. With manned aircraft giving way to guided missiles and vacuum tubes yielding to transistors, with virtually every system component changing in greater or lesser degree, often more than once, difficulties were immense and inevitable. Although declared operational in 1963 and surviving at least in part into the early 1980s, SAGE never achieved much reliability. Its real success was symbolic.

SAGE paved the way not only for the antiballistic missile systems (ABMs) of the 1960s and the Strategic Defense Initiative (SDI) of the 1980s but also for the current Worldwide Military Command and Control System. It foreshadowed their flaws as well. Inherently untestable, their ultimate capabilities remain matters of faith; each attempt to deploy such systems has evoked opposition.

POSTMODERN WARFARE, 1965–1993

In contrast to basic research, which has declined since the 1960s, mission-oriented and applied research have flourished. Military funds still support the bulk of American research and development years after the acknowledged end of the cold war. Systematic research and development geared to meet military desires has become the outstanding feature of modern military-technological development. The result has been enormous growth in the range of sophisticated gadgetry deployed on, above, and around modern battlefields.

Since mid-century the technology of so-called conventional warfare has become increasingly unconventional. Familiar weapons and equipment have been improved, sometimes to a striking degree. Retaining their basic character, tanks and guns have nonetheless acquired capabilities far beyond anything that might have been imagined in World War II. Dramatically enhanced weapons accuracy, communications reliability, and command and control effectiveness have radically altered the combat environment. Technologies barely visible in the 1940s matured in later years to reshape battle decisively. Missiles have come to figure prominently in so-called conventional warfare. Equipped with more and more sophisticated guidance and control systems, they have drastically reshaped battlefield environments and forced war machines to new levels of competence. These weapons, in sharp contrast to strategic weaponry, have periodically been tested on the battlefield.

Perhaps the most striking changes have centered on the ever-widening use of sophisticated sensors and computers to find and attack enemy forces. In contrast to such grandiose schemes as SAGE, ABM, and SDI, all of which sought to automate decision-making, efforts to automate combat have enjoyed a measure of success. The line of descent from radar-guided, computer-directed, sensor-activated antiaircraft fire in World War II to smart bombs and precision guided munitions (PGM) has been relatively straightforward. Working systematically and diligently, scientists and technologists have upgraded, diversified, and augmented guidance techniques, computer systems, and sensors, both individually and as system components.

Technology in Vietnam. Superficially, perhaps, a veteran of World War II or Korea might have found nothing too strange on the battlefields of Vietnam—aircraft, guns, tanks, and infantry still dominated operations. Appearances, however, were deceptive. Although the basic structures of combat remained largely intact, improved and novel technologies sharply altered combat. Such technologies were the direct result of military-sponsored research and development, which had brought several technologies that existed only embryonically in World War II to practical fruition. The most significant was the development and improvement of short-range electronically guided missiles and the related integration of computers and electronics with mechanical systems.

These new technologies made their full-scale battlefield debut in Vietnam, and the exigencies of combat forced further development. History persuaded the United States that technological innovation backed by immense productive capacity won wars. This became the accepted formula for victory in Vietnam. Although faith in technology ultimately proved misplaced, efforts to implement it led to striking innovations in several areas. Dramatic advances along three technological paths particularly marked the Vietnam era—helicopter operations, communications and control, and the varied technologies of detection and attack characterized as the automated battlefield.

Helicopters became the most widely broadcast image of the U.S. in Vietnam, in two distinct but complementary roles—delivering troops to combat and firepower to the enemy. Evacuation of wounded, a role pioneered in Korea, became routine in Vietnam. In 1955 the U.S. Army chose the Bell Model 204 as the winner in its design competition for a utility helicopter. Initially designated HU-1A (thus the nickname Huey, which stuck even when the prefix later changed to UH), the new turbine-powered helicopters proved faster and more versatile than the piston-engine machines they succeeded. Deliveries began in 1959, and the first Hueys reached Southeast Asia in 1962. Variously modified, they became the mainstay of army operations in the war. An extensively modified, heavily armed version, the AH-1

Huey Cobra, became the first purpose-designed attack helicopter to see combat.

Helicopters also played an important role in revolutionary advances in communications and control. Literally above the battle but linked to it electronically, helicopter-borne commanders could observe the fighting, receive information, and transmit orders to their forces on the ground. The late-1940s invention of the transistor and its subsequent development, largely financed by military money, led to communications gear dramatically reduced in size and weight compared to those of World War II and Korea.

A network of FM and VHF radio and microwave systems extended from squad to headquarters. Microwave and tropospheric systems linked stations throughout Southeast Asia, and the satellite system inaugurated in 1966 connected commanders in Vietnam to their civilian superiors in Washington. Echoing the navy's early twentieth-century experience in putting radio on its ships, the expanded communications capabilities of the 1960s proved a mixed blessing. A more secure chain of command tended to restrict the initiative of subordinate leaders.

Toward Automated War.

Military support for microelectronics and computers generated other technological capabilities that had major impacts on war fighting. The same extraordinary expansion of electronic computation that stimulated such strategic applications as SAGE also opened new opportunities for using computers in battle. In 1959 the Institute for Defense Analyses, a Pentagon think tank, assembled a panel of top scientists as the Jason Summer Study Group; it survived as the Jason Division to provide periodic assessments of key problems in military technology. In summer 1966 the problem came direct from Secretary of Defense Robert S. McNamara, who hoped to find an alternative to the costly and seemingly fruitless bombing in North Vietnam.

McNamara proposed a "fence" against North Vietnamese infiltration, partly a physical barrier of barbed wire, watch towers, and mines, but also an electronic barrier making extensive use of the new technology to locate, track, and target the enemy. A favorable response from the Jason study confirmed McNamara in his action. Despite military opposition—critics not only deemed the plan unworkable, they feared that funding such ideas might also undercut more urgent needs—McNamara went ahead. To do so, he formed the deliberately misnamed Defense Communications Planning Group (DCPG). During its five-year existence, DCPG did much to refocus major portions of the nation's military research and development effort, in the process sparking a far-reaching transformation of conventional warfare.

Although the DCPG could not avert American defeat in Vietnam, its work may well rank with the Manhattan and Polaris projects as an instance of scientific-technological ideas rapidly converted to revolutionary new or radically improved military technology. General William C. Westmoreland could by 1969 envision future fields where "enemy forces will be located, tracked, and targeted almost instantaneously through the use of data links, computer-assisted intelligence evaluation and automated fire control."

Although the flood of DCPG innovation had yet to crest when Westmoreland spoke, U.S. forces in Vietnam had already begun to deploy key elements of the automated battlefield. McNamara's original plan as modified by Jason called for two distinct but complementary efforts. The first would place remote electronic sensors to direct air strikes against traffic along the Ho Chi Minh Trail in Laos and thus restrict or prevent the movement of North Vietnamese troops and supplies southward. The second required building a more conventional fortified line, a barbed-wire fence with guard towers, minefields, and the like, supplemented by electronic sensors, to block infiltration through the demilitarized zone. Crucial developments centered on sensors and munitions.

The Electronic Battlefield.

A major part of DCPG work involved sensors, devices able to detect certain kinds of physical data, convert them to electronic signals, and transmit the results to waiting receivers. All remote sensors shared an electronic logic circuit, radio transmitter, and battery but differed in their detection units. The most common types of detectors were seismic and acoustic, the first sensing ground vibration from footfalls or passing vehicles, the latter sound from the same sources. Other remote devices detected magnetic anomalies, interruptions in self-generated electromagnetic fields, chemicals from human bodies or truck exhausts, heat through infrared sensors, or movement via small ground radar sets.

Detection led to attack from the air, aircraft directed to the appropriate zone and guided in their attack runs by continuously updated computer-analyzed data. Even bomb release was often computer-controlled. Experience showed that jet fighter-bombers, such as the McDonnell F-4 Phantom II, were too fast for the job; older jet bombers, such as the Martin B-57 Canberra, did better, but the most successful truck-killer proved to be a converted turboprop transport aircraft, the four-engine Lockheed C-130 Hercules.

Introduced to combat in the late 1960s as the AC-130, code-named Pave Spectre, the Hercules raised battlefield automation to a new level of ferocity. The AC-130 carried its own elaborate sensor systems. The fourteen-member crew monitored data from a radar able to pick up truck ignitions, a laser range finder and target designator, a low-light-level television camera, an imaging infrared device, and a ground target radar; it was also equipped with electronic countermeasures gear and a digital computer fire control system. Its armament was no less powerful: Vulcan 20mm multibarrel Gatling guns and 7.62mm miniguns, Bofors 40mm automatic guns and, in later models, a 105mm howitzer. Shortly after its introduction, according to the air force, one AC-130 destroyed sixty-eight trucks in a single hour.

Remote sensors proved so successful that they were widely adopted for a variety of tactical uses, largely forestalling the proposed McNamara fence. Spread around fire bases, for instance, they helped spot approaching enemy forces and provided enough information for defenders to call in artillery fire on map coordinates, fire support from helicopter gunships, or bombing runs by fixed-wing aircraft.

Novel or much enhanced detection devices were not limited to remote sensors. Ultimately, the most widely used was the starlight scope, deployed in sizes ranging from rifle-mounted instruments to aircraft-borne long-range devices. Magnifying starlight or moonlight as much as fifty thousand times, even the smallest version could allow a soldier to find a night target four hundred yards away. Low-light-level television cameras and thermal-imaging night vision devices joined new types of radar in helping target enemy forces.

Smart Bombs. Conventional bombs, "iron" or "dumb" bombs in the new lexicon of military technology, remained the mainstay of aerial attack in Southeast Asia, improved aerodynamically and explosively but fundamentally unchanged from those used a generation earlier. One relatively minor device of the World War II era, however, the cluster bomb, achieved far greater currency in Vietnam in a wide range of new forms that took advantage of vast advances in the technology of both materials and controls. The key idea was to spread a bomb's effect by packaging its payload in submunitions that could be more or less widely dispersed by explosive or aerodynamic forces. Such payloads included several kinds of antipersonnel or antiarmor bomblets, mines, and, toward the end of the war, fuel-air explosives. Other bombs featured more radical changes.

Munitions research and development formed the second major area of DCPG's efforts to create an automated battlefield. Innovations in bombs and missiles, like those in sensors, included the improvement of old technology as well as the development of new. Outstanding among the several products of this enterprise were so-called smart bombs. What made them smart were sensors linked electronically through microchips to aerodynamic control surfaces that could adjust the falling bomb's flight path toward its designated target. Two types of smart bombs, guided either by laser or by electrooptics, made their debut in Vietnam.

The first generation of laser-guided bombs (LGBs) were simply standard bombs to which a guidance and control unit was bolted. A sensor in the nose detected a spot of laser light projected on the target either by the attacking aircraft itself or by some other agent, such as a soldier on the ground or a spotter plane. Although more complex and costly than LGBs, electrooptical guided bombs (EOGBs), such as the Walleye, had the considerable advantage of taking care of themselves once released from the aircraft. The weapons officer on the attacking plane locked a television image of the target into the bomb's computer. When the bomb dropped, the computer compared the stored image with images received from the bomb's nose television camera as it fell, issuing signals to move the bomb's flight controls so the images matched. Accuracy multiplied.

Guided Missiles in Combat.

Vietnam became the scene of the first large-scale display of other smart weapons as well, the missiles that came to be termed precision-guided munitions. Although efforts to devise guided weapons began as early as World War I, practical designs emerged only in the mid-1950s. Unlike such World War II rockets as the bazooka or HVAR, which were on their own after firing and followed purely ballistic trajectories, the new missiles could receive commands or generate their own data and later their courses in flight. Precision derived from the same combination that made bombs smart, sensor-guided computerized control systems. Missile guidance took three major forms—passive homing, command, and active homing.

The earliest successful guided missiles operated against easy-to-spot targets, such as other aircraft or ships at sea, where relatively simple infrared or radar-passive homing systems provided perfectly adequate guidance. Engaging more difficult targets required further development. By the mid-1960s, when reliable small rocket motors and solid-state circuitry made semiautomatic guidance possible, ground tar-

gets could be successfully engaged. External systems of one kind or another using eyesight, lasers, or radar designated the target and fed through microchips to provide the commands that guided the missile to its target. Toward the end of the war in Southeast Asia, missiles carrying their own sensors, computers, and guidance logic could be launched and left to find their own targets.

Passive homing missiles began joining the U.S. arsenal in the early 1950s. First was the air-to-air Sidewinder, with infrared guidance that allowed it to home in on the heat from jet engines; steadily improved in detail and expanded in capabilities over the next three decades, Sidewinders became the most widely deployed of all air-to-air missiles. The larger, longer-ranged, and more costly radar-guided air-to-air Sparrow entered service in 1956 and likewise attained considerable longevity. An outgrowth of Sparrow technology became the first successful antiradar missile; the air-to-ground Shrike homed on enemy air defense radar and thus helped reduce the threat to aircraft from surface-to-air missiles.

Air-to-air missiles and antiradiation missiles presented relatively easy guidance problems because their targets stood out clearly in largely uncluttered surroundings. Relatively easy targeting also tended to be true for missiles used at sea against ships. This was not so for most ground targets, which had to be located and tracked amid often confusing backgrounds. Outstanding among first-generation command-guided missiles was the TOW (tube-launched, optically tracked, wire-guided) antitank missile. After launching this short-range missile, a soldier had to keep the target in the cross hairs, any movement automatically feeding control commands through the wire to the missile. Certainly not the perfect weapon, TOW nevertheless far outclassed any other infantry antitank weapon and has been deployed by many armies in vast numbers since its introduction in the mid-1960s.

Active homing missiles represented the second generation of guided missiles. The first successful fire-and-forget missile was the Maverick.

The earliest versions relied on a television camera in the missile's nose to maintain contact with the target; accordingly, it was strictly a daylight weapon. Later versions relied on laser guidance and, most recently, imaging infrared sensors. Whatever the guidance system, the attack began with the pilot or weapons officer lining the target up in cross hairs, locking it in, then releasing the missile to proceed on its own. Mavericks easily achieved direct hits in 88 percent of their test firings, and their combat performance was not noticeably inferior.

The Baroque Arsenal. Ultimately, the distinction between smart bomb and PGM ceased to matter much as their capabilities increasingly overlapped. By the time the Gulf War of 1991 began, the more important distinction had become that between projectiles needing to be guided externally to their targets and those able to find their own targets after launching, often from considerable distance. The latter group now included cruise missiles, derived in part from the remotely piloted vehicles (RPVs) that had enjoyed a degree of success in Southeast Asia and from the navy's medium-range Harpoon antiship missile deployed in the late 1970s. Their performance far outclassed that of the abortive cruise missiles of the 1950s. The best of the new generation, Tomahawk, carried terrain-matching radar so good that claims of pinpoint accuracy from hundreds of miles away seemed entirely plausible. Cruise missiles such as the Tomahawk can carry nuclear as well as conventional warheads. Other relatively short-range missiles share that capability. Relatively low-yield nuclear warheads on such missiles raised the possibility, at least in theory, of so-called tactical nuclear warfare.

The development of strategic weapons has been no less dynamic since 1970. Each leg of the deterrent triad has received dramatic upgrades, as symbolized by the MX land-based missile, the Trident fleet ballistic missile system, and the B-2 bomber. Both land-based and sea-based missiles have acquired multiple warheads, each of which can be targeted independently with increasing accuracy. Each new generation of

weapon systems improved on the performance of its predecessor, but each also demanded huge increases in funding and posed intractable deployment problems. Technological enthusiasm may have reached its pinnacle in a proposed shield against nuclear attack, the so-called Strategic Defense Initiative (SDI), dubbed Star Wars, which revived the moribund and so far futile dream of antimissile defense. After ten years and billions of dollars, the original idea of defense based on x-ray lasers vanished, and several successors did not fare much better.

Unworkability has plagued some conventional weapon systems, but their chief problems lie elsewhere. Preoccupation with technological sophistication has led to weapons of enormous capabilities and equally enormous costs. Modern aircraft devote half their weight to electronic gear, detectors and computers, collectively termed avionics. Avionics also account for much of the extraordinarily high price tags for such aircraft. Naval vessels have undergone similar evolution, and even the machines of ground combat have acquired sophisticated electronic capabilities and stunningly higher prices. Unrestrained pursuit of technical perfection has produced a baroque arsenal, possessed of extraordinary capabilities at astronomical expense.

The Gulf War seemed to mark the apotheosis of U.S. defense policy based on permanent technological revolution. High-tech warfare as displayed on television sets in the United States revealed the advanced stages of still a third military-technological revolution in the making—after the classic military revolution of the seventeenth century and the less widely acknowledged but perhaps even more decisive nineteenth-century revolution—but one the strained U.S. economy could no longer sustain without outside help.

See also COMMUNICATIONS; ENGINEERING AND SCIENCE; INDUSTRIAL MOBILIZATION AND DEMOBILIZATION; LOGISTICS; MILITARY AVIATION; THE MILITARY-INDUSTRIAL COMPLEX; *and* MILITARY MEDICINE.

BIBLIOGRAPHY

General Works

Blair, Claude, ed. *Pollard's History of Firearms* (1983).

Diagram Group. *Weapons: An International Encyclopedia from 5000 B.C. to 2000 A.D.* (1980).

Dupuy, Trevor N. *The Evolution of Weapons and Warfare* (1980).

Friedman, Norman. *U.S. Naval Weapons: Every Gun, Missile, Mine, and Torpedo Used by the U.S. Navy from 1883 to the Present Day* (1982).

Higham, Robin, ed. *A Guide to the Sources of United States Military History* (1975).

Hogg, Ian V. *The Complete Machine-Gun: 1885 to the Present* (1979).

———. *The Weapons that Changed the World* (1986).

Kaldor, Mary. *The Baroque Arsenal* (1981).

King, R. W., ed. *Naval Engineering and American Sea Power* (1989).

Lautenschläger, Karl. "Technology and the Evolution of Naval Warfare." *International Security* 8 (1983).

Macksey, Kenneth. *Technology in War: The Impact of Science on Weapon Development and Modern Battle* (1986).

McNeill, William H. *The Pursuit of Power: Technology, Armed Force, and Society Since A.D. 1000* (1982).

O'Connell, Robert L. *Of Arms and Men: A History of War, Weapons, and Aggression* (1989).

Pearton, Maurice. *Diplomacy, War, and Technology Since 1830* (1984).

Smith, Merritt Roe, ed. *Military Enterprise and Technological Change: Perspectives on the American Experience* (1985).

Van Creveld, Martin. *Technology and War: From 2000 B.C. to the Present* (1989).

Preindustrial Military and Naval Technology

Brown, M. L. *Firearms in Colonial America: The Impact on History and Technology, 1492–1792* (1980).

Howard, Frank. *Sailing Ships of War, 1400–1860* (1979).

Roland, Alex. *Underwater Warfare in the Age of Sail* (1978).

Smith, Merritt Roe. "Eli Whitney and the American System of Manufacturing." In Carroll W. Pursell, Jr., ed. *Technology in America: A History of Individuals and Ideas* (1990).

York, Neil Longley. *Mechanical Metamorphosis: Technological Change in Revolutionary America* (1985).

Nineteenth-Century Technology

Armstrong, David A. *Bullets and Bureaucrats: The Machine Gun and the United States Army, 1861–1916* (1982).

Cooling, Benjamin Franklin. *Gray Steel and Blue Water Navy: The Formative Years of America's Military-Industrial Complex, 1881–1917* (1979).

Myatt, Frederick. *The Illustrated Encyclopedia of 19th-Century Firearms* (1979).

Reilly, John C., Jr., and Robert L. Scheina. *American Battleships, 1886–1923: Predreadnought Design and Construction* (1980).

Twentieth-Century General Works

Angelucci, Enzo. *Rand McNally Encyclopedia of Military Aircraft, 1914 to the Present*, rev. ed. (1990).

Angelucci, Enzo, with Peter M. Bowers. *The American Fighter* (1987).

Batchelor, John, and Chris Chant. *Fighter: From Wood and Canvas to Supersonic Flight* (1988).

Bruce-Briggs, B. *The Shield of Faith: A Chronicle of Strategic Defense from Zeppelins to Star Wars* (1988).

De Arcangelis, Mario. *Electronic Warfare: From the Battle of Tsushima to the Falklands and Lebanon Conflicts* (1985).

Dorr, Robert F., and David Donald. *Fighters of the United States Air Force: From World War I Pursuits to the F-117* (1990).

Harris, J. P., and F. N. Toase, eds. *Armoured Warfare* (1990).

Mendelsohn, Everett, et al., eds. *Science, Technology and the Military* (1988).

Moore, John, ed. *Jane's American Fighting Ships of the 20th Century* (1991).

Polmar, Norman. *The American Submarine* (1981).

Smith, Peter C. *Close Air Support: An Illustrated History, 1914 to the Present* (1990).

Swanborough, Gordon, and Peter M. Bowers. *United States Navy Aircraft Since 1911* (3rd ed., 1990).

Taylor, Michael J. H. *Jane's American Fighting Aircraft of the 20th Century* (1991).

Twentieth-Century Technology to 1945

Constant, Edward W., II. *The Origins of the Turbojet Revolution* (1980).

Forty, George. *United States Tanks of World War II in Action.* (1983).

Friedman, Norman. *Battleship: Design and Development, 1905–1945* (1978).

Gander, Terry, and Peter Chamberlain. *American Tanks of World War 2* (1977).

Hallion, Richard P. *Strike from the Sky: The History of Battlefield Air Attack, 1911–1945* (1989).

Kennett, Lee. *A History of Strategic Bombing* (1982).

Preston, Antony. *Aircraft Carriers* (1979).

Woodman, Harry. *Early Aircraft Armament: The Aeroplane and the Gun up to 1918* (1989).

Technology Since 1945

Bright, Charles D. *The Jet Makers: The Aerospace Industry from 1945 to 1972* (1978).

Campbell, Christy. *Weapons of War* (1983).

Campbell, Christy, ed. *Understanding Military Technology* (1986).

Duncan, Francis. *Rickover and the Nuclear Navy: The Discipline of Technology* (1990).

Lightbody, Andy, and Joe Poyer. *Submarines: Hunter/Killers and Boomers* (1990).

Long, Franklin A., and Judith Reppy, eds. *The Genesis of New Weapons: Decision Making for Military R & D* (1980).

Quarrie, Bruce. *Firepower* (1988).

Silverstone, Paul H. *U.S. Warships Since 1945* (1986).

Editors of Time-Life Books, *The New Face of War: The Armored Fist* (1990).

The World's Great Military Helicopters (1990).

York, Herbert F., and Allen Greb. "Military Research and Development: A Postwar History." *Bulletin of the Atomic Scientists* (January 1977).

Strategic Nuclear Weapons and ICBMs

Baucom, Donald R. *The Origins of SDI, 1944–1983* (1992).

Beard, Edmund. *Developing the ICBM: A Study in Bureaucratic Politics* (1978).

Cochran, Thomas B., et al. *Nuclear Weapons Databook,* vol. 1, *U.S. Nuclear Forces and Capabilities* (1984).

Evangelista, Matthew. *Innovation and the Arms Race: How the United States and the Soviet Union Develop New Military Technologies* (1988).

Greenwood, Ted. *Making the MIRV: A Study of Defense Decision-Making* (1988).

Hansen, Chuck. *US Nuclear Weapons: The Secret History* (1988).

Jasani, Bhupendra M., and Stockholm International Peace Research Institute. *Outer Space: Battlefield of the Future?* (1978).

Lakoff, Sanford, and Herbert F. York. *A Shield in Space? Technology, Politics, and the Strategic Defense Initiative* (1989).

Mackenzie, Donald. *Inventing Accuracy: An Historical Sociology of Nuclear Missile Guidance* (1990).

Manno, Jack. *Arming the Heavens: The Hidden Military Agenda for Space, 1945–1995* (1984).

Martin, Laurence. *The Changing Face of Nuclear Warfare* (1987).

Peebles, Curtis. *Guardians: Strategic Reconnaissance Satellites* (1987).

Polmar, Norman, ed. *Strategic Air Command: People, Aircraft, and Missiles* (1979).

Stares, Paul B. *The Militarization of Space: U.S. Policy, 1945–1984* (1985).

Tsipis, Kosta. *Arsenal: Understanding Weapons in the Nuclear Age* (1983).

York, Herbert. *The Advisors: Oppenheimer, Teller, and the Superbomb* (1989).

The Automated Battlefield

Barnaby, Frank. *The Automated Battlefield* (1986).

Berry, F. Clifton, Jr. *Gadget Warfare* (1988).

Dickson, Paul. *The Electronic Battlefield* (1976).

Doleman, Edgar C., Jr., and the Editors of Boston Publishing Company. *Tools of War* (1984).

Friedman, Richard S., et al. *Advanced Technology Warfare: A Detailed Study of the Latest Weapons and Tech-

niques for Warfare Today and into the 21st Century (1985).

Mayer, S. L., et al. *Weapons of the Gulf War* (1991).

Richardson, Doug, et al. *High-Tech Warfare* (1991).

Robinson, Julian Perry. "Qualitative Trends in Conventional Munitions: The Vietnam War and After." In *The World Military Order: The Impact of Military Technology on the Third World*, edited by Mary Kaldor and Asbjørn Eide (1979).

Editors of Time-Life Books. *Understanding Computers: The Military Frontier* (1988).

Walker, Paul F. "Precision-Guided Weapons." *Scientific American* 245 (August 1981).

Werrell, Kenneth P. *The Evolution of the Cruise Missile* (1985).

ENGINEERING AND SCIENCE

Barton C. Hacker

Engineering began as a military specialty in antiquity, when engineers devised such ingenious machines as catapults. It was not until the eighteenth century that some in England began to call themselves civil, rather than military, engineers, and American engineers followed suit in the nineteenth century, forming their first professional civil engineering society in 1852. Through much of the nineteenth century, however, military engineers remained in the forefront of American engineering practice, promoting engineering education, building the new nation's infrastructure, exploring the country, fostering the growth of science, and helping create modern industrial management.

By the twentieth century, however, military engineering had lost much of its distinctiveness, instead taking its place as one of the lesser branches of modern engineering. The U.S. Army Corps of Engineers acquired a mainly civilian coloration as dam builder and navigation improver. Engineers within the army simply became the technical branch that constructed and destroyed fixed works.

At the same time military engineering was losing its distinct status, engineering as a whole burgeoned. During the nineteenth century, civil engineering diversified, specialized, and professionalized. Mechanical engineers formed their own professional society in 1880, electrical engi-

neers in 1884. Subdivision became a normal event, exemplified by the founding of the Society of Automotive Engineers in 1905 and the American Nuclear Society in 1954. Engineering education shifted from shop floor to classroom, engineering practice from cut-and-try to analysis and computation. By the late nineteenth and early twentieth centuries, engineering had acquired the patina of science, as well as a measure of control over innovation and production.

These refinements, even in embryo, soon commended themselves to military planners threatened by too-rapid technological change. In the twentieth century, and especially since 1950 in the United States, military demands, backed by huge defense budgets, restored much of engineering to the military fold, in practice if not in name. Contracts and specifications displaced uniforms and commands as the effective methods of exerting control.

Initially, engineering was more tightly tied to military institutions than was science, although the dream (or nightmare) of science-based breakthroughs in weaponry has a long history. The relationship between the military and science grew steadily closer as science demonstrated its military utility, beginning perhaps with eighteenth-century advances in ballistics. Its utility grew even more pronounced during the nineteenth century. Although most technological innovation still depended chiefly on trial and error, applied science and systematic innovation began to achieve impressive results.

Indeed, between the late nineteenth century and the mid-twentieth the balance was reversed. Trial and error persisted, of course, but systematic approaches across the whole range of science could produce weapons to order. Just as engineering was becoming more systematic and mathematical, science was tending toward greater practicality. Differences between applied science and scientific engineering became ever less distinct. In the late twentieth century, science spreads its mantle not only across military technology and much engineering but over virtually every area of military enterprise.

Activities as diverse as personnel management and strategic planning have joined technology as apparently subject to the rule of science. Engineering has, at the same time, expanded its domain to include the manipulation of people and social groups, as well as materials and processes. Although careful usage now requires distinguishing among science, technology, and engineering, these distinctions were rarely applicable in the past. In certain respects, however, older usages survive.

Science often serves as a convenient blanket term for a whole range of studies and practices oriented toward understanding and acting upon the world. This is especially true if practitioners stress systematic, particularly mathematical, approaches. So-called science policy studies, for example, explicitly include technology policy. Moreover, the predominantly military focus of many such studies further blurs distinctions. Military usage, in turn, consistently lumps scientific research with engineering development and product testing in a single enterprise. By the last half of the twentieth century, science as well as engineering had taken on a distinct military cast.

TOWARD INDUSTRIALIZATION

The industrial revolution and the American Revolution were coeval. Despite their break with England, the former colonies retained the language and culture of their mother country. Continuing immigration from the British Isles augmented the new republic's access to the birthplace of industrialism, continuing an already venerable American pattern. Throughout the colonial period, the European heritage loomed large, but transplanted institutions rarely flourished unchanged. American environments consistently, if not uniformly, altered knowledge and practice carried from the Old World. American engineering, scientific, and military institutions drew on European sources but always to some lesser or greater degree adjusted them to New World needs.

Engineering in the United States formally began with the founding of the United States Military Academy at West Point, New York, in 1802. The new school focused on training engineers, but military technical training proved to have many uses, outside the army as well as within. West Point graduates helped found civil engineering in the United States, both as builders and as teachers. Exploring and mapping westward across the continent during the first half of the nineteenth century, they provided the indispensable raw materials for building American science. Military engineers also filled key managerial roles in civil and military enterprises, to which railroad corporations owed a debt as great as that owed the government arsenals that pioneered interchangeable parts manufacturing. By the mid-nineteenth century, the traffic between Europe and the United States was ceasing to be one way.

Art of War versus Military Science. Superior ships and guns sustained pre-nineteenth century European hegemony, which only in the New World extended much beyond the reach of shipborne artillery. Elsewhere, Western armies had still to attain any significant edge over their opponents, but the eighteenth century marked the culmination of a long cycle in military history. Professionalizing European armies achieved a workable tactical balance within the technological confines of flintlock musket and bayonet, smoothbore artillery, and depot-oriented logistics.

the speedy development of warlike inventions and improved weapons or their prompt production in quantity. Although that ability scarcely emerged before World War I and did not become fully realized until World War II, its prospect could be glimpsed even during the course of transition.

Steam Ashore and Afloat. Steam-powered transport had far-reaching consequences for U.S. development during the first half of the nineteenth century. Railroads offered a degree of flexibility that waterways could never match, and the prewar changes were revolutionary. In 1830 the Baltimore and Ohio Railroad put thirteen miles of track into service. Competing and expanding lines laid more than nine thousand miles of track in the next two decades, mostly in the Northeast. Between 1850 and 1860, another twenty-two thousand miles of track extended the rail net to the South and West, although the Northeast retained the densest network. When the Civil War began, more than thirty-one thousand miles of track spanned the country east of the Mississippi.

Transatlantic and coastal steam-powered vessels were almost commonplace by the 1860s. Potentially, steam made the resources of Europe more readily available to both sides. Practically, it made feasible the federal blockade of the three-thousand-mile Confederate coastline. Steamers could patrol waters off southern ports more closely and more regularly than sailing ships. The price was frequent recoaling. Federal forces seized bases on the Confederacy's coast as much to maintain their blockade as to deny their use to the enemy. Armorclad warships proved invaluable in these operations. The South also relied on armorclads for defense. Although the Confederacy began without ships, it benefited from a solid cadre of Annapolis-trained officers. Unfortunately, it also lacked manufacturing facilities. Inadequate production of armor plate and marine engines hampered naval defense in the South throughout the war.

Unsolved design problems largely precluded the use of oceangoing ironclads by either side. Notoriously unseaworthy, ironclads remained restricted to protected coastal waters. Such shortcomings mattered little on western rivers, where armored gunboats played a key role in the Union's conquest of the Mississippi. Steamboats had multiplied on inland waters before the war, having solved some of the worst problems of river navigation, especially in the West. Fitted with iron plate and guns, they became valuable adjuncts to army operations.

Toward Total War. Overenthusiastic from an economic viewpoint, prewar railroad building acquired strategic significance with the outbreak of war. Understanding fully what that meant, however, took time. Unlike at least some Europeans, Americans had given little if any thought to rail's military implications. In brief, railroads allowed contending states to marshal their resources swiftly. Large bodies of troops could quickly be shifted to where they were wanted. Perhaps more important, steam-powered logistics allowed the maintenance of much larger armies than would otherwise have been feasible. Speed of troop movement and of supply emerged as the essence of rail's military utility. A defeated army falling back on its rail-heads might soon be repaired, its casualties replaced, and its losses made good. Reinforced and reequipped armies could return to fight again, as long as men and material were available. Rapidly restored armies robbed battle of its potential for prompt decision.

Dramatically increased speed of movement came at the cost of freedom of movement. Civil War armies became more and more closely tied to their railroad supply lines, the attack and defense of which came increasingly to dominate strategy. Building and wrecking rail lines became a major military function, but railroad operation remained almost exclusively a profit-making venture in private hands. It was not an easy relationship. Railroad managers professing concern for their shareholders and army officers demanding logistic support were often at loggerheads. Although the North succeeded better than the South in imposing a degree of order, the South's real problems lay elsewhere. In this as in so much else, material shortages ham-

Fortified cities almost everywhere became central to strategic planning and military engineering a crucial aspect of military organization. Siegecraft and field maneuvers alike took on a geometrical precision that eighteenth-century thinkers were wont to perceive as scientific. They talked less of the "art of war," and more of "military art and science" or simply "military science," a usage that became normal in the nineteenth century. When military schools began to appear in the mid-eighteenth century, they stressed scientific-technical training and became the model for nonmilitary schools of science and engineering.

Enlightenment military institutions underwent a sea change in the passage to America. Although the formal evolutions of British and French forces on the Plains of Abraham in 1759 testified to the persistence of well-tried forms, close-order drill and geometric precision could seldom be effectively maintained in the wilderness. Such circumstances produced a looser, more independent style that profoundly affected the conduct of war in America.

As the classic sieges of Louisbourg in Canada by British and colonial forces in 1745 and 1758 amply demonstrated, military engineering found a home in the New World. The attack and defense of fortifications did not characterize warfare only among Europeans and colonists; palisaded villages were a feature of native American life, as well. British and colonial military engineers surveyed and built roads throughout the colonies, beginning the tradition that characterized the creation of the new nation's transportation network after independence.

The American Revolution. Gunmaking along traditional lines flourished in the colonies, and colonial naval stores became a major resource of British seapower. Interactions of military and naval engineering with other preindustrial American institutions, even as limited as they were, had virtually no counterpart in science and medicine. Colonial science foreshadowed the observational preoccupations that became so marked a feature of nineteenth-century American science. It also remained distinctly provincial, if not backward, however, and had no discernible effect on military institutions.

Much the same was true of medicine, in the eighteenth century still much more art and craft than science. Military surgeons and nurses might accompany larger expeditions, but they hardly affected operations. Like all early modern armies, both British and American forces in the revolutionary war relied on camp followers as nurses. Medical services also remained little changed from earlier practices. Although the Continental army acquired a medical department, the long-standing pattern of ten deaths from disease for every death in battle showed no signs of abating.

British control of the seas dictated the shape of the American war for independence. American ships could only harass, not challenge, the enemy fleet. Ultimately, logistics proved to be the Achilles heel of the British army in America. French intervention achieved decisive results by temporarily isolating British land forces from their support. Logistics problems had earlier almost undone the American war effort. The largely agricultural colonies enjoyed ample food resources and succeeded reasonably well in building what military industry they needed almost from scratch. Distributing supplies, not finding them, was the crux of the matter for the patriots. Transportation and fortification remained constant problems for George Washington's armies, aggravated by a persistent lack of engineers.

The Significance of West Point. Scarcely had the United States achieved independence when Washington urged the establishment of a military academy, citing the want of engineers and artillerists that had plagued his army during the war. Although other motives played a part, the founding of the United States Military Academy owed much to such concerns. The same legislation that created West Point, the Act of 16 March 1802, also founded the Corps of Engineers, which would direct the new academy. Following the pattern of the European military schools founded during the preceding half-century, West Point stressed engineering and technical training.

Important as such skills might be for the army, they mattered even more for a young nation so notably lacking in them. Graduates of West Point, whether or not they remained in uniform, fanned out across the countryside to construct and maintain America's burgeoning transportation network. They surveyed roads, built forts, constructed canals, threw bridges across streams, dredged harbors, and cleared rivers. Sometimes they did the work themselves, but often they supervised others and always trained new hands, most of whom were not themselves military.

In the early nineteenth century, such on-the-job training was the way most engineers learned their trade, but West Pointers also moved into formal education as teachers of science and engineering and even as founders of engineering schools. American civil engineering owed a great deal to West Point and to military engineering. The establishment of the United States Naval Academy at Annapolis, Maryland, in 1845 did much the same for mechanical engineering as West Point had done for civil engineering.

Engineers trained at West Point took leading roles in the early years of railroad building. Perhaps more important, the army offered models of large-scale organization and techniques for coordinating large workforces. West Pointers adapted military methods to the new demands of railroad management. As the first large-scale business enterprises in the United States, the railroads in turn shaped the development of corporate organization throughout the nineteenth century. Management by staff and line, a key feature of the rising corporation, had self-evident military roots.

Military-trained engineers also came to make up a significant share of mid-level managers. Furthermore, they instructed their civilian counterparts in the new methods. Like civil engineers, potential corporate managers benefited from the fruits of military education, whether in on-the-job training in engineering projects or in more formal schooling in colleges of engineering.

Military and Naval Exploration. During the early nineteenth century, American science remained more strongly oriented toward observation than toward experimentation. The vast and little-known continent stretching west reinforced that bent. Crossing the next hill always seemed to promise a strange plant or animal, some exotic tribe, an unexpected lay of the land. A large if not entirely constant stream of specimens and notes, drawings and photographs, maps and descriptions from western exploration promoted vigorous American contributions to such primarily observational fields as astronomy, natural history, the earth sciences, and anthropology.

Even when explicitly designated scientific, however, western expeditions served other purposes as well. Identifying potential resources for exploitation was an obvious end, as was the quest for information of military value. Virtually every scientific expedition westward during the early and middle nineteenth century was also a military reconnaissance. Military organization and discipline proved invaluable in exploring a little-known and sometimes hostile land, as did the skills of the engineer. Mapmaking and building forts along the way were normal activities.

The pattern was set when President Thomas Jefferson in 1803 selected army Captain Meriwether Lewis to explore the vast new territory of Louisiana purchased from France. Lewis invited army veteran William Clark to share command of an expedition of forty people that took just under two and a half years to cross the continent from St. Louis to the mouth of the Columbia River and return. Publishing the results consumed far more time than obtaining them. During the next three decades, other military-scientific expeditions penetrated western lands, surveying, mapping, and collecting data.

Prominent among the military explorers were members of the Corps of Engineers Topographical Bureau, established during the War of 1812. Activity accelerated toward mid-century, especially after 1838, when the bureau became a corps in its own right—the Corps of Topo-

graphical Engineers—and scientists assumed larger roles in planning and staffing western expeditions. The effort was usually justified in such practical economic terms as surveying routes for a transcontinental railroad, but actual projects rarely had so narrow a focus.

The middle of the century also saw the U.S. Navy assume a major role in exploration. Although motives again were mixed, science played a larger part in the naval enterprise, and the geographical spread was far greater, ranging from the Arctic to the Antarctic, from the New World to the Old World. The U.S. Naval Observatory in Washington, founded in 1842, also became a center of research in oceanography under Lieutenant Matthew Fontaine Maury from 1844 to 1861.

West Point graduate Alexander Dallas Bache headed the Coast Survey, which was authorized in 1807 and which, besides its titular function, pioneered studies of geodesy and hydrography. Although a civilian agency, the survey made extensive use of naval officers. Benefits flowed both ways. The survey enjoyed a pool of able men, and officers gained valuable experience and knowledge that the small active navy of those years could not have provided. A disproportionately large number of senior naval officers in the Civil War had honed their seafaring skills in the antebellum Coast Survey.

Reciprocity of such direct bearing, however, was not the normal outcome of the military-scientific partnership in early nineteenth century America. The association probably benefited American science far more than it did either the army or navy. Scientists busy collecting, cataloging, and describing had as yet little to offer the armed forces. Much the same was true of engineering. Military engineers fostered engineering education, helped build the nation's infrastructure, introduced major features of large-scale management, and pioneered mass production, all of immense value to economic growth. Reciprocal benefits of any direct nature scarcely existed.

Indirect effects, however, proved enormously significant when the southern states se-

ceded from the Union. Economically, politically, and socially, the nation that divided in 1861 was very different from the Republic formed in 1789 or even the one that emerged from war in 1815. Such changes in part reflected the interactions of military institutions with American society during the preceding six decades, and they strongly influenced the nature and course of the war.

THE TRANSITION TO INDUSTRIAL WAR

The American Civil War straddled two ages. It was both the last great preindustrial war and the first major war of the industrial age. On the eve of war, the United States was not yet an industrial nation, but the process of industrialization was well under way. A key factor was steam power applied to produce and transport goods. Military engineers had once again assumed a prominent role. West Point provided many of the railroad builders, and Annapolis later began to bolster the ranks of steam engineers. Industrial capacity attained new levels of military significance as transportation improved, but in this, as in many other respects, the Civil War was distinctly transitional, and that fact strongly affected its conduct.

Before the nineteenth century, the complex interrelationship between war, science, technology, and industry so characteristic of the modern age scarcely existed. The French Revolution and the Napoleonic wars had seen the triumph of mass armies, but technologically they belonged to the past, not the future. The American Civil War occurred in the midst of far-reaching changes. Industrialization had only just begun.

In time the progressive and rapid improvement of old weapons, as well as the introduction of new ones, would become core factors in military planning and operations, but that took decades. Engineering and industry had yet to attain the scope and mastery that would allow

pered the Confederate war effort—too little track, not enough rolling stock, and insufficient means to produce more.

Militarily, railroads mattered chiefly to the final element in logistics—distribution. Equally important, although hardly clear at first to planners on either side, was production. Here, too, steam power had already begun to work massive changes in manufacturing organization before the war. In due course the patent importance of rails led eyes back to the supplies, material, and equipment they carried forward to the fighting troops. Eventually, this meant that war enlarged its scope to include not only the armies, but the resources and people that supported and sustained them. General William T. Sherman's trail of destruction through Georgia and General Philip H. Sheridan's devastation of the Shenandoah Valley prefigured a new kind of war. In this, however, as in many other ways, the Civil War was distinctly transitional— a surprisingly active intersectional trade, for instance, flourished throughout the war.

Technology, Science, and Medicine. The Civil War in America was the first full-scale war shaped in major ways by the tools and weapons of the industrial revolution. Telegraph and railroad greatly increased the pace at which events moved and combined with other technical changes to vastly extend the scope and deadliness of battle, at the same time reducing its decisiveness. New weapons multiplied the ranges at which death could be dealt, but other factors multiplied the numbers who might be killed. Agricultural mechanization permitted larger armies to be fed; industrial growth, to be armed and supplied; steam-powered transport, to be deployed and sustained.

Science played little part in these changes. Although the National Academy of Sciences was created by Congress during the war (1863), at least partly as a source of advice on war-related matters, it achieved nothing of import; many years elapsed before it became a major actor in American science. In contrast to more recent experience, the Civil War did more to disrupt than to advance science. Although not

fully evident at the time, the long-standing military support of science through exploration was one of the casualties of the war. West Point ceased being exclusively an engineering school, the Corps of Topographical Engineers expired in 1863, and the postwar Corps of Engineers itself became increasingly an executor of civil engineering projects conceived elsewhere.

Ingenuity and imagination, rather than science, marked the efforts of both sides to devise and apply new weapons and techniques. Civil War firsts—first used or first used extensively— covered a broad range: the introduction of mass production in some industries, notably clothing, and of new techniques of food preservation; the supplying and moving of mass armies by railroad and steamboat; the use of photography, telegraphy, various signal devices using flags and lamps, and aerial observation from fixed balloons; the general use of rifled small arms and the appearance of breech-loading and magazine arms, as well as early machine-gun systems; the normal disappearance of troops behind breastworks and into trenches, along with the use of wire entanglements and trench mortars; the use of land and marine mines, torpedo boats, and submarines; and the use of steam-powered armored warships. The production of swords, lances, and pikes again attests to the transitional nature of the American Civil War.

Medical care reflected another kind of transition. Again, a number of firsts may be cited, notably the use of anesthesia in front-line surgery, the establishment of an ambulance service, and the use of hospital trains. The importance of sanitation and camp hygiene was widely respected, if not always fully implemented, and became a special focus of the United States Sanitary Commission, a civilian forerunner of the Red Cross that was established in 1861 and advised and assisted the Union armies. For all that, the Civil War ended just before medicine decisively crossed the line to science; general acceptance of microorganisms as the cause of disease and thus recognition of the value of antisepsis occurred in the 1870s. Improved sanitation and medical care nevertheless sharply altered the ratio of battle-caused to disease-caused deaths. As recently as the Mexican War (1846–1848), that ratio was still 1 to 10, the same as had prevailed in the American Revolution. In the Civil War, Union armies achieved a ratio no worse than 1 to 2, and even Confederate armies under much less favorable conditions managed 1 to 3.

Rifles and Trenches. Proliferating inventions were not chiefly what mattered in the Civil War. Many were impractical, others not widely used. Technological innovation counts only to the extent that it places weapons in the hands of troops. It is only when a new device or technique is put into widespread use that its impact is felt. Steam-powered transport was one such innovation that strongly affected the course of the Civil War. Only one other Civil War first exerted an equally profound effect, although on tactics more than on strategy—rifled firearms carried by both sides.

When the Civil War began, the U.S. Army's standard arm was the Model 1855 rifle musket. Its adoption came three decades after the Springfield Armory in Massachusetts had begun its pioneering development of the uniformity system. The Confederate seizure of the Harpers Ferry Armory in West Virginia left Springfield as the only government arsenal as the war began. Its annual capacity by then stood at roughly 12,000 arms. Substantial purchases abroad marked the opening of the war, and private contracts later augmented domestic arms manufacture, but Springfield remained the Union's major source of rifled muskets. By 1865, in fact, it had become the world's largest arms factory, with an annual capacity of 300,000. The Confederacy of necessity relied more on foreign supply but managed to build a creditable arms industry almost from nothing, aided by the machinery seized at Harpers Ferry. Annual production of small arms at southern armories reached 28,000 in mid-1863, augmented by 7,000 arms from private sources.

By extending severalfold the zone of fire through which attackers must pass, rifled muskets swung the tactical balance toward defense. Smoothbore artillery with an effective range of four hundred yards far outranged smoothbore muskets. On Napoleonic battlefields massed artillery allowed attackers to decimate a defending force, clearing the way for a decisive bayonet assault. Rifled small arms reversed the advantage in the early 1860s. During the Civil War, rifled artillery failed to pick up the slack; metallurgical practice could not yet produce ordnance strong enough to withstand the pressure of a fully contained explosion, except in relatively small-caliber guns. Such guns lacked killing power, leaving rifled small arms master of the field. Defenders entrenched or sheltered behind breastworks could wreak havoc on attackers crossing open ground.

Under the new circumstances, frontal assault could succeed only at terrible cost and bayonets hardly mattered, but Civil War commanders persisted in ordering mass assaults, with usually disastrous results. Given the chance, soldiers quickly learned to dig, the spade becoming little less important than the rifle. Before it ended, the Civil War had become an engineer's war. Field fortifications, often neglected early in the war, soon became common. Troops began disappearing into the ground or behind breastworks at even brief pauses. By the final year, elaborate trench systems converted field operations into siege warfare.

FROM OUTPOST TO EMPIRE

During the late nineteenth century, the U.S. armed forces became chiefly observers of major changes in military technology and organization taking place in Europe. Both army and navy reverted to prewar levels and tasks within a few years of the close of the Civil War. Policing the frontier and patrolling distant stations again became their main functions. Military-scientific cooperation in exploration was revived during the 1870s and 1880s, although on a much smaller scale than before. The Weather Service, the Geological Survey, the Coast Survey, even the Naval Observatory, which had for varying lengths of time worked under military auspices, all became purely civilian enterprises. The

Corps of Engineers remained an army operation but grew increasingly civilianized.

In general, the close prewar links between military and scientific enterprise faded as each sought its own path toward professionalization. Professionalizing groups sought to make special schooling a prerequisite for professional entry, bureaucratic office, or masculine privilege. Armed forces, however, were not merely one more instance of a widespread nineteenth-century phenomenon. Military institutions regularly pioneered the techniques of discipline, order, and privilege that other social institutions adopted.

At one level, support for a distinctive military science reflected concerns about institutional survival during a time of flux in technique and organization. More generally, however, it showed how institutions might respond to rapid social change and became a model of such response, often implicit but sometimes overt, as in engineering. Scientific management, medical science, social science, political science, and a host of other nineteenth-century coinages, even science proper, all testify to the widely perceived value of coping with change by turning lore into systematic knowledge.

By the turn of the century, these trends had begun to produce larger consequences. During the 1880s and 1890s, the U.S. Navy began rebuilding itself as a modern sea force. Naval revival fostered economic growth, particularly in steel and related industries, and drew heavily on the growing ability of scientifically oriented engineering to produce specified armor and equipment to order. It also contributed to the rise of navalism based on an exciting new theory of sea power. The nation's imperial venture opened auspiciously with the successful naval war against Spain (1898). Sustained in part by the growing scientific competence of American medicine, U.S. forces proved capable of fighting and building in the tropics. The Panama Canal, which opened on 15 August 1914, symbolized the country's new status in the world.

Professional Officers and Scientists. By the late nineteenth century, formal schooling

had become a normal part of an officer's career, and the concept of military science had become commonplace. The link was no accident. Military science codified the underlying principles of war, which could thus more easily be taught in the classroom. It abstracted and systematized a body of esoteric knowledge suited to indoctrinating the nineteenth century's growing numbers of nontraditional candidates for officer status.

Like other professionalizing fields, notably engineering, the armed forces of the United States and Europe faced an influx of middle-class men seeking careers. Presumably lacking the genetic predisposition of their aristocratic comrades, they needed concrete and readily reproducible examples—schematic maps, war games, and rules. The so-called principles of war, for example, were a nineteenth-century innovation. Few of these teaching aids were entirely new, but their use burgeoned during the late nineteenth century and became a staple of the twentieth.

Paradoxically, military education also grew more complex and sophisticated as some of its subjects became oversimplified and standardized. The reoriented curricula of older schools in Europe and in the United States added courses in strategy and policy to the familiar tactics and engineering. At new military schools founded for that very purpose, postgraduate training became available and later was a required prelude to higher command.

The School of Application for Cavalry and Infantry, founded at Fort Leavenworth, Kansas, in 1881, marked the U.S. Army's first venture into this area; the Naval War College was established three years later in Providence, Rhode Island. Strategic and other higher military studies in the United States proliferated in the context of turn-of-the-century reform movements that affected military as well as civil society. In the twentieth century, such studies became a central feature of advanced military education. All such courses and programs pointed toward professionalization, officers educated to wield sanctioned violence responsibly.

Profound and rapid social change strongly

colored, if it did not cause, professionalization, whether of the armed forces or other corporate groups during the nineteenth century. Engineering shifted from practical training on building sites or shop floors toward increased emphasis on formal college education as a prerequisite to professional certification. Science likewise expanded its educational demands, reflected especially in the late nineteenth-century innovation of graduate programs and doctoral degrees and in the burgeoning number of professional societies. Medicine, bolstered by the success of the bacteriological revolution, emerged from a host of competing creeds to become the preeminent health profession, a claim reinforced by turn-of-the-century reforms in medical education.

Radical change justified concomitant claims to special expertise. Elaborating esoteric bodies of knowledge and technique then allowed practitioners to limit access to the field. Codified and abstracted knowledge channeled the entry of properly trained and indoctrinated candidates. During the nineteenth century, many fields shifted from apprentice and other on-the-job methods of training new members toward the use of schools or other more formal means of transmitting and perpetuating professional culture. Special knowledge, unique skill, and restricted numbers, however, counted only if a group could claim to serve higher social purposes. Promoting that claim was the key to attaining professional status. Only when society accepted professional training and competence as socially needed and wanted could the newly defined corporate group claim special social privilege, which was, of course, the whole point.

Militarized Industry. Industrialization itself owed no small debt to military interests. A career army officer and arsenal manager, Captain Henry Metcalfe, wrote the first book on factory management published in the United States. He addressed his 1885 work, an acknowledged classic of management, less to fellow officers than to corporate managers. The U.S. Navy's decision to use industrial contractors to supply armor and ordnance for its new fleet in the late nineteenth century, rather than rely on government facilities, may well mark the beginning of what has more recently been termed the military-industrial complex. From the early nineteenth century uniformity system to the late twentieth century, U.S. Air Force sponsorship of automated machine tool development, key aspects of industrial technology have emerged from military settings.

Military example may have been even more important in furthering industrialization. Discipline was the key, argued Max Weber in his treatise *Economy and Society*, first published in 1923, with military practice as its inspiration. Lewis Mumford agreed, noting in his 1934 commentary *Technics and Civilization* that military regimentation inspired the factory system and created the conditions for its implementation. Entrepreneurs and captains of industry found much to admire, and to adopt, in the regimentation and redivision of labor imposed on modernizing armies.

The sociologist Jacques van Doorn, in his 1975 essay "The Genesis of Military and Industrial Organization," has sought to link the military to the industrial revolution through the motives shared by a major architect of each. Dutch military leader Maurice of Nassau became a key figure in the early modern European military revolution when he restored drill to armies in the late sixteenth century. Efficiency engineer Frederick W. Taylor reshaped American, and eventually worldwide, industrialism when he devised scientific management in the late nineteenth and early twentieth centuries. Parallels between Maurice and Taylor were not accidental. They faced the same problem: creating a "goal-attainment organization" from a mass of socially isolated, ill-trained, and poorly motivated proletarians. Sharing a mechanistic image of human behavior, they found their common answer in regimented action. For Taylor, at least, it was a two-way street. Military models influenced his reforms and scientific management, and Taylorism, as it has often been termed, found a receptive military audience.

Regimented Schools. Similar patterns marked schools in the United States. Military concerns and money, sometimes direct, sometimes funneled through corporate intermediaries, affected higher education in many ways. Military training on campus dated to the Morrill Act of 1862, although it became institutionalized in the form of the Reserve Officer Training Corps (ROTC) only in 1916. Engineers figured prominently among supporters of this contested institution. American universities, like much of American society, for the most part welcomed such values. After he became the first head of the University of Illinois in 1867, John M. Gregory regularly cited the value of military order and drill in higher education, because it promoted discipline, built character, and generally improved the tone of the campus.

Youthful Americans would also come to enjoy such virtues, which were emphasized in secondary and even primary schools and which were later bolstered by Junior ROTC and vocational education. To many Americans, they seemed both worthwhile and desirable. Discipline derived from military training in public schools was alleged to instruct pupils in civil government and respect for law. Such lessons held no less value for adults. Militarism could be one side of the coin, but civic virtue and patriotism might be the other. In many respects, a similar pattern prevailed in Great Britain and was even more widespread on the European continent. Great as the influence of such values may have been, however, they appear to have had little direct impact on science and engineering in the universities, at least before World War I.

Commanding the Sea. Navalism, like militarism, had ambiguous meaning. Because it applied to a relatively more restricted field, however, its late nineteenth-century impact may have been all the greater. Navalism became a vital factor in international relations for a number of reasons. One was certainly the publication of Alfred Thayer Mahan's treatise *The Influence of Sea Power Upon History, 1660–1783* in

1890. The book was the fruit of his course of lectures in naval history at the recently founded Naval War College. Mahan offered a neat package of naval strength, commerce, colonies, and power that resonated in the United States and abroad.

The United States had already embarked on an ambitious naval program. Mahan offered an ideology for such endeavors, and the Royal Navy soon provided a potent symbol with the 1906 launching of HMS *Dreadnought*. The naval armaments race and the scramble for colonies intensified. Enormously fast and heavily armed, battleships and battle cruisers represented the epitome of military might as the twentieth century opened. The design was promptly emulated and improved throughout the industrialized world.

U.S. industry had never been loath to profit from military contracts. Opportunities to do so before the late nineteenth century, however, were largely limited to times of war. During peacetime the armed forces preferred to rely on their own arsenals and shipyards, but that began changing toward the end of the nineteenth century, when the U.S. Navy forged an alliance with the steel industry to promote modernization.

Rapidly developing naval technology since mid-century presented baffling problems to every navy. Screw-propelled steamships wrapped in increasingly thicker armor and mounting bigger guns for the first time provided a really large and lucrative market for a peacetime industry, provided Congress authorized a large enough shipbuilding program. The navy got its first steel ship in 1884, and its battleship program was approved in 1890. Imperial adventure soon followed.

From the viewpoint of science and engineering, what U.S. ambassador to England John Hay in 1898 called "a splendid little war" offered nothing remarkable. The Spanish-American War was largely decided at sea, where the new U.S. steam and steel navy won quick and overwhelming victories. Fighting on land against a largely unenthusiastic, if not demoralized foe, the army also won easy victories, despite appalling organizational and logistic problems.

Medicine and Empire. Medically the Spanish-American War was a near-disaster. Overall, the ratio of deaths from disease to battle deaths reached, by some reckonings, 7 to 1, which may be attributed in part to the war's brevity. Inexperienced soldiers—the regular army's strength in 1898 was less than thirty thousand, although a quarter of a million men served in the war—have always tended to have high disease rates until they learn better camp hygiene and sanitation. The war was too short to show any benefits from improvement.

Typhoid was the main killer during the Spanish-American War. An army medical research board convened after the war asked why. Walter Reed and his colleagues concluded that the disease was spread mainly by flies, by contact between persons, and by human carriers. Sanitary measures offered the best hope of controlling the disease at that point, but a decade's research produced an even better answer—vaccination with killed bacilli, which largely eliminated the threat of typhoid. Successful tests in 1909 resulted in vaccination becoming compulsory for the entire U.S. Army in 1911.

The Spanish-American War also confronted the army with tropical diseases for which it was ill-prepared. After the war, the army's responsibility for administering the new dependencies—and, in the Philippines, for suppressing insurrection—brought increased urgency to the drive to solve the puzzles of tropical disease. Army medical research boards again provided answers. The best-known was Reed's Yellow Fever Commission in Cuba, which by early 1901 had proved the disease's cause to be a mosquito-borne virus. British research in the 1890s had shown that mosquitos also transmitted malaria-causing microorganisms.

These findings did not reflect any profound breakthrough in basic knowledge; much remained to be learned about the etiology of yellow fever and malaria. What the U.S. Army Medical Department accomplished remains nonetheless important. The army acquired practical means of coping with the two main tropical diseases and a number of lesser ones as well. Antimosquito measures quickly became the basis for controlling and preventing malaria and yellow fever. Acting on the Reed commission findings, William Crawford Gorgas succeeded in reducing malaria and eliminating yellow fever in Havana by the end of 1901.

Major Gorgas then turned to a survey of the proposed site in Panama for a canal linking the Atlantic and the Pacific. Endemic malaria and yellow fever jeopardized that plan. Appointed chief sanitary officer of the Panama Canal Zone when the Corps of Engineers began work in 1904, Gorgas again succeeded; in two years malaria had been sharply reduced and yellow fever eradicated in the zone. His achievement freed the army engineers to concentrate on the task at hand, which they did to magnificent effect. Construction of the canal required ten years to complete, but the first ship passed through the Panama Canal in August 1914. It was perhaps fittingly ironic that world acclaim for this triumph of civil engineering aided by science was overshadowed by the outbreak of war in Europe earlier that month.

THE CATASTROPHE OF INDUSTRIAL WAR

World War I (1914–1918) confirmed trends clearly evident in retrospect since the mid-nineteenth century. Military institutions had changed dramatically. Repeating rifles, smokeless powder, quick-firing long-range field artillery, and machine guns multiplied firepower and extended the killing zone. Doffing gaudy color in favor of field gray or khaki, soldiers left firing lines and maneuver for ground cover and trenches. Runners began giving way to telegraph and wireless, muscle to steam and petrol. Staffs burgeoned to direct vast armies as nations prepared to put millions of men under arms. With the new giving way to the newer more quickly, almost every aspect of military life was altered, if not transformed. Equally dizzying changes marked naval technology. So rapid did the pace of change become toward the end of the nineteenth century that the ships of one decade seemed almost worthless in the next.

Military and naval novelties figured prominently, for example, in popular turn-of-the-century compendia on the progress of invention. Judging their likely impact surpassed most contemporary imaginations, however, military and civilian alike. Indeed, many have blamed the catastrophe of World War I on European armies blind to the meaning of swiftly changing technology, which may be unfair. Innovations in military technology still came mostly from nonmilitary sources, which made the flood of new or improved arms hard to control or direct. Military planners did not so much ignore problems as misjudge their magnitude. Whatever the reasons, the result was catastrophe almost beyond comprehension.

Sources of Victory. Ultimately, the war was decided by supply. The great battleships that had captured so many minds and consumed so much money before the war rarely ventured to sea, confined by fear of mines and torpedoes. The most significant naval action of the war involved submarine attacks on shipping. Despite their relatively modest capabilities by later standards, German submarines threatened on more than one occasion to deprive Great Britain of its maritime commerce and to cut its economic lifeline, especially imported food supplies. Antisubmarine tactics and the convoy system defeated the threat, but it was a close call.

Although more self-sufficient than Great Britain, Germany had to import certain crucial raw materials, as well as significant amounts of foodstuffs. It was thus a country vulnerable to blockade. Merely by existing, the Royal Navy maintained command of the sea. Blockaded and bereft of key imports, Germany improvised, sometimes brilliantly. The creation of an artificial nitrate industry to replace lost overseas sources was one of the most remarkable scientific achievements of the war, but food could not be improvised.

Throughout the war, Germany tended to re-tain an edge in tactics and operations, the Allies in management and logistics. British war production soared; perhaps more surprisingly, so did French production, despite the German occupation of France's major coal and iron region. The collapse of Russia in 1917 and its withdrawal from the war held the long-term promise of giving Germany a new breadbasket. Of more immediate importance, it augmented Germany's strong suit by freeing scores of divisions for redeployment to the western front. In spring 1918 an enlarged German army using novel infantry and artillery tactics came close to victory. Its failure owed more than a little to the intervention of fresh U.S. troops in large numbers, many of them transported to Europe in British ships and most of them equipped from Allied, especially French, factories and depots.

Americans had observed events in Europe with mixed feelings. Ambivalent though they may have been about whether to intervene, there was nothing reluctant about implementing the decision, once made. Much of the pre-1917 debate on mobilization had centered on manpower, and in the final analysis manpower was the decisive American contribution. From April 1917, when the United States declared war on Germany, until the November 1918 armistice, the U.S. Army grew from two hundred thousand to 3.5 million men, 2 million of whom reached France.

Ambitious plans to arm and equip the American Expeditionary Forces from U.S. sources proved less successful. Economic mobilization for World War I demanded an effort far beyond anything ever before attempted in the United States. It began under the auspices of the Council of National Defense, established by statute in August 1916 to coordinate industry and resources; coordination became direction as the council mutated into the War Industries Board, which came to control large parts of the economy. Although better organized than such efforts in past American wars, however, mobilization took too much time. American industry was still gearing up when the war ended, and U.S. forces fought chiefly with French ordnance and flew French and British aircraft.

Mobilizing American Science. Mobilizing science for the war effort enjoyed equally modest success. As early as 1915 the navy created a Naval Consulting Board to screen proffered inventions for value and practicality. All its members were working engineers and inventors, including Thomas Alva Edison, the chairman. Individual inventors, however, proved to have no better grasp of the scientific-technical needs of modern warfare than did most officers; vanishingly few of the suggested ideas even merited discussion.

The National Advisory Committee for Aeronautics (NACA) built on a more solid base but still failed to contribute much to the war effort. Established by Congress in 1915, NACA served a larger purpose than its name implied. In addition to advising on aeronautical policy, NACA also directed an aeronautical engineering research laboratory. The Langley Aeronautical Laboratory descended from turn-of-the-century experimental work conducted at the Smithsonian Institution in Washington, D.C. Although already a going concern on a small scale at the Smithsonian, the laboratory needed room to expand. A move to Langley, Virginia, and the building of facilities there were still under way when the war ended.

Far more broadly based than NACA or the Naval Consulting Board, a revitalized National Academy of Sciences seemed the most likely choice to centralize war research. In 1916 the academy formed a National Research Council (NRC), with members drawn from governmental, academic, and industrial research. The council sought to promote long-term basic research, as well as work on projects immediately relevant to the war.

Early in 1917 the Council of National Defense made NRC its department of research, while assigning the Naval Consulting Board exclusively to evaluating inventions. Mechanisms for shifting military funds to civilian research had not yet been devised, however, and the need for haste seemed to preclude delay. Accordingly, scientists were conscripted to work on specific projects, leaving little scope for balanced program or detached judgment. Scientific mobiliza-tion, like economic mobilization, went more smoothly than it had in the past; it was likewise only beginning to achieve results when the war ended.

Medical services displayed strikingly greater efficiency in 1917–1918 than they had in earlier American wars. Reorganization after the Spanish-American War contributed to the improvement, as did the opportunity to prepare, vouchsafed by the U.S. long-anticipated decision to enter the war. Nothing resembling the epidemics that raced through 1898 training camps afflicted the recruits of World War I. The record remained equally good overseas. Remarkably, disease accounted for but half of troop deaths in France, despite appalling conditions on the western front.

Improved medical practice and more efficient organization also continued to reduce the number of troops who died of their wounds. For the Union army in the Civil War, the ratio of deaths in battle to died of wounds had been 3 to 2. The ratio improved to 2 to 1 in 1898 and 3 to 1 in World War I. Medical supply services, indeed supply services of all kinds, also attained a level of performance notably better than in the past. They largely managed to keep up with the demands of rapidly swelling armed forces.

Toward Social Engineering. World War I imposed extraordinary demands on the economies and the societies of the belligerents. Every state had to reorganize its people and resources to sustain its home front, cope with shortages, maintain production, and keep supplies flowing to the war fronts. Bureaucratic management formerly limited to individual business firms or government agencies now applied to the entire state and displaced free-market capitalism at the center of war economies. Science took its place among the activities the state sought to control, with varying success.

In the United States these trends were less marked than in other active belligerents, chiefly because of the country's late entry. Scientific mobilization, like other aspects of the U.S. buildup, began well by the standards of former American wars but followed past patterns in

Fortified cities almost everywhere became central to strategic planning and military engineering a crucial aspect of military organization. Siegecraft and field maneuvers alike took on a geometrical precision that eighteenth-century thinkers were wont to perceive as scientific. They talked less of the "art of war," and more of "military art and science" or simply "military science," a usage that became normal in the nineteenth century. When military schools began to appear in the mid-eighteenth century, they stressed scientific-technical training and became the model for nonmilitary schools of science and engineering.

Enlightenment military institutions underwent a sea change in the passage to America. Although the formal evolutions of British and French forces on the Plains of Abraham in 1759 testified to the persistence of well-tried forms, close-order drill and geometric precision could seldom be effectively maintained in the wilderness. Such circumstances produced a looser, more independent style that profoundly affected the conduct of war in America.

As the classic sieges of Louisbourg in Canada by British and colonial forces in 1745 and 1758 amply demonstrated, military engineering found a home in the New World. The attack and defense of fortifications did not characterize warfare only among Europeans and colonists; palisaded villages were a feature of native American life, as well. British and colonial military engineers surveyed and built roads throughout the colonies, beginning the tradition that characterized the creation of the new nation's transportation network after independence.

The American Revolution.
Gunmaking along traditional lines flourished in the colonies, and colonial naval stores became a major resource of British seapower. Interactions of military and naval engineering with other preindustrial American institutions, even as limited as they were, had virtually no counterpart in science and medicine. Colonial science foreshadowed the observational preoccupations that became so marked a feature of nineteenth-century American science. It also remained distinctly provincial, if not backward, however, and had no discernible effect on military institutions.

Much the same was true of medicine, in the eighteenth century still much more art and craft than science. Military surgeons and nurses might accompany larger expeditions, but they hardly affected operations. Like all early modern armies, both British and American forces in the revolutionary war relied on camp followers as nurses. Medical services also remained little changed from earlier practices. Although the Continental army acquired a medical department, the long-standing pattern of ten deaths from disease for every death in battle showed no signs of abating.

British control of the seas dictated the shape of the American war for independence. American ships could only harass, not challenge, the enemy fleet. Ultimately, logistics proved to be the Achilles heel of the British army in America. French intervention achieved decisive results by temporarily isolating British land forces from their support. Logistics problems had earlier almost undone the American war effort. The largely agricultural colonies enjoyed ample food resources and succeeded reasonably well in building what military industry they needed almost from scratch. Distributing supplies, not finding them, was the crux of the matter for the patriots. Transportation and fortification remained constant problems for George Washington's armies, aggravated by a persistent lack of engineers.

The Significance of West Point.
Scarcely had the United States achieved independence when Washington urged the establishment of a military academy, citing the want of engineers and artillerists that had plagued his army during the war. Although other motives played a part, the founding of the United States Military Academy owed much to such concerns. The same legislation that created West Point, the Act of 16 March 1802, also founded the Corps of Engineers, which would direct the new academy. Following the pattern of the European military schools founded during the preceding half-century, West Point stressed engineering and technical training.

Important as such skills might be for the army, they mattered even more for a young nation so notably lacking in them. Graduates of West Point, whether or not they remained in uniform, fanned out across the countryside to construct and maintain America's burgeoning transportation network. They surveyed roads, built forts, constructed canals, threw bridges across streams, dredged harbors, and cleared rivers. Sometimes they did the work themselves, but often they supervised others and always trained new hands, most of whom were not themselves military.

In the early nineteenth century, such on-the-job training was the way most engineers learned their trade, but West Pointers also moved into formal education as teachers of science and engineering and even as founders of engineering schools. American civil engineering owed a great deal to West Point and to military engineering. The establishment of the United States Naval Academy at Annapolis, Maryland, in 1845 did much the same for mechanical engineering as West Point had done for civil engineering.

Engineers trained at West Point took leading roles in the early years of railroad building. Perhaps more important, the army offered models of large-scale organization and techniques for coordinating large workforces. West Pointers adapted military methods to the new demands of railroad management. As the first large-scale business enterprises in the United States, the railroads in turn shaped the development of corporate organization throughout the nineteenth century. Management by staff and line, a key feature of the rising corporation, had self-evident military roots.

Military-trained engineers also came to make up a significant share of mid-level managers. Furthermore, they instructed their civilian counterparts in the new methods. Like civil engineers, potential corporate managers benefited from the fruits of military education, whether in on-the-job training in engineering projects or in more formal schooling in colleges of engineering.

Military and Naval Exploration. During the early nineteenth century, American science remained more strongly oriented toward observation than toward experimentation. The vast and little-known continent stretching west reinforced that bent. Crossing the next hill always seemed to promise a strange plant or animal, some exotic tribe, an unexpected lay of the land. A large if not entirely constant stream of specimens and notes, drawings and photographs, maps and descriptions from western exploration promoted vigorous American contributions to such primarily observational fields as astronomy, natural history, the earth sciences, and anthropology.

Even when explicitly designated scientific, however, western expeditions served other purposes as well. Identifying potential resources for exploitation was an obvious end, as was the quest for information of military value. Virtually every scientific expedition westward during the early and middle nineteenth century was also a military reconnaissance. Military organization and discipline proved invaluable in exploring a little-known and sometimes hostile land, as did the skills of the engineer. Mapmaking and building forts along the way were normal activities.

The pattern was set when President Thomas Jefferson in 1803 selected army Captain Meriwether Lewis to explore the vast new territory of Louisiana purchased from France. Lewis invited army veteran William Clark to share command of an expedition of forty people that took just under two and a half years to cross the continent from St. Louis to the mouth of the Columbia River and return. Publishing the results consumed far more time than obtaining them. During the next three decades, other military-scientific expeditions penetrated western lands, surveying, mapping, and collecting data.

Prominent among the military explorers were members of the Corps of Engineers Topographical Bureau, established during the War of 1812. Activity accelerated toward mid-century, especially after 1838, when the bureau became a corps in its own right—the Corps of Topo-

graphical Engineers—and scientists assumed larger roles in planning and staffing western expeditions. The effort was usually justified in such practical economic terms as surveying routes for a transcontinental railroad, but actual projects rarely had so narrow a focus.

The middle of the century also saw the U.S. Navy assume a major role in exploration. Although motives again were mixed, science played a larger part in the naval enterprise, and the geographical spread was far greater, ranging from the Arctic to the Antarctic, from the New World to the Old World. The U.S. Naval Observatory in Washington, founded in 1842, also became a center of research in oceanography under Lieutenant Matthew Fontaine Maury from 1844 to 1861.

West Point graduate Alexander Dallas Bache headed the Coast Survey, which was authorized in 1807 and which, besides its titular function, pioneered studies of geodesy and hydrography. Although a civilian agency, the survey made extensive use of naval officers. Benefits flowed both ways. The survey enjoyed a pool of able men, and officers gained valuable experience and knowledge that the small active navy of those years could not have provided. A disproportionately large number of senior naval officers in the Civil War had honed their seafaring skills in the antebellum Coast Survey.

Reciprocity of such direct bearing, however, was not the normal outcome of the military-scientific partnership in early nineteenth century America. The association probably benefited American science far more than it did either the army or navy. Scientists busy collecting, cataloging, and describing had as yet little to offer the armed forces. Much the same was true of engineering. Military engineers fostered engineering education, helped build the nation's infrastructure, introduced major features of large-scale management, and pioneered mass production, all of immense value to economic growth. Reciprocal benefits of any direct nature scarcely existed.

Indirect effects, however, proved enormously significant when the southern states se-

ceded from the Union. Economically, politically, and socially, the nation that divided in 1861 was very different from the Republic formed in 1789 or even the one that emerged from war in 1815. Such changes in part reflected the interactions of military institutions with American society during the preceding six decades, and they strongly influenced the nature and course of the war.

THE TRANSITION TO INDUSTRIAL WAR

The American Civil War straddled two ages. It was both the last great preindustrial war and the first major war of the industrial age. On the eve of war, the United States was not yet an industrial nation, but the process of industrialization was well under way. A key factor was steam power applied to produce and transport goods. Military engineers had once again assumed a prominent role. West Point provided many of the railroad builders, and Annapolis later began to bolster the ranks of steam engineers. Industrial capacity attained new levels of military significance as transportation improved, but in this, as in many other respects, the Civil War was distinctly transitional, and that fact strongly affected its conduct.

Before the nineteenth century, the complex interrelationship between war, science, technology, and industry so characteristic of the modern age scarcely existed. The French Revolution and the Napoleonic wars had seen the triumph of mass armies, but technologically they belonged to the past, not the future. The American Civil War occurred in the midst of far-reaching changes. Industrialization had only just begun.

In time the progressive and rapid improvement of old weapons, as well as the introduction of new ones, would become core factors in military planning and operations, but that took decades. Engineering and industry had yet to attain the scope and mastery that would allow

the speedy development of warlike inventions and improved weapons or their prompt production in quantity. Although that ability scarcely emerged before World War I and did not become fully realized until World War II, its prospect could be glimpsed even during the course of transition.

Steam Ashore and Afloat. Steam-powered transport had far-reaching consequences for U.S. development during the first half of the nineteenth century. Railroads offered a degree of flexibility that waterways could never match, and the prewar changes were revolutionary. In 1830 the Baltimore and Ohio Railroad put thirteen miles of track into service. Competing and expanding lines laid more than nine thousand miles of track in the next two decades, mostly in the Northeast. Between 1850 and 1860, another twenty-two thousand miles of track extended the rail net to the South and West, although the Northeast retained the densest network. When the Civil War began, more than thirty-one thousand miles of track spanned the country east of the Mississippi.

Transatlantic and coastal steam-powered vessels were almost commonplace by the 1860s. Potentially, steam made the resources of Europe more readily available to both sides. Practically, it made feasible the federal blockade of the three-thousand-mile Confederate coastline. Steamers could patrol waters off southern ports more closely and more regularly than sailing ships. The price was frequent recoaling. Federal forces seized bases on the Confederacy's coast as much to maintain their blockade as to deny their use to the enemy. Armorclad warships proved invaluable in these operations. The South also relied on armorclads for defense. Although the Confederacy began without ships, it benefited from a solid cadre of Annapolis-trained officers. Unfortunately, it also lacked manufacturing facilities. Inadequate production of armor plate and marine engines hampered naval defense in the South throughout the war.

Unsolved design problems largely precluded the use of oceangoing ironclads by either side. Notoriously unseaworthy, ironclads remained restricted to protected coastal waters. Such shortcomings mattered little on western rivers, where armored gunboats played a key role in the Union's conquest of the Mississippi. Steamboats had multiplied on inland waters before the war, having solved some of the worst problems of river navigation, especially in the West. Fitted with iron plate and guns, they became valuable adjuncts to army operations.

Toward Total War. Overenthusiastic from an economic viewpoint, prewar railroad building acquired strategic significance with the outbreak of war. Understanding fully what that meant, however, took time. Unlike at least some Europeans, Americans had given little if any thought to rail's military implications. In brief, railroads allowed contending states to marshal their resources swiftly. Large bodies of troops could quickly be shifted to where they were wanted. Perhaps more important, steam-powered logistics allowed the maintenance of much larger armies than would otherwise have been feasible. Speed of troop movement and of supply emerged as the essence of rail's military utility. A defeated army falling back on its railheads might soon be repaired, its casualties replaced, and its losses made good. Reinforced and reequipped armies could return to fight again, as long as men and material were available. Rapidly restored armies robbed battle of its potential for prompt decision.

Dramatically increased speed of movement came at the cost of freedom of movement. Civil War armies became more and more closely tied to their railroad supply lines, the attack and defense of which came increasingly to dominate strategy. Building and wrecking rail lines became a major military function, but railroad operation remained almost exclusively a profit-making venture in private hands. It was not an easy relationship. Railroad managers professing concern for their shareholders and army officers demanding logistic support were often at loggerheads. Although the North succeeded better than the South in imposing a degree of order, the South's real problems lay elsewhere. In this as in so much else, material shortages ham-

pered the Confederate war effort—too little track, not enough rolling stock, and insufficient means to produce more.

Militarily, railroads mattered chiefly to the final element in logistics—distribution. Equally important, although hardly clear at first to planners on either side, was production. Here, too, steam power had already begun to work massive changes in manufacturing organization before the war. In due course the patent importance of rails led eyes back to the supplies, material, and equipment they carried forward to the fighting troops. Eventually, this meant that war enlarged its scope to include not only the armies, but the resources and people that supported and sustained them. General William T. Sherman's trail of destruction through Georgia and General Philip H. Sheridan's devastation of the Shenandoah Valley prefigured a new kind of war. In this, however, as in many other ways, the Civil War was distinctly transitional— a surprisingly active intersectional trade, for instance, flourished throughout the war.

Technology, Science, and Medicine. The Civil War in America was the first full-scale war shaped in major ways by the tools and weapons of the industrial revolution. Telegraph and railroad greatly increased the pace at which events moved and combined with other technical changes to vastly extend the scope and deadliness of battle, at the same time reducing its decisiveness. New weapons multiplied the ranges at which death could be dealt, but other factors multiplied the numbers who might be killed. Agricultural mechanization permitted larger armies to be fed; industrial growth, to be armed and supplied; steam-powered transport, to be deployed and sustained.

Science played little part in these changes. Although the National Academy of Sciences was created by Congress during the war (1863), at least partly as a source of advice on war-related matters, it achieved nothing of import; many years elapsed before it became a major actor in American science. In contrast to more recent experience, the Civil War did more to disrupt than to advance science. Although not fully evident at the time, the long-standing military support of science through exploration was one of the casualties of the war. West Point ceased being exclusively an engineering school, the Corps of Topographical Engineers expired in 1863, and the postwar Corps of Engineers itself became increasingly an executor of civil engineering projects conceived elsewhere.

Ingenuity and imagination, rather than science, marked the efforts of both sides to devise and apply new weapons and techniques. Civil War firsts—first used or first used extensively— covered a broad range: the introduction of mass production in some industries, notably clothing, and of new techniques of food preservation; the supplying and moving of mass armies by railroad and steamboat; the use of photography, telegraphy, various signal devices using flags and lamps, and aerial observation from fixed balloons; the general use of rifled small arms and the appearance of breech-loading and magazine arms, as well as early machine-gun systems; the normal disappearance of troops behind breastworks and into trenches, along with the use of wire entanglements and trench mortars; the use of land and marine mines, torpedo boats, and submarines; and the use of steam-powered armored warships. The production of swords, lances, and pikes again attests to the transitional nature of the American Civil War.

Medical care reflected another kind of transition. Again, a number of firsts may be cited, notably the use of anesthesia in front-line surgery, the establishment of an ambulance service, and the use of hospital trains. The importance of sanitation and camp hygiene was widely respected, if not always fully implemented, and became a special focus of the United States Sanitary Commission, a civilian forerunner of the Red Cross that was established in 1861 and advised and assisted the Union armies. For all that, the Civil War ended just before medicine decisively crossed the line to science; general acceptance of microorganisms as the cause of disease and thus recognition of the value of antisepsis occurred in the 1870s. Improved sanitation and medical care nevertheless sharply altered the ratio of battle-caused to disease-caused deaths. As recently as the Mexican War (1846–1848), that ratio was still 1 to 10, the same as had prevailed in the American Revolution. In the Civil War, Union armies achieved a ratio no worse than 1 to 2, and even Confederate armies under much less favorable conditions managed 1 to 3.

Rifles and Trenches. Proliferating inventions were not chiefly what mattered in the Civil War. Many were impractical, others not widely used. Technological innovation counts only to the extent that it places weapons in the hands of troops. It is only when a new device or technique is put into widespread use that its impact is felt. Steam-powered transport was one such innovation that strongly affected the course of the Civil War. Only one other Civil War first exerted an equally profound effect, although on tactics more than on strategy—rifled firearms carried by both sides.

When the Civil War began, the U.S. Army's standard arm was the Model 1855 rifle musket. Its adoption came three decades after the Springfield Armory in Massachusetts had begun its pioneering development of the uniformity system. The Confederate seizure of the Harpers Ferry Armory in West Virginia left Springfield as the only government arsenal as the war began. Its annual capacity by then stood at roughly 12,000 arms. Substantial purchases abroad marked the opening of the war, and private contracts later augmented domestic arms manufacture, but Springfield remained the Union's major source of rifled muskets. By 1865, in fact, it had become the world's largest arms factory, with an annual capacity of 300,000. The Confederacy of necessity relied more on foreign supply but managed to build a creditable arms industry almost from nothing, aided by the machinery seized at Harpers Ferry. Annual production of small arms at southern armories reached 28,000 in mid-1863, augmented by 7,000 arms from private sources.

By extending severalfold the zone of fire through which attackers must pass, rifled muskets swung the tactical balance toward defense. Smoothbore artillery with an effective range of four hundred yards far outranged smoothbore muskets. On Napoleonic battlefields massed artillery allowed attackers to decimate a defending force, clearing the way for a decisive bayonet assault. Rifled small arms reversed the advantage in the early 1860s. During the Civil War, rifled artillery failed to pick up the slack; metallurgical practice could not yet produce ordnance strong enough to withstand the pressure of a fully contained explosion, except in relatively small-caliber guns. Such guns lacked killing power, leaving rifled small arms master of the field. Defenders entrenched or sheltered behind breastworks could wreak havoc on attackers crossing open ground.

Under the new circumstances, frontal assault could succeed only at terrible cost and bayonets hardly mattered, but Civil War commanders persisted in ordering mass assaults, with usually disastrous results. Given the chance, soldiers quickly learned to dig, the spade becoming little less important than the rifle. Before it ended, the Civil War had become an engineer's war. Field fortifications, often neglected early in the war, soon became common. Troops began disappearing into the ground or behind breastworks at even brief pauses. By the final year, elaborate trench systems converted field operations into siege warfare.

FROM OUTPOST TO EMPIRE

During the late nineteenth century, the U.S. armed forces became chiefly observers of major changes in military technology and organization taking place in Europe. Both army and navy reverted to prewar levels and tasks within a few years of the close of the Civil War. Policing the frontier and patrolling distant stations again became their main functions. Military-scientific cooperation in exploration was revived during the 1870s and 1880s, although on a much smaller scale than before. The Weather Service, the Geological Survey, the Coast Survey, even the Naval Observatory, which had for varying lengths of time worked under military auspices, all became purely civilian enterprises. The

Corps of Engineers remained an army operation but grew increasingly civilianized.

In general, the close prewar links between military and scientific enterprise faded as each sought its own path toward professionalization. Professionalizing groups sought to make special schooling a prerequisite for professional entry, bureaucratic office, or masculine privilege. Armed forces, however, were not merely one more instance of a widespread nineteenth-century phenomenon. Military institutions regularly pioneered the techniques of discipline, order, and privilege that other social institutions adopted.

At one level, support for a distinctive military science reflected concerns about institutional survival during a time of flux in technique and organization. More generally, however, it showed how institutions might respond to rapid social change and became a model of such response, often implicit but sometimes overt, as in engineering. Scientific management, medical science, social science, political science, and a host of other nineteenth-century coinages, even science proper, all testify to the widely perceived value of coping with change by turning lore into systematic knowledge.

By the turn of the century, these trends had begun to produce larger consequences. During the 1880s and 1890s, the U.S. Navy began rebuilding itself as a modern sea force. Naval revival fostered economic growth, particularly in steel and related industries, and drew heavily on the growing ability of scientifically oriented engineering to produce specified armor and equipment to order. It also contributed to the rise of navalism based on an exciting new theory of sea power. The nation's imperial venture opened auspiciously with the successful naval war against Spain (1898). Sustained in part by the growing scientific competence of American medicine, U.S. forces proved capable of fighting and building in the tropics. The Panama Canal, which opened on 15 August 1914, symbolized the country's new status in the world.

Professional Officers and Scientists. By the late nineteenth century, formal schooling

had become a normal part of an officer's career, and the concept of military science had become commonplace. The link was no accident. Military science codified the underlying principles of war, which could thus more easily be taught in the classroom. It abstracted and systematized a body of esoteric knowledge suited to indoctrinating the nineteenth century's growing numbers of nontraditional candidates for officer status.

Like other professionalizing fields, notably engineering, the armed forces of the United States and Europe faced an influx of middle-class men seeking careers. Presumably lacking the genetic predisposition of their aristocratic comrades, they needed concrete and readily reproducible examples—schematic maps, war games, and rules. The so-called principles of war, for example, were a nineteenth-century innovation. Few of these teaching aids were entirely new, but their use burgeoned during the late nineteenth century and became a staple of the twentieth.

Paradoxically, military education also grew more complex and sophisticated as some of its subjects became oversimplified and standardized. The reoriented curricula of older schools in Europe and in the United States added courses in strategy and policy to the familiar tactics and engineering. At new military schools founded for that very purpose, postgraduate training became available and later was a required prelude to higher command.

The School of Application for Cavalry and Infantry, founded at Fort Leavenworth, Kansas, in 1881, marked the U.S. Army's first venture into this area; the Naval War College was established three years later in Providence, Rhode Island. Strategic and other higher military studies in the United States proliferated in the context of turn-of-the-century reform movements that affected military as well as civil society. In the twentieth century, such studies became a central feature of advanced military education. All such courses and programs pointed toward professionalization, officers educated to wield sanctioned violence responsibly.

Profound and rapid social change strongly

colored, if it did not cause, professionalization, whether of the armed forces or other corporate groups during the nineteenth century. Engineering shifted from practical training on building sites or shop floors toward increased emphasis on formal college education as a prerequisite to professional certification. Science likewise expanded its educational demands, reflected especially in the late nineteenth-century innovation of graduate programs and doctoral degrees and in the burgeoning number of professional societies. Medicine, bolstered by the success of the bacteriological revolution, emerged from a host of competing creeds to become the preeminent health profession, a claim reinforced by turn-of-the-century reforms in medical education.

Radical change justified concomitant claims to special expertise. Elaborating esoteric bodies of knowledge and technique then allowed practitioners to limit access to the field. Codified and abstracted knowledge channeled the entry of properly trained and indoctrinated candidates. During the nineteenth century, many fields shifted from apprentice and other on-the-job methods of training new members toward the use of schools or other more formal means of transmitting and perpetuating professional culture. Special knowledge, unique skill, and restricted numbers, however, counted only if a group could claim to serve higher social purposes. Promoting that claim was the key to attaining professional status. Only when society accepted professional training and competence as socially needed and wanted could the newly defined corporate group claim special social privilege, which was, of course, the whole point.

Militarized Industry.

Industrialization itself owed no small debt to military interests. A career army officer and arsenal manager, Captain Henry Metcalfe, wrote the first book on factory management published in the United States. He addressed his 1885 work, an acknowledged classic of management, less to fellow officers than to corporate managers. The U.S. Navy's decision to use industrial contractors to supply armor and ordnance for its new fleet in the late nineteenth century, rather than rely on government facilities, may well mark the beginning of what has more recently been termed the military-industrial complex. From the early nineteenth century uniformity system to the late twentieth century, U.S. Air Force sponsorship of automated machine tool development, key aspects of industrial technology have emerged from military settings.

Military example may have been even more important in furthering industrialization. Discipline was the key, argued Max Weber in his treatise *Economy and Society*, first published in 1923, with military practice as its inspiration. Lewis Mumford agreed, noting in his 1934 commentary *Technics and Civilization* that military regimentation inspired the factory system and created the conditions for its implementation. Entrepreneurs and captains of industry found much to admire, and to adopt, in the regimentation and redivision of labor imposed on modernizing armies.

The sociologist Jacques van Doorn, in his 1975 essay "The Genesis of Military and Industrial Organization," has sought to link the military to the industrial revolution through the motives shared by a major architect of each. Dutch military leader Maurice of Nassau became a key figure in the early modern European military revolution when he restored drill to armies in the late sixteenth century. Efficiency engineer Frederick W. Taylor reshaped American, and eventually worldwide, industrialism when he devised scientific management in the late nineteenth and early twentieth centuries. Parallels between Maurice and Taylor were not accidental. They faced the same problem: creating a "goal-attainment organization" from a mass of socially isolated, ill-trained, and poorly motivated proletarians. Sharing a mechanistic image of human behavior, they found their common answer in regimented action. For Taylor, at least, it was a two-way street. Military models influenced his reforms and scientific management, and Taylorism, as it has often been termed, found a receptive military audience.

Regimented Schools.

Similar patterns marked schools in the United States. Military concerns and money, sometimes direct, sometimes funneled through corporate intermediaries, affected higher education in many ways. Military training on campus dated to the Morrill Act of 1862, although it became institutionalized in the form of the Reserve Officer Training Corps (ROTC) only in 1916. Engineers figured prominently among supporters of this contested institution. American universities, like much of American society, for the most part welcomed such values. After he became the first head of the University of Illinois in 1867, John M. Gregory regularly cited the value of military order and drill in higher education, because it promoted discipline, built character, and generally improved the tone of the campus.

Youthful Americans would also come to enjoy such virtues, which were emphasized in secondary and even primary schools and which were later bolstered by Junior ROTC and vocational education. To many Americans, they seemed both worthwhile and desirable. Discipline derived from military training in public schools was alleged to instruct pupils in civil government and respect for law. Such lessons held no less value for adults. Militarism could be one side of the coin, but civic virtue and patriotism might be the other. In many respects, a similar pattern prevailed in Great Britain and was even more widespread on the European continent. Great as the influence of such values may have been, however, they appear to have had little direct impact on science and engineering in the universities, at least before World War I.

Commanding the Sea.

Navalism, like militarism, had ambiguous meaning. Because it applied to a relatively more restricted field, however, its late nineteenth-century impact may have been all the greater. Navalism became a vital factor in international relations for a number of reasons. One was certainly the publication of Alfred Thayer Mahan's treatise *The Influence of Sea Power Upon History, 1660–1783* in 1890. The book was the fruit of his course of lectures in naval history at the recently founded Naval War College. Mahan offered a neat package of naval strength, commerce, colonies, and power that resonated in the United States and abroad.

The United States had already embarked on an ambitious naval program. Mahan offered an ideology for such endeavors, and the Royal Navy soon provided a potent symbol with the 1906 launching of HMS *Dreadnought*. The naval armaments race and the scramble for colonies intensified. Enormously fast and heavily armed, battleships and battle cruisers represented the epitome of military might as the twentieth century opened. The design was promptly emulated and improved throughout the industrialized world.

U.S. industry had never been loath to profit from military contracts. Opportunities to do so before the late nineteenth century, however, were largely limited to times of war. During peacetime the armed forces preferred to rely on their own arsenals and shipyards, but that began changing toward the end of the nineteenth century, when the U.S. Navy forged an alliance with the steel industry to promote modernization.

Rapidly developing naval technology since mid-century presented baffling problems to every navy. Screw-propelled steamships wrapped in increasingly thicker armor and mounting bigger guns for the first time provided a really large and lucrative market for a peacetime industry, provided Congress authorized a large enough shipbuilding program. The navy got its first steel ship in 1884, and its battleship program was approved in 1890. Imperial adventure soon followed.

From the viewpoint of science and engineering, what U.S. ambassador to England John Hay in 1898 called "a splendid little war" offered nothing remarkable. The Spanish-American War was largely decided at sea, where the new U.S. steam and steel navy won quick and overwhelming victories. Fighting on land against a largely unenthusiastic, if not demoralized foe, the army also won easy victories, despite appalling organizational and logistic problems.

Medicine and Empire. Medically the Spanish-American War was a near-disaster. Overall, the ratio of deaths from disease to battle deaths reached, by some reckonings, 7 to 1, which may be attributed in part to the war's brevity. Inexperienced soldiers—the regular army's strength in 1898 was less than thirty thousand, although a quarter of a million men served in the war—have always tended to have high disease rates until they learn better camp hygiene and sanitation. The war was too short to show any benefits from improvement.

Typhoid was the main killer during the Spanish-American War. An army medical research board convened after the war asked why. Walter Reed and his colleagues concluded that the disease was spread mainly by flies, by contact between persons, and by human carriers. Sanitary measures offered the best hope of controlling the disease at that point, but a decade's research produced an even better answer—vaccination with killed bacilli, which largely eliminated the threat of typhoid. Successful tests in 1909 resulted in vaccination becoming compulsory for the entire U.S. Army in 1911.

The Spanish-American War also confronted the army with tropical diseases for which it was ill-prepared. After the war, the army's responsibility for administering the new dependencies—and, in the Philippines, for suppressing insurrection—brought increased urgency to the drive to solve the puzzles of tropical disease. Army medical research boards again provided answers. The best-known was Reed's Yellow Fever Commission in Cuba, which by early 1901 had proved the disease's cause to be a mosquito-borne virus. British research in the 1890s had shown that mosquitos also transmitted malaria-causing microorganisms.

These findings did not reflect any profound breakthrough in basic knowledge; much remained to be learned about the etiology of yellow fever and malaria. What the U.S. Army Medical Department accomplished remains nonetheless important. The army acquired practical means of coping with the two main tropical diseases and a number of lesser ones as well. Antimosquito measures quickly became the basis for controlling and preventing malaria and yellow fever. Acting on the Reed commission findings, William Crawford Gorgas succeeded in reducing malaria and eliminating yellow fever in Havana by the end of 1901.

Major Gorgas then turned to a survey of the proposed site in Panama for a canal linking the Atlantic and the Pacific. Endemic malaria and yellow fever jeopardized that plan. Appointed chief sanitary officer of the Panama Canal Zone when the Corps of Engineers began work in 1904, Gorgas again succeeded; in two years malaria had been sharply reduced and yellow fever eradicated in the zone. His achievement freed the army engineers to concentrate on the task at hand, which they did to magnificent effect. Construction of the canal required ten years to complete, but the first ship passed through the Panama Canal in August 1914. It was perhaps fittingly ironic that world acclaim for this triumph of civil engineering aided by science was overshadowed by the outbreak of war in Europe earlier that month.

THE CATASTROPHE OF INDUSTRIAL WAR

World War I (1914–1918) confirmed trends clearly evident in retrospect since the mid-nineteenth century. Military institutions had changed dramatically. Repeating rifles, smokeless powder, quick-firing long-range field artillery, and machine guns multiplied firepower and extended the killing zone. Doffing gaudy color in favor of field gray or khaki, soldiers left firing lines and maneuver for ground cover and trenches. Runners began giving way to telegraph and wireless, muscle to steam and petrol. Staffs burgeoned to direct vast armies as nations prepared to put millions of men under arms. With the new giving way to the newer more quickly, almost every aspect of military life was altered, if not transformed. Equally dizzying changes marked naval technology. So rapid did the pace of change become toward the end of the nineteenth century that the ships of one decade seemed almost worthless in the next.

Military and naval novelties figured prominently, for example, in popular turn-of-the-century compendia on the progress of invention. Judging their likely impact surpassed most contemporary imaginations, however, military and civilian alike. Indeed, many have blamed the catastrophe of World War I on European armies blind to the meaning of swiftly changing technology, which may be unfair. Innovations in military technology still came mostly from non-military sources, which made the flood of new or improved arms hard to control or direct. Military planners did not so much ignore problems as misjudge their magnitude. Whatever the reasons, the result was catastrophe almost beyond comprehension.

Sources of Victory.

Ultimately, the war was decided by supply. The great battleships that had captured so many minds and consumed so much money before the war rarely ventured to sea, confined by fear of mines and torpedoes. The most significant naval action of the war involved submarine attacks on shipping. Despite their relatively modest capabilities by later standards, German submarines threatened on more than one occasion to deprive Great Britain of its maritime commerce and to cut its economic lifeline, especially imported food supplies. Anti-submarine tactics and the convoy system defeated the threat, but it was a close call.

Although more self-sufficient than Great Britain, Germany had to import certain crucial raw materials, as well as significant amounts of foodstuffs. It was thus a country vulnerable to blockade. Merely by existing, the Royal Navy maintained command of the sea. Blockaded and bereft of key imports, Germany improvised, sometimes brilliantly. The creation of an artificial nitrate industry to replace lost overseas sources was one of the most remarkable scientific achievements of the war, but food could not be improvised.

Throughout the war, Germany tended to retain an edge in tactics and operations, the Allies in management and logistics. British war production soared; perhaps more surprisingly, so did French production, despite the German occupation of France's major coal and iron region. The collapse of Russia in 1917 and its withdrawal from the war held the long-term promise of giving Germany a new breadbasket. Of more immediate importance, it augmented Germany's strong suit by freeing scores of divisions for redeployment to the western front. In spring 1918 an enlarged German army using novel infantry and artillery tactics came close to victory. Its failure owed more than a little to the intervention of fresh U.S. troops in large numbers, many of them transported to Europe in British ships and most of them equipped from Allied, especially French, factories and depots.

Americans had observed events in Europe with mixed feelings. Ambivalent though they may have been about whether to intervene, there was nothing reluctant about implementing the decision, once made. Much of the pre-1917 debate on mobilization had centered on manpower, and in the final analysis manpower was the decisive American contribution. From April 1917, when the United States declared war on Germany, until the November 1918 armistice, the U.S. Army grew from two hundred thousand to 3.5 million men, 2 million of whom reached France.

Ambitious plans to arm and equip the American Expeditionary Forces from U.S. sources proved less successful. Economic mobilization for World War I demanded an effort far beyond anything ever before attempted in the United States. It began under the auspices of the Council of National Defense, established by statute in August 1916 to coordinate industry and resources; coordination became direction as the council mutated into the War Industries Board, which came to control large parts of the economy. Although better organized than such efforts in past American wars, however, mobilization took too much time. American industry was still gearing up when the war ended, and U.S. forces fought chiefly with French ordnance and flew French and British aircraft.

Mobilizing American Science. Mobilizing science for the war effort enjoyed equally modest success. As early as 1915 the navy created a Naval Consulting Board to screen proffered inventions for value and practicality. All its members were working engineers and inventors, including Thomas Alva Edison, the chairman. Individual inventors, however, proved to have no better grasp of the scientific-technical needs of modern warfare than did most officers; vanishingly few of the suggested ideas even merited discussion.

The National Advisory Committee for Aeronautics (NACA) built on a more solid base but still failed to contribute much to the war effort. Established by Congress in 1915, NACA served a larger purpose than its name implied. In addition to advising on aeronautical policy, NACA also directed an aeronautical engineering research laboratory. The Langley Aeronautical Laboratory descended from turn-of-the-century experimental work conducted at the Smithsonian Institution in Washington, D.C. Although already a going concern on a small scale at the Smithsonian, the laboratory needed room to expand. A move to Langley, Virginia, and the building of facilities there were still under way when the war ended.

Far more broadly based than NACA or the Naval Consulting Board, a revitalized National Academy of Sciences seemed the most likely choice to centralize war research. In 1916 the academy formed a National Research Council (NRC), with members drawn from governmental, academic, and industrial research. The council sought to promote long-term basic research, as well as work on projects immediately relevant to the war.

Early in 1917 the Council of National Defense made NRC its department of research, while assigning the Naval Consulting Board exclusively to evaluating inventions. Mechanisms for shifting military funds to civilian research had not yet been devised, however, and the need for haste seemed to preclude delay. Accordingly, scientists were conscripted to work on specific projects, leaving little scope for balanced program or detached judgment. Scientific mobiliza-

tion, like economic mobilization, went more smoothly than it had in the past; it was likewise only beginning to achieve results when the war ended.

Medical services displayed strikingly greater efficiency in 1917–1918 than they had in earlier American wars. Reorganization after the Spanish-American War contributed to the improvement, as did the opportunity to prepare, vouchsafed by the U.S. long-anticipated decision to enter the war. Nothing resembling the epidemics that raced through 1898 training camps afflicted the recruits of World War I. The record remained equally good overseas. Remarkably, disease accounted for but half of troop deaths in France, despite appalling conditions on the western front.

Improved medical practice and more efficient organization also continued to reduce the number of troops who died of their wounds. For the Union army in the Civil War, the ratio of deaths in battle to died of wounds had been 3 to 2. The ratio improved to 2 to 1 in 1898 and 3 to 1 in World War I. Medical supply services, indeed supply services of all kinds, also attained a level of performance notably better than in the past. They largely managed to keep up with the demands of rapidly swelling armed forces.

Toward Social Engineering. World War I imposed extraordinary demands on the economies and the societies of the belligerents. Every state had to reorganize its people and resources to sustain its home front, cope with shortages, maintain production, and keep supplies flowing to the war fronts. Bureaucratic management formerly limited to individual business firms or government agencies now applied to the entire state and displaced free-market capitalism at the center of war economies. Science took its place among the activities the state sought to control, with varying success.

In the United States these trends were less marked than in other active belligerents, chiefly because of the country's late entry. Scientific mobilization, like other aspects of the U.S. buildup, began well by the standards of former American wars but followed past patterns in ending promptly with the war. Heavily reliant on scientists in uniform, direct military research shared the fate of the armed forces. Armistice brought abrupt cuts in military appropriations and rapid demobilization.

Although the Naval Consulting Board expired, it was not without issue. In 1916 it had persuaded Congress that the navy needed a research laboratory and secured the funding required to begin building. Internal squabbling caused the laboratory to remain in limbo until 1923. The National Research Council survived the war. Although it lost whatever function in military research it may have had, it did acquire the congressional mandate it lacked during the war and maintained significant links with the scientific community.

Of all World War I science agencies, only NACA flourished in the period that followed the war's immediate aftermath. Conducting basic and applied research for military and civilian clients at the Langley laboratory, it pioneered most interwar advances in aeronautical engineering. In sharp contrast to World War I, the United States entered World War II as a leader in aeronautical design and development. No less important when the United States entered the war, NACA also became the model for organizing American scientific research.

Meanwhile, however, some less direct consequences of scientific mobilization for World War I may have been more significant. Colleges that had become enthusiastic centers for military training and education were scarcely less eager in peacetime. During the era of World War I, U.S. schools of engineering used military models in organizing research laboratories, adapted their curricula to meet military demands, and borrowed military test methods to evaluate their students.

Consequences might be as subtle as those entailed in using personality tests and job specifications created for military purposes during the war. At the other extreme lay the overt effects of research channeled by military funding. By whatever paths, military values of order, discipline, and hierarchy pervaded engineering and persisted after the war ended. Industry readily followed suit. Military techniques of classifying jobs and sorting personnel required little adjustment to suit the precepts of scientific management.

Roots of Military Mechanization. The doctrine of mechanized warfare, like the doctrine of strategic bombing, invoked the power of modern science to produce the required machines. "There is nothing too wonderful for science," exclaimed the British military theorist J. F. C. Fuller in a prize-winning 1920 essay. After serving as chief of staff in the British Tank Corps during the war, Fuller became the leading postwar advocate of mechanization. "We of the fighting services must grasp the wand of this magician and compel the future to obey us," he insisted. Although the message won converts in the United States and elsewhere, it also aroused considerable resistance. Opponents thought mechanized forces would be costly to provide, hard to maintain, prone to rapid obsolescence, and difficult to supply. Only the experience of war clinched the argument by showing conclusively that such obstacles could be overcome, adequately if not always easily.

Moving beyond that achievement, however, required finding efficient means for turning science into weapons across the full spectrum of modern warfare. In organizing for World War II, the United States largely solved that crucial problem. Instead of relying on makeshift expedients, the nation enjoyed a well-considered and effective system for making science useful to the war effort. Arrangements made to exploit science in World War II permanently transformed relations between American military and scientific institutions.

THE CLIMAX OF MECHANIZATION

World War II marked the climax of another long cycle in military history. Since the early nineteenth century, armed forces had faced a flood of new and newly improved weapons. Although some reflected military initiatives, most came from independent inventors. New weapons demanded new tactics and organization, although of just what kind was seldom obvious. Extraordinary increases in firepower both ashore and afloat outmoded traditional offensive tactics and operations, setting the stage for stalemate and the frustration of command.

In World War II further technical and tactical innovation bore fruit, yielding opportunities for generalship comparable to that in the Napoleonic wars. Mechanized armed forces wedded to the tactics of infiltration restored maneuver to battle and decisiveness to war. Striking differences in the course and outcome of the two world wars reflected the success of interwar efforts to harness scientific research to military needs. The United States was not a leader in all these developments before the war, but neither was it the laggard it had once been. In the application of science to war, it soon emerged a pioneer.

From 1940 on, the United States devised new forms for mobilizing science that succeeded beyond almost anyone's expectations. Relationships among science, engineering, and military institutions emerged from World War II utterly transformed. The reluctant military innovators of the later nineteenth century became enthusiastic seekers of technological novelty in the later twentieth. Perhaps more significant, they began finding money to support the scientific research and development engineering, as well as the testing and procurement, of the required new weapons.

Harnessing Science to War.

The new military-scientific partnership had, of course, two sides. Military institutions able to recognize the value of science and willing to support relevant research constituted only one side. By no means a minor issue, military resistance to scientific weaponeering seemed quite rational given past failures. Experience would soon show, however, that a stream of useful new devices from the laboratory could overcome most qualms.

The other side of the partnership, organizing science for the job, posed equally crucial questions. Finding scientists willing and even eager to do war research presented little problem. Every American war had produced them, and they appeared quickly after 1939 at merely the prospect of war with Nazi Germany. What was different as the United States faced entry into World War II was the organization of proper means to convert offers of help into direct research leading to engineering development of actual weapons. The solution was directed team research.

World War II has been called the physicist's war. It might better be termed the physicist's and the engineer's war. The line between scientific research and engineering development, the juncture of applied physics and science-based engineering, never easy to draw precisely in the best of circumstances, blurred beyond definition under wartime pressure. In World War II the task of dealing with unsolicited inventions was relegated to a place in the Department of Commerce, while research took center stage in the form of the National Defense Research Committee (NDRC) and the Office of Scientific Research and Development (OSRD). The result has profoundly shaped relations between American science and military institutions ever since.

The NDRC and OSRD improved or developed an extraordinary array of weapons and other products and processes useful to fighting World War II. Radar and the proximity fuse topped the list of those that most decisively affected the course of the war, but there were many others, ranging from operational analysis to blood plasma. What made the experience of World War II unique was the speed of innovation. By 1940 the United States possessed an unmatched combination of resources in science, engineering, technology, and industry. Properly organized and directed, such resources could turn ideas into weapons quickly and massively enough to alter the course of war in progress. No other nation in World War II equaled the United States across the entire spectrum of science applied effectively to war. NDRC and OSRD were the main reasons.

The NDRC and OSRD. Credit for conceiving NDRC belonged chiefly to Vannevar Bush, who became president of the Carnegie Institution of Washington in 1939 and chairman of the National Advisory Committee for Aeronautics (NACA). Bush thus found himself at the center of America's scientific establishment when war erupted in Europe. Well aware of German technical and scientific prowess, he and his colleagues received news of the German discovery of nuclear fission with great disquiet. It might mean a bomb of unprecedented power, and the prospect of such a weapon in Nazi hands terrified them. Science and technology would clearly play a major role in the coming war. Accordingly, Bush set himself the task of mobilizing science. From his viewpoint, NACA offered the most promising model for what in June 1940 became the National Defense Research Committee.

The key features of the new organization centered on the choice of problems and the means of solving them. The NDRC would not simply accept assignments from the armed forces; Bush's central idea was to keep the choice of scientific problems in the hands of scientists. War would remove money as a limiting factor, but it would also make military utility the definitive goal. That would leave the crucial decisions to science—recognizing what technological possibilities inhered in current science and judging which prospects should be pursued in light of available talent and resources. Rather than building new research facilities from scratch, NDRC contracted for research on selected problems with well-established academic and industrial organizations.

The goal of NDRC was the development of weapons useful in the current crisis. Despite its focus on applied research of immediate utility, however, it relied chiefly on academic research facilities, leaving industrial and military research organizations to pursue their own ends. Industry would be gearing up for an enormous production effort, to which it would have to devote its scientific resources; military research would presumably continue to concentrate on improving weapons already in use. Bush re-

tained administrative control of NDRC but left the technical decision-making to five research divisions: armor and ordnance, chemistry and explosives, communications and transportation, instruments and controls, and patents and inventions.

By mid-1941, NDRC was reaching its limits, and Bush devised an expanded but not fundamentally altered organization. The Office of Scientific Research and Development (OSRD) subsumed NDRC in an advisory role, joined by a new committee for research in military medicine. The five divisions of NDRC expanded to eighteen, supported by panels on applied mathematics and applied psychology. In contrast to NDRC's support through presidential contingency funds, OSRD enjoyed a line item in the federal budget; assured funds allowed the fruits of research to be developed into working prototypes for production. Perhaps most amazing, the entire structure was in place and operating effectively half a year before the United States became an active belligerent. The next four years would see the spectacular consequences.

From Physics to Hardware. Electronics became the focus of OSRD support, the Radiation Laboratory at MIT its chief research center. Radar (radio detection and ranging) was the most important of a wide range of applications that dramatically improved the integration of combat arms, the control of battlefield action, and the destruction of enemy forces. The principle of radar was known to all the major powers by the 1920s, and the U.S. Navy installed a prototype operational system on the battleship *New York* in 1938.

The real contest between radar measures and countermeasures began in the Battle of Britain during 1940. The United States soon followed Great Britain's lead and, thanks to OSRD and the Radiation Laboratory, made rapid progress. At British urging and aided by the British-invented magnetron, the United States specialized in microwave radar. The Radiation Laboratory produced 150 systems during the war to serve purposes as varied as detecting enemy planes and ships, directing guns, aiding navigation, controlling operations, locating targets, and warning of attack.

Proximity fuses were another OSRD product of great consequence, well begun before the United States was formally at war. The idea was simple: Put a tiny radar set in the nose of a bomb or shell to measure precisely when it reached a specified distance from the target; the explosive could then be reliably detonated at the set distance. When NDRC opened for business in mid-1940, the navy proposed work on radar-fused shells as a likely counter to enemy air attack. In August, NDCR's first research contract went to the Carnegie Institution for preliminary studies. A prototype fuse for five-inch shells was ready the month after Pearl Harbor. The Applied Physics Laboratory of Johns Hopkins University then completed development. Production was under way by fall 1942, and the new fuses, called VT (for variable time) reached the navy before the year ended. The new shells proved to be at least three times as effective as their closest competitor, shells fused to explode at a preset time, and as much as fifty times better than shells fused to explode on contact.

The VT fuse also marked an important step toward automation, as a sensor in a complex computer-controlled firing system. World War II forged the modern military-computer linkage. Mechanical and electromechanical analog computers had deep roots in the practical demands of compiling such products of tedious calculation as actuarial, navigational, and, by World War I, artillery firing tables. During World War II, antiaircraft fire control imposed still greater demands and more automation. Although analog computers provided most wartime firing tables, the task also promoted further development of electronic digital computers, a much speedier alternative.

Computers and radar stimulated thinking about system organization, first in Great Britain, then in the United States. Operations analysis was one result. The effective use of radar raised technical questions related to the equipment itself, in the first instance, but quickly led to other questions about organization and strategy. Systematic and quantitative approaches to problems of military tactics and strategy offered the exciting prospect of war made truly scientific. The relatively narrow focus of the war years involved NDRC and OSRD in such problems as hunting submarines and dropping bombs accurately. The OSRD's Applied Mathematics Panel played an especially prominent role in these studies. Valuable as they were, the further development of operations analysis after the war would prove even more significant.

Bodies and Minds.

Bodies and Minds. In some ways American medical achievements during World War II were the most remarkable of all. Disease, which before the twentieth century had always accounted for the vast majority of deaths in war, was all but eliminated as a significant factor in military mortality. Among the reasons for this success must be counted the work sponsored by the OSRD Committee on Medical Research, often cooperating with the National Academy of Sciences and the surgeons general of the armed forces.

Three research areas had the greatest impact: drugs, including atabrine for malaria control and the family of so-called sulfa drugs effective against many bacterial diseases; antibiotics, notably penicillin, which nicely complemented sulfa drugs in treating infectious disease; and insecticides, especially DDT, which proved enormously successful in controlling the arthropod vectors of several diseases. With few exceptions, the main emphasis was on turning substances known chiefly in laboratory contexts into mass-produced commodities. Medical innovations, like technological ones, mattered only insofar as they attained wide use.

Mortality from wounds as well as disease fell precipitously. In the Civil War, 1 of 7 wounded soldiers died, a figure that improved to 1 of 12 in World War I. The U.S. Army in World War II suffered roughly 592,000 battle casualties, of whom 208,000 died in action or before they reached an aid station. Approximately the same ratio of killed to wounded had obtained in World War I, but the ratio of fatal to nonfatal wounds improved to something closer to 1 in 143. Much of this success derived from better techniques of front-line treatment and the rapid medical evacuation made possible by motorized transport. A share of the credit must also go to the Committee on Medical Research and its work on two key threats to survival of the wounded—blood loss and infection. OSRD-sponsored research helped solve both problems. It produced methods for bringing prompt and adequate supplies of plasma and other blood substitutes, as well as refrigerated whole blood, to the edge of combat. Sulfa drugs and antibiotics went a long way toward eliminating infected wounds as a cause of death.

Another aspect of research in World War II continued the precedent set in World War I: the use of intelligence and aptitude tests to determine personnel assignments. OSRD's Applied Psychology Panel played an important role in this effort; it also studied weapon designs in relation to user capabilities, an important step in the rise of human factors engineering. The social sciences were mobilized for World War II to a degree quite unmatched previously.

Among a host of other projects, two stand out as having special significance for the postwar development of their fields. Anthropologists were called upon to evaluate the enemy, particularly the Japanese, and to consider how culture and personality might affect war- and peace-making. Sociologists, on the other hand, studied American soldiers, attempting to answer questions about adjustment to army life and behavior in combat. Not only did their findings dispel some ancient military misconceptions, their techniques and experience strongly influenced the postwar development of sociology. The militarization of the social sciences would also be a major trend in postwar America.

The Conduct of Mechanized War. However greatly the novel products of science may have affected the course of war, improved and refined older weapons and tactics most directly decided the outcome. Better guns, better tanks, better aircraft, better ships made the difference. Engineering perhaps more than science dictated the tempo of war and its ultimate results. Equally significant, military doctrine and tactics

caught up with technological change. Although much of prewar mechanized theory revealed itself wrong in detail, the larger vision of mechanized warfare proved valid—nothing resembling the trench warfare of 1914–1918 recurred.

In many respects, World War II in the air came closest to war dictated by science. Major scientific-technical advances, from radar to atomic bombs, addressed one aspect or another of air war or defense against air attack. But there was more. Fortune seemed closely to favor the side flying the latest model airplane or deploying the most recent radar measure or countermeasure. In contrast to the theorists of armored warfare, however, the prophets of strategic bombing misread the future in almost every respect. Even apart from its moral implications, air attack on enemy industry and population proved far harder to mount, more costly to maintain, and less productive of results than they had supposed.

Tactical bombing in support of ground forces, such as the interdiction of enemy supply lines, on the other hand, achieved notable success throughout the war. It was the tactical and operational uses of aircraft that mattered most during World War II. Teamed with other machines or systems, airplanes transformed the conduct of war on land and at sea from the heart of Eurasia to the far reaches of the Pacific.

Consistent success by fighter planes against heavy bombers emerged as a major factor in strategic bombing failures. Another factor was the surprising inaccuracy of high-altitude bombing, which meant that destroying a target required bombers in much larger numbers than expected. Only after a costly war of attrition, when Axis defensive aircraft and guns had become too few to counter the still growing bomber fleets made possible by U.S. productive capacity untouched by war, did attack from the air approach its promised power. At that point, the atomic bomb introduced an entirely new factor. Explosives of such power seemed to restore plausibility to strategic bombing doctrine. Relatively modest forces armed with nuclear weapons might well inflict the kind of damage that would end a war almost as soon as it began.

INSTITUTIONALIZING A NEW ORDER

World War II transformed relationships between military and scientific institutions in the United States. The plethora of useful innovations derived from wartime research lent science—the term used in its broadest sense to include not only basic and applied research but also engineering, technology, and medicine—a prestige it had never enjoyed so widely in the armed forces and in government. The experience of World War II seemed to demonstrate unequivocally that science would play a major role in future military affairs. Accordingly, scientists, especially physicists, found their expert knowledge much in demand, their services eagerly sought, and, more flattering yet, their opinions on almost any subject highly valued.

Influence flowed both ways. Wartime experience touched scientists and technologists, as well as politicians and officers. Not only had they enjoyed virtually unlimited resources, a state of affairs many were eager to see sustained, they also found themselves attracted to political and military affairs in unprecedented numbers. Relationships between American military and scientific institutions by 1945 differed markedly from what they had been before 1940. Perhaps most important, these were not the transient changes of the past. Institutions emerged after World War II to convert wartime arrangements into permanent features of American government and society.

The Manhattan Project. The military-scientific project that produced nuclear weapons by 1945 has become the paradigm of science in the service of war. It stands as a remarkable accomplishment, although engineers, both military and civilian, deserve more credit than they usually receive. The initial discovery of nuclear fission became public early in 1939. That it came from a German laboratory troubled several refugee scientists in the United States almost at once and took on ominous implications with the outbreak of war later that year. Fear of a Nazi bomb

long drove British and American nuclear research and development, although in fact the German project made little progress toward production of an atom bomb.

With a large assist from NDRC and OSRD, what became known as the Manhattan Project was fully under way by fall 1941. Nuclear research was conducted chiefly by academic teams via contracts with selected universities. Shortly after it was formed in mid-1940, NDRC took over a small, year-old, academically oriented research program on nuclear fission. Initial doubts about whether a nuclear bomb was feasible centered on whether sufficient amounts of the fissionable isotope of uranium, U-235, could be separated from uranium ore, of which 99.3 percent was nonfissionable U-238.

A year's research suggested two reasonably promising large-scale methods of obtaining U-235—gaseous diffusion and electromagnetic separation. The discovery that U-238 bombarded with neutrons could be converted into a new and fissionable element, plutonium, offered a third feasible method—chemical separation. Scientific work was then consolidated under OSRD auspices at the University of Chicago. There the main task was to prove that a chain reaction could be sustained. This task was accomplished on 2 December 1942, confirming the feasibility of using reactor-produced plutonium for a bomb.

Success had been anticipated. By mid-1942 the evidence that a bomb could be developed before the end of the war seemed strong enough to justify a major effort. In view of the project's vastly increased scope as it shifted from research and development to engineering, procurement, construction, and production, OSRD began turning the project over to the newly formed Manhattan Engineer District, U.S. Army Corps of Engineers. In three years the Manhattan Project designed, built, and operated an industrial plant that rivaled in scale the prewar U.S. automobile industry.

As part of a crash program, work on the bomb received top priority. Construction began at Oak Ridge, Tennessee, and Hanford, Washington, long before anyone knew which might be the best way to produce fissionable material, even before designs had been settled for plutonium plants or for any one of the proposed uranium techniques—gaseous diffusion, electromagnetic separation, or a third concept the navy had been funding, thermal diffusion. Pursuing all methods, scientists worked successfully with engineers to solve design and manufacturing problems as they arose.

Providing fissionable material was only part of the problem. Designing, developing, and proving a bomb under intense time pressure was something else. The task fell to the laboratory created for that purpose at Los Alamos, New Mexico, operated under contract by the University of California. Theoretical and experimental physicists joined forces with chemists, engineers, and technicians to convert a recently discovered physical phenomenon into a militarily useful weapon. Officially, work at Los Alamos began 15 April 1943; twenty-eight months later, a single U-235 bomb had devastated Hiroshima, a plutonium bomb had similarly leveled Nagasaki.

Its extraordinary success promptly made the Manhattan Project a symbol of the power of science to transform society and a gauge against which to measure other organizations. Extravagant dreams of science-based superweapons seemed to have been realized, but the new age seemed full of promise as well as threat. Military-science cooperation so successful raised hopes of larger social benefits, of problems conquered, of other dreams realized. Profound consequences flowed from both deed and symbol.

Postwar Science Policy.

Several aspects of postwar science policy bore the hallmarks of wartime experience. The Office of Scientific Research and Development ceased operations when the war ended, but it remained a model for effectively linking science and government, even in areas seemingly remote from military concerns. Much of postwar America's medical and scientific research bore the stamp of OSRD model and example.

The wartime success of the OSRD Committee on Medical Research altered the landscape of postwar American medical research. When OSRD closed, the National Institute of Health (NIH), a branch of the Public Health Service founded in 1930 to conduct research in its own laboratories, took charge of the medical committee's outstanding contracts. It soon became, in essence, the nation's central clearinghouse for medical research. Continuing its own research, NIH also administered a growing grants program directed chiefly at supporting medical schools. In 1948, Congress created the National Heart Institute, the first of the special health institutes focused on a special problem, and NIH became the National Institutes of Health. Medical research attracted strong congressional support. The agency funded with less than $3 million in 1945 disposed of a $52 million budget in 1950, and that was only the beginning.

Postwar science policy likewise reflected OSRD influence. Bush, OSRD's guiding genius, set the terms for the postwar debate over science policy in his widely disseminated 1945 report to the president, *Science—The Endless Frontier*. Backed by his wartime success, Bush won universal support for his argument that the manifold benefits of science justified public financing of research through a national foundation. Congress had, in fact, long been considering how scientific research might best be organized to serve the nation's postwar needs. In short, no one doubted the value of research. Precisely what form a research agency should take, rather than whether it should be created, became the issue.

Bush and his supporters favored something very much like OSRD writ large: federal funding for research with few strings attached, oriented toward supporting the best work without regard to distributing funds widely, meeting military and medical as well as more strictly scientific ends. His opponents preferred an organization under greater public control and less focused on the needs of the elite research centers of the eastern United States. Ultimately, they carried the day, but it took five years. The dispute delayed establishment of the National Science Foundation (NSF) until 1950, and the result was a far more modest agency than either side had intended. Military research was deliberately excluded from the purview of the new foundation, as was the medical research already adopted by NIH. Through the early 1950s, NSF remained a modest funder of academic research.

The Office of Naval Research.

The armed forces of the United States emerged from World War II with a vast array of research and development skills and organizations, all of which tended to focus on applied science, development engineering, and hardware related to the needs of their specific branch or bureau. Many of these organizations went out of business after the war, but others survived, although not always in the same form. Military funds had also supported several laboratories with close university ties, in addition to those associated with the Manhattan Project, such as the Applied Physics Laboratory at Johns Hopkins University and the Jet Propulsion Laboratory at the California Institute of Technology.

Technologically oriented applied research dominated the wartime effort, but the postwar world offered wider prospects for military uses of science, as exemplified by the altered bases of strategic planning demanded by nuclear weapons. Scientists themselves argued persuasively for the value of basic research. When postwar plans for a federal agency to support basic research were delayed, the navy filled the breach with the Office of Naval Research (ONR). Shortly after OSRD began work in the summer of 1941, the navy created its own research and development coordinating office. By 1945 that office had also taken charge of the Naval Research Laboratory and sought a statutory basis for maintaining the wartime military-science alliance. A 1946 act of Congress created ONR, which promptly began to divert funds from canceled procurement contracts into research.

Accomplishing much with relatively modest funds, ONR proved a liberal patron of academic science in the immediate postwar period. Like OSRD, the ONR adopted the research contract as its primary funding device. Accepting the inherent value of basic research, it found money for a wide range of projects without insisting they show direct links to naval needs. ONR also served as a training ground for science administrators throughout the government. Its widely admired management practices and policies helped shape the NSF after 1950. Inspired by ONR example, the other services created offices to support basic research—the Army Research Office in 1951 and the Air Force Office of Scientific Research in 1952.

The Atomic Energy Commission.

The future of nuclear energy headed the postwar agenda, and Congress singled out this area of science policy for special treatment. The reason was simple. Nuclear policy was linked too closely to national security for routine handling; in the postwar United States the bomb was the very symbol of science as military resource. Operation Crossroads, the Manhattan Project's nuclear display at Bikini in the Pacific in the summer of 1946, underlined the atom's military role. Yet hopes still ran high for the peaceful uses of a seemingly limitless source of power. Fear and hope alike colored the early decisions. Debate over what form the control of atomic energy should take was heated, the central issue whether control should be vested in military or civilian hands. Civilian control won.

The Atomic Energy Act of 1946 assigned the job to an independent agency, the Atomic Energy Commission (AEC). Five presidentially appointed civilian commissioners, one of whom served as chairman, formed the commission proper and were charged with making policy. A headquarters staff of several divisions oversaw all aspects, military as well as civilian, of nuclear research and development, procurement, production, and use. Although the 1946 act decided for a civilian commission, it nonetheless mandated a strong military presence.

The Division of Military Application became the largest component in AEC headquarters, its director by law a general or flag officer and its staff drawn from the uniformed services. Furthermore, a disproportionately large share of AEC officials, both at headquarters and in the field, were former military officers. Developing and testing nuclear weapons remained one of AEC's central functions throughout its career. Its successors, the Energy Research and Development Administration and the Department of Energy, likewise carried major military burdens.

The AEC promptly became a major patron of science, especially physics, with significant programs in the biomedical sciences as well. Following OSRD precedents, AEC directed its funding through contracts for both basic and applied research. Operating contracts also proved most useful. Formal agreements with universities enabled AEC to support and expand a network of national laboratories, beginning with those at Argonne, Illinois; Oak Ridge; and Los Alamos that were inherited from the wartime Manhattan Project. Industrial companies received contracts to manage production facilities such as those at Hanford and Sandia, New Mexico.

The Manhattan Engineer District itself dissolved at the end of 1946. Most of its assets, facilities, and workers were transferred to AEC. Military members of the wartime project became in 1947 the nucleus of a new combined agency, the Armed Forces Special Weapons Project (AFSWP). Augmenting its rosters from all branches of the armed forces, AFSWP worked closely with AEC to develop and test nuclear weapons. The AFSWP later became the Defense Atomic Support Agency, known since 1971 as the Defense Nuclear Agency.

Science and Strategy.
Among the institutional consequences of nuclear weapons was a trend toward civilianizing military strategy. Science seemed the likeliest source of answers to the novel problems posed by nuclear war. In this context, science meant chiefly the techniques of operational analysis as practiced by the OSRD Applied Mathematics Panel during World War II. Scientists, both physical and social, found themselves playing ever larger roles in strategic planning, once the almost exclusive preserve of uniformed officers.

Perhaps because of what nuclear weapons implied for strategic bombing, the air force took the lead in 1946 when it contracted with the Douglas Aircraft Company of Santa Monica, California, for Project RAND (for "research and development"), which began modestly. Initially intended to provide advice on certain relatively technical problems, it quickly expanded to become an independent nonprofit corporation. Civilian experts assumed ever larger roles in strategic planning. Physicists and engineers were joined by social scientists, especially economists, who relied upon and improved the wartime techniques of operational analysis to provide quantitative answers to critical strategic problems.

Success bred imitation. The secretary of defense and the Joint Chiefs of Staff first tried the Weapons Systems Evaluation Group, physically located in the Pentagon and commanded by a senior officer. That 1948 experiment proved a failure, unable to attract enough civilian experts. In 1956 it was replaced by the Institute for Defense Analyses, initially a university consortium, later, like RAND, a nonprofit corporation. The other services, meanwhile, followed the air force example—the army with the Research Analysis Corporation, the navy with the Center for Naval Analysis.

Military budgets dropped steeply in the five years after World War II. Relying on its monopoly of nuclear weapons and following long-standing precedents for postwar demobilization, the United States canceled most of its wartime contracts and sharply reduced its armed forces. By 1949 the euphoria engendered by victory in World War II had given way to an intensifying cold war, underscored by the Soviet Union's success, sooner than many expected, in testing its own nuclear weapons. The United States began to recast fundamentally its military and foreign policy.

The North Korean invasion of South Korea in mid-1950 marked a turning point. The Korean conflict was largely fought with World War II weapons and tactics, although jet aircraft, which had first flown in combat at the very end of World War II, now made their first large-scale appearance. Military budgets soared in response to the needs of troops in the field, but most of the money was not intended for prosecuting the war then in progress. It went instead to vastly expanding U.S. nuclear capabilities, including the crash program to develop hydrogen bombs.

The 1950 decision to proceed with H-bomb development strongly reinforced the trend toward employing civilian expertise. Thermonuclear weapons exploited the explosive fission of heavy elements to ignite the fusion of light elements, in theory multiplying explosive power virtually without limit. Conventional bombs in World War II could destroy a few hundred square yards, the fission bombs dropped on Japan a few square miles. Conceivably, destruction of such limited areas might fall within the scope of military planning based on the concept of war as a rational political tool.

Not so hydrogen bombs. Destruction measured in hundreds of square miles, a scale more nearly appropriate to a force of nature than human agency, seemed to render military experience largely irrelevant. By the late 1950s, the theory of nuclear warfare and deterrence had become the almost exclusive province of civilian experts.

Bolstering science and engineering across the board was another goal of the post-1950 military buildup. Defense Department budgets remained at a permanently high, and increasing, level even after the fighting in Korea ended. Military agencies and the AEC accounted for 70 percent of U.S. research and development funding by the early 1950s and well over 90 percent of federal funds allotted to campus research.

FROM SPUTNIK TO SDI

Whether or not fission bombs ended the war against Japan, nuclear weapons exerted their greatest effects on the future—effects much more significant for institutional development than for the conduct of war. Yet institutional changes are no less important than shifts in tactics, doctrine, or operational philosophies. Although issues related to nuclear weapons and deterrence dominated military policymaking, nuclear weapons have not been used in war since 1945.

It has not precluded war, of course, but it has kept war conventional, even if the word means no more than the absence from combat of NBC—that is, nuclear, biological, and chemical—weapons. Just as radar influenced the course of World War II far more than atomic bombs, the postwar development of electronics has affected the conduct of warfare far more significantly than has nuclear weapons development.

A decade after the end of World War II, the United States had erected an impressive if piecemeal institutional structure for turning science to military purpose. Ensuing decades brought increasingly difficult questions about the assumptions underpinning that structure and about its consequences, not only for military and scientific institutions themselves but also for American polity, economy, and society.

Consequences of Sputnik. The United States faced a military-scientific crisis after the Soviet Union launched the first artificial satellite on 4 October 1957 and another a month later, the second with a dog as passenger. Two Sputniks in one month shook the casual confidence many Americans placed in their country's scientific and technological prowess. Among the direct consequences was the formation of a new federal science agency, the National Aeronautics and Space Administration (NASA).

NASA incorporated the National Advisory Committee for Aeronautics and a number of military rocket and space projects. NASA would rely heavily on academic and industrial contractors for much of its research and development. Ostensibly a civilian agency with large military participation, all of NASA's early launch vehicles were modified missiles. NASA was never devoid of military purpose, but it has in recent years increasingly become a captive of the Pentagon.

Suddenly, after Sputnik, science advice for the president again became a high priority, and the post of special assistant for science and technology was established in the White House. Filled by MIT president James R. Killian, Jr., it was the first time a U.S. president enjoyed the services of a full-time science adviser. At the same time, the Science Advisory Committee, created in 1951 in the Office of Defense Mobilization, moved to the White House as the President's Science Advisory Committee. Given a voice at the highest levels of government, science flourished over the next decade. The decision reflected still widespread beliefs about the military potential of science and concerns about using it properly in the national interest. Much of the advice sought centered on nuclear weapons and missile development.

Pentagon reorganization in 1958 replaced the largely advisory assistant secretary of defense for research and development (established in a 1953 defense reorganization) with a director of defense research and engineering who enjoyed direct authority to approve, reject, or modify all defense research projects. Reorganization also created the Advanced Research Projects Agency (later the Defense Advanced Research Projects Agency) able to act promptly on special projects, especially in the areas of space and missile defense.

As a major supplier of research funds, the Pentagon exerted increasingly strong influence on the direction of research and even the structure of universities, which came to depend on such funds. This tendency became more pronounced with the passage of the National Defense Education Act (NDEA) of 1958, still another consequence of Sputnik's blow to national pride and the implied military threat. NDEA provided immense sums of money to channel students into courses of study the government deemed useful for national security, with a strong accent on science and engineering.

During the 1950s, there were some qualms about the progress of science and technology, especially as linked to military imperatives. President Dwight Eisenhower's farewell address in January 1961 articulated some of these concerns. His warning against the military-industrial complex was only part of the message. He also warned against the twin dangers of sci-

ence too closely entwined with government: Academic research might suffer from excessive dependence upon federal support, and government policymaking might be surrendered to a scientific-technological elite. Government in this context largely meant the armed forces.

McNamara's Pentagon.

The systems analytic approach to defense planning pioneered at RAND moved from advice to policymaking during Robert S. McNamara's tenure as secretary of defense (1961–1967). During World War II, McNamara had honed a systems approach to management and analysis while planning air force operations. After the war he brought his team and the new techniques to the Ford Motor Company, successfully reviving the moribund enterprise and rising to company president just before John F. Kennedy became president of the United States. Invited to become secretary of defense, McNamara introduced systems approaches and cost accounting to defense planning. He also brought civilian defense intellectuals, to many of whom such approaches were most congenial, from their consultancies and advisory panels into Pentagon policymaking positions. Cost accounting increasingly dictated, or at least decisively influenced, strategic choices, and fiscal planning and budget allocation became the chief means of structuring forces and procuring weapons.

The impact of such changes was not limited to matters of policy. Traditional principles of military organization began losing their unquestioned hold. The direction of armed forces increasingly came to rely on management skills rather than on command authority. Young officers might find a degree in business management more useful for their careers than training in strategy and tactics. Military professionalism lost much of its once pivotal role as civilian experts in game theory, systems analysis, and other esoteric specialties reshaped strategic planning and challenged long-standing views about the functions of armed forces. Such quantitative and systematic skills, although themselves products of military needs and support, seemed to have little in common with former notions of military expertise.

Larger aspects of American society were also affected. During the 1960s the Pentagon exerted ever greater control over the direction of American economic development. What Seymour Melman termed "Pentagon capitalism" turned the defense budget into a device for central economic planning, with profound consequences for the conduct and content of science, social as well as physical, and of engineering. Through its placement of contracts for research, development, and production, the Pentagon altered higher education and channeled key areas of technological development along lines of military interest.

The development of the automated machine-tool industry exemplifies the way military interests can transform engineering practice, even in an ostensibly civilian setting. Beginning in the 1950s, the U.S. Air Force funded research and development in techniques for controlling machine tools automatically, that is, without direct handling by workers. Among several promising methods, the air force favored numerical control. This technique emphasized the transfer of skill from worker to machine, in contrast to other methods that left greater autonomy in the hands of workers. Technological efficiency may have suffered from this choice, but it strongly promoted managerial hierarchy and control of the workforce. Such choices were nothing new. Military preferences for controlling workers, even at the expense of productivity, underwrote the expansion of scientific management at the turn of the century and promoted many of the techniques of modern management.

Hindsight and TRACES.
Escalation of the war in Vietnam put pressure on military budgets and led to questions about the payoff on military funding for research, some $10 billion between 1945 and 1965. The result was Project Hindsight, a retrospective study of weapons systems deployed as of the mid-1960s to decide just how much basic research had contributed to their success. Thirteen teams of scientists and engineers picked twenty systems then in use, tracked their development histories over the preceding twenty years, and concluded that science had played a minor role. More than 90 percent of the work had been purely technological, and most of the remainder could best be described as applied or mission-oriented research. Basic science was virtually irrelevant.

When reported in 1966, such findings threatened the rationale for military support of basic research. At least since the end of World War II, Vannevar Bush's claim that basic research in science underlay technological progress had gone largely unchallenged. That claim, in turn, underlay the scientists' justification for public support. If basic research played no significant part in advancing military technology, as Project Hindsight suggested, then science lost its claim on military resources.

Critics of these findings objected that twenty years could be too short a time for basic research to make itself felt in technological advances. Practical results might well take longer to appear. Other questions seemed equally problematic. Were the systems chosen for study the kind likely to display the results of basic research? Could a study focused on incremental improvements—almost a definition of engineering development—adequately assess the impact of major breakthroughs? Such questions, combined with deeper concerns about public support for science, led the National Science Foundation to sponsor a counterstudy called Project TRACES (Technology in Retrospect and Critical Events in Science). Conducted by the Illinois Institute of Technology, the new study concentrated on major innovations and extended the historical analysis to fifty years. The 1968 report found that academic research was, in fact, the main source of major innovations.

Although the issue has never been fully resolved, government support of basic research declined by the end of the 1960s. The armed forces became noticeably less willing to support basic research, an inclination strongly reinforced by congressional action. Controversy about science tarnished by military funds sharply increased in step with protests against the Vietnam War. In 1969 the so-called Mansfield Amendment prohibited military funding for research not directly related to military needs. Consequences were relatively minor. A Pentagon review of outstanding contracts found that only 4 percent could not meet the standard of military relevance.

Toward the Automation of War. In contrast to basic research, mission-oriented and applied research have flourished, and military funds still support the bulk of the research and development enterprise in the United States. The result has been enormous growth in the range of sophisticated gadgetry that is deployed on, above, and around modern battlefields. Qualitative changes in the accuracy of weapons, reliability of communications, and effectiveness of command and control have radically altered the combat environment. Many of these changes are the direct result of military-sponsored research and development.

Central to these changes since World War II has been the explosive growth of microelectronics, particularly computing. Initially, costly and unpredictable computers attracted little commercial interest. Military support did not demand quick returns. Despite wartime successes and indirect benefits flowing from such scientific uses as analyzing the dynamics of nuclear explosions, the huge machines of the late 1940s and early 1950s were hardly suitable for weapon systems. Automation, however, caught military imaginations. Faith in the longer-term prospects for enormously enhanced command and control mattered more than the failure-prone and hard-to-use machines currently available.

By the 1950s such prospects appeared close enough to encourage an attempt at large-scale application. Continental air defense threatened by Soviet nuclear weapons provided the problem. The answer was a centralized command and control system termed SAGE (Semi-Automatic Ground Environment). Huge mainframe computers would process incoming data from a vast network of distant radar stations, then direct interceptors against attacking bombers. Although it became operational in 1963 and survived, at least in part, into the early 1980s, SAGE was never very reliable. Probably it mattered more as symbol than system. SAGE opened the way not only for the antiballistic missile systems of the 1960s and the Strategic Defense Initiative (SDI) of the 1980s but also for the Worldwide Military Command and Control System. It foreshadowed their flaws as well. Inherently untestable, their ultimate capabilities remain matters of faith.

In contrast to such grandiose schemes, which sought to automate decision-making, efforts to automate combat have enjoyed a measure of success. The line of descent from radar-guided, computer-directed, sensor-activated antiaircraft fire in World War II to precision-guided munitions, or "smart bombs," has been relatively straightforward. Scientists and engineers have worked systematically and diligently to upgrade, diversify, and augment guidance techniques, computer systems, and sensors, individually and as system components. Primarily incremental change ultimately resulted in the qualitative transformation that General William C. Westmoreland in 1969 labeled the automated battlefield.

The complete automation of warfare may remain a more distant prospect than enthusiasts claim or critics fear, but a military revolution seems in the offing. From their earliest days, American military, engineering, and scientific institutions have interacted in manifold ways, with consequences reaching far beyond the institutions themselves. Since World War II, military managers have gained control of unprecedented resources and have learned to harness science and engineering to their wants. Imperfect as yet and enormously expensive, these new techniques have nonetheless produced a striking panoply and forced great changes throughout the armed forces. They have also transformed American science and engineering, reshaped American universities, and strongly affected almost every aspect of American society.

See also COMMUNICATIONS; INDUSTRIAL MOBILIZATION AND DEMOBILIZATION; LOGISTICS; MILITARY AVIATION; MILITARY EDUCATION AND TRAINING; MILITARY MEDICINE; *and* RESEARCH AND TECHNOLOGY.

BIBLIOGRAPHY

General Works

Durbin, Paul T., ed. *A Guide to the Culture of Science, Technology, and Medicine* (1980).

Higham, Robin. *A Guide to the Sources of United States Military History* (1975).

Higham, Robin, and Carol Brandt, eds. *The United States Army in Peacetime: Essays in Honor of the Bicentennial, 1775–1975* (1975).

Higham, Robin, and Donald J. Mrozek. *A Guide to the Sources of United States Military History, Supplement I* (1981) and *Supplement II* (1985).

Kohlstedt, Sally Gregory, and Margaret W. Rossiter, eds. *Historical Writing on American Science* (1986).

Pursell, Carroll W., Jr., ed. *Technology in America: A History of Individuals and Ideas*, 2nd ed. (1990).

Reingold, Nathan, ed. *The Sciences in the American Context: New Perspectives* (1979).

Spiegel-Rösing, Ina, and Derek de Solla Price, eds. *Science, Technology, and Society: A Cross-Disciplinary Perspective* (1977).

Van Tassel, David D., and Michael G. Hall, eds. *Science and Society in the United States* (1966).

The Colonial Period through the Civil War

Bruce, Robert V. *The Launching of Modern American Science, 1846–1876* (1987).

Calhoun, Daniel H. *The American Civil Engineer: Origins and Conflict* (1960).

Davis, Carl L. *Arming the Union: Small Arms in the Civil War* (1973).

Goetzmann, William H. *Army Exploration in the American West, 1803–1863* (1959).

Hill, Forest G. *Roads, Rails, and Waterways: The Army Engineers and Early Transportation* (1957).

Mayr, Otto, and Robert C. Post, eds. *Yankee Enterprise: The Rise of the American System of Manufactures* (1981).

Morrison, James L., Jr. *"The Best School in the World": West Point, the Pre-Civil War Years, 1833–1866* (1986).

Ponko, Vincent, Jr. *Ships, Seas, and Scientists: U.S. Naval Exploration and Discovery in the Nineteenth Century* (1974).

Taylor, George Rogers. *The Transportation Revolution, 1815–1860* (1951).

Turner, George Edgar. *Victory Rode the Rails: The Strategic Place of the Railroads in the Civil War* (1953).

York, Neil Longley. *Mechanical Metamorphosis: Technological Change in Revolutionary America* (1985).

The Late Nineteenth Century Through World War II

Baxter, James Phinney, III. *Scientists Against Time* (1946).

Bledstein, Burton J. *The Culture of Professionalism: The Middle Class and the Development of Higher Education in America* (1976).

Borden, Penn. *Civilian Indoctrination of the Military: World War I and Future Implications for the Military-Industrial Complex* (1989).

Calvert, Monte A. *The Mechanical Engineer in America: Professional Cultures in Conflict, 1830–1910* (1967).

Cooling, Benjamin Franklin. *Gray Steel and Blue Water Navy: The Formative Years of America's Military-Industrial Complex, 1881–1917* (1979).

Dupree, A. Hunter. *Science in the Federal Government: A History of Policies and Activities to 1940* (1957).

————. "The *Great Instauration* of 1940: The Organization of Scientific Research for War." In *The Twentieth-Century Sciences: Studies in the Biography of Ideas*, edited by Gerald Holton (1972).

Emmerson, George S. *Engineering Education: A Social History* (1973).

Hacker, Barton C. "Imaginations in Thrall: The Social Psychology of Military Mechanization, 1919–1939." *Parameters* 12 (1982).

Haycock, Ronald, and Keith Neilson, eds. *Men, Machines, and War* (1988).

Huntington, Samuel P. *The Soldier and the State: The Theory and Politics of Civil-Military Relations* (1957).

Jones, Vincent C. *Manhattan: The Army and the Atomic Bomb* (1985).

Karsten, Peter. *The Naval Aristocracy: The Golden Age of Annapolis and the Emergence of Modern American Navalism* (1972).

Kevles, Daniel J. *The Physicists: The History of a Scientific Community in Modern America* (1977).

King, Randolph W., ed. *Naval Engineering and American Sea Power* (1989).

Larson, Magali Sarfatti. *The Rise of Professionalism: A Sociological Analysis* (1977).

McNeill, William H. *The Pursuit of Power: Technology, Armed Force, and Society Since A.D. 1000* (1982).

Millis, Walter. *Arms and Men: A Study in American Military History* (1956).

Noble, David F. *America by Design: Science, Technology, and the Rise of Corporate Capitalism* (1977).

Paret, Peter, et al., eds. *Makers of Modern Strategy: From Machiavelli to the Nuclear Age* (1986).

Pearton, Maurice. *The Knowledgeable State: Diplomacy, War, and Technology Since 1830* (1982).

Sen, Gautam. *The Military Origins of Industrialisation and International Trade Rivalry* (1984).

Skowronek, Stephen. *Building a New American State: The Expansion of National Administrative Capacities, 1877–1920* (1982).

Smith, Merritt Roe, ed. *Military Enterprise and Technological Change: Perspectives on the American Experience* (1985).

Van Doorn, Jacques. "The Genesis of Military and Industrial Organization." In *The Soldier and Social Change: Comparative Studies in the History and Sociology of the Military* (1975).

Since World War II

Barnaby, Frank. *The Automated Battlefield* (1986).

Bellin, David, and Gary Chapman, eds. *Computers in Battle: Will They Work?* (1987).

Bruce-Biggs, B. *The Shield of Faith: The Hidden Struggle for Strategic Defense* (1988).

Duncan, Francis. *Rickover and the Nuclear Navy: The Discipline of Technology* (1990).

Forman, Paul. "Behind Quantum Electronics: National Security as Basis for Physical Research in the United States, 1940–1960." *Historical Studies in the Physical and Biological Sciences* 18 (1987).

Gilpin, Robert, and Christopher Wright, eds. *Scientists and National Policy-Making* (1964).

Herken, Gregg. *Counsels of War* (1985).

Hewlett, Richard G., et al. *A History of the United States Atomic Energy Commission*, 3 vols. (1962–1989).

Kaldor, Mary. *The Baroque Arsenal* (1981).

Kaplan, Fred. *The Wizards of Armageddon* (1983).

Kevles, Daniel J. "Cold War and Hot Physics: Science, Security, and the American State." *Historical Studies in the Physical and Biological Sciences* 20 (1990).

Lakoff, Sanford A., and Herbert F. York. *A Shield in Space? Technology, Politics, and the Strategic Defense Initiative* (1989).

Levidow, Les, and Kevin Robins, eds. *Cyborg Worlds: The Military Information Society* (1989).

McDougall, Walter A. *The Heavens and the Earth: A Political History of the Space Age* (1985).

Melman, Seymour. *Pentagon Capitalism: The Political Economy of War* (1970).

Mendelsohn, Everett, Merritt Roe Smith, and Peter Weingart, eds. *Science, Technology, and the Military*. Sociology of the Sciences: A Yearbook, vol. 12 (1988).

Mukerji, Chandra. *A Fragile Power: Scientists and the State* (1989).

Noble, David F. *Forces of Production: A Social History of Industrial Automation* (1984).

Tirman, John, ed. *The Militarization of High Technology* (1984).

Stine, Jeffrey K. *A History of Science Policy in the United States, 1940–1985*. Science Policy Study Background Report No. 1, 99th Congress, 2nd Session (September 1986).

Wilson, David A., ed. "Universities and the Military." *Annals of the American Academy of Political and Social Science* 502 (1989).

York, Herbert F., and G. Allen Greb. "Military Research and Development: A Postwar History." *Bulletin of the Atomic Scientists* (January 1977).